CITIES OF THE MIDDLE EAST AND NORTH AFRICA

CITIES OF THE MIDDLE EAST AND NORTH AFRICA

A Historical Encyclopedia

Michael R. T. Dumper and Bruce E. Stanley, Editors

Foreword by Janet L. Abu-Lughod

ABC⬤CLIO

Santa Barbara, California • Denver, Colorado • Oxford, England

Library of Congress Cataloging-in-Publication Data

    Cities of the Middle East and North Africa : a historical encyclopedia /
Michael R. T. Dumper and Bruce E. Stanley, editors : foreword by Janet L. Abu-Lughod.
        p. cm.
    Includes bibliographical references and index.
    ISBN 1-57607-919-8 (hard cover : alk. paper)   ISBN 1-57607-920-1 (e-book)
1. Cities and towns—Middle East. 2. City and towns—Africa, North. I. Dumper, Michael.
II. Stanley, Bruce E.
    HT147.5.C574 2006
    307.760956—dc22

                                            2006027503

10 09 08 07   10 9 8 7 6 5 4 3 2 1

ISBN 13: 978-1-57607-919-5 (ebook) 978-1-57607-920-1
ISBN 10: 1-57607-919-8 (ebook) 1-57607-920-1

Production Editor: Martha Ripley Gray
Editorial Assistant: Alisha L. Martinez
Production Manager: Don Schmidt
Media Editor: Ellen Rasmussen
Media Production Coordinator: Ellen Brenna Dougherty
Media Resources Manager: Caroline Price
File Manager: Paula Gerard

This book is also available on the World Wide Web as an e-book.
Visit http://www.abc-clio.com for details.

ABC-CLIO, Inc.
130 Cremona Drive, P.O. Box 1911
Santa Barbara, California 93116–1911

This book is printed on acid-free paper. ∞
Manufactured in the United States of America

This volume is dedicated to those local heroes of Middle East and North African cities who, across the millennia, have defied killing solidarities and conventional boundaries to embrace the humanity and potential of "the other" in their midst.

Contents

Preface

This volume is motivated by a simple premise: Cities need to be brought back into the analysis of the Middle East and North Africa (MENA). Long obscured by a focus on the empire or the state, their agency denied and curtailed, cities can and should receive greater attention from those interested in the region. There are many reasons for advocating this position. One of the most telling is the depth of involvement cities have with conflict and violence. As the last details on the production of this volume are being accomplished, Beirut and Tyre are exchanging bombs for rockets with Tel Aviv and Haifa. Whole districts of Beirut have been reduced to rubble, access to Tyre has been cut off, major energy and transport networks crucial to urban functioning have been destroyed, hundreds of thousands of displaced persons are on the move, while almost half of Haifa's population has fled the city.

Other cities in the region are also experiencing ongoing conflict as well: Baghdad and Basrah are torn apart by daily violence; Istanbul has experienced another explosion; Mogadishu has been conquered by forces of the Islamic Courts. It is hard to escape the conclusion that conflict among, about, and directed towards the cities of the Middle East, ongoing for five thousand years, remains a fundamental component of contemporary urban life in the region. Such events draw our attention to the cities of the region, and force us to admit that any attempt to understand the region's current dynamics without considering the urban, at least as a site for conflict and violence, misunderstands the MENA.

There are, however, many other reasons to divert attention from states and empires to cities in the Middle East and North Africa other than the fact that regional security is now primarily urban in its location, incubation, and management. Fundamentally, the processes and dynamics of conflict transformation in the region are also urban based and urban driven in their requirements. Post-conflict development, as well as sustainable economic development, also crucially depend on the vitality and involvement of cities: Just ask the people of Haifa, Beirut, Mogadishu, or Mosul. The alleviation of poverty and exclusion can not ignore the inhabitants of the shanty towns, *gecekondu,* and *bidonvilles* of Port Sudan, Algiers, Izmir,

or Nouakchott or they will not succeed. The expansion of political space in the MENA can only start from acknowledging that civil society is urban based and urban dependent, and must be nurtured by the city.

Long-term analysis of the regional future also forces an urban sensitivity. Whether it is global warming, and its implications for agriculture, urbanization and migration, or water scarcity and declining aquifers, the effects in the MENA city will be profound. Population growth, and the in-migration to cities, will dominate urban politics and the search for a voice for the disenfranchised.

Another reason to recenter the city in our understanding of the Middle East and North Africa is the obvious vitality of the region's cities. The everyday of MENA urban life drives the economy, politics, and social development of this disparate region. Young people in Cairo and Manama queue up to hear Nancy Ajram, despite the dire warnings of religious leaders and politicians about the imminent demise of society as we know it. City residents still flock to the beaches of Aqaba/Eilat, Baku, Gaza, or Casablanca for family time away from the heat of the city. Suitcase smugglers continue to ply their trade between Bandar Abbas and Dubai, Istanbul and Varna, Tangier and Tarifa despite state boundaries. Religious broadcasts from Qom are sold as DVDs on the streets of Manama, Djibouti, Marseilles, and Zanzibar. Flights still converge on Dubai and ships full of sheep leave Berbera. Architectural restoration continues in the kasbah of Nablus, on the medieval high rises of Aden, or the mosques of Timbuktu. Human rights activists still protest in Tunis and in Tabriz. The Middle East and North African city is humming, providing the buzz and hope that has always marked its city system.

It is this undeniability of the role of the urban in understanding the Middle East and Africa, no matter the policy horizon, which has stimulated the production of this volume. In a context where the power of the MENA city has tended to be ignored, misunderstood, or downplayed, the editors wished to redirect attention, to "bring the city back in," to the discussion about regional agency, decision making, and policy.

Equally, however, we felt that the city was being excluded from the historical narrative. Analysis of the Middle East and

North African city has often been disjointed, focusing on particular periods in the trajectory of a city rather than taking a perspective over the *longue durée* of a single city or of urbanism's place in regional development. Few cities in the region have been approached as a conceptual whole, and we wanted to make a statement about the usefulness of such a perspective. Likewise, the region is often framed for students through its religious or ethnic differences, obscuring the pluralistic urban reality lived by its people. A city perspective thus begins to subvert such traditional framings of the region, opening up an alternative spatial vision and approach. By examining cities as a whole, a different relationship and dynamics is revealed.

Within this volume the reader will find two primary perspectives on "the city." One stresses a city's historical uniqueness, autonomy, particularistic heritage, and trajectory. The other looks to the networks of flows and ties that link one city to another, and thus views the city through the lens of its embeddedness and ties. Both are essential to understanding the role of cities in the Middle East and North Africa.

This volume, like the urban itself, begins each narrative with human creativity, and should end with human potential. The MENA urban story contained in these pages includes significant misery, destruction, political folly, and the dominance of the powerful, but it also affirms the regenerative power and transcendence of the human spirit. Out of destruction can come renewal, learning, creativity, and openness. It is this story that the MENA city can also tell.

This story would not be told if not for the work of the wonderful production team at ABC-CLIO. Martha Gray has been a jewel, overseeing the complicated final process with understanding and skill. Alex Mikaberidze kept the project moving during its vital middle phase with kind encouragement. Anna Moore and especially Kristine Swift stepped in to keep the project from falling behind. Our thanks to them.

—The editors

Contributors and Their Entries

Kamal Abdul Fattah
Bir Zeit University
Bir Zeit, Palestine
    Jericho
    Ramallah/al-Bireh

Janet L. Abu-Lughod
New School for Social Research
New York, New York, USA
    Foreword

Aref Abu-Rabia
Ben Gurion University
Beersheva, Israel
    Beersheba

Lahouari Addi
University of Lyon
Lyon, France
    Oran

Habib Borjian
Hofstra University
Hempstead, New York, USA
    Esfahan

Kenneth Brown
Founding Editor, *Mediterraneans*
Paris, France
    Alexandria
    Algiers
    Casablanca
    Rabat/Sale
    Tunis

Michael Dumper
University of Exeter
Exeter, United Kingdom
    Acre
    Aleppo

    Damascus
    Fez
    Gaza
    Haifa
    Hebron
    Jaffa
    Jerusalem
    Karbala
    Madinah
    Makkah
    Marrakesh
    Meknes
    Nablus
    Najaf
    Nazareth
    Qom
    Tel Aviv

James Hartley
Newton Abott, United Kingdom
    Abadan
    Tangier

Laury Haytayan
Center for Conflict Resolution and Peacebuilding
Beirut, Lebanon
    Beirut

Shabnam Holliday
University of Exeter
Exeter, United Kingdom
    Bandar Abbas
    Tabriz
    Tehran

Amel M. Jerary
El-Fateh University
Tripoli, Libya
    Tripoli

Michael Pacione
University of Strathclyde
Glasgow, United Kingdom
    Dubai

Nicola Pratt
University of East Anglia
Norwich, United Kingdom
    Aswan
    Luxor
    Nouakchott
    Sfax

Simone Ricca
Architectural Restoration Consultant
Paris, France
    Amman
    Palmyra

Ahmad Abdelkareem Saif
American University of Sharjah
Sharjah, United Arab Emirates
    Sanaa
    Taif

Arthur Stanley
Fort Valley, Virginia, USA
    Ephesus
    Iznik

Bruce Stanley
University of Exeter, Huron University
London, United Kingdom
    Aden
    Aksum
    Ankara
    Aqaba/Eilat
    Ashdod
    Babylon
    Baghdad
    Baku
    Basrah
    Berbera
    Bukhara
    Bursa
    Byblos
    Cairo

    Diyarbakir
    Djibouti City
    Ebla
    Herat
    Istanbul
    Izmir
    Khartoum
    Mogadishu
    Nicosia
    Nineveh
    Nippur
    Port Sudan
    Samarkand
    Sijilmassa
    Timbuktu
    Trabzon
    Tyre
    Ugarit
    Ur
    Uruk
    Yanbu
    Zanzibar
    Zubair

Angie Turner
Economic Consultant
London, United Kingdom
    Ad-Dammam
    Buraimi and Al-Ain
    Doha
    Kuwait City
    Manama
    Muscat
    Riyadh
    Salalah

J. L. Whitaker
University of Durham
Durham, United Kingdom
    Antakya
    Hamah
    Hims
    Iskenderun
    Kirkuk
    Kufa
    Mosul
    Samarra

List of Entries

Foreword

This is an unusual contribution to the literature on cities in the Middle East and North Africa (MENA) region—deserving much applause for its ambitious decision to cover 100 cities by essays that are remarkably sophisticated and historically embedded and for the skills and energies of the editors, who have written different dovetailed introductions and, between them, have authored more than half the entries. (The rest have been written by trusted colleagues chosen for their specialized knowledge of particular subregions.)

The limited number of contributors provides a rare balance between unity of purpose—manifested by writing styles that maintain comparable levels of serious scholarly sophistication and the flexibility to vary the contents to emphasize the successive cultures and periods of greatest importance to their individual formations and transformations. Unlike the city chapters in other encyclopedias (Britannica's specialized urban encyclopedias such as the 2002 massive four-volume *Grolier Encyclopedia of Urban Cultures*), where unity is achieved by requiring individual authors to follow similar outlines, relevant or not, the present format provides an unprecedented opportunity for the authors to capture the depth and diversity of cities located within a common but hardly uniform region.

This collection strongly resists the temptation to reduce its intellectual demands on readers to their lowest common denominator. Each entry presumes some knowledge of the geographical setting and some familiarity with the long stretch of shifting imperial control, religious sects, and even dynasties. While this limits the number of its potential users, it offers rich rewards to its readers, dedicated students and scholars alike, who seek to widen their reach, to develop comparisons, and to hone better, if more limited, generalizations about cities in the MENA region.

I am particularly excited by the promise that the encyclopedia will be available on the Web. With a comprehensive index to link and sort entries into geographical, historical, and functional categories of the user's design, this book is an extremely valuable tool, not only for searching specific entries but for formulating creative and synthetic scholarly hypotheses.

My congratulations to the editors and authors for this excellent work.

Janet L. Abu-Lughod

Reevaluating the Past, Rethinking the Future

The cities of the Middle East and North Africa (MENA) evoke many vivid and colorful images. Bustling market areas and crowded caravansaries are found alongside lush, watered gardens or spacious mosque courtyards. Gray-walled and featureless twisting streets suddenly reveal a vista of an imposing mosque with the blue-and-gold ceramics of its domes and minarets flashing in the hot sun. The noise and press of heavily clad humanity and overloaded beasts can immediately give way to quiet and secluded residential areas where old men on wooden stools play backgammon with their neighbors. Next to rooftops and open spaces blistering with the dry summer heat are dark alleyways with high walls throwing a blanket of cool shade across their paths. Beside the hilltop madinah, there is a modern suburb with motorways and shopping malls. The city of the MENA region is kaleidoscopic in its range and variety. As one of the cradles of world civilizations, it boasts some of the most ancient cities of the world—Jerusalem, Baghdad, Cairo, Jericho—and some of the most modern—Riyadh, Tel Aviv, Dubai.

Despite this richness and color, the reality is, and has always been, more prosaic. Cities in the MENA region, long the center of social, economic, and political activity, are undergoing a profound crisis of growth, of service provision, and of internal social, political, and architectural change. The reality is that amid the vibrancy and variety, city officials are also struggling with overcrowding, poor infrastructure, changing economic means of production, and grand but often inappropriate attempts to ameliorate these problems but that only add to the burden and the debt. The pageantry of the cities of the region is mixed with poverty and pollution. Yet, however one wishes to perceive them, these cities are fascinating and worthy of greater study.

The study of MENA cities has also been characterized by a wide range of opinions and perspectives. To illustrate the variety of views and different points that can be emphasized, the editors have chosen to write two separate but complementary introductions. This first part of the introduction, "Reevaluating the Past, Rethinking the Future," attempts to show how the study of cities in the MENA region can be structured. It outlines the different ways in which cities in the region have been studied, examining the various phases in which different disciplines contributed to our understanding of them.

It then highlights some of the common architectural forms and environmental or logistical factors that have influenced the development of cities and, finally, some of the profound ways in which they are being transformed. The second part of the introduction, "The Wonders of Cities and the Marvels of Seeing Cities Comparatively," clarifies a range of ways to compare and contrast cities contained in this volume, offers some alternative ways beyond the geographic for thinking about the urban, and ends with a call to link the historical city with the urban world order of today.

Before looking at these issues, however, we need to first clarify a number of terms and definitions. First, what do we mean by the Middle East and North Africa? For the purposes of this volume, the editors have generally chosen to define the MENA region as stretching from Morocco to Iran and from Turkey to the Horn of Africa. This definition thus includes the twenty-two countries of the Arab League (including the Palestinian Authority enclaves in the West Bank and Gaza Strip), Turkey, Israel, Iran, and Cyprus. In adopting this definition, we need to point out some of the difficulties inherent in its usage. The usage of the term *Middle East and North Africa*, although seemingly straightforward, has been quite problematic. Why should these two distinct geographical regions, the Middle East and North Africa, be brought together as a single region? The first is in Asia, and the second, part of Africa. Surely those areas that share the Mediterranean seaboard have more in common with other Mediterranean littoral areas than with those that cluster around the Persian or Arab Gulf. There are considerable climatic and topographical differences in addition to significant linguistic and historical ones.

Part of the problem in defining the region and justifying its study as a coherent unit lies in the evolution of the term *Middle East* as a Eurocentric definition. Historically, the eastern Mediterranean seaboard and the Balkans were known as the Near East, in contrast to the Far East, defined as areas east of India. The Middle East was seen as the area in between. Then, during the First and Second World Wars of the twentieth century, Britain, the dominant power in the region at the time, established a military administration with responsibilities stretching from Iran to Libya, with its "General Headquarters Middle East" in Cairo. The term became increasingly used outside the military establishment to refer to this area and was even recognized within the region itself. By the Cold War, it had global currency. (The U.S. State Department has persisted with earlier connotations by combining two terms, with its *Near* and *Middle East* divisions, and the U.S. military has divided the same region into European, Middle East, and African commands.)

A further problem is the high degree of differentiation in the region when it is studied at a lower level, such as city level. Superficial similarities in culture, religion, and history across the region are quickly replaced by a number of subareas differentiated by geography, climate, and economy. For the purposes of studying contemporary urban change in the Arab countries of this region, Janet Abu-Lughod has delineated five types of countries whose economic makeup has a direct impact upon the functioning of cities.[1]

1. The economically marginal countries that have stagnating agriculture, little industry, and export labor (Sudan and Yemen)
2. Neocolonial countries whose economies are tied to Europe to the extent they have economic satellite status (e.g., Morocco and Tunisia)
3. The confrontation states that border Israel and whose economies have been distorted negatively from the long-running conflict (Egypt, Jordan, Syria, Lebanon, Palestinian areas, and, to a certain extent, Iraq)
4. The "Semi-Oil" states that moved from extensive agricultural production to an oil-based economy but whose development was affected by a decline in oil revenues (Algeria and latterly Iraq)
5. The rentier oil states whose oil-based economies integrated them into the world economy but that have suffered from price fluctuations affecting planning and diversification (Libya, Saudi Arabia, Bahrain, Qatar, Kuwait, United Arab Emirates, and Oman)

If one were also to consider the very different economies of Israel, Cyprus, and Turkey, the list of types and subregions within the MENA region would be very much extended. To what extent, then, is there any value in delineating a region so differentiated internally as a unit of study, and what impact does this have upon the study of its cities?

Like other area specialists of the MENA region, the editors contend that despite such internal differentiation, despite the collapse of a unitary framework like the Ottoman Empire, despite the increased hardening of borders in the twentieth century, despite the recent intrusion of Israel, despite the linguistic, ethnic, and religious differences, the MENA region is still sufficiently interlinked and shares a core of religious, linguistic, and historical experiences to offer a coherent unit of study. Clearly, the Arab core consider themselves a cultural and linguistic community sharing some collective myths and values, some experiences of resistance to colonialism, and external pressures. The reasons for including non-Arab countries (Turkey, Cyprus, Iran, and Israel) in the MENA unit are also valid. Since the rise of Islam and its spread, first through the Umayyad Empire, then the Abbasid Empire, and proceeding on to the Ottoman Empire, areas outside the core Arab areas were often integrated politically, militarily, and socially, which resulted in the region comprising a relatively homogenous cultural and political heritage. More important, perhaps, than these political structures is the shared religious tradition of Islam, a legal framework derived from a single basic source, the Qur'an, and for a time a lingua franca in the Arabic language among the commercial, political, and religious elites. In addition, the countries of the region experienced a similar pattern of economic relations with the rest of the world. Iran, Turkey, and Cyprus have much more in common with countries inside the MENA region than those outside it. The only exception is Israel, but it is a very recent arrival. Many of the cities of Palestine have a rich history prior to 1948 and continue to evolve in ways similar to those of cities of the wider Arab-Islamic hinterland today.

This introduction seeks to answer a second question: what is a city in the MENA region? Our initial response would be to respond that a city is a large urban settlement of a given minimum number of inhabitants with presumably some large historical monument such as a cathedral or mosque and with some administrative functions to indicate its importance as a national or regional center. With this flexible definition, it is clear that the size of population is only an indication, and other specific features need to be considered. The problem even with this broad definition is that it does not take historical change into account. Some cities were not always cities, while others no longer exist. Most readers would soon reflect that ancient and historical cities would not have the same population totals as a contemporary one and therefore could be excluded from the list when at points in their past history they were of great importance. Similarly, buildings decay or are demolished, rebuilt, or renovated over time; therefore, monumental features that were once important are overshadowed. In the same way, a city's role in the life of the region will change over time as new trade routes are developed or natural resources are exploited or rival cities become the seat of administration, governance, and power. The definition of what is a city, therefore, has to be flexible to take into account these changes and yet not be too broad as to make the term meaningless. This encyclopedia encompasses cities from the ancient period to the modern.

Moreover, there is a further complexity to consider. This encyclopedia is edited by two academics trained in a Western academic tradition, with contributions from people also trained in that tradition, and produced and marketed by a publishing company that also works within that tradition. Does our collective understanding of what constitutes a city reflect the patterns of urban settlement in the MENA region, or are there subtleties or refinements that also need to be included in the definition we work with? To what extent do our Western notions of city life encapsulate the urban tradition in the MENA region? Can our notions of municipal responsibilities and civic institutions be replicated, and are there other forms of organization or ways of expressing the urban that we would miss if we did not take care?

Here we touch upon an important discussion in academic circles that has been underway for half a century. The starting point for the academic debate around how best to understand and study cities was the work of the nineteenth-century German sociologist Max Weber (1864–1920). His notion of a city was based upon an ideal European type in which there was a "commune" comprising such institutions as craft guilds and chambers of commerce that "mediated" between organs of the state, such as a governor, and the populace. The debate among academics can be simply put: to what extent are cities of the MENA region like European ones, and to what extent do cultural factors such as the role of Islam as an organized religion or continuing tribal structures account for differences?

There are four main phases in the evolution of this debate. The first two focus on what the Japanese political scientist Masashi Haneda has termed the "hardware" and "software" of cities.[2] By the hardware of cities, Haneda is referring to the urban infrastructure, physical layout, and architecture. Research by academics in these fields has focused upon empirical studies of layout to identify what may be intrinsically Islamic or culturally specific to the MENA region. The results of surveys, or distillations of architectural plans, have been interpreted in a way to provide a contrast with the Weberian European model. Attention is drawn to the zigzagging narrow streets, blind alleys, the separation between the public and private space, and ethnically and vocationally segregated market areas.[3] Later academics noted that it was more than a coincidence that these studies took place during periods of colonial rule and accompanied the embedding of colonial administrative structures. And while they were empirically valuable, containing much useful basic data, their perspectives have been criticized for their loaded use of Orientalist concepts portraying the European model of a city as rational and dynamic while that of the MENA region as chaotic and stagnant. For example, R. Le Tourneau's study of the great North African city of Fez is marred by his manifestly inaccurate observation that "Fez has not changed for thousands of years."[4] This approach also saw the beginning of the academic quest for an all-encompassing definition of an Islamic city to match the Weberian European model.

The software of cities in the MENA region refers to people and their interaction. In the main it encompasses a range of political and social networks. These include tribal, religious,

or military affiliations; religious practices such as pilgrimages to tombs of holy personages or the extensive endowment system, or *awqaf;* trading patterns of the locality; and the economic interactions between the inhabitants of the city and the hinterland. Interest in these aspects was seen as an important corrective to the earlier essentialist view. Much work was carried out in identifying institutions such as guilds or networks that could be seen as "Islamic" and therefore likely to have fashioned the character and dynamic of the city.[5] These historical researchers still concerned themselves with the Weberian dichotomy but began to adopt a more textual-based methodology—that is, they were less concerned with drawings and maps but more concerned with data derived from Ottoman files; registers of the *sharia,* or Islamic court system; and *waqfiyya,* or endowment deed, documents. While some of the work by scholars such as Ira Lapidus was methodologically very rigorous, much of the work suffered from too general an extrapolation from historically specific studies. The studies of the bazaars of Aleppo in the Ottoman period did not and cannot necessarily tell us much about the suq of Marrakesh during the Al-Moravid period in Morocco.

The third main phase of debate among academics is the discussion around the usefulness of the term *Islamic,* both as an adjective and a concept, in the study of cities in the MENA region. It marks the entry of the social sciences into the debate in the 1960s, particularly the sociologists and cultural anthropologists. Their approach is to argue whether the Islamic city exists or existed at all and whether it was merely a construct devised by Western scholars that resulted in an illusory and romanticized depiction of urban forms in the MENA region. Instead, they turned to alternative terms and models to explain the pattern of relations and physical layout of cities in the region. Notable among these scholars were J. Abu-Lughod, K. Brown, and D. F. Eickelman.[6] Those adopting this third approach believed that an examination of Islamic cultural values such as *qurba,* or closeness, and their role in social networks and the distribution of residences, or the presence of Islamic law as a permeating principle in the organization of public and private space, was a more fruitful way to understand the growth and dynamics of cities in the MENA region. They, however, have been criticized for not going far enough in their rejection of the notion of an Islamic city. Their approach merely sought to be more culturally attuned to reveal the underlying rationality in the patterns of urban hardware and software derived from such sources.

The fourth approach, the anti-Orientalist critique, is more trenchant in its rejection of the idea of the Islamic city concept. As one who straddles the third and fourth approaches, Abu-Lughod has written:

> How is it that we have a large body of literature about an intellectual construction of reality called the "Islamic city" while

we have few or no articles, books, and conferences about the Christian city, the Buddhist City, the Hindu City, or the Pagan City?[7]

This position is that the values and discourses of academe in the Western world have been conditioned and framed by the monopoly of power of the Western states. In turn, the discourse has framed research that is used to consolidate and justify the West's domination of other cultures and to present the latter as defective and in opposition to those of the dominant culture. The result has been the construction of an Orient and an "ideal" of cities of the MENA region along essentialist lines that overlook, on the one hand, commonalities between the Arab-Islamic world and the West and, on the other, internal differentiation.

This view has been widely accepted by mainstream academia, and the current period in research has seen its consolidation and a process of reflection as to whether the anti-Orientalist critique is the final word in the quest of the Islamic city. Recently, there have been a number of reservations expressed about how the anti-Orientalist critique has resulted in a tendency to minimize the value of the outside perspective and the detached observer.[8] However, there is at present a perception that the variegated nature of the MENA region has been accepted and that comparative work with European cities can be useful to some extent but should not be the template upon which an understanding of cities of the MENA region be based.

Almost in parallel with these debates existed another closely related debate, one that has recently come into prominence. This latest phase is derived from two sources. First, there is the growing awareness for the need to conserve the ancient and traditional parts of many of the cities in the MENA region. As will be discussed below, the rapid changes to the infrastructure and use of cities has led to transformations in the hardware ranging from the wholesale demolition of city walls and quarters to severe neglect and inappropriate use leading to dilapidation and slum conditions. A growing awareness developed that the loss or misuse of these structures would deprive the cities of certain irreplaceable aesthetics and a sense of history and belonging. Second, there is recognition that much of late twentieth-century construction and planning has atomized society and created huge problems of alienation and dissonance. There is thus a growing interest in reviving traditional techniques of design and construction and the use of local material.

As a result, a new generation of professionals, town planners, and architects has begun to see the old quarters of the cities in the MENA region as a reservoir of knowledge of building techniques and responses to changing climatic, sociological, and logistical conditions. Akin to a seed bank, they were essential to preserve if future generations were to respond to

new challenges. Assisted and to some extent prompted by international conventions on architectural conservation and United Nations Educational, Scientific, and Cultural Organization (UNESCO) programs, and on the work of the Aga Khan Foundation, a body of technical literature (but often contextualized by socioeconomic and political data) has arisen and added to the debate.

To some extent, by focusing upon architectural issues and having to make assumptions about what values are being conserved both in the structures and the society they frame, this contribution by conservation architects reopens questions about the Islamic nature of the city. It is now widely recognized that the process of celebrating and restoring a heritage is not value free. The identification of what is the heritage of a city is usually carried out by educated professionals, bourgeois elites, and national and international funding agencies. In many cases, they will have internalized Western conceptions of an ideal city of the MENA region or at least be at variance with the needs or aspirations of the usually impoverished inhabitants of the quarters being conserved.

These, however, are micro-level policy issues that are the subject of many debates at conferences and in the literature. What is of greater relevance to this introduction is the attempt to identify certain common approaches that have confronted builders, architects, and planners in the MENA region over the ages but in a way that does not weigh it down with Orientalist baggage and dichotomies. Thus, there is recognition of the influence of the climate on both the design of the quarter or suburb and of the structure itself. Hence, the many high walls, domed roofs, covered arcades and bazaars, courtyards, rooftop terraces, wind catchers, slatted windows, and gardens are all designed to both keep out the heat and collect cooling breezes. Similarly, there is recognition of the role played by Islamic jurisprudence in determining the layout and structure of buildings. For example, the degree to which neighbors are permitted to overlook each other's houses has affected the position and style of windows as well as points of access to the house. The twisting, winding streets, with archways, cul-de-sacs, and overhanging windows, are an expression of such regulatory principles in some cities. Finally, there is awareness that modes of transportation, generally pedestrian and pack beast of burden rather than cart or coach, has been the key factor in determining the width of access routes and the nature of entry points to the city.

As has been already implied, this reevaluation of the past and how it may help in rethinking the future of the cities of the MENA region has been brought about by the rapid changes in the region since the last World War. In less than fifty years, the urban population of the MENA region has increased from 20 percent to more than 70 percent, leading to the growth of huge conurbations and megacities. In addition, there has been a dramatic increase in the population of small and medium-sized towns. Likewise, the primacy of certain cities within their states has grown tremendously. Egypt, for example, continues to be dominated by Cairo, with 12.6 percent of the total population and nearly one-third of the country's urban population. Nevertheless, regional towns such as Port Said, Suez, and Minya are becoming cities with annual growth rates of 3 to 4 percent. This pattern is replicated across North Africa and the Levant. In contrast to the mid-twentieth century, life, society, and politics in the MENA region in the twenty-first century is becoming urban life, urban society, and urban politics.

Such an accelerated process of change involves a wide range of stresses on the structural fabric of the city and the pattern of social and political behavior. It is true that increases in urbanization can be correlated with increases in per capita income, as the examples of Kuwait and Israel confirm. Nevertheless, this can be an abstract comfort for those living in substandard housing without piped water or electricity and in areas of high density. Most of the inhabitants of contemporary cities in the MENA region are experiencing not only the trauma of migration but also difficulties associated with integration as new residents and with the attendant problems of orientation, acculturation, and unemployment. This, in turn, is leading to the creation of new political and religious affiliations and constituencies that shift the balance of power and coalition of interest groups.

These all combine to produce a fragmented and possibly deeply alienated population whose demands have to be accommodated by state systems that are, by and large, defective and not up to the task of absorbing such changes. The adoption of Western planning, design, and construction techniques and values to establish mass-housing complexes on the outskirts only exacerbates the sense of dislocation. In addition, the flight of the traditional families from the old quarters of the cities to be replaced by new rural immigrants creates an environment where the congestion and overcrowding is not ameliorated and diffused by old family ties and strong communal bonds. All these processes combined have fed much of the Islamic radicalism and militancy in the MENA region. The overall result can be large squatter settlements on the margins of big cities bereft of government services and infrastructure and over which government control is weak or mediated through powerful family or religious interests. In these circumstances, the prospect for heightened conflict and tension is very likely.

Michael Dumper

Notes

1. Janet Abu-Lughod, "Urbanization in the Arab World and the International System," in *The Urban Transformation of the Developing World,* ed. Josef Gugler, 193 (Oxford: Oxford University Press, 1996).

2. Masashi Haneda, "Iran," in *Islamic Urban Studies: Historical Review and Perspectives,* ed. Masashi Haneda and Toru Miura, 235 (London: Kegan Paul International, 1994).

3. William Marcais, "L'Islamisme et la vie urbaine," in *Comptes-rendus des séances, Académie des Inscriptions et Belles-Lettres* (Paris: L. Massignon, 1928); William Marcais, "Les corps de métiers et la cité islamique," *Revue internationale de sociologie* 28 (1921); Gustave von Grunebaum, *Islam: Essays in the Nature and Growth of a Cultural Tradition* (London: Routledge and Kegan Paul, 1955), 141–158.

4. Roger Le Tourneau, *Fes avant le protectorat* (Casablanca: Société marocaine de librairie et d'édition, 1949).

5. Eliyahu Ashtor, "L'administration urbaine en Syrie médiévale," *Revista deglistudi orientali* 31 (1956): 72–128; Claude Cahen, "Mouvements populaires et autonomisme urbaine dans l'Asie musulmane au moyen age," *Arabica* 5 (1959): 225–250; 6 (1959): 25–56, 233–260; Gustave von Grunebaum, *Islam: Essays in the Nature and Growth of a Cultural Tradition* (London: Routledge and Kegan Paul, 1955), 141–158; Ira M. Lapidus, *Muslim Cities in the Later Middle Ages* (Cambridge: Cambridge University Press, 1967).

6. Janet Abu-Lughod, "The Islamic City: Historic Myth, Islamic Essence and Contemporary Relevance," *International Journal of Middle Eastern Studies* 19 (1987): 155–176; Janet Abu-Lughod, "What Is Islamic about a City? Some Comparative Reflections," in *Urbanism in Islam: The Proceedings of the International Conference on Urbanism in Islam, Vol. 1,* ed. Yukawa Takeshi, 193–217 (Tokyo: Research Project Urbanism in Islam, 1989); Janet Abu-Lughod, "Urbanization in the Arab World and the International System," in *The Urban Transformation of the Developing World,* ed. Josef Gugler, 193 (Oxford: Oxford University Press, 1996); Kenneth Brown, *People of Sale: Tradition and Change in a Moroccan City, 1830–1930* (Manchester: Manchester University Press, 1976); Dale F. Eickelman, "Is There an Islamic City? The Making of a Quarter in a Moroccan Town," *International Journal of Middle Eastern Studies* 5 (1974): 274–294.

7. Cited in Masatoshi Kisaichi, "Maghrib," in *Islamic Urban Studies: Historical Review and Perspectives,* ed. Masashi Haneda and Toru Miura, 41 (London: Kegan Paul, 1994).

8. See, for example, chapter 7 in Fred Halliday, *Islam and the Myth of Confrontation* (London: I. B. Tauris, 1996).

The Wonders of Cities and the Marvels of Seeing Cities Comparatively

There are many alternative approaches to studying the cities in the MENA region. An encyclopedia is one convenient and comfortable mechanism for gaining an overview and for beginning such an investigation. The traditional way of using an encyclopedia is to look up a single entry of interest and then move on, returning at a later date to consult another entry. However, the very presentation of information in this type of format frames the understandings of cities in the Middle East and North Africa one acquires in four crucial ways. The first is that cities are presented as discrete entities, ordered alphabetically, which delinks them from other cities with which they may be tied in vibrant networks. The very act of looking up a city alphabetically disconnects the student from the city's historical patterns of flow and exchange with other cities, stressing instead a vision of the city as an autonomous actor, bounded and self-contained.

Such framing does offer substantial benefits, in particular, being able to see the target city across time and to compare any one point in its history with any other subsequent or prior period. A city as a changing and resurgent actor, experiencing its own cycles of highs and lows, comes to the fore. The expansion and contraction, the failures of elites and leaders, the everyday of the city are nicely exposed in viewing the city as bounded and contained within itself. The ancient Sumerian word for *wall* or fortification *(uru-as* or *duru)* evolved into their word for a *city (uru);* from the very beginning of human civilization, cities have tended to be seen in this way as bounded, contained, discrete. It is important, therefore, that one approaches each city and its trajectory aware of this inherent bias toward separation and the backgrounding of connectedness. John Friedmann calls this the "historic city" perspective.[1] In fact, looking across the full trajectory of a city does provide considerable benefits not usually found in most studies of a city: what is readily available in the literature usually emerges from a concern for a particular time period or context. For example, numerous studies of Mamluk Cairo exist, but it is rarer to find a complete review from a city's founding to the present; in fact, many of the cities in this volume have never received a comprehensive study such as that available for a city such as Cairo.

The second result of presenting cities of MENA in an encyclopedia is that it is difficult to carry out comparative analysis. The cities are not framed in a comparative fashion, and so the student must do the heavy lifting to compare cities with others in the volume. If a student can transcend the limits of the encyclopedic format, however, numerous insights await him or her via the comparative process. A first simple level of comparison is, of course, provided by grouping cities of the geographic region MENA together into one package. Yet, as mentioned in the first part of this introduction, even this is not without controversy or challenge. What are the geographic boundaries of the MENA region? What insights get lost if we choose a particular geographic conceptualization of the Middle East and North Africa over some alternative? Are there better ways to define this collective that are beyond territorial and that may be more useful for analytical purposes? This is where comparison comes in, and comparison is somewhat difficult to accomplish given the encyclopedic format. The inquisitive student will want to read any particular entry with an eye out for comparisons with other cities or to approach the whole volume in a more analytical fashion to squeeze greater benefit from the work. For example, one conventional approach would be to compare cities in a particular subregion: cities around the Red Sea littoral or those in the Persian Gulf, along the Nile, or on the Mediterranean. Such an approach should highlight a range of similarities within the subregion that are obscured by a MENA perspective. Another comparison would be to seek out those commonly affected by large-scale historic events: for example, those cities incorporated into the Roman Empire in the East after 60 BC, or the cities destroyed by Temür, or those that entered the twentieth century as colonial cities. Alternatively, comparisons on the basis of roles should be particularly instructive: port cities, pilgrimage cities, capital cities, security cities. The comparison of cities caught up in particular commodity chains or transshipment networks (the Silk Road, spice trade, salt cities, drug cities, slave cities) could be insightful, as would be comparing a number of cities across time (why did Ebla and Ugarit die but Nippur, Izmir, and Baghdad continue to come back to life after destruction?). Thus, comparison of various types can take the student of MENA cities well beyond the limits of the encyclopedic format.

Third, the presentation of cities in an encyclopedic format makes it easy to lose a sense of the common themes that cities share at particular points in history: Under globalization, what is changing for all cities in the region? How did the introduction of European economic and military power in the Indian Ocean and the Mediterranean after 1500 begin to shift political power and lead to imperialism? Why has Islamist mobilization been more effective in some cities than in others? How did the split between Rome and Parthia or Byzantium and the Sassanians hurt the cities along the Euphrates? The astute reader of this encyclopedia should be able to achieve some initial insight into such questions by reading multiple entries.

Fourth, limiting one's reading to discrete city entries misses the opportunity to begin investigating fundamental questions for which we need some explanations: What forces lead to the creation of city coalitions (such as the Philistine, Ionian, Decapolis, Shia Triangle, or Phoenician city systems)? Why are certain cities more able to resist the overlordship of empires or states than others (Tyre and the Assyrians) and to retain some agency in the face of significant pressure? What factors bring a city into global prominence almost overnight while leaving others as dead ends in the world economy? What happens to cities when technology shifts their long-distance trade routes? How can cities reclaim their primacy over the hinterland once it is lost? Where does a city end and its hinterland begin? Perhaps there is no longer any such thing as a "city" that can be distinguished as separate from the regional or global political economy or the "urban."[2] Are the flows and exchange networks of cities more important than the built environment in the way people live the everyday city?

Many of the well-known travelers in history passed through cities presented in this encyclopedia, sometimes recording their impressions and comparisons. Ibn Battuta (1304–1368) is one of the best known and most widely traveled. He lived in a globalized world order, conceptualized as the Dar al-Islam, which was grounded on a network of cities stretching from his home in Tangier to Makkah, Zanzibar, Timbuktu, and Samarkand. In his *Rihla* (full title, *A Gift to Those Who Contemplate the Wonders of Cities and the Marvels of Traveling*), this fabled traveler records how he passed from one urban center to another in the company of clerics, pilgrims, merchants, and princes. Like a spider's web, the cities that were encompassed within his understanding of his world lay before him, and serendipity often drove his decision to choose one path over another. One way to understand the selection of cities in this volume is to ask whether Ibn Battuta visited this city. If he did, the city belongs in the encyclopedia. Although not every city he visited is included, and although not every city in the volume is a "Tangerine city," the theme remains significant. Ultimately, a powerful alternative to conceptualizing the MENA as a geographic or state-based concept is that of process geography, where flow and action create the boundaries rather than having them decided arbi-

trarily on a reading of rivers, seas, mountains, or temporary state regulations.[3] Thus, within this encyclopedia is imbedded an alternative conceptualization of the MENA that sees the region as emergent from an armature of cities connected by various flows of exchange, ideas, and effect. The region can be conceived as the result of lived cities and flows, connected across a range of networks, rather than seeing the region as determining the cities to be included. Thus, this volume includes a number of cities that may produce a fairly strong response: those are not MENA cities, one might say of Timbuktu, Zanzibar, Samarkand, and Baku. Yet from a flow point of view, it can be argued that they were "edge cities" for the MENA: nodes where flows of trade, religious training, credit, or guns ended or were transformed into something else. A careful comparative reading of the entries in this volume can reveal a moving set of edges to the MENA across time cycles of ebb and flow where boundaries shift as cities become included or excluded from patterns of exchange. Marco Polo cities, those mentioned by Strabo, cities visited by Leo Africanus, and Richard Burton's exotic destinations are all other ways to see edges to the MENA regions underlying city structure. One could argue that Dubai and Tel Aviv are not Middle Eastern cities because of their tight connections beyond the region rather than within its geographic definition; or that Baghdad was, during the 1990s sanctions, excluded and cut off from being a Middle Eastern city, existing in a black hole.[4]

The careful reader will also find examples of cities actively pursuing their own power and agency within national and imperial frameworks, despite our general assumptions of limited municipal control and domination. Municipal foreign policy, where cities reach out transnationally to shape and form their own destiny, has existed throughout recorded history. Examples of aggressive, proactive elites pursuing the interests of their own cities are in strong evidence in the current global context, but a comparative analysis using this volume demonstrates that this is not just a twenty-first-century phenomena related to "globalization." The reader could actually come away from this encyclopedia affirming the ongoing power of cities to overcome layers of bureaucracy and domination rather than accepting conventional wisdom that frames the historical record as one of imperial or national control over local elites. This encyclopedia is full of examples of resurgent, creative, and dissimulating cities whose actors struggle against their loss of control over their own destiny and often win. In fact, the volume might be read as a hymn to urban resilience, perseverance, and continuation, despite all the examples of violence, destruction, and restriction it contains.

There certainly is a disturbing record of violence, pain, hatred, and destruction contained in these 100 stories. Read from the point of view of conflict and conflict management, there is not a city contained here that has not been besieged, invaded, sacked, raided, or forced to offer ransom. Interestingly, some cities are more prone to destruction than others, and it is not always just the luck of the draw. Rather, political savvy on the part of local leaders, available wealth and resources, location, arrangements with other cities for protection, or depth of hinterland and water are often determinative. Read from another direction, however, many cities experienced long periods of peace and prosperity, and not just by dominating their neighbors or through naked power. Particularly, the cult or Holy Cities drew strength from a different source than did mercantile, security, or capital cities for their longevity. Vanity cities, created by emperors or kings as monuments to their glory, have various histories: some disappear without a trace after a generation or two; others are able to build a broader role and to exist into the future when the power slips away. Security cities seem, interestingly, to remain security cities across much of their trajectory; is this simply location or something more complicated? Ultimately, cities are at the core of the struggle for power in human society, and it is within them and about them that conflict occurs and where conflict transformation must also take place. This was as true in the Uruk of 3000 BC as it is in the Baghdad of 2006. If the cities of the Middle East and North Africa are to live up to their history as the central core of human civilization, they must be the sites where humans discover ways to overcome inevitable human conflict, to handle it, and to transform it into a viable urban future.

These 100 cities do not claim to represent the "top," most important, or "critical" cities in the region. Of course, there is some of that justification in the selection of many of them. But many "less important" cities are included here as well. In fact, one of the realizations that emerges from reading all these entries is that each city has a fascinating story to tell, and its trajectory is just as interesting as that of its neighbor. There are "8 million stories in the Naked City," and presented here are just a few of them; likewise, these 100 stories could be combined with 1,000 more, and it would still be enlightening reading.

So, choose to take a journey back 4,000 years to the foundations of a single historical city and watch it grow, *SimCity*-like in its evolution and development. Or start from the urban present, with its poverty, illegal cities, gray economies, and hope, and look for shared struggles. Jump from the ports of the Atlantic to the shores of the Arabian Sea, or from the oases of the central Asian steppes to the banks of the Niger Bend. Uncover dead cities forgotten by those who build houses within their ruins, explore boomtowns that appear where humans have never lived before, or watch phoenix cities reemerge again and again across millennia of human history. But remember, as you read, the people living their lives in this place and using these networks, those who built the city and called it home. Lewis Mumford, in his magisterial volume *The City in History,* looked both forward and to the past:

> If we would lay a new foundation for urban life, we must understand the historic nature of the city, and distinguish between its original functions, those that emerged from it, and those that may still be called forth. Without a long running start in history, we shall not have the momentum needed, in our own consciousness, to take a sufficiently bold leap into the future.[5]

Bruce Stanley

Notes

1. John Friedmann, *The Prospect of Cities* (Minneapolis: University of Minnesota Press, 2002), xii.
2. Ibid.
3. See Arjun Appadurai, *Modernity at Large: Cultural Dimensions of Globalization* (Minneapolis: University of Minnesota Press, 1996).
4. Bruce Stanley, "Middle East City Networks and the 'New Urbanism.'" *Cities* 22, no. 3 (2005): 189–199.
5. Lewis Mumford, *The City in History* (New York: Harcourt, 1961), 3.

Regional and Sub-Regional Maps

Middle East and North African Cities

North Africa and Egypt

Red Sea and East Africa

Eastern Mediterranean

Mesopotamia

Iranian Plateau and Central Asia

Persian Gulf and Arabia

Anatolia

Middle East and North African Cities

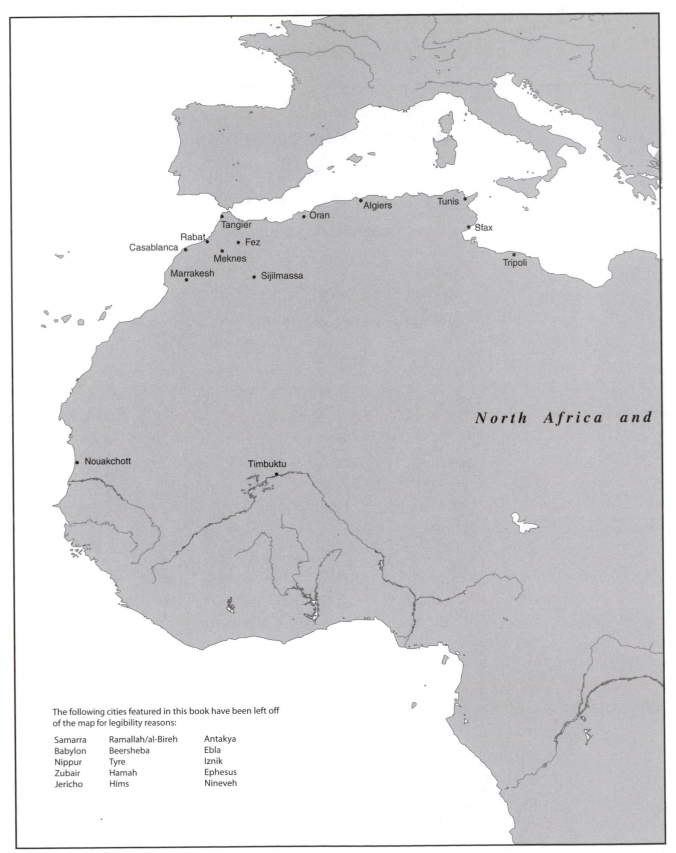

Tangier
Rabat
Casablanca
Fez
Meknes
Marrakesh
Sijilmassa
Oran
Algiers
Tunis
Sfax
Tripoli

North Africa and

Nouakchott

Timbuktu

The following cities featured in this book have been left off
of the map for legibility reasons:

Samarra	Ramallah/al-Bireh	Antakya
Babylon	Beersheba	Ebla
Nippur	Tyre	Iznik
Zubair	Hamah	Ephesus
Jericho	Hims	Nineveh

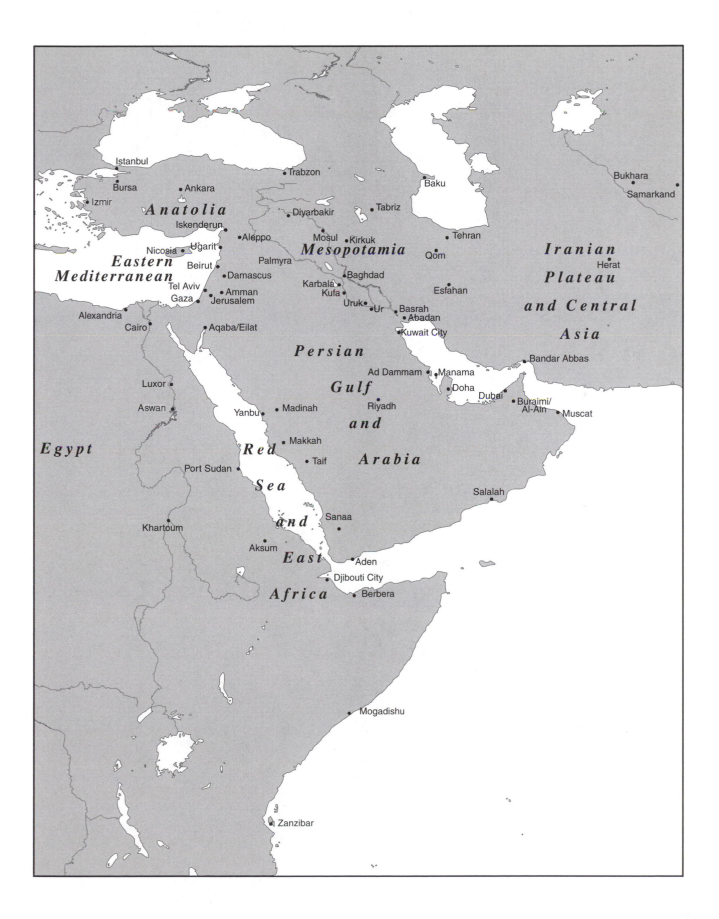

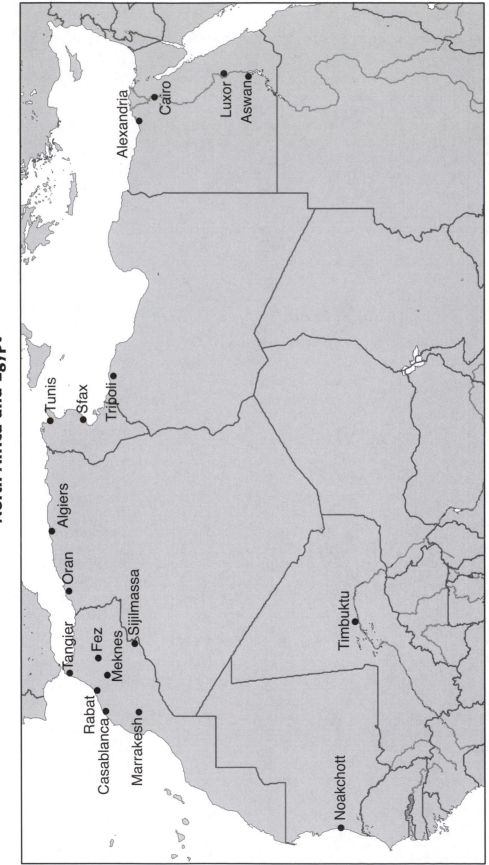

North Africa and Egypt

Tangier
Rabat
Casablanca
Marrakesh
Fez
Meknes
Sijilmassa
Oran
Algiers
Tunis
Sfax
Tripoli
Alexandria
Cairo
Luxor
Aswan
Timbuktu
Noakchott

Red Sea and East Africa

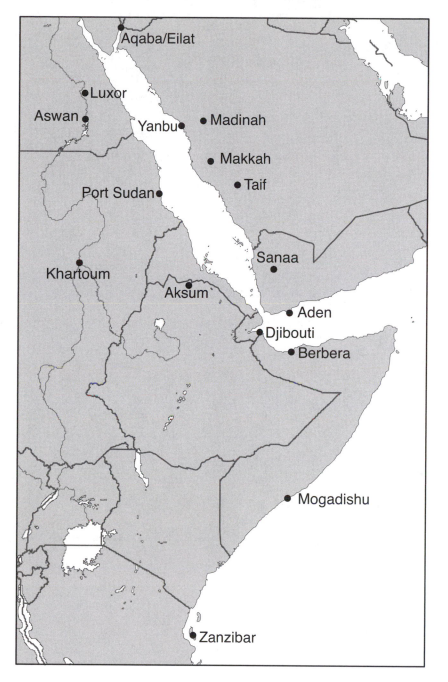

Eastern Mediterranean

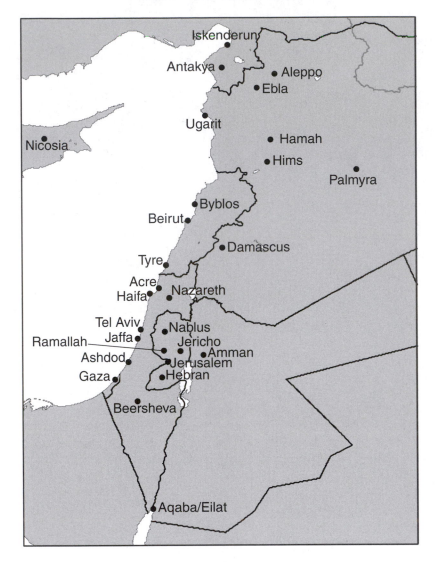

Mesopotamia

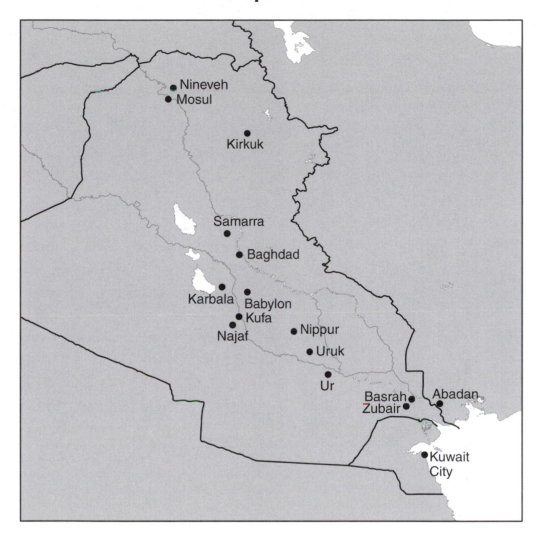

Iranian Plateau and Central Asia

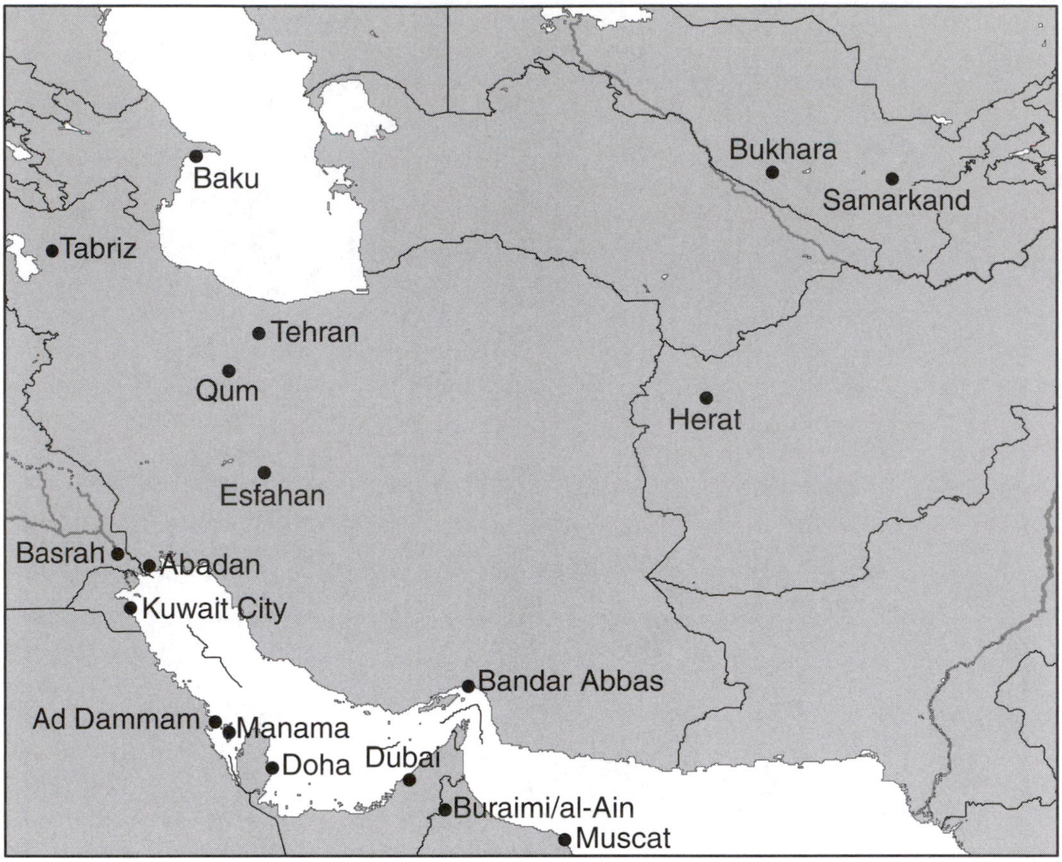

Baku

Tabriz

Bukhara

Samarkand

Tehran

Qum

Herat

Esfahan

Basrah Abadan

Kuwait City

Bandar Abbas

Ad Dammam Manama

Doha Dubai

Buraimi/al-Ain

Muscat

Persian Gulf and Arabia

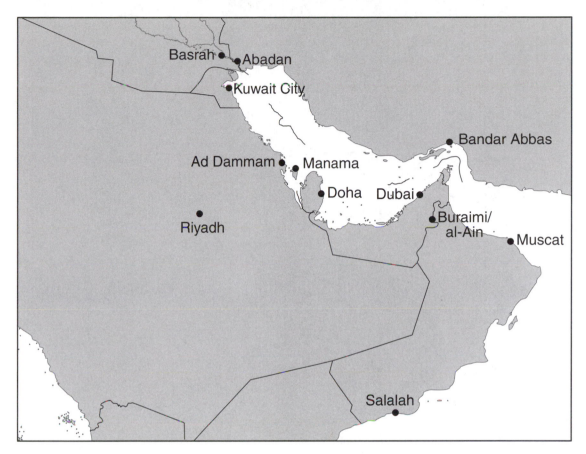

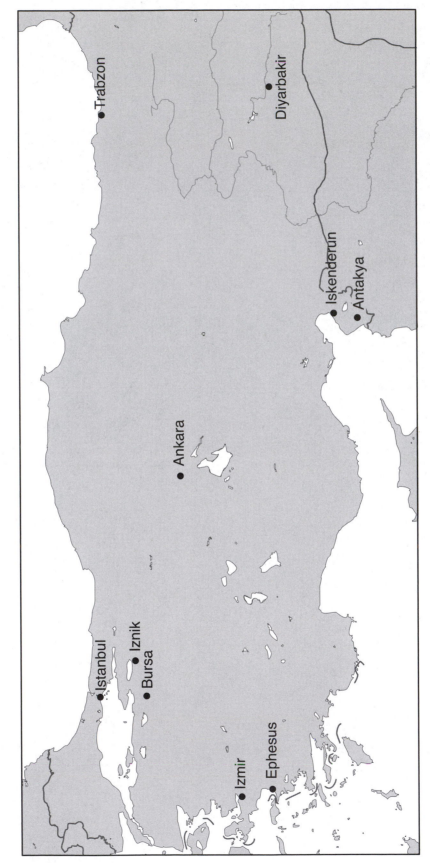

Anatolia

Trabzon

Diyarbakir

Iskenderun
Antakya

Ankara

Istanbul
Iznik
Bursa

Izmir
Ephesus

CITIES OF THE MIDDLE EAST AND NORTH AFRICA

A

Abadan
Population: 350,000 (2005 estimate)

Abadan lies on a small island just off the Iranian coast of the Shatt al-Arab just in from the head of the Persian Gulf. Until recently the site of the largest oil refinery in the world, this small city was originally known for its role as the guardian to the Shatt al-Arab and as home to Sufi monasteries and holy shrines. For the last 100 years, Abadan has been a "company town," created initially by the Anglo-Persian Oil Company (APOC) and now run by the National Iranian Oil Company (NIOC) to house the labor employed in the extraction and processing of Iranian oil. One of the most famous ports in the world, Abadan is home to a significant Arab minority and remains caught up in regional tension and conflict.

Abadan (Arabic, *Abadan*) lies in the southeastern province of Khuzistan, Iran, in the delta of the Shatt al-Arab. It is the terminus of major oil pipelines and is a key oil-refining and shipping center. Abadan Island is about forty miles long and between two to twelve miles wide, depending on the height of the tide. Abadan is not a natural island but emerged when the local rivers were linked to the Shatt al-Arab by a canal. Largely covered by salt marshes in the past, Abadan's soil remains highly salinated, and native crops are limited to dates and henna. The city lies some forty miles from the open Gulf and eight miles south of the port city of Khorramshahr (Muhammara). Until the late 1800s, there were no islands south of Abadan in the Shatt al-Arab; those that now exist have been created by silt deposits since that time.

There is little agreement on the source of the name *Abadan*. It may derive from the Arabic *abbad* (worshipers), referring to the shrines and holy sites that dot the island. An alternative foundational myth is that the town was founded between AD 695 and AD 714 by Abbad b. Hosayn Kabeti as a garrison town and subsequently was named after him. A third suggestion, by Iranian etymologists, points to the derivation of *ab* (water) and the root *pa* (to watch or guard), from which they eventually arrive at "coast guard station." As early as the campaigns of the Assyrian Sennacharib (ca. 700 BC) there is reference to an island at the mouth of the Euphrates, and Ptolemy refers to the island of Apphana. Pliny refers to the island in the first century AD, as does the great Arab geographer Yaqut (1179–1229), who mentions Abadan as the port at the mouth of the Euphrates. By the fourteenth century, Abadan was six miles from the open sea. By the 1900s, it was twenty miles from the open Gulf.

Reflecting a similar trend as its neighbor Basrah, Abadan was the site of the first Sufi *khaniqa* (guest house) and madrasa in Persia, established in 767 by Abd-al-Wahid ibn Zayd and his followers. The island remained an important center of Sufism for the next 100 years before the monastery was destroyed in 874. Despite losing the main monastery, Abadan continued to attract pilgrims to its remaining shrines, monasteries, and pilgrim hostels. As a result, the island became known as the Island of Khidr (in one version of the story, this name refers to the prophet Elias who was reputed to have lived here), and thus became a site for holiness and contemplation. The city's most imposing monuments to this day remain its shrines. Ibn Battuta, who visited the island in 1326, found a small religious community, including hermits and religious students, and considered spending the rest of his life there as a student of a master.

Abadan also played a role as a garrison town to ward off attacks by pirates or to control access into the Shatt al-Arab. For the Abbasids with their capital in Baghdad, it was one of their ports leading outward to the riches of the world. Its importance to navigation and shipping goes back to the earliest period after its founding, with the building of a wooden lighthouse in 951. Abadan's role as guardian of access into and out of the Persian Gulf has continued up to the recent Gulf wars.

In medieval times, dates formed the major crop and remained until the twentieth century the primary source of income for Abadan's inhabitants. This was backed up by the export of henna as a secondary crop, but Abadan first found international fame as a maker and exporter of cheap but high-quality straw mats (*hasir*), which were sought after as far abroad as Egypt.

The area near the mouth of the Shatt al-Arab came under Ottoman control after 1546, and the Ottoman naval base at Basrah affirmed their security interests in the area. The region was contested from 1600 to 1639 between the Safavid Empire and the Ottomans, but in the Treaty of Zohab (1639), the two empires reached the first of a series of agreements concerning their borders along the Shatt al-Arab. In 1847, within a context of increasing British and Russian political interest in the region and the modernization of the empire's central administration, the cities of Muhammara (Khorramshahr) and Abadan, despite their majority Arab populations, were deeded from the Ottoman dynasty to the Persians. The British, through their Political Resident in Basrah, retained a key interest in their hegemonic role in the Shatt al-Arab and by 1913 were reaffirming the Iranian rights to

Abadan. Again in 1937, Iraq and Iran were encouraged to clarify the eastern coast of the Shatt al-Arab as Iranian and Abadan as part of their territory. In 1975 a further agreement marked the boundary between the two states as the middle of the Shatt al-Arab, thus retaining Abadan for Iran.

Throughout most of its history, Abadan remained a small town on an island covered in hamlets and palm groves. In 1900 the island housed around 24,000 Bani-Kaab Arab tribesmen. With the discovery of the Khuzistan oil fields, and in the wake of the D'Arcy Concession of 1908, major expansion and economic growth began. With its position at the head of the Tigris and proximity to the Persian Gulf via the Port of Muhammara, Abadan was ideally suited as a site for an oil refinery and for the direct importation of equipment to supply the oil fields. APOC initially leased one square mile of the shoreline from Shaykh Khazal of Muhammara but eventually extended this to five square miles and opened a refinery in 1912, with an initial annual capacity of 120,000 tons. During World War I, two-thirds of the refinery's production went to the British Admiralty. By 1918 the capacity of the refinery increased to 1 million tons. By 1930, although the technology of the refinery was by this time seriously out of date, its capacity rose to 5 million, and by the end of World War II the recrafted Abadan oil refinery was producing more than 17 million tons annually. This culminated in 1960, when it officially became the world's biggest oil refinery, producing 21 million tons per year.

The centrality of Abadan for oil production has resulted in numerous political crises concerning control of its chief product. The first was in 1921, when Standard Oil of New Jersey, an American company, obtained an oil concession near Abadan. This threatened the British monopoly there, causing Lord Curzon to complain to the Americans about this "unfriendly" act and ask for the concession to be disqualified. Later, in 1951, what became known as the "Abadan Crisis" centered around the nationalization by Iranian Prime Minister Mossadeqh of the APOC refinery at Abadan. This led to British contingency plans for a military attack on the refinery, British warships threatening to bombard the city, and a global boycott of production from the refinery, and in 1953 the United States supported a coup against Mossadeqh in support of the Shah.

The demographic development of Abadan is inextricably bound up with the discovery and rise in importance of oil. The needs of the boomtown for young male migrant workers attracted thousands of new immigrants, including a new community of 5,000 Armenians. This company town saw the APOC and then the NIOC providing segregated housing and supplies for the workers and also attempting social engineering via control and security. In 1943 there were 25,000 employees of the oil company, representing one-quarter of the total population of 100,000. By 1950 there were more than 40,000. Almost overnight the new city of Abadan became the fifth-largest city in the country and the model of the modern industrial city in the Middle East.

This pool of oil workers meant a key political and social source of unrest and agitation. In 1929, for example, the "Abadan strike" by oil workers was the first major industrial action in the country's history, took on a decidedly anti-British and pro-nationalist tinge, and was repressed by military force. Similar themes appeared during the lead-up to the Iranian Revolution in 1979, when Abadan's 12,000 oil workers led the country's workers in the repudiation of the shah's authority. The Abadan oil workers were well organized into self-confident workers' committees, with a long tradition of trade union organizing, and they stood up to the provisional government in Tehran. The subsequent cycle of strikes, killings, and repression in Abadan played a significant role in mobilizing other cities in resisting the army and bringing on the Islamic Revolution.

One unique contingent of oil workers in Abadan during World War II were 400 Jews from Palestine who arrived in 1941 to fulfill a contract to build one part of the oil facility to supply the British war effort. Many members of this contingent were Zionists, and they used their three-year presence in Abadan to begin the first systematic effort of the Zionist Movement to proselytize the Jews of Iran and Iraq to move to Palestine.

This centrality to Iranian oil refining was not the only reason for the city's success. It also served as a shipping center for loading oil and a site for petrochemical production. After the 1960s, however, the Iranian government diversified its shipping and production sites along the Iranian coast, costing Abadan its centrality to Iranian oil. Even by the early 1920s, the APOC was having trouble with silting restricting access to the refinery, since fully loaded tankers could no longer reach the docks. Ultimately, the shipping center was relocated to Karg Island, and the refining of petrochemicals was moved to Bandar Imam Khomeini. This economic challenge to Abadan was staved off in 1966 by the creation of a joint company, Abadan Petrochemical Company, between the National Petroleum Company (NPC) and B. F. Goodrich for the production of polyvinyl chloride, dodecyl benzene, and caustic soda. Other employment opportunities appeared, courtesy of companies such as Nippon Petrochemical, or with various government and municipal services. This allowed Abadan to survive as a viable economic contributor to the Iranian economy.

From the late 1950s until the 1970s, life in this NIOC "company town" was very enjoyable for the professional elite. Dances at the Yacht Club and parties in the Caravanserai Hotel meant that some called it Iran's "Paris." The Abadan Band Club, the only jazz band in the country, played for the shah and the local elites at their events. The Braim district of the city, a gated community for foreign workers, offered luxurious grassy living for the managerial elites. In the other part of this "dual city," large housing tracts for the male workers in one-story yellow-brick houses spread out into the suburbs, with types of housing linked to the employment hierarchy. Such spatial division of labor, the formal public spaces, and the ultramodern structures marked Abadan off from almost all other Iranian cities. The Abadani accent, along with numerous English loan words, marked a local culture that was very cosmopolitan.

It was in Abadan that the infamous Cinema Rex, the acknowledged site for the beginning of the Iranian Revolution, was located. In August 1978, the cinema was locked and set on fire, resulting in the death of more than 400 people. Believing that the shah's secret service was behind the fire, mass demonstrations quickly engulfed the nation, leading to the shah's flight early the next year.

During the Iran-Iraq War (1980–1988), Abadan was a crucial early target for the invading Iraqis because of its oil production capabilities, and they sought to occupy the city. The defenders halted their advance, however, and for all of 1981 the city was under siege and bombardment, with the refinery destroyed and most of the city leveled. Iranian forces tried in January 1982 to lift the siege but failed; a second Iranian counterattack in September 1982 succeeded, at the cost of more than 10,000 casualties.

After the war, the Abadan Refinery only returned to its prewar levels of production in 1997. Thanks to the extensive damage suffered by the refinery's infrastructure, and a lack of investment by the government, Abadan no longer can be classified as the primary oil refinery in Iran. Nevertheless, by the beginning of the twenty-first century, it did seem that a revival was in progress. The first oil well dug in 1908 was still producing oil, and the area continued as a site for significant production. A special petrochemical economic zone was created in 1998 to boost local industries, increase trade, and enhance profits, and it was having a revitalization effect on the city's fortunes. Abadan produced more than 10,000 tons of goods per month, most of which were exported. The bulk of these goods was made up of oil derivatives, as might be expected, such as tires, plastics, and tar. The refinery was also increasing its production of intermediate goods, such as naphtha, destined for the petrochemical complex at Bandar Imam Khomeini.

In addition, the port of Abadan was increasingly a transshipment site for loading and off-loading of goods, and there was growth year after year. Passenger traffic via the city has also increased. The city is now shipping many goods to Basrah (vegetables and motorcycles, for example), and in early 2005 the government endorsed plans to establish a free-trade zone around Abadan and Khorramshahr to balance out similar processes occurring under U.S. leadership in Iraq (see also "Basrah"). The Petroleum University of Technology is attracting students, and the Abadan Museum is recovering from the theft of its treasures by Iraqi soldiers. Chic shops and restaurants give the appearance of develop-

ment and progress, although the "Paris" days of the period before the revolution have not returned. Since most of the city had been leveled in the fighting during 1980–1982, the government did move to redevelop the built environment of the city, particularly giving the rebuilding of homes an important priority. The upgrading of the Abadan refinery, the oldest in the Middle East, is currently in process, and an agreement was reached in 2005 to build an oil pipeline from Basrah, in Iraq, to Abadan. A new cross-border rail link has also been proposed.

Despite the economic upswing seen in Abadan and in the rest of Khuzistan Province, the city's redevelopment has been seriously hampered by a lack of available drinking water, and there have been many riots and demonstrations on this matter. July 2000 saw violent protests, brutally suppressed by the Revolutionary Guards, over the lack of available drinking water, as summer temperatures reached 125 degrees Fahrenheit.

There are still minefields around the city that have not been cleared, however, and on the edge of the city lies a huge cemetery dedicated to the martyrs of the battles to lift the siege of the city. Heroin addiction is on the increase, and babies are still born with deformities from the remaining effects of chemical weapons used in the fighting. AIDS, poverty, and unemployment remain significant problems, leading to further unrest and recent deadly confrontations with security services in the city. Some of the tension arises from the continued ethnic tensions in the city between the Arab minority and the Iranian majority. Other difficulties arise from the remaining gaps in the city's infrastructure caused by the war.

James Hartley

Further Readings
Chesney, Francis. R. *Narrative of the Euphrates Expedition.* London: Longmans Green, 1868.
Curzon, George. *Persia and the Persian Question.* London: Longmans Green, 1892.
Kemp, Norman. *Abadan: A First-Hand Account of the Persian Oil Crisis.* London: A. Wingate, 1953.
Sampson, Anthony. *The Seven Sisters: The Great Oil Companies and the World They Made.* London: Hodder and Stoughton, 1975.
Stewart, Richard A. *Sunrise at Abadan: The British and Soviet Invasion of Iran, 1941.* New York: Praeger, 1988.
Wilson, Arnold. T. *The Persian Gulf.* Oxford: Clarendon Press, 1928.

Acre
Population: 46,000 (2005 estimate)

Since ancient times, the gateway to Palestine has been considered the magnificent harbor at Acre. Now a small Israeli city with a mixed population of Palestinians and Jews, Acre has for more than 4,000 years served the hinterland of southern Syria with access to the long-distance trade routes of the Mediterranean. For a millennium a Canaanite city often under the direct rule of the pharaohs in Thebes, the city was subsequently besieged, destroyed, and rebuilt by the likes of Ramses II, King David, Ashurbanipal, Ptolemy II, Salah ad-Din, Richard the Lionheart, Napoléon, and Ibrahim Pasha. Its golden era was the two centuries it served as the key entry port and then capital of the Kingdom of Jerusalem, when Franks and Italian traders made it their link to Europe. Today its varied antiquities and monumental buildings attract many tourists, but the small fishing boats drawn up in front of its seaside restaurants are a poor substitute for the hundreds of pilgrim and grain ships that used to moor below its gates.

Acre (Canaanite, *Akko* or *Akka;* Greek, *Ace-Ptolemaïs;* Latin, *Saint Jean d'Acre* or *Acre*) is an ancient port city located on the eastern Mediterranean littoral. It sits on the northern corner of the large bay of Haifa (formerly the bay of Acre) on a small peninsula that juts out into the sea where the river Belus drains the plain of Akko; eight miles to the south, at the southern tip of the bay, lies Haifa. The city has an excellent harbor, usable under any sea conditions at any time of the year, unlike other ports, such as Jaffa, further along the coast. Thus, the site was valued for its safety and access as early as the second millennium BC. Historically Acre was the regional port for the western Galilee and its largest city. Around Acre, the coastal plain is intensively cultivated, and to the southeast stretches the fertile Jezreel Valley; directly south there were coastal marshy areas toward Haifa. Many transportation routes conversed on Acre, whether those along the coast to Lebanon, inland to Damascus, or southeast to Megiddo and the Palestinian highlands at Jenin. The great port of Tyre lies twenty-five miles to the north. Acre's walled city, surrounded on three sides by the sea, its central citadel, and the fortified harbor all helped give Acre an important military and commercial position on the coast, thus making it also a strategic prize for successive local warlords and imperial armies.

Acre is one of the oldest continuously inhabited cities in the world. Habitation on the Tel Akko site dates from before 2500 BC, and the city, known by its Canaanite name of Akko (perhaps meaning "hot sand"), appears in numerous Egyptian and Ugaritic texts over the next 1,500 years. There was strong Hyksos influence here during their domination of the coast and trade ties to Cyprus. Pliny the Elder (AD 23–79) argues that glassmaking was accidentally invented here where the river Belus runs into the Mediterranean; the river was long famous for the quality of its glass sand. Ramses II depicted his destruction of the city (ca. 1275 BC) on a relief at Karnak. By this period of the Late Bronze Age, Akko was the most important port city of central Canaan, involved in extensive trade networks around the eastern Mediterranean and with Egypt. The city was a crucial security city for the Egyptians during this time; Ramses II established a royal naval base in the city and shipped grain from the royal estates in the region. Excavations, however, demonstrate strong cul-

tural ties to Ugarit as well during the fourteenth to thirteenth century.

The archaeological record suggests a dramatic shift in the city's population after 1100 BC. It seems as if the city then became an outpost for the Sherdan Philistines at the beginning of the Iron Age, perhaps serving as mercenaries for the Egyptians or Sidonians. Canaanite cultural indications remain, and Israelite indicators start to appear as well. Thus, Akko was caught between various local and regional powers vying to control the region around Akko.

The city fell to David and the Israelites in the beginning of the tenth century. Phoenician influence returns, however, for most of the period from 900 to 700 BC. The town was captured by the Assyrians around 700 BC and virtually depopulated under Ashurbanipal; Assyrian texts note that at the time of these campaigns along the coast, Akko belonged to the King of Sidon. The city housed foreign traders and was an important cultural, commercial, and administrative center, even so. A few years later, Esarhaddon granted Akko to the Tyrians. During the sixth and fifth centuries, under the Persians, Akko was again considered the territory of a resurgent Sidon, and it played a security role for Artazerzes II; in 374 BC his campaign against Egypt was organized from Akko. Archaeological excavations demonstrate strong trade ties with Greece at this time, and Tyre remained the overlord of Akko.

In 332 BC, Akko was incorporated into the empire of Alexander the Great without a fight. Subsequently Ptolemy II, King of Egypt, seized the city in the third century BC and renamed it Ace-Ptolemaïs; he also relocated the city away from the ancient tell to its present site. The Seleucids and Ptolemies fought for control of this key port, and the city changed hands a number of times during the third and second centuries, finally falling to the Seleucids after the battle of Panias (198 BC). The Seleucids renamed it Antiochia and granted the city the privilege of asylum. It was repeatedly besieged, and in 142 BC Jonathan Maccabeus was captured in the city by the Seleucid Trypho and executed. Some sixty years later, the city, bizarrely, was attacked by Tigran II (95–55 BC), king of the Armenians, during his attempt to conquer Syria. By this time the city was autonomous and operated as an independent city-state, although Phoenicians made up a core elite, and they looked to Tyre for cultural direction (see also "Tyre").

In 48 BC, Julius Caesar incorporated the city into the Roman Empire, and, under the influence of Cleopatra, the name reverted to Ptolemaïs. Some coinage minted in the city continued to carry the Akko name in addition, indicating that the ancient traditions of the city had not been forgotten. The Romans improved its harbor, and the city grew into an important seaport, trading center, and glassmaking site. At first it was incorporated into Greater Syria but later was made a colony of Rome by Claudius ca. AD 54, perhaps because of its significance for grain transshipped from the Jezreel Valley to feed the citizens of Rome. To mark its new status, the boundaries of the city were ceremoniously plowed, and the name was changed again, this time to Germanica, to honor the defeat of the Germani.

After the permanent division of the Roman Empire in AD 395, the city, having reverted back to the Ptolemaïs name, belonged to the Eastern (later Byzantine) Empire, and by the beginning of the fifth century the city hosted a bishopric. The Arabs seized it in 636 as part of the early campaigns in Islamic expansion, and its port became known for its military usefulness to the Umayyads and for its shipbuilding industry.

It was under the rule of the Crusaders, however, that the city dramatically increased its regional importance. In 1104 King Baldwin I of Jerusalem captured it following a long siege, and then, for nearly 200 years, Acre became the point of entry for European penetration into the region and the most important military stronghold and base for the Frankish armies. The purpose of the Crusades may have been to secure access to Jerusalem, but the bridgehead was frequently Acre, given that the port was so secure. The city prospered from the influx of wealth and from being used as a base by powerful Crusader personages and orders, such as the Hospitallers and the Knights of Saint John. During truce periods between the Franks and the Muslims, its port was a center for commercial exchange between the lands of the West and the East. The multicultural nature of the city can be seen from coins, bearing both Arabic and Latin (Christian) inscriptions, discovered in its ruins. Nevertheless, political life in the Crusader domains was characterized by conflicts within and among the diverse commercial, religious, and national interests crowded together in Acre, and the constant threat to stability prevented Acre from developing into a large urban center to rival Cairo or Istanbul.

The Franks called the city Saint Jean d'Acre, which, gradually, for Westerners, evolved into Acre. The city initially was ruled from Jerusalem, but after 1191, for the next 100 years, it became the center of the rump kingdom when Jerusalem was lost. During Frankish rule, the city housed a royal mint and a royal quarter next to the port, and the walls were substantially reinforced. A new, outer harbor was constructed. Various Italian city-states established their own communes or quarters throughout the city (Genoese, Pisan, and Venetian), substantially altering its layout and built environment. The Hospitaller compound included the Palace of the Grand Master, a church, a Knight's Hall, and a rib-vaulted hospital. The Templar palace was a huge fortification and the last holdout when the city was taken in 1291.

Emigration schemes were offered to attract settlers to Acre and to its hinterland, and construction projects reshaped the city's urban plan. The landed elites often built two- to three-story *plazzi* (apartment blocks) and then leased some of the rooms to visiting merchants. It is recorded that the prices for the apartments closer to the pig market were lower than those elsewhere in the city.

By the early thirteenth century, Acre was one of the richest ports in the Mediterranean and a key center of international commerce. It may have had as many as 40,000 inhabitants. During Frankish rule, the city attracted many visitors. Abbot Nikulas, a cleric from Iceland, landed in Acre on his way to Jerusalem in 1151. Benjamin of Tudela visited Acre around 1159 and was impressed by its large harbor and the number of pilgrims arriving by ship. Maimonides was brought to the city as a boy and stayed for five months (1165). Marco Polo passed through on his way to see the Great Khan (1271). The most popular purchase for the pilgrims was special ampullae containing holy oil, all manufactured and sold in the city.

Salah ad-Din, sultan of Egypt and Syria, captured Acre in 1187. The besiegers used "Greek fire" in the attack and huge mangonel stones to batter down the walls. Richard the Lionheart subsequently recovered the city for the Franks four years later and massacred more than 3,000 of its inhabitants.

The final collapse of Crusader Acre came in 1291 after a long and bloody siege by the Mamluks. To deter any subsequent Frankish attempt to return, the Mamluks reduced the port, citadels, churches, and most other structures to rubble. In addition, they transferred district administration to Safed in Galilee, and when they eventually permitted visitors and pilgrims to visit the Holy Land, the required point of entry was the port of Jaffa, which was closer to Egypt and, because of its poorer natural defenses, easier to control. These actions ripped the heart out of this ancient city, and its population and significance declined precipitously.

The siege of Acre, 1191. From *Chroniques de France ou de St. Denis,* 1375–1400. (Erich Lessing/Art Resource)

The Ottomans succeeded the Mamluks as the dominant power in the region (1517) and took possession of Acre. A colony of French merchants subsequently built and managed the Khan al-Faranj (Inn of the Franks), one of seven such privileged trading posts that King Francis I of France founded on the coast of Syria and Palestine under the so-called Capitulations with the Ottomans.

A semi-independent governor of the province of Sidon, the Druze amir Fakhr ad-Din (1595–1634), began to revive the city by attaching it to his province and building a residence there. Yet the accounts of contemporary travelers agree that apart from the French merchants' khan and the Ottoman fort, the seventeenth-century city was little more than a "vast and spacious ruin."

By the middle of the eighteenth century, an Arab shaykh from Galilee, Dahir al-Umar, challenged the central Turkish government and carved out an autonomous entity with his headquarters in Acre. Acre's inner walls, a mosque, and the grain market are monuments to his rule. Christians were permitted to settle in the city to stimulate trade and manufacture.

However, the Ottoman central government reasserted its control over the Levant through the leadership of an Albanian Mamluk named Ahmed Pasha al-Jazzar, "the butcher," nicknamed thus for his cruelty. Dahir and his family were slain in 1775, and al-Jazzar chose Acre as his residence. With funds obtained through trade monopolies in grain and cotton and control over the countryside, al-Jazzar enhanced the fortifications of Acre with elaborate walls and moats. Bazaars, mosques, public baths, and a new main street lined with specialty shops were all built to cater to the expanding population, which during his rule reached 40,000. The Greek Orthodox and Franciscan churches and European-style hotels also date back to this period. One result of the growing prosperity of Acre was that al-Jazzar became increasingly independent of the Ottoman central government. His position and that of Acre was further enhanced when Acre repulsed a siege by Napoléon Bonaparte in 1799, which forced the French general to retreat ignominiously back to Cairo.

Al-Jazzar was succeeded by Sulayman Pasha, who, during his fifteen-year term, advanced the fortunes of the city and managed it well with the aid of his principal minister, a Jew named Haim Farkhy. Commercial life was invigorated through the construction of the Suq al-Abyad (the White Market).

However, the troubles of the region once more impinged upon the fortunes of the city when Ibrahim Bey, son and heir of Muhammed Ali of Egypt, besieged Acre in his campaign to conquer Syria (1831). The city was forced to surrender because the Ottomans were unable to send relief troops. Nearly ten years later (1840), the British organized a coalition with the Austrians and the Ottomans to end Ibrahim's Syrian adventure and put Acre under siege to force him out. During the siege, a powder magazine between the inner and outer ramparts was hit by seaborne guns, and the explosion resulted in great casualties for the Egyptians, who surrendered, and Acre was restored to Ottoman rule. Although Acre's defenses were repaired and commercial life was reestablished, the conditions of unrest had made their mark. In the latter part of the nineteenth century, the city's population declined to 10,000.

Acre was captured from the Ottomans by British troops in 1918 toward the close of World War I and included in the British Mandate of Palestine (1922–1948). Under the British, Acre took on new significance as the site of their central prison in the Middle East. The prison itself was housed in a citadel that had been built by the Crusaders in 1104. Many members of the Jewish Underground were imprisoned in the Acre citadel, including Zeev Jabotinsky, and over the course of British rule, nine people were hung there. Today the prison houses a Museum for the Jewish Resistance Prisoners, particularly stressing the dramatic escape from the Acre Prison of twenty-seven Irgun and other resistance fighters in 1947.

The first modern construction of the town began outside of the ancient walls and took place during the Ottoman period. In 1909 the German engineer Schumacher prepared a plan according to which new houses would be built outside of the town to create space for an increasing population. His plan was based on a gridiron system, and therefore construction of housing was carried out in long and narrow roads. During the British Mandate, very little construction occurred in Acre, and the rapid growth of Haifa hampered Acre's development (see also "Haifa"). During the same period, Zionist settlements sprang up in the surrounding area, and the town was enclosed from all sides with agricultural lands, thus preventing the possibility for further enlargement.

The city was captured by Israeli forces during the fighting in 1948, and most of its Palestinian Arab inhabitants fled and were prevented from returning. Although Acre was originally assigned to the Arab state in the United Nations (UN) Partition Plan for Palestine, it was subsequently incorporated into the State of Israel in 1949. Of 15,000 Palestinians in Acre before 1948, only 3,500 remained after the war, many of these refugees from other areas in Israel.

The city's Jewish population quickly grew following the end of hostilities from a few hundred in 1948 to 27,400 a quarter of a century later. Israeli planners saw the post-1948 period as an opportunity to change and replan the town, and two neighborhoods were added to Acre—one in the north and one in the east. But for the most part, residents preferred to live in the areas constructed during the mandate. Since 1948 Palestinian Arabs have been concentrated within the walled Old City.

Acre is listed only as a medium-sized town in Israel and is likely to remain so relative to the much more significant Haifa. The city's ancient port has silted up and has become secondary to Haifa's modern container port across the bay. It is used only by small fishing boats. Industries in modern Acre include a steel-rolling mill and match, tile, and plastic plants.

However, the city remains the major retail trade center for Arab settlements in western Galilee.

Today the city's main claim to fame is as a tourist attraction. The city hosts many landmarks from its long history and has been designated a United Nations Educational, Scientific, and Cultural Organization (UNESCO) World Heritage Site. The Ottoman citadel and walled fortifications are among the finest outside Istanbul. The slender minaret and shady courtyard of the al-Jazzar mosque are in good condition and still open for public worship. There are several churches dating from the Crusader period with ornate interiors. Visitors are also drawn to the tomb of Baha Allah, the prophet of the Bahai faith; he was exiled to the city with many followers by the Ottomans in 1868, served nine years in Acre Prison, and is buried in the city.

The underground Crusader ruins, in particular the Knights' Halls, are one of Acre's major sights. Accidentally exposed by a bulldozer conducting roadwork, the long-buried Crusader hall, with its dramatic vaulted ceiling, has been restored and is now the jewel of Acre's attractions. Built by the Hospitallers, the great hall's wonderful acoustics allow it to be used for a range of cultural events. Another impressive site is Khan al-Umdan (Inn of the Pillars), an eighteenth-century structure where camel caravans once brought grain and produce from Galilee to the city's market and port.

Generally speaking, economic conditions have not been good in the city. Acre is one of Israel's mixed cities, with one of the highest proportions of non-Jews, at roughly 25 percent (Christians, Muslims, Druze, and Bahais). Government attempts to consolidate a large Jewish majority in the city have been set back by a constant out-migration of discouraged Jewish residents. By the early 1970s, severe overcrowding problems had developed among the 9,000 Arab inhabitants of the Old City, where many houses were on the point of collapse. The Palestinian Arab inhabitants of the Old City are mostly employed in commerce, services, and fishing, while the Jewish inhabitants find most of their employment in the industrial zone of Haifa. Acre has experimented with joint housing for Palestinian Arab and Israeli Jews with limited success.

Michael Dumper

Further Readings

Efrat, Elisha. *Urbanization in Israel.* London: Croom Helm, 1984.

Lustick, Ian. *Arabs in the Jewish State: Israel's Control of a National Minority.* Austin: University of Texas Press, 1980.

Makhouly, Naim, and C. N. Johns. *A Guide to Acre.* Jerusalem: Greek Convent Press, 1946.

Malkin, Irad, and Robert Hohlfelder, eds. *Mediterranean Cities: Historical Perspectives.* London: Frank Cass, 1988.

Mayer, Leo A., and J. Pinkerfield. *Some Principal Muslim Religious Buildings in Israel.* Jerusalem: Ministry for Religious Affairs, Government Printer, 1950.

Philip, Thomas. *Acre: The Rise and Fall of a Palestinian City, 1730–1831.* New York: Columbia University Press, 2001.

Rubin, Morton. *The Walls of Acre: Intergroup Relations and Urban Development in Israel.* New York: Holt, Rinehart and Winston, 1974.

Ad-Dammam
Population: 1.1 million (2005 estimate)

Ad-Dammam was little known before the discovery of oil in the eastern province of Saudi Arabia in the 1930s. It played a small role in conflict over the leadership in Bahrain in the 1800s, when one of the protagonists took refuge there. Despite this brief prominence, the area remained only sparsely populated, with date palms providing one of the mainstays for inhabitants. Since oil has been discovered, the population in the area has increased tremendously, and with it the infrastructure and facilities there. Today ad-Dammam is the capital of the eastern province and is part of the conurbation including the towns of al-Khobar and Dhahran (where Saudi Aramco has its headquarters), which have also grown up as the oil industry has flourished.

Modern-day Dammam (Arabic, *ad-Dammam*) is part of the conurbation of ad-Dammam, al-Khobar, and Dhahran. The cities are located in the eastern province of Saudi Arabia, near the coast of the Persian Gulf. The area around ad-Dammam is desolate and, apart from oil, largely lacking in resources. It is surrounded by unremarkable sandy desert that is interspersed with *sabkhas,* or salt flats.

The lack of resources meant that ad-Dammam was not a prominent town, and so it does not feature widely in historical accounts of the region. The Ottomans held power there for a period in the sixteenth century, but their influence gradually declined. In the late 1700s, the as-Saud family from the Najd region made military intrusions into what is now the eastern province of Saudi Arabia as part of their efforts to spread the fundamentalist Wahhabi interpretation of Islam. At various times, the as-Saud held sway in al-Hasa, Bahrain, and Qatar, thus encompassing what is today ad-Dammam. Their influence in the area waned, however, in the first part of the nineteenth century, as the Saudi-Wahhabi alliance focused efforts on the Ottoman challenge to their authority in the Najd region.

Subsequently, in the early 1800s, what is now ad-Dammam was the site of a fort built by Rahmah bin Jabir al-Jalahimah, who was involved in a dispute over leadership of Bahrain and took refuge in the ad-Dammam area. The Khalifa tribe, which rule Bahrain today, eventually defeated Rahmah al-Jalahimah and took control over the area in 1826 (see also "Manama"). They ruled the region until 1844, when the as-Saud again moved in and conquered the Dammam area.

By the 1850s, some of the Khalifa tribe returned to the ad-Dammam area. The British intervened in 1861, attacking ad-Dammam in defense of the members of the Khalifa tribe, based in Manama. Foreign machinations did not end there—the Ottomans reasserted their authority over the eastern areas of the region, including ad-Dammam, in 1871.

The area does not appear to have subsequently thrived. When the famous J. G. Lorimor surveyed the area in the early part of the twentieth century, his *Gazetteer of the Persian Gulf* indicated that there was little in the Barr ad-Dhahran area aside from a few wells and some date groves, the latter of which were owned by members of the Bani Hajir tribe. Ad-Dammam itself he described as deserted, although remains of Rahmah al-Jalahimah's fort were still visible.

The eastern territory of the country was nonetheless attractive to the as-Saud, who had reasserted their authority in the Najd at the turn of the century and were turning their sights elsewhere as they sought to expand their holdings. The eastern area subsequently came under the control of Abdul Aziz as-Saud in 1913, when he captured Hofuf, taking control of the town from the Ottoman dynasty, which had stationed a garrison of Turkish troops there. The capture of the town gave the as-Saud effective control of the eastern region of what is now Saudi Arabia.

The eastern province, and with it ad-Dammam, became a part of the Kingdom of Saudi Arabia in 1932. But ad-Dammam remained a backwater until Standard Oil Company of California moved in during 1935 to search for oil around the Dammam Dome area. Six wells were drilled and six came up dry. But on 4 March 1938, No. 7 struck oil in commercial quantities. "Lucky No. 7," as it became known, produced over 32 million barrels of oil during its forty-five-year iconic life as the model Saudi oil well.

The flow of oil was accompanied by growth in the number of foreign oil workers, who settled in what was then known as Dammam camp. That camp was the beginnings of Dhahran, which is now the headquarters of Saudi Aramco, the largest oil company (measured by reserves) in the world. At the same time that Aramco was expanding its housing and facilities, the local towns were also growing, with al-Khobar coming officially into existence in 1942, when it was established as a municipality.

The arrival of oil money also meant that the country had the necessary funds to address the problem of water scarcity, which had until then acted as a brake on both population and economic growth in the area. Today, the ad-Dammam/Dhahran/Khobar area benefits from the government's massive investment in desalination technology, which includes the al-Khobar Desalination and Power Plant run by the Saline Water Conversion Corporation. The additional water, combined with the economic expansion and job opportunities that were created because of the country's oil industry, has been accompanied by a massive construction boom. The character of these buildings reflects their modernity—most buildings were constructed in the latter half of the twentieth century as the oil industry became more established.

That construction boom has been fueled in part by increased demand for housing. Population in the three towns has expanded from a very small base in the 1930s to, according to many estimates, more than 1 million. Although census figures are out of date, this growth has almost certainly made the ad-Dammam/Khobar/Dhahran conurbation the largest population center in the eastern province, and ad-Dammam is now its regional capital. Politically, the post of governor of the province is important, not just because of the oil sector but also because the eastern province is home to most of the country's Shi'i population.

The growth of the oil sector has also encouraged other parts of the local economy to expand. Ad-Dammam's importance as a transportation center has grown, and the city is served by the King Abdul Aziz Port in ad-Dammam, which handles non-oil cargoes for the eastern and central provinces of the country. Air travel to the city is through the King Fahd International Airport, located in al-Khobar. That facility has capacity for up to 7 million passengers per year and is the largest airport in the kingdom by area. In addition, the city is served by the King Fahd Causeway to Bahrain, which allows car travel between the two countries.

Despite the expansion of the area in recent years, the three parts of the modern conurbation have remained culturally distinct. Ad-Dammam is by far the most traditional area, while al-Khobar has a large Western population with abundant compound living. Dhahran is home to Saudi Aramco and its large and generally modern-housing gated community. Dhahran's focus on the oil sector is further emphasized by the presence of the King Fahd Petroleum and Minerals University, one of the top learning centers in the kingdom.

Angie Turner

Further Readings
Aarts, Paul, and Gerd Nonneman, eds. *Saudi Arabia in the Balance.* London: Hurst, 2005.
Al-Yahya, Eid, ed. *Travelers in Arabia: British Explorers in Saudi Arabia.* London: Stacy International, 2005.
Lippman, Thomas. *Inside the Mirage: America's Fragile Partnership with Saudi Arabia.* Boulder, CO: Westview Press, 2004.
Lorimer, J. G. *Gazetteer of the Persian Gulf.* Calcutta: Superintendent Government Printing, 1908.
Winder, R. Bayly. *Saudi Arabia in the Nineteenth Century.* New York: St. Martin's Press, 1965.

Aden
Population: 510,000 (2005 estimate)

The Yemeni port of Aden has long been one of the major entrepôts of the Middle East. With its starkly beautiful natural harbor nestled within an extinct volcano and its access to the highlands of Yemen and its products, the city called the "Eye to Yemen" would already have been significant. But given its location at the entrance to the Red Sea and its easy connections to the ports of East Africa, Aden has, for more than 3,000 years, attracted imperial attention. Whether it was the Sabaeans, Romans, Aksumites, Ayyubids, Ottomans, or British, this gateway to and from Arabia has always been open.

Aden (Arabic, *Adan*) is located on the northern littoral of the Gulf of Aden near the southern entrance to the Red Sea. Close to the southwest tip of the Arabian Peninsula, the city lies on the narrow, fertile coastal strip backed by high mountains. Access to the highlands of Yemen is via Wadi Tuban and Taiz, and to the Hadramawt along the coast to the east. Sanaa is some 260 miles to the north. By sea, Aden is an ideal starting point for overseas journeys to India, given the west-east monsoon winds, or to East Africa, with the Somalia coast and Zanzibar easily accessible. Through the Bab al-Mandab awaits Egypt, Palestine, and the Mediterranean via the Suez Canal: the port authority likes to make the point that Aden lies an equal distance between Europe and the Far East.

The city is located within a large crescent-shaped bay created by the crater of an extinct volcano. The arms of the crescent that enclose Bandar at-Tawahi (Aden Harbor or Crater Bay) are large hilly volcanic promontories, essentially islands, each with its own small harbors and bays but connected to the mainland by a narrow, sandy isthmus. The one on the right of the entrance to the bay is known as Aden Peninsula and contains the old town of Aden on its western side; the town is nestled at the base of Jebal Shamsan and has its own small harbor guarded by the rocky island of Sirah. The town has now expanded around the whole northern base of Shamsan so that it faces both outward and in toward the bay at at-Tawahi (Steamer Point) and the expanded modern harbor at Ma'alla. The western peninsula, Adan as-Sughra (Little Aden Peninsula) is the location of the oil refinery and oil harbor, Jebal Muzalqam, and was the major British military base. The mainland is an open plain backed by high mountains; to the north some six miles is the district of Shaykh Uthman, the source of the city's water.

The port of Aden is protected by these promontories from both the northeast and southwest monsoons, which allows Aden to operate 365 days of the year. As opposed to many of the Red Sea harbors, Aden has no coral reefs blocking the entrance. Billed as one of the world's top natural harbors, it offers protected anchorage to hundreds of ships. Wadi Tuban, on the mainland, is a perennial stream, and its fertile delta may have been the area of first settlement on the bay. One possible meaning for the city's name is that of residing, or preparing a place for cultivation.

The Aden of today is thus a conurbation composed of various anchorages and settled districts that once were separate villages located around the bay or on the peninsulas. The eastern peninsula, Aden Peninsula, contains most of the city's population and the old city. Little Aden Peninsula, to the west, has the city's main industrial zone.

The prehistory of the site is obscure. However, if its history is similar to that along the western Tihamah, fishing and hunting, particularly of the wild donkey, would have supported impermanent settlements starting in the Neolithic (8000 to 3000 BC) well into the Bronze Age (3000 to 1200 BC). Occasional Egyptian sea voyages to Punt (northern Somali coast) and Harappan voyages to southern Arabia during the second millennium must have stimulated interest in nearby ports with regular water and incense to sell, which Aden had. Pottery finds near the city show similarity to the Tihamah Cultural Complex, which tied the Gulf of Aden, the Eritrean, and the Red Sea Tihamah coasts together culturally about 1500–1200 BC. The growth of urbanism and political states in the highlands, particularly those of the Sabaeans, starting in the late second millennium BC, must have stimulated Aden along with it, and the city emerges into history with the early Iron Age.

It is unclear when the city was actually founded. The coast of the Gulf of Aden appears to have come under control of the Awsan confederation, an early south Arabian kingdom whose center was in Wadi Markha, ca. 900 BC, and it is around this time that Old Testament records mention the city as being a trade partner to King Solomon and to the Phoenician port of Tyre. The city may have been the main harbor of Awsan for its connections with the east coast of Africa: this may explain the fact that part of the East African shore was still called the "Awsanian Coast" long after the destruction of the Awsanian Kingdom by a Sabaean invasion after 685 BC.

Authority over Aden then appears to have passed to the nearby Qatabanians, who dominated the Wadi Tuban and the trade into the Indian Ocean as the Sabaean Empire faded. The focus for these southern Arabian kingdoms was primarily on control of the inland caravan trade, moving incense and spices from the Hadramawt into the Red Sea circuits via an inland road system: sea-based, long-distance trade was still secondary to trade by land. However, Aden may have been a major transshipment site in the cinnamon trade by this time, which is why classical writers assumed cinnamon originated in Yemen when in fact it was brought to Aden from India and the Far East.

A major shift in the significance of the south Arabian ports begins to occur during Hellenistic times, and by the first century BC, power in southern Arabia depended on a combination of highland kingdoms promoting seagoing trade via client coastal ports. Greek (Ptolemaic) and Roman demand for incense, with their power over Egypt and Palestine, facilitated this trade via the Red Sea. Another reason for this shift was the Greek and Roman realization (via Hippalus, ca. 100 BC) of the monsoon cycles in the Indian Ocean and their increased interest in dominating south Arabian trade to India. Greek coins and amphorae continue to be found in Aden, confirming the city's far-flung ties during this period.

By the time of Ptolemy's *Geography* (ca. AD 140), the topography of Aden and the land around it were very well known, and general trade had increased substantially. As a result, during the first century AD, the people of Yemen were much more prosperous, because of, according to Pliny, Rome's export of millions of sesterces to pay for their insatiable demand for incense. In that context, the rise of the Himyarian state marks a turning point for Aden's fortunes. The *Periplus Maris Erythraei* (*Circumnavigation of the Erythraean Sea,* late first century AD) implies the centrality of Eudaemon Arabia (Aden) to the Himyarite state; through Aden Himyarite ties to Rome, East Africa and the Indian Ocean trade prospered, with a great diversity of cargo transshipped through the port. The importation of horses via Aden may have been one factor in Himyarite power and their ability to unify southern Arabia under their control by the late third century AD. Certainly Aden was more important in the movement of myrrh than frankincense, since the former was found in the area or along the opposite Somali coast and so was brought to Aden for shipment, whereas frankincense primarily came from the Hadramawt and generally took other routes to market. Long-distance sea trade brought the Himyarites and the Aksumites together into an alliance at the end of the century, and this may have helped with the conversion of the Himyarites into monotheists (both Christian and Jewish) early in the fourth century.

With the conversion of the Roman Empire to Christianity, the demand for incense decreased, and this, along with internal chaos in the highlands, weakened Himyarite rule, opening the country up to Sassanian conquest around 570. Badhan, the Persian governor of southern Arabia, converted to Islam in 628, and this began a new era for Aden.

Yemen first came under the Umayyads of Damascus, and their rule was punctuated by a number of revolts. After 750 the Abbasids in Baghdad assumed authority over Yemen, although by 850 their power over Aden had devolved to more local authorities. It is from this time that a significant doctrinal split between the coastal port populations and those in the highlands begins to appear: the coastal areas remained more Sunni, with the highlands and tribes expressing more Alid and Shi'i sentiments. This may be related to the type of connections, access to resources, and diversity of population within a port like Aden.

In general, the late ninth and early tenth centuries was a period of expanding trade and connections for the city, and this attracted any political power stirring in the highlands. For example, the highlands attracted Shi'i missionaries, who sought to convert the tribes and establish a political state. At about the same time the Ismailis were spreading the faith in North Africa in what was later to become the Fatimid Empire; their early missionaries were also at work in Yemen. In 881 two missionaries traveled to Aden, where they posed as cotton merchants, using the cover of trade in the city's market to identify possible tribal allies. Soon they had moved into rural areas under tribal protection, from where they cultivated a movement. By 904 one of the two, Ibn al-Fadl, had raised an Ismaili movement in the south, captured Aden, and then marched on Sanaa. Once in power, he rejected the Ismailis and held on to power for himself until he died.

A later dynasty was the Sulayhids (1047–1138); under Ali al-Sulayhi, Aden was added to the kingdom. One indication of the contemporary prosperity of Aden was that when Queen Arwa Bint Ahmed was married to Ali's son, she received, as a dowry, the yearly revenues from Aden, which amounted to 100,000 gold dinars. Subsequently, the port was placed under the rule of the Bani Zurraye to administer for the Sulayhid state. It is from this time that slaves from East Africa were imported to cut rock for a new round of urban construction; they built Aden's extensive walls, along with five castles on the hills. These battlements protected the city until Ottoman times.

Business letters concerning Aden and its trading relations with India and Cairo during this period have been found preserved in the *geniza* (synagogue storage vaults) of Fustat (Old Cairo). Letters concerning the dealings of one Madmun ben Bundar (d. 1151), the *wakil* (trustee of the merchants or head of the Jewish marketing guild) of Aden, are revealing of city dynamics of the period. Madmun must have held great power over Aden's trade with the ports of the Indian Ocean but also over what was shipped by land to Cairo. The records show that he started a joint venture with the Muslim *wali* (governor) of Aden to create a shipping line to run between Aden and Ceylon and that he even tried to settle Jewish goldsmiths in that faraway island. His *dar* (storehouse) contained goods left behind by those shipwrecked as well as what he had bought and sold under the direction of other merchants. Madmun was a banker for the Jewish merchants of Aden, paying and receiving debts and loans. In one of his own ventures, he shipped sixty camel loads of semiprecious stones to Cairo—along with 100 fashionable robes to cover the cost of customs in ports along the way—and eight camel loads of pepper to pay for Egyptian customs and the transport of his goods to Cairo.

The Ayyubids conquered the city in 1173. Under their rule, the city was their key gateway to the Indian Ocean, and they developed a highly regulated system of rules and procedures for administering the harbor. The transparency and fairness of these regulations helped attract trade. The Ayyubids also developed a coastal fleet, the *al-'asakir al-bahriya,* which they used to guard the coast and make it safe from pirates.

Gradually, Ayyubid power declined, and their local rulers, the Rasulids, were able to break away and start their own dynasty (1229–1442). The Rasulids, Shafi Muslims, originally ruled from Aden but then shifted their capital inland to Taiz. Aden, however, remained their primary port, a mint, and the source of most of their revenue. This dynasty continued and expanded the Ayyubid regulations for the port and published a set of specific tax and customs duties, the *Mulakhkhas al-fitan,* which garnered international fame and envy from merchants and rulers around the Indian Ocean. All ships entering the port were required to produce written manifests, all goods were searched, and passengers were body searched as well.

Aden was a global emporium, cosmopolitan both in its population and in the goods it handled. Merchants from around the Indian Ocean flocked to the city. By the late fourteenth century, for example, one quarter in the city was just for the Hindu Gujarati *baniyan* (merchants), while merchants from Aden lived in the ports of China, Ethiopia, Zanzibar, and Malibar. Slaves shipped from Mogadishu were sold in its slave markets: slave girls would be prepared with frankincense and perfumes, wrapped in fine linen, and then paraded through the market by their owners, with the Rasulid Wali taking first pick for the sultan in Taiz. Horses were shipped in from Berbera for the annual horse fair; there was a government monopoly on horse sales, with the sultan getting first pick and the rest usually sold for shipment to India. Yemeni honey, grain, rose water (from Sanaa), and raisins were exchanged for pepper from Malibar or cloves, cinnamon, ginger, saffron, musk, or laudanum and opium from India, the Spice Islands, or China. Sandalwood from Java joined every kind of textile product in trade for silver, diamonds from Kashmir, coral from Libya, or rubies from India.

The area around Aden on the mainland was an important conglomeration of industrial production of glass for export; bricks, oil, and sugar were also produced for trade. Archaeological remains demonstrate regular and substantial ties to the Far East, with numerous thirteenth- to sixteenth-century Chinese celadon and blue and white porcelain. Jealous competitors, including the Mamluks in Egypt, desperately tried to redirect trade to ports under their control: after 1382 there was an intentional policy to lower customs and taxes in Jeddah to attract merchants away from Aden.

The Chinese geographers knew well the reputation and position of Aden: the city appears on the maps of Chao Ju-kuo in his famous geographic work *Chu-fan-chih* (1226). This knowledge helped the eunuch captain Zheng He visit Aden three times with his fleet during his numerous voyages for the Ming dynasty between 1417 and 1433.

Marco Polo may have visited Aden around 1293, and Ibn Battuta spent time here (ca. 1330) during this golden age. Ibn Battuta left from here for his trip down the East African coast, and it is clear he enjoyed the city. Along with his discussion of the various destinations of the ships in its harbor, he mentions the water scarcity that constantly affected the city, its famous water tanks for storing water, and the wealth of the city's shipowners.

The Tahirid dynasty controlled Aden after 1454. They continued the policy of having a fleet at Aden to guard the coast from pirates. Even so, they could not stop smuggling from the numerous small harbors around the bay, a perennial problem that haunted all rulers of the city. Twice the fleet was able to protect the city from seaborne attack, once in the 1450s and again in the 1490s.

Vasco da Gama rounded the Cape of Good Hope in AD 1497. As a result, the city quickly became enmeshed in a new, global set of economic and political dynamics. The first European to offer a personal account of Aden was the Italian Ludovico di Varthema, who published his *Itinerario* in 1511. He was impressed by the significance of the port and the way ships from all over the world, including Ethiopia, Persia, and India, sheltered in its harbor and traded for goods. Arab authors, of course, such as Ibn Majid, with his guide to navigation in the Indian Ocean, had already published excellent information about the port.

In 1513 the Portuguese captain Alfonso de Albuquerque attacked the city as part of his plan for strategic dominance in the Indian Ocean. The attack failed. Alarmed by the Portuguese threat, the Egyptian Mamluks occupied the Yemeni Tihamah and attempted to take Aden for themselves, but they too failed to capture it. The Portuguese attacked again but failed a second time.

Aden finally fell in 1538 to Sulayman Pasha, the commander of a huge Ottoman fleet. The city's fate then became shaped by the dynamics of imperial strategy crafted in faraway Istanbul rather than by its own commercial interests, and this had profound implications. The Ottomans, who had many emporia through which to trade, saw the city primarily as a barrier to European penetration of the Holy Cities rather than as an entrepôt to be promoted. Over the next century, although Aden remained involved in trade, it began to decline. The Ottomans were hated by the locals, and their governor, anticipating trouble, passed regulations stating that Arabs were not allowed to own weapons, visiting sailors were not allowed to sell their weapons to Arabs, and any Arab who bought weapons would pay with their life.

The Zaydi state in the Yemeni highlands began its rise in the sixteenth century and was able to expand into Aden, dominating the Sunni there and kicking out the Ottomans in 1630 (see also "Sanaa"). Local tribal chiefs divided up southern Yemen to rule as Zaydi representatives, and Aden came under tribal control. By the early 1600s, Aden was also in serious competition with a range of boomtowns located along the Tihamah and controlled from Sanaa. Ports like Mokka, with its easier access to the coffee-growing regions of the highlands and its ties to Sanaa's rulers, better served European trade interests. English ships shifted toward Mokka, and in 1628 the East India Company (EIC) set up a factory there.

Aden did remain central to the pepper trade, and cottons from India on their way to Egypt passed through the port; so did Egyptian opium bound for India. Aden also retained its ties with the Somali coastal towns, and a thriving trade in meat, butter, and slaves kept the Aden-Zeila and Aden-Berbera ties strong. With the rise of the Adal state along the Somali coast, and its expansion under Imam Ahmad Ibrahim al-Ghazi or Imam Gran (1506–1543), the number of Ethiopian slaves available in Aden's slave market increased

Seventeenth-century engraving of Aden. (Art Archive/Marine Museum Lisbon/Dagli Orti)

dramatically; most were shipped on to Zabid or Sanaa (see also "Berbera" and "Djibouti City").

After 1728 the Sunni population of Aden expelled the Zaydi *dawlah*, the imam of Sanaa's representative, and the chiefs of the regional tribes carved out their independence. The Abdali confederation took over Aden and declared the Sultanate of Lahj. The Zaydis did not give up the city easily, however, besieging it in 1745 for three months. The city gradually declined in importance so that by the end of the century, it was a fishing village of less than 800 inhabitants.

Mokka remained the key regional port in the late 1700s, and it served as the primary British link to Bombay. Yet, with conflict in Europe forcing the European powers to think globally about their strategic interests, the British, fearful of growing French activities in the Indian Ocean, sought a stronger foothold around the entrance to the Red Sea. Combined with their desire to gain a stronger economic position in Yemen, along with the Ottoman vacuum in the area, the British moved to establish treaty ties with the imam in Sanaa. They initially sought from him strategic control over Mokka. After 1820, when it was clear Mokka was not an option, the British shifted to the sultan of Lahj, looking for an option in Aden, al-though they received little satisfaction. By 1837, as the forces of Egypt's Muhammad Ali pacified Yemen for Istanbul, the British were finally goaded into action, fearing that all their options in the area might disappear.

Consequently, the Indian government trumped up charges against the sultan of Lahj, Shaykh Muhsin ibn Fadl, for supporting piracy. They then sent their agent, Captain Stafford Haines from the Indian navy, to take the town. After bombarding Aden from his ship on 19 January 1839, Haines forced the sultan to pay for "insults to the British flag" and then to sign a treaty accepting an annual cash payment for Aden. Aden's modern history thus begins with the British occupation of the harbor and the sultan's palace.

Resistance to the occupation began almost immediately. In November 1839, 5,000 tribesmen attacked the walls but were driven off, with 200 killed. The following May a similar attack produced similar results. These attacks were led by the Abdali. Other attacks during the 1840s were led by self-proclaimed *Mahdis* (messianic leaders) who appeared among the tribes, promoting a jihad to drive the Christians out of Muslim holy lands. Framing the occupation of Aden as a first step toward European-Christian control over Makkah and

Madinah, and given the firepower of the British, the logic required a Mahdi to drive them out. Sometimes their followers were told that they would not be harmed by Christian swords or shot. It has been argued that the subequent period after the occupation of Aden by the British produced across Yemen a messianic response, with movements within all three religious communities, Sunni, Shi'i, and Jewish, appearing until the turn of the century.

Attacks and violence continued into the 1850s, including murdering British officers and civilians, firing at British ships, and enduring periods when the town was cut off from the interior and no supplies arrived. Gradually, however, the British constructed a patchwork of agreements with tribal and subtribal leaders into a shaky edifice of protection agreements that allowed the British Political Resident in Aden to manage the city's hinterland. Particularly critical was protecting caravan passage into the interior, given that this sector had grown to become as important for the British in Aden as the port's role as a coaling station. By the end of the century, the Political Resident was intervening in intertribal conflicts, for example, forcing one of "the British tribes" to give eighty-five camels back to another tribe across the line in Ottoman territory to keep the peace with Istanbul.

Within a few years, the population of Aden increased to some 20,000 inhabitants. The city was attached administratively to India, and then the Perim and Kamaran islands were added in the 1850s. In 1850 Aden was declared a "free port" as part of the attempt to divert trade to Aden. This action did suck trade from all nearby ports and created resentment among those tribes who ended up losing much of their income. As a result, the British had to institute regular subsidies and cash payments to pacify tribal leaders. The result of all these agreements was that a dichotomy was created between Aden the port city, managed under direct control with a set of British laws and bureaucracy, versus the tribal areas outside, where British influence was maintained by payments to traditional leaders whose power and position were solidified under an indirect British regime.

The Ottomans, fearful of increasing European machinations in the Red Sea, began to reestablish direct rule over Yemen after 1849. Although it took them more than thirty years and much fighting to pacify the Zaydis, they reestablished some authority in the highlands and the Tihamah (see also "Sanaa"). At various times during this struggle, the British over the border in Aden used the port to supply illicit guns, ammunition, and even artillery to tribes in revolt against the Ottoman authorities, and the Ottomans provided funds to destabilize the tribes around Aden. As a result, Adenis were caught up in a clash of imperial interests not particularly of their own making.

In the wake of the opening of the Suez Canal (1869), Aden was able to take advantage of its new, even more centralized location on international trade circuits. In particular, it began to store supplies for steamships (coal) and later oil. The reprovisioning services for ships expanded as well, including water, victuals, and supplies. Concurrently, the city's centrality in the new communications technologies was established: Aden became a cable station on the London-to-Bombay telegraph cable. For the next 100 years, the Cable and Wireless Company staffed an office in Aden to manage the multiple cable linkages that made up the empire's strategic communication system.

One consequence of the occupation of Aden was the new ties it gave the British directly across the Gulf to Berbera and Zeila on the Somali coast. The exchange networks based on incense, livestock, slaves, and general emporium trade binding Aden and these two ports had ancient roots. After 1840 such ties increased, particularly in the supply of livestock for Aden's growing population and ship traffic. It was from Aden that Britain became increasingly involved in the political affairs of Ethiopia and Somalia, which led directly to the assumption of the Somaliland protectorate after 1884.

The Adani Indian merchant community, established after 1850, was particularly crucial in facilitating the trade to East Africa. Drawing both on the wealth of Gujarat and on their family ties to businesses in Berbera, Addis Ababa, or Zanzibar, this multireligious community used the city's centrality in the transshipment of silver around the western Indian Ocean to conduct international arbitrage. Their skill in exchanging coded telegrams with family members across the region gave them an advantage in profiting from currency fluctuations (see also "Zanzibar").

During Imam Yahya's rebellion against the Ottomans, from 1904 to 1911, Aden prospered, while Yemen was divided by war and chaos. An increasing flow of trade to the highlands entered and exited Aden, and Hodeida lost its position as the key port for Yemen. During World War I, Aden's significance as a military base was reaffirmed; British forces were able to support Sharif Hussayn's Arab Revolt from Aden, shell Ottoman positions, and support Yemen's independence under the Imam.

As northern Yemen's political system developed, Aden became a refuge and its release valve. Workers came from the north to find work in the city, and after the abortive 1948 coup against the Imam, political refugees came to Aden for its relative freedom. Students looking for higher education came south and then headed out to Cairo. Other members of the Adeni community were also on the move at this time. In 1947 there were 8,000 Adeni Jews. In 1949 and 1950, in Operation on Eagles' Wings (also called Operation Magic Carpet), Jews from all over Yemen left their homes and assembled in Aden to fly out to the new State of Israel. The Jewish Agency established camps for these emigrants; at one point there were more than 3,000 people housed in camps around the city waiting for flights. Over 50,000 Yemeni Jews ultimately left between June 1949 and September 1950.

The exodus effectively ended the Jewish community in Aden, which dated back to the second century AD. The Jews of the city had been its principal artisans and craftsmen (shoemakers, weavers, silversmiths). For more than 1,000 years, they had managed the world's diamond shipping, bringing diamonds in from India and exchanging them for gold and silver from Europe. After the British takeover of the town in 1839, Jews were granted full rights of citizenship, yet many began to leave for Palestine or America as early as 1881. It was under the pressures of independence in the highlands after 1918, and the growing concern by Adeni Muslims about events in Palestine, that tension bubbled over in the city. There were attacks on Adeni Jews in 1933, but it was the 1947 attacks, following the United Nations (UN) vote to partition Palestine, that were most devastating. More than eighty Jews were killed, synagogues destroyed, and schools and shops burned. Those who remained in Aden after the mass exodus of 1950 were again subject to attack in 1958 and at the time of the June War of 1967; as a result, the final few left with the British pullout.

In the decade after World War II, Aden prospered and became the fourth busiest harbor in the world. Yet this was a time of great regional change, and the city felt the effects. For example, the Egyptian Revolution of 1952 and the subsequent support for Arab nationalism and anti-British feelings this engendered throughout the Arab world encouraged similar reactions in Aden. Students from Aden studying abroad returned as secret members of the Arab National Movement, the Communist Party, or Baathists. The trials in the city of students for publishing articles critical of British policies just encouraged further mobilization.

The loss to the British of the Suez base (1954), along with the withdrawal from Kenya and Cyprus, also affected the city. Aden was left as the key British military base in the region, and within the tensions of the cold war, this heightened Aden's strategic significance to London, resulting in new construction and logistical requirements.

Finally, the Mossadeqh Revolution in Iran (1951–1953) and the nationalization of Anglo-Persian (British Petroleum) refineries in Iran pushed the company to find alternative (safer) havens for refining oil. Therefore, it built a new refinery in Aden in 1955 that required skilled workers and increased the need for related support services. The result was the creation of an urban workforce in Aden where there had been none before. Soon the city hosted an Aden Ports Trade Union and a national Aden Trade Union, both of which organized a large strike at the refinery in 1956. The strike encouraged political organizing and demands for independence.

Britain gradually modified the structures of its rule in Aden. The city was initially administered from British India up until 1937, when it was combined with the West Aden protectorates into a Crown colony. British allowed some voice for Adeni elites, including the Indian community, through a legislative council formed in 1955. After 1959 the Colony of Aden was transformed into the State of Aden and then combined in 1963 with the surrounding amirates into the Federation of South Arabia (FSA). For most Adenis, however, such political creations were artificial and lacked any real legitimacy, their primary purpose being to keep the conservative tribal leaders, allies of the British authority, in power.

In September 1962, there was a coup against the Yemeni Imamate, and the Egyptians quickly sent military and advisory help to the Republicans. This development had a tremendous effect in next-door Aden, immediately giving those opposed to British rule a territorial base from which to organize resistance and a source of financial and material support for armed attacks. The Arab National Movement had been organizing in Aden, creating sports clubs, cultural clubs, and student organizations; after the coup many students traveled to Taiz, were trained in military skills, and then returned to Aden to begin the armed struggle.

In June 1963, in Taiz, the National Liberation Front (NLF), the Qawmiyin, was announced, with the goal of armed struggle in Aden, independence from the British, and a unified Yemen. The NLF was a coalition, and it began to fall apart almost as quickly as it was formed. Gradually, two key groups emerged: the NLF, based more in the rural areas and led by rural commanders who pursued armed struggle, and the Front for the Liberation of South Yemen (FLOSY), based primarily in Aden city among the urban intellectuals.

Late in 1963, the insurgency began, and the NLF attacked and killed the British high commissioner. In response, the British implemented a state of emergency. Between 1964 and 1967, the number of violent incidents in Aden jumped from 36 to 3,000, and the number of British and local casualties from 36 to 1,000. At one point Crater was taken over by rebels, and a commercial airplane with passengers on board was blown up. The Aden Women's Association, publicly a social club for Arab women, distributed leaflets, hid both weapons and those fleeing the British, carried communications, and provided first aid for the rebels. The British had to bring 2,000 troops into Aden to suppress the rebellion, and in the process considerable force and torture were used. In January 1967, fighting between FLOSY and the NLF broke out in the streets of the Arab Quarter of Aden Town and continued until mid-February.

The political climate gradually shifted within Britain, and the new government abandoned its goal of keeping the base in Aden, throwing its support behind the NLF in the belief that its rural base offered a greater chance for moderate leadership. On 29 November 1967, the British withdrew from Aden and handed power over to the NLF.

The establishment of the new government led to a mass exodus from Aden. At independence, the city held 250,000 people, and it is estimated that ultimately more than 500,000 people fled the country: virtually all Adeni merchants and upper civil servants departed, as did top military officials. The new government took over a country that had twenty-nine doctors, two functioning hospitals, 250 miles of paved roads, 70 percent adult illiteracy, no industry other than the refinery, imported 60 percent of its food, and depended on huge subsidies that were no longer available. What education that was available was concentrated in Aden. It also assumed control just as the Suez Canal was closed by the June War of 1967, and the number of ships visiting the port dropped from 6,000 per year to 1,500 per year.

The NLF gradually moved to the left politically and purged its more pragmatic elements by June 1969. In November 1969, the government nationalized all major foreign commercial enterprises, including the banks, insurance, port services (but not the refinery), foodstuffs, and housing. The Three-Year Plan directed money into transportation, communications, and education. Radical land reform soon followed. In 1971 the free-port status of Aden was abolished. State retail shops, especially in clothing, were established in the 1970s, including thirty-six in Aden. A State Security Law was passed in 1975 making it illegal for any Yemeni to talk to a foreigner except on official business. An NLF Party ideological school in Aden trained more than 3,000 members.

Some outside help arrived during the 1970s. The Chinese built a textile factory in Aden that employed 1,400, built the 315-mile road between Aden and Mukalla, and staffed a hospital in the Crater District of Aden. The Cubans trained the militia and air force while providing doctors and education experts. The Russians provided 1,000 Russian advisors and were granted refueling rights at Aden, but no base facilities.

Many things went wrong along the way. By 1975 rationing of certain products was required, and there were food shortages in Aden. Every single trainee sent abroad from the refinery for further training between 1967 and 1974 failed to return; such problems were widespread, leading the government to ban emigration in 1974. Party disagreements with Saddam Hussayn in June 1979 led to Iraqi Embassy officials in Aden murdering an Iraqi Communist lecturer at Aden University.

Splits in the NLF led to President Salem Robea Ali attempting to mobilize popular radicalism à la the Chinese Cultural Revolution; as a result, there were "urban uprisings" in Aden directed at the party officials and bureaucrats enjoying their air-conditioned offices and special privileges. Ultimately, Ali failed to bring the bulk of the party leadership with him, and in June 1978 fighting broke out in and around the Presidential Palace (the former British high commissioner's residence), and he and about 200 others were killed. Subsequently, the NLF modified its structure and constitution and became the Yemeni Socialist Party (YSP). Taking a page from the Soviets, the new YSP allowed top party officials to access restricted consumer-goods shops in Aden.

With the reopening of the Suez Canal, Aden's port, and with it the economy, slowly began to turn around. The development of the Ma'alla Terminal and new deepwater berths during the late 1980s also contributed to the port's revival, as have new legal and service changes during the 1990s. The discovery of oil in the Hadramawt also made a significant contribution to government revenues, allowing it to commit to the city's development.

Political problems did not go away, however. Another intraleadership struggle broke out in Aden among factions within the YSP in January 1986. Hundreds died, and more than 60,000 people, including President Muhammad Ali, fled north to the Yemeni Arab Republic (YAR), and border tensions increased. The result, however, was surprising. Soon the refugees were allowed to return, and border tensions were calmed, and out of this process emerged serious discussions between the leaders in the south and those in the north about unification. Within the space of two years, practical results could be seen: an agreement to link Aden's power grid into that at Taiz, and a joint oil venture in the Marib basin that would ship oil to the Aden refinery. Unification picked up steam during a late 1989 summit in Aden that was followed by hundreds of joint meetings in Aden and Sanaa. The result was that on 21 May 1990, a new Republic of Yemen was declared in Aden. Sanaa was designated the political capital of the new state and Aden confirmed as its economic capital.

Within a year, the unified state faced a crucial challenge. Out of the Iraqi invasion of Kuwait and Yemeni support for Saddam came the expulsion of up to 1 million Yemeni workers from Saudi Arabia and the Gulf. Grants and loans were halted, the flow of remittances was stopped, and more than 40,000 returnees a day came across the border. Aden was one of the hardest-hit cities. Many of those outside had been Sunni, lower-class workers unaffiliated with any tribe. Many had been outside for more than a decade, living in urban settings. Thus, they congregated in Aden, a Sunni city with little tribal context. The result was that tent camps for refugees sprung up in vacant lands around the city. Perhaps as many as 40,000 people came to Aden and were temporarily housed. This influx added to a preexisting housing shortage in the city, a result of past People's Democratic Republic of Yemen (PDRY) policies. Within a few weeks, the dynamics of the city were changed: unemployment jumped to 25 percent, day-labor sites appeared on many street corners, and roads became clogged with taxis, as anyone with a car became a driver.

Unification was not easy, and the city was severely damaged during the 1994 Yemeni civil war, led by secessionists from Aden: for two months, Aden was the capital of the breakaway entity, only to be recaptured in July after heavy fighting. Many of its older buildings survived the fighting, however, and continue to grace the city. One of the oldest mosques in the city is the Aban Mosque, related to Aban ibn Uthman, a judge, scholar, and grandson of Uthman, the third caliph. This and other early mosques replicated the design and layout of the Great Mosque in Makkah. The National Museum, once the sultan's palace, is situated in Crater. The University of Aden, founded in 1975, hosts more than 20,000 students and is located on the isthmus in the Khawr Maksar District. Unfortunately, the many Eastern European–style concrete housing units built with Soviet money detract from the city's skyline.

Some of the most interesting monuments in Aden are the Tawila cisterns or tanks, often called the Tanks of Aden. Although numerous ancient cisterns are located around the city, the particular complex of reservoirs located on the heights beyond the city was a significant ancient achievement and would have helped the city service the many ships that called at its harbor. Although it is difficult to know when they were built, these huge lined cisterns, along with their accompanying dams and channel system, may date from the Himyarite period or even earlier. The United Nations Development Programme (UNDP) and the United Nations Educational, Scientific, and Cultural Organization (UNESCO) have been involved in their restoration, and they are a major tourist site.

After unification in 1990, Aden was declared the economic and commercial capital of the country, although it was not until 2002 that a serious economic and political initiative was started to reclaim Aden's role in global shipping. The Aden Medium- to Long-Term Scheme for Local Economic Development is, with World Bank help, seeking to unlock Aden's growth potential and put Aden back on the map. Infrastructural development may help: the 300-mile highway from Aden to Amran is being upgraded to a double highway. Although there is ruthless regional competition between Aden, Dubai, Salalah, and Djibouti for maritime trade and in the vessel services sector, Aden's Free Zone Authority has hopes that its ambitious plan to expand the port will restore it to a top place in the global transshipping hierarchy.

Since 1995 Aden has been the official winter capital of the country, and this has brought additional developmental aid. A key problem is meeting the future water needs of a rapidly increasing population. The country's population is projected to double within nineteen years, given the country's fertility rate, highest in the Middle East and North Africa (MENA) region; low use of contraceptives; and large population under age fifteen (50 percent). Population control is thus key to reducing poverty and to managing urban growth.

Aden's long involvement with arms' smuggling and resistance to imperial powers did not end with independence and unification. In December 1992, the first attack by al-Qaeda on U.S. interests occurred in Aden at a hotel used by U.S. servicemen; two tourists were killed. This was followed in 1998 by a failed attack in the city by British Muslims on British personnel celebrating Christmas. Since then there have been two attacks on U.S. naval ships in the port: the attack on the USS *The Sullivans* in 2000, with no one hurt, and the attack on the USS *Cole* later that same year, with seventeen American sailors killed. Today the Yemeni government is working with the

Americans on implementing counterterrorism procedures and neutralizing al-Qaeda operatives in the country. Around $22 million in U.S. military aid has gone to establish a coast guard to protect ships at anchor in Aden's harbor.

Bruce Stanley

Further Readings

Ahroni, Reuben. *The Jews of the British Crown Colony of Aden.* Leiden: Brill, 1994.

Bel, Jose-Marie. *Aden: the Mythical Port of Yemen.* Bruxells: Amyris, 1998.

Carapico, Sheila, ed. *Civil Society in the Yemen: The Political Economy of Activism in Modern Arabia.* Cambridge: Cambridge University Press, 1998.

King, Gillian. *Imperial Outpost, Aden.* London: Oxford University Press, 1964.

Kour, Zaki Hanna. *The History of Aden, 1839–72.* London: Frank Cass, 1981.

Nizan, Paul. *Aden, Arabie.* Paris: Maspero, 1976.

Paget, Julian. *Last Post: Aden, 1964–67.* London: Faber and Faber, 1969.

Walker, Jonathan. *Aden Insurgency: The Savage War in South Arabia, 1962–1967.* Staplehurst: Spellmount, 2005.

Aksum
Population: 40,000 (2005 estimate)

Aksum was the ancient capital of the only sub-Saharan African kingdom known to the Romans and Byzantines. Located on the upland area of Ethiopia, Aksum is the Holy City of Ethiopia, a city rich in tradition and fantastical monuments and central to Ethiopian national narrative and culture. It is the legendary site of the ark of the covenant, home for the queen of Sheba, and site for the coronation of kings. This key city of the early Red Sea economic system has survived plagues, famine, and periodic destruction for more than 1,300 years, and today it is reemerging as an important regional metropolis.

Aksum (Ge'ez, *Aksum*) is located on the northern edge of the Tigray Plateau at 7,000 feet on the edge of an east-west depression reachable from the east via valleys from the Red Sea coast. From Aksum there is also access to the west down into the Sudanese plains and beyond via the Takkaze Valley. The climate is monsoonal, upland savannah, with the plant cover mainly deforested because of overuse. The ancient water storage and irrigation dam systems around the city are reminiscent of early Yemenite technology, although the city has long been noted for its numerous springs. It lies about 100 miles inland and slightly southwest from the Red Sea port of Massawa and ancient Adulis, not far from the border with Eritrea.

Aksum as a city appears to date from around AD 100. However, the hinterland in which it sits has been part of a regional trading system from about 3000 BC. The region around Aksum is most probably the ancient land of Punt, known to the Egyptian pharaohs as the source of myrrh and a commercial trading partner. The earliest written records of trade with

Punt date from 2450 BC and imply an access route down the Nile. In the Egyptian record, however, there are numerous later references over the next millennium to trade with Punt by sea, which appears to have been the route of choice. Traders and ambassadors would sail up the Nile to Koptos, take the desert road via Wadi Hammamat to the Red Sea, sail down the west coast of the Red Sea to some unidentified port, then transverse inland to reach a site where all manner of goods could be obtained: the products of mines, incense, ebony wood, giraffe tails, baboons, ivory, gold, pygmies, and slaves. All the accumulated evidence suggests that Punt was in the region of upland Ethiopia, and the ports required to reach it lay along the western littoral somewhere from the current area of Port Sudan and Suwakin to Massawa or south to Djibouti.

The last regular references in the Egyptian texts to the land of Punt die out around 1100 BC. However, archaeological remains from east of the Sudanic Nile suggest the existence of regular overland trade from the Aksum region to the Nile during the next millennium. This route may have linked the Red Sea via the area of Aksum to Aswan via the Kasala region. With the rise of the Meroitic kingdom of Nubia (750 BC to AD 320), there was reciprocal trade with the Aksum area, and such trade may have extended far beyond into central Africa. Plantain banana remains, for example, discovered in an eighth-century BC grave in Cameroon, suggest a link via the Red Sea, given that the source of such bananas is East Asia.

By the time of the Ptolemies (305–145 BC), the area around Aksum was incorporated into their regular trade and security community. The port city of Adulis, thirty miles south of present-day Massawa, served as a key gateway into the highland plateau, and war elephants were a key resource the Ptolemies sought from this region. Trade along the archipelago of port cities established by the Ptolemies along the western Red Sea coast continued to increase and linked the Aksum region with Mediterranean trade as well as commerce with India and East Africa. Knowledge of the hinterland by Egypt's rulers was sparse, however, and no written evidence of overland routes to the west from this period has been discovered.

A pre-Aksumite culture, termed *Da'amat* by archaeologists, emerged in the Aksum area around 500 BC, perhaps encouraged by the trading connections that intensified at this time. This culture had ties with Sabaean culture in Yemen, showing some linguistic and artifact similarities. The Da'amat Semitic language, Ge'ez, used a South Arabian alphabet, which may have been transmitted from Arabia much earlier than the appearance of the Da'amat. The primary city for this community appears to have been Yeha, not far from Aksum.

It is out of this milieu that Aksum emerges. The site itself is located in a well-watered valley between two hills. One theory of the origin of Aksum's name is that it derives from *Ah* (Agaw for *water*) and *Siyyum* (Semitic for *chief*). Since the in-

digenous non-Semitic speakers were the Agaw over which a Semitic-speaking elite was able to impose themselves, a site known for its good access to water might naturally be derived from the authority of the "water chief" who located there. Archaeological excavations have revealed that one of the city's hills was first inhabited around 1000 BC. By the third century BC, there are examples of monolithic construction and a proto-Aksumite culture and clear indications of long-distance trade by the town's inhabitants with the Upper Nubian communities, perhaps with Meroë.

Within 300 years, the major site for the city was moved downhill into the Mai Hedja Valley between the two hills, and the city centered around a stela field constructed to memorialize dead kings. Over the next few centuries, the city's kings added additional engraved monumental granite obelisks to the site. This practice ended in AD 330, when the last few

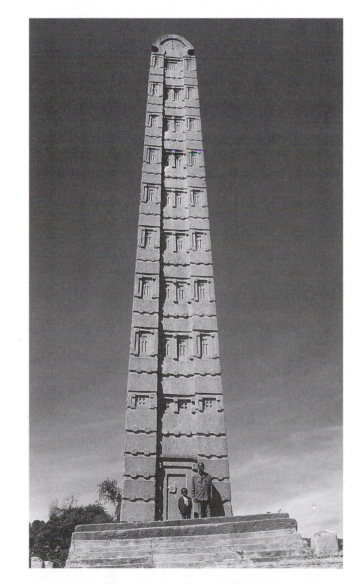

Granite obelisk, Aksum. (Maureen Dunne/UNESCO Photobank)

stelae record the conversion of King Ezana to Christianity. All told, the spectacular Mai Hedja stela field contains 126 obelisks, one of which is the largest ever recorded. A number of the surviving stelae are engraved in a unique Aksumite style, which prompted the United Nations Educational, Scientific, and Cultural Organization (UNESCO) in 1980 to declare Aksum a World Heritage Site. Greek was the language of royal inscriptions up until the fourth century, although some monumental construction includes both Greek and Ge'ez.

It is after AD 300 that the size of the city increased as its population exploded, and the city exerted its primacy over other, older cities in the region such as Yeha. At the height of its political, economic, and cultural power, around AD 500, Aksum covered approximately 250 acres, hosting perhaps 20,000 inhabitants. Today its ruins cover one of the largest archaeological sites in sub-Saharan Africa.

The city seems to emerge in tandem with the growing importance of Adulis as a key broker on the Red Sea trade between Rome's new province of Egypt and East Africa and India. According to the *Periplus Maris Erythraei* (*Circumnavigation of the Erythraean Sea,* a first-century AD pilot's guide to sailing the Red Sea), Adulis exported slaves, ivory, and rhinoceros horn, and its fleet protected the interests of Aksum. Archaeological excavation in Aksum has revealed a range of trade contacts with Roman Egypt dating from the beginning of the Common Era; with India ca. AD 220; and continuing commerce with Syria, Egypt, and Byzantium up through the seventh century. Meroë's power to the north disappeared around AD 320, perhaps because of destruction by the forces of an insurgent Aksum seeking to redirect the ivory trade from the Nile route to one based around Adulis and the Red Sea. During its early development, Aksum was not closely connected with Rome and acted as an independent agent. In fact, the kingdom participated in the great uprising against Roman power during the second half of the third century, and some of its citizens were paraded in Aurelian's triumph in Rome.

The capital city guaranteed meat for its population through the extraction of tribute in cattle from the lowland pastoralists. Two crops per year cultivated in the surrounding highlands sustained the city's inhabitants with barley, wheat, lentils, and grapes.

The state adoption of Christianity in AD 330 supplemented existing trade ties with Egypt and Byzantium with substantial religious ties as well. The conversion of King Ezana at Aksum was the result of a slave, Frumentius, who was a Syrian Christian monk captured at Adulis by pirates. Aksum adopted Christianity only five years after Constantine had made it the Roman state religion. Frumentius was appointed bishop by the Coptic patriarch in Alexandria, forever linking the Egyptian Coptic Church with the Ethiopian Orthodox community.

Under the Christian kings, the city's monumental architecture shifted to its churches and palaces rather than its stelae.

The ceremonial center of the city was moved from Stelae Park, and tradition holds that the first Church of Mary of Zion, the Ethiopian cathedral, was built in a miraculously drained lake by the earliest converts in the late fourth century. The visitor Cosmas Indicopleustes writes around AD 525 that there were a number of impressive multistory stone buildings in the city and palaces capped by square towers. The archaeological record identifies royal palaces with numerous stone thrones and villas, although most of the city was built using mud and thatch. There is a huge rainwater cistern, the *mai shum* (water chief in Semitic), dating from the Aksumite period, which held water for the citizens. Various burial mounds and catacombs dot the site as well. The city was never walled, which says something about the power and attitudes of the Aksumite rulers.

One indication of the power of the Aksum state in international trade is that the city had its own mint and produced a range of gold, silver, and bronze coins. Aksum was the first sub-Saharan kingdom to develop its own mint, reflecting a high degree of organizational control over its commercial empire. Aksum's coin production appears to have begun as early as the late third century and came to an end 400 years later in the early seventh century.

Aksum's kingdom grew in relation to the Roman Empire's needs and desires for trade but continued in the vacuum created by that empire's retrenchment. By AD 500, the city was the center of a political entity that stretched from the borders of the Atbara River in the northwest to Yemen in the south. Tight up against the Persian and Arab control of the Indian Ocean and East African trade circuits, Aksum was the quintessential independent broker, linking the Byzantines with the Indian Ocean networks. Constantine and Constantius II made overtures to the expanding power of Aksum to facilitate long-distance trade, as did Justinian the Great (527–65) when he wrote to his contemporary in Aksum, Elles-baan (Kaleb). Aksumite rulers were called *negusa nagast* (king of kings), which is why they are usually termed emperors in the Western literature.

It is unclear exactly what role Aksum played in shaping South Arabia's political trajectory. Aksum under King Ezana conquered Saba sometime between AD 300 and AD 335 and ruled it until 370. Later, around 525, Byzantium contributed an armada of ships to help the king of Aksum invade the South Arabian kingdom of Himyar. The story goes that Himyar was at that point ruled by a Jewish king, Dhu-Nuwas, who persecuted Christians in his kingdom. In response, the Aksum king Kaleb (Ella-Asbeha, AD 500–534) invaded the country and killed Dhu-Nuwas. A client king was installed to rule the country in tribute to Aksum, but a military coup ended Aksumite authority, and the Sassanians conquered the area after 570.

One way we know about Aksum during its heyday is through an important early record, *The Christian Topography,* attributed to Cosmas Indicopleustes and perhaps written around AD 547–549. The author of the topography was a Christian merchant from Alexandria, a Nestorian, who clearly was well traveled in the Nile Valley, in Sinai and Palestine, around the Red Sea as far as Cape Guardafui, and in Aksum. He and other visitors to the city report exports via Adulis including elephants, gold dust, and hides. Imports carried the eight-day journey from the coast included wine and olive oil. Another author reports seeing huge herds of elephants, perhaps as many as 5,000, corralled around Aksum ready for export. To the west, Aksum traded salt and iron, both high-value commodities. With Nubia, in addition to trade, Aksum dispatched missionaries promoting its Monophysite doctrine (AD 580).

By the end of the sixth century, the kingdom of Aksum was in trouble, although its outward forms continued well into the ninth century. In particular, shifts in regional politics began to restrict Aksum's control over trade routes. For example, wars between Byzantium and Persia between 540 and 561 and again from 602 and 632 interrupted many of Aksum's exchange flows; it also meant that the Byzantines couldn't buy the goods Aksum had to offer. With the Sassanians in Yemen after AD 570, Aksum's command of the routes in the lower Red Sea never rejuvenated. As the century came to an end, Aksum pulled back into itself and did not act aggressively to protect its interests in these areas.

The appearance of Islam and the progressive expansion of the Muslim Empire after 632 was, however, an even greater challenge to Aksumite centrality in regional trade. In quick succession, the coast of Arabia, then Yemen, then Egypt, and finally the Indian trade all became lost to Aksum and shifted to Arab control. Initial relations with Muhammad and the early caliphs were actually good. Muhammad saw Aksum as a friendly country and sent some of his first followers to Aksum in AD 615, the first *hijrah* (*flight*), for their protection. They received a favorable reception in the city, and there were regular embassies back and forth in those early years. The first commercial treaty signed by the Muslim community was with Aksum: Abd Shams ibn Abd Manaf established a commercial treaty with Aksum so that a caravan went from Makkah to what the Arabs knew as al-Habasha (Abyssinia) every winter.

Relations deteriorated, however, with the establishment of the Umayyad dynasty and its search for control over the Red Sea trade routes. Between 702 and 715, the Arabs destroyed the Aksumite fleet, and Adulis itself was captured and leveled. Without access to Adulis and the coast, and with Nile River trade redirected toward other cities, Aksumite contacts with the wider regional and international trade routes were finally severed, and the city's authority collapsed into a small area of the highlands. By the end of the seventh century, gold coins were no longer struck in the mint, and the city's population quickly declined.

Shifts in certain local factors also played a role in the city's reduced fortunes. Local agricultural production dropped at this time, probably because of a combination of factors: the accumulated effects of intensified land use and erosion in this marginal area, a climatic shift in the highlands to a dryer weather pattern in the eighth century, and a loss of authority over parts of the highlands, all of which meant that less food was available to support the city's population. In addition, by the late 700s, Beja pastoralists had immigrated into the Asmara and coastal region and were pressing on Aksumite communities as well as capturing control over incense production sites.

The result of such massive shifts in local, regional, and international contexts was disastrous for the city and for the Aksumite state. Without access to regional markets, and with little local production, its power dissipated. By the middle of the 700s, the city had shrunk to a village, and elites had fled to defensive fortifications in the mountains near their landholdings. Although the religious leadership remained in the city, the first rock-cut churches sequestered back in the mountain valleys began to appear. Aksum dropped off the maps of the Arabs and was almost totally abandoned.

Finally, around 870, the Aksumite kings shifted the capital 200 miles to the south. They abandoned Aksum both to protect their remaining authority and to find a better agricultural site to support their people. The remnants of empire eventually ended up 150 miles to the south in Lasta and Begemder and then, by the tenth century, in central Ethiopia. Aksum itself became a backwater, important only for the symbols of religious and royal authority it held. Ethiopian emperors were only occasionally crowned in the city. The leaders of the Ethiopian Church too finally abandoned the city in the mid-tenth century. It is clear that the hinterland around the city was in a chaotic state: in a letter written around 980 to the king of Nubia, the Aksum king complained that a queen of the (Jewish) Falasha, named Yudit (Judith), had led tribes who sacked the city and burned the churches, causing the king to flee from place to place.

For the next 400 years, the city was remembered primarily in legend and narrative, although it remained as a religious site. As the remnants of state authority waxed and waned far to the south in the central highlands, Aksum was only a small village, with its monuments covered in weeds. Much farther away, however, the memory of the glory that had been Aksum found a narrative home in the European legend of the lost Christian emperor, Prester John. During the Crusades (1165), just as Christian Europe was confronting the might of the Muslims, the story of a Christian "king of the Indies" surfaced. This powerful king, supposedly interested in an alliance with the pope and controlling great wealth, captured the imagination of the literati. Over the next 300 years, Christian elites fantasized about finding this king and activating a pincer movement to defeat the Muslim juggernaut. At the time, the location of India had been reduced to an obscure sense of "the east," and Ethiopia was conflated with "India" in the European geographical imagination. The high priest role assigned to the Ethiopian emperor, and his title as *jan hoi* (emperor), may have contributed to the confusion. Delegations were sent out to find Prester John in Ethiopia, and even Christopher Columbus justified his expedition to the Indies on the possibility of finding this powerful Christian emperor.

The destruction of the central city of the Aksum state may have played a role in the development of a unique Ethiopian tradition—the "mobile capital." Starting even before the fourteenth century, Ethiopian kings would move their "capital" around the various regions of their empire, establishing temporary tent cities or camps ranging from a few thousand to as many as 50,000 people. These camps would remain in place for months or more at a time, were laid out in ordered grids of social hierarchy, and contained churches, kitchens, prisons, markets, and tents for prostitutes. These wandering cities embodied the lost Aksum by containing the authority of the state and religion in one; the clergy, bureaucratic personnel, and security representatives of the state were all present. By moving around the country, both local peasantry and elites came into contact with the national leadership, the national narrative was empowered, and control over recalcitrant local leaders was reestablished.

Aksum experienced a revival during the fifteenth century. The Mary of Zion cathedral was rebuilt in 1404, the Mai Shum cistern was restored in 1426, and new quarters for citizens were constructed during the sixteenth century. Soon, reports suggest, there were eleven churches in the city, agricultural productivity had revived, and the population was on the rise.

The reasons for this revival are unknown but may be related to the revival of the Ethiopian state further to the south. As part of the resurgence of state authority in the late 1300s, a major propaganda text appeared, called the *Kebra Nagast* (*The Glory of the Kings*). In this work, legends are presented as fact tracing the lineage of the new Solomonids of Shewa (AD 1268) dynasty directly back to Menilek I, the illegitimate son of Solomon and the queen of Sheba. Aksum has pride of place in the narrative, since it was the resting place for the ark of the covenant, within the Cathedral of Mary of Zion. The *Kebra Nagast* thus makes the claim for religious sanction, historic authority, and genetic lineage for the emperor through the city of Aksum. The manuscript stresses that the Ethiopians are an elect people, establishing a new Israel. At the "end of days," the text argues, the two kings, Justinus, the king of Rome, and Kaleb, the king of Aksumite Ethiopia, will meet in Jerusalem and divide the earth between them.

In this state-creating narrative, Aksum plays a key role as the site for both religious and royal legitimacy. Thus, despite the shift in the center of authority for the Ethiopian culture to the south, Aksum remained the imagined center of the community. As a result, money and energy needed to be committed to the site to restore it to glory.

Unfortunately, the city did not have an easy ride over the next 400 years. Just as the resurgence was taking hold, the city was plundered in 1535 by the Somali Muslim invader Imam Ahmed ibn Ibrahim (known as Gragn), and the Cathedral of Mary of Zion was burned. This was quickly followed by a major famine from 1540 to 1543. It was not until 1579 that the inhabitants of the city were finally able to begin construction within the burned-out walls of the old church of a new, smaller church.

In-migration to the highlands during the sixteenth century produced the Oromo (Galla) raid on Aksum of 1611, followed fourteen years later by the locust plague of 1625 to 1627, which destroyed crops and cattle; there are even reports of cannibalism in the city during this time. Aksum again shrunk in size to perhaps as few as 1,000 people. Disasters continued with another locust plague from 1633 to 1635, combined with a cholera epidemic. There was a smallpox outbreak in 1693 and another locust plague between 1747 and 1749. Another famine is recorded for the city from 1888 to 1892. Interestingly, this four-year famine may have been exacerbated by the lengthy presence of King Yohannes and his mobile capital at Aksum earlier in the 1880s, which left a legacy of overgrazing and destruction all around the site. Given these periods of dramatic depopulation (1535–1543, 1611–1634, 1780–1855, 1888–1892), it is not surprising that the Ottomans, by this time entrenched in the Red Sea, knew little of Aksum, a town of only 5,000 people, and did not show it on their maps.

The "state project" to expand and centralize the Ethiopian empire gathered steam during the last half of the nineteenth century, and minorities had little place in the new narrative. This was particularly true in the "Holy City" of the state. Emperor Yohannes IV (r. 1872–1889) ordered his governor in Aksum to drive Muslims out of the city and to burn their religious books. If they would not agree to be baptized, they were to be exiled from the country. The Falasha as well felt the push for amalgamation; some rebelled, and around 1862 a spontaneous chiliast "March to Zion," heading for the Red Sea and Jerusalem, finally ran out of steam at Aksum.

Intrinsic to this tragic history was the city's importance to the Ethiopian state both in its religious and royal confirmation of legitimacy and in its statement of urbanism. Many European visitors during this period commented that Aksum was the only "city" in the country. Certainly as Ethiopia entered the twentieth century, it was only one of three sites with more than a few thousand inhabitants. This uniqueness meant the city was embroiled, for example, in the resistance to the Fascist invaders. The Italian air force used poison gas in their attack on the Aksum area, and many of its intellectuals were executed with the occupation. During their five-year rule over the city (1935–1941), the Italians worked to expand the municipality and established a primary school there. In this school, boys recited by heart Il Duce's life story in Italian, gave the Fascist salute, and sang Italian songs as the Italian flag was raised. Aksum was also caught up in the *Weyane,* the rebellion against the reimposition of Ethiopian rule in 1943.

With the 1974 revolution against the emperor, all that Aksum represented to the Ethiopian imperial past had to be wiped clean. The emperor was dead, the empire gone, and the traditions of the past washed away, so Aksum and its traditions were ignored and repressed by the new leftist military dictatorship of the *Derg* (committee), headed by Haile Mariam Mengistu. However, because Aksum was a small but major city in the Tigray heartland, even the Marxist-Leninists of the Derg could not wipe the city away. In fact, the city provided an important iconic component to the Tigray separatist concepts and ideology that evolved between 1974 and the 1980s into the Tigray Popular Liberation Front (TPLF). Working to overthrow the Mengistu regime, the TPLF "liberated" Aksum in 1989 on its way to forcing the dictator to flee the country in 1991. That same year, with the border with newly independent Eritrea not far to the north, Aksum ended up hosting a camp for returning Ethiopian prisoners of war.

In the post-Mengistu phase, the city has experienced a revival of religiosity and governmental attention. Tourism has been promoted and the city's spirituality and heritage celebrated. Traditions related to the Ethiopian Orthodox Church infuse modern Aksum with a sense of the sacred. For a number of days each month, priests carry a copy of the ark of the covenant, wrapped in bright cloth, around the city. The yearly Hider Zion Festival is a time of pilgrimage to Aksum, as is the joyous time of Easter. The tomb of King Basin, who supposedly ruled Aksum at the time of Jesus, and the palace of the queen of Sheba are fervently pointed out to tourists. The new Cathedral of Mary of Zion, built in 1965 by the last emperor, Haile Selassie, houses the ark of the covenant within the Mariam Tsion monastic complex.

Darker secrets surround the city as well. Reportedly, there are numerous deep caves east of the city where thousands of manuscripts from the imperial Aksumite libraries remain stored by church officials. The real ark, the story goes, may actually be housed in a monastery on an island to the south, protected by an ancient secret monastic military order, the "Sodality of the Ark of the Covent of God," whose origins date back to at least the twelfth century. And the evils perpetrated in the city during the "Red Terror of 1977," the time when Mengistu unleashed a wave of assassination and murder against students, rival leftists, and "enemies of the revolution," have still not been discussed or reconciled.

Today the city serves as a small district administrative center and has an airport and a hospital. The population of around 40,000 do get exercised about issues they see as crucial to their city: in the late 1990s, 13,000 citizens signed a pe-

tition demanding the return of the historic Aksum obelisk, looted on Mussolini's personal orders in 1937, which was raised by the Fascists in Rome. In preparation for its return, Aksum modernized its airport and strengthened two bridges over which the three sections would have to be transported. United Nations Educational, Scientific, and Cultural Organization (UNESCO) archaeologists discovered a number of ancient burial vaults under the site as they prepared for its return. Finally, in April 2005, the Aksum obelisk returned "from exile" to its restored site in the city, all financed by the Italian government.

Bruce Stanley

Further Readings

Bahru, Zewde. *A History of Modern Ethiopia, 1855–1991.* 2d ed. London: James Currey, 2001.

Garlake, Peter. *Early Art and Architecture of Africa.* Oxford: Oxford University Press, 2002.

Marcus, Harold. *A History of Ethiopia.* Berkeley: University of California Press, 1995.

Munro-Hay, Stuart C. *Aksum: An African Civilization of Late Antiquity.* Edinburgh: Edinburgh University Press, 1991.

Munro-Hay, Stuart C. *Excavations at Aksum.* London: Thames and Hudson, 1989.

Phillipson, David. *Ancient Ethiopia.* London: British Museum Press, 1998.

Aleppo
Population: 2.3 million (2005 estimate)

Home to one of the largest and most exciting suqs in the Middle East, the city of Aleppo has always been known for its trading prowess, as Shakespeare frequently acknowledged. For more than 4,000 years, the city's merchants have traveled the known world, sending silk to London, pistachios to New York, tobacco to Istanbul, silver to India, and sheep to Egypt. Dominated by its Ayyubid citadel, this second city of Syria remains the capital of the northern Levant, although its days of attracting agents from every European nation to trade in its markets are long over, replaced by industry and agricultural production.

Aleppo (Arabic, *Halab;* Turkish, *Halep*) is the principal city of northern Syria, capital of modern-day Halab Governorate, and the second-largest metropolis of Syria after Damascus. It lies on a plateau at 1,400 feet high and is located midway between the Mediterranean Sea and the Euphrates River. Aleppo has a moderate climate with short, cool, wet winters and long, hot, dry summers. Its surrounding region, parts of which are semiarid, supports extensive agriculture as well as the raising of livestock.

Today the city is connected by rail with Damascus and Beirut and traditionally by caravan route with Iraq and parts of Kurdistan and southern Anatolia. Historically, Aleppo's location made it a natural commercial depot and a busy center of traffic. Pilgrims and traders from the north also transited the city, tracing the edge of the mountains rather than the rugged coast, down through Damascus to Makkah. Though eclipsed in the modern era by the political and economic hegemony of Damascus, Aleppo preserves the essence of a traditional Arab city.

Aleppo, like Damascus, has claims to being one of the oldest continuously inhabited cities in the world. The beginnings of Aleppo can be traced to the early second millennium BC. It is referred to in the Hittite archives in central Anatolia and in the archives of Mari on the Euphrates. Aleppo was the capital of the Amorite kingdom of Yamkhad in the middle centuries of that millennium.

From 800 BC to 400 BC, the Assyrians, followed by the Persians, won control of Syria and presumably Aleppo. In 333 BC, Aleppo was taken over by Alexander the Great and remained, under the name Beroea, as part of the Seleucid Empire for 300 years. During this time, Helllenistic Aleppo was an important trading city, linking the Euphrates and Antioch. In 64 BC, Pompey brought Syria under Roman domination, and Aleppo

became part of the Roman and later Byzantine Empire until AD 637, when the Arabs captured the city and returned to calling it Halab.

In the tenth century, Aleppo was taken over by the Hamdanids, who made it virtually independent until AD 962, when it was retaken by the Byzantine Empire. It was contested frequently during the Crusader period but remained under Muslim control. Under Ayyubid rule in the thirteenth century, Aleppo was known as one of the most beautiful and dynamic cities of the Middle East.

This era abruptly ended with a Mongol attack at the beginning of 1260 BC, which in turn was followed by a long period of Mamluk rule. During the Mamluk period, trade was diverted from Aleppo to the north via Antioch and to the south through Palmyra. But when the Mongol Empire broke up, trade from east to west resumed through Aleppo. The Ottoman Turks later took over, but by that time Europe had redirected its trade through sea routes to India and China, and Aleppo never fully regained its central trading position in the northern Arabian Peninsula.

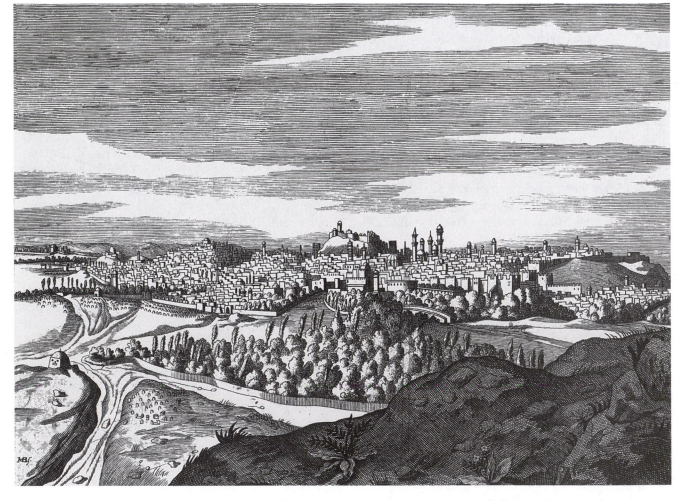

Sketch of Aleppo, 1697. (Maundrell, Henry, *A Journey from Aleppo to Jerusalem at Easter, AD 1697*, p. 1. Oxford, ca. 1703)

During the period of Ottoman rule in Syria (1516–1918), Aleppo served as the administrative capital of a large province that extended over much of northern Syria as well as parts of southern Anatolia. The city's politics were characterized by the competition for influence among local powerful figures and by periodic local clashes with the Ottoman authorities. During World War I, Aleppo's trade increased with the arrival of Armenian refugees who had fled the Ottoman massacres.

When France and Great Britain drew the boundaries of modern Syria at the end of World War I, they severed Aleppo from its natural hinterland of southern Anatolia and northern Iraq. Subsequently, after France ceded Antioch to Turkey, Aleppo also lost its Mediterranean outlet, resulting in a drastic decline in trade (see also "Antakya" and "Iskenderun").

Following the creation of modern Syria, in 1920, Aleppo continued to serve as the seat of government for the surrounding region. Local Sunni landowning families dominated the city and region's politics during the period of the French Mandate (1920–1946) and the first two decades of independence. From the 1960s, however, land reforms initiated by the new Syrian Baathist government broke up and expropriated the great agricultural estates and undermined the political clout of the former Sunni elite. The old landed notables began to be displaced by Alawi Shi'i and other minorities, who began to form a new political elite. Opposition to these developments in Aleppo and other Sunni centers led to violent clashes between Muslim organizations and the central government under President Hafez al-Assad.

In terms of urban development, the contemporary city is still based around the Citadel of Aleppo and the Old City—a long maze of narrow and mostly covered streets and arcades forming one of the largest and best-preserved suqs in the Middle East. These and the khans, madrasas, mosques, and other monumental buildings are constructed from a golden-colored limestone, which, as a result of weathering, has led Syrians to call Aleppo Halab ash-shahba (Aleppo the Grey). The Citadel of Aleppo is an enormous fortress built upon an imposing hill overlooking the Old City. The fortress became a citadel under the Seleucids, and later, Saladin's son, Ghazi, extended it to house a garrison of 10,000 soldiers. Aleppo also boasts its Great Mosque (also known as the Umayyad Mosque), built by the Umayyad caliph al-Walid. Its beautiful minaret, which rises straight from the street, dates from 1090 and is an excellent example of the great period of Islamic architecture in Syria.

The new districts, built on a European model of apartment buildings and wide streets laid out in a regular grid pattern, were constructed from the 1870s onward. Some developments in the twentieth century were later regretted. For example, in 1952 the master plan of Andre Gutton, a French architect commissioned by the city, proposed far-reaching changes to the Old City. Although the plan was not fully im-

plemented, straight streets were carved out of the old city, permitting vehicular traffic to pour into already congested quarters. The old Jewish Quarter was segmented, and in 1979 most of the Old City's northwest quarter, Bab al-Faraj, was demolished. More recently, cooperative projects between conservationists, the municipality, and international funders have resulted in more appropriate interventions in attempts to combine the modernization of the city with the preservation of Aleppo's heritage.

Aleppo has remained one of the centers of cultural life in Syria. It is noted in the country and wider region as a creative center of traditional music. The *muwashah,* a song form traced back to Muslim Spain, has been a local specialty. Hundreds of these vocal pieces—now known as *muwashahat halabeya*—were composed or preserved in the city and diffused from there throughout the region. Ottoman music has also been popular, and Turkish influences continue to distinguish local approaches to music theory. Aleppo's cuisine is considered Syria's finest. Its variety is enriched by the diverse traditions of the city's ethnic and religious minorities and draws upon the wealth of the surrounding countryside: the famous Awassi sheep and orchards of olive, nut, and fruit trees. Aleppo is particularly renowned for its pistachios, which are both exported around the world and incorporated into many sweets produced in the city.

Over the past 100 years, the population of Aleppo has grown approximately 1,000 percent. In 1900 it comprised 120,000 inhabitants, rising to 320,000 in 1950. By 1995 it was more than 1.8 million. The great majority of the residents are Sunni Muslims living alongside substantial numbers of Shi'i (Alawi) Muslims and Christians affiliated with various churches. The largest Christian minority are the Armenians, mostly descended from refugees from Anatolia who settled in Aleppo during World War I. The local Jewish community traced its origins back to pre-Islamic times and expanded in the late nineteenth and twentieth centuries. However, the Arab-Israeli conflict caused most of the community's members to leave the country in 1948, and the last remaining family left in 1994.

Aleppo's commercial role in the region has been transformed over the ages. The city's economy was traditionally based upon the trading of agricultural products, a distribution point for neighboring countries' goods as well as a market for the hinterland's products, notably cotton, grain, pistachios, olives, produce, and sheep. Since the sixteenth century, the city had been a leading center of regional and international trade linked to a wide network of markets that included cities in Anatolia, Iraq, Iran, Syria, Arabia, Egypt, Europe, and the rest of Asia. In the nineteenth century, however, much of the region's external trade was directed toward Europe, and as a result there was a shift from inland cities like Aleppo to the Mediterranean coastal towns. In addition, new boundary changes brought about by the end of the Ottoman Empire in

1918 led to Aleppo being cut off from some of its traditional markets in the region, particularly in Anatolia and northern Iraq, and narrowed still further its commercial horizons. The city's manufacturing sector, however, remained strong, and today the contemporary city is a major industrial center, producing fine silk and cotton fabric, soaps and dyes, processed foods, leather goods, and articles of gold and silver.

Michael Dumper

Further Readings

Eldem, Edhem, Daniel Goffman, and Bruce Masters. *The Ottoman City between East and West: Aleppo, Izmir, and Istanbul.* Cambridge: Cambridge University Press, 1999.

Meriwether, Margaret Lee. *The Kin Who Count: Family and Society in Ottoman Aleppo, 1770–1840.* Austin: University of Texas Press, 1999.

Russell, Alexander. *The Natural History of Aleppo.* Farnborough: Gregg International, 1969.

Tabbaa, Yasser. *Constructions of Power and Piety in Medieval Aleppo.* University Park: Pennsylvania State University Press, 1997.

Zakkar, Suhayl. *The Emirate of Aleppo, 1004–1094.* Beirut: Dar al-Amanah and El-Risalah, 1971.

Alexandria
Population: 4 million to 6 million (2005 estimate)

An age-old eastern Mediterranean metropolis of nearly two and a half millennia, Alexandria is Egypt's second-largest city; an important, burgeoning industrial center; and the country's principal port. It also has survived as a romantic myth, as "the universal metropolis," the city at the center of the world. A race against time is presently taking place between developers, bent on constructing the future, and archaeologists, preoccupied with unearthing and salvaging the past. At stake are real estate and the urgent attention to urban growth and development, on the one hand, and the ongoing discovery of an unequaled heritage, on the other hand. Beneath the contemporary Egyptian urban sprawl are layers of history: the Hellenistic city, a direct heir of Egyptian pharaonic civilization; the imperial Roman town; the city of the Late Roman Empire; the Islamic city of Arabs, Mamluks, and Ottomans; and much of the European town of the nineteenth and twentieth centuries. Alexandria is a palimpsest on which all of its ages have left their marks. It has also been seen at different times as a model of cosmopolitanism and as a microsociety planted on foreign soil and has known extraordinary cultural creativity and been a place of memory and a city haunted by legends. It has experienced ancient and modern colonization, imperialism, and nationalism in peculiar ways. Unprecedented economic booms and crises and dramatic political upheavals have determined its fate. A major turning point in its history took place there in 1956 when Jamal Abdul Nasir declared the nationalization of the Suez Canal in a speech from the city's main square. This triggered the Suez War, the tripartite invasion, and the exodus of most Alexandrians of foreign nationality. Twenty years later, Lawrence Durrell, one of the writers who had contributed immensely to Alexandrian myth, revisited the city. He wrote to a friend: "Alexandria is still full of luciferian charm and magic."

Some thirty cities in the world bear the name of Alexandria and claim the Macedonian king, Alexander the Great (356–323 BC), Aristotle's most famous pupil, as their real or legendary founder. Egypt's Alexandria (Greek, *Aleksandreia;* Coptic, *Rakota;* French, *Alexandrie;* Arabic, *al-Iskandariyya*) has a bona fide right to the claim. In 331 BC, on his way to becoming the conqueror of much of Asia and to his early death in Babylon, Alexander needed a harbor and a city to consolidate the conquest of his Mediterranean flank. It was in Egypt, beside the coastal fort-village of Rhakotis, that he chose to establish his city. Legend has it that he then presented himself to the oracle of Zeus-Ammon at Siwa in order to be proclaimed the legitimate heir to the pharaohs of Egypt and to confirm his divine origin and the promise of world conquest. The construction of the city fell to his general, Ptolemy I Soter (366–283 BC), who in 304 BC adopted the royal title and founded the Ptolemaic dynasty. Meanwhile, in 323 BC, Alexander's corpse had been brought from Asia and ceremoniously buried in the Soma, his magnificent (and still undiscovered) tomb in the heart of the new city.

The Ptolemies ushered in 1,000 years of Greco-Roman-Egyptian-Hellenistic culture before the Islamic-Arab conquest of the city in AD 642, when most of the Greek-speaking population left or became Arabicized. An Arab tradition reports that when they conquered the city, they discovered such marble streets and white houses that the light they produced was so brilliant that at night a tailor could thread a needle.

Alexandria stretches along a narrow strip of land between the Mediterranean and Lake Mariotis, 120 miles northwest of Cairo, to which it is now linked by two major highways and a rapid railway line. In 331 BC, a canal had been built connecting the city to the Nile and thereby to the pharaonic capital of Memphis. When the canal functioned in medieval times, Cairo could be reached by ship in seven days (see also "Cairo"). Today's teeming port-city, the summer seat of the Egyptian government, is one of the most popular resorts in the Middle East. Nicknamed *arusat al-bahr al-mutawassit* (the bride of the Mediterranean), its white sandy beaches extend along the Mediterranean for some 65 miles from Abukir to al-Alamein. Summers are breezy; winters temperate.

Ptolemaic Alexandria endured for 275 years (305–30 BC) before its annexation by Rome. The seat of a centralized power, it dominated all of Egypt and its environs up into the Aegean Sea. It was probably the world's greatest city and emporium of its time and played an essential role in the transmission of the Egyptian heritage personified by the god Serapis, who was protector of the town and the dynasty. The foundation of the city was considered an act of destiny: the legend of the city and the myths of its founding hero grew together. Alexander had accomplished the promise of Homer and willed the universal metropolis. According to Plutarch, Alexander had a dream that led him to order the construction of a lighthouse on the island of Pharos in the harbor of Alexandria. The "Alexander Romance" reports that an oracle had advised him to establish "a city rich in fame opposite the isle of Proteus" (i.e., the island of Pharos).

The Lighthouse of Pharos, one of the Seven Wonders of the Ancient World, completed in 283 BC, was the symbol of Alexandria's grandeur. A causeway, the Heptastadion, nearly a mile long, was constructed to connect the island of Pharos to the mainland and to divide the harbor into western and eastern harbors. The lighthouse on the easternmost part of the island, the site today of the fifteenth-century fortress of Qait Bey, stood some 400 feet high, its light supposedly visible from forty miles away. It resisted time for sixteen centuries until, in 1302, the last of a series of earthquakes brought it down. Remains from the lighthouse have been excavated underwater just off the coast over the past half century, as have relics of the royal quarters, including a colossal red-granite statue of a Ptolemaic queen representing Isis, the goddess of magic.

The Ptolemies of Alexandria established the archetype of the royal Hellenistic court, which inspired subsequent autocrats from the Roman Empire to the caliphs of Islam. The Ptolemies had enormous wealth and controlled trade in the eastern Mediterranean and overland from the Red Sea. They displayed their grandeur by luxury and opulence, in palaces, gardens, temples, stadiums and theaters, and, most notably, through the Bibliotheca (the Great Library) and the Museion (the Museum). The Bibliotheca was the first attempt in history to gather together all human knowledge. Its walls and shelves contained thousands of labeled papyrus scrolls. A center of study and research, it educated and sent out into the world some of the greatest minds of antiquity, the likes of Euclid and Archimedes. Attached to it was the Museion, a house of scholars, where the Septuagint, the Greek translation of the Old Testament, was achieved. Its translation paved the way for Christianity's spread into a large part of the Mediterranean world. The Greek language and culture and the treasures of Oriental wisdom flourished in Alexandria, and Hellenized Judaism created there some of its most important works of learning.

The Jewish community, perhaps numbering 40,000 out of a total population estimated at 600,000, enjoyed a degree of autonomy and a form of semicitizenship, and it resided in one of the five sections of this great city of the third century BC. Designed according to the Greek grid-plan model centered on the agora, the city was both a polis and a royal residence. A cosmopolitan city, its inhabitants included Macedonians, Greeks, Jews, Egyptians, mercenaries from Gaul and slaves from Nubia, adventurers, scholars, merchants, and travelers.

Its various residents lived in coexisting communities. Nonetheless, the Egyptian priestly texts insist that Alexandria is "on the edge of Egypt"; it is "the residence of the King of the Ionians ... on the shore of the Greek Sea"; but it is also "a temple of the world," and the adherents of the cults of the gods, Isis and Dionysos, among the "new pharaohs," and their courts were numerous. The Egyptian gods were thus integrated into the Greeks' view of the world.

The Roman conquest of Alexandria and its annexation to the empire took place in the period 47–30 BC. Some eighty years later, in about AD 40, the apostle Mark established Coptic Orthodox Christianity in Egypt. By AD 451, the Coptic Church he founded had become a distinct and recognized part of Oriental Orthodoxy, with its see in Alexandria. The Pope of Alexandria and the Patriarch of the Holy See of Saint Mark is currently Pope Shenouda III, and the Coptic population of the city and of Egypt, in general, remains numerous. In the period of late Roman history, Alexandria became a center of Christian theology and church government in which the patriarch of the city played a major role in the spread of the religion and in its persecution of paganism, which apparently included the destruction of the Bibliotheca in AD 391.

The Arab Muslim conquerors of Egypt integrated Alexandria into the caliphate in AD 642 and made it a Muslim city, but they also inherited a historical city and the memory of its founder, Alexander, whom they called *dhu l'qarnayn* (the man of two horns). In Arab legend, Alexander had rebuilt an ancient city associated with famous biblical figures. In doing so, he had brought it out of impiety into a time of submission to the divine will. With the Muslim conquest of the city, many of its inhabitants fled, and among those who stayed, the great majority became Arabicized and Islamized.

Throughout the period of the various medieval sultanates, Alexandria played a very secondary role to the new capital of Cairo. At various times, it was attacked by Crusader fleets. For the most part, it was an administratively autonomous zone in which the Malikite School of Law predominated because of the city's important links with the Maghreb, where Malikite law was dominant. It traded in textiles, exported linen, silk, wool, and cotton goods as far as India. At its largest, its estimated population may have reached 65,000.

Under the Mamluks (1250–1517), Alexandria was considered a *thaghar,* a frontier city, between the predominantly Muslim and Christian worlds. The general plan of the city remained as it had been in antiquity: a chessboard of eight perpendicular straight avenues surrounded by walls with four main gates. The canal link with the Nile functioned only sporadically.

After Egypt became part of the Ottoman Empire, in 1517, Alexandria's role as a center for commercial ties with European ports increased. Its commercial growth attracted rural immigrants; Muslims and Jews from the Maghreb and

Andalusia; traders from Istanbul, Italy, and Provence; and soldiers from the Balkans and Anatolia. The city expanded from its original site onto *jazira khadra* (green island), the peninsula between the two ports that connected the continent to the island of Pharos. By then the famous lighthouse had been destroyed by a series of earthquakes, and the Mamluk sultan Qait Bey had built an enormous fortress on the spot in 1477. Gradually merchants began moving beyond the walls of the city and creating new neighborhoods. The Ottoman governor Sinan Pasha, famous for his architectural feats in Istanbul, built an enormous caravansary in the new area in 1570, which attracted merchants and craftsmen. Throughout the seventeenth century, wealthy Maghrebi and Turkish merchants invested in the spice trade, coffee, and textiles, and Alexandria became an arsenal and an essential base for the Ottoman fleet.

Recent research has discovered that there had been expanding urbanism in Alexandria in the century preceding the Bonaparte Expedition of 1798. Previously it had been thought that Alexandria was a very small and poor town of 5,000 or so inhabitants when the French arrived. Now historians speak of a "modest town" of some 15,000. Apparently, the members of the expedition saw only the part of the Old City that was in ruins and failed to observe the new city that had arisen on the peninsula and outside the walls of the ancient and medieval town. Most of the population were living in neighborhoods

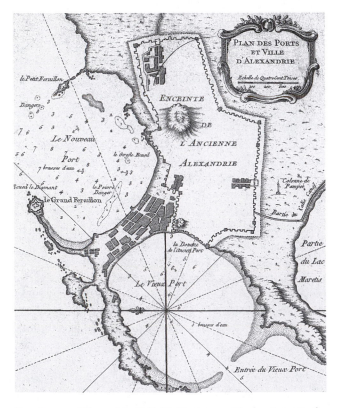

French map of Alexandria, 1764. (Bellin, Jacques-Nicolas, *Le petit atlas maritime . . .* Vol. III, pl. 86. Paris, 1764)

now referred to as the "Turkish city" and that made up a remarkably homogeneous urban ensemble. Later, when modern Alexandria boomed, the Turkish city (because of its density, narrow streets, and impasses) remained relatively intact; its Ottoman architecture and the décor of Turkish and Maghrebi mosaics were preserved in houses, mosques, and *okelles* (merchant warehouses or hotels). This patrimony, under the impact of current demographic pressure and real estate speculation, is in the process of being destroyed.

Bonaparte's stay in Egypt did not last long. Already, in August 1798, the French fleet had been decimated by the British at Aboukir, and two years later the French troops of General Kléber were beaten there by the Ottoman army. The stage was set for the next act of Alexandria's fame as a cosmopolitan city. In 1805 Muhammad Ali, originally a Macedonian merchant from Cavalla turned mercenary war chief, took the reigns of power in Egypt and became its Ottoman viceroy. He nursed imperial ambitions for which he needed a modern maritime port. He decided to resurrect and transform Alexandria to that purpose.

Between 1810 and 1839, the port was reconstructed, the city opened up to large-scale Mediterranean immigration, and the Mahmudiya Canal to the Nile dug to provide a dependable water supply. In less than a generation, a modern infrastructure had been created. At the death of Muhammad Ali, in 1839, the population had reached 100,000, and the economy, mostly based on cotton, had expanded dramatically. Alexandria was on its way once again to becoming Egypt's threshold to the world, and for the next century it would be a new Shangri-la and eventually "the Queen of the Mediterranean," an international refuge, a bustling economic center, and a cultural pole of attraction.

A new city center rose around a large and beautiful, tree-lined square. In the middle stood a monument to Muhammad Ali, with a twenty-foot-high pedestal of Tuscany marble as a base to a fifteen-foot-high bronze equestrian statue of the viceroy cast in Paris. Around the square, one found the stock exchange, elegant streets with shops and banks, and bourgeois apartment blocks in fin de siècle styles. To the west was the twin harbor with its commerce and industry. To the east stretched the corniche with its beaches and suburbs. To the north along the peninsula, the maze of lanes of the Turkish town. To the south, the catacombs of antiquity, Pompey's Pillar, and the railway station. Soon the city had gas, electricity, public transport, schools, hospitals, pensions, sporting teams, and musical groups. A railroad linked Alexandria to Cairo in 1854, another to Suez in 1858, prior to the opening of the canal in 1869; a tramway was completed in 1863. Gardens sprang into existence on the thin tongue of land bought from Bedouin between the sea and the lake.

According to a 1872 guide book, Alexandria had about 100 mosques, three Catholic churches, four Greek churches of various rites, three Protestant churches of different sects, three main synagogues, and a Coptic and a Maronite church. Each community had its own cemetery, including one for free-thinkers. The main indigenous industries were saddle working, embroidering in gold and silk, the making of jewelry, the dyeing and weaving of cotton goods, and the manufacture of pipe stems, mats, tobacco, and arms. European industries included flour mills, tanneries, oil presses, breweries, and factories for cotton ginning and soap making.

The elite of Alexandria were mostly immigrants from Europe and the Levant. They were part of a pluralistic society based on the recognition of the autonomy of the different communities that composed the population. These were determined by a combination of identities based on nationality and religion. Greeks were the largest foreign community, 37,882 in 1937; the Jewish community, some with foreign nationalities, others native Egyptians, were numerous, 40,000 in 1948. Alexandria in regard to its lifestyle and languages was at least partly a European city. Its "cosmopolitanism" came from a sense of living together and recognizing and accepting the variety of communities that shared that urban space. In 1927 the estimated population was 600,000, and of those, 100,000 were "foreigners" and possessed foreign passports. They were protected by *capitulations,* commercial treaties that exempted them from taxation and gave them immunity from judicial control by Egyptian authorities. Alexandria was a "free zone" for them. To be sure, their status was a product of imperialism and was linked to European interests. At the same time, the expansion of Alexandria throughout this period was linked to a whole series of crises and circumstances in the Mediterranean world: the "Middle East question," 1840; the Crimean War, 1854; the "cotton boom," 1863 (itself linked to the U.S. Civil War); the British occupation of Egypt, 1882; the Balkan Wars; and World War I.

In 1882 an Egyptian nationalist revolt led by Colonel Ahmad Arabi against the rule of the Khedivial dynasty that had inherited power from Muhammad Ali culminated in anti-European riots in Alexandria. These riots, in which hundreds of people lost their lives, served as a pretext for British intervention, the bombardment and occupation of the city. Most of the modern city was destroyed. Egypt became a British colony until 1922. The Egyptian government compensated the owners of property for their losses.

Four and a half million sterling pounds were paid to 4,080 claimants. The modern city was quickly rebuilt and experienced a burst of prosperity. Trade expanded, and so did the wealth of Alexandria's bourgeoisie. The city's urban morphology and architecture were increasingly modern, European in standards and techniques, and belle époque eclectic in style.

Modern Alexandria was largely created by its elite and bourgeoisie and by the dynamics of commercial exchange; an autonomous city was built by "foreigners" who were not really, or simply, "foreign." They were Alexandrian "Egyptiots": Greeks, Armenians, Sephardic and Ashkenazic Jews, Syro-Iraqis, Maghrebis, Italians, Maltese, and more. The Municipal Council of elected notables that held sway from 1890 to 1930 made Alexandria a rival to Marseille and Genoa. The Graeco-Roman Museum, founded in 1891 by an Italian archaeologist, was and is a monument to Alexandrian spirit and culture. The city functioned beautifully and apparently to the benefit of most of its inhabitants. Although many languages were spoken in the city, French was dominant among the elite and in business, a bridge across most of the communities whatever their mother tongues might be. The city was open to modernity and to cultural variety. That does not mean that there was equality and lack of conflict, especially between the dominant classes and the rest of the population, who were mostly poor Muslim and Coptic Arabs. In 1921, for example, there were serious riots and the deaths of forty-three Egyptians, twelve Greeks, and two Italians, according to the records. The Municipal Council eventually went bankrupt and was transformed into an organization nominated by the central government. There were strikes and demands for recognitions by a growing Egyptian middle class. That class was to continue to expand during World War II, which created a brief period of wealth and well-being in Alexandria and of massive immigration from the countryside. It also paved the way to a nationalist revolution.

The 1930s are considered the heyday of modern Alexandrian cosmopolitanism. An extraordinary Mediterranean urban society nurtured some of the great artists and writers of the twentieth century: Constantin Cavafis, the founder of the language of modern Greek poetry, E. M. Forster, Stratis Tsirkas, Giuseppe Ungaretti, Marinetti, Fausta Cialente, Robert Liddle, D. J. Enright, and Lawrence Durrell, among the European writers; and among the Egyptians, the actress Fatma Rushdi, the filmmakers Muhammad Bayyoumi and Youssef Chahine, the musician Bayram al-Tunsi, the poets Abdullah al-Nadim and Ahmad Rassim, the novelists Tawfiq Hakim, Edouard al-Kharrat, and Ibrahim Abdelmagid, and a whole school of excellent Egyptian painters. According to most accounts, Alexandrians in this golden age were snobbish, self-satisfied, sensual, and filled with vitality and the joy of life. Alexandria was, in the myths of its modern form, a "City of Saffron" (al-Kharrat) and had a "Spirit of Place" (Durrell). Naguib Mahfouz, Egypt's Nobel Prize–winning novelist, who spent his summers in Alexandria and wrote some novels situated there, remembers it without myths or nostalgia as essentially a European city. Greek, French, or English were heard in the streets more often than Arabic. It was a beautiful place, "so clean that you could eat off of the street." Waiters in chic hotels wore frock coats like government ministers. Such attitudes helped cultivate a climate that discriminated against Arab Egyptians.

The heart of the modern city remains Ramlah Station on Saad Zaghlul Square, with its monumental statue to the Egyptian nationalist leader, at once a terminal for tramways and a center of cinemas, restaurants, cafés, bookshops, and newspaper kiosks. It is probably there in Roman times that Cleopatra began the construction of the Caesareum for Antony that was completed by their enemy Octavius. A 1939 landmark, the renovated Cecil Hotel, where Somerset Maugham, Winston Churchill, and the British Secret Service, among others, stayed, overlooks the square. The Graeco-Roman Museum, largely unrenovated, is nonetheless or because of that still a gem, and the villas of the early twentieth century in the old Greek Quarter remain splendidly decadent. Along the twenty-mile waterfront, the corniche and the cliff road reclaimed from the sea in the early 1900s, dotted with beach huts on stilts in the golden years, continue to take the breath away, especially from inside of one of the city's racing taxis or minibuses.

The former Place de Consuls, Muhammad Ali Square, Manshieh, destroyed by the British in 1882 and then gloriously rebuilt, now carries the name of Midan at-Tahrir (Liberation Square) and needs rehabilitation. When the Free Officers took power in the 1952 revolution, it was from the port of Alexandria that King Farouk, the last of Muhammad Ali's dynasty, sailed into exile. Two years later, in October 1954, an attempt on the life of Abdul Nasir took place there while he spoke from the balcony of the Socialist Union, the former stock exchange overlooking the square. Then, once again from the same spot, on 26 July 1956, Nasir declared the nationalization of the Suez Canal. The ensuing invasion of British, French, and Israeli armies, the Suez War of 1956, led to the end of Alexandria's second golden age and its cosmopolitanism. Most of the city's Jews and British and French nationals, trapped by history, were expelled, and within a few years the very large Greek community had dwindled to less than 1,000. The exodus of the "Egyptiots," the "foreigners," marked the death knoll of Alexandrian cosmopolitanism. The system of capitulations had long been abolished by the Montreux Conference of 1937, but the privileged classes more or less had held on. The coup d'état of 1952 marked the victory of Egyptian nationalism. Egyptianization, Arabization, agrarian reform and land confiscations, state socialism, restrictions on the private sector, and the closing of the stock exchange (which had once rivaled Liverpool's) have made contemporary Alexandria a largely monoglot and Muslim city.

In 1977, during bread riots in the city, the former stock exchange burned down. It has not been rebuilt. The modern glory of Alexandria has passed away. Three or four generations of fortunes won and lost, of a city's romance that blossomed and withered, of a brief moment of recapturing a glorious past are now little more than memories. Alexandria today is a place of demographic explosion and wildcat construction. Estimates of its population vary between 4 and 6 million. Overcrowded and overwhelming, it suffers housing and infrastructural crises of unparalleled proportions. Poverty, transportation chaos, and the informal economy are rampant. Most of its residents are involved in a daily struggle for subsistence. At the same time, the opening up of the Egyptian economy in the 1970s created a boom for developers of real estate. Moreover, the city has become an industrial center because of natural gas and oil pipelines coming from Suez. These developments have also awakened the active interest of intellectuals and governments, Egyptian and foreign, in trying to save Alexandria's incredible archaeological and historical patrimony. The archaeologists, with the help of the French government, have established a Center for Alexandrian Studies (CEA) and are engaged in a race against time to save what remains of the ancient Ptolemaic capital and in salvage excavations for the restoration of ancient structures, in general.

That interest has marked the contemporary urban landscape in a forceful and promising way. In 1988 foundations were laid for a new Bibliotheca Alexandrina, a resurrection of the famed library of antiquity. It was completed and inaugurated in 2002. Built by the Egyptian government and the United Nations Educational, Scientific, and Cultural Organization (UNESCO) at a cost of $176 million, this magnificent building of more than 300,000 square feet will contain some 8 million books. It also has Internet archives, three museums, seven research centers, a planetarium, two permanent exhibitions, five art galleries, and an enormous conference center. The ambition is to put Alexandria back on the map of the world as an international center of learning and cultural diversity.

Kenneth Brown

Further Readings

Brown, Kenneth, and Hannah Davis-Taieb. "Alexandria in Egypt." *Mediterraneans* 8/9 (1996).

Canfora, Luciano. *The Vanished Library*. Translated by Martin Ryle. London: Vintage, 1991.

Cavafy, Constantine. *Collected Works*. Translated by E. Keeley and P. Sherrard. London: Chatto and Windus, 1990.

Durrell, Lawrence. *The Alexandria Quartet*. London: Faber and Faber, 1986.

Ellis, Walter M. *Ptolemy of Egypt*. London: Routledge, 1994.

Empereur, Jean-Yves. *Alexandria Rediscovered*. London: British Museum Press, 1998.

Forester, Edward M. *Pharos and Pharillon*. Richmond, VA: Hogarth Press, 1923.

Haag, Michael. *Alexandria: City of Memory*. New Haven, CT, and Cairo: Yale University Press and AUC, 2004.

Ilbert, Robert, and Ilios Yanakakis. *Alexandria, 1860–1960: The Brief Life of a Cosmopolitan Community*. With Jacques Hassoun. Translated from the French by Colin Clement. Alexandria: Harpocrates, 1997.

Jacob, Christian, and Francois de Polignac. *Alexandria, Third Century BC: The Knowledge of the World in a Single City*. Translated from the French by Colin Clement. Alexandria: Harpocrates, 2000.

Kharrat, Edwar al-. *City of Saffron*. Translated by Frances Liardet. London: Quartet, 1989.

Macleod, Roy, ed. *The Library of Alexandria*. London: I. B. Tauris, 2002.

Mahfouz, Naguib. *Miramar*. Cairo: AUC Press, 1989.

Algiers
Population: more than 3 million (2004 estimate)

Situated on the northern Mediterranean littoral of the Maghreb (northwest Africa, the far west of Islam), Algiers is the capital of Algeria, a nation that gained its independence in 1962 after 132 years of French colonization. The French virtually transformed Algiers into a European city, making it the second most important port in the Mediterranean, after Marseille. The population and space of the colonial city grew dramatically. Segregation between Europeans and Algerians was the rule, with the former enjoying the best of modern architecture and urban planning and the latter increasingly experiencing the poverty and hardships of the bidonvilles, the shantytowns. On the eve of Algerian independence, after a bitter and violent war between Frenchmen and Algerians, a secret army organization of the French (Organisation de l'Armée Secréte, or OAS) destroyed some of the infrastructure of the city. Finally, most of the more than 1 million French citizens, many of whom were from Algiers, left the country. Since 1962 Algiers has experienced enormous growing pains. The city was, as one commentator put it, for its citizens, like the French language— "war booty." Massive squatting took place in the European quarters and the kasbah, mostly by immigrants from the countryside. The end of segregation was accompanied by relative chaos in which buildings and public spaces became neglected and run down. The Algerians inherited the city of "the other" without experience of urban administration or planning. Only after decades of fluctuating economic and political instability, critical housing shortages and unemployment, and urban unrest and civil war has the city begun to emerge from the shadows of decolonization.

On the site of the coastline of today's Algiers (French, *Alger;* Spanish, *Argel;* Arabic, *al-Jaza'ir*), Phoenicians probably founded a settlement, a trading factory called Yksm, meaning "island of seagulls" or "full moons." Legend attributes its foundation to twenty companions of the mythical hero Hercules. In the second century BC, it had become a Roman colony known as Icosium. Their street plan is still reflected in the pattern of some roads, including the *rue de la Marine,* while the Bab al-Oued area of the city was a Roman burial ground. From 25 BC until AD 40, the city belonged to a vassal kingdom of Rome ruled first by Juba II and then Ptolemy. Caligula put down a rebellion by the kingdom and divided it into Mauritania-Tingitane and Mauritania-Ceasarienne, which included Icosium. The fortified city was sacked in AD 371 by a Berber prince named Firmus and disappeared from historical sources after the fifth century AD.

The site remained uninhabited until the middle of the tenth century, when Berber tribesmen founded a market town called al-Jazair Bani Mazghanna, "The Islands of the Sons of Mazghanna." The name al-Jazair refers to the rocky islets off the coast, which form a kind of natural mole. The site overlooks an arched bay near the opening of the fertile plain of the Mitidja Valley to the south and commanding to the west the Chelif Valley, the high Constantine plains, and the traditional routes to Tunisia and Morocco. A description of the town at the end of the tenth century relates that it knew some prosperity; was surrounded by a wall; and had many bazaars, freshwater, and extensive fields; and its nearby mountains were inhabited by Berber tribesmen. It exported honey, butter, and figs; its port was visited by sailors from Spain, Tunisia, and elsewhere. From the eleventh until the sixteenth century, Algiers passed from the hands of one Muslim conqueror to another, including the Almoravids; the Almohads; the Hafsids, who came from the east in the thirteenth century; and the Merinids, arriving from the west in the fourteenth century.

Lightly dominated by the Sultanate of Tlemsen, Algiers enjoyed relative autonomy under its own amirs (chiefs). It was a kind of small municipal republic governed by a civic oligarchy and a market town of modest size. The pious man who was to become the patron saint of Algiers, Sidi Abd ar-Rahman al-Thaalabi (1387–1468), lived there during that period. Few monumental buildings from that period remain today other than the Great Mosque, with an inscription from the year 1018, and a minaret furnished by the king of Tlemsen in 1324. Opposite the harbor, a small island, later known as Penon, at cannon-shot range from the town, was occupied by the Spanish ca. 1302, and from then on, exchange between the city and Spanish ports expanded.

During the Reconquista and Inquisitions in Spain, some of the expelled Muslims and Jews immigrated to Algiers. In 1529 the town and the islet of Penon were taken over by the Ottoman Turks, and the fabled pirate Khair ad-Din, "Barbarossa," established the initial *pashalik* (ruled by a pasha). Gradually, as their powers grew, Algiers was awarded the status of a *deylik* (semiautonomous city-state or political entity under nominal Ottoman authority). As a "corsair state" and Turkish regency, Algiers became the political, administrative, and maritime capital of the country. The effectively autonomous domination by the Turkish deys of Algiers, free of the control of Istanbul, continued until the French conquest of 1830.

Situated on the margins of the Ottoman and European economies, seventeenth-century Algiers was a prosperous and populous city of some 100,000 inhabitants, the chief seat of the Barbary Corsairs, infamous masters of piracy and trade. The city extended on rocky slopes descending from the kasbah to the beach, its circuit resembling a crossbow, the walls being the bow and the seashore the string. The perimeter measured along the exterior walls was some 10,000 feet and included forts and batteries; its height was about 40 feet, and it was surrounded by a ditch and flanked by towers. The city had five gates. The kasbah built on the highest point of the town became the residence of the deys. It had barracks, arsenals, the treasury, and the private apartments of the rulers. Outside the town, higher than the kasbah, was the emperor's fort. The seafront was equally protected by a series of forts.

The town inside the walls spread along the slope of the hill; at its highest point was the Jebal, an area of whitewashed houses supported by wooden shores, pressed closely together. Steep lanes with flights of steps darkened by the vaults of the houses wound up the slopes. The lower part of the town contained the favorite residences of the corsair captains, sumptuous dwellings clustered near the sea, the whole quarter a kind of arsenal of their crews. The most famous corsair captains of the seventeenth century had their palaces there as well as the mosques they endowed with their wealth. On the eve of the French conquest, there were some 150 mosques, chapels, and religious sanctuaries of brotherhoods in the town.

The population during the three centuries of Turkish domination consisted of Turks, Moors (Arab and Berber Muslims), and Jews. The Turks, who had mostly come from Asia Minor as soldiers, formed a closed aristocracy. No matter their rank, they were addressed as "Effendi," great and magnificent noblemen. When they married women of the country, the offspring, called Kuloghlus, were kept apart and excluded from public employment. The Turks were always a minority. Another group coming from abroad was composed of renegades of European origin, engineers who were artisans, pilots for the navy, and among the most illustrious corsairs. Like the Turks, their number eventually dwindled during the period from the sixteenth to the nineteenth century. The Moors made up the majority of the indigenous urban population (the *baladis*). Tradespeople and craftsmen organized in guilds; some rich, some poor, they were not permitted to participate in public affairs or serve in the army. Others, the *barranis* (outsiders), came from the countryside; these included Kabyle Berbers who were artisans and day laborers, those from the Mzab who were bakers, and so forth.

In 1830 there were in the city about 4,000 Turks, 300 renegades, 18,000 Moors (including Kuloghlus), 2,000 mostly enfranchised black slaves, 1,000 Berbers, and 4,000 Jews, who included the indigenous (Arabs and Berbers), poor and badly treated, and the "Franks" (of Italian origin, especially from Leghorn), often rich merchants and sometimes bankers of the deys and intermediaries between the regency and the European powers. In 1805 they were the objects of a riot from which they never wholly recovered. European slaves who had been captured on raids by the corsairs were also present: 25,000–35,000 in the first half of the seventeenth century, only 1,200 in 1816.

Government was administered under the supervision of the *khaznadji*, the minister of finance of the regency. Various ethnic groups and trades formed guilds ruled by amirs, all of whom were subject to the head shaykh of the town. There was an inspector of markets, another of public baths and houses of ill fame, and so forth. By all accounts, the system of administration worked well and provided security. It came to an end in 1830, disappearing along with Turkish authority.

Various European nations repeatedly tried to put down piracy, and in 1816 a British squadron accompanied by Dutch ships bombarded the city and torched the corsair fleet.

Then, on 4 July 1830, a French expeditionary corps attacked and occupied Algiers, justifying the action by saying that the dey had insulted the consul. The city surrendered to the troops the following day. By that time, the city's prosperity—which had depended on piracy—had seriously declined, and the estimated population had fallen to some 40,000.

From the beginning until the end of the 132 years of French colonization (1830–1962), Algiers underwent continuous modifications. A European city gradually came to replace the Berber, Arab, and Turkish town. By 1901 the population had increased to 138,000 inhabitants, including 69,000 Frenchmen, 11,750 naturalized Jews, and 28,250 foreign Europeans, most of them Spaniards. The harbor was greatly enlarged, and its traffic continually and dramatically grew. The territorial extension of the modern town far exceeded the limits of Turkish Algiers. Roads, barracks for the troops, and offices for the administration were built early on, often on the land of destroyed houses and religious buildings. Of all the places of Muslim worship standing in 1830, only forty-eight remained in 1862. The Ketchawa Mosque was replaced by the Catholic Cathedral of Saint Phillipe and that of Mezzo Morto was transformed into a church. The town was almost completely modernized, with European streets running across the lower part and traverse roads crossing the high town. All this aggressive tearing down and building up was already characterized by some French historians at the beginning of the twentieth century as "acts of violence."

The French had conquered Algeria with the intent to stay and to make Algiers a viable political capital. This included endowing it as a center of intellectual life and learning. Before 1900 a veritable university with schools of law, medicine, science, and fine arts had been established, with almost 1,000 students. Among the subjects taught and researched, Oriental studies occupied an important place, including the literature, languages, folklore, ethnography, and civilizations of North Africa. The accomplishments of research and scholarship were considerable. The French-built new town, with its wide boulevards and cultural edifices, eventually had its opera house, cathedrals, theaters, museums, galleries, and cafés as well as the University of Algiers.

Initially after the occupation of the city, the French built a rampart, parapet, and ditch with terminal forts, Bab Azoun to the south and Bab al-Oued to the north. These were partially demolished and replaced by a line of forts along the heights of

Bouzareah, 1,300 feet above sea level. The church of Notre Dame d'Afrique was conspicuously built there on the shoulder of the hills two miles north of the city. It is a mixture of Roman and Byzantine styles with a statue over the altar of the Virgin depicted as a black woman and a solid silver statue of the archangel Michael.

The occupation of Algiers thus had both logistic and symbolic components to the process of colonization. A violent military conquest, ostensibly intended to better control the indigenous population, destroyed most of the city. In building a European city, the French wanted a capital that would be a window of their architecture and urbanism, and to do so they employed the most famous of their architects and planners. By 1925 the creation and development of the harbor had made it the second most important French port after Marseilles in regard to tonnage. In 1930 the population had reached 246,061, the majority probably still Europeans or holding French passports. The natives lived in the "exotic and dangerous" kasbah, which was divided into four neighborhoods. The rest of the city was largely out of bounds for them. They had access to their own cafés, a football stadium, a few movie theaters, a "reserved" beach, hammams, cemeteries, houses of ill repute, and so forth. The city boasted three segregated football teams: Christian, Jewish, and Muslim. Besides the mosques, the Muslims visited the tomb of Sidi Brahim for the saint's benediction. The rest of the public space—nightclubs, casinos, the opera, and so forth—was forbidden territory. During times of political crisis and wartime, conditions worsened and brought about seclusion, control, isolation, and curfews.

Segregation was de facto and usually accompanied by racism based on origins and status. Communal solidarities were exclusive, structural inequalities and discriminations were perpetual, yet there were sometimes personal and even communal links. Put differently, two distinct, unequal societies existed side by side, the one colonial, the other colonized. Among some of the latter, the stirrings and manifestations of modern nationalism took form already in the 1920s.

Algiers' first bidonvilles—precarious, cheap, inflammable, overcrowded metal shacks—appeared in the early 1930s, a period of intense urbanization from the countryside and Kabylia. These new immigrants were considered "an army of invasion." In 1930 Europeans comprised three-quarters of the city's population. By 1954 they were 46 percent. In 1945 some

Algiers hillside. (Corel Corporation)

10,000 people out of a total of 300,000 lived in bidonvilles; in 1948 they numbered 35,000 in 120 bidonvilles.

Algiers was a colonial city, almost a creation of France, and "an ambiguous model of triumph" according to one of its historians. Until the middle of the twentieth century, the majority of its inhabitants were Europeans. Although they may have aspired to be living in a French metropolis, Algiers resembled a provincial southern city on the other bank of the Mediterranean with Paris as its center of attraction. It had a Creole-like character; even its everyday colloquial language, Sabir, had its own particular features drawn largely from French but combining elements of Spanish and Arabic. In time, these people would be called *pieds noirs* (black footed), referring to French citizens of various Mediterranean peasant origins and by extension to the Jews of Algeria. During the Algerian war of independence (1954–1962), it meant "non-Muslims," and afterward in France it was applied to the French exiles coming from Algeria.

The French city enjoyed a precarious triumph but was doomed to disappear, like colonialism, from Algeria. Yet if today's Algiers is essentially Arab Berber and Muslim, the traces of its French-dominated past run deep. Buildings of major architects—Le Corbusier, Perret, Pouillon—dot its landscape, and famous authors like Albert Camus, Kateb Yasine, and Mouloud Ferraoun, to name but a few, originated there and wrote in French.

The wars for and against France also marked the spirit of the place indelibly: the Vichy regime during World War II, when Jews had their French citizenship taken away and their children excluded from the public schools; the arrival of the Allied forces in North Africa and the establishment of their headquarters; the establishment there of Charles de Gaulle's provisional French government; the major anti-French uprising in the city in 1954, the spark that ignited the Algerian armed struggle for independence.

In 1956, following a series of general strikes led by students, Algiers was made the seat of the Committee of Coordination and Execution (CCE) of the Front de Liberation Nationale, or National Liberation Front (FLN), the independence movement that successfully mobilized men and women resistance fighters; in 1957 the city became an operational zone in what was now a war. Massive repression ensued. Tens of thousands of people were placed under house arrest, and thousands were killed or disappeared. This period has been dramatically documented in Gillo Pontecorvo's famous 1966 film, *Battle of Algiers*. In May 1958, Algiers was the principal scene of a revolt by European colonists and the French army that ushered in the end of the Fourth French Republic and brought de Gaulle back to power. Demonstrations and counterdemonstrations followed. Then, in the final months before independence, bombings by the French terrorist OAS intentionally wrecked havoc with industrial and communications facilities and destroyed most of the National Library.

Algerian independence, negotiated and confirmed in 1962, came at the price of some 1 million Algerian deaths. It also entailed an exodus for almost all of the French citizens of the country. Nearly 1 million all told left for the motherland. Many of them, perhaps 300,000, had spent their entire lives in Algiers. The city, like the French language, now became "war booty." Enormous problems, the "growing pains" of liberation from colonialism, followed in quick succession. There was massive squatting in the former European neighborhoods and in the kasbah. The exodus of the Europeans had put an end to colonial segregation and, in so doing, had created an absence of skilled labor that almost brought ordered urban life and services to a standstill.

The estimated population of Algiers on the eve of independence was 500,000, including French citizens. Around 300,000 people left in the early 1960s. Yet in the 1966 census, there were 943,551 persons living in the city and 1,648,038 in Greater Algiers. Thus, in the first four years of independence, the urban population, now almost entirely indigenous Algerians, more than quadrupled. Unchecked demographic growth and a steady flow of a rural exodus into the city created a severe housing shortage and the proliferation of bidonvilles. By the early 1990s, the shortage of housing had become critical and resulted in an occupancy rate of 8.8 persons per unit, one of the highest in the world. Life in the city was chaotic, its buildings and public spaces neglected and run-down. Its new administrators had no experience in architecture, urbanism, and town planning. The Algerians had inherited a city that had been run and controlled by "others," and they lacked the means and know-how to manage it efficiently. It has taken years to begin to regularize ownership and the collection of rents from nationalized or sequestered properties that had been abandoned and squatted. Despite the government's construction of housing projects, the shortfall in public housing now reaches several million units.

Algiers in the postcolonial decades became an impoverished city, much of it an enormous ruralized "dormitory." What was formerly the municipality of Algiers was made into a collection of municipalities, a *wilaya* (provincial government) named Algiers with an estimated population (2004) of more than 3 million. In 2000, 32 percent of the urban population was under the age of fifteen. Widespread unemployment, political and economic frustration, uncertainty and anxiety about the future, especially among the young, the militant politicization of religion, and the repressiveness of the regime pushed the country over the brink of civil war in the 1990s.

A state of emergency was declared in Algiers in 1992. Inflation, curfews, fear and violence, and attacks against secularized women characterized daily life in the city. In the struggle between Islamists and security forces, killings, bank robberies, traffic in arms, imprisonments, and the assassination of personalities in the judicial and political system and of intellectuals deemed ideological enemies of religion became commonplace. A general news blackout was imposed during almost all of the next decade. During that time, the power structure in the country managed to maintain itself at a still unknown cost in lives and destruction.

A parallel urban, informal economy of contraband and speculation grew significantly. A new vocabulary emerged: *trabendo* and *trabendistes* (respectively, the black market and its dealers); *houmistes* (homeboys, or boys from the neighborhood); and *hittistes* (those who hang out, lean against walls). In the inner-city areas, life was especially harsh and dangerous. Bab al-Oued, its walls pockmarked by bullets, was hardly safe for its own inhabitants and best approached, according to one of its young inhabitants in 1992, "like a salad: from the heart."

An Algerian film made in 1976 by Merzaq Allouache uncannily foresees many of the future developments in the city. *Umar Gatlato er-Rejla* (*Umar Slayed by Machismo*) tells the story of a young man's inability to cope with the changing nature of urban life in all its implications. He is tragically paralyzed by his machismo. Allouache's film captures the malaise of the city. It is a sad and tender portrait accompanied by an enormous affection and nostalgia for al-Jazair al-Bahja, "Resplendent Algiers," and its traditional *sha'abi* (peoples') music. Another manifestation of nostalgia is a famous song, "al-Asima" ("The Capitol"), sung by Abdelmajid Meskoud in the neotraditional mode of sha'abi in rhymed colloquial Algerian Arabic. It is a lament of an idealized Algiers of yesteryear and a "reactionary" rejection of the armies of immigrants who have descended upon the city. In effect, in today's Algiers, two-thirds of the population come from elsewhere, mostly from the rural countryside.

According to the governor of Algiers, in the last year or so the state has successfully reasserted its control over the city, establishing public services, water, gas, and electricity networks where none existed; providing lighting in public spaces; opening up more than 200 new police stations; and recruiting and training thousands of policemen. The city's territory has been extended along with increased security and public support. The government intends to make Algiers into a Mediterranean metropolis and to encourage international activities and investments.

There are some signs of normalization and movement in these directions. A few years ago, practically no cinemas, theaters, or libraries were open to the public. This is no longer the case. Cultural places and activities have restarted, and hundreds of spaces for sports have been opened. In the year 2000, fifty international theater companies and cultural groups were said to have performed in the city. The municipal authorities insist that the climate in Algiers has changed radically for the better: "The camp of hope is much bigger than the camp of death." There is no doubt that Algiers is potentially a great Mediterranean city.

Kenneth Brown

Further Readings

Berque, Jacques. *French North Africa: The Maghreb between the Two Wars.* Translated by Jean Stewart. London: Faber and Faber, 1967.

Horne, Alistair. *Savage War of Peace.* London: Macmillan, 1977.

Humbaraci, Arslan. *Algeria: A Revolution That Failed.* London: Pall Mall Press, 1966.

Quandt, William. *Between Ballets and Bullets: Algeria's Transition from Authoritarianism.* Washington, DC: Brookings Institution Press, 1998.

Reudy, John. *Modern Algeria: The Origins and Development of a Nation.* Bloomington: Indiana University Press, 1992.

Zartman, I. William. *Man, State and Society in the Contemporary Maghreb.* London: Pall Mall Press, 1973.

Zaynep, Selig. *Urban Forms and Colonial Confrontation: Algiers under French Rule.* Berkeley: University of California Press, 1997.

Amman
Population: 1.7 million (2005 estimate)

Amman is unique in the region. This modern "million" city is, in its current form, essentially a creation of the last sixty years, crafted out of the rocky hills surrounding a small village. Although built around the site of the ancient city originally known as Rabbath Ammon and then as Philadelphia, the Amman of today houses almost half of all Jordanians, has a skyline full of cranes and construction, regularly faces severe water shortages, and suffers some of the worst traffic congestion in the Middle East. Still lacking a strong sense of civic identity, Amman attracts regional visitors for its shopping, semblance of stability, and access to world markets.

The city of Amman (Aramaic, *Ammon;* Greek, *Philadelphia*), capital of the Hashemite Kingdom of Jordan, lies almost 3,000 feet above sea level on the plateau of the eastern ridge of the Jordan Valley rift, some sixty miles opposite of Jerusalem on the other side of the rift. Its rapidly growing population is daily expanding the limits of the city, resulting in a built environment that nearly touches the nearby city of Zerqa and creates a conurbation of about 2.4 million inhabitants. One out of two Jordanians lives in its metropolitan area; planning for 2030 envisions a city of 4 million over forty miles wide.

Amman greatly differs from the other urban centers of the region. Its being a modern city is the most striking characteristic of the capital of Jordan, and an almost unique feature in the millennium-old urbanized environment of the Middle East. Built on the site of the Iron Age Ammonite capital, Rabbat Ammon, and then the Hellenistic and Roman city of Philadelphia (one of the Decapolis of the first century AD), important vestiges from the Roman period are still visible in the center of Amman—including a large theater and a *nymphaeum* (garden sanctuary)—as are minor traces of the Byzantine and Umayyad periods. Its original nucleus, however, was completely abandoned between the eleventh and thirteenth centuries AD.

A new village among the ruins was actually founded only at the end of the nineteenth century, when a number of Circassian families were located around the ancient remains by the Ottoman authorities to help protect the road to Makkah. Its first municipal council was only established in 1909, and its population numbered around 2,000 inhabitants. The opening of the Hijaz Railway in 1903, and the creation of a railway station, helped Amman to prosper.

The development of Amman then becomes intimately related to twentieth-century political developments. Following the collapse of the Ottoman Empire, the whole Middle East was shared between France and the United Kingdom. Under British tutelage, the newly created amirate of Transjordan and its amir, Abdullah, needed a new capital—centrally located—to represent their new power and the new ruling elite. Transjordan, however, did not have the financial resources to develop its capital in a short span of time according to grandiose town-planning schemes like other colonial capitals, and for decades Amman remained a small urban center. During the 1920s, the first modern infrastructures of the city were built: the hospital, the central Hussayni Mosque, and the electric grid were all laid down. In 1928 Amman was officially declared the capital of the amirate, and when the country became independent and the Hashemite Kingdom of Jordan was created, in 1946, it was confirmed as the capital of the new kingdom. The city's main focal points, including the Royal Palace, the Avenues, and the National Museum, were created slowly throughout the following fifty years.

Amman developed initially on the steep hills around the river and the central valley where the Circassian village stood. The town was originally characterized by long urban

Amman, ca. 1900. (Library of Congress)

stairways climbing the hills and leading to stone villas surrounded by gardens. Traces of this phase—a few 1930s villas—may still be seen on the central hill, Jebal Amman. Then, roads were created horizontally on the city hills, the river was covered, and the valleys were gradually built up to create the busy district of "downtown Amman." Finally, the city began to extend in all directions along large avenues leading toward the neighboring cities and villages. A modern, ever-growing city, Amman now covers nineteen hills in the central region of Jordan.

Since the late 1940s, various town-planning schemes were designed for the city, but the weight of external political events and population growth has always been overwhelming, and the municipality has never been able to cope with the transformation brought by the successive waves of hundreds of thousands of refugees. Indeed, the city has grown with an extraordinary pace, expanding from 1,000 to 1 million inhabitants between 1890 and 1990. Amman has therefore developed in a rather chaotic way, with large refugee camps surrounding the nucleus of the city. Its urban growth is essentially because of the continuous influx of external immigrants more than the high birthrate of its population. Its evolution is also intimately and dramatically connected to the Arab-Israeli conflict. In 1948, following the creation of the State of Israel, tens of thousands of Palestinian refugees moved east of the Jordan River and settled in Amman. Similarly, following the June War of 1967, a new massive population transfer further altered the demographic situation in the country and in its capital.

The Palestinians in the camps surrounding the city were a particularly fertile ground for the development of the Palestinian resistance movement after 1967. All of the groups, but particularly Fatah and the Popular Front for the Liberation of Palestine, found many members in Amman. By 1969 the camps were off-limits to Jordanian security forces, and the Palestinians had established their own checkpoints in and around Amman. Finally, as Palestinians hijacked a number of airplanes and blew them up in Jordan, King Hussayn unleashed his Bedouin-based army against the Palestinian fighters, and the city was rocked in September 1970 (Black September) by fighting that lasted off and on until 1971. More than 5,000 Palestinians were killed in the fighting, and in the end the militias were driven out of the country, and the Jordanian army reestablished its control over Amman and the camps.

Since the early 1970s, following the outbreak of the civil war in Lebanon and the sudden growth of the oil revenues, the city has become an important regional financial site. The influx of capital previously invested in Lebanese banks and the money remitted back to Amman by its many Palestinian residents who moved to work in the rich oil countries has produced a construction boom and has given the city its characteristic modern and rich outlook. Entire new urban districts sprouted west of the city center after 1980. These neighborhoods, organized around a system of urban roundabouts—the "circles"—have became the symbol of modern Amman's urban development. The contradictions and divisions of Jordanian society are reflected in the actual urban fabric of the capital and have produced a city socially and geographically segregated. Wealthy West Amman, with its circles, large avenues, and the villas of the rich bourgeoisie, corresponds to poor East Amman, with its pedestrian streets, refugee camps, and limited services. The two halves seem to move further apart every year, with the central business district acting as the only common arena of interaction.

The recent origin of the city—mirroring the modern creation of the Jordanian kingdom itself—dramatically contrasts with the millenary history of other Middle Eastern cities and capitals. Amman lacks the historic depth of Cairo, Jerusalem, and Damascus and does not have a clear-cut identity and image. The cultural and social life in the city is still limited and traditional, and its "provinciality," only partially overcome by the government's plan to transform Amman into a captivating modern symbol of the country, is reflected in an amorphous and unconvincing architectural and town-planning layout and in the repetitive additions of new neighborhoods along the main road axes. The fifth, sixth, seventh, and now eighth circles are the scene for similar rich, stone-faced and walled villas and large streets, made and conceived for car traffic, according to a concept reminding one more of North American cities than of traditional Middle Eastern urban centers.

The recurrent historic pattern of refugees descending on Amman and expanding its population was repeated once more following the Gulf War of 1991. In that year, the Palestinian residents of Kuwait were expelled, and some 200,000 new refugees settled in the city. Again, following the invasion of Iraq in 2003, Amman saw a huge influx of Iraqi refugees and their wealth flood into the city, driving up prices, making hotel rooms scarce, and blocking the roads with their cars. Amman locals resent their presence, but the buzz created in the city from this latest influx of capital and activity has made Amman the virtual capital of Iraq.

Simone Ricca

Further Readings

Abd al-Rahman, Munif. *Story of a City: A Childhood in Amman.* Translated by Samira Kawar. London: Quartet Books, 1996.

Hannoyer, Jean, and Setina Shami, eds. *Amman, ville et société—Amman, the City and Its Society.* Beirut: CERMOC, 1996.

Kennedy, David. *The Roman Army in Jordan.* London: Council for British Research in the Levant, 2000.

Kirkbride, Alec. *From the Wings: Amman Memoirs, 1947–51.* London: Frank Cass, 1976.

Nevo, Joseph. *King Abdallah and Palestine.* London: Palgrave Macmillan, 1996.

Northedge, Alastair. *Studies on Roman and Islamic Amman, Vol. 1: History, Site and Architecture.* London: British Academy Monographs in Archaeology, Oxford University Press, 1993.

Ankara
Population: 3.2 million (2004 estimate)

Some cities seem to go on forever, able to reappear in very different guises and characteristics from one era to another. Ankara is one such changeling. With its roots more than 4,000 years ago in the Bronze Age, it was a trading city to the Greeks, a regional capital for the Romans, a summer resort and frontier command center for the Byzantines, a profitable textile production center for the Ottomans, and the national capital of Atatürk's new State of Turkey. The source of the unique angora wool, today its administrative and educational core provides many jobs for its huge population, and the typical urban problems of smog, illegal settlement, and health difficulties plague its population. Contemporary Ankara is a Turkish city, with all the politics of the state and its minority issues played out on its streets and in its halls of power.

Ankara (ancient, *Ancyra;* Greek, *Angora;* Turkish, *Ankara*) is located on the high plateau in the center of Asia Minor/Anatolia. The ancient city grew up at the base of a 500-foot-high steep volcanic outcropping (Atakule) located on the west bank of one branch of the Sakarya River. It is an area of low rainfall, steppe grasses, and cold winters, making Ankara's climate harsh: stifling heat in the summer and deep snow sometimes into the end of March. There were swamps around the city, which made it long a malarial zone and prone to plagues during its history. It lies at the crossroads of the key ancient east-west route, helping to link the Bosphorus with Iran and also the north-south route from the Black Sea to the Cilician Gates. There are few other cities in the area, making the city an island to be reached after the end of a long journey; Ankara thus attracted the long-distance transit trade, became an important garrison town, and attracted immigration from an extensive rural hinterland.

There are archaeological remains from Stone Age hunters, and Early Bronze Age remains continue to be found around the city, but it is in the Middle Bronze Age (ca. 2000 BC) that the city enters history. The rise of the Hittites (ca. seventeenth century BC) brought development and increased long-distance trade to the cities of the central Anatolian plateau. By the Iron Age, political dominance in the region began to coalesce around new immigrants, the Phrygians, and by the eighth century BC their core around Gordium and the nearby cities of what they called Ancyra (Ankara) and Midas City dominated much of the interior of Anatolia. Remains of their tombs and buildings dating from the eighth to the sixth century BC have been discovered during urban excavations, and they indicate luxury and wealth appropriate to the era of the legendary King Midas (r. 738–696 BC). Even at this time, the area was known for its production of textiles and the manufacture of dyes.

The Achaemenid Persians came to dominate the city sometime after 546 BC, and the Royal Road to Sardis spurred development of the central plateau. Alexander conquered the city in 334 BC after cutting the nearby Gordian knot, and the Seleucids assumed subsequent control of the central plateau. Around 275 BC, as the consequence of rebellion, mercenary employment, and defeat, members of the Galli (Celts) confederation settled around Ancyra, held it as a frontier post against the Seleucids, and established their capital in the city. Over the course of the next century, they were often at war with their neighbors and in fact were part of the Seleucid army defeated by the Romans at the Battle of Magnesia. After 188 BC, they became a vassal state of Rome, and a protectorate after 85 BC. In 25 BC, the Galatian capital of Ancyra became capital of the Roman province of Galatia Prima.

As part of a huge empire, with security and trade interests, the location of Ancyra at the center of a nascent road system meant that the city benefited from the development spurred by the empire. It became, because of location, one of the most significant urban centers in Anatolia. This east-west trade road was the busiest in the peninsula, heading across the Anatolian plateau. Travelers from Syria or the Cilician Gates, or increasingly from the Euphrates border, moved down this road heading for Nicaea, Nicomedia, Constantinople, and Europe. Every single one of the roads that led into or out of Ankara was strategically significant to the Roman Empire. With the rise of Parthian power, and then that of the Sassanians, Rome's border wars brought regular wealth and transit to Ankara. The city thus became a supply depot, a military staging area, and a command hub for much of the "east." As a textile center, its factories produced for the armies on the frontier, and its fields supplied them with grain. For the next millennium, it served such purposes for the empire.

The same roads that allowed the emperor and his armies to march east also allowed enemies to easily march west to Ankara. In 260 the Sassanians visited, soon followed by the Goths and by Zenobia of Palmyra (see also "Palmyra"). The city suffered significant damage, famine broke out, and much of the city was depopulated. By 271 the Romans were back in control of Ankara and proceeded to expand the imperial road system and fortify new borders.

Diocletian (AD 245–316) modified the administrative structure in Asia Minor, elevating the governor in Ankara to the rank of consular. A local senate ruled the city, and it was early in the fourth century that the city wall was rebuilt, new public buildings constructed (the amphitheater, for example), and the highway restored. Ankara continued to serve as a key customs center for revenue collection on both imported and exported goods.

During Diocletian's persecution of Christians, a number of martyrs came from Ankara, indicating that the city had a sizable Christian community by the early fourth century. The most famous victim was Saint Clement, who was born in the city, established an orphanage there because of his civic commitment to the city, and was executed at the base of the citadel. Saint Plato, a contemporary, became the saint of the city over the next century or so as his cult grew in importance. By the time of Constantine, Ankara was one of the most important bishoprics in Asia Minor, and there is a tradition that Ankara was the initial site considered for the First Ecumenical Council, which eventually was held in Nicaea in 325 to deal with the Arian claims (see also "Iznik"). Reportedly, theological conflicts among various groups within the city became so violent over the next few years that crowds would stampede through the streets, strip nuns and priests naked and drag them to the forum, and destroy property. Many hundreds of heretics were massacred in the city during these outrages, which lasted until 363. Corruption and lack of civil power in relation to the bishop were two reasons for the unrest.

During this time of transition, there were still pagan upper-class inhabitants in the city, and many of them sought out the best education for their sons. In particular, Libanius of Antioch, a famous teacher and rhetorician, was closely linked to the youth and fortunes of Ankara (ca. AD 350). Evidently, he had a soft spot in his heart for the city and its people, and in his correspondence he lauded Ankara's reputation for a love of learning and for the elites' willingness to turn out to hear a gifted speaker.

Ankara hosted many emperors, saints, soldiers, and pilgrims over the next three centuries as they traveled the imperial road. For Emperor Arcadius, for example, Ankara became a summer retreat for himself and the government (ca. 399). They would slowly travel out from Constantinople to Ankara at the beginning of the summer and, while living the good life there for a few months, issue laws and enjoy the dry conditions. Saint Nilus, the moralist writer, lived in Ankara during the fifth century and ran a monastery there: his letters comment on the virtues of the virgins of Ankara who devote their lives to serving the poor, the sick, and those traveling on the road. There were still members of the elite in the city who were pagan at the time, and Saint Nilus's letters argued for their conversion. New walls, a basilica, the agora, hot baths, a swimming pool, churches for Saint Plato and Saint Clement—all were built during this period.

The city had its share of troubles. A drought in the middle of the fifth century brought plague and famine to the city. Bandits prowled the roads, and there are continual reports of people being taken in by the church leaders of the city following their mugging. By the mid-sixth century, the roads on which the city depended were so unsafe that Justinian appointed a new military governor, with considerable resources and troops, to deal with the problem from his headquarters in the city. Bubonic plague appeared in 542 and killed a sizable minority of the population; it continued to reoccur over the next fifty years. Around the end of the century, the story is told, when the plague reappeared, the city fathers hired the local holy man, Theodore (soon to be Saint Theodore), to lead the whole population of the city in community prayer and to sprinkle the cattle with holy water; the plague disappeared, and the livestock were saved. Theodore is reported to have predicted an attack on the city by nonbelievers and its destruction for the period after his death (d. 613).

The Sassanians attacked and captured the city in AD 622, and their general, Sharbaraz, had all the city's inhabitants killed or sent into slavery. Many of the city's greatest buildings were destroyed, and the lower part of the city lay abandoned for centuries. Although the Byzantines drove the Sassanians out of the region in AD 628, by the mid-seventh century Ankara had barely recovered, confined to a small fortified town on the citadel. In AD 641, another unexpected enemy appeared on the central plateau: raiding parties of Muslims. By AD 646, the armies of the then governor of Syria, Muawiya, had penetrated close to Ankara, and in AD 654 they sacked the city.

In response, the Byzantines built new fortifications around the city, reorganized their by now reduced military frontier, and headquartered their military administration in the city. These fortifications succeeded in protecting the city against subsequent regular raids and large-scale attacks during the end of the seventh century and the beginning of the eighth. The city became the capital of a new province, called the Bucellarian, named after the *beccellarii* (troops) manning the frontier. Subsequent attacks by Abbasid forces occurred in 776 and again in 797, when further damage to the city had to be repaired by the emperor. One Arab legend, unsubstantiated in fact, has Caliph Harun ar-Rashid capturing Ankara and commanding that its bronze city gates be taken back to Baghdad. Two Abbasid armies under command of Harun's son, Caliph Mutasim (r. 833–842), however, actually converged on Ankara in 838, captured the city, destroyed its walls, enslaved its population, and left.

Twenty years later, the Byzantines were back, rebuilt the citadel, and consecrated the city as the new holy protector against the infidels (AD 859). An icon of Jesus protected the city gates, relics were brought from the Holy Land, and poems to the city praised "charming Ankara, the most brilliant of cities." Unfortunately, this protection was not sufficient to protect against a Christian heretic movement that temporarily captured the city in 871. Ankara came to play an iconic role in the empire's defense against the Muslim advance and was lauded in poetry for its security role. Some of its former glory and significance returned over the next century.

Ankara entered a new phase in its history with its capture by the Seljuqs ca. 1073 in the period after the battle of Manzikert. Yoruk Turkish nomads concentrated around Ankara during the last decades of the eleventh century; then more came over the next century. Although a Crusader army appeared outside the gates of the city in 1101, and captured it

from the Seljuqs, the garrison left behind found it difficult to hold out as an island surrounded by Turkoman, and the Seljuqs retook the citadel soon thereafter. They renamed the city Angora, and it was the Seljuq promotion of long-distance trade via the Anatolian east-west trade routes that revived Ankara.

Pax Mongolia had a similar effect in opening up the Anatolian routes from Europe to the east. Initially, it was the route from southern Anatolian ports to Konya, the Rum Seljuq capital, and then to Tabriz that carried the trade. When the Ilkanhids lost Konya to the Karamanids, however, the more northern route via Ankara became crucial. Then, when the early Ottomans conquered Bursa (1326), it quickly became the entrepôt anchoring the western end of this road. Along this road passed silk and spices, and it all transited via Ankara (see also "Bursa").

The Ottomans began to expand their control over the eastern trade routes with the capture of Ankara in 1354, and the city's acquisition played a key role in the rise of Bursa as an international market. The new rulers allowed the wealthier merchants of Ankara, organized in an *akhi* (form of association or professional group), significant internal autonomy. By 1401 the Ottomans captured Erzincan, and it was this threatening expansion along the trade routes that brought Bayezid I into conflict with the powerful Temür.

Upon hearing of the advance of Temür's troops, Bayezid lifted his siege of Constantinople and marched all his troops off to protect his empire from the eastern threat. The forces of the two expanding empires met at Cubuk, northeast of Ankara, in what has become known as the Battle of Ankara (July 1402). It was a huge battle, with perhaps as many as 85,000 Ottoman troops and 140,000 for Temür. The latter also had war elephants from India. In the end, the battle went against the Ottomans, Bayezid refused to flee, and he fought on until the last minute. He was captured and forced to accompany Temür's army as it campaigned throughout the Ottoman territories, collecting ransom money from the major cities. Reportedly, Bayezid's wife was made to serve naked at Temür's table, and the sultan tried to escape by digging out of his tent, so he was then kept in a cage for transport to Samarkand. He died within a few months of his capture. Temür returned east without leaving any permanent administration in Anatolia, and within ten years the Ottoman Empire was reformed and expanding. Ironically, the Battle of Ankara did have the effect of prolonging the end of the Byzantine Empire by fifty years.

The expansion of the Ottoman Empire had a positive effect on Ankara's prosperity. The city continued to support factories producing such products as soap, and it became known for its special goat's hair, mohair, taken from local sheep unique to the region. This angora was turned locally into textiles known as camlet. The angora of Ankara was very expensive, and during the late fifteenth century it became a luxury textile in great demand in Europe. The manufacture of mohair cloth had been practiced in Ankara for some centuries, and the European demand produced a revival in its local production. The Italians in particular came looking for Ankara camlets. Bursa served as the central market for the famous Ankara mohair, although as early as 1502 the Italians in Bursa would send agents directly to Ankara to buy bolts of mohair. The Florentines were famous in Lyons for their reexport of part of their mohair imports to France.

The Ankara mohair industry involved both the production of the raw wool by herdsmen in the district, whose families accompanied the herds in wagons that served as houses, and a local industry producing the yarn and textiles. Much of the hair actually went to produce buttons, but by the beginning of the eighteenth century, as the trend moved toward metal buttons, the European demand for angora declined. What was called the Celali rebellion (ca. 1600) in Anatolia harmed the Ankara merchants and producers by halting movement along the roads and even placing Ankara under siege for a time. In response Ankara refortified its city walls and moved toward a more modern fortification and away from the central citadel of the medieval period. By 1615 local merchants were well on their way to putting the industry back on its feet, and the state helped by creating a monopoly. In fact, a special tax on finished mohair cloth going through a special press constituted one of the principal revenue items collected in Ankara. Since the mohair goat was not successfully acclimatized outside of the region, Ankara was able to retain its monopoly of this craft well into the nineteenth century.

The city retained much diversity and flexibility during this period. At the end of the sixteenth century, there were around 2,500 Jewish families in Ankara, many connected with the mohair and textile trade. Muslim merchants and investors in commerce in Ankara often lent money, often for interest; acted as wholesalers for other dispersed rural craftsmen; and took goods on consignment to ship to Istanbul. A recently discovered 1592 shop inventory of a Muslim dealer in shoes, an active commodity in Ankara, is so extensive and complex that one can only conclude that the regional economy operating through the city was, at that point, very strong and vital. By 1693 English traders had a factory in Ankara to buy mohair, although the locals were not always happy with their presence: in March 1706 a mob attacked the English merchants and forced them to take refuge in one of the city's khans, where they had to wait to be rescued by the Ottoman army. An earthquake in 1688 allowed the local elites to adopt the new housing styles from Istanbul, where multistoried houses were the fashion, and the city began to lose its staid feel of single-story buildings with flat roofs.

By the early 1800s, Ankara's population may have been as high as 50,000. A list from the time of the various craft associations existing in the city demonstrates the continued centrality of textiles to the economic vitality of the city. It included tanners, catgut makers, cobblers, sandal makers, goat-hair spinners, quilt fluffers, tailors, silk spinners, cloth merchants, weavers, goat-hair sellers, goat-hair dyers, spinning-wheel makers, saddlers, skullcap makers, and rag sellers. In 1815 there were some 1,500 mohair weavers in Ankara. By the 1850s, however, most of these jobs were gone, and the mohair weavers had disappeared from Ankara. Although the government monopoly on mohair ended by the late 1830s, any privileged access to Ankara mohair yarn and to the raw mohair of the region had been long ended. European merchants routinely went directly to the nomadic tribes in the district, producing competition with local manufacturers that pushed prices through the roof. In addition, Europeans now rarely bought local products, buying only raw mohair for export. At the same time, machine-made mohair textiles imported into Anatolia drove down prices for locally finished goods.

New immigrants appeared in the city after 1860. Around 30,000 Circassians fled Russia after that year and settled along the major highway across Anatolia in cities such as Ankara. When a German concession, the Anatolian Railway Company, completed the Istanbul-to-Ankara section of the Berlin-Baghdad railway in 1893, more Circassians came to the city. The railroad contributed to a further deterioration of local handicraft, but the production of cereals on large landholdings around the city and their exportation to Istanbul helped stabilize the local economy. For a while, opium and mohair continued to travel by camel caravan via the old routes. New vineyards and gardens around the city were developed, although, when the English traveler Frederick Burnaby passed through the city in 1876, he reports that the English vice-consul in the city was surprised to see an Englishman in Angora, since few had passed through the city for many years. At the time of the First World War, Muslims made up 87 percent of the population of a city that was home to around 40,000 people. British prisoners of war were held here after 1915, and the malarial swamps made their captivity particularly difficult.

With the declaration of the nationalist struggle in Ankara in 1919, the history of this regional city took a dramatically different turn. The Grand National Assembly declared in Ankara on 13 April, and Atatürk began to create a new Turkish state. During the subsequent invasion and occupation of Anatolia by Greek, French, and British troops, Greek forces threatened Ankara for a time in mid-1921, but Atatürk defeated them at the battle of Sakarya River in August, and the tide turned. By the autumn of that year, the French were ready to negotiate a deal with the national government, and the Ankara Agreement was signed, which brought the war between France and Turkey to an end. For the nationalists, the Ankara Agreement was the greatest diplomatic triumph, since it split the French from the British and proved to the world that the Treaty of Sevres was worth nothing.

On 13 October 1923, Ankara was officially declared the capital of the new republic of Turkey, and its name was changed from Angora to Ankara in 1930. The reasons for its choice as the capital lie in Atatürk's vision of the new Turkey, different from what Istanbul represented: Ankara held little meaning for the concept of Ottoman history or ideas, and so offered a clean break with the Ottoman past; there were few existing elites that had to be manipulated or coddled, so Atatürk could shape the city as he wished; the city had no significant "Greek" associations or significance that could hinder the crafting of the concept of Turkishness vital to the new state; nor did the city have a strong minority presence but rather was significantly Turkish; and it was also at the heart of the country's communications and transport networks.

Over the next fifteen years, until his death in 1938, Atatürk built a new, modern, de novo Ankara in the image of his revolution. The city became a stage on which a new city, with new planning, new regulation, new centralization, and new state powers, could be constructed. Architects from Fascist states helped lay out the wide boulevards and streets. The vast construction projects helped create a new class of young, wealthy socialites who played in the city's hot spots and shaped its nightlife. The city in the 1930s had a buzz and a boomtown feel, with its new health centers, new education institutions, new sports fields, and cinemas. Few mosques were built, and few imams were in the city. The city was a creation of Atatürk, but he died in Istanbul, although he is buried in the huge *Anit Kabir* (mausoleum), which dominates the city.

Today Ankara is a garrison town as well as a town of government and industry. By 1970 the population had passed 1 million, growing 700 percent in three decades primarily through in-migration from rural areas. The city has grown through illegal settlements of two kinds: there are the usual urban squatter houses, *gecekondu* in Turkish, that make up the shantytowns on the southern edge of the city. But there are also thousands of *apart-kondu*, high-rise apartment blocks originally built without official licensing. To the housing problem can be added the deadly combination of a terrible climate and excessive air pollution from cars and factories. The result has been a huge problem of smog and health problems for the city's population. There is a southern middle-class area in the city (*Yenisehir*) and the old center (*Ulus*) to the north.

The city produces wine and beer, mohair, and a range of agricultural products such as sugar, flour, grains, and fruit. The University of Ankara was founded in 1946, the Middle East Technical University was established in 1956 (long a center for radical leftist politics), and Bilkent University in 1984; these are the most famous of the more than eight educational institutions in the city. In addition to the ancient fortifications of the city, the Temple of Augustus, the Roman Theater, and the Column of Julian remain from the classical period, and various churches and mosques testify to the diverse religious traditions of the city.

The city's minority population grew in the 1950s when 18 percent of all Kurdish internal immigrants moved to Ankara. Most came as migrant labor, but some also arrived as intellectuals, political activists, and students. By the 1970s, the Kurdish community in Ankara had broken into various political groups, and clashes between right- and left-leaning Kurdish parties broke out in the shantytowns of Ankara. Abdullah Ochelon, or Apo as he was known, was a student in Ankara at the time of the 1970 coup; became involved with the leftist group, the Ankara Higher Education Association (AYOD); and went on to found the Partiya Karkari Kurdistan (Kurdistan Worker's Party, or the PKK) in 1975 in the mountains. A wave of bombings occurred in Ankara in March 1990 instigated by the Partiya Islami Kurdistan (PIK), connected to the PKK.

Bruce Stanley

Further Readings
Cross, Toni, and Gary Leiser. *A Brief History of Ankara*. Vacaville, CA: Indian Ford Press, 2000.
French, David. *Roman, Late Roman and Byzantine Inscriptions of Ankara: A Selection*. Ankara: Ministry of Culture and Tourism, 2003.
Kili, Suna. *The Ataturk Revolution: A Paradigm of Modernization*. Istanbul: Turkiye Is Bankasi, 2003.
Matthews, Roger, ed. *Ancient Anatolia*. London: British Institute of Archaeology at Ankara, 1998.

Antakya
Population: 158,737 (2005 estimate)

Antakya, the classical Antioch, city of Crusader dreams and Christian authority, is both a "lost city" and a phoenix city. Much of its classical ruins now lie under tons of river silt, never to be seen again, yet its current inhabitants have reclaimed their patrimony and rebuilt a regional agricultural powerhouse in this corner of the Middle East through hard work and civil engineering. Antakya is a city where, as Libanios, born to the city, wrote ca. AD 390, you can sit "in our market place and sample every city; there will be so many people from each place with whom [you] can talk."

Antakya (Arabic, *Antakiya;* English, *Antioch;* Greek, *Antiocheia;* Turkish, *Antakya,* now also called *Hatay*) is a city in Turkey and capital of the *il* (formerly *vilayet*), or province, of Hatay. Antakya bestrides the Orontes River (Nahr al-Asi) near its mouth, where it emerges from the southwest corner of the Amuq. The quarters of the medieval city lie hemmed between the precipitous flanks of Mount Silpius and the left bank of the river, with the modern city across the stream.

Today a bustling provincial center some twelve miles northwest of the Syrian border, Antakya lies within the frontier where Turks and Kurds from the north meet Arabs from the south. Even architecturally, with its houses of stone below and timber above, Antakya smacks more of the cities of Anatolia than it does of the stone and mud cities of neighboring Syria.

For the first 900 years of its existence, Antakya was a much more important urban agglomeration than it is today. For beneath the current humble town lie the ruins of the great city of Antioch-on-the-Orontes. Around 300 BC, Seleucus I Nicator, the first of the Seleucids, founded Antioch as one of a series of new great cities designed to facilitate the control of his Syrian realm, naming it after his father, Antiochus. His son, Antiochus I Soter, made Antioch the capital of his empire, and it remained so until Pompey conquered it for Rome in 64 BC. Under the Romans, Antioch entered into its glory, for it became the capital of Syria and the Roman East, with a population in the mid-first century AD of some 300,000–500,000 souls. It enjoyed a lively commercial and intellectual life and was the main market for the rich agricultural area of the Amuq and the highlands to its south and east. Both Herod the Great and Emperor Tiberius contributed to construct its great colonnaded street.

The city was one of the cradles of early Christianity, with Peter, Paul, and Barnabas spending significant time in the city. Over the centuries, it remained central to Christians throughout the region. Constantine built one of the greatest early churches on an island in the middle of the Orontes. The patriarch of Antioch came to rank equally with his fellows in Jerusalem, Alexandria, Rome, and Constantinople within the world church. The relics of Simon the Stylite were venerated in its churches for hundreds of years, while the Crusaders discovered the Holy Lance within the church of Saint Peter.

The importance of Antioch lay in its geographical situation. The Orontes was navigable between the city and its port, Seleucia Pieria, making Antioch a great entrepôt for trade between the Mediterranean and the Orient while protecting it from attack by sea. Moreover, the city was situated at the juncture of trade routes to Mesopotamia, southern Syria, and Anatolia via the Syrian Gates (the Belen Pass over the Amanus Range) and north through the Amuq.

Nevertheless, these positive factors were countered by certain negative ones. First, Antioch was situated in the midst of an earthquake zone and suffered some seventeen earthquakes between 150 BC and AD 588, after each of which the city had to be reconstructed. Furthermore, as the administrative and commercial linchpin of the Romans in the east, Antioch was a magnet for invaders intent on supplanting them. Thus, it was taken and held by the Parthians in 40–39 BC, by the Sassanian Persian Shapur in AD 256 and AD 260, by Palmyra between AD 261 and AD 272, and again by the Sassanians in AD 540 and between AD 611 and AD 628 during their "100 years' war" with Rome.

By the time the Muslims conquered the city in AD 637–638, the various disasters of the fifth and sixth centuries had transformed Antioch into a shadow of itself. Moreover,

for the Arabs, Antakiya, as they named it, was of much less strategic and commercial importance than it had been for the Romans. For one thing, the new Islamic Empire in the east was oriented inward toward Syria, the Arabian Peninsula, and Iran, rather than outward toward the Mediterranean and Europe. Moreover, Antakiya, rather than being a coordinating center behind the north-south frontier between Rome and Persia, was situated right on the east-west frontier between Muslim and Byzantine lands. Its vulnerability to attack was evidenced by the fact that it was held by the Byzantines between AD 969 and AD 1084 and by the Crusaders between AD 1098 and AD 1268. This defenselessness was compounded by the fact that the series of disasters at the end of the classical period had brought ruin to a city once so vibrant.

Thus, under the Muslims, Aleppo acquired the role played by Antioch under the Romans because it was more inland and protected from attack and was better situated to collect the trade both from Iraq and the East, and later Anatolia and the Mediterranean as well. Under the Mamluks (1268–1517) and the Ottomans (1517–1918), Antakya became a small provincial center of only regional importance. At the end of the Ottoman period, it was capital of a *qadha'* (district) in the *sanjak* (district, region, or provincial administrative area of a state) and *vilayet* (province) of Aleppo. The changes caused by earthquakes and silting had destroyed its ports and rendered the lower Orontes unnavigable while turning the Amuq into a swamp. As a result, Alexandretta/Iskenderun, with its fine natural harbor, replaced Antakya as the main regional center and port (see also "Iskenderun").

The creation of the sanjak of Alexandretta in 1918 under Allied administration reemphasized the fact that since the advent of Islam, this region had been an ethnic frontier, first between Greek and Arab and later between Turk and Arab. It was a paradox that Antakya, though the city was situated on the farthest edge of the Syrian-Turkish boundary, had the largest Turkish population. In 1935 it was the largest city in the sanjak, with a population of 34,000, of which 58 percent were Sunni Turcophones, while other significant blocs were composed of Alawis (25.5 percent) and Christian Arabs (14.5 percent). Most Alawis and Armenians spoke Turkish as a second language. As a result of this dominance, Antakya became a center of Turkish irredentism when the conflict over the unresolved status of the sanjak post–World War I intensified in the late 1930s. It was thus only natural that this city dominated by Turks should replace Alexandretta as the capital, first of the Republic of Hatay in the summer of 1938 and then of the vilayet after its incorporation into the Republic of Turkey in June 1939.

In the intervening sixty years, Antakya has reclaimed its place as a significant regional hub by reviving its role as an agricultural city. The engineered drainage of the Amuq has allowed the city to once again exploit this rich agricultural area. The city has become a market, a processing center for the products of this revitalized region (olives, cotton, fruit, wheat, rice, and grapes), and the market hub for the people of the region. Despite Syrian irredentism concerning the city and its hinterland, cross-border trade with Aleppo has increased, and there is hope that greater cooperation may empower the whole region.

Art, culture, and archaeology continue to provide some respite to the inhabitants of the city. The Antakya International Art Festival attracts considerable regional interest, and the provincial cultural directorate promotes more than 113 local archaeological and natural sites for tourism, including the Mosaic Museum, with its restored Roman mosaics. Saint Peter's Church remains the second most holy site for the Syrian Orthodox community after Jerusalem, and pilgrims visit from throughout the region.

J. L. Whitaker

Further Readings
Brice, William C. *South-West Asia.* London: University of London Press, 1966.
Cimok, Fatih. *Mosaics of Antioch.* London: Milet, 2004.
Downey, Glanville. *Ancient Antioch.* Princeton: Princeton University Press, 1963.
Downey, Glanville. *A History of Antioch in Syria from Seleucus to the Arab Conquest.* Princeton: Princeton University Press, 1960.
Sandwell, Isabella, and Janet Huskinson, eds. *Culture and Society in Later Roman Antioch.* Oxford: Oxbow, 2003.
Slee, Michelle. *The Church in Antioch in the First Century CE.* London: Sheffield Academic Press, 2003.

Aqaba/Eilat
Population: 114,000 (both cities, 2004 estimate): Aqaba, 70,000; Eilat, 44,000

For more than 10,000 years, the freshwater and seafood available at the head of the Gulf of Aqaba on the Red Sea have supported human habitation. Located at a crucial crossroads between Asia and Africa, the current conurbation of Aqaba/Eilat is just the latest manifestation of settlement on this site; the city has changed its name and specific location across these seven millennia, ruled first by one political unit and then another. King Solomon and his Phoenician allies promoted what he called Elath for its minerals and trade potential; the Romans knew it as Aelana and emphasized its security role and access to India; for Muhammad, it was the first gateway out of the Arabian Peninsula to spreading the religion of Islam; for the British, it was key to defeating the Turks in Palestine; to the Iraqis, it was their lifeline under sanctions; and for the Jordanians and Israelis, it is a site for economic development and maybe regional peace. Since 1948 two separate cities have developed across the political boundary between Jordan and Israel. However, the cities are slowly recognizing their shared future in a confined space, and forms of cooperation are emerging. Small but central, Aqaba/Eilat is a crucial hub in regional history, reflecting the complexity and conflict at the heart of Middle East urban development.

The dual modern ports of Aqaba (Medieval Arabic, *Ayla* or *Qalat al-Aqaba;* Latin, *Aelana;* Greek, *Aila*) and Eilat (Modern Hebrew, *Eilat;* Canaanite, *Elath*) lie within five miles of each other at the northernmost point of the Gulf of Aqaba, an arm of the Red Sea. Divided by state boundaries and barbed wire, these two ports exist on a site where some form of regular human habitation has existed since before 5000 BC. Following the contours of the Great Rift Valley, the Gulf of Aqaba is part of the same geological fault line that runs from Ethiopia north through the Red Sea to the Dead Sea and Jordan River valley. At the tip of the Gulf of Aqaba, there is a natural thumbnail-shaped bay, with the Sinai mountains to the west and the Jebal al-Tih plateau beyond, the mountains of the Arabian Peninsula with the Nafud desert of northern Arabia beyond to the east, and the steep mountain pass leading down into Wadi Araba from the north opening up onto the milewide bay.

The site is a major crossroads between Asia and Africa. Aqaba/Eilat is the terminus for the ancient desert highway (the King's Highway) heading south from southern Syria and Palestine (250 miles to the south of Amman and Jerusalem); to the southwest runs the ancient spice caravan and pilgrim route to the Hijaz and Yemen; to the west the route to Suez and Cairo (270 miles); to the northwest the road to the Mediterranean at al-Arish, Gaza, and Ashdod; and to the southwest the pilgrim road to Saint Catherine's and Mount Sinai.

The Gulf of Aqaba runs 118 miles to its entrance into the Red Sea at the Straits of Tiran and is 10 to 15 miles wide between the Sinai and Arabian peninsulas. The coral reefs historically caused problems for shipping in the Gulf of Aqaba, as did the treacherous winds that often combined to wreck ships. Israel controls about 4 percent of the Gulf of Aqaba coastline, while Jordan controls 7 percent (17 miles) along the coast. Egypt and Saudi Arabia between them control the rest of the littoral.

The desert mountains around Aqaba/Eilat offer few water stations, and so the freshwater springs and oasis of Aqaba/Eilat made the site particularly attractive as a port and emporium. The oasis has always supported a modest date palm grove and date production but little other agricultural products. Shellfish and fishing, supplemented by imported grains, have been the major sources of food for the city's inhabitants over the generations. The city lies along a major fault line and experiences regular earthquakes; Wadi Shallala, which cuts through the middle of Aqaba, is probably a remnant of the earthquake in AD 1068.

More than 1,000 archaeological sites covering the period 10,000 BC to late Roman have been identified within Wadi Araba, which opens up at Aqaba/Eilat. The desert areas of the city's hinterland in the southern Negev, for example, hosted hunter-gatherer systems during the Neolithic (8000–5000 BC) and Chalcolithic (4500–3300 BC) periods; some of the Neolithic sites indicate long-distance trade in shells, perhaps passing via Aqaba/Eilat. The area clearly experienced a huge increase in population during the Early Bronze Age (ca. 3000 BC) with the appearance of a pastoral nomadic system with varying amounts of agriculture and the exploitation of copper sites. The growth of urban settlement in Egypt, Palestine, Mesopotamia, and Yemen encouraged the growth of nomadic pastoralism in the desert regions, and Aqaba/Eilat must have quickly become a settled area serving both these nascent regional urban communities and the nomads of the Sinai, Negev, and northern Arabia. By 2000 BC, there was long-distance trading through the site in metals, flint implements, ceramics and shells, and the exploitation of copper and other raw materials; the site was thus a wilderness trading outpost or entrepôt and a production and extraction point from the very beginning of its history.

Archaeological excavation suggests that post-1200 BC, new statelets emerged at the beginning of the Iron Age. Both the appearance of the Israelites on the hills of Palestine and the similar appearance of Edom on the Jordanian plateau pushed the extracting and processing of copper in the lower Wadi Araba. The first clear, written reference to a settlement on the site comes from the Old Testament, where the story of the Exodus talks about Ezion-Geber as a site in the Sinai with water and palm trees. Given the subsequent reference in the Book of Kings to King Solomon (d. 922 BC) building ships at Ezion-Geber, next to Elath, there must have been some settled habitation here in the pre-Solomon period, perhaps known to the Hebrews as they wandered in the Sinai. Whatever the pre-Israelite history of the site, King Solomon renewed Ezion-Geber/Elath around the tenth century BC as an industrial settlement to refine the ore taken from the mines in the area or shipped in from further south. The settlement had a smelter and crafted industrial production for export in addition to serving as an emporium. Solomon was in a commercial alliance with the King of Tyre, and the Phoenicians appear to have served as shipbuilders and sailors for joint expeditions headquartered in Elath (see also "Tyre"). There is some indication that the more ancient site may have been to the east, near to present-day Aqaba, with Solomon's town located further to the west. Later Judean kings, including Uzziah (eighth century BC) and Jehosephat (sixth century BC), pursued security and trade through the site. The Edomites to the northeast also controlled Aila at times during the eighth to sixth century as part of their network of trade onward to Assyria.

It was under the Arab Nabateans, however, with their commercial empire headquartered in nearby Petra, that Aila appears after the third century BC as a key port. Over the next 300 years, Aila was the major Nabatean outlet to the southern seas, and the fortunes of Petra and Aila rose and fell together.

Archaeological evidence suggests that during the Hellenistic period, the city site was again moved toward the east (perhaps because it was more protected), a gateway and walls were constructed, and trade flourished with Egypt, Yemen, and even Greece. Caravan trade from south Arabia to Palestine and Syria flourished particularly after 24 BC via a network of caravansaries, and Aila with it.

The Romans initially allowed the vibrant Nabatean commercial empire autonomy but finally incorporated Petra and Aila into the empire in AD 106. So important was Aila (Aelana) to the Romans that one of two legions placed in Palestine during the second and third centuries AD was posted at Aila: the legion X Fretensis. These soldiers were used to quarry rock and upgrade the road system, building the via nova Traiana south from southern Syria to Aelana as its terminus. Some of this road and its milestones still exist near Aqaba, with evidence of cisterns and the ruins of small forts. There is evidence of a road as well via Wadi Araba to Jerusalem.

Strabo describes in his *Geography* (AD 22), as does the famous *Periplus Maris Erythraei* (*Circumnavigation of the Erythraean Sea*, AD 55–70), the routes south from Aelana to the Arabian Peninsula. Strabo comments that it took seventy days for caravans from Aelana to return from what is now modern Yemen, bringing spices north via a series of way stations. According to Pliny (AD 77) as well as Epiphanius (ca. AD 320–402), other major routes connected Aelana to the west, crossing the Sinai to the important port of Clysma and then to the cities of the Egyptian delta. The city was also central to the expanding Roman trade with India. As an entrepôt, Aelana transshipped or exported Mediterranean wine and oil, fine ceramics, exotic stones, spices such as myrrh and frankincense, and palm wood for fuel and construction materials. It was also an important industrial production city, known for its factories of pottery, glass, and copper goods.

Under the Byzantines, the city continued to prosper as a transit site but also as a Christian center and hub for pilgrimage. The city was the site of a bishopric from before AD 325, its bishop attended the Council of Nicaea, and archaeologists have found in the heart of modern Aqaba the remains of a Christian basilica dating from the late third or early fourth century and a related cemetery. A coin horde found within the church dates from the reign of Diocletian (AD 284–305). This and other indications suggest that the Aqaba foundations are one of the oldest structures in the world built specifically as a church; certainly it is the oldest in Jordan. The church was destroyed and buried by sand during an earthquake in AD 363. Remains from the cemetery suggest these early Christians may have been Egyptian immigrants. Their diet was primarily fish and shellfish but also consisted of wheat, barley, and grapes, all imported.

The founding of Saint Catherine's Monastery at the base of Mount Sinai by Justinian (ca. 527) attracted Christian pilgrims and heightened the city's connections with Egypt. Saint

Jerome (d. 420) talks about the routes from Aila to Mount Sinai, suggesting the nine-day route first headed south along the coast and then westward across the plateau to the monastery.

During the late sixth century AD, Aila was a substantial city, with strong Byzantine walls and towers, a security city for controlling the Bedouin tribes of the desert, a major emporium for the empire, and central on the pilgrimage and trade routes that wove the Middle East and the Indian Ocean together. Ships were recruited here (ca. 525) to support the Aksumites in their troubles with the Himyarites of south Yemen. With the Persian capture of Jerusalem in 614, however, a period of decline began, since the Persians preferred their own trade routes, which bypassed Aila. The city was left to negotiate with the Bedouin tribes on its own, and its vital transit routes were unsafe for trade. The Byzantines under Heraclius recovered Jerusalem in 628 but did not reassert their control further south, choosing instead to abandon the system of *limes,* or protective forts, that had reached both to Aila and to Saint Catherine's.

The remaining inhabitants of the weakened city had little time to redevelop their links to the shrinking Byzantine Empire. In AD 630, the armies of the new Islamic faith moved out of the northern Arabian town of Tabuk and surrounded Aila. This was their first expansion out of the peninsula, and Aila was the key to the road networks leading to Palestine, Syria, and, via Sinai, Egypt. Through his generals, Muhammad offered the people of Aila a deal: they would agree not to defend the narrow passes against his forces as they transited toward Palestine, and they would pay a tribute in needed food, water, and sanctuary for his troops. In return he would not attack and destroy the city and offered protection to their ships and caravans. Given that the city had been on its own for the past fifty years, the bishop of the city accepted the arrangement, demonstrating practical sense. The expansion beyond Aila into Palestine was delayed, however, by the death of Muhammad in 632 and internal divisions within the new Islamic community. However, under Caliph Abu Bakr, an army of 7,500 men left Aila in 633 and attacked Gaza, beginning the conquest of Palestine (see also "Gaza").

Under the conquerors, a new town was soon laid out to the southeast of Byzantine Aila. It appears that the motivation may have been similar to that seen later in Fustat and Kufa, where the community of believers wanted a clean start to create a *misr,* or intentional Islamic city, laid out around the mosque as the center of the Dar al-Imara (the place of the amir, of the military) and the *Balat* (the administrative headquarters). There may have been other more prosaic reasons; the old town of Aila may have been so decayed and useless by this time that it made little sense to use the same small site.

The original Friday Mosque in the city was ordered built by Caliph Uthman around 650. This would make it one of the earliest mosques built by the new community. Under the

Rashidun and subsequent Umayyad rule (AD 650–750), the city that became known in Arabic as Ayla began to grow. The port was crucial for the new Umayyad dynasty in Damascus as their southern outlet, and the obligation of the hajj meant that Ayla expanded its pilgrimage function. The ancient track cutting across the northern part of the Tih plateau from Egypt via Clysma (Suez) became known as the Darb el-Haj. The city also hosted pilgrims coming down the Kings Highway from Syria. Thus, the city became a central node in the development and expansion of Islamic culture and urban networks, hosting numerous religious and administrative structures. Major city walls and towers defended the city, and the density of habitation increased.

The city was hit by a major earthquake in AD 748. Built on a somewhat unique geological foundation of sand and groundwater that means that earthquakes can liquefy the ground under the city, most of the city's buildings and walls collapsed. The new Abbasid leadership in Baghdad, however, instigated an immediate major rebuilding program, expanding, for example, the original mosque into a much larger Congregational Mosque. The Abbasids continued to expand the city and over the next century focused considerable attention on the safety and logistics of the hajj. As a result, Ayla became a major port for pilgrims streaming to and from the Hijaz via its Makkah Gate. A large cemetery grew up outside the gate for those who died on the journey. In addition, the city became an industrial production site for amphorae necessary for transshipment of Syrian merchandise into the Hijaz and Red Sea areas. Ayla amphorae have been found in Yemen and in Ethiopia at Aksum (and late Aksumite coins in Ayla). As the key ocean outlet for southern Syrian trade, Ayla became, in the words of the Arab geographer Muqaddasi (tenth century AD), the "port of Palestine on the China Sea." The Fatimids also invested in the city for its trading role.

In 1068 the city was hit by another major earthquake, whose epicenter was in the Gulf of Aqaba. Archaeological excavations indicate massive destruction of the city, subsidence of up to a yard, and a rising water table. A new wadi cut through the heart of the city, and little was left of the sea wall. The result was a virtual abandonment of the site and an end to its role in long-distance trade. When King Baldwin I of Jerusalem raided the town in 1116 after a seven-day ride from his capital, the remaining inhabitants fled, and there was little left of the 450-year-old city for the Crusaders to occupy. As a result, they established a small fort on a small prominence some distance from the Rashidun site and left a small contingent at what they called in Latin Elim or Helim (an adaptation of the biblical name). The Crusaders failed to develop significant trade via their conquest, although they did base a few raids on Red Sea cities from Elim, and they sent shells from the Red Sea back to Europe. Their presence in Ayla blocked overland pilgrim traffic, which under the Fatimids shifted to seaborne traffic across the Red Sea, terminating at Jeddah.

Forces of Salah ad-Din captured the fort and the new village that had grown up around it in 1170, and the Franks fled. The Ayyubids financed additional construction of the fort's defenses, and one version of the derivation of the modern name suggests that gradually a new name evolved for this new construction: Aqabat Ayla (the hill of Ayla). The Mamluks (1250–1517) understood the security value of the fort and subsequently expanded it further during their rule of the region. Pilgrimage continued, but other routes evolved, and trade moved into other paths, with the result that the town slumbered.

The Ottoman Empire assumed control of the town, and for the safety of pilgrims, after 1514. As a result, what by this time had become known in shortened form as Aqaba retained a role in providing security for the hajj but for little else. The Ottomans did build or reconstruct fifteen forts between Damascus and Aqaba along the Darb al-Shami to protect the pilgrim traffic and their water supplies, although the road through Aqaba was, during Ottoman times, a secondary route, while the major route was shifted to traverse Ma'an; in times of danger, traffic would shift back to the Aqaba option. Each year, as many as 6,000 pilgrims accompanied by 10,000 animals would traverse this road down and back to the Holy Cities. The Ottoman fort in Aqaba was built in 1515 and was the largest of those along the Darb al-Shami.

The forces of Ibrahim Pasha of Egypt occupied Aqaba in 1840, and an agreement was reached with the Ottomans that this would be legitimized as "for the protection of the Egyptian hajj." Pilgrim traffic dropped off considerably, however, because of the opening of the Suez Canal in 1866 and the Hijaz Railway in 1905, leaving Aqaba as a backwater village at the head of an unimportant branch of the Red Sea.

As so often in the past, the changing fortunes of empires and political boundaries brought Aqaba back into strategic prominence. Britain's occupation of Egypt in 1888 left unclear the boundary between the Ottoman Empire and Egypt in the Sinai. A Turkish garrison was installed in the old fort in 1892. In January 1906, British officers and Egyptian police created a crisis between British-controlled Egypt and the Turkish authorities by attempting to set up a border post at Umm Rashrash (now Eilat). Both sides reinforced their garrisons during the ensuing months, leading to the potential outbreak of hostilities. Facing a British ultimatum in May 1906, Sultan Abulhammid II accepted an administrative line (though not the legal boundary, which was to cause problems later) dividing Egyptian Sinai from Ottoman Palestine running just west of Aqaba (making Taba the border post) and north to Rafah on the Mediterranean. Anticipating conflict, the Ottomans then began to enhance their fortifications of Aqaba as part of their claims to sovereignty, although they did little else to build an infrastructure other than to lay a telegraph line. Later, but before the war, British surveyors, including a young man named T. E. Lawrence, surveyed the Sinai under instruc-

tions from Lord Kitchener, which convinced Lawrence of the strategic value of Aqaba and focused his attention on the town's fortifications.

With the outbreak of World War I, the British and Ottoman empires went to war, and Aqaba became increasingly crucial as the British attack on Palestine commenced. The town was bombarded by the French and British navies, but the Ottoman guns facing the sea maintained the defenses. Further south in the Hijaz, the Arab uprising against the Turks began in June 1916. Led by Sharif Hussayn of Makkah, the Arab forces began capturing the coastal cities and establishing their control over the Hijaz. Over the course of the next winter, they began to consider how to move beyond Arabia into the Arab urban centers of Palestine and Syria. By May 1917, the British were in the second battle of Gaza and thinking about a flanking maneuver on the east bank of the Jordan and issues of resupply. As a result, the interests of both parties converged on Aqaba, and the plan for Arab forces to take the town was approved.

Auda Abu Tayih, of the local Huwaytat tribe, and Sharif Nasir, of Madinah, led the Arab forces supported by T. E. Lawrence of the British Arab Bureau. The three, along with thirty-five Bedouins, left Wajh on 9 May, recruiting fighters as they went. By 28 June, they had a 500-strong force, which rode out of the desert from the rear of the Aqaba guns and dramatically captured the town on 6 July. They captured more than 600 Turkish prisoners, most of whom were, reportedly, later executed. Lawrence was awarded a C.B. (Companion, Order of the Bath) by the British government for this victory, while Auda and Nasir received gold payments in addition to having looted the Aqaba treasury. Aqaba then became the logistical base for guerrilla attacks on the Hejaz Railway. Enshrined and embellished in the film *Lawrence of Arabia,* this attack marked the beginning of the second phase of the Arab Revolt with its drive to Damascus and supplied a crucial motivational push to the spread of the uprising.

In the political maneuvering after World War I, Aqaba was an important prize to be gained in the negotiations. Sharif Hussayn claimed Aqaba for the Kingdom of the Hijaz, citing its natural ties with northern Arabia and Jeddah; the British wanted it associated with the new entity of Transjordan, but they initially acceded to their wartime ally. When the Saudis defeated the Hashemites in the Hijaz in 1924, Sharif Hussayn took refuge in the Aqaba area. In July 1925, the Saudis began to assemble troops to attack Aqaba and Sharif Hussayn. In response the British transmitted Sharif Hussayn to Cyprus and linked Aqaba to Transjordan under his son, Abdullah. King Abdul Aziz as-Saud rejected this development but could do little about it, with the result that Saudi claims on Aqaba, and the official boundary, remained unresolved for the next forty years, although both sides accepted that Saudi authority began two miles east of Aqaba (see also "Amman").

The rest of the coastline was also divided up during this period. In 1922 a memorandum was submitted in Geneva between Mandatory Palestine and Transjordan that set their boundary two miles west of Aqaba with a division running north to the Yarmuk River. Meanwhile, the boundary between Palestine with Egypt along the coastline remained unclear and unmarked, although the outpost of Taba, eight miles along the coast to the west of Aqaba, was considered the beginning of Egyptian Sinai. In the 1930s, Transjordanian engineers finally completed the first two-lane road between Aqaba and Ma'an.

During World War II, the British positioned troops in the port, improved the harbor, and supported some initial archaeological investigation of the area. Engineers from New Zealand assigned to upgrade the road north commented on the groves of date palms, the oppressive 130-degree heat, the white sand, and the mud huts that made up the town at that time, but most of all they commented on the road leading north, with its hairpin curves, twelve-mile assent, and dramatic vertical grade that killed the brakes and clutches on trucks.

With the 1947 United Nations (UN) vote to partition Palestine, the question of Aqaba again was on the international negotiation table. Under the UN Partition Plan, much of the Negev was assigned to the Jewish state, with an outlet onto the Gulf of Aqaba consistent with the Mandatory Palestine boundaries in the area. Once fighting broke out in Palestine after November 1947, and the new Israeli state was declared on 15 May 1948, there was little initial consideration of the Negev. Israeli-Egyptian fighting concentrated on Gaza, and it was only later that Beersheba in the northern Negev was captured by Israeli forces (see also "Beersheba"). It was only at the close of fighting, while the final cease-fire was in place during March 1949, however, that a small contingent of Israeli soldiers, driving jeeps with top-mounted guns, made a spectacular dash to the Gulf of Aqaba coast and captured a small Jordanian outpost to the west of Aqaba. Operation Uvda, this last act of the war, changed the face of the area. After subsequent negotiations, King Abdullah of Transjordan signed an armistice with Israel in April 1949 that accepted the reality on the ground of an Israeli Negev and an outlet onto the Gulf.

Israel opened a small port here in 1951, and the city of Eilat was incorporated in 1959.

As a result of the war, the Arabs blockaded the Gulf of Aqaba from 1949 to 1956 to Israeli shipping, disputing Israel's international legal rights in the Gulf. Saudi Arabia argued that the Gulf was a closed Arab historic bay and not under international law. The position taken by Israel and the United States was that it is international waters, and thus passage for Israeli ships to Eilat is guaranteed. As a result of the 1956 war, there was an agreement for Israeli free passage to Eilat, and the UN declared it an international waterway in 1958. Egypt, however, reversed its decision in May 1967 and again closed the straits to Israeli shipping, contributing to the outbreak of war in June 1967. Ultimately, Egypt recognized Israeli sovereignty in their 1979 Treaty of Peace, and there is no further question on Israeli rights to free passage through the Gulf.

Likewise, the boundary issues between Jordan and Saudi Arabia have gradually been resolved. It was not until 1965 that King Hussayn and the Saudis reached an agreement over the fate of Aqaba: in return for 2,300 square miles of Jordanian territory to the east, Saudi Arabia agreed to Aqaba as Jordanian territory and granted the Jordanians an additional 10 miles of coastline to the south of Aqaba, giving the port room to expand. This brought the Tamanieh coral reef under Jordanian control and has been a vital part of the reason Aqaba has been able to grow and develop over the last forty years.

Post-1948, with the loss of Haifa as a port available to Jordan, the country began to develop Aqaba as its only port to the world. The city hosted Palestinian refugees after 1948 and 1967; some were port workers and stevedores from Haifa and Jaffa who helped develop the Aqaba port in its early days (see also "Haifa" and "Jaffa"). Today 20,000 registered Palestinian refugees live in Aqaba, many in the poor Shalaleh area of the city, where there is high poverty and drug use.

Aqaba evolved more slowly than did Eilat. Whereas the Israelis stressed domestic and international tourism, Jordan remained focused on the port as its key transshipment site for potash and oil, with a new deepwater port built in 1961. It is really only since the Madrid Conference of 1991 that the Jordanians have started thinking creatively about Aqaba as other than a port for transit trade. An Aqaba Museum and a new urban archaeological park have helped liven up the cultural aspect of the city. The Aqaba Marine Park, along with the possibility of a future American University of Aqaba, might also change the tone of the city. In the post-Oslo period, there has been a serious push to improve the quality of the infrastructure of the Aqaba Port; a loan was agreed from the European Investment Bank to build new docks for tankers in order not to lose Iraqi business during the 1990s to Syria or to other competitors, and external investment was encouraged by a 50 percent reduction in tariffs.

Creative solutions to developing inter-Arab trade have evolved despite Israel's control of part of the coast. Long-distance hauling through the Arab world, from Cairo to Dubai, for example, cannot pass through Israel, so from the Egyptian port of Taba there is a truck ferry to carry motortrucks across to Aqaba. As a consequence of all the demand, at the Aqaba terminal hundreds of trucks may wait days for contracts for loads from Egypt. The main road out of Aqaba is thus packed with trucks heading to Damascus, Jeddah, or Baghdad, making this twelve-mile-long, steep grade out of Aqaba one of the most dangerous roads in the Middle East.

Aqaba is also aggressively tying itself into other types of regional infrastructure: plans for a natural gas pipeline from Sinai to Syria, Lebanon, and Turkey via Aqaba have been proposed; a new regional electrical grid for Egypt to sell excess electric power to Jordan and Syria, and to the Gulf Cooperation Council (GCC) via Yanbu, is far along (see also "Yanbu"). In addition, Aqaba is now the hub from the Red Sea to Palestine and Syria for Fiberoptic Link around the Globe (FLAG), the longest undersea fiber cable system in the world.

Aqaba missed out on the global tourist boom of the 1990s but is now working to catch up. New international flights, new tourism development, and a promotional push under the heading of the Aqaba Gateway Project are all geared to making Aqaba a major tourist destination. In particular the Ayla Oasis is a $1.2 billion project over the next fifteen years to provide 3,000 residential units, five hotels, a marina village, an artificial lagoon, and an eighteen-hole golf course.

Another part of the master plan revolves around the Aqaba Special Economic Zone (ASEZ). Since 2000 this new authority has sought to form the core of major regional economic development, not just for tourism but also for recreational services, professional services, multimodal transportation, and value-added industries. By providing investors with quick and flexible regulatory arrangements and world-class infrastructure, this 145-square-mile authority encompassing the city has sought to make Aqaba and its hinterland a unique entity in the region. One particular innovation is to produce industrial products within the zone for sale in the United States under the new Jordanian-U.S. Free Trade Agreement (FTA), making it legally as if they are domestic American products. Some Jordanians expressed concern about the ASEZ, worrying that Israel might gain undue control via its openness or that casinos and tourism would threaten conservative Islamic values. In response the government stressed the potential $6 billion in investment and 70,000 new jobs it expected by 2020. So far neither the worst fears nor the best projections have proved to be true.

Development has not protected the city from sanctions, quarantine, and conflict, however. In a show of gunboat diplomacy, British ships anchored off Aqaba from July to November 1958, and British soldiers temporarily disembarked in the city after the Iraqi Revolution to provide protection to King Hussayn and his government under the Eisenhower Doctrine. After 1991 there was a blockade by ships of UN states of goods bound for sanctioned Iraq.

Eilat has experienced similar cyclical processes. Between 1949 and 1967, the city was a frontier town, remote from the core of Israeli society and economy. With the capture of the Sinai in 1967, it became crucial to the administration of occupied Sinai and a popular seaside resort. Once the Sinai was returned to Egypt in 1982, Eilat reverted to its tourist and frontier aspects. In the Israeli national consciousness, Eilat remains an extraordinary place, presented as a space outside of usual Israeli life, a virtual abroad. There is a sense of life in Eilat as different (clearly encouraged by the city's tourist board), and the Eilati are perceived as strange, hippies yet cosmopolitan. The city certainly attracts a full range of visitors: it is one of the key entry points for the trafficking of women from Eastern Europe and the former Soviet Union. Many of its permanent population are French Jews, and there is significant in-migration to work in the construction industry. In 2000 Eilat began to allow Jordanian workers to enter the city for temporary work.

Eilat developed partly because of difficulties experienced by Haifa as a center for oil and refining. Haifa had been the key refinery in the Middle East, but conflict killed its regional role; Eilat developed as Israel's alternative oil transshipment center. An earlier Eilat-Haifa pipeline was replaced by 1970 with an Eilat-Ashkelon oil pipeline, which at the time was the third largest in the world. It supplied Iranian oil to the European market, particularly to Romania and to Eastern Europe. The potential of the pipeline was never fully realized, since it never operated at full capacity. In the future, Eilat hopes to finish the rail freight corridor between Eilat and Ashdod on the Mediterranean (as a cost-efficient alternative to the Suez Canal) and introduce high-speed passenger trains that can make the trip from Tel Aviv to Eilat in two and a half hours (see also "Ashdod" and "Tel Aviv"). The city remains a critical port for the importation of goods into Israel; Australian cattle shipments, for example, regularly dock at Eilat.

Early on, Eilat threw its lot heavily into tourism. The first air link between Eilat and Tel Aviv started in 1950; since 1975 there has been regular charter traffic from Europe. With the second intifada, tourist numbers dropped sharply. However, numbers have begun to turn upward, and international and domestic visitors are beginning to come back. Long-term plans include "King's City," a multimillion-dollar themed development based on King Solomon, with rides and attractions, retail shops, cafés, and perhaps casinos.

The city is a place of security and control as well. The Israeli navy has a base in Eilat and has used that base to pursue Israeli interests. The navy has interdicted smuggling operations from Eilat, for example, weapons heading to Palestine. The undercover links between Israel and the Mengistu regime in Ethiopia were fed via the Eilat-Massawa supply network for selling Israeli arms, training Ethiopian police, protecting that government, and undermining the Eritrean independence movement. Eilat was the staging base for supplying southern Sudan in its struggle against Khartoum. During the 1980s, the mayor of Eilat encouraged Durban, South Africa, its twin city, to invest in a duty-free zone in Eilat and thus circumvent the sanctions regime against South Africa, since their goods would be labeled "Made in Israel." The Egyptian navy is proud of its undercover attacks on Israeli navy ships in 1969 and 1970 in the Eilat harbor, and there are reports of a foiled Fateh terrorist attempt with a ship on Eilat in 1978.

A key development issue for both cities remains guaranteeing access to enough water. Both cities are pursuing separate projects; Aqaba is building with help from the United

States Agency for International Development (USAID) a new water supply system, and in the medium term the nonreplenishable Disi Project will meet that city's needs. Yet the development plans for the ASEZ will require an additional 30 million cubic meters of water per year by 2020 beyond what the Disi aquifer will provide. In the long run, large-scale desalination of seawater and brackish water, either by reverse osmosis or by thermal systems, appears to be the primary option. This cannot be managed by one city on its own. Thus, the politics of making water is now on the agenda for both cities. Proposals include joint desalination schemes in the Aqaba/Eilat area, and in May 2005 Israeli, Palestinian, and Jordanian representatives approved the Red/Dead Project to pump salt water from Aqaba into the Dead Sea, and using the gravity drop, freshwater is provided to all three partners. The Egyptians as well are looking to include Taba in such joint planning on water questions.

The rapid pace of development around the head of the Gulf of Aqaba to date, along with plans on the drawing boards, raises tremendous fears about the destruction of the fragile marine and desert environment. This is spurring regional discussion and cooperation. Lobster and sharks in the Gulf are both already showing signs of overfishing, and land-based pollution, particularly from the oil terminals in Eilat and the fertilizer production in Aqaba, is already a grave concern. The coral reefs four miles south of Aqaba/Eilat are already showing major damage from pollution and overexploitation. Israel projects an additional 12,000 hotel rooms; Jordan, 8,000; and Egypt, 40,000; what can be done about the sewage and pollution from 60,000 additional rooms and service?

Since Oslo there have been numerous joint "peace proposals," many of them focused on environmental cooperation to create a "Red Sea Rivera." For example, a Jordanian-Israeli Marine Peace Park is being developed as part of the effort, while EcoPeace, a consortium of Egyptian, Israeli, Jordanian, and Palestinian nongovernmental organizations (NGOs), began working together in the 1990s to promote sustainable development in the region. The Taba-Eilat-Aqaba Macro (TEAM) Area was promoted by the European Commission as a maritime gateway and tourist playground. Cooperation was envisioned on other cross-border projects as well: industrial parks near the Aqaba airport financed by Jewish investors and Arab backers, the extension of Aqaba's airport runway into Israel, the use of international facilities at Eilat for Aqaba long-distance passengers, both a highway project and a rail link to connect the two cities, joint rescue services, and cooperation on the preservation of bird sanctuaries in the Gulf of Aqaba. Many of these projects floundered on the rocks of political conflict post-2000, but some have continued working slowly to build a joint-policy approach to common problems. Ultimately, the head of the Gulf of Aqaba is a small space, where the people of four states live and share the same lim-

ited water, air and future. Conceptualizing Aqaba/Eilat as one conurbation is one component in achieving sustainable development for all.

Bruce Stanley

Further Readings

Bruce, Anthony. *The Last Crusade: The Palestine Campaign in the First World War.* London: John Murry, 2003.

Dolinka Benjamin, and Avraham Ronen. *Nabataean Aila (Aqaba, Jordan) from a Ceramic Perspective.* London: Archaeopress, 2003.

Gradus, Yehuda. "Is Eilat-Aqaba a Bi-national City? Can Economic Opportunities Overcome the Barriers of Politics and Psychology?" *GeoJournal* 54 (2001): 85–99.

Lunde, Paul, and Alexandra Porter. *Trade and Travel in the Red Sea Region: Proceedings of the Red Sea Project I.* London: British Archaeological Reports, 2004.

Sandler, Deborah, Emad Adly, and Mahmoud al-Khoshman, eds. *Protecting the Gulf of Aqaba: A Regional Environmental Challenge.* Washington, DC: Environmental Law Institute, 1993.

Ashdod
Population: 197,000 (2004 estimate)

Ashdod, located on the Mediterranean coast of Palestine, has long been an important port for trade into and out of Transjordan and the Arabian Desert as well as a stop on the Via Maris to Egypt. Though known today as the second-largest Israeli port and a city of new immigrants, ancient Ashdod was one of the key Canaanite cities, and under the Philistines it was the nominal capital of their five-city alliance. Mentioned numerous times in the Bible, the city was besieged many times by invaders, including those of the Egyptian, Assyrian, Persian, Greek, Arab, Crusader, French, British, and Israeli armies.

Ashdod (Hebrew, *Ashdud;* Arabic, *Esdud* or *Isdud;* Greek, *Azotus*) is located on the coastal plain of the eastern Mediterranean littoral, about twenty-five miles south of Tel Aviv and about seven miles north of Ashqelon, near the mouth of the Lakhish Stream. The ancient tell is inland from the coast some two miles, and there clearly was a port for the city called Ashdod-on-the-Sea (Minat al-Qal'a or Minat Isdud) to distinguish it from the city itself. The modern Israeli city of Ashdod, founded in 1956, is some three miles northwest of the tell and hosts a deepwater port built in 1965.

The earliest of the twenty-three levels of the tell dates from the Middle Bronze Age (around 1600 BC) and shows signs that the city was fortified. The city's appearance in history coincides with the period of Canaanite (Hyksos) rule over the Egyptian delta and the subsequent return of Egyptian rule to southern Palestine after 1550 BC. This was an era of intense regional trade and commerce, when many new entrepôts were established and urbanization was on the increase. During the Late Bronze Age (1550–1200 BC), Ashdod was a Canaanite city under Egyptian protectorate. The Ugarit records note its dyed textiles traded throughout the region and the fact that the city had commercial agents in Ugarit during the thirteenth century. These 300 years are clearly a time of great involvement in long-distance trade and a high-water mark for the city. Egyptian administrative or military officials were resident in the city, it had its own currency and mint, and a range of products was produced in its factories. Key trading partners were cities in Cyprus, Ugarit, the rising Phoenician cities, Egypt, and the Arabian hinterland (see also "Ugarit").

The city was destroyed during the regional upheavals before the beginning of the Iron Age (1200 BC), and when the city reemerged it was as a "proto-Philistine" city, marked by a new culture brought by these Aegean immigrants. Subsequent waves of immigration by these "Sea Peoples" brought the specific group known as the Philistines to Ashdod between 1100 and 1000 BC. Under their leadership, Ashdod quickly expanded in population, area, planned infrastructure, and power; it also developed a unique pottery form marked by graceful birds termed by archaeologists "Ashdod Ware." Gradually, in one sign of the indigenization of the immigrants, the worship of the Aegean Mother Goddess gave way in the city to the Semitic male god Dagon, worshiped by the Canaanites.

As narrated in the Bible, Ashdod was an important city during the conflicts between the emerging Israelite community in the hills and the five city-states of the Philistines along the southern coast. Starting with Samson (around 1050 BC) through to Saul and King David, Ashdod is often presented in the Israelite narrative as the iconic center of Philistine power: when captured in battle, the ark of the covenant is taken by the Philistines to the temple of Dagon in Ashdod. The archaeological record indicates that during this time, Ashdod's fortifications were significantly enhanced, and the city became one of the largest in Palestine.

Over the next 300 years, as an independent city-state, Ashdod continued to benefit from its strategic location astride trade routes both along the coast to Egypt and into the Arabian Desert. Although attacked and captured by King Uzziah of Judea around 750 BC in a conflict over control of the trade routes to the Red Sea, Ashdod's citizens rebuilt their fortifications, enclosing a city which—at its greatest expansion—included more than 100 acres. Clearly, the city at this time was an important industrial center, producing a vast range of mass-produced pottery for long-distance trade.

The Assyrians arrived around 721 BC, and Ashdod paid substantial tribute to the new hegemon. However, the leaders of this wealthy city-state appear to have valued their lost autonomy so much that a revolt occurred ten years later; a commoner named Yamani (the Greek) seized the throne and began to organize regional unrest against the new empire. A combination of the archaeological record, inscriptions from Sargon II's palace in Khorsabad in northern Iraq, and biblical references all come together to indicate what happened next.

Sargon II brought his army to southern Palestine in 712 BC to deal with the traitors and massively destroyed this Philistine city, massacring thousands of workers in their workplaces. The mutilated bodies were then buried under a layer of debris, and foreign workers were brought in from throughout the empire to assemble pottery in new factories built on top of the remains. Sargon then boasted on the walls of his far-off palace that the people of this rebellious city of Ashdod now "pull the straps" of his yoke.

The rebuilt but now substantially non-Philistine city became the administrative headquarters for an Assyrian region over the next 200 years. Evidence from the tell indicates that the Philistine cult of Dagon survived on the site and that unique cultic figurines were an important product of the pottery factories, perhaps supplying a thriving pilgrim trade. The walls were rebuilt and tributes paid regularly to Assyria; Ashdod remained involved in long-distance trade.

When the Assyrian Empire withered, Ashdod had to face a renewal of Egyptian interest in the city around 640 BC: Herodotus records the longest siege ever as that of twenty-nine years by Pharaoh Psammetichus on Ashdod, although there is little other confirmation of this report.

Ashdod's role as a regional power came to a crashing end with the invasion of southern Palestine by the Babylonian King Nebuchadnezzar around 600 BC. Its king was taken off to Babylon, the city fortifications destroyed, and the city shrank back to just the acropolis. This event marked the end of 600 years of Philistine culture in Ashdod. Over the next 300 years, the port area, Ashdod-on-the-Sea (known in Greek as *Azotos Paralios*) became more important than its inland parent. During Persian rule (539 BC), Nehemiah, the Hebrew prophet, warned the Jews against intermarriage with the evil Ashdodites. After the Achaemenid invasion, Ashdod and Gaza marked the southern frontier of the Persian Empire, with Ashdod serving as a mint for the Fifth Persian Satrapy (see also "Gaza"). Ashdod fell to Alexander the Great in 332 BC.

Worship of the Philistine god Dagon continued in a range of forms during the Hellenistic era, with Ashdod retaining some of its pilgrimage trade and cultic importance. Judas Maccabeus attacked "heretical" Jews in Ashdod in 163 BC, and in 148 BC the city fell to Jonathan Maccabeus, who destroyed the ancient temple of Dagon.

Pompey captured the city from the Hasmoneans in 63 BC. Eventually, it became part of Herod I's administration; he reportedly gave it to Salome as a gift. Salome gave it to Augustus Caesar's wife, Livia, from where it passed to the Emperor Tiberius.

Early in the Christian era, as related in the New Testament, the apostle Philip evangelized Ashdod. By the fourth century, it was the seat of a bishopric, and the holders of that role are reported to have attended the various councils of the age, including Nicaea (AD 325), Seleucia (AD 359), Ephesus (AD

449), Chalcedon (AD 451), and Jerusalem (AD 536). Archaeological evidence indicates that Ashdod was a stop on the pilgrimage trails that existed during the Byzantine period and that a Jewish community lived in the port in the sixth century AD. The Madaba Map of the sixth century AD indicates a fortified city of Minat Asdud containing a church, colonnaded street, and administrative buildings.

Ashdod passed under Arab control after their victory over the Byzantines at Ajnadain, about twelve miles from Ashdod, in AD 634. Ninth-century Syrian caravans to Egypt recorded Ashdod as the stop before Gaza, and it was the site of a medieval khan. The Arabs constructed a guard tower at Minat Asdud in the ninth century, but it did not protect the city from the Crusaders: they defeated an Egyptian army at Ashdod in August 1099. Subsequently, the Crusaders built a fortress (Castellum Beroardi) to protect the small town and harbor that remained. After the Mamluks finally drove out the Crusaders (AD 1291), they destroyed the Ashdod port to prevent a Crusader return. The harbor town was then abandoned and enveloped by sand dunes over the next 700 years, while a Palestinian village of Isdud inhabited the acropolis of the tell. At the beginning of the twentieth century, there were some 5,000 inhabitants.

During the 1948 war, Egyptian forces advanced just past Isdud along the coast, where they were stopped by the Israeli Defense Forces (IDF). Isdud was attacked by the IDF from the air and by artillery starting on 20 October 1948, the Egyptian army retreated toward Gaza, and the remaining Palestinian inhabitants were driven out of the village on 28 October, ending up as refugees in Gaza. The remains of the village and tell became agricultural lands for a local moshav. Archaeological excavations, which began on the site in 1962, dramatically transformed our understanding of Philistine history with their finds from the tell.

As part of the plan to develop the southern region of the new State of Israel, a new town and port of Ashdod was established in 1956 northwest of the remains of the old Arab village when twenty-two North African immigrants were transplanted on the sand dunes. As a "new city," it was laid out around sixteen residential zones. The deepwater port was added in 1965 and expanded starting in 2002. The strategic plan called for Ashdod to service agriculture and industry in southern Israel as its outlet to the Mediterranean, cutting transport distances to older ports like Tel Aviv and Haifa. Most of the country's orange crop is shipped from Ashdod, as are most of the copper ore, phosphates, and potash from the Negev and the Dead Sea.

Today Ashdod is Israel's fastest-growing city, with a population reaching 200,000. It has been a key site for new immigrants (Russian and Ethiopian) and has a large Haridi community, and the municipality is planning for 250,000 population. A new extension to the port, called the Jubilee Port, will double Ashdod's capacity, making it the largest in the country. The city hosts oil refineries, a major power station, and a range of major high-tech and pharmaceutical industries. There are new industrial zones and high-tech parks planned along with a free-trade zone. The city is trying to "go global," targeting the tourist trade, with a new state-of-the-art marina and an international congress center. The city, Israel's third poorest, is an important Likud stronghold, with many rank-and-file members and central committee members.

Bruce Stanley

Further Readings
Dothan, Trude, and Moshe Dothan. *People of the Sea: The Search for the Philistines*. New York: Macmillan, 1992.
Maalouf, Amin. *The Crusades through Arab Eyes*. London: Saqi Books, 2001.
Morris, Benny. *The Birth of the Palestinian Refugee Problem Revisited*. 2d ed. Cambridge: Cambridge University Press, 2003.
Tubb, Jonathan. *Canaanites*. London: British Museum Press, 1998.

Aswan
Population: 240,000 (2004 estimate)

Aswan is one of Egypt's classic boundary cities, marking an important transition historically between the floodplains of Upper Egypt and Lower Nubia. Although the border was usually farther south, Aswan thus played a key role across the millennia as a security city, although its isolation from the urban centers of Lower Egypt often meant that it was a great location for heterodoxy and resistance. Over the centuries, the shifts in political boundaries meant that the city became pluralistic, attracting Egyptians and Nubians into its markets. European visitors added to the mix during the 1800s, sitting in its Victorian-style hotel to write crime novels about "death on the Nile." Today it hosts one of the largest dams in the world and continues to be caught between resistance and development.

Aswan (Arabic, *Assuan;* Latin, *Syene*), Egypt's southernmost city, is situated approximately 600 miles south of Cairo on the eastern bank of the Nile River. Its location near the Tropic of Cancer makes the climate hot throughout the year. In wintertime, temperatures are pleasant, ranging between 74 degrees Fahrenheit during the day and 50 degrees Fahrenheit at night. In summer, temperatures rise to an excessive 106 degrees Fahrenheit during the day and 79 degrees Fahrenheit at night. Average rainfall is negligible.

Aswan sits on the banks of the Nile as it cuts between the rocky highlands of the Eastern Desert and the sands of the Sahara at a point just below the First Cataract. To the north of Aswan are the classic floodplains of the Nile, three to eight miles wide. To the south, above the First Cataract, the floodplains are disconnected and narrow, and the river is broken by numerous cataracts, meaning that the population along its banks was less numerous. The area south from the First Cataract to at least the Third Cataract has historically been known as Nubia. Thus, Aswan has always been a transition point where Nubians and Egyptians intermingle, and the city has long had strategic significance and a security role for whatever political entity dominated the area at the time. As a boundary city, Aswan's inhabitants are both Nubian and Egyptian Arab, with somewhat distinct customs and language.

There has been a human settlement in the location of Aswan from before the early dynastic period (ca. 2950–2575 BC). Elephantine Island, which is opposite the modern-day city of Aswan, in the middle of the Nile, was the location of the ancient town of Yebu (Abu). This ancient Egyptian name means "elephant town," and in the predynastic period the site may have already become a key river port for trade in ebony and ivory brought up from the south. By the late third millennium, Egyptian boats were navigating above the First Cataract to trading stations to the south. There is indication of early naval action to clear and control the Nubian population around these trading circuits. By the Third Dynasty (ca. 2700 BC), direct Egyptian trade extended as far as the Second Cataract.

For some periods during the third millennium BC, it appears that the governors of Aswan were relatively autonomous and able to mount significant trading expeditions in their own right into the south. One governor of this time, Harkhuf, is buried in the hills above the city. Harkhuf is believed to have led at least four expeditions far to the south from Aswan, bringing back huge donkey caravans filled with ivory, ebony, leopard skins, incense, mercenaries, and dancing dwarfs (see also "Khartoum").

Sometime around 1870 BC, Pharaoh Senwosret III ordered a canal cut through the First Cataract so that his warships could move south. Under the Hyksos rule (1640–1540 BC) of Lower Egypt, it appears that Aswan again fell under the control of local rulers and that it marked the boundary of their authority and the beginning of a region where neither Egyptian nor Kushite power prevailed. However, under the New Kingdom, and from this point on, Egyptian rule generally ran farther south than Aswan, often as far as the Fourth Cataract, but the boundary was generally assumed to be to the Second Cataract. Queen Hatshepsut favored the deities at Aswan and graced the temples through her contributions.

The quarries in the hills around Aswan supplied the Egyptians with fine colored granite (containing quartz, yellow and brick red feldspar, and blackish mica) for their buildings and statues. Obelisks, which can be found today in London, Paris, and New York, were also cut from the quarries here, and there remains in the bedrock a huge, unfinished obelisk that was never transported because it developed a crack.

Yebu was the starting point for the great caravan route south to Nubia and the Sudan, along which passed the commercial and military expeditions of the ancient Egyptians. Because of its location on the border between Egypt and Nubia, the area possessed great strategic importance, which continued throughout the Ptolemaic (ca. 332–30 BC) and Roman (ca. 30 BC–AD 636) periods. Rome controlled Lower Nubia through a series of forts and roads, with Syene, as they called Aswan, a key security city helping to control the region. In 24 BC, the city was raided by "Ethiopians" from the south, who drove the Jews from Elephantine Island. In 23 BC, Rome recaptured the city and placed a garrison there.

Its location on the Nile made Yebu an important center for the worship of Hapi, god of the Nile flood, and Satet (Satis), goddess of its fertility and the "Lady of Elephantine." Hapi was believed to have his home in caverns near the First Cataract. The Nile's centrality to everyday life meant that the river was constantly monitored through the use of the Nilometer, located at the southern end of Elephantine Island. For more than 4,000 years, frequent and regular readings have been taken of the water levels from the Nilometer, which was used by the rest of the country to predict harvests and to calculate tax assessments. Historically, agricultural irrigation relied on the annual flooding of the Nile, and low water levels posed a grave threat to agricultural production. Since the building of the High Dam, the Nile no longer floods annually.

Aswan's geographical position, near the Tropic of Cancer, contributed to an important scientific discovery by the great geographer Eratosthenes (ca. 273–192 BC). The city was home to a well into which the sun's rays descended perpendicularly, casting no shadow, at midday at the summer solstice. Eratosthenes deduced that this point must be the Tropic of Cancer, and by making astronomical observations from this position and from Alexandria he was able to establish the approximate circumference of the earth.

In addition to Eratosthenes, the site attracted numerous visitors across the millennia. Herodotus may have visited the First Cataract ca. 450 BC, and Strabo came with the Roman General Aelius Gallus (ca. 27 BC) to negotiate a treaty with the Merotic envoys at the Philae temple concerning Aswan as the boundary between the two entities. It is Strabo who first mentions Nubians as controlling (and raiding) much of the trade south from Syene (Aswan). The Egyptian alchemist and scholar Olympiodorus visited Syene around AD 420, collecting historical material for his books. He also acted as an envoy for the Byzantine emperor while in the region. Olympiodorus comments on the number of Nubians living in Aswan at the time.

A regular Roman presence in Lower Nubia disappeared sometime after AD 266, and Diocletian (284–304) withdrew administrative control to Aswan, although Roman coins continued to circulate far up the Nile. The city of Elephantine, as the Byzantines called it, attracted a mixed population, and by the early fifth century the government was encouraging settlement of nomadic tribes around the First Cataract.

Aswan is the final resting place of a number of significant historical figures. The governors of Aswan and other high-ranking officials from the times of the Old Kingdom to the Roman period cut their tombs out of the cliffs on the west bank of the Nile. Juvenal, the satirical Roman poet, died here in exile at the age of eighty toward the end of the first century AD. Aga Khan III, the grandfather of Karim Aga Khan and leader of the Ismaili sect of Islam for many years, had his domed mausoleum, modeled on Fatimid tombs in Cairo, built overlooking the Nile and was buried there in 1957. Aga Khan suffered from asthma and found the climate in Aswan liberating: he called Aswan the most beautiful spot on earth.

Because of its geographical remoteness, Aswan has a history of resisting the various waves of religion that swept across Egypt. It was one of the last areas to be affected by Christianity, with the cult of Isis continuing at the temple of Philae until closed down by Justinian around AD 540. But, once converted, it became a Christian stronghold. In AD 571, the Monastery of Saint Simeon was built in Aswan as a resting place for Christian travelers. The ruins of the monastery are still to be seen outside the city today. During the sixth century, the area just south of the First Cataract was a Nubian Christian kingdom known as Nobatia, which followed the Monophysite tradition and was closely linked to the Egyptian Coptic Church.

Aswan was the last area of Egypt to succumb to the Muslim conquest, when in 642 Abdallah ibn Saad captured the city and stationed a garrison there. It was from Aswan that they tried and failed to conquer Nubia in 642, and they tried again in 652. At that time, a pact or treaty was negotiated, drawing the border at Aswan. Under the Muslims, Aswan's significance increased. It became a key regional administrative capital, particularly as it dominated the trade routes to Nubia. With the significance of the holy cities and pilgrimage, Aswan became a center for controlling the caravan/pilgrimage route from the Nile to Aidhab on the Red Sea (reportedly a fifteen- to twenty-day journey) and then across to Makkah or down the Red Sea to India. Thus, Aswan became closely linked culturally and economically with the Hijaz. When Cairo's power waxed and waned over the next millennia, the mercantile elites of Aswan continued to find ways to maintain their lucrative ties with the Red Sea.

The Umayyads were driven south and west out of Egypt by the Abbasids, with a last Umayyad base in Upper Egypt lasting from 782 until 785, when the Umayyad garrison at Aswan was defeated. The Abbasids, like their predecessors over the previous three millennia, used Aswan as a base for attacking Nubia; one report has them moving from Aswan in 831 to expand their control to the south. The Fatimids had trouble south of Aswan as well, losing control over even Aswan because of Nubian attacks during the decade of the 1070s. By 1077 control had been restored, and the city's trading elite were able to raise minarets, still evident today, at the city's mosques as testaments to their wealth. The subsequent relaxation of control from Cairo allowed the emergence of an au-

tonomous Arab amirate of Aswan for a time. It took Salah ad-Din (AD 1172) to restore Cairo's control. Benjamin of Tudela, although probably never having visited the city, describes it as it was ca. 1165, prior to Salah ad-Din's invasion. He comments in particular on the extensive trading ties of the city to the south, east, and west, mentioning the export of wheat, raisins, and figs and the bringing back of slaves to its market for transshipment to Cairo. His comments suggest extensive trade in Asian goods via Aswan to the kingdoms of Alwa south of Aswan and west into Darfur and the Fezzan.

Conflicts involving the city and populations to the south did not end then, however. For example, in 1275 the Nubian king Dawud raided Aswan, and in 1365 the caliph sent an army to collect tribute from the Christian Nubians, with the army carrying boats over the Aswan Cataract to raid the riverine populations to the south. The next year, Aswan was burned by attackers of the Awlad Kanz (Kenuzi), nomads who lived south of the First Cataract; they burned the city again in 1370. In 1378, however, the governor of Aswan, Ibn Hasan, repulsed them. In 1403 there was a revolt in Upper Egypt, and Aswan was cut off from the other northern urban centers. The city was sacked by raiders in 1412 and then occupied and used as a base from which to attack caravans along the trade routes.

Starting in 1820, Muhammad Ali began to move his forces into northern Sudan, and Aswan lost its status as the key southern city of Egypt. However, it remained central to the accretion of supplies for military expeditions, providing a base for the conquest of the Sudan by Anglo-Egyptian forces under Kitchener starting in 1896.

One possible reason for the British finally invading Sudan may have been their decision to build a dam at Aswan for irrigation and plantation development, thus establishing the strategic need to control more of the Nile. The Aswan "Low" Dam was completed in 1902, with its height raised in 1907 and again in 1934. When the British completed the first Aswan Dam, the project was celebrated from the steps of the Victorian-era Old Cataract Hotel by the Khedive Abbas Helmy and Winston Churchill; subsequent visitors to the hotel have included Jimmy Carter, Princess Diana, and Agatha Christie, who wrote part of *Death on the Nile* on its terrace. The hotel, built in 1899 by Thomas Cook to house its European clients, was the wonder of the age with its electricity and services. Today it still serves visitors to the city.

Over the next fifty years, the city was primarily associated with the European tourist trade and the steady stream of archaeologists pursuing the global fad in Egyptology. Cruise ships on the Nile would stop at Aswan for guests to visit the temples and to mix with scholars like Flinders Petrie, working for the Egypt Exploration Fund.

After 1955 the sleepy town of Aswan became caught up in international politics and a global archaeological salvage project bigger than ever seen before. After President Jamal

Abdul Nasir of Egypt declared in 1955 that he wanted to build a new Aswan High Dam as a monument to national progress and independence, the city has never been the same. Although initially willing to partially fund the project, the American government withdrew support for the dam in July 1956 in an attempt to force Nasir to conform to U.S. policy goals in the region. Nasir then went to the Soviets, who agreed to help, and the construction began in 1960 as a means of guaranteeing a regulated flow of Nile water, thereby preventing famine. By 1965, 33,000 workers were involved in the project to create one of the largest dams in the world, stretching two miles across at its crest. Engineers have voted it one of the top-ten engineering feats of the twentieth century.

The construction of the dam led to the creation of Lake Nasser, the largest reservoir in the world with a surface area of 2,400 square miles. On the positive side, the dam and its reservoir have increased agricultural production by improving irrigation of already existing cultivable lands and by enabling the reclamation of large tracts of desert. The dam has also increased the production of electrical power, allowing Aswan to become an important industrial center. Under control of the Aswan Regional Planning Board, development in the area has been significant, including a chemical fertilizer plant and other chemical factories.

On the negative side, however, the building of the dam led to the flooding of a large area of land historically inhabited by the Nubian people. As a result, more than 100,000 were relocated to villages north of Aswan (such as Kom Ombo), and much of their cultural heritage was lost. In addition, many ancient temples, including Abu Simbel, were threatened with submersion and so were moved to new locations through a huge effort of international cultural cooperation. The High Dam and Lake Nasir have also caused serious environmental problems, not least of which is the need for Egyptian farmers downstream to rely on artificial fertilizers as they are now deprived of the naturally fertilizing silt that used to be deposited by the Nile as it flooded.

Just outside Aswan there continues to exist a regular camel market, one of the largest in North Africa. Sudanese animals are regularly sold here for shipment north to Cairo. The camel caravans into the city will often also carry smuggled goods: ivory and electronic equipment still make their way across the Egyptian-Sudan border for transshipment north or west.

In addition to Elephantine Island, there is also Kitchener Island, where rare and exotic flowers and trees from throughout the world are maintained, and the restored Isis Temple, saved from Philae Island when it flooded because of the dam. The new Nubia Museum houses artifacts from Aswan's history but also an extensive collection on the history of lower Nubia, lost to the dam. A new cable bridge spanning the gorge has been built, and the city now has its own local TV station. Aswan is also known for the annual migration of the rare White Storks, which stop in the area while heading to Libya.

Recent history in Aswan has also involved radical Islamist politics. Al-Jama' al-Islamiya had a base in the city, and in 1993 a series of confrontations between them and security police led to the deaths of two police and fourteen militants in the al-Rahman Mosque in the city. Despite this, the city was awarded the United Nations Educational, Scientific, and Cultural Organization (UNESCO) African City of Peace Award in 2004 for improving the living standards of its citizens.

Nicola Pratt

Further Readings
Alston, Richard. *The City in Roman and Byzantine Egypt.* London: Routledge, 2002.
Fahim, Hussayn M. *Dams, People and Development: The Aswan High Dam Case.* New York: Pergamon Press, 1980.
Friedman, Renee, ed. *Egypt and Nubia: Gifts of the Desert.* London: British Museum Press, 2002.
Hopkins, Nicholas, and Reem Saad, eds. *Upper Egypt: Identity and Change.* Cairo: American University in Cairo Press, 2004.
Jackson, Robert. *At Empire's Edge: Exploring Rome's Egyptian Frontier.* New Haven, CT: Yale University Press, 2002.
Jennings, Anne M. *The Nubians of West Aswan.* Boulder, CO: Lynne Rienner, 1995.
O'Conner, David. *Ancient Nubia: Egypt's Rival in Africa.* Philadelphia: University Museum, University of Pennsylvania, 1993.
Waterbury, John. *The Nile Stops at Aswan.* Hanover, NH: American Universities Field Service, 1977.
Welsby, Derek. *The Medieval Kingdoms of Nubia.* London: British Museum, 2002.

B

Babylon
Population: 200,000 (560 BC estimate)

Babylon was one of the most significant cities of the ancient world. Known by many around the globe because of the biblical references to the city, Babylon's iconographic role as the representative of urban decadence continues today in popular culture, while other achievements connected with the city, such as Hammurabi's Law Code or its Hanging Gardens, still fascinate the modern mind. Located in southern Iraq, the city retains its symbolic importance to both Iraqi leaders and to Christians, both east and west.

The remains of the ancient city of Babylon (Old Babylonian, *Bab-ilim;* Hebrew, *Babel;* Arabic, *Babil*) are located about sixty miles south of Baghdad in modern-day Iraq, slightly east of the Euphrates River and north of the town of al-Hillah. Its prime location, on the alluvium of southern Mesopotamia between the two powerful rivers of the Tigris and the Euphrates, and not far to the north of the marshy areas of the Delta where these rivers meet the Gulf, was crucial to its geopolitical power. Lying next to the Euphrates, and subsequently bisected by it as the city expanded, Babylon took advantage of the ease of cultivation, irrigation, transport, and management of the lower Euphrates that was not available along the Tigris.

The first mention of a city with this name is around 2300 BC, 1,000 years after the spontaneous rise of the urban-based culture and city-state system of Sumer further to the south. Under the Ur dynasties of the neo-Sumerian period (2122–2001 BC), Babylon served as a regional capital (see also "Ur"). It is not until 1894 BC, however, that Babylon enters the lists as a world city. Under the direction of Sumu-abum, an Amorite (West Semitic) tribal leader, walls were built to protect his newly captured capital.

Sumu-abum and his descendants form the First Dynasty of Babylon within the Old Babylonian Era (2000–1600 BC). Babylon's authority expanded through the conquest of neighboring city-states; by the end of the reign of the sixth king, the famous Hammurabi (1792–1750 BC), the city was the center of an extensive territorial empire, based on a vibrant city system, stretching from the Gulf to Anatolia, west to northern Syria, and east into Persia.

The Law Code associated with Hammurabi ranks as one of the outstanding developments of the rise of urban civilization in Mesopotamia. Known to us from an engraved stela, now in the Louvre, that shows Hammurabi receiving the law from the god of justice, Shamash, the code set standards for equality, fairness, and transparency that remain central to the rule of law today.

Babylon's first empire ended when Hittite invaders raided the city, perhaps in 1595 BC. After a period of chaos, a new dynasty, Kassite in origin, arose to rule for the next 400 years, with Babylon as its primary capital (1590–1155 BC). Meanwhile, the northern areas of Mesopotamia experienced tremendous urbanization and political development, with the result that a north-south dynamic, one Assyrian and one Babylonian, each based around primate cities and their city systems, began to evolve to drive regional politics over the next 700 years (see also "Nineveh").

Babylon itself became a regional religious center for the cult of its city-god, Marduk. A large ziggurat, topped by his shrine, was built at the core of the city as his dwelling place, giving rise to the biblical story of the Tower of Babel and its statement on human hubris. This religious role, when combined with the massive power of the city politically, economically, and militarily, meant that Babylon and Marduk's following evolved together, placing both at the head of the southern Mesopotamian pantheon of cities and gods. All subsequent regional kings called themselves by the title "King of the City of Babylon," and the *Enuma Elis* (the Babylonian Creation epic) stresses this link between the gods' presence and the city as the seat of political power.

This centrality meant that subsequent short-lived dynasties found they had to locate themselves in Babylon. Ultimately, however, Assyrian suzerainty was established, operating through local kingship from about 1000 BC until the fall of Assyria ca. 628 BC. Conflicts did arise from challenges presented by immigrant groups, in particular the Chaldeans, who occasionally captured the city. Finally, in 689 BC, the Assyrian king Sennacherib reportedly ordered the complete destruction of the troublesome city by having its remains thrown into the Euphrates and washed into the Gulf.

Babylon rose from the ashes, however, under the next Assyrian king, and when Assyrian domination finally ended, a Chaldean dynasty appeared in the city and began a period of expansion that quickly resulted in a new period of Babylonian empire. This neo-Babylonian period (626–539 BC), particularly during the rule of the biblically famous Nebuchadnezzar II, was the high-water mark of the city's culture and glory, seeing its power stretching to the Mediterranean, incorporating Assyria and down the Gulf into Arabia. It was the confrontation with the Egyptians, particularly over control of Syrian and Palestinian cities, that was reported in the Bible.

Map of the world, with Babylon at its center, 600–500 BC. (HIP/Art Resource)

The destruction of Jerusalem and the exile of Judea to Babylon remain today powerful images of imperial power and diaspora.

Trade routes and their control were crucial. The camel was probably domesticated prior to 1200 BC, and this allowed long-distance trade by land to supplement or even replace sea routes, and Babylon was the key entrepôt of the region. Given its agricultural productivity (based on its massive system of irrigation canals and bureaucratic management), manufacturing, cultic significance, and political authority, all the key factors of city power came together in the metropolis of Babylon. This power is well represented in one of the oldest maps ever discovered, the Babylonian world map (600–500 BC), now in the British Museum, where Babylon is presented as the "hub of the universe," surrounded by other cities.

The outer wall of Nebuchadnezzar's city was eight miles long, incorporating more than 2,000 acres, making it the largest city in the world until the heyday of imperial Rome. In fact, Aristotle, in his book *Politics* (part 3), claimed that Babylon had the "circuit of a nation" and that it took three days for some citizens to hear that the city had been captured. The Greeks of the classical period, in writing about the wonders of their world, referred to the irrigated, elevated gardens of Babylon at the time of Nebuchadnezzar as a marvel; it can only be guessed what the actual gardens were like, how extensive they were, and how they were irrigated. But it must have been impressive to see, in the middle of a dry plain, a city crowned with trees and foliage making it like an oasis.

Nebuchadnezzar II ruled for more than forty years, dying in 562 BC. His successors, through military adventures and lavish spending, quickly undermined the foundations of the empire, and the city was unprepared for the rise of the Persians. In 539 BC, the city fell to Cyrus the Great, who, legend suggests, diverted the Euphrates in order to enter the city through its soggy riverbed.

The Achaemenids allowed Babylon to continue as a key entrepôt and supported its international cult status. Herodotus, perhaps reporting from a personal visit in the fifth century, was hugely impressed by the size of its walls and moat, its multistory houses, the tower, and the agricultural system.

When the Persians were defeated by Alexander the Great (331 BC), Babylon entered a new phase in its history. It now became included in the wider Hellenic world, and older Mesopotamian and Sumerian influences began to fade. One of the main dreams of Alexander was to colonize the Persian Gulf from his new capital, Babylon. But he died (323 BC) within the city, lying in the palace of Nebuchadnezzar, before his plans were implemented. Subsequently, Babylon became part of the Seleucid Empire (312 BC), but its position as the capital was bypassed by the decision to build a new capital, on the Tigris, at Seleucia. However, within Babylon, a building program of Greek theaters and an agora added to the quality of the built environment, while major financial houses provided credit for international trade, although ships from the Gulf did shift to navigating the Tigris.

It is, however, with the rise of the Parthians (141 BC–AD 226) and their anti-Hellenistic policies, and their subsequent struggle with Rome, that Babylon lost its importance as a key trade and cultic center. Land and sea routes shifted further west, north, and south, making Babylon's geographic position no longer advantageous for international long-distance trade. Interesting remnants of high Babylonian culture, in particular some cult worship and the use of cuneiform, resonated through the region well into Sassanian times, when they ruled over a shrinking city (AD 226–637).

The Zoroastrian Sassanians persecuted, among others, the Babylonian Jewish community, which by then was almost 1,000 years old. Noted for their scholarship and religious leaders (*gaonim*, or great ones, and *amoraim*, explainers), this community was the source of the Babylonian Talmud (commentary on the Mishnah, late fifth century AD) and a schismatic sect called the Karaites (ca. AD 765), and it thrived under leaders like the philosopher and translator Sa'adiah Gaon (AD 882–942).

When the Battle of Babylon matched Sassanian elephants against forces of the invading Arabs, however, Babylon was primarily in ruins, and it was within sight of its remains that the victorious Arab armies established a temporary staging camp after their defeat of the Sassanians at Qadasiya in 637. A small town known as Babil has remained near the site ever since. Following the invasion of Iraq in 2003, American soldiers established a base, "Camp Babylon," near the ruins; they have subsequently been accused of serious damage to the city's remains.

Our current knowledge of ancient Babylon results from comprehensive archaeological excavations begun in 1899 by the German Oriental Society under R. Koldewey and later excavations by the German Archaeological Institute. As a result, extensive artifacts are now located in Berlin. The Iraqi Department of Antiquities has carried out significant reconstructions of the Ishtar Gate, the Emakh Temple, the Processional Way, and the palace complex on-site.

Bruce Stanley

Further Readings

Adkins, Lesley. *Empires of the Plain: Henry Rawlinson and the Lost Languages of Babylon.* London: HarperPerennial, 2004

Leick, Gwendolyn. *Mesopotamia: The Invention of the City.* London: Allen Lane and Penguin Press, 2001.

Maisels, Charles K. *The Emergence of Civilization.* London: Routledge, 1990.

Saggs, Henry W. F. *The Greatness That Was Babylon.* London: Sidgwick and Jackson, 1962.

Van de Mieroop, Marc. *The Ancient Mesopotamian City.* Oxford: Oxford University Press, 1999.

Wellard, James. *By the Waters of Babylon.* London: Hutchinson, 1972.

Baghdad
Population: 5.6 million (2003 UN estimate)

Baghdad, that city of flying carpets, Aladdin, and The Thousand and One Nights, *has now given way in the Western imagination to a dangerous warren of car bombs, kidnappings, and suicide bombers. Our mental image of this ancient city on the Tigris is now more likely to be of ambulance sirens, reporters embedded in the backs of Humvees, or of eerie green antiaircraft tracers threading the night sky. For many Arabs, however, it has long represented a golden age of Islamic civilization and the unity of the umma (the Muslim community as a whole); for the Ottomans, it was the symbol of their right to rule all of Islam; for Baghdadi Jews, it is now a lost community that spanned 1,300 years of culture and religious expression. This most evocative of imagined cities represents both the best and the worst of the human condition, ranging from the piles of skulls left by Temür to the heights of advanced Islamic astronomy, science, and theology during the early Middle Ages. This "City of Peace" has known little peace, located as it is in the heartland of the Eurasian system, where dreams of power and authority have always clashed with the possibilities of urban civilization.*

Baghdad (or *Bagdad*) sits astride the Tigris River in the middle of Iraq, approximately 25 miles east of the Euphrates River at the point the two rivers flow most closely together. Often portrayed as located on a *jazirah* (island) between the two rivers, the city lies at a point where the alluvial floodplain begins and runs some 330 miles southeast to Basrah and the Persian Gulf, while to the northwest is Mosul. Few geological formations mark the light brown landscape: Baghdad is the river, which sets its rhythms and, until recently, often disastrously flooded its streets and canals. Located at the convergence of roads leading east to ancient Khurasan and west to Damascus or Jerusalem, the river provides navigable access south to the Shatt al-Arab or north to Anatolia, meaning that Baghdad is easy to get to and the central node in distant transport and communication routes. Sited on a key defensible bend in the river, the city has now spread for 10 miles along both banks of the Tigris.

The city dates its beginnings from its intentional founding in 762 by the second Abbasid caliph, al-Mansur, as his new capital. However, the site and the area around it reveal archaeological remains of human habitation back to the beginnings of Mesopotamian civilization. Tell Abu Harmal, now on the outskirts of the city, was ancient Shaduppum, the administrative center for the Kingdom of Eshnunna, whose capital, Eshnunna (established around 3000 BC), is modern Tell al-Asmar, lying twenty miles northeast of Baghdad. At Abu Harmal, archaeologists have discovered ancient tablets containing laws predating Hammurabi (ca. 1792–1750 BC), fixed prices for basic commodities of grain and oil, and mathematical and geometric tablets suggesting advanced calculations. Twenty miles to the southeast along the river lies Medain (two cities): the twin ruins of Seleucia (ca. 312–165 BC), the center of Hellenistic culture of the classical age; and Ctesiphon (ca. 300 BC–AD 700), the Parthian and Sassanian capital. Thus, the location of the new Abbasid city was in the middle of a rich 3,000- year-old tradition of urban civilization and kingship.

The Arab armies defeated the Sassanians in the spring of 637 at the Battle of al-Qadisiyah, just south of modern Baghdad, and then took Ctesiphon. To confirm their rule over the valley of the two rivers, they established Basrah and Kufa in 638 as garrison cities to house Arab armies (see also "Basrah" and "Kufa"). Over the next 100 years, the struggles within Islam and the establishment of the Umayyad Empire meant that tension continued in Mesopotamia between believers about political power and how it should fit with the new Islamic faith. Out of this area of the empire emerged the Abbasid Revolution, which proceeded to defeat the Umayyad Empire in AD 750, with Abu al-Abbas declared the new caliph.

Abu al-Abbas was succeeded by his brother, al-Mansur (r. AD 754–775), who went looking for a site to establish a new capital, one that did not reflect the Arab foundations of Islam or have a separate ancient existence, like Damascus, but could symbolize the new multiethnic coalition that lay at the base of the Abbasid Revolution. Abu al-Abbas had built a palace on the Euphrates at Anbar, but al-Mansur looked farther east, to the Tigris, away from the anti-Abbasid and pro-Arab influences of nearby Kufa.

In 762 al-Mansur chose a site that, like his imperial precursors, would enable him to control the major trade, agricultural production, and communication networks in the two-rivers valley. Reportedly declaring that there was "no obstacle between us and China," al-Mansur located his new capital on the western bank of the Tigris near both a Sassanian village called Baghdad and the navigable canal Nahr Isa, connected with the Euphrates. With the help of regional architects, al-Mansur laid out a round city plan, which he named Madinat al-Salaam (the City of Peace). The Round City, as it also came to be called, had a high inner brick wall that enclosed the palace of the caliph, administrative offices, and the main congregational mosque. The next ring wall enclosed army quarters, while the third enclosed city inhabitants. All this was surrounded by a moat. It is too much to call this a major urban plan: the Round City was small in size and primarily an administrative or security complex, although it initially had quarters for different regional troops and markets for the inhabitants. The city had four gates and four major access roads. Al-Mansur employed many architects, craftsmen, and workers from throughout the Muslim world to build the new city, which was completed in four years. Above it all rose the caliph's palace, with its green dome.

However, the city's new inhabitants quickly put their own stamp on the built environment, and the City of Peace began to break through the plan. The markets were soon moved out of the Round City and relocated to the southern Basrah gate in a new area called al-Karkh. The northeast gate, leading to Khurasan, crossed a bridge of boats to the eastern bank and the growing suburb of Rusafah. The caliph's son built his palace on the eastern bank, to be followed by many others; in later years, the caliph and administration relocated in Rusafah. The city also picked up the nickname al-Zawra, since one of its inner gates was set askew (*izwarrat*).

Within thirty years, Baghdad was the premier city in Eurasia, greater in population (700,000 estimate), cultural impact, intellectual activity, and control of world trade than any other global rival. It remained the premier city in the world for the next century and a half. Yet it long remained a city of subdistricts and areas rather than an integrated entity. There were east and west Baghdad, divided by the river; there were suburban areas with their own districts, markets, mosques, and cemeteries. Such divisions still have some resonance today in the way its inhabitants live the everyday city.

The writer Yakut (ca. 891), describing al-Mansur's city 150 years after it was built, emphasized the two vast semicircles of the city, on the right and left banks of the Tigris, twelve miles

in diameter, with watchtowers on the north and south river entrances. Along the quays, Chinese ships and local rafts made of inflated skins jockeyed for position, while thousands of boats and gondolas plied the river. The caliph's palace stood in the center of a huge park with wild animals and birds. Wide streets divided the city into quarters, with each quarter overseen by a local authority responsible for its cleanliness, sanitation, and comfort, while gardens and parks were regularly swept. Homes were supplied with water via aqueducts, and the streets were lit at night. Multistoried palaces of marble were outfitted with Chinese vases and gold, and the city offered hospitals, schools, and lunatic asylums for its inhabitants.

A wide diversity of minorities and workers were attracted to the new capital. The Church of the East, what later became known as the Assyrian Orthodox Church, had been headquartered in Ctesiphon. Their head of the church, Catholikos Timetheos I, moved his residence to Baghdad in 780. Jews from Palestine and Babylon came to the new capital as well and evolved a large and stable community that lasted until the 1950s.

This flowering of Islamic civilization produced many blossoms. In particular, the city was known for its scholarship in religion, theology, and philosophy. Although often divided by the schism between Sunni and Shi'i, Baghdad produced many great religious scholars in its numerous mosques and madrasas. Crucially, two of the four schools of Islamic law were founded by inhabitants of the city. Imam Abu Hanifa (AD 699–767), founder of the conservative Hanafi branch of Islamic law, had met some of the Companions of the Prophet and was crucial in helping al-Mansur establish the city and its legitimacy, although he may have died in prison as a challenger to the Abbasid caliph. His tomb is still venerated in the city, and his school still predominates in Iraq and former Ottoman lands. Ahmad ibn Hanbal (780–855), son of Baghdad, suffered persecution for his learning, piety, and faithfulness to tradition. His concerns for orthodoxy and the Hadith profoundly shaped his followers' concerns, providing the foundations for the Wahhabi movement. His shrine has long been venerated in the Quraish cemetery.

Some 300 years later, Shaykh Abdul Qadir al-Jilani (1077–1166), a follower of Ibn Hanbal, took a religious school founded by the jurist and expanded it to establish the al-Qadiriya Sufi order. Regarded as one of the greatest saints of the Sufi tradition, this shrine of the "Sultan of the Saints" and the accompanying mosque have long been sites for pilgrimage and the source of many miracles and wonders. It is recorded that al-Jilani attracted such huge crowds with his sermons that he was forced to preach out in the open. He was famed for his conversions to Islam and for saving sinners; reportedly, many of those listening died of emotion.

One of the greatest theologians of Islam, Abu Hamid al-Ghazzali (1058–1111), began his search for the relationship between the inner and outer life when he was appointed director of the Nizamiyyah in Baghdad (1091), the most prestigious teaching post in Islamic law. Gradually developing doubts about his beliefs, al-Ghazzali left Baghdad to live the life of a wandering Sufi on the road, finally writing his *Ihya Ulum al-Din* (*Revivification of the Religious Sciences*) and the *Tibr al-Masbuk* (*An Ethical Mirror for Princes*) at the end of his career.

For the Shi'i, Baghdad had pilgrimage and holy significance as well. Within the Quraish cemetery are the four golden minarets of the Kadhmayn, the Shrine of the Two Imams. Its precinct holds the shrines of both the Seventh Imam, Musa al-Kadhim, and that of his descendant, the Ninth Imam, Muhammad Taqi al-Jawad, both revered by the "Twelvers" community. The Shi'i shrines were burned in the riots of 1051 but rebuilt. Shi'i religious scholars from Baghdad included Kulaini (d. 939), with his *al-Kafi fi Ilm ad-Din* (*Compendium of the Science of Religion*); Ibn Babuwailhi, who wrote on Shi'i law and tradition in *Kitab man l yadhuruhu l-Faqih* (*Every Man His Own Lawyer*); and al-Tusi, with his *Tahzhib al-Ahkam* (*The Correcting of Judgments*).

Baghdad was central to world science and medicine. Within the Bayt al-Hikma (House of Wisdom), a center established by Caliph al-Mamun to translate Greek scientific writings into Arabic, new advances were made in understanding the body, nature, and the cosmos. It is recorded that al-Mamun requested copies of texts held in Constantinople for the study and use of his scholars in the Bayt al-Hikma; such interlibrary loans proved crucial for the preservation of Greek scholarship. Al-Khawarizmi, the father of algebra (*kitb al-jabr*), lived and worked in the city; there was an observatory where he recorded his study of the stars.

The Abbasids worked hard to establish a strong imperial administration, remnants of which still echo throughout the region. They laid down a set of bureaucratic procedures and standards for civil servants and instituted the role of vizier (chief administrator). The empire was integrated via a royal road system and via pilgrimage roads, such as the famous Darb Zubayda, that provided security, shelter, and water supplies to pilgrims traveling from Baghdad to Makkah (see also "Makkah"). Baghdad was the center of a *barid,* or postal system of the empire, that moved royal mail quickly across vast distances.

Baghdad was also the center of fashion and high urban culture, and it sucked up the most exquisite products in the empire. The Abbasids continued the old Sassanian system of requiring a textile revenue (*tiraz,* or embroidery) from the districts of Egypt, the Caspian, and Persia. For example, 300 bales of green silk carpets and quilts, plus cotton embroidered garments, were sent from one district of the Caspian to the caliph al-Mansur as tribute; a century later, Khurasan was regularly sending 27,000 textile pieces to Baghdad. The government bought the best quality, and thus Baghdad became known for the diversity and quality of the silk textiles available in its streets. This is reflected in the numerous types of textiles mentioned in the *Alf Layla wa Layla* (*The Thousand and One Nights*) stories. The government distributed silk robes of honor, rulers would transport silk to Baghdad for sale and then donate the proceeds to the poor in Makkah, while the elite of Baghdad competed to wear the most beautiful silks from China.

Baghdad at this time was particularly known for its many great women. The writer al-Masudi mentions a number of them, for example, Zubayda, wife of Harun ar-Rashid and benefactor of the Darb Zubayda pilgrim route to Makkah. There was also al-Haizuran (also known as Khayzuran, which means the bamboo) (d. 803), wife of al-Mahdi and mother of Harun ar-Rashid, who was a *qaina* (trained professional musician slave); she was known for her political influence with both her husband and her son.

Baghdad's grandeur inspired much praise and scholarship. Ibn al-Jawzi (d. 1200), using the traditional structure of the *fada'il* (a poetry form) to catalog the praiseworthy characteristics of Baghdad, authored the book *Manaqib Baghdad* (*Virtues of Baghdad*) to honor its citizens. Khatib al-Baghdadi's (d. 1071) *Tarikh Baghdad* (*History of Baghdad*) adopted the tradition of city histories prevalent in the Muslim world to provide statistics, key information about its famous people, and a sense of the city's historical development across the generations. In twenty-nine chapters of introduction about the city, and fourteen volumes of biographic entries in alphabetical order discussing the city's key religious scholars, al-Baghdadi provided a resource on which later scholars could build.

Al-Mansur left his son Mahdi (r. 775–785) a full treasury and an empire concerned with trade. This was a time of great expansion for Islam, as it moved with the traders and merchants along the trade routes facilitated by the empire. Harun ar-Rashid, immortalized in many stories in *The Thousand and One Nights,* took over from his brother (786–809), and his rule represents the height of Baghdad's glory. After ar-Rashid died, civil war led to the first siege of the city. This yearlong siege, along with the city's capture and partial destruction, began a long process of decline.

Caliph Mutasim (r. 833–842), great grandson of Mansur, moved the caliphate out of Baghdad thirty miles north to a new capital of Samarra (see also "Samarra"). After the civil war of his other brothers, Mutasim had come to rely on Turkish slave troops to secure his rule. These forces had little of the urban Baghdadi feel, trampled women and children as they rode through the city, and raped and pillaged as they wished. Consequently, the merchant elite of Baghdad became alienated from the caliphate, and there were uprisings against the caliph's troops. Mutasim himself did not like Baghdad, being unfamiliar with the city, its customs, or its people, and so withdrew his court into a new garrison city, close enough to keep a watchful eye on Baghdad but far enough away not to be tainted by its power.

Baghdad suffered little from this move, retaining its economic, cultural, and intellectual role. Certainly, the poets, thinkers, and religious figures like Ibn Hanbal remained in Baghdad rather than move to Samarra. The city was still ten times larger than Ctesiphon had been, and its economic networks remained global: merchants still regularly left the city for China. Yet its trade routes were fragile: the Zanj Revolt of black slaves in southern Iraq cut Baghdad off from the Persian Gulf during the 870s, and they threatened to capture the city in 878.

The Abbasid capital remained in Samarra until 892, when Caliph al-Mutamid returned it to Baghdad. Yet the city went into decline over the next century. By the tenth century, the canal system had fallen into disrepair, and many of the riverside palaces had been demolished. Al-Fustat (Cairo) had replaced Baghdad as the vibrant heart of the Muslim world, and by the millennium the city had dropped behind Cordoba, Constantinople, and Cairo in population and influence. A key reason for this decline was the factional struggles that beset the capital when political control of the empire had passed from the royal family and its retainers to nonindigenous military societies. The first was when Muizz ad-Dawla entered Baghdad in AD 945, destroyed much of the city, assumed the title of Commander of Commanders, and set up the Buyid dynasty. Under the Shi'i Buyids, the first independent Shi'i school was established in the city, and its textile production, for example, the brocade known as "Baghdadi," was desired in Europe.

Tughril Beg, first sultan of the Seljuq dynasty, defeated the Buyids in 1055 and returned Sunni rule to the city. Under the influence of the exceptional Nizamulmulk as vizier, Tughril's successors Alp Arslan (1063–1072) and Malikshah (1072–1092) were able to expand Seljuq power, and Baghdad experienced a resurgence. Nizamulmulk stressed training and education as the key to a strong society and founded the Nizamiyyah in Baghdad (1067) as the key madrasa for preparing scholars of future generations. The creation of madrasas gathered speed after this, with more than thirty recorded in the city a century later. It is interesting to note that Nizamulmulk was concerned about the rise of populist street mobs in the city, particularly Hanbalis emerging from their stronghold in the Harbiya Quarter, who used mob violence to silence scholars and preachers with whom they disagreed. The city was increasingly racked by street battles between various religious groups during this time; combined with regular fires, sacking by bedouin, and floods, the ninth and tenth centuries were not easy times for the city's inhabitants.

The caliphate in Baghdad was able to carve out some political space for itself in the late twelfth and early thirteenth centuries, particularly under Caliph al-Nasir (1180–1225), and the city controlled much of present-day Iraq. Al-Nasir enjoyed showing off the head of the last Seljuq sultan on the gates of Baghdad in 1194, but he also worked hard to organize *futuwwah*, or men's clubs, one expression of popular urban Sufism, as a way of controlling the Muslim community in the city. Al-Nasir also sought to reconcile Sunni and Shi'i communities in the city, encouraging mutual tolerance.

The temporary resurgence of the Abbasid Caliphate ended in January 1258, when the Mongols appeared outside the city walls. Huleghu, one of three brothers, grandsons of Genghis Khan, led the Mongol expansion into the Middle East, committed to overthrowing the caliphate and its claim to God's authority over that of Genghis Khan. Huleghu may have offered the caliph al-Mutasim, the thirty-seventh Abbasid caliph, a deal to accept Mongol sovereignty. However, al-Mutasim was overconfident and threatened a worldwide Muslim uprising if Baghdad was invaded. Later, when the city was besieged, al-Mutasim proposed negotiation, but it was too late. The city was surrendered without resistance, but Huleghu gave the city over to plunder, which reportedly lasted forty days. The entire population was massacred, with the exception of the Christians, the coreligionists of Huleghu's wife and father. One report says the "blood of the slain flowed in a river like the Nile." Many parts of the city were burned; the canals and dikes were destroyed, making their rebuilding impossible; the grave of Harun ad-Rashid was turned out; medieval chronicles claim that the Tigris was dammed by the library books thrown into its water; and the caliph al-Mutasim and his sons were, according to various reports, either strangled, rolled in a carpet and trampled, or locked up with only gold to eat until they starved.

To Arabs the destruction of the iconic Baghdad by the enemies of Islam was a terrible, cataclysmic event. For 500 years, the city had been the center of Islam and Arab authority. For many, the sacking of the city was a punishment by God for forgetting him.

After the Mongol invasion, the city was reduced to the role of a provincial city and shrank to one-tenth of its former size. Revenues from the province dropped 90 percent, and most of the western part of the city lay abandoned. Under the Il-Khanids (subordinate Khanate), Baghdad was just one more city subservient to Tabriz and to Kublai Khan in faraway China. Buddhist temples were built in the city, although after 1295, the Mongol rulers adopted Islam, and the Buddhist traditions were ripped out. When Marco Polo visited the city (ca. 1272), there was trade, but by the time Ibn Battuta made his pilgrimage to Baghdad in 1327, he found a small city, with "no beauty in her," although the congregational mosque had been rebuilt and the Mustansiriya, where all four legal traditions were studied, was still functioning.

The city had little time to recover. The campaigns of Temür (Tamerlane or Timur-i lang) across Eurasia from 1382 to 1405 consumed Baghdad. At the time, Sultan Ahmad of the regional Turko-Mongolian Jalayir dynasty ruled the city. In 1393 Temür captured the city, and Ahmad fled; it is on this occasion that Temür ordered his cupbearer to seize all the city's wine and to pour it into the Tigris. Temür placed the city under the rule of his son, Amiranshah, and 3,000 troops, but Sultan Ahmad Jalayir retook Baghdad soon after. Consequently, Temür returned in 1401 and recaptured the city, leaving more than 100 towers of skulls dotted around the city's ruins. Sultan Ahmad regained what remained, however, shortly after Temür died, in 1405.

Baghdad took centuries to rebuild. (In fact, it was not until the twentieth century that the irrigation systems were fully restored and the population reached its former size.) For the next 350 years, Baghdad's value to empire builders lay primarily in its religious propaganda value rather than in any economic or strategic potential. For the rising Safavid Empire, Baghdad's capture in 1508 offered them, as a Shi'i power, significant legitimacy by controlling the former seat of the Sunni Caliphate. They plundered the shrines of Abu Hanifa and al-Jilani and murdered many Sunnis in the city. The Shrine at Kadhmayn was rebuilt and still attracts thousands of pilgrims each day.

For the expanding Sunni Ottoman Empire, the city's symbolic value was also significant. The Ottomans captured the city in 1534 and divided their new territory into three *vilayets* (provinces or large administrative districts): Mosul, Baghdad, and Basrah each headed by a *vali* (governor). The Safavids reconquered Baghdad in 1623 but were expelled by Sultan Murad IV in 1638, who reportedly participated in the digging of the siege trenches. At a further siege in 1683, the story is told that Sultan Mehmet IV participated in single combat with a Safavid Goliath for the fate of the city, killing the Persian with one sword stroke.

Ottoman interest in direct control over Baghdad waned after 1750, and Mamluk pashas exercised the real authority over the city. The greatest Mamluk leaders were Sulayman II (r. 1780–1802), who brought the rule of law and solid administration to the city, and Daud (r. 1816–1831), who set about modernizing the economy and infrastructure and introducing new technologies, such as the printing press. The city continued to suffer from regular floods and epidemics, however: in 1831, 7,000 homes and Daud's palace were washed away in twenty-four hours, and the subsequent famine killed 70,000 people, half the city's population.

The mid-eighteenth century was a time of dramatic change in the Persian Gulf, as the European trading companies entered the region in force and began to shape trade, local production, and communication networks for their own purposes. Basrah was the key outlet to India, with Baghdad an administrative appendage to the much more significant city to the south. The East Indian Company (EIC), for example, established a factory (trading base) in 1763 in Basrah, which until 1798 was the site of the British representation to the *pashalik* (province ruled by a pasha) of Baghdad. In particular, the Basrah resident was responsible for organizing the

Basrah-Baghdad-Istanbul section of the overland mail from England to India. Armenian merchants had long been using this same route via Baghdad to carry pearls from Basrah to Istanbul using a system of escorts and extra post-horses (see also "Basrah").

Numerous external threats to the city appeared at the close of the eighteenth century. As Napoléon Bonaparte set out for Egypt in May 1798, fear of Bonaparte's plans via the Red Sea, or the Persian Gulf, led the EIC to establish a resident at Baghdad to collect information. It is interesting that this first resident was already thinking of Britain's strategic imperial interests: he argued to London in a memorandum that Britain should send troops to Baghdad to be ready for the eventual breakup of the Ottoman Empire so that Britain could establish an independent state under British control. By 1830 the British had a full-time residence in Baghdad, linking the city into the nascent great Indian defense network in the Middle East.

The Wahhabi-Saudi alliance was also a threat to the city. They placed Baghdad under siege in 1799, and the Mamluks were forced to conclude a treaty before their withdrawal. Muhammad Ali of Egypt also articulated an interest in grabbing Baghdad from the Ottomans, though the British squashed the plan. Such threats, combined with the new commitment to imperial modernization, forced the Ottomans to reestablish central control in Iraq. Using the excuse of Mamluk mismanagement of the 1831 famine, the army massacred the Mamluks and reasserted Istanbul's direct authority over Baghdad. Subsequently, there were ten governors between 1831 and 1869. The eleventh was the best of the lot: appointed in 1869, Midhat Pasha was reform minded and laid the foundation for modern Iraq during his tenure. He reorganized the army, created codes of criminal and commercial law, secularized the school system, destroyed the city walls so the city could grow, started a newspaper, introduced modern printing presses, extended Baghdad's control over provincial areas, created an elected municipal council (1870), and reformed both the tax and landholding systems. The introduction of steamboats on the Tigris after the 1840s, the laying of the telegraph linking Baghdad to Istanbul in 1861, and the opening of the Suez Canal all brought dramatic changes. Baghdad's economy became vulnerable to the vicissitudes of the global economic and political system, local artisan crafts died away, and the city provided export cash crops to Europe and the United States.

Baghdad's inhabitants reacted in diverse ways to these developments. Many of the emergent intelligentsia and landholding elite acquired important roles in Istanbul in administration and in the Ottoman army. The surrounding tribal confederations, however, felt threatened and revolted; traffic on the river and the new telegraph line to Basrah were attacked, and between July and October 1864 Baghdad was cut off to the south by an insurgency. The revolt threatened

Ottoman control but also the Indo-European telegraph project, a key strategic concern of London. With significant British involvement and heavy Ottoman military repression, the rebels were defeated, leaving behind a legacy of British interference in local Baghdad politics and a preference for military solutions to political problems.

The city's strategic significance received a boost from the late nineteenth century with the Berlin-to-Baghdad Railway project, an ambitious plan to link the European rail system to Istanbul and then via Baghdad to the Persian Gulf. Conceived as a tool to facilitate the integration of the Ottoman Empire, it combined German capital and engineering with Ottoman labor. Sections in Anatolia were completed in 1896; the Baghdad and Basrah sections were not started until 1911, postponed by political maneuvering occasioned by British fears that the Baghdad section was part of a German strategy for military expansion toward India. The Samarra-to-Baghdad portion opened in October 1914.

With the Young Turk Revolution of 1908 and the subsequent "Turkification" of the empire, Iraqi intellectuals and young officers began to organize underground Arab societies. One such was Jamiyyat al-Ahd (the Covenant), a secret organization of Iraqi officers in the Ottoman army. This group went on to provide a core of support and then resistance to the new Hashemite monarchy.

The outbreak of World War I put British and Turkish interests in Iraq into direct confrontation. Quickly the British captured the strategically important port of Basrah but equivocated on whether to march on Baghdad. The Turkish authorities sent few supplies to the city, and by the winter of 1915 Baghdad's citizens were on the edge of starvation. A huge cholera epidemic broke out, with more than 300 dead each day. The cemeteries became full of floating coffins and exposed bodies; Christian dead were buried along the edge of the roads.

It was not until 1917 that the major British push on Baghdad could begin. Both sides saw the city as crucial in propaganda terms but lacking in any real strategic value. Thus, when Turkish forces were finally defeated in Kut in February, they fell back north to defend Baghdad. The Turks had 12,000 men and German Army Air Service planes to defend the city; the British built field railroads and flotillas of gunboats on the Tigris, and their Russian allies supported the flank. With the first British attacks, the Turks fell back to better defense lines. With a second attack on 10 March, the Turkish commander wavered, not sure what to do. His German advisors suggested a counterattack; instead, the Turks retreated northward, looting the city's food supplies to support the retreating troops. Anglo-Indian troops entered the city the next day without a fight and captured 9,000 prisoners.

The British occupation forces expected to be welcomed as liberators, but very quickly the people of Baghdad agitated for an end to the occupation. Guided by experts like Percy Cox or Gertrude Bell (the "Oriental Secretary" to the British military occupation), the British authorities began remaking the community in their own interest: they introduced new tax measures, interned ex-Ottoman soldiers, propped up Sunni elites to the exclusion of Shi'i, and ignored the Shi'i religious establishment. Most significantly, they cobbled a new country together from the three vilayets of Mosul, Baghdad, and Basrah; brought in Amir Faysal as king of their creation; and crafted a 96 percent positive referendum for his appointment.

Riots broke out in Baghdad, and mass demonstrations quickly spread to rural areas in the Shi'i south; the British blamed outside political agitators. In what became known as the Iraqi Revolt of 1920, over the next five months rebels captured towns, killed British soldiers, and agitated for an end to British occupation. In response, the British military dropped poison gas from airplanes and bombed villages, which Winston Churchill argued had an "excellent moral effect" on the locals. They also confiscated 63,000 weapons, exiled opposition leaders to Ceylon, and implemented harsh imprisonment and collective punishment regimes. T. E. Lawrence estimated that as many as 10,000 Arabs were killed in repressing the uprising.

In the interwar years, Baghdad benefited from the introduction of new technologies and communication networks. In 1921 the Royal Air Force dug a furrow all the way across the desert from Palestine to Baghdad for its planes to follow so they could find Baghdad. Imperial Airways later used this line in the sand after January 1927, when they opened the Cairo-Baghdad-Basrah sector of its Britain-to-India route. By 1924 Baghdad was connected to the Mediterranean by regular automobile and bus transport following the ancient caravan routes to Palmyra or via Rutbah Wells to Damascus. Baghdad's elites found jobs in the state administration, expanded their trade ties, and began to feel their way in the world markets. Oil production began in 1934, dumping revenues into the city. Irrigation canals were dug and expanded, increasing agricultural production. Some 900 miles of railroad track were laid in the country before 1938.

Many in the 50,000-strong Baghdadi Jewish community, for example, found work in the mandate public service and were regular participants in the political and cultural life of the city. This ancient religious group had their own quarter (Dar al-Yahud) connected to the rest of the city via the "Jewish Bridge"; their own leader (the Exilarch or Resh Galutah); ancient religious training academies; twenty-eight synagogues; and had long served as goldsmiths, pharmacists, and traders. When Benjamin of Tudela visited the community (ca. 1170), he estimated a population of more than 40,000. Under the Mamluks, the repression forced some to emigrate: this was the beginning of the Sassoon commercial empire in India and the United Kingdom, for example. As tension increased over Palestine and in World War II, there were demonstrations and attacks on members of the community. With the

Skyline of Baghdad, 1932. (Library of Congress)

creation of Israel, most Baghdadi Jews immigrated in the early 1950s and made up an important segment of Israeli intellectual and business life.

Assyrians, refugees from World War I and Turkish attacks, settled in both the Gailani Camp area of the city and in Jeelu Camp and found employment with the British occupation authorities. Other Assyrians went to work on the railroads, and gradually their communities acquired churches and expanded into new districts of the city by the 1960s.

Baghdad was a city of culture and experiment, particularly during the interwar years and following World War II. The British set up the first cinema in the city in 1917, and by the 1940s the city was hosting a budding Iraqi film industry. Traditional Iraqi music has long remained popular in Iraq, with Baghdad serving to host and support its continuation. There is a Baghdadi song tradition (al-Maqam al-Baghdadi) that still has many fans in Baghdad. In cafés in the evening as part of a populist tradition, a soloist sings couplets, and a chorus sings a reiterated refrain. The city hosted an Institute of Fine Arts, International Conferences for Arab Music, a Traditional

Music Center/Archives, and the Institute of Iraqi Music Studies. Some of the most famous contemporary Arab sculptors, poets, and writers have come from Baghdad, and its National Theater was considered the best in the Arab world. The Iraqi Museum, National Museum of Modern Art, and the Museum of Iraqi Art Pioneers all supported the claim that Baghdad was the cultural center of the Arab world.

King Faysal had to negotiate a fine line between his British backers and an increasingly alienated population. Although the country became nominally independent in 1932, the British continued to have inordinate influence in the political and economic life of the state. One of Faysal's advisors, Sati al-Husri, helped provide the theoretical basis for Arab nationalism and the Baath Party, which was to transform Iraq over the next fifty years. Al-Husri, a Syrian educator, accompanied Faysal to Baghdad in 1921 and became dean of the faculty of law at the University of Baghdad and a minister of education and archaeology. His writings called for the creation of the Arab Nation through the vehicle of national education and had a profound effect on many Arab intellectuals, including

Michel Aflaq, founder of the Baath Party. As "the philosopher of Arab nationalism," al-Husri's ideas also fed the frustrations of the new working class in Baghdad. A large general strike in 1931, led by workers from the Iraqi Railways, fed the creation of the Workers Federation of Iraq in 1932. Banned by the British and Iraqi authorities, the federation went underground, and its leaders were jailed.

Military coups occurred in Baghdad with alarming frequency, starting in 1936. The general weakness of the central government, whose power really only extended to Baghdad, was compounded by political factionalism in the military. Finally, in March 1940, Rashid Ali al-Gilani became prime minister and began to move Iraq toward a pro-Axis policy. In spring 1941, the regent Abd al-Ilah fled the country only to return with British troops to oust Rashid Ali. The exiled Palestinian leader, Haj Amin al-Hussayni tried to rally the Baghdad population to stop the invasion, but by the end of May 1941 Ali was out, the regent returned, and Nuri as-Said was installed as prime minister.

Riots and civil unrest continued, however, with uprisings in the city in 1948 and 1952. Squatter camps of thousands of landless peasants living in palm huts appeared throughout the city as in-migration from rural areas swelled the urban poor.

The Nuri as-Said government was further delegitimized by both the Anglo-American 1955 attempt to create the Baghdad Pact as part of the cold war struggle with the USSR and by the government's failure to support Nasir in the 1956 Suez War. Riots broke out in Baghdad, and secret groups formed within the military. In July 1958, a joint military-civilian coup in Baghdad brought down the monarchy, with the rebels expressing their anger by toppling the statue of Sir Stanley Maude, "the liberator" of Baghdad, invading the British Embassy, lynching the regent, killing young King Faysal II, and disinterring Nuri as-Said. Crowds looted and burned parts of the city.

A further coup in February 1963 was orchestrated, this time by the Baath Party and sympathetic military; over the next few days, significant street battles between Communists, Baathists, and Nasirites tore the capital apart, leaving more than 2,000 dead. Subsequently, televised People's Courts sentenced hundreds of "traitors" to death.

A subsequent coup in 1968 brought about control of the country by the "Tikriti" faction of the Baath. Numerous conspiracies were "uncovered," and show trials purged anyone seen as threatening the new leadership. One of the more dramatic results was the January 1969 public hanging of fourteen "Israeli spies," including several Baghdadi Jews, in front of a huge crowd of spectators.

The city experienced dramatic growth in the three decades after 1950. Its population expanded to 4 million, making it the largest Arab city after Cairo. Increased oil revenues allowed the government to spend great sums in the capital. Much of it went to education: the University of Baghdad (1957), al-Mustansiriyya University (1963), the University of Technology (1974), and the al-Bakr Military Academy. Some went into new housing projects to house bank workers, oil laborers, state bureaucrats, and military officers. Outside architects were invited to help in this process: in 1957 Frank Lloyd Wright was invited to Baghdad to design an opera house for the city, and he completed a number of other designs for the downtown as part of a "Plan for Greater Baghdad," including a rework of the grand bazaar, buildings for the university, plans for a Harun ar-Rashid Monument, and a ziggurat-shaped parking garage. The coup in 1958 meant that the plans were never implemented.

The city has been caught up in war three times since 1980. The first was during the Iran-Iraq War, from 1980 to 1988. For most of this war, Baghdad was little affected, there were few blackouts, and construction projects and expansion continued apace. It was the bombing of the city starting on 17 January 1991, however, that began a fourteen-year period of destruction, decay, and terror. On that date, Allied Coalition bombing for Operation Desert Storm began, with attacks on the Presidential Palace, the Baath Party Headquarters, and the Ministry of Defense as the coalition sought to drive Iraq out of Kuwait. In what was the largest aerial bombardment since World War II, most of the bridges across the Tigris were destroyed, electrical generation was targeted, and broadcast facilities were hammered. Civilian loss of life was high; in one incident, American bombers killed 300 civilians huddled in an air-raid shelter in a Baghdad neighborhood.

Baghdad's elite suffered little over the following twelve years of United Nations (UN) embargoes and sanctions. The city's poor, and especially the Shi'i, however, lived in increasingly desperate conditions and always under threat of the secret service. The notorious Qasr al-Niharyyah (Palace of the End), which served as a torture chamber after the 1958 and 1963 coups, continued to serve Hussayn in the 1980s and 1990s. Throughout much of the 1970s and 1980s, Saddam Hussayn's uncle and foster father, Khairallah Tulfah, was mayor of Baghdad. His vigilantes would grab women on the street who were showing too much skin and paint their legs black; his corruption finally became too much, however, and he was removed and his numerous enterprises shut down.

The city was again attacked by American bombers in late March 2003; this time troops followed up the bombing to capture the city by 9 April 2003. An influx of Iraqi exiles, civilian contractors, and private security personnel have joined the world's media in changing the face and image of Baghdad. Daily suicide bombings have killed thousands of civilians and civil servants, the city's neighborhoods are guarded by local militias, and kidnappings of schoolchildren are commonplace. The city's infrastructure remains fragile, with water, sewage, and electricity provided irregularly and chronic diseases now a regular feature in poorer neighborhoods like Sadr City.

As the occupation continues in tandem with an attempt to craft a legitimate political framework for the country, the municipalities of Iraq are becoming more autonomous in the political space that has remained open. The Baghdad municipality, led by the mayor, Ala' al-Tamim, is, among other powers, directly supervising foreign aid implementation in the city. As the violence continues, Baghdad is virtually cut off from the rest of the country, and Amman, the capital of Jordan, has replaced the capital as a site for Iraqi intercommunal debate, discussion, and agreements (see also "Amman"). With almost 25 percent of the Iraqi population living in the capital, and an annual growth rate of 2.6 percent, the UN estimates of the city's population in 2015 of 7.4 million seem low.

Bruce Stanley

Further Readings

Adams, Robert. *Land behind Baghdad: A History of Settlement on the Diyala Plains.* Chicago: University of Chicago Press, 1965.

Farouk-Sluglett, Marion, and Peter Sluglett. *Iraq since 1958.* London: I. B. Tauris, 1990.

Fathi, Ihsan. *The Architectural Heritage of Baghdad.* London: Iraqi Cultural Center, 1979.

LeStrange, Guy. *Baghdad during the Abbasid Caliphate.* Oxford: Clarendon Press, 1900.

Pax, Salam. *The Baghdad Blog.* London: Atlantic Books, 2003.

Rejwan, Nissim. *The Last Jews in Baghdad.* Austin: University of Texas Press, 2004.

Sluglett, Peter. *Britain in Iraq: 1914–1932.* London: Ithaca Press, 1976.

Stark, Freya. *Baghdad Sketches.* London: Murray, 1939.

Wiet, Gaston. *Baghdad: Metropolis of the Abbasid Caliphate.* Translated by Seymour Feiler. Norman: University of Oklahoma Press, 1971.

Baku
Population: 2.1 million (2005 estimate)

Baku, the "city of oil" and the quintessential boomtown built around oil wealth, has been known since ancient times for the black gold bubbling just below its surface. Located on the western shore of the Caspian Sea, the city of Baku is now the capital of Azerbaijan and its largest city. Visited by countless travelers over the years as a site for trade along the Silk Road, and crucial to north-south exchange between the Middle East, India, and Moscow along the Volga, Baku was early associated with Zoroastrianism and later with an icy dessert. Today the city's fame is built on the oil industry, its militant labor unions, and its association with individuals such as Stalin and Alfred Nobel.

Baku (Arabic, *Bakuya*) is located on the southwestern shore of the Caspian Sea on a bay created by the Absheron Peninsula. This forty-mile-long peninsula is the culmination of the Caucasus Mountains, jutting out into the Caspian. The mountains create a wide amphitheater, or plateau, above the bay, terracing the city nestled in the basin. Combined with numerous islands offshore, this geography created the best natural harbor on the Caspian and usable transit routes into the hinterland. Although the winds in Baku (the *khazri*) can be exceptional, there is low precipitation, and the city has a moderate climate year-round. The current administrative district of Greater Baku incorporates eleven districts, forty-eight townships, and islands near the peninsula, including a created "city," Oil Rocks, built by the Soviets sixty miles from Baku out into the Caspian and connected to the city by roads suspended above the waves. The area contains many mud volcanoes and salt lakes.

Archaeological finds indicate that the site was first inhabited during the Paleolithic period (8000 BC). Wall paintings and carvings in the surrounding mountains suggest that pastoral nomads used the site for their flocks and that reed boats plied the Caspian Sea. Burial sites have been discovered at the lowest layers of the tell dating from the pre-Zoroastrian period (1000 BC).

The first significant agglomeration appears around a Zoroastrian cultic site, called Ateshi-Baguan, dating to the seventh to sixth century BC. Exceptional natural fires occurred in this area from the seepage of oil and natural gas close to the surface. Thus, the Baku site attracted cultic practices associated with "the eternal fire." Followers of Zoroaster erected three major fire temples in the vicinity, and this attracted pilgrimage and trade to the growing city. One version of the meaning of the name is that it refers to "God's City" since Zoroastrian cultic sites cluster in the area. It appears that even at this early date, caravans of oil, extracted from open pits, were exported in all directions, linking Baku into a variety of long-distance trade and exchange networks. Herodotus (fifth century BC) talks about the region of Baku and refers to the boats used by its traveling merchants to negotiate rivers around the Caspian.

The city prospered under Achaemenid control, and this may be when the city got its name, since another version suggests that it is Persian for "windy city." Sometime between 285 and 282 BC, Alexander's former general, Seleuk, sailed these shores of the Caspian. Romans under Pompey invaded the region around 65 BC, but their control was tenuous. Later Roman monuments have been discovered in the region, including one found on the peninsula dating from the first century AD that has an inscription from the period of Emperor Germanicus. Ptolemy of the second century AD refers to Baku and to the political divisions in the area; in general, however, the Parthians held the region against the Romans.

Baku was a key city for the Caucasian Albania kingdom during the third to seventh century, and early on it became Christian; Baku was known for its Nestorian sites. Byzantine visitors in the fifth century remarked on the "flame which rises from the reef" along the edge of the sea, and it is clear that oil was being traded, in particular for medicinal purposes. The Sassanians held Baku as a vassal city with some autonomy.

The city was invaded by the Huns, the Khazars, and the Turks in the early medieval period, but it was the Arab invasion in AD 661 that brought a significant shift in fortunes. Garrisons of Arab warriors were settled in the area, including 24,000 Syrian soldiers and some Yemenis.

Arab writers of the tenth century comment on oil and salt as key products from the region traded in the long-distance trading system of Dar al-Islam. Authors such as al-Massudi report that various types of oils, including black and white oil, were being extracted in Baku and that the city was getting rich on the trade. Under the Abbasids, Baku was a small, walled city with a castle directly on the coast. Caravans came to Baku for oil from throughout the empire, with khans serving different communities, such as the ones for Bukharaians and another for those from India that still grace the city today. Interestingly, snow from this region was shipped to Baghdad during the period of the Abbasids to make a form of frozen dessert for the elite of that city.

The city was important as well as a key node on the trade route up the Volga and Don to the island of Gotland. This minor but evolving "fur route" was to have important repercussions over the next 1,000 years, given the growth of Moscow and its interest in trade to the Middle East and India. The first indication of this interest was a raid on the city by Russians in AD 913. The modern explorer Thor Heyerdahl even goes so far as to postulate Azeri settlement of Scandinavia.

The Seljuq Turks invaded Azerbaijan in the eleventh century (AD 1051–1060), leading to a general failure of Abbasid power in the area. In their place arose Shirvani dynasties. Baku was one of their key cities, and it was during their tenure that the defensive walls of the city were enhanced by Shirvanshah Manuchuhr II (AD 1120–1160). The famous Giz Galasy (Maiden's Tower), still a predominant site in the city, was built in the twelfth century over Zoroastrian foundations dating from the seventh century BC.

The dynasty worked hard to maintain and expand the power of Baku. The city became their capital in 1191 and made it a naval base. Although the city was attacked by land and by sea, the Shirvanshahs continued to spend on building fortifications, mosques and caravansaries, bathhouses, and water-storage facilities; Muhammad's Mosque, built AD 1078–1079 within the fortress, is an existing example.

Despite further massive fortress construction, such as the Sabail Castle, the city fell to the advancing Mongols in the 1200s. After a lengthy siege, Baku finally surrendered and was sacked and destroyed for resisting. Subsequently, city officials and elites worked hard to revive the city's fortunes, using strategies such as reduced customs duties to entice merchants to return to the city. This strategy appeared to work,

but the Mongols returned in 1258 under Huleghu Khan to sack the city a second time. It was around this period that Marco Polo visited the city on his way to China, commenting on the way oil was used both to light homes and for "anointing camels" suffering from mange.

During the 1300s, long-distance trade and maritime trade experienced a resurgence. Genoa and Venetian traders appeared on the Caspian and invested in linking trade through Baku to their ports on the Black Sea. Baku benefited from trade links with the Golden Horde in New Saray; with Moscow, Bukhara, and central Asia; the Middle East; and with India. Key exports for the city were oil, saffron, carpets, cottons, and salt. Baku was so important to Caspian and Caucasus trade that one European map of the period (AD 1375) named the Caspian the "Baku Sea."

Baku was incorporated into the empire of Temür and the Timurids after 1400. The Arab geographer Abd ar-Rashid al-Bakuvi (fifteenth century) commented on how the walls of Baku were washed by the waves of the sea, how the city depended on imports of wheat from nearby cities, and how the walls were strengthened by two fortified castles of stone. He also comments on the white oil used by local inhabitants for light and heat and on the 200 mule loads of oil exported from the city every day.

During the fifteenth century, a further grand period of building and development occurred. The Shirvanshah's Palace complex built during this time is now considered an outstanding example of Islamic architecture of the period, and it has been designated a World Heritage Site by the United Nations Educational, Scientific, and Cultural Organization (UNESCO). This was the time of the city's greatest wealth, and it benefited from important diplomatic links and from its cultural centrality in art and handicrafts.

In 1501 the new Safavid dynasty of Iran besieged and captured Baku. Reports of the city's defenses at the time talk about a fortress with high walls, protected by the sea and a huge trench. Significantly, the city was taken by the use of explosives under the city walls. Despite the clear indication of the power of this new technology, the city continued to have a reputation as the best-fortified city in the Caucasus.

Under the Safavids, the city continued its role in the long-distance trade in oil and as an entrepôt for transit. Archaeological finds reveal that open oil wells of up to 115 feet deep were being dug by hand in Baku at this time: a workman named Mamed Nur-oglu recorded his name on the wall upon completion of one in 1594.

Venetian and Genoese merchants continued organizing trade and making deals throughout this period. They were connected with compatriots in Kaffa and Azak on the Black Sea, key entrepôts for the Italian city-states. The newly rising State of Muscovy was also expanding its trading networks in the Caspian. Baku brokered connections between the Safavids and the Russians in an anti-Ottoman trade relationship along the longitudinal routes connecting the Indian Ocean and the Baltic.

A number of European visitors report that by the 1600s Hindu and Armenian merchants controlled trade on the Caspian. For example, the Indians in particular linked the city with the key northern port, Astrakhan, where they had a very important community until the 1700s, and with other Indian communities in central Asia and the Punjab. One indication of the significance of the Indian community of traders was the Indian temple in Baku. As early as 1784, visitors noted its presence and that it was served by Brahman priests. The Hindu community did not always have an easy time, however; there are reports of attacks on the Hindus by Muslims and of regular persecution.

By the sixteenth century, the English had appeared in Baku as well. In 1555 agents from a new Moscow company in London were sent to central Asia to report and develop trade. From 1568 to 1574, their reports mention Baku as "a town strange thing to behold, for there issueth out of the ground a marvellous quantity of oil, which serveth all the country to burn in their houses. This oil is black and called 'nefte.' There is also by the said town of Baku another kind of oil which is white and very precious, and it is called petroleum."

The expanding Ottoman Empire occupied Baku from 1578 until 1603, when the city returned to Persian control. Shortly after, the Turkish traveler Evliya Chelebi twice visited Baku (1647 and 1660) and commented that the imposing citadel protected a thriving caravan city, hosting caravans from China, Syria, and Moscow. The Muscovites traded walrus fangs, sables, and gray squirrels, he reports, in exchange for salt, oil, saffron, and silk, and ships filled with oil set sail for Iranian ports to the south. The German physician Engelbert Kampfer visited Baku in 1683, and his paintings offer an excellent indication of the nature of the city at this time.

Under Peter the Great, the expanding Russian Empire set out to turn the Caspian Sea into a Russian lake. The Russian army besieged and captured Baku in July 1723 but returned it to the Persians in 1735. New Russian-Iranian trade alliances were signed, and Baku was the key entrepôt for the regional exchange of slaves, agricultural goods, textiles, silk, and iron.

In the wake of the Safavid decline, an autonomous Khanate of Baku emerged after the mid-1700s. This independence did not last long, however. Under Czar Alexander I (r. 1801–1825), Russia moved aggressively into the Caucasus, and Baku fell to the Russians in 1806 during the Russo-Iranian War of 1804–1813. Under the Treaty of Gulistan, Baku was ceded to Russia, and the Baku Khanate was ended. The city that was incorporated into the Russian Empire was small, having only 10,000 inhabitants.

Despite its small population, the city was clearly a world city. One indication of its global interlinkage was the 1817 outbreak of cholera, which spread along the trade routes from India in the first of the great modern global epidemics. Another indication of the city's continued prominence was the growth of the carpet industry, serving changing fashion and the rise of disposable income in Europe. Baku became a center for carpet production, and producers were well aware that they needed to meet the design and quality "requirements" of a global industry.

Russian rule began to have an effect on increased trade and economic welfare in the city. New legislation, standardization, and the introduction of steamships plying the Caspian all had a powerful effect on moving Baku further up the ranks of the global urban hierarchy. During this period, the Russians affirmed the city's centrality in a number of ways: in 1859 Baku was designated an administrative center at the core of the newly created Baku province, and in 1868 telegraph communications between Baku and Tbilisi were established.

The city began its march to global oil dominance in 1823 when the first paraffin plant in the world was built in Baku to process oil extracted around the city. In 1848 Russian engineer F. N. Semyenov drilled the world's first modern oil well on the Aspheron Peninsula. The first refinery plants were built in 1859 in the suburbs of the city, ironically near the site of the Zoroastrian temple. Modern exploitation began in 1872, with the first "gusher" occurring in 1873.

The takeoff of the oil industry in Baku was fueled by both local and foreign investors. The most famous were the Nobel brothers, one of whom was Alfred Nobel of Nobel Prize and dynamite fame. In 1878 they financed a major pipeline, and in 1879 the older Nobel brothers established their own oil production company, the Nobel Brothers Oil Extraction Partnership, and they quickly went on to control 75 percent of the local industry. In addition, they were innovators: it was their company that designed and ordered the first tanker to ply the Caspian, and they went on to own a whole fleet of tankers. It was also the Nobels who introduced railroad tanker cars and tanker ports for storage. British investors were crucial to the development of Baku oil as well. The Rothschild's company was formed in 1885, and Shell Oil appeared in 1890.

Baku's central place in the evolving world system meant that innovations in the industry had a global impact. In 1884 the "Baku method" of drilling using percussion to slam the bit deeper into the ground was developed, and it quickly spread globally.

It also meant that regional and local development revolved around reticulation of the transport and supply networks for Baku. The Rothschilds financed a railway to transport oil from Baku to Tbilisi in 1883. In 1897–1907 the Nobels developed the largest pipeline in the world at the time to link Baku with Batumi on the Black Sea (549 miles). Interestingly, the oil magnates created their own association to "talk" about oil issues, the Oil Extractors Congress Council (1884), with its own magazine and library. In 1874 they supported the establishment in the city of a school for studying oil and its discovery.

By 1900 Baku was the most significant oil city in the world, the center of the global oil industry, and it serviced the largest oil field of the time. There may have been more than 2,000 oil wells in the city, producing more than 200,000 barrels per day. This meant that by 1910 the city was responsible for more than half of the oil industry's global output. Alexandre Dumas, the French author, visiting the city in the late 1850s, observed of this nascent boom that "Baku is the most turbulent city on the Caspian shore . . . [it] is indeed the commercial center of the region."

The massive growth of the oil industry encouraged unplanned and rampant growth of the city physically and in terms of population. Baku was the world's first oil "boomcity," and it suffered all the problems of a typical boomtown. One key problem was the influx of people. In 1880 the city may have had a population of more than 40,000; by 1913 that number had swelled to 400,000. Many of these immigrants were from outside Baku, either from across Russia or from further afield, and the heterogeneous mix and cosmopolitan feel of the city is still in evidence today. There was a high degree of European immigration into the city along with the oil industry. An influx of European Jews, for example, joined the local Baku community to make Baku the most important Jewish community in Azerbaijan.

Another implication of this unrestrained growth was the dramatic transformation of its built environment. In particular, the city was directly influenced by the competition of the various company owners in building villas and headquarters, many still in evidence today around its streets. The community also benefited from their involvement in supporting city institutions and innovations, gardens, and civic projects. In 1896 the first women's college in eastern Russia was built in Baku. The spin-offs into the service sector (hotels, telecommunications, transport) were tremendous and continue to influence the city today. The oil barons' concern about innovation and research laid the foundation for much of the scientific and industrial progress made in Baku over the next century. Some of the wealthiest were local investors, and they plowed back into the community much of their wealth.

However, all this growth meant that the city was virtually lawless and clearly a city of contrasts: the villas of the wealthy oil barons versus the squalid company town housing on the outskirts of the city for the immigrant labor. There were so many assassinations and murders that the oil barons had contingents of bodyguards with them wherever they went.

This lawlessness meant that dissidents from throughout Russia could find a hiding place from the czar's secret police within Baku. From 1900 to 1904, for example, the Baku Power Station was managed by a key Bolshevik, good at raising and managing funds. He was able to hide comrades on the run

within the staff of the power station, and under cover of this institution the whole Bolshevik financial network was managed and expanded.

By 1905 the boomtown was running into difficulty: ethnic and worker tension divided the city, and a downturn in production and the loss of markets to other developing sites globally meant that Baku was not as shiny as it had been. In October 1906, the Union of the Workers of the Oil Industry was established in Baku, and it became an important union leading revolutionary activity throughout Russia. The subsequent oil worker strikes of 1907 were extremely important, both for the organization of labor and for the trajectory of one young Bolshevik organizer, Iosif Dzhugashvili (Stalin). Stalin, born not far from Baku in Georgia, came to the city to organize a refinery workers strike, but local Mensheviks and Bolsheviks decided not to support him. Soon after, in early 1908, Stalin was arrested and spent a formative six months in the city prison, from where he was exiled to Vologda Province. But in 1912 he was back in Baku, trying to keep the party together. It was during this same period that Pan-Turkic and Pan-Iranian movements began to organize within the city for dominance.

The German army understood the significance of Baku, and in World War I it became a strategic objective of the general command. German troops finally were landed in Batumi on the Black Sea in June 1918. The war ended, however, before they were able to march across the Caucasus and capture the city.

With the Russian Revolution, Baku entered a difficult period. Because of the large numbers of foreign and Russian workers in the oil industry, Baku was the only city in the Caucasus to strongly support the Soviets. Outside Baku, however, 28 May 1918 was independence day for a non-Soviet Azerbaijan. Under pressure from a coalition of international forces, the Baku Soviet was forced to abandon the city in late July 1918, and Baku became a key city for the Azerbaijan Democratic Republic during its short existence from 1918 to 1920. In August 1918, 1,400 British troops arrived in Baku, invited in by the republic as part of a scheme to keep out Turkish troops. A month later, twenty-six "Baku Commissars" were killed by British troops, and Armenians were massacred by soldiers of Enver Pasha's "Army of Islam."

On 17 November 1918, a British army officer, General V. Thompson, was appointed to run Baku in what became known as the British Oil Administration. The goal was to stabilize the oil and economic situation in Baku against chaos that threatened Western interests. Thompson commented in his journal that the lack of stability in the Caucasus, particularly Georgia, was detrimental to Baku's future: the West must get the oil to Batumi or Supsa. The primacy of Baku can be noted in Thompson's observation that " the general situation in Azerbaijan depends almost entirely on the town of Baku.

Owing to its oil wealth, the town of Baku has an influence far out of proportion to its size." The British stayed only a year, leaving Baku to its fate in August 1919.

The republic sent representatives to the Paris Peace Conference, which recognized Azeri independence. But the Soviets under Lenin were not about to abandon the oil wealth of Baku. In April 1920, components of the Bolshevik army finally captured Baku and overthrew the government, and Baku was designated the capital of the new Azerbaijan Soviet Socialist Republic. It was in the wake of this takeover that Soviet policy in "the East" was crafted, starting with the September 1920 Congress of the Peoples of the East held in Baku and attended by the likes of American John Reed.

After the revolution, Soviet policy was to develop Baku as a key industrial city with a focus on the petrochemical industry. The oil industry was nationalized, and the city was expanded to include industrial and residential areas, supported by a huge building program for libraries, museums, theaters, and parks. Soviet policy also sought to control the diverse religious communities in Baku: mosques and churches were either closed or brought under national control.

Under the Soviets, some oil from Baku was sold internationally. Most of the output, however, was used to serve the expanding needs of Russia and the other republics. The industry remained innovative during this period, with the first offshore oil field in the world opening near Baku in 1923, and in 1940 the first superdeep drilling occurred in the area.

Baku came to play another role for the Soviet Union as well: that of producing hard currency through its production of two other products—caviar and carpets. Carpets and caviar were exported to Europe and the monies returned to Moscow. Ninety-five percent of all black caviar comes from the Caspian, and the industry is crucial for Baku. Ironically, it was impossible to find caviar in Baku during much of the Soviet era.

Oil rigs in the boomtown of Baku, 1926. (Bettmann/Corbis)

During World War II, the Germans, in need of oil, focused on Baku again, Hitler pushing his troops to take the city. They never made it, however, being stopped at Stalingrad. Part of the German army did capture oil fields to the north around Grozny, but Baku went on to play a key role in the industrial war effort for the Soviets: two-thirds of the country's wartime oil came from Baku, and 100 new oil products were invented.

Postwar development of Baku was dramatic. The Russians expanded offshore production with the building of the Oil Rocks city in 1947 to access the shallow pools offshore in the Caspian. They also continued industrial and scientific investment in the city, and Baku became the fifth-largest city in the USSR and an educational center. The city became known as a center for the production of oil industry equipment as well as a key site for shipbuilding and the production of electrical machinery. Baku also became crucial for chemicals, cement, foodstuffs, shoes, and textiles production. The Baku Metro subway opened in 1967, and the Soviets developed expanded oil pipelines and rail links for oil through the Caucasus to the Black Sea port of Novorossisk. Unfortunately, the city was locked into the Soviet transport and economic system so deeply that only Russian and Turkish airlines flew into the city; it was completely disconnected from the Middle East and from the expanding global order.

In the mid-1970s, the oil began to run out around the city, shifting exploration and attention offshore. Refineries operated at partial capacity, and the city's economic health began to decline. Perhaps this is one reason why Baku was a site for unrest against the Soviet regime. Certainly, by 1990 the possibilities of change were in the air, with riots and internecine attacks within the city. Gorbachev sent in Soviet troops: and on 19–20 January 1990, in what became known as "Black January," Soviet troops killed more than 200 protesters in the city.

Azerbaijani independence day was 18 October 1991, and Baku became the capital of the new country. The city holds significant primacy in the country, with more than 50 percent of the country's urban population living in Baku. Oil has continued to dominate the life of the city; for example, what became known as the "contract of the century" was signed in 1994, creating the Azerbaijani International Operating Company (AIOC). Three different groups of international companies were brought together under a plan to invest more than $1 billion to exploit three deepwater pools offshore. This marked the return of Baku to the global oil market. In addition, the pipeline debates have involved Baku in political wrangling over the routes and financing of various possible pipelines to connect central Asian and Azeri oil to the Mediterranean or Persian Gulf ports. The final decision to pursue the Baku-Tbilisi-Ceyhan route (BTC) owed much to American and Turkish interests and to Baku's need to distance itself from Moscow. The BTC, when completed, will carry 1 million barrels of oil per day to the Mediterranean.

Oil continues to move out of Baku along other tracks as well, however. Relations with Iran have improved, and so tankers on the Caspian move oil to northern Iran from the city, as do pipelines. Major refineries for Azerbaijani oil are located in Baku; for example, the Azneftyag refinery produces 60 percent of the country's output. However, its refining capacity remains underutilized, and the national government is working hard to get contracts from Russia and Kazakhstan.

Today the city has three major geographic areas: the inner core, or city (Icheri Sheher), sometimes called the "Acropolis of Baku," which is where the ancient monuments and buildings, many twelfth century, are congregated; a second area of modern buildings from the Soviet era, including the university, the museums, and the boulevards; and the sprawling suburbs, which extend up the mountain, cover the peninsula, and stretch well to the north and south of the ancient core. Some of those living in the poorest areas of the city are internally displaced persons (IDPs) from the conflict with Armenia. International nongovernmental organizations (NGOs) are currently helping more than 26,000 IDPs within Greater Baku.

Issues of Islamic fundamentalism have arisen in the city, with the three Sunni mosques accused of being avenues for Wahhabism (one report suggests 15,000 Wahhabists within Baku alone) and Saudi financial largess. Leaders of the Jeyshullah (Army of God) were convicted in 2000 of robbing the European Development Bank and of planning to blow up the U.S. Embassy in Baku. And since 2003, the government has been cracking down on all such movements, arresting Imams and protesters in this predominantly Shi'i city as well as curtailing human rights and freedom of expression.

The city faces other problems as well. Pollution in particular is of grave concern. Given the unfettered development of the oil industry over the last century, the push for chemical and petrochemical industrial production, the high use of fertilizer for agriculture, and poorly planned population expansion, the Baku region is now suffering from three interrelated environmental disasters: chemical pollution by the rivers feeding into the Caspian, offshore oil industry refuse, and rising water levels. International aid agencies are particularly concerned about the effects of these environmental problems on the health of the local population, and new projects in conjunction with the national government are set to try to tackle them.

Bruce Stanley

Further Readings

De Waal, Thomas. *Black Garden: Armenia and Azerbaijan through Peace and War.* New York: New York University Press, 2003.

Henry, James D. *Baku: An Eventful History.* London: A. Constable, 1905.

Heyat, Farideh. *Azeri Women in Transition.* London: Routledge, 2002.

Suny, Ronald G. *The Baku Commune, 1917–1918.* Princeton: Princeton University Press, 1972.

Bandar Abbas
Population: 351,000 (2005 estimate)

Bandar Abbas was the main Safavid port city in the seventeenth century and one of the grandest ports on the Arabian Sea. Strategically located at the entrance to the Persian Gulf, halfway between India and Aleppo, the city is both the descendant of the famous ancient city of Old Hormuz, which so awed Marco Polo, and the amirate of Hormuz, which flourished from 1300 to 1600 on the island nearby. The fragile opulence of Hormuz gave way to a new state-controlled port, and today Bandar Abbas is Iran's most important port and main naval base and key to its networking with the global economy.

Bandar Abbas, named after the Safavid Shah Abbas I (1588–1629), is strategically located on the Strait of Hormuz, through which flows 40 percent of the world's oil. Thirty-three miles to the south across the Persian Gulf is the Sultanate of Oman and the United Arab Emirates. Bandar Abbas, pronounced Bandar-e Abbas (port of Abbas) but commonly referred to as Bandar, is protected from the heavy sea by the islands of Hormuz, Larek, and Qeshm. The coast of the Strait of Hormuz is dotted with reefs, and the winds are notorious for going calm. Its climate is humid and hot, with 50 percent humidity and the temperature often reaching 122 degrees Fahrenheit between May and October. Traditionally, many of its inhabitants migrated out of town during the hottest periods. The city is now the capital of Hormuzgan Province, and although most of the province is desert rarely more than 820 feet above sea level, the hinterland is mountainous. The Payeh Mountains are located approximately 150 miles to the north, with its highest peak at Mount Hezar at 14,502 feet; the Zagros Mountains are approximately 150 miles to the northwest; and smaller mountains are about 100 miles to both the east and the west. From the city, there is a natural pass inland into the heart of the country, and it was this easy access route that made the port, with its natural harbor, such a desirable site. Tehran lies 920 miles to the north.

The origins of the ancient Old Hormuz, located next to Bandar Abbas, are vague. The name *Hormuz* could have derived from the Zoroastrian god Ahura Mazda or from the local word *hurmogh* (date palm). The creation of the town has been credited to Ardashir I (r. AD 226–241), the founder of the Sassanian dynasty. Ptolemy (ca. 100–ca. 178) referred to a "Harmuza" but with a different position. The earliest reference, however, is that of Nearchus, one of Alexander the Great's officers, who anchored in the district of Harmozeia at the mouth of the Anamis River (now Minab Creek).

Between the ninth and sixteenth centuries, overland trade routes linked Hormuz to Shiraz via Tarom, Forg, Fasa, Lar, Gahrom, and Karzin. The route between Hormuz and Lar was one of the country's harshest passings, winding through inhospitable mountain ranges. Although Siraf and Kish were the two ports that dominated the Persian Gulf between 1000 and 1200, by the tenth century Hormuz had established itself as an important port city for the Kerman, Sistan, and Khurasan provinces. In 1229, when the ruler of Hormuz conquered Kish, the city was considered to be the Persian Gulf's chief port city and trading center with the East, and it remained so until the Portuguese invasion. During this period it grew to approximately 200 acres. Marco Polo may have visited Hormuz in 1272 and 1293 on his journey through Iran to and from China.

With the breakup of the Ilkhanid dynasty, the Persian Gulf's islands became united by the kings of Hormuz, with Sunnis of Arab ethnicity ruling a semi-independent principality. In their advance to power, they used their navy to capture rival port cities like Kish, which was taken in 1229. By 1300, fearing attack from marauding tribes, Shah Qutb ad-Din Tahamatan moved the port and its inhabitants to the island of Jarun, four miles south of the nearest point on the mainland and twenty-five miles west of the entrance of the Hormuz Creek. Although the new port was known as New Hormuz, both the port and the island came to be simply known as Hormuz. This small but powerful trading state, controlling territory on both sides of the Gulf, used the island with its two ports (one for large ships, the other for smaller ones) as a highly defensible site, built their kingdom around it, and cleared pirates from the sea-lanes. The powers on the mainland could not take the city and did not wish to. Although the island was only rock and salt, with no good drinking water, an entrepôt grew up on the new site and hosted quarters for many different merchants, including Jews, Gujaratis, and Iranians. By charging low customs fees, the shah ruled over powerful merchant clans (such as the Baghdadi or Fali families) but did not directly participate in trade, rather extracting wealth by taxing imports. The city did serve long-distance trade, but it was also crucial to the intra–Indian Ocean trade of Iran with India and East Africa. Of particular value was the trade in horses (to southern India), jewels, pearls, and slaves for the armies of India. To the Europeans who visited in the 1400s, Hormuz was a "vast emporium of the world"; to the Chinese admiral Ma Huan, it was the best-managed port in the Indian Ocean. To Ibn Battuta, ca. 1347, it was a fine and large city, with busy markets. Unfortunately, the city-state increasingly suffered from internal strife, and by 1503 it was forced to pay tribute to Shah Isma'il I.

Although seized briefly in 1507, the city was captured by the Portuguese under the leadership of Afonso de Albuquerque (1453–1515) around 1514. These invaders recognized Hormuz as a strategic location for the foundation of their empire in the East but did not manage the city nearly as well as had its previous rulers. At first, Hormuz prospered, but gradually the corruption and heavy-handedness of their administration drove merchants away. There were a number of revolts by the local population; the one in 1522 led to the rebellion being crushed, the city being burned, and a new, young shah of Hormuz being placed on the throne to sign a new treaty with the Portuguese overlords. Although the Ottomans tried a number of times to capture the city, it was not until 1622 that the Portuguese commercial monopoly came to an end and Hormuz's importance was replaced by that of Bandar Abbas. By 1927 the site on the island was practically uninhabited, with only around 200 families.

The village of Gamru (also known as Gombroon) on the mainland, approximately thirteen miles northwest of the new Hormuz and a little west of the modern Bandar Abbas, was also under Portuguese occupation and had been developed into a successful port. Although Gamru was reportedly seized by Safavid troops as early as 1614, it wasn't until January 1622, after a three-month siege, that New Hormuz was captured by Shah Abbas I's forces, led by the Fars governor Imam Qoli Khan and assisted by the East India Company. Initially the company was reluctant to get involved in an act of war as it was against its charter. However, with the promise of privileges—opportunity to house a factory, duty-free imports and exports, half of the revenues received in customs, a monopoly of Persian silk, the Hormuz castle—they succumbed. Gamru, which lies inland up the Minau River, was renamed Bandar Abbas and became the first commercial settlement of the British in the Persian Gulf. New Hormuz was plundered to provide building materials for the new Bandar Abbas. The political appointments of sultan (the superior authority) and *shahbandar* (master of the port) were created. As these were named directly by the imperial court, they tended to reflect the rise and fall of influential groups. The year 1622 was a turning point in the history of the Persian Gulf as it marked the decline of the Portuguese and the rise of the British in the region.

Shah Abbas established Bandar Abbas as the main port of the dynasty and the Persian Gulf as part of the strategy to control silk production and its trade. Although initially an insignificant settlement of about 1,500 houses, the city was especially laid out to enable the loading and unloading of vessels. Small crafts were used for the embarkation and disembarkation of large vessels, which were able to come about five miles from the coast. A 1638 report describes two castles and a square fort defending the city's entrance. Its houses were built with burnt brick and featured wind towers. The city was at its busiest commercially between October and May, with the arrival of the caravans. Traders included those of Persian, Arab, Jewish, and Armenian origin, and in 1672 Bandar Abbas was described as an emporium visited by Moors, the English, French, and Dutch. Exports to India via Bandar Abbas included horses, gold, silver, Khorasani raw silk, brocades, and rhubarb, while imports included Asian dyestuff, spices, and Indian rice and sugar. By the 1630s, the link between Bandar Abbas and the textile-producing areas of northern India was extremely significant to the city's trade.

The latter part of the seventeenth century saw the start of a decrease in the importance of the city. The port's business was driven away by the extensive corruption of the 1640s and 1670s, the Mughal-Safavid wars of the 1650s, and famine and harvest failures of the 1660s. The Dutch, having also established themselves in Bandar Abbas, relocated to Kharg Island. By 1645 the British moved to Basrah, partly because their ships could only use the port for a couple of months per year and were vulnerable to attack. Nonetheless, 1664 saw the founding of the French East India Company (EIC) and the establishment of trading rights and factories for it at Bandar Abbas.

Although commercial activity continued during the eighteenth, nineteenth, and early twentieth centuries, the city was no longer the emporium of its glory days. The population dropped from around 12,000 at the end of the eighteenth century to approximately 5,000 in 1830. A key reason for the city's decline was the overall decline in Iran's trade caused by the Afghan overthrow of the Safavids, the subsequent Russian and Turkish invasions, and the establishment of a rival port at Bushehr by Nadir Shah (r. 1736–1747) (also known as Tahmasp Quli Khan).

Another reason for its decline was infighting among the European powers for control of the port. On 12 October 1759, for example, the French, under the leadership of Comte d'Estaing, landed in Bandar Abbas as part of their war with England. The EIC submitted, and its factory along with its contents and money were handed over; the factory was burned. The EIC temporarily moved to the Dutch factory and in 1763 completely abandoned Bandar Abbas for Bushehr.

After 1793 the city was leased to the sultan of Oman, who used the island primarily for the production of salt and kept a garrison at the fort; he reportedly made approximately $10,000 per year in revenue from customs that passed through the city, and when he visited the city he stayed in the former Dutch factory house. The city reverted back to the Qajarites midcentury following a rebellion in Muscat. During the nineteenth century, it was the export point for Kerman carpets and Khamir sulfur. Even by the end of the century, caravans were still plying the roads from the port, reaching Kerman to the north, for example, in around eighteen days. In the growing age of steam on the Persian Gulf, mail steamers would call at the port on their way to India. During World War I, the British raised a force in Bandar Abbas called the South Persian Rifles to fight the Ottomans in Basrah. In 1927 it was reported that the Bushehr-Shiraz route diverted traffic from

German map of Hormuz, 1747. (Arkstee, Johann Caspar, and Henricus Merkus, *Allgemeine Historie der Reisen zu Wasser und Lande; oder Sammlung aller Reisebeschreibungen, no. 10.* Leipzig, ca. 1747)

the city. By the 1950s, Bandar Abbas was reduced from its previous glory to a fishing port. The population was estimated at 17,000, having grown from the 1930s estimate of 8,000.

Despite Bandar Abbas being out of favor for the first half of the twentieth century, its fortunes changed dramatically during the second half. Investment in the city began in the 1930s with the establishment of a cotton-spinning mill and a road between Bandar Abbas and Kerman. It was developed as a major commercial port during the Iran-Iraq War (1980–1988) to replace Khorramshahr, which had been occupied by Iraqi forces. By the 1990s, about 75 percent of Iran's Persian Gulf imports were passing through the city. Now populated by Persian Bandaris, black Africans, and Arabs, and having a large Sunni minority, Bandar Abbas has been restored as an important port city, connected by air, rail, and road to Tehran and the rest of the country. It was from Bandar Abbas in July 1988 that Iran Air 655 left on its way to Dubai and was shot down by the USS *Vincennes;* 290 civilians were killed.

Unusually, in February 1999, Bandar Abbas hosted a group of American cruise tourists.

In addition to being a smuggling center for small ships crossing to the Arab side of the Gulf, Bandar Abbas is now home to major industries such as steel, milling cotton, fish processing, textile manufacturing, aluminum smelting, and refining. It is also the export center for the hinterland's chromium, red oxide, salt, and sulfur mines. Bandar Abbas is also home to the crackers (refining plants) that transform South Pars gas into ethylene feedstock. Recent projects include an Iranian-Indian joint-venture condensates refinery in May 2004, expansion of the refinery in June 2004, an Iranian-European joint-venture steel production plant in April 2005, and a smelter project at the end of 2005. On a regional scale, Bandar Abbas is now assuming a key role in the regional transport infrastructure as well. In November 2005, a draft agreement for the Trans-Asian Railway, which would link northern Europe to southern Asia via Bandar Abbas, was signed, thus developing a new north-south corridor to compete with ship traffic via the Suez Canal.

The port remains a center for the Iranian navy. In 1977 the shift was made from Khorramshahr to the newly completed base at Bandar Abbas, and it is now the naval fleet headquarters and principal dock facilities. A small submarine force is headquartered there, as are frigates and destroyers.

Shabnam Holliday

Further Readings

Floor, Willem. *The Economy of Safavid Persia.* Weisbaden: Reichert, 2000.

Martin, Vanessa, ed. *Anglo-Iranian Relations since 1800.* London: Routledge, 2005.

Parsa, Ali, and Ramin Keivani . "The Hormuz Corridor: Building a Cross-Border Region between Iran and the United Arab Emirates." In *Global Networks: Linked Cities,* by Saskia Sassen. London: Routledge, 2002.

Ramazani, Rouhollah. *The Persian Gulf and the Strait of Hormuz.* Alphen aan den Rijn: Sijthoff an Noordhoff, 1979.

Steensgaard, Niels. *The Asian Trade Revolution of the Seventeenth Century: The East India Companies and the Decline of the Caravan Trade.* Chicago: University of Chicago Press, 1974.

Basrah
Population: 1.5 million (2005 estimate)

Basrah is the second-largest city in Iraq, the key port for Baghdad on the Shatt al-Arab, and the first created city of Islam. Home for the development of Arabic grammar and renowned for poetry, the city has been a key trading center for 1,300 years, with its merchants and expatriate community spread widely throughout the Islamic and edge cities of Africa, central Asia, and the Indian Ocean. It is also a city of resistance, the mother of numerous Islamic sects, and a site where Arab nationalism began to flower.

Basrah (Arabic, *al-Basrah;* Medieval Europe, *Basorah* or *Bassora*) is situated in southern Iraq, thirty miles northwest from the head of the Persian Gulf. Located in a marshy floodplain created over thousands of years by the confluence of the Tigris and Euphrates rivers as they flow into the Gulf, the city has had to cope with flooding, meandering rivers, and silting throughout its history. As a result, the city has actually "migrated" over the centuries, gradually moving toward the northeast since its founding. Today "old Basrah," as it is called, lies some seven miles to the southwest of "new Basrah," which is closer to the current channel of the Shatt al-Arab. This migration has occurred for a number of reasons, including conflict and destruction. With each rebuilding, the city's elites have taken advantage of the necessity to relocate the city closer to the changing Shatt al-Arab channel. In addition, since the hinterland of the city is laced with ancient or renewed canals and ditches, the city's location has evolved as this network has expanded or contracted. The new Basrah is located on elevated land known as the "Basrah Bar": silt deposited by the Karun River running down from the Zagros Mountains into the Shatt al-Arab.

Habitation of the site and in the vicinity is very ancient. Archaeological evidence indicates that the local area was inhabited at least from the Bronze Age, and it is believed that a sequence of cities lies scattered around the plain, all within close proximity of the site under layers of alluvial silt. The Persians had a settlement in the area known as Vahishtabadh

Ardasher. When the first Arab army arrived in AD 635, they camped close to the remains of the Persian site and called it *al-Khurayba* (little ruin).

In 638 Utba ibn Ghazwan, companion of the Prophet, established a military camp on the site under the orders of Caliph Umar. Umar's reasoning appears to have been strategic: build a military camp for Arab troops on the eastern border of the nascent empire, both to keep them uncorrupted by the local community and to guard the major boundaries of the Arab desert. Basrah was thus the first city founded by Arab Muslim troops after they emerged from the Arabian Peninsula and the first city of the Islamic Empire.

As a security city, Basrah quickly grew as the supply and provision base for campaigns into Iran. Many Arab fighters from the Arabian Peninsula subsequently retired here, and the new city quickly took on a tribal and militaristic character. Companions of the Prophet, like al-Zubayr ibn al-Awwam, settled in Basrah as investors and landowners. Al-Zubayr's house in the city was famous, and he was so wealthy that when he died he left behind 50,000 gold dinars, thousands of slaves, and more than 1,000 horses. Other companions owned so much land that their daily income was more than 1,000 dirhams. These new landowners encouraged infrastructural projects; the salt marshes around the city were drained, creating fertile plains for grains and profits.

The city also quickly became a site for unrest and rebellion. The source of this unrest was the changing nature of the Muslim community as it expanded. Given the flood of new non-Arab converts to the faith, a key political question was of progenitor rights and privileges of the original Arab tribes from the peninsula. Likewise, by the time of the third caliph, Uthman, the Muslim state incorporated territory stretching from Iran to North Africa. Fundamental communal questions of legitimacy, centralization of control, land allocation, and taxation could no longer be managed as they had been in the period just after Muhammad's death. Caliph Uthman did not handle these issues well, and rebellion came to a head in 655 when dissidents from Basrah, Kufa, and Egypt joined together to murder Uthman in Makkah (see also "Kufa" and "Cairo").

Basrah was the site of the uprising against the fourth caliph, Ali, by Muhammad's widow, Aisha, and her Quraishi supporters, including al-Zubayr. Seeking to bring to justice the murderers of Uthman, the rebel forces were defeated at the Battle of the Camel outside Basrah in 658, and the uprising was quashed.

Although the city was primarily Sunni, a number of the early heterodox movements in Islam found great favor and support in Basrah. Uprisings occurred in the city in 683 and again in 701 against the Umayyads. In particular, Ibadhism, which stressed that membership in the Muslim community came by faith and not by Arab blood, evolved within the Qur'anic madrasas of Basrah around AD 720. Women played an important role in helping spread the new beliefs, as did merchant converts in the city. It is from Basrah that the first Ibadhi missionaries (*hamalat al-ilm,* or bearers of learning) were sent out to proselytize North Africa. The seeds that fell among the Berbers in what is now central Algeria and in Morocco were particularly successful. By the mid-eighth century, one of those sent out from Basrah was declared Imam, and the Ibadhi Berber (Rustum) power was born (777–909). For generations afterward, Ibadhis, long-distance trade, and Basrah were linked into merchant networks and scholar exchanges that stretched from Morocco to Oman and China.

The early city was also the home of holy mystics who inspired the Sufi tradition in Islam. Hasan al-Basri (d. 728), a *qadi* (Muslim judge or legal official) and preacher, is considered the father of Muslim mysticism. Rabi'a of Basrah (717–801), a female mystic who is revered as an early Sufi, is another example. She was born in Basrah, apocryphal stories of her visual parables illustrating the insights of Islam abound, and her poetry and teachings are still studied today.

The city was home to the invention and institutionalization of Arabic grammar. Generations of scholars developed Arab philology into a high art, and the city was famous for its school of grammarians. It is usually argued that Abul Awad al-Du'ali (d. ca. 689) was the founder of the discipline. He and the early philologists evolved their skills in concert with the study of the Qur'an and with the collection of traditions; the scholars collected poetry and verse from the Bedouin of the desert, known for their pure Arabic. Basrah was the site for this development, goes one argument, because the city was the first meeting place for the hordes of new Persian converts to Islam and the original Arab converts from Makkah and Madinah. The Arabs became so concerned that the Persians would corrupt the Qur'an with their sloppy Arabic that it was essential to train them in proper Arabic grammar.

Among other roles, the city became the point of embarkation for Iraqi pilgrims going on the hajj to Makkah. The Basrah-Makkah route, known as the Darb Zubayda, became one of the most famous pilgrimage routes in Muslim history. Under the Abbasids (750–1256), the newly developed route from Basrah to Makkah had to be laid out, provisioned with regular water via underground cisterns as well as khans built for the thousands of pilgrims, and provided with ample security. Many benefactors gave money to provide this support for the yearly procession. The most important donor to the development of this pilgrim route was the wife of the caliph Harun ar-Rashid (786–809), Zubayda (see also "Makkah").

The heyday of the city was during the eighth and ninth centuries. Baghdad was the world's largest city, the center of a world order that stretched from North Africa to Afghanistan. Basrah was the empire's key entrepôt, home to perhaps 400,000 people. Trade routes radiated out from Basrah to China, East Africa, and the Russian steppes. Given the city's constant struggle with tidal flooding and silting, the Ab-basids, to maintain Basrah's preeminent position, implemented further massive construction projects, including canals, a river port, and major water provision. Early Arab geographers described the city as a garden city, crossed by canals and gardens. The canals allowed oceangoing ships to sail up the Shatt al-Arab and unload their goods into warehouses around Basrah. Caravans as well, arriving via Persia and the Arabian Desert, unloaded in Basrah. Customs were collected at Basrah, and only then would the goods be loaded onto riverboats for the trip up the Tigris to Baghdad for distribution throughout the empire (see also "Zubair").

The stories of Sinbad the Sailor, codified in the collection *The Thousand and One Nights,* are generally assumed to originate from seafaring stories collected in Basrah from among the thousands of sailors who berthed in the city during the days of the Abbasids. Ships from the city dropped anchor in ports from Zanzibar to Malacca, returning with perfumes, precious stones, and gold. Basrahn merchants, often Persians, set up agencies and trading outposts along these long-distance routes; few traders were seen as better than the Basrahns (see also "Zanzibar").

Basrah was also a production and industrial site. It was particularly known for its glassmaking, pottery, and carpets as well as the diversity and sweetness of its dates. As a security city, it also was an arsenal for the storage and production of major military hardware. Industrial production, agricultural plantations, and long-distance trade all required creative financing, and so Basrah attracted a large Christian and Jewish community heavily involved in providing credit to support these ventures.

Basrah, with its canals, date plantations, cotton and sugar production, and seaport status, needed labor to maintain its infrastructure and support its industry. As a result, thousands of black slaves (*zanj*) from East and West Africa were brought to the Basrah area to work as forced labor and were maintained in large slave camps. The slave market in Basrah, the Suq al-Nakhkhasin, was famous throughout the empire. One rebellion was crushed in 694, but in 868, fired up by a preacher proclaiming himself a prophet, the zanj rebelled and maintained their rebellion until 883. In the process, they captured and burned Basrah in 871, leaving perhaps as many as 300,000 dead. The city remained under their control for a number of years before their strongholds in the marshes around Basrah were wiped out.

From its founding, Basrah was a city known for its scholarship, educational institutions, poetry, and musical accomplishments. Ibn Sarwan and the library he built in Basrah were renowned throughout Dar al-Islam. Many famous poets emerged from the city's creative environment. Basrah also was celebrated for its slave girls (*qayna*), who received extensive training in singing and music. After nine years of training, such slave girls were reported to have had a repertoire of more than 4,000 songs. With the fall of the Abbasid Empire,

Basrah's role as a key entrepôt decreased, although the city kept its hand in trade.

Basrah was virtually untouched by the Mongol invasion in the late thirteenth century. But with Baghdad destroyed and the Ilkhani dynasty in charge (1256–1336), regional trade routes suffered dramatically, and Basrah with them. The city's population declined, and the city shrunk in size and importance. When Ibn Battuta visited the city in 1327, he found the Grand Mosque in need of repair and, for a city renowned for its grammarians, its ulema (clerks or religious scholars who led the Muslim community) poorly trained. As a result of this decline in fortunes, and the continual silting of the Shatt al-Arab, "old Basrah" was abandoned, and "new Basrah" was founded farther to the northeast.

The city's wealth and importance revived with the establishment and expansion of the new "gunpowder empires" of the fifteenth and sixteenth centuries. To the northwest of Basrah, the Ottoman Empire emerged after 1350. As the Ottomans progressively conquered Anatolia and eastern Europe, Aleppo became the entrance from the east into this new empire. Trade routes to the Indian Ocean and East Africa were reinvigorated, and the Aleppo-Hit-Ana-Baghdad-Basrah city network became crucial to overland trade via Bursa and Venice to Europe. The centrality of the Aleppo-Basrah route is reflected in the emergence of a second route between these two cities via al-Qusayr, Karbala, Kubaysah, and Qasr al-Ihvan. Basrah welcomed goods from India, including textiles, spices, and dyes; from China and Tibet, caravans arrived with shipments of musk and rhubarb destined ultimately for Bursa.

By the early 1500s, the Ottomans expanded into Iraq, and Basrah was captured by their troops, using artillery, in 1546. Within a year, the *vilayat* (province) of Basrah was established as the seat of a *sanjak begi* (its own governor-general). The Ottomans built a new naval base in the city, emphasizing its role as a security city for the southern flank of the empire.

A second empire emerged to the southeast of Basrah in the early sixteenth century, that of the Portuguese, who captured Hormuz at the southern entrance to the Persian Gulf in 1515. The first reports of the city by Portuguese visitors appeared in 1517. With the simultaneous consolidation of Ottoman power at the head of the Gulf, the stage was set for a century of military and trade confrontation. Hormuz and Basrah squared off as key ports for each empire, and the cities and islands caught between became pawns in the "great game."

The Ottomans did not stop with Basrah but went on to capture al-Hasa and al-Qatif on the eastern littoral of the Persian Gulf in 1550. Pushing their offensive, in 1552 the Ottoman Suez fleet tried to take Hormuz but failed. The Portuguese in Hormuz responded by trying to capture Basrah in 1556 (see also "Bandar Abbas"). With their failure, Bahrain became the central point of tension and conflict between the

two empires over the next 100 years (see also "Manama"). Gradually, a modus vivendi emerged, with the Ottomans controlling the overland route to Europe, starting in Basrah, and the Portuguese dominating the sea routes to India and East Africa.

Basrah benefited from being the central command, control, and provision city for the southern frontier. For example, in 1558, 200,000 pieces of gold were sent to Basrah by the governor-general of Egypt to support the construction of a fleet in Basrah. Basrah was the key supply point for al-Hasa Province; numerous times the governor of Basrah supplied gold, lumber, ships, cannons, gunpowder, and soldiers to support the Ottoman domains further along the Gulf.

As the century progressed, overall transit trade increased. Ships came to Basrah from Hormuz every month filled with Indian goods such as spices, drugs, indigo, and Calicut cloth. Caravans of 4,000 camels accompanied by a mixture of western merchants (termed "Franks" by the Arabs but primarily Venetians), Indian Muslims, Baghdadi merchants, and Persian brokers would assemble in the city then depart for Aleppo. The city's minority communities increased, with Jews, Armenians, and *baniyans* (Hindu merchants) all involved in the long-distance trading networks as financers, merchants, and commodity brokers.

At the beginning of the seventeenth century, a new empire appeared in the Persian Gulf and threatened Basrah's preeminence. As the Safavids (1501–1722) under Shah Abbas (1588–1629) centralized their control over the Iranian plateau and coast, they clashed with the Ottomans in the Gulf. The Safavids were able to dislodge the Portuguese in Hormuz by 1622, leaving the Portuguese a toehold only in Muscat. From 1624 to 1638, the Safavids controlled Baghdad but were unable to take Basrah. One reason was that in 1624, when threatened by the Persians, the Ottoman commander of Basrah asked the Portuguese in Muscat for naval assistance. This the Portuguese provided, since Basrah had become a key trading port for what was left of their "empire." The result was the establishment of a Portuguese "factory" in Basrah and the formation of a community of Carmelite monks in the city.

With the restoration of Ottoman control over its Iraqi provinces and the signing of an Ottoman-Persian treaty known as the "peace of Zuhab" at Qasr Sirin in 1639, the Iranian-Iraqi border became fairly well agreed upon, and a period of calm followed in the Gulf. It was during this period that the emerging trading companies of the English and Dutch began to work their way into Basrah. The English first established a factory in 1645, though it was not permanent. The Dutch came at about the same time and in fact were the primary European traders in the region during most of the rest of the century. They imported textiles, pepper, nutmeg, cloves, steel, tin, sandalwood, and manufactured goods into Basrah. Of particular importance were the regular "sugar voyages" of Java sugar from Batavia to Basrah. Following the third Dutch-British war of 1672, however, Dutch power in the city began to decline.

In a demonstration of changing power structures in southern Iraq, the Muntafiq tribal confederation was able to capture Basrah in 1694 and hold it for a number of years. A revitalized Ottoman administration finally retook the city, however, and set out to restore Basrah's centrality to trade at the head of the Persian Gulf. They even went so far as to shift the Euphrates River back into its old bed, a major engineering project that helped the city that had been left high and dry by the shifting river.

During the eighteenth century, there was fierce competition between Basrah and the Iranian ports to attract and keep European trade. In 1763 the British East India Company (EIC) received permission to move its primary factory in the Gulf from Bandar Abbas to Basrah. This agreement privileged British interests to the detriment of local Basrahn merchants. It did mean, however, that during subsequent hostilities with the Persians, the Basrah governor was able to ask the British to organize "coffee ship convoys" under their flag and protection to protect the Mocha-Basrah coffee route so important to British merchants. Europeans became more involved in political and economic intrigue in the city, often subverting the local governors as well as each other's contracts and plans.

The late eighteenth century was not an easy one for the city's inhabitants. Basrah experienced a major epidemic in 1773, followed by a siege by *Zand* (Iranian) forces in 1775. As a result, the city's population plummeted from 40,000 to as few as 4,000. The Jewish community was able to persevere, however. The story goes that during the Zand occupation of the city, the sizable Jewish community was severely persecuted by the occupying army. In response, they communally prayed for a miracle. Soon afterward, his own men killed the Zand vizier, and their forces withdrew from Basrah. To this day, Iraqi Jews, although living in Israel, celebrate a special "Purim of Basrah" to remember their deliverance.

The residents for the East India Company, being poorly paid, were allowed to enter into their own private trading deals in addition to their responsibilities for the EIC. As a result, many of them became very wealthy, lived out their lives in Basrah, jointly owned ships trading out of the city, and invested in export and import ventures. Residents were not always culturally sensitive. In 1803, for example, a mob reportedly broke into the home of one of the EIC's sea captains to "rescue a Muslim woman" kept as his mistress. Their responsibilities for the EIC included spying on the French and Dutch agents in the city and maintaining their section of the overland mail route from England to India via Istanbul (Aleppo to Basrah to Bombay). Security along the route was always a problem: between 1801 and 1803, the mail was "plundered" by robbers fourteen times. Since Armenian merchants were

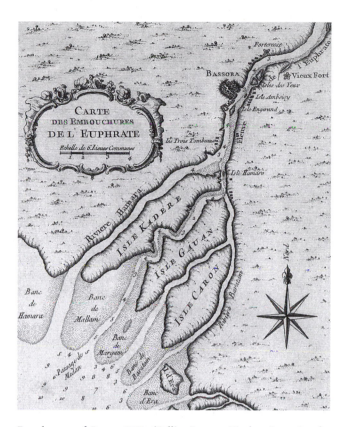

French map of Basra, 1764. (Bellin, Jacques-Nicolas, *Le petit atlas maritime. . . .* Vol. III, pl. 9. Paris, 1764)

moving pearls from Bahrain via Basrah to Istanbul using the overland mail, there was some attraction in stealing the mail packets.

With the rise of Napoléon in France, British representatives in Iraq began to worry about broader security issues, in particular French territorial designs on the Gulf. It is in this context that in 1805 we get the first suggestion by local British residents to their superiors in London that the government should establish a protectorate over an independent Iraq where security could be provided by a local force trained by the British army.

Long-distance trade through Basrah continued despite global conflict and the beginnings of industrialization. In the 1830s, the yearly Basrah-Aleppo caravan still contained 6,000 camels and transported Indian textiles, perfumes, drugs, pearls, rubies, glass, and porcelain. Grain shipments from the Basrah area to other parts of the Ottoman domains increased during this time, making the city a crucial breadbasket for the empire.

Ship traffic into the city declined in the early nineteenth century; during the 1840s, Basrah received only eighty ships (11,000 tons) per year. With the introduction of steamships, new technologies of communication, and overland transport during the middle part of the century, however, the city's fortunes experienced a dramatic reversal. By 1890 Basrah was receiving 100,000 tons of imports via its harbor; by 1913 the figure was 400,000 tons. The opening of the Suez Canal in 1869 was particularly significant for the health of the city's trading role. Instead of using the slower, overland northern Iran–Black Sea route, for example, the Iranian capital could now be quickly reached via a Tehran-Basrah connection (see also "Tehran").

Basrah experienced significant socioeconomic disruption after 1869. Much of it was self-inflicted by the Tanzimat reforms in land tenure and education, which destabilized many sectors of traditional society. Between 1910 and 1914, the Turks also implemented a number of large-scale infrastructural projects around Basrah, including extending the irrigated date plantations around the city and building the Hindiya Dam. International banks opened offices in Basrah in the early twentieth century, and the appearance of printing presses contributed to the spread of new ideas. Within the city, a new intellectual elite evolved that sought to expand their horizons through connections with the Arab world, other urban elites, and the emerging world order. These "new Basrahns" began to imagine their future via Arabism, Iraqi nationalism, or Islamic reform. In 1911 Taleb al-Naqib, a leading Sunni notable in the city, started the newspaper *al-Dustur* (the *Constitution*) and established the Reformist League of Basrah. The league and paper initially argued for Iraq's incorporation within a federated empire but soon began calling for an independent Iraq, where Sunni and Shi'i would work together for the good of the "Arab nation."

European involvement in the city became more complicated with the new century. A Russian consulate opened in 1901, and the first German consulate appeared in 1911. The Germans in particular sought influence with the Ottomans through technological projects such as the Berlin-Baghdad Railway. The British were fearful of this project for geostrategic reasons and so sought to push for a Baghdad-to-Basrah leg of the project that they might control. To sweeten their proposal, they even offered to dredge the Shatt al-Arab to allow Basrah to again host oceangoing shipping, which it had lost early in the 1800s because of silting of the channel. The German project was never fully completed, although important segments of the route were in place by the beginning of World War I, in 1914.

In the lead-up to World War I, the British in the Persian Gulf became very concerned about protecting their oil interests on Abadan Island, their privileges in Kuwait, and the route to India (see also "Abadan" and "Kuwait City"). They were fearful that German influence in Istanbul might translate into a German presence in Baghdad and Basrah, allowing a German military thrust into the Gulf. Some foreign policy officials therefore proposed, as early as 1911, that Britain attach the Basrah province to the British Empire and make it "a granary for Europe." Some political officers even suggested that settlers from the Punjab be "encouraged" to settle around Basrah, to pacify it for the empire.

On 5 November 1914, Britain declared war on the Ottoman Empire, and by 23 November soldiers from the Indian Expeditionary Force had captured Basrah. After the fall of the city, Sir Percy Cox publicly reminded its citizens that the British had "not come as conquerors but as liberators." At the same time, in private, government analysts like H. Saint John Philby and Gertrude Bell were discussing annexing Basrah.

In April 1915, the Turks mounted a significant attack to recapture Basrah, which just barely failed. During the rest of the war, Basrah served as a key regional supply base for the British war effort. To enhance the city's capacity in this regard, the British immediately began dredging the Shatt al-Arab and building a new port.

Following the war, tribal unrest emerged around Basrah. There was great dissatisfaction with the British occupation, and in 1920 this exploded in an open revolt in the rural areas, and Basrah was caught up in the conflict. Although the British were able to suppress the rebellion by aerial bombardment and massive force, the three-month uprising forced them to implement an Arab facade to their rule in Iraq. In 1922 King Faysal officially took over a semiautonomous Iraq.

Under the British Mandate for Iraq, key infrastructural developments linked Basrah to the emerging world order. By 1919 the Basrah-to-Baghdad Railway was finished. In 1927 Basrah-to-Baghdad airmail service was established, and within three years, passenger air service existed. By 1930 an express rail or bus ticket from London to Basrah could be purchased, with air or steamer connections via Dubai through to India.

Because Basrah was the second city of the new state, the state poured considerable resources into Basrah, making it central to national transport networks and to the production of dates for export from the palm plantations surrounding the city.

After the Iraqi Revolution of 1958, Basrah became an oil-exporting port. Its administrative role was enhanced as the regional capital of the Basrah Province, and the University of Basrah, established in 1964, gave the city a national educational role as well.

During the first Gulf War (1980–1988), Basrah suffered the most physical damage and the greatest number of civilian deaths of any Iraqi city. The city entered the war with 1.5 million inhabitants; at the end of the war, it housed less than 900,000. In July 1982, Iran sent five divisions to capture the city. They advanced to within seven miles of Basrah but were stopped. One thousand Iranians died each day of this attack. In 1984 the Iranians again tried to capture the city. They attacked through the marshlands and almost succeeded in cutting the major road to the south. As part of the so-called tanker war, Basrah was the site of surface-to-surface missile attacks on Iran's oil terminal at Kharg Island. Today the city is home to the "Museum for the Martyrs of the Persian Aggression" and a mile-long riverside string of statues of ninety-nine Iraqi soldiers killed in the war, all pointing accusingly toward Iran.

In the second Gulf War (1991), Basrah was again bombed. Allied pilots caught Iraqi soldiers fleeing both into the city from the south and out of the city to the north, and thousands were killed in their vehicles along al-Mutla (the Highway of Death). Today babies born in the city are still suffering congenital deformities from the effects of depleted uranium used by Allied forces.

Survivors of the retreat from Kuwait soon caught the spirit of revolt, and Basrah followed Zubair by a day in rebelling against Saddam Hussayn (1 March 1991). An Iraqi officer in Basrah led the attack on the mayor's office, the security headquarters, and the Baath Party headquarters, where prisoners were released from secret torture chambers. The rebellion in Iraq's second city inflamed other urban centers throughout the country. For a short while, before Saddam's security forces retook the city and "disappeared" thousands, the city was an open city, and exiles returned.

During the third Gulf War (2003), Basrah was the first major Iraqi city surrounded by coalition troops. British soldiers laying the siege expected an internal uprising. This did not happen, and after two weeks of targeted attacks on Baath Party and Iraqi military installations, British commandos moved in and took control of the city.

In the period after the end of formal hostilities, there have been a series of successes in redevelopment as well as continuing difficulties. Basrah Airport was quickly reopened, primarily to serve the humanitarian community, with Qatar Airways the first carrier to restart commercial services into the city. Basrah Airport also served as the site for a new phenomenon: corporate warriors. In the wake of the 2003 occupation, the U.S.-led coalition employed thousands of private military contractors to fulfill a range of tasks, including the protection of Basrah Airport and the training of Iraqi military forces.

The Basrah refinery, one of the main refineries in Iraq, is back under production postinvasion but has so far been unable to export fuel oil products because of sabotage, the theft of oil, and technical difficulties. The electrical supply to the city suffered significant damage in the war but has been restored, although Basrah has been unable to supply electricity to Baghdad because of damaged transmission lines between the two cities. For a long time, however, the wastewater and sewage treatment plants have not functioned, and the water supply is often contaminated. Basrah has already suffered a significant cholera outbreak as a result.

Basrah's location on the Shatt al-Arab and the edge of the largest marsh area in the Middle East has meant that trouble with the marshes affects the city. Saddam Hussayn ordered the marshes to be drained and poisoned in 1991 as a security

move and retaliation against the Shi'i "Marsh Arabs" (the *Madani*) and their 5,000-year-old culture. Most of the approximately 200,000 people displaced by this process moved as refugees into Basrah. In the wake of the 2003 war, there is now talk of restoring as much of the marshes as possible and perhaps restoring the Ma'dani culture as well. Nongovernmental organizations (NGOs) and international organizations are assessing the current situation and looking to develop strategies to rehabilitate the destroyed ecosystem and support those Ma'dani who wish to return.

Despite three wars, the built environment of the city still contains some remnants of the ancient city center. There is a kasbah of narrow streets and tall houses centered on courtyards, and the city's more than 1 million inhabitants retain some hope for the restoration of their lives and the city's economy.

Bruce Stanley

Further Readings

Abdullah, Thabit. *Merchants, Mamluks and Murder: The Political Economy of Trade in 18th Century Basrah*. Albany: State University of New York Press, 2001.

Dodge, Toby. *Iraq*. London: Routledge, 2005.

El-Sakkakini, Widad, and Daphne Vanrenen. *First among Sufis: Life and Thought of Rabia al-Adawiyya, the Woman Saint of Basrah*. London: Octagon Press, 1983.

Marr, Phebe. *The Modern History of Iraq*. 2d ed. Boulder, CO: Westview Press, 2003.

Tripp, Charles. *A History of Iraq*. 2d ed. Cambridge: Cambridge University Press, 2002.

Beersheba
Population: 190,000 (2006 estimate)

Beersheba is a modern frontier city, selling dreams of making the desert bloom, a home for Israel's recent immigrants, and a bright future in software and the chemical industry. But it is also an ancient crossroads, an edge city where markets arose when the Palestinian village areas touched the Bedouin seminomadic lifestyle. Lacking any built environment older than 1900, for 7,000 years the site was an oasis of springs and pasture, most famous as one of the homes of the patriarch Abraham. Its dramatic transformation to the large planned city of today makes it both a city of hope and denial, with its Bedouin heritage threatened and its future to be determined by the dynamics of mineral exploitation, nationally directed growth, immigration, and land seizures.

Beersheba (Hebrew, *Beer-sheva;* Arabic, *Bir Saba*) is situated in Wadi Saba at the juncture of the fertile plains of southern Palestine and the northern semiarid Negev. At this point, the aquifer from the southern Hebron Mountains flows close to the surface, creating numerous springs and water accessible by digging shallow wells. To the north, rainfall is sufficient for settled agriculture; to the south, pastoralism is the best use of the ecology. Numerous natural tracks to all points on the compass converge at the oasis, making the site since ancient times a crossroads for traffic heading northeast toward Hebron and Jerusalem, southwest to the coast of Gaza and thence to Egypt, south to Aqaba on the Red Sea, and east to the Dead Sea and the Jordan. Beersheba is the southernmost city on the limestone ridge that runs north to Hebron and Jerusalem and marks the watershed between the Mediterranean and the Great Rift Valley.

The archaeological record indicates periods of agricultural settlement in Wadi Saba as far back as the late Neolithic and Chalcolithic (5000–3500 BC) eras. From the eighth to the fourth millennia BC, the Negev climate was milder than today, and the area does show signs of continuous habitation. Findings at Tel Abu Matar suggest the cultivation of wheat, lentils, and other basics using floodwater farming techniques along the wadi during the fourth millennium as well as herding of goats and sheep. Unique underground structures and craft specialization are in widespread evidence for this period. Copper ore was processed at one time on the site, but the ore was not local and, like shells found in the area, was imported via long-distance trade. Evidence of metalworking and raw malachite and flint anvils suggest an advanced mineral-processing site. Artistic traditions were well advanced as well, with sophisticated ivory carvings of male and female figures. The evidence also suggests a chiefdom political organization, because of the two-tier settlement hierarchy, with smaller satellite settlements surrounding a central larger community. This Ghassul-Beersheba culture disappeared around 3000 BC.

Significant and regular long-distance trade through the site continued over the next two millennia; there are references in Egyptian texts (ca. 1900–1200 BC) to nomadic raiders of caravans in this area and of the nomadic Shasu moving their herds in the search for fodder. It is from this time that the Old Testament refers to Abraham watering his flocks at Beersheba; of Hagar and Ishmael being thrown out to wander in the wilderness of Beersheba; and of Abraham and King Abimelech swearing an oath or covenant of allegiance at Beersheba, suggesting that the city's name means either the "well of the seven (lambs)" or "the well of the oath."

Another site in the wadi, Tell Saba (Tel Sheva), sits where two major tracks intersect, giving command of the major roads and over access to the wells. Tell Saba yields up Iron Age remains, including tenth-century walls and gates, and appears to have served as an administrative site for the region during Israelite rule. Rebuilt walls, intricate water systems, and deep wells all testify to its defensive importance over the next 200 years. It is this period that is highlighted in the Tel Beersheva National Park on the site. Persian-period materials from the fourth century were also uncovered, including large numbers of *ostraca* (inscribed potsherds) referring to a range of trade goods. The personal names indi-

cate Edomites moved back and forth to the Transjordanian plateau at this time.

By the third century BC, the first indications of a Nabatean trade network in the southern Negev appear, with small defensive forts located to the south of Beersheba. At the height of the Nabatean commercial empire, from 100 BC to AD 100, regular large-scale trade from Petra to the east of Wadi Araba headed for Gaza, though there is no record that they had a trading center at Beersheba (see also "Gaza" and "Aqaba/Eilat").

Rome annexed the Nabatean trade networks in AD 106 and extended their rule as far south as Aila. The Roman road for Palestine linked Beersheba to Hebron and Jerusalem. During the Byzantine period, ecclesiastical records show a bishopric at Beersheba, and the town is indicated on the Madaba map (ca. AD 560). After the Arab conquest, however, trade and pilgrimage patterns shifted to the east, and there is little indication of any permanent structures on the site, with visitors commenting on the ruined tell.

The city reenters global history with the Ottoman takeover of the area from the Mamluks after 1514. Ottoman authority in the Negev was light, however, and it was the major tribes such as the Tarabin, al-Azazma, Tiyaha, Aheiwat, Wuheidat, and Zullam who held the key grazing grounds and water sites. They controlled the markets and trade of the region, interacting with Hebron, Maan, Gaza, and Cairo on a regular basis (see also "Hebron").

As Ottoman authority in this region cycled over the centuries, Beersheba remained a site of local importance to the Bedouin tribes of the Negev. But after Napoléon Bonaparte's occupation of Egypt (1789) and the push to dig the Suez Canal, the strategic interests of the great powers in Palestine, the Red Sea, and the Sinai began to change, and with them an increased focus on the long-distance transport routes through Beersheba. In 1841 Ibrahim Pasha and the Ottoman sultan agreed to Egyptian administration over the Egyptian hajj route through the Sinai, thus effectively granting Egypt de facto control up to a line from Aqaba to Rafah. This left Beersheba as a key oasis near the Ottoman border and strategically significant to Ottoman attempts to guarantee their continuing sovereignty in the area.

The border problem between Egypt and Ottoman Palestine was exacerbated by the conquest of Egypt by Britain in 1882. The Ottomans thus needed to secure the absolute loyalty of the shaykhs and the settlement of the nomadic Bedouin tribes on the land. By the end of the nineteenth century, the Ottoman government had been able to attain a considerable degree of internal security in Palestine. The roads were safer, and the Jerusalem council was responsible for Beersheba and served as an appeal tribunal for the nizam court held in tents in Beersheba. The Bedouin tribes had the choice of either withdrawing to the desert fastness or accepting the authority of the regime, although Bedouin in the peripheral zones and desert areas would continue to demonstrate their independence from the authorities for decades to come. Many failed to pay taxes, and internecine violence continued. These considerations led to the establishment of the new district (*qada*) of Beersheba. Thus, Beersheba was founded in 1900, as the capital of the fifth qada (the others were Jaffa, Hebron, Jerusalem, and Gaza) under the Jerusalem *mutasarriflik*. A *qaimaqam*, or dignitary, was appointed to govern the area.

The government purchased 480 acres of land from the Mhemdiyin tribe of the al-Azazma clan to establish the city, and in 1896 the leader of the clan, Shaykh Hasan al-Malt'a, donated his own large tent, which he pitched at what is now the *saraya* (government house) to serve as the administrative headquarters. The first qaimaqam, Isma'il Kamal Bey (of Ottoman origin), held his office in that tent until the saraya was built. The Ottomans appointed a team of architects to plan the new city, which was to be focused around the new government offices. Two Arab Palestinian engineers, Sa'id Effendi al-Nashashibi and his assistant, Ragheb Effendi al-Nashashibi, were joined by two foreign engineers, one Swiss and one German, and they laid out a European grid system for the city that took little notice of the surrounding topography.

During the first phase of construction (1900–1903), the Saraya House and several structures around it were built as well as an army barracks and a center for the gendarmerie. During these early years, various rooms in Saraya House were set aside to serve different purposes: on the top floor, single rooms served for the district court, the tribal court (*mahkamat al-ashar*), and the office of the qaimaqam. On the bottom floor could be found rooms for the magistrate's court, the Muslim religious court, the superintendent of police, and the city clerk. Temporary quarters for the municipality were also located in the building until a proper municipal building was built across the street. Throughout the oasis, old wells were cleaned out and fixed, and two new wells were dug.

The second stage of the city's construction commenced in 1904, during the period of Qaimaqam Assaf Belge Bey, the Damascene (1904–1906), and included construction of the municipality building, a mosque, and, afterward, a two-story school for Bedouin children, the first school in the district.

The Ottomans established their administrative center next to the ruins of Byzantine Beersheba for a number of reasons. To begin with, the oasis is central, and the surrounding area, which is flatter than most of the Negev, has more fertile soil and receives more precipitation as well; hence, the Beersheba Plain already contained a large Bedouin population. Second, the area was under the control of a friendly shaykh, al-Malt'a, which facilitated the government's functions of peacekeeping and monitoring Bedouin activities. In addition, the Tiyaha clan was located a few miles to the north, and the Tarabin clan a few to the west. Fourthly, the presence of ancient wells and the proximity to the surface of groundwater, facilitating the digging of new wells, guaranteed that the administrative cen-

ter would not want for water and in fact would be able to control an ancient intertribal irrigation area. Other reasons for the choice of the site included Beersheba's sanctity to Muslims because of its connection to Abraham and Ishmael as well as to Amro ibn al-'Aas and his son Abdullah (famous Muslim fighters).

The government encouraged the Bedouin to settle in the new city with land grants of a quarter of an acre; other settlers had to pay. The shaykhs and tribal elites were attracted enough to commit to the city, building large homes and stores for themselves. They did not live full-time in these homes, however, frequently spending time with their tribal communities and then returning to the city.

To encourage the Bedouin to participate in government, the district governor established two councils: one to govern the district (*al-majles al-idary*) and the other to govern the city (*al-majles al-baladi*). Both councils had Bedouin members. The district council included, in addition to government officials, shaykhs representing the five largest Negev clans. The municipal council also included five shaykhs who represented the same five Negev clans. The authorities appointed one of the most important shaykhs, Shaykh Hajj Ali Sliman al-Atawna, to the mayorship. He served in this post until his death, in 1922.

The Qaimaqam Assaf Bey enhanced the religious status of the district capital in 1906 with the inauguration of the large and elaborate Great Mosque, which came to symbolize cooperation between the Bedouin and the Ottoman authorities. Negev Bedouin tribes contributed more than 1,000 pounds sterling toward the mosque's construction. At the inauguration ceremony, the authorities held a great banquet for the Bedouin, at which hundreds of their newborn sons were circumcised.

Among the other municipal functions by which Assaf Bey enhanced the attraction of the city for the Bedouin were an improved water system, construction of a flour mill, and the establishment of a post office and telegraph, housed in the saraya. Since the city would only thrive by serving as a regional market and commercial center for the Bedouin who lived outside the city, Assaf Bey established an open livestock market and set Wednesday as the regional weekly market day; the weekly Bedouin market in the city still attracts Bedouin from the region as well as tourists and new Israeli immigrants. In addition, Assaf Bey built one of the most pleasant public buildings of the period, the district's first school, a two-story structure. Several of the school's Bedouin graduates would eventually go on for further schooling in Istanbul.

Early in 1914, the Germans completed a narrow-gauge railway line connecting Beersheba with Jerusalem and Jaffa. When World War I broke out in August, Beersheba served as the Ottoman command center where supply and transportation facilities were located along with workshops, warehouses, and sundry other installations used by the army.

There were large military forces in the area, and the school building was refurbished and converted into a Red Crescent hospital. General Allenby began his Negev offensive in October 1917 and on the thirty-first of the month took Beersheba after a six-hour attack. In the Zionist organization proposal to the subsequent Versailles Conference in 1919, they laid claim to the Negev, citing the biblical reference "from Dan to Beersheva" as their justification.

During the British Mandate (1917–1948), Beersheba remained the capital of the Qada and the administrative center of the Bedouin population, serving as a unifying factor that engendered a feeling of political belonging and participation. At the outset of the mandate, the authorities chose seven shaykhs, representing the five principal Negev clans, to serve as an *umad,* or council of advisors, with whom they consulted on economic affairs and to whom they listened, on occasion.

Under the British, Beersheba continued as the seat of the qaimaqam. These administrators were chosen for their knowledge of Arabic and admiration of the Bedouin lifestyle, a view that was shared by many of the British serving in the city. Beersheba also became a juridical center for the district court system and for the tribal courts. The prominence of Beersheba as a Bedouin juridical center was particularly noticeable during the tenure of the scholar Arif al-Aref as qaimaqam (1929–1939). Al-Aref enhanced the juridical efficiency of the Qada capital, succeeded in making Bedouin law less severe, and helped bring it into line with the law of the state. As of 1931, it was estimated that the city served a wider community of 100,000 Bedouin.

To preserve law and order among the Bedouin, the British established a special mobile police force, the Palestine Gendarmerie, based in Beersheba. Gendarmerie personnel, known as *hajjaneh,* would patrol the expanses of the Negev by horse and camel to make the government's presence evident. Eight additional police stations and posts, under the central headquarters in Beersheba, were put into operation.

With the founding of the town, there were 300 inhabitants listed in 1902. By 1922 there were around 2,500 people counted, including 235 Christians, 98 Jews, and 11 Druze. By 1945 the city had a population of 5,570, composed mainly of Muslim villagers from Gaza and Hebron.

At the time of the British conquest of Beersheba, a single military hospital, situated in the Bedouin school building, served the entire Beersheba region. After World War I, the British quickly built a government hospital in the city. This eight-bed hospital employed a doctor, pharmacist, and a number of nurses. The hospital and its outpatient clinic also supported outlying clinics, which the hospital's physician would visit from time to time. During al-Aref's tenure as qaimaqam, a district health officer with offices in Beersheba was appointed. He would visit encampments in outlying areas and dispense medical aid and advice.

Until the 1940s, the mandatory administration maintained five tribal schools for Bedouin boys in rural areas away from Beersheba. As in the case of village schools, tribal schools consisted of a single room and a teacher, with the instruction offered at the lower-elementary-school level; most of those who attended were the sons of the shaykhs and well-to-do tribesmen. From the 1930s, those who completed the lower forms at tribal schools could attend upper elementary in Beersheba as boarders. In 1932–1933, al-Aref revived the idea of a boarding school exclusively for Bedouin. Targeted primarily at the sons of shaykhs and notables, it was hoped that the school would provide future tribal leaders with the skills necessary for maintaining relations with government officials. Many former students of that institution have become shaykhs and professionals, among them Shaykh Hammad Khalil Abu-Rabi'a, who went on to become a Knesset member (1973–1977, 1979–1981).

All was not happy in Mandatory Palestine, however, and Beersheba was caught up in the general unrest experienced after the 1936 Arab Revolt. In September 1938, Palestinian rebels raided Beersheba; government buildings were torched and weapons taken. As a result, the police station in the city was closed. Later, the city was briefly taken over and held by rebels until December 1938. Finally, the military government retook the city and imposed martial law.

Muhammad Abd al-Hadi was the last qaimaqam in Beersheba during the British period. The British Mandate in Beersheba terminated in May 1948 as a result of a United Nations (UN) resolution (29 November 1947) to divide Palestine between Jews and Palestinians. Under the UN Partition Plan, Beersheba was the southernmost city in the Arab state, with most of the Negev directly around it allotted to the Jewish state.

The British quit Beersheba on 14 May 1948 in an impressive ceremony attended by Bedouin leaders and senior government officials. The Union Jack was lowered, and the mayor of Beersheba, Shafiq Mushtaha, raised the Palestinian flag over the saraya. Palestinian rule over Beersheba lasted only a few months. As the war in Palestine raged to the north, the Egyptian army entered the city in May 1948 and used the boarding school as their headquarters.

Count Bernadotte recommended in September that the Negev should be part of the Arab state in return for some land in Galilee for the Jewish state. This suggestion spurred the Israel Defense Forces (IDF) to solidify their hold on the area. Beersheba was bombed on 16 October and captured on 21 October 1948. The IDF officers failed to control their troops, who looted the town and drove out the remaining population. In total, by December, more than 30,000 Palestinians from the city and the surrounding areas had been kicked out or fled to Transjordan. Many more were concentrated to the east of Beersheba under military restrictions.

The city provided the base for a subsequent attack in December by Yigal Allon's troops up the ancient Roman road from Beersheba to el-Auja as they harried the Egyptian troops. The UN negotiator, Ralph Bunche, proposed an Israeli withdrawal, with the city being demilitarized and placed under an Egyptian governor. In fact, the Egyptians went so far as to designate a governor for Beersheba, but in the end they signed an armistice with Israel rather than contest the issue. Although under international pressure, Israel refused to evacuate the city, claiming that the Negev was an integral part of the Jewish state.

By February 1949, the new Israeli government was placing Jewish families in the cleared city housing. These first settlers along with soldiers garrisoned in the city made up a population of about 3,000 until 1950, when the military administration ended and the municipal council was established. The regulatory boundaries of the city were greatly enlarged to incorporate great tracks of land far beyond the city, denying the Bedouin ancient rights in the oasis. Electricity and water were finally established by 1952, and new immigrants were housed in "the new town" constructed over the next decade around eight neighborhood districts, each projected to be a neighborhood unit. Regional administration for the Negev was located in the city, and it became a major transshipment site for minerals and Eilat traffic during the last half of the twentieth century (see also "Aqaba/Eilat"). The city was thus the primate city for the region from 1950, and government commitment to development of the region and to the city has gone hand in hand.

Health care for the entire southern district, for example, rotates around the Soroka Medical Center and the medical facilities and research of Ben Gurion University. Schools for training teachers, a veterinary hospital, and a music conservatory have been located in the city. The headquarters for the Southern Command of the military is located here as well. Ben Gurion University has become a major engine for the city's development, instigating global networks, innovative training, and knowledge about the situation in Beersheba and its inhabitants. Intel built a $1.6 billion plant on the edge of the city, although other industries, for example, Motorola, Dell, the Dead Sea Works, Israel Aircraft, and Makhteshim Chemical, employ the most staff.

The various waves of Jewish immigration into Israel since 1948 have been reflected in changes in the demographic makeup of the city. Middle Eastern and North African immigrants made up the majority of early immigrants into the city. Most recently, Russians have become a major presence in the city. The massive Russian migration to Beersheba has spurred the growth of new neighborhoods since 1990. Most of the buildings built in the 1960s and 1970s are ill-suited to the desert environment, and there are few green areas of the city. As the city grew, the physical layout of the town became a hindrance on its growth and sense of unity, and traffic patterns became obstructive and difficult. As a result, master planning for the future of the city is beginning to direct new

developments, and there is a projection for a population of 500,000 by 2020. However, the city is struggling to remain economically and politically significant to the rest of the country and to maintain its frontier and innovative reputation. By 1998 the city had fallen from fourth to fifth place in city rankings by size, and estimates suggest a slide to ninth place in the future.

Beersheba still acts to deny its Bedouin heritage. By 1951 fewer than 13,000 Bedouin remained in the Negev, and more were expelled to Jordan in 1953. Following the return of the Sinai to Egypt (1978), the transfer of Bedouin from their traditional lands around Beersheba to seven "tribal" towns surrounding the city was enforced by the Green Patrol, a paramilitary police unit. Despite significant resistance to this enforced urbanization, the denial of Bedouin access to land continues, along with the destruction of homes. The Beersheba Mosque remains closed to worshipers and is scheduled to become a museum. Bedouin are discriminated against in finding employment in Beersheba, holding only 2.5 percent of all industrial jobs in the Negev (1998), and the government has discriminated in committing development funds to the new Bedouin townships. Yet in the 1990s, the Bedouin community had one of the highest population growth rates in the world (5 percent), and their respective population will have doubled by 2010, making them one-quarter of the Negev's population.

A coordinated regional development plan that incorporates the Bedouin and non-Bedouin development towns of the area together into a regional economic development plan with Beersheba seems to be an urgent requirement for the future. The city and its hinterland are currently fragmented into a collection of dysfunctional towns and unconnected rural settlements, and so developing the regional transportation networks linking the region together and with its surrounding regions (both domestically and cross-border) is a key priority. Transport development is in the cards, with the expansion of new passenger rail connections with Tel Aviv, the possibility of rail connections between Eilat and Ashdod via Beersheba to compete with the Suez Canal, and a proposed international airport. Yet, what is necessary is a new focus on human capital development that brings the Jewish and Bedouin communities together into a shared political-economic development space with Beersheba as its core.

Aref Abu-Rabia

Further Readings

Abu-Rabia, Aref. *Bedouin Century: Education and Development among the Negev Tribes in the 20th Century.* Oxford: Berghahn Books, 2001.

Lithwick, Harvey. *An Urban Development Strategy for the Negev's Bedouin Community.* Beersheba: Negev Center for Regional Development, Ben Gurion University, 2000.

Meir, Avinoam. *As Nomadism Ends: The Israeli Bedouin of the Negev.* Boulder, CO: Westview Press, 1997.

Beirut
Population: 1.8 million (rough estimate for post-2002)

Beirut is one of the oldest cities on the eastern coast of the Mediterranean. Although conquered many times across the centuries and wracked by violence, this beautiful Lebanese port city continuously reemerged, phoenixlike, from destruction, earthquake, and flame to resume its preeminent commercial role between east and west. Known most recently for the bloody civil war that divided the city for fifteen years and destroyed its urban fabric, the city was, across the centuries, part of the Phoenician expansion across the Mediterranean, home to one of the most important Roman law schools, a Crusader outpost, terminus of the medieval caravan trade, and the Switzerland of the Middle East during the 1960s. Rarely a political capital, Beirut has always been famous for the commercial savvy of its merchants, its educational opportunities, and its financial and tourist services.

There are many stories about the foundation of Beirut (Canaanite, *Biruta;* Phoenician, *Brt;* Greek, *Berytos;* Latin, *Berytus;* French *Beyrouth;* Arabic, *Beyrout*), but none are credible. The word *Biruta* originates from the ancient Semitic word for *pit* or *well,* with *Biruta* being the plural form, meaning *wells;* it is possible that the city was so named because of the abundance of wells that furnished its water supply.

Beirut is situated on a rocky peninsula bounded by the sea to the north and west and having a sheltered harbor. The climate is mild in winter and hot and humid in summer. Immediately inland, the hills rise quickly to high mountains, and so the view from the harbor is spectacular. The city is fortunate in its location, centered on the coastal road to the north and south, which facilitated contact with other Mediterranean ports. To the east, the city is linked through the mountains both via Damascus with the Euphrates and to the Palestinian mountains to the southeast.

The peninsula and the surrounding areas were initially settled during the lower Paleolithic Age 250,000 years ago. Neolithic settlements dating to the sixth millennium BC were numerous along this littoral, with findings of tools for hunting and fishing and pottery for domestic use. As the Canaanite civilization developed in Syrio-Palestine after the third millennium BC, small cities appeared along the Levantine coast, brokering long-distance trade between Mesopotamia and Egypt. Byblos (Gebail) to the north was the primary port, but others are mentioned in the texts found in Ebla dating from 2500 to 2300 BC, including one *ba-u-ra-at-tu:* Berytus (see also "Ebla"). One tradition of the founding of the city has it as a southern colony of Byblos (see also "Byblos"). During the redevelopment of Beirut in the late 1990s, archaeological excavations revealed new aspects of the city's early history:

successive city walls, dating back to at least 2000 BC, along with remains of the first acropolis and citadel and a massive city gate.

Archaeological and literary references for the city during the Middle Iron Age (900–550 BC) indicate a thriving junior member of the Phoenician city system, trading with Cyprus, the western Mediterranean, and Assyria. It was known as the Phoenician port of Berytus, and much of what has emerged about this age comes from excavations at the necropolis of Khalde, near the Beirut Airport, where more than 170 burials (ca. 900 BC) were discovered. Evidence of a local purple dye industry near the ancient harbor also suggests a vibrant trading city. The town had massive fortifications and a population known for its educational achievements. The biblical prophet Isaiah mentions the great thinkers who lived in the cities along the Lebanese coast. The historian Sanchuniathon, who lived in Beirut around 1000 BC, wrote a history of Phoenicia.

Berytus's chief divinity during this period was the female Baalat, and the city's population rejected the extensive polytheism of the age. Evidently, one ancient Phoenician custom in the cities continued during this time: for the prince of the city, in time of crisis, to take some of the most loved of his sons, dress them up as "lords" or gods, and behead them in sacrifice to the god El.

After the Assyrians, the resurgent Egyptians, and the Babylonians, Berytus passed under the rule of the Achaemenid Persians (530–333 BC). During their rule, the city was laid out along a network of streets intersecting at right angles, and this remained the fundamental orientation throughout the Hellenistic and Roman periods. A new substantial wall around a larger city was built, and further extensive urban development occurred ca. third century BC under the Seleucids.

Under the Roman Empire (after 64 BC), Beirut flourished and attained a splendor it had never known before. It was a center of Roman civilization in Syria, the most Roman city in the East. Its port was the main anchorage of the Roman galleys that patrolled the eastern Mediterranean seas. Textile production and trade enriched not only the merchants and artisans but also brought income to other citizens involved in providing lodging, transportation, and other services in support. The ready availability of agricultural products provided income for the peasants and providers of foodstuffs. The numerous travelers who passed through the city also enhanced the flow of monetary exchange both within and beyond its gates. The government and the city's religious institutions were instruments of redistribution of wealth by taxation and by the provisioning of government officials or provision for the poor. Economically, Beirut became a focal point for the commerce of the ancient world, both east and west.

Besides its commercial importance, it was in Beirut that one of the empire's most distinguished law schools flourished, attracting students from all parts of the Roman world. From the third century AD onward until 551, one of only three law schools of the Byzantine Empire world flourished in Berytus. Two distinguished professors from its faculty were invited by Emperor Justinian (527–565) to sit on commissions for the official revision of the entire legal system. This important legislative work of the sixth century AD, the *Justinian Code,* has preserved Roman law, which in turn provided the basic principles for the laws regulating many European societies in our day. Beirut was celebrated as a center of learning and important Syrian cultural center.

One of the most significant changes Beirut underwent was caused by the spread of Christianity; the early city hosted a large enough Christian community that there were six churches for its believers. By the fifth century, the Byzantines moved their administrative representative from Tyre to Beirut, which gave the city greater religious standing in the ancient world (see also "Tyre"). Under Justinian, Beirut also became a center for the new (stolen) skills of silk production; Beirut's silk factories supplied the state monopoly and shipped silk as far away as western Europe.

Destroyed by a cataclysmic earthquake on 16 July 551, which was followed by a tidal wave and fire, the city was reduced to ruins. It is estimated that 30,000 people died. These unfortunate events ended the glorious days of Beirut, and the city sank into oblivion for a long time.

The seventh century was the century of the Arab conquest of the eastern Mediterranean. Beirut held out after the fall of Damascus in September 635 because the Byzantines could supply the city by sea. But once the Byzantine army fled after the Battle of the Yarmuk, in August 636, Beirut passed into Muslim hands. The establishment of the Umayyad Caliphate, and their shift of the capital from the Hijaz to Damascus, quickly made Beirut the primary Umayyad port on the Mediterranean (see also "Damascus"). Muslims began to settle in Beirut and gradually supplanted the Christian population. One of the most prominent early Muslim personalities was Imam Abd ar-Rahman bin Amr al-Awzai, one of the most famous Islamic jurists of his time. He was an authority listened to both by the population and by the highest personalities of the state; he was always welcomed by the caliph al-Mansour.

With the establishment of Islamic control over the city, the Christians of Beirut were not harassed. When the city passed under Fatimid control (978), the religious toleration continued, and the Christians of Syria and Palestine maintained their ties with the Christians of the west, and believers were free to practice their religion. The two great powers of the time, Fatimid Egypt and Byzantium, were on good terms, as both wished to keep Seljuq incursions in check on their eastern borders. Nevertheless, in 1071 the Seljuqs captured Jerusalem and in the same year inflicted a crushing defeat on

the Byzantine army. The harsh treatment by the Seljuqs of Christian pilgrims passing from Beirut to Jerusalem helped spur the nascent crusading movement in Europe.

Beirut was not spared by the Crusaders, who sought to control all the Syrian harbors leading to Jerusalem. At the time of the first Crusader attack on the walls (1110), Beirut was a small and unassuming city, lacking the size and wealth of its neighbors along the coast. The materials for the Crusaders' siege engines were taken both from the ruins of Roman Berytus, just beyond the medieval city's walls, and from the surrounding pine forests. Its 5,000 inhabitants put up a strong resistance, but the city was finally taken; the Franks massacred all the inhabitants as a lesson for the other cities along the coast. Beirut remained under the control of the king of Jerusalem until 1187, when Salah ad-Din recaptured the coastal cities for Islam, including Beirut.

Beirut was retaken by King Aimery of Jerusalem in 1197 and experienced a 100-year golden period. Beirut was granted in fief to John of Ibelin, who ruled as the Lord of Beirut. He restored the city, built its towers again, encouraged commerce and industry, and invited the merchants from Venice, Genoa, and Pisa to invest in Beirut. After the Egyptian Mamluks defeated the Mongols at Ain Jalut (1260), Sultan Baybars signed a truce with Beirut in 1261 and reaffirmed it in 1269. Under Sultan Qalawun (r. 1279–1290), a new truce was signed with Lady Eschiva, a descendant of John of Ibelin, who ruled Beirut at the time under the authority of the Lusignan dynasty in Nicosia. The truce lasted until July 1291, when Qalawun's son, Sultan al-Ashraf Khalil, responded to provocations by Italian Crusaders who had broken the truce and besieged the city. The Frankish elite finally fled by ship, taking with them the reliquaries from the city's cathedral that had been acquired by the Crusaders while in Palestine. The Mamluk army entered Beirut, pulled down its walls, and turned the cathedral into a mosque. This put an end to Crusader rule, which had lasted longer in Beirut (171 years) than in any other coastal city.

The Mamluk sultans kept Beirut unfortified lest the Crusaders regain a foothold. They destroyed all the harbors and fortifications of the Syrian and Palestinian coast. For economic reasons, however, the Mamluks could not sustain the politics of destroyed harbors, and by the fourteenth century the decision was made to rebuild the harbor of Beirut, and the merchants from Venice restarted their business via its port.

The past glories of Beirut appeared to have ended. Beirut had no political role, and its economic role was nothing compared to what it had been under the Romans or even compared with its neighbors along the Syrian coast. The unstable political situation in the region and successive wars made it difficult for Beirut to flourish economically. Moreover, the cultural and intellectual focal point of the region lay in hinterland cities like Damascus, Baghdad, and Cairo. Yet it still played a role in the spice trade, with Venetian ships calling at the city to buy spices and pepper. With the success of the Portuguese in rounding Africa, there were serious regional shifts in the spice trade and availability. For Beirut, this meant significant problems; in 1504, for example, the Venetian galleys found no spices in Beirut. Yet the next three decades were a growth time for the city, as particularly up until 1534, the English began to visit the port and to initiate direct trade to England. They carried woolen cloth and jerseys of different colors to Beirut in exchange for pepper, spices, silks, carpets, oils, and cotton.

After the Ottomans defeated the Mamluks in 1517, Syria and Egypt were annexed to the Ottoman Empire. For the next 400 years, Beirut remained nominally within the Ottoman Empire but under shifting local rulers who often had a high degree of autonomy. The empire was divided into provinces (*willayat*) under the control of an appointed governor (*wali*), and there were local principalities in some areas. One of these kingdoms was established in Mount Lebanon (a mountainous area overlooking Beirut). In 1598 Fakhreddin II Maan was the ruler of Mount Lebanon, and the Ottoman authorities installed him as the ruler of territories between Aleppo, Palmyra, and Palestine in return for a certain sum of money. Beirut became part of the Mount Lebanon principality, and some historians claim that Beirut became the "capital" of the Fakhreddine dynasty. Many improvements were made to the city; the prince built a beautiful palace inspired by Italian architecture, for example, and he planted a forest of fir trees south of the city to improve the water supply. Another important family were the Buhturis, who had been granted the tax rights to the harbor of Beirut under the Mamluks in exchange for protection against raids from Cyprus.

Beirut factories returned to producing silk of the finest quality, which brought wealth to the city. After the death of Fakhreddine, Beirut continued to prosper economically. It served as a transit road for the silk commerce from the Shouf Mountains to Damascus. The population was modest, not more than a few thousand, and composed mainly of Sunnis and Greek Orthodox, a few Druze families, and a small Maronite community.

During the eighteenth century, the regional situation was evolving rapidly in the Orient, and the Ottoman Empire faced difficulties both within its provinces and with the expanding European powers. France, the United Kingdom, Russia, and others were interfering in the internal politics of the empire, and Beirut was caught up in these intrigues. In the Russo-Turkish War, between Russia and the Ottoman dynasty (1768–1774), the Russian fleet captured Beirut (1773), which had around 6,000 inhabitants at the time. The city was once again destabilized politically, which badly affected the economy. Merchants fled to Tripoli. After the Ottomans regained Beirut, Bashir Shehab II held the city under his rule of the

Druze principality, producing a long period of political stability and economic growth thanks to a booming silk industry. The city's population remained small, yet the European merchants who had fled returned, and the city developed again after years of instability.

During the early 1800s, the city's power and position began to grow because of numerous shifts in the city's regional administrative role. In 1832 the expansive Egyptian ruler Muhammad Ali sent troops to take over Syria, and Beirut became the provisional capital for his administration. The British and French governments set up consulates in the city, followed by other Europeans and the Americans. By 1840, however, global politics turned against the Egyptian adventure in Syria, and on 11 September 1840 an Anglo-Turkish fleet heavily bombarded Beirut at the start of a campaign to drive Muhammad Ali's forces from Syria. In the wake of the Egyptian withdrawal, ironically Beirut's administrative centrality actually increased, as the Ottomans began to use the city as a center for their own renewed control of the region. This bureaucratic significance was confirmed by the changes in 1888, when Beirut became the administrative capital of a new Ottoman willayat bearing its name. The territory of Beirut ran from Latakia to the north (in today's Syria) to Nablus (in today's Palestinian territories), an 11,000-square-mile territory. The result was that by the end of the century, Beirut housed substantial administrative offices, was accepted as the administrative center of the region, and attracted commercial services linked to the administrative offices.

This period was a time of great change. The city's travel networks were improved with the opening of a new carriage road between Beirut and Damascus in the 1860s and the subsequent development of a new narrow-gauge railroad heading inland as well. Beirut benefited from the changing politics of free trade that occurred after the 1838 Anglo-Turkish Commercial Convention struck down Ottoman monopolies and opened up internal markets to the Europeans. Beirut experienced a dramatic increase in the number of European merchants within the city.

American Presbyterian missionaries first arrived in 1820, and Beirut became their primary headquarters and area of greatest success in converting other Christians to Protestantism. The year 1834 was key, with the Jesuits returning, more Americans arriving, and the beginnings of a Catholic-Presbyterian competition for converts and institutions. New missionary schools, some acting as colleges for advanced training, were built, many with funds from American churches. The first schools for girls were established, the printing press was introduced, and new textbooks were distributed. Butrus Bustani founded a newspaper in Beirut in 1860 called *Nafir Suriya* (*Clarion of Syria*), the first political journal, which called for peace among the various sects within Lebanon.

Entrance to the port of Beirut, 1848. (Yanosky, Jean, and Jules David, *Syrie ancienne et moderne*, pl. 2. Paris, 1848)

The city's geographical position as an open gateway to the East, combined with the ingenuity of its inhabitants during the later nineteenth century, slowly brought back to its port the all-important trade from the West. Moreover, Beirut reappeared on the cultural map through the establishment of what were to become two of the most prominent universities in the region. In 1866 the Syrian Protestant College, later to become the American University of Beirut, was founded, to be followed in 1875 by the Université Saint Joseph, which later grew to include a faculty of law. These institutions made the city once again a major intellectual, cultural, and commercial center in the eastern Mediterranean world.

Beirut replaced Aleppo as the commercial focal point of the region, with the construction of the new modern harbor coinciding with the coming of the new steamers; Beirut was the first harbor capable of receiving and supporting these new steamships. It was during this period that Beirut overtook it rivals, Saida and Tripoli, which were its neighbors along the coast. The merchants began to organize, and their economic wealth was used for broader political purposes within the region.

By the end of the nineteenth century, the city's population had increased to 100,000. The newly constructed harbor attracted one-third of the commerce in Syria, much of it arriving via the new roads, which reduced the three-day trip from Damascus to just thirteen hours. Beirut gained new straight roads, public spaces, hotels, schools, two universities and hospitals, journals, political parties, and intellectual gatherings. Also during the same period Beirut experienced an expansion in banking, money lending and allied services to take care of emigrants' remittances, sericulture, the import and growing transit trade, and ventures in real estate and agricul-

tural land. During the last quarter of the century, Beirut also witnessed the Occidentalization of lifestyle and manner among its privileged classes. It was the birth of a new Beirut, to an extent that the German kaiser described it as the "rare jewel of the Sultan's crown."

The influx of new inhabitants, especially from Mount Lebanon and Damascus following the 1860 massacres of the Christians in those areas, expanded the city's population and networks. The ethnic mix of the city began to change, although the Muslim community was still the largest. Quickly a new "business" bourgeoisie, mainly Christians, emerged. These businessmen, from clans such as the Sursock, Bustros, and Pharaon, strengthened the city's business and banking relationships with the West, mainly France and Great Britain. On the other hand, Muslim businessmen were forging good ties with the hinterland of Syria, particularly Damascus. To an influential portion of its Occidentalized merchant notables and professional middle class, Beirut was Ottoman in name only, and they actually operated in a global environment. Members of this class formed new intellectual organizations with political undercurrents, looking for change and renewal; the Beirut Reform Committee, for example, formed in 1913 of eighty-six members from across the religious divides, sought a secular Syrian nation and home rule.

Such intellectual clubs and fledgling political movements had strong Arab nationalist messages, which were threatening to the Ottoman-Turkish elite. Particularly after the Young Turk Revolution (1908) within the empire, there were government attempts to repress such Arab nationalist movements within the city.

With the outbreak of World War I, Beirut lost its trade with the French and British and suffered an immediate economic crisis. Local unrest increased, and many plots against Turkish rule were hatched. As the Arab Revolt to the south, led by Amir Faysal, began to threaten the Ottomans in Palestine, the regional military governor, Jamal Pasha, instituted a repressive military occupation of the city to prevent a rearguard uprising against the Turks. On 21 August 1915, eleven Arabs were hung in Beirut's main square for sedition against the state. Another hanging, in what was subsequently to become known as Martyr's Square, occurred on 6 May 1916, when fourteen men, including both Christian and Muslim members of Beirut's elite, were hung for advocating Arab independence. Ironically, these hangings had a profound radicalizing effect on the city, with many now openly advocating Arab independence. Famine broke out, and during 1917 the dead lay in the gutters; starvation may have killed hundreds of thousands in Syria during the war. Staff of the American Red Cross provided assistance as best they could in the city prior to its capture by Allied troops on 8 October 1918. Importantly, the flag of Amir Faysal had been raised in the city on 3 October, proclaiming its allegiance to the concept of Arab sovereignty and ending 400 years of Ottoman rule.

By 1920 the destroyed Ottoman Empire had been carved up into mandates for the French and British. Based on the Sykes-Picot Agreement (a 1916 secret deal between Great Britain and France to divide the Levant between them after the war), France ended up with control over northern Syria and used military force to end the nascent Arab kingdom of Amir Faysal. France carved out two territories from its new mandate: there was Syria, but France then annexed Beirut, Tripoli, the Bekaa Valley, and the area south of Mount Lebanon to the old core of Mount Lebanon to create a new, Greater Lebanon on September 1920. Soon after, the French designated Beirut as the capital of the Lebanese Republic.

The new Mandatory Authority placed special attention on the renovation and development of Beirut. As the general headquarters for the French Mandate, the city became a showpiece of French accomplishment and its *mission civilisatrice*. The French reconstructed the harbor, tripled the number of hospitals, and restored confidence in the market for the merchants. In a few years' time, Beirut was back on its feet. The census of 1929 showed that between 1921 and 1929, hotels increased from 35 to 62, restaurants from 21 to 32, insurance companies from 26 to 45, lawyers from 86 to 111, doctors from 164 to 239, and engineers from 13 to 57, just to mention a few sectors. A new business district was built adjacent to the harbor. A district for the parliament was also built in what became known as the Place de l'Etoile. There was a real estate boom in the city and more electric power and street lighting. Radio Orient was founded as a modern communication center, linking the capital with Paris and New York. In 1929 the Beirut Airport was built, and in 1932 the Saint George Hotel was opened as a shining symbol of the French Mandate's interest in infrastructural promotion.

During this period, the population of Beirut doubled. The Sunni, Maronite, and Greek Orthodox populations all grew by more than 50 percent, while the Shi'i and Druze communities in the city tripled. Into this mix was added 28,000 Armenians and Syriacs, most fleeing from Turkey.

On 22 November 1943, Lebanon gained its independence, and Beirut became the capital of a free, independent Lebanon. However, the city did not experience a great change in fortune. Both Beirut and Lebanon were having economic difficulties because of World War II. In 1946, however, the last French soldier evacuated Lebanese soil, and the Lebanese were left on their own to figure out their own future. Administrative reforms were urgently needed from the incoming government to create a competent civil service and to introduce economic reforms.

Yet regional circumstances and Lebanese laissez-faire were enough to boost the economy in the country and to pave the way for a long period of economic prosperity. Ironically, the creation of Israel in 1948 and the disappearance of Palestine meant that Haifa Harbor, taken over by Israel, was boycotted by the Arab countries, which helped Beirut Harbor prosper. The development of oil production in the Gulf increased the income of the Gulf elite, who saved their money in Lebanese banks and traveled to Beirut to enjoy the open lifestyle. The separation of entwined Syrian-Lebanese customs into two states made Lebanon freer to decide its own financial and export-import package.

Moreover, that great asset of Lebanon, its human capital and their entrepreneurial spirit, led to the new state having a laissez-faire economic policy, which helped the Lebanese economy grow dramatically. Soon Beirut became the center for regional business in banking services and harbor traffic, which helped to spur growth in its accommodation facilities, intellectual freedom, and exotic, extravagant nightlife. Unfortunately, Beirut also became a depressed world of rural immigrants and Palestinian refugees disconnected from the growing wealth and development of the city; a "belt of misery" began to encircle the downtown, with the poor and unemployed living in shantytowns on the city's outskirts.

In 1961 the Phoenicia Hotel opened in the Ain Mraysseh area of the city, close to the well-known Saint Georges and Le Normandy. A hotel area was thus created along the seafront, and soon many other four-star hotels were constructed. Hamra Street became the trendy cinema area, with numerous theaters showing all the latest releases from Beirut, Cairo, and Hollywood.

Between 1950 and 1975, Beirut remained the primary center of Arabic media, with 27 regular newspapers published in Arabic and French and more than 760 different publications in many languages. In 1959 Lebanese television went on the air, making it the first commercial television station in the Arab world. This provided a new impetus to local filmmakers: the television series. Between 1960 and 1970, the main Arabic television programs in the Middle East were series produced in Beirut by Lebanese producers. Coproduced Egyptian movies still dominated the regional market, but there were a number of impressive Lebanese movies, like those produced in the city by Rahbani, Gabardian, and Nasri. Beirut women and their fashion and freedom became role models for Middle Eastern women, especially after the election of Miss Lebanon, Gorgina Rizk, as Miss Universe in 1970.

Thus, for most of the period between 1950 and the 1970s, Beirut embodied a phenomenon unique in the Arab world—the coexistence of different religions, philosophies, languages, and denominations. The city became known as the "Paris of the East," attracting Arab money and causes, intellectuals and opportunists, artists and prostitutes, intelligence agencies and revolutionaries. Beirut became the democratic liberal capital of the Middle East, while other Arab cites were constrained by socialist and Communist trends. Beirut, with its Swiss model of banking secrecy and extensive banking sector, was regarded as a safe haven for wealthy Arabs, especially Syrians and Egyptians. The city was the business center of the Arab world but also an intersection of international interest in the region as well as a center for the Soviet and U.S. struggle for cold war supremacy.

All this openness and mixing meant that Beirut was also the center of extreme regional political turmoil. Domestic politics were caught up in regional and global dynamics, and vice versa. In 1958, for example, regional tension reflected within the Lebanese system meant that it looked as if a leftist coup was imminent. President Shamoun asked for U.S. support, and on 15 July U.S. Marines landed on the beaches of Beirut and remained there until October; the domestic crisis calmed down, and the people of Beirut went about making money.

More significant was the role of Palestinians within the political space of Lebanon. More than 100,000 Palestinian refugees poured into Lebanon during *al-Naqba* (the disaster) of 1948–1949. By 1968 six cramped Palestinian camps housing more than 25,000 refugees were scattered throughout the city, both in the south around the airport and along the northern routes. By the beginning of the 1970s, after Black September in Jordan, Palestinian fighters established themselves in the Palestinian refugee camps throughout Lebanon and began using Lebanese territory as a base for military activities against Israel. Israeli attacks on Palestinian and Lebanese targets caught everyone up in a spiral of violence; in fact, Israeli commandos often operated with impunity within Beirut, attacking the airport in December 1968 and destroying thirteen civilian planes, kidnapping the occupants of cars driving along the Beirut Corniche, and killing Palestinian leaders in their downtown offices (1973). The increase in Palestinian military activity during the early 1970s split the people of Lebanon between those who supported their cause (mainly leftists) and those who opposed their presence in the country (mainly Christians). Thus, between 1970 and 1975, Beirut was boiling with ideas, ideologies, strikes, demonstrations, attacks, violence, and a sense of foreboding.

On 13 April 1975, the tension escalated into fighting in the capital. Palestinians and right-wing militias fought each other, with a quick escalation to general fighting throughout the country. Within Beirut both the city's inhabitants and its built environment suffered from the fighting. The greatest tragedy occurred on 17 September 1975, when downtown Beirut and the old suq of Beirut were almost entirely burnt to the ground. The British Bank, the Banco di Roma, and the harbor were looted at this time; the city center was closed off, and its businesses and ministries robbed, its civilian population forced out, and the buildings transformed into sandbagged military positions. The commercial, banking, and business functions in the heart of the city were stopped almost overnight; the hotels on its periphery were gutted, its port paralyzed, and its free zone looted. A scar, or no-man's-land, emerged through the heart of the city, dividing communities with barbed wire, sniper's nests, and neighborhood militias courting death.

Quickly, new place-names, unknown in the prewar days, began to be used and were adopted by the general public and the media. The most well-known are undoubtedly East Beirut and West Beirut, two opposing spatial units, conveniently separated by the Green Line. East Beirut was associated with all the territory occupied by the Lebanese Forces militia (a specific militia faction); it extended to the north, east, and south of West Beirut, while West Beirut could mean all the territory to the west or to the south of East Beirut. Moreover, with the development of the war, these new names became associated with political and religious affiliations. Therefore, East Beirut was considered predominantly Christian, a pro-West zone, while West Beirut was considered predominately Muslim, pro-Arab, and friendly to the Palestinians.

Some "ethnic cleansing" was conducted to destroy pockets of "others" and secure defensible enclaves. For example, between January 1976 and August 1976, when the camp fell, up to 30,000 Palestinians and Lebanese were under siege in the Tall al-Za'tar refugee camp in East Beirut. More than 3,000 people died, the rest were evicted, and the camp was razed, helping to secure a homogeneous Maronite heartland. In other examples, Kata'ib forces were evicted from the hotel district in West Beirut, and the Christians of Damur were sent packing by the National Movement. Despite these appearances of division, however, regular exchange, communication, and travel did exist, and many people lived within "the other side," confounding the superficial divisions and assumptions used by the international media.

With the destruction of the main downtown business and recreational center of Beirut, new replacement locations further into the northern or southern suburbs were found for the businesses: residential areas, considered "safe" in respect to the armaments used, were quickly transformed into commercial or business areas (Mar Elias, Mazraa, the Raouché suqs, Achrafiyyé, and Jdaidé-Antelias Kaslik-Jouniyé). Banking branches opened on both sides of the city; shopping malls were built on agricultural land. The center of many nearby villages or small towns, such as Broummana or Mansouriyye, became main areas, with shops offering goods for a sophisticated urban clientele.

The regular waves of migrants from South Lebanon moving toward the western sector of Beirut since 1978 is an example of dramatic transformations affecting the physical aspect of the city. Nearly all the rural areas in the general area of the city between Chiyah and the airport disappeared in a matter of months, replaced by housing on state- and privately owned land; all open spaces disappeared. Other refugees moved into the western part of the city proper, occupying all available residential spaces, such as abandoned or closed apartments. East Beirut, a middle- and higher-class residential area, was demographically more stable and turned more for its needs toward the newly emerging markets in the heart of Christian Mount Lebanon, while West Beirut sunk into the regional quagmire.

Israeli-Palestinian fighting continued in and around the civil war. Israel bombed targets in Beirut and off-loaded military equipment for its right-wing allies. Finally, on 5 June 1982, the Israeli Defense Forces invaded Lebanon to drive out the Palestine Liberation Organization (PLO) and reached the outskirts of Beirut in four days. They put the city under siege for nine weeks, pounding the city from the air and sea. Finally, in a negotiated settlement, PLO fighters and Chairman Arafat were forced to evacuate to Tunis.

This did not bring peace to Beirut, however; in fact, the situation worsened. The Israelis used the excuse of the Palestinian fighters' withdrawal to break their promise and to occupy the city, the first Arab capital to fall to Israeli occupation. Ariel Sharon, Israeli defense minister at the time, allowed Israel's Lebanese allies, the Phalange, to carry out a massacre of Palestinian civilians inside the Sabra and Shatila camps of Beirut (September 1982).

The Lebanese resistance to both the Israeli occupation and to the presence of American and French soldiers of the Multi-National Force supposedly monitoring the Israeli pullback in West Beirut was very fierce and led to the suicide bombings of the U.S. Marines headquarters in Ayn Mraisseh and of the French forces (October 1983). Soon after, the Americans and French withdrew, the Israelis pulled back to the south of the country, and the urban vacuum was filled by the Syrian army, which took up positions in West Beirut.

The mid-1980s in West Beirut was a time of chaos. Beirut was constantly on the front pages of world newspapers with the stories of Western hostage taking and plane hijacking. Lo-

cally, it was a period of intense internal conflict. Militias of West Beirut turned their guns on each other: Hizballah against the Amal movement; the Socialist Party against Amal. The militias deteriorated into neighborhood gangs of boys with guns, defending their city block from gangs the next street over.

Up until 1990, East Beirut had been relatively calmer than West Beirut, but it joined the chaos when the Lebanese Forces and the Lebanese army under the control of General Michel Aoun engaged in fierce street-to-street fighting. Finally facing up to the madness, Arab leaders called for an emergency rescue plan for Lebanon, and in the summer of 1990 Lebanese parliament members were called to Saudi Arabia to resolve the political conflict that had racked the country. The Taif Accord was born, with the benediction of the Arab world and the United States.

The cost of the fifteen years of war was very high and severely weakened Beirut's position in the region. The physical damage to the city was estimated to be at least $25 billion. The international airport, sewer systems, electrical grid, and telephone lines were all destroyed. The human costs were staggering; at least 170,000 people lost their lives in the fighting around the country, and 300,000 were injured. In 1975 nearly half of the country's population of 3 million lived in the city; by 1992 its population had dropped to an estimated 300,000.

The Lebanese population was facing a tremendous challenge: how to revive the country and, most importantly, how to revive Beirut, their beloved capital. The revival process kicked off in 1993 with a concert given by the Lebanese diva Fayruz in the rubble of the city. A second signal for the revival of Beirut was the appointment of the multimillionaire Rafik Hariri as prime minister. Hariri came to power with a key objective in mind: to rebuild Beirut. Not only did the Hariri government advance the resurrection of Beirut through legislation but much of the reconstruction was financed out of Hariri's own personal fortune. His company, Solidaire, carried out much of the work, and the country under his leadership borrowed heavily to get the city back up and running.

In a decade, Hariri rebuilt downtown Beirut, bringing back Lebanese Muslims and Christians to meet in the heart of Beirut, bringing back Arab and international investors, and bringing back Arab and international tourists. The project of rebuilding Beirut supervised by Solidaire, a private holding company, and the Council for Reconstruction and Development, a government entity, is scheduled to be completed by 2018. Rafik Hariri was assassinated on 14 February 2005, and he will always be remembered as a prominent pillar and builder of modern postwar Beirut. Fittingly, he is buried in Martyr's Square in the heart of the rebuilt city, some 200 yards from where he was killed.

Laury Haytayan

Further Readings

Buheiry, Marwan. *Beirut's Role in the Political Economy of the French Mandate: 1919–39.* Oxford: Centre for Lebanese Studies, 1986.

Gavin, Angus, and Ramez Maluf. *Beirut Reborn.* London: Wiley, 1996.

Hall, Linda Jones. *Roman Berytus: Beirut in Late Antiquity.* Rev. ed. London: Routledge, 2004.

Jidejian, Nina. *Beirut through the Ages.* Beirut: Librairie Orientale, 1997.

Khalaf, Samir. *Heart of Beirut: Reclaiming the Bourj.* London: Saqi Books, 2006.

Makdisi, Jean Said. *Beirut Fragments: A War Memoir.* London: Norton, 2003.

Ragette, Friedrich. *Beirut of Tomorrow: Planning for Reconstruction.* Syracuse, NY: Syracuse University Press, 1984.

Samman, Ghada. *Beirut '75: A Novel.* Little Rock: University of Arkansas Press, 1995.

Berbera
Population: 240,000 (2005 estimate)

Berbera is an ancient trading port on the northern coast of the Horn of Africa. Directly south across the Gulf of Aden from Yemen, Berbera is known as one of the hottest and most inhospitable cities in the world. Its strategic location astride the long-distance trading routes from the Red Sea to India has made it a central access point for the peoples of the Middle East and East Africa tapping into the world economy and for Europeans marching off into the interior. Known to the Egyptian pharaohs as a place to trade for myrrh and frankincense, its importance has, in the last 400 years, derived mainly from the millions of sheep, goats, cattle, and camels shipped by Somali merchants to Arabia and the Persian Gulf and from the sheepskins shipped to America. During the cold war, it started as a key Soviet naval base only to be taken over by the Americans, but today Berbera serves as the primary port for the breakaway entity of Somaliland and as an important lifeline for Ethiopian trade.

The port of Berbera (ancient Greek, *Malao*) is located on a small bay on the northwestern Somali coast 160 miles south of Aden and 130 miles southeast from the Bab al-Mandeb entrance to the Red Sea. The city lies less than 300 feet above sea level at the edge of a narrow coastal plain known as the Guban (burnt land) that runs for 150 miles parallel to the Gulf of Aden. At Berbera the steep escarpment is 4 miles distant, marking the beginning of the mountains and plateau of central Somalia. This coastal belt is very hot and arid, with little vegetation. The annual rainfall is less than one inch; from June to September the average afternoon temperatures are more than 100 degrees Fahrenheit. Heading up into the mountains, one finds within 40 miles a very pleasant zone where acacias, myrrh, aloes, gum, and other fragrant and fruit trees prosper. The mountains contain some coal, and there may be petroleum and gas in the region surrounding and offshore of the city. Ancient overland trade routes lead up from the port onto the plateau to Hargeysa and on to Harar in southern Ethiopia. South, the caravan route connects Berbera to Burko and the Haud region of the Ogaden. Along the coast to the west lies the ancient smaller port of Zayla and to the east the smaller port of Bosaso. As with the rest of the southern littoral of the Red Sea, sailors trying to reach Berbera must contend with dangerous coral reefs. In winter, winds in the Gulf of Aden may reach Force 7, making journeys by sail very dangerous.

For long periods in its history, Berbera, much like its larger twin, Aden, across the Gulf, was independent from its hinterland and deeply connected into the Indian Ocean world. It served as a central node linking the Ethiopian highlands, Arabia, Yemen and the Persian Gulf with India and long-distance trade. This was the case in 2300 BC, when the coast around Berbera and the products available from the plateau may have been the land of Punt known to ancient Egyptians. In the *Periplus Maris Erythraei* (*Circumnavigation of the Erythraean Sea*), written over two millennia later, the Greeks knew what is now modern Berbera as Malao, a place where myrrh, frankincense, other spices, and Indian copal could be acquired for importation into Arabia and Egypt. For millennia little was known of the interior behind Berbera, other than that it was a source for such products desired by the Egyptian, Greek, and Roman empires. Early in the first millennium AD, the coastal sites were under Aksumite control.

In the centuries after the Greek era, various waves of immigrants from southern Arabia moved across the Gulf of Aden and invaded the highlands, intermarrying with the indigenous inhabitants, the Gallas or Kushites. What became the Somali people is the result of this intermingling of communities across 1,000 years. A first immigrant wave may have occurred as early as 100 BC. The next wave came with the expansion of Islam starting in the seventh century when Muslim emigrants from Yemen founded an Arab sultanate with its capital at Zayla. A city called Berbera to the east of Zayla first appears in Chinese references before AD 863. These sources stress the importance of camel, sheep, and cattle herding to the people in Berbera's hinterland, while the port's trade in amber, ivory, slaves, myrrh, frankincense, and ostrich feathers was of keen interest to the Chinese chroniclers. The authors make particular reference to the mountain range that marks the boundary of Berbera's coastal plain.

In the hinterland, another major wave of the Somali people started in the tenth century. Two great clans—the Daarood Somali and the Isaaq Somali—led the migration of these nomadic pastoralists across the plateau from north to south. The latter, with their pastoralist lifestyle, settled in the arid areas of the northwest after the tenth century and used Berbera as their key regional trading fair and access point for mercantile interaction. The northern Somali appear to have had no market towns, with Berbera serving this role.

The rise of the Somali peoples as a regional political force began with the appearance of the Muslim State of Adal, founded after the ninth century. By the 1300s, the expansionist Adal has absorbed most of the Horn of Africa, including the trading city of Berbera. Berbera as a renewed and now Somali-dominated town dates from this period; the site of the city does appear to have moved slightly west over the centuries, with the original location to the east of the current harbor. The city absorbed an older village known as Bandar Abbas, and the new site houses three tombs of *sayyids* (Muslim saints) that legend says were founders of the city.

To medieval Arab writers, the people of the area were called Berber or Berberi, and the Gulf of Aden was known in Arabic as *Bahr Berbera* (the Berbera Sea) or *al-Khalidj al-Berberi* (the Gulf of the Berberi). Ibn Said (d. 1286) is the first to mention the name *Berbera* in Arabic. References of the time support the picture of Berbera as a key trading site, often making reference to a strong type of mat (*husur*), imported from Berbera, that was used as the packing material for shipment of goods from Aden to India. Ibn Battuta, in his visit to Zayla early in the fourteenth century, records that the inhabitants of the region followed the Shafi school of Islam, which they still do today.

The Adal state continued to expand and threaten its neighbors. In this context, the first use of the name *Somali* is found in an Ethiopic hymn, ca. 1400, which talks about an Ethiopian victory over these attackers. By the 1600s, Adal threatened the very existence of Christian Abyssinia. Under Imam Ahmad Ibrahim al-Ghazi (1506–1543), known in the West as Ahmed Gran, forces moved into the highlands but were repulsed by an alliance of Abyssinian and Portuguese armies. In a reversal of fortunes, Abyssinian and Portuguese armies sacked Berbera in 1518.

The Ottomans were invited into the area to help the Adal, and they used this excuse to occupy Massawa and the region in 1557. By the seventeenth century, their suzerainty over Berbera was acknowledged, but local power was exercised through various rulers, including for a time the Sharifs of Makkah.

Over the next 400 years, Berbera's life revolved around the annual trade fair that started in late October or early November and lasted until March. During this period, the city's size and population mushroomed as temporary huts were established to accommodate all the traders, merchants, sailors, and camel drivers looking to trade. Large caravans would arrive from Harar with 3,000 to 5,000 camels three or more times during the season. Traders from Muscat, Surat, Mocha, or Malucca would come by sea to exchange goods for regional produces, in particular the excellent sheep, which were renowned not for their wool but for their taste. Livestock was a crucial export to all the neighboring seaports in the Red Sea. British agents from Aden, visiting the fair in 1840, noted

other key exports from Berbera as coffee, gum arabic, myrrh, ivory, ostrich feathers, civet, wax, butter, hides, goats, and sheepskins. The influx of so many people in temporary housing led to the vicious spread of disease; by the end of each season, the huge cemetery outside of town had grown considerably.

The city's situation began to change dramatically with the projection of European naval power into the Indian Ocean. Particularly as India became more closely linked into the British Crown after 1800, the global geostrategic significance of the Bab al-Mandeb, and its key gateway dyad, Aden and Berbera, became much clearer. Interest in and knowledge of Berbera and of its hinterland rose dramatically. Europeans began to map the coast after 1802; the first map of Zayla appeared in 1810, although until 1825 Berbera remained a port rarely visited or known to Europeans. Throughout Europe there was a fascination with the "forbidden city" of Harar, the hinterland terminus for trade with Berbera, which had a reputation as a city closed to Europeans.

The incident of the trading ship the *Mary Ann* did serve to increase European interest and exposure to Berbera. In 1825 the *Mary Ann,* from India, was anchored off Berbera, seeking to trade. Local captains saw its appearance as a threat to their livelihood and evidently cut the ship adrift at night. When it drifted ashore, the ship was plundered and burnt, and some of the crew members were killed. A local shaykh saved the captain and the remnant of the crew. The Indian navy responded by sending a gunship that same year to blockade the Berbera trade fair until an indemnity was paid. Over the next few years, a naval ship continued to return to threaten the merchants of Berbera with violence unless a substantial sum was paid. The last visit, during late 1833, lasted a number of months, and the journal of one of the ship's officials, Frederick Forbes, gives the first full description of regular life in Berbera and of this application of gunboat diplomacy. Among other comments, Forbes records a game of cricket played by the sailors on the beach—the first cricket match ever played in Berbera.

Other European visitors of the time described Berbera as a poverty-stricken collection of huts with a population that cycled between 8,000 during the summer to more than 40,000 during the monsoon, when it attracted vessels from throughout the Indian Ocean world. Full of visitors, Berbera was a vibrant and crucial node in the regional trading regime, and landlord brokers, supported by local tribal elites, made the system work. The brokers would charge up to 20 percent of the value of all transactions as a form of protection payment; with these funds, local actors came to control the overland trade from Berbera into the hinterland, and foreigners were forced to deal with them as equals in Berbera. Caravans would arrive from Harar, full of goods and up to 500 slaves; following their arrival, for the next two days, the city would be abuzz with furious selling.

The explorer Richard Burton decided to visit the closed city of Harar and set out from Berbera in 1854. The description of Berbera contained in the account of his adventures, *First Footsteps in East Africa* (1856), is extremely Orientalist and patronizing, talking about the docility of the Somali and their "respect" for British power. The docile Somali in Berbera were not so welcoming in 1855 when he returned to the city to set out to discover the source of the Nile: his camp was attacked just outside the city, and Burton received a spear through his cheek, which forced him to return to England. Despite this, on through the late 1800s, numerous Europeans organized their expeditions in Berbera and then headed off to explore the hinterland of the Horn of Africa or the Nile.

In an attempt to safeguard its trade routes in a period of expanding European interest, the East India Company (EIC) established a coaling station at Aden in 1839. This brought the Indian navy and its needs into direct contact with Berbera. In particular, the navy required food for the ships that called at Aden. Quickly, Berbera became the major entrepôt for livestock raised on the western Somalia highlands and supplied across the Gulf of Aden to feed the ships calling at Aden and the community that grew around that port (see also "Aden"). The sheep trade from the interior became big business; the traders, however, were careful to provide only castrated rams so that Aden could not start its own Somali sheepherds. British political agents in Aden often visited Berbera to procure food for Aden, and arrangements were concluded with local tribal chiefs to supply cattle. Such preferential supply agreements led to security arrangements, which gradually affected the political landscape and the economy around Berbera. The first British-Somali treaty was signed in 1827, and in 1840 Britain signed a treaty with the governor of Zayla that granted harboring rights in Berbera for vessels of the East India Company. Subsequently, the EIC agent in Aden argued in 1849 that the British should occupy Berbera and restore the region to its former position as a "cultivated garden."

Competition among the ports along the coast for the increasing business with the Europeans changed local politics. The failing Zayla and the rising Berbera competed for long-distance trade connections. Sometimes local leaders were central to this competition. An example is Haji Shirmarke Ali Salih (d. 1861), who rescued the survivors of the *Mary Ann* in 1825 and went on to be an agent of the British. As the political boss of the coast, Ali Salih served as governor of Zayla for the Ottomans in the 1840s, conducted *sulha* (mediation) among the Habr Awal clan competing for control of the Berbera port, and facilitated Burton's trip to Harar. While serving the Ottomans in Zayla, he sought to shift the Harar caravan route away from Berbera to Zayla, opposed aspects of British policy, and juggled the various pressures that were threatening the autonomy of the cities of the coast.

It was not just the Europeans who were interested in Berbera. Ottoman claims to Berbera dated back to the 1500s and their defense of the Red Sea in the face of the Portuguese threat. But during the period from the late 1500s until the mid-1800s, direct rule had usually been managed by local elites under nominal Ottoman suzerainty. But with the Ottomans as the "sick man of Europe," and the Europeans translating their economic presence throughout the Middle East into military control, local powers also harbored thoughts of expansion. In particular, the Egyptians under Muhammad Ali began an imperial phase, using the umbrella of the Ottoman claims. During the 1870s, Khedive Ismail pushed Egyptian power both by land down the Nile and by sea further and further along the southern littoral of the Red Sea. The Egyptians projected their power past the Bab al-Mandeb at the end of the 1860s and raised the Ottoman flag in Berbera in 1870. Between 1874 and 1875, Egypt occupied Tajura, Berbera, and Harar; obtained a *firman* (declaration of rights) from Istanbul in which Zayla became Egyptian; and secured British recognition for its control as far as Cape Garadafuri. Britain was unhappy with this development but gradually came to see it as useful in its struggle with the French and Italians, who were also establishing treaties with local tribes along the Somali coast.

The Egyptian occupation of Berbera was short-lived, however. With the Mahdist uprising in the Sudan in 1884–1885, Egypt was forced to abandon its claims on the Somali coast, and it withdrew its troops from the city in 1884. Caught up in a global contest for colonies and geostrategic position, Britain could not afford to allow a vacuum to open up across from Aden along the new routes offered by the Suez Canal. As soon as the Egyptian troops withdrew, a British officer with a handful of police and *sepoys* (local soldiers) disembarked in Berbera and took control. The cities of Zayla and Bulhar were also occupied, and treaties were signed with six local shaykhs to protect them and to respect their independence. A vice-consul was assigned to keep order and to control the trade in the port (see also "Djibouti City").

In 1887 Britain, France, and Italy declared formal protectorates over their respective zones in Somalia, and each recognized the others' role and rights. British Somaliland came to enclose 68,000 square miles and a population of 300,000. This was Britain's first protectorate in East Africa, soon to be followed by Zanzibar, Nyasaland, Uganda, and East Africa (see also "Zanzibar").

During the next seventy-three years, Berbera, as the key city in British Somaliland, suffered greatly from neglect, distortion of its economy, and conflict. The British were unable to extract much revenue from the protectorate and thus were annually pumping monies from the Imperial Treasury into the budget. As a result, the bureaucrats in London fought any proposed allocation and were able to limit any developmental inputs into the entity. By the beginning of World War II, there were still no mines, railways, schools, or human capital development in the protectorate. In fact, to many British elites,

British Somaliland was a poor excuse for a colony and should have been abandoned. Winston Churchill made this point when he visited Berbera in 1907. As undersecretary of state, he recommended that the protectorate be abandoned, since it was unproductive, inhospitable, the people were hostile to the occupation, and the governor's residence was "unfit for a decent English dog."

Berbera did prosper as the key entrepôt for the protectorate and in fact served the whole region. As the city grew, trade was diverted from the Italian-controlled northeast to Berbera, and the port served southern Abyssinia as well. Aden became almost totally dependent on animal meat supplied via Berbera. Hides and skins were shipped to Aden as well for European and American middlemen who sought Somali sheepskins. The Somalis imported, via Berbera, guns, cotton cloth from India, and rice, as well as dates from Basrah, to supplement their diet of meat and milk. The British enlarged the harbor and provided greater security for caravans traveling throughout the region, and merchants from the Arab world and from India came to live in the city to broker livestock. The infrastructure of the city began to expand from its traditional coral limestone and began to show evidence of modern concrete brick. Somalis from the region left the country via the port to become miners, sailors, traders, or cattle dealers, both regionally as well as globally. Europeans transited the city as they set out to hunt lions, rhinoceros, and antelope.

One reason the British considered abandoning Somaliland was the resistance of the inhabitants. In particular, from 1895 until 1921, there was an Islamic insurgency led by Mullah Muhammad bin Abdullah Hassan ("the Mad Mullah"). Mullah Hassan, originally from the southeast of the protectorate, converted to the new purist Salihiyah sect in Aden in the early 1890s. Upon his return to the country in 1895, he established a Qur'anic school in Berbera. As he lived in the city, the story goes that he was offended by the attitudes and demeanor of the European community living there, in particular by the way they sought to undermine Somali cultural and religious traditions. It all came to a head one day when he was asked by a British customs official in the port to pay customs duty: Mullah Hassan responded by asking the officer if he had paid customs duty when he and the British occupation authorities had landed in Berbera: "Who gave you permission to enter our country?" Subsequently, Hassan left for the Ogaden, declared a jihad against the British, and raised an army of 3,000 tribesmen. He was able over the next six years to cut trade to Berbera to such an extent that the port ground to a halt, drive the British into defensive positions in the port cities, evade or defeat four expeditionary forces, attack Ethiopia, and force the British to consider abandoning the protectorate. In 1913 his forces even raided Berbera itself. In one communication to the British in Berbera, he wrote: "If you wish peace, go away from my country to your own. If you wish war, stay where you are."

From 1908 to 1914, the British virtually abandoned the interior of the country to Mullah Hassan. They did supply friendly tribes with weapons, which were used against other tribes in internecine warfare. One estimate is that as many as one-third of the male population of the interior died during this period of conflict. With the advent of World War I, Berbera's significance as a geostrategic site reconfirmed the British in their occupation of the northern Somali coast, and so, after 1918 they took the offensive and moved against the mullah's forces. In January 1920, they attacked his final stronghold, using airplanes for the first time in Somalia. Reportedly, the mullah's supporters, who had no idea such things existed, thought they were the chariots of Allah coming to take the mullah to paradise. Although this Somali resistance leader escaped, he finally died on the run in the Ogaden in 1921.

The expense of putting down the uprising forced the British to look for other ways to finance the protectorate. The revenues they were collecting from the commerce and transit in the port of Berbera did not even pay for the salaries of the police in the city. The city's harbor was silted up, and all stores had to be unloaded into lighters; the British could not afford to refit the harbor. As a result they tried direct taxation, which failed because of resistance. They imposed a poll tax on non-Somalis in Berbera; in response the merchants left the city. They also tried increasing customs duties at the port; trading responded by moving outside the port via illegal smuggling. They also sought to attract foreign direct investment. The Abyssinian Corporation was granted a license to build a railway from Berbera to Jigjiga in Ethiopia via Hargeysa. Mismanagement and corruption drained the funds, and the corporation disappeared. Concessions for oil exploration around Berbera were granted; no oil was found. Add to this severe droughts, particularly the one between 1927 and 1929, and the British government once again seriously considered abandoning the protectorate. They even sought to get the Italians or Ethiopians to absorb the hinterland, while they would keep Berbera.

Ironically, it was Mussolini who saved Berbera for the British. As the Italian Fascists expanded their control over Italian Somaliland in the 1930s, and went to war with Ethiopia and won, Berbera profited. The Italians pursued a modernist agenda and linked Berbera to southern Ethiopia via a modern road. This dramatically increased the traffic through the port and gave jobs to local workers. The increased demand for labor in the city attracted the rural unemployed, and the city began to boom. Modernization in Italian-controlled Mogadishu made the total lack of development in British Somaliland look pitiful. In an embarrassed response, the British began to put funds into Berbera; there was a surge of investment, and the administration committed to opening the first school (see also "Mogadishu").

All this new attention came to a halt with the outbreak of World War II. In August 1940, Italian troops marched north and captured British Somaliland. The British evacuated Berbera and retreated to Aden. Seven months later, an Anglo-Ethiopian coalition dislodged the Italians and went on to capture Italian Somaliland. For the rest of the war, the British governed both areas from Berbera.

In 1960 British Somaliland became independent. Four days later, when Italian Somaliland became independent, the two were united to form the independent Republic of Somalia, with its capital in Mogadishu. In the referendum to affirm a United Republic of Somalia, the people of Berbera rejected the merger, although it went ahead anyway.

Berbera thus lost, in the unification, its status as a capital city and its primacy. Yet the city continued to play a role in the history of the north. Because of its close dyadic link to the growing city of Hargeysa in the highlands, 117 miles away, Berbera remained the preeminent gateway for the region to the world. Soon after independence and union, Somalia signed an agreement with the Soviets to research and design a new port of Berbera. The results of their improvements were significant, and export trade via the port continued to increase during the 1970s. Berbera became crucial to the changing food demands of the Gulf States during the oil revenue boom of the 1970s, and Berbera supplied Saudi Arabia with hundreds of thousands of animals for meat. The city built extensive holding pens for livestock. There were periods, however, sometimes lasting up to a year, where the Saudis would impose a ban on cattle from Berbera, citing health reasons. Such bans hurt the city, but during such periods, trade patterns would shift to North Yemen, and livestock would illegally find their way across the Yemeni-Saudi border.

The geostrategic role of the city did not disappear and in fact was greatly enhanced during the cold war. As the Soviet navy expanded its global presence in the 1970s, Berbera became a natural point for concentration. In February 1972, the Soviets and the Somalis agreed to place a communication station at Berbera, and this was quickly followed by a Soviet dry dock. Berbera became one of the largest Soviet naval bases in the world and a security city. In 1977, however, the Soviets moved their dry dock from Berbera to Aden, and they abandoned their relationship with the Somalis for one with the new radical government in Ethiopia; in effect, Berbera was traded for Assab and Massawa. In reaction, a new American-Somali alliance, signed in 1980 and backed up by $40 million in aid, meant that Berbera was not empty for long; the American navy took over the former Soviet base in Berbera, moving into the communication facilities, the 150-bed hospital, and the housing (the Americans termed it "little Moscow") built to serve Soviet technicians. The city's

population continued to grow, reaching approximately 70,000 in 1985.

Resistance in the north against the domination and centralization from Mogadishu began in and around Berbera in 1981, when the Somali National Movement (SNM) was formed by a group of businessmen, religious leaders, intellectuals, and former army officers from the Isaaq clan. As the central government moved against the Isaaq, Berbera became caught up in the struggle. The situation intensified during the late 1980s, when the SNM adopted active rebellion; as many as 100,000 people may have died throughout the north in the subsequent fighting. Summary executions, aerial bombardment, and ground attacks by government troops occurred throughout the region and did not spare the city. The destruction of market centers and water wells and the mining of transport routes meant that Berbera suffered, and refugees moved to the city. The use of light weapons in the city proliferated, while unrest and lawlessness in the refugee camps was rampant. There were freelance bandits in control of the intercity roads, and forced enlistment into the SNM brought many males into the conflict. The security for women deteriorated dramatically, although they played a major role in keeping the linkages within society intact. Infectious diseases spread through the refugee camps, and a famine hit the north.

The fighting meant that the Berbera port was closed for animal exports from mid-1988 to 1991. During the early 1980s, the port had exported 1.2 million animals per year (95 percent of all Somali sheep and goat exports, 50 percent of all camel exports, and 60 percent of all cattle exports) as the key node in an extensive regional trading network. The more than 900 livestock merchants in Berbera were some of the most important entrepreneurs in the country, and Berbera dominated the livestock export market. The top merchants each exported between 50,000 and 150,000 animals per year. The closure of Berbera shut down the whole market and system for animal exchange and export, leading to a general collapse of the local market for meat as well.

President Barre was overthrown in January 1991, and a separate but unofficially recognized entity of Somaliland reemerged in the northwest. In May 1991, a congress of elders declared their independence from the rest of Somalia, with Hargeysa as the capital. Berbera serves as the entity's key outlet to the world.

The unilateral declaration of independence did not lead to an end of violence in the city, however. Fighting between subclans of the Isaaq broke out in Berbera in March 1992 and continued until October 1992. The city was unsafe at night, and traveling between the city and the Somaliland capital was also impossible. Significantly, a grassroots-negotiated peace agreement was signed in October 1992 that over the next decade led to a resurgence of the city. The decaying and destroyed infrastructure in the port was slowly

Aerial view of the port of Berbera. (Yann Arthus-Bertrand/Corbis)

replaced and improved, port management was professionalized, and the Berbera Livestock Merchants Association imposed order among the traders in the port.

After 1992, under United Nations (UN) Resolution 704 and Operation Restore Hope, the UN Operation in Somalia (UNOSOM) sought to restore the failed Somali state and support those in most desperate need. This involvement has been in the south of Somalia and has not really touched the breakaway north nor the city of Berbera.

Outside institutions have been involved in contributing developmental and humanitarian assistance to the city. In 1998 the UN Conference on Trade and Development (UNCTAD), recognizing the city's huge potential for maritime trade, initiated a project to revitalize Berbera, destroyed by years of civil war. UNCTAD trained Berbera port workers, managers, cargo handlers, and statistical clerks to strengthen a port that welcomed more than 800 ships in 1996. There were also investments in infrastructure. The result has been a sharp increase in cargo volume via Berbera. Much of this trade has been with the Persian Gulf via Dubai, Berbera's most important trading partner (see also "Dubai"). The Somaliland administration is looking to the future and working

to make Berbera a successful regional competitor in the ongoing "port wars."

As of 2004, the city is actually progressing despite all the indecision about the national future. One reason is the remittances flowing from Somalis abroad. Another is the health of the informal and medium-scale enterprise sector. Third, livestock and crop production are occurring, and there is limited but dependable public service provision in the city. Exports and imports via the port are twice the level they were before the war in 1988. Electrical goods landed at Berbera make their way to Mogadishu and are even smuggled into neighboring countries. Within the city, a political and security space has been created, and an economic one as well. Courts, municipal government, and support for enterprise are functioning. Berbera businesses have made loans to the administration to support the printing and distribution of new currency and to further demobilization. Few refugees remain outside the region, and the UN High Commissioner for Refugees (UNHCR) has helped most return to the city. As of 2004, there has been renewed interest in exploration for oil on- and offshore around Berbera, with American, Canadian, French, and Israeli investors seeking to get the rights in the event of gas or oil production, which would be purchased by China or Argentina.

The city's infrastructure has drastically improved during the last decade. There is an airport, water is supplied by pipe from the southern mountains, the port has an oil terminal run by the firm Total, and the European Union (EU) has sponsored the reconstruction of the Hargeysa-Berbera road and its extension on to Togwechale, on the Ethiopian border. This Berbera Corridor Infrastructure Program is part of an EU strategy to relieve the congestion in Djibouti so that needed humanitarian and developmental supplies can reach the regional hinterland. Ethiopia is receiving food shipments via the Berbera port, and Addis Ababa has made a strategic decision to use Djibouti and Berbera for its major imports rather than renew its links via Massawa. In 2004 the Berbera cement factory was reopened after being closed for ten years; the goal is to supply cement to all countries in the Horn of Africa.

The city is also in the forefront of social change. The mayor of Berbera has thrown the weight of the city behind a women's grassroots movement to get women circumcisers to give up their "weapons" of female genital mutilation. The campaign by local doctors, shaykhs, and the mayor to get the practice stopped is now taking off, and in Berbera a number of circumcisers have publicly sworn on the Qur'an to stop practicing.

Bruce Stanley

Further Readings

Ahmed, Ali Jimale. *The Invention of Somalia.* Lawrenceville, NJ: Red Sea Press, 1995.

Drysdale, John. *What Ever Happened to Somalia?* 2d ed. London: Haan Publishing, 2002.

Lewis, I. M. *A Modern History of the Somali.* 4th ed. Oxford: James Currey, 2002.

Menkhaus, Ken. *Somalia: State Collapse and the Threat of Terrorism.* London: Routledge, 2005.

Mockler, Anthony. *Haile Selassie's War.* 2d ed. London: C. Hurst, 2003.

Rebuilding Somaliland: Issues and Possibilities. Lawrenceville, NJ: Red Sea Press, 2005.

Bukhara
Population: 300,000 (2005 estimate)

The fabled city of Bukhara is one of the key central Asian oasis cities. Known throughout history primarily as a trading city on the Silk Road, it is also remembered for its role in the "great game" between the Russian and British empires of the nineteenth century. A city of many mosques and religious schools, Bukhara is renowned for its Muslim educational institutions and as a pilgrimage site, particularly for followers of the Sufi tradition. It is also one of the best-preserved medieval cities in the Middle East, beckoning tourists to Uzbekistan with its ancient suq and magnificent buildings.

Like its neighbor Samarkand, it is an edge city for the Middle East, translating cultures, ideas, products, and technology both into the region as well as outward to the Turkic steppes and to western China. Perhaps it is still possible to agree with George Gurjieff when he said, "If you really want to find the secrets of Islam, you will find them in Bukhara."

The Uzbek city of Bukhara (Uzbek, *Bukhoro* or *Bokhara*) lies 164 miles west of Samarkand and 333 miles southwest from the capital of Uzbekistan, Tashkent. It sits in the Delta of the Zaravshan River, which flows from Tajikistan, more than 300 miles away, and ends south of the city. The city lies in the basin of the Bukharan oasis, surrounded by the Kyzylkum Desert. Its hinterland is rich in mineral resources and stone, oil, and natural gas, and the river has, from the beginning of the city's history, provided irrigation for agricultural production.

The city's tell lies under the current medieval core, so it has been hard to date the earliest habitation on the site. However, there are enough indications to suggest a founding during the late second millennium BC; this would fit with the rise of an oasis urban culture throughout the Zaravshan basin around 1800 BC. Some traditions suggest that the name derives from the word *vihara*, which means *monastery* in Sanskrit; archaeologists argue that the city grew up around the site of an ancient fire temple. This would explain why the *Avesta,* the holy book of Zoroastrians, mentions the region of Bukhara as the second of seven good lands that is holy and created by the one god, Ahura Mazda.

It is unclear how extensive the city was during the next millennium, but it is clear that Bukhara was involved in long-distance trade. The remains of silk fabric dating from before 1000 BC suggest a thriving trade with China, and precious stones from the Zaravshan Valley appear in Mesopotamia. The first recorded indication of the existence of a city is when the city was captured by Cyrus the Great, the Persian king around 550 BC; the subjugation of the city-region was recorded by Darius I in 519 BC on the famous monument at Bihisutun (Behistun) in southern Iran. Bukhara was clearly a thriving city at the time, but not as significant as Maracanda (Samarkand), which became the seat of the Sogdian satrapy under the Achaemenid dynasty (559–330 BC). The city was part of the "King's Way" of cities of the Achaemenids, linking Mesopotamia with central Asia.

Alexander the Great captured the city in 329 BC in his sweep into Transoxania. Subsequently, Bukhara was incorporated into numerous empires in association with its traditionally more dominant neighbor Samarkand, making up part of a city system in the Zaravshan basin. Bukhara was, however, important enough to have its own mint in the first century AD, and records in China note ambassadors from the city paying tribute at the Tang Court in AD 618 and AD 626.

It is not until the Arab conquest of AD 709 that Bukhara began to move up the ranks in the city hierarchy and became more prominent. Qutayba b. Muslim conquered the city and founded its first mosque. This institution is often cited as the beginning of the rise of the city to its status as a center for central Asian Islamic scholarship.

The appearance of the Arabs meant that Bukhara was caught in a "great game" between the expanding Chinese Tang dynasty and the expanding Muslim Empire. In AD 751, the Chinese were defeated, however, by the Abbasids at the Battle of Talas, opening the way for Muslim dominance in the region. Under Abbasid rule in the region (AD 750–874), Bukhara and Samarkand were crucial outposts in Mawarannahr, as the Arabs called the land between the two rivers (also known as Turan). The city was an edge city, significant in the proselytizing of the nomads beyond the Syrdarya and in building trade links to the north and west (see also "Samarkand").

The Samanids (AD 862–999), a local Muslim dynasty, took power in Mawarannahr after AD 862 and designated Bukhara as their capital in AD 874. Under the Samanids, the city's commercial and cultural preeminence were unsurpassed in central Asia. The Arab geographer al-Maqdisi reports that Bukhara in the tenth century exported soft fabrics, prayer rugs, copper lamps, grease, sheepskins, and oil for anointing the head, but there is "nothing to equal the meats of Bukhara, and a kind of melon they have called ash-shaq." The Bukharan Jewish community participated in this renaissance; they were involved in winemaking in the region and in financing long-distance trade to China.

One of the most interesting cultural products of this period is the *History of Bukhara,* written by Abu Bakr Narshaki around AD 943 as a present to the Samanid ruler Ibn Nasr. The book is the earliest existing city history of what was to become a popular genre throughout Persian communities. The version that exists today was translated into Persian around 1128, abridged by another author around 1178 and presented to the ruler of Bukhara, and then supplemented by material relating to the Mongol conquest of Bukhara in AD 1220. The book is unique because it recites pre-Islamic events in Bukhara's history, discusses the city's founding, and is chronological and historical in its presentation of the city rather than being a recitation of visitors and religious figures. The book contains many stories of the early introduction of Islam into Bukhara, including the statement that the people of Bukhara had to be bribed to come to Friday prayers and that they prostrated to commands in Sogdian rather than Arabic.

Ibn Sina (Latin, *Avicenna*), the great Arab physician and scholar, was born near Bukhara (AD 980–1037). Growing up within a failing Samanid state, Ibn Sina was a child prodigy: he studied medicine and theology at the age of thirteen and was treating patients and rulers at the age of eighteen. He wrote his first book when he was twenty-one based on his research in the Royal Library in Bukhara. When the Saminid dynasty was overthrown by the Turkish Qarakhanids in 999, Ibn Sina took his medical and scholarly skills to other local dynasties in Transoxania, finally ending up in central Iran in Hamadan. After serving as the vizier in the Buyid administration, he died in Esfahan. This author of the monumental *al-Qanun al-Tibb* (*Canon of Medicine*), the preeminent medical guide of the medieval period, is quoted as saying, "I prefer a short life with width to a narrow one with length."

During this period, Bukhara was ruled by a class or group of individuals within the city called *sadr* or *sudur* (prominent men). These men held hereditary positions, collected taxes for faraway rulers, and often conducted their own municipal foreign policy. In Bukhara struggles between these leaders, the regional military leaders, and local artisans would sometimes break out, and alliances would change and shift as power dictated. A number of times, mobs would rise up and kill a particular sadr or family, accusing them of inordinate power or corruption.

The city was caught up in the dramatic changes brought on by the Mongol invasions. Genghis Khan himself led the attack on Bukhara early in 1220. After it fell, the 20,000 troops defending Bukhara were killed, and many of the city's inhabitants were forced to march on to Samarkand, where they were forced to attack that city. It may have been in Bukhara that the conqueror is reported to have said to its inhabitants, "I am God's punishment on you for your sins." Showing his contempt for Islam, Genghis also rode his horse into the great mosque and fed him from the containers for the Qur'an. He had the city destroyed, although the great Kalyan Minaret, dating from 1127, was saved.

Bukhara was also the home of the powerful Naqshbandi Sufi order. This order was founded in 1317 by a mystic born in Bukhara, Baha ad-Din al-Naqshband Bukhari, who had visionary revelations and became a famed Islamic scholar by the age of twenty. He was venerated in his lifetime, and pilgrims came to see him, seek his advice, and study with him. Al-Naqshband died in 1388 and was buried next to his school. Very quickly he was adopted as a saint and viewed as the protector of craftsmen and artists (naturally, given the prevalence of this trade in Bukhara), and pilgrimage to his grave was accorded the same significance as performing the hajj. Subsequent amirs and governors of Bukhara contributed to his school and funded new buildings, turning the area around his school and mausoleum into a religious complex and the largest center of Islamic learning in central Asia. Under the Soviets, the complex was converted into a museum for atheism, and no pilgrimage was allowed. In 1989, however, the tomb and complex were reopened and restored, and today pilgrims come from throughout Islam to visit his grave.

The Naqshbandi Sufi order is one of the oldest traditional Sufi orders, with its followers located throughout central Asia,

Turkey, and China. It initially spread through missionary activity along the trade routes. The order has traditionally concentrated on the inner spiritual life of the believer but also encouraged engagement in politics. Thus, its followers have often been able to promote the order through their substantial positions of power and influence. Today the Naqshbandiyya, as his followers are called, are the leading Sufi order in the world and are experiencing a period of growth, particularly in the United States and Britain.

The city revived under the rule of Temür, who located his capital 160 miles away in Samarkand. The Timurids financed numerous building projects in Bukhara and also promoted the city as a center for textiles and dying. The Persian Jewish community was central to this production; it was said you could tell the Bukharan Jews anywhere in central Asia by their dyed hands.

The Timurid dynasty and Bukhara fell to the Uzbek Shaybanids in 1506. From the mid-1500s, the city became the capital of their state, the Khanate of Bukhara. The Uzbeks were nomadic Turkic-Mongol tribes who invaded Transoxania from Siberia beginning in the late fifteenth century. The new Uzbek rulers interspersed with the local Tajiks, and a mutual interaction of Turkic and Persian culture emerged in the city, although the urban population remained primarily Tajik, and the language of the court was Tajik. *Uzbek* as a term came to be used to refer to the descendants of the latest nomadic wave, while *Tajik* referred to nontribal sedentary peoples of the area, whether Iranian or Turkic speaking. During the history of the khanate, Uzbeks were the ruling nobility, and Tajiks made up the bureaucracy and merchant class.

In December 1557, an English trader by the name of Anthony Jenkinson arrived in Bukhara at the head of a caravan sponsored by the English Muscovy Company. Arriving by way of the Caspian, Jenkinson wrote a journal that is a wonderful window on the new Khanate of Bukhara. He confirms that the most dangerous road in the region of the time was the caravan track from Mashhad to Bukhara, and he reports the fate of one caravan "destroyed" ten days out from Bukhara. The Balkh-to-Bukhara segment, however, was relatively easy and safe and could be completed in about two weeks, he reports. He also confirms the role of Indian merchants selling cotton textiles in the city; Bukhara was the primary destination for caravans from Mughul India. In return, Bukhara sent many products, including raw silk, once a year to Multan.

The Bukharan khans became patrons of the arts, builders of great monuments, supporters of seminaries and mosques, and Sunni orthodox promoters. It is during this period that the last of the great monuments in Bukhara were constructed. The city remained a key center for Sufi pilgrimage and a training site for Judeo-Persian poets, including Yusuf Yehudi (1688–1755).

The next 400 years were a time of division, constant encroachment by larger neighbors, and gradual loss of territory under direct control from Bukhara. The Shaybanids were overthrown by the Janid dynasty in 1599, and Bukhara lost much of its territory and grandeur under their rule. However, thanks to the connections of the Indian merchants in the city, Bukhara remained crucial from 1600 to the 1700s to the evolving Russian trade with the Punjab. It was Bukhara that turned out to be most significant to the growing international links with Siberia; Bukharan merchants had extended trade links into Siberia from the time of the grandson of Genghis Khan, Shaiban, and by the late 1600s they had built this trade into a significant commodity circuit. Black sables and fox were supplied by their communities of merchants to Iran, and they brought cottons and textiles to Siberia. They were also crucial traders to Iran: rhubarb and lapis lazuli are often mentioned, as are herbs delivered to Moscow.

A new dynasty, the Manghits, emerged after 1785 and ruled as independent amirs in what became known as the amirate of Bukhara. The amirate was small but remained significant in the economic life of central Asia, keeping ties with all the other Islamic empires and powers of the time. For example, Bukharan lambskins were prized by the Qajar elite, and Bukharan caravans would meet other caravans from Isfahan and Shiraz in Yazd to trade.

By this time, trade in Bukhara was dominated by Hindu merchants, who were spread all along the trade routes between Iran, the Volga, and central Asia. Approximately 300 well-capitalized and networked Indian merchants were the key to the city's trade with Esfahan through their brethren located in the capital of the Qajars and their compatriots in Moscow, Astrakan, and Multan. The Khanate of Bukhara received Indian cotton during this period; Jenkinson talks about Indian merchants in Bukhara selling "white cloth," and this was a crucial component of Indian trade to Iran and central Asia. One report suggests that in 1812, customs was the second-largest source of revenue for Bukhara: a key transshipment site for trade working its way into Iran or Turan.

The Khanate of Bukhara was particularly notable throughout the region, however, for its trade in slaves. Hindu Indian slaves, along with Shi'i Iranians and Christian Russians, were available in the slave market in Bukhara, as were Turkish and Persian females. Slaves were sent by rulers to each other as gifts; in the 1500s the Mughal emperor sent the khan of Bukhara four slaves skilled in masonry. Captured caravans and their merchant owners would be sold in Bukhara, and the Uzbek rulers operated much of their agricultural production on the back of Indian slaves. Jenkinson talks about the vitality of the Bukharan slave market during his visit; it is clear this market continues well into the 1800s. It appears that after the 1700s, the Hindu trade dries up, but estimates from 1821 suggest that between 20,000 and 40,000 Iranian slaves were working in Bukhara at the time; one report from the 1860s proposes 20,000 slaves in Bukhara.

The slave trade was one indication of the way Bukhara was caught up in the wider world system of the time. There are other indications, too. For example, by the late 1600s, agriculturalists in Bukhara were cultivating the new crop of tobacco and selling it throughout the region. Other consignments in caravans from Bukhara to Multan included, in addition to slaves, leather, sable (transshipped from Muscovy and Siberia), Bactrian camels (capable of carrying 50 percent more than Asian types), rubies, hunting birds, dogs, and paper. But the sale of horses was the most important to India and the foundation of a very important relationship. The trade in central Asian ponies to India and China dates back to about 200 BC. By the time of Ibn Battuta's visit along the Silk Road (early fourteenth century), Bukhara, in combination with other cities in central Asia, may have been exporting more than 100,000 horses per year to India. Droves of up to 6,000 horses would be conducted at a time, and this happened well into the 1770s. Some merchants could make more than 2,500 percent on their original investment; the horse trade was certainly of greater value overall than any European trade conducted by the European companies with India at the time.

Bukhara became caught up in the growing struggle between the Russian and British empires in the nineteenth century as they sought to promote their trade in this region. Russian expansion after Peter the Great had led to Russian military power following economic trade into the region. A "great game" of spies, traders, and secret agreements began in central Asia as the two empires sought power and influence with local elites. Bukhara dramatically reemerged into the light of the modern world in 1842, when newspapers around the globe carried the story of the capturing, sentencing, and beheading of two British military officers in the central square of the city. The officers had been held in the infamous "Bug Pit," made to dig their own graves, and publicly beheaded in front of the Ark (the amir's palace). The nationalist response among the British public produced a fact-finding mission led by one Reverend Wolff, who published his *Narrative of a Mission to Bukhara* in 1845.

Tashkent's conquest by the Russians in 1860 meant that Bukhara was essentially the last independent area between Russia and the British in India. By 1865 talks between Russia and the amirate on outstanding issues of tension had failed, and Bukharans sought to build a regional anti-Russian coalition to face the inevitable. The war party encouraged the amir to act, and he arrested all Russians in Bukhara. In response, the Russian army attacked the amirate.

In three battles, the Bukharan army was completely defeated, and on 18 June 1868 the amir signed a peace treaty that meant the loss of Samarkand and the opening up of the country to Russian merchants. The protectorate became more integrated into the Russian Empire with the opening of the Central Asian Railway in 1887 and the establishment of

Russia's customs border in 1895. The amirs were officially independent rulers, but they were often in court in Saint Petersburg and depended on the Russian military for aid in maintaining their thrones.

The opening up of Bukhara caused by the railroads and the migration of Russians and European Jews to the city produced tremendous change. Local textile manufacturing, labor intensive and built around protected markets, failed to compete with new manufactured imports. Land practices and laws began to change, and many people were put out of work. Despite these problems, Bukhara still relied on much of its old commerce and roles in the region. One British report suggests that even in the late 1800s, gold sifted from the Zaravshan River east of Bukhara still earned the city £30,000 per year. Hindu bankers and merchants in Bukhara were still the core financers in the early 1800s.

Bukhara entered the twentieth century with a built environment that was essentially still an ancient medieval city, a virtual museum of monuments. Little was done to preserve these monuments, but little was done to destroy them either. Thus, by the 1960s, when a major attempt began to catalog and restore the old city of Bukhara, much from the twelfth through the nineteenth centuries remained. Within the ancient walls, there are more than 500 important buildings or monuments, including 24 madrasas, 48 mosques, 14 caravansaries, 9 mausoleums, 4 trading buildings, the ancient Ark citadel, and many hammams. The restoration and reuse of these buildings has won major awards, including the Aga Khan Award for Architecture in 1995.

With the fall of the czars in 1917, Bukhara became just one more battleground for a range of factions fighting for political control. White Russians, the Red Army, Russian Soviets, and Muslim associations all struggled for control of the city, and fighting was intense. In 1919 a "Republic of Pan-Bukhara" was declared only to be replaced in October 1920 by a Bukharan People's Soviet Republic when the last amir, Sayid Alim Khan, was overthrown.

From 1922 to 1923, a rebellion against the Soviets took place, temporarily re-creating the amirate of Bukhara. Interestingly, this rebellion was led by Enver Pasha (1882–1922), one of the "Young Turks" who had earlier overthrown the Ottoman sultan. Enver Pasha came to Bukhara hoping to lead a Pan-Turkic movement; he tried to link with the Basmachi movement in Russian Turkestan to advance the aims of both groups. A constitution for a Republic of Turkestan was published in April 1922, but the Red Army captured Bukhara in the summer of 1922, the rebellion was suppressed, Enver Pasha was killed in August, and the Bukharan Soviet Socialist Republic was declared in 1924. In 1925 Stalin reorganized central Asia, and the Uzbek Soviet Socialist Republic was created, with Bukhara as its capital. The capital was soon shifted to Tashkent, however, and Bukhara lost its administrative role.

Under the Soviets, the city's economy, transport, and development were highly centralized and determined from Moscow. The city became a site for food production and light industry. Karakul lamb, for example, was exploited for its meat and its fleece. Traditional handicrafts such as gold embroidery and metalworking were promoted. The city was expanded by the location of a teacher training institute, a theater, and a museum. In the 1950s, the discovery of natural gas encouraged significant growth in the city-region.

With the fall of the Soviet Empire, Bukhara prospered under the new republic of Uzbekistan declared in 1991. The city was able to open up to new influences, tourists, and ideas. The city was promoted as a key tourist site by the state, it received significant international development assistance, and local civil society evolved with encouragement from international nongovernmental organizations (NGOs). The centralized authoritarian structures remain in clear control, however, and significant human rights violations have again led to growing isolation of the regime and the withdrawl of international donors.

Bruce Stanley

Further Readings

Becker, Seymour. *Russia's Protectorates in Central Asia: Bukhara and Khiva, 1865–1924.* London: Routledge, 2004.

Burton, Audrey. *Bukharan Jews: Ancient and Modern.* London: Jewish Historical Society of England, 1997.

Burton, Audrey. *The Bukharans: A Dynastic, Diplomatic and Commercial History, 1550–1702.* Surrey, UK: Cruzon, 1997.

Frye, Richard. *Bukhara: The Medieval Achievement.* Costa Mesa, CA: Mazda, 1996.

Hayes, J. R. *The Genius of Arab Civilization.* Oxford: Phaidon, 1976.

Buraimi and Al-Ain

Population: Buraimi, 60,000; Al-Ain, 300,000 (2005 estimate)

Buraimi (in Oman) and Al-Ain (in the United Arab Emirates) form two separate legal cities within the same oasis, set on the edge of the Empty Quarter in the southeastern Arabian Peninsula. Although urban sprawl has blurred the distinctions, settlements in the oasis long consisted of a number of small distinct villages. These existed before the national boundaries were suggested, and the oasis was originally known by one name, Tuwwam (also reported as Tawam and Tu'am). Known historically for its date farming and role as an oasis on the caravan track north from Oman to the coast of the Gulf, this conurbation today is a thriving and expanding urban settlement deep in the heart of the desert, boasting a university, industry, and a vibrant commercial life.

The Tuwwam Oasis lies some 100 miles southeast of Dubai and 70 miles west of the Gulf of Oman coast. It is nes-

tled up against the base of Jebal Hafiz, and there are hot springs and natural springs throughout the area. The oasis has long been cultivated by the traditional *falaj* irrigation system, which allowed the area to support considerable agriculture activity. Date farming was the mainstay of the area, organized into plantations. The economy also benefited from some trade, as the oasis's location made it a natural stopping point for those traveling from the inland side of the Omani Western Hajar to the coast of the Arabian Gulf.

Early historical accounts of the area are patchy, although there is some archaeological indication of Bronze Age habitation (2000 BC). Evidence suggests that the oasis was inhabited by Islamic times, although there is some debate about the extent of settlement prior to that period. Later historical accounts make clear that a large oasis in desolate surroundings was a desirable possession. In the early part of the nineteenth century, the Muscat-based sultan of Oman governed Buraimi (see also "Muscat"). His claim to the area was largely based on ties to the Naimi, one of the main tribes living there. But other tribes saw the attraction of the oasis, and in the 1800s members of the Bani Yas moved south from what is now the Abu Dhabi coast to Buraimi, investing some of their pearling wealth in land there.

In addition, for the first several decades of the 1800s, tribal leaders from what is now Saudi Arabia made various attempts to supplant the authority of the Muscat-based sultans. In part the Saudi dalliance was encouraged by a lack of strong control from Muscat, which was plagued by shortages of money and challenges from other tribal leaders. The Wahhabis may have also found a warmer welcome in Buraimi, where the majority of residents were Sunni, than in towns of the Omani heartland, which were largely Ibadhi. The first real Wahhabi push came at the beginning of the nineteenth century, with the Wahhabis gaining power in Buraimi. Accounts of the next fifty or so years vary, but it is clear that the Wahhabis played a role in the area, collecting *zakat* (tithes) at intervals and ruling over the local Naimi tribe for at least part of the period. In the mid-1860s, the Wahhabis were in control of the oasis, and the then Omani sultan, Thuwaini bin Said, sought to evict them. He was, however, murdered before his plans could be carried out. In the Wahhabi heartland of the Najd, meanwhile, internal political problems reduced interest in Buraimi, and although accounts vary somewhat, by the 1870s the Wahhabis had left, with power in the oasis in the hands of local tribesmen. Travelers over the next several decades reported that the Wahhabis continued to try to influence the area, but many suggested that locals were generally in charge of their own affairs.

Interest in the area was rekindled after the Second World War, as Western oil companies intensified their search for crude oil deposits in the Arabian Peninsula. By that time, two clear spheres of influence had developed in the oasis. Some villages fell under the control of Oman, and others were governed by an Abu Dhabi–appointed shaykh, Zayid bin Sultan, better known now as the head of the United Arab Emirates (UAE). The Saudi government nevertheless sought to establish sovereignty over the oasis, and in 1952 its forces occupied one village on the Omani side of the oasis, installing a tax collector there. The Omani sultan, Saeed bin Taimur, and the imam in Nizwa joined their forces with the aim of evicting the occupiers, but the British dissuaded them. Eventually, however, British patience with the Saudis wore thin, and in 1955 British officers led a band of local troops from Oman and what is now the United Arab Emirates and evicted the interlopers.

The eventual border settlement between Abu Dhabi and Oman formalized existing arrangements. Three villages—Buraimi, Hamasa, and Sara—were allocated to Oman, while another six—Al-Ain, Mataradh, Jimi, Muwaiqih, Hilli, and Qattara—were deemed to be part of Abu Dhabi. Members of the Naimi tribe were heavily represented in the villages that went to Oman, while the Bani Yas were resident in large numbers in those settlements deemed to be part of Abu Dhabi.

Although such distinctions are important on a national level, amicability has been the key to making the oasis work on a local level. The oasis today is one of the main land routes between the UAE and Oman, and the two towns are in many ways effectively one unit. There are no border controls between the two, and townspeople cross regularly from one country to the other for work and living. Major highways connect the conurbation to both coasts and allow visitors to flow in during the winter season. Although date palms are still tended, the economy has diversified. World-class hotels have been built, and Oman has established an industrial estate on its side of the oasis. Al-Ain is, however, the second-largest city in Abu Dhabi and notably more prosperous than its twin. In addition to a regional airport and various industrial ventures, Al-Ain is home to the University of the United Arab Emirates. It also hosts the largest zoo in the UAE, an Olympic-sized ice rink, a large dairy herd, a Coca-Cola bottling plant, and a major theme park. With increased prosperity has come population growth, and estimates now put the total number of residents in the oasis at close to 400,000. The majority of the residents of Al-Ain are, as in the rest of Abu Dhabi, expatriates. Buraimi, the smaller side of the oasis, has a majority of Omani nationals.

Angie Turner

Further Readings

Ghareeb, Edmund, and Ibrahim al-Abed, eds. *Perspectives on the United Arab Emirates.* London: Trident Press, 1997.

Henderson, Edward. *This Strange Eventful History.* London: Quartet Books, 1988.

Landen, Robert Geran. *Oman since 1856.* Princeton: Princeton University Press, 1967.

Walker, Julian. *Tyro on the Trucial Coast.* Durham, NC: Memoir Club, 1999.

Bursa
Population: 1,467,000 (2005 estimate)

Bursa, a bustling city in western Anatolia close to the Sea of Marmara, is most famous as the first capital of the nascent Ottoman Empire. Long before this, however, Bursa was a key city in antiquity, a health spa for the Roman elite attracted to its hot mineral springs, and "Green Bursa," with its gardens and agricultural products. Today this fourth-largest city in Turkey is the country's "Motor City," manufacturing a large percentage of the motor vehicles and spare parts produced in the country.

The city of Bursa (Greek, *Prousa;* Turkish, *Brusa* or *Burusa*), lying 60 miles southeast of Istanbul and 250 miles west of Ankara, is sited up on the slopes of Uludag, a mountain that rises more than 8,000 feet some 15 miles inland from the southeast coast of the Sea of Marmara. The contemporary city is divided by three ravines that run down the side of the mountain, splitting the city into three districts now connected by bridges. It is from the mountain that the natural sulfur springs flow, giving the city in ancient times a reputation as a site for healing. Because there are significant water resources in the region, the plains below the city are a significant agricultural production area, and the city became famous for its agricultural products, particularly fruit, such as "Bursa peaches." In addition, contained within its 22 square miles are numerous gardens and parks, hence the name "Green Bursa" in Turkish literature.

The site was probably first occupied around 2700 BC, and by 560 BC the famous Croesus, king of Lydia, controlled the area. After 556 BC, the Persians were the authority until 334 BC, when Alexander the Great captured the springs. It was not until 190 BC, however, that a permanent town was established at the foot of the mountain, legend has it, by Prusias II, the king of Bithynia, and named after him. Over the next 200 years, the city was part of a network of other city-states in western Anatolia that fought among themselves for local domination.

Intercity rivalry kept the area quite violent; in 80 BC, Julius Caesar was in the area and attacked by pirates. Finally, in 74 BC, the last king of Bithynia, Nicomedes III, bequeathed his kingdom, along with Bursa, to Rome, and the city became part of the province of Pontus. One of the more well-known regional governors was Pliny the Younger, who was appointed to root out municipal corruption and died there in AD 113. It is clear from his record that the region needed a strong hand; the problems of violent intercity rivalries still plagued the people, and there was poor city administration in Bursa.

Rich Romans loved their spa baths, and Bursa was an excellent site to take the hot springs. Consequently, the city became a resort town, with numerous baths dotted near each other. Today the area of the springs, called Cekirge, still attracts visitors to the hot mineral waters. One hammam, the Eski Kaplica (Old Spring), sits on the site of Roman and Byzantine baths. Other baths were built by various notables during the Ottoman period: for example, the Yeni Kaplica (New Spring) was built by Rustem Pasa, the grand vizier (chief administrator) of Sulayman the Magnificent, in 1552.

Under the Byzantines, the city prospered. Reportedly, even in AD 450, substantially after the empire's conversion to Christianity, there were still feasts to Artemis in the gardens around Bursa. It was a garrison city, with imperial guards stationed there in AD 562. The emperor Justinian (527–565), employing the ancient technique of transferring populations, settled Goths in the city; Justinian II (685–711) did the same thing with Slavs in 688. But it was Justinian I's decision to steal the foundations of sericulture from the Chinese that had the most long-term effect on the city's development. By the mid-sixth century, Bursa was becoming famous as a key site for silk textile manufacturing, a reputation it preserves until today. This development led to its role as a key entrepôt at the end of the Silk Road and the subsequent trade and exchange linkages that spun off from this. But why was Bursa a good location for the beginnings of silk manufacturing? Perhaps it was the interest of Justinian's wife, Empress Theodora (500–547), in the baths of Bursa that influenced his decision, or it was Justinian's palace in the gardens.

From the beginning of the next millennium, Turkish tribes migrated into the Bursa area, adding a new strand to the city's complexity. Bursa was conquered by the Seljuqs after 1071 but then was retaken by the Byzantines. It was the nascent Ottoman *beylik* (principality) of Osman Bey (1258–1326) in northwest Anatolia that returned the city to greatness; they captured the city in 1326 after a long siege and made it their first capital. As a result, Bursa holds a special place in Ottoman history as their founding city. It is here that the original members of the dynasty are buried, and it is here that the first "Bursa Period" (1299–1437) of Ottoman monumental architecture can be viewed. Although there are older Seljuq-style mosques still within the city, it is the evolving Ottoman style evident in the Yesil Mosque (Green Mosque, 1419) or the Yesil Turbi (Green Tomb) and madrasa (1424), all decorated with turquoise tiles, that epitomize the early Ottoman architecture that would culminate in the dramatic skyline of Istanbul.

Within the Hisar Quarter of the city lies the *turbes* (mausoleums) of Osman, the founder of the empire, and of his son Orhan Gazi, who captured Bursa. The current buildings in the complex are not the original, however, since these were destroyed in an earthquake in 1855. The city is also the site of mosques built by later sultans, including the Mosque of Sultan Murat II (1426) and his tomb.

The famous Muslim traveler Ibn Battuta visited Bursa in the fall of 1331, only five years after it was captured by the Ottomans. His *Rihla* (*Book of Travels*, stories of his visit) details how he met Orhan himself and was given substantial gifts by the ruler. Ibn Battuta was impressed by the sultan and found Bursa an enjoyable city. As in other cities in Anatolia, Ibn Battuta found housing and fellowship with a *fityan* association in Bursa. A fityan was something like a young men's association, combining civic pride, sports, religious training, and vocational support, under the direction of a mature civic figure (*akhi*). Their members prided themselves on their hospitality toward visitors. Although these associations had only been introduced into the city after its capture, Ibn Battuta was impressed by the members' religiosity and nobility.

As the capital of an expanding empire, Bursa quickly grew in beauty and power. It became the site of the first Ottoman mint; by 1380 it had eight hospitals serving all the religious communities in the city (Sunni, Christian, Jewish); new madrasas (religious colleges) were endowed by the ruling elite. Of particular importance were the new khans, or caravansaries, built to support the expanding long-distance trade. Within the city of today, the khans of the fourteenth and fifteenth centuries remain the center of the suq and of the tourist areas. Koza Khan (1490) is the traditional site for the end of the Silk Road. It was here that raw silk cocoons were brought to be bought and sold. In the 1400s, two key silk routes ended in Bursa: Tabriz, Erzum, and Tokat; and Makkah, Damascus, Aleppo, Konya, and Kutahya.

Most of the silk imported from Iran to Bursa was used by the local industry in the Bursa area. In 1502 it was recorded that there were 1,000 looms in Bursa, all in the private hands of the Muslim bourgeoisie. As a result, the city was very prosperous, with most of its citizens very wealthy, except, of course, the workers in the factories. These were slaves, but they often were freed and became entrepreneurs themselves. Bursa was particularly known for the brocades and gold velvets made in these factories. These luxury silks were exported to Europe, Egypt, and even back to Iran. The biggest consumer, however, was the Ottoman court. The city also produced light silks and taffeta, most of which was exported.

Spices also made their way by sea to the terminus at Bursa; the city was linked through Antalya to Alexandria, receiving spices, sugar, dyes, soap, and perfumes. The Genoese residing in Bursa then moved the spices into the European city system. By the fifteenth century, the city was also an entrepôt for cotton textiles from western Anatolia, which were transshipped to Rumeli and on to eastern Europe. Merchants were always leaving the city with rice, iron, nuts, mohair, opium, and silks bound for the Black Sea, the Crimea, and through to Russia and Poland. The city was also an importer; in 1480 Indian merchants were in Bursa selling Indian cloth and goods, while the Florentines, Genoese, and Venetians imported wool cloth to exchange for silk. The result of all this trade produced a vibrant merchant elite, willing to spend their excess cash on slaves, real estate, and monumental architecture.

As the Ottoman Empire expanded eastward, there was competition with other empires for control over the eastern trade routes. Unfortunately, Sultan Bayezid I (1389–1402) thought he could deal with the upstart Temür and sought to grab control of the silk route to Tabriz (see also "Tabriz"). In response, Temür came to settle the score, appearing outside the gates of Bursa in 1402. Bayezid's army was defeated in the Battle of Ankara, and the captured sultan was taken to Samarkand in an iron cage (see also "Ankara" and "Samarkand").

The Ottoman recovery from the wrath of Temür was speedy, however, and the empire renewed its expansion westward. As a result, Bursa was abandoned as the capital in favor of Edirne, although Bursa remained the site for the crowning of the sultan. But when Constantinople was captured in 1453 and designated the capital of the empire, Bursa was relegated to second status, with some of its population ordered to migrate to Istanbul to repopulate that city (see also "Istanbul"). Bursa continued to serve as the headquarters for military campaigns into the east of the empire, it was the formal seat of a *wali* (governor), and it was officially listed as the third capital of the empire.

As the empire expanded to the east, it competed with the rising Safavid Empire for control of the trade routes beyond western Iran. After winning the Battle of Chaldiran (1514), the Ottomans enhanced their dominance of these routes, which contributed greatly to Bursa's development. However, other cities were competing for a slice of Bursa's trade. Aleppo, for example, had a hand in the silk trade, and Armenians shifted part of their activities from Bursa to Aleppo in the sixteenth century (see also "Aleppo"). This shift in Armenian networks was significant, since the Armenians in Esfahan, Aleppo, Izmir, and Bursa monopolized the silk trade into western Europe. The city was also known for its Jewish community, some of whom were also involved in financing the silk and commodity trade. Ultimately, it was Izmir, on the coast, that surged after 1620 and began to grab Bursa's business for itself (see also "Izmir").

The late 1500s till the end of the 1600s was a period of great population growth in the city; industrialization increased, also, but so did poverty and unemployment. As a result, the number of urban pious organizations increased along with the number of students attending madrasas and local Qur'anic schools. Subsequent student riots and the Celali (Jelali) uprisings that occurred in the city can be traced back to similar social and economic difficulties. The city suffered such widespread violence and gang warfare that "gated communities" for the wealthy were established to protect them from attack. The Janissaries (the sultan's professional military) burned the city in 1607 in response to resistance.

The city's cosmopolitan nature and high level of industrialization meant that Bursa became known during the 1600s both for the positive role and status of women in the community but also for its extensive level of prostitution.

By the mid-1600s, competition to Bursa's dominant position as producer of silk textiles and purveyor of raw silk began to emerge from the European states. Centuries of Venetian dominance of the silk trade from Bursa to the west were challenged by the English, who, over the next 100 years, almost trebled their demand for raw silk to feed their new looms. Newly mechanized looms in Flanders and Italy also demanded raw silk in the Bursa market, driving up prices for local producers. Gradually, by the end of the century, the Europeans began to leave Bursa, getting their raw silk from China and Iran around the Cape of Good Hope. Although an attempt was made to actually develop local silk production around Bursa, by the 1700s local producers had lost their export market, and ironically Bursa ended up importing "Bursa" silk textiles from western Europe for local sale.

The silk industry did fight back and attempted to modernize. Steam power was introduced into the city's silk production system in 1837, and this led to a temporary revival. These innovations were more than 100 years later than similar changes in Europe, however, and it was difficult for the city to maintain its production base. Yet the silk industry survived: in the early 1900s, the city hosted a training school for silk production (called the Silk School) containing 500 weaving looms that employed 2,000 people, and it was still shipping raw silk to Lyon. Under Atatürk, Bursa silk production was protected by the state, and large industrial investment in the city meant that by 1958 the city hosted 6,000 power looms for manufacturing artificial silk.

The decline of the silk trade for Bursa was, to some extent, made up for by a shift to the global opium trade. Until the late 1700s, opium production around the city was primarily for local consumption in a paste form and sold in Istanbul. However, under the growing demand from China, and encouragement from Britain, Armenian and Jewish merchants and moneylenders began to work with local Turkish and Greek farmers to expand the crop for export, with the result that production around Bursa expanded 300 percent in fifty years. Opium was shipped by camel through Syria to Suez, where it was conveyed on American and British ships. By 1830 Ottoman opium was meeting approximately 10 percent of China's demand. The trade was profitable, with a markup of 235 percent.

Opium from the Bursa area, because of its high morphine content, was also in high demand in London and in the United States for medicinal purposes. By 1850 opium from Anatolia to these countries was worth 10 percent of all agricultural exports from the region. From 1828 until 1839, the Ottoman government ran the opium trade as a monopoly, collecting substantial revenues for the governmental budget. Under British threat, however, the monopoly was ended, and Bursa became a free market for opium, where Russians, British, and American merchants bought the product for shipment to a global market. Production in the Bursa region continued to increase well into the twentieth century. Concurrent with the opium trade was inclusion of the city in the global tobacco circuit, with its hinterland producing the majority of Turkish tobacco produced for export.

The drug connection remains today. Bursa is now caught up in the global illegal drugs trade circuit. The "Balkan" route for drugs moves drugs from southeastern Turkey to, among other sites, the Bursa suburbs or the roofs of apartment buildings, where heroin is refined before shipment to the Balkans and Europe. Cannabis is also widely available in the city.

Bursa has long celebrated its ethnic and religious diversity and developed a reputation as a city of immigrants and exiles. Jews moved to the city in large numbers after the Ottoman conquest and quickly established a synagogue. The city took in more than 50,000 immigrants from the Balkan areas of the empire, which fell to the Russians in 1878. In the census of 1892, the population of the city was 76,000, with 5,000 Greeks, 7,500 Armenians, and 2,500 Jews as key minorities. The census recorded 36 factories, 49 khans, 165 mosques, 7 churches, 3 synagogues, 57 schools, and 27 madrasas. At this time, the city was the residence of both a Greek Orthodox and an Armenian Gregorian archbishop, an Armenian Roman Catholic bishop, and a Jewish rabbi. In the early 1900s, significant numbers of Ottoman ruling family members were "exiled" to Bursa to keep them out of the politics of the capital. Today the "Natasha" trade in trafficked women from Eastern Europe includes Bursa as a stop for its illegal trafficking.

During the Greco-Turkish War of 1921–1922, significant fighting took place around the city. Greek forces, provided with weapons by France and Britain, captured the city in early July 1920. Their advanced line lay nine miles east of the city, where they were stopped. Bursa was not retaken by the Turks until two years later.

Industrialization also meant that the city became Turkey's "Motor City." Because of the city's historical role in the caravan trade, by the early 1800s its industrial base included wooden carriage manufacturing. This meant that Bursa was famous for its expertise in both design and production of the wooden as well as metal aspects of coaches. Thus, a whole network of small shops for coppersmithing, lathe masters, leatherwork, and wooden coachwork evolved, although in the Ottoman Empire, carriages were only for women. With the end of World War I and the fall of the Ottoman dynasty, the new country of Turkey began to import motor vehicles from Europe and the United States. By the 1930s, Bursa's carriage industry had shifted to automobiles, converting imported pickup trucks to minibuses or producing spare parts for the more than fifty brands of motor vehicles available throughout the country. After 1952 the requirement of joint ventures to encourage local manufacturing meant that Bursa was a natural location for the industry; today Bursa is "Turkey's Detroit," producing more than 30 percent of the automobiles manufactured in the country, more than 25 percent of all its minibuses in its four automobile plants, and much of the automotive spare parts marketed worldwide.

The combination of the hot-baths industry and the cotton textile trade has meant that Bursa is known as the home of "Turkish towels," robes, and rugs. Just as the European aristocrats came to Bursa in the period before World War I to take the baths, tourists still come to the hammams, though today it is often after skiing on Uludag, one of the most popular winter sports resorts in the country.

Bursa has a long cultural history. The city is reputedly the home of Karagoz and Hacivat, central figures in Turkish folklore and culture. These shadow-puppet characters first achieved fame in Bursa, so the city hosts an annual International Karagoz (shadow play) Festival. Bursa was also home of the sixteenth-century literary figure Lami'i Chelebi, Ottoman poet, prose writer, and thinker. Chelebi was a member of the Sufi mystic order of the Naqshbandiyya who lived his life as a hermit.

The first modern theater outside of Istanbul, the Ahmet Vefik Pasha Theater, was built in 1879 and remains central to the city's cultural life. The city nurtured some of Turkey's leading singers (Zeki Muren and Muzeyyen Senar), was home to painters (Ibrahim Balaban), and was the setting for a number of well-known novels and poems. In particular, the poet Nazym Hikmet's poem *The Legend of the Independence War* is set in Bursa's prison. Part of Bursa's intellectual life is because of institutions of learning located in the city. The American Girls School was established in the late 1800s by American Protestant missionaries, the Isiklar Military High School was established in 1845 to train modern soldiers, and the Uludao University was established in 1970.

Bruce Stanley

Further Readings

Gerber, Haim. *Economy and Society in an Ottoman City: Bursa, 1600–1700.* Jerusalem: Hebrew University Press, 1988.

Kahveci, Erol, Nadir Sugar, and Theo Nicholas, eds. *Work and Occupation in Modern Turkey.* London: Mansell, 1996.

Lowry, Heath. *Ottoman Bursa in Travel Accounts.* Bloomington: Indiana University Turkish Studies Publications, 2003.

White, Jenny. *Money Makers vs. Relations: Women's Labor in Urban Turkey.* 2d ed. London: Routledge, 2004.

Byblos
Population: 30,000 (2300 BC estimate)

The ancient seaport city of Byblos, lying on the Mediterranean coast of Lebanon, was one of most powerful long-distance trading cities of the Bronze Age (3100–1200 BC). Important as a broker for goods between Egypt, Syria, Anatolia, and Mesopotamia, Byblos was the key entrepôt for the transshipment of papyrus, timber, linens, and metals to and from Egypt by sea. Historically, this Canaanite and Phoenician city was associated with the invention of the alphabet and with a 3,000- year history of cultic worship.

Byblos (Canaanite, *Gubla;* Greek, *Byblos;* Arabic, *Jubail*) lies twenty miles north of Beirut on the Lebanese Mediterranean coast. As with some of the Phoenician port cities based around a dual harbor system, there is a hilly promontory and spring, with a small natural harbor to the north and a larger bay and estuary to the south. Inland there is a very narrow coastal strip, which quickly gives way to impressive 6,561-foot-high Lebanese mountains. Byblos was essentially the "northern" Phoenician premier city, with only Arvad as the last outpost to the north. To the south of Byblos lay its key rivals for preeminence: Sidon and Tyre.

Archaeological excavations at Byblos indicate that the site has been continuously inhabited since at least 5000 BC. By 3000 BC, the city, then known as Gubla, had grown to become the key port city along the coast of Canaan, the area between the mouth of the Orontes in northern Syria and Gaza at the gates of Egypt. It is important to note that modern conventional use makes a distinction between the Canaanites and the Phoenicians. For more than 3,000 years, the people of the cities along the Syrian/Lebanese/Palestine coast, including Gubla, called themselves Canaanites and were also called Canaanites by the Egyptians and Assyrians. The more restrictive term *Phoenicians* is a much later Greek translation of Canaanites, and its use during Hellenic times has become standardized in the Western tradition, particularly to refer to the period after the beginning of the Iron Age (1200 BC) and to the people of the specific cities along the Lebanese/Palestine coast from Arvad to Akko, including Gubla. Equally, the name *Byblos* is the first-millennium BC Greek name for the city that supplied the Greek world with Egyptian papyrus, which was called *bublos* in Greek.

Byblos has always been an important cultic site, with a long history of religious worship. Findings from the site suggest that even in the Neolithic era, inhabitants worshiped a storm god. A first-millennium BC tradition has the god El building the city walls. Around 2800 BC, a massive temple to Baalat Gebal (the goddess of Gubla/Gebal) was built in the center of the city, and she was the patron for the city and protector of the royal family. Inscriptions and finds within the temple remains suggest a strong Egyptian cultural and religious influence.

Gradually, Phoenician cities evolved a dual religious hierarchy; for Byblos it was Baal and Baalat, and the center of the city hosted a massive temple for each. By Hellenic times, these had evolved into Adonis and Aphrodite. The temple system in Byblos was marked by ritual sacrifice, an emphasis on the yearly death and resurrection of Baal, an extensive temple priesthood and support staff, sacred prostitution, and echoes of many of its rituals continued well into the Roman and Christian eras. Interestingly, Byblos' cultic role continued when it became the site of one of the earliest Christian archbishoprics, with tradition suggesting that Mark the Evangelist was the first bishop here, appointed by Peter. Even today, the Orthodox administration for the area is called the Archdiocese of Byblos and Mount Lebanon.

From 3100 BC until 1200 BC, Byblos was the central city in Canaan and the major port on the Mediterranean. It held this position primarily because of the significance of its location between the two key civilizations of Mesopotamia and Egypt, making it a classic example of the trading city. The earliest indications of its brokerage role between these two power centers comes from third-millennium BC reports concerning cedar trees being shipped to Egypt to build palaces and temples; reports of convoys of forty ships carrying wood appear quite early. The return journey brought gold and ivory used in making other export luxury goods. Byblos also owes its early significance to local sources of copper.

Written records discovered within Canaan itself are quite sparse, compared to those about Canaanite cities found in Egypt, Mesopotamia, or Ugarit/Ebla. Thus, our knowledge of Byblos is drawn from a combination of local archaeological evidence and references found among the archives in these other sites. Local excavations indicate that during the Early Bronze Age (2800 BC), Byblos had massive city walls, incorporating an area of about seven acres. Nine royal tombs from this period were discovered during archaeological excavations, and they provide a picture of an advanced and wealthy society. Across subsequent centuries, Byblos, unlike other Canaanite coastal cities, controlled a significant area of the coast itself, and the city spread southward along the bay. Byblos's territory at one point extended as far south as the Dog River, near Beirut.

The Egyptian link was always the most crucial, and what the Egyptians wanted most from Byblos was cedar. The pharaoh Cheops' (2550 BC) burial barge was partly made of Lebanese cedar, and inscriptions from this period in Egypt mention "Byblos ships" transporting wood and pine oil for use in royal funerals. Egypt purchased ships made in Byblos. Reliefs in Memphis from the Fifth Dynasty (2480–2350 BC) show Canaanite princesses arriving to marry the pharaoh, accompanied by "Byblos ships." During much of this period, Byblos was a vassal of Egypt, with Egyptian government officials located in the city and the cultural and religious life of the city clearly influenced by Egypt. Byblos appears to have been a key naval base for the Egyptians, and its shipbuilding expertise was recognized throughout the region. A copper axehead lost by an Egyptian royal lumberjack crew ca. 2500 BC has been found near Byblos. Egyptian myths about paradise have the gates of heaven barred by large gates made of Byblos wood.

Between 2500 and 2300 BC, the archives at Ebla tell us, Byblos was the primate city in an extensive Canaanite city system (Arvad, Sarepta, Akhziv, Beirut, Tyre, and Sidon). As new cities emerged in the Syrian hinterland, and the Mesopotamian city-states evolved into the first great land empires, Byblos was well placed to trade precious metals, fabrics, cedarwood, and oils to and from Egypt. Trade primacy began to attract invasion as well: Sargon I (2334–2279 BC), the first great empire builder, claimed to have invaded as far as the "Cedar Forest and the Silver Mountain" to obtain wood supplies and precious metals, which he had floated down the Euphrates for his new capital at Akkad. Later Mesopotamian rulers were no different, desiring wood and silver from Byblos for the decoration of their palaces and temples.

Byblos shows signs of being destroyed between 2300 and 1900 BC, and it appears that there was a dramatic decrease in trading around the Mediterranean. This may have been caused by an invasion by the Amorites. Byblos quickly bounced back, however, and reclaimed its place as the key Egyptian entrepôt along the coast. The so-called Temple of the Obelisks at Byblos and the royal tombs date from this time (1900–1700 BC) and demonstrate a strong cultural influence by Egypt.

The city was captured by the Hyksos in 1720 BC but was able to retain its trade preeminence and flourished by trading with the Hyksos rulers of Egypt, themselves probably Canaanite. The revolution by the Egyptian native Seventeenth Dynasty against the Hyksos resulted in a subsequent campaign to capture all of Palestine and Syria. Tuthmosis III's victory at Megiddo in 1470 BC brought Egypt back into Byblos as ruler of the region, and the city returned to its place as a crucial broker in Egypt's long-distance trade networks.

In fact, Tuthmosis III legislated annual shipments of wood to Egypt and used the shipbuilding expertise of Byblos to construct a "fleet," subsequently transported overland, for the invasion of the cities along the Euphrates. It is from this period as well that "Asiatic copper" becomes a crucial import into Egypt and Byblos a major source of its supply. Byblos had its own local sources and had long had a smelting and manufacturing capacity. Now it became a purveyor for its patron of copper from further afield. Other strategic minerals, including tin, and luxury materials, such as lapis lazuli from Afghanistan, also appear on the exchange list required by Egypt.

For the rest of the Late Bronze Age (1550–1200 BC), Byblos remained central, adding a regional administrative role under the Egyptians to its existing economic linkages. Archaeological remains prove ties with cities as far away as Ur and Mycenae (see also "Ur"). Significant archives of correspondence from Canaanite kings to the Egyptian pharaohs have been discovered in al-Amarna, and their translations provide fascinating insight into the relations between patron and client. In more than seventy letters, the kings of Byblos, including King Rib-Addi, discuss their loyalty to the pharaoh and report their tributes of ships loaded with cedarwood. Byblos traders were clearly operating trading emporia in Egypt at the time; temples to Baal in Memphis appear to testify to their existence in that city at the time of Ramses II (1228 BC).

By 1100 BC, during the time of the Twentieth Dynasty, Egypt's power over Byblos had waned, but Byblos remained crucial for meeting Egypt's need for cedarwood. This thousand-year relationship was driven by a fundamental religious component on Egypt's part, and in return, gold and silver flowed to Byblos. The discovery of a unique document, the report of Wen-Amon, an Egyptian bureaucrat sent to Byblos around 1075 BC to retrieve cedarwood, offers tremendous insights into this relationship. Of particular usefulness is the discussion of the exchange of papyrus for cedarwood and the centrality of Byblos to this regional exchange. It is also interesting to read Wen-Amon's confrontation with pirates, who robbed him of the almost seven pounds of silver with which he was to pay for the cedarwood. According to the report, King Zakarbaal of Byblos possessed an extensive papyrus library of a historical and financial nature. Five hundred rolls of papyrus were requested by the king as part of the next shipment in order to build his collection.

It is not long after Wen-Amon's visit to Byblos that the city's extreme primacy in the Canaanite city system begins to wane. The rise of Tyre, political changes to the Syrian hinterland, and the appearance of the "Sea Peoples" along the Mediterranean coast all conspired to reduce Byblos to a less prominent position regionally. In fact, by 887 BC, Tyre was powerful enough that it was able to establish colonies close to Byblos to improve its own control over the trade with Syria and Mesopotamia (see also "Tyre"). However, Byblos continued to be an entrepôt playing an ongoing role in shipbuilding; the metals and timber trade; the manufacture of textiles, garments, and luxury goods; and the papyrus trade.

Byblos' centrality made it an attractive target for the emergent Assyrian Empire. In 876 BC, Asurnasirpal II received tribute from Byblos (and other cities) at the mouth of the Orontes. The tribute list, along with subsequent Assyrian campaigns in the region, clearly shows that the Assyrians sought two things from Phoenicia: precious metals (in particular, silver) and supplies of manufactured luxury items for their palaces (perfumes, carved ivory, cloth, gold boxes, jewelry, and wooden furniture). Byblos remained a source for such items but under direct rule by Assyria. The city of Tyre, on the other hand, was allowed to remain independent to promote the overall long-distance trade that Assyria desired.

In Western conventional wisdom, Byblos has long been famous for the "invention" of the alphabet. However, Byblos' role in this crucial chapter in human history is more complex. Excavations now indicate that a proto-Canaanite pictographic form of writing was developing throughout the region as early as 2000 BC; Byblos inscriptions demonstrate a local version of pseudohieroglyphic syllabic writing around this time. At Ugarit, finds demonstrate the appearance of a cuneiform version of the Canaanite linear alphabet around 1350 BC (see also "Ugarit"). Subsequent development was quick, leading to a system of twenty-two characters by 1000 BC, which spread quickly throughout the region. The excavations at Byblos have yielded the greatest number of sources of the earliest Phoenician alphabetic inscriptions for the period between 1000 BC and 800 BC. For example, there is a graffiti warning to thieves, inscribed in a royal tomb, cursing those who would desecrate the remains. The sarcophagus of King Ahiram of Byblos (1000 BC) is inscribed with an early form of the Phoenician script. Thus, it is the abundance of sources of this particular form of the early Phoenician script that has helped designate Byblos in popular imagination as the home of the alphabet rather than any clear indication that the concept of the alphabet actually originated within the city.

Under the Assyrians and then the neo-Babylonians, the city was an occupied port functioning to meet the needs of the empire's trade policy. There are indications of an ongoing metropolitan system of elite management, which appears to have its roots as far back as 1500 BC, whereby a mercantile oligarchy operated joint large-scale shipping projects in conjunction with the political leadership. Thus, a council of elders, or "lords of the city," played a major role in governing Byblos and participated in policy decisions.

Excavations indicate the remains of a fortress in the city built during the Persian occupation (550–330 BC), and the city expanded to perhaps its greatest extent as an administrative site and security city, but it is during the Hellenistic period that the city next plays a role regionally. The city was conquered by Alexander the Great in 332 BC and subsequently provided ships for the conflict between Antigonus and Ptolemy for dominance of the region. Its naval shipyards remained important throughout its control by the Seleucid Empire (330–64 BC). Byblos absorbed Greek customs and culture and became a temple city for Adonis and Aphrodite. Interestingly, many of the stories in the Adonis narrative, derived from similar stories of Baal, are sited in Byblos. Pompey captured the city, and the temples became dedicated to Apollo and Venus. Roman temples, colonnaded streets, theaters, and baths were built, and there is some indication that the city was a Roman administrative center.

Remnants of an extensive history of Phoenicia appear in the work of Philo of Byblos, a Greek writer living in the city around AD 100 to AD 200. Philo evidently translated into Greek eight volumes of a *Phoenician History,* written by a Phoenician author who may have lived in Beirut or Tyre around 1100 BC. Portions of Philo's translation are contained in the work of Eusebius of Caesarea, writing during the next century after Philos.

Few remains from the Byzantine period have been discovered in the city, although materials recovered in Spain and from other sites in the Mediterranean indicate that Byblos was an important center for olive oil production during this period, with merchants fulfilling extensive contracts. Little evidence from the Islamic period (AD 636) has been discovered. The most impressive remains visible today date from Crusader occupation (1104), when, as part of the kingdom of Tripoli, Byblos (then known as Jubail) acquired a fortress and the Church of Saint John. The city surrendered to Salah ad-Din in August 1187.

For the next 700 years, Jubail was a local market town, with a local fishing fleet using the small northern harbor. In the mid-1800s, the French writer Ernest Renan carried out the first archaeological investigations, but it was not until 1921, with the beginning of the French Mandate over Lebanon, that systematic excavations of the city began. French excavations continued until 1975. Today visitors can visit the town and working harbor of Jubail along with the Lebanese antiquities site, which consists primarily of the Crusader ramparts, the Roman theater, and Phoenician temple remains.

Bruce Stanley

Further Readings

Aubet, Maria. *The Phoenicians and the West: Politics, Colonies and Trade.* Cambridge: Cambridge University Press, 2001.

Braudel, Fernand. *The Mediterranean in the Ancient World.* London: Allen Lane and Penguin Press, 1998.

Markoe, Glenn. *Phoenicians.* London: British Museum Press, 2000.

Tubb, Jonathan N. *Canaanites.* London: British Museum Press, 1998.

C

Cairo

Population: Central Cairo 2001, 7.2 million; Greater Cairo metropolitan region, between 11 and 17 million (2005 estimate)

For many, Cairo has always been the "mother of the world." Heir to pharaonic grandeur of nearby Memphis, the "City Victorious" of early Islam took invasion and conflict in its stride only to explode with a glorious golden age of high Islamic civilization from the eleventh to the fourteenth century. A central hub in the world's scramble for spices, coffee, sugar, and cotton, Cairo was transformed during the nineteenth century with European architecture and planning into "Paris on the Nile." Over the last century, this cultural heart of the Arab world has beat to the songs of independence, socialism, and the struggle for development. Today this megacity, largest in Africa and the Middle East, encompasses all the ubiquitous problems of decay, conservation, social welfare, and political voice emerging from the global urban condition. Every visitor across the centuries to this pulsating conurbation has commented on its monumental scale, vitality, and worldly reach. Cairo, both sacred and profane, both global and provincial, holds within its streets a virtual history of human civilization.

Cairo (Arabic, *al-Qahirah*) sits at one of the key strategic sites of the Eurasian landmass. As the Nile River races north to the Mediterranean, it emerges at this point 120 miles from the sea from between the limestone cliffs of the Giza Plateau to the west and the Muqattam Hills to the east onto a flat alluvial plain, the great fan delta. To the northwest along the Canopic branch of the great river lay the port of Alexandria; to the northeast al-Farama (Pelusium) at the mouth of the Pelusiac branch. Thus, just at this nexus, it is possible to cross from Palestine and the Levant toward Libya and North Africa, avoiding the canals and September floods of the delta. Here it is possible to unload products for transshipment after floating down the Nile from Nubia. Armies must control this point if they want to dominate both Upper Egypt and the villages of the north. It is key to trade linking Europe with the Indian Ocean and with the desert routes to Makkah, Yemen, and the Sudan: as the saying goes, everyone must pass through Cairo.

The topography of this area at the head of the delta has attracted human habitation from earliest times and strategic control by any budding political entity. Over the last 6,000 years, various sites in the immediate vicinity have had their time in the sun, then been superseded by new creations. With the rise of separate upper and lower Egyptian kingdoms, the initial boundary between them was here where the delta began. When the two kingdoms were unified ca. 3000 BC, however, there was a need for an integrative administrative and legitimating center to symbolize the union. In addition, the limestone available attracted those interested in building on a monumental scale, and the Giza Plateau to the west gave them a place away from the growing city to build the necropolis. Given the channel of the Nile at the time, the city called Memphis was established on the western bank of the Nile some fifteen miles south of modern Cairo. Sometimes called the White City, Memphis lasted as a capital, administrative center, and cult site for more than 3,500 years until the Arab invasion in AD 640, after which time ruins of the city were used to provide stone for construction on the east bank. Archaeological excavations continue beside the modern village of Mit Rahina.

Although Heliopolis (Ayn Shams) may have actually been the earliest capital of a short-lived unified kingdom (ca. 3200), it was not until the period of the Old Kingdom (2700 BC to 2300 BC) that Heliopolis, situated on slightly higher ground some twenty miles to the northeast on the east bank (what is now called the Matareya area of Greater Cairo), developed to serve the interests of the priesthood elites and that great protector god of the pharaohs, Re. This religious complex, Heliopolis or On (City of the Sun), was central to the sun cult and the spiritual heart of pharaonic Egypt. A site of pilgrimage for those from Lower Egypt and vital to learning and scholarship, it continued to attract students through to the Hellenistic era, including Plato and Eudoxus, who studied astronomy here. Heliopolis was thriving at the time of the Arab invasion and overlooked the first battlefield between the Byzantines and the Muslims for control of this strategic area.

A third site, slightly north of Memphis and across on the east bank, began to develop around 500 BC as the key strategic defensive post on the Nile. Called Babylon-in-Egypt, this security fortress marked a key crossing point of the river, and during Byzantine times it anchored the eastern end of a floating bridge across the Nile. It also defended the river entry to the Amnis Trajanus, the ancient canal that is known later as the Khalij Amir al-Mu'minin connecting the Nile to the Red Sea. Particularly during the Roman occupation after 30 BC, Babylon was the center of their military control. Babylon, still not properly excavated, lies in the area of Cairo now called Misr al-Qadimah. Nearby is a fourth site, established in the pre-Arab and pre-Muslim period by the Romans, perhaps for the provisioning of the citadel. Called Misr (citadel or fortress), this became the center of the Coptic community after 400, hosting numerous churches; the Arabic word *misr* evolved over time to imply all of Egypt. Misr had a harbor, Umm Dunain.

Thus, by the time the Arab army under the command of Amr ibn al-Aas entered Egypt in January 640, there was already a conurbation of four separate but related sites within twenty miles of each other at the head of the delta. The Byzantines focused their forces around the imposing fortress of Babylon, with its moat, high walls, and tower. The Arabs initially avoided the fortress but did capture the port of Umm Dunain. In June 640, they then took Heliopolis, about six miles away. In July the Byzantines rode out to the attack but were caught in a pincer trap and defeated. Many Byzantines were killed, and the rest fled back to Babylon. Meanwhile, Misr surrendered, and the surrounding regions were captured. The Arab army then moved to take Babylon, fearing to leave their rear exposed if they moved toward Alexandria (see also "Alexandria").

The siege began in September 640, and after a number of months, surrender terms were agreed upon. However, Heraclius, the emperor in Constantinople, failed to accept the terms, and hostilities resumed. By early April 641, the city fell, and the garrison was allowed to sail away down the Nile. In celebrating the victory, Amr ibn al-Aas held a two-day banquet for Coptic Christians from nearby Misr. The Coptic community had been dominated by the Byzantines, so they were generally supportive of the Muslim invasion. The story goes that during the first evening, the Arabs served camel's meat boiled in salt water, which the Egyptians could not eat and saw as "primitive food." The next night was delicate Egyptian food. Ibn al-Aas, also known for his poetry, drew the point with the Copts that this was why the Arabs had been able to defeat the Byzantines: they could endure hardship, while the Greeks could not.

Even before their army had taken Alexandria, the Muslims transformed their siege city into a new garrison town for their troops near to the captured fortress of Babylon. Called Fustat (tent city), this new creation (AD 640) lay on the east bank, with its back to the desert and uninterrupted lines of communication with the Holy Cities. Located in the heartland of Egypt's two most productive provinces, Fustat was a new capital, keeping the Arab military elite separated from the attractions of ancient Alexandria and providing the base for the future conquest of North Africa. The Muslims summoned the Coptic patriarch Benjamin out of the desert to resume the official leadership of the Coptic Church, now to be headquartered in Fustat. In fact, it is recorded that in the spring of 644, Amr ibn al-Aas declared that all Muslims should observe the ordinances of religion, give alms, get rid of idleness and frivolity, and take good care of their new neighbors, the Copts, since Muhammad himself had given such orders. One of the

first buildings in the new city was the Masjid al-Aas (Amr) (641), named after the general. Religious piety and tolerance were in short supply during the early years, however. The city's Arab elite soon became caught up in Muslim internecine conflict when 500 rebels from Fustat set out in 656 to murder the third caliph, Uthman.

By the ninth century, Fustat had evolved an economic role to complement its security and administrative functions. The city became the chief inland port for the country as well as a vital center of industrial production. The city grew exponentially, becoming one of the largest cities in Dar al-Islam. Its elites often had homes in Fustat, Alexandria, and Arabia and commuted among them. Successive rule from Damascus and Baghdad meant the addition of royal suburbs such as al-Askar and Helwan; monumental construction by local governors (the Mosque of Ibn Tulun, 878); and new networks of trade.

Fustat was captured by the army of the Shi'i Fatimids in 969. They established a new administrative enclave, or palace city, some three miles to the northeast of Fustat that became known as al-Qahirah (the victorious), and the Fatimid caliph al-Mu'izz arrived in 973 to make the complex his capital. For the next century and a half, Fustat and al-Qahirah coexisted, with the former maintaining its strong economic base and the latter, surrounded by walls, serving the royal court. The Fatimids built a port and a shipbuilding arsenal for al-Qahirah, making it their center of security for the country. Writing at the end of the tenth century, al-Maqdisi, the great Arab historian, considered the dual city a tremendous metropolis in every sense of the word. One reason any visitor would be impressed was the caliphal processions put on by the Fatimid rulers. Draped in brocades and fine fabrics from local factories, the caliph proceeded through the streets holding his scepter, accompanied by trumpets and a military entourage.

By the eleventh century, Cairo rivaled Baghdad in both commerce and in the arts and sciences (see also "Baghdad"). A uniquely Fatimid aesthetic emerged, based on borrowed architectural styles such as domed tombs from Iran but also on imaginative creations of their own. The Fatimids made Cairo a center of learning, with one of their most enduring creations the University of al-Azhar. The chief mosque of the city (AD 970), and built as a counterbalance to the pre-Fatimid Ibn Tulun mosque (878), al-Azhar had a library, and stipends were available for both teachers and students. Today al-Azhar offers advanced training for Muslims from across the world and ranks as the preeminent center for scholarship in the Muslim community.

This golden age of Cairo was founded on long-distance trade. The Fatimid system placed great emphasis on producing applied arts for exchange. Of particular importance were the textiles produced in Cairo's factories: state looms produced silk and woolen fabrics, although cotton and linen were specialties, since flax was the main industrial crop. The government purchased much of the product; the rest was sold for shipment up the Nile or destined for the Red Sea.

Seventy-five years after Crusaders had first arrived in the Levant, King Amalric of the Franj decided to try to capture Egypt. In a series of campaigns that lasted from 1163 until 1169, Franj armies, the troops of the Fatimid vizier Shawar, and those of Shirkuh, a Kurdish general and uncle of Salah ad-Din, struggled around Cairo for control of the capital and thus of Egypt. During a series of five invasions, numerous battles, and shifting alliances, Cairo itself was captured twice. During the second attack (1168), the local Cairenes resisted the Franj, setting fire to Fustat with 20,000 jugs of naphtha and withdrawing into the palace complex of al-Qahirah. Reportedly, the city burned for fifty-four days. The Franj withdrew, but Shirkuh and Salah ad-Din arrived six days later outside the city walls. Seizing the opportunity, they took the city, Salah ad-Din himself killed Shawar, and his uncle was made vizier. Two months later, Shirkuh died, and the thirty-year-old Salah ad-Din was acclaimed *al-malik al-nasir* (the victorious king). In 1171 Salah ad-Din declared an end to the Fatimid Caliphate and reestablished Sunni authority in the city.

Under Salah ad-Din, new, expanded walls encircled the city (three of whose gates, including Bab Zuwaylah, are still standing), with a new citadel constructed on the Muqattam escarpment at its core. Gardens graced the south and west of the city, and as the channel of the Nile moved to the west, a new port of Bulaq was created. A wider array of manufactured goods emerged from the city's factories, including parchment, tanned leather, bound books, metal objects, military equipment, furniture, prepared foods, and glass. Cairo and a rebuilt Fustat grew toward one another and shared the role of economic and political capital of the country. Records discovered within the *geniza* (repository of discarded writings) of the ancient Fustat Synagogue provide a fascinating insight into the Mediterranean trading networks of the tenth to thirteenth century and of the role of the Jewish community in facilitating both regional and global trade. The records also tell us that Maimonides (d. 1204) lived in Fustat but commuted every day the two and one-half miles to his work in al-Qahirah as the court physician.

Ayyubid control over Cairo ended in 1249 with the death of Sultan as-Salih. His widow, Sultana Sharjar ad-Durr, originally a Turkish slave, ruled the country on her own for eighty days. During this period, the Abbasid caliph in Baghdad sneeringly wrote to the amirs in Cairo that "if you have no man to rule you, let us know and we will send you one." The amirs, Turkish Mamluks (slave soldiers) of the Ayyubid as-Salih, did finally elect one of their number, Izz ad-Din Aybak, as sultan, and ad-Durr married him, marking the beginning of the Mamluk era. He ruled from 1250 to 1257, although she was the political force behind the throne. She had him assassinated but was quickly killed herself and thrown to the city's dogs.

Aybak was succeeded by Sayf ad-Din Qutuz, who led the Mamluk army out of Cairo to stop the Mongol invasion but never returned; his victorious general of the battle of Ayn Jalut (1260), Baybars, assassinated Qutuz on the return trek to Cairo and was declared sultan. This is the legendary Baybars who drove the remnants of the Crusaders from the Levant, established the four-day post linking Cairo and Damascus, and perfected the pigeon post from the city. He supported monumental architecture in the city (Mosque of Baybars, 1269) and schools.

Over the next two centuries, Cairo was at its most glorious, the largest city west of China, hosting more than 500,000 inhabitants. The Mamluk Empire (1250–1516) brought the Levant, Egypt, and Nubia together into one market and reached out across the Indian Ocean to India and China as part of a single world system of long-distance trade. Much like the role Lisbon would play two centuries later, Cairo's elites operated within a horizon that included nearly one-third of the globe.

Visitors were overwhelmed with the scale and bustle of its streets and Cairo's "restless sea of men." One Italian visitor in 1384 exclaimed that "one street has more people than in all of Florence." Only the Mamluks could ride horses, so visitors were left to find their way on foot through its more than thirty different crafts markets or to be overwhelmed by the street sellers selling cooked food (since most people did not cook at home). Pedestrians were jostled by the city's 12,000 water carriers or by its thousands of camel drivers looking for hire. Merchants marched gangs of 200 slaves imported from the Ottoman capital at Edirne to the city's markets. Nor could visitors easily find their lodgings: with caravansaries for different ethnic communities (Maghribis, Persians, Europeans, Syrians, etc.), once you found your particular khan, which could hold up to 4,000 guests, which of its 360 rooms was yours?

The city was always hosting famous visitors. In 1324 the king of the Malian Empire, Mansa Musa, passed through Cairo on pilgrimage to Makkah. His visit was so spectacular that people were still talking about it twelve years later: preceded by 500 slaves, each carrying staffs of gold, Musa gave gifts to almost everyone he met. In fact, it is recorded that he gave so much gold away that by the time he returned to the city after the hajj, he had to take out loans to finance his return home. The Tangerine Ibn Battuta first stayed in the city for about a month in 1326. While there he saw what he thought was one of the most beautiful buildings in the world, the recently constructed *maristan* (hospital) built by Sultan Qalawun, and gave up counting the number of madrasas in the city. Benjamin of Tudeh, meeting with the Jewish community in Fustat ca. 1170, found that 7,000 Jews lived there and were a vibrant part of the economic and cultural life of the city.

The city buzzed with factory production, large and small. For example, there were sixty-six *matbakhs* (kitchens or refineries) for sugar refining or paper production within Old Cairo, each employing large numbers of workers. Sugar products were consumed locally but also shipped to other Arab countries or as far away as Italy and southern France. The sultan, the largest capitalist of the age, owned many of the factories, which processed the raw product of his plantations and then sold the finished confections to the state.

As Sunnis, and as successors to the Shi'i Fatimids, the Mamluks sought to legitimate their authority within Dar al-Islam. In the wake of the destruction of Baghdad by the Mongols, and the end of the Abbasid Caliphate, Baybars "discovered" an Abbasid family member and established him as caliph in Cairo, with himself presented as his servant. This "puppet" caliphate continued in Cairo until the coming of the Ottomans.

The lengthy reign of Sultan al-Nasir Muhammad (r. 1294–1340) witnessed some of the greatest Arab literature and art of all time, contributing to the view that Cairo was *umm ad-duniya* (the mother of the world). There were a number of reasons for Cairo's creativity and reach. One was the influx of Muslim scholars, craftsmen, and rich merchants escaping the Mongol catastrophe in eastern Islam; Cairo offered a refuge for their money and their skills. In addition, Mamluk officers lived in the city rather than on rural estates, and thus they spent their money within the city on religious endowments, palaces, khans, racetracks, canals, and mausoleums, producing the most energetic surge of building that Cairo had ever known. New residential areas to the north and south of the city were added, as was the Western Canal (ca. 1313), which allowed additional orchards, farms, and palaces to be built. Since much of their monumental building was in stone, it is the domes and minarets of Mamluk Cairo that still grace the skyline today. Although the Mamluks enhanced the city's walls and expanded Salah ad-Din's Citadel, the city lacked any true center of attraction like Aleppo's citadel or Damascus's Umayyad mosque. As a result, Cairo operated more like a series of neighborhoods or self-contained communities, a dynamic that it has retained until today.

Ibn Battuta arrived back in the city in 1348 just as the Black Plague was spreading through its streets; he left after three days. Behind him lay a devastated city that suffered for decades thereafter. The Mamluks did not flee their homes in the city, fearing a loss of their power; thus, their casualty rate was so high that the civil administration and the army were decimated. From October to January 1349, 10,000 people died per day; by the time it was over, approximately 200,000 had perished, 40 percent of its population.

By 1500 Cairo's population had recovered, and demographic pressures pushed the city southward and westward to cover the area now generally termed Old Cairo. To the east and south, extensive cemeteries, known collectively as the Cities of the Dead, provided burial sites for the merged Fustat and al-Qahirah.

As early as 996, Venetians had negotiated trade agreements in Fustat. By the late thirteenth century, Europeans had become regular participants in the city's economy. As exporters and importers, they helped shape its long-distance trade networks and fashion choices. For example, the wearing of clothes made from European cloth became fashionable from the beginning of the fourteenth century. Women reportedly would wear silk and, under that, fine Rhenish cloth; by the beginning of the fifteenth century, Egyptians were wearing woolens from France and England. It was Venice, however, that was the key trading partner for Cairo, forming a de facto alliance. The fortunes of these two great trading cities rose and fell together for centuries. By the late fifteenth century, however, their dominance of the trade to Europe was challenged by the Portuguese intrusion into the Indian Ocean, and many of Cairo's networks began to shift.

The rise of the Muslim gunpowder empires of the Ottomans, Safavids, and Moguls also undercut Cairo's strategic trading networks. The Ottoman army arrived outside the gates of Cairo in January 1517, supported with superior artillery. The last Mamluk sultan, Tuman Bey, was hanged on the main gate of the city after its capture.

Under the new regime, the city ceased being the premier urban node in an empire, becoming instead a regional city serving Istanbul's interests (see also "Istanbul"). In a few sectors, however, this was not the case. As Yemeni coffee became a global commodity in the late sixteenth century, the *tuggar* (Cairene merchants) were able to monopolize much of the coffee trade. The first taxes collected on coffee in the city occurred in 1573; twenty-five years later, the coffee market equaled spices and Indian textiles in importance to Cairo's economy. Of the 360 caravansaries in Cairo at that time, 62 of them were dedicated to the coffee trade. Coffee was transported from Yemen to Jeddah, where it was transferred to Cairo-controlled shipping for transport to Cairo. There it was resold for export throughout the Ottoman Empire and Europe. More than 500 tuggar were involved in the sector.

It is interesting to note that during this time European shipping and personnel were excluded from the Red Sea north of Jeddah. Justified on religious grounds as protecting the Holy Cities from infidels, the tuggar jealously guarded their remaining primacy over the pilgrimage routes, the grain ships supplying the Holy Cities, and the coffee trade. Such defensive protection lasted only until the late eighteenth century; in 1775 the English were able to force a treaty on the Ottomans to open all the Red Sea to their ships, thus extending their commercial control from India to London. By 1793

Cairo's population reflected its decline in fortunes: it had shrunk to 250,000 inhabitants.

Bonaparte's invasion of Egypt in 1798, and the three-year French occupation of the city, marked a new phase in Cairo's history. Europeans came to dictate cultural tastes of the city's elites, to finance new technologies, and to manipulate political developments, although the French governor was assassinated in the city in 1800. Under the leadership of Khedive Muhammad Ali (1805–1848), and that of his successors Said Pasha (1854–1863) and Ismail Pasha (1863–1879), Cairo developed a European face. The grafting in of European urban forms emerged from a vision of modernization that sought to turn Egypt into a piece of Europe and to make Cairo a European city. Ismail had been deeply impressed by the Parisian Exposition Universelle of 1867; upon his return, he had a Parisian-style master plan drawn up for the city. One result of its implementation was the rejection of many older architectural styles such as the traditional *mashribaya* (wooden screens on windows), which were made illegal. Another was the wholesale destruction of the historic fabric of Old Cairo, particularly parts of the Fatimid city, which were torn down to build wide boulevards.

New European-style monumental architecture arose along the Nile: Ismail built, for example, Abdeen Palace, with a European facade to anchor the new European areas of the city, and numerous official and private structures were started. At one point, there were more than 400,000 construction workers on the government payroll. Ismail introduced waterworks and gasworks to the city, laying the new riverside district of Garden City out with 5,000 gas lamps covered with tulip-shaped glass. An opera house was built, hosting Italian troupes who sang the newly commissioned opera *Aida* supported by genuine Ethiopian slaves. An extensive system of streetcar lines connected the various suburbs. The first Arabic printing press was established in the city in 1822 and began producing scientific and literary works to supply the many new schools he opened. The construction of the Suez Canal (1859–1869) opened up the city to new influences and to European tourists traveling with Thomas Cook.

Much of this new development was financed by loans. As a consequence, the government went increasingly into debt to European investors, speculators, and governments. This resulted in the imposition of the Anglo-French debt administration (1875). Domestically, the rising intellectual elites began agitating for an end to such foreign privileges and greater political voice. Riots and demonstrations began in 1879, culminating in a revolt, led by an army colonel, Ahmed Arabi, seeking democracy and independence. The British response was military occupation of the city and internment camps in the desert.

The 1882 occupation spurred further Europeanization of parts of the city and new architecture that reflected its "colonial city" character. The city expanded both northward and westward of Old Cairo, often onto reclaimed land close to the Nile, as was the case of Garden City and Tahrir Square. Heliopolis, to the east, was modeled on Britain's new towns, while Ma'adi and Gezira, on the island with its British Officer's Club and the Palace of Ismail Pasha, were sites for villas and the elite. The city began to exhibit an east-west, traditional-contemporary division that has echoes today.

Under the British, there was an increase in in-migration to Cairo, most of it from rural areas. The city's population, 374,000 in 1882, passed the 1 million mark by the end of World War I, and by 1937 was more than 1.3 million. It thus replaced Istanbul as the largest city in the Middle East and by sheer size alone the focus of the Arab world. Many Arab Ottoman reformers fled to Cairo from the empire to gain the relative security and greater freedom of publishing in British-occupied Egypt. Rashid Rida (1865–1935), for example, arrived from Lebanon in 1897 and launched, in association with Muhammad Abduh, the periodical *al-Manar*, one of the most influential instruments of Islamic reform.

Concerns about such rapid development coalesced into the first attempts at conservation, with the establishment of

Stylized vision of the Bazaar of the Silk Mercers, Cairo, ca. 1850. (Library of Congress)

the Comite de Conservation des Monuments de l'Art Arabe in 1880. Its mission was to maintain and rehabilitate the medieval monuments of Cairo in the face of thoughtless destruction. In 1952 the Comite was disbanded and its functions assumed by the government. Another push for preservation occurred in the late 1970s with the United Nations Educational, Scientific, and Cultural Organization's (UNESCO) promotion of historic monuments and the declaration of Old Cairo as a World Heritage Site. Some 450 monuments within this area were designated for protection.

The city was home to many scholars wrestling with the future of Islam and its relation to the West. One of the most prominent was Muhammad Abduh (1849–1905). An Arab disciple of Jamal ad-Din al-Afghani, Shaykh Abduh had been involved in the Arabi Revolt but allowed by the British to resume his activities in Egypt in 1888. Abduh focused his efforts on encouraging moral reform in Egypt and in developing enlightened education. In contrast to those who rejected Islam as they adopted Western ideology, he argued that Islam could provide a belief system consistent with science and modern life and that it remained relevant today. He stressed classical Muslim-Arab heritage and that the Qur'an could be seen through modern eyes. He took the position that he would accept nothing from the West unless it passed his own rigorous standards. As chief mufti of Egypt (1889–1905), he worked to expand Egyptian education and to reempower classical Arab prose.

Expatriates experienced this period as Cairo's belle époque. The British assembled for "the season" on the veranda of the Shepheard's Hotel; at the Gezira Sporting Club; at the Mena House, below the Pyramids; or in the ice cream parlor at Gropies. The Greeks, Italians, French, and Germans also enjoyed their colonial lifestyle, in a well-established hierarchy, supported by their own little enclaves and institutions. Cairo became a center of spying activities in the lead-up to World War I. The German consulate in Cairo, with its notorious spymaster Max von Oppenheim ("the Kaiser's spy"), along with the German director of the Khedival Library in Cairo, organized the German local network.

World War I spurred increased social change and political resistance to the occupation. The war effort required Egyptian cotton, which led to food shortages and near famine in the city as food production decreased. It also brought thousands of British soldiers into the city, with all the social tensions and prostitution this entailed. Martial law, internment camps, and labor requisitions fueled the call for independence. The war also encouraged British manipulation of the future political arrangements in Arab areas. At the extraordinary Cairo Conference of March 1921, forty of the empire's top Middle East experts, including Percy Cox, Winston Churchill, and T. E. Lawrence, organized the post-Ottoman Middle East around Hashemite client states under British control: "Everybody Middle East is there," T. E. Lawrence wrote.

During the 1920s and 1930s, Cairo was the center of political activity and a hotbed of resistance. Parties like the Wafd (Delegation) of Saad Zaghlul, a follower of Arabi, organized mass demonstrations in the city, helping to force the British toward dissolving the protectorate (1922) and nominal independence (1936). The Ikhwan al-Muslimin (Muslim Brethren), founded in 1928 by Hasan al-Bana, grew to more than 1 million members committed to reviving Islam and to establishing social justice. Huda Shaarawi and al-Ittihad al-Nissai al-Misri (the Egyptian Feminist Union) took to the streets as well, pursuing both nationalism and political rights for women.

World War II brought blatant occupation back to the city as the British imposed censorship, forced the king at gunpoint to change his policy toward Germany, and threw dissidents into prison. Economically, however, the war helped Cairo expand its industrial base. With sources of supply cut off, and the increased demand created by Allied troops stationed in Egypt, domestic output rose more than 50 percent. The poor, of course, suffered, and starving mobs attacked wheat shipments in the city in 1942. In 1947 the British killed thirty demonstrators outside the Qasr al-Nil barracks in Cairo.

Toward the end of the war, Cairo hosted the preparatory meetings of the General Arab Congress to draft the Arab League constitution, which was signed on 22 March 1945. Headquartered in Cairo, the league sought to unite the Arab world politically so that its voice could be heard on key issues of concern to Arabs but also to craft a military response to Zionism. League headquarters were transferred out of Cairo in 1979 as a result of Egypt's signing of a peace treaty with Israel but were returned to the city in 1991.

Cairo witnessed much organizing, volunteering, and fundraising to support the conflict with Israel in 1948; it also was the scene of despair over the Palestinian al-Naqba (disaster). The failure was laid both at the feet of King Farouk and the occupation. Finally, the confrontation with Britain in the capital reached its climax during January 1952 with the "Black Saturday" riots, in which huge parts of the city, and particular landmarks of colonialism like the Shepheard's Hotel, were burned. Some 12,000 families lost their homes, but little changed politically. Finally, a group of "Free Officers" in the military organized a virtually bloodless coup in July 1952. The Egyptian Revolution ended the monarchy and exiled a playboy king who had recently married a sixteen-year-old and blown $150,000 in one baccarat game during his honeymoon.

Gradually, Jamal Abdul Nasir emerged as the leader of the cabal and took the country down the road of Arab socialism. This philosophy led to large-scale urban projects, a commitment to industrialization, and state control over local urban politics. Socialist housing of Soviet design and poor quality sprang up around the city, often overshadowing ancient monuments. Midan Tahrir (Liberation Square) and the Mugamma (central administrative building), for civilian record keeping, are two of the most representative of this period. Filled with college students guaranteed work upon graduation, the new satellite city, Nasir City, housed new governmental agencies. Meanwhile, older housing stock decayed, and there was little incentive for landlords to fix up their properties. The 1956 Master Plan for Cairo predicted that the city's population would be 4.5 million by the year 2000; the 1966 census recorded a population already passing 6 million.

One of the most famous architects of this period was Hassan Fathy (d. 1989). Fathy achieved cult status for his anti-establishment vision and promotion of traditional designs. Drawing on ancient mud-brick building techniques and forms, including those from Nubia, he sought to move away from imported Western visions, to craft buildings inspired by local culture and context, and to encourage the virtues of self-help.

Radio Cairo played a crucial role in the struggle for Arab legitimacy and definition after the rise of Nasir. The famous "Voice of the Arabs" broadcast Egyptian propaganda throughout the Arab world, challenging pro-Western and monarchist regimes in an "Arab Cold War" across the airwaves. Much of the content of Arab radio, including music and plays, was produced in Cairo, however, with the famous Muhammad Abd al-Wahhab and Um Kalthoum turning out the hits. The postwar period also saw the expansion of the great Egyptian film industry. Having produced its first feature film in 1923, by the 1950s "Hollywood on the Nile" was producing sixty films per year.

The city welcomed many exiles and political radicals from the decolonization struggle. The political executive of the Front de Libération Nationale (National Liberation Front [FLN]) announced the Algerian Revolution from Cairo in 1954 and mixed with other freedom fighters from across Africa who found refuge in the city. Che Guevara passed through in the early 1960s, building links between African radicals and Cuba's new leaders. Yasir Arafat, probably born in Cairo in 1929, started his political career in 1952 when he successfully ran for president of the Union of Palestinian Students in the city. The story is told that he would personally meet all Palestinian students coming to Cairo from Gaza, introduce himself, and offer his assistance in settling in. Assisted by another Palestinian, Salah Khalaf, the two started a student magazine called the *Voice of Palestine,* offered military training to Palestinian students, and generally began laying the foundation for what became the Fatah movement.

By the late 1970s, Egypt under Sadat was moving away from a socialist-directed economy and closer to the West. Within Cairo this resulted in freewheeling capitalism and less government restrictions. Illegal housing (not shantytowns but blocks of flats and illegal floors) sprung up throughout the city, unfettered by building restrictions or appropriate laws. Built on agricultural land or desert fringes, and often

linked to motorway placement, spontaneous urbanization spurred the growth of the city: 84 percent of all construction in the 1970s and 1980s was probably illegal. Rarely destroyed by the authorities, such illegal construction gradually became legalized through the provision of services. One graphic example of such expansion was the move into the Cities of the Dead. These cemeteries in Old Cairo were relatively uninhabited until the 1970s. By the end of the century, however, there may have been up to 200,000 people living among the graves. A similar situation exists with the *zebaleen* (garbage collectors), who live among the city's garbage heaps and recycle its metal and plastics.

Sadat's government sought to deal with Cairo's dramatic expansion and congestion through a new master plan, often billed as the "American Plan" because of the central role of American planners in its development. Its goal was to slow Cairo's growth by relocating population and industrialization to four new towns, or satellite cities, located around a ring road surrounding Greater Cairo. Construction began in 1977 on creations such as 6 of October City and 10 of Ramadan City. Others have been added since, including Sadat City. In the wake of the 1978 Camp David Agreement, the government was able to devote increased resources to these projects. There was little immediate effect, however, on the city's phenomenal annual 2.74 percent growth. Yet during the decade from 1986 to 1996, there was a decline in the inner-city population of central Cairo and strong growth in outlying suburbs.

One of the most dramatic events in recent Cairene history was the 1992 earthquake. Within minutes 9,000 buildings were damaged and 800 blocks of flats destroyed. More than 80,000 people ultimately were forced outward from the most densely packed core of the city to the new settlements and ring housing. Long term, the failure of the government to control illegal and thus shoddy construction, to respond quickly to the disaster, and then to clear the poor from the Old City became highly politicized and helped feed the rise of Islamist fundamentalism, as such groups stepped in to prove social support for the victims.

In the wake of the 1992 earthquake, questions of the preservation of historic Cairo reappeared on the agenda. Today there is a controversial push to turn Old Cairo into an "open-air museum," with its monuments restored and its local small industries replaced with more bazaars and tourist traps. This may involve moving tanneries like Guelud al-Madbre from the middle of Old Cairo, where it employs 10,000 people yet pollutes the area with its chemicals, out to the new cities. It may also involve moving the "undesirable" poor to other locations.

Certainly, there is a buzz of restoration work in Old Cairo; Darb al-Asfar, an ancient alleyway containing historic buildings, has been restored with money from the Arab Fund for Development. The work of the Historic Cities Program of the

Agha Khan's Trust for Culture (AKTC) is also interesting. With the Agha Khan's historic connection to Fatimid Cairo, AKTC chose to finance an eighty-acre al-Azhar Park within Old Cairo. Located in ad-Darassa, the gift of space for those densely packed into its narrow streets provided gardens, a playground, a lake, and a restaurant along with restoring monuments in the neighborhood.

Issues of unifying and empowering the administration and planning of Greater Cairo have also become important, given that the city is divided administratively between three governorates—Cairo, Giza (to the west of the Nile), and Qalyubiyya (the northern city)—and they have difficulty cooperating. There are more than thirty local and national government agencies and ad hoc committees involved in some aspect of planning and management of the Greater Cairo Metropolitan Region (GCMR) yet only one regionwide institutional entity, the GCMR Development Committee. Given that the GCMR is one of the world's largest megacities with perhaps as many as 17 million people, contains more than 25 percent of the country's population, and accounts for more than 45 percent of Egypt's gross domestic product, a high degree of coordination seems essential. Until 1992 the GCMR was the largest urban area in the world without an officially adopted development plan, and it took the earthquake to spur its adoption.

The issue of traffic congestion is high on the agenda of the GCMR. Accidents, delays, bad roads, and even the number of vehicles on the streets (446 vehicles added each day) contribute to lost revenues, pollution, respiratory-health issues, stress, and noise. There is no time of the day when the city's streets are not crowded. Add to this the problems of waste disposal (the city produces 7,000 tons of garbage per day and only 33 percent of wastewater is treated that flows into the Nile), adequate housing (20 percent of the population live in slum housing), and overcrowding (Cairo's density is sixty-nine per acre, six times that of Mexico City), and it appears that the city's politicians should be in despair.

Yet there are no lack of new plans and grand schemes. A third master plan for the city, developed with help from the French, was organized by the Mubarak government. Recent projects around the city include a new National Museum near the Pyramids, the Stock Exchange Complex, a new French University, a hi-tech research park, a third subway line, an Opera House, Media City, four new five-star hotels, and an international convention center. More than twenty private-sector communities (huge gated communities) are encircling the city with a zone of suburbs. American University of Cairo is moving out of the center to new facilities on 260 acres of land along the ring road, and the Mubarak Youth Housing project (for newlyweds) and the Future Development scheme each have 70,000 homes under construction.

Novels and short stories by Cairene authors such as Nawal as-Saadawi, Jamal al-Ghitani, and Jamil Ibrahim about life in their city have long resonated far beyond the city's boundaries. Perhaps the most famous are the novels written by Naguib Mahfouz (b. 1911). In works such as *The Cairo Trilogy*, this recipient of the 1988 Nobel Prize for Literature represented the confusion felt by the city's middle classes as their neighborhoods began to change; in *Children of Gebelawi*, he used symbolism to critique society and religion. Since he deals with the conflict between modernity and tradition, his works have generated great criticism as well; a fatwa was pronounced, calling for his assassination, and he was attacked and stabbed in 1994.

Bruce Stanley

Further Readings

Abu-Lughod, Janet. *Cairo: 1,001 Years of the City Victorious*. Princeton: Princeton University Press, 1971.

Berque, Jacques. *Egypt: Imperialism and Revolution*. Translated by Jean Stewart. London: Faber and Faber, 1972.

Dov Goitein, Shelomo. *A Mediterranean Society: The Jewish Communities of the Arab World as Portrayed in the Documents of the Cairo Geniza*. 3 vols. Berkeley: University of California Press, 1967–1978.

Petry, Carl. *The Civilian Elite of Cairo in the Late Middle Ages*. Princeton: Princeton University Press, 1981.

Poole, Stanley Lane. *The Story of Cairo*. London: J. M. Dent and Company, 1906. Repr. Nendeln, Liechtenstein: Kraus, 1971.

Raymond, Andre. *Cairo*. Cambridge: Harvard University Press, 2000.

Rodenbeck, Max. *Cairo: The City Victorious*. New York: Vintage Books, 1998.

Stewart, D. *Cairo: 5,500 Years*. New York: Thomas Crowell, 1968.

Wiet, Gaston. *Cairo: City of Art and Commerce*. Translated by Seymour Feiler. Norman: University of Oklahoma Press, 1964.

Casablanca
Population: 3,325,539 (2004 estimate)

Situated on the Atlantic coast, 200 miles southeast of Tangier and 200 miles northwest of Mogador, Casablanca spreads itself out like a great white whale. It is Morocco's primate city, its economic capital, and Africa's second-largest metropolis after Cairo. It has been a boomtown for a bit more than the last century, during which its population increased 200 percent. The French protectorate (1912–1956) chose it as the heartland of its colonial enterprise, a laboratory of town planning, retrospectively probably the greatest achievement of French colonial urbanism. Within several generations, the fishing village of Anfa was transformed into Casa, a modern metropolis and a world port of international trade. In the process of rampant urbanization, a proliferation of bidonvilles emerged onto the Casablancan landscape. Fifty years after Morocco gained its independence, the city's extremes of wealth and poverty remain sources of hope and despair.

Before the nineteenth-century growth of Casablanca (Arabic, *Dar al-Bayda*), there are only vague signs of earlier settlements. Near the present site of the city, relics have been found from a seventh-century BC Phoenician trading post and from a first-century AD Roman occupation. During the seventh-century Muslim conquest of Morocco, the Berber tribe of the Barghawata, heretics from mainstream Islam, had a base near the hill of Anfa, south of today's metropolis. In 1188, during the reign of the Almohad dynasty, the sultan Abd al-Mu'min created a port there that, according to the Portuguese historian Marmol, flourished and was called Anafe.

In the fourteenth century, the Portuguese took possession of the site. Later, it became a refuge of Muslim pirates only to be sacked by the Portuguese fleet in 1458 and again in 1515, when once more the Portuguese took it, naming it Casablanca, and holding it until its destruction by earthquake in 1755. Sometime in the late eighteenth century, the Alawite sultan Muhammad Ben Abdallah reconstructed the place, providing it with ramparts, military installations, and a customs house and giving it the Arabic name of Dar al-Bayda, the equivalent of Casablanca, "The White House."

In 1834 it was not much more than a fishing village housing 700 inhabitants. After 1850, however, Casablanca emerged as the chief beneficiary of the new, increasing European commerce with the Moroccan hinterland, and by 1866 it had a population of some 6,000, mostly adventurers and commercial entrepreneurs. The town grew, surrounded by walls with towers and four gates. The madinah had stone houses of Moorish style; several broad, irregular transversal streets; a *mellah* (Jewish Quarter); and a quarter known as Tnakar of reed and clay huts. The madinah was surrounded by a narrow girdle of vineyards and orchards of olive and fig trees.

After 1880 Casablanca began to experience the expansion of modern capitalism into Morocco's port cities, an influx of foreigners, and the beginnings of large-scale land speculation. By the turn of the century, the village was becoming a minor boomtown. Until 1907 Morocco had few natural harbors on the Atlantic. To remedy this, the Moroccan sultan Abd al-Aziz allowed the French to build an entirely artificial port, within a few years the busiest in the country and on its way to becoming a world-class port of international trade. The city's expansion accelerated rapidly. In 1907 the French invaded the coast, and in the footsteps of the military came an army of adventurers. The population then reached about 20,000; by 1912 the European population had increased from 1,000 to 20,000. In 1914 there were 31,000 foreigners (including 15,000 French, 6,000 Spanish, and 7,000 Italians), 30,000 Muslims, and 9,000 Jews. Morocco's first factory arose in Casablanca in 1908, its first labor union in 1910, and modern banks from 1912, when the French protectorate agreement was signed.

When the French resident general Marechal Lyautey made Rabat the capital of the protectorate in Morocco, there were street demonstrations in opposition to that decision in Casablanca. But it had to settle for its status as the country's economic capital, the heartland of France's colonial enterprise. The great port had been constructed and inaugurated in 1921, followed by a rapid increase in traffic and in immigration. Rail and road systems were established as well as foreign financial institutions, modern commerce, and the beginnings of light industry. (The massive export of minerals and agricultural products, the sources of great wealth, came later, in the 1930s, when the "pacification" of Morocco's interior had been completed.) Casablanca was a city on the move, a city of newcomers and adventurers who were sometimes characterized as "wolves."

The town planners and architects designed and built a magnificent European new city, its style neomauresque like that of colonial Rabat and known as *arabiasance*. A ring road of some two and a half miles enclosed an area of more than 2,500 acres, including an industrial zone, residential quarters, and a city center articulated around two large public squares, that of Place de France for commercial activities and Place Lyautey for the main administrative buildings. A network of streets and boulevards gave the modern city a fanlike shape.

The construction of what became in popular parlance "Casa" and "the African Marseille" was thanks to the city-planning genius of Henri Prost. The wide avenues, elegant buildings, and vast port were the greatest achievement of French colonial urbanism. One commentator, Susan Ossman, saw Casablanca as a laboratory for "the modernity of the Jazz Age." The Hotel de Ville designed by Marius Boyer, the cathedral of the Sacre Coeur designed by Paul Tournon, and the large cinemas were all gems of art deco.

Between the two world wars, Casablanca's suburbs spread far and wide from the city center, and early on in the period of the protectorate, rapid urbanization created Morocco's first bidonvilles. Between 1912 and 1950, the population increased to more than 700,000. Sociologists, for example, Andre Adam, often have compared Casablanca to America's "mushroom cities."

With the wartime arrival of Allied troops in 1942, an American air base was established at Nouasseur outside of Casablanca, and the influence of the United States in Morocco began to make itself felt. Hollywood added significantly to the fame of the city by the classic film *Casablanca,* which, although it was shot in a studio in California, became a metaphorical statement about a place that was both a promised land to run to and a den of iniquity to flee from.

Some attempts to create mass housing for the Moroccan Muslim immigrants from other cities and the countryside took place. In the 1920s, a superb ensemble of residences and shops, the Habous Quarter, was built to encourage the commercial elite of Fez to settle in Casablanca. It was and remains an elegant neotraditional madinah, a kind of garden city near the sultan's palace and equipped with a complete urban infrastructure of marketplace, ovens, public baths, schools, and mosques. The 1950s, a boom period for modern architecture, witnessed the extension of residential villas in the neighborhoods of Anfa and Le Polo, of office buildings, an exhibition hall, modern slaughterhouses, and places of entertainment. At the same time, another giant of French urbanism, Ecochard, designed mass housing for Moroccans. Architecturally impressive, in the shadow of proliferating bidonvilles, it proved to be too little and too late.

Resistance to French colonial rule in Morocco began in the traditional cities in the 1930s. But by the 1950s, Casablanca had become the nerve center of that resistance, and from 1953 to 1955 it was the scene of urban insurrections. The labor union movement was centered in the city and played a significant role in the campaigns for the end of the protectorate and for an independent nation-state.

In the half century since independence, in 1956, Casablanca has moved on in the same direction. The American author Paul Bowles, writing in 1982 about Morocco in general, provides an image that applies perfectly to Casa: "When France was no longer able to keep the governmental vehicle on the road, she abandoned it, leaving the motor running. The Moroccans climbed in and drove off in the same direction, but with even greater speed."

Today's Casablanca, the largest city in North Africa and one of Africa's greatest metropolises, with almost 4 million inhabitants, is the country's center of commerce, industry, finance, and its stock market. It spreads out along the corniche and its beaches and into its hinterland. The humidity of the ocean and the congestion of its traffic sadly put it into the major league of sprawling conundrums of smog and pollution. Some of its neighborhoods have become gentrified, evolved into new centers of leisure like the former working-class area of Ma'arif, with shopping malls, neighborhood businesses, expensive apartment buildings, and quality marketplaces. The expansion of the city in regard to architectural symbols includes a new prefecture; a television station (TV2M); the Sharifan Office of Phosphates; the Hassan II Mosque, on the oceanfront; a commercial center in Ma'arif, designed by the Catalan Ricardo Bofill; a museum; and impressive world-class hotels, including a Hyatt Hotel whose bar is named "Rick's Place" in honor of Humphrey Bogart's role in the film *Casablanca*. Open public spaces like the Arab League Park in the city center are places to see and to be seen for the wealthy and the burgeoning middle classes. The economically successful do not hesitate to consume conspicuously.

Casablanca is also a city of extreme poverty and potential and sometimes real social unrest. The economic disparities between rich and poor are apparently widening, and they are engraved in the physical space of the urban sprawl. Like all metropolises, Casa is hard, demanding, stressful, and a place of anonymity. A legend about one of its saints, Sidi Beliouth, recounts that when settling in the city, he tore out his eyes before going to live with savage beasts; he preferred them to humans, because they took care of him. On his death, a lion accompanied him to his tomb, and he became reputed as a saint of consolation. Another legend concerns the tomb of a tenth-

century saint buried beside a banana tree in the southwest corner of what remains of the original madinah. Sidi Bou Smara (the man of nails), passing through the city in the tenth century, asked for water to carry out his ablutions but received only insults in return. In anger he struck the ground with his walking stick, and a spring burst forth. The inhabitants insisted that he remain among them. He settled in a corner of the madinah, where he planted the banana tree that is always filled with nails placed by pilgrims who come to receive his blessing.

The original patron saint of Casablanca, allegedly of the fourteenth century, is said to be Sidi Allal al-Kairaouni (from the Tunisian city of Kairaouane), whose sanctuary tomb and that of his daughter Lalla Bagda is on Rue Traker to the north of the city center. Legend has it that the boat in which he was traveling from Tunisia to Senegal ran ashore at Casablanca. When he and his daughter died, people named the sanctuary Dar al-Bayda, "the House of the White Princess." This was later translated into Spanish as "Casa Blanca."

Historically, the king and his elite establishment, known as the *makhzen*, operated out of four "imperial" cities—Fez, Meknes, Rabat, and Marrakesh. The sultanate perpetually moved the royal capital with all its retinue among its palaces in these cities. In addition to these capitals, four Moroccan cities were considered centers of *hadara*, refined urban culture: Fez, Tetouan, Sale, and Rabat. From them came the educated doctors of the law, administrative clerks in the government, the best of musicians, cooks, and the arbiters of bourgeois taste and style. Casablanca, a late-born, essentially modern city, had none of this, no bourgeoisie, and no urban traditions. It was virgin territory, a kind of frontier town, without a preexisting society to transform newcomers into urbanites. Massive urbanization took place here in the absence of assimilation or integration into some form of an urban mold. Under the French protectorate, it was a place for adventurers, arrivistes, the hungry, and the poor, and there were quite unequal chances for the European and Moroccan immigrants who came to live and work there. The principles of urban planning based on the separation of Europeans and Muslims set down by Marechal Lyautey in the first decades of colonization could not be sustained over the long run in the face of the exuberant growth and the demographic explosion of the city.

Casablanca today looks in many places like an enormous construction site. More than half of its inhabitants are less than twenty-five years of age, and most of the first or second generations are immigrants from elsewhere in Morocco. There is no historic memory, no past; its population suffers from a kind of collective amnesia. And along with that, perhaps as a consequence and compensation, the city teems with exuberance. In the Moroccan context, it is a crossroads of people, a "mixing pot" of Arabs, Berbers, Europeans, Muslims, Jews, and Christians.

The great divide among Casablancans remains economic. The only freeway in Morocco splits the city in two and forms a demarcation line between the city center and the poor suburbs, and their ways and chances of life and death are significantly different. For the wealthy and an expanding middle class living in Casablanca's Los Angeles–like expanse, cars are a necessity and private schools for their children increasingly so. For the inhabitants of the slums and bidonvilles, any kind of education is a luxury.

Plans for the future development of the city and the eradication of its slums are on the drawing boards and in some cases in motion. These include the construction of an underground system of transportation and extended interurban freeways, and the further destruction of parts of the old madinah to build a wide boulevard from the city center to the Hassan II Mosque on the coast. That mosque at the westernmost point of the Islamic world is monumental and the only real landmark on the urban landscape. It was completed in the 1990s after five years of construction work by 30,000 laborers on a site of five acres. The prayer hall of the mosque can hold 25,000 people, and there is room on the esplanade for 80,000 more. Financed by public subscription, the complex also contains a museum and a library. It has become the main symbol of Casablanca.

What of traditional, reformist, and fundamentalist religion in the contemporary metropolis? The subject matter is immense. Clearly, the terrorist attacks carried out by Casablancan slum dwellers in May 2004 are related both to an international context and to the profound unresolved economic and political problems of the city and the country. Poverty in Casablanca is lethal, potentially and actually.

In regard to the tension or conflict between tolerant and puritanical religious beliefs and practices that one may confront in Casablanca, the legend concerning another saint, whose sanctuary-mausoleum is on a small islet just south of the city, is instructive: Sidi Abd ar-Rahman, the flautist, a pious man, decided to isolate himself along the Atlantic coast by Casablanca in order to contemplate his Creator. But unable to immerse himself in prayer, he served his master by playing a sweet melody on his reed flute. Shortly thereafter, another pious man, Sidi Bouchaib ar-Radad, hearing about Sidi Abd ar-Rahman, came to visit him and counseled him to put aside his flute and to allow himself to be guided in entering into prayer. They remained together lost in prayer for seven days. On the eighth day, Sidi Bouchaib spread his rug over the ocean and sailed away. Only after some while did Sidi Abd ar-Rahman realize that his companion had left, at which point he threw himself into the sea in an attempt to find him. Then the waves ceased, the ocean parted, and an island emerged. Seeing this miracle, Sidi Bouchaib cried out, "O Sidi Abd ar-Rahman! Forget my instructions and play your flute. Your blessedness is greater than mine!" Thus, Sidi Abd ar-Rahman remained on his island venerating God with the music of his flute until his death. His mausoleum has been visited ever since, especially by women suffering from infertility. Sometimes they organize a *lila,* a nocturnal ritual of music, dance, and trance.

The lesson of the story is that Casablanca has until now been a city of tolerance. Whether people approve of the story for its moral and aesthetic qualities or consider it as a manifestation of insupportable superstitions and practices, the place remains another of the permanent symbols on the Casablancan landscape.

Kenneth Brown

Further Readings

Cohen, J.-L., and M. Eleb. *Casablanca: Colonial Myths and Architectural Ventures.* New York: Monacelli Press, 2002.

Gershovich, Moshe. *French Military Rule in Morocco: Colonialism and Its Consequences.* London: Frank Cass, 2000.

Howe, Marvin. *Morocco: The Islamic Awakening and Other Challenges.* Oxford: Oxford University Press, 2005.

Ossman, Susan. *Picturing Casablanca: Portraits of Power in a Modern City.* Berkeley: University of California Press, 1994.

D

Damascus

Population: 1.6 million (2005 estimate for city); 3 million (2005 estimate for Greater Damascus)

Promoted as perhaps the oldest continuously inhabited city in the world, Damascus "the immortal" is certainly one of the most evocative and iconic cities in the world. Ancient by any standard, this city has been desired by emperors for its wealth and power, by artists for its architecture and light, by believers for its sacred sites, and by writers for its mystery and exotic intrigue. An oasis city serving as a desert port for the Bedouin to its east and south, this "pearl set in emeralds" was almost completely surrounded by gardens, water, and plantations, making it seem like paradise to travelers approaching from the desert. Many times a capital of expansive empires or political states, besieged and destroyed numerous times, this 5,000-year-old city is today the commercial, political, and cultural capital of Syria, with regional ambitions and complex urban problems.

Damascus (Arabic, *ash-Sham* or *Dimashq ash-Sham*), the traditional capital and chief city of Bilad ash-Sham (land of Sham), is located in the al-Ghuta Oasis at the place where the Barada River (the fold), cuts through the Anti-Lebanon Mountains to meet the desert. The city sits at the eastern base of Jebal Kassioun, with its greater part, including the rectangular ancient city, lying on the south bank of the Barada, while modern suburbs extend from the north bank. Damascus, on the edge of the desert with the mountains behind, is strategically indefensible; for some, it is a boundary city, the last Mediterranean city before the desert.

With its regular water sources, the city has always been famous for its gardens, fed by seven ancient canals catching the flow from Wadi Barada to fan the precious water out across the plain. Traditionally encircled by green gardens, this *al-Fayha'a* (the fragrant city), as it has been called, depends on the al-Ghuta and its more than 100 villages for the agricultural products that feed the city and its industries. The city is situated 55 miles east of the Lebanese capital, Beirut, and 100 miles north of the Jordanian capital, Amman.

The origins of the city remain hidden, since there have been few archaeological digs within this bustling city itself. Its colloquial Arabic name, *Sham,* is traditionally said to be derived from *Shem,* the eldest son of Noah, because he chose to live there after the biblical flood; Josephus made a similar argument when he said that Damascus was founded by Noah's great grandson, Uz. Canaanite records from the Middle Bronze Age (2000 BC) talk about a state called Apu/Upu/Apum, which must be based around Damascus, although the city itself is not mentioned in the Mari archives.

The first written reference to the city is in the reign of Pharaoh Tuthmosis III during the fifteenth century BC when, on the lists at Tel-Amarna, he cites the rulers of cities he captured at Megiddo. Over the next 300 years, the city became famous for its loyalty to Egypt.

By 1200 BC, Aramean nomads had captured the city and began calling it Dimashqa. By the end of the eleventh century BC, the city entered a new period as a growing political power in the region, forging alliances with nearby city-states and fighting with them for control of long-distance trade. In particular, the Kings Highway, the caravan road south from Damascus to the Red Sea and Yemen, became a key resource, and the kingdom of Aram, based around Damascus, sought during the late tenth and on into the ninth century to project its power south into Palestine and Jordan. Key commentaries on the dynamics of this period are the stories in the Old Testament concerning David, Elisha, and Ahab's interactions with Damascus.

Gradually, over the next century, Damascus gained preeminence within the Aram confederation, and by 853 Damascus led a Syrian-Palestinian coalition that successfully halted the advance of the Assyrian Shalmaneser III. Although Shalmaneser III sent further expeditions against Damascus in 841 and 838, and there were other expeditions, such as the 773 campaign, which captured booty from the palace of the king of Damascus, it was not until ca. 732 that the Assyrians under Tiglathpileser III finally conquered the city. It is most probable that the remains of the Aramean city lie buried under the western part of the present-day walled city.

Under the Arameans, the god of Damascus was Hadad-Rimmon, and some of the city's rulers carried the title Ben Hadad (son of the god Hadad). The city was a cult city, particularly during the ninth century, and the altar in its temple may have served as the model for the altar built by Uriah in Jerusalem. This sacred status continued into Roman times when the temple of Jupiter Damascinus dominated the same site. The importance of Damascus as a trading city may have something to do with the spread of Aramaic throughout the Middle East and its adoption as the regional lingua franca over the next millennium.

Tiglathpileser III deported many of the local inhabitants and replaced them with Assyrian settlers and garrisoned troops in the city. It is from here that Assyrian soldiers set out to deal with nomadic raiders from the northern Nefud, an early historical record of "Arabs." Damascus became a regional capital, governing sixteen districts. The city subsequently fell in 572 BC to the neo-Babylonians under Nebuchadnezzar but was soon captured by the Persian king, Cyrus, who took the city in 538 BC and made Damascus the capital and military headquarters of the fifth Persian satrapy of Syria, employing the Greek name Koile Syria for the area around Damascus. The city served as a supply station for the messengers of the Achaemenid king heading between Persia and Egypt in the fifth century BC.

Alexander the Great and his armies swept through Syria in 332 BC, and Damascus with its treasure fell without a struggle. The city subsequently became an edge city for the Seleucid Empire in its confrontations with the Ptolemaic rulers of Egypt.

By the early Roman period, Damascus fell briefly under Nabatean rule (84 BC) before becoming one of the autonomous cities of the Decapolis with its incorporation into the Roman Empire in 64 BC. Damascene merchants became middlemen of the Roman Empire, marketing and distributing products between Europe and the Parthians on the Euphrates. Damascene products, such as glassware and cloth, became renowned throughout the empire. As a consequence, Damascus became one of the most prominent cities of the Roman Empire, and a new city was built over the ruins of the ancient one.

The Romans left an important architectural and town-planning legacy in Damascus. They incorporated the earlier Aramean and Greek sectors of the city into a uniform city plan and built a broad wall encircling the whole area. Seven gates cut the wall, with each named for one of the stars in the Pleiades (Seven Sisters) constellation. One of the most famous features derived from this period was the Street Called Straight, which was mentioned in the Bible in connection with Paul's conversion to Christianity. The street still connects Bab Sharqi (the Eastern Gate) to Bab al-Jabieh (so named because the people of the village of Jabieh entered this way). Along the length of the street ran an aqueduct, while a covered colonnade stood along both sides.

The major construction in Damascus during the Roman era was the Temple of Jupiter. It was built on the same site as the former Aramean temple, and some of its remains are still standing near the entrance of the Umayyad Mosque and Suq al-Hamidiyyah. Another major project was the forum, located at the eastern side of the mosque. A colonnaded street ran between the Forum to the Temple of Jupiter, and its columns can still be found in al-Qaymariyyah Quarter.

It was during this period that Damascus became a sacred site associated with early Christianity. Tradition holds that Saul of Tarsus (Paul) set off for Damascus ca. AD 37 to imprison members of the growing Christian community there; on "the road to Damascus" he had his dramatic conversion experience. Today there are four traditional sites in the city related to Paul's time in the city, including the House of Ananias, with its underground chapel, where Catholic, Orthodox, and Muslim supplicants come to pray for assistance.

Damascus became an important center for the fledgling Christian church, and the bishop of Damascus held the second most important ecclesiastical position after the patriarch of Antioch. When Christianity became the religion of the empire, pagan worship in Damascus was banned, and the Temple of Jupiter was converted into a cathedral dedicated to Saint John the Baptist. The city's sacred character attracted scholars such as Sophronius, Andrew of Crete, and Saint John of Damascus, who furthered the reputation of its theological school. Byzantine Damascus remained much the same as it had during the Roman period, except for the large increase in the construction of churches. The city was briefly held by the Sassanians.

In mid-March 635, a Muslim army surrounded the city. They had no experience in siege warfare, and so the siege dragged on for five months. Ultimately, the city fell when a Christian bishop secretly negotiated with one of the Arab generals and helped the forces sneak over the walls at night to open the gates. Meanwhile, Arab forces on the other side of the city, unknown to the others, negotiated a surrender, and the two wings of the Arab army reportedly bumped into each other in the coppersmith's bazaar in the center of the city. Because a surrender had been negotiated, the city was not looted or destroyed. For the victors, Damascus was, even then, an iconic city. Tradition held that Muhammad, while a trader, had headed for the city but then looked down on its beauty from the mountain. At that point, he decided not to enter Damascus, noting that because it was paradise on earth, he would not enter, since man can only enter paradise once.

Damascus's golden age began in AD 661 when Muawiyah Bin Abi Sufian established himself as the fifth caliph of Islam, founding the Umayyad dynasty, which ruled the Muslim Empire for about a century. Muawiyah made Damascus the imperial capital, and it quickly became the cultural, economic, and political center for an empire that stretched from Spain to the edges of India. Each of the fourteen Umayyad caliphs made his own contribution to the city, either by building mosques and palaces, patronizing arts and sciences, or developing the administrative system. The Umayyad rulers were also responsible for the introduction of new styles of art and architecture inspired by Islam. These new styles combined with Byzantine and Persian influences to produce architectural splendors such as the Great Mosque, Damascus's greatest monument.

The Umayyad, or Great Mosque, built between AD 705 and AD 715, is the premier historical site in the city. The entire ancient Roman *temenos* (a sacred enclosure, religious platform, or holy site) was cleared of all earlier internal structures to take the new plan: a rectangular mosque with an open courtyard of white marble overlooked on three sides by a graceful two-story arcade. In the middle of the courtyard are an ablutions fountain; the domal treasury, where public funds used to be kept; and the Dome of the Clocks. The fourth side forms the huge prayer hall, with its beautiful arches and pillars.

Inside the prayer hall is a small shrine reportedly holding the head of John the Baptist, and one of the four authorized versions of the Qur'an was also kept here. One of the two minarets is dedicated to Saidna Issa (Jesus), with the tradition that he will descend upon it to judge the world. Other traditions associated with this sacred site include that prayers in the Great Mosque are equal to those offered in Jerusalem, that worship in the Damascus mosque will continue for 40 years after the destruction of the world, and that if you stayed in the mosque 100 years, your eye could never take in all of its marvels. Ibn Battuta, visiting in 1326, called it the noblest mosque in the world and commented on its beautiful Door of Hours, which was closed progressively as the afternoon ticked away.

This fourth holiest site in Islam was known in medieval times for three aspects of its design: its arcaded mihrab, its mosaics (*fusayfusa*), and its *karma* (vines) decoration. The golden mosaics, representing an idealized Damascus of the past, with gardens, bridges, and houses, lined the courtyard, with golden vines interwoven in the design. Reportedly one-eightieth of the total cost of the building went into these golden vines, most of which disappeared in the devastating fires that engulfed the mosque over the centuries: 1069, 1400, and 1893. Both its architectural form and its scheme of decoration influenced many other mosques in the Muslim world, including Umayyad Spain and Seljuq Iran. Through the centuries, craftsmen, religious leaders, and merchants established themselves around the Great Mosque, creating an interwoven religious community built around key families.

The Umayyad golden age came to a violent end in AD 750. The Abbasids occupied Damascus, killed the caliph, and put an end to the Umayyad Caliphate. The new rulers tore down all the great buildings constructed by the Umayyads and moved the capital of the Islamic empire to Baghdad, with the result that Damascus became a provincial town with a declining population and a declining role in politics and culture (see also "Baghdad"). Successive assaults and civil strife marked the next three centuries, and Damascus continued to lose its strategic importance in the empire.

In AD 969, Damascus was captured by the powerful Shi'i Fatimids of Egypt. During their century-long occupation, the Fatimids had to face internal opposition from the Sunni elites, and external opposition from enemies, which had a significant impact on Damascus's layout and spatial development. Houses were built close together, and the different quarters built fortified gates and fences for protection. Each quarter also formed local militias of young men called *ahdath* to defend residents against potential aggressors; they also often sought to overthrow Fatimid rule, considered as foreign

and heretical. One result of the division of the Old City into separate quarters was a significant increase in the number of mosques, as each quarter erected its own. By the twelfth century, there were 242 mosques in the Old City alone.

The twelfth century was a difficult period for the city's inhabitants. Under Seljuq domination, various urban groups like the ahdath and the *ruasa* (urban heads) were able to emancipate themselves from centralized Seljuq control and to carve out a significant degree of autonomy over the economic and financial life of the city, but also over its security and administration. In Damascus, the *rais al-balad* (head of the city) shared power with the appointed vizier in a fragile compromise. Such compromises often broke down; in 1149, for example, the rais assembled the ahdath and besieged the Seljuq vizier in the citadel. After considerable fighting, a new compromise was reached, and a fragile peace was restored to the city. With the coming of Nur ad-Din, who captured the city in 1154, the role of rais disappeared, and local urban elites lost power in the city.

Crusaders attacked the city in 1129 and returned to place it under siege in 1148 during the Second Crusade. When the Crusaders abandoned their siege, the corpses they left behind in their camps stank so much that even the birds were driven off by the smell.

The victories of Nur ad-Din led to a rapprochement with the Fatimid caliph in Cairo, and soon Syria and Egypt were united under Cairo's nominal authority (see also "Cairo"). Nur ad-Din was a great patron of art and architecture in Damascus, and many monuments carried his name, some of which still stand today, such as the maristan (hospital) of Nur ad-Din, the hammam (baths) of Nur ad-Din, and the madrasa (school) of Nur ad-Din. He also ordered the construction of a palace and the renovation of the city's walls and gates.

Salah ad-Din entered the city in 1174, starting the rule of the Ayyubid dynasty. For the Ayyubids, the city was sacred as well as being key to establishing legitimacy in the infighting within the dynasty. During their rule, the political elites were constantly changing, giving the city the feel that it was ruled by immigrants. Perhaps that is why two interesting phenomena emerged. One was that many Ayyubid princesses underwrote religious architecture and institutions of learning in the city. Of the 160 new religious and charitable institutions built in the city during the twelfth and thirteenth centuries, 16 percent were funded by these women, who seemed to compete to support the faith and gild the glory of their dynasty. By the thirteenth century, Damascus was a key center of Sunni religious thought and scholarship. The second phenomenon is that the Ayyubids wanted to come home to this city: Salah ad-Din, al-Adil, and al-Kamil Muhammad are all buried in Damascus along with many regional princes or rulers of the city. Visitors to the city during this period were clearly amazed by its glory: a Spanish Muslim traveler (ca. 1184) extolled the young men of the Maghrib to move to Damascus, the center of the universe. Benjamin of Tudela visited the city's Jewish community in 1170, as did Maimonides in 1267; there may have been around 3,000 coreligionists at that time, and they supported a rabbinic academy and a number of synagogues. The size of the community increased as Jewish refugees fled the Crusaders in the twelfth century and again as Jews fled Spain after 1492.

The Mongols under Hulagu occupied the city in 1260 but were soon defeated nearby at the Battle of Ayn Jallout and withdrew to be replaced by the victorious Mamluks, whose rule was one of relative prosperity. For the Mamluks, Damascus served the function of a dual capital with Cairo, and it was the second city of Islam (see also "Cairo"). Like the Ayyubids, the Mamluks loved Damascus. Sultan Baybars I died there in 1277 and was interred within his completed mausoleum in 1281. The city grew so rapidly that congestion in the Old City forced expansion beyond the walls. The Salhiyyah Quarter underwent a surge of building and developed into a town of its own, with 500 mosques, baths, and khans. Contemporary maps of Damascus show that the city had expanded to such an extent that its Old City had become completely surrounded by suburbs.

The problems of feeding a huge city are illustrated by the example of Ibn an-Nasur, a wealthy grain broker and speculator (simsar) in cereal grains of the late fourteenth century. Ibn an-Nasur had constructed a monopoly over the city's food supply and grains and could raise the prices of wheat and barley as he wanted. The year 1397 was terrible, with a drought and Turkoman raids, so the city leaders called for a public prayer for rain (istisqa). An istisqa required public preparations, with three days of fasting and prayer, followed on the third day with a community procession to a prayer ground outside the city. Evidently, Ibn an-Nasur was hated by the public, who blamed him for their misery and the lack of available food supplies, so when they saw him at the istisqa, a boy threw a stone at him. Quickly, more stones followed, and Ibn an-Nasur was killed and trampled. The crowd then cut off his head; burned his body in the square in front of the citadel; looted his house, buildings, and wine; and then went home. When the wali (city governor) returned to the city, he arrested hundreds, including the boy, gutted all of them, and paraded their bodies around the city on camelback.

In the mid-fourteenth century, Damascus was the leading center in the world for the study and teaching of astronomy. Building on foundations during the ninth century with the work of Habash al-Hasib, and continuing through the tenth and eleventh centuries, the height of the city's celestial scholarship came with the research of Ibn ash-Shatir of Damascus (ca. 1350) and his coworker, al-Khalili. They were both employed at the Umayyad Mosque, calculating local directions for prayer (qibla) and prayer times, both of which required a study of the heavens. Ibn ash-Shatir developed theoretical models to correct problems with Ptolemy's versions and cre-

ated lunar models and planetary tables. He also created one of the most spectacular sundials in the world, located on the main minaret of the Umayyad Mosque. Such creativity came to an end with the destruction of the Great Mosque when Temür sacked Damascus in 1400.

The Ottoman armies of Selim I captured Damascus in 1516, and soon all the skilled craftsmen were removed to Istanbul, which depressed much of the artisan life of the city. Yet Damascus quickly came to have particular significance for the Ottomans, certainly for their self-image as the inheritors of the caliphal and Umayyad mantles but more so for its role as the western gate to Makkah (see also "Istanbul"). For a millennium and a half, pilgrims leaving on the hajj have departed the city through the "Gates of God" in a great caravan. Assembled from Iraq, Syria, and Anatolia, and traditionally under the command of the Imarat al-Hajj (commander of the holy pilgrimage), often the pasha of Damascus, the pilgrims spent weeks in Damascus preparing for the long journey and procuring local provisions before the caravan set out. Damascus, for example, provided the preserved foods vital for provisioning the caravans, including the apricot paste made from the famous Damascus mishmish (apricots). The departure of the caravan was a religious event, as was its return; the merchandise that the pilgrims brought back from Arabia as they returned home stirred the markets of the city as well. By the mid-nineteenth century, improvements in transport and technology meant that the size of the caravan increased dramatically, and Damascus benefited proportionally. The most significant development was the Hijaz (or Pilgrim Line) Railway, built between Damascus and Makkah to facilitate the hajj.

One of the most infamous chapters in Ottoman Damascus history is the fate that befell the 1757 hajj. The caravan was attacked by Bedouin, and 20,000 pilgrims were killed or subsequently died for lack of water in the desert. The dead included the sultan's sister. Although perhaps instigated by a former governor of Damascus for political purposes, the disaster was representative of the century-long decay in Ottoman control over the city and its region that had set in by the mid-eighteenth century.

For the Ottomans, Damascus quickly became a key administrative and garrison city. For sixty years after their conquest, for example, they used the city as a base in their attempt to pacify insurgents in the Lebanese mountains. In particular, the Druze areas of the Shuf were not easily controlled, and so a number of punitive expeditions were dispatched from Damascus into the area. The Druze were viewed as heretics, and leading Damascus ulema issued fatwas to the effect that they were not Muslims or dhimmis (people of the book, or contract; i.e., Christians or Jews) and thus could be killed and their property confiscated. In 1523 the governor of Damascus and his soldiers campaigned against them, destroying forty-four villages, returning to Damascus with four

Sketch of Damascus, 1668. (Dapper, Olfert, *Naukeurige beschryving van gantsch Syrie, en Palestyn of Heilige Lant,* . . . p. 17. Amsterdam: Jacob van Meurs, 1677)

wagonloads of heads. A year later, thirty more villages were destroyed and three more wagonloads of heads brought back, along with 300 women and children as slaves. The poets of Damascus celebrated this great victory over the infidels, although it was not until 1585 that a major military campaign was able to pacify the area.

Damascus witnessed great physical changes during the Ottoman era. The greater part of new Ottoman construction took place during the first century of the Ottoman rule, when the empire was economically and militarily strong. Immediately after taking Damascus, Sultan Selim I built the Takiyyeh Mosque. Darwish Pasha was responsible for building the Silk Suq, bath, and a khan inside the walled Old City. Migrants from Palestine in particular flooded into the city, taking advantage of the Ottoman building program to find work.

One significant member of a long family line of Damascus religious figures of this age was Abd al-Ghani an-Nabulusi (1641–1731). Often called the peoples' saint, he was considered by many the outstanding Arab Sufi of his day. An-Nabulusi had memorized the Qur'an by heart by the age of five, and by the age of twenty he was teaching at the Umayyad Mosque

and writing poetry. In his later years, he wrote on Islamic theology and practice, including suggesting that smoking was permissible under Islamic law. He spoke out against government corruption and the rampages of the Turkish Janissaries (the sultan's professional slave military) in the city and was forced out of his home near the Great Mosque by neighborhood feuding, in which he participated and lost an eye.

The period from 1720 to 1830 was a chaotic and difficult time for the inhabitants of Damascus. The city was autonomous and distant from Ottoman control. During the eighteenth century, most of the governors of Damascus were chosen from the Damascene al-Azm family, which became one of the most famous families in the Arab world. Having the governorship held by a local family brought a building boom to Damascus. Dozens of baths, khans, schools, and suqs were built, most of which still remain today. The Azm Palace, built as a palatial residence for Asad Pasha al-Azm in the mid-eighteenth century, is considered a great example of Damascene houses; it is used today to house the Museum of Popular Arts and Tradition.

Yet famine, disease, and banditry were regular occurrences; anarchy ruled the city's streets; and Damascus was being drawn more deeply into the European world economy with consequent effects on society. In 1743, for example, there was no food in the city; drought struck in 1745, 1747, and 1751; locusts hit in 1746; and the plague broke out in 1743, 1755, and 1757. Natural disasters also struck Damascus: on 17 December 1759, one-third of the city was destroyed in an earthquake, with more than 20,000 killed.

Within the city, local warlords contested for control beneath a constantly rotating parade of Ottoman administrators without power or authority; armed factions battled for control of neighborhoods and political power within the city streets. Peasants and tribal groups immigrated to the city and sold their services for hire to any Sufi order, guild, quarter, or non-Muslim group. These armed gangs were then played off against the alien military units from North Africa or Kurdistan who were supposed to be supporting the Ottoman administration. The city was consistently racked by fighting, for example, between 1738 and 1743.

Citizens fluctuated between having no confidence in officials and having support for them. In 1745, for example, Asad Pasha al-Azm, the governor, failed to move against the irregular soldiers (*zurbawat*) terrorizing citizens; thus, the people reportedly derogatorily renamed him Saadiyya Kadin (Madam Saadiyya). That same year, hungry mobs chased judges out of town. Yet the people liked Asad; he was known for his tolerance for Christians, allowing them and the Jews not to wear the traditional indicative clothing of their status. Problems continued, however, and the city fell into violence again in 1750, 1753, and 1757, while in 1772 the city was temporarily occupied by Amir Yusuf Shihab, the Druze leader, whose soldiers ransacked the city. The governor of Damascus, Selim Pasha, was killed by its inhabitants in 1831.

This long century of decline was capped by the invasion of Syria by Ibrahim Pasha, son of Muhammad Ali, the ruler of Egypt. During the 1832–1840 occupation by the Egyptians, Damascus prospered and was opened to new influences, including those from Europe. With the 1840 return of the Ottomans, supported by the European powers, a new era began, as the Ottoman administration struggled to implement the Tanzimat reforms and to prevent further political intrusion by imperial powers into Syria. Yet Britain and France took advantage of the militarily weak Ottoman administration in Istanbul to make inroads into the city's economic sphere. Foreign merchants poured into Damascus to buy raw materials for processing by the new machines of the industrial revolution. By 1848 European factory-produced imports cut into local production, and the Europeans were aggressively seeking to supplement their economic clients in Damascus to build their political base. The British, for example, sought out Jews, and the few Protestants there were as clients, and Chris-

tians moved into positions as merchant entrepreneurs, particularly in textiles.

The city had a base of agriculture products, particularly in grain wholesaling, mills, presses of olive oil, sesame and molasses, and cornstarch manufacturers. In the services sector, bathhouses and coffee shops were the base of the ulema, while the merchants were involved in textiles, the most important branch of Damascus manufacturing. Yet all this appeared threatened by the changes post-1840. As a result, many Damascenes felt that the Ottoman Empire could not stand up to or stop European penetration of the region. One early manifestation may have been the first ever blood-libel accusations against the Damascene Jewish community (1840); this "Damascus Affair" attracted international attention. Another was when people in the city were so concerned about foreign intrusion that some opposed the 1850s Beirut-to-Damascus highway because it would link them more closely with Europe.

One early aspect of the Tanzimat reforms was the creation of a local council. In 1845, for example, this twelve-man body of Muslim elites was moved, based on complaints from the Jewish community about a rowdy tavern in their quarter, to ban all taverns in the city. They also considered the case of the barbers who couldn't get enough leeches since the prices set by the government were too high; therefore, they smuggled them into the city and were caught. This Majlis Shura ash-Sham al-Ali (Damascus Advisory Council), an early attempt at local authority, did represent the beginning for local governance, if ever short-lived and limited in its powers.

The internal tension in the city boiled over in July 1860 with the great massacre (*al-haditha,* as it came to be known) of 10,000 of the city's Christian citizens. Discontented soldiers, Druze forces, and urban Muslims all went on the rampage, and for a week the largely Greek Christian Quarter of Damascus around Bab Tuma was attacked. Churches, Christian businesses, and foreign consulates were all targeted; they were looted then burned. All confessions within the Christian community were affected, including the Syrian Orthodox, Armenian, Maronite, and Catholic groups. In a demonstration of its deep concern, Istanbul sent Fuad Pasha, the former foreign minister, to Damascus to restore order and to keep the Europeans from having an excuse to intervene. Once there, he gave houses to those who had suffered, placed fines on non-Christians, sent Muslim youth into the army, and arrested and executed participants in the massacres.

Damascus grew to twice its former size during the nineteenth century. The city was streamlined with new avenues, and many new suqs were constructed in residential areas, including Suq al-Hamidiyyeh, Suq Medhat Pasha, Suq Nazem Pasha, and Suq Ali Pasha, all named after the governors who ordered their construction. The French paved the road between Damascus and Beirut in 1863 and also paid for the

Hauran/Damascus/Beirut Railway, which opened in 1895. By 1880 the first graduates of new, secular judicial and educational institutions, beyond ulema control, had graduated and were beginning to reshape the city.

The concerns they developed were not necessarily those of the government in Istanbul, however. By the 1870s, there were secret societies in Damascus, composed of both Arab nationalists and Muslim reformers. One of the greatest religious reformers in Damascus was Shaykh Tahir al-Jazairi (1852–1920), sometimes called the Muhammad Abduh of Syria. He sought to reform Islam, reintroduce the Arab heritage of Islam, and to move toward national regeneration. He was sometimes called the "Shaykh of the Arab Liberals." Such men invited the famous reformer Rashid Rida to come and speak in Damascus. Rida spoke twice in the mosque in 1908 on the need for progress and looking to combine Islam and science. Although there was a confrontation with conservative ulema in the mosque, Rida's ideas found fertile ground in the city, which had become the center of the Arab national movement.

The Arab Renaissance Society (Jamiyyat an-Nahda al-Arabiyya), one of the first nationalist parties in Syria, was founded in the city in 1906. When the Committee for Union and Progress (CUP) pulled off its 1908 coup in Istanbul, there was much celebration in Damascus, and when the CUP deposed the sultan in 1909, the city offered a 101-gun salute, and public celebrations occurred throughout the city (see also "Istanbul"). Yet by 1914, disaffected notables of the landowning bureaucracy class hurt by the Young Turk slide into despotism and Pan-Turkism were the ones behind the Damascus Protocol, written and published by Damascus nationalists who supported Sharif Hussayn's 1916 Arab Revolt.

During World War I, Istanbul put the infamous Jamal Pasha (the butcher) in charge of Damascus to keep the Syrians in place. He finally moved against the Arab nationalist movement in May 1916, hanging a number of Damascus's elite in al-Marja Square. By the time the Arab Forces took the city on 1 October 1918, supported by General Allenby's Australian troops, they were greeted by a city decked out in the Hejazi flag, symbol of Arab independence.

Most of the city's elites were sympathetic to the attempts by the Hashemites to set up an Arab state, and therefore they supported Faysal, the son of the sharif of Makkah, in his bid to lead the new Arab entity. The new Syrian Congress in Damascus, in March 1920, declared Syria an independent constitutional monarchy and Faysal its king. Syrians issued their own dinars, supported resistance to French forces in Lebanon, and began to construct an administration. However, it transpired that the British had made a separate, secret agreement with the French during the war, in the form of the Sykes-Picot Agreement (1916), giving the latter the right to control Syria after the war. French control over Syria was con-

firmed when the newly formed League of Nations recognized France as the mandatory power. Thus, on 25 July 1920, French troops fought their way into Damascus, declared their mandate, deposed the new Arab government, and condemned to death leading nationalists. Faysal ended up with the British in Baghdad, Damascus's leading nationalists fled into exile, and the French created a federation of statelets, including a Damascus State declared in November 1920 (see also "Beirut" and "Baghdad").

The first governor of Damascus under French authority was a malleable Haqqi al-Azm, scion of the ancient Damascus al-Azm family. Over the next few years, al-Azm proceeded to line his own pockets and to fill the posts in the city's administration with family members and his own clients. Meanwhile, nationalist leaders began to organize an underground movement called the Jamiyyat al-Qabda al-Hadidiyya (Iron Hand Society). Their first organized protest set a pattern for subsequent protests for the rest of the mandate: after Friday prayers at the Umayyad Mosque, thousands would stream out into the Suq al-Hamidiyyah and march toward the citadel, the French headquarters, and main prison. In response, the French repressed the protest, injuring many and killing some and arresting the Iron Hand leaders and interning them on an island off the coast.

In 1925 the Syrians began their long march to independence with what was called the Great Syrian Revolt. This started in southern Syria, in Jabal Druze, but battles quickly spread to Damascus. Rebel forces used the gardens to the south and east of the capital as their base for attack. In an attempt to suppress the revolt, French warplanes indiscriminately bombed the capital, and artillery pounded the city for twenty-four hours, causing much damage in parts of the Old City. Perhaps as many as 1,500 people were killed, with more than 100 million francs in damages. The administration also used its Circassian, Armenian, and Moroccan troops in brutal repression; in one incident, twenty-four corpses were piled in al-Marja Square and prisoners made to dance around them. In retribution, two days later, the bodies of twelve Circassians, still in uniform, were discovered piled near Bab ash-Sharqi. By early 1926, the city was also encircled by a new, free-fire corridor with barbed-wire and machine-gun nests to control infiltrators. The city came under attack from the air two other times before the end of the revolt in 1927, with an additional 1,500 people killed and whole quarters of the city destroyed.

With the end of the revolt, nationalist activity in the city moved into the political arena. The city still housed the core of the Syrian nationalist movement working for independence. Many of these came together in 1928 to found the National Bloc (al-Kutla al-Wataniyya), headquartered in Damascus. By 1936 the National Bloc, along with student, ulema, and merchant leaders, was able to organize a forty-three-day strike, which began moving the French toward negotiating and accepting independence for Syria. The National Bloc was able to enforce its will within Damascus via a youth organization called al-Qumsan al-Hadidiyyah (Steel Shirts); dressed in their Fascist-type uniforms, these paramilitary cadres were dedicated to patriotic values and committed to sacrifice for the nation. By 1937 there were well more than 4,000 members in the city.

The first locally financed modern industries in the city appeared after 1928. This move toward industrialization picked up steam, and by the middle of the 1930s there were more than sixty modern factories in Damascus; by the 1940s, most new industry was being located on the outskirts of a rapidly expanding city. One growth area was fruit processing. Drawing on the gardens of the al-Ghuta, Damascus had become particularly famous for its mishmish, produced primarily as apricot paste for export. The new Syrian Conserves Company moved heavily into this business, exporting tons of dried processed fruits and vegetables annually, much of it to Palestine. Shukri al-Quwwatli, the radical nationalist leader and future president of Syria (1943), founded the company using family land and products; his involvement meant that Quwwatli became known as *malik al-Mishmish* (the Apricot King).

It was not until 1941, during World War II, that France finally recognized Syrian independence, but it kept its military presence on Syrian soil for the duration of the war. When the French did not live up to their promise to grant independence, Syrians revolted again. Damascus came under heavy bombardment in May 1945, and the parliament building was targeted. International pressure forced France to leave, however, and on 17 April 1946 the last French troops left the city.

Although the early years of independence were marked with political instability, successive coups d'état, and an attempt at unity with Egypt (1958–1961), the city grew rapidly in the postindependence period. As the seat of government, the city expanded beneath the growth of the powers of the state, the increased functions of the government, and the migration of rural population to the metropolis. Palestinian refugees also contributed to the growth of the city, congregating in camps near the city, the largest being Yarmuk Camp; at one point it hosted 200,000 refugees. By the late 1980s, the camp was also attracting poor Syrians to its cheaper housing and lower prices. Saida Zeinab Camp, south of Damascus, housed those Palestinians who fled the 1982 Israeli invasion of Lebanon or the Amal sieges of 1985.

Economically, Damascus has long been an important commercial center. Across the centuries, the city has become associated with a number of high-quality products, to which the city's name became attached. For example, sword blades forged of damascene steel, exceptionally hard and resilient, were desired by military elites across the globe for more than a millennium. Tradition says that Alexander the Great had a sword made of damascene steel, and the unique design of layered fine markings on the blade became known as "Muhammad's Ladder." Europeans could not discover the secret of its manufacture and developed many theories of how its strength was achieved; one story circulated suggesting that only if the red-hot blade was plunged into the belly of a muscular slave could it be cooled correctly and thus retain its edge. The city also gave its name to damask silk, a type of patterned silk fabric woven in Damascus.

The modern city follows a plan devised by French architects during the mandate and revised in the 1960s. Wide boulevards were laid down and along them were built concrete blocks of flats. Government buildings are concentrated in an area west of the walled city around Marjah Square and in several districts west of Salhiyyah. As the population grew, more and more of the garden and farm areas were converted to residential districts. Farming villages close by were incorporated into the city administratively and physically. Nevertheless, the government has attempted to retain green areas by zoning industry, which has slowed the loss of gardens and orchards and given Damascus a light and airy character.

Outstanding aspects of the city's physical infrastructure include the city's many suqs, the most famous of which is the Suq al-Hamidiyyah, which runs from east to west and ends at a Roman archway before the Umayyad Mosque. Another is the Citadel of Damascus, which stands on the site of the old Roman *castrum,* or military camp. The finest Ottoman monument in the city is Tekkiye Mosque complex, which was planned by the architect Sinan. The buildings that surround the mosque's courtyard were also built as accommodation for the Dervishes, known for their religious chants and whirling dances. To such ancient monuments was added the University of Damascus in 1923 and the Damascus National Museum.

Today the city is the trading center for figs, almonds, and other fruit produced in the surrounding region. Industries in Damascus include handicrafts such as the weaving of silk cloth and the making of leather goods, filigreed gold and silver objects, and inlaid wooden furniture. During the twentieth century, the city's industries produced a powerful trade union movement. By the 1930s there were large textile plants in the city, and by the 1950s the city hosted the country's most militant trade union movement, with one-quarter of all union workers in Syria in Damascus. By the mid-1980s, many of these workers were women; women made up one-quarter of all textile workers and one-third of all the tobacco workers in the city. They also worked in small-scale metalwork shops and in the assembly of electrical appliances.

The city has experienced high rates of urbanization since independence, particularly between 1980 and 1994, when the population increased 67 percent; in the mid-1990s, it was estimated that 40 percent of the population lived in informal settlements where there were environmental problems, high crime, and significant unemployment. Most of the citizens are Sunni Muslim, although large numbers of Alawites from the

Latakia region have settled in Damascus since they became more prominent in government and army service. In addition, there are significant minorities of Druze from the Golan Heights, now under Israeli control, and Palestinian refugees. There is a wide range of Christian denominations in the city, but the historic and once-flourishing Jewish population has declined through immigration to a few members.

Twenty percent of Syria's current gross domestic product comes from oil, and this is projected to run out around 2020. Damascus will have difficult times preparing for such a shift. The government is beginning to open up investment laws, and fresh investment is coming into the city, including for a new Damascus World Trade Center financed by Sharjah money. Promoting tourism has become a higher priority, and Damascus will benefit if there is an increase in visitors. Telecommunications is perhaps the next big area for investment, with the city's growing population and low penetration rate exciting investors.

Michael Dumper

Further Readings

Bahnassi, Afif. *Damascus: The Capital of the Umayyad Dynasty.* Damascus: Dar Tlass for Studies, Translation and Publication, 2002.

Barbir, Karl. *Ottoman Rule in Damascus, 1708–1758.* Princeton: Princeton University Press, 1980.

Khoury, Philip. *Urban Notables and Arab Nationalism: The Politics of Damascus, 1860–1920.* Cambridge: Cambridge University Press, 1983.

Pitard, Wayne. *Ancient Damascus: A Historical Study of the Syrian City-State from Earliest Times until Its Fall to the Assyrians in 732 BC.* Winona Lake, IN: Eisenbrauns, 1987.

Rafeq, Abdel Karim. *The Province of Damascus, 1723–1783.* Beirut: Khayats, 1966.

Tergemen, Siham. *Daughter of Damascus.* Austin: University of Texas Press, 1994.

Ziadeh, Nicola. *Damascus under the Mamluks.* Norman: University of Oklahoma Press, 1964.

Diyarbakir
Population: 750,000 (2004 estimate)

Diyarbakir, the primary city for the Kurdish community in southeastern Turkey, is an ancient trading port on the Dicle (upper Tigris) River. A city of resistance, heterodox beliefs, conflict, and scholarship, Diyarbakir can trace its history back at least 3,500 years as a key border town and security city guarding the mountain passes between Anatolia, Iraq, and Persia. With its huge basalt city walls, numerous mosques, and historic churches, the city is as proud of its remarkable resilience as it is unsure of its regional future.

Diyarbakir (ancient, *Amid;* Greek, *Amida;* Arabic, *Kara Amid* or *Diyar al-Bakr;* Kurdish, *Amed;* Turkish, *Diyarbakir*) is nestled in the mountains on the upper reaches of the Tigris River at a point where the river cuts through the Taurus Mountains to find its way to the plains of northern Mesopotamia below. Diyarbakir sits on an upland plateau of basalt rock on the west bank of the river at the edge of a large fertile valley. The ancient citadel rises some 300 feet above the bluffs overlooking the river. A gap in the Syrian range allows rain-laden clouds from the west to deposit their moisture over Diyarbakir, creating an agricultural hinterland that has always supplied the needs of the city and produced excess available for export. The city has long been known for its agricultural products, including its famous melons. The nearby mountains have provided mineral wealth, making the city the center of a rich copper-, iron-, lead-, and coal-mining industry. Through passes in the mountains, it is possible to reach the Black Sea coast, the center of Anatolia, the Iranian plateau, or the Mediterranean; downriver lies Mosul, Baghdad, and the Persian Gulf. Thus, the city has long been a key transit site, marking the intersection of river traffic and overland trade.

Some thirty miles north of the city lies Cayonu Tepesi, one of the most important Neolithic sites in the Middle East. Archaeological remains suggest habitation in the area as early as 7250 BC and demonstrate the early use of copper metal tools, a female deity cult, farming, and the domestication of dogs. It is unclear when the actual site of the city was first inhabited, but we know that the Hurri and the Hittites controlled the area during their ascendancy. But it is in early records of the Assyrians that we first hear specific reference of the city as the capital of the Aramean kingdom Bit-Zamani around the thirteenth century. In the great rebellion against Shalmaneser II in the ninth century BC, the city joined those attempting to throw off his power. Later Assyrian records contain five letters from the governor of the city of Amid, one Upah har-Bel, who writes to King Sargon II in 705 BC to complain of a lack of support.

Amid was captured by the Achaemenid Persians in 546 BC, and it became linked into the great Royal Road up the north side of the Tigris, tying the empire together. Alexander the Great captured the city known to him as Amida in 331 BC in his march through Anatolia.

It is from this time that we have our first records of the Kurds (*Cyrtii*) as mountain nomads in the region surrounding the city. The city clearly is part of the major trade routes of the area, and the Romans use the same routes for linking Amida south to Nineveh (Mosul). For the Romans, the city is known as the capital of Sophene, which was a south Armenian principality around AD 50. As the Romans expanded into the region in the first and second centuries, the city became a key frontier site in the confrontation with the Parthians. Amida became a Roman colony from AD 230 and was crucial to the confrontation with the new Sassanian dynasty. With the treaty of AD 299, the city experienced a period of peace and strengthening. It is under Constantine and his son Constantinus (324–361) that the city was elevated to a new level of regional authority and power. The foundations of the extensive walls of the city were constructed in AD 349, the Roman bridge that still stands was built, and the city was designated the capital of the Roman province of Mesopotamia. Jewish communities in the city supported the trade along the Roman road that links Zeugma on the Euphrates via Edessa, Amida, and Nisibis to Babylon and the Gulf.

Given the continued confrontation with the Sassanians, Amida's importance as a strategic site and security city was continually reaffirmed. In the mid-fourth century, the Sassanians under Shapur II attempted to take the city. The siege of Amida, reportedly employing 100,000 soldiers, lasted seventy-three days, which caused dissent in Rome on how to respond, since some parties wished to abandon that frontier and fall back to the Euphrates. Shapur II used Huns as mercenaries and finally took the city after losing one-third of his soldiers, but the lengthy engagement held up his plans and meant he could not pursue the invasion of the Roman Empire as he wished. In his anger, he ordered the destruction of Amida and all its inhabitants (AD 360). The Syrian Greek historian Ammianus Marcellinus records in his *Res Gestae* how he escaped from Amida on horseback by night just as Shapur's forces were taking the city. Emperor Julian set out to recapture the cities lost to the Persians although he died in the area in 363.

This frontier region of the Byzantine Empire became the center of Nestorian Christianity (Syro-Chaldean) after 431, with Edessa, Nisibis, and Amida all hosting the heterodox sect. The city hosted a Chaldean archbishopric, and the Church of the Virgin Mary (Meryem Ana Kilisesi) was constructed over earlier pre-Christian temple foundations. The city's shrines and saints' reliquaries, parts of the cross and ancient Bible manuscripts, attracted pilgrims, and it became a stop on the missionary trail to the east. The city became a site for great learning and Syriac theology, and its scholars played roles throughout the empire. The Byzantine court physician in the early sixth century was Aetius of Amida (AD 502–575). In his book *Iatricorum,* he deals with a range of issues, including abortion and contraception, and presents a justification for female genital mutilation. Under Justinian (527–565), the zealous monk John of Amida was appointed bishop of Ephesus and ruthlessly attacked pagan sacrifices and temples in western Anatolia. The Syriac bishop of Amida, Moro Bar Kustant, while living in Alexandria in the first half of the sixth century, accumulated an extensive library. With his death, his library was transferred to the treasury of the church in Amida, where remnants can be found today.

After two generations of peace, war with Persia returned to Amida in AD 502 with a Persian attack on the city led by King Kavadh. The role of the religious elite within the city is highlighted at the time, since monks were clearly involved in both political and military decision making. Reportedly during the three-month Sassanian siege, the monks manned the defense of the city, although the Persians found a section of wall where the monks were drunk and stormed the town; they massacred 80,000 inhabitants once they took the city. When the Byzantines mounted a return engagement ca. 503, their siege of the city lasted longer, and those inside were reduced to cannibalism.

A resurgent Byzantine Empire under Hiraclius reappeared outside Amida in 625 for the first time in generations and captured the city. The emperor spent the winter of 628–629 in Amida after the defeat of the Persians and reclaimed the pieces of the Holy Cross.

The victorious Arab armies captured the city in AD 638. In Arabic the city is called Kara Amid, or "Black Amid." Over the next three centuries it became closely connected to the long-distance trade routes of the Abbasid Empire and its new capital, Baghdad, and flourished during the eighth and ninth centuries. As the Abbasid dynasty crumbled after AD 940, however, the city's fortunes become connected with the rise of local Kurdish dynasties. In particular, the Marwanids (984–1083), with their capital in Mayyafiriqin near Kara Amid, controlled the region until the end of the century.

The Seljuqs dominated the city during the end of the eleventh century, but it passed to the Ayyubids until the Mongols under Hulagu Khan captured it in 1258. The successor state of the Ilkhanids governed the city until 1336 in a time of chaos and limited economic exchange. Just as the city was beginning to recover, Temür grabbed it in 1386. The Shi'i Qara Quyunlu, or Black Sheep, and the Sunni Aq Quyunlu, or White Sheep (1378–1502), controlled the city until the rise of the Safavids. All these invasions had a number of profound implications for the region and for the city. The first was in the ethnic makeup of the city and its hinterland. By the end of the fifteenth century, the area around Diyarbakir was significantly Turkoman and Muslim. In the mountains, the Kurds still were the majority, but the wider region progressively became Turkoman. Their control also meant a shift in the trade routes. During the fourteenth century, Tabriz became the key emporium, much more important than Baghdad for world trade (see also "Tabriz"). Under the Mongols, Asia Minor had become an important route between India and the Mediterranean. With the fall of the Mongols, and then followed by Temür's destruction of key cities along the northern route, the southern route from Iran via Syria to Bursa or Aleppo gained importance. Diyarbakir's centrality to these routes remained across this time period.

With the establishment of the new Safavid dynasty at Tabriz, the city's importance as a significant transit site increased. Shah Ismail captured Diyarbakir in 1507 and made it a provincial capital with a governor. The expanding Ottomans, however, could not leave the city in the hands of the Shi'i and conspired with the Kurdish *begs* (chieftains) to take the city. The population declared for the Ottoman sultan Selim I in 1514, and the Safavid governor, Mustafa Ustaclu Han, withdrew. The victorious Ottoman army quickly left the city, however, and Shah Ismail sent Kara Bey, the brother of the former governor, to retake it. However, the Kurdish begs protected the city until the Ottomans could return once again. From that point on, the city was incorporated into the Ottoman dynasty, and the Kurdish chiefs were recognized as local administrators and adjunct forces under Ottoman suzerainty. The largest tribes in the province were the Boz Ulus (the gray people) and the Kara Ulus (the black people); the Ottomans may have recognized more than 400 tribal chiefs and their authority in the region. Establishing these semiautonomous satraps did pay off for the Ottomans: for example, Kurdish forces came to the defense of Diyarbakir in 1515 when the city was under siege for eighteen months.

The Ottomans made Diyarbakir a *beylerbeyiligi* (provincial capital) in 1515 and recognized substantial Kurdish autonomy through local amirates ruling outside the city; the city continued to serve as the center for an administrative district under the Ottoman authorities. In the first tax census (1520), the records indicate that Diyarbakir contained, among other communities, a Jewish population of 288 households.

A miniature painting of the city, dating from 1537, exists and shows the citadel and the important mosques and churches in the city. It is contained in a manuscript entitled *A Description of the Stages of Sultan Sulayman's Campaign in the Two Iraqs,* written and illustrated by Nasuh as-Silahi al-Matraki and made during Sulayman's military campaign against Persia in 1534–1536.

Under the Ottomans, the city again prospered as part of the silk and spice routes from Iran to Europe. Iranian raw silk in particular moved in great quantities toward its terminus in Bursa, but Aleppo gradually improved as an option as well, since the southern routes were easier. The southern route went Bitlis-Diyarbakir-Mardin-Aleppo. This transport system was still caravan based around the mid-1800s, when European observers recorded that it took sixteen days to get to Alexandretta on the Mediterranean from Diyarbakir and that 600 camels would compose one caravan to Aleppo (see also "Aleppo").

A variety of goods moved the other direction as well. Caravans from Aleppo would arrive in Diyarbakir in the spring, just as the snows melted from the mountains and increased the flow of the river. These goods, supplemented with products from the city and its hinterland, were placed on *tanaquins* (flat-bottomed ships of the Tigris) and floated downriver to Mosul. Once there other ships and goods were added, and a flotilla then set out for Basrah. At that great emporium, goods could be placed on oceangoing ships and sent out to India or to the East African coast. Diyarbakir, Aleppo, and Mosul became a key triad for the Ottoman Empire, particularly as contacts with Europe via Aleppo increased during the seventeenth and eighteenth centuries (see also "Basrah" and "Mosul").

Other products and knowledge moved across this great network of which Diyarbakir was a crucial node: the city was a sheep supplier to Istanbul, and huge herds of sheep would be driven all the way to the capital. It was also a key producer of grains and grapes for Anatolia in intra-Ottoman trade. But the city also served its hinterland as a major industrial producer: its factories produced white cloth, Moroccan leather, colored (red) leather, agricultural implements, locally raised cocoons, handkerchiefs, caps, gauze, wool cloth, shoes, striped cloth, printed cloth, ironwares, stockings, and sole leather.

The economy was not always profitable, however. In 1757 the city suffered a terrible famine after locusts ate all the crops. In such times of need, Mosul often came to the aid of its sister city further upstream, providing surplus grain. At other times, as in 1859, 1897, and 1901, Diyarbakir met the needs of Mosul's starving citizens with its own surplus agricultural production.

By the late 1800s, the power of European demand, capital, and technology was beginning to affect the great long-distance trade routes and the shape of local production. European steamships on the Black Sea brought European goods to Samson on the coast, which were then shipped overland more quickly to Diyarbakir or on to Mosul. To meet increasing European demand, silk weaving in the city expanded, with the number of looms rising in the mid-nineteenth century. Although there were some attempts at industrialization, it was not until the 1900s that the looms of the city were effectively modernized. Even in 1900, however, the city reportedly had more than 600 looms, with another 1,000 located in villages surrounding the city.

The city's position on the trade routes meant that it was a site for new ideas and for resistance to central beliefs and authority. Catholic missionaries appeared in Diyarbakir and had some success among the Syriac Orthodox and Armenians after 1627, making their way along the trade routes from Aleppo in the wake of the growth of French influence in that area of the Ottoman Empire. Despite the loss of political autonomy for the Kurdish tribes surrounding the city in the late 1800s, the city became a center for Kurdish nationalism during this time. Kurdish groups formed in the city, and Kurds from Diyarbakir in Istanbul also founded societies like the Society for the Rise and Progress of Kurdistan. Ziya Gökalp, the chief ideologue for the Young Turks, grew up in Diyarbakir. As the Young Turks sought to restructure the empire and to Turkify its foundations, the Kurds around Diyarbakir became more aggressive, hostile to the Young Turks and to their ideas. Intellectuals within the city suggested a range of options, including regional autonomy for Diyarbakir.

In the wake of the Ottoman defeat in World War I, the Kurdish question appeared on the international and national agenda. What should be done, and how autonomous should Kurdistan be? Kurdish journalists from Diyarbakir argued that British protection was necessary and that the Turks could not be trusted to give autonomy to Kurds. In fact, as the Greeks and other forces invaded, the Turks could not afford to consider a Kurdish state or federated system and so took a tough line with any hint of Kurdish separateness or cultural difference. The British did interfere in the politics of the region by encouraging the creation of a separate Kurdish government; they may actually have financed Kurdish clubs in Diyarbakir during the early 1920s.

A new Kurdish movement, the Azadi (Freedom), organized the first revolt in Kurdistan in 1923. As part of the uprising, the governor of Diyarbakir was assassinated, and the new Turkish government responded by arresting many of the movement's leaders. One local religious leader, Shaykh Said, angry with Atatürk for abolishing the caliphate, took over the leadership. This Naqshbandi shaykh raised the flag of revolt in the spring of 1925, called for the creation of a Kurdish government and the reestablishment of the caliphate, and actually appointed a king of Kurdistan. Said marched with 5,000 rebels on Diyarbakir and besieged the city. Strengthened by the Seventh Army Corp headquartered within its walls, however, Diyarbakir did not fall, and Shaykh Said was caught and hanged in the city, along with forty-six others, in September 1925. Over the next few months, under a "Tribunal of Independence," 660 Kurdish nationalists were executed, many religious leaders deported from the city to western Anatolia, and surrounding villages burned to the ground. Although unrest continued in the city through 1927, this major attempt to destroy Kurdish nationalism repressed the uprising. The new central government tried to cement its control by establishing a regional teacher-training institution in the city to further the "Turkification" of the education system.

The city experienced a 25 percent loss in population at the end of the nineteenth century and beginning of the twentieth century but began to expand again by the 1930s, finally spilling outside the ancient city walls. One reason for this decline in population was the immigration of members of the Armenian and Syriac communities. There were attacks in 1895 and in 1915 on both communities, and many fled to escape the violence. The Syriac community remembers the 1915 attacks as *Sayfo* (the year of the Sword). It is from this time that the Syriac community in New Jersey, composed of silk weavers, marks its immigration from Diyarbakir. For the Armenians, they remember at least 2,500 people killed in Diyarbakir in 1895. Others consider the official numbers given by the Turkish government too conservative. What is clear is that Diyarbakir was used as a staging site for the ethnic cleansing of Armenians during the war, and more than 150,000 were transported from the city after collection. In 1870 there were approximately 14,000 Assyrians in the city; by 1966 there were less than 1,000.

Other developments were reshaping the context in which Diyarbakir operated as well. Technology reshaped regional transport links and increased economic opportunities; the city was first linked into the rail networks to extract mineral wealth from the region between 1935 and 1945. Also connected into the grid were the oil fields near Batman, regional chrome deposits, and copper mines near Ergan. Such changes did not initially affect the rural areas around the city, however. Even up until the early twentieth century, there were seminomadic migrations in the mountains, where communities would seasonally migrate across the Tigris. But with the massive mechanization of agriculture in Kurdistan in the 1950s, many Kurds left the rural areas and moved to the cities. By the 1960s, Diyarbakir began to grow quickly; 25 percent of local migrants went there. In 1930 the city had a population of 30,000; by 1970 it had 140,000. Kurds moved out of the province altogether as well; during the 1960s and 1970s, many left for Izmir or the south coast to find work; others went to Istanbul, making it the largest Kurdish city other than Diyarbakir.

The new Turkish state aggressively sought to deny the existence of minorities and so implemented policies to resettle Kurds ("mountain Turks," as the government called them) away from the southeast in order to assimilate them. This did not halt Kurdish national sentiment, and Diyarbakir was a key site for Kurdish resistance. In 1945 Kurdish nationalists held meetings in Diyarbakir; in response, government troops arrested many, and perhaps 120 chiefs were hung. Signs of a Kurdish revival appeared again in the late 1950s: in 1958 a new Kurdish publication, *Ileri Yurt* (*Forward Country*), appeared in Diyarbakir. In the early 1960s, as the government introduced a new policy of Doguculuk (Eastism), which allowed no recognition of Kurdish existence, language, or heritage, major demonstrations were held in Diyarbakir against the government. Demonstrators carrying banners saying "We are not Turks. We are Kurds" took to the city streets; hundreds were killed in the heavy army response. In 1967, 25,000 marchers demonstrated against the oppression of Kurds and demanded democratic rights.

Diyarbakir became infamous as the administrative site for the regional security apparatus, the trials of dissidents held in its military prison, the torture inflicted on detainees, and the repression experienced by its elites. By the 1970s, commandos had been dispatched to the city and the villages around to hunt for "bandits," with the resulting humiliation, rape, and torture of villagers and suspects. In October 1970, major trials were held in Diyarbakir of political leaders supporting Kurdish nationalism. New forms of resistance appeared in the area; leftist groups organized, robbed banks, and abducted U.S. servicemen. Finally, in March 1971, martial law was declared in parts of the country, including Diyarbakir, with thousands rounded up in the region and detained in the city's prison.

The violence and repression in the city got worse during the 1980s and 1990s. The coup by the military in 1980 unleashed fifteen years of confrontation and destruction in the region around Diyarbakir. As the Turkish state became more powerful under the army, the Kurdish community in the southeast responded with attempts at political expression and with violence under the leadership of the Kurdistan Workers Party (PKK). The government moved against Kurdish nationalists and politicians. The former mayor of Diyarbakir, Mehdi Zana, was tortured in the early 1980s. Death squads moved against the Kurdish political parties, and "unknown actors" assassinated many Kurdish politicians. One of the first and very prominent assassinations took place in Diyarbakir in July 1991 when Vedat Aydin, a human rights activist and lawyer, was killed in the city. At his funeral, the military shot at demonstrators, killing many. In 1993 a Kurdish member of parliament was arrested in Diyarbakir but was assassinated when the police turned him over to collaborators. The local situation was made worse in 1988 by Kurdish refugees fleeing attacks by the Iraqi government on Iraqi Kurds; 60,000 refugees fled into Turkey, many of them ending up in a government camp established in Diyarbakir. As the confrontation escalated, the city took on iconic meaning for both the Kurdish nationalists and for Turkish counterinsurgency policy in the struggle for supremacy.

The Turkish military employed collective punishment to root out the PKK. This was a period of forced evictions and the destruction of villages; by 1994 more than 3,000 villages had been evacuated or destroyed as the government took "security measures" and created "forbidden military zones" in the area around Diyarbakir. This major crackdown by the government, particularly at its height in 1993–1994, depopulated the villages of the region, and many internally displaced persons (IDPs) fled to Diyarbakir. There they lived as homeless in the city or in shantytowns on its outskirts; by the end of 1994, the city may have hosted as many as 1million IDPs.

Ironically, during the most intense period of the conflict, in 1993, Diyarbakir was one of the few places where Kurdish nationalists felt free enough to speak out. Yet they often paid a high price. As a way of moving against the nationalists, the police unleashed the militant group Hizballah, who attacked supporters of the PKK within the city, which led to street fighting and assassinations. Countrywide, in 1993, 510 assassinations were carried out. The city became so tense that both government supporters and PKK supporters warned journalists not to report from the city. In fact, during the latter part of 1993, almost all journalists closed their offices and left the city. Prisoners went on hunger strikes, and the prison served as "a university" for a new generation of Kurdish nationalists.

With the capture of Abdullah Ochelon in 1999, the decision by the PKK to disband, and the long years of repression, the overall level of violence in and around Diyarbakir began to decrease. The city remained the center of an Emergency Rule Region (ERR) with a governor's office in 2001, and the regional Turkish Secret Service (MIT) headquarters was located in the city. Diyarbakir remains a key site for regional tri-

als and imprisonment, and the Diyarbakir Bar Association and the Human Rights Association offices both report continued torture and disappearances. Gunmen killed the chief of police in January 2001, and there still is local resistance: in 2002 government troops reported capturing members of a new organization, the Kurdistan Islamic Revolutionary Front. Yet the state of emergency was lifted in 2002, and some of the villages are being resettled by IDPs from Diyarbakir, although some 300,000 IDPs still live in squalor on the edges of the city. The vast majority of the city's inhabitants are Kurds, though Turks and Arabs compose many of the state employees, and there are a few Assyrian families still in the city.

The security foundations of the city and its strategic location up against the Soviet Union and Iraq meant that the United States used the city and its region as a key communications and intelligence base during the cold war. The nearby Diyarbakir air base hosted components of the American Rapid Deployment Force in the early 1980s, and sophisticated communication equipment monitored the airwaves across the borders. Such a role for the city has continued up to the present day; in the lead-up to the 2003 U.S. attack on Iraq, the United States wanted to improve and use the air base at Diyarbakir as a staging post for attacks.

Caught up in an evolving but unsure regional future, Diyarbakir continues to try to find a way to meet the needs of its citizens. In a city where, even in 1980, there were more horse-drawn vehicles than cars, the current transport system is inadequate. The dramatic influx of refugees in the 1990s, and continued growth of more than 3.8 percent per annum, mean that the infrastructure of the city has not kept up with demand. The issue areas of clean water, housing, destruction of old buildings, energy, transport, and deteriorating environment all are problems for the city's planners. The vast majority of the city's inhabitants live in poverty. The city is seeking increased investment to meet local needs; under the Euro-Med Program, the European Union (EU) has contributed funds for major improvements in sewage and wastewater, which until recently was dumped directly into the Tigris. Ironically, the city is now a required stop for EU visitors to Turkey as a showpiece for the country's readiness, both in human rights terms and economically, to join the EU; one politician is quoted as saying that "the road to the EU passes through Diyarbakir."

The economy of the city is still built on the dual base of agriculture and industry. Animal breeding, feed and meat production, beverages, wool washing and processing, flour, wine, and textiles are all part of larger-scale production. Over the past five years, a major new industrial zone outside of the city has attracted regional industry to the city. Artisans continue to create fine gold and silver filigree jewelry, carpets, and silk in local workshops. The human capital of the city is supported by Diyarbakir University, which serves the whole region.

The city is attempting to build a tourism industry now that the violence of the past twenty years appears to be subsiding. The city pushes its historic religious sites, including the ancient Church of the Virgin Mary, with its Syriac manuscripts of ancient Mesopotamian Christianity, and the Ulu Mosque, built by the Seljuq sultan Melik Shah. The city also highlights the three and one-half miles of medieval basalt city walls, the citadel, and the house of Cahit Sitki Taranci, one of the most celebrated poets of the Republican period.

Bruce Stanley

Further Readings
McDowall, David. *A Modern History of the Kurds.* London: I. B. Tauris, 1997.
Olson, Robert. *The Emergence of Kurdish Nationalism and the Shaykh Said Rebellion, 1880–1925.* Austin: University of Texas Press, 1989.
White, Paul. *Primitive Rebels or Revolutionary Modernizers? The Kurdish National Movement in Turkey.* London: Zed Press, 2000.

Djibouti City
Population: 624,000 (2005 estimate)

Djibouti City is a port city created out of thin air by French colonialism during the late 1800s at the southern entrance to the Red Sea. Located on the northwest coast of the Horn of Africa close to the Bab al-Mandeb, this city, which gives its name to the country, started out as a security city projecting French power along vital sea-lanes. Now it is an important transshipment port for goods heading to the central Ethiopian highlands and for products being shipped to the Persian Gulf and the wider world. Most recently its role as a security city has been reemphasized by its use for the global war on terrorism and for the protection of shipping from piracy.

Djibouti City (Arabic, *Jibuti;* French, *Djiboutiville*) is located on the southern littoral of the Gulf of Tadjoura, which opens westward onto the larger Gulf of Aden. Less than 100 miles across the Gulf of Aden to the northeast is Yemen; a similar distance to the southeast along the coast lies Berbera. The city lies on three fingers of land connected by jetties, providing a large artificial harbor that constantly needs to be dredged to remain fit for modern cargo ships. The city is one of the hottest on earth, experiencing temperatures during the summer of more than 110 degrees Fahrenheit; annual rainfall is five inches. Two-thirds of the country's population live in Djibouti City, the only city in the country.

The population of Djibouti is the result of tremendous intermingling of immigrants to and migrations through the region over the last 1,000 years. The earliest inhabitants of the area were Ablé immigrants from Arabia who migrated into the area around the third century BC; their descendants are the Afar people (Arabic, *Denakil*), one of two main ethnic groups in the country. The Afar have traditionally lived primarily to the north of the Gulf of Tadjoura, and their home-

land includes what is now southeastern Ethiopia and parts of Eritrea. Afar surges to the south in the seventeenth century brought them as far south as Zayla, but the pressures of the Somali migrations toward the northwest forced them back north. To the south of the Gulf of Tadjoura, the predominant community in the modern era has been the Issa (Dir) Somalis. The product of the great Somali migrations, which began around the tenth century, they are often considered the first of the great Somali clans.

Gradually, the Gulf of Tadjoura became the line between the two communities, with Afar traditionally living on the north side of the Gulf and the Issa Somalis on the south side. Today the population of the country of Djibouti is approximately 60 percent Somali (composed of Issa, Issaq, and Gadaboursi clans), 35 percent Afar, and 5 percent other. Djibouti City, located on the southern littoral of the Gulf of Tadjoura, has had, from its beginnings in the late 1800s, an Issa majority. The number of Afar inhabitants of the city increased during the 1960s, however. As a port city, the capital, and the major site for employment, the city attracted considerable immigration from the rural areas of both communities and from a full range of other ethnic groups as well. Over the years, the city has also played host to Arabs, Indians, non-Afar Ethiopians, Greeks, Armenians, Italians, Sudanese, Chinese, French, and now the Americans.

Certainly, nearby sites were known to the Egyptian pharaohs and the Ptolemies (305–145 BC), and the small port of Zayla, southeast along the coast, is mentioned in the *Periplus Maris Erythraei* (*Circumnavigation of the Erythraean Sea*) of the first century AD. On the Djibouti City site, however, there was not habitation or infrastructure prior to French colonialism. The region was visited by Roman and Byzantine traders, and Aksum's power during the fourth to sixth century shaped local trading patterns (see also "Aksum").

The first political entities in the region grew up around trading sites established by Arab traders after the advent of Islam. During the ninth century, the first Muslim amirates emerged on the southwestern periphery of Christian Ethiopia, such as the Sultanate of Shoa (ca. 1180–1285) and its successor, the Kingdom of Ifat. These trading principalities sought to dominate the trade routes to coastal ports such as Zayla and were in constant conflict with the Ethiopian kingdom.

The region around what became Djibouti fell under the rising coastal power of Adel (AD 1500–1600), which brought together the people of the Afar and Somali to attack Abyssinia. Under the leadership of Imam Ahmed Gran, and supported by military assistance from the Ottomans, they expanded their power until stopped by a Portuguese-Abyssinian force in 1542. The Djibouti coast remained caught up in long-distance trade via Zayla, and the rise of the Harar Sultanate helped spur further intercourse between the caravans from the hinterland and the people of the coast.

The Afar had pushed as far south as Zayla, but under the effects of Somali expansion in the 1700s, they had been pushed back to the northern littoral of the Gulf of Tadjoura, leaving Zayla and Berbera the key Somali ports to the south (see also "Berbera"). North of what is now Djibouti, trade operated primarily out of Massawa.

The French arrived in the 1850s looking for a stop on the route to East Africa but also to India and their growing dominions in Indochina. The British had established themselves across the Gulf in Aden in 1839 and were building ties with Berbera (see also "Aden"). The French also wanted a strategic site close to the entrance of the Red Sea to enhance their position in global trade and to affirm their geostrategic importance. Their first acquisition was the region around Obock, on the northern rim of the Gulf of Tadjoura, when they signed a treaty with the local Afar sultan in 1862.

By the mid-1880s, ship traffic was heavy enough at Obock that the French began to look for an alternative, larger harbor, especially one that could better serve as a coaling station for their imperial traffic. They were also seeking to expand their clear authority as far south as possible, hoping to include Zayla. The French thus concluded an agreement of perpetual friendship with the Issa ruler of Djibouti and looked as if they were going to land troops at Zayla. This put them in confrontation with the British and their Issa allies. The result was an Anglo-French agreement (1888) to "draw the line" between Zayla and Djibouti, dividing the Issa community in two.

In 1888 the French laid out the new port and a grid system of streets behind it. They named the new city Djibouti (Afar for *pot*). In 1896 Djibouti City was recognized as the capital of the new French Somaliland (Côte Français des Somalis) established as the French, British, and Italians officially carved up Somali territory under a joint recognition agreement.

During the rest of the nineteenth century, the new city was a lawless and chaotic place. The French poet Arthur Rimbaud (1854–1891) visited Djibouti while he was a trader in Abyssinia during the 1880s; he labeled Djibouti as an "awful, filthy country." It quickly became known for weapons and qat (plant leaves chewed as a stimulant) smuggling and as a site to buy slaves, despite the official end of the slave trade in other ports along the coast. At one point, it took 300 camels to purchase one rifle, given that the demand for weapons was so high.

The fortunes of the city were enhanced and directly linked to those of its neighbors. Ethiopia, for example, became linked to the port with the development of the Addis Ababa–Djibouti railroad line. Started in 1894 and completed in 1897, this line cemented a "special relationship" by making Djibouti, by treaty, the official outlet for Ethiopian commerce. At times 60 percent of Ethiopia's commerce traversed this network. The critical importance of this link was later to provide the basis for Ethiopian claims to the whole territory of Djibouti in the 1960s. With Aden, by the early 1900s, Djibouti

was closely allied to that city via trading companies that controlled Djibouti's shipping schedule.

When France fell to the Germans in 1940, Djibouti became controlled by Vichy France. The British from Aden then applied a sea blockade on the port, but the Vichy forces continued to use their strategic location to report back to France by radio on British naval movements. In 1942, 4,000 British troops created a land blockade on the city as well, and in December 1942 Djibouti was handed over to the Free French, who ruled it for the rest of the war.

In the wake of the war, the winds of change that blew through the whole French colonial structure also affected Djibouti. In 1949 Issas demonstrated for reunification of British, French, and Italian Somaliland, advocating the idea of "Greater Somalia." The Afars, long favored by the French in Djibouti, supported continued French rule. The French did give the local elites in Djibouti City a voice through the new representative council that was established in March 1946. The composition and membership of the council was enlarged in 1950, although it was clear that the key ethnic divisions in the country between the Afars and the Issas were not being resolved by these new institutions.

France organized a global referendum in 1958 to see how the voters in each of its colonies felt about remaining under French rule; the majority of Djiboutians voted to remain a colony. An elected representative body was organized, though dominated by the Issa. A reorganization of the local body in 1963 helped elevate the Afar representation, known for their pro-French tendencies. It is the period from 1963 until 1976 that is known as the "Afar Domination."

Regional relations were growing more complicated as well. As the Saudi Arabian monarchy and Arab Socialist Egypt under Nasir struggled for supremacy in Arab affairs, they both played around in the Djibouti kitchen. Certain Djibouti politicians receiving subsidies from Saudi Arabia as early as the 1950s, and Nasir, via the Pan Arab Radio, sought to undermine French rule in Djibouti through support for the concept of "Greater Somalia."

The British pullout in Aden in 1967 led to a radical People's Democratic Republic of Yemen (PDRY) only an hour by boat across the Gulf, and the general decline in Aden as a port deeply affected Djibouti (see also "Aden"). Interestingly, coastal shipping, along with the regional trade network in qat, continued no matter the political changes of the 1960s and 1970s. The Djibouti airport was key to the regional qat trade. Ethiopian Air Lines would fly a daily shipment from Ethiopia into Djibouti, and cargo handlers would transfer it directly to an Aden Airways flight to Aden. The qat flights also served Djibouti City, especially meeting the demand created by the 18,000 North Yemenis who had moved there during the 1960s.

In the wake of the Algerian War of Independence, the French pullout from Indochina, and the independence and unity of Somalia in 1960, tension within Djibouti increased. Djibouti lost its role for France as a way station for shipping between France and overseas; troops and civil servant appointments were cut back, decreasing local foreign currency. By the late 1960s, the French were forced to make direct grants to the administration. De Gaulle visited Djibouti on 25 June 1966 as part of his reorganization of the French overseas departments. Significant disorders marred de Gaulle's visit to the city, and he never forgave the city's people.

One result of his visit was a decision to run another referendum on the question of the relationship with France. Scheduled for March 1967, the lead-up to the referendum witnessed considerable activities by all parties, including the French, to manipulate the results of the election. In the census of 1967, the colony had a population of 125,050. On that basis, a barbed-wire barrier was built around Djibouti City to prevent infiltration by "outsiders" or "clandestine intruders" who might "influence" the election, since already half the territory's population was concentrated within the city, and many of the inhabitants were recent Somali immigrants. This barrier was lit at night, soldiers shot people trying to enter the city, and the population of the city was investigated to see if they were actual citizens. Some 10,000 ethnic Somalis were expelled from the country around the time of the referendum, and opposition leaders were arrested. There are indications that the actual vote was manipulated. In the wake of the majority vote to retain ties to France, there were riots in the city. Many of those expelled joined the Somali Coast Liberation Front (SCLF), located across the Somali border, and they launched an armed campaign against the new local administration.

This new local administration was headed by a local premier to administer the autonomous entity, although France retained control of security and foreign affairs. The first premier was Ali Araf Bourhan, an Afar whose power base was located in the public works department and port authority in Djibouti City. One of his first acts was to replace the Somali dockworkers with inexperienced Afars; such ethnic favoritism was to mark this period of local administration and continue to be a problem for Djibouti up until the present. Under his leadership, the name of the colony was changed in 1967 from French Somaliland, resented by the Afars, to the French Territory of the Afars and Issas.

The closure of the Suez Canal caused by the June War of 1967 was a disaster for Djibouti City. Before the war, 1,000 ships per month stopped at the port. Providing services to these ships was the largest contributor to the city's revenue, followed by customs on transshipments and the transit trade to Ethiopia. With the canal closed, port traffic dropped to almost nothing, and although the city's elites responded by creating a free-trade zone in 1971, little seemed to help. Unemployment was high and chronic, and tribal clashes within the city in 1967 and "the football riots" of 1968 appeared directly related to the loss of employment. The 1969 elections were marred by violence, and terrorist attacks on the railroad line to Ethiopia and the city's train station created an atmosphere of fear. Al-Aref was twice the target of assassination attempts by Somali nationalists. The city's population doubled between 1967 and 1977, placing a great strain on social services and infrastructure. In 1970 there were attacks on Europeans, and between 1973 and 1976 the city experienced a huge crime wave. Ethnic fighting between Issas and Afars broke out in May 1975, with 16 killed and 250 injured. In response, the government imposed curfews, brought in extra gendarmerie, and expelled 1,000 illegals.

The one bright spot was the growing relationship between Djibouti City and Jeddah. With the post-1973 oil price rise, the demand for imports into Saudi Arabia was so great that the unmodernized port of Jeddah could not handle all the ship traffic wishing to dock. As a result, the Djibouti port became the backup to meet demand. Goods were off-loaded in Djibouti, stored, and then taken on smaller boats to Jeddah. The change in demand for meat resulting from increased income also helped Djibouti, which shipped sheep to Jeddah from the Ogaden. Aspects of the link with Jeddah continue today, with Saudi Arabian investors financing considerable development in the city.

The Suez Canal reopened in 1975, and everyone expected an immediate dramatic resurgence in the city's fortunes. Recovery took longer than expected, however; Aden's traffic rebounded more quickly than did Djibouti's, and few ships stopped during the first year. One reason may have been the lack of infrastructural modernization and poor human capital of the city that had resulted from the decade of decline. In 1973 there was only one native doctor in the whole city, and this problem of training was reflected throughout the employees in the port.

The violence resulting from increased pressures for independence in 1975 may have also contributed to the reluctance of shippers to visit the port. In the jockeying for position, the political parties emphasized ethnic commitments, poisoning the relationships between communities within the city. Fighting broke out, curfews were imposed, and there was a ban on public meetings. Premier al-Aref talked about the Greater Afar Project, and how "all Afars should be united under one flag." The coup in Ethiopia in 1974 did not help trade through the port, particularly as that country drifted into scientific socialism, and the transit trade withered.

A referendum on independence was offered on 8 May 1977. Ninety-two percent of the people in Djibouti City voted for it, and Independence Day was 27 June 1977. With independence, many of the city's elites fled to France, and the future of the port seemed very unclear. Sixty-five percent of the country's total income depended on port revenues, and little modernization and training had been committed to keep up with global expectations.

The new Issa-led government immediately negotiated continuing French military and economic aid to the country, initially an annual subsidy of $1.4 million. Since 1977 the French have kept 3,500 soldiers in the country, helping it to negotiate the tricky regional politics over the last quarter century. Saudi Arabia quickly came to the financial rescue of the country as well, pumping considerable aid into infrastructure and development.

The country was racked by civil war from 1991 until 1994 and again from 1997 until 2000 as various combinations of communities struggled for control of the political structure. Finally, in March 2000, the main Afar rebel group signed a peace accord with the government, and major reconstruction and investment were able to proceed throughout the country.

The city is still experiencing tremendous challenges and difficulties. One key problem is that of urban poverty. When the French cut back their troop commitments in the country, this directly produced unemployment and reduced foreign currency inflows. Today the general unemployment rate stands at 50 percent, which means half of the population lives below the poverty line. The majority of the city's inhabitants are illiterate, and AIDS is a huge health problem in Djibouti City. The city's infrastructure, water and sewage, and social service systems are overtaxed, with a noticeable increase in street children, begging, and prostitution in the streets since 2000. It is this population that is most vulnerable when natural disasters strike. Both in 2002 and again in 2004, torrential rains, floods, and high winds hit the city, washing away many homes, destroying food supplies, and killing many.

The prolonged fighting combined with regional drought meant that by 2001 the city was full of rural pastoralists, displaced persons, and economic migrants from throughout the region, seeking work in the city. The influx has meant at least 100,000 extra people in a city built for 200,000. Those looking for work are so desperate that they accept any wage, undercutting local Djiboutians. Given that the city has historically had some of the highest labor costs in the region because of the high cost of living, current wages are not enough for most workers to live on. In addition, there is a chronic lack of skilled labor; the government and donors are attacking this issue in numerous ways, including the creation of a new university in the city in 2002.

Inward migration to the city is not a new issue. Djibouti City has experienced this attraction since its creation and most significantly since independence, in 1977. Today up to 25 percent of the city's population may be illegal immigrants from Eritrea, Ethiopia, Iraq, Rwanda, Somalia, or Sudan; many of them are transiting through Djibouti, since it serves as a key transit point for those migrating (legally and illegally) to the Arab states and to the United States. There are reports of trafficking in Somali women and children as prostitutes for Arab and European countries via the port. The government regularly rounds up illegal refugees in the city and expels them from the country. During 2003, 100,000 illegal immigrants were expelled from the country, but many actually ended up in a refugee camp southwest of the city of Djibouti. One recent report suggests around 25,000 refugees still live in the city. By 1995 the city may have had a population approaching 400,000.

One of the key issues confronting Djibouti City since independence has been the linked issues of food and water. There are vegetables and dates grown in small quantities in the suburbs of Djibouti, but the country is heavily dependent on food imports to meet the needs of its citizens. Periodic locust infestations are an additional problem. Water for the city's expanding population is an ongoing policy issue. As the city has expanded, wells were drilled farther and farther from the city, and now water is piped over a great distance into the city center. As a port, Djibouti provides water to visiting ships as well. This presents the city with an interesting problem, since up to 10 percent of the city's consumption goes to ships. In fact, the visit of one large passenger liner or warship can overburden the city's fragile water supply.

The only local industry has been the production and regional sales of salt. Unfortunately, the city's residents import refined and iodized salt since there is no local refining plant. There are small indigenous exports of hides, mother of pearl, and tortoiseshell. To encourage investment and industrial development, in 1995 the entire country was designated as a free export processing zone. Until today, however, the key enterprises in the city are all shipping lines.

The harbor and port complex continue to be central to the city's future. Since the end of the civil war, in 2000, the city has gained both a new oil terminal and a new container terminal. Legislation has been passed to create a new industrial and commercial zone and money authorized to modernize the city's telecommunication installation. The European Union (EU) has finished a multiyear project to improve the human resources and infrastructure of the port. The administration and development of the port was turned over to Dubai Ports International (DPI), a key regional development company out of Dubai, that now has a twenty-year monopoly on running the port. DPI has invested $300 million into the port, believing that Djibouti has great potential as a regional hub. Under its administration, the port has dramatically improved its efficiency and is now moving quickly to becoming the key port on the southern littoral. The signs of improvement are everywhere: qat chewing within the port is not allowed, facilities are now up to international standards, and they are implementing the new International Security Procedure Standard (ISPS) Code in line with the International Maritime Organization's (IMO) security standard. Workers are better trained, and the volume of traffic per hour has doubled.

The port in Djibouti City is now 104th in the world in terms of volume; it is providing 1,100 people direct jobs, and another 2,000 indirectly, making it Djibouti's single largest employer. It is now the primary entry point for grain to the whole region, receiving huge shipments from the World Food Program to meet the humanitarian disasters in East Africa. Building on its history as a regional camel market, the legal livestock trade via the port is increasing, while the illegal livestock trade from Ethiopia into Djibouti is also on the rise.

The rehabilitation of the port is having important spillover effects into other aspects of the city's role as an entrepôt. DPI is looking to expand the city's position in the region by upgrading the international airport by creating a free-trade zone. Meanwhile, the daily distribution of qat via the airport, camel, or dhow continues through Djibouti onward to Aden, Somalia, or Europe. With the rehabilitation of the port, the importance of the railway line to Ethiopia's 30 million people has reemerged as well. Freight traffic has increased, as has passenger traffic. One hundred percent of Ethiopian coffee goes through Djibouti. Road traffic from Ethiopia to the port is also increasing. During 2002 the Djibouti-Ethiopian Commission signed a draft agreement on the use of the port for goods heading in and out of Ethiopia, reaffirming the tight relationship and mutual dependency.

In addition to such developments, the city is experiencing a number of other important changes. Work is under way, supported by the International Development Agency and Japan, to improve the water reserves (aquifers) for the city. The World Bank is funding the improvement in Djibouti City's power grid, and the joint Djibouti-Ethiopian Commission is planning to link the electrical grids in the whole region. The World Bank is even developing plans for a two-megawatt wind farm outside of the city. The city is also seeking to act as a regional hub for the importation of natural gas. The Emirates National Oil Company has recently entered into a joint venture with Djibouti to distribute gas both within the country and via Djibouti to East Africa. The exploration for oil around the city is also continuing. A mini gold rush is on as Australian companies explore for gold, and Saudi investors are putting money into hotels and tourism. The government foresees the city as a regional information and communications hub and has announced plans to create an international financial services center.

The city is also benefiting from the war on terrorism. Djibouti was created as a security city by the French in the late 1800s, and it reaffirmed that role again during the cold war, when the Americans joined with the French to spy on Soviet naval maneuvers in the Gulf of Aden. Since 1977 the French have maintained a huge Djibouti military base, for which they paid Ä18 million per year. Today, they pay Ä30 million ($35 million) for the privilege.

Although the American presence increased during the 1980s, it is in the wake of 11 September 2001 that the American presence on the fringe of Djibouti City has become much more noticeable. In return for an annual payment of $31 mil-

lion, the Djibouti government offered Camp Lemonier, near the airport, for American use. Since 2002 a U.S. expeditionary force of about 1,000 troops has used the camp—which was inherited from the French and abandoned by the Djibouti army—as a center for regional antiterrorist operations, housing for military forces, a training site for special forces and the military police, a communications center to support offshore command and control, intelligence gathering, and a key node for the new Horn of Africa task force. The CIA has conducted operations from Djibouti, including the extrajudicial killing of supposed al-Qaeda leaders in Yemen via drone planes manned from the Djibouti base. U.S. personnel based in Djibouti are also helping Ethiopia monitor its border with Somalia, training Ethiopian troops in counterterrorism, searching for pirates in the Gulf of Aden, and working to stop the illegal drug trade in the region.

Bruce Stanley

Further Readings
Alwan, Daoud A., and Yohanis Mibrathu. *Historical Dictionary of Djibouti.* Lanham, MD: Scarecrow Press, 2004.
Koburger, Charles. *Naval Strategy East of Suez: The Role of Djibouti.* Westport, CT: Greenwood Press, 1992.
Tholomier, Robert, Virginia Thompson, and Richard Adloff. *Djibouti: Pawn of the Horn of Africa.* Lanham, MD: Scarecrow Press, 1981.
Thompson, Virginia, and Richard Adloff. *Djibouti and the Horn of Africa.* Stanford, CA: Stanford University Press, 1968.
Waberi, Abdourahman. *The Land without Shadows.* Charlottesville: University of Virginia Press, 2005.

Doha
Population: 400,000 (2005 estimate)

Like many Gulf cities, Doha has seen a complete transformation over the last thirty years. The town was a pinprick before the discovery of oil and gas, and Qataris survived on income from pearling. The lack of resources did not, however, mean that there was no squabbling over this remote and uninviting peninsula. A series of conquerors held sway until about 1850, when the current ruling family (who themselves originated in the Najd region of what is now Saudi Arabia) emerged as the main local leaders. Although the peninsula probably did not appear much of a prize at the time, a wealth of hydrocarbons has meant that Qatar and the residents of its quickly expanding capital, Doha, now enjoy one of the highest per capita incomes in the world.

Doha (Arabic, *ad-Dawhah*), capital of the modern-day State of Qatar, lies on the eastern coast of a peninsula extending into the central Persian Gulf from the eastern side of the Arabian Peninsula. The entire country takes up just 4,400 square miles, and Doha is the main population center. The city has expanded to incorporate its smaller neighbor, ar-

Rayyan, into a single conurbation. The climate there is harsh—summer temperatures reach more than 104 degrees Fahrenheit, and the rocky and sandy topography is generally uninviting to agriculture.

Such conditions make it no surprise that Doha was only a small dot on the map before hydrocarbons were discovered in Qatar. There is some evidence of Stone Age settlers, but historical accounts suggest that the island was sparsely inhabited for centuries.

Qatar did, however, achieve sufficient prominence to be included in Ptolemy's second-century map, which had reference to a town believed to be the historic Zubarah. Zubarah was located on the northwestern tip of the peninsula, about forty miles from present-day Doha. The town merited mention for its role as a trading port, which it played throughout many periods in Qatari history.

Details of the subsequent centuries are sketchy at best. The Sassanians of Persia held sway over the island from about AD 300 to about AD 640. Thereafter, the island's inhabitants were converted to Islam, with Qatar then coming under the influence first of the Umayyads and then the Abbasids. The Portuguese also briefly held sway over the island during the sixteenth century before Qatar, like much of the rest of the Arabian Peninsula, came under (mostly nominal) Ottoman control.

Despite the changes in leadership, in reality Qatar held little interest for even the most intrepid of conquerors, and it remained a largely uninviting peninsula. Water sources in the interior provided some stopping points for nomads who traveled between the peninsula and watering holes in Saudi Arabia. But what settled living that there was to be made there came from pearl diving and fishing, and the current ruling family of Qatar, the al-Thani, turned their hands to these occupations when they invaded from the Najd region of Saudi Arabia in the 1750s. Official government accounts suggest that they initially settled in Zubarah, moving south to what is now Doha (meaning bay) only in the middle of the next century.

Their arrival was followed shortly by that of the al-Khalifa and al-Jalahimah tribes from Kuwait, who soon came to rule over Zubarah. These tribes used Qatar as a launching pad to conquer neighboring and more prosperous Bahrain, and they succeeded in capturing that island in 1783 while maintaining their influence over the pearling town of Zubarah.

Other outside influences also played a role in Qatar during the latter part of the eighteenth century. In central Arabia, the alliance between Muhammad bin Abdul Wahhab and Muhammad bin Saud to spread the teachings of the Wahhabist school of Islam had taken root. The as-Saud forces conquered large parts of eastern Arabia, with their influence extending to Qatar. Saudi problems with the Ottomans meant, however, that their influence over the eastern province was checked, and by the early part of the nineteenth century Saudi

influence had waned in the whole of eastern Arabia. Qatar was not immune either to the attentions of the British, whose main interest in the Gulf at that time centered on the prevention of piracy. In retaliation for such acts, Doha came under fire in 1821 from an East India Company (EIC) vessel.

As the nineteenth century progressed, the al-Thani established themselves as local leaders. By the 1850s, the al-Thani had their capital in al-Bida, the site of present-day Doha. In 1867, however, that town was largely destroyed in fighting between supporters of the al-Thani and those of the al-Khalifa in Bahrain, who decided to try to retake the peninsula. The continuing threat from the al-Khalifa encouraged the al-Thani to enter into a pact in 1868 with the British government. That accord included a British pledge of protection from the al-Khalifa.

As in other areas in the Gulf, however, the tensions between the British and the Ottomans led to conflicting alliances. In 1872 Qatar entered into an accord with the Ottomans, who promptly stationed a garrison at Doha. That relationship was not, however, always peaceful, and historical accounts show that there was fighting in 1893 between Qatari forces and the Turkish garrison. Eventually, in 1913, the Turkish forces abandoned their claims to sovereignty over Qatar. That change paved the way for a treaty between Qatar and the British in 1916, which gave Qatar the status of a British protectorate.

The British did not, however, gain a thriving metropolis; rather, Doha was a small outpost of about 12,000 souls in 1907, according to the famous British geographer, J. G. Lorimer. He describes the town as "unattractive; the lanes are narrow and irregular, the houses dingy and small." He adds that Doha had no trees of any kind and that the only small garden was one that the Turkish garrison maintained. Without even date palms, the economy was very limited at the time, and Lorimer noted that Qatar's sole export was pearls.

In these circumstances, the 1930s were a particularly difficult period for Doha and for Qatar more generally. The international pearl market collapsed during that period, as demand slackened with the world depression, and problems were aggravated by the development of cultured pearls in Japan. The first oil concession was granted in 1935, and oil was discovered in 1939. The advent of the Second World War meant that commercial production was delayed until 1949, however, and poverty and hardship continued. Eventually, however, income from oil allowed for developments in Qatar, and the country's first school was opened in 1952, followed by the first fully equipped hospital in 1959.

In 1971 the British pulled out of Qatar. Doha remained the capital of the country and the seat of government. There were some talks at the time about a federation among the smaller Gulf states, but nothing materialized. Since the British withdrawal, the al-Thani family has remained in control of the government, although there have been two subsequent palace coups. The first, in 1972, brought Khalifa bin Hamad al-Thani to power, while the second, in 1995, brought his son, Hamad bin Khalifa al-Thani, to power.

Over this period, exports of hydrocarbons have paid for the transformation of the country, and the economy of Doha remains dependent on oil and gas exports. The country's tiny population, estimated at less than 1 million, and its relatively small size mean that the wealth has had a real impact on living standards. Similarly, per capita income has skyrocketed as the country's gas-based industrialization program has progressed, and Qataris are, in per capita income terms, among the richest people in the world.

Although gas resources in particular are immense, the government is pushing for diversification into tourism and other services. A new airport is under construction on the outskirts of Doha to support the country's tourism ambitions, and in its efforts to increase its international reputation, Doha has already played host to the World Trade Organization (WTO; the latest round of global negotiations are called the Doha Round) and to the Organization of the Islamic Conference (OIC). It is hosting the 2006 Asian Games and is the venue for major international tennis and golf events.

In addition, Qatar has sought to become an education center for the Gulf region. It has established Education City in Doha, which currently houses institutions including branches of the Weill Cornell Medical College, the Virginia Commonwealth University, and Texas A&M University. These facilities are in addition to the local University of Qatar, which is also based in Doha. Qatar is also seeking to establish in Doha an onshore financial center, the Qatar Financial Centre, which aims to rival both the long-established offshore banking sector in Bahrain as well as the newly established Dubai International Financial Centre.

In a bid to broaden its media sector, Doha is now the host for numerous media organizations, including the well-known channel al-Jazeera. The city's new regional importance for media, combined with the location of the U.S. Central Command Headquarters outside the city, meant that "Camp Doha" served as the media center for press briefings by the U.S. military for the 2003 invasion of Iraq.

Qataris generally follow the Wahhabist school of Islam, which is also found in Saudi Arabia. Although the Qataris are less strict than their larger neighbors in enforcing restrictions on women's rights and alcohol, Doha nevertheless does not have a reputation as a hot spot. It does, however, have a few sights of cultural interest. As the largest city in the peninsula state, the city is the site of the country's National Museum. The collections are housed in a former royal palace, which was built in 1912. The capital also boasts the Qasr al-Wajbah (fort), the site of the 1893 battle in which the Qataris defeated the Ottoman garrison.

Angie Turner

Further Readings
Crystal, Jill. *Oil and Politics in the Gulf: Rulers and Merchants in Kuwait and Qatar.* Cambridge: Cambridge University Press, 1990.
Lorimer, J. G. *Gazetteer of the Persian Gulf.* Calcutta: Superintendent Government Printing, 1908.
Othman, Naser al-. *With Their Bare Hands: The Story of the Oil Industry in Qatar.* London: Longman, 1984.
Saud, Abeer Abu. *Qatari Women: Past and Present.* London: Longman, 1984.
Zahlan, Rosemarie Said. *The Creation of Qatar.* London: Croom Helm, 1979.

Dubai
Population: 1,299,149 (2005 estimate)

Dubai is the most populous city in the United Arab Emirates (UAE) and one of the fastest-growing metropolitan areas in the region. In contrast to major Western cities where the transition from preindustrial to industrial to postindustrial status occurred over a period of two centuries, Dubai has experienced this transformation in only fifty years. The decision by the International Monetary Fund (IMF) and the World Bank to convene their 2003 meeting in Dubai bears testimony to the city-state's remarkable progression from an insignificant fishing settlement on the Arabian Gulf to a cosmopolitan, regionally dominant, twenty-first-century city. In regional terms, Dubai's unemployment rate is less than half that of Egypt, while its gross domestic product (GDP) per capita is more than five times that of the most populous Arab state. In addition, with more than 5 million annual visitors, Dubai is now a more popular tourist destination than Egypt or India. The economic transformation of Dubai over recent decades has been accompanied by major changes in its population structure and in the pattern of urban development. More than 70 percent of the city's population are non-UAE nationals, principally a mix of other Arab nationals, Asians, and Europeans who have been attracted to and were instrumental in the economic development of the city-state. The past two decades have witnessed accelerating economic growth and explosive urban expansion that have made the city a regional command center within the global economy and a locus for a host of imaginative urban developments designed to consolidate the city's position and image as one of the leading and most progressive metropolitan centers in the Middle East.

The origins of the modern city of Dubai are rooted in the tribal culture and political history of the region. In the eighteenth century, the southern littoral of the Gulf (now the territories of Dubai and Abu Dhabi) was occupied by the Bani Yas tribe, while their historic rivals, the Qawasim, controlled the area north of Dubai (now the amirates of Sharjah and Ras al-Khaimah). The period was marked by a struggle for maritime supremacy of the southern Gulf between the two tribes, with the British allied to the Bani Yas. In response to attacks on the shipping of the East India Company (EIC) and the consequent disruption of trade with India, a British expedition was sent in 1819 to defeat the Qawasim. Subsequently, to consolidate their position, the British required the leading shaykhs along the coast , including those of the Bani Yas, to enter into a General Treaty of Peace. Not only did this secure the trade route to India but also enabled the pearling industry of the Gulf to prosper, to the benefit of Dubai, where many of the pearl fishers and traders were based.

A political change of fundamental importance for the growth of Dubai occurred in 1833, when a group of around 800 members of the al-Bu Falasah subsection of the Bani Yas tribe seceded from Abu Dhabi following a dispute with the ruler and moved to form an independent shaykhdom in Dubai. This community was ruled by Maktoum bin Buti from 1833 until his death, in 1852. Significantly, all subsequent rulers of Dubai are descended from the Maktoum family, who have exercised an ongoing and paramount influence on the development of the city-state. A second key political decision that affected Dubai's postwar growth was the decision by Britain, in 1967, to withdraw from its military bases east of Suez. This signaled the termination of the treaty relationships over the Trucial States, and on 1 December 1971 a new political entity of the UAE came into existence, comprising the former shaykhdoms of Dubai, Abu Dhabi, Sharjah, Ajman, Umm al-Qairain, Ras al-Khaimah, and Fujairah. While the administrative capital of the federation is in Abu Dhabi, Dubai has emerged as the principal economic and urban growth center, not only for the UAE but also for the other Gulf Cooperation Council (GCC) countries of Saudia Arabia, Kuwait, Bahrain, Qatar, and Oman as well as for the wider region.

For much of the nineteenth century, the pearl industry was a mainstay of the Dubai economy, which also benefited from a prevailing philosophy of economic liberalism that encouraged entrepreneurial activity. The growth of the urban economy received a major boost in 1902, when imposition of high customs duties by the government of Persia on merchants operating from their ports set in motion a transfer of the Indian trade, along with merchants, craftsmen, and their families, to the more liberal economic climate of Dubai. The interwar period proved difficult for the Dubai economy. The world recession of 1929 and the introduction of the cultured pearl by Japan undermined the economy of the Trucial States. With the demise of the pearling industry, Dubai placed even greater emphasis on trade. The outbreak of the Second World War disrupted commercial links with India, however, and the resultant economic difficulties were offset only marginally by income from aviation and petroleum exploration concessions.

Development of the oil industry, following discovery of petroleum offshore in 1966, revolutionized the economy and society of Dubai. Oil revenues enabled the government to un-

dertake major infrastructure and industrial projects that included construction of Port Rashid, the dry docks, an aluminum smelter, and the Jebal Ali Port and Industrial Area. In addition to the benefits of oil revenues, the city's growth was boosted by the entrepreneurship of the local merchant community with its network of international contacts. The commercial acumen of the city's entrepreneurs flourished during the 1980–1988 Iran-Iraq War, when Dubai's merchants engaged in a lucrative trade supplying consumer goods and equipment to Iran at considerable profit to individual traders and to the urban economy as a whole. The war also stimulated growth in the business of servicing international shipping, which found Dubai's massive dry docks a safer alternative to Kuwait or Iranian ports. Since the early 1980s, Dubai's trade with the other GCC countries and other Gulf states has expanded to make Dubai the busiest port in the region. The city's growth as a commercial entrepôt was accompanied by expansion of the banking sector. A third critical factor underpinning Dubai's postwar economic growth was the liberal economic approach of government, which sought to attract inward investment to a low-taxation, business-friendly, and politically stable environment.

Since the early 1990s, Dubai has been engaged in a process of economic expansion and diversification driven by the knowledge that oil production, having peaked at 410,000 barrels per day in 1991, is in decline and now accounts for less than 10 percent of gross domestic product. The primary objective of the 1996–2010 Dubai strategic development plan is to attain the status of a "developed economy" by the latter date. While manufacturing and trade remain major elements of the non-oil economy, the more recent emphasis on expanding the tertiary sector is evident in the importance of producer and other services, real estate, hotels and restaurants, and construction. The importance of the international "visitor economy" is reflected in the particular attention that has been focused on expanding up-market tourism, as symbolized by the development of the iconic seven-star Burj al-Arab Hotel. Further planned luxury development projects include the Palm Jumeirah (a $1.5 billion development of man-made islands in the Gulf to provide 10,000 exclusive residences, 40,000 hotel rooms, and shopping and entertainment facilities), Dubai Marina, and the World (another Gulf island development consisting of 300 private islands arranged in the shape of a world map).

In addition to strong inward flows of investment capital, the liberal open-door economic policy of Dubai has attracted a steady stream of immigrants, which has had significant impact on the sociocultural character of the city. By 1985 the number of residents had risen to 370,788, representing a fivefold increase over two decades. The population has continued to grow, albeit at a reduced rate, increasing to 689,420 in 1995 (an increase of 86 percent over the decade), to 862,387 by 2000, and to 961,000 by 2002. The rapid population growth of

Dubai's luxury hotels grace the skyline. (morgueFile)

recent decades is the result of two main factors. Of greatest significance has been immigration, fueled initially by economic expansion based on the oil industry, which created a demand for labor and expertise that could only be satisfied from abroad. The second factor, natural increase, is the result of high fertility combined with a decline in infant mortality rates and an increase in life expectancy consequent upon the introduction of modern healthcare facilities. Despite a policy of "amiratization" of the workforce since the mid-1990s based on repatriation of illegal immigrants, restrictions on entry of unskilled foreign workers, and granting priority to Emiri graduates in some state sector employment, foreign-born residents still constitute a dominant proportion of Dubai's population. In 2000, of the 862,387 inhabitants, 460,691 (53 percent) were born abroad. The influx of foreign workers has had a major cultural impact on the city, most visibly in variations in dress and language and in the growth of restaurants, shops, and other facilities to serve the needs of the immigrant populations. Immigration remains a key determinant of the urban character of Dubai.

The urban outcomes of these major historical, economic, demographic, and cultural processes are manifested most clearly in the sociospatial pattern of city development. The first half of the twentieth century was a period of slow growth and limited expansion caused by constrained economic growth and marginal increase in population. By contrast, the past twenty-five years have been a period of rapid urban expansion, in terms of both the scale and diversity of development projects and physical spread of the city, which in 2004 covered an area of 234 square miles. The annual urban growth rate is currently 3.9 percent, and the strategic plan envisages extending the built-up area by a further 193 square miles by 2015. The explosive growth of Dubai poses a number of challenges for decision makers. These include an increasing demand for housing and service infrastructure to accommodate a growing number of households and the need to provide a modern transportation system in the context of a rapidly expanding and car-dependent urban area.

Michael Pacione

Further Readings

Gabriel, Erhard. *The Dubai Handbook*. Ahrensburg: Institute for Applied Economic Geography, 1987.

Heard-Bey, Frauke. *From Trucial States to United Arab Emirates.* London: Longman, 1982.

Kazim, Aqil. *The United Arab Emirates, AD 600 to the Present.* Dubai: Gulf Book Centre, 2000.

Pacione, Michael. "Dubai." *Cities* 22, no. 3 (2005): 255–265.

E

Ebla
Population: 20,000 (2000 BC estimate)

Ebla is a classic example of a forgotten central city, once great but covered by the sands of time. What we know of the city's built environment and trade connections come from extensive archaeological investigation, which reveals a crucial city of the Bronze Age articulating trade throughout the northern Middle East via a trading league of cities. The huge tablet archives discovered in the city are one of the richest guides to the city's trade and production capacity, to its centrality in education and training of the time, and a window on Eurasian civilization in 2000 BC.

Ebla (Eblaite, *Ibla;* Arabic, *Tell Mardikh*) is located in northern Syria near the town of Idlib, thirty miles southwest of Aleppo along the primary road to Damascus. One of the best examples of a "forgotten city," until early in the twentieth century the city was unknown to modern scholars. Its existence only came to light through references to a city-state called Ebla discovered in the archives in Mari. Even then, there was no agreement on where the site might be or on the city's significance. The conventional wisdom was that northern Syria was a cultural backwater during the Early to Middle Bronze Age (3100–1550 BC): all the important civilizations or events worthy of attention were believed to be in Mesopotamia, Egypt, or Palestine.

One young Italian archaeologist, however, did not accept that northern Syria had not possessed cultures of its own. Paolo Matthiae persisted, identified the city in 1964, and led an extensive dig by the University of Rome to correct the record. The discovery of Ebla's huge palace library in 1975, virtually intact, has proved to be one of most exciting and controversial treasure troves ever discovered.

Excavations at Tell Mardikh over many subsequent seasons suggest that the site's habitation spanned six key periods. The estimate is that it was first inhabited around 3500 BC. By 3000 BC, the city was substantial in size, having both an acropolis and a lower city. Over the next millennium, it reached its zenith in area and population only to be destroyed around 2250 BC and then again around 2000 BC.

It is during the second period of the city (particularly 2500–2000 BC), and to a lesser extent the third (2000–1600 BC), that Ebla flowered as a center of a distinctive "Syrian" culture. At its height, Ebla was the hub of a hinterland that may have contained more than 200,000 people; it controlled trading emporia far afield; traded with Cyprus, Ur, and Gaza; and the city itself covered 140 acres laid out in four major dis-

tricts. It may have had a population of more than 20,000, with as many as 4 percent of its inhabitants employed as scribes.

It is in the palace archives, composing some 14,000 tablets, that Ebla and its role in Syria become clear. The clay tablets, many found in situ on shelves and lined up with reference tagging to help keep them ordered, all date from a period of a few hundred years (2500–2250 BC). No tablets were found for the period after the large-scale destruction of the city. The writing used the Sumerian cuneiform style, but it was not Sumerian. Professor Giovanni Pettinato, who deciphered this unique language, initially called it Palaeo-Canaanite since it predated known Semitic languages of Canaan like Ugaritic and Hebrew. Pettinato later decided to term the language "Eblaite," by which name it is known today.

Many of the tablets contain both Sumerian and Eblaite inscriptions, and there are many "dictionaries" or bilingual word lists contrasting words in the two languages. It is this use of the older Sumerian "international" diplomatic language in conjunction with Eblaite that allowed Pettinato to decipher the new language. It has also served to clarify scholars' understandings of Sumerian. Until the discoveries at Ebla, there existed no dictionaries of Sumerian and other languages written current with the time Sumerian was spoken, leaving pronunciations and other phonetic aspects of the language unclear. The Ebla archives, with their diversity of subjects, this dualistic style, and their vast numbers, have thus, among other contributions, improved the ability of scholars to interpret the intricacies of Sumerian.

Two particular sets of topics contained in the archives are instructive about Bronze Age Syria. First, Ebla was a quintessential trading city, and the archives reflect this through a focus on economic issues and on commercial or political relations with other cities. It is clear that Ebla imported commodities and luxury goods from sites in Afghanistan (e.g., lapis lazuli) and Egypt (e.g., alabaster vases, linen, gold, and silver). The city was a major exporter as well, and it was well known for its craftsmen, perfumes, and textiles. The products of its factories, crafted of precious metals and timber, were in great demand throughout the region. Basic agricultural products were also traded: cattle, wheat, ewes, wine, and barley are mentioned. The archives contain some fascinating revelations; for example, Ebla produced a range of beers, including one that appears to be named "Ebla," for the city.

Ebla established a complex system of trading outposts scattered far into Anatolia and toward northern Mesopotamia, and the city went to war to protect these trade routes and emporia. For some period, it controlled the city of Mari on the Euphrates. It also exacted customs duties on trade that passed within its orbit. Between 2500 and 2300 BC, the Canaanite port cities of Byblos and Sidon were key intermediaries between Ebla and Egypt (see also "Byblos"). What emerges from the tablets is the central role of Ebla in establishing and coordinating an advanced commercial city system throughout northern Syria that linked other autonomous city-states together into a trading community. This was no centralized military empire, imposed by force, but a league of cities creating wealth and welfare for their citizens, with Ebla taking the lead.

Many of the tablets in the archives have another type of focus: the city was a major education center specializing in training scribes. Because of the complexity of the syllabic cuneiform system, scribes had to learn thousands of particularized terms relevant only to law, administration, or trade. This required detailed training supported by an institutional structure. Ebla was a center for scribal education; the archives contain thousands of copybooks, lists for learning relevant jargon, and the scratch pads for students. Researchers claim, for example, to be able to follow the career of one particular scribe from his time as a lowly student through his position as a teacher and, finally, as a key administrator.

This centrality in the knowledge networks of the time meant that Ebla was a key stop on the "education trail" linking cities, and scribes attended conferences in Ebla to learn particular specialties. Clearly, the city's professionals were part of the advancement of writing, abstraction, and standardization that occurred throughout the region during this period and that soon led to the development of the alphabet.

One of the major controversies arising from the study of the Ebla archives is about their direct reference to places, events, or individuals in the Bible. Soon after the first translations of the archives were released (late 1970s), an acrimonious debate arose as to whether the archives confirmed the existence of Abraham, David, Sodom and Gomorrah, and other biblical references. These arguments occurred within the political context of the modern conflict between Syria and Israel, and the archaeologists became caught up in a global debate about the "proof" of Zionist claims to Palestine. Fantastic assertions and wild speculations in the press about the discoveries contained in the archives have led over the years to a reticence by Italian archaeologists to quickly publish deciphered texts, with the result that few translations have been made available, and the texts are closely guarded by the University of Rome. What is clear is that the archives have proved to be an outstanding source of information about the Syrio-Palestine region in the Early Bronze Age; they contain, for example, the first references to "Ugarit," to "Canaanites," and to "Lebanon" (see also "Ugarit").

The archives and the palace appear to have been destroyed by Naram-Sin of Akkad (2254–2218 BC) around 2250 BC. This fits with his claim to have destroyed Ebla, a city that had "never before been taken." The destruction layer from this event is very deep and indicates a systematic attempt to wipe out the city. At the time of the rise of the Akkadians, Ebla was the key power standing between this first territorial empire and the wealth of Cyprus, Anatolia, and the wood of the "Cedar Mountains." It is little wonder that the great imperial conqueror, Sargon, began a process of circumscribing Ebla's power, which his grandson Naram-Sin completed.

No subsequent tablet archives have been discovered in the city, and the palace was never rebuilt. The city quickly bounced back, however, and experienced a further degree of prosperity, although it never regained the heights of influence experienced during its golden era (2400–2250 BC). The city was destroyed again around 2000 BC, was rebuilt, and enjoyed another period of success before being destroyed again around 1600 BC. After this time, the city evidenced a significant loss of power and prestige, and habitation became less dense and sophisticated, with few defenses. Insignificant remains from the Persian, Greek, Roman, and Byzantine periods exist on the tell, but it is clear that after 60 BC, Ebla slipped out of remembering.

The wonderful finds in the archives at Ebla are the oldest and largest collection of tablets yet found in the Middle East. As a package, the stories they tell of life 4,000 to 5,000 years ago open a door to humanity's past that had been lost and forgotten. When examining their stories, however, it is crucial not to make the twin mistakes of confirming preexisting beliefs on the basis of their limited evidence or of interpreting their record as confirmation that the city of Ebla was the center of a great, unique empire. Neither approach will help us comprehend the contribution and uniqueness of northern Syria in the Bronze Age.

Bruce Stanley

Further Readings

Bermant, Chaim, and Michael Weitzman. *Ebla: An Archaeological Enigma.* London: Weidenfeld and Nicolson, 1979.

Gordon, C. H., ed. *Eblaitica: Essays on the Ebla.* Vol. 1–3, *Archives and Eblaite Language.* New York: NYU Center for Ebla Research/Eisenbrauns, 1991.

Matthiae, Paolo. *Ebla: An Empire Rediscovered.* New York: Doubleday, 1981.

Pettinato, Giovanni. *Archives of Ebla: An Empire Inscribed in Clay.* New York: Doubleday, 1981.

Ephesus
Population: 250,000 (AD 50 estimate)

For more than a millennium, Ephesus was one of the most important centers of Greek and Roman culture in Asia Minor. From its rise to prominence in the fifth century BC to its relative decline in the fifth century AD, it enjoyed a prestigious position within the Mediterranean community, acting as the Roman provincial capital. Home to early Christian apostles, the city became an important center for the new religion, a site for theological debate, and one of the major pilgrimage sites in Byzantium. Over its second millennium, Ephesus continued to be of influence within the region, though much reduced in importance. Today its extensive ruins attract archaeologists and visitors to western Turkey from throughout the world.

The city of Ephesus (Greek, *Ephesos;* Turkish, *Efes*) owed its significance to two vital factors: its geographic location and the great Temple of Artemis. Nestled within three small hills overlooking the western coastal plain of Anatolia adjacent to the Aegean Sea, the ruins of the ancient city are near the modern Turkish village of Seljuq. It is located approximately forty-five miles south of the metropolis of Izmir (formerly Smyrna). Situated at the mouth of the Cayster River (modern Kucuk Menderes) where it flowed into the Aegean Sea, Ephesus enjoyed an easily accessible harbor that provided a distinct commercial advantage. In addition, it was located at the crossroads of two ancient highways, the Persian Royal Road and a later Roman trade route that led eastward into the interior agricultural plateau. The second factor, nearly as important, was the beautiful Temple of Artemis (or Diana), known as one of the Seven Wonders of the Ancient World, which drew devotees and travelers alike for nearly 700 years. The Roman emperor Augustus (63 BC–AD 14) recognized the importance of these factors and designated Ephesus as the provincial capital of the province of Asia during his imperial reign. The region became one of the more important provinces of the Roman Empire.

The earliest origins of Ephesus are shrouded in mystery. Neolithic artifacts (ca. 10,000 BC) of simple tools and the bones of game birds and fish have been recently discovered. Hittite writings related to an Ahiyava Kingdom have also been unearthed, along with indications of Mycenaean influence. In 562 BC, the king of Lydia, Kroisos (Croesus), attacked and captured Ephesus, adding it to his kingdom. He is credited with building the great Temple of Artemis (Artemiseum), constructing it over an even more ancient worship site located next to a spring. As a gift to the city, Kroisos ordered the carving of huge columns, which stood along the front of the temple. On one column, unearthed in 1868 during the excavations of archaeologist John Wood of the British Museum, an inscription was found that read, "Presented by King Kroisos." Of those ancient columns, only one remains standing, marking the location of the original temple site.

As one of the Seven Wonders of the Ancient World, the Temple of Artemis is worthy of additional description. Artemis was a mythological Greek goddess, the daughter of Zeus, the king of the gods. In many of her basic characteristics, she closely resembled the Roman fertility goddess Diana. Artemis was the goddess of childbirth and female maturation. Young girls about to be married would pray to her. The

temple was of remarkable size, estimated to have been more than 300 feet long and 150 feet wide. The roof was supported by huge columns of carved figures, capped with elaborate friezes along the roofline. There is archaeological evidence of a major fire in 356 BC, but reconstruction soon followed of an even more impressive nature. The luxurious temple remained an attraction for centuries until its eventual destruction by an invasion of barbarian Ostrogoths in AD 262. Archaeological research was initiated in the temple area in 1863 by the British Museum and continues today under the Ministry of Culture of the Republic of Turkey.

In the late sixth century BC, Lydian control of Ephesus and the coastal area began to crumble under pressure from invading Persians to the east. King Kroisos was taken prisoner, and nearly all of the coastal cities were captured. The Persians united the former states of Lydia, Pamphylia, and Ionia under the name "Ionian States" and made Ephesus the capital city of the province. Ruling satraps were appointed. It was during this period that a resident of the city, Heraclitus (533–475 BC), became famous for his philosophic views. He taught that change is the basic reality of all physical existence, controlled by an unseen intelligence within created matter that he called the Logos.

In 490 BC, Ephesus joined other Ionian cities in an attempt to overthrow Persian tyranny in what became known as the "Ionian revolt." The uprising proved to be short-lived, however, and in 478 BC the Persian king Xerxes, returning from a military campaign in Greece, stopped in Ephesus to honor the goddess Artemis and, according to legend, left his children there for safekeeping. After 454 BC, Ephesus appears to have been allied with the Greek city of Athens until the Second Peloponnesian War, when it sided with Sparta. Persian and Ionian influences fluctuated over the following century until 333 BC, when Alexander the Great established Macedonian control over Asia Minor. It was said that upon his visit to Ephesus, Alexander was received as a god and savior. When he offered to assist with funding for repairs to the Temple of Artemis, the citizens refused, saying that it was inappropriate for "a god to make a temple for worship to another god."

Following the death of Alexander, Ephesus was ruled for a time by some of his subordinate generals. In 287 BC, a general named Lysimachos gained control of the region and resettled the city on the northern slopes of two small nearby hills, Coressus and Pion. The move to higher ground was occasioned by the gradual silting up of the harbor and the flooding of the early cultic sites; the low-lying area around the Temple of Artemis had already become unusable. Lysimachos encircled the city with strong walls, the partial ruins of which can still be seen today. In the second century BC, Ephesus was conquered for a brief time by the king of Pergamum, but in 133 BC King Attalus III, recognizing the power of Rome, bequeathed the city and his possessions to Roman rule.

Ruins at Ephesus, ca. 1880. (Library of Congress)

Roman rule enhanced the power and beauty of the city and brought about its golden age. Under Emperor Augustus, Ephesus was named the capital city of a newly formed province known as Asia, combining the areas of former Pamphylia and Ionia. As a provincial capital, it was the permanent location of the Roman magistrate and rapidly became the most important city and trading center of Asia. Because of its sheltered seaport and the terminus of major roads, goods arriving from the interior of Anatolia could easily be exported to Mediterranean countries. Three major shipping lanes converged on Ephesus: grain arrived from Alexandria, and military supplies, produce, commercial goods, lumber, and cattle came from Anatolia and Syria. Building construction flourished with the addition of a major aqueduct, a massive amphitheater, and numerous public and private buildings along with baths and gymnasiums. The province of Asia rapidly became one of the two most important regions of the empire. It is estimated that at its peak, the population of Ephesus numbered 200,000 to 250,000 residents, among them Roman citizens, soldiers, sailors, tradesmen, agricultural workers, and slaves.

The spread of Christianity and the eventual conversion of Emperor Constantine (AD 272–337) to Christian belief

brought major changes to Ephesus. Church building began on a large scale, and the Ephesus skyline was marked by numerous churches. In addition, the importance of the city was enhanced as a Christian center with the construction of nearby Constantinople (AD 330), now the eastern capital of the newly Christianized empire. Christianity had actually arrived in the city 280 years earlier, however; according to the New Testament, the apostle Paul traveled through that region on missionary journeys (ca. AD 50–60) and spent time in Ephesus. An interesting account of one visit is recorded in chapter 19 of Acts. The story tells of a near riot that occurred when merchants whose livelihood was dependent upon trade at the Temple of Artemis felt threatened by Paul and his preaching against idolatry. "Great is Artemis of Ephesus," they shouted in anger as Paul's friends sought to protect him from harm.

Gradually, the number of Christian believers increased, and churches were established. It is argued that by the end of the first century AD, a sizable Christian community existed in Ephesus, with its own bishop in residence. One significant tradition places the apostle John within the city in the late first century, eventually becoming its spiritual leader. It is also believed that he wrote his Gospel, Letters, and the book of Revelation there. Polycrates, a bishop of Ephesus in the late second century AD, wrote that "John's tomb was in Ephesus," and Irenaeus, the bishop of Lyon, France, claimed in AD 180 that "John had died in Ephesus." John (often referred to as Saint John) is believed to have accompanied Mary, the mother of Jesus, to Ephesus as her guardian, seeking to escape persecution from Jewish authorities. One tradition says that Mary lived her last years just outside of the city and died there.

No archaeological evidence has been found to substantiate the claim, but a small stone structure known as "the House of the Virgin Mary" is venerated today as her dwelling. Pope Paul VI and Pope John Paul II both visited the site and declared it to be a place "worthy of pilgrimage." Of greater importance, however, are the impressive ruins of two ancient churches, one the Church of Saint Mary and the other the Church of Saint John. Contemporary archaeological research and the size of the ruins of these two churches indicate the importance and grandeur of the structures that once existed there.

The traditions associating Ephesus with Saint John and Mary were rooted in early Christian belief. From earliest times, a tomb area on a hill (Ayasuluk) adjacent to the harbor was identified as the place where John was buried. Initially, small worship structures were constructed there, but in the sixth century AD (ca. AD 535) the Byzantine emperor Justinian created a basilica of impressive size. The building contained the holy tomb of Saint John and was built of brick with domes over the central crossing, plus a choir, transepts, and a nave. The historian Procopius described the church as "large and beautiful and a rival to those in the imperial city." Today the well-preserved ruins of the Church of Saint John underscore Procopius's astute observations.

The organizational structure of the early Christian movement was modeled after that of the Roman state. As a consequence, the bishop of Ephesus became the metropolitan of the province of Asia and enjoyed a measure of prestige. The city was selected as the location of three major church councils to deliberate on significant controversial issues. The first was assembled in AD 190 by Polycrates, the bishop of Ephesus, to establish an official date for Easter. The second and more famous council was called in AD 431 by the emperor Theodosius II (r. AD 408–450) to debate the teaching of Nestorius, the patriarch of Constantinople. Nestorius rejected the title "Mother of God" (*Theotokos*) in reference to Mary, the mother of Jesus, and instead called her *Christotokos* (the Mother of Christ). The doctrinal issue centered on the relationship within the human Jesus between his divinity and his humanity. Nestorius was declared a heretic and banished from the church and empire. An interesting side note is that his views became known as Nestorianism and spread eastward, gradually taking root in both India and China.

A third religious council was also held in Ephesus in AD 449, convened by the emperor Theodosius. This debate centered on the continuing controversy related to the divine versus the human nature of Jesus. A teacher named Eutyches promoted a concept known as Monophysitism, declaring that Jesus had only one single nature, which was divine. This emphasis denied the humanity of Jesus. In a famous council held in Chalcedon in AD 451, this view was rejected and condemned.

During the fourth, fifth, and sixth centuries, Rome's influence in the western part of the empire declined, and that of Constantinople to the east was on the rise. The Byzantine period brought renewed building construction and restoration to Ephesus, the Church of Saint John being a prime example. Continued prosperity in the city is evident in the extensive ruins that can be viewed today, particularly the stadium, theater, library of Celsus, the agora, and a variety of public baths and private residences. Some of these latter were quite luxurious, judging from existent floor mosaics, and multistoried apartment complexes lined the major streets. The appearance of the city in late antiquity, although altered from earlier times, must be viewed as a direct successor to that of the classical period.

The seventh and eighth centuries witnessed increasing incursions from Arab raiders to the east. In AD 654–655, the city was ravaged along with the nearby coastal city of Smyrna (see also "Izmir"). The upper agora section of the city, which had been the administrative center, appears to have been abandoned following major damage and new, more compact defensive walls built. Few facts are available from this period, but careful study of the ruins reveals a city of diminished size and wealth although continuing as an important Byzantine regional marketing and administrative center.

By the end of the first millennium, Ephesus was probably the most revered pilgrimage site in Asia Minor. Thousands of people yearly made their way from throughout the Byzantine Empire and from as far away as England to visit the city. This is because it had a multitude of saints, holy sites, reliquary, and miracles to attract pilgrims, and its location meant that it was accessible. The city was often termed Theologos, meaning "the evangelist." As a pilgrimage site, it offered numerous pleasures: regular miracles, the great cathedral, the tomb of the Seven Sleepers of Ephesus, and the tombs of Mary Magdalene and Saint Timothy. Pieces of the true Cross, clothing worn by the disciples, and the stone on which Jesus's body was prepared for burial were all available. Over the years, the number of relics and sites to visit in and around the city miraculously multiplied, drawing more pilgrims. Of particular attraction was the all-night festival in honor of Saint John. For more than 800 years, this annual miracle produced sacred dust or manna that flowed from his tomb in the cathedral to be distributed to the faithful to cure all manner of ills. Muslim pilgrims, to whom the Seven Sleepers were also significant, also made the trek to the city.

The year AD 1071 marked a major turning point for the ancient city. The defeat of the Byzantine army at Manzikert in

Armenia by the Seljuq Turks marked the end to Byzantine domination in Asia Minor. The Seljuq, followed later by the Ottomans, established their political control over the region and were accompanied by immigration of Turkic populations. By 1300 Ephesus had been pillaged of much of its stone and magnificent remains, and the city relegated to local status. As a port of the amirate of Aydin (Aydinogulu, 1300–1425), the city experienced a modest renewal of commerce, especially in trade with the Italian states of Venice and Genoa. Ibn Battuta, the famous Muslim traveler, visited Ephesus ca. 1330 and wrote that it was a commercial center of prosperous size. Other visitors of the same period wrote that the Turks charged admission to the tomb of the apostle Saint John and that part of the ruined building was a marketplace, where silk, wool, wheat, fish, and agricultural products were for sale. Western pilgrims continued to make their way to the city's ancient religious shrines, and one can still see today Latin graffiti in the ruins of the Church of Saint John dating from 1347 and 1381.

Under Muslim rule, some significant construction occurred. Still standing is the impressive Mosque of Isa Bey, dedicated in January 1375. Isa Bey was known for his interest in science and his support of learned scholars. The building measured 187 by 167 feet and consisted of two large areas, an arcaded courtyard, and a closed prayer room with two impressive domes. Western travelers were so impressed with its beauty that they supposed it was the Church of Saint John converted into a mosque. It is interesting to note that the mosque was the first major building constructed in the city since the days of Byzantine emperor Justinian, and it was the last down to the modern era. Other additions included a public soup kitchen, a candle factory, a press for linseed oil, and some outlying vineyards.

In the early 1400s, Ephesus fell to the forces of Temür. Following his rapid conquests in central Anatolia, Temür reached Ephesus in the fall of 1402, destroying the nearby city of Izmir and other coastal areas before eventually withdrawing in the spring of 1403. Nascent Ottoman influence was thus temporarily disrupted, and the coastal region of Anatolia entered several decades of turbulence and confusion.

The Ottoman Empire wielded the last major political and cultural control over Ephesus prior to modern times. It was a designated provincial administrative center, and there is evidence of modest commercial activity and minimal construction. Poverty, desolation, and general misery, however, were all noted by a variety of visitors. Apparently, none of them enjoyed their stay there. One traveler found the accommodations at a small inn so appalling that he preferred to spend the night in a nearby field. The place is described as a village built among ruins, with perhaps forty to fifty modest dwellings.

A major factor in the city's decline must be attributed to the alluvial silting of the ancient harbor at the mouth of the Cayster River. Archaeological evidence reveals continued efforts over the centuries to dredge the harbor and minimize the effect of floods and silting but to no avail. Ancient Ephesus gradually became an inland town, and each earlier harbor area had to be abandoned. New port areas were developed farther down the river. As revenues fluctuated because of shifting economic and political conditions, swamps gradually developed, exacerbating the problem. The low-lying areas gave rise to malaria, and trade shifted to other nearby port cities, such as Izmir. A variety of reasons have been proposed for the silting, among them deforestation inland, the rise and fall of sea level, pumice from volcanic activity, and the result of earthquake activity. Whatever the reasons, they occurred accumulatively over thousands of years. The ruins of ancient Greek and Roman Ephesus are now some three miles from the Aegean coast, and some two miles from the town of Selçuk, which grew up near the ruins of the Church of Saint John.

By the early nineteenth century, travelers reported abandoned ruins and the town of Selçuk to the west composed of few inhabitants. One visitor writing in 1811 reported that he could gain no rest because of the fleas and the jackals, which howled all night. The great provincial city of Roman power and prestige was no more. In 1863 the archaeologist John Wood arrived in the largely deserted village to find local farmers growing tobacco among the ruins. He began his search for the once great Temple of Artemis and thus initiated the modern era of archaeological research in the city.

Ephesus was caught up in the post–World War I struggles over the future of the Anatolian littoral. Greek forces invaded the coastal area, occupying Izmir and Selçuk in 1919. Turkish forces, led by Mustafa Kemal (Atatürk), resisted the invasion and finally moved against the Greeks. In September 1922, Turkish troops recaptured Izmir and forced a final Greek withdrawal (see also "Izmir"). At the Treaty of Lausanne in 1923, Turkey gained control of the coastal areas, and the region was incorporated into the Republic of Turkey. Today the town of Selçuk exists primarily on tourism to the national archaeological park. Under the guidance of the Turkish government, the excavations at Ephesus have continued and expanded, revealing some of the most interesting and impressive ruins of the ancient world available today.

Arthur Stanley

Further Readings

Foss, Clive. *Ephesus after Antiquity: A Late Antiquity Byzantine and Turkish City.* Cambridge: Cambridge University Press, 1979.

Koester, Helmut, ed. *Ephesos Metropolis of Asia: An Interdisciplinary Approach to Its Archaeology, Religion, and Culture.* Harvard Theological Studies 41. Cambridge: Trinity Press International, 1996.

Mitchell, Stephen. *Anatolia: Land, Men, and Gods in Asia Minor.* 2 vols. Oxford: Oxford University Press, 1999.

Esfahan
Population: 2.5 million (2005 estimate)

Because of its central position in the Iranian plateau, its mild climate, and its immensely fertile plain irrigated by the river Zayandarud, Esfahan has been an important urban center throughout most of Persian history. The city served as the capital of several provincial and imperial dynasties, above all under the Seljuqs in the second half of the eleventh century and then under the Safavids from 1597 to 1722. It was in the latter period that Esfahan grew to a celebrated world-class metropolis unmatched in the entire history of the country— "one of the greatest cities of the world" to the European traveler, Nisf-i Jihan, and "Half the World," to the Persian poet Nasir Khusraw. The imperial monuments of Esfahan today constitute one of the most significant and complete architectural complexes preserved at the heart of a modern city that owes them much of its prestige. The future of its great monuments remains, however, in doubt.

Esfahan (also spelled *Isfahan;* ancient, *Aspadana;* Greek, *Gabae;* Arabic, *Isbahan*) lies at an elevation of 5,150 feet, about 260 miles south of the capital city of Tehran. Among the population centers of the Iranian plateau, Esfahan is unique in being located in a riverine plain. An extensive irrigation system along the banks of the river Zayandarud, which crosses the city, has been functioning since time immemorial. The city has been an important trading center on a major highway running north-south between the massive Zagros mountain range to the west and the central desert on the east. Consequently, the province of Esfahan has a varied landscape of plains and hills, with equally diverse climate. In the plain of Esfahan, however, the seasons are extremely regular: hot summers and cold winters. The humidity is low, and the annual rainfall seldom surpasses five inches. No major earthquake has been reported in the last millennium—the reason so many architectural monuments in the city and its environs are still standing. Esfahan ranks, together with Tabriz, as the third-largest city in the nation, after Tehran and Mashhad.

Every Persian town has a mythical history, and Esfahan is no exception. Zoroastrian legends attribute the foundation of the citadel to King Kay Kavus. According to an ancient tradition, the city was founded before the period of the legendary Indo-Iranian hero Yama/Jam; it suffered much destruction from the Turanian king Afrâsiâb; was restored by Queen Homay, the daughter of King Bahman, son of Isfandiar; and was left untouched by Alexander the Great. The latter, according to yet another line of tradition transmitted by al-Tabari and other early Muslim historians, was the founder of Esfahan.

Esfahan is nearly as old as Persia itself. The oldest appearance of the name is Aspadana, a Greek rendering of Old Per-sian Spadana—"of or related to the army," that later developed as Spahan in Middle Persian, Sipahan and Isfahan in New Persian, and Isbahan in Arabic. The town and province were sometimes called in medieval sources by the alternate name Gay (Arabic, *Jayy*), the Gabae of Greek writers. Strabo states that the Achaemenid kings had palaces not only in Susa and Persepolis but also in Gabae, which formed, according to Ptolemy's map of Persia, the southernmost district of the superprovince of Media. There are sporadic references to Gabae/Esfahan in the Seleucid and Arsacid (Parthian) era, but more detailed data are available from the Sassanian period (AD 224–651), when Esfahan is described as a large province with 3,000 to 5,000 villages and three to seven towns—a condition that continued throughout most of the later periods.

During the Sassanian rule, the city of Esfahan comprised two adjoining towns: Gay, or Shahristan, a circular fortified town with 104 watchtowers and four gates, on the eastern border of the present city, and Juhudistan, or Yahudiyya, a Jewish settlement on the site later occupied by central Esfahan. The establishment of the Jewish colony is generally attributed to the Babylonian king Nebuchadnezzar, but a Middle Persian source attributes the founding of the colony to Yazdigird I (r. 339–420), who did so at the request of his Jewish wife, Showshandukht. In any case, the Jewish population of the city remained sizable throughout the city's history, and twenty synagogues remain in the old quarter of Jubara alone. The Jewish community is the only one that has preserved the original Median dialect of the city, otherwise overwhelmed by Persian, the lingua franca of the Iranian world and beyond.

Because of its central position, Esfahan has experienced most of the vicissitudes undergone by Persia since the Arab conquest of the mid-seventh century. For nearly a millennium, the city was incorporated into successive empires ruled by the Arabs, Persians themselves, Turks, and Mongols before the Safavids revived the essence of Sassanian Persia. For most of this period, the city held a principal position in the administrative, economic, and cultural affairs of the country. Under the Arab caliphs, Esfahan served as the capital of the al-Jibal (the mountains) superprovince, an area that covered much of ancient Media. As the temporal authority of the Abbasids waned in the tenth century, Esfahan passed under the control of the Persian Buyid dynasty, and it flourished as an extensive urban center, with splendid mansions, gardens, bathhouses, hospitals, and markets; its wealth and trade, especially its export of silk and textiles, surpassed all other cities in the jabal, save for Ray (modern Tehran). Based on a report of the daily consumption of meat in the town (2,000 sheep and goats and 100 head of cattle), its population at this time can be estimated to have been well more than 100,000. The renowned Persian traveler and poet Nasir Khusraw, who came to Esfahan in 1052, concluded his vivid account of the town by stating that Esfahan was the most populous and flourishing city that he had visited in Persian-speaking lands.

The influx of Turkic nomads from central Asia into Persia brought to power the Seljuq dynasty, whose founder, Tughril, made Esfahan the capital of his domains in the mid-eleventh century. Under his celebrated grandson Malikshah (r. 1072–1092), the city grew in size and splendor as the capital of an empire that extended from Transoxiana to the Mediterranean Sea. In those days, Esfahan had a central quadrangular *maidan* (square) surrounded by palaces, markets, and municipal, educational, and religious establishments. At the northern corner of the maidan stood the Friday Mosque, also known as the Great Mosque, which continues to be an architectural glory of the city. In this extensive complex, the two magnificent dome chambers built by Nizam al-Mulk and Taj al-Mulk, the competing viziers of Malikshah, have survived in the midst of later constructions and modifications no less worthy of artistic value.

Not long after Malikshah, the Seljuqs moved their capital to Khorasan, and Esfahan began a period of decline that continued throughout the Mongol and Timurid periods. Temür captured the city in 1387 and massacred more than 50,000 of its citizens. The city's decline was also partly caused by sectarian strifes that appear to have been a common feature of Esfahani life in medieval times. Malikshah, Nizam-al-Mulk, and a number of political and religious leaders of the city were murdered by Ismaili assassins who had grown so strong in Esfahan that they possessed two strategic suburban fortresses and collected taxes from the neighboring villages, from which 30,000 men were recruited into their uprising.

The townspeople of Esfahan were predominantly Sunni but divided into two rival sects: the Shafis, who lived in the quarter of Dardasht and were led by the influential Khujandi family, and the Hanafis, who resided in Jubara, municipally administered by the house of Saadis. It was only the treachery of the former that, in 1240, delivered the city into the hands of the besieging Mongols. Nearly a century later, when Ibn Battuta visited Esfahan (1327), the city was still split by divisions: he wrote in his *Rihla*: "Esfahan is one of the largest and fairest of cities, but is now in ruins for the greater part, as the result of the feud there between the Sunnis and Shi'i." After the adoption of Shi'ism under the Safavids, the city's internal divisions remained along similar lines but defined in different terms: factional strife arose between Haydaris and Nimatis, who dwelled, exclusively, in the aforementioned quarters of Dardasht and Jubara.

Esfahan's golden age began in 1597, when the Safavid shah Abbas the Great (r. 1588–1629) chose it as his capital and planned and rebuilt it into one of the greatest cities of the time. While the old quarters remained intact, a new quarter was added in the southern part of the city, at the center of which laid Maidan-i Shah (Royal Square), also known as Naqsh-i Jihan (Image of the Universe), an immense courtyard that measures 557 by 180 yards and is framed by a wall of blind arcades. Structures mark the four sides of this well-preserved maidan: to the south is the majestic Masjid-i Shah (the Royal Mosque, renamed the Imam Mosque after the 1979 Islamic Revolution, as was the maidan itself and many other historical monuments), clad all over by colorful tiles; to the east is the mosque of Shaykh Lutf-Allah, used by the king for his private devotions; to the north is Qaysariya, the royal bazaar's monumental gateway, which leads to the old maidan; and finally to the west of the Royal Square stands the palace Ali Qapu (Lofty Gate), a six-story building in the form of an archway that is crowned in the forepart by a large covered balcony that served as an audience hall and vantage point from which the king and his guests could watch games of polo below in the maidan. The United Nations Educational, Scientific, and Cultural Organization (UNESCO) has designated the Royal Square complex as a World Heritage Site.

It takes well more than one day for a tourist to visit the Safavid monuments of Esfahan. Not far from the Royal Square are the palaces of Chihil Sutun (Forty Columns) and Hasht Bihisht (Eight Heavens) and the architectural complex of Madar-i Shah (Royal Mother), built by the last of the Safavid kings, Shah Sultan-Hussayn, for his mother in the early eighteenth century. It consists of a madrasa, with a splendid arabesque dome, adjoined by two endowments: a lineal bazaar, which is still functioning as a two-story shopping mall, and a caravansary, which is remodeled into the modern Abbasi Inn. All these structures are within the "royal city" that stretches from the Royal Square to Chahar Bagh (Four Gardens) Avenue, another Safavid construction that traverses the entire length of the modern city. The Chahar Bagh runs southward to the Zayandarud, which it crosses by means of the "thirty-three-span bridge" built by Allahverdi Khan, the marshal of Shah Abbas. Further downstream there is yet another fine bridge, Pul-i Khwaju. Arthur U. Pope, the renowned American expert on Persian architecture, called the Pul-i Khwaju "the culminating monument of Persian bridge architecture and one of the most interesting bridges extant [because of its] rhythm and dignity"; Pope is buried in a park named after him at the foot of the bridge. To the south of the river lies the Armenian Quarter of Julfa, with more than a dozen churches dating from the Safavid rule.

Jean Chardin, who lived for ten years in the Safavid capital, offered, in his *Voyages,* a detailed and vivid description of "the greatest and most beautiful town of the whole orient," in which there were to be found followers of all religions and merchants from the whole world; Indians involved in the banking business alone numbered no fewer than 10,000. The commercial character of the Safavid metropolis can be seen in other statistics offered by Chardin: there were 273 bathhouses, 48 madrasas, 162 mosques, and 1,802 caravansaries within the city walls and 500 more caravansaries without. Accordingly, for every mosque there were more than eleven inns, a ratio that has become almost reversed today: seventy-three inns of all ranks versus more than 1,500 mosques in the district of Esfahan (2003 data). Moreover, according to Chardin, there were 12,000 to 14,000 prostitutes publicly registered, with as many more who worked on their own—in a city that was the capital of Shi'ism, attracting religious scholars and leaders from all Muslim lands. The population of this enormous city, estimated by Chardin to match that of London (i.e., ca. 650,000), grew to well more than 1 million, according to other reports, by the end of Safavid rule.

In 1722, after a six-month siege, the city fell to the Ghilzai Afghans, who sacked it and destroyed its infrastructure. For many decades afterward, most of the city was a heap of rubble, and its population dwindled to a fraction of what it had once been. During the subsequent reign of the Afsharid, Zandid, and Qajar tribes, Esfahan was eclipsed by the capital cities of Mashhad, Shiraz, and finally Tehran (see also "Tehran"). Successive massacres and famines contributed to its decline, but there was also the general economic decadence experienced by the region during the period of European imperial expansion. Land trade routes, the backbone of Persian economy, became less significant to global trade as goods were shipped more often by sea. Esfahan was left behind as a living museum of Persian civilization.

The city has been home to many contributors to Muslim and Persian cultural and religious diversity. Ibn Sina lived the last fourteen years of his life in the city (d. 1037) and completed most of his major philosophical and medical treatises there. The Bahais faith flourished in the city during the late 1800s because the Bab wrote some of his major works there in the 1840s. Hajieh Sayyideh Nosrat Begom Amin, a leading female *mujtahid* (religious authority), was born and died in the city, and she wrote her fifteen-volume study of the Qur'an here during the mid-1900s.

Esfahan had a leading role in the Constitutional Revolution of 1905, which opened a new chapter in the history of Persia. Recovery began during the reign of Reza Shah Pahlavi (r. 1925–1941), who curbed the power exerted by religious authorities and the surrounding nomads on the city. An industrial quarter was built, and the textile industry thrived once more, so successfully that Esfahan became known as the Manchester of Persia. In the following decades, Esfahan emerged as a major industrial center of the country, with large steel mills, cement factories, defense industry plants, and an oil refinery. The extensive restoration of the city's historical monuments led to the emergence of a new generation of tile makers, miniature painters, and calligraphers, among other artists. As the city grew into a center of tourist attraction, handicrafts such as metalwork, inlaying, enameling, calico, illuminating, and brocading, as well as rug weaving, flourished. The progress has continued during the years following the Islamic Revolution of 1979; however, the new demographic realities have been detrimental to urban planning as construction codes have systematically been violated in favor of a demanding population that has grown nearly threefold.

Habib Borjian

Further Readings

Blake, S. P. *Half the World: The Social Architecture of Safavid Esfahan, 1590–1722.* Costa Mesa, CA: Mazda, 1999.

Blunt, Wilfred, and Wim Swaan. *Esfahan: Pearl of Persia.* London: Elek, 1966.

Borjian, Houri, and Habib Borjian. *Abbasi Inn: Museum within a Museum.* Illustrated volume photographed by R. N. Bakhtiar, with introduction in English and Persian. Tehran: Iran Insurance Company, 1997.

Grabar, Oleg. *The Great Mosque of Esfahan.* New York and London: New York University Press, 1990.

A Journey to Persia: Jean Chardin's Portrait of a Seventeenth-Century Empire. Translated and edited by Ronald W. Ferrier. London and New York: I. B. Tauris, 1996.

Pope, Arthur U., ed. *A Survey of Persian Art.* 6 vols. London: Oxford University Press, 1938.

Welch, Anthony. *Shah Abbas and the Arts of Esfahan.* New York: Asia Society, 1973.

Yarshater, Ehsan, ed. *Encyclopaedia Iranica.* New York: Columbia University Press, 1983–present.

F

Fez
Population: 950,000 (2005 estimate)

Fez is regarded as one of the grandest and largest medieval cities in the world. Lying on the northwestern edge of the trade routes that link the Atlantic Ocean and Mediterranean Sea with the countries south of the Sahara, it was from the earliest days of the Islamic conquest a commercial, cultural, and religious center. It served as the capital city of Morocco for more than 400 years and is home to the oldest university in the country. Fez is a city that is almost unchanged through the modern ages, with Islamic traditions being nourished by the massive Kairouan Mosque, its tradition of Arab-Andalusian arts and crafts, and its vibrant medieval madinah.

Fez, or Fès (Arabic, *Fas*), is located in a narrow valley in the northern part of modern-day Morocco at the northeast extremity of the plain of the Sais. Here the waters of the eastern side of this plain enter into the valley of Sebou via the valley of the Wadi Fas and provide good communication with other parts of the region. Fez thus straddles the intersection of two of the great axes of communication. The first is the north-south axis between the Mediterranean and the Sahara and beyond to Black Africa; the second is the east-west axis between the Atlantic coast and the central Maghreb region.

In addition, the development of Fez owes much to an abundance of natural resources. The area is rich in water. Apart from the River Fez itself, which flows through the city, there are numerous springs scattered about the valley and hillsides and tributaries that have been easy to canalize and turn to urban use there. In the immediate vicinity, there are quarries that traditionally have provided building stones, sand, and lime. In addition, the Middle Atlas mountain range is close by, and its oak and cedar forests provide timber and wood of very good quality for construction and decoration. The economy of Fez was based upon textile and flour mills, oil processing, tanneries, soap factories, and other crafts. The fez, a brimless, cylindrical felt hat, takes its name from the city. The area surrounding Fez produces cereals, beans, olives, and grapes, and it is a market town for sheep, goats, and cattle raised in the region.

Founded in AD 789 by Idris ibn Abd Allah, a descendant of the Prophet Muhammad, who had fled to Morocco to escape persecution by the Abbasid caliphs, Fez is the most prominent legacy of the Islamic Idrisid dynasty (AD 788–974) and the first capital and Islamic spiritual center of Morocco. The name is reputedly derived from the pickax of silver and gold (*fas* in Arabic) that was used by Idris to trace the outlines of the city. However, it was his son, Idris II, who began the real development of the city in 809 and built the celebrated mosque of Mulai Idris. The city received its Arab-Andalusian character from waves of immigrants from Cordoba in 818 and from Kairouan in present-day Tunisia between 824 and 826, who settled on either side of the city's river.

As the city grew, important new mosques, such as the Kairouan and Andalus, were built in 859 and 862, respectively. These mosques, especially Kairouan Mosque, and the university which developed in association with it helped give Fez its stature as a prominent Islamic center of learning that rivaled al-Azhar University in Cairo. However, the relative homogeneity of the two urban settlements on either side of the river evolved into a rivalry that lasted several centuries, impairing its growth as a major city. During the thirty years between 980 and 1012, it fell under the protection of the Umayyads in Cordoba and enjoyed increasing prosperity and renown. Following this period, the rivalries between the twin towns were revived by the Zenata Berbers, who held sway in the region. However, with the arrival of the Almoravids in 1069, the two towns were united within one external wall and made into a major military base of the Almoravids in northern Morocco.

The city was once more captured in 1248 and became the capital of the Marinid dynasty. For three centuries, Fez experienced its golden age as the political, religious, intellectual, and economic leader of Morocco. The new court lived at first in the kasbah, which the Almohads had reconstructed on the site of the ancient Almoravid kasbah, in the district now called Bu Djulud. Mosques, houses, shops, flour mills, public baths, and *funduqs* (two-story lodging houses for visiting merchants) were built in such profusion that by the late thirteenth century, no more space remained within the city walls. Thus, a new royal and administrative town to the west of the ancient one was founded in 1276. This new urban center was first named the White City (*al-madina al bayda*) and is now known as Fas al-Djadid (New Fez). It consisted essentially of the palace, various administrative buildings, and a great mosque to which were added other sanctuaries, barracks, homes of dignitaries, and in the fifteenth century, a unique Jewish Quarter.

The importance of Fez as a Moroccan city declined under the Saadids (1517–1666), who chose Marrakesh as their capital (see also "Marrakesh"). Under the Alawids, Fez fared better, and its political status was rejuvenated in the period before the French protectorate was imposed on Morocco in 1912. For example, Sultan Mawlay al-Hasan (r. 1873–1894) undertook important public works in Fez. He set up a small

View of the medieval walls of Fez. (Corel Corporation)

arms factory near his palace and connected the two urban areas of Fas al-Djadid and Fas al-Bali, the madinah, which had until this time remained separated by two long walls.

Fez suffered both politically and economically under French rule (1912–1956) and by the modernization and absorption into the world economic system that came in its wake. However, protest against the French first manifested itself along religious lines. As the traditional religious center and former capital of Morocco, Fez was the place where the religious protest of the Salafiyyah movement and Moroccan nationalist agitation converged. Many important demonstrations took place there, and its leaders played an important role in the Moroccan independence movement. Indeed, the leadership of the national Istiqlal Party was dominated by the political elite from Fez. The French also left their mark on Fez in the construction of a third urban area, the *ville nouvelle,* which housed the administration and military. This area was characterized by broad avenues and low-density residential buildings.

Currently, despite a population of close to a million, Fez's importance as a primary national city has diminished. Rabat has supplanted its role as capital and administrative center,

and Casablanca has superseded it as the nation's commercial center (see also "Rabat/Sale" and "Casablanca"). Nevertheless, the leading families of Fez make up a fair portion of the Moroccan political elite, and the city itself remains an important national historical and religious center.

The pattern established over the centuries of major urban development taking place on new "greenfield" sites has meant that the city's architectural trajectory has been well preserved. This is particularly the case for Fez al-Bali, also known as the madinah or "Old Fez," which is a unique architectural and urban survivor. Much of the pattern of residence and daily life continues as it has done so for many hundreds of years. Awareness of its historical value began early during the French protectorate when the French general Lyautey put in place arrangements to protect the medieval structures against modern development. Since 1967 Fez al-Bali has been closed to cars and protected by the United Nations Educational, Scientific, and Cultural Organization (UNESCO) as a World Heritage Site. An agency for slum clearance and renovation, Ader-Fez was established and put in charge of carrying out an ambitious program of renovation consisting of the transfer of economic activities, renovation of housing, restoration of monuments, and training of supervisors and specialized craftsmen.

One feature derived from its early settlement history is that there are two distinctly different districts in Fez al-Bali. The right bank of the wadi has its roots in the Andalusian culture its original inhabitants brought with them. This quarter has a profusion of highly ornate and fine buildings. The Andalus Mosque is easily identified by its green-and-white minaret and formidable door of sculpted cedar. It dates from the ninth century and was further embellished by successive rulers. The left bank was settled by immigrants from Kairouan and brings a distinct Maghrebi culture to the quarter. The great Kairouan Mosque was the largest in the whole of Africa until the modern one in Casablanca was built in the 1990s. The mosque has been the center of Islamic learning in Morocco for more than 1,000 years, but its real growth in importance came during the tenth to twelfth century, when most of its structures were added to the rather modest original structures. The mosque is vast with many outlying courtyards and chambers, and Fez al-Bali has to some extent been built around it.

The famous Kairouan University has for eleven centuries been a religious and intellectual center whose influence has spread far beyond the confines of the region. The madrasas around the Kairouan Mosque served as former lodging houses for students coming from outside the city, and with their marble or onyx courtyards, they are eloquent architectural reminders of the city's past glories. One of the most ornate is as-Sahri Madrasa (1321), with luxurious decoration both internally and externally. The Attarine Madrasa was built in the early fourteenth century and has a beautiful bronze door opening onto an elegant courtyard with numerous examples of exquisite detail work in marble, alabaster, and cedarwood.

The gates that are part of the walls of the madinah are also noteworthy for their decorations and embellishments. Bab Boudloud, for example, a recent addition built to celebrate the unification of Fez al-Bali and Fez al-Djadid, is covered with dazzling colored tiles. The madinah itself is a labyrinth of winding alleyways housing a wide range of traditional artisan work: coppersmiths, tanners, and dyers. The famous Kissaria is the commercial center crammed with shops and stalls selling cotton fabric, silk, brocade work, slippers, cobalt blue enameled pottery, carpets, wrought iron, and fine gilt for bookbinding.

Fez al-Djadid is famous for its well-preserved Jewish Quarter, known as al-Mellah. To a large degree emptied of its Jewish inhabitants, the quarter has been taken over by rural Moroccan immigrants. The area had its own unique forms of architecture, which principally take the shape of beautifully ornate bays and windows contrasting with the plain white walls of the houses in which they were placed. The area is now undergoing detailed and extensive restoration work. The Habanim synagogue has been developed into a museum of Jewish life.

Michael Dumper

Further Readings

Bonine, M. "The Sacred Direction and City Structure: Preliminary Analysis of the Islamic Cities of Morocco." In *Muqarnas,* vol. 7. Leiden: E. J. Brill, 1990.

Burckhardt, Titus. *Fez: City of Islam.* Translated by William Stoddart. Cambridge: Islamic Texts Society, 1992.

Le Tourneau, Roger. *Fez in the Age of the Marinides.* Translated by Besse Alberta Clement. Norman: University of Oklahoma Press, 1961.

Peto, Ralph. *Ambling Down to Fez.* London: Rosemary Peto, 1981.

Smith, Charles. *Morocco as It Is: With an Account of Sir Charles Euan Smith's Recent Mission to Fez.* London: W. H. Allen, 1893.

G

Gaza
Population: 479,000 (2005 estimate)

Napoléon Bonaparte called Gaza the key to the eastern and western parts of the Arab world. As only one of hundreds of generals to attack this most ancient of Mediterranean seaports, he shares in a long tradition of appreciation for its strategic location. Today the city is best known for its role in the Israeli-Palestinian conflict and for having one of the highest population densities in the world. Currently the location of the administration for the Palestinian Authority, Gaza City is less well known for its 5,000- year history as the key entrepôt of southern Palestine and as an outlet for the spice trade traversing the Red Sea.

Situated on a low hill two miles from the east Mediterranean seashore, and twenty miles north of the Egyptian border, Gaza (Arabic, *Ghazzah*) is thought to be one of the most ancient and historic towns in the world. It is located on the climatic dividing line between the desert in the south and the Mediterranean climate in the north. This made it a vital gateway for one of the most ancient and important trade and military routes in the world, the *Via Maris* (Sea Route), which connected Palestine with Egypt along the coast. It also made the city a key entrepôt on the Mediterranean, linking the Arabian Peninsula and India with Europe via caravan routes across the Sinai.

The location also helped the city acquire a strategic status in that it formed the southern defense line not only of Palestine but of all the Bilad ash-Sham area (Syria, Lebanon, and Jordan) as well. Consequently, the city has been a battlefield for empires through the ages—various pharaonic, Assyrian, Persian, Greek, Roman, Byzantine, Arab, Crusader, and Ottoman invaders as well as the British during the First World War. Despite this it has also had a prosperous history as a flourishing market town and trading center. Along with the sliver of land known as the Gaza Strip (about 147 square miles), Gaza came under Israeli occupation in 1967. Since May 1994, it has been a largely autonomous zone under the leadership of the Palestinian Authority, which has its administrative headquarters in the city.

Canaanites established the city and called it Gaza around 3000 BC during the Early Bronze Age. The first written reference to the town of Gaza, however, is during the reign of the Egyptian pharaoh Thutmose III (r. 1479–1426 BC) when it held a garrison for his army. It is also mentioned in the Tell el-Amarna Letters (ca. 1340 BC). Several hundred years later,

Gaza was one of the five linked cities of the Philistines. It is mentioned a number of times in the Bible, especially as the site where Samson destroyed himself and his enemies by collapsing the Philistine temple. In the eighth century BC, it was conquered by the Assyrians, while from the third to the first century BC, Egyptian, Syrian, and Hasmonean armies fought for its possession. During Roman occupation, the city was called Minoa and had a strong Greco-Roman character.

In AD 635, it was the first Levantine city to be captured by the early Muslim invaders. The name *Gaza* remained unchanged, and Arab Muslims associated it with Hashim ibn Abed Manaf , the grandfather of the Prophet, who is said to be buried there after his death during one of his trading journeys. Consequently, the city became an important Islamic center. In the twelfth century, it was occupied by the Crusaders but returned to Muslim control in 1187. Its role as market town and trading center expanded under Mamluk and Ottoman rule, and many monumental buildings and fountains were built during these periods. Bonaparte stopped in Gaza on his way to besiege Acre in 1799. During World War I, the city was captured by British forces in General Allenby's push to Jerusalem in 1917.

By the terms of the United Nations (UN) plan of 1947, providing for the partition of Palestine into a Jewish state and an Arab state, Gaza was to have been included in the Arab area. In 1948 Egyptian forces defended Gaza and the surrounding area, and in the Egyptian-Israeli Armistice Agreement of 1949, Gaza and the twenty-four-mile-long by four-mile-wide strip of land held by Egyptian troops around it remained in Egyptian hands. In the course of the war, some 200,000 Palestinian refugees from the land acquired by the new State of Israel fled or were deported into the Gaza Strip, doubling the population. Gaza became the seat of the short-lived All-Palestine Government set up by the mufti of Jerusalem, Haj Amin al-Hussayni, but in practice Gaza and the Strip were administered by Egypt until 1967, with a brief interruption during the 1956 Suez War, when it was overrun by Israel.

Israeli forces occupied the city again during the Arab-Israeli June War of 1967 and introduced a military administration that lasted until 1994. Economic and civic development was severely constrained, and despite the rapid growth in population, the growth in remittances, and external donor support, per capita income of the residents remained very low in contrast to both Palestinians in the West Bank and Israelis. Political resistance to the occupation and the Israeli military response determined much of the social, cultural, economic, and political life of the city.

During the Palestinian intifada in 1987, Gaza became a center of political unrest and confrontation between Israelis and Palestinians, and economic conditions in the city worsened. In September 1993, leaders of Israel and the Palestine Liberation Organization (PLO) signed an accord that led to the evacuation of Israeli forces from the Gaza Strip. The new Palestinian Authority, led by Yasir Arafat, chose Gaza as its first provisional headquarters. The accord also led to the establishment of an elected eighty-eight-member Palestinian Legislative Council, which held its inaugural session in Gaza in March 1996.

Despite its contemporary appearance of an impoverished, poorly serviced, and congested city, Gaza has many notable historical remains and architectural features. The area of ancient Gaza was about 0.6 mile square and surrounded by a large wall with four gates in the four directions: Memas (the Sea Gate) in the west, Asklan Gate in the north, Hebron Gate in the east, and ad-Daroom Gate in the south. The town contains several distinct parts that reflect its historical development. The old historical town was built largely during the Ottoman period over the remains of earlier structures, but some features remained constant. There is a central square from which emerges the main street, Umar al-Mukhtar. This is the main longitudinal axis along which the town has developed. On both sides is the principal business center with rows of shops, some of fairly modern construction.

During the 1930s and 1940s, a new and spacious residential quarter, Rimal, was built on the sands west of the town. It contained detached houses built in European style and led to the transfer of the center of gravity of the town to an axis leading to the port, whose economic basis would thereby be strengthened. During the same period, the Zeitun and Judeide quarters were built, expanding the town toward the south, the southwest, and the east. The growth of these quarters was to a large extent caused by the activities of foreign institutions, such as the mission hospitals. The Jewish Quarter of Gaza, where about fifty Jewish families had lived until riots in 1929, expanded as well with new tenants. The refugee camps ash-Shati and al-Jabaliyya to the west and northwest, respectively, are now enormous suburbs and eclipse the city in terms of size and population density.

The principal monumental feature in Gaza is the al-Umari Great Mosque, with its large but beautiful minaret. It used to be a church built by the Crusaders in the twelfth century in the Norman style and is said to occupy the site of the first ancient temple of Marnas. Adjacent to its southern wall is the al-Qissariya Market, located in the ad-Daraj Quarter of the old city. This dates back to the Mamluk period and has vaults housing small shops on both sides of the road. Currently, it is known as the Gold Market because of the gold traded there. The Citadel of Gaza, Qasr al-Basha, also known as "Napoléon's Citadel" because of his brief sojourn there, is located in the

ad-Daraj Quarter in the old city of Gaza. It is a two-story building that dates back to the Mamluk period and was used as a police station during the British Mandate. Perhaps the most famous building, however, is the as-Sayyed Hashem Mosque, which houses the tomb of Hashim ibn Abed Manaf, the Prophet Muhammad's grandfather.

One notable feature of the city, dating from the Ottoman era, was the plenitude of water fountains established and funded by charitable donations to meet people's need for water in the dry climate. There were about 200 of them in Gaza, the most striking being that established by Behram Bin Mustafa Basha in the sixteenth century. It was renovated during the reign of Sultan Abdulhamid in AD 1893. Sadly, most of the fountains have been abandoned and are in disrepair.

Another architectural and historical feature is the Greek Orthodox Church, located in the az-Zaytoon Quarter of the old city. The original construction of the church dates from the beginning of the fifth century, while the existing structure dates back to the twelfth century. The church is characterized by its colossal walls supported by horizontal marble and granite columns and pilasters. The tomb of Saint Porphyrius, who died in 420, is in the northeastern corner. The church was renovated in 1856.

Gaza's population is composed almost entirely of Muslim Palestinian Arabs. Nearly all of the city's Jewish inhabitants left what had been a 2,000-year-old community during the early twentieth century. The massive influx of Palestinian refugees swelled Gaza's population after the creation of the State of Israel in 1948, and by 1967 the population had grown 600 percent. The city's population has continued to increase since that time, and poverty, unemployment, and poor living conditions are widespread. The Gaza Strip has one of the highest overall growth rates and population densities in the world with a density of about 5,261 per square mile. The overwhelming majority is Sunni Muslims, and the remainder are Christians.

The traditional economy of Gaza depended upon its location at the crossroads of the trade routes of the Levant and Arabian Peninsula. Toward the end of the Ottoman period, however, the ports of Jaffa and Haifa eclipsed Gaza's port, and the city lost most of its transshipment role, retaining only its fishing fleet (see also "Jaffa" and "Haifa"). After the Israeli occupation, in 1967, Gaza's port lost most of this limited income as well, and for much of the occupation it has been closed. There are Palestinian and international attempts to construct a major port to serve the Palestinian entity, but objections by Israel have so far prevented its opening. An international airport was also established in Gaza in the late 1990s, but Israeli forces have subsequently destroyed this and prevented its functioning.

The major agricultural products are citrus, olives, dates, flowers, strawberries, and other vegetables and food products, although pollution and the massive population pressures on water have reduced the productive capacity of the city's surrounding farms. Small-scale industrial production of plastics, construction materials, furniture, and textiles supplement traditional craft industries such as pottery, bamboo furniture, carpets, embroidery, tiles, and copper. In the wake of the Oslo Accords, a huge government administration has evolved, with ministries and security services employing thousands in the city. Other inhabitants are employed by the United Nations Relief and Welfare Agency (UNRWA) or the international organizations supporting development in the Strip.

Michael Dumper

Further Readings

An Atlas of Palestine. Bethlehem: Applied Research Institute, 2000.

Butt, Gerald. *Life at the Crossroads: A History of Gaza.* Epping, UK: Scorpion Cavendish, 1995.

Dowling, Theodore Edward. *Gaza: A City of Many Battles.* London: Christian Knowledge Society, 1913.

Downey, Glanville. *Gaza in the Early Sixth Century.* Norman: University of Oklahoma Press, 1963.

Efrat, E. *Urbanization in Israel.* London: Croom Helm, 1984.

Glucker. Carol. *The City of Gaza in the Roman and Byzantine Periods.* Oxford: B.A.R., 1987.

Hass, Amira. *Drinking the Sea at Gaza.* Translated by Elana Wesley and Maxine Kaufman-Lacusta. London: Hamish Hamilton, 1999.

Sabbagh, Suha, ed. *Palestinian Women of Gaza and the West Bank.* Bloomington: Indiana University Press, 1998.

H

Haifa
Population: 250,000 (2006 estimate)

Haifa, often compared to San Francisco for the beauty of its location, is a thriving Mediterranean port city. Although its roots go back some 3,000 years, well past Elijah's confrontation on Mount Carmel with the prophets of Baal, it is Haifa's status as a modern industrial city benefiting from the globalization of the twentieth century that has shaped its current environment and opportunities. Transformed by immigration and war, Haifa today struggles with the political and social issues of urban development and minority discrimination.

Haifa (Arabic, *Hayfa;* Hebrew, *Hefa*) is the third-largest city and chief seaport of Israel. Located in the northern part of the country overlooking the bay of the same name, the city lies on and around the slopes of Mount Carmel, where it dramatically meets the sea. To the northeast, seven miles across the waters of the bay, sits its economic and historical rival, Acre. Haifa is a deepwater port, sufficient for most world-class vessels. The city has thus forged its contemporary identity as an industrial port city. To the east of Haifa, on its landed side between Mount Carmel and Acre, begins the Jezreel (Zebulun) Valley, which separates Galilee from the Palestinian area known as the West Bank and which historically provided a land route to the interior of Syria. It is also excellent agricultural land, giving Haifa an agricultural base to its economy.

Until the present century, Haifa was little more than a small village, with Acre being the primary town of the bay (see also "Acre"). Known as Sycaminum (wild strawberries) during ancient times, the name *Efa* did not appear until Roman times, when a small Jewish settlement and Roman fortress existed at the city's current site. The Crusaders conquered the settlement in 1100 after a fierce defense by its Muslim and Jewish citizens and named it Caiphas. Haifa fell to Salah ad-Din in 1187 but returned briefly to Crusader rule under Louis IX of France between 1250 and 1265. It was destroyed by the Mamluks, and attempts to consolidate its development were hampered when it became an easy target for attacks by the Bedouins in the vicinity and a haven for Maltese pirate vessels.

The expansion of commercial activities in the eastern Mediterranean, especially by French merchants, encouraged the local Ottoman governor, Ahmed al-Harithi, to have Haifa rebuilt and resettled in 1631. He issued a decree granting a Carmelite priest permission to build houses in Haifa. However, Haifa still remained a haven for pirates and smugglers and was even known as "little Malta" after the pirates who found refuge in its harbor. The subsequent development of Haifa was caused by the endeavors of the two Ottoman governors who ruled the region in the second half of the eighteenth century: Dahir al-Umar and Ahmad Pasha al-Jazzar.

Dahir al-Umar conquered Haifa ca. 1760s. His primary aims were to use the port and increase his revenues from customs levied there. Because of the difficulties of defending the town, Dahir al-Umar decided to rebuild it on a site almost two miles to the southeast, and he had his soldiers demolish the old town. The new city was protected from the winds by Mount Carmel and was no longer situated on the plain but on a narrow strip of land at the base of the mountain, which made it much easier to protect; a new wall was built around it with two gates on the east and the west. Al-Umar also erected a customs house, a residence for the governor, and a mosque, known as "the little mosque," and a castle in Wadi Rushmiya with walls six and one-half feet thick. His tolerant attitude toward non-Muslims encouraged Christians to move to the town and to construct churches, while he also authorized the building of a new Carmelite monastery on top of Mount Carmel. The security that marked Dahir al-Umar's rule was reflected in the increased flow of revenues the Ottoman state came to gain from the town, especially from customs duties, while other revenues increased by 50 percent.

Al-Umar's rule was replaced in 1775 by that of Ahmad Pasha al-Jazzar ("the Butcher"), who ruled Haifa from Acre. In the middle of March 1799, Haifa fell without resistance to the forces of Napoléon Bonaparte; Bonaparte, however, retreated south two months later after failing to capture Acre. In 1831 Haifa fell to the Egyptian forces of Ibrahim Pasha and was immediately turned into an important military base for the Egyptians. During Ibrahim's rule, foreign consuls—British, French, Austrian, Danish, and Sardinian—for the first time began setting up residence in the town. This was considered as further evidence of the rise in Haifa's commercial position.

Mount Carmel was esteemed as a holy place, primarily by Christian sects. Though Elijah's cave is located on the mountain, it did not hold sufficient status to attract Jewish religious settlement. However, despite its connection to Christianity, it was not until the middle of the nineteenth century with the arrival of the Templars that habitation on the slopes above the port began to grow. In 1869 the German Templars, a Protestant group, established a colony on Mount Carmel, and this marked both the beginning of modern-day Haifa and its particular characteristics of spacious layout and cleanliness. The Templar colony was designed by the architect Jacob Shoumacher, and the settlement expanded so much that by the beginning of World War I, it made up a quarter of Haifa's area.

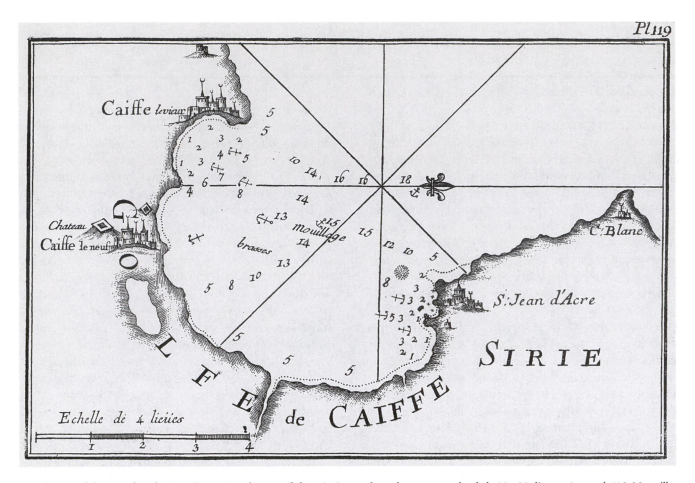

Pl.119

French map of the Bay of Haifa, 1764. (Roux, Joseph, *Receuil des principaux plans, des ports et rades de la Mer Mediterranée, . . .* pl. 119. Marseille, 1764)

In the latter part of the nineteenth and early twentieth century, the appearance of steamships resulted in a boom for Haifa, as the harbor of nearby Acre was too shallow and underdeveloped for their use. In addition to increased commercial traffic, this meant that Haifa became the embarkation point for the rising numbers of Christian pilgrims and European tourists arriving in Haifa's bay to visit the Holy Land. In response to the demand, the Templars constructed a road from Haifa to Nazareth (see also "Nazareth"). The improved roads enabled vehicular transportation from Haifa to the inland towns, encouraging higher levels of goods transport and trade. The Templars developed perhaps the first tourist industry in the country, providing rental accommodation in Haifa and goods and services required by visiting pilgrims.

In addition, the Templars were active in establishing agriculture and industry in Haifa. Among other crops, they planted groves of olive trees along the terraces of the Mount Carmel slopes. As a result, they were able to produce oil and soaps; their first oil factory constructed at the end of the nineteenth century was the forerunner of the Shemen company operating today. The Templars' well-designed neigh-

borhoods of the colony, and the opportunities for employment and trade brought about by the industrial, commercial, and agricultural development, attracted new residents to Haifa.

The Ottoman Empire was responsible for constructing in 1905 the Hijaz-Jezreel Valley Railway running from Haifa to Damascus and continuing to Makkah. This railway was of great significance to Muslim pilgrims, and it gave impetus to Haifa's growth. The construction of the railway line required many workers, and Haifa served as a development center for the railway. The city therefore attracted Arab laborers from throughout Palestine and neighboring countries to relocate to take advantage of the new job opportunities. The workers established their homes near the harbor, building generally poor-quality houses and shacks in the areas known today as Wadi Salib, Wadi Rushmiyya, and Wadi Nisnas. These extended eastward from the old central part of Haifa. When completed, the railroad established Haifa as an important export harbor in the eastern Mediterranean to which goods arrived from throughout the large hinterland serviced by the railroad. The proximity of the railroad encouraged the development of new factories in Haifa as well, as it provided the transportation of materials and products necessary for industrial operations.

The main development of Haifa, however, occurred during the period of the British Mandate for Palestine, especially in the 1920s and 1930s. The British recognized Haifa's strategic location as a primary Mediterranean port for the vast hinterland of Syria and Iraq, particularly because of its access to the railways, including the Haifa-Lod-Egypt line built in 1919. In the 1930s, the British began projects to improve and enlarge Haifa's harbor. Among the first projects were the construction of a breakwater in Haifa's bay and the commencement of harbor construction, including land reclamation from the sea. In the bay's southwest corner, a new port was completed in 1934. Between 1936 and 1939, the Kirkuk-Haifa pipeline was laid, followed by the construction of the Haifa oil refineries, adding the role of oil exportation to Haifa's capabilities. The British also developed the coastline along the bay, providing warehouses and tank farms, further establishing industrial areas with railroad access and stimulating the development of a central business district near the harbor offering commercial and financial services. Haifa was therefore established as the country's primary harbor.

As the main port in Palestine, Haifa attracted settlement by early Zionist immigrants, many stopping just off the boat. The area attracted Jewish investment: the Carmel Winery was founded before 1900, and both Levi Eshkol and David Ben Gurion worked in its vineyards as young men. The Histadrut (Zionist trade union) was founded in the city in 1920. By the late 1920s, Zionist land purchases around the bay, particularly in Haifa to create "green neighborhoods" and in the Jezreel Valley to the west, created a new class of landless Palestinian peasants and alienated the growing Arab working class in Haifa's port and industrial enterprises. Such dissatisfaction provided fertile ground for political activism, in particular the organizing of the Syrian-born Shaykh Iss ad-Din Qassam. His work among the Young Men's Muslim Association and Boy Scouts in Haifa laid a foundation for his declaration of an armed uprising (jihad) against the mandate in 1935. Qassam was quickly killed by British troops, but his supporters, Qassamites, provided the backbone for armed resistance during the Palestine Revolt of 1936–1939, and the area around Haifa was a center for resistance to the mandate all the way up until 1948. Qassam is buried in the suburbs of Haifa; his desecrated grave now lies behind a Jewish petrol station. Jewish factions smuggled illegal immigrants after World War II in through the port, and it was a major route into the country for smuggled weapons.

By 1948 the city had a population around 54 percent Jewish and 46 percent Palestinian. As soon as the UN Partition Plan was agreed upon, in November 1947, assigning Haifa to the Jewish state, sniping, terrorist attacks, and conflict broke out across neighborhood lines. In April 1948, a major offensive by the Zionist militia, the Hagana, overwhelmed the Palestinian neighborhoods of the city, with many inhabitants fleeing to Lebanon by boat. The Palestinian population of Haifa declined from more than 30,000 to around 4,000. Abandoned Palestinian housing was quickly allocated for the absorption of thousands of Jewish immigrants pouring into Israel through Haifa's port.

Today Haifa is divided into three major topographical levels. The lower city along the coast is the commercial center of the town with modern harbor facilities and its industrial zone. The middle level, Hadar HaCarmel, is an older residential zone including the poorer areas largely inhabited by Palestinians and Mizrachi Jews (those from the Arab world). On the higher reaches of Mount Carmel there are modern neighborhoods with large spacious houses with gardens and cultural facilities, along with some skyscrapers. Because of the separation between the levels, each has developed its own central business district and urban structure. Over the last few years, the city has continued to spread to the south around the edge of Mount Carmel along the coast and to merge to the north with Acre. The city does have the only subway in Israel, and a funicular carries passengers to the top of Mount Carmel.

North of Haifa's industrial zone, on the roads to the north and east, a series of small residential urban communities (*qirayot* in Hebrew) were established in the 1930s. They were originally composed mainly of small single-family homes to house industrial workers. In later years, the housing density increased as many of the small houses were replaced by apartment buildings, and residents found employment in Haifa proper. These qirayot have steadily developed a separate status from the city of Haifa, though some remain within the municipal boundary.

Haifa is renowned for a number of holy sites and places of religious significance, some of which have quite modern origins. The earliest known site is Elijah's cave, where he is said to have hidden from the prophets of Baal and King Ahab. It is on the side of Mount Carmel facing the sea and has become a pilgrimage site for believers of the three main religions. Close by is the Stella Maris Church and monastery of the Carmelite order. It serves as a pilgrimage center and houses a collection of antiquities. The monastery was used as a hospital for Bonaparte's soldiers, and a monument to French soldiers was erected in front of the church. A more recent addition to Mount Carmel is the golden-domed Bahai Shrine. The remains of Said Ali Muhammad, one of the two founders of the Bahai religion, are buried inside the shrine. The Bahais Gardens, planted in 1909, surround the shrine and are a popular outing for the inhabitants of Haifa. Also on Mount Carmel is the administrative center of the Bahai religion comprising several buildings in neoclassical style, including the Seat of the Universal House of Justice. Finally, Haifa also contains al-Kababir, a village populated by Muslim inhabitants belonging to the Ahmedi (Druze) sect and now incorporated into the Haifa municipality.

Haifa is Israel's leading industrial city. Oil from the Negev is refined here, and other major products include cement, glass, steel, and textiles. The city has excellent transport links with other parts of Israel. Israel's main naval base and port facilities for the U.S. Sixth Fleet are located here. Some 30,000 students from the prestigious Haifa University (founded in 1963) and Israel's oldest higher education institution, the Technion (Israel's Institute of Technology, founded in 1912), contribute to the area's contemporary urban buzz.

Haifa is presently undergoing a process of transition. Both economically and geographically, it is increasingly marginalized from the mainstream postindustrial processes in Israel and has experienced economic decline because of its dependence on shipping and port activities and its heavy manufacturing economic base. The transfer to Tel Aviv of almost all of the established national company headquarters, along with competition from Ashdod's deepwater port south of Tel Aviv, has accelerated this process.

As one of Israel's so-called mixed cities, Haifa demonstrates many of the problems of Israel's relations with its Palestinian minority. The population mix is officially 91 percent Jewish and 9 percent Palestinian, though the number of illegal residents is higher. Palestinians have difficulty finding housing and are cramped into neighborhoods like Halisa and Wadi Nisnas, currently experiencing increased instances of house demolition. There is employment discrimination, and they suffer from higher levels of disease, infant mortality, and school dropout rates. The city remains a magnet for Palestinians living in Galilee as the nearest large metropolitan area, with Haifa University attracting a large Palestinian student population and its hospitals providing medical assistance not available in Galilee. Politically, they have little voice in the city's municipal structure. Some organizations seek to overcome the boundaries dividing the city; Beit-Hagefen (Arab Jewish Center), for example, has been working since 1963.

The Palestinian politician Emile Habibi (1921–1996) hailed from the city; his novel *Saeed the Pessoptimist* is seen as one of the best expressions of the life of an Arab citizen of Israel. The famous Israeli academic and author A. B. Yehoshua also writes from his experience with the city. His books, such as *The Lover, Voyage to the End of the Millennium,* and, in particular, *The Liberated Bride,* deal with issues of boundaries and borders between communities.

Haifa is considered to be the only city in Israel whose leadership has maintained an adherence to traditional Zionist pioneering and socialist ideals within the context of an urban framework. By focusing on neighborhood units within the city, the political elite have aspired to make Haifa part kibbutz, part town. Shopping and cultural facilities, Histadrut (trade union federation) branches, and labor committees were all set up on a neighborhood basis, each having its political committee responsible for directing local functions. This organization was a significant factor in encouraging the decentralized structure of the city. Support for such a political organization was clearly based on the labor element of the population engaged in harbor and industrial jobs. Even with a changing population leading to a higher proportion of professional workers and businesspeople, Haifa maintains a reputation as the "red" city. The city's population has recently been shrinking at a rate of 0.5 percent per year despite being one of the top sites for Jewish immigrant absorption over the last fifteen years and taking in more than 65,000 new immigrants.

Michael Dumper

Further Readings

Bernstein, Debrah. *Constructing Boundaries: Jewish and Arab Workers in Mandatory Palestine.* Albany: State University of New York Press, 2000.
Efrat, Elisha. *Urbanization in Israel.* London: Croom Helm, 1984.
Faier, Elizabeth. *Organizations, Gender and the Culture of Palestinian Activism in Haifa, Israel.* London: Routledge, 2005.
Seikaly, May. *Haifa: Transformation of a Palestinian Arab Society, 1918–1939.* London: I. B. Tauris, 1995.
Yazbak, Mahmoud. *Haifa in the Late Ottoman Period, 1864–1914: A Muslim Town in Transition.* Leiden: Brill, 1998.

Hamah
Population: 325,000 (2005 estimate)

The ancient agricultural market town of Hamah is best known to tourists for its picturesque wooden waterwheels, many more than 500 years old. Yet this city has been the target of numerous attacks and occupation dating back to the Bronze Age. Lying in the heart of one of the most productive agricultural regions of Syria, this conservative city served as an administrative center for the Romans and for the Ottomans before producing both religious resistance to the state and movements for political change.

Hamah (Aramaic, *Hamah*) is a small city in central Syria on the Orontes River (in Arabic, Nahr al-Asi or Nahr al-Maqlub), ninety-five miles south of Aleppo and thirty-four miles north of Hims. It lies on both sides of the river just before it turns east to the plain of Asharnah. It is surrounded by steppe plateau dotted with villages whose principal crop is grain. Its most distinctive emblem is the *noria*, a great wooden waterwheel, the largest of which is some 65 feet in diameter. Dating from the thirteenth century, the noria have different names and were used to raise water from the river for both garden irrigation and domestic use, as the banks of the river rise to nearly 230 feet in height here, and much of the city lies on these heights. Hamah's population is largely Sunni Muslim, but some districts of the city are significantly Christian.

Hamah has an ancient foundation dating back to Neolithic times. Clearer archaeological evidence in the city dates from the mid-fourteenth century BC with discovered Hittite inscriptions. In the eleventh century BC, Hamah was the capital of the Aramean kingdom of Hamath and as such was mentioned in the Old Testament. It came under the rule of Solomon but later regained its independence and fought as the ally of the Aramean rulers of Damascus against the Assyrians (see also "Damascus"). After agreeing to pay tribute to the Assyrians in 738, Hamah revolted in 720 and was leveled by Sargon II.

Ruled by Assyrians, Babylonians, and Persians, it did not regain prosperity until the time of the Seleucids, who renamed it Epiphania in honor of Antiochus IV Epiphanes (r. 175–164 BC). Epiphania was conquered by the Romans under Pompey in 64 BC and remained under Roman and Byzantine rule until brought into the new Islamic state "by capitulation" in AD 636–637.

Nonetheless, even though the Orontes Valley was a bastion of Greek language and culture because of the many new Seleucid city foundations in and around it, this Greek veneer covered a Semitic core. In Roman times, Epiphania was still known to its inhabitants as well as to their Roman masters as Hamah, for a unit of Hamian archers composed one of the garrisons of the forts along Hadrian's Wall in Britain at the other end of the empire.

During the Roman and Byzantine periods and the first 450 years of Muslim domination, Hamah was hardly as important as Emesa/Hims, its nearest neighbor to the south. This was largely because the latter was a node of east-west and north-south communications. The roads that met there linked the Euphrates to western Syria, and northern Syria to Damascus and the Hijaz. Thus, after the Arab conquest, when Syria came to be divided into *junds* (military districts), Hamah was attached to the jund of Hims and remained dependent upon it until the ninth century (see also "Hims"). Although its history is obscure during this period, it was a walled market town with its ring of outlying villages. Then, under the Hamdanid rulers of Aleppo, it was drawn into the orbit of that city, where it remained until the beginning of the twelfth century (see also "Aleppo").

These were dark years, as the *atabegs* (local rulers) of northern and southern Syria struggled for predominance, while outside powers, first the Byzantines and later the Crusaders, sought to gain footholds in the interior of Syria. The Byzantine emperor Nicephorus Phocas raided the town in 968 and burned the Great Mosque. Later, all of northern Syria was nominally under Fatimid suzerainty, and during this period the Mirdasids sacked Hamah. The city then came under the sway of the Seljuqs until 1113–1114, and after the death of the last Seljuq amir it became a shuttlecock batted between competing rulers for some sixty years. Finally, after passing into the hands of the Zangids, Hamah fell definitively to Salah ad-Din in 1174–1175. Four years later, he handed it over to his nephew, al-Malik al-Muzaffar Umar. This ushered in a period of stability and prosperity as he and his descendants ruled almost continuously until 1342.

After the death of the last Ayyubid, in 1299, Hamah passed briefly under direct Mamluk suzerainty. Eleven years later, thanks to the patronage of the Mamluk sultan, Hamah came once more under the rule of the Ayyubids in the person of the famous geographer and author Abu al-Fidah, perhaps its most illustrious ruler. Unfortunately, this second period of Ayyubid rule was to be a brief one. After the son of this ruler incurred the displeasure of his Mamluk overlords, they removed him and placed Hamah once again under their direct rule, which they maintained until the coming of the Ottomans in 1517.

Hamah was quite prosperous during the Ayyubid and Mamluk periods and spread to both banks of the Orontes, with the suburb on the right bank being connected to the town proper across the river by an arcaded bridge. The town on the left bank was divided into a lower and an upper part, each of which was surrounded by a wall from the time of al-Malik al-Muzaffar Umar, and both were filled with palaces, suqs, mosques, madrasas, and a hospital, all surmounted, of course, by a citadel. Some thirty-two different-sized norias provided water for households and gardens. Moreover, a special aqueduct brought drinking water to the town from the neighboring district of Salamiyah.

Under the Ottomans, Hamah gradually became more important in the administrative structure of the region. It was first made capital of one of the *liwas* (districts) of the *eyalet* (province) of Tripoli, and then in the eighteenth century it became a *malikane* of the pasha of Damascus. After the passing of the *vilayet* (province or large administrative district) law in 1864, Hamah city itself became a *qadha'* (district) and capital of the *sanjak* (district, region, or provincial administrative area of an empire or state) of Hamah in the vilayet of Sham, or Suriye.

At the end of the Ottoman Empire, Hamah had developed into what it has remained: a medium-sized provincial town, important as the market for a prosperous agricultural area rich in cereals but that now also produced cotton and sugar beets. Yet it is also reputed to be the most conservative Sunni Muslim town in Syria. Indeed, during the French Mandate there was a saying that went, in part, "In Damascus it takes only three men to make a [political] demonstration [while] in Hamah it takes only three men to get the town to pray."

This social conservativism is closely related to a second social characteristic of this city and one that perhaps stems from the first: its notoriety as the center of great *latifundia* (estates) worked by the most miserable peasants in Syria and dominated by a few great magnate families. During the French Mandate, the district of Hamah contained within its bounds the municipality of Hamah as well as 114 villages. By an estimate made in the early 1930s, local cultivators owned outright only four of these villages while sharing ownership of only two others with a notable family.

Thus, the hinterland was severely dominated by landowning elites, which, starting in the late 1940s, led to significant class conflict as agricultural workers looked for change in this most conservative of districts. Akram Hawrani, a member of an impoverished local notable family, began to agitate for land reform and better social conditions, using as his instrument his own Arab Socialist Party (ASP). Hamah gave Hawrani and the ASP a strong base from which to participate in national politics, and the ASP soon merged with that other Syrian progressive party, the Baath, a party that was secularism and socialism incarnate. The ascent to power of this very same Baath after the revolution of 8 March 1963 sounded the death knell to the power of the landowning elite. In spring 1964, conservative forces revolted, whipped on by mosque preachers inveighing against the policies of the Baathist/ASP devil. Hamah was the epicenter of this revolt, and the new Damascus government sent tanks and troops into the crowded quarters of Hamah's old city to put down the insurrection with great brutality.

Nonetheless, the very character of this city and its inhabitants ensured that it would continue to embody opposition to what other Syrians deemed "progress." The seizure of power in 1970 by Hafiz al-Asad, a Baathist, a secularist, and, most demeaning of all, a member of a despised minority—the Alawis—was a humiliation to those who believed themselves to be the rightful holders of office. As discontent flared into revolt, Hamah again proved its epicenter. In 1982, faced with a *fin de régime*, the government in Damascus again sent troops into the city to eradicate its opponents and the city that bred them. This time they were successful but at a terrible cost, both to human life and to the stones of an ancient metropolis.

Although Hamah has recovered and its stones have been rebuilt, it has continued to be a closed provincial city. The prime reason for this continues to be that its location in the middle of the Orontes Valley does not open it to outside influences, unlike Hims, its near neighbor and great rival. The production of grains (barley, wheat, and corn) and cotton drive the life of this city, as does its industrial production of textiles. Yet there is also perhaps a psychological element. It is precisely *because* Hims is so commercial and cosmopolitan that Hamah chooses not to be, as it seeks to remain true to its heritage. Indeed, one might describe its citizens as a Syrian embodiment of Burkean conservatism.

J. L. Whitaker

Further Readings
Cobb, Paul. *White Banners: Contention in Abbasid Syria, 750–880.* New York: State University of New York Press, 2001.
Douwes, Dick. *The Ottomans in Syria: A History of Justice and Oppression.* London: I. B. Tauris, 1997.
Hawting, G. R. *The First Dynasty of Islam: The Umayyad Caliphate, AD 661–750.* Carbondale: Southern Illinois Press, 1987.
Issawi, Charles. *The Fertile Crescent, 1800–1914: A Documentary Economic History.* Oxford: Oxford University Press, 1988.
Lewis, N. *Nomads and Settlers in Syria and Jordan, 1800–1950.* Cambridge: Cambridge University Press, 1987.
Millar, Fergus. *The Roman Near East, 31 BC–AD 337.* Cambridge: Harvard University Press, 1993.
Owen, Roger. *The Middle East in the World Economy, 1800–1914.* London: Methuen, 1981.
Seale, Patrick. *Asad of Syria: The Struggle for the Middle East.* London: I. B. Tauris, 1988.

Hebron
Population: 154,714 (2003 census)

One of the most famous cities in the world, Hebron has been continuously settled for at least 5,000 years and is regarded as holy by Muslims, Jews, and Christians alike, being the burial site of the patriarch Abraham. It is one of the four holiest cities in Islam, along with Makkah, Madinah, and Jerusalem, and was both an important regional center for its market, trade, and manufacturers as well as an important pilgrimage and religious center. Long a center for conservative religious beliefs and resistance to centralization, Hebron reflects a strong tradition of tribalism and piety. It has been well preserved as a medieval Muslim town that has undergone remarkably little physical change in the last two centuries.

Hebron (Arabic, *Khalil al-Rahman* [the Friend of God] or *al-Khalil* [the Friend]; Hebrew, *Khevron*) is an ancient city in the West Bank, lying in a mountainous region twenty miles southwest of Jerusalem. There are more than two dozen springs in the area and many ancient pools and groves of oak trees. In ancient times, it was known under various names including Mamre, Kiryat Arba, and Arboa—words meaning *four*—possibly derived from its position on four hills or because the area hosted four confederated settlements in biblical times. Despite being located in the desert of Judea, its relatively high altitude (3,000 feet) grants the city cool weather during summertime and abundant rainfall in winter.

Excavations show human settlement in Hebron from as early as 3200 BC, although indications from the district suggest even earlier habitation. The ancient city was located on a tell now called Jebal ar-Rumayda, and archaeological remains indicate strong Canaanite culture. The site appears to have had cultic significance during the pre-Abrahamic (2000 BC) period, perhaps concerning myths of being the "gate to heaven," the entrance to the afterlife, or the original site of the Garden of Eden. Thus, Abraham's purchase of a burial site here just across the valley from the tell fits well with the local mythology of the site and transformed him from a pastoralist into a legal landowner. For more than 2,500 years, there has been a monumental construction over the site of what is known to Muslims as the Ibrahimi Mosque, and Jews as the

Cave of Machpelah, where Abraham acquired the cave where he, his sons, and their wives were to be buried.

Even before the Israelites arrived from Egypt and invaded the area ca. thirteenth century BC, Moses reaffirmed Hebron's cultic status by declaring that it would be one of the Cities of Refuge where sanctuary could be found, once it was captured. Hebron is where, as recorded in the Bible, Israelite spies brought back the grapes that showed how fertile the land was, and Joshua attacked the city and killed its king, Hoham. After the Israelite invasion, Hebron became a key site for the prophetic, tribal beliefs concerning Yahweh, and David ruled the city for seven years, perhaps with the support of the Philistines nearby. The Hebronites supported David as king, first of Judea and then of the combined kingdom with his capital in Hebron, but after he left to establish his capital in Jerusalem (ca. 990 BC), Hebronites felt betrayed, were antimonarchist, and participated in the revolt of his son Absalom.

Hebron was destroyed by Judas Maccabeus (164 BC), and it was King Herod who helped rebuild the city. Hebron was destroyed in the first century AD by Vespasian's troops repressing the Jewish revolt. Josephus records (AD 76) that at this time, Abraham's tomb was marked by a beautiful building, and Abraham's nearby oak attracted pilgrims. By the end of the first century, the city hosted a Christian community, and Christian pilgrims visited the city during Byzantine rule.

Muslims constructed many buildings in the city after they captured it in 635. In addition to Hebron's religious importance for Abraham's, Jacob's, and Joseph's tombs, Muhammad is believed to have passed through the city on his night journey to Jerusalem. The Umayyads and Abbasids built monuments in the city, and it was revered as the fourth-holiest site in Islam.

The Crusaders captured the city in 1100 and turned it into one of their fortresses along the spine of Palestine, calling the church they built over the site the Castle of Saint Abraham. There is a report that in 1172, the tomb wall collapsed, and certain knights entered the tomb to find the bodies of the patriarchs propped up against the wall and their shrouds deteriorating. Reverently, new shrouds were put in place and the collapsed opening was resealed.

Muslims recaptured the city in 1187 and transformed the church back into a mosque. Numerous visitors passed through during the Middle Ages, including that famous Arab traveler Ibn Battuta (1326) and Benjamin of Tudela (1170). Gradually, a tradition emerged for childless women to drop requests to Sarah down into the cave via a hole, hoping to be blessed. Pilgrims would also tear off a small part of the bark of Abraham's oak as they petitioned him for some need or another.

The city's role as market town and religious center was greatly expanded during both the Mamluk and Ottoman periods. Its rich agricultural hinterland, close to the desert region of the south and east, meant that Hebron became the center of trade for the products of both areas, specializing in grapes, raisins, vegetables, soaps, cheese, and livestock. Its role as a religious center was equally important in its development. Sharing with Jerusalem the title of al-Haramayn, or the two holy enclosures, it was given special status as an important pilgrimage center like that of Makkah and Madinah. As a result, hostels, seminaries, and many other charitable facilities were set up and supported by a network of *waqf*s (religious endowments) that channeled donations and income into the city. Much of the Mamluk city survives, and many of the buildings mentioned by the fifteenth-century traveler Mujir-ad-Din in his book on the people of Hebron were cataloged in a major 1987 survey of the city's monuments.

While Jerusalem was always the preeminent city of Palestine, the religious status of Hebron and its economic wealth often made Hebron a powerful rival, and its large families jockeyed for influence against the dominance of the Jerusalem families in Ottoman and Palestinian Arab politics (see also "Jerusalem"). Scions of Hebronite families often set up business ventures in Jerusalem, or further afield in Damascus, where they prospered. Khalilis (people from Khalil), as these entrepreneurs were called, came to control much of the economic life of Palestine and developed a reputation as the best businesspeople in the region.

Hebron became part of the Ottoman Empire in the early sixteenth century. Non-Muslims were forbidden to enter the mosque without special permission from the sultan in Istanbul; it was not until 1890 that the first Christian women were given such permission. The city did attract Christian missionaries after 1860, mainly in the form of doctors operating clinics. The story goes that one Scottish doctor saved the lives of a number of leading local notables and in return was given the honor of holding the key to the Ibrahimi Mosque for one night each year, on Christmas Eve.

The end of the Ottoman era saw the occupation of Hebron by British troops in December 1917. It became part of the British Mandate of Palestine from 1922 until 1948. The ancient but small Jewish community in the city suffered attack during the anti-British, anti-Zionist riots of 1929, and some seventy citizens lost their lives. As a result, British officials removed the remaining Jews from the city. Hebron suffered from the attention given by the British to Jerusalem as the seat of the mandate government, and Palestinian opposition to the leading representative of that administration, the mufti of Jerusalem, Haj Amin al-Hussayni, found a home among the people of Hebron. During the 1948 war, Hebron fell under the control of the forces of Transjordan, and its notables voted to become part of that kingdom in 1950. Hebronites played a key role in the economic development of the Hashemite Kingdom of Jordan during the 1950s and benefited from the city's ties with Amman.

In 1967 Hebron was occupied by Israel and became part of the West Bank territory under Israeli military administration. While the city benefited to some extent from access to the

Hebron, ca. 1910. (Library of Congress)

Israeli market and from remittances from Palestinian employment in the Gulf oil states, it suffered from poor infrastructure investment, congestion, and poor services. A predominantly conservative town, it was not at the forefront of political resistance to the Israeli occupation until the 1990s, when the opposition crystallized around militant Islamic movements. As an important religious site in Judaism, the city has also been a focus of Israeli Jewish settlement, resulting in frequent clashes between the two ethnic groups. To the north of the city, agricultural land was taken for the construction of a large Jewish settlement, Qiryat Arba, five minutes from the heart of the city. Established in 1971, Qiryat Arba was the first Israeli Jewish community to be set up in the West Bank. Today it has more than 6,000 residents and modern facilities and services. In addition, directly in the heart of the suq, a collection of houses was taken over by some fifty families who aggressively affirmed their preeminence to the Cave of the Patriarch. Violence continually breaks out between the settlers and those living in the Old City; in one of the worst cases, in February 1994, a settler from Qiryat Arba walked into the mosque and killed twenty-nine Muslim worshippers with his machine gun.

In September 1995, Israel and the Palestine Liberation Organization (PLO) signed an agreement in which Israel was to withdraw its armed forces from all Palestinian towns in the West Bank, except Hebron. Under the agreement, Hebron would generally be administered by the Palestinian Authority. However, Israel would keep a small number of troops in Hebron to guard Jewish settlers and religious sites important to Jews. In some parts of the city, Israeli troops would also patrol jointly with Palestinian police. This arrangement did not last for long, and today Israeli troops continue to guard Jews living in the city, and the suq is deserted and virtually abandoned because of the difficulties.

Hebron is one of the best-preserved medieval cities in the region, containing many architectural and historic gems. It has not witnessed the wholesale demolitions and clearances that modernity has brought to many other cities. The Old City centers around the Ibrahimi Mosque and Cave of Machpelah and is characterized by narrow, winding streets; flat-roofed and domed stone houses; bazaars and ornate mosques' vaulted arcades, winding passages, external staircases, and inner courtyards; markets; khans; *zawiyas* (lodges and mausoleums attended by Sufi mystics and pilgrims); hospices; schools; public fountains; and other monumental buildings. The Old City has no wall per se, its perimeter being formed by contiguous buildings broken by five gated entrances. Ottoman and even Mamluk buildings spill outside the confines of the Old City into the neighboring quarters, where the same traditional architecture and building patterns of narrow streets and passages prevail. Virtually the entire Old City consists of waqfs. The waqf system in Hebron, reputedly one of the oldest in the Muslim world, dates back to the seventh century, when, according to tradition, the Prophet Muhammad himself conferred the land on which Hebron was built to one of his companions: Tamim ad-Dari.

Despite impressive restoration work, however, accumulated neglect as a result of the Israeli occupation has led to deterioration of many of the quarters and buildings and its gradual abandonment. In 1967 there were 7,500 Palestinians in the fifteen quarters comprising the Old City. In 1970 there were 6,000, and in 1985 there was a dramatic decline to 1,620; by 1990 just 1,501 remained. However, in 1995 work begun by the Hebron Rehabilitation Committee succeeded in arresting the decline and revitalizing parts of the Old City with pragmatic but tasteful restoration work. The work of the committee was recognized internationally when it obtained the prestigious Aga Khan Award for Architecture in 1998.

The chief historical site in the city is the complex known to Muslims as the Ibrahimi Mosque and to Jews as the Cave of Machpelah. It houses the tombs of Abraham; his wife, Sarah; Joseph; Rebecca; Jacob; and Isaac. The external walls and paving stones are Herodian, and the size of the stone blocks has inspired the Arab legend that they were laid by Solomon assisted by jinn (spirits). The structure has been rebuilt many times. It was once a Byzantine church, a mosque, a vaulted Crusader church, and a mosque again under the Mamluks. It was the Mamluks who built the massive square masonry shrine in 1320 that is seen today around the tomb of Abraham. Inside the mosque is the mihrab, made of multicolored marble and mosaics, and two pulpits of intricate workmanship, one of which was brought by Salah ad-Din from Egypt. This combination of Crusader and Mamluk structures has made al-Haram one of the most impressive ancient monuments in Palestine.

Just across the Old City is a small hill known as Tel Hebron, or Tel Rumeida. Some Jewish scholars argue that this was the original biblical Hebron, home of Abraham and Sarah and, later, King David. There is a wall at this site dating to the days of Joshua. Recent archaeological excavations have revealed forty clay jugs, 4,000 years old, at the entrance to the area. At the south side of the tell is a tomb thought to be that of Ishai, King David's father, and Ruth, his great-grandmother. Another site of historic and religious importance is where an oak tree just more than a mile west of Hebron marks the legendary spot where Abraham pitched his tent. Excavations in 1926–1928 revealed a Herodian enclosure with a well in its southwestern corner. Local custom had held that peeling pieces of bark off the oak tree would grant a benediction. As a result of an increase in the numbers of pilgrims coming to the site, the Russian Orthodox Church, who owns the land

and the nearby monastery, has wrapped the trunk with steel braces for its protection.

Modern Hebron is the chief city for the southern half of the West Bank. While it still remains an important agricultural market city, it is also the largest industrial center in the West Bank. Plums, grains, grapes, and olives are traded and also contribute to a significant food-processing sector. The area is also known for its dozens of quarries, with stone and marble exported to Arab countries and to the building trade in Israel and the West Bank. Many of the traditional crafts of glass, pottery making, and tanning have been adapted to factory production, while light industries such as plastics, leather, furniture, and shoemaking have developed.

Up until 1948, Hebron was the capital of the administrative district with the largest number of villages of any district in Palestine. Civic importance was thus added to its other roles as a religious and commercial center. Traditionally, Hebron had comprised an inner core of the Old City and some buildings around it along the main arterial road. At the end of the nineteenth century, urban growth took place to the northwest along the road to Bethlehem and Jerusalem. During the Jordanian period, between 1948 and 1967, there was a considerable increase in population (35,000 new residents), most of whom took up residence along the Jerusalem highway. The Israeli occupation has not halted the direction of this growth but has led to congestion and overcrowding through planning restrictions and the building of Jewish settlements in the district. Since 1967 access to Hebron from the surrounding areas has become very difficult, severing the web of ties binding village and the city and killing the businesses in the suq.

Michael Dumper

Further Readings
Efrat, Elisha. *Urbanization in Israel.* London: Croom Helm, 1984.
Knohl, Dov. *Siege in the Hills of Hebron.* New York: Thomas Yoseloff, 1958.
Murphy-O'Connor, Jerome. *The Holy Land: An Archaeological Guide from Earliest Times to 1700.* Oxford: Oxford University Press, 1992.
Reynolds-Ball, E. A. *Jerusalem: A Practical Guide: With Excursions to Bethlehem, Hebron, Jericho.* London: Adam and Black, 1901.
Romann, Michael. *Jewish Kiriyat Arba versus Arab Hebron.* Jerusalem: West Bank Data Project, 1986.

Herat
Population: 300,000 (2005 estimate)

Herat, the key security city in western Afghanistan, has long been one of the most important edge cities for the Middle East. For more than 2,500 years, the city has been crucial to controlling the borders of Persia and to dominating access to the mountainous paths to India or to central Asia. Marked by its ancient citadel, the city has been captured and fought over since before the time of Alexander and is a quintessential oasis city. Renowned for the highest achievements in miniaturist painting, the city was also key to a dynamic horse and cotton trade of the early modern period. Bombed repeatedly by the Soviets, it also became key to the destruction of the Taliban regime.

Herat (Persian, *Harēv;* Greek, *Aria, Areia,* or *Alexandria Areion*) sits in the foothills of the western edge of the Hindu Kush mountain range, marking the eastern boundary of the Iranian plateau. The Hari Rud, or Herat River (also known in ancient times as the Arius), flows from the mountains in the west into the plains, creating a fertile agricultural valley and numerous oases before turning northward to die in the Kara Kum Desert. Herat grew up around the largest of the oases, at the point where travelers would break their journey between the mountains and the Iranian plateau. Numerous canals and ditches leading off from the river create a substantial agricultural zone irrigating the area. The surrounding area is semiarid, historically supporting seminomadic Dari-speaking (Persian) communities, while the oasis has traditionally been home to urbanized Tajiks and Pashtuns.

The archaeological record confirms the legends that Alexander, who understood the strategic importance of the oasis and its crossroads, founded the city fortress. This geostrategic significance has remained central to the city's history and has meant that the city had to be taken by any invaders, whether they were aiming for the mountains of Afghanistan or heading into the plateau of Iran. The city also controls a crucial north-south route, linking central Asia and western China to the Indian Ocean. It was this location at the crossroads of great civilizations that fed the city's wealth and significance.

Even in 1000 BC, inhabitants of the site were involved in a transregional trading linkage from Herat to Qandahar. Across the centuries, raw materials such as silk were exchanged, and Indian trade with Asia, Babylon, and Greece was mediated through Herat. In particular, the trade in lapis lazuli, rubies, jade, silver, and gold was profoundly Herat facilitated, and Russian amber passed through on its way to the emergent cities of the subcontinent. Such early trade laid the foundations for the subsequent Silk Road post-200 BC.

Although there are not many historical references for the period before Alexander, there are some: the Zoroastrian sacred book, the *Avesta,* for example, makes reference to the Herat area as one of the seven holy lands, and it is established that contingents from Herat fought with Xerxes at the Battle of Marathon in 490 BC. Herodotus refers to the River Akes (Hari Rud) as the center of an important region and called Herat "the pearl in the world's ocean."

It is with Alexander the Great's arrival at Herat in 330 BC after defeating Darius III that the city fully comes into the historical record. The story goes that the ruler of the city, Sati Barzan, surrendered, and Alexander left him in control of the city under the eye of a Greek garrison. After Alexander left

with his army to march on Bactra to the north, however, Barzan revolted, had the garrison killed, and prepared for Alexander's inevitable attack. After fierce fighting, the city was retaken. Alexander then built a new castle, or garrison fortification, in the center of the city to guarantee its submission, calling it Alexandria of Aria.

After Alexander's death, a Greek elite in charge of the army and tax collection and a local bureaucracy ruled Herat. The city was a polis self-governed under a council, an assembly, and officers, with its own laws, its own troops, and a right to worship local gods. Under the Greeks, Herat went by the name Areia and was the headquarters of a satrap. Numerous Greeks held the position of satrap over the next few years until the arrival of Seleucus and his final victory in 301 BC. Under early Seleucid rule, Greek immigrants to Herat and to Bactra were encouraged, granted land, and asked to serve in the army when requested. Greek culture and buildings were constructed, coins were minted, and the Greek language was used.

There is some indication that Herat may have been a frontier city for Asoka and the Maurya dynasty around 268 BC and that Buddhism found a home in the city. The Herat/Qandahar/Punjab segment of the trade route was crucial to long-distance trade of the time. This attracted the Parthians, who captured Herat around 247 BC, but it remained an important site for Hellenism, influencing the region around it. By the first century BC, Herat was part of a "royal road" offshoot for the empire, carrying traffic outward from Herat to Marv and then Samarkand and onto the Silk Road to China. Chinese raw silk and Indian goods such as precious stones, perfumes, opium, eunuchs, and pepper passed each other in the markets of Herat.

Under Chosroes I and the Sassanians, Herat experienced a great intensification of its long-distance trade. The Sassanians intentionally set out to build routes and the infrastructure for trade. Persian merchants dominated the networks into India, central Asia, and south Russia; the Persian language was the lingua franca throughout the region, and the Silk Road to China dominated Herat's existence.

The trade brought new ideas and religions to the city. Herat was the site of a bishopric by AD 424, Manichaeism found a home in the city, and the Nestorians used the city as a staging area for Christian missionaries and traders heading eastward to spread the word.

Over the next 600 years, other conquerors were interested in the city. Turkish tribes threatened the city in the late sixth century, although the Persians defeated them in a great battle near Herat in AD 589. The Arabs captured Herat in AD 650, and very quickly the city shifted to Islam as its dominant religion. Herat was captured and incorporated into the Ghaynavid Empire in AD 1030.

When the Mongols arrived in 1221, the situation changed. The city's garrison resisted, but the citizens threw open the gates. Unlike other cities in the region, the citizens were not killed. The silk weavers of Herat were shipped off to Mongolia by Genghis Khan or turned into slaves for individual Mongol elites. These artisans were often collected into *kar-khana* (large production shops) to turn out production for export. Over the next few centuries, Herat's reputation for silk weaving returned, and the city became known for this export.

The situation of Herat at the time of the Mongol invasion can be found in the *History of Herat,* by Saif b. Muhammad b. Yaqub Saifi. Discovered in 1944, this history was written between 1318 and 1322 and details the life of the city and the region during this dramatic upheaval. Saifi reports, for example, that the Mongols took Herat twice. The first time, the 12,000 defenders were killed after the city was taken, and the citizens were spared. After he moved on, however, the city rebelled, and so Genghis sent 80,000 men back to deal with the city. This time, Saifi reports, Genghis gave the following orders: "The dead have come to life again. This time you must cut the people's heads off: you must execute the whole population of Herat." It took the Mongols seven months in 1222 to retake the city. At the end of the siege, the killing took seven days, and "no head was left on a body, and no body with a head." The city's fortifications were destroyed, and its moats filled in. Then, in a final coup de grâce, two days after the troops left the city, Genghis sent troops back to kill anyone alive in the rubble. Saifi reports that much later, the city's ruins housed only sixteen people.

The Great Khan Ogedei allowed the city to be rebuilt in 1236, but it did not recover for many years, reportedly housing only 7,000 people by 1242. The Ilkhanids took the city in the Battle of Herat, in 1270, and the city was sacked again. The great traveler Ibn Battuta reports that he visited the Ilkhanid-controlled city in 1333, although his claim is questionable.

Temür captured the city in 1393, and the Timurid dynasty supported its redevelopment and the flourishing of the arts in the city. Herat became a key center for science, culture, and Islamic learning, particularly in the Sufi tradition. Important Sufi leaders lived in the city, including Shah Bahauddin.

Arts of the book, including poetry, book illustration, calligraphy, Persian miniature painting, and book binding, all flourished under the Timurids. These arts were interlinked: for example, with the evolution of the poetry of Abd ar-Rahman Jami (1414–1492) and Alishir Navai (1440–1501) and others, miniature painting absorbed new themes. The Herat art school was established in the early 1400s, drawing the top artists from Shiraz and Tabriz (see also "Tabriz"). The most well known of the painters was Kamal Ad-Din Behzad, often judged the most outstanding painter of this style. However, Herat also produced other outstanding artists, including Mirak Nakkash and Shah Muzaffar. One of the most outstanding examples of miniature painting was the illuminated manuscript, made in Herat in 1494–1495, known as the *Khamseh of Nizami;* a section of this work is now in the British Museum. Another masterpiece from this time, the miniature *Khamsa of Mir Ali Shir Navali,* resides in the Bodleian Library in Oxford. Such works demonstrate how these illustrators took the miniature painting form to its logical conclusion, employing extraordinary colors and expressing individual characterization in the human face. The fame and significance of the Herat school lasted into the eighteenth century, although by then it had lost its dynamism and its uniqueness. Under the Shaibanids in Samarkand and Bukhara, the legacy of Herat's miniaturists continued in the Bukhara school (see also "Bukhara").

This concentration of specialty and overlap of interests culminated in a reverence for the pen and the written word. Herat became a key calligraphy center based around the work of the calligrapher Sultan Ali Mashhadi, and from this specialty grew a focus on tiles and the ornamentation of mosques through cursive epigraphy. The city also became known for its historical studies and its library of historical texts.

Temür's son, Shahrukh, moved the Timurid capital to Herat and financed the construction of new monumental architecture. It was in 1405 that the city plan, which is still evident in the heart of Herat, was put in place: new fortified walls surrounding a rectangle city, the castle, or *hisar,* at its heart, each quarter composed of regular parts.

Shahrukh rebuilt the bazaar and the old citadel and established a madrasa and a convent. Shahrukh's wife, Gawharshad, was the patron for a huge religious complex in Herat, part of which still dominates the city.

During the rule of the powerful Safavids in Iran, Herat was a border city, caught up both in conflicts among the Safavids themselves and in their struggle with an emergent Afghani state. Trade remained the key to wealth for the city, and the city became linked into the new Atlantic networks as well. Trading companies of English merchants transiting through Muscovy arrived in Herat looking to capture trade from other European powers. In particular, there was a growing European demand for carpets; during the sixteenth and seventeenth centuries, Herat was known throughout Europe for the quality of its rugs and for their floral design.

Herat remained closely linked into the Iranian and Indian circuits, however. The city still sent caravans to Yazd to trade for goods from Esfahan, Shiraz, and Tehran. Horse trading remained an important moneymaker for Herat as well, as both Persian horses and Turkic horses often were driven to India via Herat. There may have been as many as 35,000 delivered per year. The profits accumulated during the 1500s and 1600s may have been crucial to the appearance of the Afghan state later in the 1700s. The horse trade via Herat continued until the late 1700s, and its scale was far greater than that of European trade with India.

Cotton from India was also part of the circulation across the regional boundaries. A 1639 report says between 20,000 and 25,000 camels annually, loaded with cotton textiles, made their way through Herat to Iran. This meant more than 5,000 tons of Indian cotton textiles sold to central Asia per year via Herat.

Herat's role in brokering transregional trade was not always guaranteed, however. It is clear that the political or security situation along the caravan routes could often swing the decision of the key merchants to shift their export routes between India and Iran from land to sea, decreasing Herat's revenues significantly for a season or two. Yet if the land route was chosen, any of the three alternative passes available for caravans making the trek to Iran from the Punjab culminated in Herat; in other words, there was no alternative except through Herat on the southern land route between India and Persia. The 360-mile link from Mashhad to Qandahar, for example, a reasonably safe route, as such routes go, passed through Herat. Reports suggest that upward of 3,000 camel loads per year transversed this route early in the sixteenth century.

Afghans monopolized the transport animals from Herat east to the Punjab but had little role to the west into Persia. The merchant capitalists providing the liquidity for this system were Indians, and Herat had a large Indian merchant community in the seventeenth century. This powerful Herat community acted as a kind of "home base" for other communities further afield; for example, the Indians in Esfahan in 1647 were originally from Herat.

Herat played a key role in the shifting political dynamics of the turbulent seventeenth and eighteenth centuries, being captured five times from 1716 to 1759. The Abdali Pashtuns first threw the Persians out of Herat in 1716 as they expanded into eastern Persia. After various internecine struggles for control of the city, the Safavid general Nadir Quli Beg captured Herat in 1731 after a long siege. As a way of controlling the Alus Abdali, Nadir incorporated many Heratis into his elite troops, and when he was assassinated in 1747, one of his Abdali retainers, Ahmad Khan, became the leader of the Afghan Abdali and declared himself *Durr-I-Durrani* (pearl of all pearls). Under Ahmad Shah Baba (Father of Afghanistan), this new Durrani dynasty expanded to capture Herat in 1749 from the Persians after another lengthy siege. At the end of the century, more internecine fighting among the Durrani led to Mahmud, the governor of Herat, rising up against his brother to capture the remnants of the Afghan kingdom. In 1805 the Qajar rulers attacked Herat, and for the next six years a ransom was paid for Herat by the Afghans. During this whole period, control of Herat was seen as crucial to the fortunes of any regional political player of consequence and thus a focus for domination and control.

In the "great game" of 1800–1920, the British and the Russians struggled for influence in central Asia, Persia, and in Herat as the center of the western province of Afghanistan. The Qajars in Tehran saw Herat as crucial to expanding their control over trade to the east (see also "Tehran"). They thus asserted their claim to the city and planned to take the city by force. This put the Persians in direct confrontation with the British, who sought to maintain Herat as part of an autonomous Afghan entity between themselves and the Russians. The situation boiled over in 1837, when a Persian army, led by Russian advisors, lay siege to Herat. A British officer, Eldred Pottinger, was an undercover spy in the city at the time. He revealed himself and offered his services to the grand vizier of Herat and was quickly put in charge of the city's defenses. The city was able to hold out until the Persians, under threat of a British invasion, withdrew the siege. Herat remained nominally under control of the Afghan amir and was finally incorporated officially into Afghanistan in 1863.

Pottinger's journal is a wonderful window on the city at the time. In particular, he comments on the significance of the 600-strong Indian merchant community in Herat in 1810, reporting that they "alone possessed capital" necessary to finance trade. For the next 150 years, the city was famous for its bazaars, handicrafts, textile weaving, cotton products, and agricultural products. By the late 1960s, it was the first stop into Afghanistan for those on the hippie trail to Kathmandu and their first taste of the seventeenth century after leaving modern Iran.

Herat remained a key city in Afghan's independent history during the twentieth century. The Herat garrison rose up against the Marxist government in 1979 and killed more than one hundred Soviet "advisors" in the city, along with their families. Thus, when this helped spark off the Soviet invasion of Afghanistan in 1979, the city was bombed numerous times by the Soviet air force, killing perhaps as many as 20,000 inhabitants; the Soviets captured Herat in 1980. It became a major key military command site for them, and they installed themselves in Alexander's citadel. Resistance by mujahideen such as Ismail Khan, the "Lion of Herat," made Herat a no-go area for the Russian military and was crucial to the eventual Soviet withdrawal in 1989. From 1992 until the city was captured by the Taliban in 1995, Ismail Khan ruled the city as the core of an autonomous region within the country, he kept Herat out of the civil war that engulfed the rest of the country, and trade and commerce with Iran flourished.

The Taliban, initially supported by Pakistan, saw Herat as important to their control of western Afghanistan, although they had difficulty controlling the Iranian and Tajik influence in the predominantly Persian-speaking city. Once in control, they instituted a reign of terror that brought the city's trade and culture to an end. Ismail was captured and kept in prison for three years before he escaped and began smuggling weapons into Herat to begin a counterrevolution from his former base. As a leader of the Northern Alliance, Ismail Khan led the attack to retake Herat from the Taliban in November 2001.

In the post-Taliban Afghanistan, Herat has become somewhat separated from the rest of the country (some call it the amirate of Herat) under the uneasy dual control of Ismail Khan, backed by the Iranians, and President Karzai, with his garrison in the citadel. Khan's 30,000-member militia was paid for by customs duties he collected; Herat's streets are clean, and the university reopened under his "governorship." Yet dissent is not allowed, and human rights abuses were cataloged by international organizations. As of 2005, Khan became minister of power, helping to manage the $10 million U.S. grant to restore power lines to Herat. The massive Maslakh refugee camp outside the city, still housing close to 100,000 people, affects the dynamics of labor in the region. Clearly, the city retains its role as a key edge city: the Iranians don't want to lose influence, while the Afghan government would like to "shift the boundary" back so that Herat is their frontier city, not Iran's. Khan's son, Mirwais Sadiq, was assassinated in Herat in March 2004, perhaps under the instigation of the central government.

Bruce Stanley

Further Readings
Ewans, Martin. *Conflict in Afghanistan*. London: Routledge, 2005.
Hopkirk, Peter. *The Great Game: On Secret Service in High Asia*. Oxford: Oxford University Press, 2001.
Johnson, Chris, and Leslie Jolyon. *Afghanistan: The Mirage of Peace*. London: Zed Press, 2004.
Lamb, Christina. *The Sewing Circles of Herat*. London: HarperCollins, 2003.
Stewart, Rory. *The Places in Between*. London: Picador, 2004.

Hims
Population: 750,000 (2005 estimate)

For 2,000 years, the city of Hims has served as a key agricultural market, production site, and trade center for the villages of northern Syria. Yet it has also provided security services to the hinterland of Syria, protecting it from the Crusaders, the Byzantines, and the Egyptians. A center for paganism, Christianity, and Islam, the city has long articulated transport flows across greater Syria while providing empires with vast foodstuffs and textiles.

Hims (English and French, *Homs;* Greek and Latin, *Emesa*) is a small city in central Syria on the east bank of the Orontes River. It lies some 125 miles south of Aleppo and 34 miles south of Hamah and is halfway on the road between Aleppo and Damascus. To the east lies the desert and to the west the southern outliers of the Jabal Ansayriah.

Hims is the market center for a large, cultivated plain devoted to the growing of grain, cotton, sugar beets, and vegetables, mostly under irrigation. This plain has supported irrigated agriculture for millennia. Southwest of the city lies Lake Hims (Qattinah), an artificial body of water created by a dam at its northern end. This structure in its original form was one of the most visible works of ancient engineering to be seen in Syria and indeed in the entire Fertile Crescent. Perhaps built by the Romans or even by the pharaohs, it created a reservoir whose water was conducted to the fields through a network of canals. However, this system had functioned in the past, and by the 1930s it had fallen into a state of extreme dilapidation and served merely to water the gardens of Hims, some 1,200 hectares. After the French Mandatory authorities reconstructed the dam between 1934 and 1938 and dug an elaborate grid of canals, this project was able to irrigate some 20,000 hectares, of which 12,000 are within the *muhafizah* (district) of Hims.

Hims is situated in a much more favorable geographical and strategic position than is its neighbor Hamah to the north because it lies in a shelf between the foothills of the Jebal Ansayriah and the Lebanon mountains to the south. This ensures that it receives the softening influences of the Mediterranean and its breezes. As a result, Hims has a much milder climate than Hamah, with higher average rainfall of eighteen inches instead of fourteen inches, but it also has greater winds. Moreover, its situation at a crossroads of north-south and east-west routes, when combined with its tradition of irrigated agriculture, has attracted human settlement from the earliest times.

In the second millennium, the prominent cities of the region were Qadesh (now called Tell Nabi Mend) to the south of the lake and Qatna (now Mishrife) located northeast of Hims, or Emesa, as it was first called. Emesa may have been founded by Seleucus Nicator (d. 280 BC), but it did not emerge into the light of history until the first century BC. At that time, Strabo speaks of one Sampsigeramus and his son Iamblichus as chiefs of the tribe (*ethnos*) of the Emesani, whose capital was the small Greek town of Arethusa (now Rastan), located on an important ford of the Orontes. Strabo seems to consider these Emesani to be among the tribes of tent dwellers (*skénitai*) who dwelt in the region south of Apamea.

During the first century AD, this dynasty rose up in the world, gaining Roman citizenship and the title of king as a result of supplying troops to aid Rome in its wars. Sometime around AD 70, this dynasty lost its kingdom, which was brought under direct Roman rule. It is impossible to discern the development of the city of Emesa and how or when the name of the tribe became attached to it. Nevertheless, it gradually acquired the attributes of a Greek city-state, starting sometime toward the end of the first century, and one can still discern traces of Roman town planning in the modern city. The process was certainly completed by the reign of Antoninus Pius (138–161), when Emesa began to strike coins.

Emesa emerges briefly into the light at the beginning of the third century, when the daughter of a prominent local family, Syrians of Greek culture who were members of the Roman elite, married a Roman senator who was to become the emperor Septimius Severus. This imperial connection brought Emesa the coveted status of a Roman *colonia*. Moreover, the last two emperors of the Severan dynasty were raised in Emesa. One of them was the high priest of the local god Elagabal. After he was raised to the purple, he brought the image of his deity, a conical black stone—possibly a meteorite—with him to Rome and set it up in the Temple of Vesta.

Thus, by the third century, Emesa was a prosperous city that had become well integrated into the Roman Orient. One reason for this might be the fact that it was a link in the eastern trade funneled through Palmyra. Certainly, in the fourth century, when Palmyra had sunk into insignificance, Emesa as well was a town of little note. Whatever its importance within the larger arena of the Roman East, it still retained local significance as the market center for villages within the region.

With its great temple dedicated to the Sun, Emesa was naturally a strong center of paganism. Indeed, perhaps the emperor Aurelian himself came here to give thanks to that deity during the course of his victories over Zenobia of Palmyra and brought this cult back with him to Rome. There are few Christian inscriptions from Emesa, although Christianity must have become well established by the fifth century. Emesa was first a bishopric, and after the miraculous discovery of the head of Saint John the Baptist nearby in 452, it was promoted to the rank of ecclesiastical metropolis.

Many Arab tribes came to settle near Emesa, or Hims, as it must now be called, in the years before the Muslim conquest. The most important of these was the Banu Kalb, thus ensuring that it became an important Yemeni center. The emperor Heraclius abandoned the town after his defeat at the battle of the Yarmuk, and the Muslims occupied it peacefully in the year 637 because the city had agreed to pay a substantial ransom.

The new rulers transformed the church of Saint John into the Friday Mosque. This was the third religion to have its cult center on this site, since the church was probably built over the temple to the Sun. Hims soon became a center of Muslim piety since some 500 of the Companions of the Prophet Muhammad came to settle there. Yazid b. Muawiya made the Hims district part of the newly formed province of Syria in 647. When he organized the frontier, he made it the capital of the *jund* (military district) comprising all of north Syria. This was because of its strategic location, although under Muawiya the northern part was hived off to form the jund of Qinnasrin. The populace of Hims took the part of Ali during his conflict with Muawiya, however, and for a long time, the city remained a center of Shi'ism.

As a bastion of the Banu Kalb, Hims became involved in their conflicts with the Qays. Indeed, the last Umayyad caliph,

Marwan b. Muhammad, who enjoyed the support of this latter faction, razed the walls of the city. The Yemeni populace of the town continued its habits of revolt under the Abbasids, and from the time of Harun ar-Rashid (796–809), the authorities sent many punitive expeditions against the town. Although Hims was quite prosperous during this period, Abbasid rule was generally unwelcome. The center of the Muslim world had shifted from Syria to Iraq, and the Abbasids were not inclined to favor the Umayyad stronghold of Syria.

With the weakening of Abbasid rule from the middle of the ninth century, Hims with its strategic position became a prize for the various dynasties contending over Syria. In a wider context, it served as an important asset in the renewed conflict between the Dar al-Islam and a revitalized Dar al-Harb. To begin with, Hims fell prey successively to the Tulunids of Egypt and the Hamdanids of Aleppo, broken by a brief interlude when its inhabitants were forced to acknowledge the suzerainty of the heterodox Qarmatians. The Hamdanids took definitive control of the city in 944 and dominated it off and on until 1016.

During most of the eleventh century, the Mirdasid shaykhs of the Banu Kilab, a powerful Arab tribe of north Syria, replaced the Hamdanids in Aleppo. Because they were inclined to Shi'ism, they did not oppose the Fatimids, who sought to extend their rule over north Syria and even Iraq from the middle of the tenth century. This precipitated a Sunni reaction spearheaded by the Seljuq Turks, and a Seljuq amir occupied Hims in 1090.

If Hims was a cat's paw for Muslim dynasties seeking to master Syria, it was even more so for foreign forces who wished to recover Syria for Christendom. For some thirty years from the middle of the tenth century, Hims was subjected to the raids and even suzerainty of the Byzantines under their great military emperors, Nicephorus Phocas, John Tzimisces, and Basil Bulgaroctonus. The Great Mosque found itself once again a church, if only briefly, and the town and its Muslim inhabitants were frequently subject to rapine and slaughter.

During the eleventh century, this Byzantine threat receded, but a new threat from the Dar al-Harb arose once again with the launching of the First Crusade in 1096. The Franks captured Antakya in 1098; looted Maarat an-Numan, halfway between Hamah and Aleppo; and besieged Hims itself. Although they were able to cut off Tartus, the port of Hims, they failed to take the city.

Hims now came under the Seljuj ruler of Damascus who made of it a huge fortified camp, a key fortress blocking the gap through which the Franks could penetrate deep into Muslim Syria. It lay in the center of a line of Muslim strongpoints that extended from Aleppo through Shayzar, Hamah, Damascus, Bosra, and Salkhad. Situated as it was on the right bank of the Orontes, it was immune to surprise attacks from the

Frankish lands to the west and was a point where the Muslims could marshal their forces and launch attacks upon their enemies.

The geographer al-Idrisi, writing at this time, notes that Hims had many fine markets, as well as paved streets, and one of the largest Friday Mosques in all Syria. As the center of a rich agricultural area, it had many gardens and orchards irrigated by canals, while the districts round about were a source of provisions, although he notes that many of these were now laid waste.

Hims, and indeed all of Syria during the 200 years that comprised the twelfth and thirteenth centuries, was subject to continual alarms and excursions as well as heavy fighting and natural disasters. During the first third of the twelfth century, the Seljuq amirs engaged in internecine fighting, during which Hims was often a prize. Moreover, they had to face a powerful rival in Imad ad-Din Zangi, ruler of Mosul and Sinjar, who was intent on extending his domains westward into Syria. This ruler and his son Nur ad-Din gradually extended their sway over Syria, with Nur ad-Din occupying Hims definitively in 1149. As a great Muslim stronghold, Hims was naturally a rallying point for the forces opposing the Second Crusade. Unfortunately, a series of earthquakes in the year 1157 did great damage to Hims as a city and as a fortress, and the tremor of 1170 proved to be the final smash of the mallet.

Yet because of its strategic location opposite the Crusader state of Tripoli, Hims was soon restored to strength. In 1164 Nur ad-Din gave Hims as an *iqta'* (fief) to Asad al-Din Shirkuh, one of his principal supporters, but reclaimed it five years later after his death. This amir was a cousin of Salah ad-Din, who seized Hims in 1175. Four years later, when he reorganized northern Syria, Salah ad-Din restored the fief to this family, who held it until 1262, thus accomplishing nearly a century of rule. During the period of Ayyubid rule, Hims remained a centerpiece of the wars against the Franks while participating in the internecine wars between the successors of Salah ad-Din and the conflicts between Mamluks and Mongols.

Nonetheless, the accession of Baybars, first of the Mamluk sultans, led to the recession and final extinction of both Frankish and Mongol threats, which resulted in the decline of the political importance of Hims. At the beginning of the fourteenth century, Hims was merely the capital of the smallest *niyabah* (province) in Syria and was included in the niyabah of Damascus. If under Mamluk and subsequently Ottoman rule (from 1516) Hims suffered political eclipse, it continued to be an important economic center, processing the agricultural and pastoral products that flowed to it from the surrounding districts. Hims was particularly famous for the weaving of wool and silk, particularly the famous cloth known as *aghabani* or *alaja,* mottled muslin run through with gold threads and used in feminine apparel. In Ottoman times, this was exported as far as Istanbul. In addition, there

were olive oil presses and water mills for wheat and sesame, while grapes and rice, grown in the surrounding marshlands from the sixteenth century, were to be found in abundance heaped up within the markets of the town. Moreover, the markets of Hims were the center of a trade in animals, where flocks of sheep and goats coming south from Aleppo met camels and cattle moving north from Damascus.

Unfortunately, despite its undoubted importance as a market center, the passing centuries saw Hims sink into a slow decline. Temür seized Hims after taking Aleppo in 1400, while during the fifteenth century, as Mamluk weakness brought insecurity to the countryside, Hims' lands suffered the ravages of Bedouin raids. In 1510 the menaces of the powerful tribe of al-Fadl b. Nu'ayr required a rescue expedition by the governor of Damascus himself. This amir then proceeded to loot the markets as payment for his "services."

The coming of the Ottomans in 1516 brought an administrative reorganization, with Hims now becoming merely one of the *liwas* (districts) attached to its old rival Tripoli. At this time, a French visitor noted that while the walls and the citadel were in good repair, within all was decay. Only the covered markets still retained their beauty. Unfortunately, the Ottomans did little to revitalize the city or give it security from Bedouin depredations. Tribal unrest during the late seventeenth and early eighteenth centuries resulted in the sacking of its suq on several occasions. Security was hardly helped by the failure to improve the city's defenses. Indeed, by the end of the eighteenth century, the Ottomans had even gone so far as to pull down all the gates of the town walls, one by one.

In 1785 the French traveler Volney gives us a snapshot of the miserable condition of this once-great city. He describes Hims as a rather large, ruined village, administratively dependent on Damascus, with some 2,000 residents, partly Muslim and partly Greek Orthodox.

The first half of the nineteenth century saw the level of Bedouin ravages of the countryside increase. The exception was the period between 1831 and 1840, when Syria came under the strong rule of Ibrahim Pasha, viceroy for his father Muhammad Ali Pasha, governor of Egypt. Hims was not happy under Egyptian rule, and in suppressing a violent revolt, the Egyptians destroyed its citadel.

Up to the 1860s, Hims was small enough with its population of between 15,000 and 20,000 people to form a discrete economic unit for the trade and processing of the agricultural and pastoral products from its satellite villages and the neighboring Bedouin. The regional economy was stimulated, however, by the efforts of the Ottoman government to extend security to the countryside. This brought expansion of settlement into the transitional zone east of the city with the foundation of new villages and the resettlement of long abandoned ones.

As Syria was drawn into the world economy in the period after 1840, Hims found itself faced with European economic competition. Although the sultan triumphed over Muhammad Ali, and forced him to withdraw his forces to Egypt, this was due less to his own efforts than to the intervention of Great Britain and other powers. As a result, European influence increased, and cheap and well-made cotton goods flooded the market. These imports were facilitated by low Ottoman tariff barriers and apparently harmed the local textile industry, which was hobbled by a handicraft method of production and numerous internal difficulties.

Happily, the destruction of an industry whose products had formed some of the most famous exports from this city for many hundreds of years was more apparent than real. The worm turned, as a growing Ottoman population brought increased demand for various types of cloth and the garments made from them. Moreover, the coming of the world economic depression that started in the early 1870s struck hard at the European textile industry, while the abolition of the internal Ottoman tariff in 1874 made local textiles more competitive. These wider factors would have had no effect, however, had it not been for the adaptability and entrepreneurial spirit of local producers. They imported European yarns of a more consistent quality and installed some advanced looms while producing a range of goods whose quality and design satisfied the needs of both the lower and upper ends of the local, the Ottoman, and even the foreign market. One British consul described Hims as the "Manchester of Syria." The number of hand looms found there rose from some 2,500 (including Hamah) in 1872 to 4,000 in 1879, 5,000 in 1902, and 10,000 in 1909.

Its economic and strategic importance was confirmed once again by the decision of the Ottoman authorities to commission a standard-gauge railway to link northern and southern Syria. The line between Riyaq Junction and Aleppo built between 1900 and 1906 was routed through Hims, and a standard-gauge branch line linked Hims and Tripoli in 1911. When the oil pipeline between Kirkuk and Tripoli was built in the early 1930s, it tended to follow in its western part the track of the ancient caravan route between Palmyra, Hims, and the Mediterranean. Following upon this came the opening of an oil refinery in 1959 to process some of the product of this pipeline for Syrian consumption.

Hims has flourished in the twentieth century as it has many times in its past, not necessarily because of its political importance within Syria. Rather, its geographical and strategic location has made it a center of agriculture and industry. Situated at the upper end of the Orontes River near the artificial lake that bears its name, and at the crossroads of important trade routes, the city and its hinterland are well placed to benefit from sophisticated agricultural projects.

The Hims irrigation scheme, the first of its kind in modern Syria, is in many ways the current incarnation of an ancient design. It has brought prosperity to cultivators and to those long-established enterprises engaged in the processing of agricultural and pastoral products.

The pipeline and its attendant oil refinery have brought a new and different stimulus to the economy. Moreover, local people have learned skills, along with habits of work and patterns of thought, that equip them to compete in the world of modern industry.

J. L. Whitaker

Further Readings

Cobb, Paul M. *White Banners: Contention in Abbasid Syria, 750–880.* Albany: State University of New York Press, 2001.

Douwes, Dick. *The Ottomans in Syria: A History of Justice and Oppression.* London: I. B. Tauris, 1997.

Hawting, G. R. *The First Dynasty of Islam: The Umayyad Caliphate, AD 661–750.* London: Croom Helm, 1986.

Issawi, Charles. *The Fertile Crescent, 1800–1914: A Documentary Economic History.* New York: Oxford University Press, 1988.

Lewis, N. N. *Nomads and Settlers in Syria and Jordan, 1800–1950.* Cambridge: Cambridge University Press, 1987.

Millar, Fergus. *The Roman Near East, 31 BC–AD 337.* Cambridge: Harvard University Press, 1993.

Owen, Roger. *The Middle East in the World Economy, 1800–1914.* London: Methuen, 1981.

I

Iskenderun
Population: 160,000 (2005 estimate)

Iskenderun is a Mediterranean port of the southern Turkish province of Hatay, located on the eastern side of the Gulf that bears its name. Established in honor of Alexander the Great, the city experienced its golden age as the port for the city of Aleppo as Europeans scrambled for the spices, silks, and products of the East after 1500. Although surrounded by marshes and prone to malaria, Iskenderun was for 400 years a key access point into the Middle East and hosted a multiethnic community. Today the city is the hub of a series of ports that serve a reemergent southern Anatolia.

Iskenderun (Arabic, *Iskandaruna;* English, *Alexandretta;* Turkish, *Scanderoon*) is located at the point on the Mediterranean littoral where the southward-trending coastline turns sharply to the west for some two and one-half miles creating a protected anchorage with a bay open to the north. It is largely sheltered from any direct swell of the Mediterranean although open to seas rising from within the Gulf of Iskenderun itself. Until the 1920s, when they were drained, marshes girded the town and rendered its climate insalubrious. Since then, it has become an agricultural and industrial center producing grain, tobacco, and fruit as well as steel and fertilizer. Moreover, its ports handle both general and specialized cargoes from Europe, the Middle East, and beyond.

Iskenderun, as its name implies, was one of the many towns established after the death of Alexander the Great and named in his honor. Its founder was probably Seleucus Nicator, who called it Alexandreia kat Isson, which was later Latinized to Alexandria ad Issum. This particular Alexandreia lay "close to Issus," which at the time of its foundation was both a small and prosperous port that coined extensively under the Achaemenids, and perhaps of more significance it was the locus of the first trial of arms between the Macedonian invader and the Great King himself. Issus lay to the north, but immediately to the south was a much older city, the Phoenician foundation of Myriandus/Myriandrus. Such was its importance that Herodotus named the Gulf upon which it lay the Myriandric Gulf.

By a process of synchronism, the new foundation replaced these towns, which both sank into desuetude. Indeed, Strabo comments that Issus was "a small town with a mooring place" while making no mention of Myriandus. Issus, which had coined extensively under the Persians, coined no more.

Yet Alexandreia itself was soon overshadowed by the creation of Seleucia Pieria, north of the mouth of the Orontes River. This magnificent new port served as the gateway to Antioch-on-the-Orontes, the most important city in the Seleucid and Roman East, while Alexandreia remained a small city or city-state on the eastern coastline of Cilicia Pedias that weathered both rises and declines in fortune. Under Antiochus IV Epiphanes, when there was a general revival of local autonomy within the Seleucid domains, Alexandreia issued a municipal coinage. It suffered during the internecine strife of the late Seleucid period as Cilicia became a nest of pirates. When Pompey came to crush these marauders, he "refounded" this city, which took the year of its renewal, 67 BC, as the first year of a new era.

Under the Romans, Alexandria ad Issum continued as a small city, typical of the Roman East, with a full panoply of municipal institutions and offices as well as debts. Between the reigns of Marcus Aurelius and Caracalla, *logistai* (public accountants who checked the accounts of public officials) were appointed by the emperor to manage the finances of the city. Alexandria played a minor part in the Christian world of the late Roman and Byzantine state. It had a suffragan bishop and is recorded as sending a delegate to the Council of Chalcedon in AD 451.

The city was once more in decline, for the geographer Abu al-Fida, prince of Hamah, writing at the beginning of the fourteenth century, notes that Iskenderuna or Bab Sikanderuna, as it was called in Arabic, was rebuilt by Ibn Abi Duwad al-Ayadh in the time of the caliph al-Wathiq but that in his own time there was not even a village on the site. When the Crusaders came to northern Syria, they certainly did not use it as a port. Rather, since the port of Seleucia Pieria was silted up, they built a new one right at the mouth of the Orontes, which they called Saint Simeon.

Iskenderuna first came into its own under the Ottomans at the end of the sixteenth century. After the Ottoman conquest of Syria in 1517, followed by that of Iraq, which was completed by midcentury, Aleppo emerged as a great international entrepôt, attracting both European traders and those from a multiethnic empire. In Aleppo was to be found not only the exotic products and spices of India, which came to the Ottoman domains via Basrah, but also products from a hinterland whose eastern anchors were Diyarbakir and Mosul. Moreover, the division of Syria into several provinces with Aleppo becoming the capital of the north gave it parity with its ancient rival Damascus (see also "Aleppo").

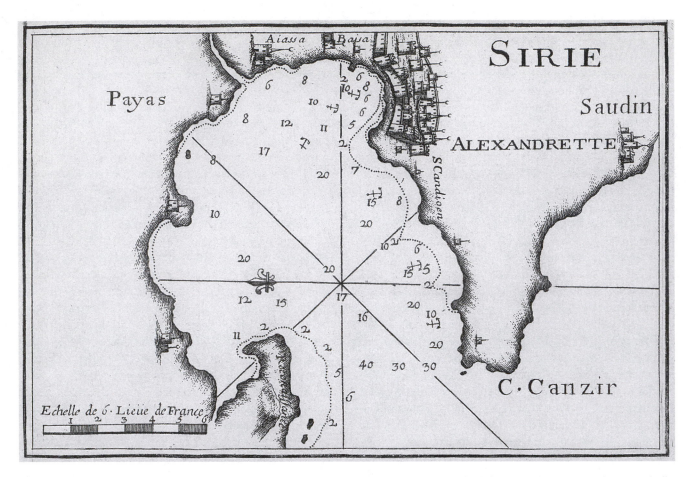

French map of Iskenderun harbor, 1764. (Roux, Joseph, *Receuil des principaux plans, des ports et rades de la Mer Mediterranie, . . .* pl. 115. Marseille, 1764)

For products from its suqs and khans to be shipped westward, Aleppo needed a port. Previously, Tripoli had been the main port on the Levantine coast, but it was insecure, and its rulers imposed vexatious exactions on European traders. Moreover, Tripoli was a minimum of eight days from Aleppo by pack animal, and since it was located in another province, this merely doubled the charges to be paid to officials along the route. At this time, the main product sent from Aleppo to Europe was shifting from black pepper to silk. Since silk was a high value, but bulkier commodity, transport costs were higher. Therefore, those who shipped from Aleppo needed a port closer to hand.

The alternative was Iskenderun, or Scanderoon as Europeans came to name it, which was located in the same province at only two or three days distance from Aleppo by caravan. Here there were no proper docks, and vessels were forced to moor in the roads and transship their cargoes ashore. Failure to develop this magnificent anchorage, the closest port for the most important trading city in the Levant, was because of its abominable climate. The town itself lay on

a narrow band of sand and shingle surrounded by malarial marshes that barred it from the cultivated land nestled at the foot of the neighboring hills. Despite these drawbacks, British, French, and Venetian mercantile interests joined those from Aleppo in pressing the Ottoman government to open a customs station there. By 1590 ships were calling at Iskenderun, and the Ottomans established the desired station at the port in 1593. The town was not confirmed as the official port for Aleppo until 1612 because of maneuvers by the governors of Tripoli, loath to lose such a sure source of revenue.

By the middle of the seventeenth century, European traders, first the Venetians, and then the British and the French, constructed and dominated a small European town, the first colonial port in the Levant. While Venetian activity did not extend much beyond 1600, the British were active until the French Revolution, with the heyday of their Aleppo trade occurring between 1660 and 1750. Generally, during this period, Iskenderun saw the passage of English broadcloth, which was exchanged in the suqs of Aleppo for Persian silk and after the disruption of silk production attendant upon the fall of the Safavids in the 1730s, for silk from Syria and Anatolia. When their market for cloth was stifled by French competition, the English sent coin. At times, other commodities supplemented silk, although most, with the exception of oak galls from Mosul and Diyarbakir, were shipped from ports other than Iskenderun.

Despite this commercial activity, Iskenderun itself remained an unhealthy and dismal place. For example, in 1764 it had only four French residents compared with forty-two at Aleppo and thirty-four at Sidon, center of the French cotton trade. Three agents sufficed to handle its commerce, controlling embarkation, debarkation, and transport: one for the British and the Venetians and two for the French. Even these sought to evade their responsibilities by remaining for long periods in Beylan, where the climate was healthier and the air more pure.

European traders and consuls were continually exercised by the inadequacy of Iskenderun as a shipping terminus. Some, driven by their memories of the classics, called for the resurrection of Laodicea ad Mare (Latakia) and Seleucia Pieria, but the pashas demurred. The French Aleppo merchants even proposed to the pasha of Aleppo to restore the port of Latakia at their own expense in exchange for a ten-year suspension of all customs dues. When their envoy extolled the advantages of this bargain for the entire region in the coming years, the pasha refused his offer, pointing out that the prospects were meaningless for him, as he was but a bird of passage—yesterday at Marash, tomorrow at Jeddah. Better a sure present without action than a risky future with it.

Moreover, caravans, which traveled the road over the Beylan Pass to the markets of Aleppo, were subject to frequent depredations from the Kurds who lived in the mountains north of that city as well as from bands of Turkoman nomads who descended from these mountains to pasture their flocks in the lowlands. They were even so bold as to raid into Iskenderun itself, drenching it with fire and blood while extorting hefty bribes from European merchants and consuls to speed their departure. Nonetheless, the Porte usually refused to authorize its pasha-governors to mount retaliatory expeditions against these brigands. All the more so, because many of the Kurdish chiefs had powerful Ottoman protection, sometimes extending into the very palace of the sultan. Even the long-sanctioned European practice of using carrier pigeons to carry political and commercial news safely between their various trading factories came under threat because the Kurds began to kill the birds to gain intelligence with which to better plan their raids. Unfortunately, even when the local pashas did send expeditions, they had little long-term effect. For example, in 1777 the pasha mounted an attack against Turkoman and Arab robbers, but the next year, circulation between Iskenderun and Aleppo was completed disrupted. Therefore, the Europeans put aside their commercial and po-

litical differences to band together and dispatched an enormous caravan of 2,000 camels, from Aleppo to Iskenderun, of which 1,300 were French. The products from the French section of the caravan were sufficient to load four large French vessels that had been waiting four or five months in harbor for cargo.

This example demonstrates the increasing preponderance of France in the Aleppo trade during the eighteenth century. Indeed, between 1776 and 1780, French goods shipped from Iskenderun outstripped the combined totals of their commercial competitors—Great Britain, Venice, Leghorn, and the Netherlands—by some 71 percent.

Iskenderun continued as the principal port for Aleppo despite its inadequacies. Yet its roadstead remained empty of vessels from the second half of the eighteenth century to the first decades of the nineteenth, not so much because of the problems of infrastructure and climate but because Aleppo itself was suffering a decline in trade. Perhaps its most important export was silk from Iran, but the collapse of Iranian silk production and the rerouting of the remainder to the Persian Gulf struck a heavy blow at Aleppine prosperity. Another factor was internal factionalism, where bitter political infighting affected the local economy. A third was the great European crisis from 1789 to 1815, which put a damper on all European trade to the Levant. A severe earthquake in 1822 followed by the introduction from Europe of cheap machine-made textiles, which hindered the sales of the local handicrafts, hardly served to improve the position of Aleppo or Iskenderun.

Starting in the 1830s there was a slow but steady revival of fortune as illustrated by the increase of the trade passing through Iskenderun. During the forty years between 1833 and 1873, both its imports and exports rose at an annual rate of around 6 percent. The principal impetus here was the Crimean War boom and the rise in exports of cotton and other commodities to record levels.

Although there were crises, particularly in the period following the two booms, the crunch came after the construction of the Egyptian railway from Alexandria to Cairo and Cairo to Suez during the 1850s and the inauguration of the Suez Canal in 1869, which had an even greater impact. Previously, the routes from Iskenderun through Aleppo and eastward to Baghdad and beyond had offered transit times and costs far less than the voyage to the east around the Cape of Good Hope. The opening of the Suez Canal eliminated this advantage.

Nonetheless, Aleppo and Iskenderun were able to recover during a second phase of growth that comprised the following forty-year period and was caused by the increase in the production and trade of their hinterland of northern Mesopotamia and Kurdistan. Thus, between 1873 and 1908, the imports of Iskenderun grew at an annual rate of 2.2 percent, while its exports rose at an annual rate of 2 percent.

This increase in the traffic of Iskenderun during the nineteenth century occurred despite the continuation of the problems of infrastructure that had bedeviled it since its inception. The first was the lack of an adequate road between Iskenderun and Aleppo, which kept transport costs high. The second was the derelict state of the port itself. Of course, one might say that if these two handicaps had themselves been remedied, the increase in the trade passing through Iskenderun would have been even greater, and Iskenderun with its natural advantages might even have outstripped Beirut (see also "Beirut").

Thus, in the second quarter of the century, the cost of goods transported by mule or camel over the seventy-seven miles between Aleppo and Iskenderun was almost the same as were the charges to ship those same goods from Iskenderun to England. In 1888 freight charges for wheat from Iskenderun to Aleppo were 50 percent of the price in Aleppo, while the cost from London to Iskenderun was only 50 percent of that from Iskenderun to Aleppo. Even more shocking was the fact that in this same year, the cost to ship licorice—a major Syrian export to the United States to flavor chewing gum and tobacco—from Antakiya to Iskenderun, a thirty-seven-mile journey, was five times greater than the charges to ship that same licorice from Iskenderun to New York.

The Ottoman response was to build a carriage road between Aleppo and Iskenderun. Graft as well as unsuitable construction methods and materials ensured that this project had to be constantly renewed, and it was described by one cynical foreign observer as a "Penelope's web." Yet when a company of Ottoman subjects, both Muslim and Christian, sought a concession to build such a carriage road, and deliberately excluded foreign stockholders to make their project more acceptable to the Porte, the government made its conditions so onerous that this company never got off the ground.

Yet the high cost of land transport between Iskenderun and Aleppo was not the gravest impediment to the success of the former as an outlet for trade. Throughout the nineteenth century, there was little progress in making the port facilities themselves more efficient and accessible. A description of the port given in 1859 could as well have been applied to 1759: a pair of dilapidated jetties, leaky lighters, deficient porterage, no portside storage facilities, unpaved streets—all contributing to damaged goods. The improvement of this superb harbor, "the best port in all Syria" as one report has it, was still limited by the presence of bogs. This made it so unhealthy that its population of under 1,000 people built their houses on stilts in an effort to escape the miasma. By contrast, the population of Beirut, the newly flourishing port of Damascus, and southern Syria was approaching 50,000. Yet the Ottoman government spent not a single para on the most important trade outlet of the *vilayet* (province or large administrative district) of Aleppo. Any enhancements, such as the jetties, were undertaken by foreigners, exasperated by its commercial deficiencies.

Forty years saw considerable advance. By now, the population had grown to some 7,000 people; the streets were paved and properly laid out, and along the seafront were stone houses and offices instead of huts on stilts. Moreover, the consuls and leading local inhabitants were starting the necessary work of drainage, and there was even a proposal to build a breakwater to protect the harbor. Finally, efforts were being made to reconstruct permanently the carriage road linking Iskenderun with Aleppo.

Thus, by the turn of the twentieth century, Iskenderun was slowly turning into a more habitable place, its population was beginning to grow, and the port was becoming more welcoming. Until the outbreak of war in 1914, the principal impetus came from the construction of the Berlin-Baghdad Railway, designed to link the markets of central Europe with Istanbul; Anatolia; northern Syria; the Mesopotamian vilayets of Mosul, Baghdad, and Basrah; the Gulf; and beyond.

Germany required a port on the Mediterranean to serve the Berlin-Baghdad Railway as a railhead for merchandise coming by sea from western Europe, and Iskenderun fit the bill. In 1911 the Germans obtained the concession to drop a branch from Toprakkale on the main line to Iskenderun. This line was built and opened in November 1913. At the same time, plans were made for a vast expansion of its port, and work started in 1912. There were to be three anchorages bounded by quays, one of which was designed to hold sixteen large ships at a time. Unfortunately, the outbreak of war ruined all these plans: the reconstruction of the port ceased while the railway line was torn up to supply lacunae elsewhere.

The coming of the Great War in 1914 thrust Iskenderun into world politics because of its important strategic location close to the Berlin-Baghdad Railway and because it appeared to give easy access to the agricultural and petroleum riches of Mesopotamia from the Mediterranean. Both Lord Kitchener, secretary of state for war, and Lord Fisher, first sea lord, advocated the British seizure of Iskenderun in preference to the assault on the Dardanelles at Gallipoli. France opposed any British operation to capture Iskenderun because it had many interests in Syria, but it could spare no troops to uphold them. Therefore, in deference to its sensibilities, the British made a political decision to shelve the "Alexandretta project." It is interesting to note that Field Marshal von Hindenburg himself believed that Allied seizure of Iskenderun and interdiction of the Baghdad Railway would have struck a mortal blow at Germany's Ottoman ally.

This entry of Iskenderun onto the world stage was but a brief one. The end of the war brought the dissolution of the Ottoman dynasty and the end of the Levant as both a political and economic unity. As a consequence of the postwar settlement, the political horizons of Iskenderun contracted to a *sanjak* (district, region, or provincial administrative area of an empire or state) of which it now served as capital. For some two years after the end of the war, France wasted blood and treasure in an attempt to wrest Cilicia from the resurgent Turkish Republic. The Franklin-Bouillon Agreement of October 1921 between the two parties allowed France a graceful withdrawal from the Cilician imbroglio while confirming the existence of a new "sanjak of Alexandretta," which the Allies had originally created by administrative fiat on 30 October 1918. This administrative unit comprised the four contiguous districts (*qadhas*) of Iskenderun, Beylan, Antakiya, and Harim (until 1 January 1925) carved from the Aleppo vilayet and lay across the linguistic and cultural frontier between Turk and Arab. This entity was administratively attached to the Syrian Mandate but had a regime that ensured equality for Turkish language and culture.

The Ottoman vilayet of Aleppo, of which Iskenderun had been a part, now found itself divided between French-mandated and Arab-dominated Syria and the newly hatched Republic of Turkey. The horrors of these years and the creation of new national entities brought population exchanges as different groups sought safe havens over the frontier. Like other towns, Iskenderun experienced a dramatic demographic shift. Just before the war, the Ottomans estimated the population of Iskenderun qadha (somewhat larger than the city alone) to be approximately 75 percent Muslim. Twenty years later, the proportions had become reversed, with a large percentage of these being Armenians who had fled Cilicia upon the withdrawal of the French.

The new political constellations that arose out of the First World War affected Iskenderun in other ways. The creation of two rival sovereignties out of a single economic zone struck a blow at the dominance of Aleppo and Iskenderun, its port. Before the war, 20 percent of Syrian exports went to Anatolia, largely via Aleppo, while 15 percent of total Syrian imports came from Anatolia. By 1932 this had shrunk to 5 percent and 10 percent, respectively, largely as a result of tariff barriers. Of course, not all of this trade went through Iskenderun. Nonetheless, if one looks at total trade through this port, the highest prewar year was 1906, with a total of 97,000 tons, which amount was not exceeded until the year 1929.

Although Iskenderun was the second busiest port in Syria after Beirut, the latter was far more active. For example, in that same year, 1929, when Iskenderun had a total trade of 98,000 tons, Beirut had a total of 445,000 tons. One reason for this was that in Iskenderun, ships still had to moor in the roads and unload their cargoes onto lighters, whereas Beirut was endowed with a modern port and docking facilities.

The failure of the French authorities to do more to promote the prosperity of Iskenderun was less caused by lack of money than by lack of political will. During the 1920s, the sanjak regularly had a budget surplus, and it was French policy to use the surpluses of the various statelets that made up the mandate for local improvements. There was, however, no money for major investments like port expansion. The extinction of the Ottoman Public Debt in 1933 released funds for a program of public works. One of the projects budgeted was the expansion of the port of Beirut, the major port of Damascus and southern Syria, but the French gave no thought to the expansion of Iskenderun, the principal port of Aleppo and northern Syria.

One can directly link this failure to invest in the port of Iskenderun to the peculiar status of the sanjak, an important piece of the mandate with a mortgage held by a foreign power who could foreclose at any time. Thus, the mandatary, with limited resources at its disposal, was naturally inclined to spend money on the Levant states over whom it held uncontested authority rather than on the sanjak, which might be whisked away at any moment.

Included in this general improvement of infrastructure was a road-building program whose goal was to provide the territories under French administration with a network of modern hard-surfaced roads. Naturally, one of the most important of these arteries was that linking Aleppo with Iskenderun. In 1934 a French journalist could boast that whereas before the coming of the mandate, the postal route between these two towns was impassable in winter while in summer required a three-day journey by horseback or carriage, now it took a mere two and one-half hours by automobile. There is a certain irony here in that the mandatary sought to bring prosperity to Aleppo and all north Syria by improving their access to the sea while failing to modernize the port that would serve as their principal gateway. In this case, one can truly say that political imperatives trumped economic rationality.

The French did use sanjak funds to make limited but important investments in the town of Iskenderun itself. One of the first acts of the French authorities was to restore the branch railway connecting Iskenderun with the former Berlin-Baghdad Railway at Toprakkale, which had been dismantled during the war. Construction of public buildings and electrification gave the city a more modern face, but the most important work done was the completion of the work of drainage that had begun under the aegis of the consuls some thirty years before. Six miles of canals dried forty-five hectares of marshes, and plantations of tens of thousands of eucalyptus trees were laid out. One happy result of these efforts was that between 1923 and 1933, the mortality from malaria fell from 57 percent of total mortality to 8 percent. Thus, after some 300 years of suffering, one of the greatest obstacles to the burgeoning of Iskenderun was finally eliminated.

In September 1936, France and a delegation of Syrian nationalists initialed a treaty that made Syria both independent and a member of the League of Nations three years after its ratification. This document contained no specific provisions for the continued autonomy of the sanjak of Alexandretta.

Turkish outrage initiated a political process that within three years brought the sanjak into the republic as its sixty-third vilayet under the name of Hatay. During the negotiations, Turkey sought as one of its immediate objectives an extraterritorial zone within the port of Iskenderun. This concession was contained within the statute of autonomy negotiated with France and the League during 1937. This was but one step and one year away from bringing Iskenderun at last within the bounds of the motherland.

Over the next decade, Iskenderun stagnated as World War II and the troubles of Palestine rocked the region. There was nearly a 25 percent population reduction largely caused by the complete and rapid exodus of its many Armenian residents, hardly keen to live once again under the domination of the Turk, who they had fled so precipitously some twenty years before. Moreover, the boundary change saw Iskenderun cut off from its hinterland by the disruption of ties with Aleppo and north Syria. Indeed, grass now grew in the cracks of the all-important Aleppo-Iskenderun highway so recently perfected. After 500 years, the city had lost Aleppo forever as its most important partner because independent Syria determined to develop its own port of Latakia, which was eventually linked to the metropolis of north Syria by both highway and rail.

Nonetheless, the 1950s found the government in Ankara with the will and the means to reorient both Iskenderun and Hatay toward the Turkish economic zone. This integration was facilitated by the Middle Eastern agricultural boom of the Korean War years and by the economic potentials of Hatay itself, now more than ever the closest and principal hinterland of Iskenderun.

Perhaps the most significant decision of the Turkish authorities was to design at long last a modern port. This port now has a breakwater 4,600 feet long that protects vessels from north and south winds and ten berths; conveyors to handle bulk ore, grain, and coal; and facilities for roll on, roll off (Ro-Ro). At present there is no container terminal, but there is a project to build one in the future. Moreover, the industrial zone, which has grown up around Iskenderun in the past forty years, has spawned its own specialized ports. Since the 1970s, two large steelworks and a phosphate factory have come into being. Each has found it desirable to build docking facilities. Indeed, the Iskenderun Iron and Steel Works (Isdamir) has constructed a small harbor with two breakwaters, six berths, and a fuel wharf. As a result, Iskenderun has finally realized the potential of its splendid anchorage by becoming the southern link of a chain of ports that stretches right around the Bay of Iskenderun to Mersina, making the entire bay one giant port. Energy, agricultural, and industrial products flowing from central and eastern Anatolia, and potentially the Caucasus, all now flow through this harbor chain.

J. L. Whitaker

Further Readings
Barker, Arthur J. *The Neglected War: Mesopotamia, 1914–1918.* London: Faber and Faber, 1967.
Davis, Ralph. *Aleppo and Devonshire Square: English Traders in the Levant in the Eighteenth Century.* London: Macmillan, 1967.
Glass, Charles. *Tribes with Flags: A Dangerous Passage through the Chaos of the Middle East.* London: Secker and Warburg, 1990.
Güçlü, Yücel. *The Question of the Sanjak of Alexandretta: A Study in Turkish-French-Syrian Relations.* Ankara: Turkish Historical Society Printing House, 2001.
Issawi, Charles. *The Fertile Crescent, 1800–1914: A Documentary Economic History.* Oxford: Oxford University Press, 1988.
Jones, Arnold H. M. *The Cities of the Eastern Roman Provinces.* Oxford: Clarendon Press, 1998.
Le Strange, Guy. *Palestine under the Moslems: A Description of Syria and the Holy Land from A.D. 650 to 1500.* London: Alexander P. Watt, 1890.
Masters, Bruce. *The Origins of Western Economic Dominance in the Middle East: Mercantilism and the Islamic Economy in Aleppo, 1600–1750.* New York: New York University Press, 1988.
Nevakivi, Jukka. *Britain, France and the Arab Middle East, 1914–1920.* London: Athlone Press, 1969.

Istanbul
Population: 10 million (2005 estimate)

Few cities in the world hold the fascination, exoticism, and mystery of Istanbul/Constantinople. Situated at the "navel of the world," straddling the shores of the Bosphorus, this city has been a site of political power, religious authority, and military control at the center of Eurasian civilization for twenty-seven centuries. For millennia, Byzantium hosted Greek and Roman authority; then, as Constantinople, it shaped Christendom for another ten centuries; as Istanbul, for five centuries it was the center of Islamic hopes and power. Today this "imperial city" is the premier world city of the Middle East and Eastern Europe, transcending the bonds of the Turkish state to rearticulate trade and culture across much of its former realm. One of the greatest urban conurbations of the world, Istanbul is not so much a national city as an eternal one, global in its civilization and in its immortality, always searching for a continent worthy of its grandeur.

Istanbul (ancient Greek, *Byzantium;* Latin, *Constantinopolis;* Turkish, *Istanbul*) lies on both sides of the southern entrance to the Bosphorus, claiming Asia and Europe as its heritage and hinterland. The city was initially sited on a small defensive peninsula sticking out from the western shore at the northern end of the Sea of Marmara at a point where water protected its heights from attack on three sides. Bounded on its northern flank by the five-mile-long Golden Horn, which is fed by two streams, those "Sweet Waters of Europe" form a natural harbor, one of the most perfect in the world, in the lee of the peninsula. There is great fishing in the Golden Horn, since the currents force sea life into the opening. Along the spine of the peninsula lie seven hills, with the first marking

Palace Point. Across the Golden Horn to the north lies Galata/Pera, long a separate entity under control of Genoese and European traders. Ferries cross the mile to Uskudar and the Asian districts of the city, lying on the shores of Anatolia/Anadolu (Greek for land of the sunrise). To the north, the narrow and treacherous Bosphorus winds its deep cut twenty miles to the Black Sea.

The archaeological records suggest that there was human habitation in the area as far back as 5000 BC, at a time when the Bosphorus was a valley with a series of freshwater lakes connecting the saline Sea of Marmara to the freshwater Black Sea. However, the fact that the city is both now so extensive and its core has remained continuously inhabited since the seventh century BC means that our knowledge from archaeology comes primarily from rescue digs. It does appear that early Greek colonists from Megara arrived at the mouth of the Bosphorus around the beginning of the seventh century and initially established a site called Chalcedon on the Asian side. Seventeen years later, according to Herodotus, another set of Megarian colonists, led by Byzas, established themselves on the European side of the entrance on the promontory on the peninsula. Byzantium, named after their leader, was a much more defensive and strategic site. The Byzantium foundation myths talk about dolphins (symbols of Apollo) marking the site and of the oracle at Delphi suggesting the colonists found the new city "across from the land of the blind," nicely interpreted as the "blindness" of the Chalcedons in missing the better site across the strait.

From the very beginning, the two colonies worked in tandem to control trade and shipping between the Greek colonies further up the Bosphorus or along the Pontos and Black Sea coast and the Aegean, although what became Byzantium was by far the more significant and strategically protected in its isolation. Excavations have revealed some pottery from as early as 500 BC, and the first walls surrounded the acropolis hill. During its first 400 years, the town gained a reputation for hard trading and heavy drinking; the female poet Moero (Myro) of Byzantium (ca. 300 BC), with her poems about love and wine, was representative of the literary references to the city. Xenophon (ca. fourth century) suggested that Byzantium was the last truly "Greek" city before reaching the colonies to its north.

The Achaemenids under Cyrus controlled the city after 546 BC; Herodotus details the bridge of boats built by the Persians so their army could cross the narrowest part of the Bosphorus to the north of the city. Byzantium accepted Persian suzerainty and was ruled by a series of tyrants, although they participated in the Ionian Revolt (497 BC), and the city was burnt in response.

During the late fifth century and much of the fourth, Athens tended to dominate Byzantium, and their protection helped the city survive a siege by Philip of Macedonia in 339. The city was repeatedly placed under siege by a further series of attackers, including the Seleucids and the Bithynians. Roman rule recognized Byzantium as a free city, a status it maintained despite its incorporation into the empire under Vespasian (AD 73). Construction continued to enhance the city, including stadia and temples.

In AD 193–196, the city was placed under a long siege by Septimius Severus because of its support for his rival, Pescennius Niger. Graphic reports of this experience, including cannibalism and failed escape attempts using crude boats made from the rafters of their homes, highlight the trauma of such an event. When it finally fell, Severus allowed the sack of the city, put most of its leaders to death, and tore down the walls. He later repented his rashness, rebuilt the city, established new walls that doubled its area, financed the Hippodrome and public baths, and generally tried to reclaim the vitality of its trading networks.

It was this resurgent city that attracted Constantine when he decided in AD 324 to establish a new capital in the east. Although he considered other options first, even going so far as to build walls and gates at Troy, the legend goes that God appeared to him in a dream and encouraged him to find another site for his capital. Another story relates that as Constantine marked out the dimensions of the new city, his couriers were flabbergasted with the huge area he was inscribing. They asked him when he would stop; his reply was that he would continue until he was told by God to halt. Some 40,000 Goth soldiers, the so-called *foederati*, provided much of the labor; pagan monuments were brought from Rome, Athens, Alexandria, Ephesus, and Antioch to beautify the city, while artisans employed the materials from throughout the empire that flowed up from the harbor. New laws and incentives to attract immigrants were propagated. On 11 May 330, the city was dedicated, and the celebrations lasted forty days.

Constantine's new land wall ran from the Golden Horn to the Sea of Marmara, enclosing some 200,000 inhabitants. This City of Constantine (Constantinople) was subdivided into fourteen districts where more than 70,000 people were provided with free bread every day. The Hippodrome was enlarged to hold 80,000 spectators, and it became the central focus of the city; eventually, emperors were crowned or executed within its circuit, and its various mobs (the Greens, Blues, Whites, and Reds) competed for control and influence in the city. The Hippodrome's political and social centrality remained for the next 1,500 years; Sigurd, king of Norway, visiting in the twelfth century, commented on the fantastical sights, from jugglers to fire-eaters, to be seen within its confines. An important later addition to the city was Emperor Julian's library, which reportedly held 600,000 volumes.

By the time of Theodosius II (r. 408–450), the city had far outgrown the limits of Constantine's wall, and it was clear that there were new dangers. Rome itself had been sacked in 410, and this was a serious warning to the Byzantine emperors. A new land wall with numerous towers was begun in 413 well to the west of Constantine's construction. Unfortunately, a violent earthquake destroyed much of this wall just as Attila the Hun was heading for the city (ca. 442), and so with great effort it was rebuilt in two months. In addition, over the next few years another wall and moat were added, creating a system of three defensive barriers running four miles from the Golden Horn to the Sea of Marmara. The city now enclosed seven hills, just like Rome, imagery that did not escape the empire's propagandists. It is recorded that the streets were illuminated at night and that a university was founded (AD 425).

One of the city's most memorable inhabitants of the time was the patriarch of Constantinople (ca. 398), later considered the city's saint. John Chrysostom, "the Golden-Mouthed," was reportedly so eloquent that the people of the city flocked to hear his sermons. It could also be that he did not hesitate to criticize the extravagance of the imperial court, contrasting it with the poverty of ordinary citizens. John preached against the immorality of the Augusta (Empress Eudoxia), the power behind the throne, but he also railed against the immoral performances of the theater, in particular the naked limbs of women that excited men so. Chrysostom was finally sent into exile, which incited his followers to riot; they burned the cathedral Hagia Sophia (Church of Divine Wisdom). Thirty years after his death, his relics were returned to Constantinople, where his coffin was reportedly opened, his body was found to have not decayed, and he opened his eyes and said "Peace be to all."

Riots in the city were a regular occurrence. On 10 January 532, Emperor Justinian was trapped in the Great Palace by a mob of Blues and Greens emerging from the Hippodrome shouting "Nika" (victory). The rebuilt Hagia Sophia was burned again in this Nika Revolt, but Justinian was able, by killing 30,000 rioters, to suppress the uprising. Their mass grave is reportedly within the confines of the Hippodrome. Within forty days, Justinian laid out a new cathedral, also called the Hagia Sophia, which still graces the city's skyline. This unique building took six years to build, was covered in mosaics and silk tapestries, and for 1,000 years was the largest church in the world.

In addition to regular urban riots, there were numerous earthquakes that destroyed much of the new monumental architecture (the period from 553 to 558 saw a number, for example). There were also severe plagues—the one in 542 ravaged the city for four months and may have killed as many as 300,000 out of its 500,000 inhabitants.

Despite such setbacks, the thirty-eight-year reign of Justinian (r. 527–565) is considered the golden age of Constantinople. In addition to the monumental architecture he commissioned, he left behind a law school and, perhaps more importantly, a state monopoly over silk production. Until this time, China monopolized the production and weaving of silk. But Justinian is famous for smuggling silkworm eggs out of China, establishing production procedures, and setting up silk-weaving factories in Constantinople.

After Justinian, the threats to Constantinople dramatically increased. In 626 the Persian king Chosroes II cooperated with the nomadic Avars to attack Constantinople and to besiege it. The Avars on the European side and the Persians on the Asian side of the Bosphorus squeezed the city between them, but the elaborate three-walled defenses, unmatched anywhere, remained too strong for the barbarians, who lacked siege craft. For five days, the Avars launched assaults against these fortifications but were repulsed with huge losses; they then left for easier pickings among the Bulgars.

The Arab Muslim armies and navy sailed unopposed up the Dardanelles in 670, landed seven miles south on the European side, and attacked the city. They too were defeated by the city walls but also by the "Greek fire" (a sprayed petroleum mixture that burst into flame) effectively used by Constantinople's defenders. Their forces withdrew to the Sea of Marmara, from where they made numerous attempts to capture the city over the next seven years. Each time they were defeated, and they finally withdrew in 677. Ever since, scholars have wondered what might have happened if the Arabs had focused all this energy and might on weaker Italy or France. Perhaps it can be argued that Constantinople's walls and Greek fire were the hinge factors that protected a weak Europe from the Arab advance, shaping subsequent world history in crucial ways.

By the twelfth century, the empire had lost much of its territory, but the capital remained a feast for the eyes and ears. Benjamin of Tudela, who visited around 1168, estimated the yearly income from customs payments alone at 20,000 gold pieces. He marveled at the number of silk garments touched with gold worn by the city's inhabitants. He and other visitors of the time commented on the multicultural aspects of the city, with its virtual tower of Babel, with all languages and races represented. The population at the end of that century may have been as much as 1 million.

The outbreak of fire remained a key problem. There were two particularly destructive infernos in 1197 and in 1198. We know about them and their devastating effects through poems written at the time. The plague regularly returned as well. When the Black Death swept the world in the mid-fourteenth century, it touched Constantinople in 1348 via Genoese trading ships. More than half of the population died.

A particularly close but problematic relationship between the two trading cities of Venice and Constantinople began with a small detail in 1082, when the Byzantine emperor Alexius I granted Venice a special relationship (the Golden Bull) as thanks for saving the Byzantine fleet and opening up the Adriatic to trade. In return, the Venetians received exemptions from tolls into the capital and full trading privileges not granted to anyone else. Tension within the city and for control of trade routes continued between the two cities for the next

350 years. For example, in 1182 competition between Italians and the Byzantine Greeks in the city resulted in a massacre of the Italians and the torching of much of their property.

The Venetians and their drive to control the eastern trade routes led to one of the greatest disasters in Constantinople's history. In 1202 Crusader forces gathering along the Lido in Venice for the Fourth Crusade were manipulated by the Venetians into attacking Constantinople, as a "temporary" diversion on their way to the Holy Land. As a result, the Venetian fleet placed the Latin army outside the city walls, where from July 1203 to April 1204 they besieged the city. When they finally captured it, they set it afire and plundered the wealth of a millennium. For three days, French and Flemish soldiers raped and pillaged: they torched the libraries and books; they stole its religious and monumental art (the bronze horses that had graced the Hippodrome for 1,000 years ended up in the Piazza San Marco); they carried away the sacred relics (bits of hair and fragments of teeth from Christ's disciples, a feather from Gabriel's wing, Saint Peter's chains, the nails of the True Cross, and some of its splinters); they raped nuns in their convents; and they ripped out the silk tapestries and silver inlay in Hagia Sophia. On Easter day, they placed a prostitute on the throne and danced around her, holding hands. The young Baldwin IX was crowned emperor of the Latin Kingdom of Constantinople, and for the next sixty years these Frankish usurpers took what they wanted from the city and did nothing to maintain its infrastructure or support its people.

The city never recovered from this Venetian treachery. The Byzantine elites waited in Nicaea to return, which they did in 1261 under the Paleologus dynasty, with the help of the Genoese navy. But the city's wealth was gone, along with its holy and martial authority. Some trade returned; European merchants continued to use Pera as a storage site for what they gained from their Black Sea trade, and the merchants carted silver ingots via Constantinople into the Black Sea and then into the steppes of western Asia as payments for the goods arriving from the east. At this point, Marco Polo's father and uncle made their first trip to China via Constantinople.

In 1301 imperial forces were defeated in a battle near Nicomedia by the cavalry of a small Turkish principality based around Eskisehir. This was the first military encounter between the Osmalis and Byzantine forces. For the next century and a half, Constantinople's remaining territory was steadily eaten away by the advance of the Ottoman Turks. By 1341 Sultan Orkhan had conquered the three Byzantine cities of western Anatolia—Bursa, Nicaea, and Nicomedia—leaving Constantinople directly in their path (see also "Bursa" and "Iznik"). By 1402 Sultan Bayazet had been besieging Constantinople for a year, while the emperor Manuel II Palaeologus was in France soliciting Christian help for what everyone expected was the final act in the loss of the city to the Muslims. Yet by July 1402, Bayazet was gone, hurrying off to the east to defend his territory from Temür; Constantinople had been granted another half century.

Sultan Mehmet II came to the throne in 1451 at the age of nineteen. By August 1452, he had completed the construction of the Rumeli Hisar on the narrow part of the Bosphorus, two miles north of the capital, thus blocking northern access to the city, and was gathering his forces to attack what was left of Constantinople. By April 1453, he had 80,000 soldiers attacking the land wall protected by a motley collection of 7,000. Mehmet's troops used the latest technology, still not in general use across Europe: siege cannon some two feet in diameter that used gunpowder to hurl 1,200-pound stone shot against the ancient walls. In another demonstration of tactical brilliance, Mehmet had seventy ships dragged from the Bosphorus over the hill of Pera down into the Golden Horn, thus circumventing the famous and ancient iron chain that protected the city's harbor. Finally, at dawn on 29 May, fifty-three days after the siege had begun, the Ottomans burst through the 1,000-year-old Edirne gate that had resisted twenty-nine sieges, and the Byzantine Empire was gone. The emperor died fighting, his body found later headless but wrapped in the imperial armor. At the last moment, a number of Venetian galleys, full of refugees who had swum out to them, escaped into the Sea of Marmara.

The sultan gave the city over to his soldiers for three days of rape and pillage, declaring that all movable property was theirs, while all "fixed" property belonged to him. Reportedly, he personally killed one soldier making off with a piece of Hagia Sophia, and he cried for what was happening to the city.

It is important to note the link between this capital of Rome and the role and mission of the Ottomans. For 800 years, Muslims had dreamed of taking Constantinople, and the Ottomans had made its capture part of their apocalyptic definition of their family. By the fifteenth century, there remained little trade or economic value to the city; its significance rather lay in its symbolic and iconic value as a focus for the Islamic imagination. Taking Constantinople empowered the Ottoman state and marked a turning point in their empire's history, allowing them to centralize their political, economic, and religious power into a single authoritarian package. The city, sometimes termed Islambul (city of Islam), subsequently attracted Islamic scholarship and devotion.

The sultan immediately put his troops to work repairing the ravages of centuries of neglect and their own depravations. The infrastructure was rebuilt: new drains, repaired cisterns and aqueducts, and new paving stones. Captives and artisans from throughout the empire were "encouraged" to migrate to the city, monumental architecture to grace the city was commissioned, and Hagia Sophia was transformed into a mosque. The Latin clergy was kicked out of the city, and a new Orthodox patriarch was invested with responsibility for thirty-six churches in the city. The Armenian patriarch was summoned to move from Bursa, and the chief rabbi was to

Sixteenth-century sketch of Istanbul. (Library of Congress)

come from Jerusalem to lead their communities in the empire from the new capital.

Mehmet's son, Bayezid II (r. 1481–1512), was the builder of what became known by its Turkish name as Istanbul, although on coins and documents its formal name remained Konstantiniyye. Bayezid developed new roads tying the city into the empire and encouraged the development of high Islamic culture. By the sixteenth century, Istanbul was the largest city in Europe and western Asia, with a population of more than 500,000, doing what this city on the Bosphorus does best: rule an empire. The monumental architecture to match the empire came to grace its skyline as well. The Sulaymaniye, the largest mosque in the empire, was built in 1557, and the Sultanahmet (the Blue Mosque), with its graceful six minarets, was built in 1617; both sought to outdo Hagia Sophia.

Istanbul was a giant, consuming city, with the rest of the empire as its hinterland. This made it unique in its relation to the government in terms of both size and political importance, forcing government economic policy to revolve around serving the city. By the mid-1600s, 250 tons of bread were baked in the city every day; 18,000 oxen killed every month; and 7 million sheep and lambs slaughtered per year, with one-tenth of them destined for that fabulous city-within-a-city, Topkapi Sarayi (Topkapi Palace). All this required 2,000 food ships to dock each year.

The financial reach and sophistication of the city was central to its place in the empire and to long-distance trade. The city benefited from the annual tributes of vassal states to the government: Bosnia and Herzegovina contributed 18,000 ducats per year, while Trebizond gave 3,000 and Moldavia 6,000 (see also "Trabzon"). Provinces provided the treasury with annual remittances; in the sixteenth century, Egypt was sending Istanbul 500,000 gold pieces every year. The state held the monopoly over basic commodities such as salt, soap, and candle wax, and detailed laws regulated daily economic life. The result of all these inflows was that when Mehmed II died, in 1481, the central treasury contained 240 million *akces* (standard Ottoman silver currency) plus 104 million gold coins.

In the sixteenth century, Greeks and Jews were the leading financiers in Istanbul, lending at 2 percent per month interest to private business, the Ottoman government, and even to foreign potentates. Many of the Jews were from Iberia or from Portuguese Marrano banking families who had fled the troubles. Many had great fortunes; in 1588 Alvaro Mendes brought 85,000 gold ducats with him when he immigrated to the city. Via their networks of agents in the leading European centers, such bankers kept Istanbul, the government, and international trade functioning.

A centralized, absolutist Ottoman administration emerged that was built around a slave-based central bureaucracy and the Janissary corps. The government took the name Sublime Porte (high gate) in the 1650s, since petitioners would cluster at the palace gates, and justice was dispensed there. The further one could work one's way through the series of gates, the greater your status and role. At the center of the palace stood the Mansion of Justice, where the sultan would dispense justice.

For Ottomans Istanbul was a holy city, ranking just behind Makkah, Madinah, and Jerusalem. This is because it was the spot where Eyup Ensari, the Prophet's friend and standard bearer, had been buried during the first Arab siege of Constantinople. Legend has it that the burial site was lost while the city remained in Christian hands for the next eight centuries. Miraculously, during the successful Ottoman siege of the city, in 1453, Eyup's tomb was rediscovered, and Mehmet the Conqueror had a *kulliye* (mosque complex) erected over the site. After Mehmet's death, it became the custom for all succeeding sultans to be girded with the sword of their ancestor, Osman Gazi, at Eyup's tomb, and then to visit the tomb of the conqueror himself in Fatih Cami (the conqueror's mosque).

The golden age of Ottoman Istanbul is usually considered the long reign of Sulayman Kanuni, "the Lawgiver," or "the Magnificent" (r. 1520–1566). This is a man who went to war on thirteen major campaigns, signed himself the ruler of thirty-seven kingdoms, was so exalted that he only gave audiences in profile, rarely wore the same clothes twice, married the slave girl Roxelana (and was faithful to her), and had four servants always with him to carry his weapons, rain gear, a pitcher of some iced drink, and anything else that he might need. Sulayman oversaw the codification of sultanic and Quranic law and worked closely with the exceptional architect, Sinan, to adorn his capital.

The citizens of Istanbul became particularly known for their participation in Sufi brotherhoods or orders. Specifically, the Naqshbandiyya order, which appeared in the city during the late 1400s, became the brotherhood of choice for the ulema, since it affirmed the significance of orthodoxy. The hold of the Naqshbandiyya over the population of the capital increased with time. In the seventeenth century, mainly the learned class were members, but by the nineteenth century every class participated through the fifty-two *takiyyas* (centers) located in the city. In the takiyyas, people could find mystic intoxication and hope for the progression of the soul toward God, but they were also taught solid Sunni tradition and expected to be virtuous.

By the 1700s, the empire was in decline, with the expanding European powers beginning to nibble off chunks of territory and control their trade as they wished. Many European aristocrats and nobility lived in exile in Istanbul. The Swedish king Charles XII, for example, sought refuge in the city in 1717. Reportedly, he became so caught up in the new fad for studying ancient Egypt that he bought an Egyptian mummy, but the Ottoman government took it away from him and stored it in the Castle of the Seven Towers, a government prison. The mummy became a regular stop on the "Grand Tour" for Europeans well into the nineteenth century.

The decade of the 1720s was a period of sensual abandon at the court, with much official hysteria and fun, with the Sa'adabat (Palace of Happiness) pleasure dome ruling palace activity. One example of this trend was tulipmania. Tulips had long been the emblem of the Ottoman royal house; as a result, the courtiers wrote poetry about them, and artisans included them in wood inlays and wove them into textiles. They symbolized romantic love, and the palace was often covered in intricate displays of the blooms.

There were also tentative moves toward "modernization" on the European model. The French helped organize, in 1720, a fire brigade in the city, while the first Turkish printing press began in 1729. Its organizers represented the nature of Istanbuli society at the time: the press was organized by an eastern European slave working with the son of the French ambassador and supported with Jewish funds. The press published seventeen books, including volumes on Turkish grammar (in French) and a treatise on syphilis, before it was closed down in 1742.

The Janissaries were a major barrier to modernization. They had started out as the slave soldiers of the sultan, the first professional army of the modern era. Over the centuries, however, they had come to value their privileges as kingmakers and upholders of tradition, and so they resisted modernization, in particular the introduction of a new musket citizen corps. By the early 1800s, they were completely out of control in the city, robbing whom they wished (including the *Kadi*, the Turkish form of *qadi,* or "judge," of Istanbul), stealing from shopkeepers, and challenging government policy. In June 1826, there was a particularly vicious revolt by the Janissaries, as they overturned their soup cauldrons in their traditional signal of rebellion. Finally, it was too much, and the sultan organized a counteruprising, unfurled the black banner of the Prophet to rally legitimacy to his side, and ordered the city's citizens to hunt them down. With glee, the citizens of Istanbul complied, killing some 10,000 of them on the first day. This was the end of this ancient core of the Ottoman military, and a new phase of standardization, professionalism, and modern tactics commenced.

Most port cities in the Mediterranean experienced considerable growth during the nineteenth century based on expanded international trade, and Istanbul was no exception. Its population increased from about 375,000 in the 1830s to more than 1 million by the beginning of World War I. There was a huge increase in the construction of private, public, business, and religious buildings throughout the city. There were also great changes in the urban infrastructure. Communication via the telegraph tied the capital into its provinces as never before, a postal service was instituted, new forms of transportation such as the steamship allowed suburbs to expand up the Bosphorus, and the city became a healthier place to live and work. Minorities became more central in mediating the city's economy, as did their European backers.

Such changes also encouraged the appearance of an independent press. In Istanbul, the Crimean War of the 1850s spurred the first journals and newspapers. By the 1870s, there were forty-seven journals in Istanbul, most of them in Greek, French, or Armenian. The first nonofficial journal in Turkish, *Ceride-i Havadis,* was founded by an Englishman in 1840. The journal gave voice both to some of the first Turkish writers in addition to introducing Western literary and nonliterary writing in translation; *Les Misérables,* for example, was serialized in 1862. Toward the end of the century, journals such as *Ahmet Midhat's Tercuman-i Hakikat* (1878) and Ibrahim Sinasi's *Tasvir-i Efkar* (1861) were contributing to the push for modern education and to the formation of a broader reading public. Sinasi, for example, called in his editorials for the right for readers to express their opinions and constantly stressed the liberal ideas of freedom, justice, equality, and constitutional government. The ideas expressed in this new medium had a powerful effect on the new secret societies that emerged during this period as they considered how to reform the empire's political system.

Beginning in the 1830s, the government embarked on a series of reforms and modernization that lasted into the 1880s. In its early period, the Tanzimat (reorganization) was top-down, instigated by the government. Within the city, there was a period of quiescence, with little organizing or political action among the people. After 1860, however, this began to shift as Istanbul became the site for all the contradictions these changes implied. The appearance of the press, the increase in European interference within the governance of the empire, and the weakening power of the government all created political space for new forms of action. Secret societies of

intellectuals and military officers, such as the Young Ottomans, began to talk about and organize for political modernization. In response, Sultan Abdelhamid II became the first sultan to enter the political arena and to attempt to manipulate popular feeling.

The 1908 revolution emerged from sporadic mutinies in the provinces fomented by young military officers, but its core and heart lay in Istanbul. The Committee of Union and Progress (CUP or Young Turks, as they became known) used the telegraph and expatriate press available to them in the capital in innovative ways to promote their ideas and to organize their movement as well as to spread their arguments along the new global information highway. Although Sultan Abdulhamid called for elections on 23 July 1908 and agreed to limit his authority, in reality little progress was made. Finally, on 13 April 1909, there was a popular revolt in Istanbul, led by religious groups and army units who supported the 1908 revolution but were disaffected with the CUP. The CUP emerged on top, however, when they occupied the city on 24 April, the sultan was dethroned, and the CUP implemented authoritarian rule. Interestingly, Abdulhamid spent the rest of his life under house arrest in Istanbul, watching boats sail up and down the Bosphorus. Huge crowds of Stambulis attended the funeral of this last great sultan in February 1918. He never lived to see what he had so eloquently predicted: the entrance of British occupying forces into the city, and the resultant breakup of the empire, as the result of Ottoman participation in World War I.

With Turkish unconditional surrender, European powers occupied Istanbul on 13 November 1918. For the next five years, they remained in the city as they schemed over possible ways to divide the Ottoman spoils. Among other plans, they contemplated transforming Istanbul into an international city. Such proposals died with the liberation of the city in October 1923 by Turkish nationalist forces under Atatürk, who immediately subordinated Istanbul to the new capital in Ankara (see also "Ankara").

In the drive to create a unified Turkish nation-state, there was no place for a cosmopolitan, pluralistic, world city like Istanbul, chaotic and commanding regional trade networks in its own right, caught up in and responsive to a global economic system. Over the next three decades, state policy sought to contain, control, and limit the city's networks, with the Ankara-based elite essentially "declaring war" on the corruption and degeneration of Istanbul. Engineering Istanbul's economic and social ties for broader political purposes was not new; the Romans, Byzantines, and Ottomans all had varied success with similar attempts. But it was the Turkish state that attempted this in its most powerful and focused form. This forced-march project involved remaking, in a generation, urban society: secularize, change the alphabet, emancipate women, industrialize, and shave off beards. Yet by the end of his life, even Atatürk had realized this strategy was not working; he was constantly drawn back to the city and died there in 1938. Today almost one-half of the country's wealth and income are generated by this conurbation, which holds almost one-fifth of its population: how can one distinguish between national and Stambuli interests?

The city's exceptional growth and expansion during the age of globalization holds within it many significant paradoxes. A growing divide between modernity and tradition resonated across the city and does to this day. A tension between the Islamic promise of this blessed city and its degeneration and estrangement from its responsibilities drives Islamists to reconquer a degenerate Istanbul. Stagnation and decay set in to many areas, as the suburbs expanded exponentially up both sides of the Bosphorus. *Gecekondu* settlements (built overnight or illegal cities), constructed by rural migrants setting up shanties wherever they could, make up more than half of the city's population and have forced the municipality to consider and reconsider its responsibilities for services. Istanbul is now, thanks to chain migration from the southeast, the "largest Kurdish city" in the world, mixing with its forty-seven other different ethnic communities. Motorways blasted away to the north, east, and west have become the core, and bane, of a city that "can not be crossed in a day" because of its incessant traffic. Perhaps the new Marmaray Bosphorus rail tunnel will decrease the city's congestion when it is finished in 2009; it may just create a megacorridor running from Izmit on the east to Tekirağ on the west. As for visitors, the city certainly attracts tourists, but it also has reemerged as "the" capital of central Asia, the Middle East, and Eastern Europe, drawing the less-well-heeled suitcase traders, who fly into its markets or disembark from its ferries, stock up, and return home laden with products to sell.

Bruce Stanley

Further Readings

Brown, Kenneth, and Robert Waterhouse, eds. "Istanbul: Many Worlds." *Mediterraneans* 10 (winter 1997–1998).

Downey, Glanville. *Constantinople in the Age of Justinian.* Norman: University of Oklahoma Press, 1960.

Eldem, Edhem, Daniel Goffman, and Bruce Masters. *The Ottoman City between East and West: Aleppo, Izmir, and Istanbul.* Cambridge: Cambridge University Press, 1999.

Freely, John. *Istanbul: The Imperial City.* London: Penguin Books, 1998.

Keyder, Caglar, ed. *Istanbul: Between the Global and the Local.* Oxford: Rowman and Littlefield, 1999.

Lewis, Bernard. *Istanbul and the Civilization of the Ottoman Empire.* Norman: University of Oklahoma Press, 1982.

Mansel, Philip. *Constantinople, City of the World's Desire, 1453–1924.* London: Penguin Books, 1997.

Pamuk, Oran. *Istanbul: Memories and the City.* London: Faber and Faber, 2005.

Runcimen, Steven. *The Fall of Constantinople, 1453.* Cambridge: Cambridge University Press, 1990.

Izmir
Population: 3.37 million (2005 estimate)

Often called "the pearl of the Aegean," Izmir (also known as Smyrna) has a long and glorious history as an Aegean port on the western coast of Asia Minor. More than 4,000 years old, the city has been fought over by Greeks, Persians, Romans, Byzantines, and Turks, even up through the twentieth century. Home to a pluralistic, multicultural, and mixed religious port community, it has hosted Sophists, Pythagoreans, Jews, Christians, and Sunnis in a cosmopolitan mix that made it unique across the history of the region. As an industrial, agricultural, and port city, this important Turkish conurbation today plays a key role in connecting the Anatolian plateau to the world economy. In the past, it was home to European merchants shipping opium, tobacco, cotton, and angora wool to meet the demands of new global fashion.

Izmir (Proto Greek, *Smurna;* Latin, *Smyrnae;* Greek, *Smirni;* Turkish, *Izmir*) is located on the western edge of Anatolia (Asia Minor) at the eastern tip of the narrow Gulf of Izmir that juts inland from the Aegean Sea. This deepwater port is nestled around the southern shore and the small fertile plain that surrounds the head of a calm and dramatic Gulf, backed by the Kemer Stream and hills, and has reminded many visitors of a gigantic natural theater; the city now extends up Kadifekale (Mount Pagos) and around to the north to include the older site of Old Smyrna (Bayrakli). Ephesus lies some 35 miles to the south, the ruins of Sardis are 45 miles inland to the east, and Istanbul is 400 miles to the northeast. Access inland to Sardis and the Anatolian Plateau is through a valley running north to the Hermus River then east. The climate is mild, and its hinterland has been called the vegetable garden of western Anatolia for its productivity. On a clear day, it is possible to see Athens from the top of Mount Pagos.

Although there are Neolithic sites in the area, and village agriculture was practiced in the valleys of the region after 8000 BC, the earliest known habitation of size in the vicinity dates from around 2500 BC, at a site now called Bayrakli (Old Smyrna), a few miles north around the coast from the current city. This site was initially on a small island, which has since become incorporated into the shore. These Early Bronze Age inhabitants were culturally part of the same community as those found around the coast as far north as Troy and coincide with the period of the founding of that city.

By the early second millennium BC, a new cultural group, the Luwians, appear in the archaeological record of southwest Anatolia, and their Indo-European language dominates the coast and the hinterland. Although the Luwians' origins continue to be hotly debated, the Bayrakli site became incorporated into this linguistic community after 1900 BC. Pottery finds dating from ca. 1400 BC, for example, suggest cultural ties to the Mycenaeans and the Aegean.

Out of the Luwian linguistic community arose a kingdom called Arzawa, which included the Bayrakli site. Concurrent with the establishment of Arzawa, the Hittites first appear in the central Anatolian written record during the sixteenth century BC, around the city of Hattusa (modern Bogazkoy), which became their capital. They adopted a cuneiform writing system for their Indo-European language and developed a scribal tradition that lasted across the next four centuries. By 1530 the Hittites went to war with the Arzawa numerous times, although it was not until the mid-fourteenth century that the Hittite Empire reached its peak. Around 1340 the Hittite king Suppiluliuma took on the Arzawa and probably conquered the area of Smyrna. Later, King Mursila II records that he had to reconquer the territory following a revolt and that he left behind governors. The swift end of the empire, however, ca. 1200, saw a general setback to trade, exchange, and cities throughout the region, and the port stagnated.

Out of the general chaos of the next 200 years, Greek colonists, the Aeolians, arrived along the coast ca. 1050 BC and assumed control over Bayrakli and the local population. They established a new city, which became known as Ti-Smurna (perhaps related to myrrh or bitter), just south of the old site along the coast, at the base of Mount Sipylus. The culture was based primarily on the extraction of agricultural surplus from locals working in the inland valleys. Archaeological remains appear in the ninth century and then pass through thirteen phases up until the classical period, starting with oval mud-brick houses, which gave way over the next 300 years to rectangular houses and to the first defensive walls. It is around this time that Homer, perhaps from Smyrna, penned the *Iliad*.

Around the end of the ninth century, a second wave of Greek invaders, the Ionians, occupied the coast and captured Smyrna and the Aeolian cities to its south. By 750 BC, the city's architecture indicates growing wealth and sophisticated construction techniques and the first signs of imports from the Levant. The city was not a large one, however, and may have only covered seventy acres of land and hosted a few thousand citizens. Part of the reason for its small size may have been that sea trade along this part of the coast had not yet developed. Another was the colonial nature of the city's relationship to the hinterland and the local inhabitants; the city lived by forced extraction or slave labor. The Ionian cities became linked together into the Panionion, a political league of Ionian cities, and the concept of the polis, or city-state, appears to have had its start here.

Ionian civilization in Smyrna reached its peak after 650 BC. Smyrna's primary temple, dedicated to Athena and founded in 690, was enlarged at the end of the century. Exquisite walls, capitals for columns, and other refinements to the temple indicate a unique prosperity among Greek cities.

The city's walls were enlarged and refined, presumably to enclose a city that was now planned and laid out on a north-south grid with perpendicular streets and strategically located markets. A number of the most extensive houses had private bathrooms and terra-cotta-lined baths. The city possessed a music culture using the lyre and clearly was in the forefront of early bronze statue manufacturing; early Ionian art motifs were already in evidence in Smyrna earlier than in other Greek cities. It also began a long history of minting coins around this time; one of the earliest shows a lion's head on a shield, memorializing the goddess Cybele, who was worshipped on the city's high places.

After the eighth century BC, trade along the coast expanded dramatically, and Smyrna grew with it. Excavations have revealed clear indications of international trade, particularly with Cyprus and, by extrapolating from the diversity of gods worshipped in the city, the existence of numerous communities of foreign traders. The Ionian cities sent out colonists of their own across the Mediterranean and into the Black Sea as far as what is now Trabzon (see also "Trabzon"). Smyrniote were, the archaeological record shows, participants in this colonization of the Pontus. By the seventh century, local production replaced many imported goods, and Ionia became a net exporter of metalwork, perfumes, painted pottery, and textiles.

Inland states like Lydia and Phrygia also developed, spurred by trade via ports like Smyrna but also by the development of trans-Anatolian routes as well as their control of inland production. Conflicts inevitably arose between Lydia, with its capital in Sardis, and the closest port city, Smyrna, which extracted customs duties and accumulated wealth at the inland city's expense. As recorded by Herodotus, after a number of attacks on the city, the Lydians under King Alyattes captured Smyrna again in 600 BC and this time destroyed the city and its walls. Strabo writes that Alyattes cleansed the city of its inhabitants, forcing them to move to the countryside.

For the next 300 years, only limited rebuilding occurred on the site, although the sanctuary was restored. The history of the region changed, however, in 546, when the Achaemenids under Cyrus captured Sardis. Despite significant resistance, indicated in the city's archaeological record by a barricaded city gate, the city-states of Ionia could not withstand the power of this centralized empire and were incorporated into the state. A provincial satrapy was established in Sardis, and that city became the terminus for the Royal Road to Persepolis and Susa. Soon they continued the road to Symrna, which became a port for trade with the Mediterranean. Smyrna served, along with other ports in the Gulf of Smyrna, as the assembly point for the invasion of Greece as well as where the remnants of the Persian fleet wintered after their defeat at Salamis (480). However, Smyrna was overshadowed by other Ionian cities, for example, Miletos.

By the early fourth century, Athens was asserting its power across to the Gulf of Smyrna and taxing imports and exports to the city at 5 percent. However, in the political situation at the time, Persia's only outlet to the Mediterranean was through the Gulf of Smyrna and the small port of Smyrna and its larger neighbor on the north coast, Phocaea. Thus, they reasserted their dominance and used the ports to build and mount an attack on rebellious Cyprus in 387.

Alexander the Great captured the city with his victory over the Persians in 334 and reportedly wintered in the area. One tradition holds that Alexander, sleeping under a tree on Mount Pagos, had a vision from Nemeseis (in Smyrna the goddess was worshipped as a double being, hence Nemeseis) that the city should be refounded on a new site, some three miles to the south along the coast from the ancient tell. After Alexander's death, the general Lysimachus gained control of Smyrna with his victory at the Battle of Ipsus (301 BC), and he laid out the new city and supported the construction of its fortress. When Lysimachus was killed in battle (281), the city came under the rule of the Seleucid Empire.

In the struggles for control of western Anatolia that wracked the region over the next century, Smyrna ended up under the rule of nearby Pergamum, and despite a number of sieges and attacks, it survived to the Peace of Apamea (188 BC) to pass under Roman overlordship. With the end of the kingdom of Pergamum in 133, the city was incorporated into the Roman province of Asia. Quickly, the city gained a reputation as a staunch friend and ally of Rome, and this reputation lasted across the next 500 years, for which it was shown great favoritism and reward. For example, in 130 BC, the city saved a Roman army from starvation and clothed its soldiers against the winter cold. In 84 BC, although under duress the city had fallen to Mithridates, its citizens did not massacre those Romans within the city as did so many other nearby cities but expelled the Mithridates garrison and supported Sulla's army in Asia. Recorded by Taitus, all this made up their claim, presented in AD 26, to the right to host the provinces' cult of Tiberius and their continued recognition as *civitas libera* (a free state). The city was home to a community of Roman traders and hosted Nemeseia, Greek games of athletic and dramatic programs dedicated to the deities, which attracted participants and audiences from across the region. Its acropolis, rising on Mount Pagos high above the city, was known as the "crown of Smyrna" for its beautiful monuments.

During the classical period, Smyrna became famous for its educational establishments and the reputation of its scholars. Around 130 BC, an eminent physician, Hikesios, founded a medical school at Smyrna. Some seventy years later, one of the teachers at the school was the medical writer Hermogenes; he reportedly lived seventy-seven years, wrote seventy-seven medical books, and was the author of a history of the city. Galen the Physician studied at the school for a time. The city also hosted many Sophists, legal scholars, and philosophers, including the rhetorician Aelius Aristides (AD 117–181) and the mathematician Theon of Smyrna (ca. AD 120). Reportedly, Aristides, a member of the Second Sophistic group, wrote such a moving letter to Emperor Marcus Aurelius concerning the destruction of Smyrna by the earthquake of 178 that the emperor cried and granted funds for the city's resurgence. Subsequently, the people of Smyrna erected a statue to Aristides as the "savior" of their city. Known for its devotion to the sophistic muses, Smyrna also hosted a *museion* (college and library) that was famous for its Pythagorean and Platonic ideology.

The writer Strabo had many fine things to say about this "first city" of Ionia in the first century BC. He talked about the city plan, its wide streets, the Homereium (shrine and statue of Homer), and the gymnasium and stadium that marked out this city of perhaps 80,000 people. He also comments on the fig-growing industry in Smyrna. Interestingly, there is still a fig industry in the city, and it was Smyrna figs that provided the basis for the nascent California fruit industry. The agora of the Roman city has been excavated and shows tripledecked stoas around the edges and a Nemeseion (temple to the goddess Nemesis) on one side. Two committees, one a People's Council and the other a smaller senate, ruled the city. Records indicate that Smyrna participated in intense intercity rivalry with Ephesus and Pergamum for top rank as the "first city of Asia" and that competitions and sacred games played a role in this rivalry, as did monumental buildings and temples to the gods (see also "Ephesus").

The city had a large Jewish community during the first century AD, and the records show regular contributions from this community to the Nemeseia games. The worshippers of Dionysos and the Pythagorean and Platonic students continued to dominate the discussions in the agora. Within this mix, the early Christian missionaries were able to find a receptive audience, and the records on the development of the church in Smyrna are more complete than for any other Christian community of the period except Rome. Paul passed through the city on his way to Macedonia in AD 55, and the church followed in the Pauline traditions of organization and doctrine. By AD 100, according to the letters of Saint Ignatius, who was conveyed through the city as a prisoner on his way to death in Rome, the community was too large to meet in one assembly, and they were holding services in house-churches. Smyrna is one of the "seven churches of Asia" included in John's Revelations, and it had many martyrs. The most famous was Saint Polycarp, bishop in AD 156, the last of those who had known the apostles. Along with eleven others, Polycarp was burned at the stake. Tradition holds that since the flames refused to touch him, he had to be stabbed to death to carry out the sentence. There were other martyrs in AD 177, and in 250 Pionius was jeered by the assembled crowds of various religious persuasions on his way to execution for his faith.

Under the Byzantines, Smyrna was a key naval base and dockyard. Following the rise of the Arab Muslim Empire, as the Arabs attempted to capture Constantinople (particularly 670–677), Smyrna was harmed by persistent naval raids along the coast although never actually captured.

Following the Byzantine defeat at the Battle of Manzikert in 1071, Seljuq Turks quickly moved to conquer Smyrna (1076). In Turkish the city was called *Izmirni* (the Smyrna). By 1080 Amir Caka Bey (Tzachas) assumed control over what became the short-lived amirate of Izmir and used the port as a naval base from which to attack Byzantine shipping. With the help of Greek shipwrights, he constructed a fleet of 100 vessels, organized his palace in Izmir much like that of the court in Constantinople, and was able, over the next decade, to establish his authority along a considerable portion of the coast. Caka Bey's son-in-law, the sultan of Nicaea, however, killed him (1092) in an attempt to unify all the Turkish beys against Byzantium (see also "Iznik"). The Byzantines, however, were subsequently able to recapture the city in 1097 when they showed up both in the Gulf with a fleet and by land with an army while supporting the progress of the First Crusade across Anatolia. With the capture and sack of Constantinople by the Fourth Crusade in 1204, the rump Nicaean Lascarid Empire used Smyrna as their key port to the Mediterranean until their recapture of Constantinople in 1261. Crucially, as part of the deal with the Genoese for their help in retaking the Byzantine capital, Michael Palaeologus agreed that Smyrna was to be completely under Genoese control.

By the early fourteenth century, the region of southwest Anatolia and the Aegean Islands were in chaos in the wake of the fall of the Seljuqs and the end of Mongol rule to the east. Into the vacuum stepped two contenders. The Aydin Turkoman dynasty arose in the southwest corner on Anatolia, conquered Smyrna in 1320, and controlled the coast from their capital at Aydin. From his naval base at Izmir, Umur Bey sent out his fleet to attack European and Byzantine shipping throughout the Aegean. To the south, the Knights of Saint John had fled the final capture of Acre (1291) to Cyprus and then moved to capture the island of Rhodes (1309). By 1319 they had progressed as far as the island of Simie. Finally, in 1344, under a coalition of Crusaders assembled by Pope Clement VI, the Knights of Rhodes, as they now called themselves, battled the amir's fleet at the entrance to the Gulf, defeated them, and then captured Smyrna, although the citadel remained in Turkish hands. The Hospitallers' rule of the city lasted until the whirlwind called Temür required the captured Ottoman sultan, Bayezid, to witness him sack Smyrna in December 1402. In the wake of Temür's return to Samarkand, Cunayd, the last Aydin ruler, resumed control, until he himself was captured and executed by the resurgent Ottomans under Murat II in 1426.

After the Ottoman conquest, western Anatolia became primarily a state farm, providing food and supplies for the capital city of Istanbul. The government came to see Izmir and its hinterland as a resource to be exploited for its fruit, grains, cottons, and woolens, which were destined for the capital city. As a result, Izmir did not grow, and around 1580 it was a small port, housing around 2,000 inhabitants. There were, however, Europeans in the form of the Ragusans, Genoese, and Venetians, for example, who were allowed limited access, via the port, to western Anatolia for some local produces (Ankara mohair and cotton) and as a transshipment route for silks from Iran. Izmir, if it counted at all in world trade, was primarily as a source of smuggled grains.

Beginning around 1600, however, the city began to grow and expand, so that within a century it was the largest city in Anatolia and the key port for the Ottoman Empire. Academics continue to disagree as to the primary reasons for its spectacular rise during the seventeenth century. Some argue the need for an alternative Mediterranean port for Iranian silk as the ancient terminus, Aleppo, was wracked by violence; others stress instead the dramatic rise in European demand for the agricultural products of the Izmiri hinterland: grain, cotton, and raisins. Other factors of importance appear to include the monopoly nature of Venetian control in the ancient emporium of Aleppo and the need of the new Atlantic powers of Holland, France, and England to develop virgin ports for their trade (see also "Aleppo"). Add the growing power of local agricultural producers interested in increasing their profits by shipping to European buyers rather than selling to government monopolies that kept prices artificially low, and you have a recipe for mushrooming growth. Whatever the combination of factors, Izmir dramatically evolved in a few decades from a regional port serving the interests of a medieval Italian trade regime into a boomtown of the world economy.

The city quickly attracted Jewish, Greek, and Armenian tradesmen (a tenfold increase in non-Muslims over sixty years) who acted as brokers or providers for the expanding foreign community in the city; the Jews, for example, placed themselves under the protection of the French consul, while the Armenians had more than 100 businesses in the city by 1610. Europeans came to live in the city to facilitate trade; in 1600 there were no consuls there, but by 1620 the English, French, Dutch, and Venetians were all represented. The English Levant Company established a factory there in 1610, and by the late 1600s it was the English who held the favorable position in the city. Known to the local Izmiris as the worst drunks of all the Europeans, the English even played out their domestic political divisions of the midcentury, between cavalier and Roundhead, in the streets of Izmir, with running battles between partisans. With its taverns open all hours and its numerous churches, Izmir had become a new beast, a "colonial port city," what the Ottomans came to call *Gavur Izmir* (infidel Izmir), floating free of Ottoman control.

Muslims from the hinterland flocked to the city for work, and other rival ports declined. Local artisans went out of business, since they could not afford the spiraling prices of basic commodities caused by European demand, and bands of local pirates and brigands organized. The Ottoman government failed to respond creatively to these developments or to protect the people of Izmir from them. Social relations throughout the region were disrupted, and the city's population spiraled; by 1650 the city's population was around 40,000.

Izmir was a huge market, with one observer in 1693 calling it "nothing but a great bazaar and fair." The growing agricultural trade of the early 1600s attracted the Iranian silk trade, so that by the last half of the century, great camel caravans arrived in the city in January, February, June, and October each year, with the best Iranian raw silk arriving en masse on the January run. The French in particular bought silk, transporting more than 600 bales to Marseille each year. For the year 1702, it was estimated that 2,000 bales of Iranian silk were brought into the city.

The city continued its growth during the eighteenth century. Despite a major earthquake and fire in 1688 (which completely destroyed the city and killed perhaps 15,000), within two years the city was back to full functionality, thanks to investment by the foreign community. There were other earthquakes in 1737, 1739, 1765, and 1778 and a major fire in 1742. Numerous diseases, brought to the city by caravan, meant that, during the eighteenth century, Izmir suffered almost continuous epidemics and plagues. Bubonic plague was the major killer and only died out in the nineteenth century; the epidemic in 1812 reportedly killed more than one-fifth of the city's inhabitants. Cholera then became the scourge of the city during the nineteenth century.

Amid such death and uncertainty, Izmir produced one of the most interesting leaders of a messianic movement, Sabbatai Zevi. Zevi's father was a Jewish immigrant to the city in the early 1600s who began by selling eggs on the street. Gradually, the family became wealthy brokers, and the third son was allowed to train for the Torah with some of the leading rabbis who had also migrated to Izmir. In the mid-seventeenth century, both Judaism and Christianity were expecting the new age to dawn and for a messiah to appear. Zevi proclaimed his messiahship in Smyrna, and as he traveled the Sabbataian movement spread from Jerusalem to Amsterdam, with both poor and wealthy following this messiah. Predicting the end of the world on 18 June, 1666, he traveled to Istanbul to be there to seize power from the sultan. Imprisoned by the Muslim authorities, he converted to Islam to escape death and died in 1676. The movement he founded was the most widespread messianic movement in Jewish history and con-

tinued in Europe for years; there were reportedly groups of believers and sects of Sabbataians in Smyrna well into the twentieth century. Other Jews in Smyrna, the so-called Portuguese (Sephardic) Jewish community in the city, were allowed in 1694 to trade under the Dutch flag, and after 1730 the Dutch allowed Jewish, Armenian, and Greek merchant families of Izmir to establish family members in Amsterdam to facilitate trade.

The mix and amounts of products passing through the port evolved over time, as did their key destinations. Increasingly, angora wool from Ankara was transshipped, and during the late 1700s cotton became the key export crop; cotton demand only declined in the 1800s with the appearance of American cotton on the global market and then briefly increased during the American Civil War. During the late 1700s, Boston was the key distribution point for opium and figs imported from Smyrna. Such trade came indirectly via Britain. With the American Revolution, however, Boston traders made directly to Smyrna and brought coffee, sugar from the Caribbean, Indian cottons, indigo, and spices to trade. Smyrna was the primary Middle East port for American skippers in the early 1800s, and although the first U.S. consul in Smyrna was appointed in 1802, he was soon withdrawn, leaving American skippers with no "capitulations" guaranteeing them favored trade with the empire and no representation. As a result, for ten years, American ships would hoist the British flag of convenience as they entered Smyrna port. With the support of the Levant Company, and the equivocal agreement of the Foreign Ministry, by 1810 American ships were carrying up to one-quarter of all trade between Smyrna and England.

With the War of 1812, this agreement ended, and American merchants temporarily disappeared from Smyrna. They returned in 1815 and traded under the American flag and a new arrangement with the Porte as "guests of the Sultan." Boston continued to be the key link to the United States. It was not until 1823 that another consul was appointed. Interestingly, Daniel Webster and Henry Clay's strong support for Greek independence in 1824 jeopardized the Boston-Smyrna trade, and many Bostonian merchants refused to serve on the Boston Committee for Greek Relief, believing their access to Smyrna would suffer.

The city attracted all sorts of Europeans, including scientists and gentlemen scholars. The Englishman William Sherard (1659–1728) was, from 1703 to 1716, the English Levant Company consul in Smyrna. He was a botanist and naturalist and created a unique botanical garden of Middle Eastern plants in a ten-acre plot outside the city. The garden attracted many of the increasing number of European "tourists" stopping in the city on the grand tour. Sherard's last will and testament bequeathed the garden, 12,000 pressed plants, and his library, manuscripts, and fortune to the University of Oxford to support a chair in botany; the Sherardian professorship at Oxford still exists today. A century later, the English gentleman scientist John Griffitt, involved in silk farming near Smyrna, helped revive Anatolian sericulture by investigating and halting the cataclysmic effects of silkworm diseases, which struck the region in the 1880s.

During the 1800s, Izmir was the major port for the export of Anatolian opium to Europe and China. The Dutch Levant Company was particularly involved in promoting this trade, and half of all Dutch exports from Izmir were in opium. Although the Ottoman government initially sought to monopolize this trade during the 1830s, their scheme broke down, and for the rest of the century, Dutch trading families, like the Van Lenneps or the Wissings, who had settled in Izmir, dominated the city's opium trade. Starting earlier with silk, they expanded to opium, often shipping it directly to Indonesia, but often fell to internecine fighting requiring intervention from Den Haag. They had their own court systems separate from that of the Ottoman state and often supported Greek insurgency. Ironically, by the end of the century, the Dutch, British, and American governments were attempting to halt the very opium trade they had earlier promoted.

As Britain sped headlong in the 1800s into the industrial age, its ties to Izmir encouraged investment in the city's infrastructure and hinterland. Money was invested in improving the port, starting in 1867, to make it larger and more efficient. British investors bought up vast landholdings around Izmir, expecting to create large plantations or colonies that would supply the industrial factories of England. It was even proposed that Scottish workers be established in colonies in the district to bring civilization and scientific farming methods to Izmir. Little came of these plans, but British investors did finance a railroad from Izmir into Anatolia to move bulk products to the port; by 1913 the line between Izmir and Aydin carried more than half of all the exports from Izmir directly to quayside.

Another increase in production and export occurred between 1897 and 1913. The export of Izmiri figs nearly doubled, tobacco exports tripled, and cotton quadrupled. The new industry of cigarette making found a home in the city and employed many women. Izmir also hosted the largest ironworks in the Ottoman world, employing 200 workers. Textile-printing factories also grew up in the city; by 1900, 1.2 million head scarves, printed on imported English cotton cloth, were shipped into the interior. The value of carpet exports also tripled, partly because six British trading companies headquartered in Izmir monopolized the whole carpet production process; 1,000 looms employing some 2,500 weavers and a host of dyers, spinners, and brokers produced most of the empire's carpets.

By the late nineteenth century, new organizations arose in Izmir to organize and regulate the production, processing, and sale of agricultural produces. There was the Tobacco Regie, a government company with monopoly rights to grow and sell tobacco, although there was the American tobacco company established in Izmir that had rights to only export tobacco. Another example was the commercial firm the Smyrna Fig Packers, which cornered the sale of raisins and figs. A word should be said about the çetes (a term for armed irregulars, bandits, brigands) who organized into informal enterprises that controlled much of Izmir's hinterland in the late 1800s and through 1922: one estimate has more than 4,000 bandits organized in numerous groups. Despite attempts by the Ottoman government to control these often mixed-religion groups or tribal-based gangs, the government never succeeded, and forced extraction of protection money was the norm.

The built environment of the city was transformed at this time. Numerous foreign schools and academies opened, as did an Alliance Israélite Universelle school. Grand villas appeared along the corniche, new hospitals were funded, a streetcar line was built, and early gas and then electric lights were installed. The Izmir of 1908 was not a segregated city, there were no walls between neighborhoods or regulations to divide the various communities from each other, and it was hard to tell to which community someone belonged, with most residents fudging conventional community boundaries. This process was helped by the fact that the city was a cultural hothouse, hosting numerous newspapers and journals in a range of languages, containing seventeen printing houses, and attracting Italian operas to its public theater. Its municipal council contained Muslims, Jews, Armenians, Greeks, and foreigners; even the fire brigade was mixed.

World War I brought an end to this unique urban environment. The Allies, parceling out the Ottoman Empire in anticipation of victory, reached a number of secret agreements concerning Anatolian territory. One, the Saint Jean de Maurienne Agreement of April 1917, committed Britain, France, and Italy to Italy's future control of southern Asia Minor, including the city and vilayet (province or large administrative district) of Smyrna. With the defeat of the empire, and the unfolding of Allied plans for dividing up Anatolia, resistance coalesced as early as December 1918, with Turkish national groups such as Mudafaai Hukuk (Societies for the Defense of Rights) organizing in Izmir and Rumelia.

In February 1919, the Greek prime minister presented the Peace Conference in Paris with a formal claim to possession of Smyrna. David Lloyd George and Georges Clemenceau backed the claim, partly to forestall the Italians, and on 15 May a Greek military division (supported by American, British, and French warships) landed at Smyrna, intending to permanently establish the "Great Idea" of Greek control of both sides of the Aegean. At the time, the city's population may have been around 300,000, with a majority non-Muslim. Local Greeks welcomed the troops, the Metropolitan of Smyrna blessed them, and then they set about massacring Turks in the city.

Ironically, the Greek army shot men wearing the fez, based on the mistaken belief that Izmiri Greeks did not wear such head-gear; as a result, a number of Greek men were killed. The invasion of Izmir produced a profound outpouring of Turkish national feeling, and it was four days later that Mustafa Kemal (Atatürk) landed in Samsun on the Black Sea coast and kicked off the Milli Mücadele (national struggle).

Although initially successful along the Aegean coast, the Greek campaign finally bogged down by 1921, and subsequent Turkish successes after August 1922 put the Greek army on the run. On 8 September 1922, the Greek army withdrew from Izmir, leaving an eerie silence the next morning as the city's population waited for the entry of the Turkish army. More than twenty Allied ships sat in the harbor and did not intervene as Mustafa Kemal rode into Smyrna on the ninth. Terror spread in the Greek and Armenian populations, which included many refugees from the interior, and many fled to the city's port, wishing to escape to the nearby ships. The pier became crammed with those wanting to escape, and there was a rush for the few public buildings designated for the "citizens" of different Allied nations (Americans assembled in the Smyrna cinema, for example).

Turkish forces went on a rampage, pillaging, raping, and executing people on the street; the metropolitan, Chrysostom, who could have escaped but chose to stay, was killed. On 13 September, a huge fire broke out, described by British reporters on the ships as a curtain of fire like twenty volcanoes. Thousands of refugees were caught between the fire and the sea, and their screams could be heard on the ships. The fire destroyed more than half the city; the disputes over who started it, Greek or Turk, continue to rage today on the Internet. For decades the marks remained visible on the city's landscape. Some of the refugees were eventually moved to the ships, and the remaining Greeks were subsequently deported from Izmir as part of the huge transfer of populations that ended the war. Izmiri Greeks ended up primarily in Athens and built a new area of that city called Nea Smirni, while many of the Turks who moved from Greece settled in Izmir. Ever since, the Greeks have called the fall of Smyrna "the catastrophe," while 9 September has been Turkish Independence Day. Ernest Hemingway, a young reporter covering the war from Istanbul, wrote a moving two-page short story called "On the Quai at Smyrna" that helped launch his writing career. Arnold Toynbee, in his book *Western Question in Greece and Turkey,* also talked about what he had witnessed in 1921 with the British. In the 1927 Turkish census, the population of Izmir was 88 percent Muslim, with 184,000 inhabitants.

At Atatürk's side as he entered Izmir was Halide Edip Adivar, an advisor to the general and a leading Turkish woman of the time. Edip was the one who stirred all of Istanbul to the nationalist cause on the day after the Greek invasion of Izmir in 1919 when she gave a resounding nationalist speech at the Sultanahmet. She went on to pen an autobiographical novel of her experiences as a nurse in the nationalist struggle after 1919 called *The Shirt of Flame* and to record her *Memoirs* in 1926. As a novelist, propagandist for Kemal, and university lecturer, Edip was one of the leading early female Turkish voices for modernization, the Turkish state, and for the participation of women in politics. In recording the events that led to the capture of Izmir, she said, "Hell seemed to be on an earth in which two peoples struggled, one for deliverance, another for destruction. There was no quarter given on either side." Cosmopolitan Izmir died in the struggle of two nationalisms.

Atatürk returned to Izmir many times. In 1923, for example, at the Izmir Economic Congress, he presented his radical policies for a European-style legal code, an end to the caliphate, and his plans to romanize the alphabet. Such social policies spurred great opposition throughout the country. In June 1926, just as he was coming to visit Izmir, a conspiracy was uncovered in the city to assassinate him. The assassination was planned by a former deputy in the national assembly who opposed the abolition of the caliphate, but Atatürk entered the city unharmed and quickly established an Independence Tribunal, housed in the Alhambra cinema. The tribunal found the conspirators guilty, and they were executed the next day. The tribunals, however, continued in Izmir, Istanbul, and Ankara and became an excuse to hang hundreds of opposition leaders throughout the country. The city hosted other types of opposition groups as well; a number of Izmiri Communists were arrested in the late 1920s but later released for political reasons relating to Turkey's relationship with the Soviet Union. Not long after, the Turkish government announced to the world that from the beginning of 1930, only letters addressed to Izmir would be delivered; if the name Smyrna was used, the letters would be returned.

Over the last half century, the fertile valleys around Izmir have been the main tobacco-growing areas in Turkey, which made it a natural headquarters for Muzer Makina, a company that builds and supplies tobacco-processing equipment. Today Izmir remains a center for growing sultanas and raisins and for viticulture for winemaking. The city is also attempting to leverage its regional role as a financial and trade center for the Aegean region to attract high-tech development; the Aegean Free Trade Zone offers tax advantages, special labor regulations, and banking services for foreign investors. As the third-largest city in the country, hosting more than 100 high-rise buildings, Izmir can claim a major role in the economic life of the country. With its Grand Canal Project, metro system, and new trade centers, the city dreams of attracting further foreign investment.

The city has significant infrastructural, urban poverty, and discrimination problems. Today the city has many squatter suburbs. Called *gecekondu* (built in a night), such illegal areas of the city are home to many rural poor working in the gray economy. Many Kurds migrated to the city during the 1970s, and it now has one of the highest concentrations of Kurds in the country; as their political status within the country fluctuated over the years, so did their status and inclusion within the city. The Romany (Gypsy) district of the slums of Izmir has been a center for resistance to municipal plans for development as they have become more organized. Izmir also has traditionally had the country's highest concentration of African Turks, descendants of African slaves who made Izmir their home.

As an industrial, agricultural, and port city, Izmir has a large working class, giving politics in the city over the years a leftist slant. In January 1980, for example, there was a strike near Izmir in an agricultural processing complex employing 10,000 workers. The strike and subsequent worker unrest spread to the shantytowns of Izmir. In response, government troops went in to crush the uprising, using armored vehicles and helicopters in pitched battles before they put down the unrest.

The city also has a high concentration of Americans. Since it was established in 1952, the Headquarters, Allied Land Forces Southeastern Europe (HALFSEE) has hosted many American service personnel and their families. Today there are approximately 1,500 U.S. military and their families in Izmir, and there is a new U.S. community center in the city. Some locals resent the inflation in housing costs that they attribute to the Americans and chafe at the restricted access to hospital and education facilities connected to their presence.

Bruce Stanley

Further Readings

Anderson, Sonia P. *An English Consul in Turkey: Paul Rycaut at Smyrna, 1667–1679.* Oxford: Clarendon, 1989.

Cadoux, Cecil John. *Ancient Smyrna: A History of the City from the Earliest Times to 324 AD.* Oxford: Blackwells, 1938.

Dobkin, Marjorie Housepian. *Smyrna, 1922: The Destruction of a City.* London: Faber and Faber, 1972.

Eldem, Edhem, Daniel Goffman, and Bruce Masters. *The Ottoman City between East and West: Aleppo, Izmir, and Istanbul.* Cambridge: Cambridge University Press, 1999.

Frangakis-Syrett, Elena. *The Commerce of Smyrna in the Eighteenth Century (1700–1820).* Athens: Center for Asia Minor Studies, 1992.

Goffman, Daniel. *Izmir and the Levantine World, 1550–1650.* Seattle: University of Washington Press, 1990.

Kastein, Josef. *The Messiah of Izmir.* Translated by Huntley Peterson. New York: Viking Press, 1931.

Iznik
Population: 17,000 (2005 estimate)

Iznik has seen many empires come and go from its site in northwest Asia Minor close to the Sea of Marmara. Founded by the Greeks in the wake of Alexander's death, the city had four great periods of glory: under first-century Roman rule, during the eighth to tenth century under the Byzantines, during the thirteenth century as capital of the Byzantine Empire in exile, and as the center for Ottoman ceramics and tile manufacture during the seventeenth century. Known in the West under its Latin name of Nicaea, the city is probably most famous for the Nicene Creed, the first great statement of Christian doctrine, which emerged from the First Ecumenical Council, held in the city in AD 325.

The city of Iznik (Greek, *Nikaia* or *Nicae;* Latin, *Nicaea*) is located in the Turkish province of Bursa, on the southeastern edge of Lake Iznik (ancient Lake Ascania). It is in the northwest plateau region of Anatolia, approximately fifty miles southeast of Istanbul across the Sea of Marmara and inland from the coast some thirty miles. The region is known for its fertile agriculture, especially its fruit and olive groves. It is believed that in ancient times the present lake was open to the Aegean Sea, providing navigation for small boats to a port just outside the city walls. That is no longer true today. Earth satellite photographs reveal that the North Anatolian Fault system extends beneath and has formed the Sea of Marmara as well as the Gulf of Izmit and Lake Iznik. Numerous earthquakes along this fault system over the centuries have closed up the entrance to the bay, creating Lake Iznik and resulting in regular major damage to Iznik's buildings and to the surrounding region. For instance, a major earthquake in AD 112 ruined much of the city: Emperor Hadrian visited there in AD 123 and directed that the city walls be strengthened and expanded along with major public buildings. In 1999 an earthquake of 7.4 magnitude heavily damaged the city of Izmit, just north of Iznik, killing at least 17,000 persons in the area.

The earliest known inhabitants of the Anatolia region were Neolithic hunter-gatherers dating to 9000 BC; Neolithic painted pottery has been found on the shores of the lake. During the Bronze Age, the Hittites (2000–1200 BC) ruled most of Asia Minor and rivaled Egypt as a Middle Eastern power. Archaeological finds in the Iznik area demonstrate a clear cultural connection between this area and central Anatolia. Other rulers controlled the area during the Iron Age, including the Phrygians of the ninth and eighth centuries and the Lydians after the seventh century, ruling the region from their capital at Sardis. Their last king, Croesus, fabled for his wealth and use of metallic coinage, was overthrown by the Persians in 550 BC, led by Cyrus the Great. From the mid-sixth century until 333 BC, most of Asia Minor was controlled by Persia, although Greek cities along the coast (e.g., Ephesus, Miletus, Priene, etc.) enjoyed a degree of autonomy. In the fourth century, Persian control declined and after 333 BC was supplanted by the Macedonian Empire of Alexander the Great. After Alexander's death, his realm was divided among his followers.

The city of Iznik (Nicaea) dates its origin to 316 BC, when it was established by one of Alexander's generals, Antigonus I, who named it after himself (Antigonia). Shortly thereafter, in 301 BC, following the Battle of Ipsus, it was renamed by another of Alexander's generals, Lysimachos, after his wife, Nikaia. Under the Selucids, the Greek name *Nikaia* (victory) underwent phonetic changes becoming first Nicea, then later Nicaea in Latin. The city prospered because of its location at the intersection of several east-west commercial roads across Anatolia and its access to Byzantium and the coast of the Sea of Marmara.

In the early third century BC, the northern region of Asia Minor along the southern coast of the Black Sea gained independence from the Selucids and divided into two provinces known as Bithynia and Pontus. Bithynia's first ruler was Nicomedes I (r. 278–250 BC). Gradually the Romans expanded their control in the region, and in 74 BC the last Bithynian ruler, Nicomedes III, bequeathed Bithynia to Roman authority. For administrative purposes, Bithynia and Pontus became united. Under the Romans, the city of Nicaea flourished and was fortified as a regional center. Engineers and administrators joined Roman merchants and planners in helping to glorify and transform the city, which attracted numerous tourists. It is estimated the Roman city walls were two and one-half miles long, thirty feet high, and included more than 100 watchtowers with four main city gates. Ruins of the Roman and Byzantine walls and gates are remarkably intact yet today. Nearby was the reputed tomb of Rome's great nemesis, Hannibal, who died in Bithynia, marked by Emperor Septimius Serverus with a marble pillar.

Nicaea was the birthplace of Hipparchus (d. ca. 127 BC), perhaps the greatest of the Greek astronomers. He is credited with discovering the procession of the equinoxes, cataloging more than 1,000 stars, and inventing trigonometry. In addition, he divided the earth sphere into 360 parts, which became the "degrees" of modern geographers, and placed his meridian, or longitude, lines on the equator at intervals of about seventy miles, roughly the dimension of a degree. One historian observed that Hipparchus used celestial phenomena common to the whole earth to locate places on the earth's surface, thus setting the pattern for man's cartographic mastery of the planet.

When the Roman Empire was divided into eastern and western sectors under the leadership of Emperor Constantine I, he established the city of Constantinople (Istanbul) in AD 330 as his eastern capital. The closeness of imperial power contributed to the growing significance of Nicaea. Constantine built a palace in the city, and the city was chosen by him in AD 325 as the location of the First Ecumenical Council. The council was called to settle a heated doctrinal argument regarding the divine/human nature of Jesus of Nazareth, and the disagreement had political as well as religious overtones. Eastern bishops and church leaders numbering more than 300 assembled in Nicaea for a two-month conference to debate the question, presided over by the emperor himself. The issue centered on the question of whether Jesus was truly the "Son of God" and therefore "equal with God," or whether, be-

cause of his human nature, he was somehow "less" than God. An Alexandrian Presbyter named Arius led a faction that contended that Jesus was a human being of "lesser substance" than God, and therefore subordinate to the Creator. The opposition, led by the bishop of Alexandria, supported by an eloquent deacon named Athanasius, contended that Jesus was of "equal substance" with God. The final decision was made by imperial edict, culminating in what is known today as the Nicene Creed. Constantine's direct involvement in the deliberations established henceforth the tradition that in matters of religion, the emperor was a lawful court of appeal. Arius was declared a heretic and was banished from the empire, but the doctrinal question continued to fester and was debated for years to come. In AD 787, another ecumenical gathering was held in Nicaea, the second to be held there. Known as the Seventh Ecumenical Council, it was called by Empress Irene to clarify the religious usage of icons and the meaning of such use in both public and private worship.

Arab attacks on the city, including in 726 and 858, occasionally led to short occupations. However, the city experienced a golden age from the ninth to the eleventh century, with significant monumental buildings and churches added to its built environment. The Monastery of Saint Hyacinthos, destroyed in 1924, lay at the center of the main Christian Quarter, with a church, fruit trees, and a well located within its walls. The city was a pilgrimage city, attracting medieval pilgrims from both the empire and further afield (for example, Saint Willibald from England in the eighth century) to view the site of the various ecumenical councils (the Church of the Fathers along with its mystical image of the "fathers" who attended) as well as the shrines of Saints Tryphon, Diomedes, John the Merciful the Younger, and Neophytos. Saint Tryphon, martyred in the city ca. AD 250, gradually became the city's patron saint, and miracles were regular occurrences at his shrine every February 1; the empire in exile used his image on its coin. The monks of the monastery had such an international reputation that pilgrims would bring other reliquary with them to deposit in the city's shrines. Muslim pilgrims also visited the city; one al-Harawi evidently came ca. 1180 to see the image of the First Ecumenical Council, since some Muslims believed Jesus himself had attended the conclave. There was a small Jewish community in the city as well.

The Seljuq Turk encroachment from the east in the eleventh century began to transform the city. In the famous battle of Manzikert in AD 1071 in eastern Anatolia, Byzantine forces were defeated by the Turks, and the emperor himself was taken prisoner. Nicaea then fell to the Seljuqs in 1078, and they held it for a decade. During this time, Turkish rule intensified in central and eastern Anatolia under the military leadership of Sulayman ibn Qutulmish, bringing with it Islamic culture and influence. He established the Sultanate of Rum (actually "Rome," i.e., Byzantine Empire) and made Nicaea his capital in 1080. Greek historians suggest that the sultan established a residence within the city of Nicaea, but others take issue with this view. Contemporary archaeologists have discovered pottery kilns in Iznik that date from this Seljuq occupation that undoubtedly influenced later artistic design. Emperor Alexius Comnenus reclaimed the city, with the help of the forces of the First Crusade, in May 1097 and rebuilt its walls with the remains of Seljuq tombs.

The erosion of Byzantine political and military power in this region continued apace over the next two centuries, abetted by the onset of the so-called Christian Crusades. Especially damaging to the Byzantines was the Fourth Crusade, in 1203, when marauding soldiers set fire to Constantinople and pillaged the capital city without mercy (see also "Istanbul"). Encouraged and supported by the doge of Venice, Enrico Dandolo, in revenge for previous insults he had received at the hands of the Byzantines, the "Rape of Constantinople" destroyed by fire and theft much of the accumulated art and wealth gathered within Constantinople over a period of nine centuries.

As a result of the invasion and the destruction of Constantinople, large numbers of the former Byzantine court fled to surrounding regions to the east across the Sea of Marmara. Soon a small principality was established in western Anatolia, with Nicaea as its capital. Composed of a variety of refugees, the "empire in exile" was able to survive for more than fifty years (AD 1204–1261) as a political entity. The founder of this fledgling empire was Theodore Lascaris, related through his wife to a former Byzantine emperor, Alexius III. Accompanied by civil and military nobility, the Constantinople patriarchate, and wealthy landowners, this tiny enclave sought to defend itself from the vicelike grip of both the East and West. During his reign, Lascaris was able to defeat the Turkish rulers of the Sultanate of Rum and reached a rapprochement with the Latin rulers in Constantinople.

The importance of this brief moment of history for the city and for broader culture in the area cannot be overestimated. The empire of Nicaea preserved the Orthodox Church and the Orthodox patriarchate, allowing them to eventually be restored to Constantinople. Noting the significance of this short-lived "empire" in Anatolian exile, it has been observed that it provided a nursery of culture that, amid political division, violent international struggle, and internal troubles, saved, protected, and continued the achievements of the former Byzantine Empire. From Nicaea the ruler Michael Palaeologus gained sufficient power to wrest Constantinople from the Crusaders' grasp and march back into the capital city in 1261. Assisted by Genoa, in an attempt to wrest the control of eastern trade from their archrival Venice, Palaeologus reestablished the throne in Constantinople for what was to become the last ruling dynasty of the Byzantine Empire.

By the end of the thirteenth century, the city may have had as many as 50,000 inhabitants. For perhaps political reasons, the city was not sacked by the Mongols, although they came close to the city in 1243 and again in April 1265. With the expansion of Ottoman Turkish control toward the end of the thirteenth century, however, Nicaea became an attractive target and a base for a number of abortive Byzantine campaigns against them. In 1301 the Ottomans captured Baphaeum, a city near Nicaea, and in 1331 Nicaea itself capitulated to their forces. The captured city was renamed Iznik (a Turkish form of Nicaea) and received financial assistance from Sultan Orhan (r. 1324–1360), since one of his wives came from the city. The Haci Ozbek Cami (mosque) was built in 1333, making it the earliest existing Ottoman mosque. A number of madrasas were founded in the city as well, including the Sulayman Pasha Madrasa, which still graces the city.

Immediately the city was cut off from its trade networks to Constantinople, and economic life declined. In addition, the Black Death hit the area in 1347, leaving behind a considerably depleted city population. A Byzantine prisoner, Gregory Palamas (archbishop of Thessaloníki), who was held in the city in July 1355, reports that many of the city's buildings were abandoned, implying that the city's population had significantly declined from its golden days of just 100 years before. Ibn Battuta, who visited around the same time, notes that most of the private homes lay in ruins, although the walls remained undestroyed and surrounded by a moat. Many of the city's Christian population immigrated to Constantinople; the skilled labor headed for Bursa, the Ottoman capital; and the remainder began to convert to Islam (see also "Bursa"). Two letters from the patriarch in Constantinople, ca. 1341, to his flock in Nicaea call on them to renounce their lapse into Islam's evil beliefs. The Ottomans converted the great Hagia Sophia, the site of the First Ecumenical Council, into a mosque.

By the end of the century, all of Asia Minor was under Ottoman control, although nearby Constantinople itself only fell to the Ottomans more than a century later, in April 1453. It was in the second half of the 1500s, however, that Iznik gained worldwide recognition. In 1514 the sultan had forced ceramic artisans from captured Tabriz to relocate in Iznik (see also "Tabriz"). With the major building programs of the mid-1550s under Sulayman the Magnificent (r. 1520–1566), the brilliant ceramic tiles produced in Iznik's factories became the decorative theme. New buildings, especially mosques, in cities such as Damascus, Jerusalem, and Istanbul required massive production of these distinctive tiles. Major technological and artistic changes were introduced that marked Iznik ceramic tiles with a unique beauty. Termed the classical age of Ottoman art, it is estimated that more than 300 pottery workshops were in production within Iznik during the city's heyday, with the city's products exported throughout the empire. By the end of the seventeenth century, however, the quality of Iznik ware had declined and production mainly moved to Istanbul. Today original Iznik tiles are treasured art objects in museums throughout the world. The Turkish government is currently sponsoring efforts to revive this ancient industry, as is the Iznik Foundation.

Following World War I, Iznik experienced turbulent times. Greek forces invaded the city in the summer of 1920, and many of the city's older sections were destroyed during intense fighting. By 1923 they had fled, leaving the city in the hands of the Turkish national army. Today the city is a small town, catering to tourists, agriculture, and a reviving interest in traditional ceramics. The cathedral Hagia Sophia, which hosted the First Ecumenical Council, is today open to tourists, but little remains of the original structure. Of interest within the church are a few partial mosaics depicting the risen Christ. Nearby is the Green Mosque, built in 1378. Its walls are of marble, and the minaret is covered with beautiful Iznik green tiles. A city museum features numerous stone carvings of Roman and Byzantine origin and a variety of artifacts. The current museum director stated in a recent interview that he believes the historic assets of the city and region warrant ad-

ditional development, but as of this date his dream is yet to be achieved. In 1962 the Nineteenth Ecumenical Council, held at the Vatican in Rome, declared Iznik to be a "holy city" and worthy of visitation.

Arthur Stanley

Further Readings

Angold, Michael. *A Byzantine Government in Exile.* Oxford: Oxford University Press, 1975.

Berardino, Angelo, ed. *Encyclopedia of the Early Church.* Translated by Adrian Walford. New York: Oxford University Press, 1992.

Danielou, Jean. *A History of Early Christian Doctrine before the Council of Nicaea.* Translated by David Smith and John Baker. London: Darton, Longman and Todd, 1977.

Denny, Walter B. *Iznik: The Artistry of Ottoman Ceramics.* London: Thames and Hudson, 2004.

Hanfmann, George. *From Croesus to Constantine: The Cities of Western Asia Minor and Their Arts in Greek and Roman Times.* Ann Arbor: University of Michigan Press, 1975.

Ma, John. *Antiochos III and the Cities of Western Asia Minor.* Oxford: Oxford University Press, 2000.

Mitchell, Stephen. *Anatolia: Land, Men, and Gods in Asia Minor.* Oxford: Clarendon Press, 1993.

Vasiliev, Alexander A. *History of the Byzantine Empire.* Madison: University of Wisconsin Press, 1964.

J

Jaffa
Population: 94,000 (1944 census)

Jaffa is an ancient port city with one of the most important natural harbors on the shores of the eastern Mediterranean. As a result, it changed hands on nearly thirty occasions, playing a significant role in the history of the region. It was destroyed and rebuilt many times until in the latter part of the twentieth century, it was absorbed by its modern neighbor, Tel Aviv. Up to that point, it saw many periods of prosperity and decline, which are reflected in its architecture and monuments. Its more recent coming to prominence was in the nineteenth century, where its role as a terminus for the overland trade route from Damascus and Nablus, and then as a point of disembarkation for tourists and pilgrims to Jerusalem, made it a cosmopolitan and vibrant place. While lacking in monumental building of great significance, Jaffa's markets and downtown harbor areas, its heterogeneous population, and its purpose as a center for transit gave it a bustling and lively character. Its eclipse as an important urban center, first by Jerusalem, and then more dramatically by Tel Aviv, has consigned it to a contemporary role as tourist area and artist colony within the greater Tel Aviv metropolis.

The ancient mound of Jaffa (Greek, *Joppa;* Arabic, *Yafa;* Hebrew, *Yafo*) lies on a 100-foot-high rocky outcrop at the southern end of a sandy plain on the eastern Mediterranean littoral and is bounded by two small rivers to the north and east. The port is the closest harbor on the Mediterranean to Jerusalem, thirty miles to the southeast via a gradual valley track. Its climate is subtropical, with contemporary average temperatures at 68 degrees Fahrenheit and an average annual rainfall of two inches falling mostly between November and April. Until the late twentieth century, its agricultural hinterland was productive and famous for its citrus fruits, grapes, and olives, from which it also derived a reputation for soap manufacture. It also was close to grain- and cotton-producing areas. It is its location on the north-south and east-west trade and pilgrimage routes, and its natural harbor, however, that provided the base of its economy and social heterogeneity. In the modern period, its harbor could not take the large ships, and it lost its role to Haifa to the north and Ashdod (nineteen miles to the south) as the shipping gateway to Palestine and Israel.

The first inhabitants of the southern end of this plain appear during Neolithic times (ca. 5000 BC), leaving behind fertility goddesses and goat bones. Chalcolithic (4000–3150 BC) structural remains and burial chambers also mark the site. By 2000 BC, a Canaanite town enclosed with large earth ramparts and a mud-brick gate marked the first urban period. Cypriot pottery and Hyksos remains indicate that by the seventeenth century the town was involved in long-distance trade and had a sizable population.

The city comes into written history when its capture in 1468 BC by Thutmose III is recorded on temple walls in Karnak. Another record suggests that the city was captured by stealth, when soldiers concealed themselves in baskets smuggled through the gates. Jaffa (Canaanite *Yafi,* meaning beautiful) then became a provincial capital during the New Kingdom, hosting royal grain silos and a massive thirteenth-century gate dedicated to Ramses II. The city evidently fell to non-Canaanite invaders ca. 1230 BC.

The city was rebuilt and became the northernmost outpost for Philistine settlers, and there are indications of a lion cult within the sacred spaces they constructed. King David captured the city some two centuries later, and during the reign of his son, Solomon (ca. tenth century), Jaffa's port was used to receive cedar timbers floated down the coast from Tyre by King Hiram for use in the temple in Jerusalem. The city gradually fell under the rule of its larger southern neighbor, Ashkelon, and was part of King Sidqia's revolt against the Assyrian king Sennacherib; he put down the revolt and destroyed the city in 701 BC.

Jaffa prospered under the Persians after 539 and was granted by them to the Sidonian Phoenicians in the second half of the fifth century. It is probably from this period that the biblical story of Jonah fleeing God from Jaffa is penned. Massive new walls were constructed, an iron industry was established, and the city was clearly involved in long-distance trade with Greece. Under Ptolemaic rule, the city became Hellenized, was the site of a mint, had some autonomy, and went by the name of Ioppe, perhaps referring to the goddess of wind (the city's harbor was reportedly difficult to enter because of prevailing winds).

During the Hasmonean revolt (ca. 165), the city was captured to serve as an outlet to international trade, and all non-Jews were exiled from the city. The city passed to Herod in 37 BC, although he undercut its economic livelihood by founding Caesarea as his port, fifty miles to the north. The city figures prominently in the stories of the Acts of the Apostles, with Peter performing a number of miracles within its gates. The Jews of Jaffa participated in the revolt against Rome, with troops of the Roman emperor Vespasian having to subdue

Jaffa twice and perpetrating tremendous slaughter (ca. AD 68). After AD 70, the city was rebuilt, settled with non-Jews, and renamed Flavia Ioppa. The town's value as a port declined in favor of Caesarea, although it continued as a mint and hosted a bishopric by the fifth century.

In the year AD 636, the town fell to the invading armies of Islam under Amr bin al-As. Under the Umayyads, the strategic importance of the old port of Jaffa reemerged, particularly so after the Umayyad ruler Sulayman bin Abd al-Malik decided to build his new regional capital inland, nearby in ar-Ramle. The centrality of Jerusalem, however, meant that Yafa, as it became known in Arabic, prospered as its key port.

In 1126 the Crusaders captured Jaffa but lost it in 1187 to Salah ad-Din. In 1191 Richard I of England recaptured Jaffa and built a citadel to protect his acquisition, but the Crusaders were forced to relinquish control for a final time in 1196. When the kings of England and France planned a new crusade in 1336, the Mamluk ruler al-Nasir ordered the harbor of Jaffa to be destroyed to prevent the Crusaders from using it as a landing point. By 1345 the town as well as its harbor lay in ruins.

For 300 years following the Crusades, Jaffa was a small working port, sparsely populated. Its main role was to serve as a port of entry for Jewish and Christian pilgrims en route to Jerusalem. A number of churches and Christian hostels were built under the Mamluks. In 1516 the Ottomans took over Palestine, and Jaffa with it. After a period of indirect rule during the 1700s, the Ottoman government tried to consolidate its control over Palestine and restore security to the port of Jaffa. As the Middle East region slowly became more closely connected with the European economy, exports from the eastern Mediterranean, particularly grain and cotton, increased; as a result, the status of port cities like Jaffa was enhanced at the expense of towns of the interior. The town's commercial activities expanded, and the harbor and its wharves were rebuilt. A mosque and an Armenian khan were also constructed. As a result of the increased prosperity and security, the number of residents rose, and by the mid-eighteenth century, Jaffa had replaced Ramle as the coastal region's pivotal city. This burst of growth and prosperity, however, was interrupted by a struggle between the central Ottoman government and its local governors during the middle of the eighteenth century over the degree of autonomy the latter was permitted. Jaffa was occupied twice (1773 and 1775), its agricultural areas laid waste, and many of its citizens executed.

European military ambitions in Palestine came right to Jaffa's door in 1799, following a siege and prolonged artillery bombardment of the city by Napoléon Bonaparte and his French army. The city walls were breached, Jaffa captured, and its treasures looted, while 4,000 prisoners were massacred. After his failure to take Acre farther to the north, Bonaparte abandoned his dream of a French eastern empire and returned to Egypt.

From 1810 to 1820, Jaffa was governed by Muhammad "Abu Naput" Syed Ali Pasha. He was known as a cruel ruler, and according to local tradition, he is said to have walked the streets of Jaffa with a club in his hand, intimidating residents with its arbitrary employment. Nevertheless, he had a vision for Jaffa, and he sought to ensure that it could compete with its rivals along the coast in Acre and Beirut. He carried out construction and extensive renovation in the city, leaving behind structures, some of which survive today. Among them are the al-Mahmudiyya Mosque; a decorative fountain, which has survived in part; and a water fountain for travelers known as "Sabil Abu Nabut," which can be seen at the entrance to Jaffa. This was another period of prosperity for Jaffa, and the city's population grew, its trade flourished, and the surrounding citrus groves were vastly enlarged.

In 1832 Egyptian troops under Ibrahim Pasha captured the city and held it until 1840. Egyptian Muslims settled in Jaffa and its environs, founding, among others, the villages of Sakhanat al-Muzariyya (Manshiya) and Sakhanat Abu Kabir (later to become Giv'at Herzl in the Israeli period). After its return to Ottoman rule, the city continued to grow in prosperity and population, becoming a key site for the export of southern Palestine's abundant fields. The city exported grains (particularly wheat), sesame, olive oil and soap, cotton, and vegetables. France was the major buyer, followed by England. After 1875 Jaffa oranges were exported to Europe from the more than 400 orange groves surrounding the city: 36 million were shipped out in 1880 alone.

The city attracted considerable in-migration after 1831, much of it from throughout Palestine but also from other parts of the Arab world. A sizable Sephardic Jewish community grew during the mid-nineteenth century as well, bringing settlers from Morocco, Turkey, Greece, and Bulgaria. These pre-Zionist immigrants formed a Council of Jaffan Jews who later found themselves in conflict with the post-1880 Ashkenazi immigrants from central and eastern Europe focused on the Zionist dream. In addition, the city attracted a number of chiliast movements from America and Germany, all feeding together to create a vibrant and cultural city in the period from 1856 to 1882.

Jaffa experienced the earliest modern infrastructural development in Palestine, supported and financed by European investors. A new road was built to Jerusalem, and the French held the concession to build the first railroad from Jaffa to the Holy City. Completed in 1892, it cut a two-day journey down to three hours. On the backs of such developments, the city welcomed an increasing flood of Victorian tourists: Mark Twain arrived early in the process, writing in his 1869 *Innocents Abroad* about the various pilgrimage sites in Jaffa and his joy in making it through the city and back onto the deck of his ship.

Jaffa from the sea, ca. 1900. (Library of Congress)

The city's expansion led to the need to broaden the city limits. Over a nine-year period (1879–1888), the Ottoman administration demolished the walls and filled in and paved their course to make a main thoroughfare around the Old City. In the surrounding area, houses, stores, khans, and storehouses were erected. The city's local Muslim and Christian elites threw themselves into these new projects and expanded their intellectual horizons. The city was the center of Palestine's budding Arab media and culture, and it hosted numerous newspapers, in particular *Filisteen,* founded in 1911 by the great Jaffa activist and visionary, Isa Daoud al-Isa (1878–1950), and the first magazine in Palestine, *al-Asmai.*

In the northern part of Jaffa, Jewish residents built the neighborhoods of Neve Zedek (1887) and Neve Shalom (1890). These were then to provide the impetus for the establishment in 1909 of Tel Aviv, the first modern Jewish city in Palestine, which was later to eclipse Jaffa. Initially planned as a residential suburb, all of Tel Aviv's first settlers worked in Jaffa. On the eve of World War I and five years after its inception, Tel Aviv could count 2,000 residents, but during the period of the British control over Palestine, it grew rapidly. In 1921 it was declared a separate town from Jaffa and formally became a city in 1934 (see also "Tel Aviv").

Jaffa produced a number of notable activists and political movements prior to and during the mandate. Shimon Moyal, for example, who was born in Jaffa in 1866 (and died there in 1915), was a Sephardic voice for tolerance between Jews and Arabs, stressing the need for Zionists at that movement's office in Jaffa to learn Arabic and to participate in the life of the Arab world. It was in Jaffa that the riots of May 1921 began, spreading to the rest of the country. Activist Palestinian women of the city formed their own movement in 1931 to participate in rallies, visit other Palestinian cities to show solidarity, and to make representation to the British high commissioner in Jaffa. The city also housed Qassimite activists, who organized strikes in the city, which helped feed the Arab Revolt of 1936. Jaffa experienced a great deal of damage between 1936 and 1939, when British forces demolished the dense heart of the Old City to provide access for armored vehicles. The Jewish community moved out, and old patterns of social interaction died.

According to the 1947 UN Partition Plan, Jaffa was meant to be included in the territory of the Arab state, but following the outbreak of war between the Zionist settlers and the Palestinians in 1948, the city was occupied by Jewish troops. All but 3,500 of the more than 70,000 Yaffawiin (Palestinian inhabitants of Jaffa) were forced to leave for Beirut or Ramallah.

After the establishment of the new State of Israel, Jaffa was incorporated into the new municipality of Tel Aviv-Yafo in 1950. However, for many years it was neglected by the municipality. Some Palestinians moved back into the city, but these were mostly refugees from other areas of Palestine. Its pre-1948 communal and political structure had been destroyed, and it became a slum on the outskirts of the richer Tel Aviv and synonymous with crime and poverty. An attempt was made in the early sixties to rehabilitate Jaffa and to restore parts of the Old City, which resulted in the creation of an artist colony and shops selling expensive kitsch, and it has become a popular venue for festivals and outdoor events. The population of the Old City and its surrounding quarters remains predominantly Palestinian Arab and has become a center for attempts to preserve Palestinian culture and restore political rights. This role was recognized by the Israeli government, and between 1967 and 1988 Jaffa became the seat of its own Muslim religious court and that of the Muslim Court of Appeal. The housing shortage means that few Palestinians own their homes, and there is a serious overcrowding problem.

While lacking in outstanding monuments of architectural heritage, a number of the quarters or features in Jaffa deserve a mention. The Manshiyya Quarter was located on the seafront just to the north of the harbor. Built by Egyptian immigrants in the nineteenth century, it was largely destroyed during the 1948 war. However, a strong symbol of its former Palestinian origins can be seen in the striking Hassan Bek Mosque and its tall slender minaret, which are familiar features in historical paintings and the current landscape of Tel Aviv-Yafo. Recently, the mosque has been partially renovated. A clock tower was erected in 1906 at the entry to the Old City in honor of the Ottoman Turkish sultan Abdul Hameed II. Its stained-glass windows each portray a different chapter in the town's history. To the southwest is Mahmoudiya Mosque, built in 1812 using columns taken from the Roman cities of Caesarea and Ashkelon. Close by is the flea market, famous for its antiques, copperware, jewelry, and bric-a-brac. Plans for the demolition of the old port of Jaffa have been submitted but not yet implemented.

Michael Dumper

Further Readings

Edbury, Peter. *John of Ibelin and the Kingdom of Jerusalem.* Woodbridge, UK: Boydell Press, 1997.

Fischer, Moshe. *Roman Roads in Judaea II: The Jaffa-Jerusalem Roads.* Oxford: BAR International Series, 1996.

Kark, Ruth. *Jaffa: A City in Evolution, 1799–1917.* Jerusalem: Ben Zvi Press, 1990.

LeVine, Mark. *Overthrowing Geography: Jaffa, Tel Aviv and the Struggle for Palestine, 1880–1948.* Berkeley: University of California Press, 2005.

Malak, Hana. *Jaffan Roots.* Jerusalem: Author, 1996.

Sherman, Arnold. *Tel Aviv-Jaffa.* London: Sterling, 1988.

Tolkowsky, Samuel. *The Gateway to Palestine: A History of Jaffa.* London: Routledge, 1924.

Jericho
Population: 42,000 (2005 estimate)

The claim is often made that Jericho is the oldest continuously inhabited settlement in the world, and that may be substantially correct. Certainly, its origins as a permanent settlement lie at least eleven millennia in the past, and although there were some centuries when the ancient tell was deserted, settlement in and use of the oasis has been continuous. The ancient town gave way to a new city during classical times located about a mile away. The modern city of Jericho grew up around a third site, beginning with a Byzantine-Muslim complex. Despite these minor variations, this "city of palms" is one of the main global landmarks in the history of human settlements, iconic in the human imagination for the story of the destruction of its walls. Although never a large conurbation, the oasis has, across the millennia, served as a winter resort, a garrison town, a garden city, a source of global beauty products and drugs, a cultic sanctuary and priestly city, a pilgrimage city, an entrepôt, and a site for political unrest.

Jericho (Arabic, *Eriha*; Hebrew, *Yeriho*) is a natural oasis, first developed by humans more than 11,000 years ago. The site lies on the western edge of the floor of the Jordan Rift Valley, up against the base of the mountains that form the north-south backbone of Palestine. The Jordan Rift is part of the far larger Syrio-African Rift system running south from Syria to South Africa, of which the Red Sea is a part. This makes it the longest, most important rift on land. Jericho is some five miles north of the northern tip of the Dead Sea, the lowest point of Earth. Jericho itself is 825 feet below sea level, making it the lowest oasis and town in the world. From Jerusalem, the drop over the fifteen-mile journey is 3,300 feet.

Jericho's oasis is the result of a constant supply of water that emerges from water-carrying rock strata lying under porous rocks exposed by the rift. All along the rift the same thing happens, making Jericho only one example, perhaps the best, of this spring system; the Jordan River is the result of the same porous rocks to the north, and similar springs occur south to Aqaba. Jericho receives on average less than 8 inches of rain per year.

Jericho sits where the streams flow out into somewhat more fertile alluvial soil, washed down from the hills around Jerusalem via the wadis lying to both sides of the site. Further away, toward the Jordan River, the soil is heavily saline, skeletal desert soil and barren. In the winter, Jericho is very warm, protected from the cold winds and snow that buffet Amman or Jerusalem. To this warm climate, available water and agricultural abundance can be added to the city's accessibility to other regions where trade can be conducted: via Wadi Qelt to the west are the Palestinian mountains, the Mediterranean, and the ancient coastal road to Egypt. To the east across a ford at the Jordan River are the Jordanian plateau and then the ancient roads to Damascus or south to Arabia via Kings Road. In other words, Jericho is unique in its history and development because of its highly favorable location and topography.

Jericho's attributes were developed by human skill, however. It is water engineering that both in the ancient past and today makes use of the water from many different springs, coordinates them, and uses this bountiful supply to create a large agriculturally productive area stretching out from the base of the mountains. Three key springs are manipulated to feed the irrigation: to the north is Ein Duq, in the middle is Ein as-Sultan, and in the south is Ein Qelt. In ancient times, this technology irrigated 5,000 acres, which was capable of supporting several thousand people; in fact, Jericho may be home to the oldest known irrigation system in the world. The oasis has always supported special crops that can't be grown elsewhere in Palestine, including papaya, bananas, sugarcane, rice, citrus, date palms, and indigo.

The earliest archaeological excavations in the oasis occurred more than 130 years ago, around 1873. Since then many archaeologists (German, British, French, American, Palestinian, Jordanian, and Israeli) have dug at various sites around the conurbation, making it the most excavated site in Palestine after Jerusalem. Kathleen Kenyon, from the British School of Archaeology (1952–1958), is probably the most famous of those excavating the site. Many of these digs have been motivated by a biblical bias, seeking to identify Joshua's walls and city, or Jewish remains, leaving much of the oasis's 11,000 years of history undiscovered, ignored, or negated.

Tel as-Sultan, the site of the most ancient settlement, has received the majority of the archaeological attention. It is here that the story of the human Neolithic revolution appears early in Jericho. As early as 9000 BC, the oasis hosted a permanent settlement on this hill near the Ein as-Sultan spring; it may have originated as a sanctuary or cultic site for hunters close to regular water and wadi flooding. By 8000 BC, mud-brick roundhouses surrounded one of the most spectacular archaeological finds of the Jericho digs: a stone tower twenty-seven feet high with an outside staircase that predates any other such discovered constructions in the Middle East by thousands of years. One estimate is that it took 100 men 104 work days to build it.

Rectangular houses, with plaster floors and stained colors, were in evidence on the tell by 7200 BC, and water cisterns and grain silos suggest an early farming community (wheat and barley). Over the next two millennia, domesticated sheep and goats appear, cattle raising was practiced by 6000 BC, and pottery was developed. At this time, the town may have housed more than 1,000 people.

Excavations reveal Jericho's participation in trading links to Anatolia, Sinai, and the Red Sea with finds of nephrite, turquoise, and cowrie shells. The area probably traded in return salt, sulfur, and bitumen and pitch. There are extensive Neolithic cemeteries around the site, including some spectacular "Jericho plastered skulls" in which clay was molded on skulls to create facial features, with colors indicating hair and cowrie shells for eyes.

The first signs of walls, defenses, and conflict appear after 5000 BC. During the Early Bronze Age, defenders repaired the walls seventeen times. The tell appears to have been destroyed around 2300 BC, for example, abandoned for a period and then experienced some reconstruction, then a period of earthquake and fire and abandonment, then limited rebuilding, and finally massive rebuilding after 1800 BC. Large cemeteries ca. 2000 BC have been found around Tel as-Sultan, with wood furniture entombed with the dead. The period around 1750 BC was the height of the golden age of Canaanite culture in Jericho.

With the appearance of settled agriculture, the need for supplemental salt in the human diet stirred a demand for traded salt, and Jericho controlled ancient salt mines on the edge of the Dead Sea. The significance of salt in society can be seen in ancient salt offerings and the sealing of contracts by an oath of salt. Thus, Jericho attracted trade and production. Even into the twentieth century, local Bedouin created artificial evaporation lagoons on the edge of the Dead Sea and carried the salt to markets in Jerusalem, Hebron, Beersheba, and Gaza.

The shores of the Dead Sea also produced bitumen, which was employed for attaching stone blades to shafts. The biblical narrative has Noah's ark sealed by bitumen, and various other ancient manufacturing processes required it. By the time of Pliny and Strabo, who comment on Jericho's bitumen, there were thousands of years of demand for this product from the city.

Jericho is most famous in the West for the biblical story of the Israelite conquest of the city. Joshua and his troops supposedly circled the walls ca. 1200 BC, blew trumpets, and the walls came crashing down. The archaeological evidence does not confirm this story, and current scholarship takes the position that the Old Testament story is most probably a foundation myth for the Israelite tribes. Likewise, the more ancient story of Lot and his wife turned to a pillar of salt ties in well with the salt production of the area.

The history of the control of the city in the first millennium BC by the kings of Israel and Judea includes events in the life of David and King Ahab and King Zedekiah's attempted escape from Jerusalem to Jericho in 587 BC when the Babylonians invaded. For Elijah, Jericho was a prophetic city associated with the sons of the prophets, and it had a certain sanctity and holiness.

In the period after the destruction of Jerusalem by the Babylonians, Jericho may have served as the capital of the region. The Achaemenids controlled the city from 525 to 332 BC, and the city served as the capital of the district. The Persians recognized the city as one of the most fertile in

Palestine, and they may have been the first to establish royal property and monopolies in the oasis. After Alexander the oasis first came under Ptolemaic rule. Royal estates produced products for Egypt, particularly balsam. The Ptolemies turned the city into a security and military town as well, housing garrisons and the elephants of their armies in the oasis. After 198 BC, it fell to the Seleucids, and their general Bacchides refortified Jericho ca. 160 BC.

The sacredness of Jericho was reemphasized after Jews rebuilt the temple in Jerusalem following their return from Babylon. In a close symbiotic relationship, Jericho became a "priestly city," with elite clerical families dominating the product of the oasis in support of the temple and the priestly community in Jerusalem. Many of Jericho's agricultural products were designated for use in the temple, and the markets of Jerusalem reportedly burst with produce from Jericho. Jericho served as a training site for priests, and many lived there for much of the year. The city also came to serve as a key spot on the pilgrim trail to Jerusalem, with Jewish pilgrims sanctifying themselves for the visit to the temple in the many *miqwa'ot* (ritual baths) of Jericho before ascending to Jerusalem. Josephus mentions the great number of pilgrims passing through Jericho well in the first century AD.

When the Hasmoneans, high priests themselves, took control of the area after the mid-second century BC, they took a keen interest in the agricultural productivity of Jericho and expanded the extensive plantations in the oasis by further aqueduct and irrigation construction. Josephus, and Strabo in his *Geographica*, talks of date palms, honey, cypress, grains, and other exotic and precious plants being grown in the oasis, with balsam in particular fetching high prices. The oasis at this time may have housed up to 10,000 people. Strabo states that Jericho had a mixed population, including Arabs, Egyptians, Jews, and Phoenicians.

The Hasmonean rulers fortified the oasis, particularly building a new complex at the entrance of Wadi Qelt, the major access route to Jerusalem. About a mile from modern Jericho, the tell of Tulul Abu al-Alayiq has now been extensively excavated and reveals a huge set of buildings spanning both the south and north side of the wadi. Two fortresses, one called Threx and the other Taurus, guarded the road and the oasis. The first winter palace on the site must have been built ca. 103 BC. Progressively enlarged, the winter palace complex came to cover three acres. A central role was given over to a huge half-acre swimming pool surrounded by wide promenades, buildings, and palace gardens.

Pompey began his conquest of Palestine in 63 BC. He appeared in Jericho with his army on his way to Jerusalem and was impressed by its large population, many fruit and palm trees, and its extensive balsam plantations. After his conquest, he divided Palestine into five districts, with Jericho being one, and placed the Maccabean Hyrcanus II (65–40 BC) over the city supported by Roman troops. As a result, over the next 600 years, Roman legions wintered in the oasis, then headed back to the highlands of Palestine and Jordan to serve.

King Herod moved to add the city to his principality in 39 BC. The story goes that the night before the attack, there was an earthquake, which he survived despite the house collapsing around him. Then, in the battle the next day, Herod was struck by a javelin but survived. Thus, he appeared to be blessed by God, and the people of Jericho opened the city to him. Still fearful of threats to his power, Herod invited his brother-in-law, the Hasmonean Aristobulus III, to the winter palace and had him drowned in the swimming pool.

Mark Antony gave Jericho to Cleopatra (ca. 36 BC) as part of her dowry, and although Herod may have wanted to drown her too when she came to the winter palace to survey her property, he worked out a deal to lease it from her for 400 talents per year. She also used the balsam from its groves to keep her skin beautiful and imported its drugs, thus setting Jericho forever on the path of a spa and beauty treatment city. Today beauty products, including salts and mud from the Dead Sea, make up a list of Jericho products famous to women around the world.

Herod instituted a substantial building program in the city, including aqueducts and canals, a hippodrome, and an amphitheater. He also expanded the winter palace, employing Roman workmen to create two huge halls, one named Caesarion, the other Agrippon, in honor of Augustus and his right-hand man, Agrippa. Both Pliny and Josephus mention that Herod benefited from the lucrative monopoly over the palm tree plantations of Jericho; the city was famous for its dates and its honey-flavored wine. To protect his investment, Herod added to the fortifications and renamed one Cypros in honor of his mother (today known as Aqabat Jabr) on the mountain overlooking the oasis. Despite the protection, Herod's slave Simeon reportedly burned the palace during a revolt just before Herod's death, although it was rebuilt and further expanded by Herod's son, Archelaus (4 BC–AD 6), before being abandoned after the death of Agrippa II.

One indication of the high degree of prosperity in the city from the first century BC through the first century AD is its extensive cemetery dating from this period. Rock-cult loculi tombs with extensive family burials demonstrate great wealth, with both coffins of wood and, later, ossuaries. Another indication was the wealth of the tax collectors in the city. Jericho was one of the richest tax districts of Roman Palestine, and the New Testament story of Jesus and Zacchaeus is only one of a number of stories about Jesus in Jericho that sanctified the site for the nascent Christian community. Pilate had a winter camp here, and at the time, Jericho was probably one of the most international and pluralistic cities in Palestine. Jewish pilgrims from Peraea (east of the Jordan) and from Galilee would assemble in Jericho to begin their trip to the temple; Jesus began his final trip to the temple and death from here as well, Luke says.

During the Jewish Revolt (AD 66–70), zealots burned the balsam groves in Jericho, and the fortresses provided them cover and temporary protection in the fighting. Pliny talks about the battle for Jericho and the Tenth Legion camping in Jericho before hauling their siege engines up the road to besiege Jerusalem. The emperor Hadrian (AD 117–138) came to Palestine in 134 to crush a revolt, and he decided to expand Jericho. Roman elites wintered in Jericho, adorning their villas with painted plaster murals similar to those at Pompeii. *Regio* Jericho (the Jericho Region) and the nearby Sea of Asphalt (Asphaltitis or Dead Sea) attracted many tourists.

The sanctity of Jericho and the starkness of the surrounding mountains attracted early Christian hermits and pilgrims. There was a bishop of Jericho by the fourth century, and Justinian had a hospice for pilgrims erected in the town and the Church of the Mother of God restored. There were many hermits' caves in Jebal Qurantul (Mount of Temptation) near the grotto assumed by tradition to be where Jesus spent his forty days of fasting. Pilgrims would descend from Jerusalem in a caravan before Epiphany (6 January) to visit both Jericho and the monastery of Saint John, Deir Mar Yuhanna, close to the Jordan River and built on a traditional site identified by the Empress Helena as the grotto where John the Baptist had lived. From there, they would walk to the Mahadet Hajleh, the bathing place for pilgrims on the Jordan. By the sixth century, a huge number of Christian pilgrims came here regularly. Both banks of the river were paved with marble, and Bedouin guides moved the pilgrims in and out of the water. This pilgrimage tradition continued up to the twentieth century, with crowds coming at Easter to bathe in the waters and to fill jars to take home to baptize those who could not make the journey. At this time, the whole district of Jericho was packed with monasteries; only Jerusalem had more. One of the most famous continues to operate today in Wadi Qelt: the Greek Orthodox monastery of Saint George (Qoziba), built in the fifth century. Attacked by the Sassanians during their invasion of Palestine in 614, many monks were killed; the monastery continues to hold the skulls and mummies of those massacred.

The road from Jerusalem to Jericho held additional sites for pilgrimage, including Khan Saliba, with its fine Byzantine mosaics, or the castle at Tala'at ed-Damm (Arabic for the ascent of blood; or Ma'ala Adummim in Hebrew, meaning ascent of the red places). Saint Jerome argued that the name derived from the blood shed here by robbers, but it could also be the red sandstone. A police post at the Khan al-Ahmar came to be known as the Inn of the Good Samaritan, although it started as a Roman military post for couriers to change horses on the way up to Jerusalem. Nearby are the ruins of the church and monastery of Saint Euthymius from ca. AD 410, one of the most important *laura* (hermit settlements) in Palestine. Euthymius spent sixty-six years in the desert and attracted devotees from across the Mediterranean.

Although the Sassanians briefly controlled the oasis after 612, the Muslim assumption of power brought significant changes. Ruling from Damascus, the Umayyad caliph Hisham (AD 724–748) built Khirbet al-Mafjar, a hunting palace one mile northeast of Tulul Abu al-Alayiq, in the eighth century. Known for its magnificent bathhouse mosaics and monumental sculpture, the palace was destroyed soon after its completion by an earthquake. Under Umayyad and Abbasid rule, the sugarcane industry of the oasis was established. After the Crusader capture of Jerusalem in 1099, Jericho became both a defensive site as well as a garden for Jerusalem, producing food for the city. The modern village of today grew up around the Crusader castle and church. The Crusaders improved the local water mills, which harnessed the dramatic flow of Ein as-Sultan, and built *tawahin es-sukkar* (sugar mills) to crush sugarcane from the oasis to make sugar for their tables in Jerusalem.

By the sixteenth century and the Ottoman conquest of Palestine, Jericho had shrunk to a small village, producing agricultural products for local and regional consumption. Known as the city of palms, its dates remained famous, but also henna, corn, and hemp were grown for export. Nablus's textile manufacturing depended on natural dyestuffs acquired from Jericho, including gall nuts (*afas*), *nila* (indigo), and *summaq* (sumac) (see also "Nablus"). Such dyes were exported as far away as Aleppo and Egypt for use in textile manufacturing; in fact, Muhammad Ali of Egypt sent merchants to Jericho in 1825 to acquire indigo seeds for his textile factories. Products from the Dead Sea such as rock oil and petroleum were exported to Egypt for use as chemicals for insecticides, coating the base of fruit trees to ward off insects, and potash was used for fertilizer.

For many centuries, the oasis had been the only town in the southern valley, and it was constantly susceptible to Bedouin raids. The Ottomans finally improved the road from Jerusalem to Jericho in the nineteenth century and begin to pay attention to security in the Jordan Valley. European tourists and pilgrims began to flow to the oasis, and the Ottomans allowed the Russians to build a church and a hospice. By the early twentieth century, there were two hotels in the city serving tourists, and it was the seat of an Ottoman *mudir* (local administrator) and a *saraya* (government building).

The Maqam al-Nabi Musa celebrations every spring also brought great crowds of Palestinian Muslims to Jericho. Started by Salah ad-Din to celebrate the liberation of Jerusalem from the Crusaders, and as a balance to the Easter caravans to Jericho and the Jordan, this pilgrimage of 10,000 chanting and singing pilgrims would annually leave al-Aqsa in Jerusalem for the Nabi Musa complex built by Sultan Baybars in 1269 just to the west of Jericho, where the prophet Moses was supposedly buried. The complex at Nabi Musa owned considerable *waqf* (religious endowment) land in Jericho, making it the largest endowment in the whole of

Palestine. The complex had rooms for pilgrims, and it was rebuilt and expanded in 1475 and again in 1820 by the Ottomans. Revived in the early 1900s under the instigation of the al-Husayni family, the Nabi Musa festivities quickly came to represent, after the 1920 British Mandate was declared over Palestine, national expression and political interests. The 1920 celebrations, for example, were used by Arab nationalists to demonstrate support for Amir Faysal, newly declared king of Syria. Speeches calling for the extension of Faysal's rule over Palestine incited the crowd. By the 1930s, religion and land issues predominated, and it became a time for delegations from all over Palestine to share ideas and to build nationalist solidarity. Finally, it became so popular that the British banned the celebrations. The Israeli military authorities did allow it to restart for a brief period in the 1980s, and Arafat continued to push for its revival until his death.

As a result of the fighting in 1948 and 1949, refugees from the Palestinian coastal towns of Ramla and Lid ended up in Jericho, establishing themselves in three refugee camps: Ein as-Sultan, Aqabat Jabr, and al-Nuwaymah. In total, more than 50,000 refugees took up residence in the oasis, dramatically changing the urban feel and context of the town. Musa al-Alami (1897–1983), the famous Palestinian nationalist, established the Arab Development Society in Jericho after 1949 and supported Palestinian orphans through agricultural production, woodworking, and redevelopment of the potential of the oasis.

Jericho was also caught up in the process of unification between Palestine and Transjordan. In December 1948, the Second Palestine Congress was held in Jericho. The Jericho Congress, as it became known, was composed of almost 1,000 handpicked Palestinian elites gathered by Amir Abdullah to confirm his annexation of Palestine to Transjordan. Delegations from Palestinian towns, military governors, representatives of various organizations, religious figures, educational leaders, and media representatives all met and proclaimed the annexation of the West Bank as a move toward Arab unity and a step toward solving the Palestine problem.

For the next four decades, Jericho was a hotbed for political organizing and unrest. Camp-town relationships in Jericho were different than in other Palestinian towns, since the refugee camp population far exceeded that of the town, and the refugees were economically and educationally superior to those from the town. It was the camps that in the 1950s became centers of the Jordanian Communist Party (JCP) and that supported the new Muslim Brethren organization. By the late 1950s, the JCP had been banned, its members tried in military courts in the city, and the organization's structure uncovered and arrested.

With the Israeli occupation in 1967, more than 70,000 refugees abandoned the camps and fled to Jordan. The Jericho mayor fled as well, creating an administrative vacuum that hurt the population of the city during the early years of the occupation. By the early 1970s, however, the municipality had assumed considerable powers for development and governance, although it was caught between the Israeli military governor and the Jordanian authorities, who continued to pay the bills. The year 1972 was important, with the first municipal elections since the occupation; the former vice-mayor defeated the former mayor in the elections and brought in a more nationalistic ticket. Abd al-Aziz as-Suwayti then set out to institute a number of public works and improvements to the city. By the late 1970s, the city was an example of one of the most aggressive cities in terms of public improvements.

It was difficult, however, to improve the lot of the city given the massive Israeli effort to construct settlements nearby. After 1967 land around Jericho was confiscated, restricted, or fenced off for security reasons, and settlements began to creep east from Jerusalem and along the Jordanian valley to constrain the city and its livelihood. New settlements, including the city of more than 50,000 called Ma'ale Adumim, now stretch most of the way from Jerusalem to Jericho. The city has been cut off from its traditional markets in Amman, Ramallah, and Jerusalem. After 1979 Israelis created their own regional councils and local communities to administer settlements and areas around Jericho, and new laws expropriated land for settlements based on archaeological rationales.

Interestingly, as early as December 1973, Jordan and Israel began talking about Jericho being the first installment in an Israeli pullback from the Jordan River. Raised repeatedly in negotiations through August 1974 as a possible first step toward a "Jericho Corridor" for Amman to Ramallah, the deal never went through and was finally abandoned with the new climate, which arose after the Rabat decisions of 1974.

Jericho's garden restaurants continued to thrive during the 1970s and 1980s with the weekend trade by Palestinian elites coming from Jerusalem to Ramallah. Many Ramallah families, such as that of Hanan Ashrawi, had long owned land in Jericho and would come for the weekend to "tend" their orange and grapefruit trees. The city also served as the gateway between the Arab world and Palestine, with the bridge across the Jordan as the only access point to the wider world for those Palestinians carrying Jordanian passports. Tourists passed through the city on organized tours to stop for an hour at Tel as-Sultan and then move on. The Israeli National Parks Authority neglected or left undeveloped other sites in the oasis, for example, Hisham's Palace, which was bereft of signs or explanations and did not appear in most ministry of tourism publications.

Jericho hosted the United Nations Relief and Welfare Agency (UNRWA) Technical Training School and clothing and textile workshops. Most employed women to work long hours, under poor conditions. This provided fertile ground for the Union of Palestinian Working Women's Committees (UPWWC), for example, which started a pro-Communist women's branch in Jericho in 1981 and by 1985 had workers committees in factories and workshops across the city. The Palestinian Federation of Women's Action Committees (PFWAC), connected with the Democratic Front, also found fertile ground here, creating a citrus fruit-juice project in the city.

The intifada (Palestinian Uprising) of 1987–1992 was supported in the city and the camps, ending with many men in prison and women working outside the home for the first time to support their families. As a consequence of the resistance, the occupying authorities began to cut off the city, building a new road system around it, and placing it under long curfews. The camps in Jericho began to revive as "displaced" persons from other areas of the West Bank made their way to the crumbling houses. Tourists bypassed the city, and the economic life of the city deteriorated.

Fortunes appeared to revive in 1993, however, in the wake of the Declarations of Principles (DOP) between the PLO and Israel. The first operational agreement to result from the DOP, the May 1994 Cairo Agreement, allowed the new Palestinian Authority (PA) to establish itself in Gaza and Jericho, being careful to say Jericho *first* and not Jericho *only* as an interim step to broader autonomy in the West Bank. Arafat returned to Jericho in 1994 via Egyptian helicopter, declaring a symbolic victory for the Palestinian people, and established a villa office in the city. This offered great hope to Jericho, and by the summer of 1994, both World Bank monies and private Palestinian investment were beginning to change the face of the city. Plans for a new twenty-four-hour casino, hotel complexes, housing, factory production, flower-export facilities, and dairy herds were all started, and some construction and training began. Saeb Erakat, a key Palestinian negotiator and minister from Jericho, played a role in the establishment of the new PA after 1994. He also taught international relations at an-Najah University and served as an editor of *al-Quds* newspaper.

Unfortunately, the boomtown atmosphere lasted only a year or two, and Jericho's future crashed on the rocks of the deteriorating political negotiations between Israel and Palestine. Since the second intifada (which began in 2000), Jericho has been confined to a small ghetto, surrounded by highways and barbed wire, where tourists and settlers whiz by on their way to Jordan, Jerusalem, Galilee, or the Dead Sea. Few choose to negotiate the checkpoints into the enclave to frequent the few remaining garden restaurants or view the shells of half-finished hotels. The Christian community continues to host a few pilgrims, but the big issue in the city is now that of water. Water pressure from the springs has decreased because of overuse by Israeli settlements and the demands of an expanding Jerusalem. Although the municipality is working on improving water irrigation schemes and distribution to farmers in the oasis with the help of international development organizations, the future of the oasis is now in doubt.

Kamal Abdul Fattah

Further Readings

Bartlett, John. *Jericho.* Guildford, UK: Lutterworth, 1982.
Kenyon, Kathleen. *Digging Up Jericho.* London: Benn, 1957.
Langfur, Stephen. *Confession from a Jericho Jail.* New York: Grove Weidenfeld, 1992.
Ruby, Robert. *Jericho: Dreams, Ruins, Phantoms.* New York: Holt, 1995.
Said, Edward. *Peace and Its Discontents: Gaza-Jericho, 1993–1995.* London: Vintage, 1995.

Jerusalem
Population: 704,000 (2004 estimate)

Jerusalem is one of the most ancient and famous cities in the world, with a unique and unusual set of circumstances that led to its growth and development. Located in the central highlands of former Palestine, the city is not itself on the ancient major trade routes that ran along the coastal plain. And despite being situated in a strategic land corridor where the continents of Europe, Africa, and Asia meet, and thus the focus of much military activity, the city was held to be of little strategic military value. To understand its significance in world history and contemporary politics, one has to recognize that it is derived from its essential character as a holy city to the three major monotheist religions of the Middle East: Judaism, Christianity, and Islam. It is the site of the earliest Israelite temple, the site where Jesus of Nazareth was crucified and buried, and the site to which the Prophet Muhammad first turned in prayer when he launched his new faith. The history and politics of Jerusalem are intrinsically tied to its central role in the ritual and practice of these religions. The result has been the evolution of a walled Old City with some outstanding monuments of great architectural value built upon layer after layer of important archaeological remains. Now a modern city claimed by two national groups, Palestinians and Israelis, the city continues to expand but suffers from ideologically led construction and planning priorities.

Jerusalem (Arabic, *al-Quds* or *Bayt al-Maqdis;* Hebrew, *Yerushalaiym*) lies in the mountains of central Palestine at higher than 1,312 feet at the conjunction of two steep-sided valleys some twenty miles from the Mediterranean coast and the port of Jaffa. It has a poor agricultural hinterland and few natural resources. Water supplies are limited, and its growth has depended upon the expansion of supplies being provided from elsewhere. Its economy has largely been based upon its holy sites, providing for clergy and servicing the large pilgrimages of all three faiths that occur throughout the year. The construction of hostels and schools (and in the twentieth century of hotels, seminaries, and colleges) has been a major economic activity. Like other holy cities in the region, the city attracts large donations and the creation of foundations and endowments to support religious sites, their staff, and welfare-provision activities. As a key administrative, cultural, and intellectual center, Jerusalem has also developed as a hub for professional services and attracted some light industry and high-technology investment. Its population has risen from 164,000 in 1946 to 266,300 in 1967 to more than 600,000 in the 1990s, roughly two-thirds of whom are Israeli Jews and the rest Palestinian Arabs.

The earliest archaeological evidence for human settlement on the site that became Jerusalem was during the Jebusite-Canaanite period around 1800 BC. These include a walled settlement, foundations of houses, water supply installations, and some tombs and caves. Following the conquest of Jerusalem by Israelite tribes under King David (ca. 1004 BC), Jerusalem acquired strategic value as being midway between the two tribal areas of Judea and Benjamin. It acted as the capital of a united Israelite kingdom. Under his successor, Solomon, there was greater construction and expansion. The Jewish Temple was built on a grand scale on a specially engineered plateau above the traditional site of the city. The fortifications were enlarged, and Jerusalem also became a commercial center, with major trading routes of that time passing through its walls. The Babylonian invasion of Jerusalem in 587 BC saw the deportation of the Israelite elite to Babylon. They were, in turn, succeeded in 539 BC by the Persians, who allowed the exiles to return and rebuild the temple but not to regain independent political control over the city. During the Hellenistic period, there was a succession of revolts by Jews against the Seleucid Greeks, one of which led to the brief reestablishment of Jewish control over the city under the Maccabeans in 141 BC.

The Roman period followed, lasting some 700 years, from 63 BC until the Muslim invasion in AD 638, and can be divided into two parts. The first period of Roman rule saw an initial regime of religious autonomy for the Jews in Jerusalem. Attempts, however, at political independence from Rome were severely crushed, culminating in the destruction once again of the temple, in AD 69–70. Finally, impatient with the constant dissension by the Jewish population, Emperor Hadrian exiled two-thirds of the city's population and made it a Roman colony, Aeolia Capitolina. It was also during this early part of the Roman period that the first Christian community was established following the execution of the Christian leader, Jesus of Nazareth. The second half of the Roman period, from the beginning of its control by Byzantium to the Muslim invasion, was of great importance for Jerusalem. The most significant event was the conversion of Emperor Constantine to Christianity. This resulted in the transformation of Jerusalem from a Roman city of very little interest to the rest of the empire into the spiritual capital of a great empire.

While Jews were allowed only an annual pilgrimage to Jerusalem, Christian churches, infirmaries, hospices, and hostels were built on an extensive scale. A further boost to the Christian presence was given by the visit of Emperor Constantine's mother, Queen Helena, in AD 336. She claimed to have found the "True Cross" and encouraged the construction of the Holy Sepulchre on the supposed site of Jesus's crucifixion. For the next 300 years, the role of Christian pilgrimage to the city became central to its economic and cultural life.

The conquest of Jerusalem (AD 638) by Umar ibn Khattab, the successor to the Prophet Muhammad and the first caliph in Islam, opened a new era of Muslim rule in the city that, save for the interruption of the Crusades, was to last until 1967. Jerusalem was of little military and strategic significance at that time, and its conquest was mainly for religious purposes. Jerusalem had been the first *qibla,* or direction of prayer, which Muslims were obliged to carry out five times per day. It was also the destination of Muhammad's "night journey" and the site where it is believed he ascended briefly to heaven, both events being recorded in the Muslim holy book, the Qur'an. The caliph Umar came to an agreement with the city's existing Christian population that in exchange for the payment of a poll tax, their property, churches, and personal safety would be assured. Jews were allowed to return for pilgrimage purposes only, but over time more and more began to settle in the city.

Under the Umayyad dynasty, between 685 and 709, the Dome of the Rock and the al-Aqsa Mosque were built in an enclosure that became known as the Haram ash-Sharif (the Noble Sanctuary). It became the third-holiest site in Islam after Makkah and Madinah. One effect of these actions was to draw pilgrims away from Makkah, where the political rivals to the Umayyads held sway. The flowering of a corpus of literature known as the *fada'il al-quds,* or the merits of Jerusalem, was part of this sanctification and prestige-enhancing process. Right up to the eleventh century, the praises of Jerusalem were sung, and it became known as the *bayt al-maqdis,* the house of holiness, from which the Arabic name for the city, *al-Quds,* is derived.

The rise of the Abbasid dynasty in 750 and the transfer of the seat of the caliphate from Damascus to Baghdad led to a relative decline in the fortunes of Jerusalem. Nevertheless, caliphal visits took place, and repairs on the holy places were carried out. There is evidence that the Christian presence continued to thrive. Diplomatic relations between Emperor Charlemagne and Caliph Haroun ar-Rashid led to the construction of many new buildings to cater to Christian pilgrims. During the Fatimid dynasty's rule over Jerusalem, Cairo became more important to Islam, and the number of Muslim pilgrims to Jerusalem declined. The Christian and Jewish role in the city increased as more became involved in the government and administration of the city. Christian pilgrimage continued to increase, having a considerable impact upon the city and causing disaffection among the Muslims. In AD 1065, nearly 12,000 pilgrims arrived in the city on a mass pilgrimage, which in those days was akin to an invasion. Thus, by the late tenth century and throughout the eleventh century, the Muslim domination of Jerusalem weakened. By AD 1099, Crusader armies had laid siege to its gates and entered the city.

Mass slaughter and expulsion of its existing inhabitants inaugurated the Crusader period in Jerusalem. This was followed by a massive program of church building. The remains of some sixty-one churches have been found dating from this period. However, no significant damage or changes were made to the Dome of the Rock, although in AD 1142 it was consecrated as a Christian church. Despite Jerusalem becoming the capital of the Crusader kingdom and an important center for Christian pilgrimage, Frankish forces did not stay and populate the city. Instead, Christian minority groups from Syria, Lebanon, and throughout the Middle East settled, establishing the heterodox nature of the Christian community in Jerusalem that survives today.

The Ayyubid period, following Salah ad-Din's capture of Jerusalem in 1187, was marked by a huge investment in the construction of houses, markets, public baths, and pilgrim hostels. Large *waqf*s (religious endowments) were set up, bringing income into the city and providing funds for the refurbishment of the Haram ash-Sharif. For the greater part of the thirteenth century, however, Jerusalem lacked any strategic or military value for the Ayyubid leaders beset by their internecine struggles. It declined to virtually the status of a village, coming to life only for the visiting pilgrim group or passing caravan.

Soon after the establishment of Mamluk rule, however, Jerusalem witnessed a flowering of Islamic culture in the city. While it remained unimportant administratively, politically, and militarily, its importance as a Muslim sacred place returned. As a home for exiled and retired Mamluk princes and dignitaries, and as a recipient of funds from large and wealthy endowments, its building work attained a level of rare architectural magnificence. Muslim pilgrimages to Jerusalem increased and became an important feature in its economy. Silk, cotton, and soap were the other main items of trade or industry in the city. The sanctity of Jerusalem to Islam was also reinforced during this period through writings of poets and religious scholars. At least thirty fada'il can be traced back to this period. Under the Mamluks, the small Jewish community in the city attained what was known as *dhimmi* status, meaning it was a recognized and protected religious minority.

A period of decline, during which Bedouins in the hinterland hampered access to the city, heralded the twilight of the Mamluk era and the dawn of the Ottoman age, which lasted until the twentieth century. Originally Turks from central Asia, the Ottomans occupied Jerusalem in 1517, with Sultan Selim receiving the keys of the Dome of the Rock and the al-Aqsa Mosque. While not building on such a grand scale or over such an extended period as the Mamluks, the Ottomans were, nevertheless, responsible for the construction of the city walls standing today. Waqfs continued to flourish, and in 1551 the Khasski Sultan Waqf, the largest waqf in Palestine, was set up. Indeed, much of Ottoman economic life of Jerusalem centered on the role of religion in the city. Revenue from the pilgrim industry, endowments, and bequests to the Christian and Jewish communities sustained a city that was some distance from ports and the trade routes of the coastal plain and lacking in natural resources or a manufacturing base.

The Ottoman period also saw the gradual emergence of European influence in the city. From the signing of the first "capitulation" treaty between the Ottomans and the French (1535) onward, European interference advanced with growing momentum. The successive capitulation treaties gave different European countries various powers over the administration of the Christian holy places, which they exercised either through the churches under their tutelage or through their consuls. By the late nineteenth century, the French and British consuls had considerable influence over political developments in Jerusalem.

European interference often focused on the privileges held by the different denominations. Greek Orthodox, Roman Catholic, Armenian Orthodox, Russian Orthodox, and later Protestant hierarchies struggled for control over the various Christian holy places and for the prestige such control would render their interpretation of the faith and their European backers. Violence and bloody clashes periodically erupted to the extent that at different points during the Ottoman era, a succession of policy decisions were finally codified into an edict, issued by Sultan Uthman III in 1757, that became the status quo. The status quo established a crude pecking order, which, since it reflected the balance of European and Ottoman power of the day, was a cause of much friction and dispute when that balance of power subsequently altered.

The nineteenth century saw the twin developments of Jerusalem as a major administrative center in the region and growing European involvement. The Ottomans made Jerusalem the administrative capital of the new province of Jerusalem. At the same time, the growing weakness of the central state allowed European influence in the city to increase dramatically, both in terms of the powers of the consuls and demographically, as a European-style "New City" began to appear outside the city walls to the east. From 1839 the British took the Jews under their wing, and a small Protestant community was created by way of conversion. The waxing power of the British Empire meant that increased Jewish immigration to Jerusalem received British protection. By the 1870s, Jewish building societies were established, and the Mea She'arim Quarter was built to the northwest of the walls. By the 1890s, these developments had proceeded to such an extent that leading Jerusalem Muslim families were protesting against Jewish immigration and land acquisition.

By the beginning of World War I, Jerusalem had become the biggest city in Palestine. The arrival of General Allenby in 1917, and the British takeover of the city marked by the establishment of the British Mandate, hastened the transformation of Jerusalem into a more European city, both in terms of physical appearance and in demographic composition and culture. The foundations upon which the modern city of Jerusalem was built can be traced back to the British Mandate administration of the city. Not since the Crusader period, 900 years previously, had Jerusalem been the administrative and political capital of such a large and coherent area. The location of government offices, legal and religious courts, and organizational headquarters in the city led to dramatic improvements in its economy, its access, and its amenities and services.

In addition, this period witnessed the growth in the Christian institutional presence and the exponential growth in the Jewish population by the end of the mandate. The boom in the construction of churches, Christian hospitals, Christian schools, and Christian guesthouses for pilgrims and the employment of Palestinian Christians from the Bethlehem and Ramallah areas all led to the construction of Christian quarters outside the walls. The influx of wealth and people these developments entailed overshadowed the Muslim community's attempts to not only represent the Palestinians in their dispute with Britain and the Zionist Jewish immigrants but also to build up their own communal infrastructure. Certainly, with reference to the early part of the mandate period, not since the Crusader period had the Christian influence in Jerusalem been so extensive. Similarly, the trebling of the Jewish population between 1922 and 1946 to slightly less than half the total population of Jerusalem was a direct consequence of British support of Zionism and the establishment of the Jewish "homeland." Disputes of access to holy places and the balance of political representation in the municipal council became the main flash points in the relations between Jews and Palestinian Muslims, and Palestinian Christians struggled against a decline in their influence over the British administration and its gradual eclipse by Jewish demographic preponderance.

The partition of Jerusalem into Jordanian-held and Israeli-held territories during the fighting that followed the withdrawal of British forces in 1948 was a tragedy for the city. While it reflected the increasing polarization between the two communities that had developed during the latter stages of the mandate, it also did nothing but entrench the divide separating them.

Over the nineteen years of the partition period (1948–1967), East Jerusalem remained static in population numbers. Having absorbed thousands of Palestinian refugees from the western part of the city, any further addition through natural growth was lost by emigration as the Palestinians sought work and security elsewhere. The Jordanian government was both unable and reluctant to invest in the economy, in the infrastructure, or in services for the city. Administrative offices were relocated to Amman, and East Jerusalem fell back onto its traditional economic base of pilgrimage and its postwar equivalent, tourism. Water and electricity supplies remained intermittent right up to 1967. Shorn of its access to the ports and agricultural wealth of the coastal plain and forbidden to develop politically as a center for Palestinian nationalism, East Jerusalem suffered a sharp decline.

In contrast, Israeli West Jerusalem was unilaterally declared the capital of the new State of Israel. The government sought to overcome its geographic disadvantages of having lost its hinterland and access to the Arabian interior by investing heavily to attract immigrants and employment. Most government offices and national institutions such as the Knesset, the Israeli parliament, a new university, and the Great Synagogue were built there. Israel had captured the main water supply to Jerusalem, and power supplies were made available from sources on the coastal plain. As a result of these activities, the population doubled to 200,000 Israeli Jews. Nevertheless, in relation to the development of other Israeli cities like Haifa and Tel Aviv, the future of West Jerusalem was precarious. Its economy was heavily dependent upon government and public sector employment. Without access to the holy places, it had little attraction for tourists, and its status as a frontline city made private investors cautious.

The occupation by Israel of East Jerusalem after 1967 up to the present has led to dramatic changes in the city as a whole. Tensions between the Palestinian and Israeli Jewish communities have been a constant theme throughout this period and reflect the broad political conflict at the national level. The Arab East Jerusalem municipality was dismissed, the mayor deported, and its area absorbed into the Israeli administration. The city's borders were then extended north to the edges of Ramallah and south to Bethlehem in a unilateral annexation of this territory (see also "Ramallah al-Birch"). Palestinians refused to recognize the legitimacy of Israeli control and have boycotted local elections since 1967.

The Israeli government adopted a policy of ensuring that the Israeli Jewish population of the city remained always at least two-thirds that of the Palestinian Arab population; large suburban estates were developed on the annexed areas on the city's east side to house Israeli Jews. They also had the effect of expropriating Palestinian-owned land and cutting off the Palestinian areas of Jerusalem from the hinterland of the West Bank, thus undermining Palestinian claims to sovereignty over East Jerusalem. Both communities sought to strengthen their institutional presence in the city through the location of hospitals, educational institutions, and cultural and intellectual activities. The Israeli Jewish community had the great advantage of government support with legal and military backing, while the Palestinian initiatives were more ad hoc and lacked coherence. Nevertheless, they managed to maintain control over most of the holy places, particularly the Haram ash-Sharif. Discussions over the future of the city between Israeli and Palestinian leaders have centered on the possibility of shared municipal frameworks. Security issues, and the issue of control over shared holy sites, have proved to be among the more difficult issues to resolve.

Given its history, Jerusalem abounds with historically important and architecturally splendid sites, and only a very few can be mentioned here. Most of the sites are contained within the Old City, whose dramatic Ottoman walls and original gates were built by Sulayman al-Qanuni, "the Lawmaker," (1520–1566). The walls partly followed the lines of Emperor Hadrian's fortifications, and the seven gates are Mamluk inspired, with an *L*-shaped entrance for defensive purposes. The eighth gate, the Golden Gate, has Roman foundations and is permanently closed. Islamic eschatology holds that it will be opened on the Day of Judgment, while in the Jewish tradition, it is the gate through which the Messiah will enter Jerusalem. Bab al-Khalil, also known as Jaffa Gate, lies beside the citadel built on Herodian foundations but extensively and ornately rebuilt by the Mamluks.

Probably the most spectacular site in Jerusalem is the Haram ash-Sharif, also known in Judaism as the Temple Mount. A large enclosure, it is the third-holiest site in Islam and was built between AD 685 and AD 709. Among other famous sites and very beautifully constructed monumental buildings included within the compound are the Qubbat al-Sakhra (the Dome of the Rock) and al-Aqsa Mosque. The Dome of the Rock is where Muslims believe that the Prophet Muhammad ascended to heaven and where Abraham attempted to sacrifice his son to God. Al-Aqsa Mosque is regarded as the place referred to in the Qur'an where the Prophet Muhammad prayed following his famous "night journey." Despite the troubled political circumstances of the present, the Haram ash-Sharif still transmits a sense of rich spirituality and peaceful reflection amid a busy and bustling city.

The subterranean areas of the Haram ash-Sharif include a large vault, known as Solomon's Stables. Although much repaired and restored by the Romans and during the Middle Ages, the vault is a Herodian creation and thought to be part of the original Jewish Temple built in 970 BC. The assumption is that it was built by King Solomon to house the ark of the covenant and the priestly Holy of Holies. All that has survived of the original Jewish Temple is the Western, or Wailing, Wall. In 1967 a Palestinian area known as the Moroccan Quarter adjacent to the wall was demolished to create a huge plaza, which is now the site of Jewish and Israeli nationalist rituals. The Old City also contains the Holy Sepulchre, the most revered site in Christendom and the place where Jesus Christ is believed to have been crucified and entombed. Christians also believe that this is the site where Christ rose after being killed. Although originally built by Emperor Constantine, the current structure dates from the Crusades. Inside is a vast collection of chapels reflecting the iconography and ritual styles of the different Christian sects that have a presence in the church. Below the Old City are also a number of water channels, the most notable of which is Hezekiah's Tunnel, which flows through the city and out again, exiting in the Kidron valley at Birket Silwan (the pool of Siloam).

Michael Dumper

Further Readings

Armstrong, Karen. *Jerusalem: One City, Three Faiths.* New York: Knopf, 1966.

Asali, Kamil J., ed. *Jerusalem in History.* Buckhurst Hill, UK: Scorpion, 1989.

Bahat, Dan. *Carta's Historical Atlas of Jerusalem.* Jerusalem: Carta, 1986.

Dumper, Michael. *The Politics of Jerusalem since 1967.* New York: Columbia University Press, 1997.

Duncan, Alistair. *The Noble Sanctuary: Portrait of a Holy Place in Arab Jerusalem.* London: Middle East Archive, 1981.

Murphy-O'Connor, Jerome. *The Holy Land: An Archaeological Guide from Earliest Times to 1700.* Oxford: Oxford University Press, 1992.

Peters, Francis. *Jerusalem.* Princeton: Princeton University Press, 1985.

K

Karbala
Population: 500,000 (2005 estimate)

This holy city of Shi'i Islam has been the center of devotion, scholarship, and pilgrimage for the global Shi'i community for 1,500 years. Centered around the shrine of the martyr Imam Hussayn, Karbala has been a consistent target of attack, capture, and religiously motivated destruction and renewal by the military forces of faraway empires. The clerics and scholars who administer and study within the precinct of this holy city often influence regional political events, and thousands of pilgrims come to this city every day, many to be buried.

Karbala (Arabic, *Karbala*) is located in the center of modern-day Iraq, on the edge of the Syrian Desert. It is connected to the Hindiyah branch of the Euphrates River by canal and lies about sixty-two miles southwest of Baghdad and forty-eight miles north of Najaf. It is one of the holiest cities in the Islamic world and the center of pilgrimage for the Shi'i, the largest Muslim sect after the orthodox Sunnis. Although there were ancient sites in the vicinity, the city grew up around the shrine of Hussayn ibn Ali, a Muslim martyr and the grandson of the founder of Islam, the Prophet Muhammad. The city became the focus of Shi'i opposition to the dominant Sunni regimes, ancient and modern. Its wealth through lavish endowments and from income derived from pilgrims has meant that the Shi'i clerical elite achieved a degree of religious and political autonomy that often led to political confrontation with state authorities, leaving an impact upon the growth and fabric of the city.

Strictly speaking, the name *Karbala* only applies to the eastern part of the palm gardens that surround the city in a semicircle. The city itself is called al-Mashhad or Mashhad al-Hussayn. Karbala has always been a particularly rich town, partly because of its possession of the shrine of Imam Hussayn but also because it has been a starting point for Persian pilgrim caravans to Najaf and Makkah and a desert port for trade for the interior of Arabia. The chief industries include the manufacture of religious goods, textiles, shoes, and the processing of cement and food. Its main wealth, however, is derived from *waqf*s (religious endowments), dedicated by Shi'i adherents from all over the world to support the shrine and the pilgrims visiting them. Thus, the shrines have become the center of the spiritual and commercial lives of the inhabitants of Karbala, whose number has steadily been growing. For example, in 1965 there were 81,500 inhabitants, and twenty years later this number more than doubled (to 184,600). During Ashura (yearly celebrations commemorating the death of Hussayn) the number swells to twice as many. Half of this population is Persian, and there is a large number of Indian and Pakistani Shi'i in residence. Many elderly pilgrims travel to Karbala and wait to die there and are catered for in special hostels and homes. Despite being rich in water and surrounded by fertile soil, Karbala was relatively poorly inhabited and prior to the Islamic period was part of a cluster of villages. Following the momentous events surrounding the death of Hussayn, however, it became a leading holy city. After the death of the ruler of the Muslim Empire, Caliph Muawiyya, in AD 680, Hussayn claimed the role of caliph. This claim was contested, however, by Muawiyya's son, Yazid, who seized power. Hussayn opposed this, and with a small band of followers of around seventy men, women, and children, he faced Yazid's far more sizable army at Karbala. Hussayn was killed, and the story of the battle and Hussayn's tragic death is central for the Shi'i version of Islam, gaining a position in the Shi'i thinking not very different from the crucifixion of Jesus Christ in Christianity. While Karbala is one of the most holy cities in the whole of Islam, it is for the Shi'i that it plays the most important role. Imam Hussayn and his brother Abbas are buried in the two great shrines in the city. Twice each year, on the tenth day of the Muslim month of Muharram and forty days later in the month of Safar, Shi'i pilgrims from throughout the region and from around the world seek to commemorate the death of Imam Hussayn in Karbala.

From these tragic beginnings, Karbala attained great importance in Shi'i piety as early as 682, when Hussayn's family was released from an Umayyad prison in Damascus. They decided to perform a *ziyara* (visitation or minor pilgrimage) to Hussayn's tomb before returning to Madinah. This was followed by a similar visit three years later by Sulayman ibn Surad, a prominent Shi'i leader from Kufa. He and his followers visited the burial site as penitents to purge themselves of the feeling of shame as a consequence of their failure to help Hussayn. Thus, the practice of visitation and ritual flagellation began and became religiously legitimized through several pronouncements by authoritative Shi'i clerics. Some went as far as to compare the virtue of a visitation to Karbala with that of the hajj to Makkah. In this way, a rival Shi'i practice arose to challenge the orthodox Sunni one, reflecting a political challenge to the Umayyad dynasty, which had kept control of the caliphate.

By 850–851, the practice of visitation by the Shi'i had become so widespread that al-Mutawwaqil, the Abbasid caliph, took action. The growing sanctity and piety connected with Hussayn's shrine had generated a radical activism among the oppressed Shi'i, and the messianic traditions related to Karbala took on subversive and revolutionary tones. Both the visitation to Karbala and the annual mourning for Hussayn were treated by the Sunni authorities as threats to their regime, and they destroyed the tomb and prohibited visits to Karbala under heavy penalties. This fear and suspicion continued to dominate Sunni thinking down through the ages, but such actions failed to completely eradicate the practice or to delegitimize Karbala as a central Shi'i holy city. Despite repeated prohibitions against pilgrims, including a banning by the caliph Harun ar-Rashid, the tomb of Hussayn was gradually added to and made more elaborate. In the eleventh century, foundations were laid for a large structure to cover the site of the tomb, and houses, markets, and a boundary wall were built around it. The famous Muslim geographer, Ibn Battuta, visited Karbala in 1326–1327 and described it as a small town lying among palm groves watered from the Euphrates.

Since the Safavid dynasty was Shi'i, during periods of Persian domination of the city, Karbala was permitted to serve its role as a Shi'i holy city. Yet tensions with the Sunnis continued. In 1801, for example, the puritanical Sunni Wahhabis entered Karbala and slew many of its inhabitants and looted the houses and bazaars. In particular, they destroyed the shrine of Hussayn and carried off the gilt copper plates and other treasures of the sanctuary. However, the city soon recovered through the contributions from Shi'i communities round the world. Under the Ottomans, Shi'i were, in general, allowed to visit the city and perform their rituals. In 1871 the Ottoman governor, Medhat Pasha, began the building of government offices and extended the adjoining marketplace beside the shrine.

During the twentieth century, Karbala's status as a Shi'i holy city was subjected to pressures from a different direction: Arab nationalism and secularism. On the one hand, improved access links and the advent of mass transportation increased the flow of pilgrims; on the other hand, the increasing inroads made by the modern state in municipal and welfare

Skyline of Karbala, 1932. (Library of Congress)

provision undercut the role of the religious authorities who controlled the city. The heterogeneous nature of the modern Iraqi state meant that Karbala functioned as a Shi'i power center separate from the Sunni-dominated state structures operating out of Baghdad. Tensions were thus inevitable, and Karbala once again began to experience restrictions and prohibitions on its religious activities, many of which were designed to curb the power and influence of its religious leadership. In 1977, for example, many hundreds of pilgrims were killed or arrested in clashes with Iraqi government forces. Tensions were exacerbated by the 1979 revolution in Iran, which brought the militant Shi'i cleric Ayatollah Khomeini to power. Khomeini had lived in Iraq for many years and had close links with the Shi'i leaders in Iraq. These tensions were not eased by the Iran-Iraq War of 1980–1989.

Following the Iraqi invasion of Kuwait and the defeat of Iraqi forces in 1991 by a United Nations (UN) coalition , Karbala was the site of a battle between Shi'i rebels and Republican Guard units loyal to Iraqi leader Saddam Hussayn. At the end of two weeks of fierce fighting, the rebels were defeated. Much of the city was destroyed, however, and subsequent renovation works were hampered by government restrictions and UN sanctions. Tensions continued into the late 1990s, with government attempts to prevent processions into the city. In both 1998 and 1999, violent incidents were reported between Iraqi pilgrims and Baath Party members and security forces enforcing the ban.

In the post-Saddam era, the freedom of religious expression has allowed Shi'i pilgrims to again come to Karbala during Ashura. In 2004 more than 5 million pilgrims descended on the city during the two key Shi'i holidays. An attack on the pilgrims left more than ninety dead. In May 2004, U.S. troops spent three weeks fighting the militias of Muqtada as-Sadr for control of the city. After significant damage to the city's infrastructure, and considerable loss of life, as-Sadr's forces withdrew.

Karbala is largely a modern city encompassing an old core with winding streets and decorated houses. At the center of this core, the prime structure of historical and architectural significance is the shrine to Imam Hussayn and his companions. The shrine is entered by wooden gates covered with glass decorations that lead to a *haram* (an enclosed sanctuary), surrounded by small rooms, or *iwan*s. These are decorated with a continuous ornamental band that is said to contain the whole Qur'an written in white on a blue background. The shrine itself is located in the middle of the haram, in a domed chamber surrounded by square-shaped structures called *rawaq*. The tomb of Hussayn is in the middle of the chamber and ringed by silver *mashrabiyya* (intricate moldings) work; at the foot of it stands a second, smaller tomb, that of his son and companion in arms, Ali Akbar. Two minarets flank the entrance of the whole sanctuary, and a third rises before the buildings on the east side of the courtyard. In one

of the corners of the haram is the Ganj-e-Shuhada, where bodies of all the seventy-two martyrs of Karbala are buried.

There are more than 100 mosques in the city, some of them Sunni. Other shrines in the city include a small building with a turquoise-tiled dome dedicated to Hussayn's cousin, Uwan, who fell with him in the battle against Yazid. Next to one of the ancient gates to the city, the Bab ad-Dhahab (Golden Gate), is the Qatl-gah, where the actual martyrdom of Hussayn took place. Karbala has many historical madrasas and libraries and is well known for the religious writings of its famous scholars.

Michael Dumper

Further Readings

Jafri, S. Husain M. *Origins and Early Development of Shi'a Islam.* London: Longman, 1979.

Litvak, Meir. *Shi'i Scholars and Patrons of Nineteenth-Century Iraq: The "Ulama" of Najaf and Karbala.* Cambridge: Cambridge University Press, 1998.

Nakash, Yitzhak. *The Shiis of Iraq.* Princeton: Princeton University Press, 1994.

Tabari, Muhammad ibn Jarir al-. *The Conquest of Iraq, Southwestern Persia, and Egypt.* Translated by Gautier H. A. Juynboll. Albany: State University of New York Press, 1989.

Tripp, Charles. *A History of Iraq.* 2d ed. Cambridge: Cambridge University Press, 2002.

Khartoum

Population: Khartoum, 1.74 million (2005 estimate); Khartoum North, 1.72 million (2005 estimate); Omdurman, 2.95 million (2005 estimate)

Khartoum is both one city and three cities, both an old city and a phoenix city, both a colonial city and an African city, both the end of the road for many and the beginning of the road for others. The capital of Sudan, it has a long history as an "almost" city prior to its establishment by Egyptian imperialism in 1821. Yet into its 185 years of existence, it has managed to cram a host of characters such as the Mahdi, Major "Chinese" Gordon, Lord Kitchener, Winston Churchill, Hasan al-Turabi, and General Ja'far Nimieri. Known to some as the "flat city" because it has so few buildings over three stories high, the city continues to struggle to integrate all its conflicting cultural and political groups, ranging from refugees and military elites to Darfurians, Nubians, Ethiopians, Eritreans, and Arabs, into one community.

Modern Khartoum is actually a conurbation, composed of three separate cities: Khartoum (Arabic, *al-Khrtum*); Khartoum North (*al-Khartum Bahri*, sometimes known as *Bahri*); and Omdurman (*Umm Durman*). Together they compose greater Khartoum, also known as "the triple capital" or the "three towns." The conurbation encompasses the spot where the Blue Nile, flowing west from the mountains of Ethiopia, and the White Nile, flowing north from the mountains of

Uganda, converge. Islands divide the channel of both rivers (Tuti Island is the largest) at their meeting point, with one bridge connecting Khartoum to the west bank of the White Nile, where Omdurman is located; another bridge connecting Khartoum to Khartoum North, located on the east bank of the Blue Nile; and one bridge linking Omdurman and Khartoum North. Parts of Khartoum are low lying and swampy, and prone to flooding, while other neighborhoods are on a slight rise and are more healthy. In fact, large-scale flooding in 1988, 1992, 2001, and 2005, for example, destroyed thousands of homes and affected more than 1 million people each time. The waterfront along the northern edge of Khartoum proper is the administrative and commercial core of the city.

The city sits near the transition from savannah and grasslands to the northern arid desert. However, from the city north to the sixth cataract of the Nile is a fertile floodplain known as the Shendi Reach that supports agriculture. To the south of the city, between the two rivers, is the fertile region known as the Gezira (from al-Jazira, the island), where most of Sudan's large cotton plantations are located. To the west of the city lies Kordufan and then Darfur, part of the Sahara, a habitat for pastoralists. To the east along the Blue Nile is the Butana savannah and southern Atbara River stretching to the Ethiopian border. The three towns thus benefit from and connect a range of diverse cultural patterns, acting as a point of convergence and change for ancient caravan routes, products, and peoples.

Archaeological excavations in the city at the site of the former Khartoum Hospital indicate that, beginning around 7000 BC, there was continuous human settlement on the site. The cultural complex revealed in these excavations, involving pottery and stone and bone tools, has been called "Early Khartoum" and was shared with communities well to the north, south, east, and west into the Sahara. Early Khartoum was an ancient aquatic way of life, a riverine culture based around fish and game. From around the sixth millennium BC, there was cultivation of wild sorghum, and after about 5000 BC cattle and small livestock were domesticated. After 3000 BC, the climate became drier, desiccation set in, and pastoralism emerged in areas away from the river. Communities were planting domesticated millet, and they were involved in long-distance trade along the Nile to Aswan.

By 2300 BC, trade with Egypt was a regular component of local life, with ebony, leopard skins, and elephant tusks being passed to the north, perhaps by a kingdom called Yam located around Shendi Reach. By the age of the New Kingdom and Thutmose I (1500 BC), the Egyptians projected their power into upper Nubia, north of the fifth cataract, and stayed there for 500 years. A kingdom known as Irem may have dominated the area of the convergence of the White and Blue Nile during this time and paid tribute to Memphis. Records become somewhat clearer with the rise of the Meroitic kingdom in the

Shendi Reach (750 BC–AD 350). Although its power waxed and waned to the north along the Nile, those to the north of present-day Khartoum continued to dominate the site of the convergence of the Nile for almost a millennium and erected towns and monuments and fortified the caravan routes in the area.

The Romans captured Egypt in 30 BC and established their frontier around Aswan and the first cataract after 23 BC (see also "Aswan"). Over the next four centuries, there were a number of expeditions against Meroë and further south. By the end of the first century BC, Roman forces had been to the fourth cataract, and 100 years later Nero dispatched Praetorian soldiers to investigate the upper Nile. With a military escort supplied by Meroë, the expedition took the White Nile branch at present-day Khartoum as far as Malakal and then returned to Rome with samples and extensive descriptions. Their story is recorded by Seneca. Subsequent Roman travelers made it just to the north of Khartoum; they left graffiti to indicate their passing. Excavations in Khartoum have recovered Roman goods, including coins, fine pottery, bronze vessels, and fragile glass.

By the sixth century, the area above the sixth cataract was controlled by a Meroitic successor state, the Nubian kingdom called Alwa (Greek, *Alodia*), whose control extended up the Blue Nile toward the Aksumite kingdom in Ethiopia (see also "Aksum"). With the arrival of Bishop Longinus ca. AD 580, as reported by John of Ephesus, the rulers adopted the Christian Monophysite doctrine and looked to the Coptic Church in Egypt for guidance. The first mention of their capital of Soba, on the north bank of the Blue Nile about fifteen miles upstream from Khartoum, is in the writings of al-Yaqubi (ca. 891). Archaeological investigations at Soba reveal that their basilicas followed Byzantine plans, and a version of Greek was used for official purposes. Trade with Byzantine Egypt was facilitated by gold brought from the Ethiopian hills, and Soba became, for the next 700 years, the key city of the region. The tenth-century Arab geographer and Egyptian ambassador Ibn Salim al-Aswani is an early source on the geography of the Khartoum area. Quoted by al-Maqrizi (d. 1442), Ibn Salim talks about his trip upriver to the junction of the Blue and White Nile, its great island (Tuti Island), and the richness of the agriculture in the area. Other visitors comment on the numerous churches and villages in the area, and there are remains located around modern Khartoum that fit these descriptions.

Islam entered the area after the eighth century with traders coming from two directions, both down the Nile and across from the Red Sea. A Muslim Quarter of Soba was established for these traders, and exchange with the Fatimid kingdom in Cairo stimulated the area. Nubian soldiers fought in the Fatimid army, and return migration may have been another source for the spread of Islamic beliefs.

By the thirteenth century, the kingdom of Alwa was gone, dissolved into local Muslim communities ruled by Nubian chiefs controlling their own section of north-south trade from their castles located south from the fifth cataract; one Mamluk emissary passed through nine separate territories on his way to Soba. Over the next century, however, Arab tribes who had been gradually migrating south after the Arab takeover of Egypt came to dominate the area. Under the leadership of Abdallah Jamma, the Abdullabi tribe established their control over the confluence of the Blue and White Nile. From their capital at Gerri (slightly north of Khartoum), they dominated both the increased trade that was moving north to Egypt and the Nubians along the Nile from the sixth cataract south. Tuti Island and the banks of both rivers around the confluence were used for agriculture and grazing.

In 1504 the Nubian Funj, who migrated from west of the White Nile to take control of the Blue Nile below modern Khartoum, established themselves at Sennar, 180 miles south of the confluence of the rivers. The Sennar Sultanate (*al-Saltana al-Zarqa,* Black Sultanate, or the Funj Sultanate) defeated the Abdullabi, who from then on ruled the area as vassals of the Funj. The Funj were most concerned with controlling long-distance trade, and the market at Sennar became the largest in the region. Gold, slaves, and ivory to Egypt left from here, and they expanded their control far into Kordufan and to the gates of Ethiopia.

The late fifteenth, sixteenth, and seventeenth centuries in East Africa was a period of religious ferment. Recent converts were searching for guidance and direction in their religious lives and so turned to more knowledgeable scholars from the Arab central lands. There were numerous Sufi (Egyptian or Arab) preachers moving through the region, establishing an (often temporary) community of followers, which evolved, upon their deaths, into sites of habitation focused around the *qubbas* (*gubbas*), or tombs, of these holy men. East Africa has many such sites of veneration, domed whitewashed buildings with huts around them. Into such a context at the beginning of the sixteenth century the saintly Maha tribe acquired, under Abdullabi and Funj patronage, Tuti Island and established themselves as the area's religious leaders and shaykhs. The Maha shaykhs were consulted by the Funj on theological and legal questions, and various members of the family established religious complexes in the area. Tuti Island became a center for the expansion of Islam in the region.

Fakih Arbab al-Agayed, for example, moved to the Mogren district of what is now western Khartoum ca. 1691 and established a *khalwa* (*zawiya*), or religious school, and mosque. His influence was widespread, and he attracted hundreds of students. His family continued the schools, and they existed at the time of the Egyptian conquest in 1821. One of Fakih Arbab's students was Shaykh Hamad (d. ca. 1730), who took

up residence in what was to become Omdurman, and a village grew up around his school there. Later, driven out by a dispute with another shaykh, Hamad reestablished himself in what is now Khartoum North, and Hillet Hamad grew up around him there; today Maha are still concentrated around his gubba in Bahri. Other Maha shaykhs established villages at Eilafun and Burri al-Lamaab, all now incorporated into greater Khartoum. Supposedly, these were the first permanent structures in Khartoum. The name *al-Khartoum* may derive from the Arabic *khrtum,* which means "elephant trunk," since this is the shape of the island at the confluence of the rivers.

By the beginning of the nineteenth century, the Funj kingdom had collapsed into political chaos. Into the vacuum stepped the new ruler of Egypt, Muhammad Ali, who ordered the imperial expansion into Sudan starting in 1820. Ismail Pasha fought his way down the Nile at the head of troops armed with modern guns and artillery. After bombarding Tuti Island, they landed at the site of Khartoum in 1821. From here they headed south and captured Sennar and then campaigned until 1823 to pacify the region. It was only then that they began to consider where to establish their administrative and military headquarters for the newly annexed territory of Sudan.

The motivation for the invasion was primarily to grab the revenues of the slave trade. But it also was long-term colonial development, and so a site was needed that could both dominate the caravan routes and also be a defensible site for the garrisons and bureaucrats of control. Although they hesitated at first, in 1826 the new governor-general of Sudan, Khurshid Pasha, established his office and a mosque at Khartoum, a site defensible from attack from the desert. In the process, Egyptian troops destroyed many of the existing mosques and gubbas located on the site, including the mosque of Fakih Arbab. Reportedly, they executed Arbab's great-grandson by tying him to the mouth of a canon and firing it.

The era of Egyptian domination in Khartoum is known as the Turkiyya (1821–1881), since the Sudanese called all colonial authorities, Egyptian or otherwise, Turki (Ottoman). By 1829 there were reportedly around 30 beehive huts and barracks for 800 soldiers in the town, and slaves were already being auctioned in the governor's house. When Muhammad Ali visited the city in 1838, there was a military hospital, staffed by European and Egyptian doctors, and consular representation. By 1840 it was a city of well more than 20,000 people, including Europeans and East Africans.

Scavenging materials from the ruins of Soba, successive pashas built a palace, government offices, warehouses for the quays, and fortified buildings. The tallest building was the mosque, made out of brick, as was the Catholic mission, built after 1856; most everything else was low mud houses or huts. The city grew with no planning or consideration for its layout, and it expanded quickly. Belgians were the first missionaries into the city, but the Franciscans soon followed and established a school for slave children bought from the slave market. By the 1870s, when the first steamships arrived, there was a three-story palace with an annex for the governor's harem, a Coptic district with a church and cemetery, grain silos, and arsenal and administrative buildings.

The new city developed a reputation as a boomtown, with everyone looking for a quick return on the slave trade, provision of services, or new schemes for agriculture. Prostitution, slavery, questionable water supply, no sewage system, high immigration rates, and constant port traffic all helped feed an unhealthy environment for Khartoum's inhabitants. There was considerable illness in the city, and the population suffered from plagues and contagious disease. One of the most severe was the cholera epidemic of 1856, and the government fled the city temporarily. Enough people died from disease that the population dropped by 1870 to 20,000. Governors did not stay long: between 1825 and 1885, twenty-five different governors served in Khartoum.

Quickly, the new city attracted the caravan routes passing east and west or north to south, and it became the hub of transport in the region. One observer in 1836 noted that all the slave caravans from Ethiopia, Sennar, and Kordofan were now converging on Khartoum. With the expansion of the regional British attack on the slave trade after 1850, international traffickers linked to the slave-trading kings in the Sahel hinterland migrated to Khartoum and found haven there that was denied them along the coast (see also "Zanzibar"). In the ivory trade, Khartoum pulled tusks from central Africa and from up the White Nile, acting as a market for resale and shipment toward Cairo. The city also played a role in the lucrative gun-running trade. From the 1840s until the 1880s, it was a central spot for selling what became known as "slave guns" transshipped throughout East Africa. In the 1860s, one report says the southern products available in the market included ivory, tamarind, civet, gold, and slaves, while the northern products included spices, paper, copper, iron, arsenic, vermilion, and Venice glass beads. Sennar, the former Funj capital to the south, lost most of its importance with the establishment of Khartoum.

From the earliest period, Ethiopians came to Khartoum and carved out a life for themselves. They were joined by many others, making it a highly cosmopolitan city, home to Copts, Muslim Egyptians, Nubians, domestic slaves, Turks, Armenians, Jews, Syrians, Algerians, Galla, and Greeks. Jurists from al-Azhar filled the legal positions. Soldiers, mercenaries, and adventurers such as Major "Chinese" Gordon and former Yankee and Confederate officers from America came to serve the pasha, suppress (or profit from) the slave trade, and command the military. West Africans, on pilgrimage to Makkah, increasingly passed through the city.

The rush for profits came to a quick end with the appearance of the Mahdi in 1881. This was the year 1300 in the Muslim calendar, and many in Sudan expected eschatological events and awaited the rise of one al-Mahdi al-Muntazar, a savior to end oppression and regenerate the faith. That year a local cleric and Sufi who had studied in Khartoum declared himself al-Mahdi and began to collect followers around him in Kordofan. Muhammad Ahmed b. Abdallah came from a clerical family and felt repelled by the sinful urban ways of Khartoum and the dominance of the Turki. His message called for the expulsion of the Egyptians and unification of the Muslim community under pure traditional Islam. As a *mujaddid* (renewer), Ahmad dressed simply, ate simply, read the Qur'an consistently, and reportedly cried when he read the holy book. He banned smoking, music, jewelry for women, and dressing "like a Turk." His followers, a motley collection of people streaming from all over Sudan to fight under his spear-and-crescent banner, were untrained and poorly armed but filled with faith. They took the title of *ansar* (supporters) and began to confront Egyptian forces. After a number of smaller successes, they unexpectedly captured the western regional capital of al-Obeid in 1883; this was interpreted as a miracle and evidence of the Mahdi's calling, further increasing his adherents. The Egyptians then sent a mercenary-led force of more than 10,000 men against him, and this expedition was wiped out by what the British derogatorily called dervishes.

The rise of the Mahdi occurred just as Britain was establishing its control in Egypt and as France, Italy, and Britain were expanding their authority over the Red Sea coast and Ethiopia (see also "Djibouti City" and "Berbera"). Thus, the situation in Sudan was perceived by them within the broader imperial scramble for Africa and their global considerations. The result was a decision by the British to abandon the province. The question then became how to evacuate both the thousands of Egyptian soldiers scattered around the province and the Europeans who had sought refuge in Khartoum. In January 1884, Major Gordon was recalled to supervise the evacuation of Khartoum.

Gordon arrived at Khartoum on 18 February to find that there were 15,000 people in the city to evacuate, including Europeans, civil servants, widows and orphans, and a garrison of 1,000 men. Quickly, he sent out 2,000 women and children on steamers, but then he delayed. Gordon sought to use his prestige and perilous position to force the Gladstone government in London to modify its decision and to retain Sudan. As the Mahdi's forces gradually encircled Khartoum, Gordon played brinkmanship with both the British government and the Mahdi, calling for a relief expedition. He strengthened the walls and defenses of the city and fortified Omdurman.

The Mahdi took the offensive and cut the Nile to the north at Halfaya. His forces then put the city under siege. During the early stages of the siege, Gordon was able to raid the area around Khartoum for cattle and supplies to maintain his stocks. Gradually, however, the noose tightened, and Gordon lost Omdurman and the north bank, and his supplies ran out. He placed mines and land torpedoes around his defenses, and to boost morale he struck medals that he handed out that said "Siege of Khartoum." The Mahdi fortified Omdurman, and it became the center of his campaign against Khartoum. He established his house here, and this led to its immediate growth, with thousands of his followers flocking to the site.

The British government finally was forced to "relieve Khartoum" and sent an army up the Nile. Aware of their imminent arrival, the Mahdi ordered a final attack on Gordon's redoubt. Finally, after 320 days, on 25 January 1885, Khartoum was attacked at dawn, and it was all was over by midday. Gordon was killed and beheaded. The Mahdi crossed from Omdurman and prayed the midday prayer in the Khartoum mosque and then returned to Omdurman. Two days later, the steamers bringing the English relief army appeared, but finding Khartoum fallen, returned downstream.

After the fall of Khartoum, the Mahdi stayed in Omdurman and ruled the state from there. He received emissaries from Muslim communities as far away as Morocco and the Saudi leadership seeking his assistance. Then, only five months after the capture of Khartoum, he suddenly sickened and died. His three caliphs buried him in the floor of his room, as he had wished. A domed tomb was built over the site, which immediately became a focus of pilgrimage.

For the next twelve years, Sudan was an independent Islamic state under Caliph Abdullah al-Taashi, the Mahdi's successor. Abdullah ordered Khartoum to be evacuated and destroyed, and the remains of Khartoum were used to build the new capital of the Mahdiyya, Omdurman. Immigrants flooded in; by 1886 thatched huts stretched four miles along the Nile, while two years later they ran for seven miles. West Africans on their way to or from Makkah on the hajj and Ethiopians who came for trade were joined by Greeks, Italians, Arabs, Indians, Egyptians, and Syrians working in Omdurman's huge market. Within a short time, it was the largest city in Sudan and by the fall of the Mahdiyya may have contained more than 100,000 inhabitants.

A form of urban planning guided the city's expansion, with quarters assigned for different tribal or ethnic groups. The caliph laid out the Friday Mosque and built the first brick house as his palace (Beit al-Khalifa). The city was laid out around the mosque and around the tomb of the Mahdi. As a holy city, infidels were forbidden to enter, and a defensive wall along the Nile protected the city.

Ultimately, the British, now in control of Egypt, decided to conquer Sudan and moved forces up the Nile, capturing towns from the caliph's forces. Finally, on 2 September 1898, just north of Omdurman at Karari, 50,000 troops of Caliph Abdullah, armed with spears and muskets, confronted the British, Egyptian, and Sudanese forces of Lord Kitchener armed with new Maxim machine guns and howitzers. Around 12,000 of the Mahdiyya forces were killed, compared to forty-eight allied forces. The caliph fled, and during a subsequent battle, he was killed. Winston Churchill, who had accompanied the expedition as an embedded journalist with the Twenty-first Lancers, called 2 September "the last great colonial battle."

Omdurman, including the Mahdi's tomb, was partially destroyed in the fighting, and some of this damage was still evident in the 1960s. Kitchener and the new Anglo-Egyptian Condominium government (agreed on in 1899) took the decision to reestablish the capital in Khartoum and to create a new, planned city, with the necessary modern infrastructure to support it. They took into account plans for military defense as well as for administration, and thus the core bureaucratic functions were placed along the river's edge, with grand gardens, avenues, and street designs that (intentionally?) replicated the shape of the Union Jack. The country was administered from Khartoum by a condominium agent, although sovereignty actually lay in the hands of the British military governor-general and his staff, Egyptians were virtually excluded from the administration.

Railways quickly encircled the city, linking Khartoum to new Port Sudan and to the south (see also "Port Sudan"). The British also laid out an arsenal and military barracks at Khartoum North, the beginning of the growth of this city. The rebirth of Khartoum required significant materials and labor, and the city imported both. There were not enough construction workers available, and so wages crept up, leading to high rural-to-urban migration; in subsequent years, there was actually a decline in agricultural production in the rural areas caused by the shift of labor. By 1900 the city was home to 8,000 people. The first regular newspaper to serve this community, *as-Sudan,* was founded in 1903 by three Lebanese businessmen, followed by *Raid as-Sudan* (*Sudan Leader*) in 1913. Sporadic violence by Mahdist forces in the countryside continued until 1919, and there were rebellions in the south; as a result, Khartoum remained the military headquarters for the country and acted as its arsenal and provisioning base.

The city benefited from the activity and spending of the war years, 1914–1918, and continued to grow during the interwar period. By 1920 Khartoum/Omdurman operated as twin or dual cities, one predominantly European, the other Sudanese. Yet Khartoum itself was also divided into a core colonial city and sprawling southern shantytowns. Down by the waterfront, Khartoum was a European city, with its shopping area run by businesspeople from Lebanon or Italy and its Egyptian Coptic or Jewish businessmen and Greek and Egyptian doctors. This was the headquarters of companies and services and housing for the Westerners. Further out were the Christian schools, schools of foreign communities, missionary sites, and Coptic schools. To the southeast, where the ground was higher and healthier, were the villas, where British administrators lived, and the higher education institutions. There was also "Little Greece," where the Greeks, who had contributed so much to building the city, had their clubs, bakeries, and churches; even the street signs had Greek on them.

To the west along the river lay "New London," containing racecourses and golf greens, the Botanical Gardens, and the zoo. It is also around the bend from where the boats coming down the White Nile dropped their cargo, making Khartoum an important inland port. The slum areas lay to the south, beyond this colonial city. "Native residential areas" like the Old Deims, the southern slums where the first construction workers had been housed, became so crowed that they housed 30,000 people in 6,000 huts. Shantytowns grew up overnight, expanding the city southward.

Slavery remained a problem well into the 1930s. In 1900 the estimate was that one-third of the residents of northern Sudan were still slaves. Although slavery was officially banned, and many slaves were freed, over the next three decades subsequent governor-generals, Gezira land barons, and religious figures colluded to move "tactfully" on the issue, with the result that various forms of slavery continued. In Khartoum, for example, the form it took was domestic and connubial slavery. Former slave women frequently ended up in the slums of Khartoum, running *anadi* (drinking houses).

By the 1920s, the city was hosting anti-British movements and feelings, spurred both by the trajectory of the Egyptian nationalist movement and a push for unity with them but also by local experiences such as the famine of 1913 and blocked avenues to Sudanese advancement. As a result, various forms of political organizing appeared in the city, including a secret society of Gordon College students and the White Flag League, which included Sudanese military officers. Sporadic demonstrations, protests, and written agitation during the summer of 1924 boiled over in November 1924, when Sudanese troops in Khartoum rebelled in support of a "unified Nile Valley." In a pitched battle, fifteen Sudanese and thirteen British were killed before the rebellion was quashed. This event was a major turning point in the city's history. It is from this point that the British began to try to "separate" Sudan from Egypt and to foster a distinct Sudanese identity. Among other responses, the British withdrew Egyptian troops from the Sudan, closed the military school in Khartoum, kicked Egyptian teachers out of the country, cracked down on the city's press, supported the creation of a National Museum and archaeological expeditions to discover the Sudanese past, and established a separate Sudan Defense Force. The Sudan Graduates Congress, created in 1938, placed its stress on achieving a separate but Arab Sudan and called for all Sudanese education to reflect Arab and Islamic values. New literary journals published in Khartoum promoted Sudanese Arab literature.

After the war, Britain's Labour Party government adopted a policy of gradual decolonization, and independence came in 1954. Khartoum's population at the time was about 100,000, with Omdurman home to 140,000. Many British and foreign inhabitants left at independence, although they were quickly replaced by a huge influx of rural migrants. The most striking fact of Khartoum's existence since independence has been its sprawling growth in size and population. From the moment of its creation, the city had attracted rural in-migration, but with independence, this trend exploded: more than 70 percent of all urban migration in the country since 1954 has gone to the three towns. The population of Khartoum increased 286 percent between 1956 and 1973 and 65 percent in the decade following that.

The surge in construction and expansion that hit in the 1950s and 1960s took the city far beyond its old boundaries. Old Deims was torn down and turned into villas built around wide boulevards for the wealthy and for foreign embassies; its inhabitants moved to overcrowded New Deims, much farther out. The University of Khartoum was founded in 1956 on the back of the development of the old Gordon Memorial College. The government made the decision to develop Khartoum North as an industrial center for the country, which meant that Khartoum North grew more quickly than the other two cities. By the mid-1960s, all the nation's manufacturing activity was in Khartoum; 90 percent of Sudan's vehicles were in Khartoum or Omdurman; and the vast majority of its rail, river, and air transport was concentrated in the tri-capital and nowhere else; head offices and commercial, trading, and service industries were all concentrated in Khartoum.

Such distorted national development meant that those who could make it to the city experienced a better lifestyle with more opportunities: per capita income was higher in Khartoum than in rural areas, people were better educated since all the higher education institutions were located in the city, life expectancy and adult literacy were higher in the three towns because of the availability of health and training opportunities, and annual incomes were more than twice that in rural areas. Most of the migrants into the city were young men looking for work in the developing industries in the city. Today such unskilled workers come to the capital to find employment in construction, services, and restaurants or to create jobs for themselves in the informal sector. One interesting segment of the city's mix was the Fulani pastoralists who brought their herds all the way across to Khartoum from central Africa on their pilgrimage to Makkah. Their goal was the cattle market in Khartoum, where they could sell their cattle to pay for the round-trip ticket to the holy cities. They often stayed in Khartoum for years before returning home.

During the last quarter of the twentieth century, the general pattern of the rural-urban migration to the capital continued to include such economic migrants. Yet Khartoum has long been a refugee city as well. Starting as early as 1915, it took in Ethiopians fleeing political unrest inside their country; postindependence it hosted refugees from the urban areas of Eritrea and Ethiopia driven out by the fighting there. The pace of flow to Khartoum and Omdurman slowed in the 1960s and 1970s as most refugees from those countries remained in border areas of Sudan. But in the 1980s and 1990s, this trend picked up again, and refugees again came to Khartoum, primarily from the urban areas of Ethiopia and Eritrea. By 1987 Sudan had the largest number of urban refugees on the continent, and most were located in Khartoum. Given such numbers, Sudanese political figures have used the refugee issue for political purposes. In 1987, for example, the commissioner for Khartoum Province gave refugees in Khartoum ten days to leave Greater Khartoum on their own; after that time, the police and government-sponsored gangs were used to intimidate them. This particular antirefugee campaign in Khartoum ended when the Islamic government came to power.

Greater Khartoum has also ended up hosting internally displaced persons (IDPs), refugees from the various conflicts within the country itself. Following the start (1983) of the rebellion in the south conducted by the Sudan People's Liberation Army (SPLA), millions of southerners ended up in Khartoum, living around the capital in displaced persons camps. Such camps, with housing constructed from tin and cardboard, were located outside the working-class districts and markets of Omdurman and south Khartoum. The largest included Angola and Mandela camps. Some of these IDPs were forcibly moved to Khartoum; for example, the students and staff of the University of Juba were moved to Khartoum, supposedly for security purposes. Add to this those displaced by the recent conflict in Darfur, and those fleeing persecution in the Nuba Mountains, and there may be as many as 4 million displaced persons living in Khartoum.

The tensions created in the city because of the marginalization of such vast numbers of refugees and IDPs, along with a 40 percent inflation rate and few social or health services, have frequently boiled over into violence on the streets. One such event was in the aftermath of the sudden death of John Garang de Mabior, the leader of the SPLA, on 30 July 2005. After years of fighting and negotiations, Garang had just recently been named vice-president of Sudan. With his death, huge protests broke out in the streets of Khartoum and Omdurman. Thousands took to the streets, setting fire to businesses and government buildings. In three days of rioting, 130 people were killed, hundreds injured, and property damaged to the tune of millions of dollars. Racial attacks based on the color of one's skin continued in various neighborhoods and involved all segments of the population.

Themes of migration, imperialism, and alienation have long been central to the work of one of Sudan's most renowned authors, Tayeb Saleh. A graduate of Gordon College in Khartoum, Saleh has primarily lived outside Sudan, but the country and the clash of cultures experienced by migrants (and displaced Sudanese in Khartoum) are key to his most famous work, *Mawsim al-Hijra ila al-Shamal* (*Season of Migration to the North*).

Bruce Stanley

Further Readings
Edwards, David. *The Nubian Past: An Archaeology of the Sudan.* London: Routledge, 2004.
Hill, Richard. *Egypt in the Sudan, 1820–1881.* London: Oxford University Press, 1959.
Holt, Peter M. *The Mahdist State in the Sudan, 1881–1898.* Oxford: Clarendon, 1958.
Lesch, Ann Mosely. *The Sudan: Contested National Identities.* Bloomington: Indiana University Press, 1998.
Niblock, Tim. *Class and Power in Sudan: The Dynamics of Sudanese Politics, 1898–1985.* Basingstoke, UK: Macmillan, 1987.
O'Connor, David. *Ancient Nubia: Egypt's Rival in Africa.* Philadelphia: University of Pennsylvania Press, 1993.
O'Fahey, Rex S., and Jay Spaulding. *Kingdoms of the Sudan.* London: Methuen, 1974.
Spaulding, Jay. *The Heroic Age in Sinnar.* East Lansing: Michigan State University African Studies Center, 1985.
Spiers, Edward, ed. *Sudan: The Reconquest Reappraised.* London: Frank Cass, 1998.
Trimingham, J. Spencer. *Islam in the Sudan.* London: Frank Cass, 1965.
Warburg, Gabriel. *Islam, Sectarianism and Politics in the Sudan since the Mahdiyya.* London: C. Hurst, 2003.

Kirkuk
Population: 620,000 (2005 estimate)

This is the oil city of northern Iraq, built on top of oil pools that for 3,000 years have fueled myth and legend about fire, hell, and brimstone. Always a multiethnic community where Arab, Kurd, Turkoman, and Assyrian intermingle, Kirkuk's struggle for control of its petroleum resources, and to command its strategic location, continues today. Whether it was the Ottomans, the Persians, the British, or the Turkish state, outsiders have always taken an interest in this city, shaping its communal relations and extracting its resources for their own ends.

Kirkuk (ancient, *Arrap-ha;* Kurdish, *Kerkuk*), a city in northern Iraq, is an important center of the oil industry. The city lies at an altitude of approximately 1,000 feet and is situated on both banks of the broad, pebble-strewn bed of the Qadha Chai, a small river that is dry except in winter or after a rainfall. The old part of the city, with its walled citadel, markets, and Muslim and Christian quarters, is set on a great rectangular tell, 120 feet in height, that overlooks the left bank of the river. Across the river, spanned by an ancient bridge of fifteen arches, is Qarwait Kalahiya, a more modern quarter with schools and hospitals, hotels, city administration offices, and the police. West of this, near the railway station, lies the suburb called Arrap-ha, built to contain the installations of the oil industry and accommodation for its workers. The city's attraction has partially been the result of its location along the main road between Baghdad and Mosul. Some 180 miles to the north of Baghdad, the city straddles the boundary between the flat or gently undulating lands to the southwest that culminate in the Jebal Hamrin and the amorphous jumble of ridges bisected by streams that rise to the gray cliffs of the Qara Dagh, the first of the mountain ranges of Kurdistan. This places it on the ethnic boundary between the mountain peoples of Kurdistan and the Arabs of the plains and desert.

Yet paradoxically, like many of the towns along the high road, it has always had a large Turkish population. The origin of these "Turkomans" is unclear: they may have been brought in from Azerbaijan or eastern Anatolia to guard this important route by any number of possible figures such as the Great Seljuqs and their successors, by Temür, or by the Ottoman sultans Selim I and Sulayman I. In centers of Ottoman administration such as Kirkuk, these Turks are Sunnis. In surrounding villages, most are heterodox and described locally as *Qizilbash* (red heads). This is a term originally used to describe the red-turbaned corps d'élite of Shah Ismail I and later came to be a pejorative term used by Sunnis to refer to the various heterodox sects of Anatolia.

Kirkuk is valued today for its petroleum. Yet for most of its history, this resource could not be exploited on an industrial scale, and so Kirkuk was noted for other things. Naturally, it has served as an agro-city, the main market for the agricultural and pastoral products of its region—wool, wheat, barley, fruit, oak gall, and gum as well as sheep, goats, and cattle. The city itself stands among gardens, orchards, and vineyards filled with fruit and olive trees, and even some cotton and rice are grown. Moreover, it is a center for the distribution of textiles and clothing for all Kurdistan, and its suqs have long been filled with mercers and drapers. Its workshops produce woolen cloth, felt used in making coats, various types of cotton material, and even some pottery.

Yet perhaps the most important role played by the city of Kirkuk throughout its history has been to serve as a defensive bastion against depredations of fierce tribes and peoples issuing from the mountains and plateaus to the east—Urartians, Medes, Parthians, and Persians from far away and Kurds near at hand. Yet unlike Mosul, to the north, it was never more than regionally important.

The Assyrians and Babylonians knew it as Arrap-ha, a name now memorialized in the modern quarter built by the Iraq Petroleum Company (IPC), near where archaeologists have found remains of this city. Under the Sassanians, the whole Kirkuk district was called Garmakán or Beth Garmai (land of warmth), because it was believed that Seleucus I Nicator, founder of the Seleucid dynasty, had raised a tower in the citadel.

After the first half of the first millennium AD, the region was a vibrant center of Nestorian Christianity, and the bishop of Karkhá acted as metropolitan of Beth Garmai, a jurisdiction that survived until the early fourteenth century. Indeed, the Chaldean (Uniate Nestorian) bishop residing in Kirkuk today still bears this venerable title. Certain Sassanian shahs inflicted terrible persecutions upon the Nestorians, including Shapur II and especially Yazdegerd II, who killed thousands in AD 445. Under Khusru II, who had a Christian chancellor, the Nestorians' situation vastly improved. After the Muslim conquest, the Arabs referred to the district as Badjarma. The Arab writer Yakut speaks of a town called Karkhína, which is probably Kirkuk.

Kirkuk itself does not emerge into history under that name until the time of Temür, when the chronicler, Ali Yazdi, mentions it in the *Zafarnama*, his history of the conqueror (ca. 1425). Kirkuk was subsequently occupied by the Aq-Qoyunlu followed by the Safavid Shah Ismail, and it then came under Ottoman sway from 1515 to 1517 in the campaigns that followed the Ottoman victory over Shah Ismail. Although the Treaty of Amasya of 1555 placed Kirkuk within Ottoman domains, it was not until 1639, when the boundary between the two powers was agreed upon, that this retrocession was apparently confirmed. For during the period 1623–1638, Shah Abbas I had seized central and lower Iraq. Nonetheless, he failed to permanently occupy the northern districts, controlling Kirkuk for only three years. Despite the "definitive" 1639 Treaty of Zuhab, the Persians sought again to seize Kirkuk 100 years later, when the future Nadir Shah besieged it unsuccessfully in 1732. The following year, he crushed the Ottoman army beneath its walls, killing the grand vizier himself. Nadir Shah finally captured and held Kirkuk between 1743 and 1746, after which time the city was returned to the Ottomans after the truce between the two antagonists.

During the eighteenth century, Kirkuk was the capital of the district of Shahrizur, but after the reforms of 1871 the *sanjak* (district, region, or provincial administrative area of an empire or state) of Kirkuk was renamed Shahrizur, while the plain of Shahrizur proper was separated off and joined with Sulaymaniyya. Despite this reorganization, Kirkuk served as an important garrison town, a bulwark against the Kurds. Because of its ethnic composition, it proved an important source of civil servants and gendarmes for the imperial administration, and even those who might not be ethnic Turks rejoiced in the appellation "Ottoman."

The British occupied Kirkuk on 7 May 1918, evacuated it a week later, and returned at the end of October just five days before the Armistice of Mudros ended the war. They then arranged during the summer of 1921 for a referendum to "elect" Amir Faysal Hussayn as king of Iraq. In true Middle Eastern fashion, he received 96 percent of the vote, with the negative vote of 4 percent coming from Kirkuk, where the Turks called for a ruler from the House of Osman, while the Kurds favored a Kurdish administration.

The resounding repudiation of their opinion drove part of the Turkish element in Kirkuk to cooperate with Kemalist officers sent to secretly operate in the Mosul *vilayet* (province or large administrative district). Starting in spring 1922, these agents sought to foment tribal rebellion to fan the embers of bitterness against the new Arab regime in Baghdad and reunite this province with the Turkish motherland from whose bosom it had been "illegally" torn in 1918. These activities were not particularly successful, forcing the new Turkish republic to shift its efforts to recover the entire Mosul vilayet onto the international stage. Thus was inaugurated the sinuous complexities of the "Mosul Question," and Kirkuk was finally and definitely incorporated into the Kingdom of Iraq only after the resolution of this imbroglio. This was achieved when the Council of the League of Nations awarded the entire Mosul vilayet to Iraq in December 1925, and the three parties accepted this by treaty six months later. Settlement of this important territorial issue, in turn, brought the calm so necessary for that successful inauguration of systematic and intensive oil exploration that has proved to be the key to the prosperity of Kirkuk today.

Since ancient times, the region has been famed for its petroleum seepages, bitumen, and sulfur. In the eleventh tablet of the ancient *Epic of Gilgamesh,* which recounts the building of the ark, a centerpiece of the Flood legend, three words for petroleum products are used within four lines:

> Three *sar* of *ku-up-ri* [bitumen] I poured over the inside wall,
> Three *sar* of *iddu* [pitch] I poured into the inside.
> The porters brought a *sar* of *šamnu* [oil] which the offering consumed,
> And two *sar* of *šamnu* which the boatmen hid.

Moreover, the existence of this resource was immortalized in the story of Daniel and the fiery furnace and by the location of his reputed tomb on the tell, which houses the ancient city of Kirkuk. During Ottoman times, some use was made of the oil seepages as matériel of war, but intensive exploitation had to await the end of World War I and the settlement of the Mosul Question.

It was on 27 October 1927 that the first oil gushed from Baba Gurgur No. 1, a well sunk in the depression of Baba Gurgur about two miles northwest of the town where perpetual fires of petroleum gas had flared for millennia. This well was an uncontrolled gusher soaring fifty feet above the derrick, drenching the surrounding countryside. It was not capped for nine days and flowed at the rate of 95,000 barrels per day.

In 1931 the IPC moved its headquarters to Kirkuk after a four-year period of preparatory activities with test drilling, scientific observation, and creation of the infrastructure necessary to underpin a modern oil industry. By the end of 1934, the Kirkuk field was in production. Here oil is found at the relatively shallow level of 2,500–2,800 feet (as opposed to the rich oil fields near Basrah, for example, where oil is found at a depth of 10,000 feet), which makes for low production costs.

Before drilling could start, the IPC was faced with still further expenses. The government of Iraq only agreed to give the company oil exploration rights provided that it build a pipeline from Kirkuk to the Mediterranean to export this national resource and to generate revenue. By 1935 the company had constructed a twelve-inch pipeline, which was a single line until Hadithah, where it divided into two branches, one going to Haifa in Palestine while the other ran to Tripoli in Lebanon. The total capacity of this pipeline was some 4 million tons per annum divided equally between Tripoli and Haifa. Until 1948 the Kirkuk field produced up to this limit, more or less, with the exception of the early war years. After the war, plans were drawn up to build an additional sixteen-inch line to Haifa with an annual capacity of 4 million tons, but construction of this line and transshipment of oil through the other one were halted with the advent of the Palestine War and the creation of the State of Israel in 1948 (see also "Haifa"). This lowered production to some 3 million tons in 1948, but the completion of another sixteen-inch line to Tripoli in 1949 allowed production to increase to 6 million tons in 1950. Moreover, the inauguration in 1952 of another thirty-inch pipeline, to Banyas in Syria, added a further capacity of 13 million tons. By 1953 production had risen to 28 million tons, and by 1970 production from the Kirkuk fields reached some 54 million tons.

The 1970s saw the construction of a new pipeline from Kirkuk to the Turkish Mediterranean port of Ceyhan. A forty-inch pipeline was commissioned in 1976, with the first tanker being loaded on 25 May 1977. The coming of the Iran-Iraq War in 1980, however, brought the closure of the two original pipelines; the pipeline to Tripoli was closed in 1981 by Lebanon because of a dispute over transit fees, while the pipeline to Banyas was closed in 1982 by Syria because the Syrian government supported Iran. As a result of these closures, the capacity of the Kirkuk-Ceyhan pipeline was expanded in 1983–1984 to carry 46.5 million tons.

Present estimates of the reserves of the Kirkuk oil field are perhaps more than 10 million barrels, with a production of some 700,000 barrels per day. Kirkuk initially produced a "light" crude, but by the 1990s overpumping produced oil with a higher sulfur content, which, if sustained, will result in permanent damage to the underground reservoirs. The regime of Saddam Hussayn sought as much revenue as possible and ordered that crude oil be injected into these reservoirs to maintain pressure so that more oil could be forced out—a practice that is still continuing. Such measures to extract oil rapidly from this aging field have had the adverse consequence of allowing water and gas to seep into the reservoirs, which in the long run will make extraction of oil uneconomic.

Because of the poor practices used to maintain pressure in the Kirkuk field, the expected recovery rate has now dropped, and attempts to maintain a high level of production without managing these reservoirs will ultimately bring an end to the illustrious history of oil production from Kirkuk.

As the nerve center of this modern industry from its very beginning, Kirkuk attracted a labor force eager to be initiated into the mysteries of the new technology. Moreover, like workers in other modern sectors of the Iraqi economy, they sought to form labor unions to assert and protect their interests. The IPC refused permission, and in July 1946 the workers went on strike for higher wages. A tragedy occurred nine days into the work stoppage when armed police attacked workers who were meeting peacefully to hear a report from the strike committee. In the ensuing melee, ten people died, clearly demonstrating that the Iraqi government had no compunction about murdering Iraqi workers to protect British interests.

In the 1947 census, the Turkomans were still in the majority in the city, with the Kurds comprising some 25 percent of the population; the rest was drawn from Syrian and Chaldean Arab Christians, Armenians, and Jews. Since then, the Kurdish population has vastly increased, becoming the majority after 1970. Kurdish immigration has commingled tensions that stem from both ethnic and class division. This mix brought an explosion in July 1959. The Kurds, poor recent migrants into the city, tended to support the Iraqi Communist Party, while the Turkomans, who were more established, prosperous, and conservative, felt threatened. Events in Mosul three months earlier, when a nationalist, pan-Arabist "counterrevolution" against the Left ended in bloody failure amid scenes of ethnic carnage, had already set the tone. In Kirkuk a minor incident lit the fuse of intercommunal conflict and resulted in the death of a considerable number of people, most of them Turkomans.

Over the years, the Arab-dominated government in Baghdad has generally had fraught relations with the Kurds, so much so that successive governments since the 1960s have instituted a campaign of Arabization in the Kirkuk region to keep its oil within the Arab sphere. This has involved forcing Kurds to register themselves as Arabs, exiling them to southern Iraq, and transferring Arab colonists from other parts of Iraq to the city. Moreover, the Baathist government redrew the boundaries of Kirkuk province—renamed Tamim (nationalization) after the nationalization of the IPC in 1972—to exclude Kurdish areas while including Arab ones. This led to bitter infighting between different ethnic groups within the city, each claiming that it alone had the right to control Kirkuk and its riches. In the post-Saddam era, this has meant bitter political battles for control of the city, including ethnic cleansing of Arab immigrants, persecution, and vigilante politics. Many Turkoman are leaving Kirkuk for Baghdad, leaving the Kurds and the Arabs to struggle for the soul of the city. Recently, an Iraqi Property Claims Commission (IPCC) has been established to help nonviolently settle conflicting claims to property within the city.

J. L. Whitaker

Further Readings
Edmonds, C. J. *Kurds, Turks, and Arabs: Politics, Travel and Research in North-Eastern Iraq, 1919–1925.* London: Oxford University Press, 1957.
Farouk-Sluglett, Marion, and Peter Sluglett. *Iraq since 1958: From Revolution to Dictatorship.* 3d ed. London: I. B. Tauris, 2001.
Fieldhouse, D. K., ed. *Kurds, Arabs, and Britons: The Memoir of Wallace Lyon in Iraq, 1918–1944.* London: I. B. Tauris, 2002.
Le Strange, Guy. *The Lands of the Eastern Caliphate: Mesopotamia, Persia, and Central Asia from the Moslem Conquest to the Time of Timur.* 1905. Repr. London: Frank Cass, 1966. (pp. 221 & 229)
Sluglett, Peter. *Britain in Iraq, 1914–1932.* London: Ithaca Press for the Middle East Center, Oxford, 1976.
Tripp, Charles. *A History of Iraq.* Cambridge: Cambridge University Press, 2000.

Kufa
Population: 123,500 (2004 estimate)

Kufa burned bright early in the expansion of the Muslim empire as one of the first cities created to house the Arab warriors in their newly conquered territory of Iraq. Home to the fourth caliph, Ali b. Abi Talib, until his assassination, the city became a hotbed of political unrest, early Shi'i belief, and insurrection. Always an edge city, caught between the draw of the Mesopotamian rivers and the Arabian desert, Kufa gradually acquired a pilgrimage and scholarship component as well as a cultural role in Islam all out of proportion to its size. Known for its grammarians and legal scholars, Kufa is still regarded by many as the Queen of the World and the royal tent of Islam.

Kufa (Arabic, *al-Kufa*) is a small town of the Najaf governorate in southeastern Iraq on the edge of the desert. It lies 105 miles south of Baghdad and 7 miles northeast of Najaf.

However unprepossessing it is today, Kufa is heir to a glorious past as one of the earliest cradles of Islam outside the Arabian Peninsula. Along with its rival Basrah, Kufa was one of the first examples of the creation of a new urban form for the nascent Islamic community. After the battle of Qadisiyya, in March AD 636, the Muslim armies under the leadership of Saad b. Abi Waqqas moved on to take Madain (Seleukia/Ctesiphon), the winter capital of the Sassanian state. Its climate and its urban character made it unattractive as a center for both the Bedouin Arabs and their leaders.

Therefore, in 638 Saad decided to create a new settlement or armed encampment (*misr*, pl. *amsár*) to house the *muqatila* (Islamic warriors) and their families on the edge of the Arabian steppe near Qadisiyya. It was placed on the principal branch of the middle Euphrates some miles northwest of Hira, the former capital of the Lakhmid vassals of the Persian shahs, which had long guarded the route to Babylon and Ctesiphon. By the late Sassanian period, the main channel of the Euphrates had shifted from its eastern branch, which flowed by Babylon, to this western one, with the former being transformed into a large irrigation canal, the Nahr Sura, during Islamic times.

For some 300 years, nearby Hira had functioned as a desert port, a "caravan city," the point of contact between Iranized officers of the Sassanian state and the great camel-herding tribes of the Arabian Peninsula as well as between Aramean peasants or city dwellers and the more humble sheep-herding tribes of the desert fringes. Kufa, on the other hand, while still on the margins of the desert, was located closer to the Sawad, the irrigated plains of lower Mesopotamia. It was on a narrow tongue of gray, gravelly sand, an advance sentinel of the desert that extended at an angle toward the Euphrates between an irrigated plain to the east and a depression to the west. Kufa was established at this particular spot to guard the great bridge of boats that crossed the river here to link the commercial high road stretching from Yemen to Ctesiphon and later to Baghdad and beyond to distant Asia.

Unfortunately, Kufa (as Najaf later) lacked a potable water supply during its first 100 years of existence, and its inhabitants were dependent on water carriers moving throughout the city to fill their needs. It was not until later that a well, called bir Ali, was dug.

The origin of the name *Kufa* given to the new settlement is somewhat obscure. The Arab historians and geographers, as was their habit, made the name a common noun designating any rounded sandy surface, but this is obviously a later linguistic reconstruction. There were both Nestorian and Syrian Orthodox bishops of Aqola/Aqula before and during the Islamic period. Moreover, this reading of the original name is confirmed by a Chinese transliteration, Ya-kiu-lo, to designate Kufa. Tabari places a locale named Aqul between the Euphrates and the houses of Kufa. Another possibility is that the name derives from the Persianized form, Kuba.

Since the Kufa site was a tabula rasa, one can see here the very process of urbanism, the creation of a new Islamic city built for those who hitherto had disdained settled life. The initial incarnation of Kufa was a geometrical military camp with tents laid out in rows. Very soon afterward, there came somewhat more permanent structures, huts constructed from the reeds found throughout the region. Then, during the first governorship of al-Mughira b. Shu'ba (AD 642–644), these huts were replaced by buildings built from adobe. It was finally under the governor Ziyad b. Abihi (AD 670–673) that kiln-fired brick was introduced as a building material, first for the citadel and the Friday Mosque, then for the private homes of the Kufan aristocracy. It was now that Kufa began to take on the aspect of a well-built permanent city. For example,

great care was taken with the Friday Mosque. Materials were brought from Ahwaz for the columns, while Aramean or Persian masons were hired to ensure that it would have a pleasing architectural form.

The initial space to be delimited, the center of the city from which all else radiated, was the main public area consisting of the Friday Mosque; the fortified palace of the governor (*qasr al-imara*); and the great square (*maidan*), which was the locus for the ceremonies that punctuated the life of the community. Finally, the importance of commerce in this bridge between "the desert and the sown" (the Bedouin lifestyle and that of the agricultural peasant) was emphasized by the construction of vaulted covered markets where each trade had its own quarter. Indeed, the markets of Kufa, both in form and in function, served as the prototype for the markets of Baghdad and for those throughout the Islamic world.

Among the trades to be found in this suq prototype, the money changers (*sayarifa*) held pride of place. One might even say that here one can discern the seed of the banking system as it later developed in the Muslim world. From the very beginning of the Muslim occupation of Iraq, Kufa administered Mada'in, the former Sassanian capital of Ctesiphon/Seleucia. Because both cities were at the nexus where the silver standard of Sassanian Iran met the gold standard of the Roman/Byzantine lands, the bankers of the Sassanian capital and its Islamic successor, Christian minorities all, handled transactions in both metals and "arbitrated" between the two standards.

Moreover, al-Mughira b. Shu'ba was from the tribe of Thaqif, whom the Prophet Muhammad had exempted from his ban on *riba* (usury) by members of the Islamic community. Although the Christian bishops of Hira were bankers for the first governors of Kufa, circumstances favored the development of Muslim banking, despite Qur'anic prohibitions. These Muslim bankers were largely Shi'i and served as financiers of the various Alid movements and conspiracies.

Fifteen avenues separating the tribal communal lots one from another radiated from this center. Private lots were given to certain famous companions of the Prophet Muhammad as a singular mark of favor. Thus, Talha, az-Zubayr, Saad and his son Umar, Abu Musa al-Ashari, al-Ashath al-Kindi, and other great figures in Islam built their mansions in the center of the city.

Other important structures in the new city outside the monumental center, the communal lots, and the private houses of the great were baths, small mosques belonging to a clan or a quarter, and, in particular, the *jabbanat* or tribal cemeteries, some dozen in number, which were not only burial grounds per se but also points of assembly, mobilization, and arming. These riddled the city, at least from the time of Ali, and were the scenes of certain famous historical events such as the revolt of Mukhtar.

Another well-known topographical feature was the so-called *kunasa*. This was at first a dumping ground west of the camp city. Then, from Umayyad times, it developed multiple functions as the unloading point for Arabian caravans, an animal market, an occasional venue for executions, and, most importantly, a fair for poets.

In contrast with Basrah, the other great Islamic urban foundation, the tribal population of Kufa was characterized by its diversity. Here settled the largest part of the muqatila, which was composed of heterogeneous tribal groups. There were large elements from Qays and Mudar that came either from large Bedouin clans—Tamim, Asad—or from those of the Hijaz—Thaqif, Sulaym, Juhayna, Muzayna. Yet, unusually, there was also a strong minority of Yemenis: both pure Yemeni tribes—Himyar, Hamdan, Hadramawt, and Madhhij—and those only recently Yemenized—especially Kinda and Bajila but also Azd Sarat and Tayyi. Certain of these Yemeni tribes (Kinda and Bajila) had already become semi-settled. The older Yemeni tribal groups had long been urbanized, and it was this element that helped spread the modes and habits of city life among tribal groups to which it was innately foreign. If one can say that in other parts of the new world of Islam—Syria, Egypt, al-Andalus—such south Arabian elements strongly influenced the formation of not only an urban but also a Muslim culture, in Kufa their impact was overwhelming.

In the first phase of its existence, Kufa perhaps contained some 20,000 to 30,000 inhabitants. One source says that Ali in his conflict with Muawiya mobilized all the muqatila of Kufa some 57,000–40,000 adults and 17,000 adolescents. When enlarging the Friday Mosque ca. 670, Ziyad ordered a building that would hold 60,000 men. To this must be added some 80,000 women and children to make a total of 140,000 Arabs registered in the district and so subject to census as those in receipt of stipends from the state. To this number, add clandestine residents, slaves, and *mawal*. At this time the registered population of Basrah numbered around 200,000, but the demographic increase of Kufa in the span of a single generation was still quite remarkable. To relieve population pressure, Ziyad sent 50,000 Arabs to Khurasan, 40,000 from Basrah and 10,000 from Kufa. Certainly, from around AD 700, the registered Arab population of Kufa remained stable or perhaps even declined. Yet this was counterbalanced by the influx of non-Arabs uprooted from the countryside, new mawali attracted by the comforts of this garrison city. This was a disorderly element, rootless and free flowing, dangerous for the tranquillity of the city. The sources report that al-Hajjaj himself, the famous Umayyad administrator notorious for his intolerance of tumult, took measures to curb this influx.

The early sedentarization of the Arabs of Kufa was successful precisely because the city was on the edge of and open to the desert and the caravans and poetry of Bedouin Arabia.

This umbilical link allowed the new settlers to acclimatize themselves slowly to a different way of life, for Kufa was formed from a recipe new to Arab history, where different ingredients, rather than clashing with one another, blended to form a single stew.

The principal event in the early history of Kufa, one that set the pattern for its future evolution, was that Ali b. Abi Talib, first cousin and son-in-law of the Prophet and last and most controversial of the *rashidun* (rightly guided) caliphs, chose Kufa as his residence. Therefore, for five years, between 656 and 661, Kufa was the capital of Islam. The murder of Ali by the Khariji Abd ar-Rahman b. Muljam elevated him into a martyr for those legitimists, the Shi'at Ali (party of Ali), who upheld the preeminence of the family of the Prophet and made Kufa a center of opposition to Umayyad "usurpation" of the caliphate. The first manifestation of discontent was the revolt in 671 of Hujr b. Adi al-Kindi, leader of the Alids in Kufa, an insurrection easily suppressed by Ziyad b. Abihi. It was at this time that Ziyad sought to facilitate the policing of the city by simplifying the plan of Kufa from a division into sevenths into one of quarters.

Kufa remained a hotbed of Alid support, so much so that al-Hussayn b. Ali was heading for it when he and a small band of followers were waylaid and slain at Karbala by the Umayyad governor Ubayd Allah b. Ziyad on 10 October 681. The aftermath of this tragedy culminated in the revolt of al-Mukhtar b. Abi Ubayd al-Thaqafi in 685–687 during the second civil war. He centered his movement in Kufa and claimed to act for Muhammad b. al-Hanafiyya, another son of Ali by a woman of the Banu Hanifa. The movement of Mukhtar is significant for the fact that for the first time in Islamic history, he relied heavily on the mawali population of Kufa for support. At this time, the term *mawali* meant those prisoners of war who had been brought to the city during the Arab conquest of their homelands and their offspring rather than the peasant immigrants who came later.

As a city, Kufa was divided between this rather inchoate mass and the *ashraf*, the proud tribal leaders from the Arabian Peninsula. Mukhtar's revolutionary program, one that gave the mawali rights to booty and stipends, did not sit well with these noble Arabs. Since he needed their support, he was forced to compromise, unwillingly perhaps, for he was unable to convince the Kufan ashraf of his sincerity. Therefore, many of them revolted against his hegemony and fled to Basrah after he suppressed their insurrection.

Moreover, it was during this revolt centered in Kufa and depending largely on mawali support that certain religious ideas, alien to the Arab idea of Islam, were first brought to the fore. Chief among them was Mukhtar's presentation of Ibn al-Hanafiyya as the Mahdi, the messiah who would come to cleanse the world at the end of time—a concept that would henceforth characterize the various branches of Shi'i Islam.

Finally, the movement led by Mukhtar provided a link between past and future, for even after its brutal suppression by the Umayyads, Ibn al-Hanafiyya retained support for his imamate, and upon his demise his followers gave their loyalty to his son Abu Hashim. According to Abbasid tradition, Abu Hashim on his deathbed transferred his rights to the Abbasid family. Thus, during the first years of Abbasid rule, Kufa, that hotbed of the Shi'i, was equally a capital for the new dynasty.

In general, Kufa was a turbulent, unruly city, always open to the lure of insurrection—and not always revolts with a doctrinal coloring. If the ashraf vigorously supported the Umayyads against the leveling program of Mukhtar, they were equally ready to oppose Hajjaj during the revolt of Ibn al-Ashath in 700–703, an insurrection based more on personal and economic grievances. Nonetheless, the unsuccessful Shi'i revolts of al-Mughira b. Said and Bayan b. Saman al-Tamimi in 737 and of Zayd b. Ali (the founder of the Zaydi branch of the Shi'i) in 740 were manifestations of that great maelstrom of religious controversy that engulfed Kufa under the Umayyads.

During the Abbasid period, the city continued its evolution, as did that Arab-Muslim civilization of which Kufa along with Basrah was one of the most important wellsprings. Under the early Abbasids, Kufa was an important city, an administrative capital where the caliphs sometimes resided but one that in the end proved untenable because of its strong Alid orientation.

In the short span of thirteen years (AD 750–763), the influx of Khurasani soldiers, mainstays of the new regime, led to some Iranization of the toponomy of the city. For example, crossroads were now called *chaharsuj*. It was now that Kufa became walled for the first time because the caliph al-Mansur encircled the city with ramparts and a moat, forcing its inhabitants to pay for this. Thus, for the first time, there arose a distinction between the city proper (*madinah*) and the suburbs because it was probable that the kunasa and some of the jabbanat were left outside the enceinte. Whether walled Kufa became the locus classicus of a proper Islamic madinah, structurally elaborate, crowded, and stifling, is a matter of question. In his account of the famous revolt of Abu Saraya in the year 814, Tabari gives such a picture of this walled and gated city while he describes the kunasa as containing dwellings like a suburb. One can see here an example of the progressive elaboration of a particular urban center from Arab military camp or town to Muslim city.

Nonetheless, al-Maqdisi , who visited and wrote about the city in the second half of the tenth century, describes it as a "splendid, charming, and beautiful metropolis with lofty buildings, very fine markets, and an abundance of supplies: it is a well-populated, prosperous place . . . all around it are palm groves and gardens." This gives us a glimpse of a Kufa that, if not still open to the desert, had at least a "green belt." Moreover, it had expanded toward Najaf to the west.

This decline of Kufa was coupled with the rise of Najaf, the city that held the tomb of Kufa's most revered inhabitant, Ali b. Abi Talib. Supposedly, his final resting place was discovered during the reign of the Abbasid caliph Harun ar-Rashid (786–809), some say by the caliph himself while hunting. Others averred that Ali was buried in a corner of the Friday Mosque at Kufa. In any case, toward the end of the ninth century, a small *qubba,* or dome, was built over the supposed site of the tomb. Soon afterward the Hamdanid prince Abul Hayjah, who governed Mosul in 904 and died in 929, rebuilt this qubba, now a dome on four columns, and adorned it with beautiful carpets and hangings. This became a place of pilgrimage under the Buyids; the great Buyid prince Adud al-Dawla wa Taj al-Milla Abu Shuja Fanna Khusraw built a mausoleum over the tomb in either 977 or 980 and was buried there along with his two sons, Sharaf al-Dawla and Baha al-Dawla.

The patronage of the dynasty of Persian Shi'i Buyids transferred the center of Shi'i devotion from Kufa to what had once been merely its suburb, while their ascendancy in Baghdad from 945 marked the end of Abbasid caliphal hegemony and confirmed the decline of such an Arab-oriented metropolis. For that other element so characteristic of this city, the desert, tribal Arab spirit with the financial and administrative structures that flowed from it also degenerated, or perhaps rather evolved, as did the Islamic empire itself. Its location on the margins of the desert had exposed Kufa to the invigorating influence of Arab and Bedouin culture but also left it vulnerable to attack from those same regions. Thus, during the turmoil at the end of the ninth century, Kufa was sacked three times by the Qarmatians, in 905, 924, 927, assaults from which the city found it impossible to recover. It is ironic that the Qarmatians were the violent fringe of a renascent Ismaili movement whose roots lay within the whirlpools of Shi'i religious disputation that had found their source in Kufa some 200 years before.

Unlike Basrah, a great port where the circuits of international trade staved off decline for a further two centuries, Kufa, bereft of its functions as a great religious center and ovary of Islam, was unable to resist being offered as an appendage to the new rulers of this nomad world (see also "Basrah"). Thus, in 996 Baha al-Dawla gave Kufa to the chief of the Bedouin dynasty of the Uqaylids as a fief. Moreover, other tribes, the Banu Asad, the Tayyi, and the newly created Shammar, settled, dominated, and ruined it. Unlike their predecessors who had formed the muqatila, they refused to abandon their nomad existence. The fate of Kufa was sealed by the founding of Hilla in 1102 near the ruins of ancient Babylon on the west bank of Nahr Sura, formerly the main channel of the Euphrates. This also signaled that the main channel of the Euphrates after having flowed past Kufa for half a millennium was gradually shifting back to its old course.

The Spanish traveler Ibn Jubayr (1144–1217) was in the area during the years AD 1182–1185 and speaks of Kufa as a ruined city regularly subject to Bedouin pillage. Orchards covered the formerly built-up area between the Friday Mosque and the Euphrates. He describes the Friday Mosque, still a magnificent site, as a home both to monuments of the Shi'i and to those from a much older world: the ark and the oven (*tannur*) of Noah, from whose mouth had boiled the waters of the Flood; the *musalla* (oratory) of Ibrahim; the mihrab of Ali; and the tomb of Muslim b. Aqil, cousin, supporter, and precursor of Imam Hussayn b. Ali, who perished in Kufa at the hands of Ubayd Allah b. Ziyad.

The Persian geographer Hamdallah Mustawfi Qazvini, who wrote around the middle of the fourteenth century, notes that Kufa was the center of an agricultural district with flourishing crops of sugarcane and cotton. Moreover, it still possessed formidable walls 18,000 paces in circumference, which had been built by the caliph al-Mansur. He also mentions the Friday Mosque and the tannur of Noah.

His contemporary, Ibn Battuta, repeats some comments of his fellow Maghribi, Ibn Jubayr, and like Mustawfi he saw the town as ruined but with some islands of prosperity within it. The qasr al-imara from where the Arab governors had once ruled was merely a foundation, but the markets were still beautiful. For him, what was most significant was the tomb of Mukhtar, newly repaired and covered with a cupola.

Such brief notices show that Kufa, once the center of Islam, was still clinging to life some seven centuries after its foundation. Under the Ottomans, it was administered from nearby Najaf under the control of the *sanjak* (district, region, or provincial administrative area of an empire or state) of Karbala. The British military *Handbook of Mesopotamia* (1917), but based on information of some ten years before, notes that the modern town "is said to be only about thirty years old." Its 3,000 inhabitants were three-quarters Shi'i Arabs with the other quarter being Persians and a few Persianized Baluchis. The *Handbook* describes the city as an agricultural center with excellent date plantations and gardens and an abundance of forage, fruits, and vegetables. Moreover, Kufa acted as a distribution hub for goods from Basrah.

In 1908 the town had some 600 houses with some 100 occupied shops and numerous storehouses and other places of business. The population was around 3,000. There was a stone bridge over the Euphrates, and six to twelve medium-sized cargo sailboats were usually anchored off the town. A horse tramway linked it to Najaf, an altogether more substantial town, with an estimated population of some 30,000 souls.

Louis Massignon visited twice, in 1908 and 1934, and in his *Explication du plan de Kufa* notes with sadness "the now deserted site of that great city which was the most *Arab* of the Muslim métropoles" where he was able to visit the few scattered remnants of past glories: the Friday Mosque, the tombs of the Shi'i martyrs Muslim b. Aqil and Hani b. Urwa, the small flat-topped mound that was said to mark the location of the qasr al-imara, and the so-called Bayt Ali.

In the twentieth century, these remains became objects of archaeological exploration. Nonetheless, Kufa as a city had itself so declined as to receive no mention in the Geographical Handbook Series of the Second World War, *Iraq and the Persian Gulf* (B. R. 524), while the *Hachette World Guides: The Middle East,* published in 1966, describe its monuments as being "of little interest."

To understand the meaning of the once great city of Kufa to the history of Islam, one must look beyond the tales of violence and turmoil to the unique cultural role it held within the Islamic commonwealth. In this it is usually compared with its rival, Basrah, that other great project of Islamic urbanism. Baghdad was the urban river into which these two streams flowed and blended.

In Kufa the twin suns around which these cultural elements orbited were Bedouin Arabism and the Islamic message, both of which excluded influences from the conquered peoples and their milieu. One of its greatest graphic contributions was the monumental "kufic" script used to inscribe the Arabic language on monuments, coins, and parchment. Its spare, angular elegance reflected the asceticism of the desert and the earnest triumphalism of the muqatila and the ashraf. Moreover, in newly founded Kufa lived Ibn Mas'ud, an early and influential *qurra* (Qur'an reciter) and traditionalist who had many disciples. The atmosphere of early Kufa led to the first elaboration of *fiqh* (jurisprudence) and *tafsir* (exegesis). Although in Kufa there was no master of spirituality comparable to al-Hasan al-Basri, there were mystics, ascetics, poets, and collectors of poetry.

Under the Abbasids, one sees a maturation of culture with the differentiation of disciplines and the appearance in Kufa of certain colossi among those founders and synthesizers of Muslim culture and law. There is Abu Hanifa (d. 772), master of canon law and progenitor of the school of law that bears his name. There is Abu Mikhnaf (d. 773), one of the first great Arab historians ar-Ruasi, to whom is attributed the first work of Arabic grammar, and Asim b. Bahdala (d. 748), who, with Hamza and al-Kisai, established three out of the seven canonical readings of the Qur'an.

In the next generation, those dying between AD 796 and 816 accepted the role of codifiers of the knowledge developed by their immediate predecessors. Thus, in law we find Abu Yusuf (d. 798) and Muhammad b. al-Hasan al-Shaybani (d.

804); in history, Hisham b. Muhammad al-Kalbi, the genealogist and historian possessed of a consummate knowledge of the Arab patrimony whose traditions he sought to collect and preserve; and, finally, al-Kisai (d. 795), the supreme exemplar of the school of grammar associated with his native city. As a rival to that of Basrah, Kufa is often viewed as a place possessed of deeper roots in the Arab environment, with a passion for grammatical anomalies and a more acute poetical sense. This was because Kufa, situated far closer to the desert world of Arabia than its rival, was more open to the influences emanating from there.

After 100 years as the capital of the Islamic Empire and center of Dar al-Islam, Baghdad for at least two generations had been attracting the best of the cultural leaders from the two older centers. Here developed an eclectic tradition in every field, one that took the contributions made by the two great amsár, digested them, surpassed them, and transmitted them to the entire Islamic world (see also "Baghdad").

For contemporary Muslims, the historical Kufa is best remembered for two things: its school of grammar and the role it played as the nursery of Shi'ism. Yet one must also recall that it was one of the first great experiments of Arab immigration and settlement, an essay in *urbanisme* where was created a new environment. Here could be played out the growing pains of a nascent religion and the culture within which it was cradled.

Of course, Baghdad did finally triumph and sucked the vital juice from Kufa, leaving it an empty husk. Yet, in closing, it might be well to recall that the Shi'i believe that at the end of time, when the Mahdi arrives once again on Earth, "Baghdad the accursed will be destroyed and Kufa will be Queen of the World after having been a dwelling of exile and waiting for True Believers." Moreover, the Hadith of Salman al-Farisi, one of the first non-Arab converts to Islam, companion of the Prophet, and true supporter of his family, asserts that "Kufa is the *qubbat al-Islam* (royal tent of Islam) [rather than its rival Basrah]; and that a time will come when the only True Believers will be those who live within her or whose hearts sigh for her."

J. L. Whitaker

Further Readings
Daftary, Farhad. *The Isma'ilis: Their History and Doctrines.* Cambridge: Cambridge University Press, 1994.
Hawting, G. R. *The First Dynasty of Islam: The Umayyad Caliphate, AD 661–750.* Carbondale: Southern Illinois University Press, 1987.
Hodgson, Marshall G. S. *The Venture of Islam: Conscience and History in a World Civilization, I: The Classical Age of Islam.* Chicago: University of Chicago Press, 1974.
Le Strange, Guy. *The Lands of the Eastern Caliphate: Mesopotamia, Persia, and Central Asia from the Moslem Conquest to the Time of Timur.* 1905. Repr. London: Frank Cass, 1966.
Morony, Michael. *Iraq after the Muslim Conquest.* Princeton, NJ: Princeton University Press, 1984.

Kuwait City
Population: 32,000 (2005 estimate for the municipality)

Kuwait City emerged in the eighteenth century as migrants from what is now Saudi Arabia settled in the area. Like many other coastal Gulf cities of the time, it became a pearling and trading center, acting as both a port city and a terminus for overland trade by camel caravan from Aleppo. Its small size and relative prosperity have meant that it has weathered threats from a number of quarters over time. In the late eighteenth century, the town saw off the Wahhabis from the Najd. In 1899 concerns about increasing Ottoman influence led Kuwait to enter into a treaty with the United Kingdom (UK), and in the early twentieth century Kuwait was again able to defeat invading Wahhabis. Oil wealth and the resulting rapid development of the country's infrastructure were the main features of the mid-twentieth century. But the Iraqi invasion of 1990 and the subsequent expulsion of Iraqi troops in 1991 forced the country to spend large sums to restore much of the earlier development work.

Kuwait City (Arabic, *al-Kuwayt*) is a coastal town located at the northwestern end of the Arabian Gulf. Kuwait's climate is dry, with average rainfall generally about four inches per year. It is also hot in the summers, with temperatures frequently reaching above 120 degrees Fahrenheit. But in common with the rest of the upper Gulf, winter temperatures can be quite chilly, falling to 5 degrees Centigrade during the day.

This generally inhospitable climate did little to attract inhabitants, and prior to the arrival of a group of migrants from Arabia in the eighteenth century, Kuwait City was just a small village with a fort. At that time, the township was ruled by the Bani Khalid tribe, whose main base was in what is now Saudi Arabia. The arriving migrants were members of the Utab tribe, hailing from the interior Najd region of present-day Saudi Arabia. By the middle of the eighteenth century, one branch of the Utab, the as-Sabah family, assumed leadership of the town and has ruled Kuwait City and the subsequent state built around it without interruption since that time.

Despite the town's small size at the start of the 1700s, a Danish explorer, Carstin Niebuhr, reported in the 1760s that it had a population of about 10,000. Like much of the coastal Gulf, the town made its living during those times from trading and pearling. For Kuwait, much of the trade was a maritime affair, and in the 1760s Niebuhr reported from his travels that there were about 800 small vessels belonging to the Kuwaitis. This trade linked Kuwait to other parts of the region, including Muscat and Bahrain (see also "Muscat" and "Manama"). Some vessels also traveled as far as India, Yemen, and East Africa, taking palm dates grown around the head of the Gulf to be traded along the way. In addition to the seafaring trade, Kuwait was the terminus for overland trade that traveled by camel from Aleppo, with some caravans between the two cities consisting of thousands of camels. This trade was particularly active during the late 1770s, when the Persian occupation of neighboring Basrah forced traders there to move some of their business to Kuwait (see also "Basrah" and "Aleppo").

This relatively prosperous town caught the attention of the fundamentalist Wahhabis, who in the latter part of the nineteenth century sought to conquer eastern Arabia. The Wahhabis were followers of Muhammad bin Abdul Wahhab, a Najdi who first preached the puritanical version of Islam still followed by many Saudis today. But the Kuwaiti townspeople, with assistance from a British East India Company (EIC) ship, managed to fight off the Wahhabi attackers, and by the early nineteenth century the Wahhabis had been driven from the area by the resurgent Ottoman authority.

The reign of the as-Sabah family continued to change hands peacefully, and trade remained the mainstay of the economy. The town appears to have prospered during the first half of the nineteenth century, with estimates of its population varying from 15,000 to 25,000.

Although Kuwait managed to maintain its independence through that time, in 1871 the city fell more heavily under the influence of the Ottoman dynasty. At that time, the Kuwaitis supported Ottoman troops who occupied al-Hasa Province, and subsequently the Ottomans provided the Kuwaiti leader with the honorific title of Ottoman governor. Although the title was only honorary, tiny Kuwait would have had little chance of challenging the authority of even the diminished Ottoman dynasty by itself. Subsequently, under Mubarak the Great, who ruled from 1896 to 1915, Kuwait sought an agreement with the UK that would ensure the city-state's continuing independence from the Ottomans. Although initially reluctant, the UK signed an agreement in 1899 after it became clear that both the Russians and the Germans were, with Ottoman blessings, planning to build railways that terminated in Kuwait. The British accord restricted Kuwait's ability to provide land to any other nationals without prior British government permission, a clause that later influenced negotiations for an oil concession.

In 1904 the British appointed a political agent to Kuwait. That city was, at the time, a reasonably diverse place, probably a result of the continuous trading partnerships that brought Kuwait into contact with many other cities. According to J. G. Lorimer, who visited Kuwait in about 1904, Arabs, Persians, Jews, and Africans all inhabited the town at the time, with the total population reaching about 35,000. Lorimer also reported that over the course of the previous thirty years, the city had doubled in geographic size.

The Kuwait economy at that time remained dependent on trade and pearling. But as with the rest of the Gulf, international oil companies became interested in concession agreements in Kuwait during the first part of the twentieth century. Kuwait eventually came to an agreement with the Kuwait Oil Company, a joint venture between the Anglo-Persian Oil Company and Gulf Oil, in 1934. In the meantime, however, the worldwide depression of the 1920s and 1930s affected Kuwaiti pearling and its merchant trading, and the overall economy went through a difficult period.

The 1930s also saw the evolution of the city-state's governing system. In 1938 the city-state elected its first Legislative Assembly. That assembly established health, police, and finance departments for the city and reorganized the customs service there.

Oil was discovered in commercial quantities in 1938, when Kuwait Oil Company found the Burgan field. World War II disrupted the company's exploitation of the area, but in 1946 the country started oil exports. The Kuwaiti government used the money it earned from the concession to improve the lives of average Kuwaitis. Throughout the 1950s, the government invested in infrastructure and services, with water desalination, electricity, and education among the top priorities for development.

In 1961 Kuwait declared itself to be an independent and sovereign state. It maintained a treaty of friendship with the UK, and shortly after declaring independence it had to call upon the British to protect it against a possible invasion by its northern neighbor Iraq, which had claimed Kuwait as a province. Despite this hiccup, Kuwait continued to develop its political institutions. In 1962 the amir promulgated the country's new constitution, which allowed for election of a national assembly. That assembly held its first session in early 1963.

Kuwait's policy makers pressed ahead with development during the 1970s, but by far the most significant economic development over that period was the 1975 decision to nationalize the Kuwait Oil Company. Full ownership gave the Kuwaiti government even greater resources to develop the local economy. The city remained the focus of the country's government, business, and financial activities. The city also hosted many expatriate workers, who participated in the boom years and growing economy. In particular, the city benefited from Palestinian immigrants, who first arrived in the city after the disasters of 1948. Other waves of Palestinian skilled workers arrived in the 1950s and 1960s, including Yasir Arafat, who worked in the city as an engineer while founding the Palestinian Fateh movement. By 1990 there were more than 400,000 Palestinians in the state, most located in Kuwait City.

The invasion of Kuwait by Iraq in 1990 and the coalition's expulsion of Iraqi troops from the country in 1991 colored subsequent events and outlooks. Substantial resources went into rehabilitation and replacement of equipment and infrastructure and into environmental cleanup. Most expatriate Arabs left the city, and the Palestinians were forced out because of Palestine Liberation Organization (PLO) support for Iraq.

Although emotional scars of the invasion remain, the city of Kuwait has recovered economically from that period. The conservative mores of most Kuwaitis means that the town is not a thriving tourism center, but its proximity to Iraq means that it has become an important transit point for people bound for post–Saddam Hussayn Iraq. Kuwait International Airport saw passenger numbers increase by 19 percent in 2004, bringing the total to more than 5 million, and there are plans to build a second terminal to handle increasing demand.

The city also has the country's main university, Kuwait University, which has several campuses spread across the city. It is also home to the recently opened American University of Kuwait. Shopping is a popular pastime, and the country has both traditional suq areas and large, upmarket shopping malls. The town also remains the governmental center for the country. In addition to ministries and the executive branch, it is the seat of the country's rather vocal national assembly.

The assembly is housed in a building designed by the architect Jorn Utzon, who was also responsible for the Sydney Opera House. Its very modern design is in fact inspired by the shape of a Bedouin tent, in keeping with the mix of modern and traditional architecture found in Kuwait City. The Kuwait Towers, which act as water reservoirs, are one of the immediately identifiable modern symbols of the city. But older houses, including the as-Sadu House and Bayt al-Bader, have also been preserved. The former is now a center for Bedouin weaving, while the latter serves as a center for display of handicrafts. Kuwait is also home to the as-Sabah Islamic art collection, the Dar al-Athar al-Islamiyah. Iraqis looted this collection during the 1990–1991 invasion and occupation, and many of the valuable pieces were lost. But some have been restored to Kuwait and are on display at the national museum.

Angie Turner

Further Readings
Abu-Hakima, Ahmad Mustafa. *The Modern History of Kuwait, 1750–1965.* London: Luzac, 1983.
Freeth, Zahra, and H. V. F. Winstone. *Kuwait Prospect and Reality.* London: Allen and Unwin, 1972.
Lorimer, J. G. *Gazetteer of the Persian Gulf.* Calcutta: Superintendent Government Printing, 1908.
Mansfield, Peter. *Kuwait: Vanguard of the Gulf,.* London: Hutchinson, 1990.
Shaw, Ralph. *Kuwait.* London: Macmillan, 1976.

L

Luxor
Population: 75,000 (2005 estimate)

The very name Luxor evokes images of ancient Egyptian wealth and power, particularly connected to the temples of Karnak and the tombs in the Valley of the Kings. For 300 years the center of a renewed Egyptian Empire, this city on the Nile is now one of the key tourist cities of the world, attracting more than 3 million visitors every year. For more than a millennium, the cultic power of this city attracted emperors and pharaohs to be inaugurated in its temples and to spend lavish amounts of money to memorialize their victories and lives. With two-thirds of Egypt's antiquities to be found in and around the city, Luxor has been molded to fit the image and "needs" of global tourism, restricting its inhabitants socially and politically within limited roles.

Luxor (ancient Egyptian, *Waset* or *Nu Amon;* Greek, *Thebes;* Arabic, *al-Uqsur*) is a bustling, medium-sized town situated approximately 420 miles south of Cairo on the east bank of the Nile River. Its picturesque location is part of its attraction, with the green fields on the edge of the Nile giving way to the pinkish sand-colored hills and the desert beyond them. The climate is dry, and average rainfall is a mere .04 of an inch. Given its desert climate, temperatures fluctuate considerably. In the winter, averages range between 42 degrees Fahrenheit and 79 degrees Fahrenheit. In summer, they may rise to 107 degrees Fahrenheit during the day and fall to 72 degrees Fahrenheit at night.

A human settlement in the location now known as Luxor has existed since the Neolithic era (ca. 5000 BC), when farmers exploited the seasonal flooding of the Nile River for the cultivation of a wide variety of crops. Waset, as Luxor was called by the ancient Egyptians, first emerged as an important power center during the First Intermediate Period (ca. 2080 BC), when it was established as the administrative center of Upper Egypt; before this it was little more than a provincial town. Since the city's god was Amun, the town was also known as Nu Amon (town of Amun), and its new bureaucratic significance increased the religious significance of Amun throughout the country.

Its geographical position contributed greatly to the town's importance, since it was close to the valuable mineral resources and trade routes of Nubia, which by the end of the third millennium were finally being directly and regularly exploited. The town also had easy access to the eastern desert and was close to the major route to the Red Sea at Qusair. In addition, its attraction was heightened by being far from the restricting power centers in the north. Location, administrative significance, and sacred capital all increasingly combined to attract wealth in the form of gold, silver, ivory, spices, and rare fauna and flora, which poured into Nu Amon. Much of this new wealth was bestowed upon the god Amun and his sanctuaries.

During the Second Intermediate period (1786–1558 BC), Nu Amon became more important, particularly with the Hyksos invasion of the Egyptian delta and the rise of the Kingdom of Kush in Nubia. During that time, the remnant Egyptian kingdom shrunk to an area around the city, pressed both from the north and south. It is from Nu Amon that the reexpansion of pharaonic power began after 1558.

The town's peak came during the eighteenth and nineteenth dynasties (ca. 1550–1196) when, for 300 years, it served as the administrative capital of the reunified country. The city also came to serve at this time as the mythological and theological center of the kingdom, since all pharaohs were perceived as gaining their legitimacy from the divine *ka,* the essence of kingship, celebrated in the Luxor Temple. Its temples, particularly that of the Luxor Temple and that of the complex at Karnak, were the most important and the wealthiest in the land, and the tombs prepared for the elite among its inhabitants on the west bank were the most luxurious Egypt had ever seen. It was claimed that the city had 100 gates; it certainly had six great temples, with two complexes on the east bank and four on the west, where the royal necropolis and Valley of the Kings and Queens were located. There are records of workmen's strikes in the city in search of better work conditions in what was perhaps the richest metropolis in the Middle East of the time. Queen Hatshepsut appears to have been the most committed to the city and spent fantastic funds on temples and construction. Amenhotep III (1403–1365 BC) founded the Luxor Temple, and on its portico he received the public accolades and the gifts of foreign ambassadors.

From the Third Intermediate Period (1085–656 BC), the center of royal activities moved back to the north. The high priests of Amun then asserted their political authority over the city and its hinterland, and Nu Amon was virtually autonomous for much of this period. Its temples continued to flourish, monarchs were still buried in the Valley of the Kings, and the town retained some importance in the administrative life of the country. It was after 1070 that there were many robberies of the tombs, with priests working hard to protect and rebury royal remains. Ultimately, private burials by elites

View from the Nile of the temples at Luxor. (Corel Corporation)

from the town often used the emptied royal tombs as repositories. The city's political influence receded only in the Late Period (ca. 715–332 BC).

Alexander conquered Egypt in 332 BC and came to Luxor and had himself invested as king in the Luxor Temple, site of pharaonic legitimation for more than 1,500 years. The name Thebes was given to the town by the Greeks, but the reason for this is not known. Under the Ptolemies, additional monuments were added to the Karnak complex. After the Roman conquest in 30 BC, they also used the Luxor Temple as a cult site to glorify the Roman emperors. When Diocletian visited the city (ca. 293), he reportedly called the local Christian leaders together within the Luxor Temple and commanded them to make sacrifices to the divine emperor. Under his rule, Thebes was turned into the capital of a new province, Thebaid, and two legions were garrisoned here. A fortress was built around the Luxor Temple to house these forces. During this classical period, Greek and Roman tourists came to the site, many leaving graffiti to mark their presence. Herodotus visited around 450 BC, commenting on the unique sourdough bread made in the city, and there were written guides to help visitors, many of whom purchased mummies and artifacts for souvenirs.

During early Christian times, Thebes was an important center for the Coptic Church, and several shrines were turned into churches. The city developed a large Coptic community, and it is here that Saint Pachomius, founder of communal monastic life, was converted and began living as a hermit. Reportedly, for fifteen years Pachomius never laid down to sleep, and he attracted a huge following. By the end of his life (ca. 346), Pachomius had founded eleven monasteries, two for women, in the Thebes area, hosting more than 3,000 monks.

The general trend for the city, however, was one of decline. Unlike the ancient northern capital of Memphis, which was superseded by Cairo, Luxor was never completely deserted (see also "Cairo"). After the Muslim conquest (642), the town became known in Arabic as *al-Uqsur*. The name derives from the Arabic word for *palaces,* which may refer to the grand, ancient Egyptian temples of Luxor and Karnak, located within and on the edge of the town. There are Mamluk remains in the city.

It was not until the survey of Napoléon Bonaparte's expedition in 1798 that the importance of Luxor's historical temples and tombs became known around the world. Since then, many excavations have been conducted, and new discoveries in and around the city continue to be made today. In the early nineteenth century, Luxor began to become a tourist attraction for wealthy Victorian travelers. This was encouraged by the inauguration of the first tourist route to the town by Thomas Cook. The discovery of a cache of royal mummies in 1881 heightened the scramble for discovery and fame around the city. In the 1880s, the European demand to discover was so great that a subscription was held in the London *Times* and the *Journal des débats* in Paris to raise money to buy out the "Arab squatters" who lived within the ruins of the Luxor Temple so that clearing of the site could begin.

By the early twentieth century, Europeans were negotiating exclusive concessions to excavate in the necropolis. For example, the British Earl of Carnarvon had the concession for the Valley of the Kings up until 1922. Together with Howard Carter, their discovery of the fabulous tomb of Tutankhamen in 1922 attracted world attention on the archaeology of the royal necropolis, and Luxor has never been the same.

Today Luxor is the most important tourist destination in Egypt and possesses good bus, rail, and air links as well as many hotels. The livelihood of Luxor's residents is highly dependent upon the tourism industry, and the pressures of international tourism have meant that the interests of the local population of the city, particularly the poor, have been ignored to make the city attractive to visitors. Since only a certain number of tourists can pass through the door into King Tut's tomb every day, Luxor's planners are targeting wealthier tourists. This has resulted in distorted development in the city, with "enclave tourism" and the clearances of poorer areas of the city of top priority. The twenty communities opposite Luxor on the west bank of the Nile have been denied building permits or developmental schemes so as to preserve the "character" of the area and to maintain an "authentic" ambiance, thus de-developing them. The World Bank's plan for Luxor's development did little to help the local poor, with more than half of its $59 million budget spent abroad on consultants and foreign contractors. The illegal ivory trade still operates in the city's suqs, as does the looting of antiquities, since local inhabitants still have problems finding work. The Theban Mapping Project, founded in 1978, has the goal of cataloging all the thousands of tombs and temples in the Luxor area, thus helping to preserve and protect these monuments to human civilization.

Over the last decade, the people of Luxor have suffered from the fluctuation in tourism revenues as the number of annual visitors has periodically dropped because of regional instability (such as the Gulf War, in 1991) and the targeting of tourists in Upper Egypt by Islamist militants throughout the 1990s. The most tragic event to affect Luxor was the killing of fifty-seven foreign tourists and three Egyptians on Luxor's west-bank site of Queen Hatshepsut's temple in 1997.

Nicola Pratt

Further Readings

Blackman, Aylward. *Luxor and Its Temples.* Rev. ed. London: Kegan Paul, 2005.

Bongioanni, Alessandro. *Luxor and the Valley of the Kings.* Rev. ed. Vercelli, Italy: White Star, 2004.

Reeves, Nicholas, and Richard Wilkinson. *The Complete Valley of the Kings: Tombs and Treasures of Egypt's Greatest Pharaohs.* London: Thames and Hudson, 1995.

Strudwick, Nigel, and Helen Strudwick. *Thebes in Egypt.* Cornell, NY: Cornell University Press, 1999.

M

Madinah
Population: 1,300,000 (2005 estimate)

Madinah, the second-holiest city in Islam, is located in the al-Hijaz Province in western Saudi Arabia. In pre-Islamic times it was known as Yathrib, and since then it has been given more than ninety names that generally denote respect and devotion. The city is most often called Madinah (Arabic for city), which is short for Madinat al-Nabi (city of the Prophet) or al-Madinah al-Munawwarah (the radiant or enlightened city), a reference to its association with the Prophet Muhammad, who is buried there. Common usage in the West is as Madinah. Once only accessible by caravan trails, the city is now an integral part of the network of modern highways and roads that connect it to Makkah (188 miles), Jeddah (230 miles), and Riyadh (512 miles). An airport has been built seven miles northeast of the city.

Madinah (Arabic, *Madinat al-Nabi* or *al-Madinah al-Munawwarah;* English, *Medina*) is situated on a flat mountain plateau at the junction of the three valleys of al-Aql, al-Aqiq, and al-Himdh. For this reason, there are large green areas amid a dry, mountainous region. The plateau is surrounded by a number of mountains that have become part of popular Islamic folklore: al-Hujaj or Pilgrims' Mountain, to the west, Salaa to the northwest, al-Eer or Caravan Mountain to the south, and Uhud to the north. The altitude of the city at 1,950 feet above sea level gives it very hot summers but moderate temperatures in the autumn and cold in winter. The city was traditionally fed by aquifers below the surrounding hills leading to the cultivation of large date palm plantations and vegetable gardens. With its fertile soil, Madinah became famous for the production of dates, and to this day palms line the streets in profusion. The current population of the city comprises Arabic-speaking Muslims who are mostly Sunni.

The Islamic and modern history of Madinah is closely intertwined with its role in the genesis of Islam and the hajj (pilgrimage) trade and with the creation of extensive endowments (known as *awqaf*) this centrality engendered. Huge numbers of pilgrims and wealthy patrons of good works ensured that the city remained at the epicenter of Islamic activity and prosperity. While it never eclipsed Makkah as the center of Islam, at the same time its role as the second-holiest city of Islam has never been in doubt. Although Madinah came to prominence with the introduction of Islam to the region, its roots date back hundreds of years into the pre-Islamic era. The earliest history of Madinah is obscure, but it is probable that the Arab tribes of Aws and Khazraj were then in occupation of the area. It is also known that some Jewish tribes settled in the city in pre-Christian times. The main influx of Jews seems to have taken place as a result of their expulsion from Palestine by the Roman emperor Hadrian about AD 135. The availability of food and water made Madinah an important reprovisioning point for the caravans that plied the commercial routes from the southern part of the Arabian Peninsula along the Red Sea to Syria and Egypt. Its inhabitants sold food to these passing caravans and engaged in long-distance trade.

Before the Prophet Muhammad's flight from Makkah to Yathrib, as Madinah was then known, the city notables were familiar with the Prophet's reputation for honesty and sincerity. They therefore sent envoys to him asking that he intercede in a dispute between the two powerful tribes (Aws and Khazraj) of the city. As a result of his mediation, many notables turned to Islam and were followed by other converts. Following the growing threat to their fellow Muslims in Makkah by the Quraysh tribe, the people of Yathrib offered a safe haven to them. From AD 620 onward, groups of Muslims came to live in Yathrib until in September AD 622 the Prophet Muhammad himself left Makkah for Yathrib, an event known as the *Hijrah* (migration).

The Prophet's arrival in Yathrib was a defining moment in the history of Islam. It signified both the creation of the first Islamic state and the rapid expansion of the new faith beyond its origins in the Hijaz. The city became known as Madinat al-Nabi, and the date of the Prophet's arrival there marked the first year of the Islamic calendar. Following a period of consolidation of the young Islamic community in Madinah, in AD 630, Muhammad and his followers entered Makkah and incorporated the holy shrine of Kaabah into the new Islamic faith.

While the Holy Mosque in Makkah was the spiritual center of Islam, Madinah became the administrative hub of the new Islamic state during the Prophet Muhammad's lifetime. It was from here that the successful campaign to convince the tribes to abandon idolatry was waged. It was also in Madinah that the Prophet's companions compiled the verses of the Holy Qur'an and collected the Hadith (teachings and sayings of the Prophet) that would serve as the basis of *sharia* (Islamic law). And it was also in Madinah that the Prophet died, on 8 June 632, and where he was buried in his house adjoining the mosque. After his death, the first three caliphs, Abu Bakr as-Siddiq, Umar Ibn al-Khattab, and Uthman Ibn Affan, continued to administer the expanding Islamic nation, which had by now spread to Persia and Syria, from Madinah. In time Caliph Abu Bakr and Caliph Umar were buried in a separate chamber next to the Prophet. Caliph Uthman and several members of the Prophet's immediate family were buried at the nearby Baqi Cemetery.

Madinah grew rapidly until AD 661, when the Umayyad dynasty transferred the capital of the caliphate to Damascus. Thereafter, Madinah was reduced to the rank of a provincial town, ruled by governors appointed by the distant caliphs. Little is known about the physical development of the city during this period up to the arrival of the Ottomans in AD 1517. It appears that native rulers enjoyed a fluctuating measure of independence interrupted from time to time by the depredations of the sharifs (rulers) of Makkah. Indeed, ongoing local disputes and conflicts severely affected the prosperity of the city (see also "Yanbu"). At the same time, the city became a political refuge during both the Umayyad and Abbasid periods, and a measure of its lack of strategic and commercial value lay in the fact that no city walls were built around the city until the arrival of the Fatimids. This relative tranquillity is also regarded as one cause of its growing eminence in Islamic intellectual life during this period.

The Ottomans occupied Madinah in AD 1517, but because of the difficulty in transporting significant number of troops to the city, in the main, they ruled through proxies. Thus, Ottoman suzerainty over the city was largely nominal for some time before the puritanical Wahhabi sect first took over the city in 1804. The Ottomans retook Madinah in 1812 and remained in effective control until the revival of the Wahhabi movement under Ibn Saud a century later. The protection of the traditional annual hajj caravan from Damascus to Makkah, which also passed through Madinah, was an important symbolic duty of the Ottoman Caliphate. Successive sultans expended great efforts in ensuring the safety of this annual caravan without it being attacked by desert Bedouin. Between 1904 and 1908, the Turkish administration in Istanbul built the Hizaj Railway from Damascus to Madinah in an attempt to ensure Ottoman control over the hajj but also to strengthen its administrative and military control over the Hijaz area. A railway station and terminal yards were built and added to the prosperity of the city. Ottoman rule came to an end during World War I, when the sharif of Makkah, Hussayn, revolted and put the Hijaz Railway out of service with the assistance of the British officer T. E. Lawrence (Lawrence of Arabia). Hussayn later came into conflict with Ibn Saud, and in 1925 the city fell to the Saudi dynasty. The establishment of the Kingdom of Saudi Arabia in 1932 united the Arabian Peninsula and led to a revival of the pilgrimage trade to Madinah. Following the influx of petrodollars during the 1970s, Madinah has undergone massive developments that have transformed the city into a modern metropolis receiving pilgrim flows in excess of 1 million pilgrims per annum.

Among the original architectural features of the city were the double walls that surrounded the city and that were flanked by bastions and accessed by nine gates. The chief building within is the Masjid-an Nabawi (Prophet's Mosque), which contains the tombs of Muhammad, his daughter Fatima, and the caliphs Abu Bakr and Umar. Legend has it that to decide on the location of the mosque, the Prophet Muhammad let loose his camel, and where it came to rest was the site of the new mosque. The original mosque had a spacious yard, and its walls were made of bricks and clay. Half the roof was covered with palm fronds, while the other half was left open. Part of the building became a refuge for the faithful who had no homes. On the eastern side, apartments were built to house the Prophet and his family. The new mosque was surrounded by the shops and stalls of all kinds of merchants, and it soon became the political and economic as well as the spiritual nucleus of the city. The pilgrimage to Makkah, which usually includes an additional excursion to Madinah, was buttressed by the tradition that the Prophet Muhammad himself endorsed such a journey. A Hadith cited by both Bukhari and Muslim includes the advice that "a prayer performed in the Prophet's Mosque is better than a thousand prayers in any other place except Masjid al-Haram in Makkah."

Additions and improvements were undertaken by a succession of caliphs and rulers. For example, the chamber of the Prophet's wives was merged into extension work carried out during the time of the Umayyad caliph al-Walid Ibn Abd al-Malik. Fire twice damaged the mosque, first in AD 1256 and again in AD 1481, and rulers of several Islamic countries contributed to the costs of its rebuilding. Sultan Selim II (r. 1566–1574) decorated the interior of the mosque with mosaics overlaid with gold. Sultan Muhammad built the dome in 1817 and in 1839 painted it green. Sultan Abd al-Mejid I initiated a project for the virtual reconstruction of the mosque in 1848 and completed it in 1860. This was the last renovation before the modern expansion in 1953–1955.

The most recent restoration and expansion program of the Prophet's Mosque was launched by King Fahd in 1985. A unique feature of the 1985 expansion project was the development of the twenty-seven main plazas capped by sliding domes that can be rapidly opened or closed according to the weather. The development of the surrounding open areas and the seven newly constructed entrances ensure the smooth passage of pilgrims into the mosque. However, this was carried out at the expense of preserving some of the charm of the old city and surrounding walls. The mosque is now fully air-conditioned, and the system pumps 17,000 gallons of chilled water per minute through pipes into the basement of the mosque, where it is used to cool air circulating throughout the complex. A labyrinth of service tunnels, drainage systems, and supply networks also now crisscrosses the area to accommodate the service equipment and other maintenance works, including an underground parking facility designed to hold nearly 5,000 cars. The mosque and courtyard and roof space now allow more than 700,000 visitors to pray simultaneously.

Other main features in the city include the Jannat-al-Baqi Cemetery lying to the east of Madinah. Several companions of the Prophet Muhammad and renowned Muslim holy men are buried there. At the time of the Wahhabi conquest of 1925, the cemetery was denuded of all the domes and ornamentation of the tombs, but the ruins have been tidied up with simple concrete graves in place of the old monuments and enclosed by a wall. Another famous mosque, the Masjid Quba, is about two miles southwest from Masjid an-Nabawi. This is the first mosque in the history of Islam whose foundation stone was laid down by Prophet Muhammad himself on his migration to Madinah. Finally, the Masjid Qiblatayn (the Mosque of the Two Qiblas) is situated to the northwest near the valley Aqiq. In this mosque, the Islamic faith holds that God directed Prophet Muhammad, who was in the middle of a prayer, to turn his face from the al-Aqsa Mosque in Jerusalem, Islam's first qibla (direction of prayer), to the Kaba in Masjid al-Haram in Makkah.

Part of the economic activities based upon the pilgrimage trade includes an unusual state enterprise known as the King Fahd Holy Qur'an Printing Complex. Built on more than thirty-seven acres and employing some 1,500 scholars, artists, and technicians, the complex produces annually more than 14 million copies of the Qur'an in Arabic and six other major languages as well as audiocassettes, CDs, and videos of recitations of the Qur'an. These are mostly for distribution to visitors to the two holy mosques and for donations to mosques, religious institutions, schools, and universities throughout the world.

The modernization of Madinah has not been as rapid as that of other Saudi Arabian cities such as Jeddah and Riyadh. Expansion and development has involved the complete demolition of the old city wall and the incorporation of the historic areas with the now built-up pilgrim camping ground (al-Manakh) and the Anbareya Quarter. As Madinah expanded in the late twentieth century, the provision of adequate water supplies was addressed by laying massive pipes to bring in water from desalination plants along the Red Sea. In addition to the income derived from the religious-based economy, Madinah continues to support the cultivation of fruits, vegetables, and cereals. The city is especially well known for its date palms, the fruits of which are processed and packaged for export. Of the 500 varieties of dates produced in the kingdom, some 120 are cultivated in the environs of Madinah, in particular the popular variety known as the Ajwa. Madinah was also famous in early Islamic times for metalworking, jewelry, and armory industries. These industries were never large scale, and such enterprises were largely connected to agricultural technology.

Michael Dumper

Further Readings
Esin, Emel. *Mecca the Blessed, Madinah the Radiant.* 2d ed. London: Paul Elek Production, 1974.
Makki, Muhammad. *Medina, Saudi Arabia: A Geographic Analysis of the City and Region.* Amersham, UK: Avebury, 1982.
Umari, Akram. D. al-. *Madinan Society at the Time of the Prophet,* Herndon, VA: International Institute of Islamic Thought, 1981.

Makkah
Population: 1.4 million (2005 estimate)

Makkah is the birthplace of the Prophet Muhammad, founder of Islam, and the most sacred of the Muslim Holy Cities. Makkah was an important classical trading center, located on the main caravan routes connecting the southern parts of the Arabian Peninsula with the Middle East, North Africa, and Europe. However, its predominant role over the past seven centuries has been that of the center of Islam and the site of the annual hajj in which millions (formerly hundreds of thousands) of pilgrims come to perform their weeklong ritual. Its sacred nature has had a fundamental effect upon the urban development, character, and economy of the city, with the whole city devoted to the accommodation, transit, and servicing of pilgrims and to support for students and scholars of Islam.

Makkah (English, *Mecca*) lies inland in western Saudi Arabia, in al-Hijaz Province, some forty-five miles east of the Red Sea port of Jeddah. Located in rugged terrain of bare volcanic and granite rock, the narrow, sandy flood bed of the Wadi Ibrahim (Valley of Abraham) winds into the city, which is surrounded on three sides by mountains, some nearby topping 3,000 feet; this topography has meant that the city can suffer from flash floods. To the east of the city via a high pass is access to Taif and the Najd beyond. There is little natural vegetation in the area, and the city has always depended on imported foodstuffs, such as grains and dates, to support its population. The famous Zamzam spring long provided the sweet water for pilgrims.

By the time the Romans captured Egypt, the east coast of the Red Sea was already known for its caravan trade in incense. The Nabateans at Aila and Petra operated at the northern end of a caravan network that passed frankincense and myrrh from southern Arabia via Yemen along the oases of the Hijaz into the Mediterranean circuits at Gaza or to Damascus (see also "Aqaba/Eilat"). Makkah appears to have evolved as an early node in this link between Yemen and the Nabateans, using its freshwater and topographical access to allow its inhabitants to make a living. The first mention of the city may be by the Alexandrian geographer Ptolemy, who in the second century AD identified a city in this area of the Arabian coast called Macoraba. Arab writers paint a picture of a pre-Islamic

Makkah operating within the interstices between the Sassanian and Byzantine empires to the east and north, the Aksumite Empire across the Red Sea, and the remnants of the Himyarite and Saba kingdoms in Yemen (see also "Aksum").

Makkah itself was taken over by Qusay ibn Kilab and his Quraish tribe around the beginning of the fifth century AD. The Quraish elite were merchant traders, organizing caravans to Aila and Gaza, Damascus, and Aden. They put money into buildings in the town, introduced a new economic and political organization to the community, and developed its relations with surrounding tribes; Quraish elites even owned vineyards and property in Taif (see also "Taif"). The city was regularly supplied with grain from Yemen; perhaps participated in the exchange of silk along the caravan routes; and traded cloth, wines, raisins, slaves, and animals. Its merchants attended regular trade fairs and promoted their own, like the large one nearby at Ukaz. The annual fair at Ukaz became famous for large poetry readings and competitions. The best compositions were often written on cloth in gold letters and hung in the Kaabah and known as *mu'allaqaat* (hung ones). By 570 the city was important enough to be the target of attack by Abraha, the Abyssinian general in Yemen, who brought elephants for the assault, but the attackers were consumed by the plague, and the city was saved; 570 became known in the Qur'an as the year of the elephant.

While an important trading center, Makkah was also a site of religious significance well before the Prophet Muhammad adopted it as the center for his new religion, Islam. The presence of a large black stone, presumably a meteorite, had become a regional sacred site, a *haram,* and gradually a number of religious practices had grown up associated with the site. The stone was housed in a tentlike structure, known as the Kaabah, which became increasingly ornate over time. By the sixth century AD, although the Kaabah was associated with the biblical Abraham, it had been transformed into a shrine for the worship of idols, and a tradition of pilgrimage to the Kaabah was well established. When the Quraish captured the town, they assumed the entire *sharaf* of Makka: all the official responsibilities and obligations relating to the Kaabah and the organization of the substantial pilgrimage associated with it.

It was into this milieu that the Prophet Muhammad was born in Makkah in the year of the elephant. His life was to have not only a profound impact upon the world but specifically on Makkah. Despite growing up in a pagan society, Muhammad was interested in monotheistic beliefs. In AD 610, at the age of forty, he entered into a period of retreat in a mountaintop cave called Hira and received the first of a series of revelations that became the Qur'an. The essence of the revelations was an exhortation to abandon idolatry and embrace the one god, Allah. As a result of his preaching, wisdom, and pragmatism, a following grew around Muhammad, and the new religion was known as Islam. He encountered strong resistance from the wealthy tribes in Makkah, however, particularly the dominant Quraish. They saw Islam's monotheism and condemnation of idolatry as a threat to their position and prosperity, which was partly derived from the presence of idols in the Kaabah and the many pilgrims who came to Makkah to worship them.

They forced Muhammad to leave the city for Madinah in AD 622. This journey, known as the *Hijrah* (migration), was later designated as the first year of the Islamic era (see also "Madinah"). In the remaining ten years of his life, the Prophet's message spread across Arabia and was embraced by its inhabitants. In the year 630, he personally returned to Makkah and removed the idols from the Kaabah and rededicated it as the House of Allah, to which Muslims all over the world are required to face when praying five times per day. In 632, shortly before his death, Muhammad led a large caravan of pilgrims from Madinah to Makkah to perform the hajj, which consisted of a circumambulation of the Kaabah seven times, as was laid down in the Qur'an. He thus conferred upon Makkah the role of the spiritual center of the Islamic world.

Makkah never became the seat of government for the Islamic empires that followed the spread of Islam. It always remained a spiritual and pilgrimage center, with the government and administration passing between Damascus, Baghdad, and Cairo. Its role and status in Islam and relative inaccessibility allowed it a considerable autonomy. Indeed, as the ancient caravan routes passing along the Red Sea coast and through Makkah fell into decline with the opening of new sea routes and a more northerly land route, the city lost its commercial significance. The economy and life of the city became increasingly centered around pilgrimages to the Kaabah and donations of Muslim rulers and benefactors. One result was that much of the real estate of the city became endowed as *waqf* (religious endowments), and the wealth of the Islamic world flowed into the city. Many endowments across the Islamic world finished off their dedications with "for the poor of Makkah and Madinah," and funds were sent accordingly. Hostels, seminaries, orphanages, mosques, and schools were all supported by an international network of endowments and administrators.

Nevertheless, control over the *haramayn,* as the twin Holy Cities of Makkah and Madinah are known in Islam, was an important legitimizing element. Both the Umayyad dynasty based in Damascus and the Abbasids in Baghdad were assiduous in gaining and maintaining possession of Makkah and winning over the religious and political elite to their side. In AD 1269, the city came under the control of the Mamluks, and in 1517 it fell to the Ottomans. During all of these eras, city rulers were chosen in the main from the sharifs, or descendants of Muhammad, who retained a strong position in the surrounding area. For various periods, these local rulers were able to carve out considerable autonomy for themselves, and the amirate of Makkah would dominate life in the conurbation of Makkah, Madinah, Yanbu, and Jeddah.

With the fall of the Ottoman Empire after the First World War, Makkah was contested between the Hashemite sharif Hussayn and the powerful Wahhabi family of as-Saud from central Arabia. King Abdul Aziz as-Saud entered the city in 1925, and it became part of the Kingdom of Saudi Arabia.

The urban development of Makkah is centered around the al-Haram Mosque, the central mosque housing the Kaabah. Although compact and densely populated, the old city area stretches to the north and southwest of the mosque. Mountain ranges to the east, south, and west have circumscribed growth in those directions, but in the second half of the twentieth century Makkah expanded along the roads to the north, northwest, and the mountain pass to the west. Expansion was accompanied by the construction of new streets in the old city, and houses close to the al-Haram Mosque have been razed so that open spaces and wide streets surround it.

There are four main squares, each with modern-day fountains. In the Old City area, traditional buildings are constructed out of local stone and reach two or three stories. Slum districts can still be found in various parts of the city comprising mostly destitute pilgrims who remained in Makkah after completing a pilgrimage. In the past, Makkah was reliant on a limited supply of subterranean water drawn from wells that restricted its demographic growth. However, a pipeline was built to transport water from desalination plants at Shuaybah on the Red Sea. Makkah is not richly endowed in resources. Arable land is limited, and almost all food for the city must be imported. Vegetables and fruit are brought daily from surrounding areas, and over the centuries the provision of food from the grainaries of Muslim empires for the Holy City has been a key responsibility of its conquerors. Industry is limited and includes the manufacture of textiles, furniture, and utensils. As described below, the mainstay of the city's economy centers around its holy site and servicing the annual tide of pilgrims who come to the city.

The main sites in Makkah are naturally connected to its role in Islam. The al-Haram Mosque complex has undergone many changes since the time of Muhammad, but the core remains the Kaabah, the holiest shrine in Islam, with its cube-shaped, one-room stone structure. In AD 638, the caliph Umar Bin al-Khatab, during the course of repairing some extensive flood damage, enclosed the courtyard around the Kaabah at the same time, extending the mosque's area considerably. His successors continued the practice of enlargement

Pilgrims circling the Kabbah in Makkah, ca. 1910. (Library of Congress)

to accommodate the increasing number of pilgrims; the size and layout achieved in 918 AD, however, was then maintained for more than 1,000 years. The Ayn al-Zamzam is a sacred well inside the precincts of the al-Haram Mosque. Muslim tradition has it that Allah provided this water for Hagar, mother of Abraham's son Ishmael, when he was crying of thirst. The water is supposed to have special qualities and is much sought after by pilgrims as a souvenir and remedy for ailments.

The pilgrimage of hajj to Makkah is one of the five "pillars of Islam" and incumbent on every Muslim able to do so. It takes place in the first ten days of Dhu al-Hijja, the last lunar month of the Islamic calendar. The rituals performed by the Prophet Muhammad during his last visit to Makkah in 632 form the basis of the pilgrimage, which has been conducted every year since by Muslims. They comprise the donning of a simple white towel to accentuate the humbling nature of the hajj, an overnight stay in Muzdalifa and Mina, a ritual slaughter, the ritual stoning of the devil, and the circumambulation of the Kaabah in an counterclockwise fashion. It is a time for abstinence, prayer, and quiet reflection. In addition, lesser pilgrimages are performed throughout the year. Muslims also conduct the al-Umrah, the minor pilgrimage to Makkah, which can be performed at any time of the year outside the hajj season. A popular time for the al-Umrah is during the month of Ramadan, and large numbers of worshippers and pilgrims gather at the al-Haram Mosque.

During the medieval period, the hajj was often an expensive and hazardous undertaking. En route pilgrims had to pay a variety of taxes to local rulers and port officials, and many areas were unsafe to travel because of brigandage. Indeed, it was partly to ensure the safety of pilgrims, as well as for economic reasons, that an annual pilgrimage caravan was introduced. Such caravans, involving thousands of people and animals, set off from Damascus, Cairo, or Baghdad and were accompanied by armed guards. Many died on the way from attack or disasters; others died in Makkah itself because of poor sanitation, overcrowding, poor crowd control, and limited medical facilities. The cemetery to the north of the city holds the remains of many thousands of such pilgrims.

The latter part of the twentieth century saw a crisis in the organization of the hajj. Numbers have increased exponentially as mass systems of transport became available, and both costs and journey times fell dramatically. From a figure of a quarter of a million pilgrims in 1960, there were more than 1.5 million in the mid-1990s. Projected growth figures range as high as 3.7 million pilgrims per year for the first decade of the twenty-first century. These existing and projected numbers have necessitated a complete overhaul of the traditional organization, the layout of the city and the services provided. The majority of pilgrims arrive by commercial jets at a special Haj Terminal built in Jeddah. A fleet of buses move the pilgrims from the airport to Makkah, where they are distributed among the thousands of hotels and hostels and the tent cities erected for the duration of the pilgrimage.

The hajj is the cornerstone of the economy of Makkah. Preparations begin months in advance, and once it is over, the clearing operations continue also for some months. The city and the pilgrimage sites are cleaned and prepared for the next year, provisions are replenished, and machinery and equipment are checked and maintained. Large quantities of food and water are distributed throughout the tent complexes and along the route of the pilgrims from the Holy Mosque to the nearby holy sites in Arafat, Muzadalifah, and Mina and back to Makkah. In contrast to the tradition of centuries, the tens of thousands of sheep sacrificed at the conclusion of the pilgrimage are no longer slaughtered out in the open by family groups but processed at nearby abattoirs and factories. Unhygienic conditions and the frequency of accidental fires caused the Saudi authorities to intervene and establish safer systems for such large numbers of pilgrims. The meat is canned and distributed worldwide among the needy, including victims of famine and natural disasters.

Over the years, the Saudi government has had to invest heavily in new facilities and infrastructure to cater to the increase in pilgrims. The present al-Haram Mosque dates from AD 1570 and comprises a central quadrangle surrounded by stone walls, the inner sanctuary around the Kaabah paved with marble. Aware that the existing structures could not support the growing numbers of worshippers, King Abdul Aziz initiated a refurbishment and expansion program. Construction continued over twenty years, with surrounding districts of the Old City demolished, and when the work was finally completed in 1976, the enlarged mosque and courtyard complex could accommodate 300,000 pilgrims.

In 1988 King Fahd initiated another phase of expansion. This was a multibillion-dollar program of modernization to make the places of pilgrimage more accessible to growing numbers. The western wing of the existing mosque was enlarged to hold more than 1 million worshippers. Two very tall minarets were added to complement the seven existing ones. Newly laid floor tiles were made of specially designed heat-resistant marble, and the whole structure is cooled by one of the world's largest air-conditioning units. In addition, escalators have been incorporated alongside a number of fixed stairways in the northern and southern sides of the building to improve the flow of pilgrims and minimize congestion. Excavating a two-story basement for overflow prayer space and utilities also created further space. The project was completed in 1992.

The city has not only been obliged to cope with this dramatic rise in pilgrims but also with the accompanying traffic problems the additional transportation has caused. The initial response by the Saudi authorities was the wholesale construction of motorways and car parks. This had an adverse impact upon the environment to the extent that all of the sixteen miles between Makkah and the Plain of Arafat was being taken up. It also threatened to erode the spirituality of the experience of the pilgrimage. To counter these developments, the Saudi authorities placed quotas on the amount of pilgrims each country could send and limited vehicular access for Saudi nationals.

The population of Makkah is heterogeneous, comprising not only the original Arab inhabitants but also the descendants of pilgrims who settled in it over the centuries. Virtually all the ethnic groups of Islam can be found in Makkah, and there is a tendency for national and ethnic groups to live together in the same districts of the city. There is a ban on non-Muslims entering the city that accentuates its Islamic character. The population fluctuates according to the times of the year and the influx of pilgrims. Most inhabitants are concentrated in the Old City and its environs.

Michael Dumper

Further Readings

Didier, Charles. *Sojourn with the Grand Sharif of Makkah.* Cambridge: Oleander, 1985.

Dodd, Edward, and Rose Dodd. *Mecca and Beyond.* Boston: Central Committee on the United Study of Foreign Missions, 1937.

Hurgronje, Christiaan. *Makkah, A Hundred Years Ago.* London: Immel, 1986.

Ibn Duhaysh, 'Abd al-Malik ibn 'Abd Allah. *The Holy Haram of Makkah and the Boundary Marks Surrounding It: A Historical and Field Study.* Lucknow, India: Department of Arabic, Lucknow University, 1990.

Sugich, Shadiya. *Living in Makkah.* London: Macdonald, 1987.

Yafi, Abdullah al-. *Management of Haj Mobility Systems: A Logistical Perspective.* Amsterdam: Johannes Enschede, 1993.

Ziehr, William. *The Ancient World: From Ur to Mecca.* London: Orbis, 1982.

Manama
Population: 165,000 (2004 estimate)

The existence of freshwater from underground aquifers has made Manama an attractive location for settlement for thousands of years. Throughout much of its history, it was a trading center as well as being famous for its pearls, and it has thus periodically caught the attention and come under the control of major powers. British interest in Bahrain was initially sparked by trading and piracy concerns, and for most of the nineteenth and twentieth centuries the United Kingdom (UK) played an important role in local politics. Bahrain's dwindling oil resources have also influenced Manama's development; pushed to diversify economically, the city has become a major financial center for the Gulf region.

The city of Manama (Arabic, *al-Manamah*) is located on the northeastern end of the main Bahraini island, close to the western central littoral of the Persian Gulf. In a region where water is a scarce commodity, the area around Manama has long been known for its underground aquifers, producing an oasis that attracted settlers and provided the main source of fresh drinking water. In addition, Manama lies in a relatively fertile area of the island, in a plain able to support cultivation of date palms and other hardy vegetation. The city is the capital of the island nation-state of Bahrain.

Oasis farming and fishing in the area around Manama may be as old as the beginning of the third millennium BC. By 1500 BC, the island was clearly a key trading center for the Gulf region, taking advantage of its ideal location between Mesopotamia and the Indus Valley. Alabaster vases from Egypt and Syrio-Palestinian pottery have been found around Manama. Bahrain is generally thought to be the site of the ancient civilization of Dilmun, which existed sometime after 2500 BC, and artifacts from that civilization have been found in what is now present-day Manama. A British archaeologist, T. Geoffrey Bibby, and his Dutch colleague, Peter Vilhelm Glob, first posited the link between Dilmun and Bahrain in the 1950s. Dilmun is itself perhaps most famous for its role in the ancient *Epic of Gilgamesh,* where it was known as an island where immortality could be found; it may be the original site for the concept of the Garden of Eden. It is from this period (2300–1000 BC) that the majestic burial mounds of Bahrain, estimated to number more than 170,000, began making their appearance, ultimately forming one of the largest cemeteries in the world.

The Dilmun commercial network lasted for about 2,000 years, eventually giving way to the Assyrians in about 700 BC. Assyrian rule was relatively short-lived, ending after just a century. The Babylonians followed, faring somewhat better, with the Greeks temporarily conquering the island in about 300 BC. They chose to rename it Tylos, apparently after two ships from Alexander the Great's fleet that visited the island. Pliny, in his first century AD writings, refers to Tylos and to the pearls it produced as well as to its cotton fields.

The Parthians and then the Sassanian Persians governed the island during the first half of the new millennium, and new religious beliefs spread through the area. By AD 410, there was a Nestorian bishopric near to Manama and a major monastery, making it the oldest seat of Christianity in the Gulf. The Nestorians were deeply involved in pearl diving, even asking their bishop if divers needed to observe the Sabbath. Bahrain fell to the Muslim armies in AD 630, and one of the earliest mosques in the Gulf was established here (the Khamis Mosque), perhaps as early as the late seventh century. Soon the Muslim community was involved in long-distance ocean trading; Chinese coins dating from the 650s to ca. 1200 have been found in the city.

In 1330 the forces of Hormuz conquered the island, and it is a manuscript from 1345 that first mentions a town called al-Manamah (the place of dreams). Manama gradually became a center for Shi'i scholarship and ulema training, and Bahrain provided many of the leading Shi'i clerics in Persia and Iraq over the next three centuries. These local ulema were deeply involved in the pearl-diving trade as capitalists and merchants, and they also financed production of grain in the city's hinterland.

The first time Manama fell out of the control of regional powers was in 1521, when the Portuguese, with support from their new Hormuzi allies, conquered it as part of their broader inroads into the Gulf region (see also "Bandar Abbas"). The Portuguese were interested in expanding their trading empire, controlling the spice trade that passed through the key Gulf ports, and thus set up forts in coastal areas. Their legacy to greater Manama includes Qalhat Bahrain (Bahrain Fort), which is also known as the Portuguese Fort. According to the Bahrain National Museum, the fort, which is one of the main tourist attractions on the outskirts of the city, was built on the site of at least two earlier forts.

Despite their fortifications, the Portuguese did not last a full century in Manama, with the forces of Shah Abbas taking the island in 1602. Under the Safavids, the official yearly value of Bahraini pearls was 600,000 ducats, produced by more than 2,000 pearling dhows. The island also produced a continuing wealth of Shi'i scholars, who predominated in the mosques of Persia. During the 1700s, the whole region experienced increased insecurity, and all the towns on the island declined in population and wealth. With the death of Shah Karim Khan (1779), remaining Persian control over the Gulf disappeared, and mainland Arab tribes were able to expand their elite domination over the sites of key revenue production along the Arab coast, whether pearling, harbors, customs, trade, or shipping. One Sunni tribe, the al-Khalifa, originally from the southern Najd, initially migrated to Kuwait, and then in the late 1700s moved from there, along with a Kuwaiti family, the al-Jalahimah, and captured Qatar. From Qatar, in 1789, the two families launched an invasion of nearby Bahrain. After their capture of the island, the two tribes fell out, with the al-Khalifa remaining in Bahrain and the al-Jalahimah moving back to Qatar. Today the al-Khalifa continue to rule an island that has a 70 percent Shi'i majority.

It was the British and their interests in Indian-Ottoman transit trade through the Gulf, however, that shaped much of the city's trajectory over the next two centuries. By 1820 the British had employed their naval power to control Arab "piracy" along the Arab littoral of the Gulf. Increasingly restrictive treaty arrangements were forced on the Arab shaykhs along the coast; the al-Khalifa signature on a General Treaty of Peace in 1820 was followed by subsequent treaties over the rest of the nineteenth century, as the British consolidated their position in Manama.

Eventually, in 1900, the British government appointed a political agent to Manama to represent their interests. That position was initially to be temporary, but it became permanent at the end of the year. Subsequently, the United Kingdom built a permanent residence for the political agent in Manama between 1901 and 1902, and the British played an important role in policy formulation in the coming decades. In particular, they helped bring the slave trade to a close in the city and used their naval power to protect the al-Khalifa family from Persian irredentism.

The pearling trade continued to dominate economic life in the mixed community of Manama during the early part of the twentieth century. Each year, during the pearling season (July to October), 15,000 local divers would go out from Manama en masse on fleets of more than 400 *dhows* (local sailing ships) ceremoniously blessed by the amir to the beat of drums and chants. The city's pearl market was full of Indian pearl brokers looking to buy from the boat captains for shipment to Bombay. The profits from this trade did not lead to great prosperity for the city, however, and the famous observer of the Gulf, J. G. Lorimer, described Manama in 1908 as "damp, squalid and depressing." Subsequently, the situation worsened—the worldwide depression of the 1920s, combined with the introduction of cultured pearls from Japan, led to the collapse of the global pearl market, badly affecting the economy of Bahrain.

Manama was not a dying city, however. Commercial fishing out of the city's harbor provided some regular income; observers during the interwar years describe thousands of fish drying in the sun along the Manama Pier. The city also was a dry dock for hundreds of dhows needing repairs, and the harbor continued to handle the export of Bahrain's famous dates, particularly the khalas variety. The energy of the city attracted American missionary doctors, who established the American Mission Hospital in 1903, one of the first of its kind in the Gulf. In 1929 Imperial Airways made the area north of Manama a stop on the first regular seaplane route from London to Brisbane.

Standard Oil of California (Socal) discovered oil on the island in 1932, and by 1934 Bahrain had become the first Gulf state to export crude. This early discovery of oil not only relieved the immediate problems of the collapse of the pearl market, but it also allowed for economic development of the country much earlier than that which occurred in other Gulf states. Immigrants from southern Persia and India worked the new oil industry; the small Jewish community welcomed new arrivals, all expanding the mixed ethnic and sectarian population of the city.

In 1935 another factor that has influenced Manama first came into play. In that year, the British navy moved its Gulf operational headquarters to Juffair, a few miles southeast of Manama. In 1949 the U.S. Navy also started using these port facilities. The relationship with the British navy was to last until 1971; the United States continues to use the military facilities in the city's suburbs as a base for the Fifth Fleet. Aside from the security relationships that have developed from the foreign military presence, the foreign troops have brought money and a more liberal lifestyle to the city, helping it to attract a global clientele.

On the political front, the British continued to play an important role in Manama's development into the second half of the twentieth century. In 1946 the British government moved the headquarters of its Political Resident, the senior UK official in the Gulf, to Manama from Bushire in Iran. This move put Manama at the center of the political map for the Gulf, as the British Political Resident was responsible for relations with the government of Bahrain and, through political agents stationed in other Gulf states, for ties with other treaty countries in the region. In 1960 the city housed 62,000 people and was still surrounded by date palm plantations and small villages.

By the late 1960s, however, the political relationship that had dominated Manama's development for more than 100 years was changing, and with it the city's built environment. Budget pressures in the United Kingdom forced the withdrawal of British troops in 1971, and in August of that year Bahrain became independent. Manama became the capital of the independent nation-state of Bahrain. It remains both the seat of government for the country and the main commercial center for Bahrain, now housing more than 35 percent of the country's population within its ten-square-mile boundary. The University of Bahrain was established in the city in 1986, and major industry has located around its edges.

Although Bahrain was the first Gulf state to discover oil, its reserves are relatively limited, and dwindling oil resources have forced the diversification of the Bahraini economy. As key to this development, Manama has become a financial center for the Gulf region. The explosion of the financial services industry in the city began in earnest after the outbreak of the civil war in Lebanon, where many banks had previously maintained their Middle East headquarters. During the 1980s, the city intentionally sought to attract bank headquarters and regional offices; today more than 175 banks have branches in the city, making it the financial center of the Gulf Cooperation Council (GCC). Islamic banking has taken off in the city as well (twenty-six Islamic banks, five Islamic insurance companies, and thirty-seven Islamic mutual funds located in Manama), and Manama has become known as a hub for the Sharia-compliant finance, insurance, and bond markets. Competition for Manama's financial role is growing, however. Dubai has established its own International Financial Center, and Doha has recently announced plans for a financial center. To try to keep pace, Manama is building the $1 billion Bahrain Financial Harbor, located on reclaimed land along the seafront. The city also is attracting transnational corporations: American Express and Chevron have both chosen to locate their regional headquarters in the city. As a result of the influx of expatriates, Manama is more than one-third non-Bahraini, with a very cosmopolitan feel.

Bahrain has also sought to promote itself as a tourist destination, and Manama has been particularly successful in attracting weekend tourists from neighboring Saudi Arabia. Excellent transportation links contribute to this success; in 1986 a fifteen-mile-long causeway between ad-Dammam and Manama was completed, allowing more than 3 million visitors per year to travel between the mainland and the island. Manama boasts a number of five-star hotels, which add to its appeal as a tourist destination.

Attractions on the outskirts of the capital are helping to increase tourist interest. In 2004 the country opened a Formula One (F-1) racetrack and held the first ever F-1 race in the Gulf region. Tourists are also attracted to older parts of Manama, with its covered bazaars and centuries-old houses with central courtyards and wind towers. The old commercial heart of the city was Bab al-Bahrain (the gate of Bahrain), today the site of government offices near the old suq. The area is to be redeveloped, and a consultant has been appointed to make proposals.

Although such developments encourage tourism, Manama is not without problems that could act as a brake to the sector. In particular, tension between the ruling Sunni al-Khalifa and the majority Shi'i population (which is at least in part the result of the economic hardship and the need for political reform) is sometimes a problem. In 1981 there was a failed Shi'i coup attempt, while as late as 2004 Shi'i protests in Manama about developments in Iraq were harshly handled by the security services, and several were injured.

The long history of liberal and early development during the twentieth century has meant that Manama has experienced a number of firsts in the Gulf. The city housed the region's first cinema, its first radio station, and the first printing press. Today the largest megaplex cinema in the Gulf is being built. With its large and articulate working class, and huge number of foreign workers, Manama has also had a history of labor unrest. The first labor strike in the Gulf hit the city in 1938, formed around the Right to unionize and to elect a legislative council.

Angie Turner

Further Readings

Adawy, N., and O. Al Hassan. *Bahrain: Gateway to the Gulf.* Gulf Center for Strategic Studies, 1996.

Lawson, Fred H. *Bahrain: The Modernization of Autocracy.* Boulder, CO: Westview Press, 1989.

Lombard, P. *Bahrain: Civilisation of the Two Seas.* Exhibitions International, 1999.

Lorimer, J. G. *Gazetteer of the Persian Gulf.* Calcutta: Superintendent Government Printing, 1908.

Vine, P. *Pearls in Arabian Waters: The Heritage of Bahrain.* London: Immel Publishing, 1994.

Marrakesh
Population: 823,154 (2004 census)

Marrakesh is the traditional southern capital of the kings and sultans of Morocco and a major trading center for the western Maghreb region. A fascinating mix of Berber, Arab, and African ancestry, the people of Marrakesh see themselves as the real traditional Morocco, a city where trade meets politics and authority. For foreigners, the city's magic, captured in song and story, lies in its breathtaking location beneath the High Atlas Mountains, its red and pink buildings and walls, and the exoticism of its snake charmers, teeth pullers, and drummers in Djemâa al-Fna Square. As the gateway to the Sahara via ancient caravan routes, Marrakesh has cycled through numerous periods as the capital of Moroccan dynasties only to be sidelined under new political authorities who moved their capitals elsewhere. Known to Europeans during their age of exploration as Morocco City, Marrakesh eventually lent its name to the country itself, and today it continues to attract visitors to its Sufi shrines and sunny climate.

Marrakesh is situated on the fertile Haouz Plain, 30 miles from the foot of the High Atlas Mountains, some 150 miles south of Casablanca and 100 miles inland from the Atlantic port of Safi. Although rainfall is low, the city benefits from aquifers fed by the snows of the Atlas, making it an oasis city. Long served by a system of long subterranean tunnels that bring this water to the surface by taking advantage of the very slight slope upon which the city is built, the city has been able to create extensive gardens and date plantations. Marrakesh used to be the starting point for caravans heading south through the high Tishka Pass (8,000 feet) to the Sahara to trade with Timbuktu. They brought back chiefly gold and Sudanese slaves, for whom Marrakesh was an important market. Modern-day industries include the processing of fruit, vegetables, and palms; tanning; and the manufacture of wool, flour, building materials, and handicrafts, notably leather goods and carpets. In the mountains are mines extracting copper, lead, and graphite.

Straddling as it does the nomadic and settled regions of Morocco and being formerly a major slave market, the population is heterogeneous. It is mainly derived from nomadic tribes of Berbers and Arab-Berber origin. In addition, there is much mixing with sub-Saharan and Sudanese populations. A Berber dialect is much in evidence in Marrakesh although the language of the tribes around the city is Arabic. While a solidly Islamic city, there is a small Jewish *mellah* (quarter) that dates back to the 1550s, when Jews were forced to move into the area of the sultan's stables.

Marrakesh has long been famous for its devotion to the cult of saints, with shaykh veneration and spirit possession holding a strong place in popular culture. During the twelfth century, the city was famous for attracting "Shaykhs of the Way," Sufi teachers from Spain and the Maghreb. For example, Abu Yaza, considered the spiritual father of Moroccan Sufism, was a teacher in the city, and Abu al-Abbes as-Sibiti, the famous Sufi, died in the city in 1204. Thus, dotted around the city are numerous pilgrimage sites of *walis* (holy men) who are buried in various cemeteries. Not all of these Sufi shaykhs are accepted by the orthodox but are nevertheless rooted in Berber history and society. Today inhabitants of the city still continue an ancient tradition of "doing the tour" of the various sites scattered around the city. Both men and women will often set out on such daylong excursions as a form of relaxation and enjoyment.

Marrakesh was founded ca. 1062 by the Berber Almoravid dynasty, who sought to control the lucrative caravan trade across the Atlas range and through the Sahara. There were few inland urban conurbations at the time, and so Marrakesh was created as part of an intentional policy of control and imperial domination. Abou Bakr, head of the Almoravids, undertook the construction of a kasbah, and by 1126 the madinah was surrounded by walls stretching for twelve miles, with nine gates and 202 towers.

The challenge of the Berber Almohad dynasty under Abu al-Mumin brought them to the gates of the Almoravid capital in 1147. Both the defenders and the besiegers employed European Christian mercenaries in the siege: 12,000 Castilian horsemen participated with the attackers, while a contingent of Frandji (Franks or Europeans) betrayed their Almoravid employers and opened one of the gates. The victorious troops looted the city and destroyed most of its monuments. Marrakesh then became the capital of the Almohad dynasty, which stretched from the Atlantic Ocean to the frontiers of Libya and from Andalusia to the Sahara. As a result, the city prospered, and many fine monumental buildings were constructed. Abu al-Mumin began the construction of the Koutoubia Mosque, which his grandson Yacoub al-Mansour adorned with a striking minaret that is still standing today. An administrative district was constructed outside its walls, a substantial *khettara* (underground irrigation canals) system was developed, and Andalusian-style buildings arose to grace the city. The city housed both minority Christian and Jewish communities during this period, although numerous pogroms and massacres befell one or both groups at various times under Almohad rule.

Marrakesh was to remain the capital of the empire until the collapse of the Almohad dynasty in 1269, when the conquering Marinids decided to rule from Fez (see also "Fez"). They sacked the city a number of times and massacred minorities. As a result, Marrakesh lost its preeminent position in the Maghreb region. Its marginality and vulnerability can be seen in the way it was nearly captured by the Portuguese in 1515 and the fact that it was beset by repeated famines.

With the rise to power of the Saadids in the sixteenth century, Marrakesh, captured in 1525, again became the capital.

Industrial production flourished, and trade guilds controlled the textile and leather production. It was during this time that the Europeans first made a substantial appearance in the city. They came for many reasons, including to purchase the famous Moroccan leather produced in the tanneries of the city. The English in particular were welcomed as a counterbalance to Portuguese power along the Atlantic coast. It is from this time that the European term for Marrakesh, *Marroch,* gradually came to be applied to the whole country.

The Saadid sultan al-Mansur particularly sought to expand the reach and power of Marrakesh. It is from the city that the invasion of Timbuktu and Mali was launched on 16 October 1590 by 23,000 troops equipped with English cannon and muskets. During the thirty-year occupation of Timbuktu, al-Mansur was able to extract enough gold that he became known as Sultan adh-Dhahabi (the Golden). The Sudanese ulema in Timbuktu paid the greatest price, however. For their resistance, al-Mansur had them and their families exiled to Marrakesh, stole their books and destroyed their ancient Islamic libraries, and extracted gold from their treasuries in taxes (see also "Timbuktu").

Marrakesh again suffered another period of decline when the successors to the Saadids, the Arab Alawites, shifted their capital to Meknes (see also "Meknes"). However, some infrastructural development took place under Sidi Muhammad Ben Abdallah, who rebuilt and restored the walls, the kasbah, and palaces and mosques as well as creating new gardens.

By the nineteenth century, Marrakesh was again on the decline, although it did regain some of its former status in 1873, when Moulay al-Hassan I was crowned there. The city was the power base for the 1907 rebellion of Moulay Abd al-Hafid against his brother, the sultan Abd al-Aziz, who he accused of allowing too much European influence into the country. It was al-Hafid, however, who became sultan in 1909, who was forced to accept a French protectorate in return for his throne.

One reason for the problems experienced by the city during the end of the nineteenth and beginning of the twentieth centuries was that power was located in the hands of a series of local Berber warlords, or Grand Caids de Sud, who ruled the city from their tribal homes in the Atlas Mountains although often held court in the city. Nominally under the sultan at Rabat, and then under the French protectorate, these Caids used thugs to expropriate agricultural surplus from the peasants of the Haouz, extracted corvée, and imposed a Caid tax on the merchants of the city (see also "Rabat/Sale"). The tales from the al-Glawi court in Marrakesh during the end of the nineteenth century caught the imagination of Europeans and made the exotic Marrakesh an idealized city of Oriental excess. The most powerful of these pashas was the last, al-Hajj Thami al-Glawi. Ruling the city for fifty years, he controlled all of southern Morocco; upon his death, in 1956, his al-Glawi tribe owned 45,000 acres of the best farmland surrounding the city.

Under the French protectorate (1912–1956), the city became a major agricultural entrepôt and center of light manufacturing. There was considerable investment in irrigation technologies and agriculture, and the population of the city increased from 70,000 in 1912 to 215,000 in 1952. The French constructed a *ville nouvelle* (a new colonial town) outside the walls, laid out in the modern gridlike pattern with shady boulevards and low-density residential areas. Under the colonial administration, new academic opportunities arose in the city. One example was the Alliance Israélite Universelle (AIU), a Franco-Jewish organization established in Paris in 1860 to work for the emancipation of Jews. The AIU established a network of schools in Morocco, including Marrakesh, to train Jewish students in French and secular subjects. Graduates of the school in Marrakesh went on to participate in the Moroccan Jewish migration to Israel and America that occurred in the 1950s.

The modern city is now graced with beautiful gardens, such as the Menara Gardens in the south. The city's population experienced a relative decline in the mid-twentieth century at the expense of the great Atlantic cities of Morocco. Yet tourism has increased dramatically and ensured the city's continuous prosperity. The importance the state attaches to the city was symbolized in April 1994 when it was chosen as the location for the signing of the international General Agreement on Tariffs and Trade (GATT), which established the World Trade Organization. In 2001 the city played midwife to the Marrakesh Accords, implementing the Kyoto Protocols. The city's development has not been without problems, however. Worker unrest broke out in a leftist uprising in the city in March 1973 against the authoritarian government of King Hassan, and the government's close association with the Americans has meant the nearby Benguerir air force base hosts a U.S. military presence, which has been resented in the city.

The heart of Marrakesh remains the madinah, with its densely populated twisting alleyways and covered bazaars. Despite the congestion, Marrakesh is graced with numerous monuments that are outstanding for their architectural and historical value. In 1985 the United Nations Educational, Scientific, and Cultural Organization (UNESCO) recognized the World Heritage significance of the madinah and kasbah of Marrakesh. Among the grandest buildings in the suq is the Koutoubia Mosque, which was begun in the early twelfth century. The mosque took its name from the Arabic word for books, *kutub,* because there was once a book market nearby. With a 230-feet-high square minaret topped by three golden orbs, the mosque is visible from a great distance in every direction. The decorations of its upper parts reveal colors that change with the sunlight.

The madrasa of Ali Ben Youssef, built ca. 1570, is another example of striking architecture. The madrasa is a remarkably well-preserved fourteenth-century Quranic school that was once the largest such institution in the Maghreb. As many as 900 students once lived in the upper-level rooms arranged around inner courtyards. The madrasa also contains a small mosque, whose beautiful carvings and plasterwork designs continue to delight visitors.

Within the madinah can also be found the remains of the al-Badi Palace, built in the sixteenth century. The major construction work went on for sixteen years, involving craftsmen from all over the Mediterranean, and it was regarded as the most beautiful palace in the world. The palace was ransacked in the seventeenth century for the materials to complete another palace at Meknes. Today an annual folklore festival is held in the grounds during May or June.

Another two outstanding palaces deserve mentioning, both built more recently (in the nineteenth century). The Dar Sidi Said Palace, with its planted courtyard, is now an arts and crafts museum housing an important collection of Moroccan antique crafts. Another palace, the al-Bahia, was originally built in the 1880s as a harem's residence and contains most of the elements that together make up iconic Moroccan architecture: carved wooden ceilings, tiled lower walls, painted ceilings, fountains, interior courtyards, and marble.

Marrakesh is also home to one of the Maghreb's most extensive royal mausoleums. The Saadid Tombs is a huge necropolis created by the sultan Ahmed al-Mansur in the late sixteenth century as a burial ground for himself and his successors. There are more than sixty intricate indoor tombs, with many more located outside among the gardens. The central mausoleum, the Hall of Twelve Columns, which contains the tombs of Ahmed al-Mansur and his family, has a vaulted roof, *mashrabiyya* (carved wooden screening traditionally used to separate the sexes), and columns of gray Italian marble.

In addition to the monumental buildings of princes and scholars, Marrakesh is a commercial and trading center. This can be seen in the bazaars of the madinah but more famously in Djemâa al-Fna Square. Djemâa al-Fna is a centuries-old meeting place of regional farmers and tradesmen, and it has always been more than just a market. With gates leading out into the suq, and flanked with mosques and a series of cafés, its stalls of bric-a-brac are accompanied by open-air entertainment. Particularly in the late afternoon and on into evening, the square fills with all sorts of buskers and performers, including storytellers, snake charmers, acrobats, dancers, musicians, monkey tamers, fortune-tellers, henna ladies, tooth pullers, and astrologers. For centuries, troupes of performers have passed through the Djemâa al-Fna, performing for a day or a week, then moving on to other towns. Contributions are expected, since it has long been considered a religious duty to support such traveling groups. The view and atmosphere at sunset is an important feature of Marrakesh life and a main selling point for tourism.

In such a colorful, hip, and cosmopolitan city, it is not surprising that Marrakesh has attracted its share of poets and artists. Al-Mouatamid, poet and king of Seville, wrote his most beautiful poems during his exile in Marrakesh, and the famous poet Hafsa Ben al-Haj visited the city. The philosopher Abu al-Walid Ibn Rushd (Averroes, 1126–1198) lived in Marrakesh, where he wrote several of his best-known works. More recently, Marrakesh has become famous for the international Marrakesh Folk Festival, whose highlights are exhibitions of Moroccan Berber dance. Today the city retains its playground image with the opening in 2005 of the largest club complex in Morocco, hosting the biggest sound system in Africa.

The city is also buzzing with foreign real estate investors. Marrakesh is currently a hot international property site, attracting second-home buyers from Europe who want investment property in exotic sunny locations. This real estate boom has meant that all the *riads* (older town houses) within the suq have been bought up and converted to hotels, restaurants, and celebrity hideaways, and the city is experiencing a boom of villa expansion in its undeveloped outskirts.

Michael Dumper

Further Readings
Bovil, Edward William. *The Golden Trade of the Moors.* 2d ed. London: Oxford University Press, 1968.
Fernea, Elisabeth Warnock. *A Street in Marrakech.* Garden City, NY: Anchor Press, 1976.
Gershovich, Moshe. *French Military Rule in Morocco.* London: Frank Cass, 2000.
Mayne, Peter. *The Alleys of Marrakesh.* Harmondsworth, UK: Penguin, 1957.
Meakin, Budgett. *The Land of the Moors.* 1901. Repr, London: Darf, 1986.
Shatzmiller, Maya. *The Berbers and the Islamic State.* Princeton: Markus Wiener, 2000.
Slymomovics, Susan. *The Walled Arab City in Literature, Architecture and History.* London: Frank Cass, 2001.
Terrasse, Henri. *History of Morocco.* Casablanca: Ed. Atlantides, 1952.

Meknes
Population: 587,000 (2005 estimate)

Meknes, the smallest of the four imperial cities of Morocco, served as the capital of the country from 1675 to 1728 under the early Alawites. The construction of a huge palace by Moulay Ismail, the founder of the dynasty, after his overtures in marriage to the daughter of Louis XIV of France were rejected has given it the epithet of the Moroccan Versailles. Nevertheless, despite some periods of grandeur and great influence, Moulay Ismail never succeeded in making Meknes the great imperial city he planned it to be. Meknes did not achieve a sustained dominant role in Moroccan urban life of that of its sister cities and rivals, Marrakesh and Fez. Today it remains in essence an exquisite outdoor museum to frustrated courtship.

Meknes lies on a high plateau overlooking the fertile plain of the Agdal basin in north-central Morocco, west of the Middle Atlas. Today's city is split into two halves by the gorge of the Bou Fekrane River, with the madinah (old town) on one side and the French colonial town, the *ville nouvelle,* on the other. Its hinterland is very fertile, composed of good soil, and the city and its surrounding area have excellent water supplies. Thus, it sits in one of the best agricultural districts of Morocco. Agricultural products that flow into the city include citrus, olives, and cereal crops. It is eighty miles east of Rabat and some thirty-five miles southwest of Fez and located at a crossroads for travel to the mountain resorts. Its geography and location have meant that for more than 2,000 years conurbations on the site have played a security and strategic role as a border city between the north and south of the region.

Meknes enjoys relative wealth and is one of modern-day Morocco's fastest-growing cities. The population is composed of many distinct ethnic groups: Shorfah, Bwakher, Berbers, and Jews. The Shorfah are descendants of Moulay Idris, the first Muslim conqueror of Morocco. While retaining some ancient privileges, they generally form an impecunious aristocracy in the city. The Bwakher, descendants of a black African guard of Moulay Ismail, were for many decades fiercely independent but in the twentieth century took up the trades of blacksmiths and mat makers. Jews traditionally formed about a quarter of the population until the mid-twentieth century, when many immigrated to Israel. The Berbers are the largest population group in Meknes. They were largely former mountain dwellers, and the colorful clothes of the Berber women, with their short skirts, leather gaiters, and wide-brimmed hats, give the city a distinctive feel. The population of Meknes is subjected to seasonal fluctuations as artisans return to their villages to assist in the harvest.

Habitation on the site goes back to at least the third century BC; archaeological finds indicate an indigenous Berber town, with magistrates, temples, and its own writing system. It was a trading city, as indicated by significant finds of Carthaginian/Punic products. This Mauritanian kingdom was ruled by Juba II under indirect control from Rome until the empire took direct control in AD 40.

The city was renamed Volubilis, and it became the southernmost garrison city for the new Roman province of Mauritania Tingitana. Beyond the city were a defensive ditch, a few military garrisons, and then the Berbers. A temple to Saturn was built over an older temple to local gods, and remains of a House of Venus, hot-water springs piped into baths, and exceptional bronze and marble sculptures indicate considerable wealth and power. It was a large city, and its remains today are some of the best-preserved Roman ruins in Morocco. In the second and third centuries, the cultivation of wheat and olive oil in the region brought further prosperity. This wealth can be seen in remaining monuments such as the Victory Arch (ca. 217), in honor of the Roman emperor Caracallas, or the valuable house mosaics depicting Bacchus on his chariot. The city was connected via a fortified Roman road with the coastal cities to the east and with Tingis (Tangier) (see also "Tangier").

By the reign of Diocletian (284–305), however, the expense of maintaining North African positions forced a pullback of Roman legions, and in 285 the city was peacefully abandoned by the Roman military. The local Berber Baqates tribe assumed power, continuing to use Latin names and titles. It remained Roman in culture and ties, and archaeological remains indicate a Jewish presence from at least the third century AD. Early Christian objects have been found, and a martyr is reported in the city in 298. Trade with tribes to the south continued as the city's lifeblood, and by the early seventh century the Christian community was quite sizable, there were new city walls, and the city remained a functioning power in the region.

By the eighth century, the city appears to have fallen under the control of a Berber tribe known as the Maknassa, from whence the name may be derived, although there is also the suggestion that Meknes was the name of a citadel founded on the site of a reduced town that existed by this time. This pluralistic city welcomed Moulay Idris, great-grandson of the Prophet Muhammad and the father of Islamic Morocco, in 788 and received some benefit from its nearness to Fez, the new capital founded (789) by the Idrisid dynasty (788–974); the city is also only twenty-five miles from Mount Zerhon, where Moulay Idris is buried (see also "Fez").

As the new Berber dynasty of the Almoravids arose in the eleventh century, they needed a military base south of Fez to guard the caravan routes to the Sahara, and so they developed Meknes to serve this role. The city fell to the Almohads in 1150, who reinforced its security role, and during the thirteenth century the city prospered: an aqueduct, several bridges, a kasbah, and mosques were built. The water supply was improved, and the famous Madrasa Djadida was constructed and is still standing today, as the Madrasa Bou Inaniyya. Under the Marinids, Meknes continued its role as an industrial center, producing olive oil; revenues from the oil presses in Meknes paid for new mosque construction in Fez.

The city did not come into its own, however, until the Alawite dynasty, still reigning today, adopted it as their capital in 1673. Under the founder, Sultan Moulay Ismail (1672–1727), a massive wall enclosed the city, with twenty imposing and ornate gates. When the daughter of Louis XIV, the princess of Conti, refused his hand in marriage, the young sultan determined that he would build a palace that would rival Versailles in splendor and elegance. An ambitious building program was started, and a huge separate enclosure reserved for the sultan containing two palaces, one for the sultan and one for his wives and 500 concubines, was constructed reportedly using Christian slave labor. By robbing materials from nearby Volubilis, the palaces were built as a series of gardens connected by pavilions supported on marble columns. There are in total forty-five separate pavilions within the grounds as well as four mosques and twenty domed tombs containing the graves of sultans and their families.

To provide for the palace, there was a huge granary, a storehouse, and magnificent stables. For example, one remarkable feature of the palace was the deep wells constructed in the Dar al-Ma (House of Water). Beside it are the large vaulted rooms of the Heri as-Souani, which served as the storehouse for the city's food reserves as well as storage for fodder for more than 12,000 horses. The household was financed by a tax on the Jews of the city and by gifts from the tradespeople of Meknes's market. The palace also contains the mausoleum of Moulay Ismail, made of several open rooms decorated with mosaics of enameled ceramic. The mosque within the mausoleum contains two clocks that were offered by Louis XIV of France to Moulay Ismail when he refused the marriage of his daughter to him.

Moulay Ismail's rule was confirmed by his new creation, the Abid al-Bukhari, a slave army composed of black slaves collected from around Morocco and forged into a separate professional army loyal only to him as a sharifan (descendant of the Prophet) and their paymaster. By 1678 the Abid garrison had 14,000 soldiers; by the time Ismail died, in 1726, there were 150,000. The sultan housed his guard near Meknes in Mashrah ar-Raml; this base camp also housed the bought or confiscated slave women he collected to be their wives. The Abid were his shock troops or occupation force, and their role as a political force in Meknes continued up until the French protectorate. A very interesting book, which appeared in London in 1745, tells the story of Thomas Pellow, a twelve-year-old ship's boy from Cornwall, who was captured by Barbary corsairs, converted to Islam, and became a soldier in Moulay Ismail's Abid army. He married one of the camp women, became an interpreter, and finally returned to England in 1738 to publish his tale.

The imperial city was completed by Moulay Ismail's son Moulay Abdallah (1727–1757) and his grandson Sidi Mohamed ben Abdallah (1757–1790). After the death of Moulay Ismail, however, the imperial city gradually lost its use as a royal residence, partly because of the devastating earthquake of 1755. When, in the nineteenth century, Meknes ceased to be an imperial capital in preference to Fez, it became neglected. However, the sultan would often meet foreign consuls, housed in Tangier, in Meknes. The painter Eugene Delacroix traveled as part of an official French mission to the sultan in 1832, and his sketches and paintings of life at the court in Meknes are a fascinating window onto that period of the city's history. Delacroix reports that it took them ten days to make the journey under armed escort, that no European could address the sultan directly but only through a Jewish interpreter, and that the delegation was confined to their rooms for the three days it took for the sultan to finally meet with them.

It was not until the reign of Moulay Hassan at the end of the nineteenth century that Meknes was restored and revived. The period of French rule (1912–1956) saw the construction of a new colonial city across the Wadi Bou Sekrane opposite the imperial palace, and the city became a regional command center for French troops. After independence, the city housed the Royal Military Academy (Dar al-Beida). It was around a cadre of Berber officers and generals who had studied together at the academy or served in the Meknes area that the failed military coup attempt against King Hassan was organized in July 1971.

In addition to tourism, the modern city is known for its industrial production, including agricultural products such as palm oil and distilling. In addition, the city has a reputation for the manufacture of carpets, textiles, painted wood furniture, and a unique handicraft tradition in multihued embroidery based around a geometric star pattern.

The heart of the madinah of Meknes lies to the north of the Place al-Hedim and the Great Mosque. Smaller than the madinah of Fez, the madinah of Meknes is also quieter and not among the finest in Morocco. The *kissaria,* the commercial heart of the madinah, is located just behind the Great Mosque. Built in the fourteenth century, it is an open market flanked by handicraft workshops. South of the Great Mosque is the Place al-Hedim. Once a vibrant marketplace with entertainers and colorful stalls, al-Hedim has suffered from modern attempts at restoration and renovation. To the south is the Bab Mansour al-Aleuj, a monumental gateway decorated with beautiful green mosaics. It is considered one of the finest and most ornate gates of all North Africa. It was completed in 1732 during the reign of Moulay Ismail.

Situated on the north side of the Place al-Hedim is the Dar Jamai, now the Museum of Moroccan Arts. Built in 1882 to be the residence of the Jamai family, it is a fine example of Moroccan and Andalus architecture and gives an insight into the lifestyle of the wealthy families of Meknes. It is known for its famous cupola hall, richly decorated with enameled ceramics, painted wood, and sculptured plaster. It was used as a military hospital under French rule and became a museum in 1920. To the west of the Place al-Hedim is the Jewish Quarter, or *mellah.* The old mellah was located on a sloping hillside, and the Jewish community acquired a new site in the 1920s. The first houses were built in 1924, and a synagogue was inaugurated there in 1926.

The ancient pilgrimage site of the mausoleum of Moulay Idris, founder of the first Muslim dynasty in the Maghreb, still plays a part in the life of the city. The mausoleum was built upon two mountainous peaks some twenty miles from Meknes and completely renovated by Moulay Ismail at the beginning of the eighteenth century, and believers make the pilgrimage to his grave to ask for intersession for health or conception problems. A yearly pilgrimage from Meknes occurs in August and September, in which a large number of the city's inhabitants and tribes of the region celebrate the founder of the country.

Today the city is moving forward both politically and in terms of infrastructure development. There are plans for a new world-class stadium in the city, for larger industrial projects, and for dramatic upgrading in rail access to the city. Although Meknes has experienced political unrest, such as in 1981 when riots over economic conditions and International Monetary Fund (IMF) conditionality rocked the city, in 2003, in an attempt to demonstrate new openness and transparency, the new king, Muhammad, allowed an opposition candidate to become mayor of the city.

Michael Dumper

Further Readings

Bovil, Edward William. *The Golden Trade of the Moors.* 2d ed. London: Oxford University Press, 1968.

Doumou, Abdelali. *The Moroccan State in Historical Perspective, 1850–1985.* Dakar: CODESRIA, 1990.

Gershovich, Moshe. *French Military Rule in Morocco.* London: Frank Cass, 2000.

Meakin, Budgett. *The Land of the Moors.* 1901. Repr. London: Darf, 1986.

Shatzmiller, Maya. *The Berbers and the Islamic State.* Princeton: Markus Wiener, 2000.

Slymomovics, Susan. *The Walled Arab City in Literature, Architecture and History.* London: Frank Cass, 2001.

Terrasse, Henri. *History of Morocco.* Casablanca: Ed. Atlantides, 1952.

Mogadishu
Population 1.2 million (2005 estimate)

The city of Mogadishu has a long and glorious past but is best known for its most recent, bloody history. One of the most dangerous cities in the world over the last sixteen years, Mogadishu's name is now connected in popular culture with the disaster of American and United Nations (UN) involvement there during the early 1990s as represented by the movie Black Hawk Down or with its potential as a hiding place for al-Qaeda and terrorism. Yet during the thirteenth and fourteenth centuries, it was the jewel of western Indian Ocean trade and a center for Islamic learning. Through its port passed grain for southern Arabia, sesame oil for East Africa, and ivory for the pianos of America. Today, still chaotic and dangerous, it hosts the most advanced Internet cafés on the African continent and is the hub of the global Somali diaspora.

Located on the southern Somali coast of the Indian Ocean just north of the equator, the port of Mogadishu (Somali, *Muqdisho;* Italian *Mogadiscio;* Arabic *Muqdisho*) has been an edge city for the Middle East for 1,500 years. It is situated at a point of transition, where to the north lie semiarid conditions good for camel pastoralism and to the south better-watered grasslands and an interriverine basin excellent for cattle and agriculture. Caravan routes linked the city by road with Kenya, Ethiopia, and Berbera on the northern coast. Mogadishu lies at the southern end of the monsoon flow from Aden; from here, one waited for a different wind that blew south to Kilwa. This part of the East African rim has long been known as the Benadir Coast (from the Persian *Bandar,* or ports), with Mogadishu linked with its smaller sister cities to the south, Merca and Brava. The derivation of the name *Mogadishu* is unclear; one suggestion is that it is Somali for "imperial seat of the shah" (*maqad shah*) or Swahili for "last northern city" (*mwyu ma*). Neither seems to reflect the origins of the city in an earlier period.

The city grew up around a good natural harbor whose entrance is marked by dangerous coral reefs to the north and south. Inland from the port, it is a short ten miles to the Wabi Shabeela (Shabelle River) running parallel to the coast. Along the coast, the area is dry, receiving on average just seventeen inches of rain per year. Regional drought is always a possibility; and since Mogadishu depends on the import of food from both the Shabelle region and from Somali pastoralists in the more arid north, the city has frequently suffered problems of food security and famine. Inland from the city are deposits of uranium, salt, manganese, and copper.

Small settlements have existed along this stretch of the East African coast from prehistoric times, attracted by the protected harbors, water, fishing, and trade up and down the coast. It is not, however, until the end of the first century AD that we begin to get the smallest glimpse in the written record that there was settlement and trade along the Benadir Coast. The *Periplus Maris Erythraei* (*Circumnavigation of the Erythraean Sea*) implies that there was trade via Egypt through the Red Sea to the north Somali coast at this time, and perhaps down the East African coast, but little else. Ptolemy also suggests such trade as far south as Pemba; we know the Romans pursued trade along the East African coast looking for ivory, ostrich feathers, and gold. Certainly, over the next three centuries the area around Mogadishu witnessed interaction between peoples from the hinterlands and traders coming from Egypt, Arabia, Persia, and India. Such visits were seasonal, undertaken at great risk, and depended on the permission of the African leader. The Parthian, Byzantine, and Sassanian empires all sought trade in East Africa, gradually increasing the density of interaction around Mogadishu.

By the fifth century, regular trade was reaching increasingly farther to the south and was bringing gold and ivory out of the hinterland, then up the coast to nascent gateway Benadir ports, and from there into the trade circuits of the Indian Ocean, Red Sea, and Mediterranean. In the regional oral tradition and in the first Arabic materials, it is clear that pre-Islamic visitors from southern Arabia (Hadrami) and traders from Persia were regular visitors and that a few began to mix with the local *zanj* (Arabic for the African or black inhabitants).

It is really with the spread of Islam after AD 632, however, and the historical writings produced during its early expansion that Mogadishu as a specific site appears in the written record. As Muslims began to travel along the Benadir Coast, they recorded their visits or told others what they had seen. The expanding Islamic empire sought trade with the local population, producing a quick expansion and intensification in Mogadishu's trade linkages to Yemen, the Red Sea, and the Persian Gulf. It also meant that the city's role as a gateway to the south as far as Sofala in what is now Mozambique developed; for the next 600 years, Mogadishu became a key gateway to southern trade, and the city exploited the ivory and gold of the Sofala coast via a network of small feeder ports, perhaps as many as thirty-seven by AD 1300. Reports of 1,000 Omani vessels trading with East Africa in the tenth century, when Oman was ruled by the Qarmatians of Bahrain, affirms the deep ties developing between the Benadir and the Middle East (see also "Zanzibar").

Middle Eastern traders brought Islam with them along the long-distance trade networks in East Africa, but there were also other immigrants carrying their religion with them in their baggage. An important group were Islamic heretics escaping persecution. As theological conflict and schism shook early Islam, religious refugees migrated to the edges of their known world for safety or for economic opportunity. Kharijites and Shi'i arrived in Mogadishu before the thirteenth century. This is probably the source of the earliest East African tradition of the *Shirazi* (a generic term for Persians or Arabs, those who come from Shiraz). One tradition, contained in the *Kilwa Chronicle,* says that Mogadishu was "founded" by seven brothers from al-Hasa migrating from the Persian Gulf during the tenth century; other traditions suggest earlier Shirazi migrations. The number seven was a mystical number for the Shi'i who had broken with the orthodox Sunni community, and in this foundational myth they fled first to Yemen and then south to Mogadishu. Many in this early immigrant wave were Hadrami, but others came too, from Yemen, Oman, the Hijaj, and the Persian Gulf.

Despite the tradition that Muslim immigrants "founded" the Benadir ports, it is now widely accepted that there were preexisting communities here with African leadership who welcomed these exiles, although the Arab traders had to gain permission to stay, and they had to settle in particular quarters of the town. Tribute was paid, and disagreements often arose over conflicting cultural understandings about land

rights, but intermarriage and assimilation occurred rather quickly, and the Muslim minority in towns such as Mogadishu slowly began to grow.

A third type of Muslim immigrant came from families particularly known for their religious learning and status. Such personages were quickly able to become leaders of the city's fledgling Muslim community. For example, members from a Yemeni clan noted for their scholarship, the Banu Qahtani al-Wa'il, arrived in Mogadishu and were installed as the *qadis* (judges) of the town as well as the *khatibs* (preachers) of the Friday Mosque. They exploited their special status to become a religious dynasty in the city, obscuring families of earlier settlers, although it appears that non-Arab Africans retained political control.

The expanding communities of Muslims along the East African coast continually attracted regular travelers from the Islamic world, and their stories made it into early Arabic writings. Al-Massudi (915–957) was the first to write about the East African coast (Bahr al-Zinj) in his *Muruj al-Dhahab Wa Ma'adin al-Jawhar.* Al-Idrisi (1100–1166), in his *Kitab Nuzhat al-Mushtaq fi Ikhtiraq al-Afaq,* mentions Mogadishu as an important entrepôt, centered between the eastern and western Indian Ocean production zones. Ibn Said (1213–1286), in his *Kitab Bast al-Ard fi al-Tul wa a- Ard,* talks about Mogadishu as the largest Islamic center on the coast and called it "a city of Islam" (Madinat al-Islam).

As soon as expanding Muslim communities in East Africa collected enough wealth, they rushed to build a stone mosque. Mogadishu has two mosques bearing thirteenth-century dates, a clear indication that by that century the city's Muslim community was large and had money to donate to such construction. Archaeological excavation suggests four major stone building periods in the city's history, the first in the twelfth century.

A new wave of Middle Eastern immigrants arrived in the thirteenth century, centered on the Abu Bakr b. Fakhr ad-Din clan. It is at this point that the political structure became dominated by Muslims and by recent immigrants, since the people gave the sultanate of Mogadishu to this clan, who were recognized by the Banu Qahtani. Between them the two clans divided the political and religious leadership of the city. As late as the nineteenth century, Qahtanis were still holding the posts of the city's qadi and khatib.

For Mogadishu the period from 1300 to 1500 was its golden age. The city experienced dramatic growth in population, wealth, commercial power, and control over the hinterland and coast. The yearly monsoons regularly brought new arrivals from throughout the Indian Ocean and the Middle East. Many stayed; many moved on, only to return. An urbanized culture based around coastal Islam emerged on the back of the city's role as a key emporium. In particular, the city attracted increasing migration from the Red Sea area. Among the clans who arrived were the sharifan Makhzumi clan from Makkah (they paid for a minaret to be built in the city), while others arrived from Yanbu (see also "Makkah" and "Yanbu").

The city's fame spread as far as China. Mogadishu is mentioned in a Sung-era (960–1279) book on foreign countries as a place of trade for the Persians. Ming dynasty (1368–1644) records note the city as a destination for trade in bananas and sugarcane picked up in the Maldives. These records also note that the city was known for its export of cloth. The Chinese eunuch Cheng Ho visited the city twice, once in 1417 to 1419 and again in 1421 to 1422 on trading voyages for the emperor; perhaps he was seeking deals in sandalwood, ebony, ambergris, and ivory mentioned by the thirteenth-century Arab author Yaqut as available in the city's markets.

The famous Arab traveler Ibn Battuta visited Mogadishu during its heyday (1332). His observations focus on its by now well-established Muslim community, centered around a madrasa (he stayed in student housing), legal scholars, and sharifan families. He mentions the city's trade with Syria and Egypt, the latter enshrined in the surname of a judge at the time, al-Misri (the Egyptian). A Genoese monk, Leonis Vivaldi, may have also visited the city around the same time (1320).

Another indication of the continued immigration of families from the Middle East are the tombs of Persian immigrants that can still be seen in Mogadishu and in the naming of various quarters of the city; one is still called Shashiya or Shanshiya. Ibn Khaldun, in his writings, suggested that immigrants from central Asia around Tashkent (Shash) dispersed as far afield as Mogadishu, which may be the source of the name for this quarter.

It should be noted that many of the Arab immigrants to Mogadishu after AD 1250 claimed to be descendants of Muhammad via his son-in-law, Ali. Thus, as sharifans or Alawiya/Alids, they both claimed and were usually granted special religious and social status. This *baraka* (legitimacy) allowed these immigrants to immediately integrate into the Muslim communities at the top levels of the elite, marrying leading women from the African or Arab families and often establishing their own political leadership. In such circumstances, proving the genealogical claim was crucial; consequently, officials termed *naqib al-ashraft* (marshal of the nobility) throughout the Muslim world had the job of checking the genealogical claims of Alids. As late as the early twentieth century, there was reportedly a naqib al-ashraft in Mogadishu, the position held by a particular family across the generations. These immigrants were often believed to be special agents of Allah's protection or miracle workers, and they were actively sought out as immigrants by a city's elites for the religious significance and blessing they could bring to the community. Once arrived, Alids often acted as mediators between other clans (*sulha*); certain families from Mogadishu

became famous throughout the Indian Ocean world for their role as peacemakers. These Alid clans also participated in regional networks (*tariqa*) of Alawiya reserved for descendants of Ali. Such networks were just another way the elites in Mogadishu accessed trade and resources around the Indian Ocean rim.

Often younger members of these new immigrant families would then move on to other cities in the Indian Ocean. As a result, the leading families of Mogadishu had blood ties to Kilwa, Mombassa, the Comoros, Madagascar, or the Seychelles. Such secondary migration often produced subsequent return migration to Mogadishu; records indicate returnees from Gujarat, Indonesia (Aceh), and Zanzibar.

The commercial centrality of the city can be read in the fact that it minted its own coins after 1300. For the next 400 years, Mogadishu coins of copper and silver facilitated regional trade. During the 1500s, coins from the city adopted the Ottoman style of monogram, or *turghra*, showing connection with the expanding Ottoman Empire. Other coins circulating in the city were from China, south India, Sri Lanka, and Venice.

The height of Mogadishu's power occurred just as one of the greatest migrations in human history brought the Somali peoples into contact with the city. For more than 1,000 years, Somali clans had been migrating from the shores of the Red Sea south, and they began to arrive near Mogadishu in the thirteenth century. A second wave of Somali immigrants, the Ajuran, created a political structure (sultanate) on the lower Shabelle basin between 1500 and 1650 and moved to take over the political structure of Mogadishu. An Ajuran family, Mudaffar, established a dynasty in the city, thus linking the two entities together; for the next 350 years, the fortunes of the interior and of the urban port became the fortunes of the other.

During this time the Portuguese also arrived along the East African coast (1498) and began to establish an economic and military presence along the trade routes of the Indian Ocean. Over the next 250 years, they played a key role in shaping regional dynamics, although the Benadir Coast remained outside their direct control, and Mogadishu was able to retain its autonomy within the Indian Ocean trading world.

In the 1600s, a new wave of Somali immigrants, the Abgaal, moved both into the Shabelle basin and into Mogadishu, and the city's Mudaffar dynasty collapsed. A new political elite, led by the Abgaal Yaaquub imams, with ties to the new leaders in the interior, moved into the Shingaani Quarter of the city. Remnants of the Ajuran lived in the other key quarter of the city, Xamarweyn. Ajuran merchants began to look for new linkages and regional trade opportunities since the Abgaal had commandeered the existing trade networks. Consequently, ties to Luuq in southern Ethiopia, and to the new Omani rulers in Zanzibar, became a particularly

Ajuran source of trade and strength, with caravans regularly leaving the city for southern Abyssinia and Harar in the Somali north.

By the sixteenth century, Mogadishu's golden age was in a slow decline as the dynamics of Indian Ocean trade shifted elsewhere. The city's population shrank, its income decreased, some older quarters of the city were abandoned, and key trading networks passed first through other cities. This does not mean that the city disappeared from the trade routes or life of the Indian Ocean: Ching dynasty (1644–1911) coins circulated in the city, Mogadishu was the only mint functioning along the East African coast, the city traded via Aden with Cambay, and Gujarati money funded the city's trade. Mogadishu traders still lived abroad in entrepôt like Malacca to conduct trade. Specialized cotton textiles for the Egyptian market were produced in the city's factories. Exports of slaves, cattle, and ivory left the port for Zanzibar or the Red Sea, while slaves from Abyssinia were imported along the caravan routes for use in the textile factories. Other waves of Arab and Persian immigrants arrived in the city in the late 1500s and early 1600s, refreshing its ties to the Middle East (see also "Aden").

The East African coast, and Mogadishu with it, entered a new phase at the end of the 1700s. New imperial actors were appearing in the ports, with inordinate military power and global economic interests. The first to appear were the forces of the imams of Muscat. Starting in the mid-seventeenth century, their ships raided the Benadir ports and extended their "protection" over the coast. They were particularly interested in expanding trade in slaves and ivory, and so Muscati traders reached out, via the Mogadishu gateway, into the interior. Somali caravanners aiming for the new states of the interior assembled in the city and then headed out in long camel trains, carrying guns for trade (see also "Muscat"). The hand of the Omanis was light, primarily evidenced by taxes collected on the export of slaves to India, the Gulf, or the French plantations in the Mascarenes. At the beginning of the nineteenth century, the city contained around 200 stone houses and hundreds of huts.

With the expansion during the 1820s of Zanzibar's role in the Omani commercial empire, control over Mogadishu became more political and centralized. For example, in 1823 an Omani fleet heading to capture Mombassa stopped in Mogadishu, kidnapped two community leaders, and imprisoned them in Zanzibar to impress on the city's merchants the need to conform. Clearly, they did not listen, since Mogadishu was bombed and sacked by an Omani fleet in 1828. As a result, the city leaders sued for peace and submitted to Sultan Seyyid Said.

Over the next fifty years, an increasing number of Europeans visited the city and left their impressions of its streets and people. Through their eyes we see a city graced by four minarets but starkly divided into two major quarters. Almost like two separate towns, with open space between and dividing walls, the Xamarweyn section was home for the merchant elites with trade ties to the wider world, to the Ethiopian highlands, and to Zanzibar. Shingaani, the other half of the town, was where the religious elite, the imam, and those connected to the sultan of Geledi in the interior lived.

Europeans commented on the tremendous numbers of Arab dhows in the harbor, bringing sugar, molasses, dates, salt fish, and arms to the port in exchange for ivory, gums, and textiles. Mogadishu's factories produced *futa benaadir,* a locally woven cloth that they traded both to the interior and to the Red Sea. Custom demanded that strangers to the city should be "held" under the control of local mediators or brokers (*abban*), whose job it was to keep them safe and under control.

The city suffered a number of setbacks during the mid-nineteenth century. In 1835 there was a bad epidemic of plague and drought, producing a famine in the city; a terrible cholera epidemic killed many inhabitants in 1858. In the interior, uprisings of the Baardheere *jamaaca* (jihadists) disrupted Mogadishu's export ivory trade from 1836 to 1843, ruining many merchant families. Conflict inside the city over succession for the role of imam (1842–1843) required the intervention of the sultan of Geledi, who appeared outside the city with 8,000 warriors to mediate the conflict. To strengthen his claim of ultimate suzerainty over the city, Sultan Said of Zanzibar sent a governor to Mogadishu in 1843 who arrived to take control of the city with two soldiers. At that time, the city had around 5,000 inhabitants, including slaves.

The latter part of the nineteenth century witnessed a resurgence in the wealth and population of Mogadishu. There were two main reasons for this expansion. The first was the development of a plantation economy on the Shabelle River to produce grain and sesame for the global market. Beginning around 1800, Somali landowners from the city started importing Bantu slaves from farther south to cultivate millet, sorghum, and sesame on their rural land. By the 1840s, on the back of this slave labor, they were providing most of the grain for southern Arabia and Oman and more than half of the sesame oil for transshipment from Zanzibar. This expanding "grain coast" required intensive labor for cultivation, so non-Somali, non-Muslim Bantu speakers were imported on large slave dhows up the coast. As many as 4,000 slaves were imported annually through Mogadishu. Slaves were cheaper than camels, and so they came to be used for cultivation and herding in the hinterland but also within the city itself to turn the sesame oil mills, as domestic servants, and as concubines. By the late 1800s, Mogadishu was a "slavery city," with as many as two-thirds of the city's population in bondage, a development that indicates a dramatic shift in the social relations of production within the city.

The second reason for the growth of Mogadishu was the ties to the Zanzibar Sultanate and, through it, to the global economy. American, British, and French trade with Zanzibar stimulated the cities of the Benadir Coast, particularly the demand for ivory gathered in southern Ethiopia for use as piano keys. Nor could the nouveau riche in Zanzibar get enough of what the Somali pastoralists offered: hides, ghee, and meat.

Preempting the two-pronged expansion of the Egyptians down the Nile and via the Somali coast, the sultan of Zanzibar made his role in Mogadishu "official" in 1871, establishing a *garesa* (garrison house) for his soldiers and flying his flag. The Somali clans from the hinterland, however, continued to hold the real economic and political power in the city. That was, at least, until the British and the Italians began to carve up their "areas of influence" along the Somali coast during the 1880s. The Imperial British East Africa Company (IBEAC) moved up the coast from what is now Kenya, and the Italians expanded their claims south from the Gulf of Aden and the interior of the Horn of Africa. These Italian claims were based on, among other things, Italian explorations in Somalia during the late 1800s. For example, in 1891 the Italian explorer Luigi Robecchi-Bricchetti left Mogadishu and crossed the Horn of Africa to Berbera (see also "Berbera").

Because of its new overlordship over the sultan of Zanzibar, the IBEAC was able, in 1889, to sublet rights in the hinterland between the Benadir ports to Italian charter companies. This quickly led in 1892 to the sultan actually ceding the ports of Brava, Merca, and Mogadishu themselves to Italy for twenty-five years, subject to a fixed annual rent. Italy finally acquired complete title to the coastal area in 1905 by purchasing outright all rights from the sultan of Zanzibar; Italian Somaliland was born.

The new Italian administrators were immediately faced with a number of crucial tasks. The first was to break the power of the Somali landlords and clans of the hinterland and to open up the region to Italian companies. Resistance was fierce, however, and in a number of battles, the clans defeated Italian troops. Italian companies failed to be attracted to the area, and in general the projection of Italian influence outside the cities failed miserably.

A second task was to restructure the slave-driven economy. In 1903 Mogadishu had 6,700 inhabitants, 31 percent of them slaves. On the landed estates held by the city's elites in the Shabelle Valley, slaves provided all the labor. Slave caravans still arrived in the city, and the royal commissioner himself purchased girls as concubines. Under political pressure from home, the local administration finally suppressed the slave trade after 1910.

The city remained physically and socially divided into the twentieth century, with Shingaani and Xamarweyn separated by a wall and having separate markets and mosques. Yet to-gether the city celebrated the Persian solar New Year as *Istaaqfurow* (the Pharoah's festival) or *dabshiid,* and the slave dances of the Bantu became an important cultural tradition in Mogadishu. The city served as a key Islamic center with Qur'anic schools (*duksi*), which prepared Qur'anic teachers to serve the Islamic community of East Africa.

After taking Ethiopia in the 1930s, the Italian Fascists included Mogadishu in their new Africa Orientale Italiana (AOI). The Fascist administration established a number of new institutions in the city, including the Institutio Magistrale, teacher training centers, and institutes for industrial arts and public health. They also established special troops of Somalis, the Zaptie, to control and intimidate the population. Italian colonists were encouraged to settle in the city, creating an elite Italian minority in control of the economic and political heights of society.

The AOI ceased to exist five years later. After the beginning of World War II, British and Ethiopian troops set out to remove the Italians from the Horn of Africa. British troops under General Cunningham marched north from Kenya and captured Mogadishu in February 1941. They then headed on to Addis Ababa, and the Italians surrendered the Horn of Africa in November 1941.

Following World War II, the British sought to withdraw from Italian Somaliland but were concerned about potential Soviet agitation in the region. Thus, they and the Americans pushed the United Nations (UN) to legitimize a renewed role for a rehabilitated Italy. Italy, too, had residual imperial aspirations; together these factors helped produce a decision by the UN to award Somalia as a trusteeship territory to Italy. Somalis resisted this decision, leading to clashes in Mogadishu in January 1948 in which fifty-two Italians were killed. Nonetheless, on 21 November 1949, the UN passed Resolution 289, which approved a ten-year mandate for the Italians to guide the Somalis to independence.

In April 1950, the Italians established in Mogadishu the Italian Trusteeship Administration (Amministrazione Fiduciaria Italiana in Somalia [AFIS]) and set out to create a state structure inspired by the Italian model of a centralized state. Assisted by an advisory council appointed by the UN (1954–1957) and composed of an Egyptian, a Colombian, and a Filipino, the AFIS stumbled its way toward creating the institutions of independent government. There certainly was resistance from Somalis; the Somali Youth League (SYL), for example, one of eight national Somali parties based in Mogadishu, was opposed to the Italian presence and organized anti-Italian activity. There was resistance as well from old Italian colonialists and Fascists in hiding. Mogadishu was a postwar haven for Italian Fascists fleeing the new Italy, and the Italian community in Mogadishu, both old and new, resisted the AFIS, the introduction of Somali power, and the loss of their authority. Within such a context, the Egyptian representative to the UN Advisory Council, Kamal ad-Din Salah, was assassinated in the city in 1957.

The AFIS was consistently short of funds, and so there was a speedy but underfunded process of Somaliazation to the local administration. Yet the AFIS gave preferential treatment to Italian companies and investors in new banana plantations, and Italian enterprises quickly gained control of most of the key sectors of the economy. By 1960 little development had occurred in the city; for example, there were no formal credit institutions so important for development.

The Somali Republic was created in 1960, and within five days British Somaliland had joined to produce a united Somalia. Mogadishu was declared the capital of the new state although southern Somalis dominated the city, it had few connections to the northern coast, and all the state institutions were concentrated in the capital. The business elite from Mogadishu tended to shape national decision making and to focus state funds on the city's needs and development.

The development of the city's infrastructure moved quickly during the next decade. The port was extended in the late 1960s, and an international airport was built outside the city. The National University of Somalia was established in 1970 with technical assistance from Italy; hence, lectures were in Italian. The key landmarks remained the Arba-Rucun Mosque (the Mosque of the Four Pillars); the cathedral the Italians had built directly next to it; the Fakr ad-Din Mosque, dating from 1269; and the Garesa Palace. The city's population rose to around 191,000 by 1970.

In October 1969, General Muhammad Said Barre carried out a coup d'état. The adoption of scientific socialism in 1970 (abandoned in 1980) led to the nationalization of banks, schools, insurance firms, imports, and wholesale trade within Mogadishu along with the creation of a huge security apparatus. Under the 1974 Treaty of Friendship and Cooperation with the USSR (terminated in 1977), Mogadishu experienced an invasion of Soviet military, security, and bureaucratic personnel. After 1979, when the United States became a key ally of Somalia, Mogadishu witnessed an invasion of U.S. military personnel as U.S. troops took over former Soviet military bases.

Mogadishu had long been a major export gateway for the Somali livestock trade. During the 1970s and 1980s, the city's transshipment of sheep and cattle was a key foreign-exchange earner for the whole country. Large export traders from the city monopolized most of the country's trade and invested their profits back into the city. The city hosted a large national cattle market, and the state supported projects to maintain the interests and profits of these key elites: huge modern holding pens, quarantine stations, and improvements in the deepwater port, all built with foreign aid. The city was also important for its industries, such as processed food, leather, wood products, beverages, and textiles. The oil refinery and chemical factories also contributed to Mogadishu's attraction to rural workers. There were costs, however. The massive slaughter of sheep and cattle created one of the worlds' worst records for shark attacks, since the blood from the abattoirs was dumped directly into the sea off the city's beaches.

The years of the Barre dictatorship were terrible ones for Somalia, with famine, the Ogaden War, civil war in the northwest and northeast, huge human rights violations, and millions of refugees and internally displaced persons (IDPs). But Mogadishu was relatively uninvolved in these developments. It was only in the late 1980s that an underground movement began to organize in the city against the regime. Educated young men who had studied or worked in the Middle East oil states returned to the city ready to use political Islam to overthrow the dictatorship. Small cells of Muslim Brotherhood and Islamic study groups finally coalesced into al-Ittihad al-Islamiya and worked for change.

In January 1991, Barre and his cohorts were pushed out of Mogadishu by the United Somali Congress (USC), affiliated with the Hawiye clans, moving up from the south. A violent civil war quickly developed in the south among former members of the regime and diverse militias vying for power. The result was both a huge refugee migration from the south to Mogadishu and the spillover of the fighting into the streets of the city itself. Between 1991 and 1992, as many as 500,000 may have died in the southern region, and perhaps 1.7 million people (more than one-third of all people in the south) were displaced. Some 250,000 refugees fled to camps within Mogadishu, and aid agencies became their only source of support.

The fighting in Mogadishu in late 1991 and early 1992 intensified, with an estimated 14,000 people killed in the city itself. Most of the city's residents and the IDPs were displaced; schools and hospitals were targeted in the early fighting, and later what was not destroyed was looted and shipped to surrounding countries. Factions led by Farah Aidid and Ali Mahdi fought for control of the northern part of the city, mobilizing more than 30,000 armed men and boys. Ali Mahdi had more supporters, but Aidid's forces had the heavy weaponry: old artillery, antiaircraft guns, antitank recoilless guns, mortars, and even air-to-air missiles taken from MiG-17 fighter bombers and mounted on the back of pickup trucks for use against ground forces.

Civilians fled the city, decreasing the city's population from its pre-1991 level of 1.25 million to around 700,000. Because rival Hawiye militias controlled the city, non-Hawiye inhabitants of the city fled, reducing the diversity and pluralism of the city's population. Those who remained shuttled from one part of the city to another as the fighting shifted from neighborhood to neighborhood. The university was destroyed, as was most of the city's housing, and the aid agencies, including the UN, finally pulled out, since they could not

War-ravaged Mogadishu, 1992. (David Turnley/Corbis)

move around to deliver aid. Italy was the last Western country to suspend economic aid and to evacuate its embassy.

Famine set in throughout the south and in Mogadishu among the IDPs. The International Committee of the Red Cross (ICRC), which was one of the only remaining aid donors, was forced to make huge payments to militias to protect the delivery of aid (reportedly $100,000 per week); these payments actually fed the war economy and discouraged disarmament or reconciliation. In such a context, the pressure on the UN to act finally became intense, and so "Operation Restore Hope" was born. In December 1992, the United States led a multinational force into Mogadishu to protect the delivery of humanitarian aid to the needy.

Unfortunately, the United Nations Operation in Somalia (UNOSOM) had problems from the beginning and never accomplished its goals. The whole project was poorly organized; the rationale for the force was vague and continued to shift; and few of the team members understood Mogadishu, Somali society, or the dynamics on the ground. The distribution of aid attracted refugees to the city as well as attracting the militias. As a result, the forces on the ground got caught up in the

spiral of violence and became players rather than legitimate mediators.

On 3 October 1993, a bloody battle between U.S. troops and Somali militias left hundreds wounded and killed 18 U.S. service personnel, 1 Malaysian soldier, and approximately 1,000 Somalis. These events, depicted in the subsequent book and movie *Black Hawk Down,* caused such a reaction in the United States that the Clinton administration pulled U.S. troops out of UNOSOM in March 1994. The operation remnant went from bad to worse, with militias taking what they wanted. Adid financed his war against Ali Mahdi both by selling off what he had looted in Mogadishu (wires, plumbing, roofing, and office equipment) and by taking it from the UN. For example, a Zimbabwean contingent within the city was attacked; 1 soldier was killed, while the others were stripped to their underwear. As the militia left, they confiscated more than $2 million of automatic weapons, mortars, and armored personnel carriers. Soldiers from other countries sold trucks, tankers of gas, and so forth to anyone with cash, and $3.9 million in cash disappeared from the UN compound. Five different times, UNOSOM threatened to pull out, hoping the threat would elicit cooperation from the warlords in delivering aid; nothing worked. After spending $4 billion, the UN finally abandoned Mogadishu and the mission to Somalia in March 1995. The militia conflict began to slow down as the city ran out of things that could be sold or commandeered.

Since 1995 the UN has hosted numerous conferences and peace meetings outside the country to try to reach a cease-fire and to begin a process of nation building inside the country; each agreement collapsed soon after. The entrenched warlords within Mogadishu, like Hussayn Aidid, son of the late general Farah Aidid, had little interest in supporting these political solutions. The city's business community, on the other hand, desired a restoration of order and a decrease in violence. As a result, they broke with the warlords in 1997 and began to organize the city and their security on their own. For example, they began funding a Sharia militia and court system to maintain security at the port, the major roads, and the main markets.

By 2000 this same Mogadishu business community had become strong enough to try to organize national politics; in fact, they acted as a shadow Somali state. They funded a new UN-supported national conference at Arta that produced a Transitional National Government (TNG), they paid the TNG's budget, and had one of their own members appointed as president. In return, they expected significant profit from the restoration of the national administration to Mogadishu and the subsequent inflow of foreign aid and government contracts.

The TNG established themselves in Mogadishu in early 2001 and began to assert their power in the city. Yet by the time of the events of 11 September 2001, the TNG was in trouble. They had been unable to establish even limited control across the city, and security was no better than it had been before their appearance. The militia leaders were unwilling to cede any power, and the TNG had no revenues of its own. In fact, they could not even control their own supporters: in 2001 Mogadishu businessmen, on whom the TNG relied, imported millions of dollars of counterfeit Somali shillings, enhancing their wealth, which was held in dollars. The hyperinflation that resulted generated huge street protests and riots.

Other players also shaped the city's urban dynamics. Al-Ittihad built an effective organization in Mogadishu and ran the sharia court system, which has provided a modicum of rule of law in the capital over the last decade. Islamic aid agencies' and Saudi-Gulf money were distributed via al-Islah, who created new Islamic schools throughout the community.

The U.S. Navy interdicted ships along the coast, placed the city under aerial surveillance, and sent commandos into a Mogadishu hospital to capture a Yemeni suspect for interrogation in Guantanamo Bay. The United States also froze the assets of al-Barakaat, the largest of Somalia's *hawala* (informal money transfer) enterprises because of fears that it was being used by al-Qaeda. AT&T shut down the entire telecommunication network, cutting Mogadishu off from the world. These actions harmed hundreds of thousands of Somalis who could no longer expatriate funds back into Mogadishu.

Life in the city continues to be very dangerous and difficult. Gunmen high on their daily fix of the narcotic qat (flown in fresh daily from Kenya) still control the streets from the backs of their pickup trucks and divide up the neighborhoods into control zones. The northern part of the city remains the sector where clan warfare is worst; the southern part of the city is more peaceful and more modern, with mansions and safe streets. In May and June 2004, rival groups clashed in the city over disputed business territories, with more than 100 people killed. For three years, day laborers have been smashing the wall around the U.S. Embassy to get the iron rods within the concrete to sell; for this they make about $1.20 per day, half of which goes to one of the seventy different gunmen who control specific sections of the wall. Bus drivers entering the city must pay protection money at six different checkpoints as they take passengers into the city center. There is no central electricity; power is supplied either through small generators or via neighborhood providers. All the clubs in the city have been closed, and most have become refugee camps. Wedding parties are held in secret and surrounded by armed guards because of the threat that gunmen will burst in and rob the guests and happy couple. One percent of the city's population is HIV positive, and there are no medicines for them. Since the old central market has been destroyed, a new, makeshift market, the Barkara, is where one goes to buy passports, weapons, or quick transport out of the country via small planes to Nairobi.

There are some important signs of emergent grassroots order in the city, however. Islamic courts settle disputes. Somali doctors working abroad got together in 1998 and set up a hospital in Mogadishu. Fourteen civil society groups presented a united eight-point appeal for neighborhood peace to the warlords and traditional leaders and then went on strike at hospitals, schools, and the university to emphasize their commitment for change.

Economically, Mogadishu also seems to be on the move. A new business district has emerged, and business there is booming, with new office buildings and the import of large electrical goods on the increase. Water, electricity, schools, and even university training are available in the calmer southern sector of the city via private companies, if one has enough money. Coca-Cola is back in Mogadishu, combining social projects in the community, a multiclan investment formula, and a private militia into a "risk protection" package so it can operate. A small airline company has started ferrying people to regional neighbors, and a local harbor in the northern suburbs handles shipments from abroad. The city has the fastest and most advanced telecommunications in Africa or the Middle East, with three phone companies in fierce competition for business. The city is full of mobile phone masts soon to handle the 3G standard, new Internet cafés offer wireless service, and surfing the net is $.50 per hour, cheapest in Africa.

Essentially, Mogadishu perhaps has prospered economically exactly because there was no government. No licenses to operate are required, there is no government monopoly, no customs are collected, and there are no taxes. Bills are paid and contracts enforced via the traditional clan system and the hawala connections to Dubai. The ideal free market is alive and well in Mogadishu.

Yet businesses must pay huge outlays for protection. Armed guards are required for every office to guard all employees and to protect the money and merchandise. Businesspeople must pay so the planes importing their goods are not shot down. There is no quality control, so consumers don't know if the purchased goods are five years out of date. The port remains closed because of conflicts between militias for control of its potential revenues; late in 2004, a ship chartered by a Somali businessman to bring food and fuel from Dubai attempted to dock and was fired upon and ordered to leave.

On into 2005, the militias in the city continued to act with impunity, shaping the city as they wished. The Italian wargrave cemetery with its 700 graves was dug up and the human remains dumped near the Mogadishu airport so that one of the militias could build a mosque and fortification on the site. The city's police chief, who supported the disarming of the militias, began to investigate the issue but was assassinated in late January. Yet the Islamic court presence grew, beginning to ban cinemas and prohibiting the celebration of the new year.

Under both domestic and international pressure, the national government, the Transitional Federal Government of the Somali Republic, tried again to convene in Mogadishu in early 2005. They formed in Nairobi and tried to have ministries begin operating under the cover of African Union (AU) troops. The Islamic Courts Union in the city vowed, however, to resist the AU peacekeepers with their new and expanding militias and to create an Islamic state. By mid-2006, the Islamic court militias had driven out most of the warlords, the TNG was only a minimal presence in the city, and violence and destruction spread across neighborhoods. The warlords formed a new coalition, backed this time by American money and support, and attempted to retake the city. American involvement, to the tune of $150,000 per month, was motivated by fear that the success of the Islamic court militias will open the door to al-Qaeda support, and the city will become a training ground and haven for global terrorism. As a result, America has been supplying this new "anti-terrorism alliance" and creating a backlash within the city. Ethiopia and

Eritrean governments have also been supplying weapons to their own allies, as have the Italians, choosing to support the transitional government.

Meanwhile, the population of the city continues to rise, although the roads became packed again with refugees fleeing the city during the fighting in the summer of 2006. The city remains a magnet for those looking for jobs or displaced in other parts of the country. People move in and out of the city depending on events in the hinterland but also according to seasonal and climatic conditions. Up to 25 percent of those in Mogadishu are IDPs who live in 200 camps scattered throughout the city. There are certainly more than 1 million people in the city, and the real number may be as high as 2 million. Estimates suggest that the city will house 2.5 million people by 2015.

Bruce Stanley

Further Readings

Alpers, Edward. "Muqdisho in the Nineteenth Century: A Regional Perspective." *Journal of African History* 24, no. 4 (1983): 441–459.

Jama, Abdurahman D. *The Origins and Development of Mogadishu, AD 1000 to 1850: A Study of Urban Growth along the Benadir Coast of Southern Somalia.* Studies in African Archaeology. Uppsala, Sweden: Uppsala University, 1994.

Lewis, Ioan M. *A Modern History of Somalia.* Athens: Ohio University Press, 2002.

Stevenson, Jonathan. *Losing Mogadishu: Testing U.S. Policy in Somalia.* Annapolis, MD: Naval Institute Press, 1995.

Mosul
Population: 1.17 million (2005 estimate)

For one and a half millennia, the ancient city of Mosul has commanded the point where the mountains of Anatolia and Iran give way to the plain of the upper reaches of the great Tigris River. From here, it was linked to the cities of the Iranian plateau, the centers of Anatolia, and the inland cities and ports of Syria. Long known for its religious diversity and ethnic pluralism, Mosul now offers the world its oil and strategic location.

Mosul (Arabic, *al-Mawsil*) is the third-largest city in Iraq. It is located in the northern part of the country and lies on the west bank of the Tigris, opposite the ruins of Nineveh, the ancient Assyrian capital. It derives its name from the fact that several of the arms of this river combine (*waṣala*) here to form a single stream. Mosul is a place of meetings in more than just the geographical sense. As a hub of communications and trade, it acts as a node of contact for different peoples and religious groups. Built on a plateau jutting out into the alluvial plain of the Tigris, which undercuts its ancient walls, Mosul, like Nineveh before it, dominates the plain. From here in past times, caravan trails either led west and north to Syria and the great international entrepôt of Aleppo or meandered south to Baghdad, the Persian Gulf, and India. When traveling south from Mosul, voyagers had the option of going by land or by water down the Tigris. If they chose the latter, they would ride on a *kelek,* a boat of inflated skins used for cargo both on the Tigris and Euphrates.

When the Germans decided to build the Berlin-Baghdad Railway, they had it follow one of the old caravan trails between Aleppo and Baghdad, with Mosul as the major station in northern Iraq. At the end of the First World War, this line was still unfinished, and the first through-trains from Baghdad to Istanbul via Mosul did not leave until July 1940.

Because of its location on major trade routes, and on the frontier linking the forbidding mountains of Kurdistan and the plains of the Jazira, Mosul has always been a major commercial center for its region, whether it is the Islamic province of al-Jazira, the Ottoman *vilayet* (province or large administrative district) of Mosul, or northern Iraq. As a market center, or agro-city, that handled and processed products for its hinterland, the Assyrian plains, and the mountains of Kurdistan, it has always had local industries for food processing and leatherworking. The latter made use of the gall from the oak trees of Kurdistan. In medieval and Ottoman times, Mosul was famous for its jewelry, arms, carpets, and especially textiles. Indeed, the French and English term for its fine cloth, *mousseline* (muslin), declares its origin. With the opening of an oil refinery in 1976, Mosul has kept up with the times by contributing to what has become Iraq's principal source of foreign exchange.

For similar reasons, Mosul and its surrounding plains and mountains have attracted diverse peoples and religious communities that have sought refuge here throughout history. Of course, there is the usual mix of Arab and Kurd, nomads and sedentary peoples, peasants and townsmen, most of them Sunni Muslims. A closer look shows that here flourishes a heterogeneous mixture of religious communities.

First come disparate groups of Christians. The oldest are Nestorians and Syrian Orthodox established since the days of the Sassanians. Next come their Uniate counterparts, Chaldeans and Syrian Catholics, who professed allegiance to Rome in the sixteenth century to gain French consular protection. Finally come the much smaller groups of Armenian Orthodox, Latin Catholics, and Protestants, which stem from emigration and missionary enterprise.

Second come other communities, remnants of older beliefs who have sought refuge in the mountains surrounding the city. The largest are the Yezidis, the devotees of Malak Ta'us, the Peacock King, with their villages in Jebal Sinjar and the mountainous district of Shaykhan across the Tigris where lies their principal shrine, Shaykh Adi. Much smaller are the Mandaeans, boat builders and silversmiths, a Gnostic remnant from the days of early Christianity, and the Shebeks.

These Kurdish peasants are perhaps Shi'i, although they have no mosques. Their neighbors believe them to be a remnant of the Mongol invasions of Hulagu or Temür.

Thus, Mosul, the city and the region, has had a long and contentious history. When the Muslims conquered the Sassanian territories in Mesopotamia, they found two fortresses on opposite sides of the Tigris. The citadel on the east bank bore the name of Nineveh, the storied Assyrian capital (see also "Nineveh"). That opposite was probably a Nestorian monastery founded ca. 570 AD, around which the shah Khusraw II Parviz built a number of buildings. In 641 the Muslim general Utba b. Farqad, who raided up the east bank of the Tigris, first seized the fortress of Nineveh before crossing the river to subdue its counterpart. There, in some Sassanian gardens nearby, he founded a new town, which he named al-Mawsil.

His successor made Mosul into a camp city (*misr*) and built the first Friday Mosque. The greatest early benefactor of the city was the caliph Marwan b. Muhammad, who made it the capital of the Jazira province. He built walls, roads, a bridge of boats over the Tigris, and a Friday Mosque, a building approvingly noted by the traveler and geographer al-Maqdisi some 230 years later.

After the decay of Abbasid power, Mosul came under the rule of the Arab tribal dynasties of the Hamdanids and the Ukaylids. This "Arab interlude" from 906 to 1096 was followed by a Turkish one: first the Seljuqs (1095–1128); then the Zangids, Turkoman *atabegs* (local rulers) of Mosul and Sinjar; and finally Badr ad-Din Lu'lu', "the pearl sultan." It was under the Zangids and Badr ad-Din that Mosul saw a resurrection of its fortunes after years of decay, with the construction of beautiful buildings and gardens along with the restoration of its fortifications, long in disrepair.

The rule of the Turkish atabegs was brought to an abrupt end by the Mongol invasion of Hulagu Khan. The city was spared an initial sacking because of the diplomacy of Badr ad-Din but finally met its fate in 1261 after his son took the wrong side and lost his life in battle. The Mongol interlude culminated in rule by Temür, who not only did not sack the city but showed it great favor. Rule by the Turkish dynasty of the Aq Quyunlu was followed briefly by that of the Safavids, from 1508 to 1535, when they were defeated by the Ottoman sultan, Sulayman the Magnificent. Thus began the period of Ottoman rule, which lasted until 1918 and at nearly 400 years was the longest of any dynasty.

Direct Ottoman control waxed and waned. Short-tenured pashas (for example, between 1638 and 1700, there were forty-eight of them), whose aim was to make as much money as possible during their tenure, ruled the *sanjak* (district, region, or provincial administrative area of an empire or state) of Mosul, long a subdistrict within the *eyalet* of Diyarbakir (see also "Diyarbakir"). Then, for approximately

100 years, the *pashalik* of Mosul was held almost continuously within the family of Abd al-Jalil, whose founder had defended the city heroically when it was besieged by Nadir Shah in 1743.

In 1834 the Ottoman government deposed the last Jalili pasha and imposed a closer control over the sanjak—not very successfully. Finally, in 1879 the sanjak of Mosul was elevated into a separate vilayet encompassing the lands of ancient Assyria. By this time, the city had returned to its state under the Seljuqs, dirty and run-down, with its most recent set of walls breached in many places. Its disparate populace did not live happily together, and sectarian strife between Muslims and Christians and among the various Christian *millets* (recognized communities) themselves was endemic.

Yet for Mosul and its vilayet, a new day was dawning because of the prospect that large quantities of oil—needed to power battle fleets—might exist there. During World War I, British forces, after a disastrous start, conquered most of the three vilayets that made up Mesopotamia. They entered the city of Mosul itself *after* the signing of the armistice of Mudros in order to ensure their control of the resources of this particular vilayet. Although the Mosul region was claimed by France under the terms of the Sykes-Picot Accords, after the end of the war Clemenceau agreed to the request of Lloyd George that the vilayet be included within the British sphere of influence, provided that France would have equal access to its petroleum resources.

In its turn, the new Turkish Republic sought to establish its claim to the oil-rich province and to incorporate Mosul and its vilayet into the new state. After much contention, a judgment of the League of Nations Council awarded Mosul to Iraq in 1925. For Iraq, control of this region was vital to both its security and to its economic prosperity, but attachment to the new Iraqi state brought a diminished importance to its largest northern city. The creation of Iraq, with its capital at Baghdad, meant that the nation was focused there rather than on now-subordinate provincial centers. Moreover, the vilayet of which Mosul had been the proud capital since 1879 was subdivided into four *liwas* (districts), Mosul, Sulaymaniya, Kirkuk, and Arbil, and in 1969 the Mosul liwa was further subdivided into two new districts, Nineveh (Ninawa) and Duhuk.

Because of its location in the north, close to the perennially rebellious Kurds, Mosul, an essentially conservative city, was spared much of the political agitation, which finally culminated in the overthrow of the monarchy in 1958 and ushered in the regime of Abd al-Karim Qasim. Moreover, much of the surrounding land was acquired by local notable families who were not in sympathy with the aims of the revolution. In March 1959, these elements combined with local Arab nationalists and certain disgruntled military supporters of the dictator to stage an attempted coup. This was brutally suppressed after four days of fighting but has become enshrined in the iconography of the Iraqi Baath Party.

Two vignettes concerning the city help illustrate its unique history. During the rule of Temür, the Gur Khan himself came to Mosul to seek the intercession of Nabi Jirjis (Saint George) and Nabi Yunus (the Prophet Jonah). These two prophets, one a Christian saint, the other a Jewish prophet, so granted the wishes of this pious Muslim and fearsome ruler that he lavished rich gifts on their shrines.

Six hundred years later, in 1979, there was a mirror of this scene. Adnan Khairallah, the favorite cousin, brother-in-law, and defense minister of the Iraqi strongman Saddam Hussayn, who saw himself as the Temür of his age, came to Mosul. He visited the famous Syrian Orthodox monastery of Deir Mar Matta on Jebal Maqlub to seek intercession from the saint for his wife to have a baby. His intercession was successful, and in 1980 and 1981 Saddam himself came to this monastery and endowed it with great gifts. Thus, a Christian saint so granted the wishes of two pious but ruthless Muslims that they lavished great gifts on his sanctuary.

During Saddam's rule, Mosul's social fabric was "readjusted" through ethnic cleansing of Kurds, Assyrians, and Turkomans and a policy of "Arabization" for the city. As a result, in the post-Saddam era, intercommunal tensions among "returnees" from these communities and Arab "settlers" have divided the city and undercut any attempt to restore security to what many now believe to be the second-largest city in the country. The kidnapping of the Roman Catholic Archbishop of Mosul by insurgents in early 2005 is just one indication of the tension among communities in a city that once epitomized the best in multiethnic urban relations of the Middle East.

J. L. Whitaker

Further Readings
Batatu, Hanna. *The Old Social Classes and the Revolutionary Movements of Iraq: A Study of Iraq's Old Landed and Commercial Classes, and of Its Communists, Ba'thists and Free Officers.* Princeton: Princeton University Press, 1978.
Fattah, Hala. *Politics of Regional Trade in Iraq, Arabia, and the Gulf, 1745–1900.* Albany: State University of New York Press, 1996.
Issawi, Charles. *The Fertile Crescent, 1800–1914: A Documentary Economic History.* Oxford: Oxford University Press, 1988.
Khoury, Dina Rizk. *State and Provincial Society in the Ottoman Empire: Mosul, 1540–1834.* Cambridge: Cambridge University Press, 1997.
Luke, Harry. *Mosul and Its Minorities.* London: Martin Hopkinson & Company, 1925.
Owen, Roger. *The Middle East in the World Economy, 1800–1914.* London: Methuen, 1981.
Robinson, Chase. *Empire and Elites after the Muslim Conquest: The Transformation of Northern Mesopotamia.* Cambridge: Cambridge University Press, 2000.
Shields, Sarah D. *Mosul before Iraq: Like Bees Making 5-Sided Cells.* Albany: State University of New York Press, 2000.
Sluglett, Peter. *Britain and Iraq, 1914–1932.* London: Ithaca Press for the Middle East Center, Oxford, 1976.

Muscat
Population: Muscat 25,000 (2005 estimate); Greater Muscat 650,000 (2005 estimate)

Muscat, a jewel on the rim of the Indian Ocean to sailors and a hellhole of heat to British political agents, has long inhabited a different world from its Omani hinterland. A city of extensive ethnic pluralism, polyglot traders, and heterogeneous religions, for more than two millennia this small port welcomed the world, and for the last 500 years it has been the key entrepôt of Oman. Then, for most of the twentieth century, its political leaders cut the city off from outside influences, literally locking the wooden gates at night and enclosing the city behind its medieval walls. Today Muscat has thrown open those gates, quickly but thoughtfully modernizing its infrastructure and human resources, and is working to rebuild its ties to the globalized world order.

Muscat (Arabic, *Masqat*) is a seafaring city, and at different periods in its history, merchants and sailors have brought prosperity to this coastal region. Situated on the western littoral of the Arabian Peninsula, outside the entrance to the Persian Gulf at the southern end of the al-Batinah coast on the Gulf of Oman, Muscat is uniquely positioned to interact with the Indian Ocean and its trade routes, since sailing ships had to hug the Arab rather than the Iranian coast to enter the Gulf. Muscat sits on a crescent-shaped harbor, crammed into the base of the Hajar Mountains, with promontories embracing the harbor on either side. This makes it one of the most attractive sites for a city in the region but also extremely hot during the summer months. Most foodstuffs had to be imported: fish was the staple diet. Since the inhabitants of the al-Batinah coast tended to concentrate along the littoral around small harbors, the city is actually an amalgamation of several small hamlets clustered together but effectively divided until the last few decades by mountainous terrain. Today Muscat has been incorporated into the Governorate of Muscat, a conurbation that also includes the ancient ports of Mattrah, as-Seeb, and Quriyat.

As early as 6000 BC, the coastal area around Muscat was occupied by small fishing communities deriving their sustenance from the sea and from exchange with the interior. An uncovered cemetery site suggests that by the fourth millennium BC, this stretch of coast hosted a sizable community, with complex political and social structures. Seed and plant remains from the same period indicate that the inhabitants were already using nonnative cultivars such as sorghum and palm dates brought to the area from southwest Iran and eastern Africa, demonstrating ancient participation in a conveyor belt of movement and exchange around the Indian Ocean.

For the early urban centers of Mesopotamia of the third millennium, Oman was most probably Magan, a source of copper and metals, while pottery remains indicate exchange with southwest Iran, Bahrain (ancient Dilmun), Susa, and the Indus Valley. Over the next 1,000 years, the area exported metals, marine products, pearls, and hard dark stones for making idols to its neighbors. Rulers of Magan paid tribute to the Assyrians in the seventh century BC, and the area fell under control of the Achaemenid Empire after 550 BC, with regular messages exchanged between Oman and Persepolis; Maganite contingents fought in Xerxes' army in 480 BC, according to Herodotus. Seleucid influence after Alexander gave way to Parthian garrisons and then Sassanian control. There is the possibility that Ptolemy (first century AD) makes the first recorded reference to Muscat in his *Geographike Hyphegesis*.

Migrations from the first century AD on brought Arab tribes, most prominently from Yemen, into the interior of Oman, and by the fourth century AD they had seized control from the Persians of what was by then the town of Muscat. The main port on the al-Batinah coast, and the center of Oman, was Sohar, to the north of Muscat. Sohar remained the key Persian town after the migrations, while smaller ports to the south were Arab. During the fifth century, Persian Christians fleeing persecution migrated to the area, and Arab Christians were located along the Omani coast. Although some in Oman converted to Islam while Muhammad was alive, it took a swift military campaign through the area (633) to solidify Sohar and Muscat's commitment to Islam in the year after the Prophet died.

With the Abbasid Empire and its trade links to the Indian Ocean, Muscat grew in importance, serving the likes of Sinbad the sailor and his crew as they made their last stop for water before leaving Arabia or first made port upon arriving back in home waters. Muscat became an increasingly important trading city, first as a port for ships traveling to China and subsequently as an active player in growing trade between the Gulf and East Africa. Indian citrus fruits first came to the Middle East via the ports of Oman, eventually reaching the Mediterranean via the trade networks. Local smelting factories produced metal ingots for export. Muscat was a second-tier city, not as significant as Sohar, Kish, or Hormuz, but it continued during the ninth to sixteenth century as part of a network of ports at the head of the Gulf and outside it that served the Middle Eastern trading networks (see also "Bandar Abbas").

The Portuguese fleet under Albuquerque captured the city in 1507 and then burned everything. They then established an imposing fort and an equally imposing prison that still overlook the main palace. They governed Muscat for more than a century, using it as a stopping-off point in their trade routes and as a naval base. Its location on the Indian Ocean meant that the port served an important role for these Europeans that it had not served before, and the city's status increased, particularly after their loss of Hormuz (1622) to

Shah Abbas. Although there were revolts (1522), attacks by the Ottoman fleet on the city (1546, 1551), and Safavid plans for its capture (1622), the Portuguese held on until 1650, when Arabs from the interior of Oman under the Ya'rubid dynasty, supported by Hindu merchants (*bayan*) inside the city, placed Muscat under siege and finally managed to dislodge them. Over the next several decades, the citizens of Muscat prospered, as the city's location controlling the entrance to the Gulf and Oman's role as a regional shipping power meant that the port continued to play a role in Indian Ocean trade, and it became a naval base for imperial expansion. The Dutch VOC opened a factory here in 1670; smuggling to the Iranian coast was big business because of the difference in customs fees, while worldly sailors and mercenaries ran afoul of the puritanical laws about drinking and whoring.

The period between 1718 and 1744 was characterized by internal political squabbling and numerous uprisings and sieges of the city. The Ya'rubi ruler Saif ibn Sultan enraged his subjects with his drunkenness and attitude toward the Qur'an and so was twice deposed only to return with help from Nadir Shah's fleet and army, who then remained as overseers. Finally, the governor of Sohar, Ahmad ibn Said, rebelled, captured Muscat from the Iranians by a ruse, and was declared imam, thus founding the al-BuSaid dynasty that rules Oman today. Persians were kicked out of the city but returned as traders later in the century. In the 1780s, the ruler of Oman at that time, Hamad bin Said, moved his capital from the interior to Muscat, thus making it the central city of the country. Under the al-BuSaid, however, the division between Muscat and the tribes of the interior widened, with interior leaders focused on internal and religious matters. The al-BuSaid were, in contrast, secular leaders with some experience in commerce, and their own interest in trade helped to dramatically increase the prosperity of the city in the latter part of the eighteenth century. The city was essentially a detribalized site, looking outward to its extensive trading links, and highly cosmopolitan. The pearl trade, grain and cloth shipments from India, dates, and slaves competed with horses and sugar brought in from the highlands. Local Baniyan merchants provided the financing and worshipped in two Hindu temples.

From the turn of the nineteenth century, however, Muscat and Oman started a gradual decline. One reason was the result of British efforts to reduce the slave trade, which had been a mainstay of Muscat commerce. As the century progressed, Muscat-based sultans found themselves increasingly in debt and with little control over the interior of the country. Their reliance on the British for financial and military support grew, and the British used this opportunity to increase their influence over Omani policy. The introduction of the steamship and telegraph undercut local merchant elites and shifted trade routes to other ports; consequently,

some merchants shifted to illegal slaving, gunrunning, and smuggling. The city's population dropped from around 50,000 to 8,000. In 1873 a treaty was signed abolishing slavery, although its end in the city did not come until 1963. From 1873 until 1963, when slavery actually ended in the city, the flagpole in the compound of the British residence was used for manumission: slaves seeking freedom would clasp the flagpole and then be given a certificate in Arabic and English, signed by the sultan and granting their freedom. For example, in 1890 thirty-two fugitive slaves were freed in this way. The compound was the home for the British political agent, who served as informal foreign policy advisor for the sultan.

Another reason for the decline in the city's fortunes was the shift of al-BuSaid political and economic power to Zanzibar. During the nineteenth century, the ruling al-BuSaid empire in East Africa expanded, and with it the significance of Zanzibar expanded. Though it was initially ruled from Muscat, by 1840 the centrality of Zanzibar to the dynasty's power and wealth were such that Said b. Sultan (r. 1806–1856) moved his capital to the island and did not return for a visit to Muscat for eleven years (see also "Zanzibar"). It was Sultan Said who sent his personal yacht, the *Sultanah,* to New York with gifts for President Van Buren. Arriving in 1840, the ship's visit began a long period of American-Omani friendship. Some of the gifts became part of the first collection housed in the new Smithsonian Institution in Washington, D.C. With Said's death in 1856, conflict between his sons for control of the Omani empire allowed British interference, which resulted in 1861 in the separation of the Omani state into two sultanates, one based in Muscat, the other in Zanzibar, both dominated by Britain.

By the end of the nineteenth century, the sultan's power did not extend into the hinterland, where the Ibadhi imamate's authority resurfaced. The city itself was besieged in 1895 by tribes under their influence. In 1932 a new sultan, Said bin Taimur, came to power. He sought to reduce the influence of the British and, more generally, the influence of the outside world. The city was confined by its seventeenth-century walls, and the three gates of the city were closed and locked at night. A single hospital, founded in 1893 by the Dutch Reformed Church of America, provided the only modern health care. The outside world seemed to always intrude, however: in 1943 a Japanese midget submarine torpedoed a merchant ship in the harbor.

Consequently, under the sultan's reign, Muscat became closed and insular. In part, the isolation was the result of policy, but it was equally the result of poverty. Oil was not discovered in commercial quantities until 1962, and it was not until the latter part of that decade that oil exports started. As a consequence, travel to the sultanate remained as difficult as it had been in the preceding several centuries, with Muscat accessible only by sea except for the most intrepid cross-country traveler. Few ships stopped there, and few foreigners had contact with the country.

Sultan Said was overthrown in 1970 by a bloodless coup, which brought his Sandhurst-educated son, Qaboos bin Said, to power. The change in leadership in Oman heralded a number of policy initiatives, and Muscat has undergone a serious transformation. The head of the city's municipality has been granted ministerial rank, indicating the importance that the government places on the capital region.

Foremost among the developments has been the improvement of internal and external transportation linkages. The heretofore isolated townships of Muscat and Mattrah have been joined by a modern road system and, together with other expanding residential areas, now form the capital of Oman. The country's largest airport, Seeb International Airport, is located on the outskirts of the city. Muscat is also served by Mina Qaboos (Qaboos Port), which handles a substantial amount of cargo destined for use within the country, and Mina Fahal, which serves as the country's port for export of petroleum products.

Other services are also based in Muscat. The country's major teaching hospitals are located there, as is the only state-owned university. These two factors, which have improved health care and provided greater educational opportunities, have contributed to a 4 percent annual expansion in the city's population.

The main organs of government are also located in Muscat. In addition to ministerial headquarters, the country's *Majlis ash-Shura* (an advisory council elected by partial suffrage) and the *Majlis ad-Dawla* (an appointed advisory council) hold their sessions in the capital. The country's first and largest industrial estate is located on its outskirts, and most business families also have their main offices in the city. As business has tended to focus on wholesale and retail trade of imported goods, Muscat has again become the center of the country's consumer commercial trade.

Muscat's good external transportation linkages are combined with its natural beauty and sites of historical interest. These factors have led to a concentration of larger hotels in the capital area, which has become the focus of the new tourism industry. Although there has been an effort to promote other sites within the country for tourism, Western tour groups in particular tend to base themselves in Muscat.

This concentration of wealth and government resources in Muscat led to some concerns about regional jealousy, and in recent years the government has worked to ensure development in areas outside the capital. That decision reflected the need not only to ameliorate any feelings of a bias in government spending but also to stem rural-urban migration, which has put increasing pressure on employment opportunities and services in Muscat. The city's population remains highly diverse, with foreign labor mixing with the different strands making up the Omani community: Baluch, Hindus, Zadjalis, Persians, and Zanzibaris. The questions of employment and population will probably ultimately determine the length of Muscat's current prosperity. The government is moving to address those problems on a national level, but results have, at best, been mixed. Although Muscat is not likely to revert to the backwater that it was in the 1960s, it may see another gradual decline as high population growth combines with limited resources and living standards fall.

Angie Turner

Further Readings

Clements, F. A. *Oman: The Reborn Land.* London: Longman Group, 1980.

Landen, Robert Geran. *Oman since 1856: Disruptive Modernization in a Traditional Arab Society.* Princeton: Princeton University Press, 1967.

Lorimer, J. G. *Gazetteer of the Persian Gulf, Oman and Central Arabia.* Calcutta: Superintendent Government Printing, 1908.

Morris, James. *Sultan in Oman.* London: Faber and Faber, 1957.

Potts, Daniel. *The Arabian Gulf in Antiquity, Parts I and II.* New York: Oxford University Press, 1990.

Skeet, Ian. *Oman before 1970: The End of an Era.* London: Faber and Faber, 1985.

N

Nablus

Population: 135,000 (2005 estimate)

Often considered the second city of Palestine, Nablus's history stretches back more than 4,000 years. Under the Romans, it became a retirement home for legionnaires, with baths, racecourses, and temples. Situated at the base of the cultic Mount Garizim, where the Samaritans have worshiped for millennia, the city remains home to a small community of these heterodox Jews. Occupied by the Crusaders, the Mamluks, and the Ottomans, the city's Old City and suqs reflect the building programs of these rulers and is one of the most important districts for historic buildings in Palestine. The city has long profited from its reputation for sweets and soaps, while today it struggles with the continuing effects of resistance to Israeli occupation.

Nablus (Arabic, *Naablus;* Hebrew, *Shechem*) lies approximately thirty miles north of Jerusalem and is a major commercial center and marketplace in the occupied Palestinian territories currently known as the West Bank. An ancient city with archaeological remains from nearly every epoch in the history of the region, its location at the crossroads of a major east-west road connecting the Mediterranean coastal plain with the Syrian hinterland and the primary Palestine north-south mountain road gave it an important trading and strategic importance. Its layout is based upon a former Roman city structure, with medieval Arab constructions on top and modern developments mainly to the east and west. Often eclipsed by Jerusalem, its rich archaeology, colorful history, feisty political independence, and commercial skills are often overlooked. The boundaries of the Old City are now indistinct, and there is no city wall. However, the core area can be discerned by gates in the streets leading to a maze of narrow lanes, vaulted in places to afford shelter from the sun and the rain, and the bustling market streets, known as the kasbah.

Nablus lies between two key mountain ridges emanating from Jebal 'Ibal and Jebal Jarzim and at the entry of a depression that runs down to the Mediterranean Sea. The site has abundant water, which has remained key to the vitality of the city. The topography of the Nablus district can be divided into four parts: Jordan Valley, the eastern slopes, mountain crests, and western slopes. The highest point in the district reaches 3,000 feet above sea level, at Jebal Ibal, while the lowest elevation is 1,100 feet below sea level at the southeast cor-

ner of the district. It has hot, dry summers and moderate, rainy winters.

The city has always been the trading center for the surrounding region, in which grapes, olives, and wheat are grown and livestock is raised. The chief products of Nablus were olive oil, soap, and wines. Today Nablus is considered the major commercial, industrial, and agricultural center in the northern West Bank. With the hinterland producing a surplus of olives, the manufacture of olive oil soap, produced from olive oil and caustic soda, is a Nablus specialty. Some of the city's soap factories have been operating for more than 250 years. Nablus is also the commercial hub for the small Palestinian economy, and in 1995 the embryonic Palestinian Security Exchange, now trading twenty-eight companies, was set up in the city.

The origins of Nablus can be traced to the Canaanite period of the Middle Bronze Age (2500 BC). The city is mentioned, for example, in the Tel Amarna letters of the pharoanic period as well as in the reports of Thutmose III. It is also mentioned in the Old Testament as a place where Abraham purchased land and established an altar; the indications are that it was already a substantial settlement when he arrived. Its main development as a city, however, clearly began during the Roman period. The Roman emperor Titus rebuilt the city in AD 70 for veteran legionaries to settle and called it Flavia Neapolis (from which the present name derives) in honor of his father, the emperor Flavius Vespasian. The town acquired all the civil and religious structures of a Greco-Roman city, with colonnaded streets leading to an agora, hippodrome, temples, and basilicas. The city was watered by above and underground aqueducts and fountains and protected by ramparts. On the slopes of Jebal Ibal, there are remains of a Roman necropolis. Traces of this Roman city have been excavated, and a length of an aqueduct survives to the west of the town.

In the fourth century, Neapolis was partially Christianized and became the seat of a bishopric. However, the early Christians had to struggle against the remnants of the Samaritans, a heterodox Jewish sect, who dominated the district. The emperor Zeno expelled the Samaritans from Jebal Jarzim and built a church on its summit ca. AD 485. In 521 a confrontation between the two religious communities resulted in the death of the Christian bishop and some priests and the destruction of many churches and monasteries. The Byzantine emperor Justinian restored Zeno's Church in 531, and remains of this octagonal church were excavated in 1928. Justinian made a concerted effort to reduce the power of the Samaritans, and eventually they fled across the Jordan River, where, in a decisive battle, they suffered huge losses. Nowadays, only a small community of about 200–300 Samaritans live on the lower slopes of the mountain. The present-day Samaritans celebrate their feasts of Passover, Pentecost, and Tabernacles on top of Jebal Jarzim.

In AD 636, Nablus fell to the Arabs and became part of the Umayyad Muslim dynasty. By all accounts the city flourished as a trading center, taking advantage of being on an important route between Damascus and Gaza and on to Egypt. The Damascus connection became the linchpin of its economy, and close links between the two cities continue to this day. The famous tenth-century geographer al-Maqdisi reported that the city was named "the little Damascus." He also wrote of its extensive marketplace. During this period, the Jami' al-Kabir, or Great Mosque, was built.

Following the occupation of Palestine by the Crusaders in 1099, Nablus fell under their control. The knights of the Hospitallers built several churches and a royal palace, which became the residence of Queen Melisende from 1152 to 1161. A surviving Crusader structure is a fortified tower located in the middle of downtown Nablus. During the reconquest of the region by Salah ad-Din in 1187, Nablus was badly damaged in his assault on the city. There was further serious damage in 1202 when an earthquake struck the city. However, many Crusader buildings remained in use and were adapted to Muslim purposes, mostly by the conversion of churches into mosques (Jami'al-Kabir, Jami' al-Nasr). The Crusader hospital remained in use during all this period.

In 1260 and 1280, Nablus once again was attacked, first by invading Mongols and then by nomad tribesmen whose power had increased in the wake of the collapse of the Ayyubid administration. Nonetheless, the period of Mamluk rule (1260–1516) is regarded as a prosperous one. Local produce was exploited in the manufacture of cotton goods, sweets, and soap. Today cotton is no longer manufactured, but Nablus, like its twin, Damascus, is still renowned for sweets manufacturing, particularly the famous Nablus *kanafi* (cheese and sugar dessert). Most of all, the city has been known for its soap made with pure olive oil. The Mamluks were great builders, and foundation inscriptions still in place indicate a building boom of some significance. The most notable include Jami' al-Khadra (the Green Mosque, which may be a converted Crusader building), the tomb of Shaykh Badr, and a public bath, the Baydari Hammam.

During the Ottoman period, Nablus became a district capital under the control of the governor of the province of Damascus. District governors and city administrators were able to use their positions to achieve considerable wealth,

Stylized vision of Nablus in the mid-nineteenth century. (Library of Congress)

and many built grand palaces. Prominent among these are the palaces of the Abd al-Hadi, Hashim, Nimr, and Touqan families, described by nineteenth-century travelers as fortresses guarded with huge iron gates, similar to those to be found in Italy. The largest palace was the Touqan Palace, which was said to accommodate more than 1,000 armed militia members. Many of the religious buildings in Nablus also date from the Ottoman period. The further expansion of the olive oil soap industry can be seen by the fact that by 1882 there were no fewer than thirty soap factories in the city. Interestingly, all of these were built of stone with vaulted ceilings, since timber had become scarce in Palestine during the nineteenth century.

During the British Mandate (1922–1948), Nablus suffered a major earthquake, which led to the departure of many of the inhabitants from the central core districts to outlying areas, although some new building to the north and west of the Old City had already been undertaken before 1927. The arrival of the motor car encouraged further emigration from the Old City to the slopes of the overlooking mountains, where access by vehicular traffic was easier than the partly stepped streets of the kasbah. Also during this period, Nablus became a center of Palestinian resistance to British rule as well as to Jewish Zionist immigration. It was here that the first attacks on Jews led to the beginning of the 1936 Arab Revolt, and the people of Nablus were deeply involved in using their ties in Jordan to smuggle weapons and money into the country.

After the 1948 Arab-Israeli war, the city fell under Jordanian authority, and two refugee camps for Palestinians from the coast were built near it. The influx of refugees provided a considerable impetus for expansion, and it strengthened the city's economic and social ties with Amman, the capital of Jordan; in fact, many of the city's elites established strong ties to the Jordanian monarchy that have continued into the present. The regional road leading to the east was expanded, and the town began to spread out in a new direction. In 1967 the Israeli army occupied Nablus, and a third refugee camp added to the city.

Despite restrictions on travel and other commercial activity, the city grew and retained its position as the second-largest Palestinian city on the West Bank after Jerusalem. Nablus became an important intellectual, cultural, and political center, but the Israeli military occupation hampered municipal activities, and the provision of basic infrastructure and amenities was poor. An-Najah University was created in 1977 from the progressive development of a local private high school started in 1912, and this university has now become the largest in Palestine, with more than 10,000 students.

The city has continued its role as a center for political resistance and organization. Surrounded by Israeli settlements, during the first Palestinian intifada, it was a site for regular clashes with the Israeli occupation troops, and the Nablus Prison was notorious for the torture that occurred there. As a result of the Oslo Peace Accords between the Palestine Liberation Organization (PLO) and Israel, Nablus came under the jurisdiction of the Palestinian Authority (PA) in December 1995, and the Nablus Municipality began an ambitious program of renovation. It improved the city's water network, partially developed its electricity network, and began paving the city and treating sewage problems. However, in April 2002, Nablus was reoccupied by Israel, causing severe damage to the historic core of the city, with sixty-four heritage buildings suffering severe structural damage or being destroyed. The Israelis claim that the city continues to serve as the nerve center of militant Palestinian organizations and anti-Israeli activity. The construction of the Israeli Wall has cut off parts of the city's traditional hinterland, and confrontations continue regularly both along the wall and within the city.

In addition to the historical monuments already mentioned, Nablus contains many other structures of note. Among these are the cloth market, Khan al-Tujjar, considered one of the finest examples of such markets in all of the country; the al-Manara clock, built at the beginning of the twentieth century; the Old Saraya, which acted as offices for the Turkish government; and the Khan al-Wakala.

Nablus was also famous for its Turkish baths. The oldest working Turkish bath in Palestine is the Hammam ash-Shifa, located in the Old City. This bath was constructed early in the Ottoman period and was recently restored as part of the city's renovation program. The hammam was damaged by the Israeli incursion in 2002.

The Jami' al-Kabir is the largest mosque in Nablus and is marked by a beautiful arch that can be seen at a prominent street corner of the city. A legend passed on by the city's inhabitants claims that this is the site where Joseph's brothers showed their father, Jacob, the blood-stained coat of many colors to convince him that his favorite son was dead. Close by, about a mile south of the city center, lies the supposed tomb of Joseph and the Well of Jacob, his father. The site, as a shared Muslim and Jewish site, has become the source of much Palestinian-Israeli friction. Tradition has it that this well was also where Jesus Christ is said to have met the Samaritan woman who offered him a drink of water. The Crusaders restored the well that now stands within the walled complex of a Greek Orthodox monastery.

The majority of the city's population is Muslim. In addition, there is a small but well-integrated minority of Christian Palestinians in the city along with the now small number of Arabic-speaking Samaritans. The refugee camps, comprising more than 30,000 people, have become part of the urban fabric of the city, and their people contribute both to its manufacturing industry and to its political radicalism.

Michael Dumper

Further Readings

Doumani, Beshara. *Rediscovering Palestine: Merchants and Peasants in Jabal Nablus 1700–1900.* Berkeley: University of California Press, 1995.

Efrat, Elisha. *Urbanization in Israel.* London: Croom Helm, 1984.

Moors, Annelies. *Women, Property and Islam: Palestinian Experiences 1920–1990.* Cambridge: Cambridge University Press, 1995.

Najaf
Population: 502,000 (2005 estimate)

Najaf is one of the holy cities of Islam and is the burial ground of Imam Ali, cousin and adopted son of the founder of Islam, the Prophet Muhammad. As such it has been, since the ninth century, a focus for pilgrimage, particularly for the Shi'i sect in Islam. It quickly attracted Shi'i scholars and religious leaders, and so for more than 1,000 years it has been one of the leading centers of Shi'i learning in the world. Students from around the world come to Najaf to attend its seminaries and schools, and for centuries pious believers have sought to be buried near Imam Ali; thus, the cemeteries around the city have grown into perhaps the largest graveyard in the world. Particularly since the eighteenth century, Najaf has often been in rivalry with that other Shi'i center of scholarship, Qom in Iran. Although a number of leading clerics have been assassinated during political struggles, important clerical families from the city have reemerged in post–Saddam Hussayn Iraq to restore Najaf to a position of power and religious authority, particularly within Iraq but also into Lebanon and the global Shi'i community.

Najaf (Arabic, *an-Najaf*) is situated in south-central Iraq, southwest of the western branch of the Euphrates River. It is ninety-nine miles south of Baghdad and fifty miles from Iraq's other holy city, Karbala. *Najaf* in Arabic means an elevated spot without access to water, or dry land, and the city is situated on a high plateau on sandy soil overlooking a wide basin. Unlike its sister city, Karbala, which is well watered and is known for its gardens, Najaf is a desert city, looking to the open arid areas of the Najd to its southwest. Over the years, the city has had regular problems with water shortages and drought, often experiencing years of little rainfall and dry wells. It is, nevertheless, a wide spacious city with airy courtyards designed to keep the desert heat in check. Its location means that tribes from the desert come to Najaf as their regional market. Kufa, some six miles down the road, is older but significantly smaller (see also "Kufa").

For millennia prior to the Muslim invasions, there were sites of habitation scattered around this area of Mesopotamia. However, a shrine on this site was established in the eighth century by the Abbasid caliph Harun ar-Rashid (r. 786–809) over what he regarded as the revealed tomb of Muhammad's son-in-law and the fourth caliph, Ali ibn Abi Talib. Ali had been assassinated in AD 661 in the doorway of his recently completed mosque in nearby Kufa, and the site of his burial was kept hidden by his family and followers (the Alids and early Shi'i) from the Sunni Umayyad and early Abbasid caliphs. Legend has it that Harun ar-Rashid, who happened to go hunting outside Kufa, stumbled across a small piece of raised ground where his dogs refused to chase down a stag. The caliph determined that this was the tomb of Ali and had a structure constructed. As a result, very quickly devotees of Imam Ali, and pilgrims to the tomb, began to settle down around the monument (Hazrat Ali), and the city emerged organically.

A number of Shi'i scholars from Kufa migrated to Najaf and established a base from which to teach and spread Shi'i traditions. Its development as a Shi'i pilgrimage center and a center of learning was encouraged by the support and patronage it received from a number of Shi'i rulers, such as Muhammad ibn Zayd al-Alawi (d. 900), the ruler of Tabaristan. He initiated the construction of the dome over the shrine and the Sufi prayer hall nearby. Sultans of the Shi'i Buyid dynasty (950–1055) contributed by adding the arched halls and hospices that provided residence for the students who came to study in Najaf. In the eleventh century, Shaykh al-Ta'ifah al-Tusi, a great Shi'i scholar and leader of the community, was expelled from Baghdad and decided to establish his own school, or madrasa, in Najaf. His teachings were based on a text-oriented Shi'i curriculum that came to predominate, and present-day Shi'i *mujtahids* (revered theological scholars) regard themselves as the intellectual descendants of al-Tusi's madrasa.

By the fifteenth century, Najaf had replaced Kufa as the locus of Shi'i activities and scholarship. However, this centrality did not last long. Najaf had to struggle against other rising centers of Shi'i learning; with the establishment of Shi'ism as the state religion of Iran under the Safavid dynasty in the early 1500s, there was a flow of Shi'i scholars from Iraq and Lebanon to Iran with the result that Iranian madrasas, particularly at Qom, came to rival those of Najaf. This shift in power within the Shi'i community meant that by the late 1600s, Najaf was almost in ruin and not very important (see also "Qom").

But a number of factors helped restore the city's fortunes. With the decline of Esfahan and the end of Safavid power in Iran, along with the 1722 Sunni Afghan attacks on the country's cities, Persian Shi'i leaders fled to Iraq and Najaf (see also "Esfahan"). Later, Nadir Shah's policies did little to restore Shi'i as opposed to state power. When the city came under significant pressure from the Wahhabi-Saudi alliance in the Najd after the mid-eighteenth century (twice being besieged), the Persian clerics in the city moved to construct a network of tribal support and pilgrimage from the areas of southern Iraq. It is during this time that the great conversions of southern Iraqi Arab tribes to Shi'i Islam occurred, and the Najaf clerics projected their power into the politics of the region. Najaf became a border city, trading with the Wahhabis but never sure of their intentions. During this time, the city suffered from considerable drought and water access problems, although this did not halt its growth as an important center for scholarship, pilgrimage, and religious activities. During the Ottoman period, more madrasas were established so that by the end of the nineteenth century there were around twenty schools in the city.

As a center of Shi'ism, Najaf derived considerable income from pilgrimages, endowments, and corpse internment, which gave the religious hierarchy both power and autonomy. The chief *majiat* at Najaf received so many contributions that he was able to distribute in 1918 £100,000 in charity. In one interesting example, under what was known as the Oudh Bequest coming from India, between 1850 and 1918 the British transferred 6 million rupees from India to Najaf and Karbala to subsidize poor and junior clerics in these cities. In Najaf 73 percent of the recipients were Persian or Indian clerics, while the rest were poor citizens. By 1914 the city hosted more than 8,000 students from throughout the Shi'i world.

There are traditions in the Hadith that suggest that Ali will intercede with Allah for supplicants. Traditions also suggest that the shrine contains the tomb of Adam, the first man, and also that of one of the sons of Noah, who refused to enter the ark and thus died in Najaf. There is also the tradition that Abraham bought land in the Wadi as-Salaam (Valley of Peace) that runs through the present city, predicting that it would be from here that 70,000 of those buried in the valley would be guaranteed entrance into paradise and would then be able to intercede with Allah for others. Imam Ali is reported to have said that Wadi as-Salaam was a part of heaven. One result of all this sanctity is now one of the city's most striking features: its location as the site of perhaps the largest cemetery in the world. Over the centuries, the bodies of millions of Muslims have been brought here for burial from all over the world. It is estimated that annually more than half a million corpses are shipped to the city for burial near to Imam Ali, and a small contribution is collected. The cemetery stretches for miles; as a result, the city is surrounded by a vast City of the Dead and is approached through the cemetery. It is possible to drive a car down "streets" between the tombs, some of which are simple and small, but others are huge and the size of small mosques. Many famous clerics and holy men are buried there.

Such wealth and numbers meant that, like its sister city, Karbala, Najaf became a rival power center to the Sunni and Ottoman administration based in Baghdad (see also "Karbala"). Najaf also stretched its legitimacy and authority into Iran; relations were close enough that during the 1903–1905 movement in Iran against Russian and British influence, Najaf supported the struggle with petitions and demonstrations. A few years later (1909), mujtahids in Najaf organized a jihad movement against the Russian presence in Iran. There was frequent opposition to centralizing reforms by outside authority, and in 1915 the city went into open revolt, and the Ottoman Turks were driven out; the city remained autonomous until the British captured the city in August 1917. In 1918 the British governor of the city was assassinated, and Najaf participated in the 1920 uprising against the British occupation. In response, the British besieged the city and cut off its water in an attempt to subdue the uprising.

During such troubles, one of the significant features of Najaf architecture can come into play: the *sirdabs* (deep cellars) in the city's houses. These cellars can be up to five stories deep, entered via narrow staircases dropping away sharply. Often used as places of concealment during times of oppression, they are now used as larders for keeping foods cool or for wells for the house. Indeed, the older houses of Najaf are well adapted to the desert climate with their courtyards, balconies, high vaulted ceilings, and thick walls, which both allow the air to circulate and block the desert heat.

The rise of the modern Iraqi state headquartered in Baghdad meant that for the next thirty years, the Shi'i religious leaders in Najaf were quiescent, and they adopted the traditional position of shunning politics. Improved access links and the advent of mass-transit systems such as air travel and intercontinental highways consolidated, however, the city's role as a center for pilgrimage. At the same time, the Iraqi state undermined the power and semiautonomous role of the clergy by providing municipal and welfare provision. Steps were taken to develop Najaf as a modern city; in 1931 five gates were opened in the city walls, and a wide square was designed for the southern part of the city, around which were built palaces, houses, cafés, gardens, schools, and a hospital. This new district was called al-Ghaziyah.

However, following the revolution in 1958, and the radicalization of national politics, the Shi'i leadership in Najaf felt challenged by atheist political forces and began to organize politically. Although some clerics remained indifferent to national politics, others founded the Jamaat al-Ulama, a coalition of leaders to counter antireligious trends in society. A key goal became resistance to the rise of Communist political influence in the country (and its appearance in Najaf during the 1940s and 1950s among the young members of some of the leading religious families). A related concern was the decline in their power. Restrictions on students, for example, meant that by 1958 there were less than 2,000 students in Najaf, and only 300 of them were Iraqis. Money stopped flowing in, and by the end of the decade the clerics had to ask for donations to keep the city's shrines going.

As a result, clerics in Najaf helped found the Da'wa Party (the call) and supported the *al-Adwa* (the lights) monthly journal. Other Najaf clerics made weekly public radio broadcasts, and later there was a fatwa against membership in the Communist Party. Behind much of this was the rising light of

Muhammad Baqir as-Sadr, a junior scholar in 1958 but whose father-in-law was acting president of Jamaat and whose older brother was a mujtahid and senior member of the coalition. As-Sadr was deeply involved in this expansion of the political role of the Najaf clergy.

As-Sadr also realized the need to radically reform the *hawza* (scholarly community) in Najaf. Religious students were exempt from military service, and many students, ranging in age from twenty to sixty, stayed in the colleges for many years, since there was no "time limit" for graduation. Thus, when he assumed responsibility for the city's educational system, as-Sadr set out to change the curriculum, revise and develop new texts, improve and require student attendance, and move toward a graduate requirement system.

From 1964 to 1968, Baghdad's politicians hesitated to move against Najaf and its clerical power base. It is during this honeymoon that they allowed Ayatollah Khomeini's exile from Iran to Najaf in 1964, which became an important turning point for the city. Khomeini stayed for twelve years, building considerable networks and connections within the Arab Shi'i community, although his sojourn also heightened the struggle between Qom and Najaf for leadership of Shi'i Islam, especially after Khomeini returned to Iran.

With the Baathist coup of Abu Bakr in 1968, however, more direct confrontation began. The Baathists sought to control the power of the Shi'i leadership in Najaf through a range of tactics: they expelled non-Iraqi students from the hawza and kept track of the remaining few hundred Iraqis; they cut trade to Najaf, removing its role as a desert market town; they diverted income flowing into the city from charities; they denied pilgrim traffic, thus cutting income; they limited corpse traffic, thus decreasing income to the clerics; they controlled the madrasas, limiting the power of the clerics; and, finally, they sought to reorient the tribes toward Baghdad. The city's fortunes were also hurt by a sustained drought around Najaf in the mid-1970s, since this harmed the rural populations and decreased the flow of income into the city. In such a context, it is no wonder that Qom's status in the Shi'i world began to surpass that of Najaf.

In response to political pressure, as-Sadr moved to create a stronger structure for the leader, or Marjaliyya structure, so as to protect the hawza from the Baathists. Saddam Hussayn then began in 1974 to limit the annual processions in remembrance of Imam Hussayn. These outpourings of grief and remembrance traditionally spanned four days, when observants would walk from Najaf to Karbala on pilgrimage. In 1977 the Baath tried to completely ban the processions on twenty Safar. In response, full-scale riots broke out in Najaf, and as-Sadr issued a fatwa prohibiting Muslims from joining the Baath Party. Saddam then tried to win over the city with substantial gifts of new buildings and rebuilding older ones, and he actually visited the shrine in 1979. He called himself

the grandson of Imam Hussayn and was able to get some of the clerics from the city to support him.

The 1979 Islamic Revolution in Iran marked another turning point for the city of Najaf. When Khomeini returned to Iran, he publicly called on Iraqi Shi'i to support as-Sadr and encouraged him to stay in Najaf and to fight the Baath regime. This call caused many of as-Sadr's supporters to take to the streets in a show of resistance to the regime; to as-Sadr's chagrin, it exposed them to the Baathists, who were waiting for such an opportunity.

Saddam Hussayn had as-Sadr arrested. In response, as-Sadr's politically active sister, known as Bint al-Huda, gave a fiery speech in the Shrine of Ali, calling on Shi'i to take to the streets in his support, and the *bazaaris* (shopkeepers) in the city went on strike. The Baathists did release him into house arrest, but thousands of his supporters were arrested and executed around the country. Finally, seeing little alternative, as-Sadr came to see himself as a martyr and called on the Iraqi people to resist the regime and to work to bring about an Islamic state like that in Iran. The end was not long in coming. This leader of Najaf and his sister were both arrested, taken to Baghdad, and killed in 1980.

The Iraqi invasion of Iran in 1980, and the eight-year war with Iran, dramatically affected Najaf. One obvious way was in the burials in the city of the young Iraqi men killed on the front. In 1983, at the height of the Iran-Iraq War, there were sixty coffins an hour moving through the Imam Ali Mosque for burial in Wadi as-Salaam. Another leading Najaf clerical family, the al-Hakim, represents the fortunes of the city during this time. Ayatollah Mohsen al-Hakim had been a leading cleric in the city in the 1970s. His son, Muhammad Bakr al-Hakim, after imprisonment and torture, fled the country for Iran in 1980 and supported their revolution via the Supreme Council of the Islamic Revolution in Iraq (SCIRI). Early in the war, he visited prisoner-of-war (POW) camps in Iran and tried to get Iraqi Shi'i to support a revolt against Saddam. In response, the Iraqi Baathists moved against his family in Najaf. In April 1983, Saddam Hussayn invited Najaf clerics to come to Baghdad; most refused. So, in May 1983, ninety members of the family, ranging in age from nine to seventy-six, were arrested, and six of them, all clerics, including three brothers of Muhammad, were executed in front of other family members. One relative was then sent to Tehran to warn Muhammad to stop his activities against the regime. Muhammad Bakr al-Hakim, upon returning to Najaf following the U.S.-led invasion in 2003, was killed by a car bomb in August 2003.

Najaf was on the front line in the Gulf War of 1991 as well. The defeat of Saddam's army in March 1991 by the coalition of forces led by the United Nations (UN) precipitated an uprising in the city the day after the cease-fire against Baghdad in which the Shi'i of the south took a leading role. "Saddamites" were rounded up and murdered, while tribal leaders assembled with their militias in Najaf in order to "march on Baghdad" against Saddam. After six days, the Revolutionary Guards responded in force and brutally repressed the uprising after destroying much of the city and the shrine, looting and massacring many civilians.

Throughout all these trials, the city remained an important market town and grain center for the tribes around it. Thus, in 1993 Saddam came to visit Najaf and demanded a show of support. It was here that local tribes were first required to perform tribal dances (*hosa*) and theatrical productions with tribal flags and guns as a demonstration of allegiance and acceptance of his authority. Such gestures were not enough to keep the city's clerics in line, however. Although the government had recognized Ayatollah Muhammad Sadiq as-Sadr (cousin of the murdered cleric) as grand ayatollah in 1992, hoping he could be manipulated by Baghdad, by 1998 as-Sadr had begun distancing himself from the government in Friday sermons and urging people, against government wishes, to attend mass prayer gatherings. Finally, in 1999 Muhammad Sadiq as-Sadr was assassinated following Friday prayers in Najaf along with two of his sons. It is his picture that dominates Sadr City, the volatile Shi'i Quarter of Baghdad renamed for this martyr (see also "Baghdad").

In the post-Saddam era, Najaf has been a site of considerable tension and conflict over the intertwined issues of power among its clerics and confrontation with the occupying Americans. Ayatollah Abd al-Majid al-Khoei, brought back from exile by the Americans in an attempt to reshape clerical politics in Najaf, was immediately stabbed to death in April 2003 upon his return. The leading power in the city is now the seventy-six-year-old Ayatollah Sistani, providing unique moral authority in a community unsure of its power and position. Sistani, originally from Qom, came to Najaf to study and has lived in the city ever since. Although he remains an Iranian citizen, and speaks Arabic with a Persian accent, he has built up a power base in the city. Sistani retained his distance from Khomeini, found his own funding, and used that to support groups and clients. From his office in Najaf there now radiates out a network of schools, libraries, hospitals, charities, and technology centers across Iran and Iraq. Like many of the other clerics, he lives a few hundred yards from the entrance to the shrine. It was Sistani who orchestrated thousands of supporters onto the streets to keep the Americans focused on one-man, one-vote elections at the announced time schedules. It was also Sistani who returned from his sickbed in London to halt the fighting around the shrine that had broken out between the Mahdi army and the Americans in August 2004.

Many students question, however, if Sistani is a real leader like the thirty-year-old clerical upstart, Moqtada as-Sadr, son of the murdered Muhammad Sadiq as-Sadr. As-Sadr pledged

to purge Najaf of Iranian influences, putting him in direct conflict with Sistani, and to rid Iraq of American and British troops. In 2003 as-Sadr, a modest cleric playing on his Sadrist heritage, created his own militia, the Mahdi army, and in both March and August 2004 large-scale fighting broke out in the city between them and the Americans. Their base was the Wadi as-Salaam Cemetery, where, during the August 2004 fighting, more than 300 fighters were killed. On into 2005, the Americans were involved in various cleanup operations; for example, since the fighting in Najaf, the U.S. government has disbursed more than $1.9 million to 2,600 Najafi residents as condolence payments (*solatia*) to those injured, or to those who lost family members in the fighting, or to cover collateral damage to houses. In addition, the U.S. military continued to collect weapons from the cemetery. Cemetery workers would collect weapons from the graves in Wadi as-Salaam and pile them on the side of the streets through the graveyard. By mid-2005, the U.S. military reportedly had collected 1,258 weapons and 10,000 munitions, including six guided missiles, from the Valley of Peace.

Ironically, the end of Saddam has reempowered Najaf. The American liberation of the hawza has sparked tension in three arenas: within Iraq, tension with Qom and Iranian Shi'i, and closer ties and links to southern Lebanon and the Shi'i there. Musa as-Sadr, trained in Najif and cousin of Muhammad Baqir as-Sadr, who came to Lebanon in 1960, was the father of the Shi'i Amal movement (1975) in southern Lebanon. Although he disappeared and was presumed killed in 1978 on a trip to Libya, the close connections between Najaf and Lebanese Shi'i continue today, with numerous new hawza being founded around Sidon since the fall of Saddam.

The shrine of Imam Ali, rebuilt many times, is an imposing structure and has long captured the imagination. The large central dome, covered in gold leaf, is flanked by two tall minarets and can be seen from a great distance. The interior is inlaid with blue tiles intertwined with gold and white marble. The complex includes, in addition to the shrine, an enclosed sanctuary, or *haram*, a small hospital, baths, and a media center. There are reports that in the post-August 2004 period, the Iraqi government and the Americans began to clear out some of the damaged buildings around the shrine to create a larger open space for control and security; members of the local community resisted this process, since no one in the city was consulted and the buildings around the shrine have historical and cultural significance.

Michael Dumper

Further Readings
Litvak, Meir. *Shi'i Scholars of Nineteenth-Century Iraq: The "Ulama" of Najaf and Karbala*. Cambridge: Cambridge University Press, 1998.
Nakash, Yitzhak. *The Shi'is of Iraq*. Princeton: Princeton University Press, 1994.
Young, Gavin. *Iraq, Land of Two Rivers*. London: Collins St. James Place, 1980.

Nazareth
Population: 63,000 (2005 estimate)

Nazareth is situated in the Galilee region of Israel where the most southerly hills of the Lebanon range drop sharply to the plain of Esdraelon. It was the home of Jesus and that of his parents, Joseph and Mary. As such it became an important city in the history of Christianity and the site of many religious buildings, not least the largest Christian edifice in the Middle East—the Basilica of the Annunciation. Currently a medium-sized city in the modern State of Israel, its role as a predominantly Arab Christian city is being challenged by demographic and planning transformations over the last half century in which tensions with the Muslim and Jewish populations have come to the fore. However, as a result of its distance from the coast, its isolation from important trade routes of the interior, and its mountainous hinterland, Nazareth never achieved the status of other major religious cities of the world, and its monumental structures are consequently comparatively modest.

Nazareth (Arabic, *al-Nasira;* Hebrew, *Nazaret*) lies on the edge of the lower Galilee hills, just at the point where they fall off into the Valley of the Jezreel. The city is nestled in a bowl between surrounding hills at 1,200 feet above sea level, and its edge was marked by a small valley that produced a spring. Modern settlement has taken place up and all along the hillsides, especially to the north. The result is that the city is spread out in the shape of an amphitheater surrounded by well-clad hillsides and vegetation. The city lies along routes to the west that reach the Mediterranean at Mount Carmel and southeast to Afula and on to the Palestinian mountains at Jenin or the Jordan Valley.

The ancient history of Nazareth is obscure. The lower Galilee and the valleys below long hosted numerous Canaanite sites, and Megiddo and Akko were well-established urban centers closely tied with Egypt across the Middle and Late Bronze Age (2000–1200 BC). There are numerous Early Iron Age (twelfth to eleventh century BC) settlements nearby as well, but there are no clear indications of settlement on the site itself. The city is not mentioned in the Old Testament, but it is referred to several times in the New Testament (for example, Luke 1:26 and John 1:46). The name may refer to a young shoot or a new flower.

Scholarship has traditionally argued that Jesus's Nazareth was an isolated community of around 1,000 persons, cut off from the urban centers of Palestine. However, recent research suggests that it was not such an insignificant village as traditionally argued. Excavations near the spring, now known as Mary's Well, suggest a Roman bath, unusual if it was an isolated village. Some authors are also advocating a close connection between Nazareth and the Hellenistic-Roman city of Sepphoris, four miles away. Given the high investment in new construction in Sepphoris during the first century AD, perhaps carpenters from nearby villages found work in the urban center and enjoyed its theaters and Greek discourse. After the destruction of the temple in Jerusalem in AD 70, Sepphoris took in many Jewish immigrants from the south and became the center of rabbinic scholarship and the place where the Mishnah was codified. Nazareth would have been a nearby Jewish village, providing handicrafts and agricultural products to that city of 20,000. Interestingly, Nazareth is not mentioned by Josephus (first century AD) or in any of the Talmudic writing from this period.

Like Sepphoris, Nazareth remained predominantly a Jewish town during the first four centuries of the common era, and the village's boundaries were marked by Jewish tombs that have been discovered in the city. But gradually a Jewish Christian community appeared in the village, perhaps focused around members of Jesus's family. There are indications that both Sepphoris and Nazareth hosted substantial communities of followers of Jesus from the first century; graffiti, amulets, and other indications of Christian belief have been discovered. Nazareth had a synagogue, which appears to have become a synagogue church and then a grotto shrine after the mid-fourth century. After Constantine's conversion to Christianity, Nazareth became a stop on the pilgrim trail for such travelers as Saint Jerome. Although Constantine did not build a Basilica here, by the end of the fourth century the grotto shrine had been incorporated into a Church of the Annunciation, which pilgrims visited. Two hundred years later, visitors remark on seeing both the Church of the Annunciation and a Church of the Nutrition on the site where Jesus was brought up. By this time, most Jews had migrated out of the lower Galilee, having left after the earthquake of 365 and the general Christianization of the lower Galilee post-Constantine.

Palestine was conquered by Muslim-Arabs in AD 637, but despite the revered position of Jesus in the Qur'an, little of historical significance occurred in Nazareth during the early Islamic period. Limited pilgrimage to Christian sites was permitted, but it did not thrive as a holy city like Jerusalem, and many of the religious sites such as the Church of the Annunciation fell into disrepair. The Saxon pilgrim Wilhebald (725) notes the existence of only one church, that of the annunciation, in the town.

Following the conquest of Palestine by the Crusaders (1098) and the establishment of the Latin kingdom, the role of Nazareth changed dramatically. The Franks paid special attention to the city, and the church was quickly rebuilt (1101). Major repairs were also carried out on the Church of the Nutrition, also known as Saint Joseph's House. At the same time, the Greek Orthodox erected the Church of Saint Gabriel near the Virgin's Well, and the Archiepiscopal See of Scythopolis was also transferred to Nazareth, indicating the growing importance of the city in church affairs.

On the same day as he defeated the Franks at the nearby battle of Hittin (4 July 1187), Salah ad-Din forced the remaining Crusaders, and their accompanying European clergy, to leave the town. In 1229 Frederick II was able to negotiate a corridor of access for pilgrims coming from Acre. In 1251 the king of France, Louis IX, and his queen came to celebrate mass in the grotto. In 1263, however, the Mamluk sultan Baybars, in his final push to kick the Franks out of Palestine, completely destroyed all the Christian buildings in the city and placed the town off-limits to Latin clergy. Nazareth soon dwindled to the status of a poor village, and by 1294 pilgrims reported finding only a small church protecting the grotto. Its population remained Christian, however, matching that of other Christian villages in the Galilee hills.

In the fourteenth century, a few friars belonging to the Roman Catholic Order of Franciscans were permitted to establish themselves in Nazareth, setting up quarters among the ruins of the Basilica. Their stay over the next 300 years was punctuated with persecutions, executions, and finally eviction in 1548. However, in 1620 Fakhr ad-Din, amir of the Druze, who controlled this part of Palestine and Lebanon in the early Ottoman period, allowed them to build a small church over the Grotto of the Annunciation, and they began to organize pilgrimage tours to surrounding sacred sites. The region, however, suffered from banditry, and the Franciscan monks were often kidnapped and held for ransom by Bedouin from the area. The Franciscans nevertheless remained near the grotto, and in 1730 the powerful Shaykh Dhahir al-Umar authorized them to erect a church; this building stood until 1955, when it was demolished to make way for the construction of the existing basilica.

Napoléon Bonaparte's troops captured Nazareth on 31 March 1799 during their campaign in Palestine. On 17 April, Bonaparte visited the holy sites and reportedly considered making his general Junot the duke of Nazareth. However, he reconsidered after realizing how close "Junot of Nazareth" would sound to "Jesus of Nazareth." During his occupation of Syria (1830–1840), Ibrahim Pasha of Egypt opened up the territory to European traders and missionaries. Although he was kicked out by the Ottomans, the door remained open, and European money and institutions flowed into Nazareth. From 1845 to 1870, the Bedouin leader Aqiili Agha dominated political and security dynamics in Galilee, and under his rule the Christians of Nazareth were protected during the troubles and pogroms of the 1860s.

The first medical missionary into the city was Kaloost Vartan, an Armenian from Istanbul, sponsored by the Edinburgh Medical Missionary Society. Vartan arrived in 1864 and died in Nazareth in 1908 after creating the Scottish "hospital on the hill" and its nursing training center. In 1896 the Society of Saint Francis de Sales was allowed to establish an orphanage in the city, since the sultan favored the French. By the end of the nineteenth century, Nazareth had become a strong Christian Arab town hosting well-funded communal projects, a growing European community, and the construction of new religious buildings.

Until the beginning of British rule in Palestine in 1919, the population of Nazareth was mainly Christian, most of whom were Greek Orthodox, with a Muslim minority. During the British Mandate period, the town became an administrative center for the mandate government, and the construction of new medical and educational institutions drew in both professional and manual sectors of the regional workforce. Migration from other Galilee villages to Nazareth picked up steam, with the result that Nazareth became the largest Arab urban center in Galilee, eclipsing Shafa'amr, Tiberias, and Acre (see also "Acre"). Many Muslims were among those who moved to the growing city, and this represented a challenge to the Christian elites. The Arab Cigarette and Tobacco Company hired many of the fellah displaced by Zionist land purchases in the Jezreel.

The city also became an intellectual center and a focus of resistance to Zionism. The followers of Shaykh Izz ad-Din al-Qassam found support in the community during the 1936–1939 Arab Revolt, and the hated British District Commissioner of Galilee, Lewis Andrews, was assassinated, along with his police escort, in front of the Anglican Church in September 1937 by four Qassimites. Women in the city organized a branch of the Arab Women's Association in 1930 to work for Palestinian independence, and the Arab Workers Congress dominated by the Communists had a branch in the city by the early 1940s.

Under the Peel Commission recommendations of 1937, Nazareth was allocated to the proposed Arab state, and the UN Partition Plan of 1947 placed Nazareth within the Palestinian Arab territory. As civil war broke out in Palestine after November 1947, Nazareth quickly became a haven for Palestinians of the region (some 5,000) escaping from the hostilities. After the first cease-fire in the 1948 war, the infamous Israeli Plan Dalet tasked the Golani Brigade with besieging Nazareth, and they captured it from Fawzi al-Qawuqji and the Arab Liberation Army on 16 July 1948. The city ended up not experiencing the mass expulsion by Israeli forces of civilians that had occurred in other cities. Its population grew rapidly over the next decade, and the Muslim population came to exceed that of the Christian Arab one.

For nearly twenty years, until 1966, the population of Nazareth remained under martial law, which restricted the citizens' freedom of movement. They also experienced massive expropriation of surrounding land owned by its inhabitants. This land was used for the establishment in 1957 of Nazaret Illit (Upper Nazareth) as a Jewish development town. Since that time, it is quite legitimate to speak of two Nazareths or even of a divided city.

Upper Nazareth was established as a Jewish urban counterweight to Palestinian Arab Nazareth in view of the fact that at the time of the establishment of the State of Israel, there were practically no Jews living in the center of Galilee. It became a national priority of the new Israeli government to dilute the concentrations of Palestinian Arabs in the Galilee region.

The new town was located on the slopes above the existing Palestinian Arab Nazareth, mostly to the east, with extensions on the north and south. Nazareth is inhabited exclusively by Palestinian Arabs, while Upper Nazareth is overwhelmingly (90 percent) Jewish. While the two towns are physically contiguous and linked by a single local bus service, they are totally separate in terms of jurisdictional authority and administration. The two municipalities rarely cooperate, although both derive their authority and budgets from the Israeli Ministry of the Interior. Contrasts in infrastructure and development features of the two cities are pronounced. Upper Nazareth is a modern, well-designed town with spacious, relatively low-cost housing developments, industrial areas, well-equipped schools, parks, and recreational facilities. On the other hand, Nazareth has poor-quality and high-density housing, with potted roads, inferior schools, and limited infrastructure amenities and no industrial plants, all largely because of a small municipal budget.

One implication of such developments has been the ongoing struggle of the Nazareth municipality with the national government over land expropriations, planning issues, and budget allocations. Up until 1975, the city had a Labor Party–sponsored mayor, which produced an unrepresentative, corrupt municipality. In the 1975 elections, however, Tawfiq Zayyad, of the Rakah Communist Party (and a poet), was elected with a 67 percent majority. The city began to take a confrontational approach to working with the Israeli national government to improve things for the Palestinian Nazareth community. By March 1976, the Arab population of Galilee took to the streets to protest the confiscation of land, and the national government responded with force. Nazareth experienced huge demonstrations, and six Palestinians were killed in Galilee. On 30 March, *Yawm al-Ard* (Land Day) has since been celebrated annually in the city as a day of resistance to general discriminatory policies of the Israeli government. As the "Arab capital of Israel," Nazareth continues to be a site of tension. In October 2000, police snipers shot a number of protesters, with thirteen killed throughout Galilee on the same day. The Orr Commission, publishing its findings on the events in 2003, found that the stain of discrimination still prevents the Palestinian minority from receiving equal land and housing rights in Galilee.

Over the years, the population and residential changes within the city have resulted in a decline in the dominance of the traditional Christian families over municipal politics. As the increasingly politically active Muslim population of the city has found its voice, political clashes have occurred. Most

recently, tension surfaced (or was encouraged by outsiders) over land adjacent to the basilica and what this meant about control over religious sites in the city. The divisions are not just Muslim-Christian, however; they also can include Maronite, Greek Orthodox, Coptic, Catholic, Adventist, Islamist, and Communist. Yet its citizens daily cross confessional boundaries in their work and friendships, with the stigma of being a nonintegrated minority within the state more important than that of their religious differences.

Architecturally, Nazareth is a good example of a Mediterranean mountain town, with a mix of Middle Eastern styles belonging to different eras. Nevertheless, apart from the basilica, the city has never attracted the investment or political interest to produce monumental buildings of outstanding architectural merit. The centerpiece of the city is the historical suq, which was the commercial heart of the Old City and included workshops for traditional artisan crafts. A project to restore the suq offered some promise but has never been extended to surrounding housing or business establishments, meaning that it has failed to produce significant change. At the foot of the ridge close to the main transport intersections is a large concentration of traditional two-story houses of Galilee stone, with tile roofs, patios, and inner courtyards, most of which were built in the 1800s or the early 1900s. Ill-conceived attempts at renovation have left many derelict, with little effect on the pressing needs for housing in the Old City. Further up the hillside, construction is less dense, and houses date from the early 1900s and later. On the upper part of the slope and spaced even more widely apart are massive modern edifices with concrete frames and columns.

As the home of Jesus for thirty years before he began his ministry, Nazareth offers many sites commemorating his early life with Mary and Joseph. Many of them have scant archaeological evidence for their existence but nevertheless are deeply rooted in local legend and church tradition. The most important shrine is the Grotto of the Annunciation, where, according to the New Testament, the archangel Gabriel announced to the Virgin Mary that she would be the mother of Jesus. The grotto now lies within a new Basilica of the Annunciation, completed in 1955. Denounced by some who see its profile as a "rocket that is about to take off," this is the largest Christian church in the Middle East and can be seen from every corner of the city. The interior of the current church is unapologetically modern, with a bare concrete structure and an austere minimalist interior. However, the sparseness is softened and contrasted by colorful mosaics and panels of artwork donated from Roman Catholic communities from all over the world intended to signify the universality of the Catholic Church.

Other important religious structures in Nazareth include the Church of Saint Joseph, built in 1914. This follows the outline of a medieval church on the same site based upon the tradition that it enclosed an underground chamber identified as the carpentry workshop of Joseph. The Convent of the Sisters of Nazareth lies on top of a Jewish necropolis containing one of the best examples of a tomb sealed by a rolled stone. The masonry structures are medieval and probably belonged to a Crusader monastery or convent. After the expulsion of the Franciscans, the Muslims used the site as a place of worship.

The Church of Saint Gabriel is a Greek Orthodox church that took the place of a round medieval church, which was itself an adaptation of an earlier Byzantine edifice. The church is on the site of the spring that feeds the Virgin's Fountain a few feet to the southeast; the site was an important place of pilgrimage for both Byzantines and Crusaders. Finally, within the marketplace itself is a structure of thick, curved stone walls but rough and unadorned, known as the Synagogue Church. This is reputedly the site of the ancient synagogue where Jesus preached as a young man and stands adjacent to a Greek Catholic church.

Michael Dumper

Further Readings

De Haas, Jacob. *History of Palestine: The Last Two Thousand Years.* New York: Macmillan, 1934.

Emmett, Chad. *Beyond the Basilica: Christians and Muslims in Nazareth.* Chicago: University of Chicago Press, 1995.

Gibbons, John. *The Road to Nazareth: Through Palestine Today.* London: Hale, 1936.

Murphy-O'Connor, J. *The Holy Land: The Indispensable Archaeological Guide for Travellers.* Oxford: Oxford University Press, 1992.

Rabinowitz, Dan. *Overlooking Nazareth: The Ethnography of Exclusion in Nazareth.* Cambridge: Cambridge University Press, 1997.

Schick, Robert. *The Christian Communities of Palestine from Byzantine to Islamic Rule.* Princeton: Darwin Press, 1995.

Nicosia
Population: 254,032 (2001 estimate: 206,200, Greek side; 47,832, Turkish side)

Nicosia, the capital of the island state of Cyprus, is currently a divided city, split between Greek Cypriot and Turkish troops all watched over by the blue berets of the United Nation (UN). Although Cyprus is now incorporated into the European Union (EU), Nicosia has always been an integral part of the cultural, political, and economic life of the eastern Mediterranean and thus very much a Middle Eastern city. Whether one focuses on its Crusader heritage, Roman villas, Venetian walls, British government buildings, or its Ottoman caravansaries, this most cosmopolitan of cities retains its 2,500 year links with its neighbors across the sea and looks forward to the day when the barbed wire and checkpoints will disappear and the city will once again be reunited.

Nicosia (Greek, *Levkosia;* Turkish, *Lefkosa;* Latin, *Nicosia;* Arabic, *Niqusiya*) is located on the northern bend of the small Pediaios River (now a seasonal wadi) in the heart of the Mesaoria (between the two mountains) Plain in the center of Cyprus. To its southwest lies easy access to the mineral-laden Troodos foothills; to the northwest or northeast lies access to the coastal harbors. Thus, Nicosia lies at a central point of intersection at the heart of the island, with access in all directions. The view to the north reveals the northern range of the Kyrenia Mountains, with the "five-fingered mountain," Pentadaktylos, in the distance. The site is surrounded by good agricultural land, and up until the fifteenth century there were still large tracts of forest where elites would go hunting within easy range of the city.

Near to the Nicosia site there have been found Neolithic (6000–3000 BC) remains and some of the oldest pottery on the island. During the excavation for the Cyprus Hilton, Bronze Age tombs were found in the area of the Ayia Paraskevi, indicating that there was settlement along the river as early as 2400 BC. Certainly, by 2000 BC, the organized extraction and shipment of copper from the nearby mountains made this site a crossroads for donkey caravans heading to the coasts, where the ore was carried to northern Syria. This central valley, with the Nicosia site, was to remain at the confluence of island events up to the present.

By 1700 BC, the first urban areas were appearing along the coasts, and as far away as Babylon, the demand for copper from Alashiya (Cyprus) was constant. This demand meant that the region around what is now Nicosia was caught up in a long-distance commodity chain of copper production that affected the area's development. Copper-smelting workshops appeared in the Nicosia area between 1700 and 1400 BC. Port cities like Enkomi on the east coast thrived under the demands and power of Egypt and Ugarit (see also "Ugarit"). By 1300 BC, there was probably a village on the site, part of the "Copper Road" of the ancient Middle East.

Around 1200 BC, local island control of copper extraction, production, and shipment appears to have given way to outside dominance of mercantile interests. It is from this time that a strong Mycenaean and then Aegean cultural influence comes to dominate the north and west coast of the island, with immigrants taking control of those ports and the political leadership of the hinterland. On the east coast, by the mid-eleventh century, Phoenician immigrants had established Kition and Salamis (which replaced Enkomi) as gateway cities, with copper production and trade as essential to their contacts to the expanding Assyrians. Thus, the center of the island was caught in a tug-of-war between the urbanizing east and west coasts and the pull of their trade networks to the Aegean or the Canaanite cities of Syria and Palestine. Gradually, a number of city-states emerged, speaking Arcado-Cypriot and strongly influenced by Peloponnesian culture.

By the time of the establishment of Assyrian suzerainty over the island around the period of Sargon II (721–705 BC), seven kingdoms are recorded as paying tribute. Forty years later, Ashurbanipal (668–627 BC) received tribute from more, including one Ledroi. Clearly identified now as lying under the current streets of Nicosia, over the next 1,000 years the name of Ledroi or Ledra reoccurs in reference to a small city-state on the banks of the Pediaios River. The size and significance of the town must have cycled over that millennium; there are few references after Ashurbanipal until the fourth century BC, when it had grown into a more significant city-state with cultic shrines to Baal-Hammon and Aphrodite, and then sinks again during the Roman area, insignificant enough to have been bypassed by the Roman road system on the island.

After the Achaemenid (526 BC) conquest of the eastern Mediterranean, both Cyprus and the Levantine coast were administered together as a unit, with the Phoenician Cypriots centered in Kition managing an extensive copper extraction network throughout the island. The Cypriot towns joined the Ionian Revolt against Persia in 499 BC but were strongly repressed by the Persians and the Phoenicians in Kition. Alexander the Great won Cyprus when he defeated the Persians at Issus in 333 BC, and Paphos became the island's Hellenistic capital rather than Kition.

Since Nicosia is today a large city, it has been difficult to carry out systematic archaeological investigations to discover the earliest history of the city. However, what is known comes from emergency studies when new construction is in process. Such analysis suggests that the development of a town on this site dates from at least the fourth century BC. One foundational myth has the city founded by Lefkon, a scion of the Ptolemaic dynasty of Egypt, sometime after 305 BC—hence, the Greek Levfkosia. An alternative has the town named for the local poplar tree, the Lefki, which would have once marked the banks of the river.

The island came under Roman rule in 58 BC and formed an integral part of the Roman Empire with Paphos as its capital. The evangelists Paul and Barnabas (a Cypriot Jew) visited Cyprus around AD 46 and converted the Roman proconsul, Sergius Paulus. Christianity spread on the island (Barnabas may have been martyred in Salamis in AD 61 and tradition has his tomb marked by a monastery in Famagusta), and it is possible that by the time of Constantine (d. AD 337), a majority of the island's inhabitants were Christian. Certainly, there was a large early church hierarchy located in the cities of Cyprus, and Ledra was the site of a bishopric; in the years after Constantine, there are records of a Saint Macedonius as bishop in Ledra, and later a Saint Triphyllius, whom Saint Jerome (d. 420) named the most eloquent bishop of his time. After 431 the Byzantine emperor accepted that the Cypriot church was autonomous and rated its own archbishop, or

exarch, of the Cypriot Orthodox church, ecclesiastically independent from other archbishops. Salamis was the capital of Byzantine Cyprus and the location of the archbishop.

The constant struggle between the Byzantine Empire and the Sassanians (224–651) led in 617 to a Sassanian invasion of the island. In 649 Muslim forces invaded the island and established a tribute structure; they returned in 654 following a revolt in its key cities. Conflict between the Byzantines and Arabs over Cyprus was nominally ended in 688 with a novel agreement between Justinian II and the Umayyad caliph Abd al-Malik for the island to be neutral ground between them. Further Arab naval attacks on port cities occurred, however, in AD 743, 806, and 911. The result of such attacks appears to have been the migration of the coastal populations inland, where they could establish stronger defenses. It is from this time that Leucosia begins its rise to primacy.

By the eighth century, Leucosia or Nicosia was the seat of the archbishop for the island. This central role for the faith in the whole island contributed to the gradual growth of the city as a Christian religious center. This religious centrality was confirmed by political centrality, with the city becoming the capital of the island after 965, when Byzantine forces retook the island and established their court system and governmental bureaucracy in Leucosia. By the time of the Crusades, the city had a wide reputation for Christian learning and scholarship.

In 1184 the island's then Byzantine governor declared himself independent of Constantinople and ruled Cyprus from Nicosia as emperor. However, he was cruel to the local population and made enemies of the various monarchs and aristocrats assembling in the eastern Mediterranean for the Third Crusade. In fact, it was the English king, Richard the Lionheart, on his way to the Crusade in 1191, who decided to teach the upstart a lesson and captured the island in three days. Richard entered Nicosia without opposition but had no interest in remaining in the city, so he sold it and the surrounding island to the Knights Templars. The Knights quickly established themselves in the castle of Nicosia, despite local resistance, and massacred the majority of the citizens. Subsequent rebellion encouraged the Templars, in turn, to quickly move on, and they sold the island to Guy de Lusignan, who founded the Lusignan dynasty (1192–1489), ruling from Nicosia as "Lord of Cyprus."

Through fifteen subsequent rulers, this dynasty maintained Latin/Frankish control over the local Orthodox community. A Latin see was established in the city and the Orthodox church bureaucracy driven outside the walls. There was Orthodox resistance, with uprisings in the capital over the years and, in 1231, Orthodox clergy burned at the stake. Finally, in the fourteenth century, an ecumenical council agreed to an end to the fighting, and Nicosia became a city for churches from many denominations and sects. Churches for the Dominicans, Franciscans, Augustinians, Carmelites, Benedictines, Carthusians, Greeks, Armenians, Jacobites, Maronites, and Nestorians were all subsequently part of the diversity of the city's composition.

For different periods during their rule, the Lusignan rulers also held the title "King of Jerusalem," although Jerusalem was held by the Muslims and there was little left of the Crusader kingdoms along the coast. In 1285, for example, the seventeen-year-old John was crowned king of Cyprus in Nicosia and then immediately crossed to the port of Tyre, where he was crowned king of Jerusalem (see also "Tyre"). John died a year later and was succeeded by his fourteen-year-old brother, Henry, crowned in the cathedral in Nicosia on 24 June 1285. The dynasty spent great monies on developing the city and its fortifications; some of that money came from the excommunication, imprisonment, and confiscation, ordered by the pope in 1312, of the remnants of the Knights Templars' headquarters on the island.

For the European powers, Cyprus was a key forward military and economic base targeted at the heart of the Muslim-held Holy Land, and it grew very wealthy from long-distance trade. As a result, Nicosia was often a staging site, conspirator's nest, and a city of spies for invasion plans, competition, and logistics. In the Battle of Nicosia on 24 June 1229, the Franks fought among themselves for control of the kingdom. In 1365 Peter I, the then Lusignan king of Cyprus, organized a "crusade" by European knights from Nicosia directed at Antalya and then Alexandria (see also "Alexandria"). Even Venice and Genoa competed for control of the trade from Famagusta to the east, which led to fighting back and forth across the island and through its towns during the thirteenth and fourteenth centuries. All this intrigue and attention meant that Europe knew of the city and its significance: Dante mentioned Nicosia in his *Paradiso* in 1305, using its standard Latin name at the time, Nicosia.

By the late fifteenth century, the Lusignan dynasty had little to offer the Cypriot people or its European allies, and the last queen, Caterina Cornaro (r. 1474–1489), ceded Cyprus to Venice in 1489. The Venetians then ruled the island through a series of military governors sited in Nicosia and established extensive sugar plantations run by slaves or Greek serfs to produce cash, much of which ended up as fantastic villas in the old quarters of Nicosia. The island became known for its vineyards, cotton plantations, and fields of sugarcane.

With the rising threat of the Ottoman dynasty, the Venetians promoted Nicosia as the last Christian bastion to the Ottomans and rebuilt its medieval walls between 1567 and 1570 in a new modern style appropriate for the gunpowder age. Employing an eleven-pointed star with moat and projecting bastions, the 2.8-mile-long walls and three gates (Kyrenia, Famagusta, and Paphos) are still largely intact and one of the few remaining examples of sixteenth-century European military fortifications. Unfortunately for the declining Venetian commercial empire, the Ottomans were little deterred by the new walls and finally turned their attention in 1570 toward this last remaining Venetian outpost. One rationale for the shift in their interest may lie in the supposed desire of the new sultan, Selim the Sot, for that famous Cypriot wine.

The Ottomans sent 50,000 troops into a siege of Nicosia that lasted six weeks; when Nicosia was captured, the Ottoman generals allowed eight days of rape, pillage, and massacre of the inhabitants of the city, resulting in 20,000 casualties. Venetian survivors were sent into slavery, while the Greek underclass were "freed" from Venetian rule, with some reportedly thanking their Ottoman invaders. The Ottomans immediately began to move immigrants from Anatolia into the valleys and towns of Cyprus. Although some churches were turned into mosques, the new rulers reestablished the Greek archbishop, kicked out the Latins, and allowed the Orthodox to build a number of new churches. As Ottoman governors came and went through the gates of the city, over the next 300 years the archbishop became increasingly important politically and economically in the life of the island, and more power gravitated to Nicosia.

Ottoman control of Nicosia became less sure as the revolt on the Greek mainland picked up steam in the 1820s. Local support for Greek independence was crushed in 1821 with the public hanging of the archbishop in the main square, but the structures of mercantile power were shifting as well, undermining Ottoman control. By the early 1800s, European merchants were leaving the island only to be replaced by Levantine Catholic merchant families with networks linking Nicosia to Aleppo, Istanbul, and Izmir. The numbers of this new merchant class were swelled in the 1830s by prominent Christian and Jewish merchant families fleeing to Nicosia to avoid the Egyptian invasion of Syria. Nicosia was famous for its silks and gold embroidery.

City life was precarious, no matter where you were on the socioeconomic ladder. The city experienced numerous earthquakes over the years, for example, with the one in 1741 being particularly devastating, with minarets falling and cracks in the walls of the city. An extensive cholera epidemic hit in 1835 and a huge fire in 1857. As late as 1860, African slaves were delivered across the Sahara to Tripoli and then transported to Nicosia for sale in its market.

The patterns of life in Nicosia changed on 1 July 1878, when Britain peacefully assumed control over the island. Under the 1878 Cyprus Convention, secretly negotiated between the Ottomans and their ally, the British Empire, England would occupy and administer the island to protect the Ottomans against possible Russian aggression. The fact that controlling Cyprus might facilitate the defense of the new British lifeline to India, the Suez Canal, was not mentioned. There was to be a regular "Tribute" paid by Britain to the Porte

Layout of the unique Venetian walls for Nicosia, 1615. (Beauvau, Henry de, *Relation iournaliere du voyage du Levant.* Nancy, 1615)

in recognition of Istanbul's continued sovereignty. The tribute was never paid, and the issue caused great resentment in Nicosia.

At the time of the British takeover, Nicosia's population was around 11,000 people, with perhaps as many as half coming from a Turkish background. Over the next forty years, however, the city's demographics changed dramatically as new government offices, increased trade with the Middle East, increased immigration from the countryside, and an infusion of Armenians and British workers decreased the Turkish percentage in the city and increased its multiculturalism. From the beginning, the archbishop called on the British to facilitate *enosis,* or unity, with Greece and to commit themselves to leaving the island.

Others were calling for British political support as well. In 1902 Theodore Herzl proposed to Joseph Chamberlain, the British colonial secretary, that the new Zionist Movement could temporarily set up a Jewish political home in British-controlled Cyprus. Chamberlain rejected Cyprus as a home for the nascent Zionist Movement but encouraged other British-controlled territories, such as Uganda, as possibilities.

Although formally under the Ottomans until 1914, with the outbreak of World War I the island was annexed by the British when the Turks allied with Germany, and Cyprus became a Crown colony. Following the war, the new Turkish government and the Greek government began supporting their respective communities on Cyprus, with the Greek majority advocating enosis with Greece as the subsequent stage beyond British occupation and the Turkish minority beginning to propose *taksim* (partition) if the British withdrew. This caught the colonial administration in an increasingly chaotic political situation. In addition, a growing Communist movement and frustration with the insensitivity of the colonial administration combined to destabilize the local political space.

When the British announced new taxes for imperial defense just as the global depression was hitting Cypriot pocketbooks, Nicosia's population went into the streets. During October 1931, riots resulted in the death of six civilians, many wounded, and the British government house in Nicosia being burned to the ground. Reportedly, the loss of the government's house was of no great concern to the new governor's wife, who had mistaken the house for the stables upon her arrival. In response, the colonial administration cracked down ruthlessly: thousands were thrown into prison, political and human rights were suspended, the number of security personnel was increased, the flying of Greek and Turkish flags was banned, the teaching of Greek and Turkish history was curtailed, religious leaders were exiled, and the church hierarchy was placed under government control.

During World War II, the island hosted aircrews and naval bases for the advancement of the war effort, it narrowly avoided a German paratrooper invasion, and Cypriots served in the British army. When these soldiers came home after the war, they expected a greater political voice in Cypriot affairs and advocated for an end to British rule. When the British continually postponed Cypriot independence for the sake of cold war strategic necessity, resentment began to build, and Greek Cypriots began to mobilize. Attempts at intercommunal dialogue and debate over the island's political future were organized by Mayor Dervis, but the British heavy-handed restrictions killed such approaches. With the voice of the new outspoken Archbishop Makarios encouraging "enosis and only enosis," a violent movement, the National Organization of Cypriot Fighters (EOKA), organized within the Greek Cypriot community and launched a campaign of bombings and assassinations on 1 April 1955. Government offices in Nicosia were a prime target, as were British officials. Makarios envisioned an urban guerrilla movement against the British, and many Nicosia inhabitants were underground members of EOKA. Glafkos Clerides, the president of the Cyprus Republic after 1993 and a Nicosia native, went by the nom de guerre Yperides as he went about his business as a British-trained lawyer defending EOKA fighters arrested by the British.

Despite a yearlong cease-fire in 1957, the struggle for union with Greece continued, and EOKA reemerged in 1958 better organized and more violent than ever. Attacks on British officials; fighting in the streets of Nicosia against a new Turkish underground movement, Turk Mudafa Teskilat (TMT); and killing of Greek Cypriot leftists all marked the next two years in the city. Gradually, the city became increasingly divided into enclaves, and people rarely crossed into the other's space.

Political negotiations on the island's future began in Zurich and London to reach a compromise between enosis and taksim. The result was a new Republic of Cyprus declared on 16 August 1960 with Nicosia as its capital. Archbishop Makarios, building on his position as *ethnarch* (head of the nation) and leader of the national movement, became the president of the republic. Britain retained access to two military bases, and Greece and Turkey agreed to be jointly responsible to preserve the republic.

Although there were formal arrangements for power sharing, within two years of independence, militias had re-

newed their underground mobilization and arms acquisition and were linking to their respective mainland Greek or Turkish military supporters. During a politically charged discussion on revising the nascent constitution, on 21 December 1963, a police check of Turkish Cypriot civilians' papers led to the death of two Turkish Cypriots. Almost immediately, rival militias began fighting within the streets of Nicosia, hostages were taken, and the violence quickly spread around the country, leaving more than 1,000 Turkish and 200 Greek Cypriots dead. Following an armistice, many Turks from surrounding villages fled their homes and ended up in the Turkish Quarter of Nicosia, living in tents or cramped many to a room. By May 1964, the United Nations (UN) established a peacekeeping force in Cyprus (UNFICYP), and the blue berets first appeared in the city's streets to maintain the cease-fire.

Although unrest and violence continued over the next decade, it was not until July 1974 that large-scale violence returned to the streets of the capital. A small group of EOKA recidivists, supported by the new junta in Athens, attempted to assassinate President Makarios because he was no longer sufficiently committed to enosis. Makarios just managed to escape death in the attack and fled the partially destroyed Presidential Palace in Nicosia into the arms of the British military, who whisked him out of the country. The EOKA member Nicos Sampson declared himself provisional president and began moves to unify with Greece. In response, Turkey invaded the island on 20 July, and by the time of the cease-fire they controlled the northern 37 percent of the island. Nicosia itself was caught up in the fighting and ended up divided by barbed wire and machine-gun emplacements facing each other across its ancient narrow streets and lanes.

In late 1974, the UNFICYP's mission was extended and expanded to include supervising cease-fire lines, providing humanitarian service, and monitoring the buffer zone, which cuts across the island and through the heart of Nicosia. The line within the city is now called the "Green Line" and is marked by watchtowers, high concrete walls, and one key crossing point; the UN troops patrol the Green Line through the city on bicycle. Subsequent to the cease-fire, 60,000 Turkish Cypriots and a much smaller number of Greek Cypriots were exchanged across the dividing line, effectively partitioning the country, the capital, and the population of the island. Sporadic shooting across the line kept the city on edge, and no one was immune from the disaster; just before the end of that year, U.S. Ambassador Roger Davies was killed by a sniper.

Over the last thirty years, there have been numerous attempts to resolve the problems and reconstitute a federal government. Most plans were rejected by one side or the other, although the UN's attempts during 2003 and 2004 to gain acceptance for UN Secretary General Kofi Anan's plan came closest to succeeding. A Turkish state in the north was declared but remains unrecognized by the international community, and since 2004 Cyprus has been a member of the EU.

The heart of the city remains Eleftheria (Freedom) Square, but visitors may also see the restored Palace of the Archbishop; the Gothic cathedral, Agios Ioannis (Saint John), built in 1662; or the Chrysaliniotissa Church, the oldest Byzantine church in the city (1450). The former Saint Sophia Basilica (ca. AD 1228), housing the tombs of the Lusignan monarchs, is now the Selimiye Mosque and crowned by two tall minarets. The city hosts a number of museums, including the Cyprus National Museum and others dedicated to folk art and to the 1955–1959 national struggle. A number of large khans, including the Buyuk Khan and Kumardjilar Khan (both sixteenth century) have been preserved, and many public water fountains built by the Ottomans grace street corners.

Today Nicosia continues to play both a commercial and administrative role. There are a number of small industries located around the southern rim of the city on three industrial estates and in eighteen industrial zones. These factories produce textiles, processed food, clothing, leather, pottery, and footwear. Despite being divided, the city remains the economic heart of the island, with all the financial institutions, including the Cyprus Stock Exchange, located within its boundaries. As of 2001, the city hosted more than one-fourth of the country's population.

Under United Nations Development Programme (UNDP) auspices, a master plan for Nicosia was developed by architects and sociologists from both sides. The plan suggests how to rebuild the unity of the city once the barriers come down and includes a vision of a binational university. This master plan has remained one of the only points of continuous contact between the two sides as Nicosians express their hope for thoughtful and conflict-aware urban planning. Certainly, after 2003 there was a move to open up free access across the divided city, and the demand for such access has been expressed in peace demonstrations by the city's inhabitants on both sides of the Green Line.

Bruce Stanley

Further Readings

Calotychos, Vangelis. *Cyprus and Its People: Nation, Identity and Experience in an Unimaginable Community, 1955–1997.* Boulder, CO: Westview Press, 1998.

Crawshaw, Nancy. *The Cyprus Revolt.* London: Allen and Unwin, 1978.

Durrell, Lawrence. *Bitter Lemons.* New York: Dutton, 1957.

Foley, Charles, and W. I. Scobie. *The Struggle for Cyprus.* Stanford: Hoover Institution Press, 1975.

Holland, Robert. *Britain and the Revolt in Cyprus, 1954–1959.* Oxford: Clarendon, 1998.

Karageorghis, Vassos. *The Civilization of Prehistoric Cyprus.* Athens: Athenon, 1976.

Stefanidis, Ioannis. *Isle of Discord: Nationalism, Imperialism and the Making of the Cyprus Problem.* New York: New York University Press, 1999.

Nineveh
Population: 200,000 (650 BC estimate)

The most powerful and well-known of the early northern Mesopotamian cities, Nineveh is associated in Western literature, art, and popular culture with Jonah and Nahum of the Old Testament. Capital of the Assyrian Empire from 705 to 612 BC, Nineveh was the largest of the Assyrian cities and surrounded by a wall seven miles long. The Book of Jonah gives the population as 120,000, though current estimates suggest anywhere from 75,000 to 300,000. Covered in tiled reliefs and shaded by winged bulls, the city's monumental scale continues to overwhelm visitors to the museums. At its height, the city of Nineveh was the premier city of an empire that stretched from southern Egypt to central Iran and from Anatolia to the shores of the Gulf.

The remains of Nineveh (Syriac, *Ninua*) are located on the edge of the modern city of Mosul in northern Iraq. The site is on the east bank of the Tigris River, at the point where the Khawsar (Khosr) River enters the Tigris. This places it thirty miles south of the beginning of the mountains, at a natural crossing point on the Tigris for roads west to Syria and the Mediterranean, roads north to Kurdistan, and south to the Gulf. The steppe area here is moist rather than dry, making highly productive rain-fed agriculture possible. Prehistoric sites appear near Nineveh as early as the eighth millennium, and excavations at Nineveh itself show continuous site habitation starting around 6000 BC.

With the beginning of the Chalcolithic era (late seventh millennia BC), there is a dramatic rise in the numbers of inhabited sites, in their sizes, and in population growth throughout the northern Mesopotamian area. Housing size grows very quickly between 5800 BC and 4500 BC, grain storage is sophisticated, quality pottery with standardized forms is used throughout the region, and evidence of regional trade into Anatolia is evident. However, this is not yet indicative of an urban culture structured around city systems. It is in the south, with its indigenous urban process, where the first cities and city systems appear, and only later does the north follow with its own distinct urbanization cycle.

Dramatic developments in urbanization, the emergence of city-state hierarchies, and advances in production and culture mark the Ubaid and Uruk periods in southern Mesopotamia (5500–3350 BC). In the north, however, an urban system does not arise until much later, in the late fourth millennium. In general, when urbanism does appear in the north, there are fewer cities, spaced farther apart, and of a smaller size than evident in the southern urban culture, which emerged more than 1,500 years earlier.

Historical finds from the Nineveh V level (2800 BC) include beautiful local pottery and Sumerian weapons. It is only

Stylized sketch of how ancient Nineveh on the Tigris might have looked. (Ridpath, John Clark, *Ridpath's History of the World,* New York, 1901)

with the inclusion of the territory around Nineveh into the first great Mesopotamian territorial empire of Sargon I and his Akkadian dynasty (2254 BC), however, that written records begin to be available for the north. During the neo-Sumerian era (2100–2000 BC), the specifics of Nineveh are hidden. It is clear that the Ur III kings controlled northern Mesopotamia under regional commanders (*ensi*). However, the role and power of Nineveh at this time is unknown. Generally, this is a period of flux, with significant migration into the north by the Amorites, a western Semitic people, and the beginnings of the rise of new power centers in Anatolia, Egypt, and Iran. Over the next 300 years, the Amorites established themselves as rulers in northern Mesopotamia, and one leader, Samsi-Addu, and his sons concentrate power into the first Kingdom of Upper Mesopotamia or the "first Assyrian Empire" (1800 BC). During this time, independent Nineveh was incorporated into this city system and became associated with the fate of the key city of Assur, some sixty miles to the south along the Tigris. Assyria, as the region became known, extended its economic reach along the trade routes into Asia Minor, northern Syria, and Kurdistan. In particular, prior to 1750 BC, Assur had trading bases in Cappadocia for strategic metals, importing tin in exchange for their gold, silver, and copper.

The region fell to Hammurabi around 1758 BC, but around 1700 BC the "father of Assyria," King Adasi, restored Assur's independence from Babylon, and the small kingdom continued under a succession of rulers while larger forces raged around it. Other immigrant groups, however, composed of Indo-Europeans and Hurrians, subsequently established a presence near Nineveh, went on to establish the kingdom of Mitanni based between northern Syria and northern Iraq, and began to extract tribute from the kings of Assur after 1500 until 1360 BC.

With the appearance of King Ashur-uballit I (1365–1330 BC), Assyria and Nineveh with it begin their dominance of the Middle Eastern stage. Ashur-uballit quickly incorporated much of the territory of the failed Mitanni entity, and by his death Assyria had become the key power in northern Mesopotamia. Nineveh was the cultic center for the worship of Ishtar, and Assyrian kings over the next 500 years contributed to rebuilding the city's temples after earthquakes and to expanding the size and appearance of the shrine. Assyrian kings built summer palaces in Nineveh, and the city profited from its special alliance with the capital of the empire.

It is from the time of the last great Assyrian dynasty, that of Tiglathpileser III (744–728 BC), Sargon II (721–705 BC), and his son Sennacherib (705–681 BC), that Nineveh emerges as the core city of the empire. Tiglathpileser reorganized the army, brought solid administration to the empire, and built the most efficient empirewide communication system until the Roman era. Sargon II, conqueror of most of Palestine and Syria, moved the capital from Nimrud to a new planned city, Dur-Sharrukin. With his untimely death, his son Sennacherib chose to abandon his father's partly completed city and to establish his capital in ancient Nineveh. Before coming to power, Sennacherib had spent considerable time in Nineveh, up until then a "royal residence," so he was familiar with the city. The city retained its ancient cultic significance and was actually more strategically based for controlling trade routes to the Mediterranean and into Anatolia than other Assyrian cities.

Sennacherib built a massive administrative center within the city and laid out, with considerable planning, a new capital unlike any seen up to that time. The king invested in extensive urban development projects, including water distribution systems, parks, street redevelopment schemes, and population redistribution. Labor was supplied by defeated peoples from throughout the empire, including those from Palestine mentioned in the Bible, who were forcibly transferred to the capital. The ruins of the seven-mile-long walls he built remain impressive today. Zoos, canals, experimental tree nurseries: all were part of the urban redevelopment scheme to immortalize the wealth and power of this empire, which stretched from the Nile to the Caspian and from Lake Van to the Gulf.

Sennacherib's grandson, Ashurbanipal (668–627 BC), continued the neo-Assyrian dynastic tradition of grand buildings in Nineveh covered with reliefs and fine decorations. Many of these reliefs are on display in London or Paris, where the precision of their detail and the lavishness of their scale continue to overwhelm visitors. It is Ashurbanipal's library, however, that has been the source of most amazement and information in the modern era.

With the death of Ashurbanipal, the empire went into fast decline, through a combination of civil war and the challenge of peripheral states. In the summer of 612 BC, a combination of Babylonians and Medes brought a huge army to the gates of Nineveh (see also "Babylon"). The archaeological remains demonstrate that a strong defense of the city gates was given, but it was not enough, and the city fell. The victors burned the city, destroyed its major palaces, flooded it in a symbolic act of final destruction, and claimed to have carted away its ashes.

Nineveh failed to arise from this tragedy. The destruction was so severe that Herodotus does not mention the city, and 200 years after its fall, passing generals did not even recognize the destroyed walls as belonging to Nineveh. Some inhabitants evidently lived on the site in the Seleucid period, and within the destroyed walls a Christian monastery, later turned into a mosque, is dedicated to Nabi Yunus (the prophet Jonah).

Our knowledge of the Nineveh site comes primarily from two rounds of excavations. Starting in the 1840s, the French consul in Mosul dug within the walls. Later European teams toured the magnificent Ashurbanipal reliefs in Paris and London, exciting the European imagination and leading to the founding of the Assyrian Excavation Fund and a more structured excavation in Nineveh under the direction of the British Museum. It was the discovery of thousands of clay tablets from Ashurbanipal's royal library, however, that has been the greatest legacy of this first phase, which lasted into the early twentieth century. Many of the tablets were bilingual, which allowed those working to decode the Sumerian language to advance more quickly. The legacy of this vast library, accumulated by an enlightened monarch concerned with preserving his own 2,000-year culture, is a window into the ancient urban past.

A second major set of excavations by the Iraqi Ministry for Antiquities and some reconstruction of walls and gates continued up until the Gulf War of 1990. Reports from the late 1990s indicated that inhabitants of Mosul, in their search for cash to survive the international sanctions, were raiding the Nineveh site for its antiquities, and in the post–Saddam Hussayn era, the vulnerability of the site to robbery has continued.

Bruce Stanley

Further Readings
Leick, Gwendolyn. *Mesopotamia: The Invention of the City.* London: Allen Lane and Penguin Books, 2001.
Pollock, Susan. *Ancient Mesopotamia.* Cambridge: Cambridge University Press, 1999.
Roux, George. *Ancient Iraq.* 3d ed. London: Penguin Books, 1992.
Van de Mieroop, Marc. *The Ancient Mesopotamian City.* Oxford: Oxford University Press, 1999.

Nippur
Population: 30,000 (2000 BC estimate)

In the southern Mesopotamian city system that arose in the early days of cities, Nippur played the role of the cultic center of a flexible system of gods that grounded both politics and religion for the Sumerian civilization. As the city of Enlil (who was the storm god, king of the lands, and god of power and authority), Nippur was at the religious heart of the system and the site where the gods assembled in council. Although there were shrines to Enlil in other cities, as a "temple city" comparable in significance to Jerusalem, Rome, or Makkah, Nippur held the key shrine for this premier deity, and he was the patron of the city's fortunes and power. This cultic centrality remained across Nippur's 6,000 years of existence, attracting wealth, scholarship, and administrative libraries. The vast tablets and written remains found in the city make it one of the most important cities, and holy sites, in human history.

The remains of Nippur (Arabic, *an-Nuffar*) are located today between the Tigris and Euphrates rivers in the mid-Mesopotamian zone, about sixty miles north of Ur, seventy miles southwest of Baghdad, and a few miles northeast of ad-Diwaniyah in southern Iraq. For much of Nippur's history, however, a branch of the Euphrates ran through the city, and canals bisected the city at different times. The river shifted to the west by the time of the Arab conquest, and today the tell is some twenty miles distant from the river.

Nippur's first remains date from the Hajji Muhammad phase of the Ubaid period (5000 BC), and the belief is that even then, the city had a central shrine, located on the spot over which all subsequent cultic construction was built. Evidence from the Early Dynastic and Akkadian periods (2960–2164 BC) suggests an elevated temple platform, city walls, and a greatly expanded city on both sides of the river. By 2000 BC, the city covered as much as 320 acres.

Interestingly, the city appears to have been abandoned in the years after the death of Hammurabi and the fall of the Old Babylonian kingdom (ca. 1720 BC), possibly because of an environmental crisis such as a shortage of water. For more than 300 years, sand dunes encroached up to the sanctuary. Beginning during the Late Kassite period, in southern Mesopotamia rebuilding began, and the city became a major provincial governorship, central for regional administration. A new canal was dug to bring water from the now-shifted Euphrates back through the city, and there is evidence of a moat in front of a new city wall. By the thirteenth century, new temples had been built over the old holy sites, and the city expanded to cover most of its old scale. A recently discovered map of the city dating from 1250 BC confirms the findings of the archaeologists of the layout of the city at this time.

With the end of Kassite rule, Nippur appears to have lost its administrative functions, and it shrank to a small community around the ziggurat site. However, it is clear that the religious centrality of this temple city continued. Rulers of subsequent dynasties found it necessary, as had those of past kingdoms, to return to the city and to link their legitimacy with its ancient traditions and gods. Even 2,000 years after its heyday, rulers in Mesopotamia claimed that they had been crowned in Nippur "by Enlil," and they all carefully recorded their contributions to refurbishing Enlil's shrine within the city.

Once again the city was revived by a change of empire: with the rise of the Assyrians, the city again became an administrative site for a regional governor, and Ashurbanipal and Shamash-shum-ukin (668–627 BC) rebuilt the ziggurat and the city walls. By the time of Nebuchadnezzar II (604–562 BC), however, the city is much smaller than previously, although there are indications of substantial, well-decorated temples around the holy site.

Again, the city expanded during the Achaemenid period (539–331 BC) and is clearly linked into the long-distance trade routes of the empire. The vitality of the city continues into the Seleucid period, but it is under the Parthians, and particularly from AD 100 to AD 242, that the city again becomes a major player in the whole region, with extensive walls and strategic fortifications, temple construction, and huge public buildings.

Its fortunes remain bright through the Sassanian, Umayyad, and into the Abbasid period, with occupation layers covering a larger area than 1,000 years earlier. A Christian bishopric was evidently located in Nippur. After AD 800, how-

ever, the city quickly lost its importance, perhaps as part of the general environmental and political shifts in the region during this time, and by AD 1250 only a small aspect of the site, well away from the main religious sites, is occupied. There was some slight revival during the Ilkhanid and Timurid periods (ca. 1350–1450), however.

Into the modern period, there were villages around the site, and when the University of Pennsylvania archaeologists arrived on the tell in 1889 to begin the first American excavations in the Middle East, they employed local Nuffarians as workers. Work on the tell was suspended from 1900 until 1948, at which time University of Chicago expeditions began extensive studies that lasted until the Gulf War. Scholars remain hopeful that they can return to the site in the near future.

The findings of these excavations have been phenomenal. Because Nippur never produced its own dynasty or attempted to rule the other cities in the region, and considering that it served as the religious navel of the southern Mesopotamian universe, the city never suffered the regular systematic destruction experienced by its neighbors. As a holy city, and with more than 100 temples, it became a depository for gifts, pilgrimage offerings, and symbolic decoration. One temple was rebuilt more than seventeen times between 3200 BC and AD 100. Nippur also served as a key regional capital; thus, it was a depository for governmental records. As a result, the city serves as a fantastic laboratory for archaeological excavation. Expeditions have discovered thousands of artifacts, tremendous amounts of pottery, and useful natural specimens of bones, pollen, and seeds.

In particular, however, it was the tablets, deposited within Nippur as the central holy city, that have proved most exciting to archaeologists. More than 100,000 tablets have been recovered from the site, covering the full scale of Sumerian and subsequent religious, economic, political, administrative, and literary output. This is the site that has presented us with the Creation myth, the Flood epic, and *The Epic of Gilgamesh*. One estimate calculates that more than 80 percent of all our knowledge of the Sumerian literary tradition emerges from the Nippur finds. This sacerdotal library with its epic tales, myths, hymns, prayers, and lists of gods also contained scientific texts. Nippur is, consequently, both one of the richest sites for understanding Mesopotamian history but also the standard for all other sites in the region, providing a baseline for stratification and dating.

Nippur's fortunes were completely tied to the primacy of Enlil in the Sumerian pantheon. Enlil had blessed Nippur, and in one of the hymns to Enlil it says that Enlil built Nippur with his own hands as his very own city. Enlil was not always the first of the gods, but his elevation to primacy may have occurred after Mebaragesi, king of Kish (2700 BC), built a temple to Enlil in Nippur. Quickly, Enlil evolved into the force that separated the earth from the sky through the power of his breath and the strength of his word. As the creator of the world, and following his victory over the forces of Chaos, Enlil continued to decide the fate of humans through his leadership of the council of the gods as the "Lord Wind." As a result, Enlil "chose" those who were to rule Sumer and Akkad and sanctified their rule. This narrative, clearly serving the interests of Nippur and the priests located there, was resilient enough to still be the cornerstone of the neo-Babylonian new year festival 2,000 years later.

Around 2550 BC, Enlil's temple had its first "rebuilding" by the reigning Sumerian king, establishing a pattern that was to last at least 2,000 years whereby rulers legitimized their rule over the region by contributing to the sanctuary at Nippur, thus gaining the backing of the priests of Nippur. Ur-Nammu, of the Ur III dynasty (2112–2095 BC), erected a ziggurat in Nippur in addition to ones in other cities. Even Hammurabi, who sought to supplant Enlil as head of the pantheon with the Babylonian god Marduk, felt compelled to embellish the sanctuary of Enlil (see also "Ur" and "Babylon").

The hegemony of Nippur can also be seen in other ways. For example, Mesopotamian rulers continually granted Nippur special protection from the taxes and responsibilities imposed on other cities. The Assyrian kings made a point of releasing Nippur from these responsibilities as part of their demonstration of commitment to the gods of ancient Sumer.

Nippur never produced kings and never produced a dynasty that ruled the Sumerian city-state system, but it was the center of a Mesopotamian system of tithes and contributions that brought it great wealth and power. During the Ur III dynasty, a rotation of monthly tax contributions from other cities brought food and goods to a "state" storage site near Nippur. This economic centrality brought in goods from long-distance trade, and archaeological excavations have discovered goods from Greece, Egypt, the Indus valley, and the Caspian in Nippur's remains. Nippur's cultic centrality and temple monuments also made it a site for pilgrimage; directions for finding one's way around named streets within the city have been discovered among the tablets in the city's archives.

Finally, the city was hegemonic in the region thanks to its command of knowledge. Nippur was the site of writing, a center for training and supporting scribes. Scribe schools flourished throughout its history, and their copybook lessons are scattered throughout the tell.

Bruce Stanley

Further Readings

Bottero, Jean, Elena Cassin, and Jean Vercoutter, eds. *The Near East: The Early Civilizations.* New York: Delacorte Press, 1965.

Leick, Gwendolyn. *Mesopotamia: The Invention of the City.* London: Allen Lane and Penguin Books, 2001.

Maisels, Charles Keith. *The Emergence of Civilization.* London: Routledge, 1993.

Roux, George. *Ancient Iraq.* 3d ed. London: Penguin Books, 1992.

Van de Mieroop, Marc. *The Ancient Mesopotamian City.* Oxford: Oxford University Press, 1999.

Woolley, C. Leonard. *The Sumerians.* London: Norton, 1965.

Nouakchott
Population: 800,000 (2005 estimate)

Few other cities in the world have grown so exponentially from just more than 300 inhabitants to almost 1 million in forty years. And few other cities have the permanent water shortages experienced by this created capital built on sand. With one face looking to a future based on offshore oil, the other to a past constructed on the trans-Saharan salt trade, the people of the Mauritanian capital of Nouakchott struggle with complex urban problems, such as shantytown life, soaring crime rates, ethnic conflict, and unemployment, but also with their unique problems: the structures of slavery as well as fighting the sand dunes that relentlessly seek to reclaim their city. As a Middle East/North African edge city, its diversity is both an asset and a curse.

Nouakchott (Arabic, *an-Nouakshut;* French, *Nuakchott*) is the capital city of Mauritania and the largest city in the Sahara. It is located three miles inland from the coast of the Atlantic Ocean and is approximately equidistant from Mauritania's southern border with Senegal and its northern border with the disputed territory of the Western Sahara. The vast majority of Mauritania consists of desert. Indeed, the dunes to the north and east of Nouakchott encroach upon the city. The climate in Nouakchott is mostly warm and dry. The city suffers from dust storms nine months of the year, perhaps leading to the name, which means "place of the winds," and it rains on average only six days per year.

The city is located on the southwestern edge of the Sahara, close to the point where the Sahel, a semiarid area, begins. Under different historic paleoclimates, the area has had more or less rain, but the site has always marked an edge: the point at which North Africa meets the sub-Sahara. Baobab trees, relics of the last wet phase, until recently still grew north of the city, and older citizens remember eating their fruit and leaves. The city sits along the ancient coastal Imperial Highway, which linked the mouth of the Senegal River to the Mediterranean via the trans-Saharan trade routes at Azuqqi (Akjoujt). To the east lies the oasis city of Awdaghust, that great caravan city of the eighth through the fourteenth century, serving as the gateway to the golden triangle between the Niger and the Senegal rivers. South along the coast is the ancient salt city of Awlil, which was shipping sea salt to Timbuktu and Jenne well before the ninth century. North along the coast lies the first Portuguese slave port, Arguin, dating from 1461.

The site of Nouakchott was chosen as the capital of Mauritania in 1957. The city was laid out two miles southwest of the *ksar* (small colonial fort) and its surrounding village of 324 inhabitants, which served as a stop-off point on the coastal route between Rosso, to the south on the Senegal River, and Atar, to the northeast. The city was constructed on what appeared to be fixed dunes, to protect the city from the flooding of the Aftout as-Saheli (a vast coastal depression to the north of the Senegal River Delta), which almost surrounds the city and used to flood the village, causing serious damage. Despite the country's Islamic traditions, Nouakchott was planned in a way similar to other colonial cities, with a strict separation between the "traditional" neighborhoods and the "modern" city; the mosque and the suq, for example, are located more than half a mile apart from one another.

In 1957 the city was constructed for an anticipated population of 15,000. By 1969 the population of Nouakchott had surpassed 20,000, and by 1987 it was approximately 600,000. Today it is home to more than one-third of the country's total inhabitants, with some estimates placing the population at more than 1 million. The city is the political and administrative capital of the country, and many citizens are employed in the state sector. It is home to the National School of Administration (built 1966), National Institute of Advanced Islamic Studies (built 1961), National Library, National Archives, and the University of Nouakchott (built 1981).

The city has an international airport and a port. The port, located about 3 miles west of the city, consists of two jetties: one for small vessels (Wharf Quay), built by the French during the 1960s, and the second (Port of Friendship Quay), for larger vessels, built by China during the late 1970s. The port is one of the entrance points used by Malian businesspeople to transport goods along the 684-mile paved "Road of Hope" to their landlocked country. Iron ore, phosphates, and copper are exported from the port. Wheat, sugar, rice, and other foodstuffs are imported. While there has been a steady increase in the port's activity, it remains less busy than the port of Nouadhibou to the north. In addition, people in Nouakchott work in light industry, construction, fishing, and in the traditional craft sector. Sea salt is still produced to the north and south of the city, while Internet cafés, called *cyber-thes,* dot the city.

The official language of the country is Arabic, while Wolof and Soninke are recognized as national languages by the constitution. Many applicable legal texts exist only in French, which is widely spoken across the public sphere. The language spoken by all ethnic groups is Hassaniya, which is a form of Arabic that has encorporated Berber vocabulary. It is said that the Moors (Arabs) constitute approximately 35 percent of the population, and they dominate the city's positions of power and authority. The remaining 65 percent is composed of indigenous African groups and former slaves (*Haratins*).

Around 5000 BC, the southern Sahara around and inland from Nouakchott experienced a wet period, and Stone Age hunters tracked a range of savannah animals; nearby rock art drawings record this diversity. After 2500 BC, however, progressive desiccation dried up what had been savannah, shallow lakes, and swampland, and the Sahara extended ap-

proximately to where the city is located today. Archaeological studies have found Late Stone Age (2000 BC) remains along the coast, suggesting that this area hosted small hunter-gatherer communities, and there are indications of goat and sheep species from North Africa being kept in this area by this time. A small copper-mining and -refining industry developed inland after the ninth century, and by 500 BC, early Berbers from the north arrived in the southern Sahara via the coastal routes on horses and began to introduce Punic technology, including iron making, to the local Soninke desert-edge communities. Over the next millennium, successive waves of Berber pastoralists and traders brought irrigated agriculture and date palm growing to the western oases of the southern Sahara.

The domestication of the camel meant that by the early centuries of the first millennium AD, trans-Saharan trade became much easier, and a range of routes developed to link the coast of Mauritania directly north to North Africa or northeast via oases to Tunisia or Libya. The camel-herding Znaga Berbers migrated into the southern Sahara after the fourth century. Thus, by the time the Arabs arrived in North Africa in the late seventh century, an existing network of trans-Saharan trade, with Berber tribes providing the connection across the Sahara, linked the Mediterranean and the local complex communities west of the Niger Bend and along the Senegal River. By the tenth century, the Empire of Ghana, based in the triangle between the Senegal and Niger rivers, was expanding, and the first Islamic entity in the area, called Takrur, was emerging on the Senegal River. Arab writers began to record stories of Bilad as-Soudan (Land of the Blacks) and its gold.

Regional trade for the desert-edge communities on the far west coast revolved around salt production and its long-distance trade to the interior for needed commodities. The Banu Gudala, who controlled the coast north of the Senegal River in the area of present-day Nouakchott, were on the periphery of these expanding inland trade networks, since at this time there was little maritime trade. Traders did circulate, however, and the Gudala elite adopted Islam. The story goes that one Gudala leader, while stopping in Kairouan on his return from the hajj, requested from a famous Muslim shaykh that he assign one of his students, a scholar-cleric, to return with him to the Gudala and help set his people on the correct path for their new religion. This is how in 1039 Abdallah Ibn Yasin, spiritual founder of what became the Berber Almoravids, began his mission in the southwest corner of the Sahara around Nouakchott. The stories suggest that Ibn Yasin's vision of purification, reform, corporate prayer, and true Islam was too strict for his new flock, however, and he was expelled.

Some traditions hold that the preacher then retreated to an island off the coast, perhaps near to Nouakchott, to found a *ribat* (militant monastic community) called Aratnanna.

Other interpretations of the records do not stress the physical ribat but interpret its meaning as a doctrine, style of fighting, or codified belief. Whatever the actual form, Ibn Yasin attracted a core of followers, whom he called *al-Murabitun* (followers of the ribat). Ibn Yasin then agreed to an alliance with the Gudala's fraternal enemies to the northeast, the Lamtuna confederation. Their leader, Yahyah bin Ibrahim, accepted Ibn Yasin's ribat, and together, sometime after 1054, they set out in a jihad to conquer the unbelievers. The Gudala were massacred, Awdaghust and Sijilmassa as two ends of the trans-Saharan trade route were captured (see also "Sijilmassa"), and although Ibn Yasin died soon after (1059), the Almoravids subsequently swept across northern Morocco and into Spain; by 1090 they controlled, from their new capital in Marrakesh, an empire stretching from Awlil to the south of Nouakchott almost to Barcelona (see also "Marrakesh"). Gradually, in the interface between the desert and the Sahel, a joint Berber-Soninke culture evolved around the oasis cities and along the salt routes, with strong social traditions of vertical and horizontal segmentation.

After the thirteenth century, Arabs of the Banu Hassan tribe began to move into the southern Sahara, and by the fifteenth century these warrior elites had replaced the Berber Znaga in the position as warriors (*hassan*), relegating the Znaga primarily to the position as clergy (*zawaya*); the Berber language was replaced with Hassaniya, a version of Arabic. The Banu Hassan came to dominate most of the oasis cities and the salt, gold, and slave trade via their amirs (military rulers), and later the southwestern Sahara became divided among different amirates. It is they who became known to Europeans as *Maure* (Moors) and still make up much of the elite in Mauri(tanian) society.

After AD 900 until 1900, the Mauritanian coast—from Awlil and N'Teret in the south past Nouakchott north to the island of Arguin—produced sea salt through evaporation, which linked this area into the great Saharan salt caravans heading to Awdaghust and Timbuktu (see also "Timbuktu"). Beginning with the Portuguese after 1441, there was a European presence along this coast; the Portuguese captured their first twelve African slaves to take back to Lisbon just to the north in 1441, and by 1444 they were grabbing fishermen from this coast in midnight raids from their caravels. By 1461 they had built Castello Arquim on the island of Arguin to try to divert the trans-Saharan slave trade through its doors. The Dutch joined them in the area in 1621 with their own station, and then from 1633 to 1678 they ran their operations from the captured Portuguese factory.

By the early 1600s, the French were establishing their settlement at Saint Louis on an island in the Senegal River. The coastal salt trade routes thus became modified for use for the Atlantic trade and for the gold desired by the Europeans, and the center for long-distance trade began to shift toward the Atlantic coastal ports. Caught between the "caravel and the caravan," the coast around Nouakchott became controlled after 1630 by the Banu Hassan, who created the amirate of Trarza and participated in the trade of Atlantic gum arabic and slaves, trans-Saharan slaves, horses, and gold.

Throughout the nineteenth century, France, Spain, and Britain competed along the Atlantic coast for export opportunities and access to African markets. Until the mid-twentieth century, the Mauritanian towns of Atar (northeast of Nouakchott) and Rosso (on the Senegal River, in southern Mauritania) were major commercial towns. During this period, the area of Nouakchott had little commercial significance, but various nomadic tribes seasonally used its water and pastures, while *takhredient* (freed slave fishermen working for the Banu Hassan overlords) lived in small villages along the coast.

By the end of the nineteenth century, France had begun to penetrate Mauritania, and it fully colonized the country by 1920. The first French military post was erected at Nouakchott in 1903. This post was abandoned in 1908 as the French moved farther east, but they reestablished the post in 1929. The French administered the colony from Saint-Louis, an island in the middle of the Senegal River, and invested practically nothing in developing the country's infrastructure or administration. Mauritania was principally a buffer zone for the French, protecting their more valuable assets in Senegal and Mali (then called Soudan). ·

Since Mauritania was administered by the French from Saint-Louis, the country did not possess a capital city. After Morocco gained independence, in 1956, King Muhammad V began to express irredentist desires to create a "Greater Morocco," which would have included a large part of Mauritania. There were some sympathizers for this idea among Mauritanian Moors, who saw Morocco as the Moorish homeland. However, the French and the majority of the Mauritanian governing council were against this idea, and they made hasty preparations to choose a Mauritanian capital city to try to win the loyalty of the Mauritanian people. The assistance of Jamal Abdul Nasir in dampening Moroccan claims resulted in the naming of the major street in the new capital after him.

The members of the preindependence Mauritanian governing council recommended the site of Nouakchott as a prospective capital. Other, more obvious choices were rejected for political and strategic reasons. Rosso was considered by the Moorish majority to be too associated with Senegal and the southern Mauritanians (who were of Pulaar, Wolof, and Soninke ethnicities). On the other hand, the port town of Nouadhibou was considered too far north for the southern Mauritanians. It also suffered from very poor transport links to the rest of the country. Finally, Atar was too vulnerable to attacks from Morocco. Nouakchott was thus chosen as a site for the new capital, being centrally located between the country's Moorish north and the African south. It also had reasonable transport links, being located on the old "Imperial Road." The first stone was laid on 5 March 1958.

In November 1960, Mauritania became an independent nation under President Mokhtar Ould Daddah, with Nouakchott as its capital. At independence, there were fewer than fifteen university graduates in the whole country. Even by 1965, the only newspaper in the city was a mimeographed bulletin published by the Peoples' Party, distributed weekly in Arabic (500 copies) and French (800 copies).

In 1968 Nouakchott witnessed violent protests against the continued racial discrimination felt by the population of southern Mauritania, who did not speak Arabic. The protests were suppressed, and it was made illegal to discuss racial conflict. Arabization, a postindependence process to empower the Moorish elite in positions of power continued, and Arabic was made the official language. Race riots took place again in Nouakchott and Nouadhibou (Mauritania's second city) in 1987, following the arrest of twenty prominent southerners for the distribution of a tract in French entitled, "Manifesto of the Oppressed Black Mauritanian: From Civil War to National Liberation Struggle, 1966–86." Following the riots, thirteen people involved were also jailed, and elements of Islamic law, part of a new process of Islamicization, was introduced. Tension continued to grow throughout 1988, until in 1989 a border incident between Senegal and Mauritania led to lynchings of Senegalese and Mauritanian southerners in Mauritania and violence against Mauritanians living in Senegal. As a result, curfews were introduced in Nouakchott and Nouadhibou, and the army policed the streets of Dakar, Senegal.

The government in Nouakchott has also had to deal with problems on its northern borders. After Spain withdrew from Western Sahara, ceding the territory to Morocco, Mauritania, and the Spanish-installed Sahrawi council, Mauritania became embroiled in a war with the Polisario Front (a guerrilla movement fighting for the independence of the disputed Western Sahara). In June 1976 and July 1977, the Polisario Front mounted raids on the outskirts of Nouakchott and shelled the presidential palace. The war crippled Mauritania economically and proved to be a huge embarrassment, finally bringing down the president, Mokhtar Ould Daddah, in July 1978. The new regime brokered a peace deal with the Polisario one year later.

The large growth in Nouakchott's population is principally because of the recurring droughts in the Sahara since 1969, which have paralyzed the rural and, particularly, the pastoral economy and forced people to migrate to the capital city. The city grew by 20 percent on average per year during the 1970s, and between 1977 and 1978 it grew 100 percent to more than 200,000 people. During the 1980s, the government offered incentives for immigrants to return to the rural life, with little success. Also during the 1980s, the World Bank claimed that

Nouakchott's uncontrolled urbanization growth was among the highest in Africa.

This has created a crisis within nomadic Moorish society. Despite the large concentration of a sedentarized population, urban lifestyles coexist in Nouakchott with nomadic traditions. For example, Mauritanian Moors often erect tents in their gardens or next to their apartment blocks as places to receive guests. People keep goats to be able to drink fresh *zrig* (a drink made of fermented milk, water, and sugar). The large majority of Nouakchott's inhabitants wear the traditional, robelike boubou rather than European dress.

Rapid urban growth has brought Nouakchott many of the social problems associated with other African cities. There are substantial *kebes*, or bidonvilles, dotted around the capital, many inhabited by poverty-stricken ex-slaves and their descendants. One estimate suggested that 40 percent of the city lived in such illegal housing, often constructed from old car parts, cardboard, and roofing materials. Few inhabitants have access to running water or electricity. The average pay is $1 per day, and much work in the agricultural sector is seasonal, with no work between January and July; bread riots broke out in the city in 1995 and lasted for three days. Unemployment, chronic health problems, drug addiction, and prostitution are significant issues for the municipality. But there are other problems as well. Malaria appeared in the city for the first time in 2003, and the locust plague of 2004 was the worst in fifteen years, stripping the city's gardens and fields of all greenery.

There is now a permanent water shortage in the city. Even before the site was chosen for the capital, there were water shortages in the area. Although the city was sited partially to make use of the nonrenewable Trarza aquifer, and planned for 80,000 utilizing that supply, the population pressures now mean that water is overused and very expensive. Trucks, donkeys, and standing water pipes provide water for the less-well-off areas of the city, and water restrictions have led to a decrease in the number of urban gardens in the city; diarrhea among the young remains a huge health problem. One solution may be the Aftout Saheli Project, partially funded by the Islamic Fund and the World Bank, which plans to bring water to the city from the Senegal River.

The government has committed to other new projects for the city, including upgrading slums, creating employment, establishing community microcredit schemes, and empowering community groups, although many in the city are cynical about the potential of such projects to modify the municipality's fundamentals. The city government has been broken up into nine districts, together composing the new urban conurbation of Nouakchott, as one way to make it more responsive to its citizens. New transport links are beginning to connect the city more easily to other parts of the country: the new 300-mile road to Atar has cut travel time to seven hours, although this is only if government workers are employed full-time to keep sand dunes off the road.

The economic situation declined so badly in the late 1970s because of the sustained drought, the war in Western Sahara, and the global decline in copper and iron-ore prices that one way the pressures surfaced was in a series of coups d'état. Ould Daddah was overthrown in 1978, and then there was one in 1981 and another in 1984, which brought Colonel Ould Sid Ahmed Taya to the presidency. There was a coup attempt in 1996 and another in 2003. Large protest demonstrations in the city during June 2005 were aimed against the president, and in August 2005 another military coup finally succeeded while Taya was out of the country for Saudi's King Fahd's funeral. A seventeen-member Military Council for Justice and Democracy now rules in his place, and its members have committed themselves to opening the country to democracy, to holding national elections by March 2007, and to continuing the diplomatic recognition of Israel that began in the 1990s.

Slavery remains inherent in the social structure of the city. Although slavery has been legally banned a number of times during the twentieth century, including in 1981, it was not criminalized, and nothing was done to modify the culture of slavery that underpins the very foundations of society. Many thousands of persons in the city are still discriminated against in employment and education as a result of their status as slaves or former slaves. Al-Hor and SOS Esclaves are two organizations of ex-slaves that work for change under very difficult circumstances of denial and harassment of civil society groups working to expose the issue. A new law passed in 2003 punishing any slave owner with fines or imprisonment may have some effect, however.

The future remains unclear. Oil revenues may bring some relief. Offshore drilling forty miles west of the city was ex-pected to start in late 2006, with Mauritania becoming Africa's fourth oil supplier. Global terrorism has put the city on the map with fears that the country may be a base for training jihadists. The post-2001 American-led Pan-Sahel Initiative against terrorism resulted in U.S. soldiers training a Mauritanian rapid-reaction force in counterterrorism tactics; the new Trans-Sahara Counter Terrorism Initiative (TSCTI), started in 2005, is better funded and more comprehensive in scope. Its concern is with Islamist terrorists using traditional caravan routes across the desert for smuggling or access to safe havens; this has already produced joint parachute operations to the east of the capital. Human rights activists were fearful that President Taya was using the link with the Americans to justify a crackdown on his opposition, especially when he cited terrorism as the reason for a series of major arrests. Fifteen young Mauritanian soldiers were killed in the far north of the country in June 2005 by members of an Algerian-based group, the Salafist Group for Preaching and Combat, who cited the Mauritanian ties to the Americans for their attack.

Nicola Pratt

Further Readings
Bovill, Edward W. *Golden Trade of the Moors.* 2d ed. London: Oxford University Press, 1968.
Pitte, Jean-Robert. *Nouakchott: Capitale de la Mauritanie.* Paris: Publications du Departement de Geographie de l'Universite de Paris-Sorbonne, 1977.
Savage, Elizabeth, ed. *The Human Commodity: Perspectives on the Trans-Saharan Slave Trade.* London: Frank Cass, 1992.
Stewart, C. C., and E. K. Stewart. *Islam and Social Order in Mauritania.* Oxford: Clarendon Press, 1973.
Webb, James L. *Desert Frontier Ecological and Economic Change along the Western Sahel, 1600–1850.* Madison: University of Wisconsin Press, 1995.

O

Oran

Population: 770,000 (2005 estimate); more than 1.2 million in the greater Oran area

The birthplace of Algerian raï, hip-hop, and rap music, the port city of Oran offers one face to the Mediterranean and another to the interior of the country. For more than a millennium, this city has served both as a naval base and as a key commercial entrepôt for trade. Famous for its role as the city of Albert Camus's The Stranger *and* The Plague, *Oran's sons and daughters have shaped Algerian-French culture, just as 130 years of French occupation transformed the city's population and character through settlement and racism.*

Oran (Arabic, *Wahran;* French, *Ouahran*), capital of Oranie, the westernmost district of Algeria, is the second city in the country, facilitated by its substantial infrastructure of ports and roads. Oran is a port city on the Gulf of Oran and located in the most fertile portion of the country, known as the tell. This region borders the coast and extends inland for about 150 miles into the Tellian Atlas. Although there are only a few plains of small size along this coast, such as the Cheliff, between Algiers and Oran, these areas are very fertile, permitting cereal cultivation. For the most part, the mountains descend down to the coast; to the east and west of the city, the desert encroaches.

Unlike the other Oranais cities of Mascara or Mostaganem, Oran was never a center of commerce or of religious culture. Neither did it really have as much of an effect on the region as Tlemcen or, in fact, cities like Nédroma, Mazouna, or even Kalaa, which could be said to have been more significant in the social and cultural life of the region than Oran.

Paleolithic finds near Oran indicate ancient habitation along the coast. Phoenicians created trading posts along the littoral, and by the third century BC the area was under the rule of the Carthaginians. Roman rule looked to the coast to provide grain for the imperial capital, and there are ruins in the area, although Roman rule was focused farther to the east around Cirta. The Vandals and then the Byzantines controlled the area until the Arabs began their conquest of North Africa in the raids of 681.

The city itself was reportedly founded (ca. AD 940) as a trading city by the traders of the Andalusian Umayyads looking for an entrepôt on the coast. One theory suggests the city is named for the last two lions (*waherain*) who lived near the site when the city was established, remnants of the African lions that used to roam the region. Under the Almohads (1152–1246), Mers el-Kébir served as a key naval port and arsenal. The Zayyanids took Oran after this and ruled the city from nearby Tlemcen, using the port as their key outlet to the world and particularly to Spain, where they had strong connections. It also served as an access point for trans-Saharan routes to the Sudan. It was these connections that enticed persecuted Jews to migrate from Spain to Oran and for other refugees, both Jewish and Muslim, to choose Oran after 1492.

As it expanded into North Africa after 1492, Spain occupied the city in 1509 and used it as a garrison town. Two hundred years later, the bey of Mascara, operating under Ottoman suzerainty, captured Oran. The Spanish returned, however, in 1732, which is when they built the Cathedral of Saint Louis. This area of the North African coast is prone to earthquakes, and a large one hit in 1791, killing more than 30,000 people and destroying most of the city. It is at this point that the Spanish decided to abandon the city.

Into the vacuum came the bey of Mascara, who set himself up in Oran to lay siege to the *beylick* to the west held by the bey of Tlemcen. This placed the town back under the Ottomans, who claimed sovereignty but essentially allowed the local rulers along the coast to do as they pleased. This attracted the attention of the French, who captured the town in 1831. At the time there were reportedly only 3,000 souls in the town, and it was less important than Mers el-Kébir, six miles to the west. Soon after the occupation, the city was wracked by cholera and then by smallpox, which killed a good part of its population.

Local resistance to the French occupation of Oran was led by the famous Algerian leader Abd el-Kader (1808–1883), the new bey of Mascara. He besieged the French in the city and negotiated a treaty where, as lord of the interior beyond Oran, he was able to organize national resistance to their occupation.

Early in the French occupation of Oran, there was an open French invitation for settlers to come to the city and many Spanish peasants, particularly from around Valencia, came. They ended up in competition with preprotectorate Moroccan migrant labor, which moved east from the Rif Mountains, and within the city fighting would often break out. For example, in 1879 dockworkers from both groups fought across the city. This Spanish community did not assimilate, instead retaining substantial ties with the towns from where they had come. It was Spanish farmers and colon labor that planted the vineyards and orchards that subsequently made Oran famous. As the power of the Spanish increased in the city, anti-Semitism increased, and the Dreyfus Affair in the metropole set a context for attacks on the city's Jewish community.

The Mosque of the Pasha, Oran, ca. 1870. (Library of Congress)

The French began a series of administrative and physical changes to the city. They made Oran capital of a French department, modernized the port, and upgraded the Mers el-Kébir naval base into one of the most important for the French Mediterranean fleet. It was during this period that Oran became known to some as the "little Paris" of North Africa. They constructed new roads along the old Roman roads, east to west, and at Oran laid rail tracks into the interior (1868). Such improvements did not prevent the epidemics from returning, however: between 1861 and 1872, there were two cholera plagues, one typhus plague, and one smallpox plague. There was a famine in 1868 and a rebellion in 1871.

One of the leading proponents of a French Algeria, Eugene Etienne (1844–1921), was from Oran. A top colonialist in the Chamber of Deputies in Paris from 1881 to 1919, Etienne was a leader of the Parti Colonial, served as a colonial undersecretary, was a journalist, and shaped French policy in Africa. He never saw himself as a representative of the Algerian Muslim community and was openly hostile to their participation in the politics of the country.

During the mid-nineteenth century, the town drew indigenous populations from the surrounding countryside as well as Europeans from France and Spain. The indigenous people were dispossessed of their land, while the gradual concentration of landed property during the later part of the century forced the majority of Europeans to abandon the agricultural land on which they had settled since their arrival from Europe. These Europeans chose to live in the suburbs of Oran, which comprised Mediterranean-style houses just one or two stories high. In this way, the suburbs of Gambetta, Saint-Eugène, Delmonte, Saint-Antoine Boulanger, Eckmül, and others were populated by *pieds-noirs*—French settlers born in Algeria—among whom the most commonly spoken language was Spanish.

Muslim Algerians were concentrated in the *village nègre* (called *ville nouvelle* after 1945) and Lamur, a shantytown constructed on farmland belonging to a colonist called

Lamur, who employed some of them. This quarter was known in Arabic as *al-Hamri* (mud), because it did not have paved roads. Other shantytowns also existed at Planteurs and Ras al-Aïn, built on the hill overlooking the town.

Thus, as the city entered the twentieth century, Oran remained a colonial town, just as it had been under the French occupiers. It was the only town in Algeria where the pieds-noirs were more numerous than the indigenous people of the area. This strong European presence has left its imprint in the city's architecture. Oran does not have the allure of Arab cities such as Tlemcen, Algiers, or Constantine; it is more Mediterranean with its low houses and its rectangular apartment buildings, which give it the cachet of a French provincial town. By 1954 the city was the largest in Algeria, with much of its growth since 1900 having come from the in-migration of the Muslim community. The city's French citizens looked to Paris, however: Yves Saint Laurent, for example, left the city after high school to study fashion design in Paris.

Oran witnessed a number of key actions of World War II. In July 1940, the British navy shelled the French warships holed up in Mers el-Kébir to prevent them from falling into the hands of the Germans. Two years later, under Operation Torch, 40,000 American troops landed to the east and west of the city and fought their way into the center against Vichy French forces. The city was captured on 10 November 1942.

The city played its role in the Algerian Revolution from 1954 to 1962. The Front de Libération Nationale (National Liberation Front [FLN]) was particularly active in the city, organizing large demonstrations and attacks. Ben Bella, the first president of the independent state, was from the area around Oran, and he got his start when he robbed the Oran Post Office (1950) to gain funds for his underground resistance group. Houari Boumédiène, who overthrew Ben Bella in a coup in 1965 and served as president until his death in 1978, had served as commander of the Oran military district for the FLN army up until 1960.

During those heady days of revolution and independence, Oran continued to serve as a key port for the country. Under the Evian Agreement, the French were allowed to lease Mers el-Kébir for fifteen years. Thus, there was the irony, in 1963, of a Cuban tank battalion unloading in the Oran port to head off in support of Algeria in their brief 1963 War of the Desert against Morocco, just under the noses of French troops. These were the first Cuban troops in Africa and the beginning of an aggressive Cuban-Algerian relationship (that lasted until the coup against Ben Bella) to support revolutionary movements in Africa with weapons shipped via Oran.

Upon independence in 1962, the populations of the older quarters occupied apartments in the suburbs, which had already been swelled by migration from the surrounding countryside. As a result, over the next decade, the town's population doubled, although by the first half of the 1970s there was still accommodation available for use by workers re-cruited for the industrialization program launched by President Boumédiène. But by the end of the 1970s, the city was experiencing a housing crisis because of the combined effect of population growth and the continuing exodus from the countryside.

Consequently, the city evolved according to its own rules and not those of the urban planners. The colonial order, with its inequalities and hierarchies, was succeeded by a postcolonial disorder manifested in the degradation of the urban fabric with buildings in ruins, highways not maintained, commerce in an anarchic state, and film theaters turned over to traders. New shantytowns, referred to by the press as "precarious housing" or "anarchic construction," have appeared. Once a family group settles in a place and builds makeshift housing, it is soon followed by other families, giving rise to quarters of several hundred people where there is no running water, electricity, or paved roads. These quarters all carry the same name: *bni ou skout* (build and keep quiet).

The authorities proved unable to face up to the enormous tasks bequeathed by colonization, from maintaining streets and buildings to developing infrastructure such as schools and commercial facilities. This situation led to a rapid deterioration in the fabric of the city. In an attempt to deal with the housing issue, the state hastily built, on the town's periphery, numerous housing projects. These projects were poorly planned, and living conditions there are difficult; there is little commercial activity, schools are far away, and public transport is inadequate. At the same time, certain residential peripheries (Saint-Hubert, Canastel) have seen the construction of luxury villas belonging to well-to-do tradesmen, industrialists, and senior officials.

With independence, more than 200,000 of the city's inhabitants, Europeans and Jews, left for France. With more than half of its population gone, the city took a long time to recover its vitality. Yet by 1970, half of the country's industry was located between Oran and Algiers, and soon there was discussion about an auto manufacturing plant in the city.

The city has long been known for its music. Within this port city, Arabic, Spanish, Jewish, and Berber music had long been blended into new forms. By the middle of the twentieth century, musicians like Reinette L'Oranaise (the little queen from Oran), who learned to sing and play classical Arab music in the city, were making their own contributions to Arab-Andalusian music. Two decades later, what had long been a local form of giving advice or an opinion, *raï*, about social issues, love, or drinking, and essentially a port-city bar culture of dancing, came to the world's attention as a flamenco-style Arab popular music, also known as raï. Having its base in the slum areas of the city as a form of resistance, this music spread throughout the Algerian diaspora on cassettes, and by 1985 festivals of raï were held. Although most of the singers fled to France after 1990 because of attacks on its worldliness and its incitement against religious beliefs, famous sons of Oran, like the "king of raï," Cheb Khalid, continued to challenge social morals and conventions. Some have paid with their lives for their devotion to free expression: Rachid Baba Ahmed, one of the early promoters, singers, and producers of raï music, was murdered outside his record store in Oran in 1995, it is assumed by Islamists. A decade later, Oran remains home to alternative music: more than forty rap groups record in the city, the band members hang out on its beaches, and the musicians mix French, English, and Arabic together into musical poetry about their city and its social problems. A compilation of music by the city's groups was issued in 2000 and called *Wahrap* (a play on the Arabic name of the city, Wahran, and the word "rap").

The city has also produced its authors, often writing in French rather than in Arabic. One of the most famous was Albert Camus (1913–1960). It is in Oran that he developed his style, and his experience growing up in its "invincible summer" shaped all his works. Both *The Stranger* (*L'Etranger*) and *The Plague* (*La Peste*) are set in the city, and he expressed his disillusionment with French policy in Algeria via his essays and stories. Emmanuel Roblés (1914–1995), the novelist and playwright, was born here, as was Helene Cixous (b. 1937), the feminist writer. Another more recent author is Assia Djebar (b. 1936). In her collection of short stories called *Oran: Langue Morte (Oran: Dead Language),* she represents the horrors and difficulties of living through the civil war of the 1990s and the tensions it produced within families and for intellectuals.

Profoundly affected by the political crisis that plagued the country after 1992, Oran served as a refuge for numerous villagers fleeing terrorism and military violence. This influx increased unemployment and engendered social violence, which pervaded the daily life of the town both at a collective and individual level. The city voted overwhelmingly for the Islamic Salvation Front (FIS) in December 1991. Although Algerian feminists marched in the city in January 1992 to protest against the FIS victory, for the rest of the decade many intellectuals and social activists went quiet during the troubles. The university was divided over the question of women and veiling, most of its cultural and social events were suspended, and many faculty members left the country.

One of the reasons for this generalized violence was probably the increase in poverty and the scarcity of resources, which meant that many social groups felt their survival was at stake. The town's landscape is characterized by scenes not envisaged by it planners—women with babies in their arms sleep in the streets, children aged five to fifteen wander in groups searching for food and shelter, and dozens of beggars move up and down the pavements.

The city remains an important port (exporting methane, natural gas, and petroleum), financial city, and industrial city (wine, for example), and the municipality is pushing tourism as part of its development plan. The city continues to suffer from water scarcity, however. A major project to deal with this, the Mostaganem-Arzew-Oran (MAO) project, has been started, which includes the Cheliff Dam, east of the city. In addition, the government has recently approved the construction of a desalination plant that will provide 100,000 cubic meters per day.

Yet Oran is succumbing to an evolutionary trajectory that the authorities appear powerless to stop. Under the weight of numbers, urban life has deteriorated to such an extent that the traffic, pollution, noise, hygiene, and security are factors making one forget the beauty of the sea on which, as Albert Camus wrote, Oran has turned its back.

Lahouari Addi

Further Readings

Horne, Alistair. *A Savage War of Peace.* Rev. ed. London: Papermac, 1987.

Lazreg, Marnia. *The Eloquence of Silence: Algerian Women in Question.* London: Routledge, 1994.

Schade-Poulson, Marc. *Men and Popular Music in Algeria.* Austin: University of Texas Press, 1999.

Smith, Tony. *The French State in Algeria, 1945–1962.* Ithaca, NY: Cornell University Press, 1978.

Valensi, Lucette. *On the Eve of Colonialism: North Africa before the French Conquest, 1790–1850.* New York: Africana, 1977.

P

Palmyra

Population: 200,000 (AD 270 estimate); 50,000 (2005 estimate)

Palmyra, a city of palms lying on the edge of an oasis in the eastern Syrian desert, almost brought down the Roman Empire in AD 271. Led by a beautiful warrior queen, Zenobia, this ancient caravan city known to the Assyrians and Babylonians rose to world greatness and then fell, comparatively overnight, although whispers of its past continued well into the sixteenth century. Today the vast ruins of this 5,000-year-old desert city attracts busloads of tourists wishing to imagine themselves as supplicants in the Temple of Bel or to watch the sunset from the spot where Monty Python's Life of Brian was filmed. No ancient city in the Middle East has yielded so many sculptures, texts, inscriptions, or architectural remains to flood the museums of the world.

Palmyra (Semitic, *Tadmor*) lies in the Syrian Desert, about 137 miles northeast of Damascus, halfway between the Mediterranean Sea and the Euphrates River. Snuggled up against the eastern edge of mountains around an oasis where the Efqa Spring bubbles up from the base of Jabal Muntar, the ancient Tadmor sits at a crossroads of the most southerly group of caravan routes that traverse the Fertile Crescent linking Syria and the river basins of Mesopotamia. Easily accessible today by the rapidly developing Syrian road system, it may be reached from both the capital and Homs. From Palmyra the road continues east toward the Euphrates River and Iraq.

Known as the "Bride of the Desert," this ancient city grew in the heart of the Syrian Desert around a large oasis renowned for its luxuriant vegetation. An extensive irrigation system of underground aqueducts, or *qanat* (covered irrigation channels), also fed the gardens around the city. The oasis attracted a diverse collection of animals, including, well into the medieval period, lions. The ancient name of the city, known from early antiquity, is Tadmor, probably related to a Semitic root meaning "to protect." It was known as Palmyra in Hellenistic times and during the Roman period but returned to its original name following the Arab conquest in AD 634.

The language spoken in Palmyra was an Aramaic dialect with strong Arab influences, known as Palmyrene, possessing its own alphabet. In addition, Greek was also frequently spo-

ken and written in the city, as was Latin, though to a lesser extent. Greek became the preeminent language during the Byzantine period, while, since the Umayyad period, Arabic became the language used in the city.

The specific origins of Tadmor are unclear. Human presence in this site was most probably connected to the existence of a rich source of sulfurous water—the Efqa Spring—around which Palmyra grew throughout the centuries. Flint remains around the oasis suggest Neolithic occupation, and archaeological soundings under the Temple of Bel have found traces of cultic use on the site dating from the Bronze Age (2300–2200 BC). The city is first cited as Tadmr in the archives of the city of Mari dating from the second millennium BC. Assyrian records of the first millennium indicate that the city was an Aramean city and that it was dominated by nomadic tribes that regularly "caused problems" for the Assyrians.

As a Seleucid city, Palmyra prospered during the Hellenistic period, and the records show that it provided troops in the conflicts with the Ptolemies. Much of its early trade was with Seleucia, from where much of its fashion and art derived. In the chaos that marked the end of that empire, Syrian city-states arose that looked more to the Parthians than to nascent Rome. Although Mark Antony raided a Palmyra (41 BC) that was considered under Parthian control at the time, its rise to international relevance as a major international trade center really only began in the first century AD.

Its fortune was intimately connected to the overall political situation of the time, and Palmyra's fame rose after the fall of its caravan-controlling neighbor to the south, the Nabatean Empire, in AD 106. As the key desert trade routes to Mesopotamia, Persia, and India shifted to the north around the Fertile Crescent, Palmyra was ideally situated to act as a shortcut across the desert. By guaranteeing safety, water, and organized caravans, the city benefited from the unresolved and continuous tension between Rome and the Parthian Empire that allowed the city to carve out a quasi-independent status.

The city's revenues emerged from two sources. Of primary importance were the customs duties collected for luxury items, such as silk, transshipped via Palmyra as a *portorium* (port where transit tax was paid). Secondly, the city's own tax law brought revenues into the city from the salt fish, wheat, olive oil, unguent, slaves, and bronze statues that the city imported. Personal wealth for the merchant princes of the four key tribes of the city came from the caravan trade, where they

293

served as caravan leaders and speculators. Palmyra merchants owned ships in the Persian Gulf, regularly traveled to India to trade, and lived in cities to the east to facilitate trade back to their home. Fashion reflected these ties to the Persian Gulf; women of the city wore strings of pearls, sourced in the Gulf and an Oriental fashion not found in the Greco-Roman world. The leaders of the merchant class clearly spent considerable sums on the promotion and development of their city and received public statues and recognition in return.

The personal connections of the Severian imperial family (AD 193–235) with Syria, and the Roman conquest of Dura Europos, located on the Euphrates some 124 miles east of Palmyra, drew the city more into the Roman sphere. By the time of Caracalla, Palmyra had obtained the status of a Roman *coloni* and was one of the main urban centers of the East. Throughout most of the Roman-Parthian frontier wars, Palmyra was able to defend its status as a nonpolitical commercial center, in control of numerous villages and satellites, and to maintain regular troops to protect the desert routes from Bedouin attack. Dura, as the junior partner, and Palmyra worked together to facilitate the trade to and from the East and to maintain its safety. Palmyrene camel corps served in the imperial army.

Its fortunes declined following the Sassanian conquest of the Parthian Empire (AD 224) and the progressive development of an alternative trade road passing to its north. In the mid-third century, when Rome's influence decreased and the internal weaknesses of the central power made it difficult to control the border areas, the fortune of local clans increased. Septimus Odeinat belonged to one of the leading political families of the town and was able to organize and lead a strong army of Palmyrene archers and cavalry that reconquered, in the name of Rome, the territories Rome had been forced to relinquish. Under Odeinat's rule, Palmyra became a regional power.

Following the sudden death of Odeinat in 268, his wife, the famous queen Zenobia, acceded to power as tutor of her son Wahballat. Her extraordinary personality is forever woven into the fame of the city, though she actually caused its partial destruction and contributed to its decline. Zenobia sensed a weakness in Rome's control and began to expand Palmyra's power throughout the region. Excellent at self-promotion, Zenobia claimed descent from Cleopatra and dressed in armor. She sent her armies to conquer Egypt in 270 and attacked the Anatolian cities. Zenobia crowned herself Augusta and named her son as emperor. Her actions appeared to threaten the very integrity of the Roman Empire.

The Romans couldn't tolerate the challenge and under the new emperor moved with a strong army to rein in the rebellious queen. In 272 Emperor Aurelianus reconquered Antiochia and moved toward Palmyra. After he besieged the city, Zenobia was captured and taken to Rome, where, legend has it, she was paraded through the streets in golden chains. It is unclear whether she was killed in Rome or lived out her life as a matron on the Tiber. Palmyra quickly rebelled against Rome, however, and their army returned and partially destroyed the city in 273.

The end of Zenobia's brief rule marked the beginning of the decline of Palmyra. The shifting balance of international powers and the change of the main traffic routes made it less and less important and transformed the previously world-famous commercial center into a peripheral town. As long as there was caravan traffic and an oasis, however, the city continued to exist.

There was another brief phase of development of the city after Emperor Diocletianus signed a peace treaty with Sassanian Persia in 297 and reorganized the road and defensive network of the region. The *strata diocletiana* to link Damascus with the Euphrates was constructed, and legions were assigned to the city to man the protective forts (*limes*). As a result, the last extension of the city, known as Diocletianus Camp, was built and surrounded by a walled enceinte.

In the Late Roman period, the city turned to Christianity, and it is recorded that a bishop of Palmyra, one Marinus, took part in the Council of Nicaea in 325. The ancient temples of Baalshamin and the ancient Temple of Bel were transformed into churches, and at least two new Christian basilicas were built in the city. The city retained a certain importance in long-distance trade during the Byzantine period, and Justinian had it garrisoned and refortified.

In 634 Palmyra was conquered by Muslim forces led by Khalid ibn al-Walid, general of the first caliph, Abu Bakr. Khalid was recalled by Abu Bakr from Iraq to help capture Syria, and he made a legendary forced march with little water across the desert to take the city from the Byzantines. By this time, the city's role was relatively marginal in Syrian affairs.

In the twelfth century, the inhabited area had shrunk so dramatically that all of Tadmor could be enclosed within the compound of the Temple of Bel. The external walls of the *temenos* (a holy precinct) were restored and partially rebuilt, while the imposing *propylea* (monumental gateways to the temple) were destroyed and transformed into a fortified gate (AD 1132–1133), reusing most of the Roman masonry. It was around this time that Benjamin of Tudela visited the city, reporting that it contained a community of 2,000 Jews.

The forces of Temür paused long enough on their way to Damascus (1401) to rough up the city, and under the Ottomans the decline continued as Tadmor became a minor backwater town. The village of Palmyra remained constrained within the compound till the twentieth century. In 1929 the French mandatory power decided to evacuate the residents to restore the temple and to create a new airy modern city close by.

The imposing ruins of the city cover an area of approximately six square miles. This vast field of ruins is dominated by the silhouette of the Ibn Maan fortress perched on a high hill overlooking the city. The citadel was built in successive building campaigns from the thirteenth century to the seventeenth century. Besides making it strategically significant, its setting makes it a wonderful spot from which to appreciate the vast expanse of the ruins spread out below. As a result, local drivers make significant profit from taking tourists up the mountain to catch the sunset across the desert. Scenes from the Monty Python movie *The Life of Brian* made use of the citadel as a backdrop.

Surrounded by the Syrian Desert, the green mass of the oasis, with its 500,000 trees (date palms but also olive trees and pomegranates), delimits the ancient urban center, whose white and golden limestone columns create a majestic tableau. A large Hellenistic city wall, whose traces are still visible, encloses the whole oasis and the city, leaving outside only the necropolises. Such an extended area, however, was never wholly urbanized. The original nucleus of the city probably extended between the Efqa Spring and the Temple of Bel, but most of the area within the walls was not built up. In the first and second centuries, the Roman city grew north of the Hellenistic settlement, along the small wadi that crosses the site.

Three major necropolises surround the city. The most extraordinary among them, which has attracted the attention of the foreign visitors since the "discovery" of the city in the late seventeenth century, is the Western necropolis, characterized by its tower tombs that dot the so-called "Valley of Tombs." Though in Palmyra one might also find *hypogea* (underground tombs) and funerary temples, the most characteristic feature of the city's necropolises are undoubtedly these extraordinary monuments. The tower tombs consist of a square tower, resting on a larger stepped base, built according to a regular and relatively repetitive scheme. The oldest examples date back to the Hellenistic period and were built of irregular stone blocks; the later examples, however, were carefully constructed and had a richly decorated interior. Hundreds of corpses could be buried in these structures, which had up to four main levels reached by a spiral staircase built between the central core and the outer walls. The richest among them were spacious enough to have large central chambers on each floor containing funerary sculptures and a particularly elaborate carved and painted ceiling.

Starting from the late second century, hypogeum-style tombs became the most frequent form of burial, and tower tombs ceased to be built. These underground galleries generally have a *T*-shaped plan and host many tens of loculi directly carved into the rock. The burial zone was reached through a large stone staircase leading underground, the access to which was closed by imposing stone doors. One of the most ornate hypogeum-type tombs has been removed and rebuilt in the Archaeological Museum of Damascus, where it is now housed in a purposefully built underground room.

Within some tombs, archaeologists have found well-preserved textiles dating from the second century AD. Han period Chinese silks with intricate patterns clearly indicate the substantial long-distance trade that linked Palmyra via the Silk Road with the Far East. Fine local Syrian linen and wool weaving suggest an advanced local textile technology that may have been exported.

Within the enceinte of the Hellenistic city wall, the most evident urban features are the striking mass of the Temple of Bel and the extraordinary colonnade. This urban axis is not regular and straight but follows instead three different directions, as it was built within previously urbanized areas. Palmyra, in fact, did not develop according to precise plans, neither in its Hellenistic phase, nor later during the Roman period. Instead, it grew in an almost chaotic way, with small partially independent quarters built according to diverse orientations, which extended to create a continuous urban space. The large Roman axis, built between the second and third centuries, therefore, had to comply with the existing urban fabric. Long colonnades were typical of the Oriental Hellenistic and Roman cities. They played not only a decorative function but also constituted the actual core of urban life where most of the commercial and public activities of the city took place. In Palmyra creative architectural solutions had to be designed to accommodate the colonnade within the preexisting urbanized area and to connect its three segments. An elliptic square, with an imposing *tetrapylon* (structure with four gates, reerected by the Syrian Antiquity Department with concrete columns) skillfully connects its two western segments, while an extraordinarily decorated triangular archway links the road to its southernmost part leading to the monumental entrance of the Temple of Bel. The opening of the colonnade caused the partial demolition of the preexisting *temenos* of the Temple of Nabu, one of the largest religious complexes in the city. The traditional features of Roman cities, the theater and the thermal baths, opened onto the medium section of the road parallel to the small wadi crossing the city.

A new city wall, enclosing a much smaller area, was built at a later stage, possibly during the rule of Zenobia. It incorporates all the largest constructions and defines an urban area organized around the axis of the colonnade. This wall, strengthened by square towers, follows the line of the central wadi and had an evident defensive function. Many vast and elegant patrician mansions have been found by archaeologists in this part of the city. They all have the traditional plan with central courtyard and *peristilium* (arcade that surrounds the garden). Other important mansions, whose rich mosaic floor decorations dating from the third century may now be seen in Palmyra's and Damascus's archaeological museums, were located southwest of the ancient city center along the oasis limits. Some among them were inhabited until the ninth century.

The Temple of Bel rises on an ancient cultic site, leveled and enlarged to create the flat basis of the religious compound. It was built between AD 17 and AD 32 and officially inaugurated on 6 April 32. The central temple is surrounded by a large temenos mostly built during the second century. The precinct had an imposing outer facade with a high stone wall decorated with regular windows and niches, while its internal facade was characterized by continuous galleries supported by a double row of columns. The outer facade was dominated by a powerful propyleum, preceded by a monumental flight of steps and a great pillared portico leading into the temenos through three large and richly decorated gates. There was a second, lateral entrance for the animals—a ramp leading to the sacrificial altar passing under an arch built beneath the colonnade.

In the religious sphere, the culture of Palmyra was influenced both by the Greco-Roman Mediterranean culture as well as by Mesopotamic and Iranic civilizations, though it also had its own specific traditions. The original principal divinity of the city, worshipped in the Temple of Bel, was the god Bol (assimilated to the Phoenician divinity Bel and later to Zeus). Other main deities were the triad Nabu, Iarhibol, Aglibol; the Arab goddess Allat; and Baalshamin, master of heavens, whose origin is Canaanite. The caravan gods, Arsu and Azizu, representing the horse and camel as well as the divine stars that protected caravans, were particularly popular in the city.

In the Byzantine period a church was created within the Temple of Bel, and a few remains of Christian paintings on the internal walls are still visible. Following the Arab conquest, the church was transformed into a mosque, and a small mihrab was carved in its southern wall. The mosque remained active until the forced eviction of residents of Palmyra from the Temple of Bel compound during the French Mandate in 1929, when the temple was restored.

Sculpture in Palmyra embodied the multiplicity and syncretism of the city, showing a unique synthesis of Western and Oriental elements capable of producing a wholly original style in which the Hellenistic, Parthian, and Roman codes mingle. In the many carved funerary reliefs and statues found in the city, Oriental elements, like Parthian-style dresses, rich ornamentation, and frontal representation, coexist with more classical vocabulary.

At the end of the seventeenth century, the attention of European travelers and researchers began to "rescue" Palmyra and its ruins from oblivion. A group of Europeans tried to reach the ruins in 1678 but were turned back by a Bedouin attack. Thirteen years later, another group, English merchants based in Aleppo, reached the city and were able to describe its ruins. The diaries of this expedition, and the record they made of Greek inscriptions from the monuments, were published in 1695 and constitute the first European document known about the city.

At the beginning of the eighteenth century, Cornelius Loos, an architect, visited the ruins of Palmyra and made the first graphic survey of the site. Forty years later, in 1751, two Englishmen, Robert Wood and James Dawkins, visited Palmyra and prepared, with the support of an Italian architect, Giovanni Battista Borra, detailed drawings of its ruins, including a number of precisely surveyed stone-carving details. Their work was published in 1753 with the title *The Ruins of Palmyra.* Their book was an incredible success and had an enormous influence on architects in England and all over Europe, becoming one of the reference manuals of the century. By portraying a diverse and oriental form of classical art, which was dramatically different from the ruins of Rome that had served until then as models and rules for neoclassical architects, Wood and Dawkins' work introduced new and original features into British neoclassicism. "Palmyra ceilings," for instance, directly inspired by Wood's drawings, became a relatively common feature in late eighteenth-century English countryside mansions.

The West's fascination with the East drove many other voyagers to the Syrian Desert during the nineteenth century. Among them, the extraordinary figure of Lady Hester Stanhope, who dreamed of reviving the legend of Palmyra and the legacy of Queen Zenobia, is worth mentioning. She visited Palmyra in 1813 at the head of a large caravan, the first European woman ever to reach the desert city. In the following years, many other travelers made the trek and visited its ruins, though the area was still dangerous and unsafe because of possible Bedouin attacks.

Scholars were also attracted. The Marquis de Vogüe toured the city in 1853 and first deciphered Palmyra's inscriptions. In the twentieth century, Western scholarship continued to pay attention to the ruins of Palmyra, and the main European powers all sent scientific expeditions to the city. In 1900 the Russian Archaeological Institute of Constantinople studied the site and discovered the famous Palmyra Tariff, the longest text in the Palmyrene language found in the city. The German missions invested the site between 1902 and 1917, measuring and mapping the whole area. In the years after World War I, the site was intensively studied. And during the 1930s, the French mandatory administration undertook a large restoration operation campaign focusing on the rescue of the Temple of Bel.

The whole oasis and the ruins of the city were declared a protected archaeological park during the French Mandate, and the modern Syrian state conferred special status on the site, investing large efforts in its preservation and restoration. In 1982 Palmyra was inscribed in the United Nations Educational, Scientific, and Cultural Organization (UNESCO) World Heritage List, reaffirming its extraordinary signification for mankind's heritage.

The modern city of Tadmor was founded during the French Mandate in the early 1930s, when the villagers who lived amid the ruins of the Temple of Bel were removed by force and relocated to a new settlement nearby. Since then, the town has grown in size and population. The town plan, designed by the French Mandate administration, was organized around the Archaeological Museum and the "neoclassical" building of the City Hall. This scheme is now almost unrecognizable, as in recent years the city has grown in a rather chaotic manner and is threatening the large protected perimeter of the archaeological area. The Efqa Spring, which once flowed through the modern town, has now dried to a trickle because of modern population demands. Laborers from the new city found employment in nearby salt works.

In May 1941, British troops and soldiers from the Free French invaded Syria from Transjordan against Vichy French forces. Stopped by Vichy troops outside Damascus, a contingent performed a flanking movement and attacked and eventually occupied Tadmor from the desert, thus threatening the Vichy rear and forcing the troops to withdraw from the capital.

Today the city is the supply and logistics center for accessing the Palmyra gas reserves discovered in the area. Under control of the Syrian Petroleum Company, the national government is attempting to exploit, with foreign assistance, the Palmyra field for domestic electricity generation.

Modern Tadmor is also infamous as, in the words of one Syrian writer and inmate, "the kingdom of death and murder." The city is the location for Tadmor Prison, which houses primarily political prisoners of the Syrian regime. Built initially by the French as military barracks, Tadmor Prison was the scene in 1980 of a massacre of approximately 500 Ikwan (Muslim Brethren) prisoners. Following a botched assassination attempt on the life of President Hafiz al-Asad, his brother, Rifat al-Asad, brought his special commandos to the prison and massacred those associated with the Ikwan's rebellion against the regime. According to reports, the prison is still used to house long-term political prisoners and as a site for torture and executions.

Simone Ricca

Further Readings

Browning, Iain. *Palmyra*. London: Chatto & Windus, 1979.

Butcher, Kevin. *Roman Syria and the Near East*. London: British Museum Press, 2003.

Dirven, Lucinda. *The Palmyrenes of Dura-Europos*. Leiden: Brill, 1999.

Drijvers, H. J. W. *The Religion of Palmyra*. Leiden: Brill, 1976.

Isaac, Benjamin. *The Limits of Empire: The Roman Army in the East*. Oxford: Clarendon Press, 1993.

Pollard, Nigel. *Soldiers, Cities and Civilians in Roman Syria*. Ann Arbor: University of Michigan Press, 2000.

Richardson, Peter. *City and Sanctuary: Religion and Architecture in the Roman Near East*. London: SCM Press, 2002.

Segal, Arthur. *From Function to Monument: Urban Landscapes of Roman Palestine, Syria and Provincia Arabia*. Oxford: Oxbow Books, 1997.

Port Sudan
Population: 1 million (2005 estimate)

Port Sudan, the major port for the country of Sudan on the Red Sea, started life as a colonial city, a creation of a consortium of British Empire officials and cotton capitalists hungry for an outlet for Sudan's "white gold" to the world. Only 100 years old, the city now has all the attributes of a large industrial port as well as all the internal politics of ethnic differences, immigrant communities, and conflicts that come from urbanization and regional migration. The city is evolving toward a wider regional role as the central outlet for much of the production and imports moving through East Africa as well as continuing to serve African Muslims heading to Makkah on the hajj.

Port Sudan (Arabic, *Bandar es-Sudan* or *Shaykh Barghut*) lies on the western Red Sea coast about 35 miles north of the much older port it replaced, Sawakin. It lies about 500 miles by rail northeast of Khartoum, 700 miles south of Suez, and 170 miles southeast across the Red Sea from Jeddah. The city lies to the south of the port, which is accessible by sea through the coral reefs via a broad channel, giving way to various quays and well-developed docks on both sides of the harbor. Off of Port Sudan, the Red Sea is at its widest and also reaches its greatest depth, of 3,324 yards, with 50 yards visibility. The city's climate is very damp and hot, with temperatures reaching well above 90 degrees Fahrenheit throughout most of the year, and disease is always a possibility. Annual rainfall is minimal, around four inches. Before AD 1000, it was wetter in the area, but across the last millennium it has been drier. In the central business district, the city has the wide avenues and grid layout of a colonial city, and the major buildings reflect colonial monumental design. Behind the expanding shantytowns is an arid plain marked by little vegetation, and inland lies a line of hills that contains the city.

This area of the Red Sea coast has long been a site for water ports and harbors. The first historical references to harbors and ports in the Port Sudan area are found in Egyptian inscriptions referring to voyages to the "land of Punt"; the first of these voyages may have taken place before 2450 BC. Herodotus (fifth century BC) makes reference to pharaohs conquering ports along the Erythraean Sea (the Red Sea), and biblical references to the land of Sheba may also refer to ports of call near to the modern site of Port Sudan. The Ptolemies (305–145 BC) were the first authority to actively develop ports south of Berenike along the African littoral of the Red Sea, and some of them were used for capturing war elephants. It may be that Port Sudan is the same as Port Soteira mentioned by Strabo (ca. AD 20) and what Ptolemy (ca. AD 130) termed Port Theon Soteriron, but the link is unclear.

This coastal area of the Red Sea has long been home for the Beja nomads, who were its indigenous inhabitants. Entering the area between 4000 BC and 2500 BC, the Beja primarily spoke a Hamitic language, To Bedawie, though some came to speak Tigray because of their connections to the Tigray in the highlands. Port Sudan was built right in the middle of their territory, and in the city the Beja are the predominant ethnic grouping. In the region around Port Sudan, they make up the majority. All other ethnic groups now in the city immigrated into the area during the last 150 years. By the late 1990s, it was estimated that there were about 2 million Beja (Bujah in Arabic) in Sudan and Eritrea, with a few in southeast Egypt.

The Ottomans controlled this area of the coast beginning with the capture of Sawakin in 1517. By the nineteenth century, however, with the strong position held by the British in Aden, the growing French interest in Djibouti after the 1850s, and Egyptian expansionism into this area after the 1820s, this last remaining part of the littoral became caught up in global politics (see also "Aden," "Djibouti City," and "Berbera"). Sawakin came under direct Egyptian rule in 1865.

Of particular importance for Port Sudan's development was the transformation of Sudanese politics along the Nile and its spread into the Red Sea region with the rise of the Mahdi (divinely ordained leader) Muhammad Ahmad ibn as-Sayyid abd Allah. The Mahdist movement emerged in 1881, and by 1885 the Mahdist forces had captured Khartoum. One of the Mahdist generals, Osman Dinga, was from Sawakin, and he started in 1883 to raise the rebellion among the Beja along the Red Sea coast. His troops defeated two Egyptian columns near Tokar, 100 miles south of the future Port Sudan, and linked this region into the Mahdist state.

Sawakin came into British hands in 1879, right before they took control over Egypt. Horatio Kitchener was appointed governor in Sawakin in 1886, and by 1891 Osman Dinga was driven out of Tokar by an Anglo-Egyptian force. With the defeat of the Mahdist forces by Kitchener in 1898 at the Battle of Omdurman, the Anglo-Egyptian condominium over Sudan was established (see also "Khartoum").

During the first five years of the Anglo-Egyptian condominium in Sudan, two key forces drove the planning for the Red Sea coast: first, the need to establish security along the Red Sea shipping lanes, and second, the desire to develop agricultural production, particularly cotton, within Sudan. A key need was to expand the Sudan Military Railway to the coast. A second came from the British Cotton Growing Association (BCGA), whose goal was to promote sources of cotton within the empire. In 1903 the BCGA wrote to the Foreign Office, arguing strongly for a new port to be built along the Red Sea. The BCGA was already pushing the Gezira Scheme for irrigation and cotton growing in northeast Sudan; the construction of a new, modern port so that their cotton could

pass to the global market was "very important to them." These two factors together conspired to produce the plan for creating Port Sudan. Construction began in 1904.

The site chosen was the Mersa Shaykh Barghut, a harbor named for the saint whose tomb is prominent on the northern headland. Over the first six years, the condominium spent 1 million pounds sterling to develop the town and port. A customshouse and railroad were crucial, as were basic port facilities. Hundreds of miles of roads and thousands of miles of telegraph lines were laid throughout the Sudan during the first five years of the condominium, and much of it was part of the work to link Port Sudan to Khartoum. From 1900 to 1914, transport development accounted for 75 percent of the government's capital expenditure in the country.

In building the new port, city, and railroad, the condominium could not use slave labor: in 1899 slavery was made illegal in the country, and one of Britain's moral justifications for taking over the Sudan had been to end slavery. Yet they needed labor badly for construction and new development. As a result, they brought in unskilled labor to build Port Sudan, including workers from Yemen and the Hijaz. To run the port, they needed skilled labor, and Greek and Italian skilled labor was imported. At one point, the Foreign Office even considered importing Indian Muslims to work on the railway. Although in the end they did not, from the very beginning, Port Sudan became a "city of immigrants," since many of the laborers stayed in the Red Sea province after working on the project.

Port Sudan officially opened in 1909, and it immediately attracted considerable trade. Initially, the greatest export via the port was gum arabic. During the period of the Mahdiyya, Sudan's export of gum had been halted, but in the early 1900s it rapidly reemerged as the country's main export and was central to government revenue. Quickly, the port was also handling ivory, raw cotton, sesame, cereal sorghum, hibiscus, coffee, cooking oil, molasses, and grain. British steamers, which had been transiting the Red Sea since the 1840s, stopped at the new port. So did Italian and German steamers coming through Suez. Gradually, cotton's importance increased, and by the mid-1920s there was a major boom, and cotton surpassed gum export.

By 1935 Port Sudan was a key node in the transport system for East Africa. Trade occurred both north to Suez and south to Aden as well as east to the Hijaz and west beyond Khartoum. Oil reached all parts of East Africa via Port Sudan in the mid-1930s: bulk petroleum was moved from Port Sudan to Khartoum by railroad tankers where it was siphoned at quayside into bulk river barges and taken south to Juba from whence it was hauled by tanker lorries to northeast Congo and far southern Sudan.

Such rapid and distorted development had its costs, however. Port Sudan, with its new immigrant wage labor, became a hotbed for resistance and unrest. In August 1924, there was general labor uprising in the Sudan, sponsored by the White Flag League (WFL). When the league's leader, Ali Abd al-Latif, was arrested and sent off to prison, cadets of the military school in Port Sudan rioted. Egyptian Railway Battalion workers staged a demonstration at the railway station. Civilians, including postal and customs clerks, and military contingents continued to demonstrate when other WFL leaders were transported out of Port Sudan. The clandestine workers section of the WFL continued to organize and direct the uprising. Finally, British troops were sent in, and two warships threatened the city. By the time the countrywide demonstrations ended, Sudan had passed through a major watershed in its history, particularly because the Sudanese began to see themselves as separate from developments in Egypt and that their own history was theirs to shape.

Strikes were not unusual in the Port Sudan dockyard. Another large one occurred in 1938. By this time, the authorities were looking for villains under the bed; in particular, they saw the evil hand of Soviet communism working its way into the city via Soviet commercial links and brokers around the Red Sea. Starting in 1931, British intelligence actively sought out Communist agents in the port among the migrant labor.

By the beginning of World War II, Port Sudan was large enough and sufficiently integrated into the regional economy that it played a key role in the Red Sea theater. The city suffered more damage from Italian air raids than any other town in the region, and at one point it was attacked by an Italian submarine. The port was used as a base for minesweeping and patrol work in the Red Sea, and the two tugs that operated out of the port composed the first Sudanese navy. The Allies shipped vital petrol inland from Port Sudan, although the city was cut off at times because of events farther away toward the Bab al-Mandeb. Despite these temporary cutoffs, the city expanded its transshipment role as well as hosting many new industrial production sites to support the war effort.

Port Sudan's regional significance was again underlined with the reopening of the Suez Canal in 1975 and the dramatic events of the second oil price rise during the end of the decade. As the Saudis and Gulf Arabs began to reap the increased windfall from their oil, discussions surfaced about building an alliance between Saudi money and Sudanese land and labor. The idea of remaking Sudan into the breadbasket of the Arab world was explored, and Port Sudan was the crucial broker in the middle of this process. Cooperation across the Red Sea would bring Sudan into the modern age. In fact, huge investments were made in the city by Arab investors: new spinning and weaving factories were built in Port Sudan to process local materials and produce, peanut (ground nut) exports increased, local mining was expanded, the airport

was upgraded, oil and natural gas in the Red Sea off Port Sudan began to be exploited, and Sudan started shipping bulk sugar through the port. A new 500-mile pipeline from Port Sudan to Khartoum was built, along with a Port Sudan refinery. Even the Soviets got into the act, building a huge grain elevator in the port.

Unfortunately, much of this potential and investment was wasted. Many of these projects were not finished on time, the country's debt increased dramatically, revenues went down, poor prior planning showed itself, corruption ate away at profits, Sudanese labor was siphoned off to the Gulf, and land prices skyrocketed. Combined with the reappearance of internal conflict within Sudan, and the huge refugee and internally displaced problem, Sudan's economy went into free fall. Port Sudan continued to function, but the period from 1980 to 2000 was a difficult one for the inhabitants of the city.

Port Sudan was hit hard by the post-1974 civil war in Ethiopia. Starting in 1975, Ethiopians fled to Port Sudan to seek jobs and refuge. By 1983 more than 50,000 refugees were living in and around the city, making up to one-sixth of the population. Three-fourths of the refugees were below the age of thirty, and only half of those of school age attended school. Locals accused them of straining medical facilities, forcing up housing costs, and causing water shortages. Whatever the truth, the city's infrastructure was stretched. In response, international donors set up projects in Port Sudan. The UN High Commission for Refugees (UNHCR) came in during 1981 with $2 million of support for Eritrean refugees, the French set up three clinics, the Ford Foundation supported small-scale industrial creation, and the African Center for the Constructive Resolution of Disputes (ACCORD) sponsored microcredit projects for women working in the informal economy.

The presence of so many refugees, particularly ones related to the Beja tribal confederation, upset social and political relations within the city. For example, the Ethiopian Popular Liberation Front (EPLF) was very active within the refugee community living in Port Sudan. They established their own schools and literacy programs, worked to resolve conflicts within their own community, and created a physical rehab center for 170 men and women maimed by war.

In another example, the area around Port Sudan was used by Jewish and Israeli organizers to smuggle Ethiopian Falasha Jews out of Ethiopia. Falasha were encouraged to flee the chaos in Ethiopia following the 1974 Ethiopian Revolution and to join thousands of other Tigray and Eritrean refugees in refugee camps in eastern Sudan; from there they would be smuggled to Israel for a new life. A small-scale effort was mounted between 1979 and 1984. With the assistance of the U.S. Central Intelligence Agency (CIA), the process went into high gear in the summer of 1984. Port Sudan was one assembly and demarcation point for this mass exodus called "Operation Moses" and "Operation Sheba" by its proponents. Approximately 17,000 Falasha passed through eastern Sudan on their way to Israel by the end of operations in 1985.

The influx of refugees was not the only problem for the city. A significant regional drought between 1983 and 1985, combined with governmental neglect of the pastoral sector and rising grain prices, forced many of the Beja into famine by the deaths and forced sales of their livestock. As a result, thousands of Beja came down from the hills onto the Port Sudan–Kassala highway to beg. By 1986 international agencies were still feeding 300,000 people a day. The government repressed any suggestion of famine, terming it simply a "problem of Ethiopian and Chadian refugees."

The Port Sudan population grew dramatically during this period. In 1956 there were around 50,000 people in the city. By 1984 the city held more than 300,000 people, in 1993 perhaps 800,000. Seventy percent of today's population, whether Sudanese, migrant, or refugee, live in slum areas or shantytowns, known as *deim*, that surround the port and suburbs. In these "fourth-class residential areas," people from as far away as West Africa squat illegally on the fringe of official slums, living in packing crates and cloth shelters sometimes located on rubbish dumps. The deim lack water, electricity, proper roads, and sanitation.

Ethnic divisions within the city have been exacerbated by the lack of jobs and poor economic conditions. The top of the city's urban economy is run by northern Arabic-speaking Sudanese from the Nile. They are recent immigrants to the area following the creation of the city. The Beja compete for lower-paid jobs and self-employment; below them are the other migrant groups, like the Nuba or Beni Amer, followed by the refugees.

The majority of Nuba men in Port Sudan are daily wage laborers, with a few having skilled employment. Some Nuba women offer prostitution and illegal alcohol to get by. The Nuba have historically been persecuted in Port Sudan and have low status, yet as a community the Nuba have shown a strong and militant unity in their districts within the slums. The Beni Amer are also having difficulty, since they are seen as Eritreans and have a reputation for being cunning and treacherous.

These two groups, fighting for similar places toward the bottom of the urban ladder, battled each other within the city at different times: in 1986, for example, Nuba versus Beni Amer ethnic fighting led to the torching of whole neighborhoods and ethnic cleansing. Eight hundred houses were destroyed, and thousands were displaced.

Such ethnic-directed violence is not new in Port Sudan. Nubians were attacked in 1977–1978, Christian Eritreans were the target in 1982–1983, and there was urban rioting in 1986. Clashes and killings involving the Beni Amer occurred

again in 2003. It could be argued that the political economy of Port Sudan maintains strong ethnic divisions that can manifest themselves violently; in a mainly squatter city, such violence can be peculiarly effective. The poor have been unable to unify and direct their anger at the Arab elite and have ended up fighting among themselves.

Port Sudan was also caught up in the fighting with the Southern Peoples Liberation Army (SPLA). Starting in 1983, the SPLA went after an oil pipeline project connecting the south to Port Sudan's export terminal, which they claimed was exploiting the resources of the south. The key contractor was Chevron, a U.S. multinational. The SPLA first attacked foreign technicians. Later they attacked the Chevron camp and held British hostages for two days. In December 1983, they shot an American worker. And in February 1984, they attacked again, killing three foreigners. Chevron shut down its work on the Port Sudan pipeline. In the late 1990s, the SPLA also targeted the Port Sudan–Khartoum road and warned companies and citizens not to use the road since it was a "military operations zone."

This same road to Port Sudan is now famous as having been "improved" by Osama Bin Laden. In 1993 he was the construction engineer whose company worked to shorten the road from Khartoum to Port Sudan from about 700 to 500 miles. Bin Laden employed mujahideen who had fought with him in Afghanistan to help build the road in order, he said in an interview, to "improve the lives of the Sudanese."

In the twenty-first century, Port Sudan is hoping for improvement. Much hope is being placed in new economic development. The city certainly appears to be articulating a wider region of East Africa today: after March 2002, for example, Ethiopia consolidated almost all of its exports via Port Sudan and is linking its rail and road networks directly to the city. More and more livestock are being shipped to Saudi Arabia, cotton is still king in northeast Sudan, and the new oil terminal has increased export capacity. The pilgrimage route to Makkah continues to do brisk business, there is a new international hotel in the city, and there is talk of attracting direct air links to Europe. This might bring the scuba divers and tourists to the Red Sea. Jacques-Yves Cousteau often came to Port Sudan since he valued the pollution-free waters off the coast.

Bruce Stanley

Further Reading

Jok, Jok Madut. *War and Slavery in Sudan.* Philadelphia: University of Pennsylvania Press, 2001.

Lesch, Ann Mosley. *The Sudan: Contested National Identities.* Bloomington: Indiana University Press, 1998.

Nicall, Fergus. *The Mahdi of Sudan and the Death of General Gordon.* Stroud: Sutton, 2005.

Voll, John, Richard Lobban, Robert Krona, and Carolyn Fluehr-Lobban. *Historical Dictionary of the Sudan.* Lanham, MD: Scarecrow Press, 2002.

Q

Qom
Population: 1 million (2005 estimate)

To many Iranians, Qom is the true capital of the Islamic Republic. Mother of the Islamic Revolution, the city of blood and uprising, this alter ego to Tehran traces its heritage as a pilgrimage site back two millennia and as a challenger to political elites back almost as long. Like its Iraqi counterparts Najaf and Karbala, this Shi'i holy city has a scholarly and training role that can be traced back 1,000 years. The city hosted the rise of Ayatollah Khomeini, succored resistance to imperial powers, and raised the red flag of martyrdom. Today its power influences Lebanon and Iraq, and it touches millions of Shi'is around the world via the Web, pilgrimages, and its seminary graduates.

Qom (also *Qum* or *Qhom*) is a city in central Iran and the administrative center of Qom Province. It is located about 75 miles south of the capital city of Tehran and 158 miles north of Esfahan; it lies at the junction of all the road and rail routes linking southern Iran with Tehran. The city was built inside a natural basin some 3,084 feet above sea level and beside the Qom River, which flows from the Zagros Mountains to the west of the city. Nearby are two salt lakes into which the river drains. Winters are not very cold, but summer temperatures frequently exceed 104 degrees Fahrenheit. Rainfall is sparse and very irregular; with this semiarid climate, the region is not renowned for its agricultural production, which has depended on irrigation through traditional *qanat* (covered irrigation channel) systems.

The history of Qom is ancient but obscure and may begin around 1000 BC. An Iron Age site near Qom, Shamshirgah, may reveal additional clues to this early period. The city was known for its trade in saffron, and there is evidence that Alexander the Great destroyed what was known at the time as Kumandan (for its *kum,* or walls) during his campaigning through Persia (330 BC).

Qom has been a center for religious activity throughout its history, serving initially as the site of a Zoroastrian fire temple under the Parthians and then during the Sassanian dynasty (AD 224–641). When the Sassanian king, Kubad I (AD 488–531), restored the city to prosperity, it may have served as a regional administrative center. Even after the Muslim invasion of Persia in 643, the Qom area remained a center for Zoroastrian religious practices for at least another 200 years.

Qom became a focal point of Shi'i Islam following the deaths of Imam Ali (661) and then Imam Hussayn in 680 at the hands of their Sunni opponents. In AD 685, Arab followers of the two imams took refuge in Qom to escape Umayyad persecution. In the course of the next century, most of Qom's native population converted to the Shi'i Islam of the Arab immigrants. Subsequently, the presence in Qom of a large community of Shi'i Muslims led Fatima, the sister of Reza, the Eighth Shi'i Imam, to stop in the city on her way north; unfortunately, she became sick and died (816) and was buried in the city. Her tomb soon became a site for pilgrimage for the Shi'i, which in turn led to Qom developing as a center of Shi'i learning between the ninth and the sixteenth centuries. As such, it was a site of resistance to political authority, particularly that of the Abbasids or Sunni princes. The city was thus attacked in 825 and again a few years later after another rebellion.

Under the Shi'i Buwayhids (950–1055), Qom prospered, with theological seminaries established in the city. By the twelfth century, the first major shrine to Fatima the Pure, as she became known, was built over the saint's grave. Just toward the end of Sunni Seljuq rule, Hasan as-Sabbah was born in the city; he went on to found and lead the Ismailiyah (Assassins) movement.

Seljuq rule in central Iran gave way to various *atabeg* (local rulers) principalities and Mongol invasions; through it all, Qom maintained its sacred nature for Shi'i and for some Sunni rulers. Despite their doctrinal disagreement with the nature of the city, a number of Sunni rulers between 1300 and 1490 resided in Qom for part of each year. Temür captured the city (ca. 1381) and massacred most of its inhabitants.

In the sixteenth century, the Safavid dynasty (1501–1722) proclaimed Shi'ism the official state religion, and Qom became an object of royal patronage. Four Safavid shahs are buried in a mosque behind Fatima's shrine, known as the Hazrat-i Masumah (the Pure Saint), which was rebuilt and embellished by successive shahs, although it was then destroyed by Afghan invaders in 1722. Subsequently, its dome was plated with gold by the ruling Qajarites during the nineteenth century, and a mirrored gateway was added. Many theological colleges were endowed, and several shahs and senior Persian officials had elaborate mausoleums built next to the shrine. By 1850 the shrine to Fatima the Pure had become one of the most important Shi'i religious sites in Iran, second in pilgrimage only to the shrine in Mashhad to her brother, Imam Reza.

While Qom prospered as a pilgrimage destination, its reputation as a scholastic center and place of Shi'i learning declined in the nineteenth century. By 1900 there were few outstanding theologians teaching in Qom, and its seminaries and colleges were largely inactive, yet even then, in the declining days of the Qajar dynasty, the city was a site for political resistance and organization. One reason for the decline may have been the dramatic effect of the 1870–1871 famine on the population of the city. Without rain for two years, the city suffered from exorbitant bread prices. There were bread riots and cannibalism, and dead bodies lined the roads. The city's population dropped from 25,000 to 14,000. This was followed by the cholera epidemic of 1904, brought to the city by clerics on pilgrimage.

Qom's revival as a center for religious studies began in 1920, when the first of several prominent Shi'i theologians immigrated to the city. Many of the clergy who arrived during the early 1920s came from the important Shi'i centers in Iraq, Najaf, Kufa, and Karbala, which had fallen under British colonial rule in 1918 (see also "Najaf," "Kufa," and "Karbala"). Increasing state control over their activities and the dominance of Sunnis from Baghdad in the postcolonial administration led them to seek an environment that was more supportive of their work. As a result, hundreds of seminary students flocked to Qom to study at the new colleges. One was a young student who later became known as Ayatollah Khomeini, the leader of Iran's Islamic Revolution of the late 1970s.

The city's reemergence as a theological center coincided with the rise of the Pahlavi dynasty (1925–1979), a monarchy ruled by shahs who not only espoused an overt anticlericalism and secularism but who also, in the city's later stages, looked to the glories of Iran's pre-Islamic past for inspiration. Qom became a base for challenge to Tehran, to external influence, and to its domestic policies. The city became the site for the largest seminary in the country. Interestingly, during the 1952 crisis, the clerics in the city supported the shah rather than Mossadeqh and prayed for his return to the country; the *bazaaris* (shopkeepers) in the city went on strike for Mossadeqh. In 1963 tensions between the Iranian government and the clergy, led by an outspoken teacher in the city, Khomeini, led to major antigovernment demonstrations in Qom following his arrest; protesters shouted "Either death or Khomeini" at the Savak (internal security) commandos in the city. The ensuing brutal repression created a deep cleavage between the regime and Qom's clerics and students. Following imprisonment he was exiled (1965) and took up residence in Najaf in Iraq. It was during this time that another student, Musa as-Sadr, received his training in Qom before heading off to southern Lebanon, where he helped organize the Shi'i of Lebanon into a political and military force before his disappearance in 1978 (see also "Tyre").

Qom remained the center of opposition to the Pahlavi regime, and during the 1970s there were frequent clashes with government forces culminating in numerous riots and strikes. Sixty percent of the country's *talabehs* (theology students) were studying in Qom, and although Khomeini was in exile, many were under his influence. His taped speeches were broadcast from the loudspeakers of the mosques, leading some to call the Iranian Revolution the "cassette revolution." The turning point came in 1975, when on the twelfth anniversary of his arrest 1,000 clerical students took over the madrasa Faizieh Qum near the Shrine of Fatima, raised the red flag of Shi'i martyrdom, and broadcast Khomeini tapes. When commandos finally suppressed the takeover, a number of students had been killed and hundreds injured. The cycle of mourning ceremonies began a process that culminated in a larger massacre of students in January 1978, which served as the key spark for the final mobilization of the country against the shah. It is said that the Iranian Revolution was nursed in the schools of Qom, but the city's *bazaaris* also became involved; resistance soon spread across Iran, and in 1979 the shah was forced into exile.

Khomeini returned in triumph to Qom and established an Islamic republic. Although the capital remained in Tehran and Khomeini was obliged to settle there, Qom was seen as the spiritual heart of the revolution and of the Islamic republic. As a result, over the last twenty-five years, considerable funds have been spent on renovating its mosques, seminaries, shrines, and public buildings. New infrastructure projects have been undertaken, including the construction of a toll expressway connecting Qom and Tehran.

Qom is a city of seminaries, and a scholastic atmosphere pervades the whole city; there are more than 20,000 clerics within the holy precinct. Students usually study within a madrasa, organized around a central courtyard with a small fountain in the middle, where they often gather when they leave their second-floor classrooms, which are carpeted with Persian rugs. The students wear robes of blue, brown, or black. Often, when university students in Tehran march for more freedoms, the seminary students in Qom respond by marching for greater orthodoxy. The first theological school for women was established in Qom in 1984. The holiness of the city and its significance can still be seen in the number of corpses shipped to the city for burial in its cemeteries.

When Muhammad Khatami, a graduate of Qom's seminary, decided to run for a second term as president in 2001, a cabal of leading clerics denounced his supporters as proponents of a "cultural of liberalism" and came out in support of another of their own, Ali Fallahian, who is much more conservative. Certainly, a Qom old-boy's network pervades the country's Council of Guardians and manages the judiciary and intelligence services. To many in Iran, the majority of political power in the country resides in this city, not in Tehran. Qom may also be the capital of southern Iraq post–Saddam Hussayn: Ayatollah Ali as-Sistani, based in Najaf, is a key shaper of internal Iraqi politics. Most of his assistants and supporters are in Qom, where he lived in exile during the years of Saddam. Qom is the base for Shi'i Internet promotion; seminary students from around the world are translating all the basic Shi'i literature into twenty-seven languages and making it available online through Web sites hosted in the city. During the time of Saddam, Qom was supported by the Iranian state partly as a response to his promotion of Najaf; in the post-Saddam era, what will be the relationship between the two Shi'i holy cities of Qom and Najaf?

Qom is home to a population of great ethnic and linguistic diversity. Like other pilgrimage cities around the world and as a center of Islamic learning, there is a constant flow of immigrants to the city. From the earliest days of Islam, a significant number of Arabs were added to the original Persian inhabitants, and intermarriage over the centuries has led to a heterogeneous population mix. Other notable immigrant groups include the Khaladj, who speak an archaic Oriental Turkish and who arrived in the area between the eleventh and fourteenth century. Their names were transferred to the mountains of Khaladjistan to the east of Qom. Since the Islamic Revolution, there has been a tremendous increase in the city's population, partly because of a construction boom and because of a major expansion in enrollments at the theological colleges. Youth thus make up a huge proportion of the city's population; reportedly, the "hidden attractions of Qom" include poor women who migrate to Qom to act as temporary wives (prostitutes) for the men of the city. It is in the cemeteries of the city where such arrangements are agreed and consummated.

Because of its role as a key transportation hub for the country, Qom is a major trading center. It also hosts many types of factories. During the eighteenth and nineteenth centuries, major glassmaking factories were located here, and the region became known for its carpets. Qom is particularly famous for Ghaliche rugs, which are small rugs made of silk that are usually hung on the walls rather than used as floor coverings. There are oil and natural gas fields in the area, which are bringing in additional income, although they are not of the highest quality or size. Local products include cotton, nuts, and opium poppies, and the city is known for a sweet pastry called *sohan*. A major source of income for the city remains, nevertheless, its extensive and wealthy endowments and income brought in by students and pilgrims.

Michael Dumper

Further Readings

Daniel, Elton L. *The History of Iran.* Westport, CT: Greenwood Press, 2001.

Fischer, Michael M. J. *Iran: From Religious Dispute to Revolution.* Cambridge: Harvard University Press, 1980.

Keddie, Nikki. *Iran: Religion, Politics and Society.* London: Frank Cass, 1980.

Keddie, Nikki, ed. *Religion and Politics in Iran: Shi'ism from Quietism to Revolution.* New Haven, CT: Yale University Press, 1983.

Shaked, Shaul. *From Zoroastrian Iran to Islam: Studies in Religious History and Intercultural Contacts.* Aldershot, UK: Variorum, 1995.

R

Rabat/Sale
Population: 1,919,322 (2004 estimate)

The royal and administrative capital, Rabat, "the pearl of Morocco," overlooks the Atlantic Ocean and the mouth of the Oued Bou Regreg, where it faces the city of Sale. During the French protectorate (1912–1956), Rabat was made the country's capital. The colonial authorities, urban planners, and architects intended it to be a showcase of the protectorate and a masterpiece of planning. They were partly successful. Today, a half century after independence, the agglomeration of "the Two Banks," Rabat/Sale, Morocco's second-largest city, lies midway along an urban belt stretching from the cities of Kenitra to the industrial capital of Casablanca. It manifests most of the problems of uncontrollable massive urbanization.

In the area of contemporary Rabat/Sale (respectively, Arabic, *Ribat al-Fath;* and Arabic, *Sala;* English, *Salee*), there is evidence of much earlier habitation. The district of the Bou Regreg includes undated Neolithic remains, neo-Punic relics of a fourth-century BC Carthaginian trading post, and some ruins and inscriptions of a Roman settlement, Sala Colonia; these are on the left bank of the river on a site called Chellah (Arabic, *Shalla*), where a fourteenth-century cemetery of the Muslim Merinid dynasty remains intact, including some impressive mausoleums, on an amazingly beautiful site. The name *Sala* may derive from a Berber or Punic term for *rocks* or *precipice.* This Roman frontier town was along the *limes* (protective forts), the last outpost of Rome's North African empire. According to the historian Pliny (AD 39), this outpost bordered a desert infested by elephants.

In the late fifth century AD, Vandals destroyed the Roman town, and when the Arab conquerors arrived around 690, Sala was inhabited by Berbers, perhaps Christians, who resisted unsuccessfully the eventual establishment at the beginning of the ninth century of the Muslim Sharifan dynasty of the Alawis with its capital at Fez (see also "Fez").

The first Muslim city in the area, Sala, on the right bank of the river, was founded around 1030 by a tribe called the Banu Ashara and soon thereafter conquered by the Almoravid dynasty. The Moroccan Arab historian al-Zayyani recounts a foundation myth according to which Sala was the first city in Morocco built by the Berbers. According to the myth, a Himyarite, at the time of Alexander the Great, led the Berbers from the east. At Sala, his horse, which had stopped whinnying since entering Tunisia, suddenly emitted a loud neigh, sounding like "Sla." The Himyarite ordered the construction of a citadel where his foot had struck ground. The Berbers settled there and named it Sala.

Rabat, on the right bank and overlooking the ocean, initially rose as a citadel in 1150, a staging point for the invasion of Spain. Its Arabic name, *Ribat al-Fath,* means "citadel of the conquest." A *ribat* is a religious retreat, a kind of monastery or fortress castle, and there had probably been one on that site (where the present-day kasbah of Udaya now stands) since the eleventh century, when an alleged 100,000 *murabitun* (holy warriors) lived there along a frontier protecting Sale from the Barghwata, an indigenous Berber dynasty.

In 1195, when the Almohad sultan Yaqub al-Mansur left to invade Spain, he ordered the construction of an enormous city ringed by monumental walls extending to the river and ocean, almost four miles in length and enclosing an area of more than 1,000 acres. The city was completed in 1197 and included most of what was to become the old and new cities of Rabat. After the victories in Spain, al-Mansur added magnificent buildings, a bridge to Sale, and the Hassan Mosque, which was intended as the largest mosque of western Islam with 302 marble columns, ninety-four stone pillars, and a massive square minaret. Begun, but never completed, the minaret still towers today over Rabat/Sale. The sultan, on his deathbed in 1199, is said to have confessed that he regretted building Rabat, because it was a waste of the public treasury. In any case, within fifty years of his death, the royal city had decayed and virtually disappeared except for its magnificent walls and minaret until its refoundation 350 years later in the seventeenth century by immigrants from Spain.

In the seventeenth century, the Atlantic had replaced the Mediterranean as the main center of global trade routes and of conflict. The activity of piracy on the high seas boomed, and Rabat attracted both Muslims expelled from Spain and naval warriors from Algiers and Tripoli. The final edict of expulsion from Spain in 1609 brought large numbers of immigrants to Morocco. Some of these Moriscos and Marranos, Muslims and Jews, respectively, who remained in Spain after the Reconquista and continued to secretly practice their religions reached Rabat. They arrived in two waves: firstly, Hornacheros (from the inland town of Hornachos), who joined the sultan's army and were quartered in the kasbah of Udaya where they soon established an independent corsair "republic," and secondly, from throughout Spain, poor Andalusians, who settled in the madinah of Rabat, the Arab town, and who soon established a city-state, another corsair "republic" alongside that of the Hornacheros. Their combined population was around 6,000, and the whole area was called Sala Jadida (New Sale). An additional internal rampart was built within the walls laid down by al-Mansur. The Andalusians' urban plan, a grid pattern, consisted of four main streets running north and south and two major arteries, east and west. The decorative arts in construction were those brought from Spain, and so were many aspects of the way of life—clothing, food, music. The population included renegades, adventurers, and bandits, among others.

Corsair activity had to do with trade and privateering; it was a livelihood and a way of life. Between 1618 and 1626, ships operating out of the Bou Regreg captured 6,000 prisoners and goods worth 15 million pounds sterling. In 1661 the sultan of the Alawite dynasty reestablished the authority of the *makhzan,* the Moroccan state, over the three republics of the Bou Regreg (including Sale) and ended their piracy on the seas by making it a state enterprise. Thereafter, Rabat became one of the four royal capitals of the sultanate, a regular stopover for the court, and for tax collectors, on the annual itinerary between Fez and Marrakesh (see also "Marrakesh"). The kasbah of Udaya housed a garrison of loyal troops, two palaces were built, and Rabat became an "imperial" city. The location was increasingly strategic as the mountainous regions between the other capitals became unsafe. However, the end of piracy and the beginning of European hegemony were to usher in gradual colonization.

On the eve of the plague that struck Morocco in 1799, Rabat and Sale had a combined population of 25,000–30,000. Rbatis and Slawis, inhabitants of Rabat and Sale, respectively, were considered as possessors of *hadara,* of urban culture and refinement. The two cities' Jewish communities, integrated and economically important, had been moved out of the madinah proper into *mellahs,* separate Jewish quarters. By 1830 and the beginning of the French conquests of North Africa, international trade, and the scramble for colonies, Morocco's incorporation into the world economic system had been set in motion on the way to its final reduction to the status of a French colony. By the end of the nineteenth century, Rabat had become the country's third-largest urban agglomeration and industrial center after Fez and Marrakesh.

De facto colonization had occurred by the beginning of the twentieth century. In 1908 Rabat's population was 20,000–25,000. A French traveler described it as "the pearl of Morocco." Sale had about 10,000 inhabitants and was something of a jewel itself.

The form of Rabat resembled a trapezoid, a compact quasi-geometric shape lacking suburbs or dependencies other than palace and military outposts and accessibility by small boats across the river to Sale. The built-up area covered some 222 acres; its interior and exterior walls remained impressive. Gates, external and internal between the quarters, were closed at night and taxes collected on goods entering

and leaving the city. The city was policed and had an autonomous and thriving marketplace. Suwaiqa (the little market) traversed the main commercial quarter with its regular sequence of specialized markets. There were half a dozen major mosques, thirty-two secondary ones; twenty-six Qur'anic schools, shrines, and religious orders; and places for the care of the sick and accommodations for travelers. Beyond the walls, some gardens, and orange groves, the land was unsettled, almost a tabula rasa.

By March 1912, when the protectorate was officially declared by the Treaty of Fez, France already controlled the central core of the country—Rabat, Sale, Meknes, Fez, and Casablanca. The process of "pacification" was to continue from 1907 to 1921. Marechal Lyautey, the first resident general (1912–1925), disembarked at Casablanca on 13 May 1912, went directly to Fez to meet with the sultan, and intended to make Fez the capital of the protectorate. A year later, however, because of a lack of submissiveness in Fez, the French decided on a coastal location to prevent encirclement, and Rabat became Morocco's capital (see also "Casablanca").

Lyautey had a vision. He wanted to "conserve," "rescue," and "restore foundations." He had a policy of urban development, and it was elaborated by one of France's most illustrious planners, Henri Prost, who worked with the marechal from 1913 until 1923 and then again with other residents general from 1931 until 1951. Their policy of urban development had three principles: (1) minimal alteration to indigenous quarters, which were to be preserved and protected; (2) creation of a cordon sanitaire around "native reservations" by a greenbelt of open land; and (3) design and construction of a model modern city. The same master plan was to be applied to the *villes nouvelles,* new (European) towns in Rabat, Marrakesh, Fez, Settat, and Meknes (see also "Meknes").

In fact, it proved impossible to construct a cordon sanitaire in Rabat because foreigners already had moved in and bought land just beyond the city walls. Otherwise, the plan was followed, often making use of an elaborate system of laws and regulations, for example, to convert vast public domains into private freehold. The result was that Rabat became two coexisting but not interpenetrating cities based on the "natural" segregation of economies and cultures and buttressed by laws. Janet Abu-Lughod called it "a system of cultural and religious apartheid" that was justified in moral and practical terms. For E. Levi-Provencal, French Rabat in 1936 was "a masterpiece, famed throughout the world, of successful town planning and architecture."

Lyautey and Prost did nonetheless succeed in establishing a zone of *nonedificandi,* of forbidden construction, 820 feet in width just outside the walls of the madinah of Rabat. It is today the major boulevard meant to separate the madinah and the European city. From the Tibin Gate of the madinah, a wide ceremonial street extends to the as-Sunnah cathedral mosque and the gate leading to the palace complex. Just to the east of the palace and on the opposite side of the ceremonial road and on the heights stood La Residence, the administrative zone of the French protectorate then and the place of the independent Moroccan government offices today.

The ville nouvelle, the European city of Rabat, rose on the land between the interior and exterior ramparts and to the south. It encircled and strangled the madinah, which had no space in which to expand. In the long term, the growing Moroccan population, which increased tenfold during the first decades of the protectorate, had to settle in bidonvilles on the outskirts of the ville nouvelle. The sale to individuals of expropriated domainal and *habus* (pious endowments; *waqfs* in the Arab East) lands for "public purposes" paid for the infrastructure of roads, lighting, water, and drains in the ville nouvelle.

By 1946 urbanism had turned sour: the port was moribund, with industry virtually nonexistent with the exceptions of brick making and food conservation; the bidonvilles had expanded to include one-third of the Moroccan Muslim population. Rabat had become a city of administration, goods and services, largely privileged Europeans, and mostly proletarianized Moroccans. In the period from 1912 to 1951, the population of Rabat/Sale increased from 40,000 to more than 200,000. Three-quarters lived in Rabat. They included about 42,000 Europeans, 10,000 Jews, and 100,000 Muslims. Most of the phenomenal increase in the Moroccan population took place as a result of immigration from the hinterlands. The urban density of the madinah and bidonvilles grew alarmingly. A rigid and self-perpetuating system of class stratification and almost complete physical separation along ethnic lines had taken root.

Meanwhile, Sale had lost much of its specificity and become incorporated into the colonial system: as a subsidiary dormitory, the "backyard" of Rabat. Its population almost doubled in the decade of 1951–1961. Large-scale subsidized housing to reabsorb the bidonvilles of the two cities had begun, but it never has caught up with population growth.

Morocco gained its independence in May 1956. The sultan, Muhammad V, returned from his imposed exile, a result of a nationalist struggle that had begun in the 1930s. Rabat became the official capital, the site of the royal palace, the parliament, the administration, the military, and foreign embassies. The economic capital of the country, Casablanca, lay fifty miles to the south. With independence came a massive emigration of foreigners, and in the process of decolonization the extremes of social and physical space separations were mitigated. Aside from the sometimes significant distinction between Arabs and Berbers, Morocco was 99 percent religiously homogenous.

Demographic growth and urbanization did not perceptively slow down. In 1971 Rabat/Sale had a population of 523,000, half of them immigrants: in Rabat 367,000, an increase of 62 percent since 1952; in Sale 156,000, an increase of 105 percent over the same two decades. The agglomeration was now Morocco's second-largest city after Casablanca with its 1.5 million inhabitants. Forty percent of the population was in government employment. Half of the remainder lived from petty trade and menial services. The rest were unemployed or quasi employed. The city lacked a generative economic base other than tourism and artisanship.

Urban problems did not abate: land shortage, inflation, and a lack of basic utility lines were endemic. The cost-of-living increase in Rabat between 1973 and 1975 at 31 percent was the highest in Morocco. In 1975 the estimated population of Rabat/Sale had grown to 750,000, and today, thirty years later, it hovers around 2 million. The transformation of bidonvilles into housing projects is at best piecemeal, partial, and informal. Some new and impressive middle-class housing has taken place: Yaqub al-Mansur and Hayy Riyad in Rabat, Hayy Salam and Sala Jadida in Sale. Four to five times as much land is now occupied as in 1970. Sites once considered peripheral and without value are now in the middle of the expanding and projected metropolis. Rabat/Sale is an enormous building site, construction a race against time.

Despite the numbers, density, and poverty, Rabat and Sale still seem provincial; the center of the ville nouvelle, apart from the encroaching madinah at some points, seems unchanged from forty years ago. The airport is small and modest. There are traffic jams at noon because so many people still go home for lunch with the family and a ritual siesta. What is visually new and apparent is the growing presence of women in public and their economic activity.

With all that and the widening gap between a small elite and an expanding number of the urban poor, Rabat remains one of the loveliest cities of the Arab world, its site magnificent and extraordinary. The views of the ocean, the Oued Bou Regreg, and the two opposing historical cities can be breathtaking. It has charm and extensive green plantings and parks, spacious modern quarters, and an involuted, ungentrified, though seeping out at the edges madinah with pockets of real beauty. The air is clean, the climate agreeable, the summer ocean breezes refreshing, the palette of colors pleasing to the eye.

Kenneth Brown

Further Readings

Abu-Lughod, Janet. *Rabat: Urban Apartheid in Morocco.* Princeton: Princeton University Press, 1980.

Brown, Kenneth. *People of Sale: Tradition and Change in a Moroccan City (1830–1930).* Manchester and Cambridge: Universities of Manchester and Harvard, 1976.

Ennaji, Mohamed. *Serving the Master: Slavery and Society in Nineteenth Century Morocco.* New York: St. Martin's, 1999.

Ramallah/al-Bireh
Population: 57,000 (both cities, 2004 estimate)

Ramallah/al-Bireh, a conurbation of two cities ten miles north of Jerusalem, is best known as the temporary capital of the Palestinian Authority and the gravesite of the Palestinian president Yasir Arafat. However, its roots lie across 5,000 years as a crossroads for travelers heading east down to Jericho and for pilgrims heading south to Jerusalem. It is also the ancestral home for a large and vocal Palestinian community in the United States, known as "the Bride of Palestine" because of its garden restaurants and springs, and the media and education heart of the Palestinian nation.

The conurbation of Ramallah/al-Bireh lies along the central Palestinian mountain spine, ten miles north of Jerusalem and around thirty-five miles inland from the Mediterranean coast. It is a crossroads, with the major north-south mountain road from Lebanon to Egypt running through it and an east-west road rising up from Jaffa passing through the town, then descending to the east to the oasis city of Jericho. Nestled among the mountains, it lies in a watershed area, with many towns and villages scattered in its hinterland. The climate is moderate, with an annual rainfall similar to that of Frankfort or London. Ramallah/al-Bireh sits 3,000 feet above sea level, making it cool in summer and not too cold in winter. The towns receive snow; historically, there have been white Christmases and some white Easters. Most snow lasts no more than three days. The Palestinian mountains are predominantly limestone, and so the valleys around the city have many springs. Some parts of the city are named for the spring in that area: Ein Munjid or Ein Misbah, for example. Bireh (*bir* means "well") has water on its flat plateau, and a good climate has meant that there have long been settlements in the area across thousands of years. It was possible to grow both trees and field crops around the city. The Bible talks about grapes, figs, and olives from this area; in the fields, there were wheat, lentils, tomatoes, cucumbers, and zucchini. The crops are Mediterranean (garlic) but also temperate crops as well (cherries, pears, apples, and plums).

It appears that the earliest settlement was probably about 5,000 to 6,000 years ago. Given that the site is only a half day on foot from ancient Jericho, it is logical that the site housed very early settlements. Archaeological investigations at Tell an-Nasbeh, to the south of Ramallah, show a Canaanite town from around 3000 BC. Slightly north, the current site may have been called, in Canaanite, *Ram* (high place) or *Beit* (altar) of *El* (God). It appears that the first concentration was in Tell an-Nasbeh, with smaller patterns of settlement scattered away near walled fields. In the immediate vicinity of Ramallah/al-Bireh, British archaeological surveys indicated as many as ten Canaanite settled areas.

From the earliest times, traders, shepherds, and warriors moved through the area passing to the north or south. Many languages, peoples, and their gods traveled this road: Canaanite, Babylonian, Egyptian, Aramaic, and Assyrian. Abraham was the most famous, stopping at Beit El, the Bible reports, to set up an altar and to sacrifice to El. If Abraham were a historical figure, he would have been similar to other nomadic patriarchs, moving across the Ramallah/el-Bireh area, interacting with the local Canaanite villagers, and eventually moving south toward Hebron sometime in the early second millennium BC. The city's importance as a cult sanctuary is retained in the current name, Ramallah, with the ancient Canaanite/Aramaic word *Ram* linked with the Arabic word for God, *Allah,* thus creating a city name that is half ancient, half Arabic.

Excavations by al-Quds University archaeologists have uncovered remnants of a two-story Roman tower in the city, and other excavations have shown remains of a Roman/Byzantine church. The remains are not appropriate for a village but rather for a town; both must be interpreted to mean that there was a substantial settlement on the site during the Roman/Byzantine occupation of Palestine (64 BC–AD 636).

The conquest of Palestine by the Muslim forces of the caliph Umar (634 – 644) occurred in AD 636, and the records mention Ramallah. Because of the significance of Jerusalem in Muslim beliefs, Ramallah/al-Bireh experienced a resurgence, particularly under the Umayyads, as indicated by the increasing number of remains and finds identified throughout the city. Al-Bireh, for example, has a khan for travelers along the road. Thus, the cycles appear to have been Canaanite settlement; a Roman site, with perhaps more than 1,000 inhabitants; and, during the Islamic period, a similar number of inhabitants.

Over the next 1,300 years, as politics and security allowed, Ramallah/al-Bireh was a famous stop on the pilgrim trail for both Muslim and Christian pilgrims. Travelers would often spend the last night of their journey to Jerusalem in Ramallah and then move south in the early dawn to see the Holy City lit by the first rays of the sun. For millions of pilgrims across the centuries, the expectation generated by a final pause in Ramallah/al-Bireh before heading to Jerusalem was the highlight of their journey of faith. Today the experience can often be the same for those arriving for the first time via the Lod Airport and driving over the Ramallah/al-Bireh crest, or coming up from the Jordan River Bridge, as they strive to catch that first glimpse of al-Quds.

The Crusaders captured Ramallah/al-Bireh when they took Jerusalem in 1099, and they established Frankish settlements in the area. There are remains of a Crusader church, and the written records mention both cities as sites for settlement. The Crusaders appeared to have loved the town; it was close to Jerusalem but also a good production site for things to sell in Jerusalem, and the weather was more pleasant than in the capital.

By early Ottoman times (1516–1918), Ramallah is mentioned as a village in conurbation with two others: al-Bireh and Beit Unia. These records always mention the town as a mixed city, housing both Christians and Muslims. The Ottoman archives also record sixteenth-century Ramallah as a prosperous agricultural town, sitting at the core of other villages that depended on it and its connections to Jerusalem.

The oral traditions of the founding of Ramallah appear to relate to this period around the sixteenth century. The story is told of a clan of five Christian Arab brothers from east of the Jordan fleeing from Karak and founding Ramallah *de nuvo*. The tradition goes on to say that their good Muslim friends joined them and founded al-Bireh. Ramallah families are proud of their ancestry back to one of the five brothers. The truth may more likely be that there had always been Christian communities here, even before the Crusaders, and that the East Bank immigrants settled among the local Christians.

There were no known battles in the immediate vicinity of Ramallah/al-Bireh, but the town was clearly always viewed by military leaders as defensively significant to Jerusalem. It was one of the first places occupied or where defenses were established; thus, its security or war history has always been directly connected with that of the Holy City.

Both because of its role as a crossroads and its agricultural productivity, Ramallah/al-Bireh became a feeder city for Jerusalem. This was true for agricultural products, which would be taken to the markets of Jerusalem, and for manufacturing. People from the city were always going to Jerusalem for work and returning home when they could. The city became the hub of a collection of eighty-eight villages and towns that fed into Ramallah/al-Bireh for markets and travel connections, making it a key regional center in its own right.

Soon after the Ottoman takeover, it appears as if Ramallah/al-Bireh began developing as an educational center as well, a role that has grown and expanded until today the city is the educational capital of the Palestinian community. It seems as if there were elementary schools connected with the Greek Orthodox Church as far back as the sixteenth century. Records exist indicating that teachers were paid money in 1706 to teach Arabic and Greek to students. In the mid-1800s, however, a great burst of educational activity began that put Ramallah/al-Bireh on the educational map.

Ramallah's rapidly expanding urban fabric. (Ricki Rosen/Corbis)

After 1834, during the rule of the Egyptian prince Ibrahim Pasha, Palestine was opened to European interests, including religious ones. As a result, there was a huge influx of Western church representatives and missionaries into the area, resulting in the development of schools and hospitals. Ramallah/al-Bireh was attractive thanks to its tradition of Greek Orthodox schools, its mixed Christian and Muslim community, its relative prosperity, its closeness to Jerusalem, and a relative tolerance toward outsiders and new ideas. Ramallah/al-Bireh Christians were already in touch with family members who had begun to immigrate abroad, and these networks facilitated a range of contacts and flows of ideas that marked Ramallah/al-Bireh as different.

In 1848 the first missionary school was opened, closely followed in 1858 by one established by the Latins. In 1869 Eli Jones, of the American Quakers, came to the area and began setting up a number of Friends schools. One reason the Quakers chose Ramallah/al-Bireh was their concern to empower local village girls so they could acquire jobs working for elite families in Jerusalem. By 1889 the Friends Girls School had been established, followed by the Friends Boys School in 1901. In 1875 the Protestants established a school for boys, and in 1891 the Lutheran German Girls School was created.

The combination of early immigration, educational opportunities, English-language training, and networks to Europe and America together meant that more and more Ramallah/al-Bireh graduates began to look globally for economic opportunities. By the end of the nineteenth century, the first Ramallah/al-Bireh communities were established in the United States; Palestinian Quakers ended up in Havertown, Pennsylvania, for example, thanks to the Quaker connection, and formed the first "Ramallah Club." Aziz Shaheen traveled to America in the early 1900s and was one of the city's first immigrants to make a million dollars. Like many others after him, he brought that money back to Ramallah/al-Bireh, where much of it was donated to the further development of schools and universities.

By the beginning of the twentieth century, the city had the reputation as the place to go for advanced education (high school education being the top rung available within the country at the time). Many of these students came from all over Palestine (and gradually the Gulf) as boarding students, living in Ramallah/al-Bireh and adding their diversity to the city's mix. The nearby village of Birzeit got its own high school, and the students from the Lutherans' and the Friends' schools mixed in Ramallah's streets. Muslims, Christians, and Jews attended the schools as boarders (the last Jewish students left with the Arab Revolt in 1936). Close friendships across confessional boundaries tied many of the graduates together into alumni networks that provided support and jobs in Detroit, Los Angeles, Houston, and the Gulf long after the students had moved on. Often they moved on to the American University of Beirut (AUB), and Ramallah/al-Bireh has always had a close link to Beirut, to AUB, and to the intellectual life and politics of Beirut as a result. The graduates of the city's schools became leading educators, politicians, and business elites throughout Palestine and in their adopted countries. Farhat Ziadi, for example, was a professor of Arabic at Princeton and helped lay the foundation for the study of Arabic in the United States.

The ripple effects of this educational hothouse role continue until today. In the 1960s, the Birzeit high school evolved into a two-year diploma college and finally into Birzeit University in 1970, the first university in Palestine. The Friends' schools still provide innovative education to Palestinian students, many heading abroad for further training. The openness of the city, a reputation it still has today, means that it is attractive to young people, students, and intellectuals pursuing new ideas and global contacts and more open lifestyles.

By the beginning of the twentieth century, Ramallah/al-Bireh had a few thousand inhabitants, and by 1912 there were 5,000. The Ottomans finally began to take an interest in developing the economic and governance potential of their Palestinian towns, and so in 1902 Ramallah was designated a municipality. The road from Jerusalem to Ramallah/al-Bireh had been upgraded in the late 1800s but not the road north to Nablus. Finally, in 1903 the governor of Jerusalem sacrificed a sheep to open the new road north from al-Bireh to Nablus.

Unfortunately, the new road system made it easier for invaders to move quickly through the country as well. With the outbreak of World War I, the British and their new Arab allies began attacking Ottoman Palestine, and General Allenby captured Jerusalem in 1917 (see also "Jerusalem"). The Friends Boy's school in Ramallah was commandeered by the Turks as a hospital during the fighting. Residents of Ramallah/al-Bireh recalled the sight of retreating Turkish soldiers streaming north through the city trying desperately to make it to Nablus to regroup.

The establishment of the British Mandate in Palestine (1920–1948) brought significant development and prosperity to Ramallah/al-Bireh. The mandatory bureaucracy in Jerusalem required trained bilingual staff; Ramallah/al-Bireh graduates were readily available and capable. Diplomats, military personnel, and government bureaucrats looking for leisure spots to spend their money gravitated to the garden restaurants and open atmosphere of the city. As the number of immigrants abroad increased, their remittances flowed back into the families of the city, and spending on land and education increased; new villas were built on the outskirts, and the old, cramped small houses of the city center were abandoned. Industry increased, and agricultural production expanded. Waves of immigrant workers, particularly from Hebron, came during the 1920s and 1930s to work for the mandate or to work for the expanding production; these immigrants moved into abandoned houses in the center, where many of their descendants still live today (see also "Hebron").

The boomtown feel of Ramallah/al-Bireh during the mandate attracted the nascent media of the country and spurred cultural development as well. One of the earliest Palestinian newspapers, *The Mirror,* was established in the city in 1919. Ramallah was chosen as the site for the Palestine Broadcasting Service. The British built a radio-broadcasting tower taller than the Eiffel Tower to broadcast to all of Palestine. Radio Street today is one of the most vibrant and quickly developing areas of the city, home to ministries, nongovernmental organizations (NGOs), a range of private Palestinian media, and new banks.

Ramallah/al-Bireh played a role in the growing struggle with the Zionist community in Palestine during the mandate. Key citizens of the city sought to promote the Palestinian cause globally, drawing on their training and experience: Fuad Shatara, in the early 1900s, was in New York City and served as president of the Palestine Anti-Zionism Society. He sent a letter to Lord Balfour asking him to listen to the Palestinian case against Zionism. Shatara went on to become the president of the Arab League. Khalil Totah, an early Palestinian Quaker educator, moved to the United States in 1944 to become director of the Institute of Arab American Affairs, which sought to inform Americans about the situation in Palestine. It was during this time that the city was designated a security site by the British, who built one of their infamous Tagget Buildings in Ramallah as a security prison and military headquarters.

During World War II, Ramallah/al-Bireh experienced the war primarily through the blackouts imposed by the British on the city but also through its many Ramallah/al-Bireh immigrants to America who served in the U.S. military.

A key turning point for the city was the war of 1947–1948 between the Palestinians and the Zionists and the resulting political developments of the *al-Nakba* (the disaster) as it unfolded on into the 1950s. After the United Nations (UN) decision for partition (November 1947), refugees began to pour into the city, particularly after the fall of Lydda and Ramleh during April 1948; many children lost their lives during the exodus up into the Ramallah/al-Bireh hills. The Jordanian Arab Legion took over Ramallah/al-Bireh soon after 15 May 1948; their presence helped block the Israeli plan to capture Ramallah, and they also worked to prevent an exodus of scared civilians from the city.

The city benefited from the Palestinian refugees who came to the city in 1948. With the loss of Haifa and Jaffa, Ramallah/al-Bireh became one of the largest cities in what remained of Palestine. Refugees camped out in four areas that later became the refugee camps al-Jelazon, Kalandia, al-Amari, and Kadoura, which today together house around 30,000 refugees. The fundamental social fabric of the city changed as a result and evolved from being a small town to having regional and international connections, including new eating habits and less traditional social relations.

In response to the tragedy, the middle-class women of Ramallah/al-Bireh sought ways to help the new arrivals. New civil society institutions were formed to help the refugees. For example, Inaash al-Usra, founded by Um-Khalil, provided training and cultural and microenterprise support for women. Embroidery cooperatives to help the refugee women to make and sell traditional Palestinian cross-stitch embroidery flourished. Ramallah/al-Bireh was famous for its traditional red on black or white embroidery (every Palestinian town or village had different styles or colors of such embroidery that often marked the women's dresses). The Ramallah/al-Bireh Cooperative provided thread and fabric to the refugee women and then sold the product (pillowcases, dresses, tablecloths, runners) to, usually, international visitors. This traditional Ramallah/al-Bireh embroidery gradually became known internationally—through the work of these and other cooperatives—as typically Palestinian and to evolve new nationalistic forms beyond the traditional stitch patterns of flowers, cypress, or birds into representations of the Palestinian flag, maps of Palestine, or other patterns with nationalistic meaning. In another form of support for the refugees, the UN Relief and Welfare Agency (UNRWA) set up both men and women's teacher training colleges (now four-year colleges) in the city. All this voluntary activity helped mark the city out as a key site for civil society organizing and social action.

During most of the twentieth century, the Ramallah side remained a primarily Christian town. In 1945 the city held 5,000 people, mainly Christians. By 1961, after the refugee influx, there were more than 16,000. In the central square, or al-Manarah, there was a fountain surrounded by five lions, perhaps memorializing the five brothers who founded the city. Under the Jordanians, the city, called "the Bride of Palestine," became a summer resort, attracting the wealthy from Kuwait, the Gulf, and Jordan to its lovely hotels and garden restaurants. There were many Western foreigners as well, including diplomats, NGO staff, and education volunteers. The Jordanians also used the Muqataa (Ramallah Prison, the former Tagget building) to house security detainees and as a military headquarters.

Immigration continued through most of the twentieth century. By 1946, 15,000 of the original 6,000 residents of Ramallah had left to the United States, and this expanded the exposure of the Ramallah Club from Detroit to Los Angeles; the al-Bireh Association experienced a similar development. Today the Ramallah/al-Bireh community is one of the largest and most active individual Arab communities in the United States.

Israeli troops captured Ramallah/al-Bireh on 7 June 1967. The clock on the tower in the middle of town remained for years locked at 10:15, the time the first soldiers appeared. Over the next thirty-nine years, Ramallah/al-Bireh has remained a key center for significant resistance to the occupation. Early on, the Ramallah and al-Bireh mayors secretly facilitated Arafat's attempt to establish an underground resistance movement during July and August 1967.Israeli security services discovered Arafat was hiding out in Ramallah, however, and surrounded the house where he was hiding. The noise created by his landlady resisting the soldiers alerted him, and he escaped that night across the Jordan River. Later, the Israelis deported many of the leading intellectual and political leaders of Ramallah/al-Bireh. Both Nadim Zaru, the Ramallah mayor, and Abu Jawad Saleh, the mayor of al-Bireh, for example, were deported to Amman. The deputy mayor of al-Bireh was deported in 1973. The city was also used as a large prison; in 1982 three editors of East Jerusalem papers were placed under town arrest in Ramallah, unable to get to their offices and manage their newspapers. The Muqataa and the Ramallah Police Station became infamous as sites for torture and mistreatment. In 1980 a car bomb placed by Israelis cost the Ramallah mayor, Karim Khalif, a key spokesman for Palestinian political rights, his right leg.

Birzeit University, which the Israelis called the "intellectual center of Palestinian nationalism," was closed for months at a time, and students were beaten and imprisoned, faculty deported, books confiscated, and buildings trashed. Underground classes would continue, however, meeting around the city in basements, churches, and mosques. The Communist Party had long had a strong branch in Ramallah; in the wake of the occupation, the city became a center for secular leftist resistance groups like the Popular Front for the Liberation of Palestine (PFLP) and the Democratic Front for the Liberation of Palestine (DFLP). Ramallah/al-Bireh women were very important to the struggle for self-determination; through political activism and via the development of a vibrant NGO movement, Ramallah/al-Bireh women made the city a key center for women's rights, social change, and national resistance.

Ghassan Kanafani's short novel, *Return to Haifa,* written in 1969, has refugees from 1948 who had lived those twenty years in Ramallah going back to Haifa to see their old home. In the end of the novel, they return to their lives in Ramallah, distressed about how little the broader Arab world really understood the Palestinian struggle.

The occupation also changed the landscape around the city. To the north, the Israelis confiscated hundreds of acres to build the settlement of Beit El, which became an administrative and security headquarters for the occupation. West of the city, new settlements were established, cutting off villages from their fields and from Ramallah/al-Bireh. The issue of water has always been very important for the city, which was known for its good water. With the occupation, the city lost control over its water supply. Israel sunk a deep well near the city's key water supply, Ain Samiya, and used that water for

supplying settlements; the city thus became dependent on Israel for its water needs.

Ramallah/al-Bireh crucially changed with the Oslo Agreement. Before 1992, at its heart, the conurbation was just two linked towns; afterward, it changed in size, in function within the community, and in the mix of its population and density. With the first Israeli withdrawal from the city proper in 1995, Ramallah/al-Bireh became the center for the Palestinian Authority (PA) in the West Bank, housing the offices of the Legislative Council, the executive branch, security forces, ministries, and the Central Statistical Bureau. This has also meant the appearance of embassies, like the new $1 million Chinese Embassy, and many delegations. The Muqataa became the headquarters of the president of the PA and the place where the Israelis confined President Arafat for the last few years of his life. He died in November 2004, and it now houses his temporary tomb.

After 1993 many Palestinian Americans began to return, to bring money back, and to consider investing or taking up residence again for good. As the political process ran into trouble after 1996, this return movement tended to dry up, with Ramallah/al-Bireh citizens continuing to immigrate to the United States, Canada, and Australia. Rural migration from throughout Palestine to the city continues, however, and the city is now attracting educated Israeli Palestinians as well. Many young couples move to the city to find work and to experience a more open lifestyle.

With all this immigration, money, and new responsibility, the built environment is shifting daily. Ramallah/al-Bireh is now the financial center of Palestine, housing the central offices of the Arab Bank, the Jordan Bank, the Cairo-Amman Bank, the Palestine Bank, and seven others. Major reinsurance headquarters are here, as are two of the three main Palestinian newspapers (*al-Ayyam* and *al-Hayat al-Jarideh*). Housing projects and cooperatives, hotel projects, and high-rise offices dot the skyline; new restaurants (from Chinese and Italian to traditional grills), clubs, bars, and dance clubs have all made Ramallah/al-Bireh into a vibrant city with a high percentage of young people studying and working. Ramallah grew up the hill along the main roads in the direction of al-Bireh, bringing the two towns together into a single seamless conurbation. The city is the media capital of the country, hosting TV studios, Web radio stations, and broadcast channels. The Greater Ramallah/al-Bireh metropolitan area now includes Beit Unia and is home to more than 140,000 people. The links to Jericho in terms of business development, agricultural production, and financial flows make these two cities closely tied.

The city is alive culturally as well, hosting Palestinian artists, a new state-of-the-art cultural center, cinemas, theaters, and art galleries. The Ramallah/al-Bireh International Film Festival, backed by al-Jazeera and the British Council, is putting the city on the international events map. Restoration of the old "grand villas" with their unique architecture and beautiful tile work has attracted international architectural attention.

Israeli forces have returned to the city a number of times since 1995, attempting to control the unrest and mobilization that emanates from a city transformed into a large prison by closures, settlements, checkpoints, the Separation Wall, and travel restrictions. Much of the natural hinterland of the city remains cut off and under Israeli control, stifling the city's development; a number of the older industries in the city have died (Silvana Chocolates and Tako Tissues, for example) to be replaced by service industries and businesses not bound in the same way by physical boundaries and constant closures.

Kamal Abdul Fattah

Further Readings

Amiri, Suad. *Sharon and My Mother-in-Law: Ramallah Diaries.* London: Granta Books, 2005.

Barghouti, Mourid. *I Saw Ramallah.* London: Bloomsbury, 2004.

Hass, Amira. *Reporting from Ramallah.* Brooklyn: Autonomedia, 2003.

Pringle, Denys. *Fortification and Settlement in Crusader Palestine.* Aldershot, UK: Ashgate, 2000.

Shaheen, Azeez. *Ramallah: Its History and Its Genealogies.* Birzeit, Palestine: Birzeit University, 1982.

Riyadh
Population: 4.2 million (2006 estimate)

Riyadh is now a large, modern capital city, but until 200 years ago it was just a small and little-noticed desert oasis town. The harsh conditions of the Najd region in which Riyadh is located made it unattractive to conquerors, and although the oasis was on trade caravan routes, contact with the outside world was relatively limited. An alliance between the founder of the conservative Wahhabist sect of Islam and the as-Saud tribe in the mid-1700s eventually brought the town to prominence as the seat of the as-Sauds, and it was declared the capital of Saudi Arabia in the first part of the twentieth century. The subsequent advent of oil wealth has allowed the Saudi government to transform what was a walled mud-brick town at the start of the twentieth century into a modern city with the infrastructure to support its more than 4 million inhabitants.

Riyadh (Arabic, *ar-Riyadh*) is one of the oasis centers of the Najd area in the center of the Arabian Peninsula in what is now Saudi Arabia. The regular supply of water there meant that from the earliest times, the area was populated, with date palms providing one of the mainstays of diet. Although oil wealth and desalination have extended considerably the limits of the city, the surrounding countryside remains a harsh mixture of sandy desert and mountains. The name may derive from the Arabic *rawdah,* meaning a place of gardens and trees.

The modern city is thought to be on the site of a collection of ancient towns known as Yamamah. The Banu Hanifah tribe settled the Yamamah area in pre-Islamic times, with the largest town in the region called Hajar. Yamamah was the site of a fierce battle after the advent of Islam, pitching the Banu Hanifah against Abu Bakr's troops. During the battle, a large number of Abu Bakr's troops who had memorized the Qur'an were killed, an event that, according to some accounts, led Abu Bakr to consent to the writing down of the Qur'an.

Historical mentions of the region are nevertheless brief, and the harsh conditions and long distances meant that the Najd was not subjected to control for great lengths of time by outside conquerors. Indeed, much of the population of the Najd region were *bedu* (seminomadic herders), adding a further difficulty for outsiders who might have had ambitions to conquer the region.

There was, however, some contact with the outside. As an oasis with some settled population, the area that is now Riyadh was along some trade caravan routes. Trade caravans linked the area with places as distant as Baghdad and Makkah, and through time locals traded with the Arabs in the towns along the Gulf coast in al-Hasa. In addition, settled oasis areas in the Najd region had extensive contact with local bedu tribes.

Relative to Makkah and Madinah and to coastal cities such as Jeddah, however, Riyadh, called at that time Muqrin, was a small backwater that attracted little attention. That situation changed somewhat in the late 1700s and early 1800s as Najdis, led by Muhammad ibn Saud, sought to spread their influence. The as-Saud tribe hailed from the small town of ad-Diriyah near Riyadh, and in 1744 that family had linked up with Muhummad ibn Abdul Wahhab, the founder of the conservative Wahhabist sect of Islam that still dominates present-day Saudi Arabia. The pact between the two led to military efforts to spread the tenets of Wahhabism.

By the late eighteenth century, the as-Sauds had captured Riyadh and established control over a substantial portion of the Najd. By the early nineteenth century, their forces had raided the shrine of Imam Hussayn in Karbala in Iraq, and they subsequently destroyed what they considered un-Islamic monuments in Makkah and Madinah (see also "Karbala," "Makkah," and "Madinah").

Ottoman rulers were, unsurprisingly, concerned about the growth of as-Saud influence, which covered many areas that were at least under their nominal control. Ibrahim Pasha led a force into Arabia that, by 1818, managed to capture ad-Diriyah and Riyadh. The leader of the as-Saud was taken captive and sent to Constantinople, where he was executed. By the mid-1820s, however, the as-Saud had regrouped sufficiently to recapture Riyadh from the Ottomans. Ad-Diriyah had been sacked in the earlier Ottoman military action, and the as-Saud consequently named Riyadh their capital.

Although the Ottomans continued to exert some influence over the area for years to come, the real threat to as-Saud leadership in Riyadh over the next several decades was family infighting. Despite the (sometimes murderous) squabbling, the as-Saud managed to maintain its hold over Riyadh, and in the latter part of the nineteenth century the family was based in that town. In 1891, however, the leader in Riyadh, Abd ar-Rahman as-Saud, was forced to flee the city with his family as a rival tribe, the as-Rashids, took over.

The ar-Rashid hegemony was, however, short-lived. In 1902 Abdul Aziz as-Saud (also known as Ibn Saud), the founder of modern-day Saudi Arabia, captured the city. The tale of that conquest is now legendary. With only about forty "companions," Ibn Saud waited one morning until the Rashidi governor and his contingent of bodyguards left Qasr al-Masmak (Masmak Fort) in the center of the city. They sought unsuccessfully to capture him outside the fort, and as the governor escaped into the compound, Ibn Saud's forces followed, capturing Masmak and the city. A spearhead from that fight remained in the historic door of the fort for years after the city's capture. Ibn Saud subsequently used Riyadh as a staging point for his further military efforts to conquer the rest of what is now Saudi Arabia.

Accounts of Riyadh at the turn of the century suggest that the city was surrounded by a high earthen wall that had nine gates through which all visitors and residents had to traverse. The women's market was hidden behind a row of butcher's shops, and slaves played an important role in the city's economy and in the royal household. By modern standards, it was a small outpost; the population in the early years of the twentieth century was estimated at about 8,000.

Foreign visitors to the city were few in those days. Among those who did make the journey was the British political agent for Kuwait, Captain William Shakespear, who visited Riyadh in 1914. Captain Shakespear was an enthusiastic amateur photographer, and he took a number of photographs during his stay. Those snapshots are among the earliest of the city, and many are now on display at al-Turath, a Riyadh-based cultural institution.

In 1932 the city was named capital of Saudi Arabia, and the conqueror of the state, now King Abdul Aziz, ordered construction of the Murabba Palace, which acted as his official residence. Riyadh's population at the time was estimated at about 30,000. The increase in numbers since the turn of the century probably reflected a number of factors, including the enhanced role of the city in the affairs of the country and the need for proximity to the king to benefit from the largess that he distributed.

The king's resources were significantly increased as oil income started to flow into the kingdom after World War II. Substantial investment consequently went into development of the infrastructure of Riyadh. By the mid-1950s, the old walls of the city and most of the old mud-brick buildings had been knocked down to make way for modern buildings. The increased resources, both in the city's infrastructure and more generally in better health care, meant that the city continued to grow in population, with the population reaching an estimated 169,000 in 1962 and 650,000 in 1974.

Despite Riyadh's status as capital of the country, for years many government activities remained in the more cosmopolitan and commercially oriented Red Sea city of Jeddah. Under King Abdul Aziz's successor, his son King Saud, most government ministries made the move to Riyadh in the mid-1950s. The exception was the foreign ministry, which remained in Jeddah with most foreign embassies. In 1975, however, the Saudi government decided that the foreign ministry and foreign diplomatic missions should move to Riyadh and embarked on the development of a new diplomatic quarter. As infrastructure and buildings there were completed, many foreign missions moved into the quarter in the 1980s, making Riyadh the seat of the country's foreign relations.

By that time, the population of the city had grown to about 2 million, and it has continued to expand, with the government estimating the total at about 6 million by 2007. The size of the city has also increased to about 600 square miles. The tremendous growth in population (over 8 percent per year during the late 1990s) has been enabled by the use of desalinated water, which is piped to the city from Jubail on the Gulf.

Very little of the old city remains, but the government has made some effort to preserve and rebuild some of the major sites of the early twentieth century. Qasr al-Hokm, which served as the headquarters for Ibn Saud after he conquered Riyadh, has been rebuilt on its original site. In addition, some efforts have been made to preserve the Masmak fort, which is now used as a museum in the King Abdul Aziz historical complex. Also in the complex are the Iman Turki bin Abdullah Mosque, which has been rebuilt, and the Murabba Palace, King Abdul Aziz's residence in the 1930s, which has been restored. The Thumairi gate, one of the original nine gates into the city, has also been restored, although the growth of Riyadh means that it is now in the town center.

As capital of modern-day Saudi Arabia, Riyadh has reasonable domestic and international transportation links. In addition to an extensive road network, a railway connects Riyadh to Ad-Dammam in the Eastern Province, and the government has recently hired consultants to advise on an expansion of that network to Jeddah. Air links are also to the standard expected of a modern capital; the King Khaled International Airport (the world's largest in square miles), which is served by more than two dozen airlines, handled more than 9 million passengers in 2003. The city has also sought to establish its credentials as a cultural center for the Middle East, and in 2000 it was named the United Nations

Educational, Scientific, and Cultural Organization (UNESCO) Arab Cultural Capital. Among the preeminent cultural institutions in the city is the King Faisal Center for Research and Islamic Studies, the branch of the King Faisal Foundation charged with working to preserve Islamic culture.

As the capital of the country, Riyadh's economy is dependent on the government sector. Figures from the Riyadh Development Authority, which is responsible for planning within the capital area, suggest that about 40 percent of jobs in the city are with the government sector. Although many of these jobs are in ministries at the national level, there are also a number of levels of bureaucracy responsible for governing Riyadh itself. In addition to the Riyadh Development Author-

ity, the capital falls under powers of both the Riyadh Municipality and a regional governor. This dependence on the state is a far cry from Najd of a century ago, where independence and self-sufficiency were keys to survival.

Angie Turner

Further Readings

Facey, William. *Riyadh: The Old City.* London: Immel, 1992.

Helms, Christine Moss. *The Cohesion of Saudi Arabia.* London: Croom Helm, 1981.

Peterson, J. E. *Historical Dictionary of Saudi Arabia.* London: Scarecrow Press, 1993.

Philby, J. B. *Arabia of the Wahabis.* London: Constable, 1928.

Rasheed, Madawi al-. *A History of Saudi Arabia.* Cambridge: Cambridge University Press, 2003.

S

Salalah
Population: 160,000 (2005 estimate)

From supplying frankincense for the temples in Rome to being the only port between Singapore and Western Europe that can handle the largest class of container ships, Salalah certainly has a long but restrained history in between. Oman's second-largest city, but clearly different in style and climate from Muscat, as the capital of Dhofar Province, Salalah faces the Arabian Sea and perhaps an autonomous future much like it has for the last 2,000 years.

Set in the southern province of Dhofar, the town of Salalah presents a striking contrast to the rest of Oman. The town is naturally green and lush, with coconut palms and banana trees found in local gardens and along the roadside in abundance. The city owes much of its uniqueness to position—the Dhofar region just manages to catch the tail end of the Indian Ocean monsoon each year, giving the area an entirely different climate than the rest of the country. The monsoon, which is locally known as the Khareef, brings rain for about three months starting in June, and a low cloud cover descends over the area. One of the results is that, while Muscat swelters with temperatures in excess of 100 degrees Fahrenheit in the summer, Salalah's average maximums are generally around 85 degrees Fahrenheit.

Geography also plays a role in Salalah's uniqueness. The city is located on a narrow coastal plain, part of a strip that runs for about 30 miles. Just about 9 miles inland, the plains meet the Qara Mountains, a strip of limestone mountains that contain numerous caves, including Tawi Atayr sinkhole, one of the largest in the world. Beyond the mountain is a high plateau area that eventually gives way to the Empty Quarter. Salalah lies more than 620 miles southwest from the Omani capital Muscat, and its relative isolation has meant that the city developed separately from the rest of Oman. Different tribes dominate the area, many of which are bound by family connections to the Hadramawt in what is now Yemen. In addition, Salalah inhabitants have traditionally adhered to Sunni Islam, in contrast to Omanis living up the coast in Muscat and inland in the Jabal Akdar region, where Ibahdism played a greater role. In trade terms, Salalah has long been connected with India and eastern Africa; its dhows still carry local cargo to Zanzibar and Somalia (see also "Zanzibar").

One early source of wealth in Salalah was frankincense, dried gum resin from the tree of the same name. Unique to the area around Salalah, for more than 2,000 years the resin captured a high price and is perhaps best known in the West as one of the gifts given by the three wise men to Jesus at birth. More generally, however, overland exports of the incense reached other Arabs in Gaza, Iraq, and Egypt, while sea trade meant that Dhofari frankincense was available in far-away Asian ports. Egyptian and Roman demand for temple use kept the workers in far-off Dhofar busy year-round; Pliny the Elder and Ptolemy both knew exactly where frankincense came from. Frankincense trees are still an important feature of the landscape in the Dhofar, but the market for this incense has diminished over the centuries and now plays only a minor role in the economy of the region.

There are few written records or archaeological indications to tell us of the city's ancient history. Numerous archaeological sites are continually being discovered, and recent investigations suggest that there were larger towns along the ancient "Frankincense Trail" than were expected. However, there was little sedentary habitation prior to the Islamic era. It is known that Salalah was largely independent until 1829, when Said bin Sultan, the Omani ruler, moved to take control of the city. But it took, because of resistance from the locals, a second expedition from Muscat in 1879 to establish firmly Omani jurisdiction over Salalah and the surrounding area, and even then the city remained relatively isolated from the rest of the country. That isolation made it attractive in the twentieth century as a retreat from the political pressures in Muscat, and Said bin Taimur, the father of the current sultan, lived there during the last dozen years before he was deposed in 1970. Holed up in al-Hisr (the fortress), Said communicated with his officials via radio and whiled away the hours with his harem under the watchful eye of slaves and eunuchs. In many ways, the sultan treated the area (termed the "dependency of Dhofar") as a personal fiefdom, leading to local frustration with his leadership. There were no hospitals or clinics, no schools, and no right to travel or to build houses for the inhabitants of the city.

Disenchantment with Sultan Said's rule eventually led to revolt in the Dhofar. By the late 1960s, rebels backed by the Communist-inspired People's Democratic Republic of Yemen (PDRY, the former South Yemen) were finding increased success in their attacks against government forces and had tried to assassinate the sultan while he was reviewing his troops. In 1970, when Sultan Qaboos took over, a full-scale civil war was raging in the south, and Salalah had occasionally come under siege and mortar fire. The old sultan imposed strict repression on Salalah's population, including encircling the city with barbed wire and propping up enemy corpses in the corner of the suq as a lesson to the community. Eventually, however, Omani troops, aided by British, Iranian, and Jordanian forces, put down the Popular Front for the Liberation of Oman (PFLO), with the last shots of the war fired in 1975.

Government efforts did not focus exclusively on a military victory. The new sultan also sought to win the loyalty of southerners through a hearts-and-minds campaign, and these efforts continued after the war. Qaboos has worked to incorporate southerners into his administration, and considerable money has been spent on developing the city and surrounding area. Unlike any city other than Muscat, Salalah is home to the full complement of government departments. The Omani navy has a base in Mina Salalah (Port Salalah).

Agriculture, fishing, and livestock husbandry continue to be important parts of the area's economy, but investment in major infrastructure in recent years aims to shift the focus to more industrial enterprises. In the late 1990s, the Omani government decided to build a container port in the city with the hope of creating large transshipment trade through the area. The port, now one of the top-twenty transshipment ports in the world, has four operating berths and the latest cargo handling equipment, making it a regional competitor to Dubai and Aden (see also "Dubai" and "Aden"). The private sector partners in the venture are now pushing for expansion, stressing Salalah's strategic location close to the sea-lanes and its clean security record.

In addition, a free-trade zone is in the works, along with new world-class hotels and telecommunication technology. Industrial parks, using natural gas imported via the regional Dolphin Project, are planned, and international lenders are willingly granting money for local projects. Efforts are also being made to develop tourism in the town, which is the center of the annual Khareef Festival during the summer months. Picturesque dhow traffic has remained in the port, and new promotion schemes such as "Archaeological Caravans" have helped increase tourism 10 percent each year over the last decade.

As with other parts of Oman and the Arabian Peninsula, improvements in health care in recent years have led to increased population. The population of Salalah now stands at about 160,000, with about two-thirds of that total being Omani nationals. The figures make Salalah the largest city by far in the Dhofar and the single largest urban area outside of the Muscat governorate. There are indications of worker unrest: Indian workers protested in the late 1990s about their misuse and lack of wages.

Angie Turner

Further Readings
Landen, Robert Geran. *Oman since 1856.* Princeton: Princeton University Press, 1967.
Morris, James. *Sultan in Oman.* London: Faber and Faber, 1957.
Peterson, J. E. *Oman in the Twentieth Century.* London: Croom Helm, 1978.
Townsend, John. *Oman.* London: Croom Helm, 1977.
Zarins, Juris. *The Land of Incense.* Muscat: Sultan Qaboos University, 2001.

Samarkand
Population: 366,000 (2004 estimate)

Samarkand is one of the most famous oasis cities of central Asia, just across the mountains from Iran and on the edge of the Turkic steppes. It is also close to the western cities of China and the northwestern cities of the subcontinent. As a result, it has long been one of the edge cities of the Middle East, reflecting Middle Eastern culture and religion outward and introducing new cultures, technology, and ideas into the region. An important prize for numerous conquerors across the centuries, it is most famous as the capital of Temür and the Timurid Empire of the fifteenth century. Today it is the second city of Uzbekistan and a key United Nations Educational, Scientific, and Cultural Organization (UNESCO) World Heritage Site with its numerous monuments and the uniquely beautiful Registan.

Samarkand (Sogdinian, *Maracanda*) is located on the banks of the Zarafshan (Sravšan) River in a long valley or basin, nestled up under the high Zarafshan Mountains. Throughout its history, the city has been surrounded by numerous irrigation ditches, dams, and waterways, making its hinterland very fertile and verdant, although the region is extremely arid. Today the city is still the center of a huge agricultural production zone.

The city lies at the intersection of five great cultural zones: Russian, Turkic, Chinese, Persian, and Indian. All have mixed together in Samarkand over the centuries to create what Edgar Allen Poe called the "queen of the earth" and the ancient Arabs the "Eden of the East." Crucial valleys lead up and over the mountains at this point: to the southwest lies the low passes out onto the plains around Bishkent or the road west to Bukhara. Northeast lies the passes across to Tashkent and the Fergana Valley. The ancient six gates of the city led to all points of the compass; in particular, the city was one of the key nodes on the ancient Silk Road to and from China, and it was also critically situated for the "fur" route north to the Urals and the southeast road to India.

Up until the Arab conquest, the region of which Samarkand is the urban center had a number of names, depending on whose cultural influences are being emphasized. The Persians knew the area as Sogda or Sogdiana. Located between the Amudarya and the Syrdarya rivers, Sogdiana was first recorded in the archives of the Achaemenid dynasty of Persia. Archaeological excavations, however, indicate that settlement around the fertile oasis at Samarkand may go back to the second millennium BC. Along the whole "foothill zone," caught between the mountains to the south and the Kara Kum Desert and steppes to the north, there are oases and areas where irrigation can support human settlement. The first cities appear in the Zarafshan valley around 1800 BC, and a distinct oasis culture, linked with Mesopotamia, Egypt, northern India, and China, emerges. From the beginning, these oasis cities, linked into a regional city system, were caught up in the world system of the time, depending on long-distance trade to provide political stability and the continuity of wealth.

Soviet archaeologists argued that Samarkand itself was founded in 530 BC. Current archaeological finds are questioning, however, this traditional view that urban settlement and civilization in this area on the edge of the Middle East did not emerge until the Early Iron Age. Little archaeological investigation has been done around Samarkand, and it is only now, in the post-Soviet era, that international funding and teams are beginning to illuminate the Bronze Age in this area of central Asia.

When Cyrus the Great conquered the Sogdiana region from the Medes after 550 BC, he captured its thriving, well-established key city Maracanda (Samarkand). It is recorded that Darius (522–486 BC) made the city the capital of the Sogdiana satrapy and that Samarkand supplied lapis lazuli and carnelian for the construction of the palace at Susa. Under the Achaemenid dynasty (559–330 BC) the city was walled, with a central fortress, seven and one-half miles of fortifications, and an irrigation infrastructure creating an agricultural hinterland far beyond the walls. The city was part of the "King's Way," linking Babylon through Nishapur to Samarkand and beyond to China.

Sogdiana was eastern Iranian in culture and language, and the Zoroastrian religion was founded among the oasis cities of the region in the middle of the first millennium BC. The key text of the religion, the *Avesta*, mentions Sogda as the "second of the good lands and countries" created by the one god, Ahura Mazda.

We know little about Maracanda in the intervening years until Alexander the Great captured it in 329 BC following a fierce battle on the outskirts of the city. Although Alexander's army destroyed most of the city, Maracanda became his base for operations in the area beyond the Oxus (Amudayra) River; hence, it became known in western geography as Transoxaina. The chronicles record that Alexander, after drinking heavily one night in the palace at Maracanda, accidentally killed his own commander in chief, Clitus. Alexander is not remembered fondly in the Zoroastrian community: he is cursed for destroying one of the only remaining copies of the full and ancient *Avesta* by throwing it into the river at Samarkand.

In the turmoil after Alexander's death, Maracanda was incorporated into the territory of the Seleucid Empire, and the region, including northern Afghanistan, became known as Bactria. The Hellenization of the region progressed, but the fame and significance of the Sogdian peoples were not subsumed. It appears, for example, that the Sogdians were great traders and entrepreneurs and that various versions of their language became the lingua franca of the Eastern trade routes during the period from 400 BC until AD 700. There is an argument that the Sogdians were the crucial cultural formers of the region through their trade and linguistic dominance and their far-flung outposts and entrepôts. Sogdians had trade representatives throughout the Chinese domains, although they referred back to "headquarters" in Maracanda. The Sogdian language was based on Aramaic but written vertically. By the second century BC, Samarkand was the key city in central Asia—powerful in its own right though under distant rule—and a central node in a far-flung trading system.

One reason for the central role of the Sogdians was the new openings to the East. It was under Emperor Wu-ti (141–87 BC) of the Han dynasty that the Silk Road was created in his search for trade to the west. The Sogdians already controlled the routes to Persia and Anatolia, so they now had a new opportunity to be brokers in an expanded long-distance trade network. The Chinese expanded westward into Xinjiang Province in 103 BC, and this stabilized the access and security across the Pamir Mountains. In return, the Sogdians set up delegations in cities throughout China. It is interesting to note that the Chinese were also seeking the "heavenly horses" of central Asia: Samarkand participated in the long-distance trade in horses as well as silk for the next 800 years.

Greek dominance in the region did not last, and Bactria was overrun by nomadic groups from what is now western China. The emergent power was the Kushans (50 BC–AD 250), a Turkic people who adopted an Iranian language written with the Greek alphabet and who believed in Buddhism. We do not know if they conquered Samarkand, but their influence throughout Sogdiana was felt primarily in cultural forms.

The Sassanians conquered the region around AD 260, and Samarkand became a regional center for them, hosting a royal governor. It was during their rule that the city became a key site for Manichaeism, and it is from Samarkand that the religion spread further into central Asia. Nomadic invaders, the Hephtalites (White Huns, AD 400–550), controlled Samarkand for the next 150 years before they were replaced by a western Turkic tribal group, the Qaghan, who defeated the Hephtalites in an alliance with the Persians. The Qaghan (AD 550–650) ruled Samarkand until defeated by the Chinese under the Tang dynasty. The Tang created a protectorate, received tribute from Samarkand, and made it a regional administrative post but did little to protect the city from the expanding Arab armies of the Umayyads, who finally captured Samarkand around AD 710.

By this time, the older core of the city had become known as Afràsiàb, and archaeological remains from the tell suggest a high degree of artistic creativity and splendor. Murals from this period depict the full range of cultural influences mixing in the city, and they stress the three virtues at the core of Samarkand's regional role: wisdom, riches, and bravery.

This ebb and flow of the Persian, the nomadic, and the Chinese influences are a hallmark of the Samarkand narrative. Throughout it all, the Sogdiana identity, centralized around the influence of Samarkand, continued, and they remained key players in the wider world articulated by long-distance trade. Sogdian language kept the Silk Road functioning from a base in the Chinese capital Changan, all the way to Constantinople, where a delegation visited in AD 568 to discuss trade. They had colonies in the Crimea, left inscriptions to guide travelers into northern Pakistan, and took gifts to Bangkok for the Buddha, and there are indications that they had representatives in Sri Lanka and Canton. Communities of Sogdians integrated into Chinese society, produced excellent silver and gold luxury goods, and were often put in charge of textile manufacturing for export or of the production of decorative tiles. Sogdians may have introduced new types of fruits and vegetables to China, their music and dance was influential at court, and their writing forms and words crept into the Chinese, Mongol, and even Korean and Japanese languages. Samarkand was a key site for the minting of coinage: the archaeological record from Moscow to China confirms this significance.

In the period from AD 200 to AD 712, Samarkand was a diverse religious community as well as key hub in the trade routes between Byzantium, the Middle East, and China. Every kind of religion had a home in the city, including Buddhism, Zoroastrianism, Manichaeism, Judaism, and the Nestorian Christians. Around AD 650, a Buddhist monk, Hsuan-tsang, visited Sa-mo-kien, as he called it, commenting on its tolerant and vibrant pluralistic community. He also says the people loved their wine and food, often dancing in the streets. Reports suggest that the entrepreneurial nature of the city was so strong that young men were expected to go out into the world to seek their fortune along the Silk Road. Samarkand was the seat of a metropolitan see for the Nestorians by this time and had a reputation as a key gateway city for Nestorian missionaries from Iraq taking the Silk Road into China.

Thus, when the Arab Muslims arrived in 710, they found a high urban culture, well connected into the far reaches of the Eurasian landmass, and skilled in trade, production, and entrepreneurship. The city flourished within a hinterland of agricultural production, including cotton, watered by an advanced irrigation system. With the Arab conquest, the network of trade routes that emanated from Samarkand became included within the broader Muslim Empire. The "border" with the steppe moved to the north along the Syrdarya River, and Islam began to find a foothold in the city. After 751, with the rise of the Abbasid Empire with its Persian composition, Samarkand benefited from a new solidarity and universalistic ethic that connected it to cities as far afield as Rabat and Tangiers.

One of the first and most significant products the Arabs discovered in the city was paper, which was produced in Samarkand to a high quality. From here its use spread throughout the Muslim world. Products of Samarkand began to appear throughout the empire, and the fame of its cotton and muslin fabrics heightened demand. Contemporary reports note the following exports from the city: silver-colored fabrics, large copper vessels, artistic goblets, tents, stirrups, bridle heads and straps, satin, red fabrics known as *mumarjal,* silks, hazelnuts, and horses.

Samarkand became a place of pilgrimage for Muslims early after the conquest. Out of many holy sites around the city, two are exemplary. The shrine of Qassam ibn Abbas, a cousin of the Prophet Muhammad and reportedly instrumental in introducing Islam to Transoxiana, is located in the city. Another is the shrine for the Islamic saint Muhammad ibn Ismail al-Bukhari. Known for compiling the most authoritative Hadith (600,000 sayings of the Prophet Muhammad), al-Bukhari's grave, as does that of Ibn Abbas, continues to draw believers from throughout the region.

Fairly quickly, direct Abbasid control from Baghdad dissipated, to be replaced by local autonomous dynasties nominally under the caliphate. The Iranian Samanids (AD 862–999) came to power along the Zarafshan River, and Samarkand became even more significant as a key link along numerous trade routes. In particular, it is during this period that trade with European Russia and the Volga intensified. One indication is that the majority of all Muslim coins discovered in Russia are from the Samanid period, most probably minted at Samarkand. The silver was certainly mined in the Zarafshan valley.

The Samanids were overthrown around AD 1000 by their Turkish mercenaries. The tenth century had witnessed a significant new migration into the region of Turkic tribes that was to progressively change the composition and dynamic of the Middle East. Over the next 200 years, Samarkand came under the control of a succession of Turkish dynasties, including the Seljuqs and the Khwarizm-Shahs. Their rule was a distant one, and the city was able to dominate a city system of other cities in the Zarafshan basin. During this time, the city, perhaps home to more than 500,000 people, was seen as the chief Muslim city in central Asia, famous for its scholarship and dramatic architecture. A visitor who recorded his impressions of the city was Benjamin of Tudela, who proposed a figure of 50,000 for the Jewish community in AD 1170.

It was in AD 1220, however, that Genghis Khan took the city as the Mongols marched across the world. The city was a headquarters for resistance and so was savagely destroyed after its capture and most of its population massacred and its artisans exiled to Mongolia. Even by ca. AD 1270, when Marco Polo reports he saw the city, Samarkand had not recovered. Long-distance trade shifted away from Samarkand to the south, partly because of the rise of factional conflict within the Mongol elite after the death of Genghis Khan.

The city's fortunes revived, however, with the rise of the infamous Temür (AD 1336–1405). Born fifty miles south of Samarkand, Temür-I-Leng (the iron one who limps) was a prince of a small Turko-Mongolian tribe within the broader Chagatai confederation that controlled Transoxiana. By 1369 he had overcome all rivals to the control of the Chagatai, dedicated himself to restoring the Mongol Empire, and established his capital at Samarkand. Through ruthless campaigning, war, and mountains of skulls, by 1399 his empire reached from Moscow to Delhi and included Persia and the Caucasus. In 1401 Temür took Damascus and Aleppo and then captured Baghdad. He deported all the artisans from these cities back to Samarkand, where they worked at a fevered pitch to complete his monumental constructions throughout the city. After capturing Anatolia in 1402, he next set his sights on the Ming dynasty in China. He left his capital toward the east with a huge army in December 1404, but he did not get far, dying 250 miles from home in early 1405. His embalmed body was sent back to the city in an ebony coffin, and he was buried in his family mausoleum.

The Samarkand of 1405 was the pride of the Muslim world. Its major monuments remain, even today striking testament to the skills of the imported artisans from throughout the Muslim world and to the drive of Temür and his successors to construct edifices of symbolic power and beauty. Within its five-mile-long walls, the core of the city was the Registan, a huge public square surrounded on three sides by religious complexes of mosques, khans, and madrasas. Built at different times by members of the Timurid dynasty between 1370 and 1500, these beautiful buildings "held up the sky" with their huge portals, twin minarets, thousands of blue tiles, and carved marble. Emblazoned on one building is the Arab proverb, "If you want to understand us, examine our monuments." In 1888 Lord Curzon called the Registan "the noblest public square in the world . . . no European spectacle indeed can adequately be compared with it."

The beauty, magnificence, and cultural significance of Samarkand at the height of Temür's rule is recorded by a Western visitor, Ruy Gonzalez de Clavijo, who came to Temür's court as a diplomat from Spain in 1402. He speaks in his memoirs of the technological sophistication of the city, palaces of four stories, the large and diverse bazaar, and its numerous fountains. He comments as well on Temür's drive to complete buildings in the shortest possible time,

One portal to the great Registan Square in the heart of Samarkand. (Corel Corporation)

using both the threat of death and his own presence on-site to inspire the builders. At one point, as de Clavijo noted, the conqueror called an assembly of the tribes. In response, within a few days 20,000 yurts quickly appeared on the outskirts of Samarkand, expanding the city by at least 200,000 people.

What de Clavijo does not note is the interlinkage of architectural themes and borrowing that flowed from the Muslim community's connections to Samarkand and from Temür's policy of bringing artisans from the conquered cities to his capital.

For example, the beautiful turquoise dome of the Gur Amir, Temür's mausoleum, was based by its Damascene architects on the dome of the Umayyad mosque in Damascus that Temür had burned; these Samarkand domes went on to inspire the onion domes of orthodox Moscow's Kremlin and, through Shah Jahan, Temür's descendant, the Taj Mahal. The motifs in the tiles throughout the city show a dramatic mixture of Chinese and Persian influences and are considered some of the finest decoration in Asia.

Temür's tomb in the Gur Amir continues themes stressed during his life: his cenotaph is the largest slab of green jade in the world; his tombstone is inscribed with the saying, "When I rise from the dead, the whole world will tremble"; and the tomb lists his (fictitious) genealogy linking him both directly to Genghis Khan and to Ali, the son-in-law of Muhammad.

Under Temür's grandson, Ulugh Beg (AD 1394–1449), Samarkand was the center of an intellectual community and of artistic productivity unrivaled in the Middle East. The city housed one of the most important Islamic universities of the time. Ulugh Beg, known as a scholar, poet, astronomer, and mathematician in his own right, taught at the university, and he founded one of the most important celestial observatories in the world. Using his huge marble sextant and other innovative instruments, Ulugh Beg and his staff, over the period from AD 1408 to AD 1437, regularly took star observations in a scientific manner, routinely evaluated the results, and published their data, thereby making Samarkand the astronomical capital of the world in the early fifteenth century.

The Timurid dynasty was overthrown in 1500 by Turkic Uzbek invaders. Samarkand continued, however, as a key trading city, connected to the east with the powerful Ming dynasty. Ming archives record merchant caravans, customs fees, and tribute from Samarkand arriving consistently throughout the fifteenth and sixteenth centuries. During this period, however, the city slips in significance and is buffeted by political decisions made elsewhere. Chinese, Mughal Indian, and Persian power competed for the city, with the city passing from one ruler and local coalition to another. Out of these transitional Uzbek tribal alliances, three political entities, or khanates, emerged in the region by the mid-1700s: Bukhara, Khiva, and Kokand. Samarkand was controlled by Bukhara (see also "Bukhara").

The Khanate of Bukhara was deeply involved in global trade during this time, and Samarkand benefited as well. Hindu bankers and merchants served as the driving force for this trade, working their networks with other Indian communities as far afield as Esfahan, Tabriz, Astrakhan, Moscow, Multan, Lahore, and the Deccan (see also "Esfahan" and "Tabriz"). The city was very pluralistic, containing a range of quarters for different communities: Christian, Jewish, Hindus, Afghans, and Gypsies.

Samarkand participated in a number of trading circuits that were important to its wealth. One was horses: thousands of horses were shipped through the city to India from the 1400s until the late 1700s. Another was slaves. From the time of the Timurids, Indian slaves had been important to the agricultural plantations around Samarkand, and the city functioned on the back of thousands of slaves in homes and the market. By the 1700s, they were Iranian slaves. When Samarkand was annexed by Russia, there were 10,000 slaves in the city, indicating the role they played in the economic and cultural history of the city.

A third important export was fruit and nuts. The fresh- and dried-fruit and nut trade contributed to Samarkand's positive trade balance for more than 300 years. Fruit from the agricultural plantations around the city was shipped by camel caravan to the Mughal wealthy of the Punjab. Samarkand melons, apples, pears, almonds, pistachios, and grapes ended up on breakfast plates in Multan. Caravans of fruit from Samarkand regularly went as far south as the Deccan well into the 1800s. Akbar, the Mughal emperor, tried to cut this trade by resettling fruit growers from Samarkand in the Punjab, but the trees did not prosper, and the attempt failed.

By the early 1800s, Russia was on the borders of the Bukharan Khanate and showed aggressive designs on the territory. Many of the religious and military leaders of the Bukharan Khanate wanted to fight the threat from Russia. The amir was finally forced by this hawkish elite to proclaim a holy war of defense (March 1868), and he marshaled his forces at Samarkand. In response, the Russian army, looking for an excuse, moved into Bukharan territory. The key battle took place outside the walls of Samarkand, where the Russians were victorious and captured the city on 2 May 1868. As part of the peace agreement, Samarkand was ceded to Russia, while the rest of the khanate became a protectorate, although it retained a degree of autonomy until 1917.

The Russians quickly made changes to the ancient city. They linked Samarkand to the railroad networks in 1896, and it became an agricultural export city, shipping a range of products including wine, cotton, fruit, rice, and tobacco into the Russian Empire. It also became a site for the manufacturing of leather, shoes, silk, and clothing. The Russians tore down the old city walls and began construction of new areas of the city.

Following the success of the Red Army in the area, Samarkand was briefly the capital of the Uzbek Soviet Socialist Republic (AD 1924–1930), after which the capital was moved to Tashkent. During the Soviet era (1924–1991), Samarkand remained the center for a regional agricultural production district and for small industry serving the Soviet economy. It was known for tea, textiles, fertilizer, tractor and vehicle parts, and, interestingly, cinema apparatus. The city hosted Uzbek theater, a university, and seven other higher education training centers. A small Jewish community continued the traditions of central Asian Jews, although most have now left since the country's independence in 1991. During World War II, Samarkand was a way station for supplying the nationalist Chinese from the Middle East.

With the independence of Uzbekistan in 1991, Samarkand has begun to revitalize, thanks to tourism and foreign direct investment. Samarkand serves as the administrative capital for one of the thirteen provinces in Uzbekistan. Donors such as the Asian Development Bank and the World Bank are lending the government millions of dollars to improve the city's infrastructure. Outside universities are setting up training facilities and working to improve the quality of education available to local students. International nongovernmental organizations (NGOs) are working with local charities to improve civil society and to enhance opportunities for women in business. There are numerous Internet service providers and Web design and bank start-ups, indicating an investment boom by local entrepreneurs.

The city has also benefited from the government's new national narrative that stresses Temür as the key national hero and the Timurid spirit as crucial for development. The city is a regional transport hub and is becoming more important as new links are created with Uzbekistan's neighbors to the south. New chemical-processing plants, funded by the Japanese, are making their mark in central Asia.

The city still has difficulties, however. The merchants in the bazaar are facing tremendous pressure from the government to modernize, standardize, and turn over more taxes, processes they are resisting. Tajikistan, the upstream riparian neighbor on the Zarafshan River, is increasing its water demands, threatening to cut the flow around Samarkand available for irrigation. The push to be a leader in the chemical sector is deepening an already dangerous urban level of pollution. And the drive for tourism is threatening the monuments: in its attempt to attract tourist cash, the government is pursuing inappropriate and temporary repairs to the historical landmarks, endangering their character and stability. Human rights and freedom of expression remain very tightly controlled by the Tashkent regime, and observers have noted increased repression after 2005; corruption is also a major problem in the city.

Bruce Stanley

Further Readings
Belenitsky, Aleksander. *Central Asia.* Cleveland: World Publishing, 1968.
Blunt, Wilfrid. *The Golden Road to Samarkand.* London: Hamish Hamilton, 1973.
Christian, David. *A History of Russia, Central Asia and Mongolia.* Cambridge: Blackwell, 1998.
Grousset, Rene. *The Empire of the Steppes: A History of Central Asia.* Translated by Naomi Walford. New Brunswick, NJ: Rutgers University Press, 1970.
Hiebert, Frederick. *Origins of the Bronze Age Oasis Civilization in Central Asia.* Philadelphia: University of Pennsylvania Museum Publications, 1995.
Hookham, Hidda. *Tamburlaine the Conqueror.* London: Hodder and Stoughton, 1962.
Knobloch, Edgar. *Beyond the Oxus: Archaeology, Art and Architecture of Central Asia.* London: Ernest Benn, 1972.

Samarra
Population: 100,000 (2006 estimate)

Of all the created monumental capitals scattered throughout the Middle East, Samarra seems one of the most tragic and wasteful. Sited less than 100 miles north of Baghdad, the city was, for the Abbasid caliphs, a "folly," an ill-conceived political and social disaster that bankrupted a vast empire. Partly a retreat from the politics of the court, Samarra's golden age lasted just fifty years, and then its huge palaces and vast mosques were raided for materials. Although it became a Shi'i shrine city, it never recovered its glory, and today it is a regional market on the road to the north and a site for resistance to the U.S.-led forces.

Samarra (Greek, *Souma;* Syriac, *Shumara*) is a town on the east bank of the middle Tigris River in Iraq, 78 miles north of Baghdad, 193 miles south of Mosul, and 30 miles south of Takrit. It serves as a trade and administrative center for its region with a certain amount of industry and handicrafts as well as an agricultural market. During the 1950s, the government built a barrage north of Samarra designed to control the spring flood of the Tigris by diverting the waters into the depression of the Wadi Tharthar west of the river. This led to an increase in the size of the town as the peasants from the floodplain moved onto the steppe land among the ruins of the Abbasid city. Thus, Samarra covered an area of some 86 acres in 1924, increasing to 300 acres in the 1970s.

Until the caliph al-Mutasim decided to build a new capital there in AD 835, the site of Samarra had been lightly occupied. The area was the locus of the Chalcolithic Samarran culture, and in 690 BC Sennacherib refounded the city of Surmarrati. Perhaps this was located on the fortified site dated to the Assyrian period found at al-Huwaysh opposite to the modern town. Ammianus Marcellinus speaks of the town Sumere on the Tigris, one stage from where the emperor Julian died.

There were both Nestorian and Monophysite Christians in the region, for each had a bishopric of Tirhan, which was probably located east of the Tigris opposite Takrit. This is somewhat confirmed by Yaqut, who said that when al-Mutasim decided to build his capital, he bought the land for his palace from a monastery called al-Tirhan.

It was supposedly the Sassanian ruler Khusraw Anushirvan who constructed the Qatul al-Kisrawi (cut of Khusraw), a northern extension of the great Nahrawan Canal during the sixth century AD. At its head lay a Sassanian military and administrative center, called by the Arabs Kharkh Firuz. This project, and a further canal built by the caliph Harun ar-Rashid, improved the fortunes of the Samarra region. Nonetheless, agriculture hardly developed around Samarra despite such infrastructural improvements, for here the chief occupation was hunting.

It was the isolation of Samarra from the tumults of Baghdad, as well as the attractions of the chase, that determined al-Mutasim to move his court there. Just months before his own death, al-Mamun, his brother and predecessor, had proclaimed as doctrine the Mutazilite theory that the Qu'ran was created. Therefore, upon his accession in 833, the new

Abbasid caliph found the populace of the capital bitterly angered by the persecution of such esteemed theologians as Ahmad b. Hanbal over their refusal to adhere to the new orthodoxy. Quite aside from this ideological conflict was the fact that the caliph's own bodyguard clashed frequently with the civilian inhabitants of the capital. To these cultivated citizens of Baghdad, this army of foreign slaves, Turks, and other peoples were brutal soldiers, un-Arabized and non-Muslim, who spoke incomprehensible and barbarous languages.

Yet more important than these specific factors impelling a change of residence was the role played by the palace as residence and locus of caliphal power under the Abbasid regime. When he succeeded or sometimes even while he had been crown prince, a new caliph sought to distinguish himself and his rule from that of his predecessors. Since the palace was both the incarnation and symbol of that power, the new incumbent either built an entirely new residence or went further to build an entirely new palace-city in a district, often insignificant and uninhabited, upon which he could place his own stamp. Moreover, there were often sound strategic reasons for doing so.

Thus, al-Mansur, the great grandfather of al-Mutasim, built his new Round City near the village of Baghdad to establish a new capital for the new dynasty in a district that possessed a strategic location in the center of the rich province of al-Iraq. Here the courses of the Tigris and Euphrates approached one another, caravan routes met, and the climate was healthy and nonmalarial (see also "Baghdad"). Ar-Rashid, father of al-Mutasim, built a city beside the town of Raqqa on the all-important Syrian frontier with the Byzantine Empire, naming it ar-Rafiqah (the companion). Al-Mutasim himself chose Samarra.

New caliphal capitals received new names, felicitous ones to sanctify the new foundation and the new era they inaugurated. Thus, the Round City was named Madinat as-Salaam (the city of peace), while the palace complex at ar-Rafiqah became Qasr as-Salaam (the palace of peace). The caliph named his new creation Surra Man Raa (he who sees it is happy) in a play on the name Samarra.

The palace complex of al-Mutasim was called Dar al-Khilafa, or Dar al-Khalifa, or Dar as-Sultan, or Dar Amir al-Muminin. It covered an area of 300 acres and was subdivided into the public palace—Dar al-Amma—where the caliph held audience each Monday and Thursday, and the private palace—al-Jawsaq al-Khaqani—which was home to the rulers and their families. It is notable that the name of the private palace, Manor of the Khaqan, includes within it the Turkish title for a supreme ruler, which shows the influence the Turkish *ghulams* (slave soldiers) were already beginning to exercise in the new capital. Moreover, the name given locally to the new city, Askar al-Mutasim (the military camp of al-Mutasim), indicates both its purpose as a place to house the

ghulams away from a civil populace and the probably temporary nature of this foundation.

The palace complex included gardens and a polo field. An avenue, some two miles in length, linked it to the main town, which included markets and a Friday Mosque built by this caliph. The caliph spared no pains to embellish his new construction, bringing marble from Antioch and Laodicea in Syria and importing vast amounts of teak from India and palm beams from Basrah. Across the river on the west bank, the caliph laid out extensive parks with plants and trees from all over Dar al-Islam and beyond.

Scattered round were the cantonments of five separate guard units, each under its own leader. Of these, three were composed of Turks, one was a unit of Arabs from the Nile Delta and the Western Desert (the Maghariba), and the last was a unit of Ushrushaniya from Ushrushana, a mountainous district between Samarkand and Farghana. These were recruited and under the leadership of the Afshin al-Khaydar, prince and hereditary ruler of Ushrushana who had been one of the principal mainstays of al-Mutasim since he had governed Egypt for al-Mamun.

The death of al-Mutasim in 842, and the accession of his son Harun al-Wathiq, brought a first crisis in the affairs of the seven-year-old metropolis. Its populace wondered whether the new ruler would abandon the city as his uncles had abandoned Qasr as-Salaam, built by his grandfather, or whether he would stay. In any event, al-Wathiq decided to remain. Moreover, he focused on the economic development of the city, building a port as well as a new palace for himself named Qasr al-Haruni along the banks of the Tigris.

It was during the reign of his brother and successor Jafar al-Mutawakkil (847–861) that Samarra reached the height of its prosperity. The city expanded to an occupied area of thirty-five square miles with a circumference that, according to the geographer al-Maqdiasi, was one day's journey. The caliph was a lover of architecture and built a new Friday Mosque as well as some twenty palaces costing nearly 300 million dirhams. The new mosque, the largest in the world, was built between 849 and 851 and was part of an eastern extension of the city into the old hunting park. It measured 784 by 512 feet with seventeen aisles in the prayer hall and with a triple portico around the courtyard. The mihrab was decorated with glass mosaic, while the walls were lined with panels of dark blue glass. The mosque was placed within an outer enceinte that measured 1,227 by 1,453 feet, with covered porticoes for additional believers during the Friday prayer. It was approached by three avenues, each 171 feet wide.

Its minaret, the famous Malwiyah, rises to a height of 171 feet and has a square base and a spiral staircase to the top. Its construction was influenced by that typical Mesopotamian construction, the ziggurat. The caliph himself rode up the staircase on a white Egyptian donkey.

Early photograph of the ancient mosque and minaret (ca. 851) in Samarra. (Hulton-Deutsch Collection/Corbis)

The city center was focused on the Askar al-Mutasim and had seven parallel avenues, one of which lay along the banks of the Tigris and held the quays where docked the river transport that served as the chief means of supplying this massive conurbation as well as the cantonments of the Maghariba.

Within this central district, its principal thoroughfare (al-Shari al-Azam, later named the Darb al-Sultan) followed the route of the main road between Baghdad and Mosul. Along it lay the *diwan* (administration) of the land tax (*kharaj*), the caliphal stables, the slave market, police headquarters, the main prison, and the main markets, which surrounded the Friday Mosque built by al-Mutasim. Finally, at the end of this avenue, west of the Dar al-Khilafa, lay the residences of the great palace servants.

This avenue was some seven miles, or three *farsakhs*, in length. To appreciate the significance of this distance, it is well to remember that the Arab geographers generally fixed the length of a day's caravan journey at five farsakhs. Moreover, in some sections, the Shari al-Azam reached a width of 200 ells

(322 feet) so that it was more like an extended *maidan* (a great square) than a great processional way.

The old central avenue built by al-Mutasim was narrowed from 197 feet to 33 feet and ended at the southern entrance of the Dar al-Khilafa, around which were the palaces of the principal Turkish amirs. To the east of this, along the other four main axes of the city, were to be found the barracks of the different regiments of guards.

Although Mutawakkil made Samarra into one of the largest and most beautiful cities in the Islamic Empire—indeed, in the world—he finally became dissatisfied with a foundation that owed its origins to his predecessors. First, he moved briefly to Damascus in AD 858, but it was too far from the core of his power in Iraq and Iran. Then, the next year he decided to build a city north of the former Sassanian administrative center at Kharkh Firuz. This city, called al-Jafariyya, al-Mahuza, or al-Mutawakkiliyya (on the coinage), was only occupied for two years, from 859 until the assassination of the caliph in 861. Here al-Mutawakkil erected another mosque, now called Abu Dulaf, with a similar style of minaret and only slightly smaller in area than the one he had ordered constructed at Samarra. Still, it is the second-largest mosque in the world.

Unfortunately, the new capital was soon found to have a problem. The thirty-mile canal and aqueduct that supplied the city with water from the north proved so badly leveled that water hardly flowed. Although this would have led to the slow strangulation of this city in any case, the assassination of its founder and eponym led to the immediate transfer of the court a few miles south to its old haunts.

The reign of al-Mutawakkil saw enormous expenditure, not only in the extension of Samarra and the building of his new capital but also in maintenance of his court. Moreover, while living in Samarra, isolated amid his regiments of Turkish guards, the caliph found himself increasingly at the mercy of soldiers who in a land far from their own homes gave their principal loyalties to their own leaders. His death in a plot involving his Turkish guard commanders and his heir led to the making and unmaking of four caliphs in nine years (861–870). This involved armed insurrections within the city itself on three occasions.

Although Samarra remained the Abbasid capital until 892, it continued to lose importance as both an administrative and an urban center. The caliph al-Mutamid was very much under the control of his able brother al-Muwaffaq, who had close ties with the Turkish regiments and removed these forces from Samarra to keep them under his thumb as he grappled with the various crises besetting the Abbasid regime. Therefore, Samarra became a gilded cage for the caliph where he could indulge in pleasures of the senses, among which was the erection of a palace—al-Mashuq (the Beloved)—on the west bank of the Tigris. After the caliph died in Baghdad in 882, his body was returned for burial to the city where he had wasted so much of his life. The center of power returned to Baghdad, and Samarra began to decline.

The city was looted several times between 887 and 895, and there was massive depopulation. Nonetheless, the center of the original city around the markets was still occupied, as were the satellite towns of al-Kharkh and al-Matira to the north and south of the city. When the caliph al-Muktafi sought to resettle Samarra in 903, he found the great palace of al-Jawsaq a ruin and gave up the attempt.

Samarra continued to molder. When al-Maqdisi visited it some eighty years later, he noted that Samarra had become a ruin field where one could walk two or three hours without coming upon an inhabited place. Moreover, he indicated that the mosque of al-Mutawakkil, which "used to be considered superior to the mosque of Damascus," had fallen from this high estate.

Despite its ruinous state, Samarra over the centuries was transformed into a center for Shi'i pilgrimage because the Ab-

basid caliphs sought to keep the imams, descendants of Ali b. Abi Talib, under close surveillance. Therefore, both the Tenth Imam, Ali al-Askari or al-Hadi (r. 835–868), and his son al-Hasan al-Askari, the Eleventh Imam (r. 868–874), were brought to Samarra and lodged near the mosque of al-Mutasim in Askar Mutasim, from whence they derived their *nisba* (names indicating relationships). Even more significant was the fact that the Twelfth Imam, Muhammad al-Qaim, went into occultation (*ghayba*) in Samarra in 874, disappearing in a cleft commemorated by the Sardab al-Mahdi.

The first elaboration of the double shrine over the tombs took place in 945 at the hands of the Hamdanid ruler Nasir ad-Dawla, and the Buyids continued this work. There were frequent rebuildings, of which the most important in medieval times were in 1054 by Arslan al-Basasiri and in 1210 by the caliph an-Nasir li-Din Allah, which was celebrated by an inscription in the Sardab. The shrine as it appears today, with a tiled dome over the double tombs of the imams and a smaller gilded dome over the Sardab, is principally the work of the Qajar ruler Nasir ad-Din Shah in 1869.

Despite its role as a pilgrimage center, Samarra did not revive. The shifting of the course of the Tigris south of Samarra to the east during the twelfth and thirteenth centuries led to the rerouting of the Baghdad-Mosul highway to the west of the Tigris, which brought a loss in trade. In the early part of the fourteenth century, Mustawfi, the Shi'i pilgrim and geographer, noted that Samarra was mostly a ruin. He did, however, remark on the marvelous spiral minaret of the Friday Mosque.

The city was not walled until 1834, when a charitable donation enabled a barrier to be put up using Abbasid bricks as material. The wall built was fifteen-sided, crenellated, and polygonal, pierced by four gates facing north, south, east, and west. There was a semicircular bastion at each salient angle. The wall seems to have kept people out: the British population estimate for the city in 1920 was 2,000. It was not until the 1960s that the city broke the 25,000 mark.

Samarra was founded by al-Mutasim ex nihilo to take his court and entourage away from densely populated Baghdad, where civil strife between his own bodyguard of semicivilized non-Muslim Turks and the sophisticated local populace led him to fear for his own safety. Like preceding generations of his family, however, he also sought to assert his individuality by creating a new center of power through construction of a unique capital where he could impose his own stamp upon history untrammeled by precedent.

For the caliph, it did not matter particularly that the site of his new creation was isolated and not particularly well watered, for over the millennia the inhabitants of lower Mesopotamia/Iraq had learned to make do and create a paradise where none had existed before. Indeed, al-Mutasim and his son al-Wathiq in particular endeavored to make the new city a going concern and give it permanence by supplying it with an economic as well as an architectural foundation.

Under al-Mutawakkil the previously well-ordered, rational plan of urban expansion took on an aspect of extravagance and even megalomania. The caliph, seeing the Islamic Empire slipping from his control to that of his amirs, could only assert his power by means of extravagant (and expensive) building projects within a sphere that was definitely his own. Unfortunately, the vast elongation of the city along the banks of the Tigris created an urban agglomeration that could not sustain itself because of problems of urban transport, soil infertility, and principally of dearth of water and an inadequate *qanat* (covered irrigation channels) system. This building folly culminated with the construction of Jafariyya/al-Mutawakkiliya, which was only inhabited for two years before being abandoned.

This climax under al-Mutawakkil was followed by political and social disaster, contraction, and finally abandonment with a return to Baghdad. Even the transformation of Samarra into a center for Shi'i pilgrimage could not arrest a decline that had as much to do with locational, spatial, and environmental factors as it did with politics.

With the invasion of Iraq in 2003, Samarra became famous for its resistance to American troops. There were three significant operations in and around the city over the next three years, including the 2004 street fighting against insurgents that drove thousands of the city's citizens out of the area. In 2002 the population was estimated at 200,000; by 2006 it was less than half that number. The Americans also constructed a seven-mile-long wall around the city to control attacks, although many American soldiers report that Samarra is perceived as one of the worst assignments they can receive. In early 2006, a huge car bomb destroyed the golden dome of the al-Askari shrine. Many Shi'i blamed Sunnis for the destruction, and Sunni mosques throughout Iraq were attacked.

One might well ask why Baghdad succeeded as a great urban agglomeration while Samarra failed. Both were new caliphal foundations designed to mark off a new era. The fact that the former was situated in a healthy and fertile district in the center of al-Iraq where caravan and river routes met gave it an undoubted advantage.

Their return to Baghdad, however, did not rid the caliphs of their grandiose building habits. Indeed, from the time of the Buyids, when the caliphs were even more powerless than their predecessors of a century or two before, the Abbasid rulers could only assert themselves by building great palace complexes, also subsumed under the name Dar al-Khilafa, where they lived in splendid isolation from the world. Such palaces inevitably acted as a centrifugal force on a city whose Daylami or Turkish amirs had the locus of their power situated elsewhere. It was only the development of public institu-

tions like the madrasa during the eleventh century that brought a unifying force to counteract the divisiveness promoted by separate palace complexes, each relatively sufficient in itself. Thus, Baghdad entered a renaissance while its former rival continued to slumber on in isolation and decadence.

J. L. Whitaker

Further Readings

Adams, Robert McCormick. *Land behind Baghdad.* Chicago: University of Chicago Press, 1965.

Le Strange, Guy. *The Lands of the Eastern Caliphate: Mesopotamia, Persia, and Central Asia from the Muslim Conquest to the Time of Timur.* 1905. Repr. London: Frank Cass, 1966.

Robinson, Chase F. *A Medieval Islamic City Reconsidered: An Interdisciplinary Approach to Samarra.* Oxford: Oxford University Press, 2001.

Rogers, J. M. "Samarra: A Study in Medieval Town Planning." In *The Islamic City: A Colloquium,* edited by A. H. Hourani and S. M. Stern, 119–155. Papers on Islamic History 1. Oxford: St. Anthony's, 1970.

Sanaa
Population: 2 million (2005 estimate)

Located inland on the southwestern tip of the Arabian Peninsula, Sanaa is the political capital of the Republic of Yemen. Essentially closed to visitors until 1962, this is an ancient city whose rich cultural history continues to survive despite much political and physical change over the centuries. Local tradition holds that the city was initially erected by Sham, son of Noah, and that it is the oldest city on Earth; the archaeological evidence is of continuous habitation on the site from around the first century BC. This "pearl of Arabia" is one of the most architecturally exotic and visually fascinating cities in the region, with a unique intact medieval core of more than 6,500 multistoried houses built before the eleventh century, some of the earliest mosques on the peninsula, the ancient market, and more than twelve hammams. Today its sprawling, modern new city, growing at more than 11 percent per year, threatens this core, despite significant international attempts to preserve this United Nations Educational, Scientific, and Cultural Organization (UNESCO) World Heritage Site.

Sanaa (also known as Sana or Sanaa) is situated in the center of the northern highland zone in an elevated plateau that rises 7,200 feet above the Red Sea. The city lies in a fertile valley on the plateau surrounded by higher mountains, giving it two short rainy seasons and historically supporting rain-fed agriculture around the city; today qat and grapes are grown in the Sanaa basin. This plateau is often considered the ancestral heartland of the Arabs and was home to sedentary tribes controlling established territory. The city straddles an ancient caravan crossroads linking the plateau via mountain passes and wadis with the *tihamah* (coastal plain) to the west and south, the southern highlands, and the Hadramawt to the east.

Saba—or the Sabaeans—is the name of a political community dating from the first millennium BC whose capital was the town of Marib, about 117 miles east of Sanaa. The first written evidence of this tribal confederation may be found in the Old Testament with the reference to the queen of Sheba's (Saba) visit to King Solomon around 960 BC. There is also a reference in Genesis to a town called Azal, which may be Sanaa, thus linking the site to one of the supposed descendants of Noah via his son Shem. Other references to Sabean rulers don't appear until the records of the neo-Assyrian kings Sargon II and Sennacherib, ca. 715 BC and 685 BC, respectively. Over the next 600 years, there are numerous indications of the Sabaean domination over the Sanaa basin but little evidence of extensive habitation on the site. The height of Sabaean power appears under Karib al-Watar (ca. 430 BC), and it is after this point that other local kingdoms begin to assert their autonomy. These caravan kingdoms end up competing for control of the spice trade routes across the plateau, and as the competition heats up, the earliest inscriptions of a town called Sanaa appear (ca. 180 BC).

Sabaean power reemerges during the first century AD, and conflicting evidence suggests that Sanaa may have been founded at this time by Karib al-Watar Yuhanim I, king of Saba. This would place its emergence just as the maritime trade was outproducing the overland trade, and the port cities of the Tihamah were attracting wealth to the rising southern power of Himyar. Inscriptions discovered in the temple of Awa in Marib suggest that it was during the reign of the brother kings Ilisharah and Yazal when the importance of Sanaa in the Sabaean state was at its peak, which is in line with Muslim sources. From the end of the second century, Marib and Sanaa played parallel roles in the political life of the Sabaean state: Marib served as the headquarters for campaigns eastward against Hadramawt and northward against the Bedouin, while Sanaa was the headquarters for campaigns against the Himyarites and westward toward the Red Sea coastal areas. Having dual capitals was significant for repulsing conquerors but also served to maintain a complex network of trade routes tying the Indian Ocean, the Red Sea, the Arabian Peninsula, and the Mediterranean together. Certainly, the Sabaean kings of this time consistently stressed Sanaa and its palace (citadel) of Ghumdan as a dynastic headquarters on a parallel with Marib; the city's name may derive from the word for arsenal quarter or fortified place.

By the third century AD, Saba's power was spent. Somewhere around AD 280, Saba's entire domain, including the small town of Sanaa, was absorbed into the expanding Kingdom of Himyar, with its capital at Zafar. Archaeological finds indicate that around this time a wall was built around Sanaa, but the city slips from the written record after AD 299.

The ancient cult in Sanaa was paganism, which was a reflection of the socioeconomic circumstances that prevailed at that time. Yemenis were mainly farmers and traders who paid great attention to astronomy to regulate navigation and irrigation. Therefore, they worshipped the trinity of the Moon, Sun, and Venus. This Sabaean national cult of al-Muqah remained down to the beginning of the fourth century, firmly rooted in al-Muqah's shrine at Marib. In Sanaa the divinity of the tribal confederation of Sumay was Talab Riyam, represented by an ibex and revered as the protector of flocks. Remains of a temple dedicated to him have been found near Sanaa. Within the region, however, the fourth century was a time of great change, with the ancient polytheistic cults being swept away and replaced by a monotheistic type of belief. In consequence, the temple of al-Muqah at Awa was abandoned, and there is no epigraphic mention of Sanaa between the fourth to sixth century.

The expanding political power of Aksum and Byzantine Christianity in Yemen was marked by aggressive proselytizing and conversion starting under the Byzantine emperor Constantine II (350–361). The Aksumites occupied parts of the region for the next 200 years, referred to themselves as rulers over the peninsula, and minted coins for use in Yemen (see also "Aksum"). The force of these imperial powers may be one reason that the Himyarite state began to turn to Judaism, which spread through the region and become the main religion of Sanaa. Trade also contributed to the introduction of Judaism into Sanaa as merchants carried the religion along the trade routes and via Jewish settlements concentrated in cities and oases such as Sanaa, Najran, and Yathrib (see also "Madinah"). The spread of monotheism based on Christianity and Judaism may be the reason that local legend gives Sanaa the nickname Madinat Sam (Shem's city) and has Shem, son of Noah, founding the city in antiquity.

Tradition also holds that early in the sixth century, Dhu Nuwas of Sanaa (AD 515–525) was converted to Judaism and boldly moved against local Abyssinian centers of power and their Christian allies. In the zeal of his new faith, this Himyarite leader massacred Christians in Najran. In response, the Byzantine emperor Justin (518–527) used this pretext to instigate his Christian allies in Aksum to invade Yemen under the pretext of protecting Christians, although it is just as likely that the struggle with the Sassanians for control of long-distance trade was also a rationale.

Led by General Abraha, the Aksumites killed Dhu Nuwas (ca. 528) in battle. Subsequently, however, Abraha, with support from local elites, rebelled and proclaimed himself king of Himyar and Saba (AD 547). The Aksumites failed twice in their attempts to depose him. Abraha had a cathedral, Ghurqat al-Qalis, built in Sanaa as a center of Christian pilgrimage and pushed the spread of Christianity in the region.

He also reportedly used the city as a staging area for his attempt to destroy the Kaabah in Makkah in 570–571. Although his attack is remembered for his use of elephants, it was unsuccessful, and Abraha died on his return to Sanaa.

Today little remains of al-Qalis other than its foundation wall. The site, however, remains a tourist stop on the lowest part of the Tinsmith's Lane opposite the Jewish synagogue. From the remaining octagonal ground wall it seems the cathedral was modeled on the Church of the Nativity in Bethlehem, which has a domed octagonal chapel, and the west-to-east orientation parallels the orientation of Aksumite churches in Ethiopia. From its description in various manuscripts, it was a magnificent piece of art, contemporary with the other great Byzantine churches of the period such as Hagia Sophia.

The Himyarite kingdom survived the Abyssinian invasion and continued to rule over Sanaa even after the Sassanian invasion of 571. Khosrow I sent an expeditionary force to Yemen that advanced as far as Sanaa and dislodged the Aksumites, who were allies of the Byzantines. The Persian general who captured Sanaa reportedly raised his standard above the gate and commanded that it never be lowered. A native prince, the legendary Sayf ibn Dhi Yazan, was appointed as the Sassanian vassal.

Sanaa struggled hard to emerge as a preeminent trading city in the region. To advance their claim, the powers that ruled Sanaa established caravansaries; minted coins in gold, silver, and bronze; imposed regulations and market codes to regulate caravans' passages; and concluded protection agreements with the tribes along the routes. In addition, they established well-guarded settlements along the roads to escort and protect their caravans. Among the main trade stations these caravans used was Makkah, and Sanaa and Makkah fostered good bilateral trade relations between their cities (see also "Makkah"). Sanaa was one of ten regional markets in Arabia at fixed times of the year in the pre-Islamic era, attracting traders and buyers to its annual market. The ancient core of the city's markets was organized around key *samaser* (khans or caravansaries), where traders offered their goods. Today the *jambiah* (traditional Yemeni dagger) market continues to attract many visitors, and the medieval homes built by the merchants dominate the Old City's skyline.

The dense network of trade and ties to Makkah may be one of the reasons behind the easy and early acceptance of Islam by the people of Sanaa. Within six years of the *hijrah* (622), Sanaa had embraced the new religion, and one of the first mosques for the new faith was built in the city under plans directly approved by the Prophet Muhammad. Constructed in a field belonging to the Abna (the Persian governor at the time Islam came to the Yemen) west of the Ghamdan citadel, this Great Mosque remains one of the most prominent early Islamic monuments in existence. Since then,

the mosque, with its 183 pillars raided from the different eras of pre-Islamic Sanaa, has undergone significant alterations and additions, making it the largest mosque in the city.

Sanaa's primacy in the region began to grow when it became the capital for the new Zaydi Shi'i dynasty after 893. Yahya bin al-Hussayn, a Shi'i claimant in the Hijaz, was invited to the Sanaa basin to help resolve a local tribal conflict. He immigrated along with a group of Alids and their families. These immigrants became the nucleus for a religious aristocracy with its base in the northern highlands and its capital in Sanaa. Iman al-Hadi, as al-Hussayn became known, founded the Zaydi *dawa*, whose descendants ruled until 1962. Despite occupation by Sunni empires and leaders like the Ayyubids (1173–1228) and Rasulids (1228–1381), Sanaa provided the imams with a base to rule over a majority Sunni community.

The existing city wall was rebuilt in 861 by King Ibn Yufir and expanded by the Ayyubids; by the mid-nineteenth century, the city wall measured some five and one-half miles in circumference. The city walls were 12 feet thick and made of clay, and on the outward side, they were dressed in stone. Small, round, semicircular towers projected from the wall as bastions at roughly 120-foot intervals; some of them were battlements, and some were entirely built of stone. Part of the city wall and most of its traditional seven gates are still standing and have been renovated; Bab al-Yaman, the southern gate, is particularly spectacular. The city has many mosques with gilded domes—those in which imams had been buried—and many still-in-use public baths, some dating back to pre-Islamic times.

From the medieval period to the present, Sanaa has continued to grow. It has long been a populous city, with fine dwellings, often five to nine stories high, most of them decorated with plaster, burned brick, and dressed stones. The streets were clean, and parks and gardens were everywhere. Imam ash-Shafi (768–820) wrote, "Sanaa must be seen." Ibn Rustah wrote in the tenth century of the grandeur of the city, with its multistoried houses and their decorations as well as its delicious food. The city was divided into quarters, mainly named after the mosque in that quarter. Each quarter also had its own market (more than forty specialty markets within the suq), and each market was governed by the chief shaykh, who was elected by the merchants. The duties of the shaykh were laid down in the *qanun* (law) and regulated by the *hakim* (governor). Like the Islamic *muhtasib* (market inspector), the shaykh's key duty seems to have been to keep an eye on weights and measures. This hierarchical administration of markets within the city was very innovative and continues to function today.

Up until the medieval period, all three main Islamic sects (Sunnis, Ismailis, and Zaydis) could be found within the city. By the modern period, however, the Zaydis made up the vast majority of Sanaa's inhabitants. Non-Muslim minorities like

Sanaa's medieval downtown skyline. (Tibor Bognar/Corbis)

Jews and the Hindu Baniyans also constituted part of Sanaa history. Jews have lived in the city from as early as the third century, and over time they created their own quarter in the city (Qal-Yahud), based around the early synagogue near the Ghumdan citadel. The Jews of Yemen were well known for their specialist skills, including in pottery and jewelry. In the long history of Sanaa, the normally good relations between Jews and Muslims were, from time to time, disturbed by unhappy events: the looting of Jewish property; the excessive zeal of some officials; the temporary expulsion of Sanaa's Jews in 1679; or the excitement created by messianic movements among the Jews themselves, such as during the messianic troubles of the seventeenth century. In general, the common culture of both Muslims and Jews of Sanaa, and their tolerance of each other, was impressive. The mass migration of Yemeni Jews to the new State of Israel occurred between 1948 and 1950, leaving only a few hundred members of this ancient community in the country.

Hindu merchants and traders, the Baniyan, first appeared in Sanaa during the days of al-Mutawakkil Ismail (r. 1655–1656), though they must have settled in the ports of the southern Arabia littoral much earlier. A town or market in southern Arabia without them was rare, to the extent that they settled in every market, and people turned to them to purchase items, to borrow money, and to give property on condition that the gain should be divided between them.

The Ottomans controlled Sanaa twice. Their first reign began in 1538 and lasted until 1602, when the imams reasserted their authority and kicked out the Ottomans. While Sanaa was ruled by the Ottoman pasha, European captains calling at the ports of Mocha or Aden would visit Sanaa to solidify their special privileges or capitulations for trade; with the reassertion of the imams, most of these visits ended (see also "Aden").

The Ottomans reappeared on the coast in 1835 in the guise of Muhammad Ali's Egyptian troops, and by 1870 Turkish forces were back in the city. Under the mandate of the Tanzimat reforms, the Ottoman administration began to modernize the country, introducing new roads, planning, schools, and hospitals, although in very limited quantities. The Ottomans felt they were in a rush to solidify their claim to the country, surrounded as they were by an expansionist Egypt, British interests in Aden and Berbera, and imperialist Italian and French presence along the Somali coast (see also "Berbera" and "Djibouti City").

Imam Yahya came to power in 1904. In the wake of the demise of the Ottoman dynasty (1918), Yemen under his leadership tried to secure its independence by staying away from international involvement and avoiding regional Arab politics. Yahya implemented a policy of isolationism, preventing foreign investment, cracking down on local liberal movements, allowing few people to travel abroad, and carrying out no infrastructural investment into roads, communication facilities, hospitals, or banks. He closed the schools for girls opened by the Turks and supported no school system.

As a result, Sanaa became a hotbed for intellectual rebellion and antiregime organizing. Various groups working underground to free Yemen, reform the imamate, or bring modernization appeared in the city during the 1930s. The Fulaihi madrasa, for example, which attracted Islamic scholars from throughout the country, generated the Fatat al-Fulaihi (the youth of Fulaihi). This group of scholars would read smuggled books prohibited by the imam. Another, the Hait al-Nidal (the committee of the struggle), was committed to the introduction of reforms; in 1936 most of its leaders were imprisoned by the imam. The Shabab al-Amr bil-Maruf wal-Nahi an al-Munkar (the youths for the enjoining of good and the forbidding of evil) issued a manifesto in 1941 calling for a Yemeni *nahda* (renaissance), a parliament, and a Constituent Assembly (al-Jamiya al-Tassisiya), with Islam being the means to raise Yemen from its backwardness.

Imam Yahya repressed such movements, fearing their threat to his rule. The response was his assassination in February 1948. When his son, Imam Ahmad, took over, many of the Free Yemeni leaders were executed, and liberal civil dissent died with them.

Although Imam Ahmad (r. 1948–1962) opened up the country and committed to some reforms, political and economic change moved too slowly for those who wanted to join the twentieth century; riots and demonstrations in Sanaa in 1961 calling for change and reform were indications of the deep unrest among the city's population. One week after Imam Ahmad died, in September 1962, republicans inside the military pulled off a coup in the city and began to ally themselves with Nasir's radical Egypt.

Saudi support for the rural tribes committed to restoring the imamate led to a violent eight-year civil war pitting urban republican Sanaa against much of the rest of the country. By the time Egyptian troops withdrew from the country in 1968, the country was exhausted, and an arrangement was reached between the republicans and the royalists to establish a presidential system. Unfortunately, coups and assassinations continued, destabilizing the country and the capital Sanaa with it. Today the country, reunited with Aden into a single Yemen (1990), remains under the control of its longtime ruler Ali Abdullah Salih.

Despite the dramatic political changes that Sanaa has witnessed, many of its antiquities and old features still survive. The most famous are the remains of Ghumdan Castle (ca. 200 BC), which must have been, both technically and aesthetically, one of the grandest achievements of pre-Islamic civilization. Sitting on elevated ground on the ancient tell, this royal palace for the Sabaean and Himyarite kings of Yemen was destroyed in the time of the third caliph, Uthman (ca. 655). The descriptions of the castle before its destruction mention that it had twenty levels and four sides, each in a different colored stone—one side white, one black, one green, and one red. It had copper lions at each corner that roared when the winds passed through the statues. The lights from its alabaster windows and roof allowed visitors to see flying birds. The remains of Ghumdan lie near the Grand Mosque in old Sanaa, and today it is used for storing grain and arms.

Sanaa today hosts the country's administrative offices, including the presidential office, the government, the parliament, and the supreme court. The government bureaucracy still is the largest employer. Increasingly, Sanaa has expanded far beyond the Old City wall, which still surrounds old Sanaa. The continuous migration from the rural areas to Sanaa has had, unfortunately, a negative impact on the limited infrastructure and resources, in particular the water, and hence the level of services. The United Nations Educational, Scientific, and Cultural Organization (UNESCO) has launched an ambitious program for maintaining and renovating the Old City, which was designated a World Heritage Site in 1988. The economic activities are basically services, construction, and agriculture in the valleys around the city. The gross domestic product (GDP) growth in 2002 was estimated at more than 3 percent, with 35 percent of the workforce unemployed.

After the revolution of 1962, destruction of parts of the medieval physical fabric of the city began, including the demolition of parts of the city wall and seven of the gates to allow modern traffic to enter. The ancient "butterfly" shape to the old city and its walls, which in 1962 had enclosed a population of 35,000 within 1.2 square miles, has now given way to a sprawling modern conurbation that has doubled in population every six years and consumed the agricultural fields that had surrounded the old city. Ameliorating the thoughtless destruction of the medieval heritage has been one key objective of attempts at rebuilding, restoration, and preservation by international funding.

In addition to the dramatic population growth of the city, the influx of remittances by Yemeni laborers working in the oil industry in neighboring Saudi Arabia has helped place considerable stress on the Old City's historic buildings and its inadequate infrastructure. Wealthier residents fled to the new sections of the city, creating an uncontrolled housing boom, while poor rural immigrants crammed into the Old City, and the built environment deteriorated. Despite post–civil war central planning and five-year plans, the city's infrastructure, particularly water and sewage provision, are dangerously overstretched, leaving today's city struggling both to meet basic needs and to retain its glorious heritage and unique architecture.

Ahmed Abdelkareem Saif

Further Readings

Lewcock, Ronald B. *The Old Walled City of Sanaa.* Paris: UNESCO, 1986.

Niebuhr, Carsten. *Travels through Arabia.* Translated and abridged by R. Heron. Edinburgh: Heron, 1792.

"Part III. The Modernization of an Islamic City: The Case of Sanaa." In *The Middle East City: Ancient Traditions Confront a Modern World,* edited by Abdulaziz Saqqaf. New York: Paragon House, 1987.

Rathjens, C. *Jewish Domestic Architecture in Sanaa, Yemen.* Jerusalem: Israel Oriental Society, 1957.

Sergeant, R. B., and Ronald Lewcock, eds. *Sanaa: An Arabian Islamic City.* London: World of Islam Festival Trust, 1983.

Sfax
Population: 340,000 (2005 estimate)

Sfax has been known for more than 2,000 years as a key port for central Mediterranean trade. For the Romans, it was grain. For the Byzantines and Abbasids, Sfax was the olive oil port. For the Ottomans, it was slaves and gold. To the French, it was land for colons establishing plantations. To Rommel and Montgomery, it was a supply base from which to invade Egypt or Sicily. Since independence, its port and phosphates works have supported the Tunisian economy but also provided a hotbed for labor unrest and political organizing.

Sfax (Arabic, *Safaqis*) is Tunisia's second city and is located on the Mediterranean coast of the olive-producing area, known as the Sahel, which extends from the Gulf of Hammamet in the north to the Gulf of Gabès in the south. Off the coast of Sfax are a group of islands called the Iles Kerkenna. The city is located approximately 178 miles south of Tunis. The climate is mild and relatively dry, with average temperatures of 53 degrees Fahrenheit in winter and 78 degrees Fahrenheit in summer. Average annual rainfall is 7.75 inches.

The city consists of two districts or parts: the madinah and the newer colonial town of European and business construction. The madinah is surrounded by walls dating from the ninth century. Until 1832 no Europeans were allowed to enter. Many of the mosques and private houses inside the madinah are excellent examples of seventeenth- and eighteenth-century architecture, though some are considerably older. The Great Mosque, with its lofty minaret, was built in 849 and rebuilt in 981, with modifications during the eighteenth century. Located within the madinah is a busy suq.

The site was first settled by the Phoenicians between the eleventh and ninth century BC and became part of the Carthaginian Empire. After Carthage fell to the Romans in 146 BC, the Romans called the town Taparura. Six miles to the south was another town, named Thaenae (Thina); together they were incorporated into the Roman Empire as part of Africa Proconsularis. Julius Caesar won a major battle outside the city walls in 46 BC against the forces of Cato the Younger and King Juba. More than 80,000 troops were involved in the fighting and more than sixty war elephants. During these times, Sfax was part of the commercial networks linking the Mediterranean basin and the interior of Tunisia. For the Romans, the plains of Byzacium outside Taparura produced much of the grain required by their capital city. Pliny the Elder (ca. AD 60) reported on the fecundity of the area, saying it produced yields of 100 to 1. By the fourth century, the area had been shifted to olive oil production and become the foremost oil supplier to the empire, and the city's elites accumulated great wealth and political power in Rome from this production.

The city became part of the Vandal Empire in North Africa after 439 until the Byzantine invasion in 533. With the end of Byzantine control after 656, Islam began to supplant Christianity in the urban areas. For the next 200 years, the area around Sfax was unsettled, with trade routes interrupted by nomadic tribes and by the struggles between the Arabs and the Berbers. Not until the ninth and tenth centuries, particularly under the Aghlabids, did Sfax prosper again economically. Sfax, like Kairouan and Gabès, became an important market and manufacturing center as it lay at the end of a trans-Saharan caravan route. Slaves and other sub-Saharan commodities, such as ivory, ebony, ostrich feathers, and gold dust, were shipped via Sfax's port to other parts of the Abbasid Empire, and the harbor filled with ships from Naples, Venice, Genoa, Pisa, and Marseilles. The city's fame as a center for the manufacture of olive oil and cloth (both cotton and woolen), and as a fishing center, continued unabated. As a reflection of its prosperity, the city's ramparts were erected in the ninth century.

Early in the eleventh century, the trans-Saharan trade began to decline, and regional commercial activity shifted toward trans-Mediterranean trade. As a seaport, Sfax benefited from this trend. Under the al-Muwahhids (1160–1227), trade with Europe was increased. Among the commodities traded in the city were salt, copper, and glass beads from Venice; wine from France, Greece, and Spain; European cloths; and local products, including cotton and woolen cloths, olive oil, coral, and pottery. Pisan and Genoese consuls lived permanently in the city in *funduqs* (two-story lodging and storage houses for visiting merchants) established for trading purposes From the eleventh century onward, however, Europe gradually gained a stranglehold over Mediterranean commerce, resulting in the exclusion of North African Muslims from all but the most minimal participation in legitimate trade.

Autonomy from European influences was not easy. Sfax was one of the ports occupied by the Spanish between 1535 and 1574; the Jewish community in the city suffered disproportionally during this occupation. By the 1770s, Arab merchants in Sfax were still deeply involved in domestic trade within the Ottoman Empire, but 56 percent of all their shipping was handled by European flag carriers. Sfax was home to Barbary corsairs of the bey of Tunis during the eighteenth and early nineteenth centuries, inviting retribution; Venetian ships bombarded Sfax twice in late 1785, for example. The city remained, however, a major production and trading port throughout this period. The modernizing prime minister, Khair ad-Din (r. 1873–1877) did begin a number of experiments with land reform around Sfax, handing state land to peasants for olive production.

French marines invaded Sfax in July 1881. Sfax was to prosper again economically under the French protectorate (1881–1956), despite being bombarded and pillaged by the occupation troops and later made to pay an indemnity equivalent to about a quarter of a million pounds. Under the protectorate, Sfax was one of five provincial headquarters. The French developed phosphate mining in Gafsa starting in 1896, which provided materials for the Societe industrielle d'acide phosphorique et d'engrais established in Sfax. Moreover, olive cultivation was substantially extended. On the outskirts of Sfax, in 1892, the French established new olive plantations on the *terres sialines* (lands that were originally owned by the Siala family and returned to the bey of Tunisia in 1871). A decree of 1892 arranged for the transfer of some of these lands to Europeans or local people at ten francs per two and one-half acres on condition that plantations were developed upon them. The city's economic importance was increased by French improvements to the country's infrastructure; as a result, Sfax became linked to the rest of the country by rail. The city's present harbor was constructed between 1895 and 1897 by the French Compagnie des Ports de Tunis, Sousse et Sfax.

The city attracted French settlers and financiers who took over the olive and cotton plantations. It also attracted nomads from the Sahel, who became wage laborers. Thus, the city's population began to grow with rural in-migration; shantytowns and crime began to appear, and the labor force in the port and the phosphate mines also grew.

During World War II, Sfax was occupied by German and Italian troops. The city was General Erwin Rommel's staging point for his drive to the Nile in May 1942 (Operation Aida). British General Bernard Montgomery captured the city on 10 April 1943. The story goes that Montgomery had bet U.S. general Dwight D. Eisenhower's chief of staff a new B-17 bomber if he could take Sfax before 13 April. Eisenhower duly provided the bomber to Monty. The port subsequently was the staging point for the invasion of Sicily later in the year.

Since independence, Sfax has continued to grow economically. The city possesses the second-busiest port in the country. For most of central-southern Tunisia, the city is the most important center for exports and distribution. It is linked to all major towns in Tunisia via road and rail. The major export to pass through its port is that of phosphates brought from Metlaoui and Redeyef (in the region of Gafsa) by train. In addition, salt, seafood, and agricultural products, predominantly olive oil, are exported. The most important destination for exports is Europe, often via flights from its international airport.

Aside from a commercial port, Sfax possesses a busy fishing port, producing approximately 25 percent of the country's seafood per annum and exporting another 10,000 tons. Sponges were a crucial export for many years. Moreover, the governorate of Sfax is an important industrial center (second only to the Tunis region). The most important manufacturing sectors are textiles and clothing, agro-industries, and mechanical and chemical industries. Sfax is also an important agricultural producer and accounts for 40 percent of national olive oil output and 30 percent of almond output. Despite the fact that rainfall in and around Sfax is lower than the average usually required for agricultural cultivation, proximity to the sea causes condensation, allowing for the cultivation of olives without irrigation.

The large wage-labor population in the city has provided a fertile ground for labor organizing and political movements. In 1956 and again in 1962, the workers at the port and phosphate mines went on strike and expressed their displeasure with national policies. In 1984, in response to the International Monetary Fund (IMF) and its directed doubling of bread prices, Sfax residents rioted for four days, helping to start a nationwide uprising that forced the government to cancel the increase. In 2001 the head of the Regional Union of Workers Congress of Sfax presented a public call for greater democracy in the country.

Since the 1970s, the coastal areas close to Sfax have been developed with hotels for tourism. However, the city is geared more toward commerce and industry than to tourism. Today the Sfax Regional Development Authority seeks to attract private investment, including foreign direct investment (FDI), to the city and its governorate through investment incentives, ensuring that Sfax is part of the global economy. One way it will do that is via oil concessions. The company Eurogas has a 45 percent stake in the offshore Sfax oil and gas pool, which is expected to produce significant revenues for the city.

Nicola Pratt

Further Readings

Anderson, Lisa. *The State and Social Transformation in Tunisia and Libya, 1830–1980.* Princeton: Princeton University Press, 1983.

Henry, Clement. *The Mediterranean Debt Crescent.* Gainesville: University Press of Florida, 1996.

King, Stephen J. *Liberalization against Democracy: Local Politics of Economic Reform in Tunisia.* Bloomington: Indiana University Press, 2003.

Perkins, Kenneth. *A History of Modern Tunisia.* Cambridge: Cambridge University Press, 2004.

———. *Tunisia: Crossroads of the Islamic and European World.* Boulder, CO: Westview Press, 1986.

Sijilmassa
Population: 100,000 (AD 1000 estimate)

For 650 years, the oasis city of Sijilmassa was the key entrepôt, or broker city, linking the Mediterranean and the Muslim world with the gold and slaves of West Africa. Located in the Maghrib al-Aksar (western Maghrib, what is now south-central Morocco), this autonomous city-state monopolized control of goods shipped north from Ghana and Mali across the Sahara and was the assembly point for the huge twice yearly caravans heading south across the desert to Timbuktu. By AD 1350, as much as one-third of all the gold circulating in Europe and the Muslim world had passed through the gates of Sijilmassa, and hundreds of thousands of black slaves destined for slave markets around the Mediterranean first glimpsed the city as they emerged out of the Sahara between AD 757 and AD 1400. The first spiritual home in North Africa of Kharijite exiles fleeing the Abbasid persecutions, it became a site for religious dissent, incubator for puritanical religion, nursemaid to numerous dynasties, and a pilgrimage site up to the twentieth century.

The ruins of Sijilmassa (Arabic, *Sijilmasiyah* or *Madinat al-Amira*) are located about 200 miles southeast from Fez across the eastern High Atlas Mountains on the edge of the large Tafilalt Oasis. A journey of eight to ten days by camel south from Meknes or Fez through the mountain pass at 6,561 feet, Sijilmassa was the last city before the true Sahara. The geography allows a clear assent north into the mountains along the Wadi Ziz and over the pass into the fertile plains of Morocco or directly south into the desert along the preeminent trans-Saharan route through the salt mines of Taghaza to the middle Niger.

The ruins of the city run for some 4 miles along the east bank of the Ziz River, which flows through this largest of Mo-

rocco's oases. Fed by the Ziz and Rheris rivers, the Tafilalt Oasis covers some 233 square miles, is 80 miles in circumference, and is the farthest point where water from the Atlas Mountains reaches into the Sahara. Fed by the abundant water lying just below the surface, the oasis supports significant agricultural production, including grain, fruit, and vegetables. The most important product is dates, and those from the oasis developed a worldwide reputation.

There is some dispute about the origins of the city. Leo Africanus, the great sixteenth-century traveler, reported in 1515 that the local legend was that Romans had founded the city, though recent archaeological investigation has found no evidence of this. Sedentary peoples may have settled the oasis as early as the fourth century BC, depending on irrigated agriculture and herding for a living. Certainly, the Tafilalt Oasis would have quickly become a key transfer site for caravan traffic across the Sahara when the capability had developed. However, it may have taken from AD 100 to AD 300 before organized mobile tribes of camel nomads came to dominate the long-distance trade of the desert, although evidence for long-distance trade in the region is weak for this early period. The Tafilalt Oasis would have been a perfect spot for Berber inhabitants of the mountains and hills of the pre-Saharan zone to meet nomads working the trans-Saharan trade. It also may have served as a site for Berber-organized resistance to Roman urban authority further northeast in the *limes* (protective forts).

The city itself, however, dates from the eighth century AD and is directly linked with the arrival of the Arabs, Islam, and the region's incorporation into the wider trading and cultural network of the Eurasian city system. Sijilmassa was the second city founded by Muslims in North Africa after Kairouan, and it was intentionally created to control the north-south and east-west trade in the region. Because Sijilmassa lies at the confluence of the trans-Saharan and east-west steppe routes leading to Algeria, Tunisia, and ultimately to Cairo, building a city on the site of an older trading market nurtured by a lush agricultural hinterland made great sense. There was already long-distance trade in gold across the Sahara; with the incorporation of this region into the broader Muslim polity, there was an explosion of trade with West Africa.

Kharijite refugees from the Abbasid persecution arrived in the Berber areas of the western Atlas around the 720s. Traveling in small bands of religious believers, they were looking for protection and support through local affiliation. The Berbers likewise were looking for a way of being Muslim but independent of the Arab elites establishing themselves throughout urban Morocco. Kharijite sectarianism fit in well with the political needs of the Berber chiefs for legitimation, resistance, and central control of long-distance trade. Idris ibn Abdallah, for example, descendant of the Prophet, arrived in central Morocco in the mid-700s and established a political link with the Arawba tribe. The religious legitimacy of Kharijite sectarianism combined with the first attempts at a Berber state project to produce the Idrisid state (AD 789–926), constructed around a local city system supported by the agricultural hinterlands north of the Middle Atlas.

In a similar context, south of the Atlas Mountains, Berber tribal leaders supporting an Arab Kharijite leader named al-Yasa founded Sijilmassa in AD 757. The city was independent and flourished through a combination of elements: its control of the trans-Saharan trade; a Berber-Arab leadership; a religious ideology of zeal, legitimacy, and resistance; and links into the developing state project north of the High Atlas. The founding of Fez by the Idrisids in AD 808 had an important effect on the spectacular early development of Sijilmassa (see also "Fez").

The city's built environment quickly developed under the strong hand of the founding coalition. Al-Yasa ruled the city-state from 790 to 823 and is responsible for much of its early monumental and defensive construction. He was part of the Midrar dynasty, which ruled the city for the next 200 years, establishing what has become known as the Tafilalt Kingdom. Despite Idrisid attempts to control the city-state, Sijilmassa resisted, using its monopoly over southern trade to guarantee its wealth and autonomy.

Under the Midrar dynasty, Sijilmassa developed into a crucial entrepôt. Ibn Hauqal (AD 967) talks about the size of its layout and its formidable city gates. Al-Bakri (AD 1068) comments on the monumentality of its buildings; al-Massudi (tenth century) comments on its minting of all the gold from the Sudan; others wrote about its control and organization of the trade to the south or east to Tahert.

Sijilmassa played an important part in the rise of the Fatimid Empire in North Africa (AD 930–1062) as well. Ubaid Allah al-Mahdi, the first publicly identified leader of the Fatamid line, fled from Syria, found refuge in Sijilmassa, and established an alliance with Abdullah as-Sufi. It was in the city that they declared the rebellion against Abbasid rule in North Africa. In September AD 909, the army of al-Mahdi then headed for Kairouan, which soon became the capital of the new empire. It was al-Mahdi's grandson who captured Egypt and established Cairo for the Fatimid Caliphate (AD 973, see also "Cairo"). Sijilmassa's association with the Ismailis contributed to the city's importance as a pilgrimage site up to the twentieth century.

Sijilmassa was the site of further sectarianism and rebellion over the next thirty years. After a long civil war, the Fatimid iman al-Muizz could report that his general Jawhar had captured Sijilmassa in September 958 from the Midrarid dynastic "pretender" to the Fatimid throne, Ibn Wasul, and that Ibn Wasul had been carried off in an iron cage.

The next and more successful state project in Morocco had profound implications for the independent city-state. Sijil-

massa traded extensively with the oasis city of Audoghast, far to the southwest across the Sahara and close to the Senegal River. In fact, trade between the two cities was so extensive that Ibn Hauqal reported in the tenth century that one Sijilmassa merchant owed 40,000 gold dinars to another merchant of Audoghast. Around AD 1039, Audoghast was the capital of the Sanhaja Berber confederation, which had recently converted to Islam. One of its chiefs, Yahia ibn Ibrahim, returning from the hajj and invited the radical preacher Abdullah ibn Yasin of Sijilmassa back to the Western Sahara. There Ibn Yasin founded a *ribat*, a fortified outpost for preaching and conversion to his radical vision of Islam. In 1042 Ibn Yasin led an army of his new disciples, initially composed of Sanhaja Berbers of the Western Sahara, out of the ribat in a jihad against other Berber tribes who rejected his austere and purist interpretation of Islam. This army, known as the al-Murabitun (people of the ribat), became known to the Christians of Spain as the Almoravids (AD 1062–1147, see also "Nouakchott").

After subduing the tribes of the Western Sahara, Ibn Yasin led his swelling and fanatical army north. Their first stop was his hometown of Sijilmassa, where the Almoravids defeated the city's army, killed the amir, and established a garrison. The people of the city, members of the Zenata Berber confederation, soon rebelled against the puritanical regime, and Ibn Yasin returned to suppress the revolt and crush the Kharijite faith. He then used the city as a base to quickly organize his growing army and attacked across the Atlas range to take the cities of central Morocco. Although Ibn Yasin was killed in 1057, the Almoravid army under Yusuf ibn Tachfin went on to capture all of Morocco. In 1062 Yusuf founded Marrakesh and took Fez, in 1079 he reached Tangier and invaded Andalusia, and by 1102 he ruled from Madrid to Senegal (see also "Marrakesh" and "Tangier").

Taking Sijilmassa was crucial to the nomadic strategy of monopolizing the key gold trade routes and their resources. With the control of these routes, the Almoravids were able to weaken the urban centers of the north and the coast, leading to their incorporation into the new empire. Sijilmassa became an important mint for gold dust brought from West Africa, and its coinage became the medium of exchange as far away as Muscovy, Bukhara, Aqaba, and Zanzibar. Given the wealth of its merchant traders, the city's elite were key allies to the Berber nomads, and Sijilmassa was able to retain a degree of mercantile autonomy under these political-religious patrons and prospered as a city.

Its merchant traders spread throughout Dar al-Islam and West Africa, facilitating trade with their hometown. Many would start from the city with cheap coral beads made in Ceuta, load up with salt in Taghaza, and then end their journey along the Senegal in the silent trade of salt for gold. Gold, slaves, animals, and ivory were shipped north, and cowries, salt, sugar, horses, books, textiles, metal goods, and military hardware were shipped south.

Monumental architecture, city walls, public baths, and grandeur were the legacy of this period. The city's water supply was technologically sophisticated and dependent on extensive dams and infrastructure to channel the rivers. Early on, a wall surrounded the city, but later a wall was built to surround the whole oasis. Under the distant dynasties, the city served as an administrative *diwan* (administration) for the collection of taxes and customs duties.

Sijilmassa continued its tradition both as a refuge for those persecuted for their religious beliefs and as a magnet for those seeking to make money. Around 1,200 descendants of Muhammad's son-in-law Ali were invited by Sijilmassa citizens to settle in their city; the immigrants allegedly brought with them the cloak of Muhammad. In the 1300s, foreign merchants were well represented: Genoese traders had a *funduq,* or walled trading house, in Sijilmassa. These same Genoese provided important cartographic information about West Africa to the cartographer Giovanni di Carignano for his famous 1320 map. Jewish merchants found a home in the trading community funding the trans-Saharan caravans. Their network of coreligionists along the major North African and trans-Saharan routes was a crucial facilitator in building Sijilmassa's monopoly. They also were important artisans, providing specialist skills as metalworkers, jewelers, tailors, cobblers, and carpenters. Their community prospered, and the Tafilalt Abuhatzira family in particular became regionally known for their piety and rabbinic influence. Their yeshiva also attracted students from throughout the region. Within this mix of Berber, Arab, Muslim, and Jew, African slaves, often linked to the religious institutions in the city, provided the menial labor for the date plantations and villas of the merchants.

A confederation of religious opponents to the Almoravids soon arose to challenge for control of Morocco. The Almohads (AD 1130–1269) quickly captured Marrakesh in 1147 and went on to take all of Muslim Spain and North Africa by the 1170s. Within less than a century, however, their dynasty was overthrown by the Berber Merinids or Banu Merin (AD 1258–1465), who captured Marrakesh from them in 1269. Unfortunately for Sijilmassa, the Merinids took a different attitude to the cities under their control than did their predecessors. Rather than supporting semiautonomous urban development and encouraging merchants to expand trade, the Merinids shifted trade to the coasts, supported the creation of alternative urban centers, and imposed heavy taxation on the trading elites. Because the state was fierce but weak, there was significant civil war during their rule, and Sijilmassa, a key jewel in the crown, suffered siege and destruction in 1311–1333, 1361–1363, and 1387.

The great traveler Ibn Battuta visited the city in 1352. He spent four months there outfitting his team for the two-month-long winter caravan crossing to Mali (see also "Timbuktu"). While in Sijilmassa, Ibn Battuta records his astonishment upon discovering that his host, a Sufi scholar named Muhammad al-Bushri, was the brother of another Sufi he had befriended in China. Ibn Battuta also notes that the caravan's "managers" were Masufa Berbers, holding a monopoly in the oasis over the guides, guards, and drivers for the trans-Saharan trade.

Sijilmassa, geographically removed from the core of Maghreb Arab urban development, experienced a degree of autonomy during this period. But the rise, internal conflict, and fall of these centralizing dynasties between AD 1000 and AD 1400 also ate away at the city's monopoly of the gold trade. The centralizing states had revenue concerns, and as overall trade expanded and their need for gold dramatically increased, they opened up numerous routes to the east and south other than those articulated by Sijilmassa. They also tightened the net on the city's revenues. By the late fourteenth century, the city's wealth, importance, and control of trade had been diluted, challenged by other sites, pillaged by the Merinids' direct taxation, and threatened by privileges granted to other tribal confederations. According to Leo Africanus, the city dates its destruction to 1393, when the citizens rose up against the Merinid governor, destroyed the defensive walls, fell out among themselves, and moved into small village fortresses, or *qasr,* around the oasis. The city was abandoned and quickly fell into ruin.

Once Sijilmassa was abandoned, although some merchants in the oasis remained involved in long-distance trade, the key regional caravan *point de départ* shifted southwest to Tinduf, where it remained until the early twentieth century. Over the next 200 years, conflict between Spanish, Portuguese, and Muslim powers for control of the maritime trade in gold from West Africa diminished the importance of all trans-Saharan routes. The Tafilalt Oasis went through a shift in technology and water supply, changing the demography of the oasis to that of numerous villages rather than a single urban center. Although the Grand Mosque was reconstructed between 1430 and 1460, when the traveler Leo Africanus twice passed through the oasis between AD 1510 and AD 1515, he was struck by the ruins of Sijilmassa and the site's desolation.

Although the city itself was destroyed, the inheritors of the Sijilmassa legacy, the people of the Tafilalt Oasis, remained crucial to developments in Moroccan history. By the early 1600s, the Alawite family, those descendants of Ali who had migrated to the city around 1200 from Yanbu, reemerged as an Arab political-religious force to challenge for control of Morocco. Trading on their sharifan heritage, the religious legitimacy of the Tafilalt site, their domination of the agricultural production of the oasis, and their desire to maintain what was left of the Tafilalt control of trans-Saharan trade, the

Alawites burst into the chaos of the Moroccan political arena. By AD 1666, they controlled the country, and they remain today the dynasty in control of the Moroccan state. Thus, the present king Muhammad traces his ancestry to Sijilmassa. Elites from Tafilalt are particularly revered political advisors to the dynasty.

As Alawite power grew in the seventeenth century, they sponsored monumental rebuilding in the oasis. The Grand Mosque was enlarged, and significant water management projects along the Ziz were undertaken. Much of the required labor for these projects was supplied by black slaves: the second Alawid sultan, Mulay Ismail (1672–1727), reportedly owned 150,000 black slaves, either for use in his army or as state laborers. Most of these slaves had been transported across the Sahara, and their first stop, before the great slave market of Marrakesh, was Sijilmassa.

Two major tribal confederations came to control the Tafilalt region after 1700. One was the Ait Atta Berber confederation, one of the largest in Morocco. Known for their warrior skills and ferocity, they extracted protection payment from the qasrs throughout the oasis, dominated the palm and date agriculture, and monopolized the remaining caravan trade. The other was the Dawi Mani Arab tribe, which owned date groves in the oasis. Between them, these two tribes offered the strongest resistance to the French imperial encroachment after 1900. Using flintlock muskets made by Jewish gunsmiths in the oasis, and later acquiring Remington and Winchester rifles from European arms traders, the Ait Atta attacked French Foreign Legion outposts established by the French occupation in the Tafilalt region. Such resistance to the loss of their autonomy and livelihood continued well after the 1907 invasion.

Although the Tafilalt Oasis is home to some 80,000 people today, and agricultural production continues apace, Sijilmassa itself is a set of ruins along the Ziz River. Yet the site was included in the first "List of 100 Most Endangered Sites" issued by the World Monuments Fund in 1996. This is partly because of the unbaked-brick Grand Mosque located on the central tell of the ruins. Rebuilt in 1796, the Grand Mosque requires regular preservation to maintain its structural integrity. The site also receives visitors and pilgrims; numerous tombs of Sufi saints and holy men remain, as do tombs of Jewish holy men from the Abuhatzira family that still attract visitors from among the descendants of the Tafilalt Jewish community, which emigrated to Israel en masse in 1973.

Bruce Stanley

Further Readings

Africanus, Leo. *Description de l'Afrique.* Translated by A. Epaulard. Paris: Adrien-Maisonneuve, 1957.

Boone, James L., J. Emlen Myers, and Charles L. Redman. "Archaeological and Historical Approaches to Complex Societies: The Islamic States of Medieval Morocco." *American Anthropologist* 92, no. 3 (September 1990): 630–646.

Bovill, Edward W. *The Golden Trade of the Moors.* Princeton: Markus Wiener, 1995.

Lightfoot, Dale R., and James A. Miller. "Sijilmassa: The Rise and Fall of a Walled Oasis in Medieval Morocco." *Annals of the Association of American Geographers* 86, no. 1 (March 1996): 78–101.

T

Tabriz
Population: 1.7 million (2005 estimate)

Few cities have suffered as much devastation from earthquakes and attack as Tabriz. Located in the northwest corner of Iran where Turkey, Iraq, Azerbaijan, and Armenia (and formerly Russia) meet, this city of the Silk Road has been destroyed and rebuilt many times over the last 2,000 years. As capital of the Ilkhanid, Black Sheep Turkoman, and Safavid dynasties, the city was graced by numerous exquisite monuments, few of which survive today because of the ravage of earthquakes or invaders like the Mongols, Temür, or the Russians. Home of the famous school of Persian miniature painting of the great artist Bihzad, eulogized by the Sufi poet Rumi, and incubator for the Constitutional Revolution in Iran in 1908, the city remains one of Iran's great urban centers.

Tabriz is situated 4,600 feet above sea level in a valley at the foot of the volcanic Sahand mountain range, which stretches between Tabriz and Maragheh in northwest Iran. At the base of the triangular valley is the Aji-chai plain, which slopes toward Lake Umiya, through which flows the Aji River into the center of Tabriz. Located 403 miles northwest of Tehran, 193 miles southeast of Bazargan on the Iran-Turkey frontier, and 360 miles north of Kermanshah, the city has, historically, been ideally situated to be a major trade center. It has been subject to earthquakes and invasions from and military occupations by competing dynasties throughout its history because of its strategic position between Turkey, Russia, Azerbaijan, and Iran. This has resulted in the constant destruction and reconstruction of the city and its monuments, few of which still exist today.

A variation of the city's name is Tibriz, which may be the local dialect's version. Now, however, the city's name is exclusively Tabriz, which can be translated as "making fever run" or "that which makes the heat disappear," suggesting a connection with the volcanic nature of its location. The main language is Azeri, a Turkish dialect, although Persian is the lingua franca.

The origins of Tabriz are unclear. There is a debate on whether Tabriz is associated with the ancient Media. The northern Pahlavi text *Tavrez* hints that the city has a pre-Sassanian (AD 224–651) or pre-Arascid heritage. A fourteenth-century Armenian historian suggested that Tabriz was founded by the Arshakid Armenian Khosro (AD 217–233) in revenge against the Sassanian king Ardashir (AD 224–241) for killing the Parthian king Artabanus. According to another legend, the city was built in AD 791 by caliph Harun ar-Rashid's wife, Zulaikha. However, it is reported by both al-Baladhuri (d. AD 892) and Ibn al-Faqih (d. AD 912) that the city was rebuilt by the ar-Rawwad al-Azdi family, whose sons were responsible for the city's walls, perhaps following its destruction by an earthquake. W. B. Harris reports that the site of Tabriz is not that of the original city. Although the city was totally destroyed by an earthquake in 858, it was described as a fine town a century later only to be ruined again by the 1042 earthquake.

The Mongols first presented themselves at Tabriz's walls in winter 1220–1221 and again in 1222. Not until 1224, however, with more support from Mongolia, did they finally manage to force the surrender of the Ildegizid Atabeg Ozbeg b. Pahlawan and the Khwarizms. The Khwarizm Jalal ad-Din returned to the city in 1225, but in 1231 the Mongols reconquered Tabriz and the province. The Mongol Ilkhanid ruler Abaqa (1295–1282) made Tabriz the capital of the Ilkhanid Kingdom, under the suzerainty of the Mongols. It remained the capital until Uljaytu, the eighth Ilkhanid ruler, moved his administration to Sultaniyya. It is possible that Marco Polo traveled through Tabriz during the latter part of the thirteenth century on his journey through Iran to China.

It was during the reign of Ilkhanid Ghazan Khan (r. 1304–1316) that Tabriz flourished and became a world city. Even though Ghazan Khan destroyed its temples, churches, and synagogues, being a recent convert to Islam, new walls were erected, enlarging the city threefold, and the city's bazaar, now considered one of the Middle East's oldest and largest bazaars, was developed. As part of his administrative reforms, Ghazan Khan was also responsible for the introduction of Iran's uniform monetary system as well as a failed attempt to introduce paper currency in the city. Ibn Battuta visited in the early fourteenth century and was dazzled by its display of precious stones. Suburbs to the east, Rashidiyyeh or Rab'-i Rashid (Rashid's Quarter), were developed under the patronage of the vizier Rashid ad-Din (1247–1318). To the west, around Ghazan Khan's tomb, which housed a hospital, mosque, library, and institutions of learning, grew up the district of Sham. Ilkhanid Tabriz's only remaining monument, Masjed-e Ali Shah, was built around 1310 by the vizier Taj ad-Din Ali Shah. It was adapted in 1809 to form part of the citadel and, standing ninety-two feet high, is now known as Arg-e Ali Shah (Ali Shah's fortress/citadel) or Arg-e Tabriz (Tabriz's fortress/citadel).

This period also witnessed the rise of Tabriz as an important literary center. Rashid ad-Din wrote *The Compendium of*

Landscape painting of the Ilkanid Ghazan Khan at Tabriz, ca. 1295. (Corel Corporation)

Histories, which integrated Mongol, Muslim, Chinese, Indian, and European history. The *Shah Nameh, Life of Alexander,* and the fables of *Kalila wa Dimna* were copied and illustrated by the famous artists of Persian miniatures in the city. The famous Kamal ad-Din Bihzad (1460–1535) established his school in Tabriz late in his life, and his followers carried on the tradition for years. Jalal ad-Din Muhammad Rumi (1207–1273), the Sufi Persian poet, eulogized Tabriz in his six-volume poem, *Masnavi-ye Manavi (Spiritual Couplets).* Mahmud Shabistari (1288–1321), who was famous for his rhyming couplets *Gulshan-i Rāz (The Secret Rose Garden),* written around 1311, lived and worked in Tabriz.

Tabriz was also capital under the Qara Quynulu Jahan Shah (king of the world, r. 1436–1467). The Qara Quynulu (Black Sheep Turkoman) Empire included eastern Anatolia; northwestern, western, and central Iran; and Iraq. However, the Aq Quynulu (White Sheep Turkomans), who defeated Jahan Shah, temporarily transferred the capital to Amid (see

also "Diyarbakir"). It was moved back in 1472 by Uzun Hassan (r. 1453–1478). Although severely damaged by the 1778 earthquake, the exquisite entrance to the 1465 Masjed-i Kabud, or Blue Mosque, part of a complex built by Jahan Shah's wife, Khatun Jan, still remains. The mosque possessed pools fed by a canal and a domed square hall and decorated mihrab with floral designs. The mosque also housed a hospice for Sufis.

Uzun Hassan's death in 1478 was followed by civil war and the establishment of Tabriz as the Safavid capital by the dynasty's founder, Shah Ismail I (r. 1501–1524). Within a decade, the Safavids had conquered the rest of Iran. Claiming to be the Mahdi and the divine fire of the hidden imam, Ismail made Twelver Shi'ism the state religion. Fearing Ottoman attack, the capital was once again moved, this time to Qazvin, by his successor Shah Tahmasp I (r. 1524–1576).

The Safavid dynasty's bullion, sourced from Ottoman territory, was reminted in Tabriz's mint. It was mainly the Armenians who carried the bullion to the city; after they had sold their silk in Aleppo and Izmir, they would return to Tabriz in October with the bullion (see also "Aleppo").

As the Ottomans and Safavids struggled for hegemony in the region, Tabriz was often caught up in the fighting, and it changed hands a number of times. Nonetheless, it flourished, with the population increasing from approximately 300,000 in 1500 to 550,000 in 1673. A famous seventeenth-century Tabrizi was the physician Maqsud Ali Tabrizi, a translator for the Mughal emperor Jahangir (r. 1605–1627). His translations from Arabic to Persian include Shams ad-Din Muhammad ibn Mahmud Shahrazuri's (thirteenth-century) sayings of thirty-four pre-Islamic and seventy-seven post-Islamic scholars and physicians.

Tabriz was seized from the Ottomans by Nadir Shah (r. 1736–1747), the first king of the Afshar dynasty. Mashhad became the capital and Tabriz the regional seat of the northwestern part of his empire. Following Nadir Shah's death in 1747, his nephew, Ibrahim Khan, emerged from the succession struggle with the crown and proclaimed himself king in Tabriz. Karim Khan Zand's dynasty (r. 1760–1779) followed, but little is known of Tabriz during this period.

Tabriz reemerged to significance during the Qajar reign (1781–1925), even though Tehran was their capital (see also "Tehran"). The 1830s witnessed the revival of the Trabzon-Tabriz trade route, which had been active at the beginning of the nineteenth century as an alternative route for exporting Gilan's silk. Although at its height in the 1850s and 1860s, with two-fifths of Iran's trade, by the 1900s the route fell from favor as other routes through Russian Transcaucasia and the Persian Gulf ports emerged (see also "Trabzon"). Because of the city's proximity to the Russian frontier, the city was made a regional military center. It was momentarily occupied by the Russians during the Russian-Iranian War (1826–1828).

Tabriz was the site for the trial and execution of Sayyid Ali Muhammad Shirazi, the Bab (the gate), who founded the Bahai religion. Proclaiming his prophethood in 1844, the Bab said he was announcing the coming of the great prophet, the Bahá Ulláh, or hidden imam. In a time of messianic expectation, his declaration was a threat to the Qajar regime, followers fought with troops of the authorities, and the Qajar leaders tried him in front of religious authorities and the crown prince. After his execution by firing squad in 1850, his body was taken to Haifa, where he was entombed in the Shrine of the Bab (see also "Haifa").

In the late nineteenth century, the city came to play an important role in Iran's social and political movements. Tabriz was now Iran's second city, with an estimated population of 200,000 (1895). In reaction to the concession of a tobacco monopoly to the British, it became home to the first demonstrations (1891) of the tobacco protest movement. The protests spread to Mashhad and Esfahan and culminated in the boycott of tobacco nationwide (see also "Esfahan"). Furthermore, because of the city's position as an international trade center, with a more modernized economy, Tabriz led in the uprising known as the Constitutional Revolution. In 1900 and 1901, secret societies distributed *shabnamehs* (night letters or antigovernment leaflets) in the city's streets. On 23 June 1908, the day Tehran's *majlis* (parliament) was bombarded, open rebellion broke out in Tabriz.

Many Tabrizis were important figures during the Constitutional Revolution: Sattar Khan (1868–1914) led Iranians from Azerbaijan, Gilan, Bakhtiar, and Tehran in protest against Muhammad Ali Shah Qajar's abolishment of the constitution; the cleric, politician, and journalist Haji Mirza Hassan Tabrizi, known as Hassan Roshdiyyeh, as a member of the Maref Association was active; the famous poet Iraj Mirza (1874–1927), whose work includes *Mother* and *Zohreh va Manuchehr,* was also active; and the linguist, historian, reformer, and philosopher Ahmad Kasravi Tabrizi (1890–1946) also joined the Constitutional Revolution. He was critical of the clergy and a supporter of democracy. After a failed assassination attempt by the Fadain-e Islam, he was stabbed to death. His work includes *The 18 Year History of Azarbaijan, The Constitutional History of Iran, The Forgotten Kings, The 500 Year History of Khuzestan, A Brief History of the Lion and Sun,* and *Sheikh Safi and His Progeny.*

Following the 1780 earthquake, new boulevards, mosques, caravansaries, and large gardens were built in the city. New construction also included work on four of Tabriz's churches: the rebuilding of Saint Mary Church (Kelesa-ye Maryam-e Moghaddas) in 1785; the building of Holy Serkis Church, in the Banvan neighborhood, in 1821; the renovation of Saint Serkis Church, in the Armenian Quarter, in 1845; and Able Mary Church, in the Miar Miar Quarter, in 1910. In 1868 Haj Vali Memar-e Tabrizi constructed Constitution House, which was used as a gathering place for the leaders, activists, and sympathizers of the Constitutional Revolution. Tabriz of the time was described by W. B. Harris as a walled city with eight principal entrances, one of which had been recently opened to allow European carriages to pass through and thus avoid the narrow streets and bazaars.

Tabriz changed hands yet again when the Russians occupied the city in 1915, expelling an Ottoman-Kurdish force. During their occupation, the Russians added to Tabriz's strategic position by extending the Tiflis-Julfa Railway to the city in 1916. With the Russian Revolution, their troops withdrew, allowing the Ottomans to briefly return.

In the 1930s, under the Pahlavis, Tabriz developed into one of Iran's most important commercial centers, with a population of 260,000. Its industries included high-quality leather for both Iranian and European markets, cotton yarns and woolen goods, soap, cigarettes, and beer. The carpet industry, having been revived in the latter part of the nineteenth century, established Tabriz as a center for export to Europe. The districts' dried fruits and almonds were exported to Europe via Julfa, Tiflis, and Batoum. Development included new wide streets, public gardens, and a town hall. The railway was extended to link Tabriz to both Turkey and Tehran.

In 1941 the Soviets occupied Tabriz and northwestern Iran. On 10 December 1945, the city was proclaimed the capital of the autonomous regime of the Firqah-i Dimukrat-i Azerbaijan (Democratic Party of Azerbaijan) under the leadership of Seyyed Jafar Pishavari. The nationalist nature of the partition was reflected in the nationalization of banks and the establishment of the Azerbaycan Universiteti (University of Azerbaijan) in 1946 (renamed the University of Tabriz in 1979). Following pressures from the United States and the United Nations (UN), the Soviets gave in, and the Pahlavi imperial army reasserted control on 12 December 1946. A famous Tabrizi of this period is the socially and politically motivated Azeri writer Samad Behrangi (1939–1967), famous for his children's book, *Mahi-ye Siyah-e Kuchaloo* (*The Little Black Fish*).

Tabriz is now the capital of Iran's Eastern Azerbaijan Province and was the country's second-largest city until the 1970s. Having been enhanced as a linking city by the Turkey-Iran rail route, Tabriz continues to be a major trade center, especially for trade between Turkey and Iran. More recent famous Tabrizis include Ivan Alexander Galamian (1903–1981), one of the twentieth century's most influential violin teachers, whose most notable pupils include Itzhak Perlman, Pinchas Zuckerman, Michael Rabin, and Violaine Melançon; founder of the analytical philosophy of medicine, Kazem Sadegh-Zadeh (b. 1942); and footballer Karim Bagheri (b. 1974), who was responsible for Iran's comeback against Australia in the 1998 World Cup qualifier.

Shabnam Holliday

Further Readings

Bahari, Ebadollah. *Bihzad, Master of Persian Painting.* London: I. B. Tauris, 1996.

Kolbas, Judith G. *The Mongols in Iran: Chinqiz Khan to Uljaytu, 1220–1309.* New York: Routledge, 2005.

Raby, Julian, and Teresa Fitzherbert, eds. *The Court of the Il-Khans, 1290–1340.* Oxford: Faculty of Oriental Studies, 1996.

Shaffer, B. *Borders and Brethren: Iran and the Challenge of Azerbaijani Identity.* Cambridge: MIT Press, 2002.

Werner, Christoph. *An Iranian Town in Transition: A Social and Economic History of the Elites of Tabriz, 1747–1848.* Weisbaden: Harrasowitz, 2000.

Taif
Population: 350,000 (2005 estimate)

Taif contradicts all the images one may have of a city on the Arabian Peninsula. It is green, with fresh grapes and oranges available, a fresh cool breeze, and rose farms in the surrounding hills. This "little bit of Syria" in western Saudi Arabia has always been a resort town, serving political leaders from the Red Sea cities with a summer home away from the heat and sticky atmosphere of the coast. Today, during the summer, it becomes the official capital of Saudi Arabia. Fifteen hundred years ago, it was little different, with the elites of Makkah owning land and vineyards in the oasis. Although its inhabitants at first drove the Prophet Muhammad out of town, this city quickly became a junior partner in the expansion of the Muslim community. Its resort feel has attracted conferences and summits, and the Saudis have found it convenient as a site for regional diplomatic negotiations in and among the delights of horse racing and shopping in its suqs.

Taif (Arabic, *at-Taif*) is located some seventy miles to the east of the Saudi Red Sea port of Jeddah, high up in the mountains separating the Hijaz from the Najd heartland of the Arabian Peninsula. The city lies at 4,800 feet above sea level in an oval basin just below rugged ridges with high mountain peaks in the distance. The basin is a large oasis, marked by numerous hand-dug wells and orchards but without the palms of oases in the desert. The city faces north down the valley and is bisected by Wadi Wajj. Blessed by high altitude and low humidity, Taif was the only place in the Hijaz where water might freeze, noted the geographer al-Istakhri (ca. tenth century AD). Pine trees, fruits, and water remind visitors of the beauties of Mount Lebanon or Syria. Grape vines, introduced after the fourth century from Syria, produced grapes used for renowned wine or were processed into Taif raisins, considered a delicacy throughout the Middle East.

Through the oasis passed the ancient incense route, which led from the Hadramawt to Petra and Gaza and the historic caravan route connecting Makkah via Najran to Sanaa. Until only recently, reaching the city was a difficult task; most of the tracks up the mountains were too steep for camels, and even

with donkeys, one had to walk part of the way. Today Jeddah is two hours by car. Barren volcanic and granite rocks host forests of juniper and wild olive as one nears the city. The great Wadi Aqiq flows north toward Madinah, and in the past flash floods have carried bushes from the mountains far toward the plain. The city itself has always suffered from runoff and flash flooding, given that Taif receives the highest precipitation in Saudi Arabia.

Taif is an old resort town, an ancient station on the caravan routes, and an even older oasis settlement. There are archaeological remains in the basin that date back before 2000 BC. Ancient dams and irrigation systems testify to continual use for agricultural production. The few superficial excavations that have been carried out have revealed little about the evolution of the city, but since there are many Nabatean and Thamudi inscriptions carved on stones on the outskirts of the city, we know that it goes back to the first millennium BC. The site was probably inhabited by Amalikites (ca. 1500 BC) and known as Wij, which is still the name of a fertile valley within the city of today. Since then, because of the fertility of the land, moderate weather, and the availability of water, many tribal confederations have captured and controlled the oasis for a time, including the Thamudis, Azds, Mudhir, Adwan, Hawazin, and Thaqif.

The word *Taif* appears to derive from the root word meaning *enclosure* and thus may refer to the city walls encompassing the city. Taif acquired this name after the Thaqif tribe defeated and expelled the Hawazin bani amir from the oasis and then built a wall to prevent their being forced out. This walled area was called Madinah Jahiliyah and controlled the oasis in the pre-Islamic period.

The Thaqif remade the oasis to support a substantial agricultural community. They developed irrigation canals, improved cropping, regulated the rights and liabilities of farmers and landowners, and exported their agricultural products. These technologies and social patterns were rare in the Hijaz, although they were similar to those that existed farther south in Yemen at the time. Taif does represent, of sorts, climatically a northern outpost of Yemen. This is one reason that at times the boundary of Yemen was seen as being at Taif.

The agricultural community high in the mountains evolved close relationships with Makkah in the lowlands. The Qur'an refers to Makkah and Taif as the *al-Qariyyatain* (the two cities), an expression that clearly implies a dyadic link between them. Taif was strongly linked with Makkah in two key ways. The first was via commercial exchange. Their economic cooperation manifest itself in the export of almost all of Taif's crops exclusively to Makkah, in particular its famous brewed wine. Makkah produced no agricultural products of its own and so was dependent upon Taif as its breadbasket or for the grain imported via Taif from Yemen. In return, wealthy Quraishi merchants invested heavily in the farms and estates of Taif, where they used to spend their summers.

Taif thus became a strategic city for the Hijaz: its gateway to Yemen and the Najd, its breadbasket, its vacation paradise. Whatever the political entities of the time, it was crucial that they command the strategic town of Taif if they wanted to control the coast. Such centrality attracted, for example, Mundir III of Hirah, a client of the Persians, who controlled the city after AD 531.

In the pre-Islamic period, there was another link between the two cities, which manifested itself in religious competition. The Thaqif worshipped the goddess al-Latt, and they struggled to attract pilgrims to the al-Latt shrine in Taif rather than to the Kaabah of Makkah. It was among the sacred trees of the shrine (the *haram*) that the killing of animals or humans was banned. This competition had a religious component but also a source in the revenues generated from such pilgrimage. As a result, when the Abyssinian general Abraha marched on the Kaabah in 570, the Thaqif supported the expedition, and a key Thaqifi leader acted as guide for the Abyssinian army through their territory to Makkah. Relics of this idol worship are still in the vicinity.

The combination of trade, agriculture, and pilgrimage meant that Taif was a good site for a regular market or fair. Nearby was the Ukaz Fair, one of the most famous in all of Arabia. As part of a regular cycle of fairs throughout the year, Ukaz attracted merchants from Yemen, the coast, and the far north. Included in this colorful spectacle of the suq were poets and singers who came to participate in talent contests. These contests produced some of the most famous *qasidah* (odes), including the *Seven Muallaqat* (suspended, perhaps, because the best were suspended in Makkah on the Kaabah), the best of the best. Some of these pre-Islamic poems make reference to the city walls and villas of Taif. The fair continued into the eighth century, after which its function was replaced by larger urban markets and changing caravan routes.

Around 620 the Prophet Muhammad visited the Ukaz Fair, and what he had to say sparked interest in some of the traders from Yathrib (Madinah). Later, before his migration to Madinah, Muhammad, accompanied by his adopted son Zeid, visited Taif to preach but was refused even a hearing and was stoned as he was driven out of the city. The Prophet, supported by a crowd of warriors, returned in 630 and laid unsuccessful siege to Taif for almost a month. In 631 the head of the tribe embraced Islam, which resulted in his assassination by his own people. Quickly, however, the city changed its mind and sent a delegation to the Prophet and indicated their willingness to embrace Islam. The Prophet, stressing the diplomatic immunity of ambassadors, did not hold their earlier antagonism against them and welcomed them into the community (see also "Makkah" and "Madinah"). Interestingly, the men of Taif evidently complained about one aspect of the oath of Islam, the requirement to refrain from *zina* (generally translated as "adultery"). They argued that, as merchants, they were often gone from home for long periods and that

flexible arrangements in relations with their wives were acceptable among their community. Some also sought to retain al-Latt during a period of transition; Muhammad would have none of it, and the idol was destroyed.

By the time of caliph Abu Bakr, the people of Taif were clearly a key part of the Muslim community: in 633 they were included in a call to a jihad against the Byzantines. The Abdullah ibn al-Abbas Mosque, where Muhammad's first cousin is buried, was the first mosque in the city; today its ruins are an archaeological site. Nearby is a cemetery where martyrs of the attack on the city in AD 630 are buried, and the tombs of two of Muhammad's sons are also located here.

Taif was home to many historic personalities during the rise of Islam. For example, there was Ummayyah bin Abi as-Salt, a famous monolithic poet who imagined himself a prophet. When Muhammad declared his own prophecy, the competition did not destroy Muhammad's appreciation of his poetry. Tradition holds that the rise to power of the Umayyad dynasty was the work of caliph Muawiyah and three other political geniuses (*duhat*), two of whom were from Taif: al-Mughirah bin Shubah and Ziad bin Abih, Muawiyah's half brother. Also, two of the most prominent Umayyad military leaders, al-Hajjaj bin Yusuf and Muhammad bin al-Qasim, were from Taif. Al-Hajjaj abandoned his school in the city for the sword in defense of the Umayyad Caliphate and its control of the Hijaz. There was also Aishah bint-Talhah, one of the most famous beauties of the Umayyad age and the talk of the Taif resort elite. She refused to veil herself, saying that Allah had given her this face, and by showing it in public the people would recognize his generosity. In addition, there was al-Harith ibn Kaladah, the "doctor of the Arabs," the first scientifically trained doctor in the Hijaz.

Although Muawiyah moved his capital to Damascus, he evidently missed his old Hijazi base. He and his brothers all invested heavily in landholdings in Taif and in its agricultural infrastructure, building dams, improving its canals, and increasing its production. Muawiyah is reported to have said that happy is the man who can "see spring in Jeddah, summer in Taif, and winter in Makkah." Another similar saying was that "all good men want to visit Makkah, but they want to die in Taif."

Taif was on the great pilgrimage route from Syria to Makkah. Pilgrims would stay the night in the city, then head down to the Holy City; the site of *meeqat* (point on the route defined for *ihram,* or putting on the white seamless garments) is not far from Taif.

In 1815 J. L. Burckhardt, the most famous early European explorer to enter Makkah in disguise, visited Taif for an extended visit. While there he presented himself to Muhammad Ali, the sultan of Egypt, who was in the city while on campaign against the Wahhabi rebels in the Hijaz. Ali gave "Shaykh Ibrahim ibn Abdullah," the disguised Burckhardt, a gift of money.

At the beginning of the First World War, Taif was still the summer resort for the sharif of Makkah, but it also housed a garrison of Turkish troops. Given its strategic importance, Taif was thus one of the four cities attacked on the opening day of the Arab Revolt by Sharif Hussayn's troops in June 1916. During the three-month siege, the story goes that the Egyptian officer in charge of the Arab artillery kept trying to kill the Turkish commandant, whose movements were revealed by a spy. Each time the Egyptian targeted the room where the commandant was reported to be, he had just moved on. Finally, the commander was so shaken by this sequence of near misses that he surrendered the garrison.

Once World War I was over, Sharif Hussayn and King Abdul Aziz as-Saud began testing each others' resolve, and the point of confrontation revolved around Taif. Amir Abdullah, commanding for his father the sharif, attacked the as-Saud forces first (1919) and was defeated in battle. The population of nearby Taif was so fearful of a follow-up attack by the Wahhabi troops that most of the Makkahans in Taif fled; the story goes that only one old sharifan lady stayed behind, arguing that she knew Ibn Saud's royal family, and she could not expect that she would be mistreated by such a man. Although Ibn Saud did not follow up this victory with an attack on Taif, he did launch his final assault on the Hijaz in September 1924 by attacking the city. His Wahhabi troops did kill those who resisted and drove out 3,000 city residents the following day. The Hashemites accused Ibn Saud of a massacre in the city. Subsequent European visitors to the city found it virtually deserted.

Quickly, however, the city was repopulated, and it has grown outward in all directions along the major entrance routes. Gradually, most of the central garden and agricultural plots have been taken up, the city walls were torn down, and today there is a key problem of water management and distribution. In 1948 the population was 20,000; today it is approximately 350,000 in the winter; during the summer, the town is invaded by "the summer people," around 300,000 visitors, who flood into the city, taking up all the hotel space and even setting up tents on its outskirts. Ibn Saud sometimes stayed near Taif in a tent city erected for his use.

One of the most beautiful buildings in the city is the Palace of Shubra, a four-story villa built for Ali Pasha, the ex-sharif of Makkah. With its marble and delicate woodwork, surrounded by beautiful gardens, it remains today one of the key monuments in Taif. King Abdul Aziz as-Saud died here in 1953. Other palaces dot the landscape; King Khalid, marking the end of an era, died in his summer palace in Taif in June 1982, while the new king, Fahd, built his own palace in the city soon after.

As the summer seat of power, Taif was often where the personal largess of the king was handed out to recipients by special committees going door-to-door with cash. In the late afternoons, horse racing and networking are the key pastimes.

People come for the feel of the air, saying that it has a distinct quality and smell. It is a city of bright colors and design, hosting innovative buildings, parks, and shopping complexes.

The city is particularly known for its rose water and rose perfumes, or attar. This perfume or essence is distilled from millions of rose petals collected from rose farms in the mountains surrounding the city. Known as "Arabia's Rose," the city has hosted this unique industry for more than two centuries, and its product has great potency, causing high demand by pilgrims on the hajj. The various distilleries located in the city compete with each other over quality and character of this "essence of Taif." The leftover mash is fed to cows, producing milk with a slight rose flavor.

As U.S.-Saudi military cooperation deepened in the 1960s, the Saudi air force base at Taif became a major logistical hub for the standardization and improvement of the Saudi military. Taif received a significant upgrade, with new facilities, shelters, and training sites all focused to support their responsibilities to cover Makkah, Madinah, and Jeddah.

As an accepted site for political networking, Taif has also hosted negotiations and mediation. In 1934 the Treaty of Taif settled the boundaries between Yemen and the new kingdom of Saudi Arabia. This agreement was one of the only boundary settlements in the peninsula that was not negotiated with the "guidance" of the British government. In 1977 the Carter administration tried to meet with representatives of the Palestine Liberation Organization (PLO) in Taif to discuss Palestinian participation in peace talks with the Israelis. In 1981 the city shared the Third Islamic Summit with Makkah, hosting thirty-seven nations focused on Palestine. A negotiation that succeeded occurred in 1988, when leaders of the Afghan mujahideen met directly for the first time with Soviet leaders to plan the transition to local rule after the Soviets pulled out.

The best-known agreement negotiated in the resort is the Taif Accord (1989), which brought an imposed, negotiated end to the Lebanese civil war. Under the auspices of the Arab League, hosted by Saudi Arabia and guaranteed by its money, with acceptance of Syrian strategic hegemony in Lebanon and with the support of the United States, Lebanese parliamentarians met for three weeks in the resort during October. They agreed to a modified power-sharing arrangement for Lebanon, and although fighting in Lebanon continued for a few more months, the war drew to a close in 1990, with the Taif Accord providing the framework for Syrian dominance well into the new century. Soon after, from August 1990 to spring 1991, Taif served as the home for the Kuwait government in exile during the Iraqi occupation of Kuwait.

The city is now open to non-Saudi tourists. Starting in 2001, the government allowed pilgrims on the Umrah to travel to other spots in the kingdom other than the holy cities. Taif quickly became one of the key places on the pilgrim list, primarily for its gardens and shopping rather than for any religious meaning. The city has witnessed some troubles. The most recent was the shootout in June 2004, when security forces killed two suspects from the earlier bombing of al-Khobar in May.

Ahmed Abdelkareem Saif

Further Readings

Niblock, Tim. *Saudi Arabia.* London: Routledge, 2005.
Peterson, J. E. *Saudi Arabia and the Illusion of Security.* London: Routledge, 2005.
Raheed, Madawi al-. *A History of Saudi Arabia.* Cambridge: Cambridge University Press, 2002.

Tangier
Population: 600,000 (2004 estimate)

The port of Tangier, situated on Morocco's northern Atlantic coast, directly overlooks the entrance to the Mediterranean through the Strait of Gibraltar and is the easiest entrance to North Africa from Spain. As a result, Tangier has been of strategic importance for thousands of years, beginning with Phoenicians and Carthaginian traders, and later the British and American fleets, and lasting until today's European Union (EU) struggle with illegal migration. One of the key "international cities" of the twentieth century, Tangier attracted migrants, artists, beatniks, and those seeking freedom of expression and lifestyle from all over the world, becoming known for its drugs and counterculture.

Tangier (Arabic, *Tanjah;* Spanish, *Tanger*) is a port city located along the southern coast of the narrow Straits of Gibraltar on the Atlantic side of the entrance to the Mediterranean. Thus, it is the last coastal site before heading out into the Atlantic on the North African littoral or the first southern port before entering the inland sea. With its natural deepwater harbor, and its crescent-shaped town plan with the sea in front and the Rif mountain range behind, the city inhabits a beautiful setting and has always attracted transient shipping. The port lies nine miles southwest across the strait from Tarifa.

The port was a small Phoenician staging post perhaps as early as the tenth century BC, but it was Carthaginian traders who developed the site as one of the farthest outposts of their commercial empire. Shards of pottery and other ceramics from the tell date Carthaginian occupation as early as 500 BC. The site became known as Tingi, perhaps in relation to the myth of a great giant who opened the straits between the Atlantic and the Mediterranean. Such a story became associated with Hercules in Greek and Roman mythology, but in Berber the term may refer to Tingi or Antaeus, son of Poseidon. It is probable that Tingis was a key staging point for the Carthaginian explorer Hanno's voyages of discovery that pushed down the African coast looking for gold in the fifth century BC.

The site was controlled by the local kingdom of Mauritania (146 BC–AD 40) but then passed under Roman control as the capital of Mauritania Tingitana, their farthest province in North Africa. Under the Romans, a key military road was built across the province, linking Tingi to Sale to the southwest, which facilitated the significance of Tingi as a security site and as an entrepôt for slaves, animals, citrus wood, and ostrich feathers. Strabo refers to the city in his first century *Geography,* as does Pliny fifty years later.

Under Diocletian in the late third century AD, the province was reorganized and shrank to a small colony centered on Tingis. Prior confrontations with the tribes beyond the Roman *limes* (frontiers), and the borders they marked, had been resolved primarily through *collegia* (negotiations), but by the end of the third century it finally reached such a point that it was cost-effective to reduce Roman exposure back to the primary ports along the littoral. Christianity spread to the city by the late third century, and it may have been a site of a bishopric. Two early Christian saints, Saint Marcellus and Saint Cassian, were beheaded in Tingis in 298. Marcellus was a Roman centurion who publicly rejected the carrying of the army standards since they proclaimed Diocletian as a god, and Cassian was a court reporter who refused to record the punishment of death against Marcellus.

In the fifth century, the Vandals swept into North Africa led by their chief, Gaiseric, who used Tangier as a staging post from which to launch his attacks against the rest of Africa. The town passed under nominal Byzantine control after 533, becoming a backwater for the next few centuries. As the Arab army moved into northwest Morocco after 680, Christians and Berbers sought refuge in Tingis. Led by General Uqba, the Muslims appeared outside the city gates in 682, but it was not until the city was captured by Musa ibn Nuayr in the early eighth century that the city became an important edge city for Islam. Most Tangerines were cosmopolitan, generally Arab and Sunni, and they fell into conflict with the indigenous Berber tribes of the interior, who joined with the Kharijite rebellion. The Kharijites took control of the city in 739, which spurred a period of religious and economic growth.

Moulay Idris founded his kingdom in 788, and Tangier benefited from governmental concern to develop the infrastructure of the region. The subsequent Idrisid dynasty came into conflict with the Andalucian remnants of the Umayyads, who saw themselves as the true Muslim dynasty, and the city was caught up in the middle of this struggle, which continued for the next 150 years. Finally, weakened by conflict and infighting, the city fell to the Fatimid dynasty from Tunisia, which took control in 958.

For the next 400 years, Tangier passed under many different administrations, and various factions struggled to gain control of this important port and the trade routes between southern Europe and Africa that passed through its streets. The city fell under the al-Moravids, then the al-Mohads, who wiped out the large Jewish population of the city; next came the Tunisian Hafsid dynasty, and later the Marinids. Each of these dynasties left their mark on the city, as the influx and mix of religious beliefs and tribes laid the foundations for what was to become one of the world's most liberal cities.

In 1325 Tangier's most famous son, Ibn Battuta, set out at the age of twenty-one on a pilgrimage to Makkah. This Tangerine was gone twenty-nine years, visiting most of Dar al-Islam and traveling more than three times the distance covered by his relative contemporary Marco Polo. When he did return, a scribe put down his travels in a tome that became known as *The Marvels of Cities and the Wonders of Wandering* (Ridla). It is because of the fame of the traveling Ibn Battuta that many people have heard of the city of Tangier.

Italian traders often called at Tangier during the medieval period. Starting in the thirteenth century, the Genoese were preeminent, and they would refit in the port as they mapped the African coast to the south. By the fourteenth century, Tangier had become a major gateway into the North African Muslim world for European traders exchanging spices and cloth for cereals and sugar goods. As with all conduits of trade, Tangier grew wealthy and cosmopolitan as merchants made the city a trading and finance center. The Venetians were particularly central to the control of the city's trade into Europe and encouraged the importation of goods from across the Sahara. The city became an autonomous amirate of Tangier in 1421, but unfortunately, the level of commercial activity brought the city to the attention of the empire-building European powers, and given the crusading goals of Prince Henry the Navigator, the Portuguese tried in 1437, with eighty ships and 15,000 men, to take the city. They failed but tried again two decades later, and the city surrendered in 1457.

Thus, this port of trade became a pawn among the Atlantic empires over the next 500 years, with little control over its own destiny. Tangier became a victim of realpolitik when it passed back and forth between the Spanish and Portuguese during the sixteenth century. Even at this time, the city had acquired a reputation for spies and political intrigue; the Swedish engineer Bechman, for example, worked in the city for the English king Charles II to protect the restoration. Finally, in 1662 the English acquired the city when, along with Bombay and 2 million crowns, Tangier was acquired as part of the dowry of Catherine of Braganza when she was wed to King Charles II. This was the first English colony in Africa. The famous English diarist Samuel Pepys, who, although based in London, became Tangier's treasurer and secretary in 1664, is reported to have said that Tangier was "the most considerable place the King of England hath in this world." Pepys traveled to Tangier in 1683 to facilitate the evacuation of the English mission there when their rule ended.

Tangier's position, as the trading jewel in the crown of English possessions and thorn in the side of the Portuguese, did not last long, however. In 1679 Moulay Ismail of the new sharifan Alawite dynasty laid siege to the town and eventually forced a British retreat; as they were leaving, the British reduced the city to rubble. Ismail led a detailed program of reconstruction, yet a lack of money, a shift of key trade to other ports, and political will meant that the city entered a period of decline until, by 1810, the population was estimated at only 5,000.

In 1777 Morocco was the first government in the world to recognize the new nation of the United States, beginning a long diplomatic history between the two countries. At the center of this history continued to be Tangier, the diplomatic capital of the country and the port where foreigners interacted with Morocco. American shipping began calling at Tangier before the revolution, and the Moroccan sultan negotiated a treaty with the United States in 1786 that was signed by Thomas Jefferson. The United States established a consulate in the city, and in 1821 Sultan Moulay Sulayman gave a villa in the madinah to the Americans for their legation. This was the first U.S. property abroad, and the beautiful American Legation building in Tangier remains today U.S. property, although now a museum and library dedicated to U.S.-Moroccan friendship. James Simpson, for example, was the U.S. consul general in Tangier who helped save the crew of the U.S. merchant brig the *Commerce* after they were shipwrecked on the Saharan coast in 1815 and made slaves by local tribes.

By the beginning of the nineteenth century, autonomous corsairs out of Tangier were attacking American shipping and holding the sailors of many nations for ransom. In response, U.S. commodore Preble sailed into Tangier harbor in 1803 and pulled off a daring rescue of American prisoners. Even by the end of the century, such problems continued to resurface: Jon Perdicaris, an American adventurer attracted to the city by its reputation for excitement and danger, was kidnapped in May 1904 by Ahmed al-Raisuli, said to be "the last of the Barbary pirates."

The year 1845 marked a turning point in the city's interaction with the European empires. In just another of a collection of "gunboat diplomacy" actions taken against the city by Europeans, the French navy bombarded the city in 1844, and half of its Jewish population fled. Spain went to war with Morocco, and under the resultant Treaty of Tangier, the defeated Moroccans opened the city to foreign merchants and canceled the tribute they had been required to pay. Indeed, Morocco's first privately owned bank, the Pariente Bank, opened in 1844 in Tangier. This was followed in 1856 with a treaty with England that opened the city to free trade and flooded the country with tea and sugar. It was during this period that Giuseppe Garibaldi lived in the city while in exile.

Tangier's renaissance as an economic and diplomatic center began in the mid-nineteenth century, as the various European diplomatic missions struggled for influence in the city that served as the Moroccan diplomatic capital. By the early twentieth century, the Europeans were looking to take over the country: France's Tangier delegation was pro-annexation, and were strong advocates for a French colonial takeover of the country. Kaiser Wilhelm II's unexpected visit to the city in March 1905 raised the specter of European war over Morocco's fate, prompting President Roosevelt to become involved in helping to resolve the quarrel.

The result of the complex negotiations was that the city of Tangier was carved out of Morocco and placed under a shared international condominium by the 1906 Algeciras Conference. The city was granted special status, and the town and the surrounding territory were placed under an international commission, with the sultan of Morocco, Abd al-Aziz (r. 1894–1907), as its nominal ruler. In this way, because of the complexity of European and imperial interests in the city, various entrenched positions could be retained, and the city would retain its distinctive international character. Meanwhile, the country of Morocco surrounding the Tangier Zone became a French protectorate under the Treaty of Fez in 1912 and part of the French Empire (see also "Fez").

After World War I, Britain, France, and Spain signed an official protocol (1925) providing for the shared international administration of the security of the city; eventually, there were more than twenty countries, including the United States, the Union of Soviet Socialist Republics, Belgium, Sweden, and the Netherlands, participating in this condominium. The neutral zone covered 225 square miles and was administered by an international assembly of twenty-seven members, a Committee of Control, and a European administrator. By this time, the cosmopolitan population of Jews, Arabs, Spaniards, French, and others made Tangier an international city quite unlike any other, and this innovative form of international administration required the diplomatic corps stationed there to participate together in its administration and shared security patrols. This unique international agreement, which was in effect until 1956, continues to be cited in international law as a key precedent to twenty-first-century humanitarian law, to United Nations (UN) authority for collective intervention, and as a precedent for the joint international administration of space, the oceans, and Antarctica.

In 1929 Spain was given preeminent police powers in the city. With the rise of fascism in Spain, this meant that Tangier became a halfway house for Gypsies and other "deviants" fleeing from Franco; by the late 1930s, the city was also a haven for eastern Europe Jews fleeing from the Nazis. From the beginning of World War II, the Spanish consolidated their police powers and basically unilaterally administered the city. For the whole period of the war years, the city was a place of welcome and refuge but also a place of dead ends, restrictions, and frustrations. Any and all things human could be found in

the city, and spies and double agents frequented its bars and cafés. It was this unique characteristic of the city that was enshrined in the classic movie *Casablanca;* just as Tangier was the inspiration for the film, so was the Café de Paris the model for Rick's Café.

Foreigners have always played a part in the development of the city and in its representation. During the 1800s, the city became a site for European artists to have their first brush with the exotic "other": Louis Tiffany, for example, painted a landscape of market day outside the walls of Tangier in 1873, as did Henri Matisse in his *Window at Tangiers.* The kasbah and the mysterious "white city" became a haven for artists of all persuasions, reaching its peak in the 1950s, when nearly half the population was comprised of foreigners. Indeed, much of Tangier's international fame can be placed at the door of writers and artists such as Allen Ginsberg, Jack Kerouac, Eldridge Cleaver, Jean Genet, Paul Bowles, William Burroughs (who wrote *The Naked Lunch* there), Francis Bacon, playwright Joe Orton and his lover Kenneth Halliwell, and musician Brian Jones, then of the Rolling Stones, who recorded the *Master Musicians of Jajouka* in the city.

Tangier's fortunes began to change when it lost its unique international status and was reincorporated into Morocco in 1956. The offshore banking and finance centers left for Spain and Switzerland, and with the money went a great deal of the expatriates, who today number under 2,000. New districts, filled with recent in-migration from rural Morocco, have grown up on the outskirts: illegal slums for unskilled rural laborers or those attracted to "suitcase smuggling" of pharmaceuticals across the straits. Now primarily a Berber city, the city has experienced more than a 3.5 percent annual growth rate over the last two decades.

Politically, Tangier continues to be the site for regional agreements and discussions of trade. In 1958 the city hosted the first meeting of Algerian (Front de Libération Nationale [National Liberation Front—FLN]), Tunisian (neo-Destour) and Moroccan (Istiqlal) political parties to discuss a North African Economic Community. On the twenty-fifth anniversary of this moribund agreement, the three states met again in Tangier in 1989 to recommit themselves to the concept of the Grand Maghreb, which became known as the Arab Maghreb Union.

Although much of the wealth has gone, and with it a great deal of the international glamour, Tangier is still a destination for the artistic and bohemian. As in the time of Ibn Battuta, the tomb of the holy man Sidi Jabou, saint of the sea, still attracts visitors to his seaside rock to pray for a child or blessings. To the west of Tangier lies the old madinah, which is the home to two ancient marketplaces, the Grand Socco and the Petit Socco (*socco* being the Spanish word for *suq*). Selling everything from *djellebas* (Moroccan robes) to the leather goods for which Morocco is famous, the marketplaces have been the focus of the old town for many centuries. Dominating the heart of the city is the kasbah, which houses the Sultan's Palace (now a museum of Moroccan history) and the Museum of Antiquities, in what used to be the kitchens. Outside the madinah is the Sidi Bouabid Mosque, with its huge tiled minaret. The city is home for the contemporary Moroccan novelist and recipient of the 1987 Prix Goncourt, Taher Ben Jalloun, who wrote about his hometown in his novel *Harrouda,* calling it a site of "contraband and *kif*" (cannabis), a city of female smugglers open to the world.

It is unclear where the future for this "shoulder of Africa" lies. There is talk of building a second port to deal solely with commercial traffic, which would create a more attractive aspect in that part of the town, and a trans-Saharan road is currently under construction that will link Tangier with Lagos. The road will provide a financially attractive alternative to the current method of flying goods across North Africa. The city's elites are taking up cricket and golf and "going global" in their business connections. Until Tangier regains its economic strength, however, it remains a popular tourist destination. Lured by its history of sexual and social freedom, and by its site as the closest "exotic other" just across the straits, Tangier's location means that it will always be a European's first stop on the African continent and an African's last stop before Europe.

James Hartley

Further Readings
Bourgia, Rahma, and Susan Gilson, eds. *In the Shadow of the Sultan: Culture, Power and Politics in Morocco.* Harvard: Harvard University Press, 1999.
Bowles, Paul. *Tangier Journal, 1987–1989.* New York: Norton, 1998.
Green, Michelle. *The Dream at the End of the World: Paul Bowles and the Literary Renegades in Tangier.* London: HarperCollins, 1992.
Harris, Walter. *Morocco That Was.* London: Blackwood and Sons, 1921.
Hopkins, John. *The Tangier Diaries: 1962–1979.* London: Arcadia Books, 1997.
Landau, Rom. *Portrait of Tangier.* London: Robert Hale, 1952.
Lane-Poole, Stanley. *The Barbary Corsairs.* London: T. Fisher Unwin, 1890.
Mackintosh-Smith, Tim. *Travels with a Tangerine.* London: Pan Macmillan, 2002.

Tehran
Population: 7 million (2005 estimate for city); 20 million (2006 estimate for Greater Tehran)

Established as the capital of Iran by the Qajars in 1786, and the center of Iran's revolutions in the twentieth century, Tehran is best known as the vibrant hub of modern Iran. Although its rise to power has really only spanned the last three centuries, the city has long been celebrated for its trees, climate, religious shrines, and underground homes. An industrial powerhouse, Tehran is also the political and social heart of the country, hosting its major governmental institutions, cultural centers,

and dissident movements. The dramatic rise in its population has brought in its wake all the urban problems of overworked infrastructure, major traffic congestion, pollution, and health problems, but the job as mayor of Tehran remains a political launching pad for politicians and for social change.

Tehran (Arabic, *Tihran;* French, *Téhéran*) lies in north-central Iran, astride the strategic corridor connecting western Iran with Khurasan. The city is situated on the southern slopes of the Alborz (or Elburz) mountain range, which separates it from the Caspian Sea, some 50 miles to the north. The city has expanded within a natural basin surrounded by mountains and desert; to the northeast overlooking the city is the Alborz's Mount Damavand (18,639 feet), the highest peak in Iran; to the east is the Gorgan Steppe; to the south, Iran's central desert, Dasht-e Kavir. These dramatic topographical features have hemmed in the physical growth of the city. The city's residents try to leave the city as often as possible in the heat of summer, when temperatures often reach above 100 degrees Fahrenheit. The dominating To-Chal ridge (12,904 feet) is a popular destination for skiing and picnicking, as are the Caspian beaches, only a three-hour drive away. Shiraz lies 350 miles to the south, Baku 300 miles to the north, and Bandar Abbas on the Persian Gulf coast is 600 miles to the southwest. The city was long known for its gardens and vegetation; in the seventeenth century, it was described as the town of plane trees.

Tehran was originally a village on the northern outskirts of the ancient city of Ray (also Rahga, Rages, Rayy), which was inhabited 8,000 years ago and subsequently called Cheshmeh Ali after the First Shi'i Imam. The city's northeast suburb of Qeytariyeh was likely to have been an occupied site during the sixth millennium BC. The earliest references to a town called Tehran include as-Samani's citation of his ancestor Muhammad bin Hammad Abu Abdollah Hafez Tehrani Razi's (d. 874–875 or 884–885) writings on the Hadith, Khatib Baghdadi's (d. 1071) mention of well-known Tehranis, and Ibn Balkhi's praises of the quality of Tehran's pomegranates in his *Farsnameh* (written ca. AD 1111). It is not until 1220, however, that Tehran itself is mentioned in Yaqut Hamavi's testimony, completed by Zakariya Qazvini in 1275, as a large village of gardens, orchards, and vegetable gardens. The records of the Mongol invasion (1220) mention a "Tehran" being captured. Many of its homes were built underground, possibly to protect against invading foreigners. As late as 1818, Ker Porter also referred to the underground nature of the Tehran homes.

It was not until the Mongols destroyed Ray that Tehran began to grow in size and significance. It was witness to the comings and goings of Iran's conquerors and dynasties over the next 400 years. The Safavid shah Tahmasp I (r. 1524–1526) constructed Tehran's *arg* (citadel), towers, and fortifications and developed the bazaar, now six miles long, which created an economic and political powerhouse for trade at the core of the city. The arg was later renovated by Karim Khan Zand of the Zand dynasty (r. 1750–1777) and under the Qajars became their official residence, known as the Golestan Palace; this palace was later used by the Pahlavis for royal receptions and for the coronation of the shah.

Shah Abbas, the most eminent Safavid shah (r. 1571–1629), built Tehran's first palace, Chahar Bagh (four gardens) (ca. 1580s). Shah Soleyman (r. 1667–1697) had a *divan khaneh* (imperial secretariat) built in a *chenarestan* (plane tree orchard). Shah Tahmasp II resided in Tehran in 1725 but fled on seeing the approach of the Afghans, who occupied the city and built the Darvazeha-yi Dawlat (state gates) and the Darvazeha-yi Arg (citadel gates). Nader Shah of the Afshar dynasty (r. 1736–1747) assigned his son, Reza Qoli Mirza, as governor of Tehran in 1741.

The proximity of the city to their grazing and hunting grounds in Mazandaran-Gurgan, the home of their Turkoman followers, made Tehran a convenient capital for Agha Muhammad Khan Qajar in 1786 as the dynasty was established. Tehran became a city of great importance and has remained so until today. It was from the Qajar capital that Iran was united for the first time. Fath Ali Shah (r. 1779–1834), the second Qajar shah, was responsible for the building of the city's *soltani,* Moezz o-dowleh, and Haj Seyd Azizollah mosques and for cultural development. The Qajar dynasty was renowned for paintings on lacquered and enameled objects featuring traditional flora and fauna designs and portraits of the shah and leading courtiers. In literary terms, however, Tehran still lagged behind its competitors Esfahan, Shiraz, and Kashan, although the first Persian newspaper, *Karghaz-i akhbar,* was founded in the city in 1837. Also during this period, Bahá Ulláh (Hussayn Ali Nouri), who came to be the founder of the Bahai faith, was born on 12 November 1817 in the city.

During Naser ad-Din Shah's reign (r. 1848–1896), there were several significant developments in Tehran. Now a walled city, it developed into one of Iran's largest urban conurbations with bazaars, mosques, and palaces; its population grew from 15,000 in the 1790s to 100,000 at the end of the nineteenth century, and the city began to expand outside of its walls. The city was the site of important political events: it witnessed the persecution of the Babis in 1850, after an attempt on the shah's life, and the mass movement against a concession of a tobacco monopoly in 1891. Culturally, Tehran also grew in importance. Dar al-Funun, the first Western high school, was founded in 1851–1852 and was to play an important role in the development of typography and lithography. The first state newspaper, *Ruznama-yi dawlat-i aliyya-yi Iran,* was established by the great reformist Prime Minister Amir Kabir during this time.

The socioreligious movement that came to be known as the Constitutional Revolution (Enghelab-e Mashroteh) in 1905–1906 is another crucial turning point in the history of Tehran. In response to the growing encroachment of foreign powers (especially Russia and Britain) on Iran's domestic and foreign affairs, and on the autonomy of the Qajars, a movement of elites and religious figures finally burst out, calling for a constitution modeled on that of Belgium with a *majlis* (parliament) and limited suffrage. This initial constitution became the basis of the Iranian constitution until 1979. The 1905 revolution is often referred to as the first step in Iran's political development toward democracy. Tehran for the first time became the country's center of political, intellectual, and publishing activity. A celebrated figure during this period was Tehran-born Mirza Ali Akbar Ghazvini, known as Dehkhoda (1879–1956). He wrote the famous Persian-language encyclopedia *Loghat-nameh,* and along with its founder, Mirza Jahangir Khan Shirazi, worked on the newspaper *Sur-Esrafil,* which played an important political and literary role. Using the language of common people, it aimed at exposing the despotism and corruption of the Qajar shahs. It was the first of its kind to be sold on street corners.

During the Pahlavi dynasty (1925–1979), Tehran achieved even greater dominance within the country. Having deposed Ahmad Shah Qajar, the majlis of Iran proclaimed Reza Khan as shah in 1925. In the 1930s, Reza Shah developed national communications with better roads and the Trans-Iranian Railway linking Tehran to the Persian Gulf and the Caspian Sea. The first bus company was founded by Muhammad Ghobei. Wider streets followed the grid of *qanats* (covered irrigation channels), which distributed water from the Alborz to the city. Building projects were supported by brickworks and building industries in southern Tehran. The population increased from 210,000 in 1922 to 540,000 in 1940. Modern education reforms included the founding of the University of Tehran in 1934; famous students from the university have included Seyyed Muhammad Khatami and the 2003 Nobel Peace Prize winner, Shirin Ebadi.

The city's process of modernization, urbanization, and industrialization continued under Tehran-born Muhammad Reza Shah (r. 1941–1979), when his father was forced to abdicate by Britain and the Union of Soviet Socialist Republics during their occupation of Iran in World War II. Tehran became an international metropolis; its population increased from 1.5 million in 1956, when it constituted 26.2 percent of Iran's urban population, to 3 million in 1966 and 6 million in 1980. The state led an industrialization drive in the mid-1950s bringing considerable growth into the city's manufacturing industries, 30 percent of which were in Tehran and its hinterland. Now Tehran is home to more than half of Iran's industry, including the textiles, sugar, weaponry, automobile, electronics, chemical, and cement industries.

Tehran has a north-south division, along Khiyaban-e Enghelab (the Avenue of the Revolution, known as Shah Reza before 1979), which mirrors the city's political and social

Skyline of Tehran, 1997. (Brian A. Vikander/Corbis)

stratification. Unlike the southern part of Tehran, the northern section of the city is associated with the privileged middle classes because of its better water supply and climate. It now includes the villages of Golhaq, Tajrish, and Shemiran, which were aristocratic summer retreats and now house the residences of major foreign embassies, and is marked by extensive parks. The district's *maseels* (canals and seasonal rivers) channel away excess water from the Alborz. In Tajrish can be found the Shi'i religious shrine of Imam Zadeh Saleh, the son of the Seventh Shi'i Iman and saint Musa al-Kazim.

During the post–World War II period, Tehran experienced political events of a national and global scale. The emergence of political parties, a free press, and trade unions characterized political liberalization in the early part of the last shah's reign. In 1951 Prime Minister Muhammad Mossadeqh (also Mossadegh) nationalized the oil industry; the subsequent overthrow of Mossadeqh was orchestrated in the streets of Tehran by the Central Intelligence Agency (CIA) and a few military officers. The 1960s and 1970s witnessed the revival of high-quality textiles and other Iranian handicrafts and a proliferation in the city of critical thought in art, cinema, and literature. Tehran-born intellectuals included feminist Forough Farokhzad (1934–1967), whose poetry and award-

winning films continue to influence artists today, and Jalal Ale-Ahmad (1923–1970), whose *Gharbzadegi* (*Westoxification*) identifies the West as the cause of Iran's failings. Ali Shariati's (1933–1977) lectures at Tehran's Hosseini-ye Ershad Institute led him to be arrested by the authorities.

On 12 December 1978, more than 2 million people filled Tehran's Azadi Square (previously Shahyad Square) in protest against Muhammad Reza Shah. This protest was the culmination of a long process of growing unrest and was triggered by an article in the official press attacking Ayatollah Seyyed Ruhollah Khomeini (1900–1989). Despite the shah's subsequent call for a more moderate constitution, Khomeini's supporters called for his abdication. The shah fled Iran on 16 January 1979, and Khomeini arrived in Tehran's Mehrabad Airport from exile in Paris on 1 February 1979, where an estimated 6 million people welcomed him. The Islamic Republic was created, Khomeini took on the title "Supreme Leader," and the events leading up to it came to be referred to as the Islamic Revolution. Abolhassan Banisadr (b. 1933) became Iran's first president in 1980. In reaction to U.S. refusal to hand over the shah for trial in Iran, a group of students took fifty-two Americans hostage for 444 days at Tehran's American Embassy in November 1979. This event came to be known as the Iran hostage crisis and has influenced Iranian-American relations ever since.

The visible impact of the 1979 revolution on Tehran includes gender segregation on buses; conversion of royal palaces into museums and parks; the changing of street names, many of which now memorialize the martyrs of the Iran-Iraq War (1980–1988); proliferation of murals illustrating the Islamic Revolution and anti-American slogans; and compulsory *hejab* (head covering) for women. The year 1992 saw a new urban policy with the construction of urban freeways, renovation of southern districts with cultural centers and sports facilities, and new tower blocks in northern Tehran. Although Tehran's population has continued to grow with in-migration from the provinces, in the early 1990s the growth slowed down to an annual 1.4 percent rather than the phenomenal 10.28 percent experienced during the mid-1970s. The physical decay of the central districts of the city illustrates the effects of decentralization and suburbanization.

The election of Seyyed Muhammad Khatami (b. 1943) as the country's president by 70 percent of the votes cast in 1997 had a dramatic effect on Tehran's political and social life. There was a proliferation of newspapers and periodicals, a growth of nongovernmental organizations (NGOs), an expansion of the contemporary art community, and relaxed rules regarding hejab. Tehran-born Abdol Karim Soroush (b. 1945) called for the separation of the clerical establishment from organized political activity. Tehran became home to a metro system, and Borj-e Milad (Milad Tower), part of the Tehran International Trade and Convention Center, is Iran's tallest tower (1,034 feet); it is expected to replace the 1971 marble Azadi (previously Shayhad) Monument as the symbol of Tehran. In 2005 Mahmoud Ahmadinejad, the mayor of Tehran, was elected president of Iran.

Shabnam Holliday

Further Readings

Ansari, A. *Modern Iran since 1921: The Pahlavis and After.* Edinburgh: Pearson Education, 2003.

Keddie, Nikki. *Qajar Iran and the Rise of Reza Khan, 1796–1925.* Costa Mesa, CA: Mazda, 1999.

Madanipour, Ali. *Tehran: The Making of a Metropolis.* New York: Wiley, 1998.

Tel Aviv
Population: 370,000 (2006 estimate)

Tel Aviv has been called a "city without a history" because of its creation, de novo, from the sands along the Mediterranean in 1909. Created with the goal of being the first "all-Jewish city" of the modern era, Tel Aviv remains an enigma, both within Israel and for its residents. Founded not by plans but by pioneers, a European city on the edge of the Orient, a child of Jaffa but now its boss, a secular city in conflict with the spiritual Jerusalem, a garden city with pollution problems, a city of crime and culture, Tel Aviv defies categorization. Certainly, it aspires to global city status with its financial institutions, diamond exchanges, Bauhaus architecture, and high-tech industries, but its poor find little joy in its development.

Tel Aviv, officially known in the contemporary period as Tel Aviv-Yafo, is located in the center of Israel on the shores of the Mediterranean. It spreads nine miles along the coast and two to four miles inland. Tel Aviv has two rivers: the Yarkon, which runs from east to west and flows to the sea, and the Ayalon, which runs from south to north and flows into the Yarkon River. Tel Aviv's climate is subtropical, with average temperatures at 68 degrees Fahrenheit and an average annual rainfall of two inches. The rainy season is between November and April, and there are sixty-four rainy days annually on average. Tel Aviv shares boundaries with six towns—Bat Yam and Holon in the south, Ramat Gan and Givataym in the east, and Herzliya and Ramat Hasharon in the northeast—and the greater metropolitan area incorporates more than 2.7 million people.

Founded in Ottoman Palestine in 1909, it is considered to be the first city established by Jews in modern times as new settlers arrived during the late nineteenth century. The early history of Tel Aviv is closely linked to Jaffa, which ultimately was eclipsed by Tel Aviv and is now one of its suburbs. Despite its predominantly Palestinian Arab population, in the late nineteenth century Jaffa became a center of Zionism. In 1891 a general committee for the *yishuv* (Jewish community in Palestine) was established. During the first wave of Jewish immigration (known as the First Aliyah), Jaffa became home to the Palestine bureau of the World Zionist Organization, the central committees of different labor movements, and headquarters for various sports and educational groups. With the establishment of Tel Aviv in 1909, the major Jewish organizations moved to the new city, signifying a geographical shifting of a society and culture that had been developing in Jaffa for almost thirty years.

Thus, the specific and unique character of Tel Aviv arose from the Zionist ideological background as well as the material expectations of its founders. The ideological background influenced the act itself of the creation of Tel Aviv, its character, and its development. Zionism needed urban settlement, and the Zionist organizations realized the importance of Tel Aviv for overall Zionist aims in Palestine. Aid in financing Tel Aviv was received from the Jewish National Fund, the main funder of Jewish Zionist settler activity in Palestine. In fact, the largest single area of investments in the interwar period was Tel Aviv. The funds expended in its construction constituted about one-half of the total Jewish investment in Palestine during these years.

In mid-1906, following a series of complaints and concerns expressed by Jews living inside Jaffa, it was proposed that a new community be established outside Jaffa as a residential area for Jewish workers (see also "Jaffa"). From this suggestion quickly emerged a housing association (Agudat Bonei Batim), which solicited interest and then purchased land east of Neve Tzedek away from the beach. Neve Tzedek was already a Jewish community, built up around a brick factory and houses owned by a Sephardic Jew from Algeria; the new area was to be beyond that, "on the sand."

The housing association divided the land into sixty plots to be granted to the first subscribers of the association. In the spring of 1909, a lottery using shells encoded with the numbers of the housing lots was held on the beach, and the first families, primarily from Russia and Poland, set to work. Quickly the association built the first public building, the Herzliya High School, and it accepted its first students into all-Hebrew classes soon after.

The new community was based on a vision of a new Jewish city that would be independent and created de novo from the sand. Hebrew would be the language of its streets, and its layout would have green spaces and open parks and be very European in feel. In fact, the visionaries drew on the work of Ebenezer Howard and his Garden City movement in England for their inspiration. After considerable discussion, the name of the city was agreed to as Tel Aviv, drawing on the title used by Nahum Sokolow for his translation of Zionism's founding book, Herzl's *Alteneuland*. Sokolow was linking the idea of a tell as an old mound of historical remains of a city with the season of spring (*Aviv*) and the concept of renewal and birth.

In only five short years, Tel Aviv had grown to 2,000 inhabitants. World War I marked a temporary halt to its growth, but with the implementation of the British Mandate in Palestine (1923–1948) and the initially open British attitude toward Jewish immigration, waves of Jewish emigrants had their first sight of Palestine through the city's new port (1936). This "baby of Zionsim" was declared a town in 1921 and formally became a city in 1934.

The allocation of green areas was given high priority by the first city planners. The founders of Tel Aviv envisaged it as a garden city, a dream that unfortunately could not be sustained because of Tel Aviv's fast growth. Its mayor, Meir Dizengoff, having requested the help of the Zionist Organization in the matter, was referred to Patrick Geddes, Scottish biologist and sociologist and one of the fathers of modern city planning. In April 1925, Geddes drew up a master plan for the development of north Tel Aviv, which gave clear preference to green and open spaces. At that time, Tel Aviv was a small town with a population of about 25,000. Geddes presented a report showing his concept of a large garden city of about 100,000. The dwelling places would be cottage style, built in the center of the plot with a flower garden in the front and a vegetable patch in the back. Although his plan was not fully implemented, it served as a general blueprint for many years, and

the prioritization of green areas continues to serve as a guideline in all master plans.

The first Yemeni immigrants settled in the city in the 1930s, and German immigration caused by the rise of Nazism created a "little Berlin" neighborhood to add to many others. The Habime National Theater was established in the city in 1931, and the Mograbi Opera House expanded the city's cultural offerings. A casino was built out into the water on stilts, and the city became the center of the Hebrew press in the country.

Following World War II, the city underwent further development, partly as a result of the growing communal conflict between Palestinian Arabs and Jews, and with another wave of Jewish immigration prior to 1948, Tel Aviv had become the largest city in Palestine.

Tension between the Jewish community and Palestinians bubbled over a number of times. In 1921, 1929, and 1936, there were riots and confrontations across neighborhoods in Jaffa and Tel Aviv. In November 1945, there was further violence. As the city was the center for the Zionist Organization, the city also saw considerable confrontation with the British. In particular, the Stern and Irgun gangs were involved in a number of incidents: in January 1945, a British judge was kidnapped from his courtroom in Tel Aviv; in April of that year, seven officers were killed at a military base in the city; and in June 1946, the British Officers Club in the city was attacked and six British officers kidnapped. Underground munitions factories operated in the city, and by the end of 1947 Britain had little authority or presence in Tel Aviv, and the Jewish community members were managing all their own affairs.

In May 1948, David Ben Gurion, surrounded by the leaders of the Jewish organizations headquartered in the city, proclaimed the State of Israel at a meeting held in the Tel Aviv Museum. For the next seven months, Tel Aviv was the provisional capital of the new state until west Jerusalem was proclaimed the capital in 1949 (see also "Jerusalem"). During the war of 1948–1949, Tel Aviv served as the key port for new immigrants, who were taken off the boats, given a gun, and headed off to the front. The city was bombed by Egyptian aircraft after 15 May until early June, when the first Israeli air force planes engaged in a dogfight over Tel Aviv, shooting down two attackers. Jaffa was captured by Jewish forces prior to the declaration of the state, with most of its more than 60,000 Palestinian inhabitants fleeing to the West Bank or Lebanon.

Jewish immigrants were quickly moved into the empty houses in Jaffa, and that city was officially incorporated with Tel Aviv in 1950, forming the conurbation of Tel Aviv–Yafo. Other Palestinian villages in the area were seized: Tel Aviv University is partially built on Shaykh Muwanis's land. In 1950 the government of Israel declared that Jerusalem was to be the capital of the State of Israel and transferred its official

Tel Aviv high-rises along the beachfront. (morgueFile)

buildings and legislature to Jerusalem. This was not recognized by the international community, however, and all but two countries have kept their embassies in Tel Aviv.

The Tel Aviv Stock Exchange was established in the city in 1953, and this, along with earlier developments of financial institutions, meant that Tel Aviv became Israel's financial center. The stock exchange has flourished, experiencing strong rates of growth particularly during the dot-com boom of the 1990s. Today the city hosts 51 percent of all banking jobs in the country, thereby asserting its clear supremacy over Jerusalem and Haifa. Tel Aviv has been able to consolidate its position as a preferred location for high-tech industry, given this sector's dependence on all the services in which the city excels—financial services, expert manpower, and research and development institutions. The planned extension of Atidim Science-Based Industrial Park, which will provide space for new enterprises, will help to extend Tel Aviv's role in this sector. The Diamond Exchange, founded in 1921, is also located here, and the city remains a crucial player in the global diamond circuits.

More than half of Israel's industrial plants are found in the Tel Aviv metropolitan area, including textiles, diamond polishing, food processing, and furniture production. All the major bus and truck companies have their headquarters here, and it is a transport hub for the country via the airport and railway systems.

With its sandy beaches close to the city center and forty-four hotels, the city is also the core of the Israeli tourist industry. The tourist business provides work for 17,000 people, one-third of whom are employed in the hotel sector. The city's direct income from tourism totals $55 million annually, depending on tourists from other places in the country but also from Europe and the former Soviet Union.

Tel Aviv is also a major center for higher education. Tel Aviv University, founded in 1953, has thirteen faculties and 25,000 students and is the largest university in the country. An orthodox Jewish university, Bar-Ilan University, was founded in 1955. Rabbinical and theological institutions (yeshivas), primarily concentrated in the Bene Berak area of the city, serve students from Jewish communities throughout the world.

For aficionados of the Bauhaus, art deco, and eclectic styles of architecture, which flourished in Europe prior to World War II, Tel Aviv is an outdoor museum. Jews who emigrated from Germany were influential in promulgating the minimalist, functional architectural style inspired by the works of Le Corbusier and Erich Mendelsohn, which also suited the socialist philosophies that informed much of the public sector in pre-state Tel Aviv. Currently, about 1,500 buildings are marked for historic conservation out of 4,000 buildings designed in this style within the "White City" area of the city. Some good examples of conservation can be viewed in the area between Rothschild Boulevard and Montefiore Street, where financial companies and institutions, architectural firms, and law firms have rehabilitated some of these special buildings, breathing new life into them. In 2003 the United Nations Educational, Scientific, and Cultural Organization (UNESCO) designated the "White City" as a World Heritage Site.

Tel Aviv is not only Israel's business capital, it is also a bustling cultural center, offering an impressive concentration of museums, art galleries, theaters, cinemas, restaurants, sidewalk cafés, pubs, and shopping centers. On most nights, the city is buzzing with visitors from Jerusalem and the hinterland walking along the corniche and frequenting the nightlife. It has been said that "while Jerusalem prays, Tel Aviv plays," and the city retains its reputation for crime, prostitution, and as the general sin city for the country. In the summer, the municipality sponsors outdoor events and festivals, which take place against the backdrop of the promenade, Tel Aviv port, or the Old City of Jaffa. The three largest museums in the country operate in the city—the Eretz Israel Museum, the Tel Aviv Museum of Art, and the Museum of the Diaspora, and almost one-half of all performing arts performances in the country occur here. The city is the country's center for classical music (the Israel Philharmonic Orchestra and the Israel Opera) and for many of its theater companies. It is the site for Kika Rabin (Rabin Square), the former Kings of Israel Square, where Prime Minister Rabin was assassinated in 1995; it is this square where most of the major political rallies in the country's history have been held.

Given all these attributes, Tel Aviv is an attractive place of residence. Yet problems continue. Housing supply falls consistently behind demand, with the result that property values are high, thus making the city's available residential accommodations unaffordable to the large majority of aspiring buyers. Indeed, over the past twenty years, apartment prices in Tel Aviv have consistently been the highest in the country, some 20 percent higher than those in Jerusalem. In addition, the city experiences a high crime rate, and drug use is high. The Russian mafia has reportedly moved into the city, bringing trafficking and money laundering. The city has 10,000 prostitutes, more than 70 percent of them from the former Soviet Union. The city was the target of Saddam Hussayn's rockets during the Gulf War in 1991, and numerous terrorist attacks during the last fifteen years have made its citizens cautious about going out to its cafés.

Michael Dumper

Further Readings
Efrat, Elisha. *Urbanization in Israel.* London: Croom Helm, 1984.
Goldscheider, Calvin. *Israel's Changing Society: Population, Ethnicity and Development.* Boulder, CO: Westview Press, 1991.
Kellerman, Aharon. *Society and Settlement: Jewish Land of Israel in the Twentieth Century.* Albany: State University of New York Press, 1993.
LeVine, Mark. *Overthrowing Geography: Jaffa, Tel Aviv and the Struggle for Palestine, 1880–1948.* Berkeley: University of California Press, 2005.

Timbuktu
Population: 20,000 (2006 estimate)

The fabled, unattainable city of Timbuktu, representing in the European imagination the farthest reaches of the world, has served for thousands of years as a meeting point for West African and North African cultures. It was part of the city system of Dar al-Islam, a noted site of universities and Islamic training, and an entrepôt for the salt, gold, and slave trade across the Sahara. It is an edge city for the Middle East and North Africa, home to Arab traders, a river port city, and the "city of 333 saints."

Timbuktu (French, *Tombouctou*) lies at the farthest northern point of the great Niger Bend in north-central Mali. Its importance derived from its location at the meeting of the river and the Sahara. Although today the city is seven miles from the course of the Niger, in its heyday in the fourteenth century the river flowed closer to the city, and canals brought water to its edge. In fact, the city was served by its own port on the river, known as Kabara. The Niger flooded seasonally (mid-July to December), and during the dry season (March to June), navigation on the river was difficult. Today sand dunes encroach upon its streets, but 1,000 years ago the city was situated on an area of savannah, hosting numerous sweet-water wells. Timbuktu is not surrounded by any agricultural heartland and long needed to import almost all of its key supplies.

Trans-Saharan trade over the centuries followed three key routes: a western route linking Morocco through Mauritania to the Senegal River, a central route that had its terminus on the Niger Bend around Timbuktu, and an eastern or "Egyptian" route through what is now Gao farther down the Niger River. Sparse archaeological evidence of luxury exchange along the far western route from Morocco to Mauritania exists for the first millennium BC, and a few literary indications, for example, in Herodotus, tell of interaction across the eastern route. A number of limited remains and references from the Roman era suggest sporadic links between West Africa and North Africa across all three routes. It is conventional wisdom, however, that it was the domestication of the camel after the first century AD that made direct, regular long-distance trade across the Sahara along all three routes possible.

Trade between the communities of the savannah (what the Arabs called *Bilad as-Sudan,* or Land of the Blacks) and the Mediterranean eventually developed because both had evolved extensive city systems of their own and were reaching out to expand trade and profits. The Berber nomads of the desert, quickly adapting the new "technology" of the camel, became the brokers between these two urban systems and facilitated regular trade along a range of commodities. Gold from the south was exchanged in the north for dates, corn, and manufactured essentials needed by the Berbers. Luxury goods from the north, along with copper, were exchanged for gold in the south. With the creation of the Kingdom of Ghana (AD 622–1203), its merchant elites aggressively sought out regional and interregional trade opportunities. A dense agricultural and urban community developed in the upper Niger over the next 400 years, blending production, distribution, and technology into an integrated and sophisticated city system. By AD 1000, the empire of Ghana incorporated territory from the Senegal River to the Niger Bend, including the site of Timbuktu and oases in the middle of the Sahara. Boat traffic capable of carrying up to seventy tons plied the river, moving goods downriver from the Niger inland Delta. It was during this period that merchants sought a controlled site to facilitate more stable trans-Saharan trade, and Timbuktu was founded as a result of the push of West African urbanism. In particular, it was the city of Jenne, farther west up the Niger toward the inland Delta and situated in a rich agricultural zone, that was Timbuktu's key twin. This huge city, built on regional trade, worked in tandem with the port of Timbuktu to facilitate the trans-Saharan trade and the expansion of regional networks.

An alternative narrative suggests that it was the expansion of Islam under the Arabs into North Africa after AD 700 that was the crucial factor in the establishment of Timbuktu. This argument stresses the need for gold on the part of the new Arab polities along the western Mediterranean, in particular the Umayyad dynasty in Andalucia or the later Fatimid Caliphate (AD 910), which encouraged the Tuareg Bedouin to reach out to the kingdoms along the Niger. Timbuktu is thus the result of Arab urbanism's push, Arab financial backing of the venture, and a Tuareg need for a trading site at the edge of the desert; Timbuktu was the perfect site to establish such an outpost.

Various foundational myths are proposed for Timbuktu. Most support the belief that the name comes from that of a woman, Tin Abutut, who lived at a well a few miles from the

Niger. The most interesting proposal is that her name means "the lady with the big navel." The site, some distance from the river, may have been chosen since being directly on the water was unhealthy for camels because of the West African disease trypanosomiasis. Sources suggest that the city was founded by the Massufa Sanhaja (one tribe from among the Sanhaja Berbers from the southern Sahara) around AD 1100.

The first phase of the city's development saw settlers from both the Niger inner Delta and from oases in the Sahara creating a pluralistic community of merchants and Bedouin. By AD 1100, the outpost had grown into a key market town of perhaps 10,000 inhabitants where the goods of the Niger inland Delta met the goods transshipped from the Mediterranean, profiting both communities. Expanding on the addition of a second wave of immigration from other trading emporia in the region, the city became a pluralistic mix of Arab, Berber, Tuareg, Songhay, Berabish Moor, Fulani, and Wangara traditions.

A range of commodities traded along regional and trans-Saharan circuits were mediated by Timbuktu: slaves, ivory, horses, skins, cloth, kola nut, pepper, weapons, rice, and foodstuffs such as dried fish and fish oil. Gold in quantities of more than 4,400 pounds per year moved north out of the city, along with grain. Copper and brass moved south from North Africa. Later, the core commodity moving south was salt from the Sahara itself. The Tuareg initially controlled the salt mines of the mid-Sahara around Teghaza and used their monopoly to supply much of West Africa. Although salt was available in the region, the eighty-pound salt blocks marketed by the Tuareg were purchased by the West African elites for spices and curing. This ethnic control of trade routes is representative of the socioeconomic dynamics operating out of Timbuktu, which comprised a number of de facto ethnic monopolies that sought to maintain control of sites, resources, production, and logistics to benefit a particular ethnic community. Such patterns produced numerous trade wars, raids, and reprisals, many of which influenced Timbuktu's economy directly.

The Ghanan Empire declined after 1076 and finally disappeared in 1203. In the vacuum of the upper Niger, the Malinke expanded their control during the late thirteenth century. The most famous Mali emperor or sultan, Mansa Musa (1307–1332), captured Timbuktu around 1325. It was Musa who built the first monumental buildings in the city, sponsored Islamic scholarship in Timbuktu, and encouraged scholars from the Arab heartland to come to the city to teach (see also "Cairo").

Malian power waned by the end of the fourteenth century, and the city passed under Songhay control. From their capital in Gao, the Songhay Empire (1490–1591) ruled a vast stretch of the middle Niger as far west as Jenne, but Timbuktu was the jewel in the crown, serving as the economic, cultural, and religious heart of the empire. In tandem with Jenne, Timbuktu prospered under the extraordinary expansion brought about by Askia Muhammad (r. 1493–1529), who ruled one of the largest empires in African history and a vast network of long-distance trade.

A debate exists over the degree of autonomy this powerful city exercised within the empire. Conventional wisdom stresses the autonomy of Timbuktu and its long history of independence as a merchant city-state. This view suggests that although an imperial Songhay bureaucracy and governorship existed within the city, it was really the ancient municipal position of the *qadi* (the Muslim judge or legal official), in association with the clerical and merchant elite of the city as *jamā'a* (or association of the learned), that made key decisions. In fact, this view argues, Timbuktu held primary influence over Gao rather than the other way around.

An alternative view, however, stresses the military power of the imperial administration contained in the more than 3,000 horsemen and foot soldiers (armed, the traveler Leo Africanus tells us, with poisoned arrows) under the governor's command. The city even hosted a Hi-koi (commander of canoes) responsible for managing both the military traffic and business commerce along the river. This argument also stresses the Songhay taxation system, which reaped tremendous revenues from the transit trade of Timbuktu. The city was central to the empire's networks, and keeping centralized control over its policies and inhabitants was crucial to the empire's existence.

Whatever the direction of influence, it is clear that Timbuktu retained a high degree of autonomous municipal structure, centered around a core triangle composed of hereditary families holding the qadi position, the merchants, and the ulema associated with Sankore. The city certainly pursued imperial policy at this time: for example, its elite supported one of four brothers in a civil war of succession in 1586, crowning him as *askia* (ruler) only to have him defeated by the last of the other brothers, who then took substantial revenge on the scholars and elites of the city.

The city maintained its links with other cities through the personal networks of its merchants. These market networks often were organized into trading associations, or *dyula*, based on ethnic and class groupings, which provided support, capital, and trust to maintain the links required for long-distance trade. Timbuktu was served by merchant communities or merchant houses in the Sijilmassa Oasis at the northern Moroccan edge of the Sahara, communities in Gao and Jenne, and in other Saharan port cities and Niger sites as far south as Nigeria and the modern Ivory Coast (see also "Sijilmassa"). This commercial clientism facilitated trade, especially on the gold circuit, where secrecy concerning the source of the gold was crucial to its producers. In addition to facilitating trade, merchant networks were often involved in establishing prices or making sure that gouging did not occur.

These merchant linkages were often intensified by religious ties and theology, bringing a particular interpretation of Islam and entrepreneurship together into a single trading philosophy; Timbuktu, with its dual merchant and Islamic ethos, benefited from this ideological package, which promoted trade. Hereditary family roles in the city were legitimized by this framework. The Kunta merchant clan, for example, played a key role in Timbuktu history for more than 300 years, serving in various religious and administrative roles to promote the city's welfare.

The city was valued by its inhabitants and by regional conquerors for its key entrepôt role, controlled by the local Arab elite. However, the city also hosted some limited industrial production, generally associated with the black slaves, or *bela*, of the Tuareg. Trade-relevant products included leather, baskets, and cotton cloth. Leo Africanus reports that weaving was very prevalent. The city also profited from its slave market. Many of the estimated 9.3 million black slaves (primarily women) transported across the Sahara from AD 800 to AD 1900 would have passed through the slave market in Timbuktu. The great traveler Ibn Battuta reports his own problems buying and selling female slaves while in the area, and he returned to North Africa in the company of a caravan transporting 600 female slaves.

Ibn Battuta also noted the monetary system of the period on his visit to Timbuktu in 1353. He makes the earliest reference to the use of cowries (*cypraea moneta*) for currency in the sub-Saharan city system. These small cowries, imported from the Maldives via Persia and the Sahara, were used in Timbuktu from the 1200s until the early twentieth century. The other major currency supporting Timbuktu's trading network was the *mithqāl*, valued at around 4.72 grams of gold. Mithqāls and gold dust were in use in Timbuktu until the French occupation. The exchange rate, despite seasonal variation, was approximately 3,500 cowries to the mithqāl. It is interesting to note that, during a particular period of Tuareg domination and frequent raids of the city, Timbuktu had to pay regular ransom. For the year 1738, the ransom was 1,500 mithqāls, but it was reportedly paid in cowries because gold was scarce that year. Other forms of exchange also included iron bars, salt slabs, and copper rings and bars. Ibn Battuta reports that he purchased a slave for 25 mithqāls, or 28,750 cowries, which was too expensive, he complained. By the 1800s, the average price of a slave was around 75,000 cowries.

One reason for the reputation of the city was its academic and educational complex, around which evolved a religious elite. The Jingarey Ber Mosque (the Mosque of the Friday Prayers) was initially commissioned by Sultan Musa on his return from the hajj in 1325. The tradition is that Jingarey Ber was built by the Andalusian architect Abu Ishap al-Touwaidjin, who was enticed to the city by Sultan Musa with promises of a vast fee in gold. Sankore Mosque, built somewhat later around 1400, served as the core of an Islamic university. It is

Seventeenth-century sketch of Timbuktu. (Stapleton Collection/Corbis)

unique in its architecture, centered around a pyramidal mihrab. By the mid-sixteenth century, under the Songhay Empire, the university was organized around separate colleges under the authority of an imam. Students associated themselves with one imam following an extensive course of study that centered around the Qur'an but also included history, philosophy, mathematics, or even astronomy and medicine. At its height, the complex may have hosted more than 25,000 Muslim scholars; today there are about 15,000. The city's reputation for scholars, saints, and holy men derives both from its role as an incubator for local religious talent and for its role in attracting in-migration from even the Holy Cities to its educational institutions. The city's scholarship and pietism spiraled outward, touching minor clerics and holy men in the city's hinterlands, throughout the Niger Bend, and across the trade routes of the Sudan and Sahara.

Its Muslim scholars developed a deserved reputation throughout Dar al-Islam, going on the hajj, teaching in the madrasas of Makkah and Madinah, and showing up as students in Spain, Morocco, or al-Azhar. And there is no doubt that the city's Islamic elite were crucial in the spread of Islam throughout sub-Saharan Africa. Scholars such as the Sufi Alfa-Hashim, who taught in Madinah from 1907 to 1931, were only the latest in a long line of holy men to emerge from Timbuktu. This give-and-take within Dar al-Islam is well represented by the visit of Ibn Battuta but also by the pilgrimage of political leaders from the region, starting as early as the twelfth century. Both Mansa Musa's hajj and that of Askia Muhammad in 1497–1498 were remarkable events in Makkah.

Regional leaders understood the religious centrality of the city and gave great sums to rebuild or enhance its mosques and madrasa; Askia Muhammad had the Sankore Mosque rebuilt, and he sent one of his sons there to study. A successor, Askia Daud (1549–1582), studied under an imam, supported the copying of manuscripts, paid for slaves for the scholars at Sankore, and had new libraries built. Such beneficence did not shield political leaders from scholarly rebuke, however. In one surviving epistle to Askia Muhammad, a Moroccan scholar warns that a proper Muslim ruler would never allow the display of public nudity that he had found in Timbuktu.

Still today the city hosts numerous libraries of ancient manuscripts. In its heyday, it was known as "the city of books." The city literally lived off of its books: a tradition of translation and copying of manuscripts developed in the city, leading to numerous production facilities for this purpose. The scholars published their own books, which were sold throughout the Islamic world. Private collections were held by many scholars; Ahmad Baba (d. 1627) is quoted as saying that his collection of 1,600 books was one of the smaller ones in Timbuktu. Askiya Daud reportedly established public libraries. Finally, books were an important component in the trans-Saharan trade, with Moroccan books being shipped to Timbuktu on a regular basis. Leo Africanus makes this point when he says that in Timbuktu there is "a great demand for books, and more profit is made from the trade in books than from any other line of business" (see also "Marrakesh").

Although Songhay was the common tongue in the city, Arabic was the language of the elite, used for Qur'anic instruction, bureaucratic administration, legal documents, family records, and regional trade. Regional histories became a well-developed art form, and two particular manuscripts have been preserved and tell us much about the history of Timbuktu during its height: *Tariqh al-Sudān,* by as-Sadi, and *Tariqh al-Fattāsh,* by Ibn al-Mukhtar. As-Sadi's work remains today a fundamental source of information about the situation of Timbuktu in the long-distance trading networks of this period. Gradually, by the 1700s, local languages became expressed in the Arabic script (Kaswahili, Hausa, Songhay); this expansion of literacy was particularly attributable to the work of the scholars of Timbuktu. It is only now being discovered that letters and documents in Arabic script exist that were written in the Americas by African slaves from this region.

The greatness of Timbuktu began to wane with its capture from the north in 1591 by a Moroccan mercenary army composed of Andalusian renegades. Their use of firearms, the first appearance south of the Sahara, overwhelmed the local defenders, and the city passed under the control of the expansionist Saadid dynasty of Morocco. The Saadids, seeking to drive back the Spanish and to profit from the growing Atlantic political economy, sought to monopolize the gold and salt trade across the Sahara in response to Spanish incursions along the West African coast. They also required the gold to resist the incursions of the Ottomans from Algeria. Thus, taking Timbuktu was a strategic necessity for enhancing Moroccan status in the world political economy. Interestingly, the pretext for the invasion was a request by Sultan al-Mansur to Askiya Ishaq II for a tax of one mitqāl on each load of salt brought to Timbuktu across the Sahara, claiming it would be a contribution to the army of Islam. With Ishaq's refusal, the invasion was launched and the city taken.

This major incursion, Muslim against Muslim, marked a turning point in the history of the city. Timbuktu's fate was now in the hands of political and economic necessities that were global rather than regional or local. This new scale is reflected in the equipment brought to bear on the city: cast-iron cannons from England, 500 mounted gunmen, 2,000 musketeers. In other words, a force equipped with all the cutting-edge technology of the age attacked Timbuktu. In fact, Sultan al-Mansur briefed his troops before they left, suggesting that they were "modern" and that it will be "easy for us to wage a successful war against these people and prevail over them."

The pasha Judar, who led the army, set up residence in Timbuktu, and the city became the pivot for supply and attack outward. New roads and a fortress were built in the city with forced labor. A harsh regime of tax and confiscation were imposed on its citizens, and residents were required to supply timber and to build canoes in support of the occupiers. Resistance hardened, and the Moroccans executed many inhabitants. A large revolt occurred for two months in 1591, finally subdued with great loss of life. The qadi sent a petition to the sultan, complaining of the brutality of the Moroccan forces and their violation of Islamic law. Finally, the pasha had enough of elite resistance in the city, and in October 1593 he moved forcefully against Tuareg, ulema, scholar, and merchant elites, killing many, exiling others, confiscating their property and homes, and destroying the educational institutions. It is at this point that the scholar Ahmed Baba was deported to Marrakesh, along with many of the manuscripts in the city. It is argued that this was a key turning point for all Sudanic civilization; it certainly marked the beginning of the decline of Timbuktu.

The Moroccan adventure did not go well, however. Initial technological superiority deteriorated under the effect of disease, political infighting, and coordinated Songhay resistance. A new pasha, appointed by the sultan, died in Timbuktu in 1596, perhaps poisoned by his own general. Over the next sixteen years, Timbuktu continued to suffer from occupation, with a range of arbitrary laws imposed and a responsive cycle of regular rioting and retaliation.

The end of Moroccan direct control came from an unexpected quarter. In a coup d'état, the military leader Ali took control of the army and assumed the title of pasha. The Saadidian sultans stopped sending troops and weapons to Timbuktu, and by 1630 the colony was independent and had been indigenized through marriage, fraternization, and the return of merchant power in the city. Songhay never reemerged to rule the area, and local petty kingdoms formed in its place. Morocco ultimately gained little from the colonization attempt, with the sultan Zidan, son of al-Mansur, commenting to the famous historian Ahmad Baba of Timbuktu that the expedition of 23,000 soldiers had produced nothing.

Timbuktu and the middle Niger slid into decline during the next 200 years as a combination of factors contributed to a decrease in the sub-Saharan trade, including division and conflict in the North African termini, intrusion of European powers in West African ports, the new gold sources available to Europeans in America, and the lack of a central power in the Sudan. Although the salt, gold, and slave trade continued, long-term drought and famine in the region over the next 150 years also contributed to the decline in the importance of the city. The city was captured by the Tuareg and remained under their control until the coming of the French.

Timbuktu was caught up in the appearance of the West African jihad movement of the 1700s. Before this time, Islam in the region had two forms: that of the urban merchant class and that of the royal court. The rural and local poor did not follow Islam. The jihad movement added a rural militant Islamic trend and led to a period of expansion of kingdoms in the region. Timbuktu, captured numerous times during this era, was viewed by the movement as a place of sin, impurity, and non-Islamic practices.

Yet because of its reputation as a center of Islamic learning and a source for legitimacy, the city was treated by the new states as a closed enclave on the periphery. Restrictions were certainly imposed. At one point, for example, the growing of tobacco, the playing of games and music, and the flaunting of signs of luxury were all forbidden. But the rulers understood the importance of the city in the salt trade, and when the city rebelled, its deviance was contained while maintaining its function as an entrepôt. For example, in 1844 the ulema and merchants fomented a rebellion. The response was a two-year economic blockade of the city. The conflict ended in an agreement of autonomy in return for the recognition of nominal rule and the payment of taxes. It was during this period that the great Sankore University library was burned, erasing many significant works of Islamic scholarship.

European society began to hear about the fabled wealth of the city of Timbuktu through various sources. The Almoravid Empire in the late eleventh century acquired gold via Timbuktu, and the Christian states in the Mediterranean depended on their gold dinars sourced from Timbuktu. It is estimated that more than half of all the gold in medieval Europe was imported across the desert, most via this city. A Spanish map of 1375 has the king of Mali holding a gold ingot, sitting on a throne in the approximate position of the city, thus reflecting the stories of Sultan Musa's visit to Cairo in 1324. In 1447 Italian merchant Antonio Malfante, in reviewing cities in the "land of the blacks," talks about Thambet (Timbuktu) and the role of *piroque* (boats) in its trading networks. In 1506 King João II of Portugal sent seamen to assess the overland or water routes to Timbuktu, that imagined city of the interior. Leo Africanus in particular is credited with launching the European interest in the city; he visited the city twice around 1512, and his *Description of Africa,* published in Italian in 1550, was widely circulated. In 1620 Englishman Richard Jobson reported hearing of a city called Timbuktu,

whose roofs were covered in gold, far into the interior of West Africa. The Scotsman Mungo Park visited the city in 1796. In one report, contained in a book entitled *An Account of Timbuctoo and Hausa, 1820,* a merchant recounts that the city was surrounded by a moat and a high mud wall, with three gates into the city: one facing the river, a second facing the desert, and a third facing Makkah.

In 1824 the Geographical Society of Paris offered a prize of 10,000 francs for the first European to visit and report back from Timbuktu. Rene Caille, a Frenchman, took up the challenge, disguised himself as a Muslim, and reached the declining city in 1828. He recorded that Timbuktu was "one of the largest cities I have seen in Africa," although he was disappointed that it did not live up to his expectations as the fabled city of gold. Heinrich Barth, the great German explorer, commenting on the Timbuktu of 1853, noticed that the caravan trade was currently suspended because of fighting among the Berbers in the Sahara. Barth is remembered for discovering a copy of the *Tarikh al-Sudan* within the city and transmitting the text to the European audience.

The French army entered Timbuktu in 1893. They had established the port of Saint Louis on the Senegalese coast in 1659 but did not really move inland until General Louis Faidherbe became governor of Senegal in 1854. Under the push of the French military, and the "scramble for Africa" signed in the Berlin Agreement, France moved into the middle Niger. Mali, including Timbuktu, became independent in 1960.

Today young tourists visit the city in large numbers to say they have been, but few tourists stay longer than a day or two. The city is hot, desolate, and encroached by dunes. Although Timbuktu is an administrative center for the Malian state, the impoverished national government has little money to spend "in the north." Public services are almost nonexistent, the new airport lacks dependable flights, and there is one Internet café in the city. Local elites participate in a new grouping, the Action Committee for the North, which seeks to alter national government neglect of the region.

The city suffered in the 1990s from the civil war that flared up to the north between the Tuaregs and the Songhay. Although refugees remain from the fighting, a relative calm now exists in the north, but Timbuktu has shrunk to around 20,000 inhabitants.

City elites have been able to generate substantial international interest in city preservation. Significant international monies have flowed into two major restoration projects: support for some of the seventy or so private libraries in the city, with their outstanding collections of Islamic manuscripts dating back more than 1,000 years, and United Nations Educational, Scientific, and Cultural Organization (UNESCO) support for the restoration of the Sankore University, Sidi Yahia Mosque, and Djingareyber Mosque, all three facing imminent destruction by desertification. The local community members have constantly been involved in maintaining the *banco,* or earthen walls, of their mosques: every two years the community participates in a citywide work scheme to restore the covering to the shrines.

Bruce Stanley

Further Readings

Ajayi, J. F. A., and Michael Crowder, eds. *History of West Africa.* Essex: Longman Group, 1985.

Brook, Larry, and Ray Webb. *Daily Life in Ancient and Modern Timbuktu.* Minneapolis: Lerner, 2000.

Fremantle, Tom. *The Road to Timbuktu.* London: Constable and Robinson, 2005.

Jenkins, Mark. *To Timbuktu: A Journey down the Niger.* London: Robert Hale, 2002.

Miner, Horace. *The Primitive City of Timbuktu.* New York: Doubleday, 1965.

Saad, Elias N. *Social History of Timbuktu.* New York: Cambridge University Press, 1983.

Sattin, Anthony. *The Gates of Africa: Death, Discovery and the Search for Timbuktu.* London: HarperCollins, 2004.

Trabzon
Population: 240,000 (2006 estimate)

For more than a millennium, Trabzon, one possible home of the legendary Amazons and a major entrepôt of the southeastern Black Sea, was one of the key cities on the Silk Road from Persia. Europeans struggled for "position" in the city to dominate the transit trade to Moscow and Venice, while slaves from the Caucasus were sold in its markets, and its grain fed Constantinople/Istanbul. Site of an alternative Byzantine capital city, and one of the earliest Greek colonies of the Iron Age, Trabzon has always been an outpost for security in the region, and the city remains today a crucial trade gateway for the people of the Caucasus and the eastern Black Sea.

Trabzon (Greek, *Trebizond;* ancient Greek, *Trapezus*) is a port city on the southern Black Sea littoral of northeast Turkey. Close to the mountain vastness of the Caucasus, Trabzon is the first large port city to the west. It lies on a bay encircled by the rugged Pontic Mountains, which separate it and its fertile plains off from the Anatolian plateau. The site is a high tablelike promontory facing the sea, protected by steep drops on two sides and the ancient harbor on the east; in Greek *Trapezus* means *tableland* or *flat top,* and the citadel is located at the highest point. Through the Zigana Pass to the southwest (6,543 feet) and then the Kop Dagh (8,823 feet), it is possible to reach via Erzurum to the key hinterland city of Tabriz. Ancient mining in the mountains along the Pontic coast generated gold and iron ore, while tea, tobacco, and hazelnuts (the nut of Pontus) have been key regional cash crops. Around Trabzon the Caucasus flora and fauna begin to give way to Mediterranean themes, including lower annual rainfall, pine trees, and a few olive trees. Today housing has consumed most available agricultural land, and the city has spread along the coast and south along the mountain pass into the interior.

Archaeological evidence for Trabzon's early history remains limited. Literary evidence in the form of Eusebius's argument for 756 BC as the founding of the city by Milesian colonists from Sinope is the standard assumption, although some contend that it was not until a century later that Trapezus was founded. Clearly, even then there was long-distance trade across the mountains linking the Iranian plateau with the Black Sea; thus, a third argument suggests that Mycenaean Greeks probably knew of locals on the site from the Late Bronze Age, as represented in the legend of Jason and the Golden Fleece (twelfth century BC), but only founded Trapezus as an emporium by the early eighth century to facilitate the trade in processed iron ore and silver that locals were extracting and processing from the mountains inland of the site. As the Greeks progressed into the Iron Age, Trapezus may thus have been one of their earliest colonies on the Black Sea, an outpost required for their technological development in the post-Homeric period.

These small Greek colonies controlled little of the hinterland but were enclaves of Greek culture that looked down on the local inhabitants as backward, exotic, and barbaric; hence, the stories are told of the Amazonian women in the vicinity of Trapezus and the search for the source of silver controlled by the Urartu in the interior. The invading Cimmerian tribes captured Trapezus and used the area as their base to raid Asia Minor until they were defeated by the neo-Assyrian Ashurbanipal (668–626 BC). Gradually, the Black Sea (*Pontus Euxinus* to the Greeks) became a Greek lake, with trade among its Greek colonies.

Cyrus, the first Achaemenid, captured the city around 546 BC. Under this first Persian dynasty, the eastern Black Sea coast became a separate satrapy. Darius (522–486 BC), interested in arboriculture, promoted, among other plants, the spread of the famous nut of Pontus to Greece. Assassination and brotherly intrigue quickly ate away at the power of the empire; when Artaxerxes II was challenged in battle by Cyrus his brother, the latter was killed (401 BC), and the Greek soldiers in Cyrus's army made their way north across Armenia. This "lost army of the Ten Thousand," glorified by the participant Xenophon, finally ended up in Trapezus, shipped their injured and old home on the city's ships, and walked the rest of the way back to Greece.

The southern Black Sea coast fell to Alexander the Great with his victory over the Achaemenids at Issus (333 BC). Upon his death, the Seleucids established their empire to the south, while an independent kingdom of Pontus was founded, by Mithridates I Ctistes, that included Trapezus as a key port. Over the next 200 years, Pontus, Armenia, and a shrinking Seleucid state together held the uneasy middle of Asia Minor against the expanding Romans to the west and the rising Parthians to the east. Mithridates VI Eupator (132–63 BC) of Pontus, in particular, created an increasingly powerful kingdom that challenged Rome and forged an alliance with Armenia. After 90 BC, Tigran the Great of Armenia, along with his father-in-law, Mithridaes, held off the Romans until they faced Pompey and his legions sent in 69–66 BC to subjugate the two insurgents. They were defeated, and Trapezus came under direct Roman rule.

The new region of the empire was called Pontus Polemoniacus. It is from this time that the Roman cult of Mithraism may have begun in Pontus and Trapezus. Plutarch argues that Mithraism spread from the proselytizing of Pontic pirates defeated by Pompey in 67 BC. An alternative is that local Zoroastrian forms of the Mysteries of Mithras practiced in Trapezus spread throughout the empire via the Roman sailors and legionnaires who were stationed in the city over the next 200 years, ending up as far away as an altar on Hadrian's Wall in northern England.

The Romans used Trapezus as their security hub for the eastern edge of the empire. They created a naval arsenal in the city and based the Pontic fleet in its harbor; from here, Pliny (AD 110–112) wiped local pirates off the southern Black Sea. The Romans sent convoys out from Trapezus to repress the Armenian revolt of AD 57. Under Vespasian (69–79), Trapezus was the end anchor for the expanded coastal fortifications of the empire along the Black Sea coast, the northernmost end for the Cappadocian *limes* (forts) that protected the Euphrates edge to the south, and the "gate to Armenia." The importance of the city for the defense of the empire was reinforced by Diocletian when he took the trouble to base the Pontica legion at Trapezus after 284. The eastern caravan trade entered the city on an eight-meter military road that ended in Trapezus, and this Roman road remained essentially unchanged until 1938, when the railway bypassed Trapezus.

Under the Romans, the city flourished as a major trading city linked directly along the coast to Byzantium. In the middle of the city stood a monument dedicated to Hadrian, who ordered the harbor, hippodrome, and theater constructed, and the temple of Hermes and Philesios. By the first century AD, Trapezus had both Christians and Jews. Peter's first letter in the New Testament is written to Christians in Pontus, tradition has it that Saint Andrew preached from a cave here, and Eugenios was martyred during the time of Diocletian and then was adopted as the city's patron saint. Locals were recruited into the legion here. Greek remained the key language in daily and official use, especially among the Christians.

The first indication of future trouble came in 134, with the invasion of the Alani, an Iranian nomadic tribe, into eastern Anatolia and Trapezus. A century later, ca. 257, allies of the Goths, the Borani, streamed south through the Caucasus, sacked Trapezus despite its reinforcement to legionary strength, and seized much of the eastern Pontic fleet. It took the city another century to recover.

Under the Byzantine emperors, Trebizond's importance waxed and waned with the power of the imperial armies.

Under Justinian I (AD 527–565), with the reexpansion of the empire toward the gates of Armenia, Trebizond's importance increased as a garrison and edge city for the empire. For the next 500 years, the city remained part of the empire, closely linked via the sea with Constantinople (see also "Istanbul"). Early Arab writers wrote about the bahr al-Trabazunda (Sea of Trebizond) as something they hoped to capture, but they never threatened the city, and the Black Sea remained open to trade between Trebizond and the other Greek cities around the littoral.

The fortunes of the city started to change with the arrival of the Turkomans into the area, beginning in 1048 with raiders who pillaged Armenia, Erzurum, and Trebizond. The new Comnenus dynasty in Constantinople (1081–1185) at first had little to do with Trebizond, which continued operating as an autonomous city. In 1139–1140, however, John Comnenus reasserted the direct control of Byzantium over Trebizond.

The sack of Byzantium in 1204 by the Latins during the Fourth Crusade reinvigorated Trebizond's fortunes. The grandsons of the emperor Andronicus I Comnenus escaped to the port and established their authority over the city, with Prince Alexius Comnenus assuming the position of emperor. Trebizond became the center of a new Empire of Trebizond, and generations of the Grand Comneni, as they became known, ruled over the city until the Ottomans finally captured it in 1461. Thus, the Comneni became the longest ruling family of the Byzantine Empire.

Under this family, the city became a regional power, trading throughout the Black Sea and far up into Russia. As an independent city-state on the Black Sea, Trebizond imported and exported a full range of goods. Many of the goods it exported were reexports that had arrived in the city via long-distance trade. Others were grown or produced locally in the hinterland of the city. Products for which the city became known included silver, iron, and alum mined from either the Pontic Mountains or the Caucasus; various kinds of cloth; silk, of course; and black wine. The transit trade was also a great moneymaker for the city elites, since they collected taxes on all goods that entered and left the city.

The first half of the thirteenth century saw the Black Sea rocked by political unrest; in 1214 Sinope fell to the Seljuq Turks, and Trebizond was forced to pay tribute to retain its autonomy from the sultan of Iconium. Michael Palaeologus was able to restore the Byzantine Empire in Constantinople (1261) but failed to regain former Byzantine possessions in the Crimea, which now paid tribute to the Empire of Trebizond. The Venetians sought trade in the Black Sea but found it advisable to unload their cargo at Constantinople rather than venture into troubled waters.

Worse was to come, however. Between 1240 and 1250, the Mongols appeared in the Caucasus, conquered all Armenia and Erzurum, and invaded Asia Minor. Trebizond joined a military alliance with the Sultanate of Iconium and the Empire of Nicaea to defend their independence, but it proved futile: the combined Seljuq-Trebizond forces were defeated by the Mongols. The emperor of Trebizond made a speedy peace with them and, on condition of paying an annual tribute, became a Mongol vassal.

The inclusion within an empire linking Iran, central Asia, Russia, and China dramatically facilitated both long-distance caravan trade and shipping on the Black Sea. Anatolia emerged as the key east-west trading highway of the Eurasia system. As Tabriz became a dominant center for trade with both East and West, Trebizond acted as its outlet to the world economy; in tandem, this dynamic dyad facilitated international long-distance trade stretching from China to London (see also "Tabriz"). As the junior partner, Trebizond adopted the weights-and-measures system of Tabriz. Because of this centrality, Trebizond was able to mesh both its sea routes and its land routes and to prosper. The Italians rushed in, jockeying for control of these trading opportunities; Michael Palaeologus granted the Genoese exclusive rights to Black Sea trading and seven years later allowed the Venetians to return. It was Genoa, however, that helped Trebizond to quickly supplant Egypt and the Levant as the terminal for the Indian spice caravan. Italian merchants were so desperate for the goods arriving in Trebizond that they were willing to wait up to three months for the arrival of the caravans from Iran and China. In the 1300s, the Genoese in the city were exempt from taxes and had many factories there. There were so many Venetians in the city that by 1319 they had been allowed to build their own church, houses, warehouses, and quay, all funded by a tax on the local Venetians. The sea route to Constantinople was significantly shorter and more secure than the land route, so fine cloths from Flanders and Florence were imported via Trebizond to the elites of Persia, and Persian silks, and some from China, passed through on their way to the courts of Europe. This is the time (ca. 1290) when Marco Polo claims to have returned via Trebizond from his stay in China.

The city's centrality in the trade networks of the day exposed it to all sorts of invasions and difficulties; the Black Death hit the port in the fourteenth century, wiping out many of its artisans and sailors. The conflicts for position between the Genoese and the upstart Venetians often broke out into fighting within the city and among their ships on the Black Sea. Troops of the Anatolian Turkoman sultanates often raided the city; it was burned in 1344, for example, though quickly rebuilt. As the boundaries of the "empire" contracted, its survival became dependent upon intrigue and fortunate marriages: daughters of the Grand Comneni became brides for Georgians, Armenians, Turks, and Greeks in the politics of alliances and city defense.

The struggle between this remnant of Hellenism and the expanding world of the Turkomans often found its creative expression in epic poetry. Both communities produced famous epics during this period that capture much of the life of the times and of the conflict between them. The famous *Digenes Akrites* cycle, for example, is a comprehensive picture of the Byzantine world in Asia Minor and of frontier life with its brave deeds and incessant warfare. Similar in form to *The Song of Roland* or *The Poem of the Cid,* which present legends from the struggle between Christianity and Islam, this epic of Basil Digenes was written down in the fourteenth century but appears to derive from Diogenes, a leader who fell in Asia Minor in 788 fighting the Arabs. The stories share many themes with the tales of *The Thousand and One Nights,* and parts appear to have been written during the tenth century. The hero is an *akritai:* defender of the outposts of the empire, an autonomous ruler of the marchlands, who devotes his life to the struggle with the Muslims and mountain robbers. Digenes was a famous Byzantine hero, and until recently his "grave" on the outskirts of Trabzon was still venerated for its ability to protect babies against evil spells.

The Turkomans in the area around Trebizond had their own collection, *Dede Korkut,* one of the greatest folk epics of the fourteenth century. This prose collection is believed to be the oldest surviving example of the *Oğuz Turkoman* tales, which describe tribal life in eastern Anatolia in epic style. This collection is a major source of information for the history of the time.

The rise of the Ottoman Turks, first from Bursa, then from Edirne, and finally in Istanbul, reshaped the fortunes of Trebizond. With Bursa as the central political core of the new empire, the silk trade shifted toward western Anatolia, and the trade routes moved south as well (see also "Bursa"). Trebizond became one of the last remaining Greek port cities outside of Byzantium itself, autonomous in its highly defensible position. Although the Ottomans placed the city under siege by land and sea numerous times during the fourteenth century, the city was not captured and continued to trade with Constantinople and other cities on the northern Black Sea littoral as well as with its Turkish enemies.

The conqueror Temür rushed through the region in 1390 and captured most of the cities in the area. However, uniquely, Trebizond survived because of an early alliance with him by its ruler, Alexius III. In the wake of Temür's death, the remnants of the Ottoman Empire reemerged and began to reconquer the lands they had held before his appearance. By 1450 their naval power, both in the Mediterranean and in the Black Sea, was formidable, and in 1454 the Ottoman fleet sailed along the southern Black Sea coast, forcing all powers along its shores, including the Comnenus kingdom of Trebizond, to pay tribute in recognition of Ottoman suzerainty.

The final conquest of Constantinople in 1453 by Mehmet II (the Conqueror) left only isolated remnants of the once-glorious Byzantine Empire. However, Mehmet sought them out as well, wishing to leave none "among the Byzantine Greeks who could be named King" to threaten Ottoman claims. Thus, he attacked the Comnenus after he had dealt with Palaeologus. Emperor David gave him the excuse he wanted: David helped forge a Muslim-Christian alliance to ward off Mehmet's impending attack. Mehmet led his troops by land and also sent a navy against Trebizond in 1461, and their appearance caused David to exclaim "Woe! Thunderation! What an army!"

Emperor David surrendered the city without a fight and agreed on a peace treaty. The emperor, his whole family, and court officials, along with their gold and precious personal possessions, were conveyed in a special ship to Istanbul, where they were kept under house arrest. The people of the city fared less well: men and women were enslaved, divided between sultan and dignitaries; young boys were placed in the Janissaries; and many of the rest of the city's inhabitants were deported to Istanbul to repopulate that decimated city. Albanians were forcibly transferred from Albania to Trebizond in the late fifteenth century for resettlement. David had not learned his lesson, however. He conspired with his former allies from house arrest, and so the sultan threw him into prison, and two years later he ordered David, his brother, and his seven sons and nephew to be killed and their bodies thrown to the dogs.

The fall of the Byzantine Empire and of its last bastion, Trebizond, produced an extensive migration of Byzantine intellectuals to the key Christian economic centers of the time, particularly to Italy. A good example is Bessarion of Nicaea, an influential Byzantine humanist. Born and educated in Trebizond at the beginning of the fifteenth century, Bessarion ended up in Constantinople, where he studied Greek poets, orators, and philosophers but also religious teachings, and he became a monk. As archbishop of Nicaea, he advocated a reunification of the Latin and Greek Church, a radical idea at the time. When his ideas were rejected by the Orthodox community, Bessarion moved to Rome, became a Latin cardinal, and had a profound influence on the Italian renaissance through his advocacy of an understanding of non-Christian literature and thinking. In particular, his extensive personal library became the core of the Bibliotheca Marciana in Venice. The fall of Constantinople to the Ottomans was a major blow to his world, and he advocated a Venetian crusade against the Turkish threat to Europe. In his final years, Bessarion wrote the lengthy *Encomium,* a eulogy to his native city, Trebizond.

As the Ottoman domains continued to expand for the next century, the city grew as well. Called Trabzon in Turkish, the city was considered exceptionally beautiful by Mehmet II, who valued the skills of its artisans; when he needed a world map on which to plan his military campaigns, he turned to Amirutzes of Trabzon to create it. The Ottoman elite also adopted the city as a site for relaxation and contemplation. Endowments to construct Islamic public buildings began to reshape the city's built environment. The mausoleum of Gulbahar, wife of Sultan Bayezid II (1481–1512), was built during this early surge of Islamic construction and still graces the city today. The fact that Sultan Sulayman the Magnificent (r. 1520–1566) was born in the city while his father Selim was governor meant that it received considerable architectural attention from Sulayman and his descendants. However, the records show that during this time Trabzon also experienced food security problems and suffered a chronic wheat and barley shortage.

Although Trabzon had lost much of the silk trade to Bursa, as the Black Sea became a Turkish lake and closed to Latin ships, Trabzon benefited. Twenty years after the conquest of Constantinople, the Genoese in the Black Sea were gone. The Black Sea's ports became the "Nursing Mother of Constantinople," providing the capital with all necessities and foodstuffs, and Trabzon was one of the key ports. The city was also closely linked with Caffa in the Crimea: city merchants would send shiploads of consolidated goods across to the north, where the demand for arak, wine, hazelnuts, and ship's masts was insatiable. By the early 1500s, Moscow and Poland were in direct, regular connection to Trabzon, where its wine was in high demand.

Around 1600 the English began to expand their trading presence in the empire, and they lobbied hard for access to Trabzon as a conduit for the Persian silk trade. In fact, in 1609 some English ships snuck through as far as Trabzon in spite of the ban, but this was rare. By the end of the century, Iranian silk was moving again across the northern Erzurum-Trabzon road because of plague and uncertainty in Mesopotamia, including Arab attacks along the Baghdad route; Trabzon was back in the silk business. Trade into and out of Trabzon was dominated by a powerful merchant class of Muslims as well as an expanding group of non-Muslims.

The seventeenth century was a period of conflict and development both to the north of the Black Sea and to the south, and the city played both a security role as well as that of an entrepôt. As the Ottomans continued to expand during the first part of the century, Trabzon supplied the advancing armies with grain and military supplies; and as the Ottomans ended up on the receiving end during the seventeenth century, the same was true. For example, in the various confrontations with the Safavid Empire, Trabzon handled extensive cargoes of grain from the river ports on the Danube for haulage to the southern front. In the wars with Hungary, Trabzon shipped cannonballs from Kigi, outside of Erzurum, across the Black Sea and up the Danube to support the troops. In the early 1600s, violence came directly into Trabzon, when Cossack raiders attacked the city's trading partners in the Crimea and then unexpectedly appeared by boat in the city's harbor and ransacked the city. The city recovered, however, and throughout the 1700s, its trade expanded, including ship's masts, copper products, and foodstuffs. Iron from Russia joined Persian silk in transiting the markets of the city destined for all points of the globe.

Dramatic shifts in Black Sea trade toward the end of the eighteenth century led to important changes in the composition of the city's merchant class and in the life of the city. The Kucuk Kaynarca Treaty of 1774 between the empire and Russia was a fundamental turning point in Ottoman history, since it led to an opening up of all the empire's cities to Western and Russian influence. In particular, however, it meant an end to the empire's domination of the Black Sea, allowing the Russians into the cities of the region. The result was increased trade and new opportunities for the non-Muslim minorities to make a living in long-distance trade. It also directly led to population growth in the port cities around the Black Sea.

By the early part of the nineteenth century, Russian money and arms had helped create a semiautonomous Trabzon, where tax collection by Istanbul did not occur and regular contact was not maintained. In the Ottoman-Russian War of 1828–1929, Russian forces advanced along the Black Sea coast as far as Trabzon; the Adrianople Treaty, which ended the war, confirmed Russia's rights and privileges and expanded the commercial freedoms of its citizens throughout remaining Ottoman domains. Not to be left out, other European powers began to move into the port cities of the Black Sea and to demand similar privileges. Trade through and out of Trabzon increased dramatically with these changes, increasing more than 200 percent in the next few years, yet it was not the local elites who benefited. The English came to dominate the trading life of the city with their transit trade to Persia, and by the time of the Anglo-Ottoman Commercial Convention of 1838, Trabzon's trade had increased another 400 percent. The Crimean War of 1853–1856 also served to help the expansion of the city's trade networks, since much of the material requirements of the war were met via the port.

Concurrent with these shifts in the city's importance and centrality came fundamental changes in technology. The first steamship services opened in the city in 1836, when a British steamer service linked Istanbul via Samsun with Trabzon; within four years, companies from four other countries were also plying the route. By the end of the century, there were ten companies operating through the city. As in the Persian Gulf or the Red Sea, the introduction of steamers brought about an overall increase in trade but shifted power and wealth away from local Muslim shippers and the coastal sailing ships, which reverted to carrying local coastal bulk goods between regional ports. The shift in power to the Europeans allowed Greek and Armenian families to tag along, receiving many of the new jobs as representatives of the companies, insurance brokers, and transshippers that became available. Thus, their future in the city became tied with that of the European powers, for better or worse.

The development of the shipping lines into Trabzon facilitated the last gasp of the white slave trade in the city. Trabzon had long been a key port for the Circassian and Georgian slave trade, with trade from smaller ports into Trabzon, where slaves were consolidated for shipment to Istanbul, Izmir, the Levant, and Egypt. British, Ottoman, French, and Austrian steamers from Trabzon to Istanbul regularly carried slaves: if there were fifty Circassian passengers on a ship, perhaps up to one-third may have been slaves. British steamers were preferred by the dealers for their large size and better deck conditions, but British companies would sometimes refuse to carry large groups of Circassians. The traders would then shift the cargo to French and Ottoman government ships that would carry them.

Under pressure from the Europeans, in 1855 the grand vizier issued an official order to the Trabzon garrison to halt the slave trade, and the British and French navies backed up that order with regular visits to the port. Subsequent to the order, dealers continued to use various techniques and tricks to avoid the ban: for example, small sailboats crammed with up to 220 slaves were used in transporting Circassian slaves from the Caucasus to Trabzon, from where they were smuggled out in various ways. Since sailing in the eastern Black Sea is extremely hazardous, many lives were lost in these illegal operations. It is reported that in the early 1860s demand for such transport was so high that sailboat captains could extract a transportation fee of one child per thirty persons, chosen by lots.

Despite international attempts, it is recorded that even in the early 1870s there was still a slave-dealer guild in the city that illegally kept the trade going and monopolized the price. In 1879 Trabzon officials reported that they were still confronting strong demands from Abaza slaves (Abkhazians) to be freed from their bondage. The Europeans found that the trade was so difficult to halt because often Circassian girls were sold by their own, poor families, and within the Ottoman system such women often rose to great roles or became wives of the grand vizier.

The fantastic expansion of Trabzon's trade leveled off in the 1870s. Alternative routes via the Caucasus and Russia, the construction of the Ankara-Erzurum Railway, and the growing significance of the Iranian port of Khoramshahr after the opening of the Suez Canal in 1869 meant a gradual end to caravans and slow land travel (see also "Ankara"). The English, with their strong base in Trabzon, saw their profits drop off, and slowly their presence in the city began to fade.

The decade between 1914 and 1924 saw the very social fabric of the city torn up and dramatically reworked. Trabzon was a principal site for attacks and massacres of its Armenian community in 1915. Officials in Trabzon were involved in organizing attacks on Armenians, and there are reports that Armenians were put into boats in the port and taken out into the Black Sea and drowned. The U.S. consul in Trabzon reported how boats would set out with Armenian passengers and return a few hours later empty, and in one case he said 3,000 children were drowned. Cemal Azmi, the governor of Trabzon for part of this period, later reportedly boasted that

Trabzon on the Black Sea coast, ca. 1915. (Library of Congress)

he had contributed to the subsequent rich harvest of anchovies: Trabzon is famous for its anchovies, a staple of the
poor in the area. The U.S. consul also reported the systematic
rape and forcible prostitution of Armenian girls in the city by
police and public officials.

In November 1914, the city was bombarded by the Russian
navy, and in April 1916 a combined Russian navy and army
attack captured the city. Over the next two years, some religious and business leaders from the Greek community cooperated with the occupation, creating resentment in the Turkish majority. With the Russian Revolution, the Erzincan
Armistice (December 1917), and the chaos in the Russian
army that ensued, Russian troops began to withdraw from the
city in January 1918. Local "Laz" Turkish militias immediately attacked Greek citizens, and a process of attack, ethnic
cleansing, and refugees fleeing to churches for refuge began.
The Greek community organized resistance and an ad hoc
structure and controlled parts of the city. Armenian fighters
appeared in Trabzon hoping to support local Greeks and to
ethnically cleanse the Turks from the city. Georgian Bolsheviks attacked local landowners, and some communes were
established in the city. Outsiders blew up an ammunition
depot in Trabzon, killing hundreds of local people. By the
time a contingent of Turkish soldiers showed up on 24 February 1918, there was little that they could do to restore order.

As the Russian forces melted away, the resulting vacuum in
the Caucuses and eastern Anatolia opened the door for various irredentist and ethnically based schemes for new political entities, and the city descended into chaos. The Greek
community, led by Orthodox religious leaders like Trabzon
Metropolitan Chrysanthos Lain, began calling for an independent Pontus Greek state and argued their case to a sympa-

thetic audience at the Paris Peace Conference. Weapons were
acquired from Russian and Greek sources, and underground
arsenals were created. Under pressure from the Paris Peace
Conference, the rump Istanbul government agreed to a study
to investigate the treatment of Christians in Trabzon to
"prove" that there were not massacres and mistreatment
going on. Finally, to restore order, Mustafa Kamal was appointed by the Istanbul government to head the regional
army, and he landed in Samsun in 1919.

Over the next two years, the chaos and localized fighting
got worse. The Pontus Society, a new organization evolving
from a Greek resurgence society founded in 1904 among
graduates of the American school in Merzifon, launched a series of armed attacks on New Year's Day, 1920, to create a Pontus state running from Samsun through Trabzon to the Georgian border. Their flag, modeled on the Greek blue and white,
was carried by various militias in the mountains and in the
city. Meanwhile, the Turkish majority were also organizing
politically to express their claims: the sixteen delegates to the
Erzurum Conference made a strong emotional case for action
to retain the region for Turkey, and the Trabzon Muhafazai
Hukuk Cemiyeti (Society for the Protection of the Rights of
Trabzon) lobbied for action in Istanbul. Under the stillborn
Treaty of Sevres (1920), an Armenian state was envisioned
that would have included Trabzon. The United States, in fact,
told the Turks to begin to mediate over Trabzon in expectation of the city's inclusion.

Finally, in April 1920, the Turkish national parliament created the Central Army to crush the rebels, and Kamal and
General Kazim Karabekir Pasha finally brought the region
back under control. One technique was to forcibly exile Greek
men between the ages of fifteen and fifty; many of Trabzon's

citizens were marched to central Anatolia. There were also 174 Greeks executed. Another tactic was to establish a Turkish Orthodox Church of loyal "Turkish" Christians. In the end, the rebellion was crushed by 1923, with perhaps as many as 12,000 Greeks and 2,000 Turks killed.

Between 1923 and 1924, about 1.4 million Greeks were forcibly uprooted from Asia Minor and settled in Greece as part of the compulsory exchange of populations contained in the peace treaty. Many of the deportees came from Trabzon. The Greeks of Pontus were taken to northern Greece near the Bulgarian and Yugoslavian borders, where they remain today. Interestingly, they had a tradition of mummers plays, primarily performed at Christmastime, involving going from house to house. As many as fifty of these Pontic Greek mummers plays are still remembered and performed. In fact, the English term *mummers* may have been borrowed from Trabzon during the thirteenth century in the wake of the Fourth Crusade.

The modern city of Trabzon has received considerable development attention and planning under the modern Turkish state. The French architect J. Lambert prepared a city plan in 1938, although much of it was overtaken by unplanned growth of the city. Port facilities were improved, and the city became home for the Black Sea Technical University from 1963. The decades of the 1960s and 1970s witnessed the greatest population growth for the city, with a growth ratio of more than 50 percent.

There was another spurt of in-migration after the fall of the Soviet Union, as traders from the Caucuses made Trabzon their key entrepôt. Today Trabzon is host for a world trade center, the second one in Turkey after Istanbul. With its international airport and extensive health, educational, and commerce facilities, the city is becoming a crucial transnational door for the whole region. Tourists from the former Soviet Union are also arriving, attracted by the ancient city walls, the palace of the Grand Comneni, and converted Byzantine churches such as the Hagia Sophia and the Panaghia Chrysokephalos (the Cathedral of the Comnenus). The city is also a site for regional political dialogue: in 2002 the presidents of Turkey, Azerbaijan, and Georgia met to discuss and sign new regional cooperation agreements concerning transportation corridors, oil and gas pipelines, communication projects, and the fight against terrorism and organized crime.

Bruce Stanley

Further Readings

Ascherson, Neal. *Black Sea.* London: Vintage, 1996.

King, Charles. *The Black Sea: A History.* Oxford: Oxford University Press, 2004.

Miller, William. *Trebizond: The Last Greek Empire.* 1926. Repr. Amsterdam: Adolf Hakkert, 1968.

Pavliuk, Oleksander, and Ivanna Klyupush-Tsintsadze. *The Black Sea Region: Cooperation and Security Building.* Armonk, NY: M. E. Sharpe, 2003.

Tsetskhladze, Gocha, ed. *Colloquia Pontica 1: New Studies on the Black Sea Littoral.* Oxford: Oxbow Books, 1995.

———. *North Pontic Archaeology.* Leiden: Brill, 2001.

Tripoli
Population: 1.8 million (2006 estimate)

Since the time of the Phoenicians, trade along the Libyan coast of the Mediterranean has been drawn to the natural harbor of Tripoli. Trans-Saharan trade also quickly found its way to this entrepôt, with caravans composed of thousands of camels making their way north to meet Roman, Byzantine, Arab, or Spanish ships. Home for Roman grain and emperors, the city became the capital of Italy's Libyan colony when the Italians returned after 1911. Famous as one of the Barbary strongholds, Tripoli fought with the nascent American state, with its invasion enshrined in the "U.S. Marine Corps Hymn." Today the city is the busy and expanding capital of Libya as well as the White City of fame and legend.

Tripoli (Arabic, *Trabulus al-Gharb*), capital of Libya, is the largest and busiest city in the country today. It is located in northern Libya on the Mediterranean coast. The Jebal Nafusa mountain range to the south of Tripoli has always served as a natural border between the desert and the sea. Tripoli is uniquely situated where the Sahara Desert meets the Mediterranean Sea. Its large sheltered area of anchorage has made it one of the most important trading ports in the southern Mediterranean. Tripoli is also the only seaport along the shortest trans-Saharan trade path from interior Africa to Europe. This strategic location, as well as its mild climate, has made Tripoli a valuable asset to fighting powers since the beginning of history.

Tripoli was first established by the Phoenicians around the sixth century BC. At the time, this oasis was inhabited by various Libyan coastal tribes, who are said to be ancestors of today's Berber population in northern Africa. Initially, the Phoenicians used this oasis as an intermediate sailing port to the West. Eventually, it became a Phoenician settlement and later a town under the name Oea. Oea, together with several other coastal towns, made up the Carthaginian Emporia. Until the Second Punic War (210 BC), Oea was under the rule of Carthage, and the inhabitants of this area were called Libyphoenices. After the defeat of Carthage (149 BC), Tripoli fell under Numidian rule.

This lasted until 46 BC, when Caesar annexed Numidian territories, declaring Africa Nova. Under the Romans, the western part of Carthaginian Emporia became Tripolitania. It included three towns: Sabratha, Leptis, and Oea. The name *Tripolis* was derived from the Greek word *tri,* meaning *three,* and *polis,* meaning *towns.* Throughout the Roman period, Tripolitania referred to the area of these three towns, that is, Sabratha, Leptis, and Oea.

As a part of the Roman Empire, and especially during the second century AD, Tripolitania flourished. The wealth of this zone depended upon three factors: agriculture, maritime commerce, and trans-Saharan trade. Eventually, trade from interior Africa to the Mediterranean coast gained importance, making the coastal port of Oea a significant center for exchange. Gold, ivory, slaves, and exotic animals for Roman circus fights were all brought from the Chad area to Oea. Here they were exchanged for Roman luxury products. Later, when the use of camels became popular as a means of trans-Saharan transportation, trade boomed, allowing the town of Oea as well as Leptis to prosper.

In addition to trade, the reign of Septimus Severus, the first native of Tripolitania to become emperor of Rome, had a big effect on the status of this region. This African emperor from Leptis ruled the Roman Empire from AD 193 to AD 211. He was popular among the people of Rome as well as the people of his home area of Tripolitania. Because of Septimus Severus's connections to elites on both sides of the Mediterranean Sea, Oea as well as Sabratha and Leptis thrived and experienced what some historians refer to as an early golden age.

After 297 the name Tripolitania was shortened to Tripolis. Later, under the rule of the Augusti, Oea was given several privileges, which made it grow into an important center. At the same time, the conditions in Leptis and Sabratha slowly deteriorated. With this dominance of Oea over the other two neighboring towns, eventually Tripolis started to refer to Oea alone. In time, around the fifth century AD, Oea was called Tripolis. This name, with slight Arabic deviations, has remained the name of this city until today.

In 423 when Boniface, Roman general of Africa, was suspected of disloyalty by Rome, he asked assistance from the Vandals in Spain. After he reconciled with Empress Placidia, however, the Vandals, once invited into the area, refused to leave. This marked a new era. The Roman Empire was in decline, and the Vandals took advantage of its fading power. After three decades of fighting, the Vandals finally defeated the Romans and took Tripolis in 455. They remained in control of the town until 533.

The reign of the Vandals in Tripolis was not marked with glory. Quite the contrary, this town shared the fate of other neighboring towns, which dramatically declined under their rule. The economy and the people suffered severe hardships, and the population of Tripolis declined from approximately 30,000 to 7,000.

The Byzantine army conquered the town in 533, but their rule did little to improve the situation of the people of Tripolis. Many of the Byzantine officials were Greek-speaking foreigners who had difficulties building good relations with the town dwellers. Theaters and amphitheaters became fortified residences. The harbor was also fortified. A few churches were built, more to serve the Byzantine garrisons than the people. In brief, there are no indications that Byzantine rule in Tripolis did anything to stop the deterioration of the city.

In AD 645, after a two-month siege, the Arab commander Amr ibn al-Aas entered Tripoli, and the Islamic era began. Unfortunately, the city continued to experience unrest, fighting, and war. First, the unrest was mainly sparked by the local, then called Berber, population of Tripoli, who would not accept Arab and Muslim rule. Later, however, the Arabs themselves fought over Tripoli, and its political alliances shifted among different administrative centers such as Damascus, Baghdad, Kairouan, and Cairo.

Under the Umayyads, Rufai ibn Thabit al-Ansari was appointed as the first Muslim ruler of Tripoli (667). Struggle for control of the city continued for centuries, however. Not until Haroun ar-Rashid, the Abbasid caliph, appointed Ibrahim al-Aghlabi in 800 to rule the area did Tripoli experience some peace. Ibrahim al-Aghlabi established a new *imara* (administration) with its capital in Kairouan, and he placed his son, Abdullah Ben Ibrahim Ben al-Aghlab, as ruler of Tripoli. The Aghlabids remained in control of the city for about a century, and Tripoli had a chance settle down. The city wall was rebuilt as well as several mosques and Qur'anic schools. Arab Islamic culture flourished, and most of the Berber population converted to Islam.

Fights over the city started again around 909, as Aghlabid rule weakened and other families and tribes sought to replace them. First, the Fatimids stepped in and remained in control of Tripoli from 909 until 972. More significantly, however, was the reign of the Berber tribe Beni Ziri (Zirids), who, together with their relatives the Beni Khazroun, ruled Tripoli from 972 until 1027. During the almost sixty years of their reign, Tripoli was an independent city-state for the first time in its history. Just as the foundation of a regularized political system was being established, however, the city was retaken by the Fatimids in 1030.

During this time, Tripoli became increasingly important as a center for the trans-Saharan caravan trade, which attracted increased foreign interest in the city. As Arab power weakened, the Normans from Sicily conquered the city and ruled between 1146 and 1158. The Arabs regained control of the city, however, first under the al-Mohadids (AD 1160–1230) and later under the long rule of the Hafsids (1230–1510). Spanish troops conquered the city in 1509 but only remained until 1539, when they left the city in the hands of the Maltese knights of Saint John of Jerusalem, who continued until 1551. In 1551 the expanding Ottoman Turks under Captain Dargut surrounded the city by the sea and captured it, with Dargut appointed the first Ottoman pasha of Tripoli. Ottoman suzerainty over the city lasted, with only slight interruption, until the Italian invasion in 1911.

Initially, the people of Tripoli were happy to have the city under Muslim rule again. Slowly, however, the pasha imposed Turkish superiority, which made their rule unpopular among the citizens of the city. In 1711, when Ahmad Pasha Karamanli seized power, he became the first son of Tripoli, although of Turkish origin, to rule the city. Ahmad Pasha paid taxes to Constantinople, accepting their overall authority, but had sole power of the city. Although the French attacked and destroyed Tripoli in 1728, Ahmad Pasha rebuilt the city.

Karamanli rule lasted until 1835, effectively giving Tripoli independence for more than a century. In the post-Napoléon era of British dominance in the Mediterranean, the pasha of Tripoli became an ally of the British, and their consul in Tripoli began reporting on the rich trans-Saharan trade between Tripoli and the "Sudan" kingdoms of Bornu, Hausa, and Sokoto. Ivory, precious stones, gold, and slaves were brought to Tripoli and sold to countries north of the Mediterranean. This ancient trade was one of the two key financial foundations for the city's autonomy.

The city's second financial resource at the time was through "war against aggressors" as perceived locally or "piracy" as perceived abroad. As one of the six North African states or so-called Barbary States, Tripoli under the Karamanlis had signed treaties with some foreign powers allowing their ships free passage along the Tripoli coast, but the ships of other nontreaty states were liable to be captured and held for ransom by the corsairs. The new nation of the United States initially paid tribute to guarantee free passage but then refused payment in 1800. In response, Yusef Pasha Karamanli declared war on the United States in 1801. For the next four years, in what has become known as the Tripolitan War, the nascent U.S. Navy fought with Tripoli ships, including engagements where the USS *Philadelphia* was captured (1804). Finally, in August and September 1804, an American fleet, led by the USS *Constitution,* bombarded the heavily defended harbor of Tripoli, followed by a U.S. land expedition along the coast. A treaty of peace was finally signed between Tripoli and the United States in June 1805, ending the tributes and opening Tripoli to U.S. trade. It is from this time that the "U.S. Marine Corps Hymn" includes the phrase "from the shores of Tripoli."

By the 1830s, in the face of European imperialist expansion in North Africa, the Ottomans moved to reassert their direct authority and claim to Tripoli. They captured the Karamanli leaders and deported them to Istanbul, and Tripoli fell again under direct Ottoman rule. Despite some legislative and administrative reforms, this second Ottoman period in Tripoli was an unhappy one. Pest, drought, and discrimination brought development within the city to a standstill.

The Italian colonial power defeated the Ottomans and took control of the city in 1911, and some of the people of Tripoli hoped for change. The long-awaited change, however, did not happen. Tripoli, the declared capital of Italian Libya, became divided into sections. The old city belonged to the people of Tripoli, while a new city, outside the old city walls, was developed for the Italian occupiers and new settlers. Schools and churches were built to educate the locals and make them Italian. The elites of Tripoli, who were considered by the majority of the local people as Italian agents, followed in the Italian footsteps and adopted an Italian way of life.

Eventually, the Italian part of Tripoli flourished. The local population resisted and as a result suffered concentration camps and deportation. They hung all their hopes on the likes of Umar al-Mukhtar, the famous freedom fighter, hoping he would reach Tripoli and kick the Italians out. In the meantime, they remained impoverished within the old city or moved out to the slums.

After World War II and the defeat of the Fascist powers, Tripolitania, with Tripoli at its core, became a British protectorate, with British and American army bases. The victorious Allies finally agreed to bring Tripolitania and Cyrenaica together into a new federated state, and Libya became independent in December 1951 under the pro-British head of the Sanusiyah, Sidi Muhammad Idris al-Mahdi as-Sanusi. Under King Idriss, as he became known, Libya became a constitutional monarchy, with Tripoli as its capital, although his preference was for the Cyrenaican city of al-Bayda. Considering the new state's meager financial resources, it was difficult to establish the needed infrastructure for a modern capital city, since at the time of its independence Libya was among the poorest countries in the world. Tripoli did not start to thrive until after the discovery of oil in 1958. Then education and health care became more accessible to most of the people, and construction projects within the city began to increase. British and American political influence remained substantial, particularly through the continued presence of their military bases in the country.

When on 1 September 1969 Colonel Muammar al-Qaddafi took power through a military putsch, different priorities were set. The foreign presence in Tripoli was ended, including American, British, Italian, and French military bases and civilian institutions. The goal was to take Tripoli back to its Arabic and Muslim roots; hence, all bars, casinos, and theaters were shut down. Later, as a result of the escalating Palestinian-Israeli conflict and adamant anti-Western policies toward the new government, the British and American embassies were shut down. In due course, Libya became the Socialist People's Libyan Arab Jamahirya, although Tripoli remained the capital. Under socialism, trade, which was the heartbeat of Tripoli for centuries, became insignificant. Other factors also isolated the city: internal politics between 1979 and 1992; the U.S. bombing of Tripoli in April 1986; and United Nations (UN) economic, flight, and arms sanctions (1992–1999) all hurt the economic and social life of Tripoli. During this period of isolation, little was introduced into the city in the way of modernization, and the pace of development slowed considerably. On the other hand, public schools and hospitals were opened to all sectors of the population for free, increasing literacy among young men and women to 100 percent and improving health care and awareness. Water from the Great Man-Made River, originating from the south of Libya, reached most houses of Tripoli. Throughout this time, the city remained home to government ministries, some foreign embassies, the country's main television and radio station, and the most important university of the country, al-Fateh University.

When the UN embargo was lifted in 1999, things started to change in the capital city. After years of hibernation, the people of the city started to wake up. This was partly encouraged by political steps to improve relations with Western powers, most importantly with the United States. By 2003 the attempts to make up for lost time were becoming obvious: new reforms were introduced, investment opportunities were encouraged, and socialism was de-emphasized. Agricultural production such as olive oil, oranges, and dates as well as local industry such as iron and steel, tobacco, and textile factories were updated. Private shops, universities, and hospitals were reopened. Foreign investors as well as visitors were allowed to enter the country despite the lack of an adequate infrastructure. Drastic changes have occurred, sometimes too quickly, in Tripoli, which for decades had witnessed very little change.

Today the 3,000-year-old city of Tripoli is striving to live up to its great potential. It boasts of an ethnically and religiously homogenous population (ca. 90 percent Arab Muslims), the capital city is growing rapidly, and its people are doing what they have always done best—making business with the outside world. A simple walk through the city of Tripoli today reveals many remnants of its many phases of history. Monuments of the city's glorious and troubled past are still standing: the Roman arch of Marcus Aurelius, the fortress, the original mihrab of the mosque of Amr ibn al-Aas inside the Ahmad Pasha Mosque, the Catholic Church of Santa Maria, Dargut Pasha's Turkish Bath, Yusif Pasha Karamanli's house, the Italian piazza outside the old Turkish city wall, and modern Tripoli developing along the shore. With ongoing projects to renovate its old city as well as to modernize and clean its new part, Tripoli aims to reclaim its old title and become once again the White City.

Amel M. Jerary

Further Readings

Hare, John. *Shadows across the Sahara: Travels with Camels from Lake Chad to Tripoli.* London: Constable, 2003.

London, Joshua. *Victory in Tripoli.* Hoboken, NJ: Wiley, 2005.

Mattingly, David. *Tripolitania.* London: B. T. Batsford, 1995.

Pennell, C. R., ed. *Piracy and Diplomacy in Seventeenth Century North Africa: The Journal of Thomas Baker, English Consul in Tripoli, 1677–1685.* London: Associated University Presses, 1989.

Todd, Mabel Loomis. *Tripoli the Mysterious.* New York: Grant Richards, 1912.

Tunis
Population: 984,000; Greater Tunis, 2.1 million (2006 estimate)

With the heritage of three millennia of urban civilization reaching back to the Phoenicians and their capital at

Carthage, Tunis manifests almost all aspects of Mediterranean history. It lies on a gulf of the North African coast, midway between Gibraltar and the Dardanelles, at the crossroads of the Saharan routes of Africa. The development of Tunis after the arrival of its Muslim conquerors is associated with the destruction of Carthage, which may be considered as its ancestor. The Muslim-Arab city that arose became the capital of Tunisia in the thirteenth century and remained for centuries thereafter a model of Islamic urbanism. As a French protectorate from 1881 to 1956, Tunis grew into an urban agglomeration containing several cities: the original Arab madinah, a new European space that became the city center, and a number of gourbivilles (shantytowns of rural migrants). Since Tunisia's independence, these disparate parts of the city have changed in different ways without forming a coherent, integrated whole.

Tunis (Spanish, *Tùnez;* Arabic, *Tûnis, Tûnus, Tûnas*) is the Arabic name of both the country of Tunisia and its capital, also called *al-hadira* (the city par excellence) and nicknamed *al-khadra* (the Green City). The origin of the name probably comes from the Berber root *t-n-s,* which can be found in other North African toponyms and means "stopping place" or "encampment," and it suggests that the site was initially founded by the indigenous North African Berber-speaking population. In the eleventh century BC, the Phoenicians of Tyre had established trading posts along the shores of the Mediterranean, probably including posts at Tunis and its neighbor, Carthage (see also "Tyre"). In 814 BC, the princess Elyssa and a number of Tyrian aristocrats, said to be fleeing the tyranny of Pygmalion, founded Carthage, in Punic *qart Hadasht* (new city); it was to become the uncontested capital of the Phoenician colonies of the west after Alexander the Great took Tyre in 332 BC. Carthage was one of the richest cities in the world of antiquity and eventually the home of the likes of Jugurtha, Hannibal, and Saint Augustine. In its heyday, it was the greatest sea power in the Mediterranean, colonizing the coasts of Africa, Spain, the Balearuics, Sardinia, and Sicily. The city, with an estimated population of 300,000, was a model of Hellenistic urbanism.

Carthage and Tunis were so close to one another that one may consider them variants of the same city. A day's march separated the Punic capital, situated on a peninsula along the shores of a gulf, from the hilltop settlement at the far end of the lagoon. The first mention of Tunis in the historical record is in 395 BC, when, according to Diodore of Sicily, 200,000 "Libyans" revolted against Carthage and took the town of "Tunes." Greek and Latin historians often refer to it as a modest fortification within view of and an ally of Carthage. Both cities were destroyed by Rome following the Third Punic War in 146 BC and then reconstructed by the emperor Octavius. Carthage became the capital of Roman Africa, the granary of the empire. For some while, it was ruled over by vassals, including the legendary Berber rebels Masinissa, Jugurtha, and Juba I and II, who briefly established Numidian kingdoms.

Roman Carthage prospered, enjoying the munificence of Hadrian and Anthony. With its port and forum in the upper city and its temples honoring the gods of Rome often assimilated to the Carthaginian Pantheon (Jupiter, Junon, Minerva, Tanit, and Saturn), it was also a cosmopolitan place of Berbers, Greeks, Syrians, Jews, and slaves from throughout the Mediterranean. The city reached its apogee in the second century AD before a series of revolts and the decadence of the empire set in. From the third century AD, Christianity began to spread into the area, especially the schismatic Donatist movement. When the Vandal armies arrived in 439, Carthage became the capital of their empire. A century later, in 533, it was conquered by the Byzantines and renamed Karthago Justiana. Although it maintained its cosmopolitan character and Latin culture, by then it had ceased to be an important city. Tunis, meanwhile, had been destroyed by the Romans and then revived, apparently as a relay post. By the sixth century, its inhabitants had become Christians, but as long as Carthage existed, it remained a small fortress town.

With the rise and spread of Islam in the seventh century, the conquest of the Eastern Maghreb was completed by the occupation of Carthage. In 698 the Muslim armies, fearing attacks from the sea by the Byzantines, destroyed the city and its infrastructure in its entirety. They chose to establish themselves in the inner area of the lagoon on the eastern side of a hillock between the gulf and a salt marsh on a defendable site protected from attacks and to transform the fortress town of Tunes into a Muslim-Arab city. Arab historians date its birth as 9 March 699 and attribute its foundation to the Umayyad general Hassan ibn al-Numan. An arsenal and shipyards were then built, it is said by 1,000 Coptic workers brought from Egypt, and a canal was dug between the sea and the gulf at Halk al-Oued (La Goulette).

Like Carthage, medieval Tunis was located between the ancient caravan routes of the Sahara and the edge of a large gulf where the western and eastern parts of the Mediterranean, midway between the Dardanelles and Gibraltar, come together. Initially, the city took on essentially military and maritime functions, but the presence of hundreds of thousands of soldiers encouraged its development and the integration of its indigenous and Arab inhabitants under the banner of the religion of Islam. During the following centuries, Tunis remained a secondary city, the capital being initially Kairouan, then Mahdiya. Nonetheless, Tunis developed and because of frequent rebellions gained a reputation as a "seditious city." Reconstructed ramparts with five gates, an impressive kasbah and cathedral mosque with surrounding markets and residential neighborhoods, hammams, and caravansaries were built up during the ninth century. The city had cottage industries, commercial and agricultural activities, and centers of learning.

During the eleventh century, the country was conquered by the Fatimid caliphs, Ismaili Shi'i who had risen in Kairouan before moving east to conquer Egypt and establish their capital in Cairo (see also "Cairo"). At midcentury their amir in Kairouan rebelled and pledged allegiance to the Abbasid caliph in Baghdad. As a consequence, the Fatimids expedited the migration of the Banu Hillal and Banu Sulaym, turbulent nomadic tribes from the Egyptian delta, to put down the rebellion. These tribesmen destroyed most everything in their paths and created a situation of general anarchy with the result that a multitude of local rulers came to power. Tunis became for almost a century a small, independent principality governed by the Banu Khurasan and incorporating a growing population of refugees from other cities.

In 1159, almost four centuries after the Muslim conquest of the country, Tunis was conquered by the Almohades Sultanate based in Morocco. Promoted to and ever since then the capital of Ifrîqiya, medieval "Eastern Barbary" (i.e., Tunisia), the city became one of the gems of Islamic urbanism. In 1227 the governor of the city rebelled against the Almohadis and established the Hafsid Caliphate, which was to dominate the country from Tunis for the next three centuries. It was also the time of the Eighth Crusade, when in 1270 Saint Louis died and was buried in Carthage (and where centuries later a church was to rise in his commemoration). During this period, the madinah, the Muslim-Arab city, assumed its classical character and grew into the form and structure that it maintained until the eve of the French protectorate (1881–1956).

At the center of the circular city stood al-Zaytuna, the monumental mosque, one of the Maghreb's most beautiful examples of Islamic architecture. Surrounding it were the suqs, markets, and bazaars, these in turn encircled by continually expanding residential neighborhoods. A second communal mosque named after and near one of the seven city gates, Bab al-Bahar, the gate of the sea, was built late in the thirteenth century. Under the regime of the Hafsid dynasty, madrasas, zawiyas (lodges and mausoleums attended by Sufi mystics and pilgrims), a hospital, and several new suburbs with their funduqs (hotels and wholesale houses for foreign merchants) complemented the urban landscape. The patron saint of Tunis, Sidi Mahrez, was buried in one of the most impressive zawiyas that dominated the city, as was another reputed saint, Sidi Bil Hsan. The population probably reached 100,000 and included Christians and Jews, the former living in the southern suburb of the city, the latter residing in their own neighborhood within the walls, the hara, the Jewish Quarter.

In the sixteenth century, the corsairs of Algiers and the Spanish fought over Tunis until troops loyal to Istanbul won dominance over the country, which in 1574 became an Ottoman province. In the mid-seventeenth century, its governor established the dynasty of the Murad beys, to be succeeded, in turn, by the Hussaynid beys in the early years of the eighteenth century. Under the beys, immigrants arrived from various provinces of the Ottoman Empire, Turks by descent or conversion as well as Moriscos and Marranos fleeing from Spain or coming from Leghorn (Livorno), merchants from France and England, and slaves (6,000 in 1654), many of them prisoners taken by the corsairs of Tunis.

Commerce in the city remained important until the early nineteenth century, when the Kingdom of Tunis was forced by the European powers to end piracy and to open the country widely to European influences. Already in the eighteenth century, immigration of merchants, especially French and English, had increased substantially and served to expand the city's limits and play a major role in its trade. This diversity of peoples living in Tunis gave the city a cosmopolitan quality. Its main industries were the production of *chechias* (woven woolen caps), the weaving of silk, the casting of metals, and the manufacture of pottery. Trade with Marseille, Leghorn, Morocco, Makkah, and sub-Saharan Africa flourished. And piracy—brigandage and the accompanying commerce in stolen goods and kidnapped persons—was in its golden age. The madinah of Tunis was a serene city, characterized by respect for convention and habit. Its tone and tenor were set by the *baldis*, the deeply rooted urban and profoundly civilized elite.

A new city began to develop in the decades leading up to the protectorate, a consequence of immigration and projects of modernization, reform, and construction by the Hussaynids. To the north of the city, the beys expanded the Bardo, their administrative center and residences, building palaces and gardens, a military academy, and a treasury mint, all within a surrounding wall flanked by towers. A secondary school with a partly modern curriculum, as-Sadiqiya, was created by a reform-minded minister in 1875 and situated in a renovated building in the center of the madinah. In 1858 Muhammad Bey created a municipality, its council chosen from among notables and entrusted with administering the city's finances and public spaces. Government-funded constructions went up in different suburbs. Along the coasts to the north and south, officials and wealthy notables began to build villas and summer homes. In 1860, when the French consul received the authorization to build a new House of France outside the ramparts, a new European city was born.

The foreign colonies grew as a result of waves of immigrants fleeing the poverty of Malta, Sicily, Sardinia, and rural areas of inland Italy. They constructed houses and businesses in the suburbs where they lived, employing European architectural designs according to their habits and tastes. The bey Hussayn b. Mahmud authorized their construction of the Church of Sainte-Croix on the site of a former hospital. They opened schools and a hospital, extending substantially the area of the city. Soon the walls that surrounded the city came down, and nothing separated any longer the development of

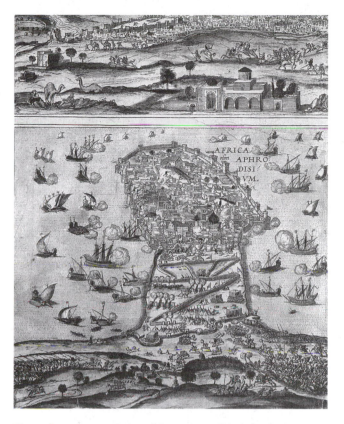

Sixteenth-century engraving of the capture of Tunis by the Ottomans in 1574. (Art Archive/Musée des Arts Africains et Océaniens/Dagli Orti)

the future new European city. The immigrants strengthened a variety of urban activities, especially maritime trade in the export of grains, olive oil, woolens, skins, wax, and the import of manufactured goods: textiles, metals, wood, and commodities like sugar, coffee, rice, and spices. In the 1870s, an English company received the concession to construct railway lines connecting the capital to the northern suburbs of La Goulette and La Marsa and to Bardo; the company ceded the concession to Italians in 1880. A French company at the same time had received the concession for railways to the Algerian frontier and to the Sahel region of Tunisia. Thus, on the eve of the French protectorate, Tunis had two railway stations, an Italian one to the north and a French one to the south.

The establishment of the French protectorate in 1881 marked a turning point in the city's history: the rapid expansion of the European population and the modernization of the urban infrastructure, administration, transport, commerce, industry, and sanitation. Colonial rule was legitimated in the name of "order," "management," and "hygiene." The *ville nouvelle* (the new European city) became Tunis's city center, taking the place of the madinah. A new municipal council with a European majority had as its aims the preparation for European immigration, the development of a colonial economy and infrastructure, and the provision of the amenities of a modern city.

European immigration and urbanization originating from the Tunisian countryside took place concurrently. By World War I, Tunis had a population of about 150,000, including some 70,000 Europeans (44,237 Italians, 17,875 French, 5,986 Maltese, 1,381 Greeks, a few Spaniards, and others), 65,000 Muslims, and 20,000 Jews. Colonization brought a modern administration and a multiplication of state employees, development of rail and road communication, and a modern port at the edge of the city that is linked to La Goulette and the open sea by a six-mile canal across the waters of the lagoon. The port joined to the railways allowed for the export of phosphates, iron, and lead, as well as agricultural products, and for the import of fuels, machines, and manufactured products. The establishment of banks and credit facilities supported the development of commerce, internally and externally, as well as modern industries, especially for food and building materials.

Tunis became a kind of twin city. The madinah conserved its traditional Muslim-Arab character, but it was devalued, its culture and way of life considered archaic and underdeveloped. This view was not specific to the Europeans but largely shared by the young activist nationalists opposed to colonial rule.

Juxtaposed to the madinah, the new city, with its planned landscape of vertical and horizontal arteries, checkerboard fashion, had emerged. Residential buildings sprung up with speed, inhabited by Europeans and Tunisian Jews able to leave the overpopulated and unsanitary hara in which they had lived. Most buildings were eclectic, beaux arts styles dominant in France. The new city, which came to resemble a provincial French town, spread to the east, where the development of the port had made it possible to gain land from the lagoon and to the south and north. The new city center ran from west to east along Avenue de la Marine, where the former consulate of France now became the Residence Generale of France and where one found the cathedral, administrations, banks, headquarters of companies, theaters, hotels, and cafés. On either side were mixed areas of apartments and industrial enterprises that extended to the outer areas of the city bordering on the countryside, where the wealthy lived. The extension of urban space was accompanied by the construction of a network of an underground sewage system, water pipelines, and gas and electric lines. Belvedere Park was planted on nearly 250 acres of land within the new city, which also had a tramway system, initially horse drawn, then electrified, and an infrastructure of schools, clinics, hospitals, and research institutes, all for the usage and pleasure of Europeans.

Between the two world wars, the population and the space of the city continued to expand from 171,600 in 1921 to 219,500 in 1936 in the city and from 21,300 in 1921 to 38,500 in the surrounding suburbs (88,800 Muslims in 1921, 110,000 in 1936; 22,600 Jews in 1921, 32,300 in 1936; 81,500 Europeans in 1921, 115,600 in 1936). The traditional industries and crafts practiced by Tunisians continued the decline that had begun with the onset of the protectorate. The madinah and the two large suburbs attached to it changed little, if at all. The first urban development plan for Tunis in the 1930s stipulated that the madinah should retain its character and that all construction must conform to architectural and decorative requirements. Meanwhile, the new city experienced a construction boom of public buildings like the Municipal Casino and the monumental building of the French consulate and of private ones in the way of company headquarters, hotels, and high-rise apartment buildings. Expansion of urban space took place to the north beyond Belvedere Park with the new residential area of el-Menzah. But the most significant change was the emergence around the madinah of a belt of *gourbivilles* (slum neighborhoods made up of barren, rural-like constructions, erected without planning permission on lands without ownership or title, and lacking any collective services). Gourbivilles like Djabal Lahmar, Mallasin, and others were inhabited by poor rural families; by 1946 some 50,000 people who had migrated to the capital, hoping to improve their lives, resided in these gourbivilles, which may be considered a third type of city within the city.

During World War II, Tunis was occupied by Axis forces for almost two years, and it provided the base for their final stand in Africa. As a consequence, the city suffered some destruction from the fighting and aerial bombardments, and a number of its Jewish inhabitants were arrested by the Nazis and sent to concentration camps in Europe. During the war and subsequently, several satellite towns grew up around Tunis at the same time as extensive construction was taking place in its suburbs. On the eve of Tunisia's independence, in 1956, the population of Greater Tunis had grown to 561,117 (261,600 Muslims, 38,900 Jews, and 160,500 Europeans). The gourbivilles surrounding the madinah contained more than 100,000 inhabitants.

Independence led to the departure of most of the European and Jewish population. It was followed by a substantial increase in the number of Tunisian Muslims living in the capital. In 1976 the urban population had grown to 679,603, and by 1994 Greater Tunis had surpassed 1,250,000. The newly independent nation-state had Arabicized the public sector and multiplied the number of personnel; local industries developed, especially in textiles, plastics, and electronics; and higher education expanded significantly. Some of the traditional urban landmarks of Tunis were destroyed or transformed in the name of modernization and town planning. At the same time, the statues that symbolized colonial rule were taken away, and in the urban toponymy the hallmarks of France and its history and heroes were replaced by Tunisian figures of the national movement and Third World heroes.

Public and private housing construction took place on a massive scale. Planned and regulated areas of apartments and villas had risen to the north connected to the city center by freeways, while to the west gourbivilles were being restructured by the municipality with the help of the World Bank. To the northwest, housing projects swallowed up agricultural lands, and to the south the beach suburbs near the industrial areas grew denser. The policy of the government and its president, Habib Bourguiba, was to modernize the country quickly and to combat underdevelopment. In terms of urban planning, this has meant investing in the new city, neglecting the madinah, and eradicating the gourbivilles.

Ambitions of making Tunis into a thriving Middle Eastern capital city replacing the commercial centrality of Beirut have only partly succeeded. From 1979 to 1990, Tunis was the headquarters of the Arab League, but the hopes of that providing an unprecedented boom to urban development were not realized. Nonetheless, a new generation of buildings, including a number of skyscrapers, has appeared on the urban horizon: government offices, hospitals, schools, banks, commercial companies, and hotels.

The architecture of modern Tunis has been almost entirely inspired by contemporary European models and styles. Only in the suburban villas of the new bourgeoisie does one find real or imagined traces of traditional Islamic architecture. The madinah of Tunis, once idealized and immortalized in the paintings of Delacroix and Macke, covers about one square mile and is now densely populated by more than 150,000 people. Although it has been considered one of the best preserved Arab-Muslim cities in the world and classified since 1979 by the United Nations Educational, Scientific, and Cultural Organization (UNESCO) as a World Heritage Site, its heritage remains unrecovered. The madinah is mostly a residual, impoverished, and desacralized space inhabited by uprooted peasants who are sometimes capable of resisting demolitions and forced expulsions.

Some Tunisian urban historians call the neglect of the madinah "collective amnesia." The powers that be seek another urban image for Tunis, drawing on the pre-Islamic past of antiquity and projecting into imagined modernities. Carthage has resurged as the predecessor of Tunis. The distant past is honored, the Berber Jugurtha seen as resistant to Roman colonialism, and the Punic hero Hannibal nationalized, his name used for a television station created in 2005. A sign of the ambiguities of the capital's ambitions and identities are the names of its new international airport, "Tunis-Carthage," and its national football team, the Carthage Eagles. But the heritage remains multidimensional. In the ruins of the Roman coliseum of Carthage, inhabitants of Tunis spend summer evenings enjoying, among other things, the singing and dancing of a local star, Habouba.

Kenneth Brown

Further Readings

Flaubert, Gustave. *Salambo.* Translated by Powys Mathers. London: Folio Society, 1940.

Ibn Khaldun, Abd ar-Rahman. *The Muqaddima.* 2d ed. Translated by F. Rosenthal. London: Routledge and Kegan Paul, 1967.

Perkins, Kenneth. *A History of Modern Tunisia.* Cambridge: Cambridge University Press, 2004.

Perkins, Kenneth. *Tunisia: Crossroads of the Islamic and European Worlds.* Boulder, CO: Westview Press, 1986.

Woodford, Jerome. *The City of Tunis: Evolution of an Urban System.* Cambridge: Middle East and North African Studies Press, 1990.

Tyre
Population: 30,000 (1200 BC and 2005 estimate)

One of the greatest cities of the classical Iron Age Mediterranean, and the epitome of the entrepôt city in the Middle East, Tyre is the best known of the Phoenician cities. The mother of Carthage, valiant struggler against Alexander, the source of purple for the emperors of Rome, a jewel in the crown of the Crusader states, center of resistance to the Israelis, this most ancient "Queen of the Mediterranean" today primarily serves the south of Lebanon rather than plays on the international stage as a global city. Yet in its glory, this island city rose in magnificent grandeur high above the waves of the Mediterranean, the sun sparkling off the golden roofs of its palaces and temples, its harbors packed with ships from throughout the known world.

Tyre (Arabic, *Sur;* Latin, *Tyros;* Hebrew, *Zor*), founded initially on the larger of two islands lying directly off the southern Lebanese coast in the Mediterranean, is twenty miles south of Sidon (Saida) and ten miles north of the Lebanese-Israeli border. It now lies at the tip of a small peninsula connected to the mainland, which is the result of sediment that has accumulated since Alexander the Great built a causeway out to the island city during his siege. The site is opposite the middle of the deltaic plain of the Litani River and had a small, natural harbor on the northern side of the island. Classical references to Tyre are often unclear whether they were referring to the island city or to the "new" city on the coast, including fortifications and the Ras al-Ain spring, which provided water for both parts of the city.

It is often claimed that Tyre is one of the world's oldest cities and that it has been continuously inhabited. Neither is correct. Finds on the tell suggest that the city was founded around 2800 BC; this fits very well with Herodotus's suggestions about the origins of the city. There are signs of habitation on the site dating back before 3000 BC. However, it appears that at some point after its initial founding, the island site was abandoned and not reoccupied until ca. 1600 BC.

Recent discoveries of a sunken city, Yarmuta, some 1,500 feet off the coast indicate that the Lebanese coastline has been receding over the centuries. Yarmuta is older than Tyre, and it is possible that Tyre reemerged as the key coastal city in this area of the lower Lebanon coast after Yarmuta was inundated ca. 1600 BC.

From the beginning, Tyre was involved in long-distance trade, but it was overshadowed by the primate central Canaanite coastal city of the time, Jubail (Byblos), which dominated trade with Egypt, Ugarit, and Mesopotamia (see also "Byblos"). Tyre became more significant in the regional records during the Late Bronze Age (1550–1200 BC); trade and diplomatic correspondence between Abi-Milki, king of Tyre, and the Egyptian pharaoh tells of the dispatch of cedarwood to the Egyptian ruler. The archives at Tel Amarna in Egypt contain numerous letters from the monarchs of Tyre discussing political unrest in the region and despairing over Egyptian indifference.

Tyre, like the other Canaanite cities of the coast, was involved in the trade of copper, tin, cedarwood, iron, and purple dyed cloth. As cities especially preferred by Egypt, they expanded their manufacture of luxury items made of precious metal, glass, faience, or boxwood. Driven particularly by Egypt's temple-induced demand for timber, Egyptian hegemony over the coastal cities as far north as Ugarit during the Late Bronze Age facilitated the growth of state-sponsored interregional trade and empowered cities like Tyre (see also "Ugarit"). Tyrinian merchants and woodworkers lived and worked in Egypt's capital, Memphis, at this time.

As with so many of the other cities in the region, Tyre experienced a period of dramatic socioeconomic and political change at the end of the Bronze Age (ca. 1200 BC). Egyptian power waned, the "Sea Peoples" invaded the coastal area, and scholars generally agree that new forms of political structures begin to appear throughout the region. Significantly for those cities along the southern Lebanese coast, the preeminent Canaanite city to the north, Ugarit, was destroyed, never to reemerge. Regional trade routes with Cyprus and the Aegean disappeared for a time, and long-distance trade with Assyria shifted to the southern Lebanese ports like Tyre with the appearance of the Aramaic Semites in the Syrian hinterland. New powers appeared in the south, in particular the Philistines and the Israelites, with the Philistine navy raiding and circumscribing trade as far north as Sidon. It is out of this chaos that scholars mark the beginning of the age of the "Phoenicians." This Greek term is used to refer to the inhabitants of those cities along the Lebanese coast (Tyre, Sidon, Beirut, Byblos, and Arkad) that began to evolve as a separate city system from their neighbors to the north or south. Over the next 800 years, this community of cities evolved a separate Canaanite subculture (1200–332 BC) termed Phoenician. Operating much like the later maritime trading city systems of Italy (Venice, Genoa, and Pisa) or the Hanseatic League of northern Germany, these cities used their maritime trading networks as their key survival strategy (see also "Beirut").

During the Early Iron Age (1200–900 BC), Tyre was a second-tier city, less significant than Byblos or Sidon. In fact, Sidon claimed on its coins and in its regal titles that it was the "mother of Tyre." There may be some truth to the claim; Sidon colonists may have helped restart Tyre around 1150 BC. It is clear, however, that Tyre was beneficially nested within the nascent Phoenician city system, which interacted with other emergent city systems like Philistia and those based around Kition on Cyprus. The city was soon able to embark on a period of urban renewal and physical expansion. However, Tyre remained vulnerable because of its continued dependence on the mainland and the limited size of its navy. Additionally, when compared to Sidon, since its networks linked it more closely to Egypt, as chaos hit Egypt, Tyre suffered a greater loss of trade.

The ascendancy of King Hiram I to the throne of Tyre (969–936 BC), however, marks the beginning of a dramatic rise to status as the Queen of the Mediterranean, surpassing its two northern rivals. Over the next seven centuries, Tyre was the key entrepôt in the eastern Mediterranean, coming to dominate all other ports in the Levant. Part of the reason lies in the return of Egyptian unity and economic expansion. Another lies in the intentional search by Hiram and subsequent kings of the city to expand their economic opportunities and connections.

Hiram was a classic entrepreneur, always looking for ways to expand and develop Tyre's opportunities and centrality in trade. Tradition holds that Hiram was the one who linked the two islands together, on which the city sat, to allow for greater expansion. Archaeological evidence supports this claim: the city is built on one main rocky island and a linked smaller island, which initially held a cultic center to the god Melkart (King of the City). Hiram understood the city's need for a larger base so built a causeway to connect the two islands. In his time, the main harbor of the city was on the north side and called the "Sidon" harbor since it faced Tyre's neighbor to the north. Once the islands were linked and the city expanded (two and one-half miles in circumference), a breakwater was built to the south of the island, creating the "Egyptian" harbor. This dual harbor system, connected by a canal through the city, allowed even more space for ships and quays for unloading, giving Tyre a comparative advantage over its rivals. Quickly, the city added multistory housing, fantastically decorated palaces and temples, and huge 150-foot-high walls for protection. By the end of Hiram's rule, this island city had the highest population density, most urban lifestyle, and significant pollution (from its dye factories) of any city in the Middle East.

The city's power was based on three foundations: maritime trade links, factories for production of key exports, and its geopolitical location at the edge of two key land routes—through Palestine to the Red Sea and across the desert to the Euphrates. Unlike Sidon, which had a significant agricultural hinterland and iron ore deposits, Tyre's hinterland was limited; it only incorporated, according to Pliny, nineteen miles. It was able to surpass Sidon, however, on the basis of its trade networks and its aggressive merchant policies.

Tyre, as the hegemonic city of the Phoenician city system, began to establish colonies and trade routes of its own. This expansion occurred in two phases. The first phase saw the city building alliances with neighbors to expand and develop land routes throughout the Middle East. One of the best known of these alliances was with Kings David and Solomon of the newly emergent Kingdom of Israel. As recorded in the Bible, Hiram developed a commercial alliance with his southern neighbor, Solomon, that had four components: provision of cedarwood and craftsmen for the building of the temple and palace in Jerusalem, cooperation in developing and protecting the land route to Eilat on the Red Sea, regular maritime expeditions through the Red Sea to Yemen and Ethiopia, and joint venture capital and cooperation in commercial links (see also "Aqaba/Eilat"). Both kings were looking for new revenues and opportunities, and they evolved an advanced degree of cooperation to exploit the southern trade routes to Arabia and East Africa. The relationship between the two men had other components as well. Biblical records and records from Tyre both confirm that Hiram and Solomon were involved in a series of wagers concerning riddles; they sent each other riddles and bet whether the other could solve them.

The alliance with Israel continued to some degree for the next century. Ethbaal of Tyre gave his daughter Jezebel to Ahab, king of Israel (ca. 865 BC). Between believers in Baal, the chief god of Tyre, and the followers of Yahweh, there was great struggle for primacy of belief among the population of the region. Elijah's confrontation on Mount Carmel (Haifa) with the priests of Baal may have been partly to do with economic control of the coast and of trade routes (see also "Haifa").

Other aspects of Tyre's expansion onto the Levantine landmass included trade emporia close to their rival in the north, Byblos; exclusive connections with Assyria; and a hegemonic dominance over Sidon. This strategy began to fail, however, with the rise of centralized Assyrian power in the hinterland after 900 BC: trade routes to the south and east became blocked. It appears that the kings of Tyre then began to exploit their second option, which was to build on their maritime networks, which extended to Cyprus, and to move beyond them, establishing trade colonies in the middle and west of the Mediterranean. The key dyad of Tyre and Sidon was the driving force for this expansion westward; colonization was survival. The city made money off of its manufacturing, off of customs duties and transshipment fees to its colonies, and off of the strategy of "buy cheap, sell high" throughout the Mediterranean.

The best known of Tyre's colonies was Carthage, founded around 800 BC, but there were many others, such as Utica, Nora, and Sulcis (see also "Tunis"). These "daughters" offered Tyre both sources of raw materials and demand for its products. Minerals from these outposts would pass through Tyre and then be transshipped to Assyria, Egypt, Palestine, and Arabia. There was a very close link with Cyprus, and often during the Assyrian period, Tyre is presented both as head of the Phoenician cities and lord over Cyprus.

This basic strategy served the city well for almost 1,000 years. Tyre became so crucial to competing territorial empires surrounding it that a high degree of autonomy was virtually guaranteed; the city was too valuable to confine or destroy. When there was a balance of power among rival empires, Tyre had a very high degree of autonomy; when one hegemon became dominant, Tyre's autonomy would decrease significantly yet be reaffirmed and legitimized despite its subservience.

From the ninth century on, Assyria was the dominant hegemon in the region, and Tyre paid tribute during much of the next 200 years; there were times, however, when it sought to end this dominance. Around 876 BC, Asurnasirpal required the first tribute; Tiglathpileser III, however, had to march against a rebellious Tyre in 738 BC. Under Shalmanezer, Tyre revolted again, was besieged, and held out five years. When Esarhaddon (680–668 BC) came to the throne, Tyre rebelled and held out against another siege. In 664 BC, Tyre was attacked by Ashurbanipal, who captured the city. From this period on, Tyre operated as part of the Assyrian Empire and continued its commerce under the empire's umbrella.

When the Assyrian yoke disappeared, around 630 BC, Tyre exploited its independence, and scholars call this the golden age of the city. It is the great city of this period to which Ezekiel prophesied, saying, "Perfect in beauty . . . who is there like Tyre?" The city was known for its poets, scholars, historians, and scribes; historiography about the city was available in its regionally famous library and archives.

Subsequent rulers found it regularly necessary to suppress this rebellious city. Nebuchadnezzar II of Babylon, after taking Jerusalem, reportedly besieged Tyre for thirteen years (585–572 BC). This could only be possible because of the ability of Tyre's navy to supply the city completely from the sea and the Babylonians' lack of a navy (see also "Babylon"). The results, however, were a draw, and both sides decided to sign a treaty of submission. Tyre passed under Persian control in 538 BC under Cyrus II.

One of the most well-known attempts to capture Tyre was by Alexander the Great. A detailed report of the siege can be found in the writings of Arrian. As Alexander moved south along the Mediterranean coast, only Tyre and Gaza resisted. Tyre and its navy provided the core of the Persian fleet, and Alexander saw Tyre as the key to defeating Persia's ability to spoil his conquests. Tyre on its island held out for more than seven months, finally falling in July 332 BC, when Alexander had a causeway built out to the fortress city. Arrian reports that Alexander allowed his soldiers to slaughter more than 7,000 men of the city; 2,000 others were crucified along the coast, and as many as 30,000 of its inhabitants may have been sold into slavery. The Macedonians imported colonists to repopulate the city, and sailors and shipbuilders of Tyre subsequently accompanied Alexander on his march to the east.

In the struggles for the spoils after Alexander's death, Tyre was a prize hotly and continually contested by the Ptolemies of Egypt and the Seleucid dynasty of Persia. It was not until 198 BC that Tyre settled down to remain under Syrian and Seleucid control. Interestingly, Tyre did not initially suffer from the founding of the new port of Alexandria. In fact, both flourished from the expansion of trade to the west and beyond the Pillars of Hercules. However, when the Ptolemaic emperors diverted the Red Sea trade to Alexandria by rebuilding the canal that linked the Nile and the Red Sea, Tyre's 800-year domination of the spice trade from Arabia came to an end (see also "Alexandria").

With the rise of Rome and their "Punic" wars with Carthage, Tyre supported its "daughter" city, even hosting Hannibal after he fled. Pompey captured Tyre in 64 BC, and the city came under the peace of Rome. When Rome was torn by conflict, however, Tyre was often seen as a key prize for the antagonists. Reportedly, Cleopatra asked Antony to give Tyre to her when it was part of his domain, but he refused, reaffirming its autonomous status. During the Roman era, Tyre was able to retain its ancient rights of autonomy and even was awarded the title and rights of a "metropolis" and "colony" having *Jus Italicum* (certain rights and privilages granted favored provincial cities).

Although Jesus probably never visited the city, which lay not far from Galilee, his disciples did; by ca. AD 55, Paul was able to visit a church in the city, and a little more than 100 years later Tyre hosted its own bishopric. Scholarly debates raged throughout the Mediterranean during the third century between neo-Platonists and Christians, and the leading protagonists, Porphyry and Methodius, bishop of Tyre, were both natives of the city. The city was the scene of conflict among various religious groups, including the ancient believers in Hercules (Melkart), Jove, Christians, and Jews, and many Christians were executed in the arena.

The Romans expanded the city's ancient manufacturing base in producing purple dye and cloth but reaffirmed the tradition that only royalty were allowed to "wear the purple." After Constantine's conversion to Christianity, a great basilica was built in Tyre; a description tells of the exceptional marble, cedarwood, and bronze fittings of this beautiful temple. Reportedly, subsequent Christian leaders persecuted Jewish inhabitants of the city, and massacres of Jews are reported well into the seventh century.

Tyre fell to the advancing Arab army in AD 635 and became the key Arab port on the Levantine coast. It was from Tyre in AD 647 that Muawiyah launched his invasions of Cyprus, Malta, Rhodes, and Crete. Tyre served as an administrative center, the site of the arsenal, and the key embarkation port for Muslim attacks on the Byzantines. Visitors throughout the Abbasid period comment on the massive but beautiful walls, thriving harbor full of ships, the iron chain across the harbor mouth to protect the ships at night, and the cosmopolitan nature of the city, including its prostitution and street magicians. One of the new industries in Tyre during this period was the production of sugar, which was shipped throughout the Mediterranean from its port.

After the Crusaders took Jerusalem in 1099, they sought to capture Tyre as a key gateway for their support from Europe. Although they attacked and besieged the city numerous times, it was not until AD 1124 that they were finally successful, in particular, because of the support of the Venetian fleet, which blockaded the city from the sea. After a three-month siege, the citizens of Tyre were starving, and they finally agreed to surrender the city on 29 June.

Uncharacteristically, the Crusaders allowed Jews and Muslims to continue to practice their faith in the city, and they supported the continuation of its manufacturing and long-distance trade. By this time, the city was particularly known for its glass, pottery, and textile production. Rabbi Benjamin of Tudela records ca. 1160 that on his visit, the iron chain still protected the harbor, the production of Tyrian glass and purple dye continued, and ships from "the whole world" were docked in the port. In 1185 the Muslim author Ibn Jubair reported a similar sight, commenting, "There is none more wonderful among the maritime cities."

Salah ad-Din was not as successful with his siege of the city as had been Alexander. Following his capture of Jerusalem and most of the coast, Salah ad-Din initially besieged the city in November 1187 but withdrew in January 1188. In subsequent fighting, Tyre remained in Crusader hands; in fact, it became the burial site, within the cathedral, for the German emperor Frederick Barbarossa after he drowned (1189). It also reportedly remained the site of a mint and of a slave market. Not long after, Conrad, the ruler of Tyre and scheduled to be soon crowned king of Jerusalem, was killed within the city by "assassins" under orders of the "Old Man of the Mountain" (1192) or perhaps from Salah ad-Din.

The city's trade suffered during its control by the Crusaders. It was unable to trade with the Syrian hinterland, and the rising power of the Italian trading states, in particular

Venice, limited its options overseas. It also suffered from being caught in the middle of internal conflict among the Crusaders. Various factions fought each other for control of the city, and it was repeatedly besieged by various Christian armies. Gradually, Acre, farther to the south and more central to the focus on Jerusalem, came to dominate the coast, serving as the key gateway for Europeans into Palestine (see also "Acre"). Internecine fighting over control of the city continued, with a large sea battle between Venetians and Genoese occurring directly off the city in 1260, and Venetian galleys attacked the city in 1264.

Such intercommunal violence, combined with the withering of support from Europe and the rise of the Mamluks in Egypt, marked the final end for the Crusaders in Palestine. The sultan sent his troops against the coast, Tyre's governor fled the city, and the city surrendered to them in 1291. The Mamluk troops massacred or sold into slavery all the remaining inhabitants, burned the city, and destroyed its walls.

The destruction of the city was so complete that pilgrims and visitors to the area were shocked by the desolation compared to their expected image of this once-great city. Ibn Battuta, the great Arab historian, visited in 1355, writing that little remained of its once-monumental walls. Little had changed by 1751, when a European visitor counted ten people living in the ruins. In 1799 Napoléon Bonaparte's general Vial visited and found a small village.

A few decades later, Ibrahim Pasha's attempt to take Syria was ended by European pressure; in 1840 Tyre was bombarded by ships of the English and Austrian navies as they used gunboat diplomacy to send Ibrahim back to Egypt. The remains of the city continued to host a small village (6,000 people), but it was of more interest to the Europeans than to local leaders; the Germans sent an excavation team in 1874 to find the remains of Emperor Frederick Barbarossa, but they were unsuccessful, while the French under Renan sponsored the first archaeological expedition (1880). During the French Mandate, Poidebard began the process of reclaiming the historical record of this fabulous city (1939).

With the French occupation, Tyre became incorporated into the newly enlarged Lebanon. As the largest city in the south, it began to grow concurrent with the development of the villages in its hinterland. The civil war within Palestine after November 1947 directly affected the city and its security as Palestinian refugees began to escape from Haifa, Safad, and other places in Galilee during spring 1948. By September 1949, more than 100,000 Palestinian refugees were established in new refugee camps throughout southern Lebanon, and they looked to Tyre as the regional market for supplies and jobs.

Tyre grew rapidly; today there are around 30,000 inhabitants, and the city serves a hinterland of more than 100,000 people. After 1970, with the influx of Palestinian fidayeen into southern Lebanon from Jordan, Tyre became directly caught up in the Palestinian struggle with Israel. As a result, Tyre was bombed by the Israeli navy and experienced street fighting within the old market. The city was invaded by Israel in 1978 and again in 1982 as the Israel Defense Forces (IDF) raced for Beirut. It remained under the control of Israel's allies until the withdrawal of Israel from southern Lebanon in 2000. Large areas around Tyre (about seventy square miles) remain mined zones, with abandoned villages, fields, and deforested zones.

Tyre has also played a role as the central city for the Shi'i community in southern Lebanon. Musa as-Sadr, the Iranian cleric who is credited with empowering the Shi'i community as a political force with the establishment in 1975 of the political movement Amal, first came to Tyre as a judge in 1959 (see also "Qom").

Slowly the city is redeveloping. Significant amounts of international assistance and new projects have begun in the south, and Tyre has benefited from this influx of aid. The city is now reconnected to the rest of the country through the new coastal highway, and goods are being shipped from the port. The Lebanese Tourism Ministry is planning on tourists returning to Tyre's archaeological sites, and plans for new hotels and facilities to bring back the "Queen of the Mediterranean" have been approved. In 1987 Tyre was declared by the United Nations Educational, Scientific, and Cultural Organization (UNESCO) a World Heritage Site in an attempt to halt the damage of war and robbery to the city's ancient remains.

Bruce Stanley

Further Readings

Aubet, Maria E. *The Phoenicians and the West.* 2d ed. Cambridge: Cambridge University Press, 2001.

Katzenstein, H. Jacob. *The History of Tyre.* Jerusalem: Schocken Institute, 1973.

Shanahan, Rodger. *The Shi'a of Lebanon.* London: I. B. Tauris, 2005.

Shirley, Janet. *Crusader Syria in the 13th Century.* Aldershot, UK: Ashgate, 1999.

U

Ugarit
Population: 8,000 (1600 BC estimate)

Ugarit was the northernmost Canaanite city-state, and during the Bronze Age (3100–1200 BC) it was one of the most important coastal trading cities in the eastern Mediterranean. Situated on the Syrian littoral, Ugarit prospered because of its strategic location, brokering trade (particularly metals) and its manufactured goods to six subsystems: Egypt, Cyprus, the Aegean, Anatolia, the upper Euphrates, and Babylonia. When the city was destroyed in 1190 BC, after 1,000 years of significance, it disappeared, never to rise again. Amazingly, modern scholars were unaware of the city's significance or even its existence until its name appeared in translations from cuneiform tablets discovered at Tell al-Amarna in Egypt. It was not until 1931 that the city itself was identified in Syria, and its centrality to the Canaanite subsystem began to emerge.

The ruins of Ugarit (Arabic, *Ras as-Shamra);* are located on the Syrian coast, seven miles north of modern Latakia, on a headland known in Arabic as *Ras as-Shamra.* Excavations indicate that Ugarit was inhabited as far back as the Early Neolithic Age (6500 BC). Pottery finds from strata covering the Chalcolithic period (5250–3000 BC) demonstrate similarities with discoveries in Jericho, while remnants of al-Ubaid pottery, the first dominant style from lower Mesopotamia, strongly suggest that even during this era the inhabitants of this site were participants in a system of exchange stretching to Palestine and to the nascent city system of the lower Euphrates.

During the Early Bronze Age (3000–2100 BC), Ugarit strata indicate a broadening exchange with Mesopotamian civilization. The Akkadian Empire (2340–2230 BC) reached out as far as the Syrian coast in its search for wood from what was called "the Cedar Forest" (perhaps the cedars of Lebanon) and metals from the "Silver Mountain" (mines in southeast Anatolia), and Ugarit may have been a key point in this search for resources. Archival finds from inland Ebla dating from before 2500 BC refer to the "Canaanites," and the first reference to the city of Ugarit dates from about 2200 BC, also in the Ebla records (see also "Ebla").

Around 2250 BC, a systemic set of crises brought to an end both the Old Kingdom of Egypt and the Akkadian Empire in Mesopotamia. Large population migrations of Amorites, speakers of Northwest Semitic, made their way northward, and the Levantine coast was not immune to their raids and destruction. Throughout the region, it was a time of change and crisis. Ugarit Level III shows dramatic evidence of decline and decay during this period.

When Ugarit reappears on the world stage during the Middle Bronze Age (2100–1750 BC), it is as a key Canaanite entrepôt, brokering trade between a revitalized Mesopotamia under the Ur III dynasty or that of Hammurabi in Babylon and the Middle Kingdom of Egypt. Akkadian-inscribed cylinder seals from this period have been found in Ugarit, indicating trade ties with Babylonia (see also "Ur" and "Babylon").

It is the dramatic increase in Egyptian influence in Ugarit during this period that is most remarkable, however. The Twelfth Dynasty of the Middle Kingdom placed great attention on the Canaanite cities as the important edge or frontier cities of its power, and Ugarit was the most northern of these outposts. Ugarit and Byblos are the key city dyad for Egyptian influence and trade (see also "Byblos"). Central was the Egyptian interest in wood, ships, and luxury goods, and gifts were regularly exchanged to keep these exchanges flowing. Through Ugarit, indirect linkages between Egypt and Crete were maintained, and objects from the Aegean headed to Ugarit for reexport to Egypt. Numerous finds in the city strata itself testify to the closeness with Egypt: statues of the wife of Pharaoh Sesostris II (r. 1897–1878 BC), sphinxes from the 1842 to 1797 BC period, and a stela dedicated to what was probably an Egyptian ambassador to Ugarit during this period. There is evidence as well of Cretan-Minoan presence in the city. Minoan civilization was expanding, and it appears that there was a close link with both Ugarit and Byblos during its development.

It is during this period that the first major building projects appeared in the city. Temples to Dagan and Baal, both important in the Semitic pantheon, were constructed along with a significant wall system. The strata indicate that the city was involved in international trade in a range of sectors, including olive oil (a major export for Ugarit over the next 600 years) as well as in copper, bronze, perfumes, and horses. Interestingly, the king of Ugarit wrote the king of Mari around 1800 BC to request permission for his son to visit the famed palace at Mari, which during the Old Babylonian period was the largest palace of the time. Its 260 courts and chambers covered an area of about two and one-half acres. Around the same time, the king of Byblos reports to the Egyptians that the palace at Ugarit is much larger and grander than his own. A "king list" discovered in Ugarit indicates that the first kings of Ugarit appeared at the end of the third millennium and that Yaqarum was the founder of the dynasty.

A second cycle of disaster and confusion struck the Middle East in approximately 1780–1590 BC. This was the era of the Hyksos invasion of Egypt, the fall of the first Babylonian dynasty, and changes in political order throughout the region. Ugarit was caught up in the wider chaos, and as Egyptian power faded, the city slipped under the tutelage of the Hurrians. Ugarit weathered the changes fairly well, however, and the city expanded during the rest of this period. City planning, stone houses, and new temple complexes marked its expansion of wealth and power, although the numerous remains of military equipment hint at a dangerous rise in regional violence. Contacts with Cyprus and the Euphrates cities are indicated by numerous remains and suggest continued long-distance trade (see also "Nicosia").

Ugarit once more became an important edge city with the return of Egyptian power under the New Kingdom. Tuthmosis II (r. 1492–1479 BC) completed the conquest of the Canaanite port cities, and Ugarit was incorporated into a system of naval bases along the coast. Although Amenophis II (r. 1427–1400 BC) stationed Egyptian troops in Ugarit to help control an insurrection in the city, the city benefited from Egyptian stability and security over the region. It was during this period that construction of the massive palace began, and over the next 200 years it was expanded to incorporate more than ninety rooms fed by its own underground water system.

By the beginning of the next century, the kingdom of Mitanni, along the northern Euphrates, and the Egyptians reached a peace agreement cemented by marriage, allowing Ugarit to expand outside the city walls, with large villas and warehouses marking this transition. Evidence from this new quarter suggests that the perfume trade was an important component of the city's wealth.

The city continued to prosper into the mid-1350s, until a number of crises and difficulties occurred in quick succession. An earthquake or tidal wave, followed by a great fire, hit the city and destroyed many of the major buildings. Secondly, the Hittites had established themselves in central Anatolia and expanded their power southward from Cilicia. Letters from the king of Ugarit to the pharaoh, discovered in al-Amarna in Egypt, report how the political leaders of the region had switched sides and reported tribute of gold, purple cloth, and silver being paid to the Hittites.

Yet this king of Ugarit, Niqmaddu (1360–1330 BC), appears to have walked the fine diplomatic line between the two powers, and he continued to remain both autonomous and prosperous at the same time. The Hittites did not occupy Ugarit, although there is evidence that there was a Hittite ambassador in the city and that Ugarit sent a contingent of soldiers to fight with the Hittites against the Egyptians at the Battle of Qadesh, near Ugarit, in 1286 BC. With the subsequent peace treaty between the two superstates, Ugarit continued to prosper in the interstices between them. Remains from the strata of this period include the truly significant archives of the ambassador-bureaucrat Rapanu. His house of thirty rooms with its private library is only one of a number of separate archives found throughout the site.

Hittite power in the region began to wane by the middle of the century, and the last king of Ugarit was Ammurapi, who reigned from around 1225 BC until the destruction of the city, probably around 1190 BC. Interestingly, in the destruction strata, archaeologists discovered a number of clay tablets still in the kiln, suggesting that these were the last words of the city prior to the apocalypse. These final testaments imply that the Hittite Empire could no longer protect or control Ugarit, that famine existed throughout the land, and that enemy ships were raiding along the coast. Ugarit had sent ships and troops to help others, the tablets report, and was then unable to fend off attackers in their absence.

Although the destruction layer is very extensive, it is not enough to attribute the end of Ugarit to this one event. There are indications of decline prior to the destruction and of changes that were occurring in the region and across Ugarit's trade routes that made it difficult for the city to subsequently reemerge. For example, the importance of copper and bronze was decreasing, and Ugarit had built its trade routes significantly on sourcing them. Additionally, the region went into a third cycle of decline, often termed the "crisis of 1200," which involved a range of political and social processes, including the decline in long-distance trade and a loss of contacts with Crete and Cyprus. Conventional wisdom suggests that the intrusion of the "Sea Peoples" along the coast from Ugarit to Gaza may have been a key factor in the destruction of Ugarit and its dominance. However, there is evidence that Ugarit may have employed at least one faction of the Sea Peoples, the Shardana, as mercenaries or royal retainers before the height of the invasions, and thus the Sea Peoples may not be entirely or even significantly to blame for the gradual downturn in the region.

Excavations indicate that there was some habitation of the Ugarit site after 1190 BC, but the remains are very sparse. Clearly, the city's strategic importance for trade is taken over by a rejuvenated Byblos, the rise of the Kingdom of Tyre and Phoenicia, and a shift in trade patterns both to the north and south over the next 400 years.

Although Greek and Arab seafarers knew the nearby harbor as Minet el-Beida, "White Harbor," the city itself disappeared from human memory until 1929, when a French team under C. F. A. Schaeffer began digging in the area after a Syrian farmer reported finding a necropolis. Numerous seasons of investigation occurred into the 1970s, and the site today is open to the public under the Syrian Department of Antiquities.

Much of what is known of Ugarit, and of its networks, comes from the tremendous number of clay tablet archives discovered throughout the city. These archives represent the major source of knowledge about the Canaanites and their culture, religion, and politics. Many of the tablets were written in the lingua franca of the day, Akkadian, and focus on international relations among city-states and expanding territorial empires. Others, however, are about local legal or commercial issues. A good number are poems, myths, and legends, and it is easy to see significant links with Mesopotamian mythology.

Crucially, it is the area of religious and social practice where the Ugarit archives have provided the most interesting insights. Given that the Western world's understanding of the Canaanites and their religion has been refracted through the lens of the Israelite narrative in the Old Testament, Ugarit literature offers an important context for this material. Its significance lies both in its age (it was written before the Israelites emerged as a community) and in the fact that the Israelites emerged from the Canaanite cultural milieu dominated by Ugarit.

As with other Semitic peoples, the Canaanites had El as the supreme god and ruler of their pantheon on the "mountain of the gods." In the Ugarit archives, El has the characteristics of an elderly god, benevolent and compassionate yet aloof. He is depicted as the father of Dawn and Dusk through union with his consort, Asherah, mother of the gods and the source of life. In Ugarit, many other gods were worshiped as well, befitting a trade emporium and primary city. Yet it was Baal, the storm god and warrior son, who shared the primary place, along with Dagan, the god of grain and renewal, in dual temples at the center of the city.

Some of the archival finds were written in a local Ugaritic script. Within a year after their discovery, in 1930, the first translations of this unknown script were published. It turned out to be highly significant: it was an early alphabetic script (fourteenth century BC), consisting of thirty cuneiform signs, used to express alphabetic rather than syllabic values. Given the city's role as a key crossroads, it makes sense that separate regional discoveries moving toward the development of the alphabet during the early second millennium may have come together in Ugarit and, through this city, shared with the broader world. In the Ugarit archives, there are many examples of "word lists": these are not dictionaries but reference lists for thousands of words (flora, fauna, names of gods, classes of society, etc.). Scribes used them to learn their cuneiform words through association from one word to another. Particularly in Ugarit, there were many examples of quadrilingual lists, giving the same words in Sumerian, Akkadian, Hurrian, and Ugaritic. It was these finds that allowed scholars to break the Ugaritic script so quickly and these lists that indicate more clearly than anything else the centrality of this city for trade and exchange during the Bronze Age.

Ugarit's economic networks were very dense, which meant that its port was always full (150 ships, by one report). Unlike most of the other Canaanite coastal cities, the city controlled substantial territory inland (more than 1,300 square miles).

Its closest trade links were with cities along the Levantine coast, in particular with Arwad and Byblos. Its connections into the silver-rich southern Anatolian regions, however, gave it a resource unavailable to other Canaanite cities, making it both a market and rival for those farther down the coast. During the Hittite domination, these northward connections became even closer, in particular those with the Cilician port of Ura and with Carchemish. Economic ties with Cyprus were also important. Mycenaean traders were also established in the Ugarit port. Such links placed Ugarit centrally into a dense network that connected Knossos to Susa and upper Egypt to Anatolia and Mycenae into a single Middle Eastern system, with Ugarit at its core.

The links into Anatolia, with its silver, lead, copper, tin, and iron, made Ugarit the major mineral importer and exporter of the Late Bronze Age. It specialized in shipping such minerals among the various subregions, using ships that could carry between 200 and 400 tons. Silver was the core of the economy, and prices in Ugarit were set in silver weight.

Ugarit is thus what could be called a "port of trade," with a professional association of traders under the authority of the state. Such trading cities were usually kept neutral and autonomous by surrounding powers to facilitate long-distance trade. Ugarit was such a port of trade (as was Byblos, and during the next millennia, Tyre). There were key trading houses or families who played both diplomatic and commercial roles for the government. Private speculation is recorded, finding its indication in the fact that in Ugaritic, the word *brother* also means *company*. There was a monetary economy in Ugarit, and merchants paid for purchases in coinage of silver *sicles*. A trade association evidently existed, and basic capitalist instruments for financing trade were available.

The archives indicate that numerous cities had commercial missions or representatives in Ugarit including Ashdod, Akko, and Knossos (see also "Ashdod"). Ugarit had missions in other cities as well. Some of these appear, like Beirut, for example, to be administrative offices for offshore production; the Beirut mission was primarily to oversee bronze working. Ugarit was a major producer of luxury goods (filigree and purple cloth) for Mesopotamia and raw materials (trees) for Egypt.

Bruce Stanley

Further Readings
Curtis, Adrian. *Ugarit: Ras Shamra.* Cambridge: Lutterworth Press, 2000.
Gates, Charles. *Ancient Cities.* London: Routledge, 2003.
Pardee, Dennis. *Sbl-Writings from the Ancient World: Ritual and Cult at Ugarit.* Leiden: Brill, 2002.
Wyatt, Nicholas. *The Mythic Mind: Essays on Cosmology and Religion and the Old Testament.* Rev ed. London: Equinox, 2005.
———. *Religious Texts from Ugarit.* Sheffield, UK: Continuum International, 2002.
Young, Gordon D. *Ugarit in Retrospect.* Winona Lake, IN: Eisenbrauns, 1989.

Ur

Population: 34,000 (2600 BC estimate); 65,000 (2030 BC estimate)

Of all the earliest cities in history, it is Ur "of the Chaldees" that stands out in the minds of the general public as the quintessential "first city." Part of the first emergent city system of Sumer in southern Mesopotamia during the fourth century BC, this city is most famous as the original home of the patriarch Abraham. Its iconographic role in our perceptions is heightened by the translation of the word Ur, which means city in the Sumerian language. Yet it also was the capital for a number of successful dynasties during the first 3,000 years of urbanism, a central cultic city of worship and pilgrimage, and a key entrepôt for trade between Mesopotamia, the Gulf, and beyond for more than three millennia.

The ruins of Ur lie just north of what was then the shoreline of the Persian Gulf and a few miles west of the ever-changing course of the Euphrates. On the edge of the alluvium, the tell at Ur is about 10 miles from an-Nasiriyah in southern Iraq and about 140 miles northwest of Basrah.

Ur and its sister cities, in particular Eridu and Uruk, began to emerge around 5500 BC within twenty miles of each other, with Ur the most southern of those in this settlement system founded by the Ubaidians. Beginning from a small fishing and marsh exploitation village, by 4000 BC Ur's inhabitants were raising cattle, goats, sheep, wheat, barley, and dates. The city's inhabitants built and maintained an extensive system of canals, on the average two miles long, and used boats for moving supplies up and down the Euphrates. The city expanded in size to twenty-five acres.

By 3350 BC, city specialisms, cult identities for each city, and a hierarchy of cities of different sizes had developed within this rapidly urbanizing area of southern Mesopotamia. Ur was less than half the size of Uruk during this period and remained significantly smaller for the next 1,000 years. But it profited from its location as the city closest to the entrance to the Gulf and from its involvement in the city system led by Uruk (see also "Uruk").

Ur emerges as a key player in the political life of the southern city-state system during the period of the first Ur dynasty (2670 BC), when it became the capital of Sumer under the king of Ur, Mesanepada. Numerous archaeological finds covering this era suggest that the city was a cultic site for the Moon god Nanna, with an extensive priesthood hierarchy and a complex economic system built on trade and manufacturing. More than 1,800 burials have been excavated from this period, including the so-called Royal Tombs of Ur. Evaluation of the contents and their implications reveal a sophisticated religious-political culture, rich in luxury trade goods and precious metals, able to command the allegiance of retainers willing to commit suicide to support their patrons in the afterlife. In the suburbs of Greater Ur, which stretched for up to four miles, craft production sites for the manufacture of clay figurines, stone amulets, pottery, cylinder seals, reed mats, chariots, and metal goods have been discovered, providing a complex picture of a thriving division of labor and a system of government-driven production.

Sargon I of Akkad, the first territorial emperor in history, added Ur to his conquered cities around 2340 BC. In the wake of his empire, a second dynastic period at Ur of four kings is recorded in the *Sumerian King List*, although archaeological excavation has told us little about this period, probably because of the massive subsequent building campaigns within the city over the next 300 years.

It is during the Ur III dynasty (2112–2004 BC) that the city reached the greatest extent of its power, and wealth. Under the dynasty's founder, Ur-Nammu, Ur quickly reemerged in this new era of empires to control territory and trade from the lower Gulf to the Turkish mountains. This "neo-Sumerian" renaissance marks a new degree of territorial power and state bureaucracy unseen in the 2,000 years of previous urban history in southern Mesopotamia.

New forms of city system interaction emerged: marriages of convenience were signed to expand Ur's power, and ambassadors were sent to conduct negotiations with other cities for open trade. The dynasty's five rulers conducted extensive monumental building programs, and it is during this period that Ur's massive ziggurat, the ruins of which still mark the southern Iraqi plain, achieved its greatest scale.

One of the most remarkable achievements of this dynasty was the promulgation of the world's first extant legal code, a copy of which is currently held in the Museum of the Ancient Orient in Istanbul. Called Ur-Nammu's Code, this collection of verdicts shows particular concern with the maintenance of irrigation and agriculture, the core of the power and wealth of Sumerian civilization. It also contains verdicts on divorce, bodily injury, corruption, adultery, and the treatment of slaves. The material clearly reflects a functioning legal system run by trained judges, with testimony under oath, compensation, and a concern that the punishment should fit the crime.

During the height of Ur III, the city expanded to more than 220 acres in size. Some estimates of its population at this time are as high as 250,000 inhabitants, though most current projections are significantly lower. From the extensive archaeological evidence, we know that there was city planning, with regularized streets, two-story row houses of a standard size of around twenty-seven by thirty feet, and street drainage systems. Plumbing in many houses included inside bathrooms, piped water, and sewage systems.

The empire was highly centralized, with the king at the center, although there were approximately forty regional centers where both judicial and bureaucratic power was exer-

Stylized sketch of the ruins of Ur in the eighteenth century. (Ridpath, John Clark, *Ridpath's History of the World,* New York, 1901)

cised. Of particular concern to Ur was the administration of the economic flows into the city. Archaeological evidence from more than 24,000 translated tablets indicates a highly efficient system of provision through contracts, risk taking by private entrepreneurs and "bankers" to support long-distance trade, standardized measures and a silver-based monetary system, and huge state-owned "industries" in textiles (wool and linen), leather, and fish. The capital was provisioned by grain shipments from far to the north via canals, and a system of cattle and sheep markets under the bureaucratic control of the state and temple hierarchy but depending on a public and private partnership to meet its need for meat. Large gangs of labor were organized to harvest crops from the south to north during harvest season. Long-distance trade was maintained with Bahrain, Oman, the Indus, and the Turkish plateau (see also "Manama"). An education system for training the scribes operated to supply the empire with trained bureaucrats for maintaining this complex system.

Ur at this time was a melting pot of ethnic groups within its urban environment, combining old Sumerian speakers with a newer Akkadian elite. Around this time as well, the Se-

mitic Amorites appear within the city lists as new tribal immigrants. A city culture of literature, music, labor specializations, monumental buildings, and formal language marked it off from the rural areas around it. It is clear that the city dwellers were fearful of those "outside the city," and trouble with tribal invasions inspired the ruler Shu-Sin to build a defensive wall to keep out the nomadic hordes.

The end of the Ur III dynasty is recorded in graphic detail in a range of documents, including poetic eulogies or "lamentations" for the city after its fall. Ultimately, invading Elamites from the west destroyed the weakened city and carried off the king ca. 2004 BC.

The city was quickly rebuilt and actually grew in size over the next few hundred years. It also remained a key cultic site for the Moon god. It was never again to become the primary city in the Mesopotamian city system, however, as its political authority passed to others. When the northern cities came to power under the Assyrians, Ur served as their southern regional administrative center (see also "Nineveh"). Nomadic immigrants to the region, in particular the Chaldeans, filtered in around 900 BC, gradually taking power in the southern cities. Their neo-Babylonian king Nebuchadnezzar II rebuilt many of the ancient monuments in Ur, including the ziggurat, partly as an affirmation of its continuing cultic and symbolic role as a preeminent "first city" in the Mesopotamian urban narrative. This continuing spiritual significance of the city is demonstrated with the revival of Nanna's cult by the neo-Babylonian king Nabonidus (556–539 BC), who appointed his eldest daughter high priestess in Ur.

Under subsequent occupations by the Persians, little is recorded of the city. The last evidence of inhabitation comes from 324 BC, which mentions the city as being controlled by Arabs.

Our extensive knowledge of the city's history, architecture, plan, and people comes from the major excavations carried out by the British Museum starting in 1919 and joined slightly later by the University of Pennsylvania. The Iraqi Ministry of Antiquities has continued the work, partially rebuilding Ur's ziggurat.

Bruce Stanley

Further Readings

Leick, Gwendolyn. *Mesopotamia: The Invention of the City.* London: Penguin Press, 2001.

Maisels, C. K. *The Emergence of Civilization.* London: Routledge, 1993.

Pollock, Susan. *Ancient Mesopotamia.* Cambridge: Cambridge University Press, 1999.

Van de Mieroop, Marc. *The Ancient Mesopotamian City.* Oxford: Oxford University Press, 1997.

Woolley, C. Leonard. *The Sumerians.* New York: Norton, 1965.

Woolley, C. Leonard. *Ur of the Chaldees.* London: Ernest Benn, 1929.

Uruk
Population: 80,000 (2800 BC estimate)

The first human settlements that can be termed cities appear in southern Mesopotamia around 4000 BC. Within twenty miles of each other in what is now southern Iraq, the three cities of Eridu, Uruk, and Ur were the most prominent settlements within an emergent city system, sharing a common culture that evolved into the first urban civilization. Of the three, Ur takes a slower path to prominence and political power, while Eridu, cultic city for the key Sumerian god Enki, comes to be viewed in Sumerian myth and literature as a holy city, the site of power that brings order from chaos. Eridu, however, never attained the size or power of its two sisters. It is Uruk, with its overwhelming size, cultural force, and political organization, that became the first "primary" city in history. This is the primordial city of myth, where writing began, and the largest city in the entire world for generations. For the next 3,000 years, Uruk remains a key actor within this southern city system, retaining its cultic centrality until 100 BC and only gradually losing its power into the era of the Islamic conquests.

Uruk (biblical, *Erech;* Greek, *Orchoi;* Arabic, *al-Warka*), this "mother of all cities," was located on the Euphrates River close to what was then its outlet into the Persian Gulf. Today the site, Tel al-Warka, is seven miles from the river, halfway between Baghdad and Basrah, near the Iraqi town of as-Samawah.

Archaeological excavations indicate that Uruk began as a small settlement around 5300 BC. Initially smaller than Eridu, by 4000 BC it had grown to a few acres. The most dramatic growth came over the next 750 years during the Uruk period. By 3300 BC, through a combination of urbanization, administrative development, and cultic centrality, Uruk reached 250 acres, with perhaps as many as 35,000 people. It had become twice as large as its next-largest neighbor.

This phenomenal growth continued. During the Early Dynastic period (2960–2365 BC), Uruk may have had a population of between 50,000 to 80,000, covering more than 1,100 acres (1.56 square miles). Ur, by comparison, covered 25 to 35 acres. A city on this scale would not be seen again for 2,000 years.

The city walls were also part of its claim to primacy. City walls first appeared in southern Mesopotamia before 3000 BC, perhaps because of the increase in intercity warfare. Uruk's walls at their greatest extent stretched for more than six miles, were more than twenty feet high, and were punctuated by guard towers and gates. Walls were crucial to the concept of the city in Sumeria, and the iconographic representation of "a city" is of a wall. In the literature as well, it is the city wall that defines and marks civilization. This is best seen in *The Epic of Gilgamesh,* where the city walls of Uruk are crucial to the creation of the city. Uruk's walls were often praised in the literature, with reference made to how they were created by the primordial gods. For the Sumerians, cities with their walls were to be respected because of the tight link between a city's god, its political power, and its well-being. This is one reason victories in conflict with other cities were often memorialized with statements that refer to destroying the defeated city's walls.

Part of the power of Uruk was also to be found in the pervasiveness of its cultural reach. For 500 years (3500–3000 BC), during what is called the Uruk period, this city was the center of a dominant urban cultural package, and included a particular pottery style, cylinder seals, architecture, decorative arts, and pictographic writing. This culture was influential from northern Syria across to Susa in Iran and throughout the southern urban heartland. This cultural influence is closely related to the extensive commercial networks the city developed; this first world "trading empire" saw the city drawing goods from as far away as southern Anatolia. It is suggested that this urban culture profoundly effected the development of urbanism in northern Mesopotamia, encouraging the dramatic shift there after 3200 BC from village to urban forms.

The city had an important cultic role in the region as the city of two gods: An(u), the father of the gods, and Inanna,

"Queen of Heaven" (and of the storehouse, carnal love, and war). As a result, the city had two temples, which at one point dominated the core of the city, taking up as much as one-third of the total area within its walls. Excavations indicate at least seven progressive temple enlargements or redefinitions over the centuries, with extensive decorations, brightly colored walls, and gradual development of a ziggurat. Successive rulers of the region, from the Ur III dynasties down through the Assyrian kings to Parthian rulers, all felt it important to restore, expand, or contribute to the cultic architecture in Uruk as part of their "priestly duties" as king.

It is the development of writing that is most closely connected to Uruk and its early hegemonic role. The first pictographic writing appears around 3100 BC, discovered at Uruk IV level. These forms have evolved from basic pictures but are not yet the Sumerian cuneiform, which reaches its classic form somewhat later. This earliest writing evolved to keep track of exchanges and products and provided a permanent record of these transactions crucial to the maintenance of the city-state. Uruk texts attribute the invention of writing to the lord of Uruk, Enmerkar.

One of the reasons Uruk is perceived as the primordial city is *The Epic of Gilgamesh,* which is one of the greatest literary products of Sumerian civilization. Discovered in Nineveh in the library of Ashurbanipal, the stories were copied before 1500 BC and probably refer to an actual king from Uruk's early dynastic history, perhaps around 2700 BC (see also "Nineveh"). This model city, the mother of all cities, deserves the comments of *The Epic of Gilgamesh* when it exclaims: "Look at its wall which gleams like copper, inspect its inner wall, the likes of which no one can equal! … Go up on the wall of Uruk and walk around." It is interesting to note that a form of urban municipal governance for Uruk is evident in the epic, with reference to two types of city assemblies: one of elders and another of men of the city. Both appear to have a role in making decisions about actions concerning the city. Inscriptions found at other sites confirm the existence of an urban decision-making system in early Mesopotamia, although archaeologists continue to debate the degree of "democracy" such references may indicate.

Uruk never comes to dominate the later territorial empires of the next 2,500 years in Mesopotamia. It continues as an important city during the empires of Sargon the Great, Ur III, and Assur's rise in the north, but never again is it a primary city. However, its role in Mesopotamian cultural and religious tradition is constantly acknowledged by subsequent rulers, whether Assyrian, neo-Babylonian, or Persian. Uruk, for example, along with other ancient cult centers, is granted special status by the Assyrian kings: protection from taxes and a release from corvée and military duties. The size of the city does shrink, however, over the centuries; by the sixth century BC, Uruk had shrunk to 275 acres, with approximately 12,500 inhabitants.

Translated tablets suggest that during the neo-Babylonian era, a form of corporatist identity structured Uruk society, with guild-type structures negotiating with the sanctuary elites and the sanctuary making representation to the king. Three groups of craftsmen are mentioned: carpenters, metal engravers, and goldsmiths. Interestingly, the agreement appears to indicate that these hired craftspeople agree to work only for this one temple and not to take on any extra work.

Under the Seleucids (305–126 BC), Uruk enjoyed some prosperity; impressive monuments were constructed, including additions to the Anu ziggurat and new temples to the city's two gods. Contrary to expectations, they were in Babylonian style rather than showing Greek influences. By this time there was a Greek community in Uruk, but older Babylonian customs and laws continued. Given the Seleucid interest in astronomy, it was also a time for a revival in Babylonian astronomy and in translating the ancient texts concerning the heavens.

Uruk was inhabited during the Parthian period (250 BC–AD 227), and these rulers also looked to older Babylonian forms rather than classical Greek ones. It appears that the remaining ancient temple complex at Uruk was destroyed around 100 BC, but it was replaced by a Greco-Iranian temple to the Iranian god Gareus and perhaps a temple for Mithra.

During the Sassanian period, Uruk was a center for agricultural production as well as for manufacturing; glass slag found north of Uruk suggests large-scale industrial output. Finally, what was left of Uruk was taken over by Arab armies after they had defeated the Sassanians at Qadisiyyah in AD 637. By then, agricultural production began to slip, population shifted to the new cities of the Muslim conquerors, and changes in the flow patterns of the Euphrates left Uruk to dry up like the rest of the region.

Modern-day investigation of the Uruk site began in 1850 with small-scale studies by British officials. The first formal excavations began, however, under the Germans in 1912 and continued off and on through 1990. Much of the site remains unexplored, however, and our knowledge of the full scope of the city remains incomplete.

Bruce Stanley

Further Readings

Algaze, Guillermo. *The Uruk World System.* Chicago: University of Chicago Press, 1993.

Kovacs, Maureen, trans. *The Epic of Gilgamesh.* Stanford: Stanford University Press, 1989.

Leick, Gwendolyn. *Mesopotamia: The Invention of the City.* London: Penguin Press, 2001.

Maisels, Charles K. *The Emergence of Civilization.* London: Routledge, 1993.

Pollock, Susan. *Ancient Mesopotamia.* Cambridge: Cambridge University Press, 1999.

Roux, Georges. *Ancient Iraq.* 3d ed. London: Penguin Books, 1992.

Van de Mieroop, Marc. *The Ancient Mesopotamian City.* Oxford: Oxford University Press, 1999.

Y

Yanbu
Population: 188,430 (2004 provisional census)

Yanbu is a port city on the western Red Sea coast of Saudi Arabia. A growing industrial and development town re-created since 1975 out of the oil wealth of the kingdom, Yanbu has ancient roots in the Red Sea trading and pilgrimage routes. The city is famous for its role during the spread of Islam as well as its contribution to the Arab Revolt against the Ottomans during World War I.

Yanbu (Arabic, *Yenbo, Yanbu al-Bahr,* or *Madinat Yanbu al-Sinaiyah*) is located on the eastern Red Sea littoral approximately 200 miles northwest of Jeddah, 460 nautical miles southeast of the Suez Canal, and 100 miles west of Madinah. The natural harbor is sheltered by the mainland to the north, and like most ports along the Red Sea it has coral reefs blocking much of its entrance. Today there is a mile-long channel to enter the massive new complex that now stretches for miles along the coastline, making it one of the world's largest industrial ports. The post-1975 city is located to the south of the commercial port.

The city's story begins around an oasis of springs some thirty miles inland from the Red Sea coast up the Wadi al-Yanbu, underneath the al-Hijaz (or as-Sarat) Mountains. This oasis, known as Yanbu (it flows out) because the water flows easily from the earth, is located on one of only six passes through the al-Hijaz (the barrier) Mountains, which connect Madinah to the Red Sea. The export of dates from the oasis, travelers heading from the coast to Madinah, and the flow of water down the wadi to the sea all contributed to human settlement around the natural harbor, which became known as Yanbu al-Bahr (Yanbu on-the-sea), over time becoming more important than its inland progenitor.

The first references to the area around Yanbu are in Greek surveys of the Red Sea that mention the Kinaidokolpites, or Kinana tribe, living on the Arabian coast from Yanbu south toward Jeddah. Egyptians had traveled the Red Sea for millennia prior to this, but their references were primarily to the western or African littoral and to harbors along that coast to "Punt"; the eastern coast was viewed as dangerous and not worthy of mention. Alexander the Great had other ideas, however, and sent a naval officer, Anaxikrates, to make a survey of the Arabian coast around 324 BC. With the rise of the Ptolemies in Egypt (305–145 BC), the Red Sea, or the Erythraean Sea as they knew it, becomes better represented in the written record.

By the time of the Roman conquest of Egypt (30 BC), there was a thriving long-distance trade route in incense operating along the east coast caravan routes. Under an Arab trading monopoly, frankincense and myrrh were carried overland from Dofar via Yemen and Yanbu into Nabatean circuits up to Aqaba and then to Gaza for shipment throughout the Mediterranean (see also "Salalah" and "Aqaba/Eilat"). Rome disputed Arab control and began to subvert Arab dominance. Augustus sent an expedition in 25–24 BC under Aelius Gallus to invade the south Arabian coast in an attempt to control long-distance trade to India and southern Arabia. Gallus assembled his force not far from what he knew as Iambia (Yanbu) to deal with Arab tribes that were "troubling" trade. At various times, Yanbu may have come under Nabatean control (first century BC to AD 111) as their power south of their southernmost port, Leuke Come, ebbed and waned.

By the time Strabo (63 BC–AD 23) wrote about the Red Sea, there were 120 ships annually sailing directly to India from Myos Hormos on the Egyptian Red Sea coast. Such private enterprise still avoided the Arabian coast; the famous *Periplus Maris Erythraei* (*Circumnavigation of the Erythraean Sea*), written perhaps between AD 55 and AD 70 by a Greek merchant trader, presents the north Arabian shore as dangerous and controlled by vicious pirates.

With the rise of the Aksumite Empire in the interior of what is now Ethiopia, patterns of trade around the Red Sea shifted. By AD 300, the empire dominated both sides of the sea, and Roman influence was in decline. Around AD 330, Aksum became the second Christian state, with close ties to the Coptic Church in Egypt and to the newly Christian Byzantine Empire. At one point, the king of Aksum sent attackers against the Arab coast around Yanbu, declaring that "I waged war from Leuke Come to the land of the Sabaeans" to stop pirate and tribal raids on Aksum's sea and overland monopoly over the incense trade.

By AD 500, it was the Arabian side of the Red Sea that was urbanized and involved in trade, while the African coast was desolate. What we know of the basin in the mid-sixth century is contained in a work by Cosmas Indicopleustes called *The Christian Topography.* Cosmas relates the geography of the Red Sea apparently based on personal visits to its shores and describes the region's commerce with India and China. What emerges from his writing is that Yanbu was embedded in an Arab city system built around oasis cites, port cities, tribal control, long-distance trade, and a monetized economy, and the Byzantines wanted to dominate that trade. After 527 the emperor Justinian created a number of Arab client kingdoms in northwest Arabia, including the Ghassanids, a Byzantine phylarchy headquartered in the Golan who controlled Palestine and parts of the northern Arabian coast as far south as the port of Leuke Come, north of Yanbu. It appears, however, that the Byzantines were unable to dominate Yanbu, the northernmost of a set of autonomous free cities caught between the Greeks and Yemeni kingdoms to the south.

Yanbu was always viewed as the point of division between the northern Red Sea and the central district of the coast. This was partly because of wind patterns making it much more difficult to make progress north against the winds after Jeddah; it was also because of the geography of access across the mountains to the oasis cities beyond, since for travelers heading north, Yanbu was the last access point through to the interior routes. Heading south from Aqaba, the traveler had two options: either the overland route following the oases or the coastal route, stopping at Yanbu because of its water and natural harbor. Jeddah was the next major harbor to the south and the next point of easy access through the mountains. Thus, Yanbu evolved as the junior partner to Jeddah, and the two cities thrived or declined in tandem.

There was a strong Jewish community in Yathrib (Madinah) during the early seventh century, there were other Jewish communities in the area, and these communities were in touch with coreligionists in Palestine and Egypt. There was also regular trade and traffic across to Berenike (Bernice) on the Egyptian coast and from there along the ancient "Elephant Route" inland to the Nile. All this implies that Yanbu was located at an important crossroads and was part of a large, vibrant regional city system. Certainly, the people of Yanbu were religious: the city was known as a site for idols and cult sanctuaries to southern Arabian gods such as Manat and Suwa.

The people of Yanbu also became known as the first converts to Islam. The Djuhayna, or Beni Kelb tribal confederation, with Yanbu as their key town, controlled the coastal road between Makkah and Syria in the early seventh century. After the Prophet Muhammad's hijrah to Madinah (622), they were, the tradition says, the first tribe to support him. They provided spies for his first attacks on Qurishi caravans heading to Makkah, fought to protect his agents and supporters, and helped mediate with the Qurish. As a result, Muhammad recognized their fief over Yanbu and its water and commended them on their faithfulness to his cause; tradition holds that the Prophet claimed that if believers ever needed refuge, they should seek it around Yanbu, and if a believer was looking for a wife, he should seek one among the women of Yanbu. Yanbu is also the site where Muhammad's faithful gray mule, Duldul, is buried.

In the early period of the Islamic empire, Yanbu became known as a site of wealth and power. According to the author al-Massudi, the fourth caliph, Ali ibn Abi Talib, owned property in Yanbu. This was because the city benefited from the prestige and power of Makkah and Madinah, which were central players in a number of key circuits: the expanding hajj pilgrim routes; the flow of corn subsidies from Egypt to the Holy Cities, the incense routes north to the Mediterranean, and the Indian-Egyptian trade. By the time of the early Muslim empires, there were two major alternative trade routes north between Makkah and Madinah and then further along the network. The first was the Darb as-Sharki, which worked its way east of the mountains. The second was the Darb as-Sultani, which followed the coast. Yanbu was a key part of the Darb as-Sultani route, linking with Madinah through Wadi al-Safra.

By the late tenth century, the power of key merchant and religious families in Makkah, Madinah, and Yanbu was such that each evolved into an amirate based around a hereditary family leading the community's interests. The autonomy of these city-states varied, depending on the power of far-off Islamic empires in Damascus, Baghdad, or Cairo, but they were able to retain a high degree of independence across hundreds of years. Their own subjects called the local princes sultan or sharif, institutionalizing sharifan dynasties in this area. Occasionally, the regional pattern was upset, as when, in the mid-twelfth century a Zaydi imam from Yemen, Ahmed ibn Sulayman, was able to expand his control as far north as Yanbu. Quickly, however, Yemeni control receded, and the three cities continued about their business.

In particular, Yanbu was a site for resistance and heterodox beliefs. The city became known as the epicenter of Shi'i activity in the Hijaz and Wadi al-Yanbu as devoted to Zaydism. During the Abbasid period (750–1258), as well as under the Ayyubids (1169–1260), Shi'i dominance in Makkah was repressed. Yanbu was able to serve as a nearby site for the Zaydi religious exiles.

In fact, at the end of the twelfth century, Qatada ibn Idris, born in Yanbu in 1146, was able to capture control of Makkah (1201) and found a new dynasty of sharifs, the Banu Qatada (Banu Hasan), based on a restoration of the Zaydi dominance in the region. After strengthening the fort at Yanbu, Qatada went on to conquer Madinah and Taif to create, with Yanbu and Makkah, a sizable principality (see also "Taif"). He killed the last of the Haswashim sharifs and installed himself as sharif: all sharifs of Makkah since have been from his lineage. The current king of Jordan, Abdullah, is thus one of his descendants. Despite assassination and violence by subsequent Mamluk generals at various times over the next 150 years, Makkah's rulers remained primarily Zaydi; this is primarily because of their protected base in Yanbu, from which the faith was able to continue to return to authority in Makkah.

Conflict among these free cities also occurred over trade questions. Merchants using the free cities as part of their long-distance trade networks had a range of alternative ports available to them, which sometimes meant intercity tension. Between 1394 and 1396, for example, during a period of political unrest in the amirate of Makkah, Yemeni merchants shifted their Indian trade from Makkah's port of Jeddah to Yanbu al-Bahr. In 1396 the new ruler of Makkah, seeking to attract the Yemeni merchants back to Jeddah and thus revive his customs income, slashed taxes collected at Jeddah by a third. In response, the Yemeni merchants returned to Jeddah, abandoning Yanbu. A similar dynamic occurred between 1413 and 1418: political unrest shifted trade north to Yanbu, and a change in tax structure shifted it back to Jeddah. In general, Jeddah held primacy over Yanbu because of its link with Makkah as the primary Holy City.

Yanbu was the home for the first Hasani-alid Shurfa (sharifans) who arrived in Sijilmassa, Morocco, in the thirteenth century. Whether invited by pilgrims or attracted by a special deputation from Sijilmassa requesting their immigration since they were Banu Hasan, they found support in the Tafilalt Oasis (see also "Sijilmassa"). Their descendants went on to create two sharifan states in Morocco. The first was the Saadids (Banu Saad), who captured Marrakesh in 1524 (see also "Marrakesh"). The second was the Alawids, who founded, under Mawlay ar-Rashid in Fez (1666), the modern Moroccan state (see also "Fez"). Currently, King Muhammad of Morocco thus traces his claim of sharifan authority from his Yanbu origins.

By the 1500s, the number of ports along the central and northern Arabian littoral had consolidated into only a few; Yanbu al-Bahr, for example, replaced ad-Djar, another port one day's journey farther south, as the key port for supplying Madinah's grain and receiving pilgrims. Yanbu also continued to be known for the export of dates grown in the oasis.

The Ottomans arrived in the Red Sea at the same time as the Portuguese. After 1503 the new Portuguese power in the Indian Ocean threatened traditional Egyptian long-distance trade via the Red Sea to India, and the Mamluks looked powerless to stop them. In 1513 the Portuguese actually captured the island of Kamaran off the Yemeni coast not far to the north of al-Hudaydah, and every year their ships raided shipping along the littoral. They even tried to take Aden in 1513 but failed (see also "Aden"). By 1517, however, after defeating the Mamluks in Syria and Egypt, the Ottomans received the grateful allegiance of the Holy Cities, which were fearful of a Portuguese invasion. In fact, two days after this allegiance was given, the Portuguese fleet attacked Jeddah. Quickly the Ottomans took on the mantle of providing security for the Red Sea trade routes and immediately built a fleet for the Red Sea. Headquartered in Jeddah, the fleet and the new governor of the Hijaz imposed their will on the amirates of Yanbu, Madinah, and Makkah and by 1525 had captured Yemen, Suakin, and Aden (1538), thus blocking Portuguese plans to control the Red Sea routes to India. In 1540 the Portuguese did retaliate, sending a fleet into the Red Sea that killed the garrison at Suakin and tried to take Suez.

The Ottomans, via the Egyptian treasury, supplied Makkah, Madinah, and Yanbu with all essential foodstuffs and provisions to maintain the region and the hajj. Cash, grain, arms, and soldiers were all shipped from Cairo via Suez or Bernice via Yanbu or Jeddah (see also "Cairo").

Despite their largess, the Ottoman domination was not an easy period; there was much resistance from local tribal and urban elites to Ottoman decisions. For example, when a certain Yusuf was appointed governor of Jeddah and Shaykh al-Haram by Ibrahim Pasha in Cairo in late 1667, he had to take 500 troops with him to secure his post. The sharif at the time, Hammuda, disputed his appointment, and Yusuf was defeated near Yanbu and died in prison.

By the 1550s, there was an increase in the spice trade through the Red Sea, particularly the movement of pepper, ginger, and cinnamon. This made the Red Sea the most crucial long-distance trade route for Asian trade. Yanbu suffered in comparison with Jeddah as a port, partly because the passage of large ships north of Jeddah was very dangerous. As long-distance trade involved larger and larger ships, Yanbu's importance decreased as Jeddah's increased. However, since a large amount of the spice trade that landed at Jeddah or came north overland from Aden continued by caravan on to Damascus and Aleppo, Yanbu retained a significant regional transit role.

With the capture by the Dutch of the spice-producing islands of the East Indies, the transit trade in spices via the Red Sea dried up. This did not kill Yanbu and the role of the Arabian port cities, however. They retained a role in the import of Indian cottons, and fairly quickly the city was able to participate in the evolving trade of a new global commodity: coffee from Mocha.

Yanbu was caught in a vise between two new regional states during the early nineteenth century. From 1788 to 1803, the sharif of Makkah struggled to protect the Holy Cities from the rising power of the Saudi-Wahhabi state emerging in the Najd. By 1803, however, Amir Saud captured the Holy Cities and imposed his puritan version of Islam; by 1807 they were turning back pilgrims from Syria and Egypt. As a result, in 1811 an Egyptian task force sent by Muhammad Ali landed in Yanbu to deal with the Saudi-Wahhabi occupation. The Egyptian forces quickly defeated the Saudi forces around the Holy Cities, and Yanbu was incorporated into an 1832 grant of the coast to Muhammad Ali by the Ottoman Porte. Under pressure on other fronts, the Egyptians withdrew in 1840, leaving the Ottomans in nominal control of al-Hijaz.

With the opening of the Suez Canal in 1869, and the introduction of new technology such as steamships into the Red Sea (1840) and telephones (1896), Yanbu was bypassed by the long-distance trade routes. The Hijaz Railway followed the traditional overland pilgrim route north from Madinah and also bypassed Yanbu. The Ottomans did, however, establish a number of municipalities in al-Hijaz as part of their administrative reforms, and Yanbu became a recognized city in 1870.

Yanbu may be best known to cinema buffs from its significance in the film *Lawrence of Arabia*. In July 1916, Yanbu was the site of the assembly of 8,000 Arab forces under Amir Faisal during the early days of the Arab Revolt against the Ottoman Turks. As the sharifan family attempted to train and organize their nascent army, Yanbu provided them with an assembly point that could both keep pressure on the Turkish division isolated in Madinah as well as give them port access to the supplies and gold provided by the British navy. As dramatically represented in the film, it was from Yanbu that the guerrilla campaign to cut the Hijaz Railway supplying Madinah was launched. It was also the point from which the move north on Aqaba and then on to Damascus began in January 1917. Yanbu has thus taken on a somewhat iconic role as the place from which modern Arab independence was launched.

Yanbu benefited financially from its incorporation into the Saudi kingdom in 1925. With the defeat of the Hashemites, the Red Sea ports were immediately linked into a much larger market including the Najd and subsequently al-Hasa, and their scope of operation and trade links greatly improved. The new Saudi government was willing to spend money on the city: Yanbu hosted one of a chain of wireless stations created in 1925, was designated the site of a commercial tribunal established in 1931, and had an international post office by 1939. Up until the 1970s, however, the built environment changed little, and the city retained its reputation for local traditional Red Sea coral-block architecture.

Yanbu's fortunes altered dramatically when it was chosen in 1975 to be the site for one of the most ambitious urban development projects in the world. Along with its twin on the east coast, al-Jubail, Yanbu was designated as a showpiece of model urban development for the Saudi Kingdom. Under the direction of the Royal Commission for Jubail and Yanbu, the two cities were developed from scratch to begin diversifying the industrial base of the kingdom; Yanbu was conceived as the kingdom's outlet to the Mediterranean, Europe, and the Americas; Jubail would be the door to Asia. This urban development project represented the largest single investment ever undertaken in world history ($250 billion over the first ten years).

The 1975 five-year plan called for Yanbu to become a city of 135,000 residents, connected by a superhighway to the capital in Riyadh and on to Jubail. New housing for 20,000 families was constructed along with telecommunications, hospitals, recreation, education, and electric and sewage infrastructure. A Master Gas System (MGS) that made use of previously burnt gas waste was built to fuel the city's growing, energy-hungry industrial sector.

Although the overall pace of Yanbu's development has slowed over the last twenty years as the kingdom has experienced revenue and budgetary difficulties, the city continues to grow and its industrial base to expand. Interest-free loans are offered to private businesses to locate in Yanbu, and the continual upgrading of the port has made it one of the most sophisticated deepwater ports in the world, much larger than its rival, Jeddah. The city is the major port for unloading the massive grain and food imports required by the kingdom. Fifty-six industrial plants are in operation, most of them related to petrochemicals or hydrocarbon-based industries. Yanbu is now the site of a naval base, and it offers the region an advanced education and training complex. All this comes at a cost, however: the city expends more than $200 million per year to maintain its infrastructure to support all this industry.

Yanbu's oil terminal receives oil shipped to the city via huge 800-mile-long pipelines crossing from the oil fields of the kingdom's east coast. This terminal can export 3 million barrels per day. Three large refineries and a petrochemical complex can also process oil for export. Another pipeline brings liquefied natural gas to the city. The key contractors for so much of this development have been American companies; for example, Bechtel was the key U.S. contractor for the petrochemical complex.

In the midst of such dramatic development, the city continues to retain one of its oldest responsibilities: receiving pilgrims through its new passenger hall in the port. Tourist promotion for scuba and water sports is on the rise, and the city has great plans to develop desert tourism as well. Such plans have been hurt by terrorist attacks in Yanbu on Western targets in the city. In May 2004, five Western engineers working under contract for Exxon were killed, and an attack on the Yanbu International School was averted.

Bruce Stanley

Further Readings

Al-Rasheed, Madawi. *A History of Saudi Arabia*. Cambridge: Cambridge University Press, 2002.

Graf, David F. *Rome and the Arabian Frontier*. Aldershot, UK: Ashgate, 1997.

Menoret, Pascal. *The Saudi Enigma*. London: Zed Press, 2005.

Naval Intelligence Division. *Western Arabia and the Red Sea*. Rev. ed. London: Kegan Paul, 2005.

Pampanini, Andrea. *Cities from the Arabian Desert: Building of Jubail and Yanbu in Saudi Arabia*. Westport, CT: Greenwood Press, 1997.

Taylor, Jane. *Petra and the Lost Kingdom of the Nabataeans*. Cambridge: Harvard University Press, 2005.

Z

Zanzibar
Population: 220,000 (2005 estimate)

Zanzibar, the name of both a city and the island off the east coast of Africa on which it sits, has long conjured up images of exoticism and exploration. Certainly, the city made its way into Western imagery through the travel writing of Richard Burton and Henry Morton Stanley in the last half of the nineteenth century. But it is the city's importance as a key edge city, mediating between East African communities and the Middle East for more than 1,000 years, and as a world emporium for trade in slaves, ivory, and spices that made its reputation long before Dr. David Livingston arrived. The city is representative of a whole archipelago of trading ports, stretching along the East African coast as far south as Kilwa, which had strong Arab, Persian, and Islamic ties; experienced Arab imperialism; and was linked by clerics and scholarship to the holy cities, making it a vital part of the Middle East and North African city system.

The island of Zanzibar (Arabic, *Zanjibir;* Swahili, *Unguja*), twenty-five miles off the coast of Tanzania across the Zanzibar Channel, is fifty miles long and about twenty-five miles wide. Its near, smaller neighbor, Pemba Island, is often considered in tandem with it. The city of Zanzibar lies on the western coast of the island, about halfway down its length, on a peninsula creating a sheltered natural harbor. The island is a coral island, so no part of the city rises more that 100 feet above sea level. Zanzibar is the island's major urban center, its key port, the location for regular ferry transport across to the mainland capital, Dar as-Salaam, and the administrative center for government functions. The hinterland of the city is lush agricultural land, divided into plantations for cash crops such as cloves, coconuts, and bananas. These important commodities are the product of high average rainfall from the monsoon patterns over the Indian Ocean and plenty of groundwater.

Conventional wisdom has suggested that urban culture and settled habitation along the East African coast was the product of urban Arab and Somali immigrants into the Zanzibar region around AD 700. Revisionist theories are now emerging, however. Post-1990 archaeological investigation of pre-Islamic East African sites has brought to light a much earlier indigenous Bantu Iron Age culture along the coast by AD 100. Investigation so far suggests little about the actual foundations of the city of Zanzibar, but it is clear that a nearby site of Unguja Ukuu was inhabited by the end of the first century

AD. An Iron Age culture thus linked Bantu-speaking Hadimu and Pemba peoples in the vicinity of Zanzibar city into a regional trading system for iron ore, grain, fish, shell products, and salt.

Yet even earlier fragments hint that the Zanzibar region was part of a thriving long-distance trade system much earlier. Controversial evidence suggests that copal found in Tell Asmara in Mesopotamia was imported from Zanzibar around 2400 BC. The region appears more solidly into human history 2,500 years later in Roman literary references in the famous *Periplus Maris Erythraei* (*Circumnavigation of the Erythraean Sea,* AD 55–70) and writings of Ptolemy (second to third century AD), which imply that the Zanzibar coast was the farthest southern market for Roman goods. To the Romans, the people were known as the Azanians and a source for ivory and spices. Archaeological remains of gold- and silver-in-glass beads and Roman coins appear to confirm an AD 100 to AD 300 trading link of this region with the Roman world. This trading link may have first emerged via an overland route from the Nile to the coast at Zanzibar, only later to be supplemented by transoceanic links to the Mediterranean via the Red Sea around Cape Guardufai.

Excavations at Unguja Ukuu suggest that by the seventh century AD this site on Zanzibar Island was part of a thriving Indian Ocean city trading system with imports arriving from the Middle East, India, and the Byzantine world. Sailors from Zanzibar may have been trading around the north Indian Ocean coast, and although the evidence remains controversial, by this time there appear to have been Arab, Persian, and Somali traders living along the Zanzibar Channel, bringing their culture into the mix. Trade routes certainly reached far into the East African interior and, by the eighth century, to the Comoros islands and Madagascar to the south.

Immigrants from the Persian Gulf intermingling with indigenous Bantu speakers may have founded the city as early as AD 750. Chronicles tell of emigrations from Shiraz in Persia or from Oman to the western coast of the island. The potential of the port, easy access outward to the Indian Ocean, and its protection from attack were the major reasons for the site's popularity. The Arab geographers of the time called the area *Zanj i-bir* (the black coast) in reference to its inhabitants.

Islam arrived to Zanzibar with the Arab and Persian traders. The writer Ali al-Massudi records a Muslim community here before AD 950, and the Kizimkazi Mosque, the first monumental building in the city, was built in AD 1107 by those from Persia who had intermarried into Bantu society and came to be known as Shirazi. Later, subsequent waves of

Yemeni, Omani, and Red Sea immigrants brought other versions of Islam, including Ibahdism, to the city, although the Shafi school of Sunni Islam was dominant. There was also secondary migration from Zanzibar, which created new clan networks with places farther south such as Kilwa, Madagascar, and the Comoros. Many of these immigrants were from prestigious Arab linages linked to Ali. This gave them a degree of status, or *baraka,* in the expanding Arab and Muslim community of the city.

By the tenth century AD, Zanzibar was a true edge city for the Middle East because of intermarriage and the interaction of ideas, values, dress, religion, political identity, and economic trade. Arabic was the key language of trade, and the extended Arab and Persian clan connections linked Zanzibar through the Persian Gulf with China. The Chinese manuscript *Chu-fan-chi,* of the thirteenth century, mentions Zanzibar as a place of trade for the Persians, and there is some indication that Chinese fleets may have visited Zanzibar in the late fourteenth century; certainly, gifts from the Zanzibar coast were presented to the Chinese emperor around this time.

The *Hudud al-Alam* (AD 982) suggests that Siraf, the key trading port on the Persian Gulf, had wooden buildings made from wood brought from "Zangibar." Although Mombasa was the larger city at this stage, Zanzibar mediated the gold exports from Kilwa to its south and was in direct contact with the Buyid court in Shiraz. The city had its own dynasty of sultans, coins were minted in the city, and the Muslim city-states along the coast attracted visitors like Ibn Battuta, who passed through the Zanzibar Channel on his way to Kilwa in 1329. Slave labor from the Zanj coast was important in maintaining the plantations of the Abbasids, and when they rebelled, as in the Zanj Revolt (869–883) around Basrah, it created havoc for the empire. During the twelfth century, Aden and Kish went to war to dominate the slave trade from East Africa, and in the wake of the Mongol invasions, Hormuz monopolized trade with Zanzibar (see also "Aden" and "Bandar Abbas").

With the arrival of the Portuguese after 1495, life in the East African port city system changed dramatically. On the return from his voyage to India in 1499, Vasco de Gama visited Zanzibar, and despite significant resistance the Portuguese captured the city early in the sixteenth century. It must be noted that the Portuguese misunderstood the complex cultural melting pot that was emerging in Zanzibar; they were deeply impressed by the advanced state of trade and civilization among the East African trading city-states, and they attributed this to the Arab (Moor) influence, with which they were familiar in North Africa. In the Portuguese mind, the local African community was relegated to that of a peripheral role, and the Arabs were seen as the elite and founders of these city-states. Black Africans were viewed as lacking the ability to have established such complicated social systems.

The Portuguese ruled Zanzibar from their key trading center, Mombasa. With their extensive trading forts up and down the coast, the Portuguese sought to control the gold trade. They failed, however, never managing to control more than one-third of the flow; the rest remained in Arab-Muslim hands.

By the late sixteenth century, the wealth of the East African coast attracted other trading states. The first English ship reached Zanzibar in 1591, and the reemergent Omani state began to conquer the coastal cities starting in the mid-1600s. Zanzibar fell to the sultan of Oman by the end of the century (see also "Muscat").

The Omanis pursued expansionist policies for the city, encouraging its trade and the city's built environment. They built the Old Fort to protect their investment and were responsible for invigorating the slave trade from Zanzibar to provide non-Muslim labor to their date plantations in Oman. As an entrepôt for traders and merchants from throughout the Indian Ocean, Zanzibar evolved an Indian community (*baniyan*) that gradually came to finance much of the trade to the Persian Gulf and India. Surat was a key long-distance trading partner, and Zanzibar transshipped slaves, rice, live cattle, and smoked meat from Madagascar to the Ottoman, Safavid, and Mughal empires.

The slave trade continued to grow, with slaves shipped to Arabia as well as to the Mauritius and Reunion islands for their emerging plantation economies. The demand for slaves grew to such a point that the Arab slavers moved deeper and deeper into the interior, creating a commercial empire based on slavery and ivory. By the late 1700s, they had outposts as far inland as Malawi. Arab Zanzibari agents would establish alliances with local tribes and provide them with guns to help them capture slaves. Captured slaves would then be marched to the coast in huge caravans of 1,000 slaves or more, sometimes forced to carry ivory tusks for sale to Europe and China. Slave ships on the coast would transport the captives to the huge slave market at Zanzibar. In this way, Zanzibar came to dominate a commercial empire, similar to that of Venice, of sites, alliances, and flows throughout East Africa, covering the coast from Kilwa (Mozambique) in the south to Mogadishu in the north and stretching as far into the interior as the Great Lakes (see also "Mogadishu"). From Zanzibar, caravans into newly established trading and slave assembly towns like Ujiji on Lake Tanganyika spread Islam and firearms into the Great Lakes region of Africa. A popular saying of the time suggested that "when the flute plays in Zanzibar, all of Africa dances."

European trading interests reemerged along the East African coast just as the Omani Empire was reaching its peak. Together, the conjunction of interests of the Europeans and the Omanis meant that the period from 1800 to 1860 was the "golden age" of Zanzibar; after that time, until the establishment of the Zanzibar protectorate under the British, Zanzibar was fighting to retain its trading empire against the encroachment of the Europeans.

Much of the city's success was thanks to the activities of Sultan Said ibn Sultan, who came to power in Oman in 1804. Sultan Said sought to build Omani trading power, and he focused on Zanzibar as its engine. There were four key strategies for the city: expand its centrality in the slave, ivory and spice circuits; make the city his administrative center; empower the city through technology, modernization, and monumental architecture; and link the city's power with that of the Europeans.

Sultan Said enhanced the city's centrality in the slave and spice trade by expanding the slave market in Zanzibar to the point that it handled 8,000 slaves per year. He introduced clove production to the island in 1812 and reorganized the land into huge plantations, worked by slave labor, for production and export. Slaves were sent off to Muscat to work the date plantations there and to work the pearl beds in the Persian Gulf. Such strategies put Zanzibar at the center of the key circuits of East Africa: by the 1850s, 90 percent of all the cloves in the world came from Zanzibar (the Europeans called it the Spice Island), and the French depended on slaves from Zanzibar to keep their sugar-producing colonies in the Indian Ocean viable.

Sultan Said encouraged close contact with the emerging Atlantic powers. In 1827 he signed a trade treaty with the United States, and the United States opened a consulate in Zanzibar in 1833. In fact, Sultan Said was responsible for the first Arab ship to visit the United States: the *Sultana* arrived in New York in 1840 to purchase guns, china, and cloth. Sultan Said allowed a British consulate in Zanzibar in 1841, and the French received the same privilege a few years later.

Sultan Said also sought to expand his power by shifting his capital from Muscat to Zanzibar. This occurred in 1832, with the result that the city experienced its greatest period of construction. In just a few years, the mud and wattle houses of the city were significantly replaced by stone construction, and the city expanded to the north, south, and east. Because Zanzibar was the administrative capital, money poured into infrastructure development, monumental building, and the construction of villas. Luxury goods flooded the city, and the latest technologies were in demand. As a result, by the beginning of the twentieth century, this intense cosmopolitan development had produced a varied and complex architectural heritage and a cityscape representing an amalgam now known as Swahili urban culture.

The mixture of slaves and Europeans was ultimately disastrous for Zanzibar's empire in East Africa. Slavery was banned throughout the British Empire in 1812, and the Royal Navy became the instrument for enforcing this norm globally. The policy was a direct challenge to the strategy of the Omanis to build Zanzibar's power on the back of the expansion and control of the slave trade. Ironically, Zanzibar's trade in slaves was growing just as Britain was attempting to enforce its new policy, and the inevitable clash of interests worked its way out across a number of decades, starting in 1822. In that year, the British forced the sultan to sign the Morseby Treaty limiting the slave trade to only parts of the Indian Ocean, particularly Oman. By midcentury, a second imposed treaty limited the slave trade to Zanzibar. Finally, in 1873 the British blockaded Zanzibar and forced the closure of the slave market. Soon a cathedral was built over the spot, and British ships based at Zanzibar patrolled the coast attempting to catch smugglers.

In 1862 a treaty was signed in Paris between Britain and France to respect the independence of Muscat and Zanzibar. The motivations of this treaty are interesting, as it reflected the growing imperial concerns of the two empires with East Africa. France had been seeking for twenty years to expand its positions along the coast and was also attempting to support its plantation owners in Reunion Island, who needed to import slave labor to work the sugar plantations. Thus, France had little interest in halting the slave trade yet did not wish to antagonize the British. The French worked hard to get the sultan of Zanzibar to agree to allow France to export slave labor from Zanzibar to Reunion despite his treaty obligations with the British. The result was a new French proposal to "free" slaves and then to entice them to Reunion as "enrolled" workers. While this process continued, thousands of slaves were freed overnight and then shipped off to Reunion the next day. For a while Sultan Said allowed the free exit of his subjects. The British applied significant pressure, however, and the process was cut off. In response, a new scheme was hatched on Reunion to establish a French Roman Catholic depot for collecting freed slaves; providing hospitals, doctors, and priests for these ransomed slaves; and then sending them to Reunion for further "religious instruction." In fact, the leader of the scheme argued that the priests would ransom, educate, teach the habits of work, and finally introduce the ex-slaves into the civilized life of Reunion. There they would be persuaded to work on the plantations. In fact, French Roman Catholics did arrive in Zanzibar in 1858, but the scheme never worked, and the British, concerned about how the appearance of the clerics could lead to claims of a French protectorate (as they had in Lebanon and China), limited the effectiveness of the plan.

The British expanded their economic exposure in East Africa during this period, which had profound implications for the sultan of Zanzibar. The expansion of the commercial activity of the Imperial British East Africa Company (IBEAC) in Uganda meant that the sultan received substantial lease payments from the IBEAC, which did give him important autonomy in his activities, but it also delegitimized his sovereignty over these areas.

The illegal slave trade continued, despite the British application of gunboat diplomacy. Although slightly diminished in scale, the trade shifted away from the Zanzibarian port cities and empowered local Somali tribes, who managed a smaller overland route running from Kilwa north to the Red Sea (see also "Berbera" and "Djibouti City"). These tribes resented the loss of their major livelihood and blamed the Omani overlords in Zanzibar for caving in to European pressure. Their dissatisfaction was one factor in the progressive loss of Zanzibar's trading empire after 1875 along the Benadir coast.

In addition to the lucrative slave trade, there was another, even more profitable circuit, which was sited in Zanzibar. This was the ivory trade. Although transshipment of ivory from the Zanzibar region dates back to the Roman period, the dramatic increase in global demand after 1800 became centered in Zanzibar. By the 1850s, there were three East African caravan routes into the interior. The most popular and central one originated in Zanzibar and ended in Ujiji on Lake Tanganyika, from where a series of secondary routes reified outward to related Arab-run outposts and assembly camps. This six-month journey might win an Arab trader 18,000 pounds of ivory, carried back to Zanzibar in caravans of up to 2,000 professional porters. Traders would carry outward from Zanzibar 20,000 yards of cloth (for example, *merikani* cotton, from America), beads or wire, and even opera glasses, depending on the fashion of the day in the interior, and trade them for tusks. Female tusks in particular were prized in Zanzibar for sale to the American market for billiard balls. The Indian merchants in Zanzibar who financed this trade expected to make more than 100 percent profit. The Chinese, Indian, European, and American demand for ivory was insatiable during the nineteenth century, making the trade of 400,000 pounds per year out of the Zanzibar market worth around £150,000, triple that of the yearly sale of cloves. In 1891 Zanzibar provided more than two-thirds of the world total; in 1894, 80 percent of their export went to America.

The financial core of Zanzibar's wealth was its new immigrant Gujarati Muslim community, working in partnership with the sultan and his expansionist policies. Through their strong agent and commercial networks linked to the newly powerful port of Bombay, Zanzibar became engaged in a vibrant expansionist chain of credit and exchange both around the Indian Ocean and globally. By 1860 there were 6,000 Gujaratis in Zanzibar, and they effectively controlled all import and export into the city. They also controlled the collection of customs. By providing credit to Arab traders and to their patron the sultan, the Gujaratis were the financial engine for the expansion of the slave and ivory trade, the development of the spice plantations, and the push into the Great Lakes. They also became the distribution agents for all the new goods flowing into East Africa from European, American, Japanese, and Indian traders. Although much of their profit was repatriated to Bombay, some remained to finance new buildings and villas, helping to transform the built environment in Zanzibar.

As the effective capital of East Africa, and because of the regular slave and ivory trade with the Great Lakes region, Zanzibar was the natural starting point for European expeditions of discovery into central Africa. The first expeditions were those of German explorers in 1844. In 1857 Burton and Speke assembled their expedition to the source of the Nile in Zanzibar. In 1866 Dr. David Livingston lived in Stone Town for a number of months before setting out for Lake Tanganyika. His house, containing some of his effects, is a city museum today. And in 1871 Henry Morton Stanley assembled his expedition to search for Dr. Livingston in the city. Stanley returned a number of years later to form his expedition to cross the continent, emerging two years later on the Congo coast.

Sultan Said died in 1854, and his three sons struggled for control of his imperial legacy. The British finally imposed an agreement on the family, called the Canning Agreement, in 1861, which divided the empire into two independent entities: one governed from Muscat, the other from Zanzibar. In 1870 the youngest son of Said, Barghash ibn Said, became sultan of Zanzibar and ruled over the collapse of his father's power in East Africa.

This was a period of wealth, opulence, extravagance, and intrigue in Zanzibar. The city had a population in excess of 70,000. Under Barghash's rule, Zanzibar continued to extract wealth from its virtual monopoly on the international clove trade and from customs revenues from the transshipment of goods and slaves. The sultan owned forty-five plantations himself, invested in ivory, and was a weapons broker. With his wealth, Barghash maintained a harem of ninety-nine concubines, reportedly requiring five in his bed each night. He also spent lavishly on the city's infrastructure, seeking to demonstrate all the forms of a modern state: the sultan made a grand trip to England in 1875 to visit Queen Victoria, returning to the city with telephones, electric lights, and ice-cream makers. In 1881 the first steam locomotive in East Africa was introduced for the sultan's private railway from the city to his summer palace. He spent money to have a steam-driven navy, and he encouraged British companies like the British India Steam Navigation Company to start monthly service between Aden and Zanzibar in 1872. Seven years later, Zanzibar had telegraph service via Aden to Europe. He financed the construction of the Bait al-Ajaib (House of Wonders), the largest building in the city and the first to have electric lights and an electric elevator.

It was not just the European empires of the British and Germans that began to threaten the commercial empire of Zanzibar in the 1870s but also an expansionist Egypt. Under Khedive Ismail, Egypt had been expanding its influence up the Nile and into Somalia in a bold attempt to take over the

Early photograph of the sultan's palace on the Zanzibar seafront. (Library of Congress)

ivory trade and to enlarge its colonial territories. By 1870 Ismail was in control of the Somali coast as far as Ras Asir (Cape Guardafui) and was expressing further designs on Ethiopia and the southern areas of Somalia under a claim to represent the Ottoman caliph. In 1875 Egypt launched an invasion into nominal Zanzibari territory from two directions: one under Gordon moving from the Nile toward the coast, the other a naval task force moving down the southern Somali littoral. The naval group was accompanied by 500 troops under command of a mercenary, a former American Confederate officer. This task force attacked and captured the port of Brava, less than 100 miles south of Mogadishu, which flew the sultan of Zanzibar's flag. Quickly, the Ottoman flag was run up the pole, and the sultan's troops were disarmed. The task force then proceeded farther down the coast, ending as far into Zanzibar territory as Kisimayu on the Juba River, where an Arab governor and a fort represented the sultan's interests.

This crisis did not last long, however. The sultan used his new telegraph connections via Aden to cable London for support, and the *Times* ran the cable along with a call for Britain to force the Egyptians out. The sultan also ordered a large consignment of rifles to help him defend his territory. The Foreign Office quickly forced the Khedive to withdraw, using British control of the Egyptian budget and debt as a fulcrum to move Ismail and threatening the Egyptian forces in Brava with a Royal Navy cruiser. The task force was withdrawn, and the crisis ended. Its significance should not be understated, however. It was this clash of Middle East protagonists in East Africa, conflict between an expansionist Egyptian territorial empire and a decaying Omani commercial empire, that helped encourage the British into East Africa, as they sensed a security and economic vacuum that they had the power and interest to fill. How different the region might have subsequently looked had Ismail had financial autonomy and the two Arab empires been able to design and enforce a mutual boundary between themselves.

In the four years before Barghash died, in 1888, the political situation of Zanzibar declined precipitously. In 1884 the Germans lay fraudulent claim to land on the mainland, following it up with gunboat diplomacy to annex these territories. In response, the British and French negotiated an agreement in 1886 on East African spheres of influence with the Germans that left Zanzibar with no mainland territory.

Zanzibar became involved in one other important trade circuit during this period that deserves mention. The sale of secondhand and discarded weapons from the states of Europe to East Africa had been going on throughout the mid-nineteenth century. Muskets were prevalent across the interior by the 1860s, and Burton writes of 13,000 being shipped through Zanzibar in one year. However, with the dramatic improvements of the post-1860s in rifle and ammunition technology, arms dealers saw East Africa as a key market for the latest weapons, particularly as a component of the slave trade. Weapons, ammunition, and gunpowder were shipped into the interior to be used for the forcible acquisition of slaves or for trading for slaves or ivory. By the 1880s, both European and Arab traders were delivering up to 100,000 firearms into the interior per year. Zanzibar became a key transshipment site; during the first six months of 1888, the Zanzibar Customs House handled 1 million bullets and 69,000 pounds of gunpowder.

In response, the European powers sought to embargo this trade, fearing resistance to their economic and political plans for colonization. They had some reason for concern: clearly, Arab nationalists along the coast, in the interior, and in Zanzibar were considering various violent forms of response to regain autonomy from the new occupation. Uprisings did break out though never in a coordinated fashion. Zanzibar was a source of smuggling, and the sultan circumvented the embargo by having weapons from Europe shipped to Muscat and then reshipped down to Zanzibar. The embargo was short-lived, but a trade triangle did develop: dates or weapons from Oman were carried by dhow to Aden; traders slipped into Djibouti harbor to pick up arms, which would then be carried down the Somali coast to disembark around Brava; then traders would sail into Zanzibar empty to pick up return freight to the Persian Gulf. This arms trade had the participation of the French and made much money for the Belgium and English arms manufacturers. Estimates are that during the last fifteen years of the nineteenth century, more than 1 million firearms were delivered into East Africa.

In 1890 the British took over Zanzibar and Pemba, declaring the Zanzibar protectorate and making all slavery illegal. A key motivation appears to have been expanding German influence in the city and the fear that the Germans threatened British commercial interests. Another rationale may have been the dream of some consular officials; a number had grandiose schemes to make Zanzibar the future Hong Kong of East Africa. Thus, the British jumped into a political arrangement that was not necessarily desired: empire by the imperialism of free trade, it might be called. There was also a convenient political vacuum. By destroying the slave trade, the British had shifted the balance of power in Zanzibar: the Arab elite lost their livelihood with the destruction of the slave trade, the sultan's power was undermined, the Indian financiers controlled the spice plantations, and former slaves were converted into impoverished laborers on the plantations.

Despite the loss of political autonomy, other dynamics originating in the city continued to shape East Africa. The city's economic centrality had meant a cultural and ideological primacy as well. By the late nineteenth century, the city was the center of a vibrant and complex Swahili Muslim civilization, which stretched along the trade routes deep into the Congo and south to Mozambique. Swahili poetry from Zanzibar shows a deft combination of Hadrami verse forms and Bantu traditions.

As the capital of the only Muslim state in the region, Zanzibar had a long tradition as a center for Islamic training, higher education, and scholarship. Qadis and muftis from south Arabia taught local ulema in its madrasa. As Swahili spread as the lingua franca of the region, Islam followed. In fact, the city became the center for the expansion of Sufism in the region: the Alawiya, Shadhiliya, and Qadiriya Sufi brotherhoods (*tariqas*) were all represented. The sultan's name was mentioned in Friday prayers (*khutba*) even to the west of the Great Lakes.

One variant of the Qadiriya found a home in Zanzibar. The Uwaysiya, founded by Shaykh Umar Uways al-Barawi (1847–1909), used the city as its base into East Africa during the late nineteenth century. Agents carried out missionary activity into the mainland as far as eastern Congo. They converted Bantu speakers to Islam and Muslims to Sufism. The shaykh was assassinated in 1909 for advocating tolerance of local beliefs about the worship of saints. The Uwaysiya Qadiri became a major Islamic movement in East Africa and, of note, in Indonesia as well, and it is still expanding today, retaining its links to Zanzibar as a source of support and authority.

Interestingly, Sultan Barghash and his son Khalifa were members of this Sufi sect: for Ibahdis, this was highly unusual and may be interpreted as part of the political necessities that emerged in the late 1880s as the sultans of Zanzibar sought ways to generate resistance to the encroachment of the Europeans into their empire. The Uwaysiya were involved in political intrigue against the Germans in Tanganika after 1891, supported rebellions organized by Arab elites against the Belgians in eastern Congo, and helped to propagate the "Makkah Letter," a propaganda device urging the Swahili community to rise up against European rule, which was prophesied to end in the near future. The German authorities forcefully repressed these "Islamic agitators" against the "proper" rulers of Tanganika.

During World War I, the city witnessed the sinking of the Royal Navy cruiser HMS *Pegasus* in the harbor by the German cruiser *Konigsberg*. After the war ended, Britain took over former German territory and finally ended the last remnants of the underground slave trade.

Over the colonial period, the city gradually lost its significance in the region, being replaced by Dar as-Salaam. The British maintained a separate administration on the island, with the Parliament controlled by the Arab elite under the sultan. Former smuggling routes for the slave trade became routes to smuggle goods from Zanzibar to the Tanganyika mainland, where customs were higher.

After World War II, the city's political, economic, and social situation deteriorated even further. Much of this became apparent in the general strike of 1948, initiated by the mainland immigrant African laborers on the city's docks. With the end of slavery, the island had recruited mainland workers to provide menial labor on the plantations or for domestic service in the homes of the Arab, Indian, and European elite. By 1948, with the general downturn in Zanzibar's economy caused both by poor clove crops and by its replacement by Dar as-Salaam, the situation of the African workers in general in the city declined dramatically: their housing was deplorable, wages decreased, only 12 percent of students were African, and the British continued to exclude them from the political system.

Urban unrest was sparked by a number of key events but was also encouraged by charismatic mainland organizers. One in particular was Abbas Othman, otherwise known as Jomo Kenyatta, who would go on to become the first president of Kenya. Although the strike lasted only three weeks, it was significant as the first all-African political expression of community power and for the divisions with the Arab and Indian communities it engendered. This trend toward African solidarity reached its fulfillment in the events of 1963–1964 with the revolution by the African population against the Arab and Indian elite.

Interestingly, the British became concerned at this time about anti-British feeling among Zanzibar's Arab community, who were unhappy about British colonial policy in Egypt and Palestine. There was evidently significant reaction to Zionism and to the emergence of Israel along with a growing sense of Arab nationalism and anti-imperialism. Fear of this insurgent Arab nationalism led to a go-slow policy by the British administration to local political change and a decision not to modify the political arrangements that favored the Arab minority. The Zanzibar National Party (ZNP) represented Arab interests and had a platform of independence and Arab cultural dominance for the island.

As Africa moved toward decolonization during the late 1950s, unrest was very strong in Zanzibar. The British finally offered a change in the administration of the island in 1961, with the ZNP winning elections that year. In the lead-up to independence in 1963, the ZNP again won, and the country was declared independent under their leadership in December 1963. The sultan was reinstated as state sovereign.

The African majority, however, was very radicalized and rose up in a coup in January 1964. Violent attacks against Arabs and Indians convinced the minorities that their situation was precarious, and many left the city quickly; the last Arab sultan fled the island to Oman. By the mid-1960s, few of the city's Arab and Indian population remained.

In place of the sultan, Shaykh Abeid Amani Karume, the first African leader for 500 years, was declared president of Zanzibar and Pemba. Karume and the new president of Tanganyika, Nyere, met and declared an Act of Union between the two entities in April 1964. Within this arrangement, Zanzibar is semiautonomous, with its own president and House of Representatives. Zanzibar City is the administrative center and seat of the government.

For the next thirty years, Zanzibar experienced radical politics. The Afro-Shirazi Party was declared the only legal party, quickly nationalized the clove and coconut plantations, and established small landholdings. Trade unions were outlawed, strikes were repressed, and human rights ignored. East Germany and China were Zanzibar's major allies and donors. Strong socialization failed, however, and the economy remained weak. Beginning in 1985, a governmental commitment to a free market emerged, but the political system has continued to be chaotic.

Zanzibar City had long been divided into two major sections: Stone Town, with its European, Arab, and Indian communities, and Ngambo, meaning "the Other Side" (of the drainage canal), for the indigenous African and mainland immigrant communities. Stone Town has long had waste treatment systems, lighting, indoor plumbing, and high land prices; Ngambo had none of these. President Karume quickly pursued a radical socialist agenda of state transformation after the revolution, and his vision was worked out in the shaping of the city's built environment between 1964 and 1977. A socialist urban transformation policy was implemented, employing a master plan of Soviet-inspired block concrete housing in Ngambo, which destroyed the Swahili culture and lifestyle of the community. Funded, built, and modeled on the German Democratic Republic's monumental socialist design concepts of the 1960s, the cityscape of Ngambo was transformed under the "New Zanzibar Project," in which everyone in Zanzibar and Pemba would soon be organized into ten new towns. Stone Town, viewed as representative of evil colonialism, was allowed to deteriorate, and Ngambo was slated to become the example of what the socialist state could accomplish.

After destroying much of the existing low-rise housing, forced labor was used to build thousands of concrete apartment blocks inappropriate to the Swahili family. Today these areas of the city have been reterritorialized by the community and refashioned through adaptation and transformation in important ways to mesh them with society's patterns.

Today a tourist boom to Zanzibar is the major source of hard currency for the government, along with an influx of expatriate workers. The Swahili cultural legacy is primarily seen in the built environment of the city. Stone Town, one of the last remnants along the East African littoral of a medieval city, is being revived through the joint efforts of the Aga Khan Foundation and the United Nations Educational, Scientific, and Cultural Organization (UNESCO), which designated the complex a World Heritage Site.

Bruce Stanley

Further Readings

Bennett, Norman R. *A History of the Arab State of Zanzibar.* London: Methuen, 1978.

Bhacker, Reda. *Trade and Empire in Muscat and Zanzibar: Roots of British Domination.* London: Routledge, 1992.

Cooper, Frederick. *From Slaves to Squatters: Plantation Labor and Agriculture in Zanzibar and Coastal Kenya.* New Haven, CT: Yale University Press, 1980.

Farsi, Abdalla Saleh. *Seyyid Said Bin Sultan: Joint Ruler of Oman and Zanzibar.* New Delhi: Lancer Books, 1986.

Nicolini, Beatrice. *Makran, Oman and Zanzibar: Three-Terminal Cultural Corridor in the Western Indian Ocean, 1799–1856.* Translated by Penelope-Jane Watson. Leiden: Brill, 2004.

Sheriff, Abdul. *Slaves, Spices and Ivory in Zanzibar.* London: Currey, 1987.

Zubair
Population: 300,000 (2005 estimate)

Zubair is a town in southern Iraq not far from the larger city of Basrah. During the incorporation of southern Iraq into the world economy during the eighteenth and nineteenth centuries, Zubair functioned as the "desert port" for Basrah, the market town where caravans and Bedouin coming out of the deep western desert, or southeast from Aleppo, met traders from the fertile areas of the Shatt al-Arab Delta. Known also as a pilgrimage site for its graves of Muslim holy men, the city is now infamous for the "Highway of Death," where American pilots killed thousands of Iraqi soldiers during the 1991 Gulf War.

Located approximately eight miles to the south of modern or "new Basrah," Zubair (Arabic, *az-Zubayr*) is now effectively a suburb of its larger neighbor and part of a conurbation that extends along the major north-south highway. It lies twenty miles north of the Kuwait-Iraq border on the edge of the tidal floodplain for the Shatt al-Arab. In Abbasid times (AD 758–1258), Zubair lay within a large agricultural area, irrigated by an extensive series of canals, and directly next to "old Basrah." As Basrah progressively moved to the northeast as the Shatt al-Arab shifted, Zubair was left behind to evolve its own identity (see also "Basrah"). Today the canals have silted up, although the area can be flooded by tidal surges as far as the Basrah-Zubair road, and in the recent past boats have sometimes been required to reach the town. A new canal, the Khor al-Zubair, links the city with Umm al-Qasr thirty miles away. In 1947 the city housed approximately 18,000 people; today it is home to around 300,000.

The city grew up around the mosque dedicated to the Companion of the Prophet, Zubair ibn al-Awwam, whose grave lies within. Al-Awwam was a cousin and close companion of Muhammad; the Prophet termed al-Awwam the "first to raise the sword of Islam" and "Disciple of the Messenger of Allah." Zubair was married to the eldest daughter of Caliph Abu Bakr but was most famous as the commander of the dissident army led by his sister-in-law, Aisha, the wife of Muhammad, during her abortive revolt in Basrah. Al-Awwam was slain at the Battle of the Camel (AD 658) and was buried where he fell, hence the town of Zubair.

The city also houses the grave of the early Muslim mystic, Hasan al-Basri (AD 642–728). Al-Basri, one of the most revered of the early preachers of Islam, was an outspoken critic of the Umayyad caliphs. He stressed religious self-examination (*muhasabah*) and earned a reputation as a dynamic speaker and insightful teacher.

Zubair quickly became a site for pilgrimage, and over the centuries a community evolved to serve the faithful. The city also was the scene of intense theological debate and disagreement. Al-Basri's grave site meant a strong Sufi tradition of veneration along with a Sunni tradition intermingled within the city, and the Shi'i presence in the region also contributed a component. The ancient Basrah Jewish community also added diversity to the area.

Starting around the fifteenth century, Zubair became a gateway or staging site for Basrah caravans leaving for the southwestern desert. The caravans attracted traders, and the city gradually became known as a regional market center. Bedouins from the surrounding region would come to the city in the winter and spring to exchange camels and horses for grain, coffee, henna, rice, and ghee brought in from India via Basrah. Tribal merchants would also buy coffee, dates, and sugar for trade deeper into the Najd. The city evolved a horse market for animals from central Arabia and Iraq. Most of these horses were destined for India and points farther afield via Basrah.

It also produced a range of agricultural products from its hinterland that were sold in its own markets, moved into the desert, or shipped to Basrah or Muhammara. Local products included vegetables, fruit, dates from local plantations, and cooking oil.

The city evolved during the 1700s from this regional market role into an edge city between the Najd and the emerging global economy because of two factors: in-migration from the Najd and expansion of the long-distance trade routes outward through Basrah and southern Iraq into the wider world system. Zubair was located between the expanding British Empire in the Gulf, the expanding Ottoman Empire moving south from Baghdad, and the new Wahhabi-Saudi state in the Najd. As a free port brokering trade among these three polities, Zubair was able to expand and enhance its trade, production, and market role. For merchants in the region, Zubair meant no officials, no restrictions, and only a single flat fee to pay.

Building on its pilgrimage and caravan base, the in-migration of Najdis over the period 1750 to 1900 was crucial to the city's expansion. Immigrants into the city came in a number of waves and for various reasons. Some, seeking religious freedom, fled from the Wahhabi-Saudi expansions of the 1770s or 1820s. In fact, anti-Wahhabi tribes driven out of the Najd in the late 1700s who settled in Zubair provided troops for the Baghdadi Mamluk Ali al-Kahya's attempts to control and resist Saudi expansion.

Other immigrants fled economic hardship, seeking respite from the droughts and high price cycles of the central Najd, particularly between 1870 and 1874. Finally, others came to the city fleeing conflict and occupation: some fled the civil war among the Saudis between 1865 and 1876, while others came to the city from al-Hasa (the eastern coast of the Arabian Peninsula) after the Ottomans invaded al-Qatif in 1871. As a result of this in-migration, Zubair's citizens employed Eastern Arabic, rather than the dialect of nearby urban Basrah.

From the 1780s until 1900, Zubair was a boomtown as the region's trade with and linkage into an expanding world economy intensified. The city's heyday was in the early to mid-1800s; British visitors called it opulent and noted that it was home to the richest merchants in the region. Zubair's environment was healthier than Basrah's since it was not as close to the water or marshes. The city's primary attraction was that, like Kuwait, it was a free port, without many controls, where its elites were concerned only to "do business" in as unrestrictive an environment as possible. This served the interests of many regional actors of the time. Through its close dyadic link to its neighbor, Basrah, Zubair became that city's *bab* (gate) to the trade routes of the Najd as well as the fort protecting Basrah from the tribes of the desert. For the Saudis, Zubair, along with Kuwait, was a free port where tribal merchants could obtain goods brought from India. The city also served the needs of the large and powerful Muntafiq tribal confederation with their autonomous status along the Iraqi-Najd boundary. For the British merchants making new inroads into the area, access to Zubair proved crucial for making new contacts and links into the Najd.

Of particular significance to the city was the international trade in dates. Zubairi merchants would come to Basrah to buy dates at the big yearly date market and then take them back to Zubair for distribution throughout the Najd. Zubairi merchants also financed part of the trade, operating an extensive credit system for dealing with risk in the industry, including futures trading. They also conducted arbitrage in currencies during the short date season.

The premier merchant family in Zubair was the Zuhair family. They used the city as their base, interlinking to other networks via family "agents" located in Aleppo, Basrah, and Baghdad. The Zuhairis fought hard to protect their investments, the city's autonomy, and its control of trade from encroachment by the Ottomans, the British, the Wahhabi-Saudi confederation, and tribal confederations like the Muntafiq. This often meant that Zubair was in conflict with the nearby Basrah administration. The two cities cycled through close and then conflictual relations, depending on who was gaining dominance in either city. Tensions would often erupt with the Wahhabi-Saudi coalition over control of the central Najd trade routes or within the city among key local families and the émigré elites from the Najd tribes. Regional actors like the shaykh of Kuwait, Basrah officials, or Muntafiq elders would intervene in support of various factions in the city. As a result, during the 1800s, the city suffered from a series of assassinations: for example, the shaykh of Zubair was assassinated over political and economic issues in the late 1800s directly related to expanding Ottoman control in the city. At one point, there was a siege of the town, and Zuhair family members were arrested and sent into exile by the Najd coalition.

During the 1870s, to regain their control of the city, the Zuhairis turned for support to the Ottomans. Once returned to power, however, the Zuhairis resisted the Ottomans, who then directly intervened. After a battle for control of the city, the victorious Ottomans installed their own governor and ended the city's autonomous status. By the last years of the nineteenth century, Zuhair family members were representing the city in the Ottoman parliament, and the Iraqi border with British-controlled Kuwait was fixed south of the city (see also "Kuwait City"). Najd merchants retained some power, however, and were able to resist Ottoman regulation in the city. For example, until the early 1900s, they were able to restrict competition by keeping Christian and Jewish merchants out of the city. Zubair also became a key smuggling site.

After the 1850s, Zubairi merchants were increasingly hurt by the growing centralization and regulatory burden imposed by the Ottomans in Baghdad and Basrah. They were also affected by competition with the British in the horse and grain trade, which decreased Zubairi control over trade with India. Caught between the three power centers, and confronting the expansion of state power in the region, this free port began to hemorrhage its elites. Many merchants were ruined, while others fled to competing entrepôts where they had a base or contacts. The city's role was gradually taken over by other cities along other routes. The Ottomans attempted, however, to revitalize local agricultural production at this time, with some success. They reorganized and improved the canal system in the area, making the Zubair hinterland a primary rice and grain production zone.

With the Iraqi Mandate after 1920, Zubair was officially cut off from its traditional networks of trade in the Saudi and Kuwait markets and became incorporated into a Baghdad-controlled state economy. Being close to the border, however, meant that it was the first stop for the huge smuggling industry, which operated across the porous borders. "Saudi" tribes would travel to Zubair to buy local rice and grain; the Iraqi government finally ended this trade in the 1950s to increase their hard currency. Smuggling continues today, with Coalition Forces reporting after the 2003 invasion that daily smuggling of diesel fuel from the Khor al-Zubair storage tanks to Kuwait is taking up to one-third of all the production of the Basrah refinery.

Zubair is now the site for the giant "Zubair field" of heavy oil, which has the potential to produce 220,000 barrels per day. This field was heavily damaged in the Iran-Iraq War (1980–1988), when there was fierce fighting in the marsh areas around Basrah. Since then the field has been mothballed, and it requires new technology to get it up and running. After April 2003, foreign companies were contracted to refit the field and get it pumping. Natural gas is also present around the city, and the city is the site for a fractionation plant for natural gas liquidification (NGL) and for liquid propane gas (LPG) storage.

Zubair's location on the major north-south highway also placed it in the line of fire for any conflict between Kuwait and Iraq. The Iraqi Fifty-first Mechanized Division was headquartered in the city, and it was the site for launching the August 1990 attack on Kuwait. Western hostages were briefly held in the city prior to the outbreak of the 1991 Gulf War, and the city suffered tremendous infrastructural damage from American bombing after hostilities commenced. The "Highway of Death," littered with hundreds of destroyed Iraqi army vehicles and the bodies of thousands of fleeing Iraqi troops, ran up to the city gates. Today the city's children are being maimed from unexploded cluster bombs, and depleted uranium (DU) continues to spread cancer and birth defects throughout its population at a rate higher than anywhere else in the country. Zubair was one of the first Iraqi cities captured by coalition forces in spring 2003. The remains of more than 200 Iranian prisoners of war dating from the 1980s were found in a city torture chamber in May 2003.

Zubair is a predominantly Sunni city surrounded by a Shi'i rural population. In the wake of the 1991 Gulf War, the southern uprising against Saddam Hussayn started in Zubair and spread throughout the south before it was brutally repressed by Iraqi Republican Guards. Thousands of Zubairi citizens are still missing from that period.

Bruce Stanley

Further Readings

Alnasrawi, Abbas. *The Economy of Iraq: Oil, Wars, Destruction of Development and Prospects.* Westport, CT: Greenwood Press, 1994.

Fattah, Hala. *The Politics of Regional Trade in Iraq, Arabia, and the Gulf.* Albany: State University of New York Press, 1997.

Sacker, Stephen. *On the Basra Road.* London: London Review of Books, 1991.

Thabit, Abdullah. *Merchants, Mamluks and Murder: The Political Economy of Trade in Eighteenth Century Basra.* Albany: State University of New York Press, 2001.

Glossary

Abu (Arabic) father of [someone]

ain (Arabic) spring or water source

al-Hasa (Arabic) eastern part of the Arabian Peninsula, including the coast and littoral of the Persian Gulf, having an Arab Shi'i majority

Alawi (Arabic) Shi'i religious sect found in Turkey, Iraq, Syria, and Lebanon

al-Naqba (Arabic) the disaster; the Palestinian term for the loss in 1948 and 1949 of their homeland to the new State of Israel and the resulting Palestinian refugee diaspora

amir/emir (Arabic) general or commander of an army, naval force, or military group; prince or tribal chief

ansar (Arabic) initially supporters or helpers; used first to refer to those from Madinah who first supported the Prophet. Now often used for those supporting Islamist movements or committed to a struggle

ayatollah (Arabic and Persian) leading Shi'i religious leader; one acknowledged by other clerics as a top scholar

bab (Arabic) gate to a city or door

bahr (Arabic) ocean or large body of water

baniyan (Sanskrit) Indian merchant caste, often from Gujarat, located throughout the Arabian sea ports, and sometimes in inland entrepôt, financing and facilitating trade; also used for Hindu merchants

bayt (Arabic) house or household

Bedu/Bedouin (Arabic) seminomadic or nomadic pastoralists living on the edge or within arid desert; having a strong tribal structure; herding sheep, goats, or camels

Berbers (Arabic) the indigenous people of north Africa who struggled against the Romans and Arabs and now are minority cultural and linguistic communities throughout North Africa

bey (Turkish) district governor or head of a division of troops; particularly used in North Africa under the Ottomans

bidonvilles (French) term for shantytowns initially made from bidon (tin cans); used in relation to illegal districts that have grown up in urban areas of North Africa

bilad/balad (Arabic) homeland or country

caliph (English form of Arabic *Khalifa*) successor, vice-regent; the ruler of the Muslim community sanctioned by God to rule

caliphate (English) the institution of political and religious leadership of the Muslim community

colonia (Latin) farm, colony; came to mean a key outpost of the Roman Empire in a conquered territory

dar (Arabic) house or storehouse, building, place, tribal territory

Dar al-Islam (Arabic) abode of Islam; country or area where the law of Islam is established and the ruler is Muslim

Darb (Arabic) road or route, such as the Darb az-Zubaida, the pilgrim road that ran from Kufa to the Holy Cities

deylik/beylik (Turkish) semiautonomous city-state or political entity, under nominal Ottoman authority, ruled by a dey or bey. More often used in North Africa to refer to a corsair state of the sixteenth to nineteenth century

dhimmis (Arabic) people of the scripture, obligation or contract; Christians, Sabeans (Zorastrians) or Jews who came under Muslim rule and thus had certain duties and rights toward and from Muslims

diwan/divan (Arabic/Turkish) a policy council of the highest army and government officials meeting with the caliph, sultan or ruler

Druze (Arabic) a small religious community, mainly in the mountainous areas of Lebanon, Israel, Jordan, and Syria, that broke off from Islam in the eleventh century

entrepôt (French) transhipment port or city where long-distance trade brings goods to market for storage and sale or further transhipment

fidayeen (Arabic) fighters or strugglers who are willing to sacrifice, often their lives, for their cause. Used primarily in relation to the Palestinian groups that sprang up after 1948 to struggle against Israel

funduq (Arabic) primarily a North African term for large buildings in a city constructed around a central courtyard used to house visiting merchants and to store their goods; also khan or caravansary

geniza (Hebrew) storage vault for important records of medieval Jewish communities, often in synagogues. The discovery of the Fustat (Cairo) geniza in the nineteenth century revealed tremendous records of medieval trade and transactions around the Mediterranean and the Middle East

ghazi (Turkish) fighter or volunteer, usually confronting Christian forces, who expands the Muslim faith. Used particularly in Western Anatolia after the Seljuq invasion to refer to the small bands of warriors that established principalities along the frontier with the Byzantine Empire

Hadith (Arabic) tradition. Used particularly to refer to the teachings and sayings of the Prophet Muhammad, accumulated after his death; often used as a guide to correct or righteous behavior

Hadramawt the southern central area of the Arabian Peninsula, now eastern Yemen, which faces onto the Arabian Sea

hajj (Arabic) one of the obligations on all Muslims, to go to Makkah to perform the rituals of the faith; pilgrimage to Holy Cities

hammam (Turkish) a public bath; often called a Turkish bath, many of which existed in cities throughout the Middle East, particularly during the Ottoman period. Often built with funds given by a particular family or ruler

haram (Arabic) forbidden or sacred; often enclosed, private, restricted space, often refers to Muslim religious areas as in Jerusalem, Makkah or Madinah; as **hareem** also used for area of seclusion for women

Hijaz (Arabic) western coastal area of the Arabian Peninsula where the Holy Cities of Makkah and Madinah are located

Hijrah (Arabic) emigration or flight. Term usually used to refer to Muhammad's move from Makkah to Madinah in AD 622. Marks the beginning of the Muslim era "After the Hijra" (AH)

ibn/ben (Arabic) son of [someone]

imam (Arabic) spiritual leader; a Muslim religious leader or cleric. In Shi'i Islam, the term *imam* is often used for the leader of the righteous community, the one who will lead politically and spiritually

intifada (Arabic) rising up or uprising. Used in relation to the Palestinian uprising against the Israeli occupation starting in 1987. Now used to refer as well to the "second intifada," which started in 2000

jami (Arabic) mosque or gathering place for the Muslim community during Friday prayers

Janissary/Janissaries (Turkish) new troops; Ottoman sultan's professional slave military corps; initially composed of Christian children taken as slaves and brought up in the military to serve as the key shock troops of the Ottomans

jebal (Arabic) mountain

jihad (Arabic) to struggle for the faith; holy war, not necessarily physical, against the forces trying to overturn Muslim community or personal belief

Kaabah (Arabic) the holy cube-like structure at the center of the great mosque in Makkah; built of local stone covered with a yearly-renewed black curtain

kasbah/casbah (Arabic) the old heart of a city; the enclosed or medieval core where the streets may be more crowded and narrow, with older houses and markets

khan/caravansary (Turkish) building used to house merchants, goods, and their animals while on the road or at the end of the journey. Large khans were often built in the middle of a city's suq as the gift of rich families or elites

kitab (Arabic) book

kulliye (Turkish) a mosque complex, often containing the mosque, public kitchens, schools, tomb and hospice

Kurds the mountain people who inhabit the border areas of southeast Anatolia, northern Iraq, northwest Iran, and parts of Azerbaijan. They speak various dialects of Kurdish and have a sense of being part of the Kurdish community, composing some 27 million people

limes (Latin) frontier, particularly the line of forts protecting that boundary of the Roman Empire

liwa (Arabic) administrative district within a province; other administrative divisions of various sizes used by Muslim authorities included **muhafizah, qadha, malakane, eyalet, jund,** and **niyabah.**

madrasah (Arabic) school, college, or religious training institution for students

Mahdi (Arabic) the guided one or savior; one called by Allah to lead the community. The assumption was that the Mahdi would appear in times of crisis

Mamluks (Arabic) slave soldiers. Term particularly used in relation to the Turkoman military slaves of the Ayyubids in

Egypt, who took power as sultans and started their own dynasty (1250–1517)

majlis (Arabic) initially meaning a reception room, the term is now used most often to refer to an assembly or parliament that meets to consult on policy

Maronites A Christian sect, primarily in Mount Lebanon, followers of the monk Maro, of the fifth century. Their power base in the mountains and association with the French gave them power under the French Mandate and in the creation of modern Lebanon, with the president of Lebanon traditionally drawn from the Maronite confession

masjid (Arabic) mosque and place of worship

madinah (Arabic) city or town. When lowercased, *madinah* refers to the older heart of Middle East or North African cities. Used as the proper name *Madinah*, it refers to the Holy City in the Hijaz where the Prophet Muhammad is buried

maidan (Persian) large square in the center of a city; more often used for Persian or central Asian cities

mellah (Arabic) separate Jewish quarters of medieval, usually North African cities

mihrab (Arabic) the niche in a mosque indicating the direction of prayer toward Makkah

millet (Turkish) Ottoman administrative structure and system based around identified religious communities whose leaders were responsible to the government for their communities and often for various administrative functions within their communities

misr/amsar (Arabic) garrison cities, founded by Muslims to house their troops in newly conquered areas. Basrah, Fustat (Cairo), and Kufa are examples

mujtahid (Arabic) religious authorities, doctors of Islamic law and jurisprudence

murabitun (Arabic) those who have committed to a particular creed, or formed a community around a religious leader; used in various ways through Muslim history to refer to movements emerging from a sect or place of retreat

nabi (Arabic) prophet

nahda (Arabic) the renaissance or reawakening; often used in relation to the Arab awakening in literature, nationalism, and intellectual debate that emerged after the 1840s in the Levant

nahr (Arabic) river

Najd (Arabic) middle-arid central desert area of Arabian Peninsula; location of the capital of Saudi Arabia, Riyadh

Nestorians Christian sect, followers of Nestorius (d. 451) that blossomed throughout Iraq, Iran, and the central areas of Asia. Spread by a strong missionary tradition along the Silk Road as far as China

pasha (Turkish) regional governor

pashalik (Turkish) regional governorate or administrative region; in North Africa came to refer to autonomous regions nominally under Ottomans but ruled by powerful local families or pasha

polis (Greek) city-state or political community, often acknowledged as autonomous by imperial powers

qadi/kadi (Arabic) Muslim judge or legal official

qanat (Arabic/Persian) covered irrigation channels, part of an irrigation system or scheme, frequently in oases, to expand the irrigated area

qasr (Arabic) castle or fortified site, often in the middle of a city, to protect against attack

qubba (Arabic) dome or arch; came to mean a domed shrine, often housing the tomb of a holy man or saint

Qur'an (Arabic) the holy book of Islam that records the word of God as delivered to Muhammad

Rashidun (Arabic) the rightly guided caliphs; the first four successors or caliphs after Muhammad (Abu Bakr, Umar, Uthman, Ali)

ribat (Arabic) fortified Muslim monastery, religious retreat, or sanctuary. The term is often used in North Africa to refer to sites where students also served as military forces

sanjak (Turkish) district, region, or provincial administrative area of an empire or state

saraya (Arabic) headquarters of the regional or district administration; often applied to the actual building or complex

satrap/satrapy (Old Persian) protector of the kingdom; a person appointed as regional or provincial governor. Thus, the administrative area of the Achaemenid Empire came to be called a satrapy; these divisions generally continued to the end of the Sassanian Empire

sayyids (Arabic) descendants of the Prophet, hence forming a nobility throughout Islam

shaykh (Arabic) patriarch of the tribe, the leader of the community; often used in relation to a tribe or clan but sometimes also referring to a religious leader, saint, or holy man

sharia (Arabic) Islamic law and duties as derived from and revealed in the Qur'an. There are four major schools or traditions spread throughout the Muslim world (Hanafis, Malikis, Shafis, and Hanbalis)

Sharif/Sharifan (Arabic) noble one who is a descendant of the Prophet Muhammad through his daughter Fatima and his son-in-law, Ali. Also called Alids. The term came to be used in particular to refer to the political leader or mayor of Makkah, who was responsible for the political and social well-being of Muslims in the Holy Cities. It also came to be used for families who were descendants of the Prophet, thus acquiring particularly revered status

Shi'i (Arabic) the second largest grouping, sect, or community in Islam. Followers of Ali, who believe that he was the rightfully designated caliph. Now the majority belief in Iran, with minority communities located throughout the Muslim world

Sufi (Arabic) Muslim mystic; often a member of particular Sufi order or follower of a particular saint

sultan (Arabic) military and political ruler or sovereign, often appointed by the caliph or Muslim religious leader, to protect and rule the community. Used more often in Turkish or Turkoman context

Sunni (Arabic) the largest community of believers in Islam (90 percent); the orthodox majority belief

suq (Arabic) market area of a city; there could often be a number of suqs, each for different specialties or products

tariqa (Arabic) literally, path or way; came to refer to the complex system of Muslim religious orders networked around the world

tell (Arabic) mound created from the remains of cities or buildings accumulated over time. Archaeologists will often dig a tell over a number of seasons to trace back the history of habitation on a particular site

turbe (Turkish) mausoleum or conical tomb for saints or sultans in Ottoman or Turkoman areas

ulema (Arabic) clerics or religious scholars who lead the Muslim community

umma (Arabic) the Muslim community as a whole

vilayet/wilayat (Turkish/Arabic) province or large administrative district

villes nouvelles (French) new colonial (European) towns added to cities like Fez, Rabat, Marrakesh, and Meknes in North Africa by the French

vizier/wazir (Turkish/Arabic) all-powerful minister or chief bureaucratic official, initiated under the Abbasid caliph and used through the end of the Ottoman Empire

wadi (Arabic) valley or water course, often dry until the rainy season

Wahhabis (Arabic) followers of Muhammad bin Abd al-Wahhab (d. 1792), a Najdi imam who first preached the puritanical version of Islam still followed by many Saudis today

wali/vali (Arabic/Turkish) initially used to refer to a protector, hence governor or appointed official; later, particularly in North Africa, *wali* is used to refer to a local saint or mystic

waqf/awqaf (Arabic) religious endowments; lands or buildings endowed by pious elites for public purposes

wilaya/willayat/vilayet (Arabic/Turkish) provincial government or provincial district

zakat (Arabic) obligation on Muslims to tithe money to the poor or those in need; an alms tax

zanj (Arabic) African or black inhabitants of the East African coast; black slaves brought to Muslim cities

Timeline
Dynastic and Imperial Ages

I. Neolithic to Iron Age

II. Alexander to Muhammad

III. Muhammad to the Rise of the Gunpowder Empires

IV. European Imperialism to the State Project

I. Neolithic Age to Iron Age

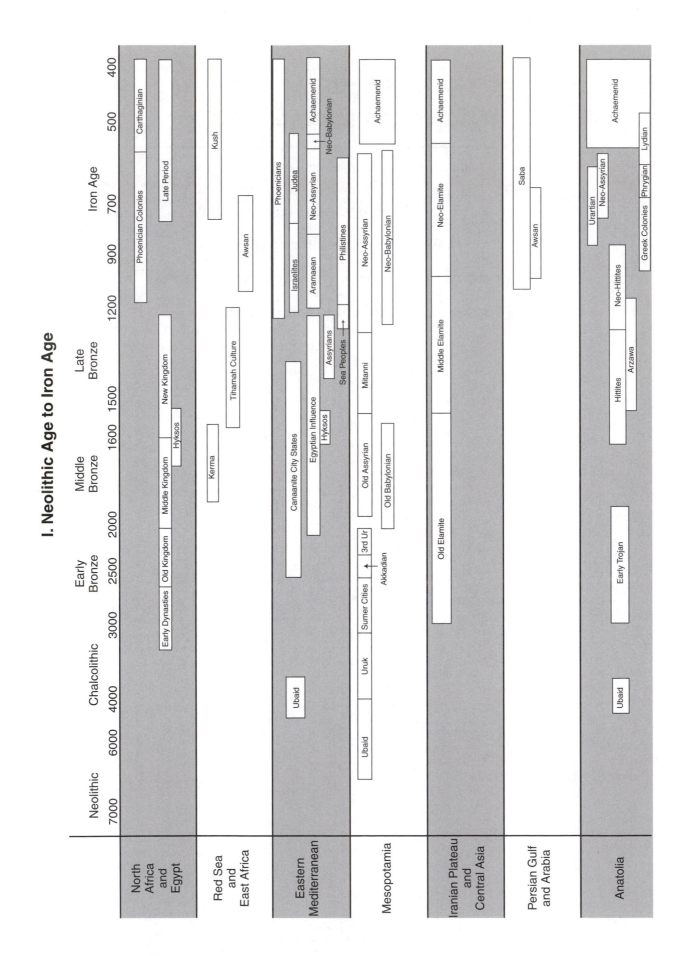

II. Alexander to Muhammad

	300 BC	200	100	0	100	200	300	400	500	AD 600

North Africa and Egypt: Carthaginians · Mauritania · Rome · Vandals · Byzantine · Macedonian & Ptolemaic · Rome · Byzantine

Red Sea and East Africa: Macedonian & Ptolemaic · Rome · Byzantine · Kush · Meroitic · Aksumite

Eastern Mediterranean: Phoenician · Ptolemaic · Seleucid · Parthian · Rome · Byzantine · Sassanian

Mesopotamia: Macedonian/Seleucid · Parthian · Sassanian

Iranian Plateau and Central Asia: Seleucid · Greco-Bactrian · Parthian · Sogdian · Sassanian

Persian Gulf and Arabia: Qataban · Saba · Hadramawt · Himyar · Sassanian

Anatolia: Macedonian/Seleucid · Galatian · Rome · Byzantine

III. Muhammad to the Rise of the Gunpowder Empires

AD 700 · 800 · 900 · 1000 · 1100 · 1200 · 1300 · 1400 · 1500

North Africa and Egypt
- Umayyids — Abbasids — Idrisids — Aghlabids — Fatimids — Al-Moravids — Zirids — Al-Mohades — Marinids — Zayyanids — Hafsids — Ottomans
- Umayyids — Abbasids — Fatimids — Ayyubids — Burji Mamluks — Burji Mamluks — Ottomans

Red Sea and East Africa
- Aksumites
- Ziyadids — Hamdanids — Early Solomonic — Solomonids
- Somali Migrations — Mamluks — Ottomans
- Ayyubids — Somali States — Portuguese
- Swahili Coastal City States — Portuguese

Eastern Mediterranean
- Umayyids — Abbasids — Fatimids — Crusader States
- Seljuqs — Ayyubids — Bahri Mamluks — Burji Mamluks — Ottomans

Mesopotamia
- Umayyids — Abbasids — Buyids — Ilkhanids — Jalayirid — Qara & Aq Quyunlu
- Safavids

Iranian Plateau and Central Asia
- Umayyids — Abbasids — Samanids — Seljuqs — Khwarizm — Ilkhanids — Timurids — Safavids
- Mongols

Persian Gulf and Arabia
- Umayyids — Abbasids — Ziyadids — Qarmatian — Ayyubids — Tribal Rule — Rasulids — Ottomans
- Portuguese

Anatolia
- Byzantine — Rum Seljiqs — Ottomans
- Nicaea

IV. European Imperialism to the State Project

	AD 1600	1700	1800	1850	1900	1920	1950	1990

North Africa and Egypt

- Saadid
- Ottoman Corsair States
- Alawites
- France
- Spain and France
- States
- Moroccans in Songhai
- French →
- Muhammad Ali and Descendants
- Italy
- Europeans in Western Sudan
- British
- Ottomans

Red Sea and East Africa

- Sennar Kingdom
- Egypt | Mahdi
- Anglo-Egyptian rule
- States
- Ethiopian Kingdom
- Italy
- States
- Portuguese
- Islamic Amirates
- Omani
- British Rule
- Adel Sultanate
- Amirates
- European Rule
- States

Eastern Mediterranean

- Ottomans
- Ibrahim Pasha
- British / French Mandates
- States
- Israel / Palestine

Mesopotamia

- Ottomans
- British
- State

Iranian Plateau and Central Asia

- Safavids
- Qajars
- Pahlavi
- Khanate of Bukhara
- Russia
- Soviet
- States

Persian Gulf and Arabia

- Portuguese
- Safavids
- Arab Tribal Rule
- British
- States
- Ottomans
- Zaydis
- Ottomans
- Wahhabi

Anatolia

- Ottomans
- European and Greek Invasion
- State

Index

About the Editors

MICHAEL R. T. DUMPER is currently a Reader in the department of politics at the University of Exeter, United Kingdom. His research interests are the permanent-status issues of the Middle East peace process, religious institutions, and the urban politics of the Middle East. He is currently researching comparative perspectives on refugee repatriation programs and on the impact of conflict on the urban environment of Jerusalem. Dr. Dumper has served as a consultant to the European Union on Palestinian refugees and on the future status of Jerusalem. Major publications include *The Politics of Sacred Space: The Old City of Jerusalem in the Middle East Conflict* (Lynne Rienner, 2001) and *The Politics of Jerusalem Since 1967* (Columbia University Press, 1996).

BRUCE E. STANLEY is currently a professor of international relations as well as the provost of Huron University in London. He is also a research fellow in the department of politics at the University of Exeter, United Kingdom. His research interests include Middle East urban history, conflict resolution, and Middle East political economy. He is currently researching Middle East city networks in the world system and post-conflict development in Middle East cities. He has served as a consultant to the European Union on conflict resolution in the region and on Palestinian civil society.